Romer

External Plan Northwood

Bruce

8 B-6 (c) Total current assets, $741,223

8 B-7 (c) One-year interest charge originally included in face amount, $13,200

9-1 No key figure

9-2 (a) May 31 inventory, $280

9-3 (a) Sept. 30 inventory balance, $3,450

9-4 (b) (4) Jan. 15 LIFO inventory, $18,500

9-5 (a) (2) FIFO cost of goods sold, $18,100

9-6 (c) LIFO cost of goods sold, $18,700

9-7 (a) (1) Average cost shrinkage loss, $567

9-8 (a) (2) LIFO cost of goods sold, $303,480

9-9 (b) (3) LIFO cost of goods sold, $7,420

9-10 (a) Gross profit rate, 1992, 43%

9-11 (b) (3) Gross profit, $264,144

9-12 (b) (1) Turnover rate, FIFO, 2.4 times

10 A-1 (c) Total cost of equipment, $91,200

10 A-2 Depreciation for 1995, (b) $36,000; (c) $33,750

10 A-3 (a) Depreciation for 1996, (3) $15,000; (4) $11,520

10 A-4 (c) Total 1994 depreciation for tax purposes, $210,656

10 A-5 Gain on disposal of moving van, $4,000

10 A-6 No key figure

10 A-7 (c) (2) Taxable gain on disposal, $2,320

10 B-1 (a) Total cost of equipment, $220,720

10 B-2 Depreciation for Year 2, (b) $65,600; (c) $64,800

10 B-3 Depreciation for 1993, (b) $15,000; (d) $26,664

10 B-4 (a) Accumulated depreciation: Machine C, $36,000

10 B-5 Gain on disposal of truck, $1,000

10 B-6 No key figure

10 B-7 (c) (2) Taxable gain on disposal, $1,360

CP-3 (a) Total assets: Alpine, $494,400; Nordic, $496,200; (b) revised net income: Alpine, $225,000

11-1 No key figure

11-2 No key figure

11-3 (a) Total current liabilities, $375,403

11-4 (b) Interest expense on Midwest Bank note, $3,200

11-5 (b) Interest expense on Sun National Bank note, $4,704

11-6 (c) Total current liabilities, $337,656

11-7 (c) Unpaid balance, $8,331

11-8 (c) Jan. 1, 1995, unpaid balance, $539,370

11-9 (b) Total payroll cost, $22,553

11-10 (b) (4) Employer's total payroll costs, $479,051

11-11 (c) Total payroll cost, $15,706

12 A-1 (b) Total assets, $220,800

12 A-2 (a) Net income, $54,000; (c) total assets, $217,720

12 A-3 (a) (4) Pascal's share, $28,000

12 A-4 (c) Stein's share, $26,100

12 A-5 (c) Bonus to Ritter, $30,000

12 A-6 (c) Bonus to Kim, $60,000

12 A-7 (a) Cash to Nix, $11,600

12 B-1 (b) Total assets, $277,800

12 B-2 (a) Net income, $54,500; (c) total assets, $175,500

12 B-3 (a) (2) Martin's share, $58,000

12 B-4 (a) Conrad's share, $102,600

12 B-5 (c) Bonus to Lee, $70,000

12 B-6 (d) Debit to Spence, Capital, $22,500

12 B-7 (b) Cash payment by Merit, $18,000

13-1 No key figure

13-2 No key figure

13-3 No key figure

13-4 No key figure

13-5 No key figure

13-6 (a) Profit under percentage-of-completion, 1993, $3,000,000

13-7 No key figure

13-8 No key figure

14 A-1 (b) Dec. 31, 1994, retained earnings, $1,937,000

14 A-2 (a) Total stockholders' equity, $15,370,000

14 A-3 Total stockholders' equity, $2,063,000

14 A-4 (b) Total stockholders' equity, $1,082,560

14 A-5 (b) Total assets, $1,512,100

14 A-6 (g) Book value per share, $27.60

14 B-1 (b) Dec. 31,1994, retained earnings, $1,490,000

14 B-2 (a) Total stockholders' equity, $3,405,000

14 B-3 Total stockholders' equity, $2,112,000

14 B-4 (d) Total stockholders' equity, $890,200

14 B-5 (b) Total assets, $1,352,950

14 B-6 (i) Net income, $2,168,000

15 A-1 (a) Income before extraordinary items, $13,620,000

15 A-2 (b) Retained earnings, $7,230,000

15 A-3 (a) Net income, $336,000

15 A-4 (1) Total stockholders' equity, $743,600

15 A-5 Retained earnings, Dec. 31, $874,500

15 A-6 (b) Total stockholders' equity, $8,792,800

15 A-7 (a) Total paid-in capital, $4,990,000; (b) retained earnings, $874,000

15 B-1 (a) Income before extraordinary items, $11,820,000

15 B-2 (b) Retained earnings, $7,940,000

15 B-3 (a) Net income, $265,000

15 B-4 (1) Total stockholders' equity, $4,578,000

15 B-5 Retained earnings, $346,600

15 B-6 (b) Total stockholders' equity, $9,318,000

15 B-7 (a) Total paid-in capital, $3,228,000; (b) retained earnings, $469,800

(continued on inside back cover)

Accounting: The Basis for Business Decisions

Robert F. Meigs
San Diego State University

Walter B. Meigs
University of Southern California

Accounting:
The Basis for
Business
Decisions

Ninth Edition

McGraw-Hill, Inc.

New York ■ St Louis ■ San Francisco ■ Auckland ■ Bogotá ■ Caracas ■
Lisbon ■ London ■ Madrid ■ Mexico ■ Milan ■ Montreal ■ New Delhi ■
Paris ■ San Juan ■ Singapore ■ Sydney ■ Tokyo ■ Toronto

ACCOUNTING
THE BASIS FOR BUSINESS DECISIONS

1 2 3 4 5 6 7 8 9 0   DOW   DOW   9 0 9 8 7 6 5 4 3 2

ISBN 0-07-041385-1

This book was set in Century Schoolbook by York Graphic Services, Inc.
The editors were Alan Sachs and Linda Richmond;
the designer was Joseph A. Piliero;
the production supervisor was Phil Galea.

Drawings were done by Vantage Art.
R. R. Donnelley & Sons Company was printer and binder.

This book is printed on acid-free paper.

Cover Photo Credits: Chicago Skyline, Donald C. Johnson; Stock Exchange Columns, David Pollack; International Currency, Ted Horowitz; all courtesy the Stock Market. Hands On Computer courtesy Superstock.

Library of Congress Cataloging-in-Publication Data

Meigs, Robert F.
    Accounting, the basis for business decisions/Robert F. Meigs,
  Walter B. Meigs.—9th ed.
      p.   cm.
      Includes index.
      ISBN 0-07-041385-1
      1. Accounting.   I. Meigs, Walter B.   II. Title.
  HF5635.M4887   1993
  657—dc20   92-31501

INTERNATIONAL EDITION

Copyright © 1993, 1990, 1987, 1984, 1981, 1977, 1972, 1967. 1962

Exclusive rights by McGraw-Hill, Inc. for manufacture and export. This book cannot be re-exported from the country to which it is consigned by McGraw-Hill. The International Edition is not available in North America.

When ordering this title, use ISBN 0-07-112717-8

Contents

v

Preface

This text is an introduction to the field of accounting and to the use of accounting information as a basis for business decisions. It is intended for use in the first college-level accounting course, which usually spans either two semesters or three quarters.

OUR GOALS IN THIS NINTH EDITION

We have tried to accomplish many things in this ninth edition. Among our most important goals have been to:

1. Provide students with a better understanding of the environment in which accounting information is developed and used.
2. Shift emphasis from the preparation of accounting information to its interpretation and use.
3. Retain a course structure which meets the specific content requirements of most colleges and universities.

Providing Students with a Better Background

If students are to appreciate the nature of accounting, they first should have a basic understanding of the business environment. We find, however, that many introductory students lack this background. Often the introductory accounting course is also the students' first course in the business curriculum.

We give increased attention to explaining business practices before discussing accounting issues. Our focus is upon *current* business and accounting practices, not those of the past. For example, virtually every business with external reporting obligations now uses a perpetual inventory system. Yet many accounting textbooks continue to emphasize periodic systems. We emphasize *perpetual* inventory systems.

For purposes of illustration, textbooks traditionally assume the use of simple, manually maintained accounting records. Such records do not meet the needs of most modern businesses. We, too, find it convenient to use simple accounting records as the basis for many illustrations. However, we also explain how the information is processed in a computer-based environment.

Attention is given throughout the text to the role of *professional judgment* in both the development and interpretation of accounting information. We explain in some depth the codes of professional ethics developed by the American Institute of Certified Public Accountants and by the Institute of Management Accountants. We also discuss audits, reviews, and the independent auditors' potential liability to the users of financial statements.

Shifting to a "User Orientation"

Today, relatively few introductory students will become professional preparers of accounting information. All, however, will become life-long information **users.** For this reason, we have shifted our emphasis significantly from the preparation of accounting information to its interpretation and use.

This shift in emphasis affects the text in several ways. For example, we have added new assignment material designed specifically to develop students' critical thinking skills and communication skills.

A user-oriented approach also affects topical content and emphasis. Topics relevant to basic business decisions now are addressed, even if these topics traditionally have been deferred to later accounting courses. Examples of such topics include accounting for postretirement costs, audits and reviews, "window dressing," and many of the disclosures which accompany financial statements.

Throughout the text, attention is given to analytical ratios and financial relationships. The chapter on analysis of financial statements now serves primarily as a review.

Increased attention also is given to the use of accounting information **by management.** No longer is this topic addressed only in a group of "managerial" chapters; it now is integrated throughout the text.

Some "traditional" accounting topics relate primarily to the preparation of accounting information and are of little significance to the information user. Examples include reversing entries, manual special journals, and alternative methods of recording accruals and deferrals. In our user-oriented approach, such topics are given less emphasis. Often they are presented in Supplemental Topic sections or in an appendix.

Preserving a Proven Course Structure

Some universities are experimenting with radically different approaches to the introductory accounting course. We have *not* embarked upon such a path. We have great respect for the existing structure of the introductory course, which has evolved from decades of experience and research. We recognize that many students transfer credit for this course from one institution to another. Some standardization of the curriculum is therefore essential.

We regard our changes in this ninth edition as *evolutionary,* not *revolutionary.* Faculty acquainted with our past editions will find much that is familiar.

ELEMENTS OF THE TEXTBOOK

This ninth edition is accompanied by more in-the-text learning aids than ever before.

Chapter Introductions and Learning Objectives

Each chapter begins with a brief overview and a set of basic learning objectives. These learning objectives then are integrated with the text discussions and are summarized in the End-of-Chapter section.

Cases in Point

A distinctive feature of past editions has been the use of short **Cases in Point,** which are based upon actual events. Many new Cases in Point have been created for this edition as part of our increased focus on the contemporary business environment.

Supplemental Topics and Appendixes

A new feature in the structure of this edition is the inclusion of short **Supplemental Topic** sections at the end of several chapters. These Supplemental Topics are closely related to the content of the chapters in which they appear.

Students always should read the Supplemental Topic sections, as these discussions will enhance their overall understanding of the chapter. Instructors, however, may decide whether these topics are of sufficient general interest for inclusion in class discussions, homework assignments, and examinations. [Assignment material and examination questions relating to Supplemental Topics are preceded by an asterisk (*).]

In contrast to the Supplemental Topics, the four **Appendixes** at the end of the text provide self-contained coverage of specialized topics. We consider coverage of the Appendixes optional; students are not expected to read the appendixes unless assigned by the instructor.

Pedagogical Use of Color

The four-color design of this text is used as a learning aid. For example, a light green background shading is used in illustrations of *accounting records,* whereas a light blue background is used in illustrations of *financial statements.* Red often is used to *highlight* key elements of an illustration.

End-of-Chapter Reviews

Each chapter is followed by a variety of learning aids, including a **Summary of the Chapter Learning Objectives,** a **Glossary of Key Terms,** and a series of **Self-Test Questions.** Most chapters also include a **Demonstration Problem,** with a complete solution.

Each chapter summary concludes with a paragraph explaining the relationships between that chapter and upcoming topics. This device aids students in viewing accounting as an integrated information system, rather than as series of separate topics.

Assignment Material

One of the distinctive features of this ninth edition is the increase in the quantity and variety of the assignment material. Increased emphasis is placed upon the development of students' analytical abilities and communication skills. Much of the new assignment material is based upon the operations of well-known companies.

Five categories of assignments accompany the text. These are (1) Discussion Questions, (2) Exercises, (3) Problems, (4) Cases and Unstructured Problems, and (5) Comprehensive Problems.

Discussion Questions are short and usually call for expository answers. In addition to developing writing and communication skills, these questions explore students' conceptual understanding of accounting.

Exercises are short assignments, usually focusing upon a single concept. We have greatly increased the number and the variety of Exercises. By enabling instructors to cover basic concepts quickly, we hope to allow more time for discussing in class such assignments as our Cases and Unstructured Problems.

Problems are longer than the Exercises and address several concepts at one time. Most chapters contain both an *A* and *B* problem series, each providing thorough coverage of the chapter. A few chapters contain a single—but longer—series of problems. The single series accommodates a greater variety of assignments.

Cases and Unstructured Problems emphasize the development of analytical skills and communication skills. They also provide a wealth of assignment material well suited to in-class discussions.

To encourage the use of these assignments, we have developed Cases and Unstructured Problems covering a wide range of time requirements and difficulty levels. Many of our Exercises and Problems also call for analysis and the use of judgment.

We consider our six ***Comprehensive Problems*** to be among the most useful assignments in the text. Each of these problems ties together concepts presented over a span of chapters. Two of the Comprehensive Problems are similar in scope to a "practice set," and another involves the analysis of an actual annual report.

Most chapters contain several problems designed for solution using the AIM General Ledger or Spreadsheet packages. These problems are identified by the computer disk symbol shown in the margin. A red symbol (▣) identifies problems for the general ledger package; a blue symbol (▣) identifies problems for the spreadsheet package.

A ***Checklist of Key Figures*** for Problems and Comprehensive Problems appears on the front and back inside covers of the text. The purpose of these check figures is to aid students in verifying their problem solutions and in discovering their own errors.

The Flexibility of PRIMIS

Accounting: The Basis for Business Decisions, Ninth Edition, and selected supplementary materials are available on the McGraw-Hill/Primis custom publishing database. Any materials on the database can be configured and created to your specifications. The Primis database includes several McGraw-Hill accounting texts, selected Harvard business cases, and articles from various journals.

NEW AND EXTENSIVELY REVISED CHAPTERS

Many chapters in this ninth edition have been revised significantly. Almost every chapter contains greater emphasis upon the use of accounting information and more assignment material than ever before. Among the changes in topical content which will be noticed most readily are:

Chapter1, "Accounting: The Language of Business," has been rewritten to provide a more comprehensive introduction to the process of financial reporting. We have added discussions of such topics as reporting requirements of publicly owned companies, auditing, and professional ethics. Also included is a new discussion of the nature and sources of generally accepted accounting principles. Career opportunities in accounting are discussed in a Supplemental Topic section at the end of the chapter.

In *Chapter 4,* we have revised the format of the work sheet. Our goal is to focus upon the *accounting processes* illustrated within the work sheet, not to present the document itself as a component of the accounting cycle.

Chapter 5, now entitled "Merchandising Activities; Classified Financial Statements," exemplifies many of the changes in this ninth edition. The opening pages of this chapter illustrate our concerted effort to explain business practices before discussing the accounting treatments accorded those practices.

In keeping with contemporary business practices, this chapter now emphasizes *perpetual inventory systems*—the type of system used in every large business organization. Periodic systems still receive thorough coverage; in fact, we have added an explanation of a "shortcut" periodic system that is used by many small businesses.

The final portion of Chapter 5, "Introduction to Classified Financial Statements," typifies our increased emphasis upon the *use* of accounting information.

Chapter 6, "Accounting Systems, Internal Control, and Audits," emphasizes the capabilities of computer-based accounting systems, rather than the use of manual special journals. Among the new features of this chapter are examples of how data bases tailor information to meet the needs of different decision makers. New elements of this chapter also include discussions of financial and operational audits, and the related topics of employee fraud and management fraud.

Chapter 8, "Accounts Receivable and Notes Receivable," now includes discussions of the goals of credit management, accounts receivable turnover rates, strategies for quickly converting receivables into cash, and disclosure of concentrations of credit risk. These additions illustrate our increased emphasis on the use of accounting information by management, as well as by persons outside of the business organization.

Our coverage of notes receivable with interest included in the face amount has been moved to a Supplemental Topic section, as such notes are held primarily by financial institutions.

Chapter 9, "Inventories and the Cost of Goods Sold," has been revised extensively in light of our emphasis upon perpetual inventory systems. Also included are discussions of the just-in-time concept, inventory turnover rates, and the objectives of efficient inventory management. The nature and significance of large LIFO reserves are discussed as a Supplemental Topic.

Chapter 10, dealing with plant and equipment, includes extensively revised coverage of trade-ins and a new Supplemental Topic section addressing depreciation for income tax purposes.

Our coverage of liabilities, contained in *Chapters 11* and *16,* has been revised extensively. *Chapter 11* now focuses upon the types of liabilities *common to most business entities,* including long-term installment debt. ***Chapter 16,*** in contrast, addresses those types of liabilities found primarily in the financial statements of large, publicly owned corporations. This format completes our coverage of accounting for unincorporated businesses in the first semester. It also heightens students' awareness of the differences in the business environments of small businesses and of large corporations.

Our coverage of liabilities also has been expanded in terms of topical content. Chapter 11 now includes long-term installment debt, disclosure requirements relating to financial instruments, and increased emphasis on loss contingencies and commitments. Extensively revised coverage of payroll liabilities now appears as a Supplemental Topic.

In Chapter 16, new or expanded coverage is given to topics which, because of their materiality, are relevant to the users of corporate financial statements. Examples include deferred income taxes and an employer's obligation for postretirement benefits.

Chapter 13, "Accounting Concepts, Professional Judgment, and Ethical Conduct," is new to this edition. One objective of this chapter is to review at one time many of the generally accepted accounting principles discussed throughout the text. Another objective is to look in some depth at key elements of the AICPA and IMA (formerly NAA) codes of professional ethics.

Chapter 18, "Income Taxes and Business Decisions," has been revised along more conceptual lines and is no longer dependent upon the tax rates and regulations of a specific year. (We have also integrated throughout the textbook discussions of basic income tax concepts which affect business decisions.)

Chapter 20, "Analysis and Interpretation of Financial Statements," has been revised to reflect our emphasis of this topic throughout the textbook.

Chapter 22, "Cost Accounting Systems," contains new coverage of activity-based costing, just-in-time inventory systems, and total quality management.

SUPPLEMENTARY MATERIALS

This text is accompanied by a large number of supplementary learning and teaching aids. These supplements are listed below and in the graphic illustration at the end of this preface. A complete description of these materials is contained in the ***Instructor's Guide.*** If you would like information and costs on the supplemental materials, please contact your local McGraw-Hill representative. We value both your interest and our supplements.

For the Student:

Self-Study Guide, co-authored by Mary A. Meigs
Accounting Work Sheets, Group A Problems, Chapters 1–15
Accounting Work Sheets, Group A Problems, Chapters 14–26
Accounting Work Sheets, Group B Problems, Chapters 1–15

Accounting Work Sheets, Group B Problems, Chapters 14–26
Blank Forms for Problems and Cases
Accounting Information Manager: A General Ledger Program by John W. Wanlass
Accounting Information Manager: A Spreadsheet Program by John W. Wanlass
MicroGuide Computerized Accounting Tutorial by Jean Gutmann
Manual Simulations and Applications:
  Premium Foods Corporation: A Financial Statement Analysis Case by Christie W. Johnson
  The Next Dimension: An Accounting Cycle Application by Mary A. Meigs
  Facts-by-FAX: An Accounting Cycle Application
  Color Copy Co.: An Accounting Cycle Application
  Echo Paint Co.: A Small Business Application with Forms by Richard A. Wright
  Executive Woodcraft: A Managerial Accounting Application by Ronald W. Hilton
  Printer Recharge, Inc.: A Corporate Practice Set by Phillip Ricci and Wanda G. Spruill
Computer-Based Simulations and Applications:
  CYMA General Ledger Package: Shadow Mountain Hotel
  CYMA General Ledger Package: Authenticity and Facts-by FAX
  Echo Paint Co.: A Small Business Application with Forms, by Richard A. Wright
  Remington Restaurant Supply: A Computerized Accounting Cycle Application
  Electronic Spreadsheet Application to Accompany the Premium Foods Corporation Financial Statement Analysis Case by Christie W. Johnson

For the Instructor:

Annotated Instructor's Edition by David Marcinko
Lecture Video Series
Case Study Videos for Analysis and Critical Thinking
Instructor's Manual / Critical Thinking Guide to Accompany Case Study Videotapes by Mark S. Bettner
Solutions Manual
Overhead Transparencies: Solutions to Problems and Exercises and Selected Text Exhibits
Solutions to Applications
Test Bank (Manual and Computerized Versions)
Achievement Tests and Comprehensive Examinations (four series)
Instructor's Guide and Answers to Achievement Tests by David Marcinko
Electronic Classroom Presentations by Glenn Owen
Interactive Solutions Software
Teaching Transparencies
Report Card: Electronic Grading Software
Financial Statement Analysis Problem Set and Software

CONTRIBUTIONS BY OTHERS

The ninth edition has benefited from a number of perceptive reviews. We wish to express our sincere thanks to these reviewers, who are listed at the conclusion of this Preface.

We also want to thank the following individuals, each of whom has authored supplements which accompany the text: **Mark S. Bettner,** *Bucknell University;* **Jean Gutmann,** *University of South Maine;* **Ronald W. Hilton,** *Cornell University;* **Christie W. Johnson,** *Montana State University;* **David Marcinko,** *SUNY, Albany;* **E. James Meddaugh,** *Ohio University;* **Mary A. Meigs,** *San Diego State University;* **Glenn Owen,** *University of California, Santa Barbara;* **John W. Wanlass,** *DeAnza College;* **Richard A. Wright,** *American River College;* **Phillip Ricci** and **Wanda G. Spruill,** *SUNY, Geneseo.*

We owe a special debt to Mary Meigs. Professor Meigs has authored or co-authored the Study Guide, the Test Bank, and several of the accounting applications which accompany this edition. She also has participated in virtually every stage of this project. Her contributions have improved the text and the supplementary materials in many ways.

Our special thanks also go to **James M. Emig,** Villanova University and **Roger A. Gee,** San Diego Mesa College for assisting us in the proof stages of this edition with detailed reviews of the end-of-chapter assignment material.

We appreciate the expert attention given this book and its many supplements by the staff of McGraw-Hill, especially **Alan Sachs, Linda Richmond, Judy Howarth,** and **Debbie Emry.**

The assistance of **Jawade Anwar, Melody Gritton, Jeannette Haley,** and **Tom Templeton** was most helpful in preparation of the manuscript.

Robert F. Meigs

Walter B. Meigs

Acknowledgments

REVIEWERS CONTRIBUTING TO THIS EDITION

Sarah L. Adams, California State University, Chico
Linda Anderson, Cabrillo College
Shelby D. Bennett, University of North Carolina, Asheville
Dorothy Binger, Tallahassee Community College
Gary R. Bower, Community College of Rhode Island
Barry Buchoff, Towson State University
Carol E. Buehl, Northern Michigan University
Don E. Collins, Ithaca College
Ellen Cook, University of Southwest Louisiana
Anita Ellzey, Hartford Community College
Larry W. Goode, Missouri Southern State College
Edward S. Goodhart, Shippensberg University
Debra Goorbin, Westchester Community College
Gisela Halpern, El Camino College
Geoffry D. Heriot, Greenville Technical College
George A. Johnson, Radford University
W. P. Lam, University of Windsor
L. R. Loschen, Eastern New Mexico University
Johanna D. Lyle, Kansas State University
Gary B. McCombs, Eastern Michigan University
Edward J. McDonnell, Los Angeles City College
Rene Manes, Florida State University
Roger E. Martin, Keene State College
Timothy D. Miller, El Camino College
Greg Mostyn, Mission College
Barbara J. Mull, Hartford Community College
James F. Newman, State University at Stony Brook
Sharon R. Parrish, Kentucky State University
Barbara Saar-Gregorio, Nassau Community College
Nancy L. Saltz, Lynchburg College
Robert Sanborn, University of Richmond
Robert J. Shepherd, University of California, Santa Cruz
Norman D. Stevens, College of Marin
Gwen Totterdale, University of Hawaii
Joyce Strawser, CUNY-Baruch College
James F. Ward, University of Notre Dame
Jane K. Ward, The University of Northern Iowa

TEXTBOOK AND STUDENT SUPPLEMENTS
(New or expanded features are shown in blue)

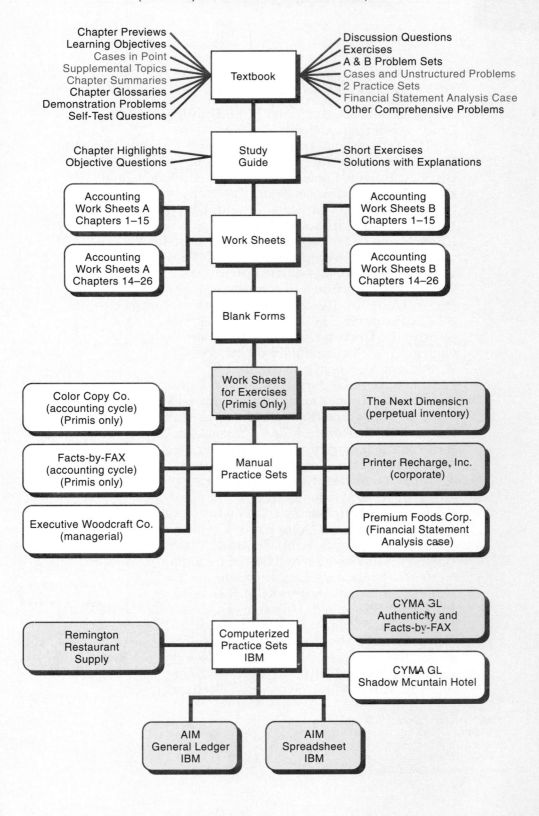

Chapter Previews
Learning Objectives
Cases in Point
Supplemental Topics
Chapter Summaries
Chapter Glossaries
Demonstration Problems
Self-Test Questions

Textbook

Discussion Questions
Exercises
A & B Problem Sets
Cases and Unstructured Problems
2 Practice Sets
Financial Statement Analysis Case
Other Comprehensive Problems

Chapter Highlights
Objective Questions

Study Guide

Short Exercises
Solutions with Explanations

Accounting Work Sheets A Chapters 1–15

Accounting Work Sheets A Chapters 14–26

Work Sheets

Accounting Work Sheets B Chapters 1–15

Accounting Work Sheets B Chapters 14–26

Blank Forms

Work Sheets for Exercises (Primis Only)

Color Copy Co. (accounting cycle) (Primis only)

Facts-by-FAX (accounting cycle) (Primis only)

Executive Woodcraft Co. (managerial)

Manual Practice Sets

The Next Dimension (perpetual inventory)

Printer Recharge, Inc. (corporate)

Premium Foods Corp. (Financial Statement Analysis case)

Remington Restaurant Supply

Computerized Practice Sets IBM

CYMA GL Authenticity and Facts-by-FAX

CYMA GL Shadow Mountain Hotel

AIM General Ledger IBM

AIM Spreadsheet IBM

SUPPLEMENTS FOR INSTRUCTORS
(New or expanded supplements are shown in blue)

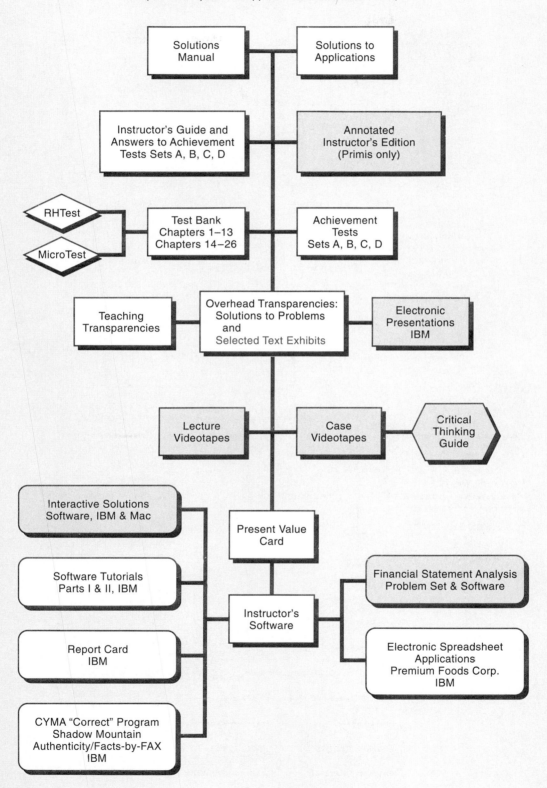

The Accounting Cycle

In these first four chapters, the continuing example of Roberts Real Estate Company is used to illustrate the concepts of double-entry accrual accounting for a small, service-type business. Accounting for a merchandising concern will be introduced in Part 2.

Also included are two Comprehensive Problems. The first of these focuses upon the nature of double-entry accounting and the interpretation of a balance sheet. The second provides a review of the entire accounting cycle.

1 Accounting: The Language of Business

The primary purpose of this introductory chapter is to explore the nature of accounting information and the environment in which it is developed and used. We emphasize the financial reporting process, including the roles played by financial statements, generally accepted accounting principles, independent audits, and professional judgment. A basic financial statement—the balance sheet—is illustrated and discussed. We explain the nature of assets, liabilities, and owner's equity, and why a balance sheet always "balances." We also introduce Roberts Real Estate Company, which is used as a continuing example throughout the first four chapters.

This chapter concludes with a discussion of career opportunities in accounting.

After studying this chapter you should be able to meet these Learning Objectives:

1 *Define accounting, financial reporting, and financial statements.*

2 *Explain the phrase "generally accepted accounting principles."*

3 *Describe and prepare a balance sheet; define assets, liabilities, and owner's equity.*

4 *Describe the accounting principles involved in asset valuation.*

5 *Indicate the effects of various transactions upon the accounting equation and the balance sheet.*

6 *Use a balance sheet in evaluating the short-term solvency of a business organization.*

7 *Explain the concept of adequate disclosure.*

8 *Identify factors contributing to the reliability of financial statements.*

9 *Identify several areas in which accountants must exercise professional judgment.*

*10 *Describe various career opportunities in accounting.*

---

* *Supplemental Topic, "Careers in Accounting"*

WHAT IS ACCOUNTING?

OBJECTIVE 1
Define ac-
counting,
financial
reporting,
and finan-
cial state-
ments.

Some people think of accounting as a highly technical field which is prac-
ticed and understood only by professional accountants. Actually, nearly
everyone practices "accounting" in one form or another on almost a daily
basis. ***Accounting is the art of interpreting, measuring, and communicating the results of economic activities.*** Whether you are paying
your phone bill, balancing your checkbook, preparing your income tax return, or managing an international corporation, you are working with accounting concepts and accounting information.

Accounting has often been called the ***language of business.*** Such
terms as ***assets, liabilities, net income, cash flow,*** and ***earnings per
share*** are but a few examples of technical accounting terms widely used
throughout the business world. Every investor, manager, and business
decision maker needs a clear understanding of accounting terms and concepts if he or she is to participate and communicate effectively in the business community.

The use of accounting information is not limited to the business world.
We live in an era of accountability. An individual must account for his or
her income and must file income tax returns. Often an individual must
supply personal accounting information in order to qualify for a loan, to
obtain a credit card, or to qualify for a college scholarship. The federal
government, the states, the cities, and the school districts all use accounting information as the basis for controlling their resources and measuring
their accomplishments. Accounting is just as important to the successful
operation of a government, a social program, or a church as it is to a business organization.

The study of accounting should not be limited to students majoring in
accounting or finance. Everyone who engages in economic activity—***which
means everyone***—will benefit from understanding the nature, significance, and limitations of accounting information.

The Purpose of Accounting

The basic purpose of accounting is to provide decision makers with information ***useful in making economic decisions.*** These decisions concern
the allocation and use of scarce economic resources, such as money, land,
and labor. The manner in which we allocate and use economic resources
shapes the world's economies. Resource allocation decisions determine
prices, wages, the goods and services we produce, the adequacy of our food
supplies, the quality of our transportation systems, and which countries
will prosper or suffer economic decline.

Our primary goals in this text—and in this introductory course—are to
develop your understanding of accounting information and your abilities to
use this information effectively in making economic decisions.

Just as there are many different types of economic decisions, there are
many types of accounting information. The terms ***financial accounting,
management accounting,*** and ***tax accounting*** often are used in describing the types of accounting information most widely used in the business community.

Financial Accounting—"General-Purpose" Information Financial accounting refers to information describing the financial resources, obligations, and activities of an economic entity (either an organization or an individual). Accountants use the term ***financial position*** to describe an entity's financial resources and obligations at one point in time, and the term ***results of operations*** to describe its financial activities during the year.

Financial accounting information is designed primarily to assist ***investors*** and ***creditors*** in deciding where to place their scarce investment resources.[1] Such decisions are important to society, as they determine which companies and industries will receive the financial resources necessary for growth, and which will not.

However, many ***other*** decision makers also make use of financial accounting information. A company's managers and employees constantly need such information in order to run and control daily business operations. For example, they need to know the amount of money in the company's bank accounts, the types and quantities of merchandise in the company's warehouse, and the amounts owed to specific creditors. Financial accounting information also is used in income tax returns. In fact, financial accounting information is used for so many ***different purposes*** that it often is called ***general-purpose*** accounting information.

Management Accounting Management (or managerial) accounting involves the development and interpretation of accounting information intended ***specifically to aid management*** in running the business. Managers use this information in setting the company's overall goals, evaluating the performance of departments and individuals, deciding whether to introduce a new line of products—and in making virtually all types of managerial decisions.

Much "management accounting" information is financial in nature but has been organized in a manner relating directly to the decision at hand. However, management accounting information often includes evaluations of "nonfinancial" factors, such as political considerations, the possible effects of various actions upon the environment, the company's public image, and worker productivity.

The enormous storage capacity of computers enables large companies to maintain integrated ***management information systems,*** which provide decision makers with both financial and nonfinancial information. Financial information, however, comprises the largest component of every management information system. The reason is simple: by definition, ***every economic decision involves financial considerations.***

Tax Accounting The preparation of income tax returns is a specialized field within accounting. To a great extent, tax returns are based upon financial accounting information. However, the information often is adjusted or reorganized to conform with income tax reporting requirements.

---

[1] FASB, *Statement of Financial Accounting Concepts No. 1,* "Objectives of Financial Reporting by Business Enterprises," (Norwalk, Conn., 1978), para. 30.

The most challenging aspect of tax accounting is not the preparation of an income tax return but rather *tax planning.* Tax planning means anticipating the "tax effects" of business transactions and structuring these transactions in a manner that will minimize the income tax burden.

Focus of This Text   In this textbook, we begin by introducing the basic concepts of financial accounting. These discussions will emphasize both the process of *financial reporting* to investors and creditors and the usefulness of financial information to an organization's management and employees. In later chapters, our emphasis will shift toward management accounting and the use of accounting information in specific types of managerial decisions.

Major income tax concepts are discussed at various points throughout the text, and Chapter 18 is devoted entirely to this topic. Comprehensive coverage of income taxes, however, must be deferred to more advanced accounting courses.

Remember that the fields of financial, management, and tax accounting are *closely related.* Thus, we often address financial reporting requirements, management's information needs, and income tax considerations within a single chapter. Our emphasis throughout this text will be upon the accounting information developed in *profit-oriented business organizations.*[2]

THE FINANCIAL REPORTING PROCESS

All of the accounting information developed within a business is available to management. However, much of the company's financial accounting information also is used by decision makers *outside* of the organization. These outsiders include investors, financial analysts, investment advisors, creditors (lenders), labor unions, government agencies, and the public. Each of these groups either supplies money to the business or has some other interest in the financial health of the organization. A labor union, for example, needs information about a company's financial strength and profitability before negotiating a new labor contract.

Supplying general-purpose financial information about a business to people outside the organization is termed *financial reporting.* In the United States and most other industrialized countries, large "publicly owned" business organizations are required by law to make much of their accounting information public, that is, *available to everyone.*[3] These countries also have enacted laws to ensure that the *public information* provided by these organizations is reasonably *complete* and *reliable.*

Small businesses are *not* required to provide general-purpose financial information to persons outside the organization. In fact, many small busi-

---

[2]   The accounting practices of governmental agencies and other "not-for-profit" organizations differ in a number of ways from those of profit-oriented organizations. "Not-for-profit" accounting is a specialized topic and is addressed in advanced accounting courses.

[3]   A company is "publicly owned" whenever ownership "shares" in the company are offered for sale to the general public. Public information about a business can be obtained by writing to the company's corporate secretary.

nesses do not make such information available. However, banks and other creditors often *insist* upon receiving this information as a condition for making loans to the business.

Financial Statements

The principal means of reporting general-purpose financial information to persons outside a business organization is a set of accounting reports called *financial statements.* The persons receiving these reports are termed the *users* of the financial statements.

A set of financial statements consists of four related accounting reports that summarize in a few pages the *financial resources, obligations, profitability,* and *cash transactions of a business.* A complete set of financial statements includes:

1 A *balance sheet,* showing at a specific date the *financial position* of the company by indicating the resources that it owns, the debts that it owes, and the amount of the owner's *equity* (investment) in the business.

2 An *income statement,* indicating the *profitability* of the business over the preceding year (or other time period).

3 A *statement of owner's equity,* explaining certain changes in the amount of the owner's equity (investment) in the business. (In businesses which are organized as corporations, the statement of owner's equity is replaced by a *statement of retained earnings.*)

4 A *statement of cash flows,* summarizing the cash receipts and cash payments of the business over the same time period covered by the income statement.

In addition, a complete set of financial statements includes several pages of *notes,* containing additional information which accountants believe is *useful in the interpretation* of the financial statements.[4]

The basic purpose of financial statements is to assist users in evaluating the *financial position, profitability,* and *future prospects* of a business. In the United States, the annual (and quarterly) financial statements of all publicly owned corporations are *public information.*[5]

In deciding where to invest their resources, investors and creditors often compare the financial statements of many different companies. For such comparisons to be valid, the financial statements of these different companies must be reasonably *comparable*—that is, they must present similar information in a similar format. To achieve this goal, financial statements are prepared in conformity with a set of "ground rules" called *generally accepted accounting principles (GAAP).*

---

[4]   A complete set of financial statements, along with the accompanying notes, is illustrated in Comprehensive Problem 5, which follows Chapter 20.

[5]   In *annual* financial statements, the time period covered by the income statement, statement of retained earnings, and statement of cash flows is one year. In *quarterly* statements, the period covered in these statements is a quarter of a year (three months). The balance sheet reflects what the business owns and owes at the *end* of the time period covered by the other statements.

Financial Statements and Income Tax Returns The Internal Revenue Service (IRS) requires businesses and individuals to file annual income tax returns designed to measure taxable income. ***Taxable income*** is a legal concept defined by the United States Congress, and Congress frequently makes changes in these laws and regulations. In many instances, income tax laws are similar to generally accepted accounting principles; but in other cases, they are quite different. Therefore, an income tax return is a special accounting report, separate from the company's financial statements. A company's income tax return is sent only to tax authorities such as the IRS; it is ***not*** public information.

The Functions of an Accounting System

Most business organizations have an accounting system for preparing financial statements, income tax returns, reports to managers, bills to customers, and other types of accounting information. An accounting ***system*** consists of the personnel, procedures, devices, and records used by an entity in developing accounting information and in communicating this information to decision makers. Accounting systems often make use of computers and other electronic devices, as well as handwritten forms and records. In fact, the accounting system of any large business organization includes all of these components.

In every accounting system, the economic activities of the organization are ***recorded*** in the accounting records. Next, the recorded data are ***classified*** within the system to accumulate subtotals for various types of economic activities. Finally, the information is ***summarized*** in accounting reports designed to meet the information needs of various decision makers, such as investors, managers, and governmental agencies.

The "Transactions" Approach to Recording Economic Activity Accounting reports summarize information which has been recorded in the accounting system. In recording economic activities, accountants focus upon ***completed transactions***—that is, events that (1) cause an ***immediate change*** in the financial resources or obligations of the business and (2) can be ***measured objectively*** in monetary terms.[6] Examples of transactions include purchasing or selling goods or services, receiving cash, and making cash payments. The recording of transactions in an accounting system may be performed in many ways, such as writing with a pen or pencil, using a cash register, or entering data through a keyboard.

The primary strength of this "transactions approach" lies in the ***reliability*** of the information that is recorded. The recorded information is based upon past events, for which the financial effects upon the business can be measured with a reasonable degree of ***objectivity***.

In another respect, accountants' emphasis upon transactions ***lessens*** the usefulness of accounting reports. Some important events are not recorded in the accounting records, because they do not meet the definition of

---

[6] Accountants use the term ***objective*** to mean neutral, free from bias, and verifiable in amount. The concept of ***objectivity*** is a generally accepted accounting principle and has a profound effect upon accounting practices and accounting information. This concept is discussed further on page 17 and at many points throughout the text.

a transaction. For example, the death of a key executive, a technological breakthrough by the company's research department, or the introduction of a new product by a competitor are not "transactions," and therefore they are not recorded in the accounting records. These events may cause significant *future* changes in the financial resources and obligations of the business, but they do not cause *immediate* changes. In addition, the financial effects of these events cannot be measured with much objectivity.

The preceding events are examples of important "nonfinancial" information. Although these events are not recorded in the accounting records, they are recorded elsewhere in the management information system. In addition, these events are disclosed to persons outside of the business organization through press conferences, notes to the financial statements, or the news media.

Internal Control

The decisions made by management are based to a considerable extent upon information developed by the accounting system. Therefore, management needs assurance that all the accounting information it receives is accurate and reliable. This assurance is provided by the company's *system of internal control* (or *internal control structure*). A simple example of an internal control procedure is the use of serial numbers on checks issued. Accounting for an unbroken sequence of serial numbers provides assurance that every check issued has been recorded in the accounting records.

A *system of internal control* includes all measures used by an organization to guard against errors, waste, and fraud; to assure the reliability of accounting data; to promote compliance with management policies; and to evaluate the level of performance in all divisions of the company. In short, a system of internal control includes all of the measures designed to assure management that the entire organization *operates according to plan.*

Audits of Financial Statements

What assurance do outsiders have that the financial statements issued by management provide a complete and reliable picture of the company's financial position and operating results? In large part, this assurance is provided by an *audit* of the company's financial statements, performed by a firm of *certified public accountants (CPAs).* These auditors are experts in the field of financial reporting and are *independent* of the company issuing the financial statements.

An *audit* is an *investigation* of a company's financial statements, designed to determine the "fairness" of these statements. Accountants and auditors use the term *fair* in describing financial statements which are reliable and complete, conform to generally accepted accounting principles, and are *not misleading.*

As part of the audit, the CPAs investigate the quality of the company's system of internal control, count or observe many of the company's assets, and gather evidence both from within the business and from outside sources. Based upon this careful investigation, the CPA firm expresses its *professional opinion* as to the fairness of the financial statements. This opinion, called the ***auditors' report,*** accompanies the financial statements distributed to persons outside the business organization.

Auditors do not guarantee the accuracy of financial statements; they only express their expert opinion as to the fairness of the statements. However, CPA firms stake their reputations on the thoroughness of their audits and the dependability of their audit reports. Over many years, audited financial statements have established an impressive track record of reliability.

Annual Reports

As part of the financial reporting process, large business organizations prepare ***annual reports*** for distribution to investors and to anyone requesting a copy. Included in these annual reports are audited financial statements for each of the last several years. These ***comparative*** financial statements enable users to identify trends in the company's performance and financial position. Annual reports also include the auditor's reports on the comparative statements and discussions by top management of the company's financial position, profitability, and future prospects. In addition, they contain much nonfinancial information about the company's objectives, products, and operations.

CASE IN POINT   McDonald's Corporation devoted much of a recent annual report to the company's concern for the environment. Included in the report were discussions of the company's programs for solid waste management, resource conservation, and recycling. (The annual report was printed entirely on recycled paper.)

Financial Reporting: A Multimedia Process

Although financial statements are the ***primary*** means of financial reporting, they are not the ***only*** means. Information about a business is also made available to outside decision makers through news conferences, press releases, annual reports, and filings of public information with governmental agencies. In addition, many financial analysts, investment advisory services, and business magazines continually evaluate the financial position, profitability, and future prospects of publicly owned companies. Many such evaluations are readily available to the public at little or no cost.

CASE IN POINT   Financial analysts share their views with the public every Friday night on *Wall $treet Week,* a television program broadcast over PBS. Weekly business magazines, such as *Barrons, Business Week,* and *Forbes,* also publish evaluations of the financial position, profitability, and future prospects of many publicly owned companies.

The Use of Computers in Accounting Systems

Computers are tools widely used by accountants for recording, processing, and storing accounting information. In addition, the use of computers helps make accounting information **more useful to decision makers.** First, computers enable accountants to assemble information and deliver it to decision makers far more quickly than is possible in a manual system. Of even greater importance, computers enable accountants to classify and summarize data **in many different ways.** For example, the daily sales reports prepared for the manager of a large department store may be most useful if sales are summarized **by department.** In sales reports prepared for the store's merchandise buyers, however, it may be more useful to summarize the daily sales **by product.** Thus, computers assist accountants in tailoring accounting reports to the needs of specific decision makers.

The Distinction between Accounting and Bookkeeping

Persons with little knowledge of accounting may fail to understand the distinction between accounting and bookkeeping. **Bookkeeping** refers to the daily operation of an accounting system—that is, recording and classifying routine transactions. Bookkeeping is a skill that an individual might acquire within a few weeks or months. Most bookkeeping functions can be performed most efficiently through the use of a computer.

A professional accountant must have a far broader range of knowledge and skills than a bookkeeper. For example, accountants need an understanding of financial reporting requirements, income tax regulations, and the regulatory requirements affecting specific industries. They should be able to design accounting systems and systems of internal control, interpret and record complex transactions, and assist managers in interpreting all types of accounting information. Most importantly, accountants must be able to exercise **professional judgment** in order to resolve problems that do not have "official" solutions.[7]

Accounting is more than a skill—it is a **profession.** To become a professional accountant requires a formal education, experience, and a commitment to continually updating and expanding one's knowledge.

GENERALLY ACCEPTED ACCOUNTING PRINCIPLES (GAAP)

OBJECTIVE 2
Explain the phrase "generally accepted accounting principles."

Generally accepted accounting principles (or **GAAP**) are the "ground rules" for financial reporting. These principles provide the general framework determining **what information is included in financial statements and how this information is to be presented.** The phrase "generally accepted accounting principles" encompasses the basic objectives of financial reporting, as well as numerous broad concepts and many detailed rules. Thus, such terms as **objectives, standards, concepts, assump-**

---

[7] In large part, it is the need for individual practitioners to exercise **their own judgment** in resolving problems which distinguishes "professions" from other occupations. Throughout this text, we will emphasize those situations which require accountants to exercise their professional judgment.

tions, methods, and ***rules*** often are used in describing specific generally accepted accounting "principles."

We already have discussed two concepts embodied in generally accepted accounting principles: ***comparability*** (among different companies) and ***reliability.*** In this chapter we will discuss six other generally accepted accounting principles: the ***entity principle,*** the ***cost principle,*** the ***going-concern assumption,*** the ***objectivity principle,*** the ***stable-dollar assumption,*** and the ***concept of adequate disclosure.*** These and other accounting principles will be considered further at many points throughout this book.

Let us emphasize, however, that ***there is no comprehensive list of generally accepted accounting principles.*** In fact, new accounting principles emerge continuously as business organizations enter into new forms of business activity.

The Nature of Accounting Principles

Accounting principles are not like physical laws; they do not exist in nature awaiting discovery. Rather, they are ***developed by people,*** in light of what we consider to be the most important objectives of financial reporting. In many ways generally accepted accounting principles are similar to the rules established for an organized sport, such as football or basketball. For example, accounting principles, like sports rules:

- Originate from a combination of tradition, experience, and official decree.
- Require authoritative support and some means of enforcement.
- Are sometimes arbitrary.
- May change over time as shortcomings in the existing rules come to light.
- Must be clearly understood and observed by all participants in the process.

Unfortunately, accounting principles vary somewhat from country to country. The phrase "generally accepted accounting principles" refers to the accounting concepts in use in the United States. However, the principles in use in Canada, Great Britain, and a number of other countries are quite similar. Also, foreign companies that raise capital from American investors usually issue financial statements in conformity with the generally accepted accounting principles in use in the United States.

Several international organizations currently are attempting to establish greater uniformity among the accounting principles in use around the world.

Organizations Influencing Accounting Practice

Many organizations play an active role in developing generally accepted accounting principles and in improving the quality of financial reporting in the United States. Among the most influential of these organizations are the Financial Accounting Standards Board, the American Institute of Certified Public Accountants, the Securities and Exchange Commission, and the American Accounting Association.

Financial Accounting Standards Board (FASB) Today, the most authoritative source of generally accepted accounting principles is the Financial Accounting Standards Board, known as the FASB. The ***FASB*** is a highly independent rule-making body, consisting of seven members from the accounting profession, industry, government, and accounting education. Lending support to these members are an advisory council and a large research staff.

The FASB is authorized to issue *Statements of Financial Accounting Standards,* which represent official expressions of generally accepted accounting principles. To date, the FASB has issued over 100 such *Statements,* along with a number of *Interpretations* and *Technical Bulletins.*

In addition to issuing authoritative *Statements,* the FASB has completed a project describing a ***conceptual framework*** for financial reporting. This conceptual framework sets forth the FASB's views as to the:

■ Objectives of financial reporting.

■ Desired characteristics of accounting information (such as relevance, reliability, and understandability).

■ Elements of financial statements.

■ Criteria for deciding what information to include in financial statements.

■ Valuation concepts relating to financial statement amounts.

The primary purpose of the conceptual framework is to provide guidance to the FASB in developing new accounting standards.[8] By making each new standard consistent with this framework, the FASB hopes that its official *Statements* will resolve accounting problems in a logical and consistent manner. (The conceptual framework itself is not "officially binding" upon companies engaged in financial reporting, as are the FASB's *Statements.*)

The FASB is part of the private sector of the economy—***it is not a governmental agency.*** The development of accounting principles in the United States traditionally has been carried out in the private sector, although the government, acting through the Securities and Exchange Commission, exercises considerable influence.

American Institute of Certified Public Accountants (AICPA) The AICPA is a professional association of certified public accountants. Prior to the creation of the FASB, committees of the AICPA were responsible for defining generally accepted accounting principles.

The AICPA participates actively in many aspects of accounting. For example, it has developed a ***code of professional ethics*** to be followed by all of its members. In addition, a committee of the AICPA establishes the professional ***auditing standards*** to be followed by CPAs in auditing financial statements. The AICPA also conducts research into accounting issues and makes its findings known to the FASB.

Securities and Exchange Commission (SEC) The SEC is a governmental agency with the ***legal power*** to establish accounting principles and finan-

---

[8]   FASB, *Statement of Financial Accounting Concepts No. 1,* "Objectives of Financial Reporting by Business Enterprises," (Norwalk, Conn., 1978), p. 4.

cial reporting requirements for publicly owned corporations. In the past, the SEC has tended to adopt the recommendations of the FASB, rather than to develop its own set of accounting principles. Thus, accounting principles continue to be developed in the private sector but are given the *force of law* when they are adopted by the SEC.

To assure widespread acceptance of new accounting standards, the FASB *needs* the support of the SEC. Therefore, the two organizations work closely together in developing new accounting standards. The SEC also reviews the financial statements of publicly owned corporations to assure compliance with its reporting requirements. In the event that a publicly owned corporation fails to comply with these requirements, the SEC may initiate legal action against the company and the responsible individuals. Thus, the SEC "enforces" compliance with generally accepted accounting principles.

American Accounting Association (AAA)   The AAA is comprised primarily of accounting educators. The Association has sponsored a number of research studies and monographs in which individual authors and Association committees have taken positions on various accounting issues. However, the AAA does not have any official authority to impose its views; its influence stems only from the prestige of its authors and the persuasiveness of their arguments.

The AAA also sponsors the Accounting Education Change Commission, which currently is seeking new and innovative ways to enhance accounting education.

"Authoritative Support" for Accounting Principles   To qualify as "generally accepted," an accounting principle must have "substantial authoritative support." Principles, standards, and rules set forth by the official rule-making bodies of the accounting profession, such as the FASB, automatically qualify as generally accepted accounting principles. However, many concepts and practices gain substantial authoritative support from *unofficial* sources, such as widespread use or recognition in textbooks and other "unofficial" accounting literature. Thus, the phrase "generally accepted accounting principles" includes more concepts and practices than appear in the "official" literature.

FINANCIAL STATEMENTS: THE STARTING POINT IN THE STUDY OF ACCOUNTING

The preparation of financial statements is not the first step in the accounting process, but it is a logical point to begin the *study* of accounting. Financial statements convey to management and to interested outsiders a concise picture of the profitability and financial position of a business. These statements—each less than a page in length—summarize the thousands or even millions of transactions recorded during the year in the company's accounting system. Thus, financial statements are the *end product* of the accounting process. The student who acquires a clear understanding of the nature and content of these statements is in a better position to appreciate the objectives of the earlier steps of recording and classifying business transactions.

The three most widely used financial statements are the **balance sheet,** the **income statement,** and the **statement of cash flows.** In this introductory chapter and in Chapter 2, we shall explore the nature of the balance sheet, or **statement of financial position,** as it is often called. Once we have become familiar with the form and arrangement of the balance sheet and with the meanings of technical terms such as **assets, liabilities,** and **owner's equity,** it will be as easy to read and understand a report on the financial position of a business as it is for an architect to read a blueprint for a proposed building. (We shall discuss the income statement in Chapter 3, and the statement of cash flows later in the course.)

The Balance Sheet

OBJECTIVE 3 Describe and prepare a balance sheet; define assets, liabilities, and owner's equity.

The purpose of a balance sheet is to show the **financial position** of a **given business entity** at a **specific date.** Every business prepares a balance sheet at the end of the year, and most companies prepare one at the end of each month. A balance sheet consists of a listing of the assets, the liabilities, and the owner's equity of a business. The **balance sheet date** is important, as the financial position of a business may change quickly. A balance sheet is most useful if it is **relatively recent.** The following balance sheet shows the financial position of **Vagabond Travel Agency** at **December 31, 1994.**

A balance sheet shows financial position at a specific date

VAGABOND TRAVEL AGENCY
Balance Sheet
December 31, 1994

Assets		Liabilities & Owner's Equity	
Cash	$ 22,500	Liabilities:	
Notes receivable	10,000	Notes payable	$ 41,000
Accounts receivable	60,500	Accounts payable	36,000
Supplies	2,000	Salaries payable	3,000
Land	100,000	Total liabilities	$ 80,000
Building	90,000	Owner's equity:	
Office equipment	15,000	Terry Crane, capital	220,000
Total	$300,000	Total	$300,000

Let us briefly describe several features of this balance sheet. First, the heading sets forth three things: (1) the name of the business entity, (2) the name of the financial statement, and (3) the balance sheet date. The body of the balance sheet also consists of three distinct sections: **assets, liabilities,** and **owner's equity.**

Notice that cash is listed first among the assets, followed by notes receivable, accounts receivable, supplies, and any other assets that will **soon be converted into cash or consumed in business operations.** Following these relatively "liquid" assets are the more "permanent" assets, such as land, buildings, and equipment.

Liabilities are shown before owner's equity. Each major type of liability (such as notes payable, accounts payable, and salaries payable) is listed separately, followed by a figure for total liabilities.

Finally, notice that the amount of total assets ($300,000) is *equal* to the total amount of liabilities and owner's equity (also $300,000). This relationship *always exists*—in fact, the *equality of these totals* is one reason that this financial statement is called a *balance* sheet.

The Concept of the Business Entity   Generally accepted accounting principles require that a set of financial statements describe the affairs of a specific business entity. This concept is called the *entity principle.*

A *business entity* is an economic unit that engages in *identifiable business activities.* For accounting purposes, the business entity is regarded as *separate from the personal affairs of its owner.* For example, Vagabond is a business organization operating as a travel agency. Its owner, Terry Crane, may have a personal bank account, a home, a car, and even another business, such as a cattle ranch. These items are *not involved in the operation of the travel agency* and should not appear in Vagabond's financial statements.

If the owner were to intermingle his or her personal affairs with the transactions of the business, the resulting financial statements would fail to describe clearly the financial position and operating results of the business organization.

Assets

Assets are economic resources which are owned by a business and are expected to benefit future operations. Assets may have definite physical form, as do buildings, machinery, and an inventory of merchandise. On the other hand, some assets exist not in physical or tangible form but in the form of valuable legal claims or rights; examples are amounts due from customers, investments in government bonds, and patent rights.

One of the most basic and at the same time most controversial problems in accounting is determining dollar values for the various assets of a business. At present, generally accepted accounting principles call for the valuation of assets in a balance sheet at *cost,* rather than at appraised market values. The specific accounting principles supporting cost as the basis for asset valuation are discussed below.

OBJECTIVE 4
Describe the accounting principles involved in asset valuation.

The Cost Principle   Assets such as land, buildings, merchandise, and equipment are typical of the many economic resources that will be used in producing income for the business. The prevailing accounting view is that such assets should be recorded at their cost. When we say that an asset is shown in the balance sheet at its *historical cost,* we mean the dollar amount originally paid to acquire the asset; this amount may be very different from what we would have to pay today to replace it.

For example, let us assume that a business buys a tract of land for use as a building site, paying $100,000 in cash. The amount to be entered in the accounting records as the value of the asset will be the cost of $100,000. If we assume a booming real estate market, a fair estimate of the sales value of the land 10 years later might be $250,000. Although the market price or economic value of the land has risen greatly, the accounting value as shown in the accounting records and in the balance sheet would continue unchanged at the cost of $100,000. This policy of accounting for assets at their cost is often referred to as the ***cost principle*** of accounting.

In reading a balance sheet, it is important to bear in mind that the dollar amounts listed do not indicate the prices at which the assets could be sold nor the prices at which they could be replaced. One useful generalization to be drawn from this discussion is that a balance sheet ***does not*** show "how much a business is ***worth***."

The Going-Concern Assumption   It is appropriate to ask ***why*** accountants do not change the recorded values of assets to correspond with changing market prices for these properties. One reason is that the land and building being used to house the business were acquired for ***use*** and not for resale; in fact, these assets cannot be sold without disrupting the business. The balance sheet of a business is prepared on the assumption that the business is a continuing enterprise, a "going concern." Consequently, the present estimated prices at which the land and buildings could be sold are of less importance than if these properties were intended for sale.

The Objectivity Principle   Another reason for using cost rather than current market values in accounting for assets is the need for a definite, factual basis for valuation. Accountants use the term ***objective*** to describe asset valuations that are factual and can be verified by independent experts. For example, if land is shown on the balance sheet at cost, any CPA who performed an audit of the business would be able to find objective evidence that the land was actually valued at the cost of acquiring it. Estimated market values, on the other hand, for assets such as buildings and specialized machinery are not factual and objective. Market values are constantly changing, and estimates of the prices at which assets could be sold are largely a matter of personal opinion.

At the date an asset is acquired, the cost and market value usually are the same. The bargaining process which results in the sale of an asset serves to establish both the current market value of the property and the cost to the buyer. With the passage of time, however, the current market value of assets is likely to differ considerably from the cost recorded in the owner's accounting records.

The Stable-Dollar Assumptions   Severe inflation in several countries in recent years has raised serious doubts as to the adequacy of the conventional cost basis in accounting for assets. When inflation becomes very severe, historical cost values for assets simply lose their relevance as a basis for making business decisions. Much consideration has been given to the use of balance sheets which would show assets at current appraised values or at replacement costs rather than at historical cost.

Accountants in the United States by adhering to the cost basis of accounting are implying that the dollar is a ***stable unit of measurement,*** as is the gallon, the acre, or the mile. The cost principle and the stable-dollar assumption work very well in periods of stable prices but are less satisfactory under conditions of rapid inflation. For example, if a company bought land 20 years ago for $100,000 and purchased a second similar tract of land today for $500,000, the total cost of land shown by the accounting records would be $600,000. This treatment ignores the fact that dollars spent 20 years ago had far greater purchasing power than today's dollar. Thus, the $600,000 total for cost of land is a mixture of two kinds of dollars with very different purchasing power.

After much research into this problem, the FASB required on a trial basis that large corporations report supplementary data showing current replacement costs and price-level adjusted data. However, after a few years, the cost of developing and disclosing such information in financial statements was judged to be greater than the benefits provided. Consequently, the disclosure requirement was eliminated. At the present time, the stable-dollar assumption continues in use in the United States—perhaps until challenged by more severe inflation sometime in the future.

Liabilities

Liabilities are debts. All business concerns have liabilities; even the largest and most successful companies find it convenient to purchase merchandise and supplies on credit rather than to pay cash at the time of each purchase. The liability arising from the purchase of goods or services on credit is called an ***account payable,*** and the person or company to whom the account payable is owed is called a ***creditor.***

A business concern frequently finds it desirable to borrow money as a means of supplementing the funds invested by the owner, thus enabling the business to expand more rapidly. The borrowed funds may, for example, be used to buy merchandise which can be sold at a profit to the firm's customers. Or the borrowed money might be used to buy new and more efficient machinery, thus enabling the company to turn out a larger volume of products at lower cost. When a business borrows money for any reason, a liability is incurred and the lender becomes a creditor of the business. The form of the liability when money is borrowed is usually a ***note payable,*** a formal written promise to pay a certain amount of money, plus interest, at a definite future time.

An ***account payable,*** as contrasted with a ***note payable,*** does not involve the issuance of a formal written promise to the creditor, and it does not call for payment of interest. When a business has both notes payable and accounts payable, the two types of liabilities are shown separately in the balance sheet, with notes payable usually listed first. A figure showing the total of the liabilities should also be inserted, as shown by the illustrated balance sheet on page 15.

The creditors have claims against the assets of the business, usually not against any particular asset but against the assets in general. The claims of the creditors are liabilities of the business and have priority over the claims of owners. Creditors are entitled to be paid in full even if such payment should exhaust the assets of the business, leaving nothing for the owner.

Owner's Equity

The owner's equity in a business represents the resources invested by the owner (or owners). The equity of the owner is a ***residual claim,*** because the claims of the creditors legally come first. If you are the owner of a business, you are entitled to whatever remains *after the claims of the creditors are fully satisfied.* Thus, owner's equity is equal to the *total assets minus the liabilities.* For example, using the data from the illustrated balance sheet of Vagabond Travel Agency (page 15):

Vagabond has total assets of	*$300,000*
And total liabilities amounting to	*80,000*
Therefore, the owner's equity must equal	*$220,000*

Suppose that Vagabond borrows $20,000 from a bank. After recording the additional asset of $20,000 in cash and recording the new liability of $20,000 owed to the bank, we would have the following:

Vagabond now has total assets of	*$320,000*
And total liabilities are now	*100,000*
*Therefore, the owner's equity **still** is equal to*	*$220,000*

It is apparent that the total assets of the business were increased by the act of borrowing money from a bank, but the increase in total assets was exactly offset by an increase in liabilities, and the owner's equity remained unchanged. The owner's equity in a business *is not increased* by the incurring of liabilities of any kind.

Increases in Owner's Equity   The owner's equity in a business comes from two sources:

1 Investment by the owner
2 Earnings from profitable operation of the business

Only the first of these two sources of owner's equity is considered in this chapter. The second source, an increase in owner's equity through earnings of the business, will be discussed in Chapter 3.

Decreases in Owner's Equity   If you are the owner of a sole proprietorship, you have the right to withdraw cash or other assets from the business at any time. Because you want to see the business succeed, you will probably not make withdrawals that would handicap the business in operating efficiently. Withdrawals are most often made by writing a check drawn on the company's bank account and payable to the owner. Other types of withdrawals also occur, such as taking office equipment out of the business for personal use by the owner or using cash belonging to the business to pay the personal debts of the owner. Every withdrawal by the owner reduces the total assets of the business and also reduces the owner's equity.

In summary, decreases in the owner's equity in a business are caused in two ways:

1 *Withdrawals* of cash or other assets by the owner
2 *Losses* from unprofitable operation of the business

Accounting for these types of transactions will be explained and illustrated in Chapter 3.

The Accounting Equation

A fundamental characteristic of every balance sheet is that the total dollar amount of assets is **equal to** the total of liabilities and owner's equity. As stated earlier, the equality of these two totals is one reason for calling this financial statement a **balance sheet.** But **why** do total assets always equal the total of liabilities and owner's equity? The answer can be given in one short paragraph.

The dollar totals on the two sides of the balance sheet are always equal because these two sides are merely two views of the same business property. The listing of assets shows us **what resources** the business owns; the listing of liabilities and owner's equity tells us **who supplied these resources** to the business and how much each group supplied. Everything that a business owns has been supplied to it by the creditors or by the owner. Therefore, the total claims of the creditors plus the claim of the owner equal the total assets of the business.

The equality of assets on the one hand and of the claims of the creditors and the owner on the other hand is expressed in the equation:

The basic "accounting equation"

$$\text{Assets} = \text{Liabilities} + \text{Owner's Equity}$$
$$\$300,000 = \$80,000 + \$220,000$$

The amounts listed in the equation were taken from the balance sheet illustrated on page 15. A balance sheet is simply a detailed statement of this equation. To illustrate this relationship, compare the balance sheet of Vagabond Travel Agency with the above equation.

To emphasize that the equity of the owner is a residual element, secondary to the claims of creditors, it is often helpful to transpose the terms of the equation, as follows:

Alternative form of equation

$$\text{Assets} - \text{Liabilities} = \text{Owner's Equity}$$
$$\$300,000 - \$80,000 = \$220,000$$

Every business transaction, no matter how simple or how complex, can be expressed in terms of its effect on the accounting equation. A thorough understanding of the equation and some practice in using it are essential to the student of accounting.

Regardless of whether a business grows or contracts, this equality between the assets and the claims against the assets is always maintained. Any increase in the amount of total assets is necessarily accompanied by an equal increase on the other side of the equation, that is, by an increase in either the liabilities or the owner's equity. Any decrease in total assets is necessarily accompanied by a corresponding decrease in liabilities or owner's equity. The continuing equality of the two sides of the balance sheet can best be illustrated by taking a brand-new business as an example and observing the effects of various transactions upon its balance sheet.

Effects of Business Transactions upon the Balance Sheet

Assume that James Roberts, a licensed real estate broker, decided to start a real estate business of his own, to be known as Roberts Real Estate

OBJECTIVE 5
*Indicate the
effects of
various
transactions
upon the
accounting
equation
and the bal-
ance sheet.*

Company. The planned operations of the new business call for obtaining "listings" of houses being offered for sale by owners, advertising these houses, and showing them to prospective buyers. The listing agreement signed with each owner provides that Roberts Real Estate Company shall receive at the time of sale a commission equal to 6% of the sales price of the property.

The new business was begun on September 1, when Roberts deposited $180,000 in a bank account in the name of the business, Roberts Real Estate Company. The initial balance sheet of the new business then appeared as follows:

Beginning balance sheet of a new business

ROBERTS REAL ESTATE COMPANY
Balance Sheet
September 1, 19___

Assets		Owner's Equity	
Cash	$180,000	James Roberts, capital	$180,000

Observe that the equity of the owner in the assets is designated on the balance sheet by the caption, ***James Roberts, capital.*** The word ***capital*** is the traditional accounting term used in describing the equity of the proprietor in the assets of the business.

Purchase of an Asset for Cash   The next transaction entered into by Roberts Real Estate Company was the purchase of land suitable as a site for an office. The price for the land was $141,000 and payment was made in cash on September 3. The effect of this transaction on the balance sheet was twofold: first, cash was decreased by the amount paid out; and second, a new asset, Land, was acquired. After this exchange of cash for land, the balance sheet appeared as follows:

Balance sheet totals unchanged by purchase of land for cash

ROBERTS REAL ESTATE COMPANY
Balance Sheet
September 3, 19___

Assets		Owner's Equity	
Cash	$ 39,000	James Roberts, capital	$180,000
Land	141,000		
Total assets	$180,000	Total owner's equity	$180,000

Purchase of an Asset and Incurring of a Liability   On September 5 an opportunity arose to buy from Kent Company a complete office building which had to be moved to permit the construction of a freeway. A price of $36,000 was agreed upon, which included the cost of moving the building and installing it upon the Roberts Company's lot. As the building was in excellent condition and would have cost approximately $80,000 to build, Roberts considered this a very fortunate purchase.

The terms provided for an immediate cash payment of $15,000 and payment of the balance of $21,000 within 90 days. Cash was decreased $15,000, but a new asset, Building, was recorded at cost in the amount of $36,000. Total assets were thus increased by $21,000, but the total of liabilities and owner's equity was also increased as a result of recording the $21,000 account payable as a liability. After this transaction had been recorded, the balance sheet appeared as shown below. (Remember that cash is always the first asset listed in a balance sheet.)

ROBERTS REAL ESTATE COMPANY
Balance Sheet
September 5, 19__

Totals increased equally by purchase on credit

Assets		Liabilities & Owner's Equity	
Cash	$ 24,000	Liabilities:	
Land	141,000	Accounts payable	$ 21,000
Building	36,000	Owner's equity:	
		James Roberts, capital	180,000
Total	$201,000	Total	$201,000

Note that the building appears in the balance sheet at $36,000, its cost to Roberts Real Estate Company. The estimate of $80,000 as the probable cost to construct such a building is irrelevant. Even if someone should offer to buy the building from Roberts Company for $80,000 or more, this offer, if refused, would have no bearing on the balance sheet. In a balance sheet, most assets are valued at their *cost,* not at their current market values.

Sale of an Asset After the office building had been moved to the Roberts Company's lot, Roberts decided that the lot was larger than was needed. The adjoining business, Carter's Drugstore, wanted more room for a parking area, so, on September 10, Roberts Company sold a small, unused corner of the lot to Carter's Drugstore for a price of $11,000. Since the sales price was computed at the same amount per square foot as Roberts Company had paid for the land, there was neither a profit nor a loss on the sale. No down payment was required, but it was agreed that the full price would be paid within three months. In this transaction a new asset, Accounts Receivable, was acquired, but the asset Land was decreased by the same amount. Consequently, there was no change in the amount of total assets. After this transaction, the balance sheet appeared as follows:

ROBERTS REAL ESTATE COMPANY
Balance Sheet
September 10, 19__

No change in totals by sale of land at cost

Assets		Liabilities & Owner's Equity	
Cash	$ 24,000	Liabilities:	
Accounts receivable	11,000	Accounts payable	$ 21,000
Land	130,000	Owner's equity:	
Building	36,000	James Roberts, capital	180,000
Total	$201,000	Total	$201,000

In the illustration thus far, Roberts Real Estate Company has an account receivable from only one debtor, and an account payable to only one creditor. As the business grows, the number of debtors and creditors will increase, but the Accounts Receivable and Accounts Payable designations will continue to be used. The additional records necessary to show the amount receivable from each individual debtor and the amount owing to each individual creditor will be explained in Chapter 5.

Purchase of an Asset on Credit A complete set of office furniture and equipment was purchased on credit from General Equipment, Inc., on September 14 for $5,400. As the result of this transaction the business owned a new asset, Office Equipment, but it had also incurred a new liability in the form of Accounts Payable. The increase in total assets was exactly offset by the increase in liabilities. After this transaction the balance sheet appeared as follows:

ROBERTS REAL ESTATE COMPANY
Balance Sheet
September 14, 19__

Assets		Liabilities & Owner's Equity	
Cash	$ 24,000	Liabilities:	
Accounts receivable	11,000	Accounts payable	$ 26,400
Land	130,000	Owner's equity:	
Building	36,000	James Roberts, capital	180,000
Office equipment	5,400		
Total	$206,400	Total	$206,400

Total increased by acquiring asset on credit

Collection of an Account Receivable On September 20, cash in the amount of $1,500 was received as partial settlement of the account receivable from Carter's Drugstore. This transaction caused cash to increase and the accounts receivable to decrease by an equal amount. In essence, this transaction was merely the exchange of one asset for another of equal value. Consequently, there was no change in the amount of total assets. After this transaction, the balance sheet appeared as follows:

ROBERTS REAL ESTATE COMPANY
Balance Sheet
September 20, 19__

Assets		Liabilities & Owner's Equity	
Cash	$ 25,500	Liabilities:	
Accounts receivable	9,500	Accounts payable	$ 26,400
Land	130,000	Owner's equity:	
Building	36,000	James Roberts, capital	180,000
Office equipment	5,400		
Total	$206,400	Total	$206,400

Totals unchanged by collection of an account receivable

Payment of a Liability On September 30, Roberts Real Estate Company paid $3,000 in cash to General Equipment, Inc. This payment caused a decrease in cash and an equal decrease in liabilities. Therefore the balance sheet totals were still in balance. After this transaction, the balance sheet appeared as follows:

ROBERTS REAL ESTATE COMPANY
Balance Sheet
September 30, 19—

Totals de-creased by paying a liabil-ity

Assets		Liabilities & Owner's Equity	
Cash	$ 22,500	Liabilities:	
Accounts receivable	9,500	Accounts payable	$ 23,400
Land	130,000	Owner's equity:	
Building	36,000	James Roberts, capital	180,000
Office equipment	5,400		
Total	$203,400	Total	$203,400

The transactions which have been illustrated for the month of September were merely preliminary to the formal opening for business of Roberts Real Estate Company on October 1. Since we have assumed that the business earned no commissions and incurred no expenses during September, the owner's equity at September 30 is shown in the above balance sheet at $180,000, unchanged from the original investment by Roberts on September 1. September was a month devoted exclusively to organizing the business and not to regular operations. In succeeding chapters we shall continue the example of Roberts Real Estate Company by illustrating operating transactions and considering how the net income of the business can be determined.

Effect of Business Transactions upon the Accounting Equation

A balance sheet is merely a detailed expression of the accounting equation, *Assets = Liabilities + Owner's Equity.* To emphasize the relationship between the accounting equation and the balance sheet, let us now repeat the September transactions of Roberts Real Estate Company to show the effect of each transaction upon the accounting equation. Briefly restated, the seven transactions were as follows:

Sept. 1   Began the business by depositing $180,000 in a company bank account.

2   Purchased land for $141,000 cash.

5   Purchased a prefabricated building for $36,000, paying $15,000 cash and incurring a liability of $21,000.

10   Sold part of the land at a price equal to cost of $11,000, collectible within three months.

14   Purchased office equipment on credit for $5,400.

20   Received $1,500 cash as partial collection of the $11,000 account receivable.

30   Paid $3,000 on accounts payable.

The table below shows the effects of each of the September transactions on the accounting equation. The final line in the table corresponds to the amounts in the balance sheet at the end of September. Note that the equality of the two sides of the equation was maintained throughout the recording of the transactions.

	Cash	+	Accounts Receivable	+	Land	+	Building	+	Office Equipment	=	Accounts Payable	+	James Roberts, Capital
Sept. 1	+$180,000		–0–		–0–		–0–		–0–		–0–		+$180,000
Sept. 3	–141,000				+$141,000								
Balances	$39,000		–0–		$141,000		–0–		–0–		–0–		$180,000
Sept. 5	–15,000						+$36,000				+$21,000		
Balances	$24,000		–0–		$141,000		$36,000		–0–		$21,000		$180,000
Sept. 10			+$11,000		–11,000								
Balances	$24,000		$11,000		$130,000		$36,000		–0–		$21,000		$180,000
Sep. 14									+$5,400		+5,400		
Balances	$24,000		$11,000		$130,000		$36,000		$5,400		$26,400		$180,000
Sept. 20	+1,500		–1,500										
Balances	$25,500		$9,500		$130,000		$36,000		$5,400		$26,400		$180,000
Sept. 30	–3,000										–3,000		
Balances	$22,500	+	$9,500	+	$130,000	+	$36,000	+	$5,400	=	$23,400	+	$180,000

FORMS OF BUSINESS ORGANIZATIONS

In the United States, a business enterprise may be organized as a *sole proprietorship,* a *partnership,* or a *corporation.* Generally accepted accounting principles apply to the financial statements of all three forms of organization.

Sole Proprietorships

A business owned by one person is called a ***sole proprietorship.*** Often the owner also acts as the manager. Roberts Real Estate Company, the company used in our illustration, is a sole proprietorship owned by James Roberts. This form of business organization is common for small retail stores, farms, service businesses, and professional practices in law, medicine, and public accounting. In fact, the sole proprietorship is by far the most common form of business organization in our economy.

From an accounting viewpoint, a sole proprietorship is regarded as a business entity ***separate from the other affairs of its owner.*** From a legal viewpoint, however, the business and its owner are not regarded as separate entities. Thus, ***the owner is personally liable*** for the debts of the business. If the business becomes insolvent, creditors can force the owner to sell his or her personal assets to pay the business debts.

Partnerships

An unincorporated business owned by two or more persons voluntarily acting as partners (co-owners) is called a ***partnership.*** Partnerships, like sole proprietorships, are widely used for small businesses. In addition, some very large professional practices, including international CPA firms, are organized as partnerships. As in the case of the sole proprietorship, the owners of a partnership are personally responsible for all debts of the business. From an accounting standpoint, a partnership is viewed as a business entity separate from the personal affairs of its owners.

Corporations

A corporation is the only type of business organization recognized ***under the law*** as an entity separate from its owners. Therefore, the owners of a corporation are ***not*** personally liable for the debts of the business. These owners can lose no more than the amounts they have invested in the business—a concept known as ***limited liability.*** This concept is the principal reason why corporations are the most attractive form of business organization to many investors.

Ownership of a corporation is divided into transferable shares of capital stock, and the owners are called ***stockholders.*** Stock certificates are issued by the corporation to each stockholder showing the number of shares that he or she owns. The stockholders are free to sell some or all of these shares to other investors at any time. This ***transferability of ownership*** adds to the attractiveness of the corporate form of organization, because investors can more easily "get their money out" of the business.

There are many more sole proprietorships and partnerships than corporations, but most large businesses are organized as corporations. Thus, corporations are the ***dominant form*** of business organization in terms of the dollar volume of their business activities. In addition, it is primarily corporations that distribute their financial statements to investors and other outsiders.

Reporting Ownership Equity in the Balance Sheet

Assets and liabilities are presented in the same manner in the balance sheets of all three types of business organization. Some differences arise, however, in the presentation of the ownership equity.

Roberts Real Estate Company is a sole proprietorship, owned by one person. Therefore, the owner's equity section of the balance sheet includes only one item: the equity of the proprietor, James Roberts. If the business were a partnership with two or more owners, we would use the term ***Partners' Equity*** instead of Owner's Equity and would list separately the amount of each partner's equity in the business. If the business were organized as a corporation, the caption used in the balance sheet would be ***Stockholders' Equity.*** It is ***not*** customary in a corporation's balance sheet to show separately the equity of each stockholder. In the case of large corporations, this clearly would not be possible, as these businesses often have ***several million*** individual stockholders (owners).

In the balance sheet of a corporation, stockholders' equity is subdivided into two general categories: (1) capital stock and (2) retained earnings.

Capital stock represents the amount which the stockholders originally *invested in the business* in exchange for shares of the company's stock. *Retained earnings,* in contrast, represents the increase in stockholders' equity which has accumulated over the years *as a result of profitable business operations.*[9]

The three methods of reporting ownership equity in the balance sheet are illustrated below:

In a Sole Proprietorship

Ownership equity as reported in a balance sheet

Owner's equity:

Dale Nelson, capital .... $ 50,000

In a Partnership

Partners' equity:

Pamela Barnes, capital	$40,000	
Scott Davis, capital	35,000	
Total partners' equity		$ 75,000

In a Corporation

Stockholders' equity:

Capital stock..	$5,000,000	
Retained earnings	3,278,000	
Total stockholders' equity		$8,278,000

THE USE OF FINANCIAL STATEMENTS BY OUTSIDERS

Most "outside" decision makers use financial statements in making *investment decisions*—that is, in selecting those companies in which they will invest resources or to which they will extend credit. For this reason, financial statements are designed primarily to meet the needs of creditors and investors.[10] Two factors of concern to creditors and investors are the *solvency* and *profitability* of a business organization.

Creditors are interested in solvency—the ability of the business to pay its debts as they come due. Business concerns that are able to pay their debts promptly are said to be *solvent.* In contrast, a company that finds itself unable to meet its obligations as they fall due is called *insolvent.* Solvency is critical to the very survival of a business organization—a business that becomes insolvent may be forced into *bankruptcy* by its creditors. Once bankrupt, a business may be forced by the courts to stop its operations, sell its assets (for the purpose of paying its creditors), and end its existence.

---

[9]   If the business operates *unprofitably,* retained earnings can become a *negative* amount, indicating the extent to which the unprofitable operations have *decreased* the stockholders' equity. The implications of negative retained earnings are discussed in Chapter 14.

[10]   In this context, *creditors* include everyone to whom the business owes money. One may become a creditor of a business either by lending it money or by providing goods and services with payment due at a later date. *Investors,* on the other hand, are those persons having or considering an *ownership* interest in the organization.

Investors as well as creditors are interested in the solvency of a business organization, but they are even more interested in its ***profitability.
Profitable operations increase the value of the owners' equity*** in the
business. A company that continually operates unprofitably will eventually exhaust its resources and be forced out of existence.[11] Therefore, most
users of financial statements study these statements carefully for clues to
the company's solvency and future profitability.

The Short Run versus the Long Run   In the short run, solvency and profitability may be independent of each other. A business may be operating
profitably, but nevertheless run out of cash, and thereby become insolvent.
On the other hand, a company may operate unprofitably during a given
year, yet have enough cash to pay its bills and remain solvent.

Over a longer term, however, the goals of solvency and profitability go
hand in hand. If a business is to survive, it must remain solvent and, in the
long run, it must operate profitably.

CASE IN POINT   Throughout the 1980s, the business activities of Donald
Trump were enormously profitable, increasing Trump's net worth by several billion dollars. Yet in June 1990, the billionaire became insolvent; he
did not have enough cash to meet a scheduled interest payment to his
creditors. After days of around-the-clock negotiations with numerous
banks, Trump was able to borrow enough cash to make his operations solvent again—at least for the moment. Had he not been able to arrange
these "eleventh-hour" loans, Trump's creditors might have forced portions
of his financial empire into bankruptcy.

Evaluating Short-Term Solvency   One key indicator of short-term solvency
is the relationship between an entity's ***liquid*** assets and the liabilities
requiring payment ***in the near future.***[12] By studying the nature of a company's assets and the amounts and due dates of its liabilities, users of
financial statements often may anticipate whether the company is likely to
have difficulty in meeting its upcoming obligations. This simple type of
analysis meets the needs of many ***short-term*** creditors. Evaluating long-
term solvency is a more difficult matter and is discussed in later chapters.

In studying financial statements, users should ***always*** read the accompanying notes and the auditors' report.

*OBJECTIVE 6
Use a bal-
ance sheet
in evaluat-
ing the
short-term
solvency of a
business
organiza-
tion.*

The Need for Adequate Disclosure

The concept of adequate disclosure is an important generally accepted accounting principle. Adequate disclosure means that users of financial
statements are informed of any facts ***necessary for the proper interpretation*** of the statements. Adequate disclosure may be made either in the
body of the financial statements or in ***notes*** accompanying the statements.

*OBJECTIVE 7
Explain the
concept of
adequate
disclosure.*

---

[11]   The concept of profitability is discussed further in Chapter 3.

[12]   "Liquid" assets are those expected to be converted into cash or consumed in business operations within a short period of time; from a short-term creditor's point of view, by the time payment
is due. By definition, cash is the most liquid asset.

Among the events that require disclosure are significant financial events occurring *after* the balance sheet date but before the financial statements have been issued to outsiders. For an example, let us refer to the December 31, 1994, balance sheet of Vagabond Travel Agency, illustrated on page 15. Assume that on January 4, *1995,* the building owned by Vagabond was completely destroyed by fire. As the building existed at the end of 1994, it properly is included in the balance sheet date of December 31. However, users of this balance sheet need to be informed that the building *no longer exists.* The destruction of this building should be disclosed in a note accompanying the financial statements, such as the following:

Note 7: Events occurring subsequent to the balance sheet date

On January 4, 1995, a building shown in the balance sheet at $90,000 was destroyed by fire. The Company does not insure against this type of loss. The financial effects of this loss will be reflected in the Company's 1995 financial statements.

In addition to important "subsequent events," many other situations may require disclosure in notes to the financial statements. Examples include lawsuits against the company, due dates of major liabilities, assets pledged as collateral to secure loans, amounts receivable from officers or other "insiders," and contractual commitments requiring large future cash outlays.

There is no comprehensive list of the items and events that may require disclosure. As a general rule, a company should disclose any financial facts that an intelligent person would consider *necessary to the proper interpretation* of the financial statements. Events that clearly are unimportant *do not* require disclosure.

The Reliability of Financial Statements

OBJECTIVE 8
Identify factors contributing to the reliability of financial statements.

Why should decision makers outside an organization regard financial statements as being fair and reliable? We already have identified three factors: (1) companies' systems of internal control, (2) the concept of adequate disclosure, and (3) audits performed by independent accounting firms. In the United States, *federal securities laws* provide additional assurance as to the reliability of financial statements.

Federal Securities Laws   The federal government has enacted laws requiring that the financial statements of publicly owned companies be prepared in conformity with generally accepted accounting principles, including the concept of adequate disclosure. Any person who *knowingly causes such financial statements to be misleading* may face criminal penalties and may also be held financially responsible for the losses incurred by anyone relying upon the statements. These securities laws apply to the management of the company issuing the statements and also to the independent auditors.

Management's Interest in Financial Statements

The management of a business organization is vitally concerned with the financial position of the business, and also with its profitability. Therefore, management is anxious to receive financial statements as frequently and as quickly as possible, so that it may take action to improve areas of weak performance. Most large organizations provide managers with financial statements on at least a monthly basis.

However, managers have a special interest in the ***annual*** financial statements, as these are the statements most widely used by decision makers outside of the organization. For example, if creditors view the year-end balance sheet as "strong," they will be more willing to extend credit to the business than if they regard the company's financial position as weak.

A strong balance sheet is one that shows relatively little debt and large amounts of liquid assets relative to the liabilities due in the near future. Management can—and does—take steps to make the year-end balance sheet look as strong as possible. For example, cash purchases of assets may be delayed so that substantial amounts of cash will be on hand at the balance sheet date. Liabilities due in the near future may be paid or replaced with longer-term liabilities.

These actions are called ***window dressing***—legitimate measures taken by management to make a business look as strong as possible at the balance sheet date. Users of year-end balance sheets should realize that while these statements are "fair" and "reliable," they may not necessarily describe the "typical" financial position of the business. In its annual financial statements, almost every company tries to "put its best foot forward." Many creditors, therefore, regard monthly balance sheets as providing a more typical picture of a company's financial position.

COMPETENCE, INTEGRITY, AND PROFESSIONAL JUDGMENT

OBJECTIVE 9 Identify several areas in which accountants must exercise professional judgment.

The preparation of accounting reports is not a mechanical task that can be performed by machine or even by well-trained clerical personnel. A characteristic common to all recognized professions—such as medicine, law, engineering, architecture, and accounting—is the need for individual practitioners to resolve many problems with their own ***professional judgment.*** The problems encountered in the practice of a profession are often complex, and the specific circumstances unique. Consequently, no written set of rules exists to provide answers in every situation.

In preparing the financial statements of a large business organization, the company's accountants and its independent auditors must make many "judgment calls." For example:

■ What constitutes "adequate" disclosure?

■ At what point should a business in financial difficulties cease to be viewed as a going concern?

■ What types of investigative procedures are necessary to assure auditors that a company's financial statements represent a "fair" presentation?

■ Which efforts by management represent legitimate "window dressing," and which are inappropriate actions that would make the financial statements misleading?

Unfortunately, judgmental decisions ***always involve some risk of error.*** Some "errors in judgment" result from carelessness or inexperience on the part of the decision makers. However, others occur simply because future events do not work out as anticipated.

If the public is to have confidence in the judgment of professional accountants, these accountants first must demonstrate that they possess the characteristics of **competence** and **integrity.**

Professional Competence   Both the accounting profession and state governments have taken steps to assure the public of the technical competence of certified public accountants. CPAs are licensed by the states, in much the same manner as states license physicians and attorneys. The licensing requirements vary somewhat from state to state, but in general, an individual must have a college education with a major in accounting, pass a rigorous examination (the *Uniform CPA Examination*), and have several years of accounting experience. In addition, most states require all CPAs to spend at least 40 hours per year in "continuing education" programs throughout their professional careers.

Beginning in the year 2000, the AICPA will require its new members to have completed 30 semester hours of college work **beyond** a bachelor's degree—that is, a fifth year of college. Many states are amending their licensing laws to include this new educational requirement.

Integrity and Ethics   *Integrity* means honesty and a strong commitment to ethical conduct—doing the "right thing." For a professional accountant, integrity is just as important as competence. However, it is far more difficult to test or enforce.

Associations of professional accountants—and also the state governments—have taken steps to encourage and enforce integrity within the profession. For example, several professional associations have developed **codes of professional ethics** for their members.[13] These codes are intended to help professional accountants fulfill their professional obligations with integrity.

One concept found in all professional codes of ethics for accountants is that accountants must **never knowingly be associated with misleading accounting information.** In fact, a professional accountant should **resign his or her position** rather than become involved in the preparation or distribution of misleading information.

Professional accounting associations investigate the backgrounds of individuals applying to take the professional competence examinations. These examinations also include questions testing the applicants' knowledge of professional ethics. In addition, most states include the AICPA's *Code of Professional Conduct* in their licensing requirements for CPAs. Thus, violations of this code may cause a CPA to lose his or her license to practice public accounting.

Of course, the basic concept of ethical conduct—acting with honor and integrity—**applies to management** as well as to professional accountants.

---

[13]   In accounting, codes of professional ethics have been developed by the American Institute of Certified Public Accountants (AICPA), the Institute of Management Accountants, and the Institute of Internal Auditors.

The users of financial statements should recognize that the reliability of these statements is affected by the **competence, integrity,** and **professional judgment** of the management, accountants, and auditors involved in the financial reporting process. But as we have previously stated, audited financial statements—and the accounting profession—have established an impressive track record of reliability. More than any other factor, the competence and integrity of professional accountants ensure the fairness and reliability of financial statements.

■ ■ ■ ＊ *Supplemental Topic*
Careers in Accounting

THE ACCOUNTING "PROFESSION"

OBJECTIVE 10
Describe various career opportunities in accounting.

Accounting—along with such fields as architecture, engineering, law, medicine, and theology—is recognized as a "profession." What distinguishes a profession from other disciplines? There is no widely recognized definition of a profession, but all of these fields have several characteristics in common.

First, all professions involve a complex and evolving body of knowledge. In accounting, the complexity and the ever-changing nature of the business world, financial reporting requirements, and income tax laws certainly meet this criterion.

In all professions, practitioners must use their professional judgment to resolve many problems and dilemmas. Throughout this text, we will point out situations requiring accountants to exercise professional judgment.

Of greatest importance, however, is the unique responsibility of professionals **to serve the public's best interest, even at the sacrifice of personal advantage.** This responsibility stems from the fact that the public has little technical knowledge in the professions, yet fair and competent performance by professionals is vital to the public's health, safety, or well-being. The practice of medicine, for example, directly affects public health, while engineering affects public safety. Accounting affects the public's well-being in many ways, because accounting information is used in the allocation of economic resources throughout society. Thus, accountants have a basic "social contract" to avoid being associated with misleading information.

Accountants tend to specialize in specific fields, as do the members of other professions. In terms of career opportunities, accounting may be divided into four broad areas: (1) public accounting, (2) management accounting, (3) governmental accounting, and (4) accounting education.

PUBLIC ACCOUNTING

Certified public accountants, called **CPAs,** offer a **variety of accounting services to the public.** These individuals may work in a CPA firm or as sole practitioners.

The work of CPAs consists primarily of performing **independent audits, income tax work,** and **management advisory services** (management consulting). Some CPAs also offer bookkeeping services to small businesses, but many do not.

We have already discussed the role of independent audits in the financial reporting process (see pages 9–10). For many years, auditing has been the principal function of CPAs. Today, however, tax work and management consulting are separate areas of specialization which are rapidly growing in importance.

Providing **management advisory services** is, perhaps, the fastest growing area in public accounting. The advisory services extend well beyond tax planning and accounting matters; CPAs advise management on such diverse issues as international mergers, manufacturing processes, and the introduction of new products. The entry of CPAs into the field of management consulting reflects the fact that **financial considerations enter into every business decision.**

A great many CPAs move from public accounting into managerial positions with their client organizations. These "alumni" from public accounting often move directly into such top management positions as controller, treasurer, chief financial officer, or chief executive officer.

MANAGEMENT ACCOUNTING

In contrast to the CPA who serves many clients, the management (or managerial) accountant works for one enterprise. Management accountants develop and interpret accounting information designed specifically to meet the various needs of management.

The chief accounting officer of an organization usually is called the **controller,** in recognition of the fact that one basic purpose of accounting data is to aid in controlling business operations. The controller is part of the top management team, which is responsible for running the business, setting its objectives, and seeing that these objectives are achieved.

In addition to developing information to assist managers, management accountants are responsible for operating the company's accounting system, including the recording of transactions and the preparation of financial statements, tax returns, and other accounting reports. As the responsibilities of management accountants are so broad, many areas of specialization have developed. Among the more important are the following:

Financial Reporting Management is responsible for a company meeting its financial reporting obligations. Therefore, some management accountants specialize in preparing financial statements and other reports for outsiders. This specialty requires an in-depth knowledge of generally accepted accounting principles.

Design of Management Information Systems Designing an efficient information system is a most challenging task. Management accountants specializing in this area need expertise to be knowledgeable about external reporting requirements, the information needs of managers, and the means of achieving adequate internal control. In addition, they must be familiar with the latest computer hardware and software and be able to develop a satisfactory system **at a reasonable cost.** Systems design is not a one-time effort; large organizations continuously expand and improve their information systems.

Cost Accounting Knowing the cost of each business operation and cf each manufactured product is essential to the efficient management of a business. Determining the per-unit cost of business activities and of manufactured products—and interpreting this cost data—comprise a specialized field called ***cost accounting.***

Financial Forecasting A financial forecast (or budget) is a plan of financial operations for some ***future*** period. Actually, forecasting is much like financial reporting, except that the accountant is estimating future outcomes, rather than measuring past results. A forecast provides each department of a business with financial goals. Comparison of the results actually achieved with these forecast amounts is one widely used means of evaluating departmental performance.

Income Tax Accounting Many companies rely primarily upon CPA firms for tax planning and the preparation of income tax returns. Large companies, however, usually maintain ***tax departments*** and perform some of these functions "in house."

Internal Auditing Large organizations usually maintain a staff of ***internal auditors.*** Internal auditors are charged with studying the system of internal control and evaluating the efficiency of many different aspects of the company's operations. As employees, internal auditors are not "independent" of the organization. Therefore, they ***do not*** perform independent audits of the company's financial statements.

Professional Certification for Management Accountants Management accountants are not required to be licensed as CPAs. However, they voluntarily may earn a Certificate in Management Accounting (CMA) or a Certificate in Internal Auditing (CIA) as evidence of their professional competence. The requirements for becoming a CMA or CIA are similar to those for becoming a CPA.

Careers in management accounting often lead to positions in top management—just as do careers in public accounting.

GOVERNMENTAL ACCOUNTING

Governmental agencies use accounting information in allocating their resources and in controlling their operations. Therefore, the need for management accountants is similar to that in business organizations. However, governmental agencies generally do not have "investors" and, therefore, do less financial reporting. Also, they do not prepare income tax returns.

The accounting standards used in government differ significantly from those in the business world, because earning a profit is not an objective of government. Universities, hospitals, churches, and other ***not-for-profit*** institutions also follow a pattern of accounting similar to that of governmental agencies.

In addition to managerial accounting positions, government offers other career opportunities, such as the following:

The GAO: Who Audits the Government?   The General Accounting Office (GAO) audits many agencies of the federal government and also some private organizations doing business with the government. The GAO reports its findings directly to Congress. Congress, in turn, often discloses these findings to the public.

GAO investigations may be designed either to evaluate the efficiency of an entity's operations or to determine the fairness of accounting information reported to the government.

The IRS: Audits of Income Tax Returns   Another governmental agency that performs extensive auditing work is the Internal Revenue Service (IRS). The IRS handles the millions of income tax returns filed annually by individuals and business organizations, and it frequently performs auditing functions to verify data contained in these returns.

The SEC: The "Watchdog" of Financial Reporting   The SEC works closely with the FASB in establishing generally accepted accounting principles. Each year large publicly owned corporations must file audited financial statements with the SEC. If the SEC believes that a company's financial statements are deficient in any way, it conducts an investigation. If the SEC concludes that federal securities laws have been violated, it initiates legal action against the reporting entity and responsible individuals.

Many other governmental agencies, including the FBI and the FDIC (Federal Deposit Insurance Corporation), use accountants to audit compliance with government regulations and to investigate suspected criminal activity. People beginning their careers in governmental accounting often move into top administrative positions.

ACCOUNTING EDUCATION: CAREERS AS FACULTY MEMBERS

So many attractive career opportunities exist for accounting majors that most graduates move directly into public accounting, management accounting, or governmental accounting. An interesting alternative, however, is to embark upon the graduate study and research necessary to become an accounting faculty member. The demand for qualified accounting faculty is intense. Individuals with these qualifications are highly mobile; there are positions to be filled in virtually every state and every country.

Accounting faculty positions offer opportunities for research, consulting, and writing and an unusual degree of freedom in developing individual skills. Accounting educators contribute to the accounting profession in many ways: one, of course, lies in effective teaching; another, in publishing significant research findings in professional journals; and a third, in influencing top students to pursue careers in accounting.

Many accounting faculty have the opportunity to take "leaves of absence" from their university positions. During these leaves, the faculty members may enhance their professional knowledge by conducting research, working in public accounting, or working with organizations such as the FASB, AICPA, or SEC.

ACCOUNTING AS A "STEPPING-STONE"

We have mentioned that many professional accountants leave their accounting careers for key positions in management or administration. An accounting background is invaluable in such positions, because top management works continuously with issues defined and described in accounting terms and concepts.

An especially useful "stepping-stone" is experience in public accounting. CPAs have the unusual opportunity of getting an "inside look" at many different business organizations.

END-OF-CHAPTER REVIEW

SUMMARY OF CHAPTER LEARNING OBJECTIVES

1 **Define accounting, financial reporting, and financial statements.**
Accounting is the art of interpreting, measuring, and communicating the results of economic activities. Financial reporting means supplying general-purpose financial information about a business to decision makers *outside* the organization. This information is usually in the form of financial statements. Financial statements are a set of four related accounting reports that describe the *financial position* of an organization and the *results of its operations* for the preceding year (or other time period).

2 **Explain the phrase "generally accepted accounting principles."**
Generally accepted accounting principles are the concepts, standards, and "ground rules" used in the preparation of financial statements.

3 **Describe and prepare a balance sheet; define assets, liabilities, and owner's equity.**
A balance sheet is a financial statement showing the *financial position* (defined in terms of assets, liabilities, and owner's equity) of a business entity at a specific date. However, a balance sheet does *not* show how much a business currently is worth.

Assets are economic resources owned by the business, liabilities are debts or financial obligations of the business, and owner's equity is the residual claim of the owners to the assets of the business.

4 **Describe the accounting principles involved in asset valuation.**
Most assets are valued in accordance with the *cost principle.* This generally accepted accounting principle indicates that the valuation of assets in a balance sheet should be based upon historical cost, not upon current market value. Three other accounting principles supporting the valuation of assets at cost are the *going-concern assumption,* the *objectivity principle,* and the *stable-dollar assumption.*

5 **Indicate the effects of various transactions upon the accounting equation and the balance sheet.**
A transaction which increases total assets must also increase either total liabilities or owner's equity. Similarly, a transaction which de-

creases total assets must decrease either total liabilities or owner's equity. Some transactions increase one asset while decreasing another; such transactions do not change the total amounts of assets, liabilities, or owner's equity.

6 Use a balance sheet in evaluating the short-term solvency of a business organization.

One step in evaluating the short-term solvency (debt-paying ability) of a business is to compare the amount of liquid assets with the amount of liabilities coming due within the near future.

7 Explain the concept of adequate disclosure.

Adequate disclosure means that financial statements should include any financial facts necessary for the users to *interpret* the statements properly.

8 Identify factors contributing to the reliability of financial statements.

Factors contributing to the reliability of financial statements include the objectivity principle, the concept of adequate disclosure, systems of internal control, audits by independent CPAs, federal securities laws, and the judgment, competence, and integrity of professional accountants.

9 Identify several areas in which accountants must exercise professional judgment.

Accountants must rely upon their professional judgment to resolve many issues arising in accounting practice. Examples include: What constitutes "adequate" disclosure? How should a transaction be recorded when no "official" accounting principles seem to apply? At what point should a business in financial difficulty cease to be viewed as a going concern?

*10 Describe various career opportunities in accounting.

Career opportunities in accounting include public accounting, management accounting, governmental accounting, and accounting education. Public accountants render auditing, income tax, and management advisory services to a variety of clients. Management accountants fill the needs for accounting information within one specific organization. Governmental accounting careers include management accounting and various types of auditing. Accounting education provides career opportunities in teaching and research.

A characteristic of an accounting textbook is that each new chapter builds upon those which have come before. For example, in the next three chapters we will expand our Roberts Real Estate Company example to illustrate double-entry accounting, the use of accounting records, and the measurement and reporting of business income.

Our basic goals in this textbook are to help you develop your abilities to *understand* and to *use* accounting information. Throughout this course, you should focus upon the usefulness—and the limitations—of the accounting information available to decision makers.

---

*   *Supplemental Topic, "Careers in Accounting"*

KEY TERMS INTRODUCED OR EMPHASIZED IN CHAPTER 1

Note to Students: Each chapter includes a glossary explaining the key accounting terms introduced or emphasized. You should review these glossaries carefully; an understanding of accounting terminology is an essential step in the study of accounting. These terms will appear frequently in later chapters, in problem material, and in examination questions. (Because of the broad and introductory nature of Chapter 1, this glossary is longer than those in later chapters.)

Accounting equation   Assets are equal to the sum of liabilities plus owner's equity (A = L + OE). This equation is reflected in the format of the balance sheet.

Accounting system   The personnel, procedures, records, forms, and devices used by an organization in developing and communicating accounting information.

American Institute of Certified Public Accountants (AICPA)   The national professional association of certified public accountants (CPAs). Carries on extensive research and is influential in improving accounting standards. Also develops auditing standards and administers the *Uniform CPA Examination.*

Annual report   A document issued annually by publicly owned corporations to their stockholders. Includes audited financial statements for several years, as well as nonfinancial information about the company and its operations.

Assets   Economic resources owned by an entity.

Auditing   Performing an investigation enabling the auditors to express an independent opinion (auditors' report) as to the fairness and completeness of a set of financial statements.

Balance sheet   The financial statement showing the financial position of an entity by summarizing its assets, liabilities, and owner's equity at one specific date.

Business entity   An economic unit that controls resources, incurs obligations, and engages in business activities.

Capital stock   Transferable units of ownership in a corporation.

Certified Public Accountant (CPA)   An independent professional accountant licensed by a state to offer auditing and other accounting services to clients.

Corporation   A business organized as a separate legal entity and chartered by a state, with ownership divided into transferable shares of capital stock.

Cost principle   The widely used principle of accounting for assets at their original cost to the current owner.

Creditor   A lender; an entity to which money is owed.

Disclosure ("adequate")   The accounting principle of providing with financial statements any financial facts necessary for the proper ***interpretation*** of those statements.

Fair   A term used by accountants to describe a set of financial statements that are complete, not misleading, and prepared in conformity with generally accepted accounting principles. Auditors express their opinions as to the "fairness" of financial statements.

Financial accounting   The development and use of accounting information describing the financial position of an entity and the results of its operations.

Financial Accounting Standards Board (FASB)   An independent group that conducts research into accounting problems and issues authoritative pronouncements as to "generally acceptable" accounting principles.

Financial position   The financial resources and obligations of an organization, as described in a ***balance sheet.***

Financial reporting The process of periodically providing "general-purpose" financial information (such as financial statements) to persons ***outside*** the business organization.

Financial statements Four related accounting reports that concisely summarize the current financial position of an entity and the results of its operations for the preceding year (or other time period).

Generally accepted accounting principles (GAAP) The accounting concepts, measurement techniques, and standards of presentation used in financial statements. Examples include the cost principle and objectivity.

Going-concern assumption An assumption by accountants that a business will operate indefinitely unless specific evidence to the contrary exists, such as impending bankruptcy.

Internal control All measures used within an organization to assure management that the organization is operating in accordance with management's policies and plans.

Liabilities Debts or obligations of an entity that have arisen from past transactions. The claims of creditors against the assets of a business.

Objectivity principle Accountants' tendency to base accounting measurements upon dollar amounts that are factual and subject to independent verification.

Owner's equity The excess of assets over liabilities. The amount of an owner's net investment in a business plus profits from successful operations which have been retained in the business.

Partnership An unincorporated business owned by two or more persons voluntarily associated as partners.

Profitability An increase in owner's equity resulting from successful business operations. (This concept is discussed further in Chapter 3.)

Public information Information which by law is available to the general public. The annual financial statements of large publicly owned businesses are public information.

Publicly held corporations Corporations in which members of the general public may buy or sell shares of capital stock.

Retained earnings The portion of the owners' equity in a corporation that has accumulated as a result of profitable business operations.

Securities and Exchange Commission (SEC) The federal agency with the legal power to establish financial reporting requirements for large, publicly owned corporations. Also enforces federal securities laws, bringing legal action against possible offenders.

Sole proprietorship An unincorporated business owned by an individual.

Solvency Having the financial ability to pay debts as they become due.

Stable-dollar assumption An assumption by accountants that the dollar is a stable unit of measure, like the mile or the gallon. A simplifying assumption that permits adding or subtracting dollar amounts originating in different time periods. Unfortunately, the assumption technically is incorrect and may seriously distort accounting information during periods of severe inflation.

Stockholders Owners of capital stock in a corporation; hence, the owners of the corporation.

Stockholders' equity The ***owners' equity*** in an entity organized as a corporation.

Transaction An event that causes an immediate change in the financial position of an entity and that can be measured objectively in monetary terms. In current practice, transactions serve as the basis for recording financial activity.

Window dressing Legitimate measures taken by management to make a business look as strong as possible at the balance sheet date.

DEMONSTRATION PROBLEM FOR YOUR REVIEW

The accounting data (listed alphabetically) for Crystal Auto Wash at September 30, 19___, are shown below. The figure for Don Johnson, capital is not given, but it can be determined when all the available information is assembled in the form of a balance sheet.

Accounts payable	$14,000	Land	$58,000
Accounts receivable	800	Machinery and equipment	65,000
Building	52,000	Notes payable	29,000
Cash	9,200	Salaries payable	3,000
Don Johnson, capital	?	Supplies	400

INSTRUCTIONS

a Prepare a balance sheet at September 30, 19___.

b Does this balance sheet indicate that the company is in a strong financial position? Explain briefly.

SOLUTION TO DEMONSTRATION PROBLEM

a

CRYSTAL AUTO WASH
Balance Sheet
September 30, 19___

Assets		Liabilities & Owner's Equity	
Cash	$ 9,200	**Liabilities:**	
Accounts receivable	800	Notes payable	$ 29,000
Supplies	400	Accounts payable	14,000
Land	68,000	Salaries payable	3,000
Building	52,000	Total liabilities	$ 46,000
Machinery & equipment	65,000	**Owner's equity:**	
		Don Johnson, capital*	149,400
Total	$195,400	Total	$195,400

* Computed as total assets, $195,400 − total liabilities, $46,000 = Don Johnson, capital, $149,400

b The balance sheet indicates that Crystal Auto Wash is in a ***very weak*** financial position. The highly "liquid" assets—cash and receivables—total only $10,000, but the company has ***$46,000*** in debts due in the near future. Based upon this balance sheet, the company appears to be insolvent.†

---

† Perhaps the company can generate enough cash from its daily operations to pay its debts. A balance sheet does not indicate the ***rate*** at which cash flows into the business. A recent ***statement of cash flows*** would be useful in making a more complete analysis of the company's financial position. Also, as this business is organized as a sole proprietorship, creditors may look to the personal solvency of the owner, Don Johnson. He is personally liable for the debts of the business entity.

SELF-TEST QUESTIONS

The answers to these questions appear on page 56. (Note: In order to review as many chapter concepts as possible, some self-test questions include more than one correct answer. In these cases, indicate **all** of the correct answers.)

1   A "set" of financial statements: (Indicate all correct answers.)
  a   Is intended to assist users in evaluating the financial position, profitability, and future prospects of an entity.
  b   Is intended to assist the IRS in determining the amount of income taxes owed by a business organization.
  c   Includes "notes" disclosing items necessary for the proper interpretation of the statements.
  d   Is intended to assist investors and creditors in making decisions involving the allocation of economic resources.

2   Generally accepted accounting principles: (Indicate all correct answers.)
  a   Include only the official pronouncements of the standard-setting organizations, such as the FASB, the SEC, and the AICPA.
  b   May include customary accounting practices in widespread use even if not mentioned specifically in official pronouncements.
  c   Eliminate the need for professional judgment in the preparation of financial statements.
  d   Change and evolve as business organizations enter into new forms of business activity.

3   Which of the following statements is **not** consistent with generally accepted accounting principles relating to asset valuation?
  a   Assets are originally recorded in accounting records at their cost to the business entity.
  b   Subtracting total liabilities from total assets indicates what the owner's equity in the business is worth under current market conditions.
  c   Accountants assume that assets such as office supplies, land, and buildings will be used in business operations, rather than sold at current market prices.
  d   Accountants prefer to base the valuation of assets upon objective, verifiable evidence rather than upon appraisals or personal opinion.

4   Arrowhead Boat Shop purchased a truck for $12,000, making a down payment of $5,000 cash and signing a $7,000 note payable due in 60 days. (Indicate all correct answers.)
  a   Total assets increased by $12,000.
  b   Total liabilities increased by $7,000.
  c   From the viewpoint of a short-term creditor, this transaction makes the business less solvent.
  d   This transaction had no immediate effect upon the owner's equity in the business.

5   A transaction caused a $10,000 **decrease** in both total assets and total liabilities. This transaction could have been:
  a   Purchase of a delivery truck for $10,000 cash.
  b   An asset with a cost of $10,000 was destroyed by fire.

  c   Repayment of a $10,000 bank loan.

  d   Collection of a $10,000 account receivable.

6   Which of the following factors contribute to the *reliability* of the information contained in financial statements? (Indicate all correct answers.)

  a   The competence and integrity of professional accountants.

  b   Federal securities laws and the SEC.

  c   Systems of internal control and audits by independent CPA firms.

  d   The concept of adequate disclosure.

7   Which of the following statements relating to the role of professional judgment in the financial reporting process are valid? (Indicate all correct answers.)

  a   Different accountants may evaluate similar situations differently.

  b   The determination of which items should be "disclosed" in notes to financial statements requires professional judgment.

  c   Once a complete list of generally accepted accounting principles is prepared, judgment need no longer enter into the financial reporting process.

  d   The possibility always exists that professional judgment later may prove to have been incorrect.

*8   Which of the following statements regarding accounting careers is the *least* valid?

  a   Management accountants, CPAs, and the SEC all participate in the process of financial reporting.

  b   The principal function of internal auditors is to issue reports on the "fairness" of their company's financial statements.

  c   Careers in accounting education often involve research and consulting.

  d   A background in accounting may serve as a useful "stepping-stone" to positions in top management.

ASSIGNMENT MATERIAL

DISCUSSION QUESTIONS

One objective of these questions is to give you an opportunity to demonstrate and develop your *communication skills.* Therefore, we ask that you answer each question in your own words.

1   In broad general terms, what is the purpose of accounting?

2   Why is a knowledge of accounting terms and concepts useful to persons other than professional accountants?

3   What is meant by the term *financial reporting?* What impact, if any, does financial reporting have upon our economy?

4   What is *public information?* What does this concept have to do with financial reporting?

5   In general terms, what does a set of *financial statements* describe? Identify the specific statements and other information that comprise a complete *set* of financial statements.

---

*   Supplemental Topic, "Careers in Accounting"

6 Are financial statements the **only means** by which decision makers outside of management obtain information about the financial position, profitability, and future prospects of a business?

7 Define the term **business transaction.** Give several examples of business transactions, and several examples of important events in the life of a business that **do not** qualify as "transactions." What is the relationship between business transactions and the information contained in financial statements?

8 Explain briefly why each of the following groups is interested in the financial statements of a business.

   a   Creditors

   b   Potential investors

   c   Labor unions

9 What is the purpose of a **system of internal control?**

10 What is the purpose of an **audit?** Would a large corporation or a small sole proprietorship be more likely to retain a CPA firm to perform an annual audit? Explain.

11 Are computers essential to the operation of an accounting system? Briefly describe several ways in which computers help make accounting information **more useful** to decision makers.

12 Distinguish between **accounting** and **bookkeeping.**

13 The following questions relate to the term **generally accepted accounting principles.**

   a   What type of accounting reports are prepared in conformity with these principles?

   b   Why is it important for these principles to be widely recognized?

   c   Where do these principles come from?

   d   Give two examples of generally accepted accounting principles relating to the valuation of assets.

14 How do accounting principles become "generally accepted"?

15 With respect to financial reporting, what is the importance of the **FASB?** Of the **SEC?**

16 Explain briefly the concept of the **business entity.**

17 State briefly the purpose and content of a balance sheet. Does a balance sheet show how much a business is currently "worth"? Explain.

18 Why is owner's equity considered to be a **residual claim** to the assets of a business organization? Can the owner's equity in a business be a **negative** amount? Explain.

19 The owner's equity in a business arises from what two factors? What two factors can cause decreases in owner's equity?

20 State the accounting equation in two alternative forms.

21 Why are the total assets shown in a balance sheet always equal to the total of the liabilities plus the owner's equity?

22 Can a business transaction cause one asset to increase without affecting any other asset, liability, or the owner's equity?

23 Give examples of business transactions that would:

  a Cause one asset to increase and another asset to decrease, with no effect upon liabilities or owner's equity.

  b Cause both total assets and liabilities to increase, with no effect upon owner's equity.

24 Assume that a business becomes insolvent. Can the owner (or owners) of the business be held personally liable for the debts of the business? Give separate answers assuming that the business is organized as (a) a sole proprietorship, (b) a partnership, and (c) a corporation.

25 One objective of every business is to operate profitably. What other primary objective must be met for a business to survive? Explain.

26 What is meant by the term **adequate disclosure?** Give several examples of items that may require "disclosure" in financial statements.

27 Describe at least four factors that contribute to the **reliability** of financial statements.

28 What is meant by the phrase "a **strong** balance sheet"?

29 Describe the term **window dressing.** Why should users of financial statements be aware of this concept? Explain.

*30 Identify four broad areas of **career opportunities** in accounting. Is an accounting background of any use to an individual who does not intend to make a life-long career in accounting?

*31 What are the principal types of services rendered by CPAs? Why is experience in public accounting especially useful as a "stepping-stone" to a career in the top management of a business organization?

EXERCISES

EXERCISE 1-1
Accounting
Terminology

Listed below are twelve technical accounting terms emphasized in this chapter.

Financial reporting	Audit	Insolvent
Financial statements	Assets	Balance sheet
Corporation	Liabilities	Owner's equity
Sole proprietorship	SEC	GAAP

Each of the following statements may (or may not) describe one of these technical terms. For each statement, indicate the term described, or answer "None" if the statement does not correctly describe any of the terms.

a Obligations of an entity arising from past transactions.

b An investigation by independent accountants intended to assure outsiders of the fairness of a company's financial statements.

c The organization primarily responsible for developing new accounting principles by issuing *Statements of Financial Accounting Standards.*

d The process of distributing general-purpose financial information to persons outside a business organization.

e Economic resources owned by an entity.

---

* Supplemental Topic, "Careers in Accounting"

f   Accounting reports describing the financial position, profitability, and cash transactions of a business entity.

g   Being able to meet financial obligations as they come due.

h   A form of business organization in which the owners are *personally liable* for all debts of the business.

i   Assets minus liabilities.

j   The "ground rules" for presenting information in financial statements.

k   The financial statement indicating the profitability of the business for a period of time.

**EXERCISE 1-2
The Accounting
Equation**

A number of business transactions carried out by Green River Farms are shown below:

a   Purchased a computer on credit.

b   The owner invested cash in the business.

c   Purchased office equipment for cash.

d   Collected an account receivable.

e   Sold land for cash at a price equal to its cost.

f   Paid a liability.

g   Returned for credit some of the office equipment previously purchased on credit but not yet paid for.

h   Borrowed money from a bank.

Indicate the effects of each of these transactions upon the total amounts of the company's assets, liabilities, and owner's equity. Organize your answer in tabular form, using the column headings shown below and the code letters *I* for increase, *D* for decrease, and *NE* for no effect. The answer for transaction **a** is provided as an example:

Transaction	Assets	=	Liabilities	+	Owner's Equity
a	I		I		NE

**EXERCISE 1-3
Financial
Reporting**

A major focus of this course is the process of financial reporting.

a   What is meant by the term *financial reporting?*

b   What are the principal accounting reports involved in the financial reporting process? In general terms, what is the purpose of these reports?

c   Do all business entities engage in financial reporting? Explain.

d   How does society benefit from the financial reporting process?

**EXERCISE 1-4
Generally
Accepted
Accounting
Principles**

Generally accepted accounting principles play an important role in financial reporting.

a   What is meant by the phrase "generally accepted accounting principles"?

b   What are the major sources of these principles?

c   Is there a comprehensive list of generally accepted accounting principles? Explain.

**EXERCISE 1-5
Audits of Financial Statements**

The annual financial statements of all large, publicly owned corporations are audited.

a   What is an audit of financial statements?

b   Who performs these audits?

c   What is the basic purpose of an audit?

EXERCISE 1-6
Accounting
Organizations

Describe the roles of the following organizations in establishing generally accepted accounting principles.

a The FASB

b The AICPA

c The SEC

EXERCISE 1-7
Who? What?
When?

At the end of 1994, the accountant for C. Abrams & Sons, a construction company, prepared a year-end balance sheet with the following heading:

ABRAMS CONSTRUCTION
Statement of Financial Position for the Year 1994

INSTRUCTIONS

a Identify any errors in this heading.

b Prepare a corrected heading.

EXERCISE 1-8
The Nature of
Assets

Define *assets.* Give three examples of assets other than cash that might appear in the balance sheet of (a) **American Airlines** and (b) a professional sports team, such as the **Boston Celtics**.

EXERCISE 1-9
The Nature of
Liabilities

Define *liabilities.* Give three examples of liabilities that might appear in the balance sheet of (a) **American Airlines** and (b) a professional sports team, such as the **Boston Celtics**.

EXERCISE 1-10
Accounting
Principles and
Asset Valua-
tion

The following cases relate to the valuation of assets. Consider each case independently:

a World-Wide Travel Agency has office supplies costing $1,700 on hand at the balance sheet date. These supplies were purchased from a supplier that does not give cash refunds. World-Wide's management believes that the company could sell these supplies for no more than $500 if it were to advertise them for sale. However, the company expects to use these supplies and to purchase more when they are gone. In its balance sheet, the supplies are valued at $500.

b Zenith Corporation purchased land in 1955 for $20,000. In 1994, it purchased a similar parcel of land for $300,000. In its 1994 balance sheet, the company valued these two parcels of land at a combined value of $320,000.

c At December 30, 1994, Lenier Company purchased a computer system from a mail-order supplier for $14,000. The retail value of the system—according to the mail-order supplier—was $20,000. On January 7, 1995, the system was stolen during a burglary. In its December 31, 1994, balance sheet, Lenier showed this computer system at $14,000 and made no reference to its retail value or to the burglary.

INSTRUCTIONS

In each case, indicate the appropriate balance sheet valuation of the asset under generally accepted accounting principles. If the valuation assigned by the company is incorrect, briefly explain the accounting principles that have been violated. On the other hand, if the valuation is correct, identify the accounting principles that justify this valuation.

EXERCISE 1-11
Using the Ac-
counting Equa-
tion

Compute the missing amount in each of the following three lines.

	Assets	=	Liabilities	+	Owner's Equity
a	$279,000		$171,000		?
b	?		112,500		$ 75,000
c	615,000		?		285,000

EXERCISE 1-12
Preparing a
Balance Sheet

The night manager of Majestic Limousine Service, who had no accounting background, prepared the following balance sheet for the company at March 31, 1994. The dollar amounts were taken directly from the company's accounting records and are correct. However, the balance sheet contains a number of errors in its headings, format, and the classification of assets, liabilities, and owner's equity.

MAJESTIC LIMO
Manager's Report
8 PM Thursday

Assets		Net Worth	
Cash.........................	$ 19,000	Accounts receivable..........	$ 41,000
M. Johnson, capital...........	48,000	Accounts payable	24,000
Automobiles	96,000	Notes payable................	86,000
		Interest payable	5,000
		Supplies	7,000
Total	$163,000	Total	$163,000

INSTRUCTIONS Prepare a corrected balance sheet, including a proper heading.

EXERCISE 1-13
Preparing a
Balance Sheet

The items appearing in the balance sheet of Banners by George at December 31, 19__, are listed below in random order. You are to prepare a balance sheet (including a complete heading). Arrange the items in the sequence shown in the balance sheet illustrated on page 15 and include a figure for total liabilities. You must compute the amount for Chris George, capital.

Land.........................	$135,000	Office equipment	15,100
Cash.........................	18,150	Accounts payable	21,900
Accounts receivable..........	28,350	Building.....................	105,000
Chris George, capital	?	Notes payable................	97,500

EXERCISE 1-14
Effects of
Business
Transactions

For each of the following categories, state concisely a transaction that will have the required effect on the elements of the accounting equation:

a Increase an asset and increase a liability.

b Decrease an asset and decrease a liability.

c Increase one asset and decrease another asset.

d Increase an asset and increase owner's equity.

e Increase one asset, decrease another asset, and increase a liability.

EXERCISE 1-15
Interpreting the
Effects of
Business
Transactions

Five transactions of Lau Architectural are summarized below in equation form, with each of the five transactions identified by a letter. For each of the transactions (a) through (e) you are to write a separate sentence explaining the nature of the transaction. For example, the explanation of transaction **a** could be as follows: Purchased office equipment on account at a cost of $6,800.

	Cash	+	Accounts Receivable	+	Land	+	Building	+	Office Equipment	=	Accounts Payable	+	Tom Lau, Capital
				Assets						=	Liabilities	+	Owner's Equity
Balances	$13,000		$39,000		$65,000		$55,000		$23,000		$42,000		$153,000
a									+6,800		+6,800		
Balances	$13,000		$39,000		$65,000		$55,000		$29,800		$48,800		$153,000
b	−4,200										−4,200		
Balances	$ 8,800		$39,000		$65,000		$55,000		$29,800		$44,600		$153,000
c	+10,500		−10,500										
Balances	$19,300		$28,500		$65,000		$55,000		$29,800		$44,600		$153,000
d	−300								+1,900		+1,600		
Balances	$19,000		$28,500		$65,000		$55,000		$31,700		$46,200		$153,000
e	−5,000												−5,000
Balances	$14,000		$28,500		$65,000		$55,000		$31,700		$46,200		$148,000

EXERCISE 1-16
Forms of Business Organizations

QWIK Software Company has assets of $850,000 and liabilities of $460,000.

a Prepare the ownership equity section of QWIK's balance sheet under each of the following *independent* assumptions:

1 The business is organized as a sole proprietorship, owned by Johanna Schmidt.

2 The business is as a partnership, owned by Johanna Schmidt and Mikki Yato. Schmidt's equity amounts to $240,000.

3 The business is a corporation with 25 stockholders, each of whom originally invested $10,000 in exchange for shares of the company's capital stock. The remainder of the stockholders' equity has resulted from profitable operation of the business.

b Assume that you are a loan officer at Security Bank. QWIK has applied to your bank for a large loan to finance the development of new products. Is it likely to matter to a lender whether QWIK is organized as a sole proprietorship, a partnership, or a corporation? Explain.

EXERCISE 1-17
Professional Judgment

Professional judgment plays a major role in the practice of accounting.

a In general terms, explain why judgment enters into the accounting process.

b Identify at least three situations in which accountants must rely upon their professional judgment, rather than upon official rules.

*EXERCISE 1-18
Careers in Accounting

Four accounting majors, Maria Acosta, Kenzo Nakao, Helen Martin, and Anthony Mandella, recently graduated from Central University and began professional accounting careers. Acosta entered public accounting, Nakao became a management accountant with **IBM**, Martin joined a governmental agency, and Mandella (who had completed a graduate program) became an accounting faculty member.

INSTRUCTIONS

Assume that each of the four graduates was successful in his or her chosen career. Identify the types of accounting *activities* in which each of these graduates might find themselves specializing several years after graduation.

---

*   *Supplemental Topic, "Careers in Accounting"*

PROBLEMS

Group A

PROBLEM 1A-1
Preparing a Balance Sheet; Computing Owner's Equity

Listed below in random order are the items to be included in the balance sheet of Pearl Beach Resort at December 31, 1994:

Sailboats	$ 15,200	Buildings	$225,000
Land	210,000	Cash	14,600
Accounts receivable	4,800	Furnishings	29,100
Accounts payable	13,500	Notes payable	320,000
Equipment	9,200	Nancy Moore, capital	?

INSTRUCTIONS

Prepare a balance sheet at December 31, 1994. Include a proper heading and organize your balance sheet similar to the illustration on page 15. (After "Buildings," you may list the remaining assets in any order.) You will need to compute the amount of owner's equity.

PROBLEM 1A-2
Recording the Effects of Transactions

Water-Wise Landscaping was organized on September 1 of the current year and had the following account balances at December 31, listed in tabular form.

	Assets			=	Liabilities		+	Owner's Equity
	Cash +	Land +	Building +	Office Equipment =	Notes Payable +	Accounts Payable +		J. Green, Capital
Balances	$14,800	$50,000	$45,000	$22,500	$32,000	$25,300		$75,000

Early in January, the company carried out the following transactions:

1 The owner, J. Green, deposited $20,000 in personal funds into the bank account of the business.

2 Purchased land and a small office building for a total price of $80,000, of which $30,000 was the value of the land and $50,000 was the value of the building. Paid $20,000 in cash and signed a note payable for the remaining $60,000.

3 Bought a Xerox copying machine on credit for $9,500 (30-day open account).

4 Obtained a loan from Gulf Coast Bank in the amount of $18,000. Signed a note payable.

5 Paid the $9,500 account payable originating in transaction 3.

INSTRUCTIONS

a List the December 31 balances of assets, liabilities, and owner's equity in tabular form as shown above.

b Record the effects of each of the six transactions in the tabular arrangement illustrated above. Show the totals for all columns after each transaction.

PROBLEM 1A-3
Preparing a Balance Sheet; Effects of a Change in Assets

!HERE COMES TIGER! is the name of a traveling circus owned by Tiger Hayes. The ledger accounts of the business at June 30, 1994, are listed below in alphabetical order.

Accounts payable	$ 17,400	Notes receivable	$ 2,400
Accounts receivable	8,900	Props and equipment	59,720
Animals	126,040	Salaries payable	6,500
Cages	16,400	Tents	42,000
Cash	21,680	Tiger Hayes, capital	?
Costumes	21,000	Trucks	42,460
Notes payable	120,000	Wagons	28,100

INSTRUCTIONS

a Prepare a balance sheet by using these items and computing the amount of the owner's capital. Organize your balance sheet similar to the one illustrated on page 15. (After "Accounts Receivable," you may list the remaining assets in any order.) Include a proper balance sheet heading.

b Assume that late in the evening of June 30, after your balance sheet had been prepared, a fire destroyed one of the tents, which had cost $11,200. The tent was not insured. Explain what changes would be required in your June 30 balance sheet to reflect the lost of this asset.

PROBLEM 1A-4
Preparing a Balance Sheet; Effects of Business Transactions

The balance sheet items of The Original Malt Shop (arranged in alphabetical order) were as follows at the close of business on September 30, 1994:

Accounts payable	$ 8,500	Land	$55,000
Accounts receivable	1,250	Kay Martin, capital	54,090
Building	45,500	Notes payable	?
Cash	7,400	Supplies	3,440
Furniture & fixtures	20,000		

Throughout October, the business will be closed for remodeling. The transactions occurring during the first week of October were:

Oct. 3 Martin invested an additional $30,000 cash in the business. The accounts payable were paid in full. (No payment was made on the notes payable.)

Oct. 6 More furniture was purchased on account at a cost of $18,000, to be paid within 30 days. Supplies were purchased for $1,000 cash from a restaurant supply center which was going out of business. These supplies would have cost $1,875 if purchased under normal circumstances.

INSTRUCTIONS

a Prepare a balance sheet at September 30, 1994. (You are to compute the missing figure for notes payable.)

b Prepare a balance sheet at October 6, 1994.

PROBLEM 1A-5
Preparing a Balance Sheet; Discussion of Accounting Principles

Melonie Austin, owner and manager of Old Town Playhouse, needs to obtain a bank loan to finance the production of the company's next play. As part of the loan application, Austin was asked to prepare a balance sheet for the business. She prepared the following balance sheet, which is arranged correctly but contains several errors with respect to such concepts as the business entity and the valuation of assets, liabilities, and owner's equity.

OLD TOWN PLAYHOUSE
Balance Sheet
September 30, 1994

Assets		Liabilities & Owner's Equity	
Cash	$ 18,600	**Liabilities:**	
Accounts receivable	156,200	Accounts payable	$ 4,600
Props and costumes	1,800	Salaries payable	28,200
Theater building	13,500	Total liabilities	$32,800
Lighting equipment	8,500	**Owner's equity;**	
Automobile	12,000	Melonie Austin, capital	10,000
Total	$210,600	Total	$42,800

In discussions with Austin and by reviewing the accounting records of Old Town Playhouse, you discover the following facts:

1 The amount of cash, $18,600, includes $12,000 in the company's bank account, $2,100 on hand in the company's safe, and $4,500 in Austin's personal savings account.

2 Accounts receivable include $6,200 owed to the business by Artistic Tours. The remaining $150,000 is Austin's estimate of future ticket sales from September 30 through the end of the year (December 31).

3 Austin explains that the props and costumes were purchased several days ago for $14,800. The business paid $1,800 of this amount in cash and issued a note payable to Actors' Supply Company for the remainder of the purchase price ($13,000). As this note will not be paid until January of next year, it was not included among the company's liabilities.

4 Old Town Playhouse rents the theater building from Kievits International at a rate of $1,500 per month. The $13,500 represents the rent paid through September 30 of the current year. Kievits International acquired the building seven years ago at a cost of $126,000.

5 The lighting equipment was purchased on September 26 at a cost of $8,500, but the stage manager says that it isn't worth a dime.

6 The automobile is Austin's classic 1955 Porsche, which she purchased two years ago for $9,600. She recently saw a similar car advertised for sale at $12,000. She does not use the car in the business, but it has a personalized license plate which reads "PLAHOUS."

7 The accounts payable include business debts of $3,700 and the $900 balance of Austin's personal Visa card.

8 Salaries payable includes $25,000 offered to Mario Dane to play the lead role in a new play opening next December and also $3,200 still owed to stage hands for work done through September 30.

9 When Austin founded Old Town Playhouse four years ago, she invested $10,000 in the business. She has shown this amount as her owner's equity in order to comply with the cost principle. However, Live Theater, Inc., has offered to buy her business for $30,000, and she believes that perhaps the owner's equity should be changed to this amount.

INSTRUCTIONS a Prepare a corrected balance sheet for Old Town Playhouse at September 30, 1994.

b For each of the nine numbered items above, explain your reasoning in deciding whether or not to include the items in the balance sheet and in determining the proper dollar valuation.

Group B

PROBLEM 1B-1
Preparing a Balance Sheet; Computing Owner's Equity

Listed below in random order are the items to be included in the balance sheet of Mystery Mountain Lodge at December 31, 1994:

Accounts receivable	$ 7,800	Furniture	$ 47,800
Cash	19,300	Snowmobiles	15,700
Accounts payable	35,800	Equipment	18,400
Daniel Craig, capital	?	Notes payable	339,000
Buildings	296,000	Land	115,000

INSTRUCTIONS Prepare a balance sheet at December 31, 1994. Include a proper heading and organize your balance sheet similar to the illustration on page 15. (After "Buildings," you may list the remaining assets in any order.) You will need to compute the amount of owner's equity.

PROBLEM 1B-2
Recording the
Effects of
Transactions

The items making up the balance sheet of Travel Connection at December 31 are listed below in tabular form similar to the illustration of the accounting equation on page 25.

		Assets			=	Liabilities		+	Owner's Equity
	Cash +	Accounts Receivable +	Automobiles +	Office Equipment =		Notes Payable +	Accounts Payable +		D. Hall Capital
Balances	$9,500	$58,400	$9,000	$3,800		$20,000	$25,200		$35,500

During a short period after December 31, Travel Connection had the following transactions:

1 Bought office equipment at a cost of $5,700. Paid cash.
2 Collected $4,000 of accounts receivable.
3 Paid $7,200 of accounts payable.
4 Borrowed $10,000 from a bank. Signed a note payable for that amount.
5 Purchased an automobile for $15,500. Paid $3,000 cash and signed a note payable for the balance of $12,500.

INSTRUCTIONS a List the December 31 balances of assets, liabilities, and owner's equity in tabular form as shown above.

b Record the effects of each of the five transactions in the tabular arrangement illustrated above. Show the totals for all columns after each transaction.

PROBLEM 1B-3
Preparing a
Balance Sheet;
Effect of a
Change in Assets

Shown below in random order is a list of balance sheet items for Valencia Farms at September 30, 1995:

Land.........................	$305,000	Fences & gates	$ 18,650
Barns and sheds	43,500	Irrigation system	11,180
Notes payable................	295,000	Cash.........................	9,285
Accounts receivable..........	12,425	Livestock	67,100
Citrus trees	42,600	Farm machinery..............	23,872
Accounts payable	42,830	Walter Berkeley, capital.......	?
Property taxes payable	5,075	Wages payable	1,010

INSTRUCTIONS a Prepare a balance sheet by using these items and computing the amount for Walter Berkeley's capital. Use a sequence of assets similar to that illustrated on page 15. (After "Barns and sheds," you may list the remaining assets in any order.) Include a proper heading for your balance sheet.

b Assume that immediately after this September 30 balance sheet was prepared, a tornado completely destroyed one of the barns. This barn had a cost of $18,400 and was not insured against this type of disaster. Explain what changes would be required in your September 30 balance sheet to reflect the loss of this barn.

PROBLEM 1B-4
Preparing a Balance Sheet; Effects of Business Transactions

The balance sheet items for Gremlin Auto Wash (arranged in alphabetical order) were as follows at June 30, 1994:

Accounts payable	$ 4,000	Land	$40,000
Accounts receivable	300	Notes payable	46,000
Building	20,000	Supplies	2,800
Cash	4,600	Susan Young, capital	?
Equipment	26,000		

During the next two days, the following transactions occurred:

July 1   Young invested an additional $15,000 cash in the business. The accounts payable were paid in full. (No payment was made on the notes payable.)

July 2   Equipment was purchased at a cost of $9,000 to be paid within 10 days. Supplies were purchased for $500 cash from another car-washing concern which was going out of business. These supplies would have cost $900 if purchased through normal channels.

INSTRUCTIONS **a** Prepare a balance sheet at June 30, 1994.
b Prepare a balance sheet at July 2, 1994.

PROBLEM 1B-5
Preparing a Balance Sheet; Discussion of Accounting Principles

Hollywood Scripts is a service-type enterprise in the entertainment field, and its owner, Bradford Jones, has only a limited knowledge of accounting. Jones prepared the balance sheet below, which, although arranged satisfactorily, contains certain errors with respect to such concepts as the business entity and asset valuation.

HOLLYWOOD SCRIPTS
Balance Sheet
November 30, 1994

Assets		Liabilities & Owner's Equity	
Cash	$ 940	Notes payable	$ 67,000
Notes receivable	2,900	Accounts payable	29,800
Accounts receivable	2,465	Total liabilities	$ 96,800
Land	70,000	*Owner's equity:*	
Building	54,326	Bradford Jones, capital	63,080
Office furniture	6,848		
Other assets	22,401		
Total	$159,880	Total	$159,880

In discussion with Jones and by inspection of the accounting records, you discover the following facts:

1   One of the notes receivable in the amount of $700 is an IOU which Jones received in a poker game about two years ago. The IOU bears only the initials B. K., and Jones does not know the name or address of the maker.

2   Office furniture includes an antique desk purchased November 29 of the current year at a cost of $2,100. Jones explains that no payment is due for the desk until January and therefore this debt is not included among the liabilities.

3 Also included in the amount for office furniture is a typewriter which cost $525 but is not on hand, because Jones gave it to his daughter as a birthday present.

4 The "Other assets" of $22,401 represents the total amount of income taxes Jones has paid the federal government over a period of years. Jones believes the income tax law to be unconstitutional, and a friend who attends law school will help Jones recover the taxes paid as soon as he completes his legal education.

5 The asset land was acquired at a cost of $34,000 but was increased to a valuation of $70,000 when a friend of Jones offered to pay that much for it if Jones would move the building off the lot.

INSTRUCTIONS

a Prepare a corrected balance sheet at November 30, 1994.

b For each of the five numbered items above, use a separate numbered paragraph to explain whether the treatment followed by Jones is in accordance with generally accepted accounting principles.

CASES AND UNSTRUCTURED PROBLEMS

CASE 1-1
"Nonfinancial"
Information

In 1987, **The Procter & Gamble Company (P&G)** discovered Olestra, a product which greatly reduces the fat content and calories in potato chips and other fried foods. The product is believed to have great market potential, but as of 1990, the Food and Drug Administration had not yet approved its use and sale.

INSTRUCTIONS

a In 1987, would the discovery of Olestra and its future sales potential have been recorded in P&G's accounting records and reflected in the company's financial statements?

b How did investors, creditors, and other interested people learn of this discovery and its potential benefit to P&G?

CASE 1-2
Reliability of
Financial Statements

In the early 1980s, **Chrysler Corporation** was in severe financial difficulty and desperately needed large loans if the company were to survive. What factors prevented Chrysler from simply providing potential lenders with misleading financial statements, making the company look like a risk-free investment?

CASE 1-3
Ethics and
"Window
Dressing"

The date is November 18, 1994. You are the chief executive officer of Flowerhill Software—a publicly owned company that is currently in financial difficulty. Flowerhill needs large new bank loans if it is to survive.

You have been negotiating with several banks, but each has asked to see your 1994 financial statements, which will be dated December 31. These statements will, of course, be audited. You are now meeting with other corporate officers to discuss the situation, and the following suggestions have been made

1 "We are planning to buy the WordMaster Software Company for $5 million cash in December. The owners of WordMaster are in no hurry; if we delay this acquisition until January, we'll have $5 million more cash at year-end. That should make us look a lot more solvent."

2 "At year-end, we'll owe accounts payable of about $12 million. If we were to show this liability in our balance sheet at half that amount—say, $6 million—no one would know the difference. We could report the other $6 million as stockholders' equity and our financial position would appear much stronger."

3 "We owe Delta Programming $3 million, due in 90 days. I know some people at Delta. If we were to sign a note and agree to pay 12% interest, they'd let us postpone this debt for a year or more."

4 "We own investments that cost us $2 million, but today they are worth at least $6 million. Let's show them at $6 million in our balance sheet, and that will increase our total assets and our stockholders' equity by $4 million."

INSTRUCTIONS Separately evaluate each of these four proposals. Your evaluations should consider ethical and legal issues as well as accounting issues.

CASE 1-4
Using a
Balance Sheet

Sun Corporation and Terra Corporation are in the same line of business and both were recently organized, so it may be assumed that the recorded costs for assets are close to current market values. The balance sheets for the two companies are as follows at July 31, 19__:

SUN CORPORATION
Balance Sheet
July 31, 19__

Assets		Liabilities & Stockholders' Equity	
Cash	$ 18,000	**Liabilities:**	
Accounts receivable	26,000	Notes payable (due in 60 days)	$ 12,400
Land	37,200	Accounts payable	9,600
Building	38,000	Total liabilities	$ 22,000
Office equipment	1,200	Stockholders' equity	98,400
Total	$120,400	Total	$120,400

TERRA CORPORATION
Balance Sheet
July 31, 19__

Assets		Liabilities & Stockholders' Equity	
Cash	$ 4,800	**Liabilities:**	
Accounts receivable	9,600	Notes payable (due in 60 days)	$ 22,400
Land	96,000	Accounts payable	43,200
Building	60,000	Total liabilities	$ 65,600
Office equipment	12,000	Stockholders' equity	116,800
Total	$182,400	Total	$182,400

INSTRUCTIONS **a** Assume that you are a banker and that each company had applied to you for a 90-day loan of $12,000. Which would you consider to be the more favorable prospect? Explain your answer fully.

b Assume that you are an investor considering purchasing all the capital stock of one or both of the companies. For which business would you be willing to pay the higher price? Do you see any indication of a financial crisis which you might face shortly after buying either company? Explain your answer fully. (It is recognized that for either decision, additional information would be useful, but you are to reach your decision on the basis of the information available.)

CASE 1-5
Preparing a
Balance Sheet
(Instructor Participation)

You are to prepare a *hypothetical* balance sheet for an entity (or type of entity) specified by your instructor. Include in your balance sheet the types of assets and liabilities that you think the entity might have, and show these items at what you believe would be realistic dollar amounts. (Note: The purpose of this assignment is to help you visualize the types of assets and liabilities relating to the operations of a specific type of business. You should complete this assignment ***without*** referring to an actual balance sheet for this type of entity.)

CASE 1-6
Using a Balance Sheet (Instructor Participation)

Obtain from the library the ***annual report*** of a well-known company (or a company specified by your instructor).

INSTRUCTIONS

From the balance sheet, notes to the financial statements, and auditor's report, answer the following:

a What CPA firm audited the company's financial statements, and did the auditors consider the financial statements a "fair" presentation?

b Select three items in the notes accompanying the financial statements and explain briefly the importance of these items to people making decisions about investing in, or extending credit to, this company.

c Assume that you are a lender, and this company has asked to borrow an amount of cash equal to 10% of its total assets, to be repaid in 90 days. Would you consider this company to be a good credit risk? Explain.

ANSWERS TO SELF-TEST QUESTIONS

1 a, c, d   2 b, d   3 b   4 b, c, d   5 c   6 a, b, c, d   7 a, b, d   *8 b

---

*   *Supplemental Topic, "Careers in Accounting"*

2 Recording Changes in Financial Position

In this chapter we illustrate the accounting cycle—the procedures used by a business to record, classify, and summarize the effects of business transactions in its accounting records. The transactions of Roberts Real Estate Company, as described in Chapter 1, are now recorded in the company's general journal and posted to the general ledger accounts. The preparation of a trial balance is illustrated, and the uses and limitations of the trial balance are discussed. The chapter concludes by comparing the accounting procedures applied in manual accounting systems with those in computer-based systems.

After studying this chapter you should be able to meet these Learning Objectives:

1 *Describe a ledger account and a ledger.*
2 *State the rules of debit and credit for balance sheet accounts.*
3 *Explain the double-entry system of accounting.*
4 *Explain the purpose of a journal and its relationship to the ledger.*
5 *Prepare journal entries to record common business transactions.*
6 *Prepare a trial balance and explain its uses and limitations.*
7 *Describe the basic steps of the accounting cycle in both manual and computer-based accounting systems.*

The Role of Accounting Records

Many business concerns have several hundred or even several thousand business transactions each day. It would not be practical to prepare a balance sheet after each transaction and it is quite unnecessary to do so. Instead, the many individual transactions are recorded in the accounting records, and, at the end of the month or other accounting period, a balance sheet is prepared from these records. In this chapter, we shall see how business transactions are analyzed, entered in the accounting records, and classified for use in preparing a balance sheet. In later chapters, we shall also see that the accounting records contain the data necessary to prepare an income statement, income tax returns, and other financial reports.

THE LEDGER

OBJECTIVE 1
Describe a ledger account and a ledger.

An accounting system includes a separate record for each item that appears in the balance sheet. For example, a separate record is kept for the asset cash, showing all the increases and decreases in cash which result from the many transactions in which cash is received or paid. A similar record is kept for every other asset, for every liability, and for owner's equity. The form of record used to record increases and decreases in a single balance sheet item is called an **account,** or sometimes a **ledger account.** All these separate accounts are usually kept in a loose-leaf binder, and the entire group of accounts is called a **ledger.**

Many businesses use computers for maintaining accounting records; they store data on magnetic discs rather than in ledgers. However, an understanding of accounting concepts is most easily acquired by study of a manual accounting system. The knowledge gained by working with manual accounting records is readily transferable to any type of automated accounting system. For these reasons, we shall use standard written accounting records such as ledger accounts in our study of basic accounting concepts. These written records continue to be used by a great many businesses, but for our purposes they should be viewed as conceptual devices rather than as physical components of an accounting system.

The Use of Ledger Accounts

A ledger account is a means of accumulating in one place all the information about changes in a specific asset, a liability, or owner's equity. For example, a ledger account for the asset cash provides a record of the amount of cash receipts, cash payments, and the current cash balance. By maintaining a Cash account, management can keep track of the amount of cash available for meeting payrolls and for making current purchases of assets or services. This record of cash is also useful in planning future operations and in advance planning of applications for bank loans.

In its simplest form, an account has only three elements: (1) a title, consisting of the name of the particular asset, liability, or owner's equity; (2) a left side, which is called the **debit** side; and (3) a right side, which is called the **credit** side. This form of account, illustrated on the following page, is called a **T account** because of its resemblance to the letter **T.** More complete forms of accounts will be illustrated later.

T account: a ledger account in simplified form

	Title of Account	
Left or debit side		*Right or credit side*

Debit and Credit Entries

An amount recorded on the left or debit side of an account is called a ***debit,*** or a ***debit entry;*** an amount entered on the right or credit side is called a ***credit,*** or a ***credit entry.*** Accountants also use the words ***debit*** and ***credit*** as verbs. The act of recording a debit in an account is called ***debiting*** the account; the recording of a credit is called ***crediting*** the account.

Students beginning a course in accounting often have erroneous notions about the meanings of the terms ***debit*** and ***credit.*** For example, to some people unacquainted with accounting, the word ***credit*** may carry a more favorable connotation than does the word ***debit.*** Such connotations have no validity in the field of accounting. Accountants use ***debit*** to mean an entry on the left-hand side of an account and ***credit*** to mean an entry on the right-hand side. Thus, debit and credit simply mean left and right, without any hidden or subtle implications.

To illustrate the recording of debits and credits in an account, let us go back to the cash transactions of Roberts Real Estate Company as described in Chapter 1. When these cash transactions are recorded in an account, the receipts are listed in vertical order on the debit side of the account and the payments are listed on the credit side. The dates of the transactions may also be listed, as shown in the following illustration:

Cash transactions entered in ledger account

		Cash			
9/1		180,000	9/3		141,000
9/20		1,500	9/5		15,000
	181,500		9/30	*159,000*	3,000
9/30 Balance		22,500			

Each debit and credit entry in the Cash account represents a cash receipt or a cash payment. The amount of cash owned by the business at a given date is equal to the ***balance*** of the account on that date.

Determining the Balance of a T Account The balance of a ledger account is the difference in dollars between the total debits and the total credits in the account. If the debit total exceeds the credit total, the account has a ***debit balance;*** if the credit total exceeds the debit total, the account has a ***credit balance.***

In our illustrated Cash account, a rule has been drawn across the account following the last cash transaction recorded in September. The total cash receipts (debits) recorded in September amount to ***$181,500*** and the total cash payments (credits) amount to ***$159,000.*** These totals, called ***footings,*** are entered in small-size figures just above the rule. (Notice that these footings are written well to the left of the regular money columns so that they will not be mistaken for debit or credit entries). By subtracting the credit total from the debit total ($181,500 − $159,000), we determine that the Cash account has a debit balance of *$22,500* on September 30.

This debit balance is entered in the debit side of the account just below the rule. In effect, the horizontal rule creates a "fresh start" in our T account, with the month-end balance representing the *net result* of all the previous debit and credit entries. The Cash account now shows the amount of cash owned by the business on September 30. In a balance sheet prepared at this date, Cash in the amount of $22,500 would be listed as an asset.

Debit Balances in Asset Accounts   In the preceding illustration of a cash account, increases were recorded on the left or debit side of the account and decreases were recorded on the right or credit side. The increases were greater than the decreases and the result was a debit balance in the account.

All asset accounts *normally have debit balances;* in fact, the ownership of cash, land, or any other asset indicates that the increases (debits) to that asset have been greater than the decreases (credits). It is hard to imagine an account for an asset such as land having a credit balance, as this would indicate that the business had disposed of more land than it had acquired and had reached the impossible position of having a negative amount of land.

The fact that assets are located on the *left* side of the balance sheet is a convenient means of remembering the rule that an increase in an asset is recorded on the *left* (debit) side of the account, and also that an asset account normally has a debit *(left-hand)* balance.

OBJECTIVE 2 State the rules of debit and credit for balance sheet accounts.

Asset accounts normally have debit balances

Any Asset Account

(Debit) Increase	(Credit) Decrease

Credit Balances in Liability and Owner's Equity Accounts   Increases in liability and owner's equity accounts are recorded by credit entries and decreases in these accounts are recorded by debits. The relationship between entries in these accounts and their position on the balance sheet may be summed up as follows: (1) liabilities and owner's equity belong on the *right* side of the balance sheet, (2) an increase in a liability or an owner's equity account is recorded on the *right* (credit) side of the account, and (3) liability and owner's equity accounts normally have credit *(right-hand)* balances.

Liability and owner's equity accounts normally have credit balances

Any Liability Account or Owner's Equity Account

(Debit) Decrease	(Credit) Increase

Concise Statement of the Rules of Debit and Credit   The use of debits and credits to record changes in assets, liabilities, and owner's equity may be summarized as follows:

Asset Accounts	*Liability & Owner's Equity Accounts*
Increases are recorded by **debits**	*Increases are recorded by* credits
Decreases are recorded by credits	*Decreases are recorded by* **debits**

Double-Entry Accounting—The Equality of Debits and Credits

The rules for debits and credits are designed so that *every transaction is recorded by equal dollar amounts of debits and credits.* The reason for this equality lies in the relationship of the debit and credit rules to the accounting equation:

Assets = Liabilities + Owner's Equity

If this equation is to remain in balance, any change in the left side of the equation (assets) *must be accompanied by an equal change* in the right-hand side (either liabilities or owner's equity). According to the debit and credit rules that we have just described, increases in the left side of the equation (assets) are recorded by *debits,* while increases in the right side (liabilities and owner's equity) are recorded by *credits.*

OBJECTIVE 3
Explain the double-entry system of accounting.

   This system is often called *double-entry accounting.* The phrase "double-entry" refers to the need for both debit entries and credit entries (equal in dollar amount) to record every transaction. Virtually every business organization uses the double-entry system regardless of whether the company's accounting records are maintained manually or by computer. In addition, the double-entry system allows us to measure net income at the same time we record the effects of transactions upon the balance sheet accounts. (The measurement of net income is discussed in Chapter 3.)

   Double-entry accounting is not a new idea. The system has been in use for more than 600 years. The first systematic presentation of the double-entry system appears in a mathematics textbook written by Luca Pacioli, a friend of Leonardo da Vinci. This text was published in 1494—just two years after Columbus discovered America. Although Pacioli wrote the first textbook on this subject, surviving accounting records show that double-entry accounting had already been in use for at least 150 years.

Recording Transactions in Ledger Accounts: Illustration

The use of debits and credits for recording transactions in ledger accounts now will be illustrated using the September transactions of Roberts Real Estate Company. Each transaction will first be analyzed in terms of increases and decreases in assets, liabilities, and owner's equity. Then we shall follow the rules of debit and credit in entering these increases and decreases in T accounts. Asset accounts will be shown on the left side of the page; liability and owner's equity accounts on the right side. For convenience in following the transactions into the ledger accounts, the letter used to identify a given transaction will also appear opposite the debit and credit entries in the ledger. (This use of identifying letters is for illustrative purposes only and is not used in actual accounting practice.)

Transaction (a) Roberts invested $180,000 cash in the business on September 1.

Recording an investment in the business

Analysis	Rule	Entry
The asset Cash was increased	Increases in assets are recorded by debits	Debit: Cash, $180,000
The owner's equity was increased	Increases in owner's equity are recorded by credits	Credit: James Roberts, Capital, $180,000

Cash		James Roberts, Capital	
9/1 (a) 180,000			9/1 (a) 180,000

Transaction (b) On September 3, Roberts Real Estate Company purchased land for cash in the amount of $141,000.

Purchase of land for cash

Analysis	Rule	Entry
The asset Land was increased	Increases in assets are recorded by debits	Debit: Land, $141,000
The asset Cash was decreased	Decreases in assets are recorded by credits	Credit: Cash, $141,000

Cash			
9/1 180,000	9/3 (b) 141,000		

Land		
9/3 (b) 141,000		

Transaction (c) On September 5, Roberts Real Estate Company purchased a building from Kent Company at a total price of $36,000. The terms of the purchase required a cash payment of $15,000 with the remainder of $21,000 payable within 90 days.

Analysis	Rule	Entry
A new asset, Building, was acquired	Increases in assets are recorded by debits	Debit: Building, $36,000
The asset Cash was decreased	Decreases in assets are recorded by credits	Credit: Cash, $15,000
A new liability, Accounts Payable, was incurred	Increases in liabilities are recorded by credits	Credit: Accounts Payable, $21,000

Purchase of an asset, with partial payment

Cash				Accounts Payable		
9/1	180,000	9/3	141,000		9/5	(c) 21,000
		9/5	(c) 15,000			

Building	
9/5 (c) 36,000	

Transaction (d) On September 10, Roberts Real Estate Company sold a portion of its land on credit to Carter's Drugstore for a price of $11,000. The land was sold at its cost, so there was no gain or loss on the transaction.

Sale of land on credit (no gain or loss)

Analysis	Rule	Entry
A new asset, Accounts Receivable, was acquired	Increases in assets are recorded by debits	Debit: Accounts Receivable, $11,000
The asset Land was decreased	Decreases in assets are recorded by credits	Credit: Land, $11,000

Accounts Receivable	
9/10 (d) 11,000	

Land			
9/3	141,000	9/10	(d) 11,000

Transaction (e) On September 14, Roberts Real Estate Company purchased office equipment on credit from General Equipment, Inc., in the amount of $5,400.

	Analysis	Rule	Entry
Purchase of an asset on credit	A new asset, Office Equipment, was acquired	Increases in assets are recorded by debits	Debit: Office Equipment, $5,400
	A new liability, Accounts Payable, was incurred	Increases in liabilities are recorded by credits	Credit: Accounts Payable, $5,400

Office Equipment			Accounts Payable	
9/14 (e) 5,400			9/5 21,000	
			9/14 (e) 5,400	

Transaction (f)   On September 20, cash of $1,500 was received as partial collection of the account receivable from Carter's Drugstore.

	Analysis	Rule	Entry
Collection of an account receivable	The asset Cash was increased	Increases in assets are recorded by debits	Debit: Cash, $1,500
	The asset Accounts Receivable was decreased	Decreases in assets are recorded by credits	Credit: Accounts Receivable, $1,500

Cash			
9/1 180,000	9/3	141,000	
9/20 (f) 1,500	9/5	15,000	

Accounts Receivable		
9/10 11,000	9/20	(f) 1,500

Transaction (g)   A cash payment of $3,000 was made on September 30 in partial settlement of the amount owing to General Equipment, Inc.

	Analysis	Rule	Entry
Payment of a liability	The liability Accounts Payable was decreased	Decreases in liabilities are recorded by debits	Debit: Accounts Payable, $3,000
	The asset Cash was decreased	Decreases in assets are recorded by credits	Credit: Cash, $3,000

	Cash				Accounts Payable		
9/1	180,000	9/3	141,000	9/30	(g) 3,000	9/5	21,000
9/20	1,500	9/5	15,000			9/14	5,400
		9/30	(g) 3,000				

Running Balance Form of Accounts

T accounts are widely used in the classroom and in accounting textbooks, because they provide a concise conceptual picture of the financial effects of a business transaction. In actual practice, however, most businesses prefer to use the ***running balance*** form of ledger account. This form of account has special columns for recording additional information, as illustrated below with the Cash account of Roberts Real Estate Company:

				Cash			Account No. /	
Date		Explanation	Ref	Debit		Credit		Balance
19 —								
Sept	1			180,000 00				180,000 00
	3					141,000 00		39,000 00
	5					15,000 00		24,000 00
	20			1,500 00				25,500 00
	30					3,000 00		22,500 00

The ***Date*** column shows the date of the transaction—which is not necessarily the same as the date the entry is recorded in the account. The ***Explanation*** column is needed only for unusual items, and in many companies it is seldom used. The ***Ref*** (Reference) column is used to list the page number of the journal in which the transaction is recorded, thus making it possible to trace ledger entries back to their source. (The use of a ***journal*** is explained later in this chapter.) In the ***Balance*** column of the account, the new balance is entered each time the account is debited or credited. Thus the current balance of the account can always be observed at a glance.

The "Normal" Balance of an Account   The running balance form of ledger account does not indicate specifically whether the balance of the account is a debit or credit balance. However, this causes no difficulty because we know that asset accounts normally have debit balances and that accounts for liabilities and owner's equity normally have credit balances.

Occasionally an asset account may temporarily acquire a credit balance, either as the result of an accounting error or because of an unusual transaction. For example, an account receivable may acquire a credit balance because of overpayment by a customer. However, a credit balance in the Building account could be created only by an accounting error.

Sequence and Numbering of Ledger Accounts   Accounts are usually arranged in the ledger in *financial statement order,* that is, assets first, followed by liabilities, owner's equity, revenue, and expenses. The number of accounts needed by a business will depend upon its size, the nature of its operations, and the extent to which management and regulatory agencies want detailed classification of information. An identification number is assigned to each account. A *chart of accounts* is a listing of the account titles and account numbers being used by a given business.

In the following list of accounts, certain numbers have not been assigned; these numbers are held in reserve so that additional accounts can be inserted in the ledger in proper sequence whenever such accounts become necessary. In this illustration, the numbers from 1 to 29 are used exclusively for asset accounts; numbers from 30 to 49 are reserved for liabilities; and numbers in the 50s signify owner's equity accounts. Numbers in the 60s represent revenue accounts and numbers from 70 to 99 designate expense accounts. Revenue and expense will be discussed in Chapter 3. The balance sheet accounts used thus far in our Roberts Real Estate illustration are numbered as shown in the following *chart of accounts:*

Account Title	Account No.
Assets:	
Cash...	*1*
Accounts receivable..	*4*
Land...	*20*
Building..	*22*
Office equipment	*25*
Liabilities:	
Accounts payable	*32*
Owner's equity:	
James Roberts, capital	*50*

System for numbering ledger accounts

In large businesses with hundreds or thousands of accounts, a more elaborate numbering system is used. Some companies use an eight- or ten-digit number for each ledger account; each of the digits carries special significance as to the classification of the account.

Sequence of Asset Accounts   As shown in all the balance sheets we have illustrated, cash is listed first among the assets. It is followed by such assets as marketable securities, short-term notes receivable, accounts receivable, inventories of merchandise, and supplies. These are the most common examples of current assets. The term *current assets* includes cash and those assets which will quickly be converted into cash or used up in operations. Next on the balance sheet come the relatively permanent assets used in the business (often called *plant assets*). Of this group, land is listed first and is followed by buildings. After these two items, any order is acceptable for other assets used in the business, such as automobiles, furniture and fixtures, computers, lighting equipment, store equipment, etc.

THE JOURNAL

OBJECTIVE 4
Explain the
purpose of a
journal and
its relation-
ship to the
ledger.

In our preceding discussion, we recorded business transactions directly in the company's ledger accounts. We did this in order to stress the effects of business transactions upon the individual asset, liability, and owner's equity accounts appearing in the company's balance sheet. In an actual accounting system, however, the information about each business transaction is initially recorded in an accounting record called the ***journal.*** After the transaction has been recorded in the journal, the debit and credit changes in the individual accounts are entered in the ledger. Since the journal is the accounting record in which transactions are ***first recorded,*** it is sometimes called the ***book of original entry.***

The journal is a chronological (day-by-day) record of business transactions. The information recorded about each transaction includes the date of the transaction, the debit and credit changes in specific ledger accounts, and a brief explanation of the transaction. At convenient intervals, the debit and credit amounts recorded in the journal are transferred ***(posted)*** to the accounts in the ledger. The updated ledger accounts, in turn, serve as the basis for preparing the balance sheet and other financial statements.

Why Use a Journal?

Since it is technically possible to record transactions directly in the ledger, why bother to maintain a journal? The answer is that the unit of organization for the journal is the ***transaction,*** whereas the unit of organization for the ledger is the ***account.*** By having both a journal and a ledger, we achieve several advantages which would not be possible if transactions were recorded directly in ledger accounts:

1 **The journal shows all information about a transaction in one place and also provides an explanation of the transaction.** In a journal entry, the debits and credits for a given transaction are recorded together, but when the transaction is recorded in the ledger, the debits and credits are entered in different accounts. Since a ledger may contain hundreds of accounts, it would be very difficult to locate all the facts about a particular transaction by looking in the ledger. The journal is the record which shows the complete story of a transaction in one entry.

2 **The journal provides a chronological record of all the events in the life of a business.** If we want to look up the facts about a transaction of some months or years back, all we need is the date of the transaction in order to locate it in the journal.

3 **The use of a journal helps to prevent errors.** If transactions were recorded directly in the ledger, it would be very easy to make errors such as omitting the debit or the credit, or entering the debit twice or the credit twice. Such errors are not likely to be made in the journal, since the offsetting debits and credits appear together for each transaction.

The General Journal: Illustration of Entries

OBJECTIVE 5
*Prepare
journal en-
tries to re-
cord com-
mon busi-
ness trans-
actions.*

Many businesses maintain several types of journals. The nature of operations and the volume of transactions in the particular business determine the number and type of journals needed. The simplest type of journal is called a **general journal** and is shown on the next page. A general journal has only two money columns, one for debits and the other for credits; it may be used for all types of transactions.

The process of recording a transaction in a journal is called **journalizing** the transaction. To illustrate the use of the general journal, we shall now journalize the September transactions of Roberts Real Estate Company which have been discussed previously.

Efficient use of a general journal requires two things: (1) ability to analyze the effect of a transaction upon assets, liabilities, and owner's equity and (2) familiarity with the standard form and arrangement of journal entries. Our primary interest is in the analytical phase of journalizing; the procedural steps can be learned quickly by observing the following points in the illustration of journal entries:

1 The year, month, and day of the first entry on the page are written in the date column. The year and month need not be repeated for subsequent entries until a new page or a new month is begun.

2 The name of the account to be debited is written for the first line of the entry and is customarily placed at the extreme left next to the date column. The amount of the debit is entered on the same line in the **left-hand** money column.

3 The name of the account to be credited is entered on the line below the debit entry and is **indented,** that is, placed about 1 inch to the right of the date column. The amount credited is entered on the same line in the **right-hand** money column.

4 A brief explanation of the transaction begins on the line immediately below the last account credited. This explanation includes any data needed to identify the transaction, such as the name of the customer or supplier. The explanation is not indented.

5 A blank line should be left after each entry. This spacing causes each journal entry to stand out clearly as a separate unit and makes the journal easier to read.

6 An entry which includes more than one debit or more than one credit (such as the entry on September 5) is called a **compound journal entry.** Regardless of how many debits or credits are contained in a compound journal entry, **all the debits** are entered **before any credits** are listed.

7 The LP (ledger page) column just to the left of the debit money column is left blank at the time of making the journal entry. When the debits and credits are later transferred to ledger accounts, the numbers of the ledger accounts will be listed in this column to provide a convenient cross-reference with the ledger.

In journalizing transactions, remember that the **exact title** of the ledger accounts to be debited and credited should be used. For example, in recording the purchase of office equipment for cash, **do not** make a journal entry debiting "Office Equipment Purchased" and crediting "Cash Paid

	General Journal			Page /
Date	**Account Titles and Explanation**	**LP**	**Debit**	**Credit**
19 —				
Sept 1	Cash		1 80 0 00	
	James Roberts, Capital			1 80 0 00
	Invested cash in the business.			
3	Land		1 41 0 00	
	Cash			1 41 0 00
	Purchased land for office site.			
5	Building		36 0 00	
	Cash			1 50 0 00
	Accounts Payable			2 1 0 00
	Purchased building to be moved			
	to our lot. Paid part cash;			
	balance payable within 90			
	days to Kent Company			
10	Accounts Receivable		1 1 0 00	
	Land			1 1 0 00
	Sold the unused part of our			
	lot at cost to Carter's Drugstore.			
	Due within 3 months.			
14	Office Equipment		5 4 00	
	Accounts Payable			5 4 00
	Purchased equipment on credit			
	from General Equipment, Inc.			
20	Cash		1 5 00	
	Accounts Receivable			1 5 00
	Collected part of receivable from			
	Carter's Drugstore.			
30	Accounts Payable		30 00	
	Cash			30 00
	Made partial payment of the lia-			
	bility to General Equipment, Inc.			

Out." There are no ledger accounts with such titles. The proper journal entry would consist of a debit to *Office Equipment* and a credit to *Cash.*

A familiarity with the general journal form of describing transactions is just as essential to the study of accounting as a familiarity with plus and minus signs is to the study of mathematics. The journal entry is a **tool** for **analyzing** and **describing** the impact of various transactions upon a business entity. The ability to describe a transaction in journal entry form requires an understanding of the nature of the transaction and its effects upon the financial position of the business.

Posting

The process of transferring the debits and credits from the general journal to the proper ledger accounts is called ***posting.*** Each amount listed in the debit column of the journal is posted by entering it on the debit side of an account in the ledger, and each amount listed in the credit column of the journal is posted to the credit side of a ledger account.

The mechanics of posting may vary somewhat with the preferences of the individual. The following sequence is commonly used:

1 Locate in the ledger the first account named in the journal entry.

2 Enter in the debit column of the ledger account the amount of the debit as shown in the journal.

3 Enter the date of the transaction in the ledger account.

4 Enter in the reference column of the ledger account the number of the journal page from which the entry is being posted.

5 The recording of the debit in the ledger account is now complete; as evidence of this fact, return to the journal and enter in the LP (ledger page) column the number of the ledger account or page to which the debit was posted.

6 Repeat the posting process described in the preceding five steps for the credit side of the journal entry.

Illustration of Posting   To illustrate the posting process, the journal entry for the first transaction of Roberts Real Estate Company is repeated at this point along with the two ledger accounts affected by this entry.

Note that the ***Ref*** (Reference) column of each of the two ledger accounts contains the number 1, indicating that the posting was made from ***page 1*** of the journal. Entering the journal page number in the ledger account and listing the ledger account number in the journal provide a ***cross-reference*** between these two records. It is often necessary to refer to the journal entry in order to obtain more information about an amount listed in a ledger account. A cross-reference between the ledger and journal is therefore essential to efficient use of the records. Another advantage gained from entering in the journal the number of the ledger account to which a posting has been made is to provide evidence throughout the posting work as to which items have been posted. Otherwise, any interruption in the posting might leave some doubt as to which entries had been posted.

Journalizing and posting by hand is a useful method for the study of accounting, both for problem assignments and for examinations. The manual approach is also followed in many small businesses. One shortcoming is the opportunity for error that exists whenever information is being cop-

Journal

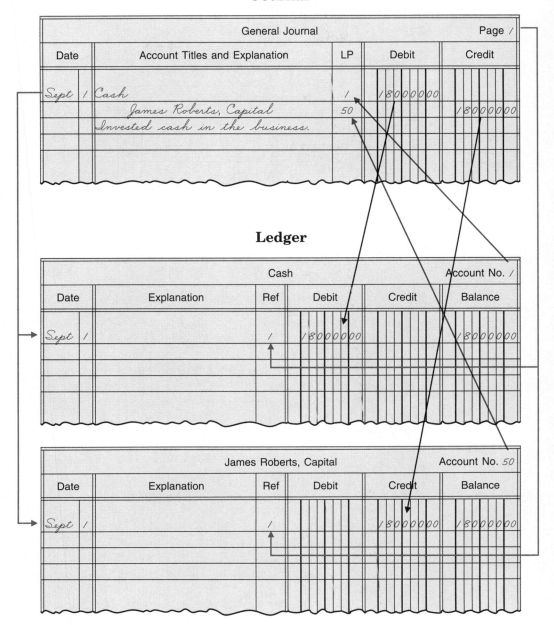

Ledger

ied from one record to another. In businesses having a large volume of transactions, the posting of ledger accounts is performed automatically by computer, which speeds up the work and reduces errors.

Ledger Accounts after Posting After all the September transactions have been posted, the ledger of Roberts Real Estate Company appears as shown on pages 72 and 73. The accounts are arranged in the ledger in the same order as in the balance sheet, that is, assets first, followed by liabilities and owner's equity.

To conserve space in this illustration, several ledger accounts appear on a single page. In actual practice, however, each account occupies a separate page in the ledger.

Ledger showing September transactions

		Cash				Account No. 1
Date	Explanation	Ref	Debit	Credit	Balance	
19 —						
Sept 1		1	18000000		18000000	
3		1		14100000	3900000	
5		1		1500000	2400000	
20		1	150000		2550000	
30		1		300000	2250000	

		Accounts Receivable				Account No. 4
Date	Explanation	Ref	Debit	Credit	Balance	
19 —						
Sept 10		1	1100000		1100000	
20		1		150000	950000	

		Land				Account No. 20
Date	Explanation	Ref	Debit	Credit	Balance	
19 —						
Sept 3		1	14100000		14100000	
10		1		1100000	13000000	

		Building				Account No. 22
Date	Explanation	Ref	Debit	Credit	Balance	
19 —						
Sept 5		1	3600000		3600000	

Office Equipment					Account No. 25
Date	Explanation	Ref	Debit	Credit	Balance
19 —					
Sept 14		1	5 4 0 0 00		5 4 0 0 00

Accounts Payable					Account No. 32
Date	Explanation	Ref	Debit	Credit	Balance
19 —					
Sept 5		1		2 1 0 0 00	2 1 0 0 00
14		1		5 4 0 00	2 6 4 0 00
30		1	3 0 0 00		2 3 4 0 00

James Roberts, Capital					Account No. 50
Date	Explanation	Ref	Debit	Credit	Balance
19 —					
Sept 1		1		1 8 0 0 0 00	1 8 0 0 0 00

THE TRIAL BALANCE

OBJECTIVE 6
Prepare a trial balance and explain its uses and limitations.

Since equal dollar amounts of debits and credits are entered in the accounts for every transaction recorded, the sum of all the debits in the ledger must be equal to the sum of all the credits. If the computation of account balances has been accurate, it follows that the total of the accounts with debit balances must be equal to the total of the accounts with credit balances.

Before using the account balances to prepare a balance sheet, it is desirable to **prove** that the total of accounts with debit balances is in fact equal to the total of accounts with credit balances. This proof of the equality of debit and credit balances is called a **trial balance.** A trial balance is a two-column schedule listing the names and balances of all the accounts **in the order in which they appear in the ledger;** the debit balances are listed in the left-hand column and the credit balances in the right-hand column. The totals of the two columns should agree. A trial balance taken from the ledger of Roberts Real Estate Company follows.

ROBERTS REAL ESTATE COMPANY
Trial Balance
September 30, 19__

Cash	$ 22,500	
Accounts receivable	9,500	
Land	130,000	
Building	36,000	
Office equipment	5,400	
Accounts payable...		$ 23,400
James Roberts, capital.......................................		180,000
	$203,400	$203,400

Uses and Limitations of the Trial Balance

The trial balance provides proof that the ledger is in balance. The agreement of the debit and credit totals of the trial balance gives assurance that:

1 Equal debits and credits have been recorded for all transactions.

2 The debit or credit balance of each account has been correctly computed.

3 The addition of the account balances in the trial balance has been correctly performed.

Suppose that the debit and credit totals of the trial balance do not agree. This situation indicates that one or more errors have been made. Typical of such errors are (1) the posting of a debit as a credit, or vice versa; (2) arithmetic mistakes in balancing accounts; (3) clerical errors in copying account balances into the trial balance; (4) listing a debit balance in the credit column of the trial balance, or vice versa; and (5) errors in addition of the trial balance.

The preparation of a trial balance does not prove that transactions have been correctly analyzed and recorded in the proper accounts. If, for example, a receipt of cash were erroneously recorded by debiting the Land account instead of the Cash account, the trial balance would still balance. Also, if a transaction were completely omitted from the ledger, the error would not be disclosed by the trial balance. In brief, *the trial balance proves only one aspect of the ledger, and that is the equality of debits and credits.*

Despite these limitations, the trial balance is a useful device. It not only provides assurance that the ledger is in balance, but it also serves as a convenient stepping-stone for the preparation of financial statements. As explained in Chapter 1, the balance sheet is a formal statement showing the financial position of the business, intended for distribution to managers, owners, bankers, and various outsiders. The trial balance, on the other hand, is merely a working paper, useful to the accountant but not intended for distribution to others. The balance sheet and other financial statements can be prepared more conveniently from the trial balance than directly from the ledger, especially if there are a great many ledger accounts.

Locating Errors

In the illustration given, the trial balance was in balance. Every accounting student soon discovers in working problems, however, that errors are easily made which prevent trial balances from balancing. The lack of balance may be the result of a single error or a combination of several errors. An error may have been made in adding the trial balance columns or in copying the balances from the ledger accounts. If the preparation of the trial balance has been accurate, then the error may lie in the accounting records, either in the journal or in the ledger accounts. What is the most efficient approach to locating the error or errors? There is no single technique which will give the best results every time, but the following procedures, done in sequence, will often save considerable time and effort in locating errors.

1 Prove the addition of the trial balance columns by adding these columns in the opposite direction from that previously followed.

2 If the error does not lie in addition, next determine the exact amount by which the schedule is out of balance. The amount of the discrepancy is often a clue to the source of the error. If the discrepancy is *divisible by 9,* this suggests either a *transposition* error or a *slide.* For example, assume that the Cash account has a balance of $2,175, but in copying the balance into the trial balance the figures are *transposed* and written as $2,157. The resulting error is $18, and like all transposition errors is *divisible by 9.* Another common error is the *slide,* or incorrect placement of the decimal point, as when $2,175.00 is copied as $21.75. The resulting discrepancy in the trial balance will also be an amount *divisible by 9.*

   To illustrate another method of using the amount of a discrepancy as a clue to locating the error, assume that the Office Equipment account has a *debit* balance of $420, but that it is erroneously listed in the *credit* column of the trial balance. This will cause a discrepancy of two times $420, or $840, in the trial balance totals. Since such errors as recording a debit in a credit column are not uncommon, it is advisable, after determining the discrepancy in the trial balance totals, to scan the columns for an amount equal to exactly *one-half* of the discrepancy. It is also advisable to look over the transactions for an item of the exact amount of the discrepancy. An error may have been made by recording the debit side of the transaction and forgetting to enter the credit side.

3 Compare the amounts in the trial balance with the balances in the ledger. Make sure that each ledger account balance has been included in the correct column of the trial balance.

4 Recompute the balance of each ledger account.

5 Trace all postings from the journal to the ledger accounts. As this is done, place a check mark in the journal and in the ledger after each

figure verified. When the operation is completed, look through the journal and the ledger for unchecked amounts. In tracing postings, be alert not only for errors in amount but also for debits entered as credits, or vice versa.

Some Tips on Record-Keeping Procedures

Dollar signs are not used in journals or ledgers. Some accountants use dollar signs in trial balances; some do not. In this book, dollar signs are used in trial balances. Dollar signs should always be used in the balance sheet, the income statement, and other formal financial reports. In the balance sheet, for example, a dollar sign is placed by the first amount in each column and also by the final amount or total. Many accountants also place a dollar sign by each subtotal or other amount listed below an underlining. In the published financial statements of large corporations, the use of dollar signs is often limited to the first and last figures in a column.

When dollar amounts are being entered in the columnar paper used in journals and ledgers, commas and decimal points are not needed. On unruled paper, commas and decimal points should be used. Most of the problems and illustrations in this book are in even dollar amounts. In such cases the cents column can be left blank or, if desired, zeros or dashes may be used. A dollar amount that represents a final total within a schedule is underlined by a double rule.

THE ACCOUNTING CYCLE: AN INTRODUCTION

OBJECTIVE 7
Describe the basic steps of the accounting cycle in both manual and computer-based accounting systems.

The sequence of accounting procedures used to record, classify, and summarize accounting information is often termed the ***accounting cycle.*** The accounting cycle begins with the initial recording of business transactions and concludes with the preparation of formal financial statements summarizing the effects of these transactions upon the assets, liabilities, and owner's equity of the business. The term ***cycle*** indicates that these procedures must be repeated continuously to enable the business to prepare new, up-to-date financial statements at reasonable intervals.

At this point, we have illustrated a complete accounting cycle as it relates to the preparation of a balance sheet for a service-type business with a manual accounting system. The accounting procedures discussed to this point may be summarized as follows:

1   **Record transaction in the journal.**   As each business transaction occurs, it is entered in the journal, thus creating a chronological record of events. This procedure completes the recording step in the accounting cycle.

2   **Post to ledger accounts.**   The debit and credit changes in account balances are posted from the journal to the ledger. This procedure classifies the effects of the business transactions in terms of specific asset, liability, and owner's equity accounts.

3   **Prepare a trial balance.**   A trial balance proves the equality of the debit and credit entries in the ledger. The purpose of this procedure is to verify the accuracy of the posting process and the computation of ledger account balances.

4 Prepare financial statements. At this point, we have discussed only one financial statement—the balance sheet. This statement shows the financial position of the business at a specific date. The preparation of financial statements summarizes the effects of business transactions occurring through the date of the statements and completes the accounting cycle.

In the next section of this chapter, and throughout this textbook, we will extend our discussion to include computer-based accounting systems. In Chapters 3 and 4, we will expand the accounting cycle to include the measurement of business income and the preparation of an income statement.

Manual and Computer-Based Systems: A Comparison

In our preceding discussion, we have assumed the use of a manual accounting system, in which all the accounting procedures are performed manually by the company's accounting personnel. The reader may wonder about the relevance of such a discussion in an era when even many small businesses use computer-based accounting systems. However, the concepts and procedures involved in the operation of manual and computer-based accounting systems are *essentially the same.* The differences are largely a question of whether specific procedures require human attention, or whether they can be performed automatically by machine.

Computers can be programmed to perform mechanical tasks with great speed and accuracy. For example, they can be programmed to read data, to perform mathematical computations, and to rearrange data into any desired format. However, computers cannot think. Therefore, they are not able to *analyze* business transactions. Without human guidance, computers cannot determine which events should be recorded in the accounting records, or which accounts should be debited and credited to record an event. With these abilities and limitations in mind, we will explore the effects of computer-based systems upon the basic accounting cycle.

Recording Business Transactions The recording of transactions requires two steps. First, the transaction must be *analyzed* to determine whether it should be recorded in the accounting records and, if so, which accounts should be debited and credited and for what dollar amounts. Second, the transaction must be *physically entered* (recorded) in the accounting system. As computers do not know which transactions should be recorded or how to record them properly, these two functions must be performed by accounting personnel in both manual and computerized systems.

Differences do exist, however, in the manner in which data are physically entered into manual and computer-based systems. In manual systems, the data are entered in the form of handwritten journal entries. In a computer-based system, the data will be entered through a keyboard, an optical scanner, or other input device. Also, data entered into a computer-based system need *not* be arranged in the format of a journal entry. The data usually are entered into a *data base,* instead of a journal.

What Is a Data Base? A data base is a warehouse of information stored within a computer system. The purpose of the data base is to allow information that will be used for several different purposes to be entered into the computer system *only once.* Data are originally entered into the data base. Then, as data are needed, the computer refers to the data base, selects the appropriate data, and arranges them in the desired format.

The information that must be entered into the data base is the same as that contained in a journal entry—the date, the accounts to be debited and credited, the dollar amounts, and an explanation of the transaction. However, this information need not be arranged in the format of a journal entry. For example, in a data base, accounts usually are identified by number, rather than by title. Also, abbreviations such as "D" or "C" are used to indicate whether an account should be debited or credited. Once information has been entered in the data base, the computer can arrange this information into any desired format, such as journal entries, ledger accounts, and financial statements.

Posting to Ledger Accounts   Posting merely transfers existing information from one accounting record to another—a function which can be easily performed by a computer. In a computer-based system, data posted to the ledger accounts come directly from the data base, rather than from the journal.

Preparation of a Trial Balance   Preparation of a trial balance involves three steps: (1) determining the balances of ledger accounts, (2) arranging the account balances in the format of a trial balance, and (3) adding up the trial balance columns and comparing the column totals. All these functions involve information already contained in the data base and can be performed by the computer.

Preparation of Financial Statements and Related Disclosures   The preparation of a balance sheet and of the related disclosures are two very different tasks. The balance sheet—like the trial balance—consists of account titles and dollar amounts taken directly from the ledger. Hence, a balance sheet may be prepared automatically in a computer-based system.

Making the appropriate *disclosures* to accompany a set of financial statements, however, is a very different matter. Determining the items to be disclosed and wording the appropriate notes to the financial statements are tasks requiring *professional judgment.* Therefore, appropriate disclosures *cannot be prepared automatically by a computer;* they must be prepared carefully by people with *sound judgment,* as well as extensive knowledge of generally accepted accounting principles and financial reporting requirements.

At this point, our discussion of financial statements is limited to the preparation of a balance sheet. The preparation of an income statement involves additional procedures which will be discussed in the following chapter.

In Summary . . .   Computers can eliminate the need for copying and rearranging information which already has been entered into the system. They also can perform mathematical computations. In short, computers eliminate most of the "paper work" involved in the operation of an accounting system. However, they *do not* eliminate the need for accounting personnel who can analyze business transactions and explain these events in conformity with generally accepted accounting principles.

The differences in manual and computer-based systems with respect to the accounting procedures discussed in this chapter are summarized graphically in the flowcharts below. Functions which are performed by accounting personnel are printed on a white background, and tasks which can be performed automatically by the computer are printed on a gray shaded background.

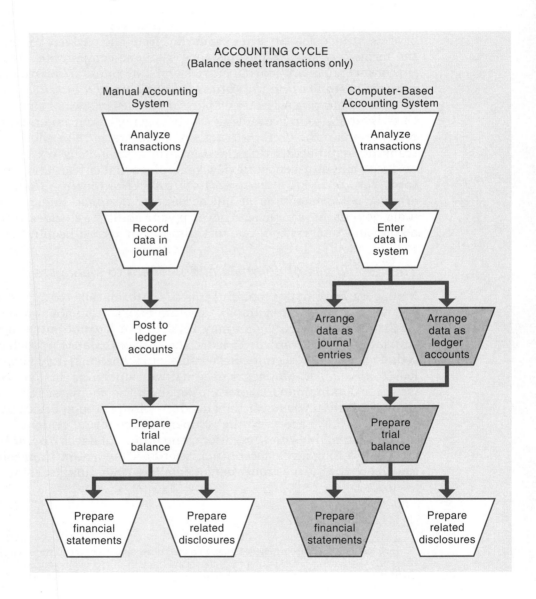

ACCOUNTING CYCLE
(Balance sheet transactions only)

JOURNALS, LEDGERS, AND ACCOUNTING EDUCATION

In this chapter, our discussion of journals and ledgers has focused upon the simplest forms of these accounting records—a manually maintained "general" journal and T accounts. While these records might be sufficient for a very small business, most organizations use more complicated and more efficient types of journals and ledgers. An increasing number of organizations use computer-based accounting systems. Even when a manual system is in use, the recording of transactions can be done much more quickly in "special journals" than in the two-column general journal.[1] The formats of accounting software differ somewhat from one package to the next; also, the formats of special journals vary from one company to the next.

However, general journal entries and T accounts *illustrate the effects of transactions upon the financial position of a business* more clearly than do accounting software displays or entries in special journals. Despite their limited use in accounting practice, general journal entries and T accounts remain the preferred method of illustrating the effects of business transactions in accounting classrooms and accounting textbooks.

As a student, you should view general journal entries and T accounts as *tools for analyzing transactions and illustrating their financial effects,* not elements of actual accounting systems. Remember, our primary goal in this course is to develop your ability to *understand and use* accounting information, not to train you in record-keeping procedures.[2]

The Usefulness of Journals and Ledgers to Managers

Managers continually make use of the information contained in the accounting records. For example, to obtain information about a specific business transaction, managers may refer to the journal entry in which the transaction was recorded. To learn the current balance in such critical accounts as Cash, Accounts Receivable, and Accounts Payable, managers look to the ledger. Managers need not wait until financial statements are issued to obtain financial information about the business. They may obtain this information whenever they need it—often through desktop computers with "read only" access to the company's accounting system.[3]

In contrast, investors, creditors, and other outsiders *do not* have direct access to a company's accounting records. They obtain financial information about the business only *periodically*—when financial statements are issued.[4]

---

[1] Special journals are journals designed to record *one* particular type of transaction quickly and efficiently. By having several different kinds of special journals, a business may be able to record efficiently *all* types of transactions that *occur frequently.* Special journals will be discussed further in Chapter 6.

[2] Although the format of accounting records varies from one business to the next, a student who understands the basic concepts of double-entry accounting should have little trouble in learning to understand and use the accounting records of any specific organization.

[3] "Read only" is an internal control that allows users of a specific computer terminal to read data, but not to alter the data or input new data into the system.

[4] Certain financial events may be disclosed to outsiders between financial statement dates, through such media as press conferences. Still, managers have far more timely access to most accounting information than do outside decision makers.

END-OF-CHAPTER REVIEW

SUMMARY OF CHAPTER LEARNING OBJECTIVES

1 Describe a ledger account and a ledger.

A ledger account is a device for recording the increases or decreases in one financial statement item, such as a particular asset, a type of liability, or owner's equity. The ledger is an accounting record which includes all the ledger accounts—that is, a separate account for each item included in the company's financial statements.

2 State the rules of debit and credit for balance sheet accounts.

Increases in assets are recorded by debits and decreases are recorded by credits. Increases in liabilities and in owner's equity are recorded by credits and decreases are recorded by debits. Notice that the debit and credit rules are related to an account's *location in the balance sheet.* If the account appears on the *left-hand side* of the balance sheet (asset accounts), increases in the account balance are recorded by *left-side entries* (debits). If the account appears on the *right-hand side* of the balance sheet (liability and owner's equity accounts), increases are recorded by *right-side entries* (credits).

3 Explain the double-entry system of accounting.

The double-entry system of accounting takes its name from the fact that every business transaction is recorded by *two sets of entries:* (1) debit entries to one or more accounts and (2) credit entries to one or more accounts. In recording any transaction, the total dollar amount of the debit entries must equal the total dollar amount of the credit entries.

4 Explain the purpose of a journal and its relationship to the ledger.

The journal, or book of original entry, is the accounting record in which business transactions are initially recorded. The entry in the journal shows which ledger accounts have increased as a result of the transaction, and which have decreased. After the effects of the transaction have been recorded in the journal, the changes in the individual ledger accounts are then posted to the ledger.

5 Prepare journal entries to record common business transactions.

The effects of business transactions upon the assets, liabilities, or owner's equity of a business are recorded in the journal. Each journal entry includes the date of the transaction, the names of the ledger accounts affected, the dollar amounts of the changes in these accounts, and a brief explanation of the transaction.

6 Prepare a trial balance and explain its uses and limitations.

In a trial balance, separate debit and credit columns are used to list the balances of the individual ledger accounts. The two columns are then totaled to prove the equality of the debit and credit balances. This process provides assurance that (1) the total of the debits posted to the ledger was equal to the total of the credits, and (2) the balances of the individual ledger accounts were correctly computed. While a trial balance proves the equality of debit and credit entries in the ledger, it does **not** detect such errors as failure to record a business transaction, improper analysis of the accounts affected by the transaction, or the posting of debit or credit entries to the wrong accounts.

7 **Describe the basic steps of the accounting cycle in both manual and computer-based accounting systems.**

At this stage of our study, the steps in any accounting system are (1) record transactions in a journal, (2) post the information to the ledger accounts, (3) prepare a trial balance, and (4) prepare financial statements and the related disclosures. In a manual accounting system, all four steps are performed by accounting personnel. In a computer-based system, steps *2, 3,* and *4* (excepting ***disclosures***) are performed automatically by the computer.

We will expand our discussion of the accounting cycle in the next two chapters to include steps relating to the measurement of net income. For the introductory student, Chapter 2 is one of the most important chapters in the textbook. Journal entries and T accounts will be used as instructional devices throughout the study of accounting. The topics of double-entry accounting and the accounting cycle serve as "building blocks" for much of the material presented in later chapters.

KEY TERMS INTRODUCED OR EMPHASIZED IN CHAPTER 2

Account A record used to summarize all increases and decreases in a particular asset, such as Cash, or any other type of asset, liability, owner's equity, revenue, or expense.

Accounting cycle The sequence of accounting procedures applied in recording, classifying, and summarizing accounting information. The cycle begins with the occurrence of business transactions and concludes with the preparation of financial statements. This concept will be expanded in later chapters.

Credit An amount entered on the right-hand side of an account. A credit is used to record a decrease in an asset and an increase in a liability or in owner's equity.

Data base A storage center of information within a computer-based accounting system. The idea behind a data base is that data intended for a variety of uses may be entered into the computer system only once, at which time the information is stored in the data base. Then, as the information is needed, the computer can retrieve it from the data base and arrange it in the desired format.

Debit An amount entered on the left-hand side of an account. A debit is used to record an increase in an asset and a decrease in a liability or in owner's equity.

Double-entry accounting A system of recording every business transaction with equal dollar amounts of both debit and credit entries. As a result of this system, the accounting equation always remains in balance; in addition, the system makes possible the measurement of net income and also the use of error-detecting devices such as a trial balance.

Footing The total of amounts in a column.

Journal A chronological record of transactions, showing for each transaction the debits and credits to be entered in specific ledger accounts. The simplest type of journal is called a general journal.

Ledger A loose-leaf book, file, or other record containing all the separate accounts of a business.

Posting The process of transferring information from the journal to individual accounts in the ledger.

Trial balance A two-column schedule listing the names and the debit or credit balances of all accounts in the ledger.

DEMONSTRATION PROBLEM FOR YOUR REVIEW

Stadium Parking was organized on July 1 to operate a parking lot near a new sports arena. The following transactions occurred during July prior to the company beginning its regular business operations.

July 1   Sylvia Snyder opened a bank account in the name of the business with a deposit of $45,000 cash.

July 2   Purchased land to be used as the parking lot for a total price of $140,000. A cash down payment of $28,000 was made and a note payable was issued for the balance of the purchase price.

July 5   Purchased a small portable building for $4,000 cash. The purchase price included installation of the building on the parking lot.

July 12   Purchased office equipment on credit from Suzuki & Company for $3,000.

July 28   Paid $2,000 of the amount owed to Suzuki & Company.

The account titles and account numbers used by Stadium Parking to record these transactions are as follows:

Cash	*1*	*Notes payable*	*30*
Land	*20*	*Accounts payable*	*32*
Building	*22*	*Sylvia Snyder, capital*	*50*
Office equipment	*25*		

INSTRUCTIONS   **a**   Prepare journal entries for the month of July.

b   Post to ledger accounts of the three-column running balance form.

c   Prepare a trial balance at July 31.

SOLUTION TO DEMONSTRATION PROBLEM

a

General Journal   Page 1

Date		Account Titles and Explanations	LP	Debit	Credit
19__ July	1	Cash	1	45,000	
		Sylvia Snyder, Capital	50		45,000
		Owner invested cash to begin business.			
	2	Land	20	140,000	
		Cash	1		28,000
		Notes Payable	30		112,000
		Purchased land. Paid part cash and issued a note payable for the balance.			
	5	Building	22	4,000	
		Cash	1		4,000
		Purchased a small portable building for cash.			
	12	Office Equipment	25	3,000	
		Accounts Payable	32		3,000
		Purchased office equipment on credit from Suzuki & Co.			
	28	Accounts Payable	32	2,000	
		Cash	1		2,000
		Paid part of account payable to Suzuki & Co.			

b

Cash					Account No. *1*
Date	Explanation	Ref	Debit	Credit	Balance
19 —					
July 1		*1*	*45000*		*45000*
2		*1*		*28000*	*17000*
5		*1*		*4000*	*13000*
28		*1*		*2000*	*11000*

Land					Account No. *20*
Date	Explanation	Ref	Debit	Credit	Balance
19 —					
July 2		*1*	*140000*		*140000*

Building					Account No. *22*
Date	Explanation	Ref	Debit	Credit	Balance
19 —					
July 5		*1*	*4000*		*4000*

Office Equipment					Account No. *25*
Date	Explanation	Ref	Debit	Credit	Balance
19 —					
July 12		*1*	*3000*		*3000*

Notes Payable					Account No. *30*
Date	Explanation	Ref	Debit	Credit	Balance
19 —					
July 2		1		112000	112000

Accounts Payable					Account No. *32*
Date	Explanation	Ref	Debit	Credit	Balance
19 —					
July 12		1		3000	3000
28		1	2000		1000

Sylvia Snyder, Capital					Account No. *50*
Date	Explanation	Ref	Debit	Credit	Balance
19 —					
July 1		1		45000	45000

c

STADIUM PARKING
Trial Balance
July 31, 19__

	Debit	Credit
Cash	$ 11,000	
Land	140,000	
Building	4,000	
Office equipment	3,000	
Notes payable		$112,000
Accounts payable		1,000
Sylvia Snyder, capital		45,000
	$158,000	$158,000

SELF-TEST QUESTIONS

Answers to these questions appear on page 101.

1 According to the rules of debit and credit for balance sheet accounts:
  a Increases in asset, liability, and owner's equity accounts are recorded by debits.
  b Decreases in asset and liability accounts are recorded by credits.
  c Increases in asset and owner's equity accounts are recorded by debits.
  d Decreases in liability and owner's equity accounts are recorded by debits.

2 Which of the following statements about accounting procedures is *not* correct?
  a The journal shows in one place all the information about specific transactions, arranged in chronological order.
  b A ledger account shows in one place all the information about changes in a specific asset or liability, or in owner's equity.
  c Posting is the process of transferring debit and credit changes in account balances from the ledger to the journal.
  d The end product of the accounting cycle consists of formal financial statements, such as the balance sheet and the income statement.

3 On March 31, the ledger for Manor House Cleaning consists of the following:

Cleaning equipment	$27,800	Accounts receivable	$21,000
Accounts payable	15,700	Cash........................	6,900
M. Poppins, capital	20,000	Salaries payable.............	9,600
Office equipment	2,000	Cleaning supplies	2,600
Automobile..................	7,500	Notes payable...............	22,500

In a trial balance prepared on March 31, the total of the credit column is:
  a $67,800   b $93,100   c $25,300   d $65,300

4 Sunset Tours has a $3,500 account receivable from the Del Mar Rotary. On January 20, the Rotary makes a partial payment of $2,100 to Sunset Tours. The journal entry made on January 20 by Sunset Tours to record this transaction includes:
  a A debit to the Cash Received account of $2,100.
  b A credit to the Accounts Receivable account of $2,100.
  c A debit to the Cash account of $1,400.
  d A debit to the Accounts Receivable account of $1,400.

5 The following journal entry was made in Dixie Stores' accounting records:

Cash...	12,000	
Notes Receivable	48,000	
Land		60,000

This transaction:
  a Involves the purchase of land for $60,000.
  b Involves a $12,000 cash payment.
  c Involves the sale of land for $60,000.
  d Causes an increase in total assets of $12,000.

ASSIGNMENT MATERIAL

DISCUSSION QUESTIONS

1 In its simplest form, an account has only three elements or basic parts. What are these three elements?

2 At the beginning of the year, the Office Equipment account of Gulf Coast Airlines had a debit balance of *$126,900*. During the year, debit entries of *$23,400* and credit entries of *$38,200* were posted to the account. What was the balance of this account at the end of the year? (Indicate debit or credit balance.)

3 What relationship exists between the position of an account on the balance sheet and the rules for recording increases in that account?

4 State briefly the rules of debit and credit as applied to asset accounts and as applied to liability and owner's equity accounts.

5 Does the term *debit* mean increase and the term *credit* mean decrease? Explain.

6 What requirement is imposed by the double-entry system in the recording of any business transaction?

7 Explain precisely what is meant by each of the phrases listed below. Whenever appropriate, indicate whether the left or right side of an account is affected and whether an increase or a decrease is indicated.
   a A debit to the Land account
   b Credit balance
   c Credit side of an account
   d A debit of $200 to the Cash account
   e A debit of $600 to Accounts Payable
   f A credit of $50 to Accounts Receivable

8 For each of the following transactions, indicate whether the account in parentheses should be debited or credited, and give the reason for your answer.
   a Purchased a copying machine on credit, promising to make payment in full within 30 days. (Accounts Payable)
   b Purchased land for cash. (Cash)
   c Sold an old, unneeded typewriter on 30-day credit. (Office Equipment)
   d Obtained a loan of $30,000 from a bank. (Cash)
   e James Brown began the business of Brown Sporting Goods Shop by depositing $20,000 cash in a bank account in the name of the business. (James Brown, Capital)

9 For each of the following accounts, state whether it is an asset, a liability, or owner's equity, and whether it would normally have a debit or a credit balance: (a) Office Equipment, (b) John Williams, Capital, (c) Accounts Receivable, (d) Accounts Payable, (e) Cash, (f) Notes Payable, (g) Land.

10 Why is a journal sometimes called the *book of original entry?*

11 Compare and contrast a *journal* and a *ledger.*

12 What is a *compound journal entry?*

13 Since it is possible to record the effects of business transactions directly in ledger accounts, why is it desirable for a business to maintain a journal?

14 What purposes are served by a trial balance?

15 In preparing a trial balance, an accounting student listed the balance of the Office Equipment account in the credit column. This account had a balance of $2,450. What would be the amount of the discrepancy in the trial balance totals? Explain.

16 Are dollar signs used in journal entries? In ledger accounts? In trial balances? In financial statements?

17 List the following five items in a logical sequence to illustrate the flow of accounting information through a manual accounting system:

   a Information entered in the journal

   b Preparation of financial statements

   c Occurrence of a business transaction

   d Debits and credits posted from journal to ledger

   e Preparation of a trial balance

18 Which step in the recording of transactions requires greater understanding of accounting principles: (a) the entering of transactions in the journal or (b) the posting of entries to ledger accounts?

19 List the procedures in the ***accounting cycle*** as described in this chapter.

20 What is a ***data base?*** How does a data base relate to the preparation of journal entries and ledger accounts in a computer-based system?

EXERCISES

**EXERCISE 2-1
Accounting
Terminology**

Listed below are nine technical accounting terms introduced in this chapter:

Ledger	*Account*	*Data base*
Posting	*Credit*	*Double-entry*
Trial balance	*Debit*	*Journal*

Each of the following statements may (or may not) describe one of these technical terms. For each statement, indicate the accounting term described, or answer "None" if the statement does not correctly describe any of the terms.

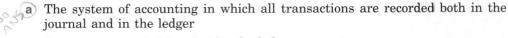

a The system of accounting in which all transactions are recorded both in the journal and in the ledger

b An entry on the left-hand side of a ledger account

c The process of transferring information from a journal to the ledger

d The accounting record in which transactions are initially recorded in a manual accounting system

e Information stored in a computer-based accounting system which can be arranged into any desired format

f A device that proves the equality of debits and credits posted to the ledger

g The accounting record from which a trial balance is prepared

EXERCISE 2-2
Double-Entry and the Accounting Equation

A number of transactions are described below in terms of the balance sheet accounts debited and credited:

1 Debit Cash, credit Accounts Receivable.
2 Debit Accounts Payable, credit Cash.
3 Debit Cash, credit Tom Hill, Capital.
4 Debit Equipment, credit Accounts Payable.
5 Debit Land, credit Cash and Notes Payable.
6 Debit Accounts Payable, credit Equipment.

INSTRUCTIONS

a Indicate the effects of each transaction upon the elements of the accounting equation, using the code letters *I* for increase, *D* for decrease, and *NE* for no effect. Organize your answer in tabular form using the column headings shown below. The answer for transaction 1 is provided as an example.

Transaction	Assets	=	Liabilities	+	Owner's Equity
1	NE		NE		NE

b Write a one-sentence description of each transaction.

EXERCISE 2-3
Double-Entry Accounting: Debit and Credit Rules

Analyze separately each of the following transactions, using the format illustrated at the end of the exercise. In each situation, explain the debit portion of the transaction before the credit portion.

a On April 2, Ginger Denton organized Metro Insurance Agency by opening a bank account in the company name with a deposit of $80,000 cash.

b On April 11, the new business purchased an office building in an industrial park for a total price of $128,000, of which $72,000 was applicable to the land and $56,000 to the building. A cash down payment of $34,500 was made and a note payable was issued for the balance of the purchase price.

c On April 21, office equipment was purchased on credit from ADR Company at a price of $6,400. The account payable was to be paid on May 21.

d On April 29, a portion of the office equipment purchased on April 21 was found to be defective and was returned to ADR Company. ADR Company agreed that Metro would not be charged for the defective equipment, which had cost $950.

e On May 21, the remaining liability to ADR Company was paid in full.

Note: The type of analysis to be made is shown by the following illustration, using transaction **a** as an example:

a (1) The asset Cash was increased. Increases in assets are recorded by debits. Debit Cash, $80,000.

   (2) The owner's equity was increased. Increases in owner's equity are recorded by credits. Credit Ginger Denton, Capital, $80,000.

EXERCISE 2-4
T Accounts

Enter the following transactions in T accounts drawn on ordinary notebook paper. Label each debit and credit with the letter identifying the transaction. Prepare a trial balance at June 30.

a On June 8, Lynne Jones opened a bank account in the name of her new business, Bluegrass Company, by making a bank deposit of $82,000 cash.

b On June 12, land was acquired for $36,000 cash.

c On June 14, a prefabricated building was purchased from E-Z Built Corporation at a cost of $40,800. A cash payment of $10,200 was made and a note payable was issued for the balance.

d   On June 20, office equipment was purchased at a cost of $7,100. A cash down payment of $1,100 was made, and it was agreed that the balance should be paid within 30 days.

e   On June 26, $3,400 of the amount due E-Z Built Corporation was paid.

**EXERCISE 2-5
Effects of Debits and Credits on Ledger Account Balances**

The first six transactions of South Pacific Travel Agency appear in the following T accounts.

Cash				Office Equipment			
(1)	60,000	(2)	20,000	(3)	20,000	(4)	5,000
(6)	2,300	(5)	15,000				

Accounts Receivable				Notes Payable			
(4)	5,000	(6)	2,300			(2)	100,000

Land				Accounts Payable			
(2)	72,000			(5)	15,000	(3)	20,000

Building				Michael Chan, Capital			
(2)	48,000					(1)	60,000

For each of the six transactions in turn, indicate the type of accounts affected (asset, liability, or owner's equity) and whether the account was increased or decreased. Arrange your answers in the form illustrated for transaction *(1),* shown here as an example.

	Account(s) Debited		Account(s) Credited	
Transaction	*Type of Account(s)*	*Increase or Decrease*	*Type of Account(s)*	*Increase or Decrease*
(1)	*Asset*	*Increase*	*Owner's equity*	*Increase*

**EXERCISE 2-6
Recording Transactions in a Journal**

Enter the following transactions in the two-column journal of Jenkins Sporting Goods. Include a brief explanation of the transaction as part of each journal entry.

Nov. 1   The owner, Dan Jenkins, invested an additional $40,000 cash in the business.

Nov. 3   Purchased an adjacent vacant lot for use as parking space. The price was $98,500, of which $28,500 was paid in cash; a note payable was issued for the balance.

Nov. 12   Collected an account receivable of $4,500 from a customer, Jean Krieger.

Nov. 17   Acquired office equipment from Tower Company for $7,600 cash.

Nov. 21   Issued a check for $764 in full payment of an account payable to Hampton Supply Co.

Nov. 28   Borrowed $25,000 cash from the bank by signing a 90-day note payable.

EXERCISE 2-7
**Journal Entries
to Illustrate
Effects of
Transactions**

Prepare general journal entries to illustrate the effects of each of the following transactions upon the financial statements of Seacoast Airline. You are to determine appropriate account titles.

Jan. 4   Purchased two seaplanes from Scout Aircraft at a total cost of $790,000. Paid $390,000 in cash and signed a note payable to Island Bank for the remainder.

Jan. 8   Purchased spare parts for the new planes from Breckwoldt Aviation. The parts cost $17,600, and were purchased on account.

Jan. 12   Issued to Earl Scoggins, the owner of Scoggins' Flight School, a $500,000 note payable in exchange for a parcel of waterfront land and a floating aircraft hangar in Columbus Bay. The current value of the land is appraised at $300,000, and of the floating hangar, $200,000.

Jan. 15   Returned to Breckwoldt Aviation $4,300 of the aircraft parts purchased on January 8. The return of these parts reduced by $4,300 the amount owed to Breckwoldt.

Feb. 2   Paid the remaining balance owed to Breckwoldt Aviation from the purchase on January 8.

EXERCISE 2-8
**Relationship
between Journal and Ledger
Accounts**

Transactions are recorded ***first*** in a journal and ***then*** posted to ledger accounts. In this exercise, however, your understanding of the relationship between journal and ledger is tested by asking you to study some ledger accounts and determine the journal entries which probably were made by the company's accountant to produce these ledger entries. The following accounts show the first six transactions of Gutierrez Construction Company. Prepare a journal entry (including written explanation) for each transaction.

Cash					Notes Payable			
Nov. 1	60,000	Nov. 8	33,600		Nov. 25	10,000	Nov. 8	100,000
Nov. 30	35,000	Nov. 25	10,000					

Land				Accounts Payable			
Nov. 8	70,000			Nov. 21	480	Nov. 15	3,200

Building				Joe Gutierrez, Capital			
Nov. 8	63,600					Nov. 1	60,000
						Nov. 30	35,000

Office Equipment			
Nov. 15	3,200	Nov. 21	480

EXERCISE 2-9
**Preparing a
Trial Balance**

Using the information in the ledger accounts presented in Exercise 2-8, prepare a trial balance for Gutierrez Construction Company at November 30, 19__.

EXERCISE 2-10
**Uses and Limitations of a
Trial Balance**

Some of the following errors would cause the debit and credit columns of the trial balance to have unequal totals. For each of the four paragraphs, write a statement explaining whether the error would cause unequal totals in the trial balance. Each paragraph is to be considered independently of the others.

a   A payment of $400 to a creditor was recorded by a debit to Accounts Payable of $400 and a credit to Cash of $40.

b   A $540 payment for a new typewriter was recorded by a debit to Office Equipment of $54 and a credit to Cash of $54.

c   An account receivable in the amount of $800 was collected in full. The collection was recorded by a debit to Cash for $800 and a debit to Accounts Payable for $800.

d   An account payable was paid by issuing a check for $350. The payment was recorded by debiting Accounts Payable $350 and crediting Accounts Receivable $350.

EXERCISE 2-11
Uses and Limitations of a Trial Balance

The trial balance prepared by Discount Plumbing Service at June 30 was not in balance. In searching for the error, an employee discovered that a transaction for the purchase of a calculator on credit for $380 had been recorded by a ***debit*** of $380 to the Office Equipment account and a ***debit*** of $380 to Accounts Payable. The credit column of the incorrect trial balance has a total of $129,640.

In answering each of the following five questions, explain fully the reasons underlying your answer and state the dollar amount of the error if any.

a   Was the Office Equipment account overstated, understated, or correctly stated in the trial balance?

b   Was the total of the debit column of the trial balance overstated, understated, or correctly stated?

c   Was the Accounts Payable account overstated, understated, or correctly stated in the trial balance?

d   Was the total of the credit column of the trial balance overstated, understated, or correctly stated?

e   How much was the total of the debit column of the trial balance before correction of the error?

EXERCISE 2-12
Steps in the Accounting Cycle; Computerized Accounting Systems

Various steps and decisions involved in the accounting cycle are described in the seven lettered statements below. Indicate which of these procedures are mechanical functions that can be performed by machine in a computerized accounting system and which require the judgment of people familiar with accounting principles and concepts.

a   Decide whether or not events should be recorded in the accounting records.

b   Determine which ledger accounts should be debited and credited to describe specific business transactions.

c   Arrange recorded data in the format of journal entries.

d   Arrange recorded data in the format of ledger accounts.

e   Prepare a trial balance.

f   Prepare financial statements (a balance sheet).

g   Evaluate the debt-paying ability of one company relative to another.

EXERCISE 2-13
Manual vs. Computer-based Systems

For each of the following steps in the accounting cycle, explain whether the step requires human judgment or whether it can be performed automatically by a computer in a computer-based accounting system.

a   Record transactions as they occur.

b   Post recorded data to ledger accounts.

c   Prepare a trial balance.

d   Prepare a balance sheet and related disclosures.

EXERCISE 2-14
Different Uses for Journals and Ledgers

Briefly explain the usefulness of journal entries and of ledger accounts:

a In the operation of an accounting system.

b From the viewpoint of business managers who are **not** personally responsible for maintaining accounting records or preparing their company's financial statements.

c From the viewpoint of an accounting student or an accounting instructor (assuming **general** journal entries and T accounts).

PROBLEMS

Group A

PROBLEM 2A-1
Recording Transactions in a Journal

Elizabeth Carver, a certified public accountant, resigned from her position with a large CPA firm in order to begin her own public accounting practice. The business transactions during September while the new venture was being organized are listed below.

Sept. 1 Carver opened a bank checking account in the name of her firm, Elizabeth Carver, Certified Public Accountant, by depositing $32,000 which she had saved over a period of years.

Sept. 10 Purchased a small office building located on a large lot for a total price of $91,200, of which $48,000 was applicable to the land and $43,200 to the building. A cash payment of $18,240 was made and a note payable was issued for the balance of the purchase price.

Sept. 15 Purchased a microcomputer system from Computer Stores, Inc., for $4,680 cash.

Sept. 19 Purchased office furniture, filing cabinets, and a typewriter from Davidson Office Supply Company at a cost of $3,960. A cash down payment of $720 was made, the balance to be paid in three equal installments due September 28, October 28, and November 28. The purchase was on open account and did not require signing of a promissory note.

Sept. 26 A $140 monitor in the microcomputer system purchased on September 15 stopped working. The monitor was returned to Computer Stores, Inc., which promised to refund the $140 within five days.

Sept. 28 Paid Davidson Office Supply Company $1,080 cash as the first installment due on the account payable for office equipment.

Sept. 30 Received $140 cash from Computer Stores, Inc., in full settlement of the account receivable created on September 26.

INSTRUCTIONS

Prepare journal entries to record the above transactions. Select the appropriate account titles from the following chart of accounts:

Cash	Office equipment
Accounts receivable	Notes payable
Land	Accounts payable
Building	Elizabeth Carver, capital

PROBLEM 2A-2
Analyzing
Transactions
and Preparing
Journal Entries

The Tool Shed was organized to rent trailers, tools, and other equipment to its customers. The organization of the business began on May 1, and the following transactions occurred in May before the company began regular operations on June 1.

1 On May 1, Mark O'Brien opened a bank account in the name of his new company with a deposit of $70,000 cash.

2 On May 3, The Tool Shed bought land for use in its operations at a total cost of $75,000. A cash down payment of $15,000 was made, and a note payable (payable within 90 days without interest) was issued for the balance.

3 On May 5, a movable building was purchased for $16,000 cash and installed on the lot.

4 On May 10, equipment was purchased on credit from Ace Tool Company at a cost of $14,100. The account payable was to be paid within 30 days. (The asset account is entitled Rental Equipment.)

5 On May 31, a cash payment of $20,000 was made in partial settlement of the note payable issued on May 3.

INSTRUCTIONS

a Prepare an analysis of each of the above transactions. The form of analysis to be used is as follows, using transaction **1** above as an example:

1 (a) The asset Cash was increased. Increases in assets are recorded by debits. Debit Cash, $70,000.

(b) The owner's equity was increased. Increases in owner's equity are recorded by credits. Credit Mark O'Brien, Capital, $70,000.

b Prepare journal entries for the above five transactions. Include an explanation as a part of each journal entry.

PROBLEM 2A-3
Preparing a
Trial Balance
and a Balance
Sheet

Environmental Services is a weather forecasting service which provides information to growers and dealers in perishable commodities. Its ledger account balances at November 30 were as shown in the following alphabetical list.

Accounts payable	$ 7,000	Land	$ 85,200
Accounts receivable	16,700	Notes payable	145,000
Automobiles	14,600	Notes receivable	2,400
Building	110,000	Office furniture	12,900
Carl Ford, capital	129,650	Office supplies	850
Cash	17,650	Property taxes payable	1,060
Computer	18,800	Salaries payable	3,740
Computer software	5,450	Technical library	1,900

INSTRUCTIONS

a Prepare a trial balance with the accounts arranged in financial statement order. Include a proper heading for your trial balance.

b Prepare a balance sheet. Include a subtotal for total liabilities.

PROBLEM 2A-4
Posting to
Ledger Ac-
counts; Prepar-
ing a Trial Bal-
ance and a
Balance Sheet

Mei Yi is a veterinarian. In January, she began organizing her own animal hospital, to be known as Animal Care Center. Mei Yi has prepared the following journal entries to record all January business transactions. She has not posted these entries to ledger accounts. The ledger account numbers to be used are: Cash, 1; Office Supplies, 10; Land, 20; Building, 25; Medical Equipment, 27; Notes Payable, 30; Accounts Payable, 31; and Mei Yi, Capital, 50.

General Journal				*Page 1*
Jan	2	Cash..	60,000	
		Mei Yi, Capital..........................		60,000
		Investment in business by owner.		
	4	Land..	45,000	
		Building....................................	115,000	
		Cash....................................		40,000
		Notes Payable..........................		120,000
		Purchased land and building.		
	7	Medical Equipment	7,480	
		Accounts Payable		7,480
		Bought equipment on credit from Medco, Inc.		
	8	Office Supplies...............................	590	
		Accounts Payable		590
		Bought supplies from Miller Supply.		
	13	Accounts Payable	1,400	
		Medical Equipment		1,400
		Returned defective medical equipment to Medco, Inc., for credit on account.		
	18	Accounts Payable	590	
		Cash....................................		590
		Made payment of liability to Miller Supply.		

INSTRUCTIONS

a Post the journal entries to ledger accounts of the three-column running balance form.

b Prepare a trial balance at January 31 from the ledger accounts completed in part **a.**

c Prepare a balance sheet at January 31, 19__.

PROBLEM 2A-5
Preparing Journal Entries, Posting, and Preparing a Trial Balance

Ann Ryan, a licensed real estate broker, on October 1 began the organization of her own business, to be known as Ryan Land Company. The following events occurred during October:

Oct. 2 Ann Ryan opened a bank account in the name of the business by depositing personal savings of $35,000.

Oct. 6 Purchased land and a small office building at a total price of $98,500, of which $64,000 was applicable to land and $34,500 to the building. The terms of the purchase required a cash payment of $29,500 and the issuance of a note payable for $69,000.

Oct. 15 Sold one-quarter of the land at its cost of $16,000 to a neighboring business, Village Medical Clinic, which wanted to expand its parking lot. No down payment was required; Village Medical Clinic issued a note promising payment of the $16,000 in a series of five monthly installments of $3,200 each, beginning October 30 (ignore interest). As the land was sold at the same price per square foot as Ryan Land Company had paid to acquire it, no gain or loss results on this transaction.

Oct. 20 Purchased office equipment on credit from Buffington Company in the amount of $5,280.

Oct. 30 Paid $3,440 as partial settlement of the liability to Buffington Company.

Oct. 31   Received the first $3,200 monthly installment on the note receivable from Village Medical Clinic.

The account titles and account numbers to be used are:

Cash	1	Office equipment	26
Notes receivable	5	Notes payable	30
Land...............................	21	Accounts payable	32
Building	23	Ann Ryan, capital	50

INSTRUCTIONS   a   Prepare journal entries for the month of October.

b   Post to ledger accounts of the three-column running balance form.

c   Prepare a trial balance at October 31, 19__.

**PROBLEM 2A-6
Preparing
Journal En-
tries, Posting,
and Preparing
a Trial Balance**

After playing several seasons of professional football, George Harris had saved enough money to start a business, to be called Number One Auto Rental. The transactions during March while the new business was being organized are listed below:

Mar. 1   George Harris invested $140,000 cash in the business by making a deposit in a bank account in the name of the new company.

Mar. 3   The new company purchased land and a building at a cost of $120,000, of which $72,000 was regarded as applicable to the land and $48,000 to the building. The transaction involved a cash payment of $41,500 and the issuance of a note payable for $78,500.

Mar. 5   Purchased 20 new automobiles at $8,600 each from Fleet Sales Company. Paid $40,000 cash, and agreed to pay $32,000 by March 31 and the remaining balance by April 15. The liability is viewed as an account payable.

Mar. 7   Sold an automobile at cost to Harris's father-in-law, Howard Facey, who paid $2,400 in cash and agreed to pay the balance within 30 days.

Mar. 8   One of the automobiles was found to be defective and was returned to Fleet Sales Company. The amount payable to this creditor was thereby reduced by $8,600.

Mar. 20   Purchased office equipment at a cost of $4,000 cash.

Mar. 31   Issued a check for $32,000 in partial payment of the liability to Fleet Sales Company.

The account titles and the account numbers used by the company are as follows:

Cash	10	Automobiles	22
Accounts receivable	11	Notes payable	31
Land...............................	16	Accounts payable	32
Buildings	17	George Harris, capital	50
Office equipment	20		

INSTRUCTIONS   a   Journalize the March transactions.

b   Post to ledger accounts. Use the running balance form of ledger account.

c   Prepare a trial balance at March 31, 19__.

Group B

PROBLEM 2B-1
Recording
Transactions in
a Journal

In May, James Colby, a physician, decided to open his own medical practice. During May, the new business engaged in the following transactions:

May 4   Colby opened a bank account in the name of his medical practice, James Colby, M.D., by depositing $36,000 cash.

May 16   Purchased a small medical office. The purchase price was $95,400, which included land valued at $50,000 and a building valued at $45,400. A cash down payment was made for $21,000, and a note payable was issued for the balance of the purchase price.

May 19   Purchased office furniture on account from Modern Office Company, $2,340.

May 22   Purchased medical supplies for cash from Denton Labs, $1,630.

May 23   Returned to Denton Labs $225 of the medical supplies purchased yesterday as these items were not exactly what Colby had ordered. Denton Labs agreed to refund the $225 within 10 days.

May 30   Made an $1,170 partial payment on the account payable to Modern Office Company.

May 31   Received the $225 refund from Denton Labs for the supplies on May 23.

INSTRUCTIONS   Prepare journal entries to record the above transactions. Select the appropriate account titles from the following chart of accounts:

Cash	*Land*	*Notes payable*
Accounts receivable	*Building*	*Accounts payable*
Medical supplies	*Office furniture*	*James Colby, capital*

PROBLEM 2B-2
Analyzing
Transactions
and Preparing
Journal Entries

Yoko Toyoda is the founder and owner of Perfect Portraits, a photographic studio. A few of the company's business transactions occurring during July are described below.

1   On July 2, purchased photographic equipment for $2,525, paying $750 in cash and charging the remainder on the company's 30-day account at Camera Supply Company.

2   On July 7, Yoko Toyoda made an additional investment in Perfect Portraits by depositing $5,000 cash in the company bank account.

3   On July 9, returned to Camera Supply Company $400 of photographic equipment which did not work properly. The return of this equipment reduced by $400 the amount owed to Camera Supply Company.

4   On July 25, collected cash of $900 from customers in settlement of accounts receivable.

5   On July 31, paid the remaining $1,375 owed to Camera Supply Company.

INSTRUCTIONS   a   Prepare an analysis of each of the above transactions. The form to be used is as follows, using transaction **1** as an example:

     1 (a) The asset Photographic Equipment was increased. Increases in assets are recorded by debits. Debit Photographic Equipment, $2,525.

     (b) The asset Cash was decreased. Decreases in assets are recorded by credits. Credit Cash, $750. A liability was incurred. Increases in liabilities are recorded by credits. Credits Accounts Payable, $1,775.

   b   Prepare journal entries, including explanations, for the above transactions.

**PROBLEM 2B-3
Preparing a
Trial Balance
and a Balance
Sheet**

The ledger accounts of Black Mountain Golf Club at September 30 are shown below in alphabetical order.

Accounts payable	$ 15,340	Lighting equipment	$ 52,900
Accounts receivable	1,300	Maintenance equipment	36,500
Building	184,200	Notes payable	390,000
Robert Jones, capital	384,060	Notes receivable	24,000
Cash	14,960	Office equipment	1,420
Fences	23,600	Office supplies	490
Golf carts	28,000	Sprinkler system	50,000
Land	375,000	Property taxes payable	2,970

INSTRUCTIONS

a Prepare a trial balance with the ledger accounts arranged in the usual financial statement order. Include a proper heading.

b Prepare a balance sheet at September 30, 19___. Include a subtotal showing total liabilities.

**PROBLEM 2B-4
Posting to
Ledger Ac-
counts; Prepar-
ing a Trial Bal-
ance and a
Balance Sheet**

After several seasons of professional tennis competition, Jim Hand had saved enough money to start his own tennis school, to be known as Winners' Tennis College. During July, while organizing the business, Hand prepared the following journal entries to record all July transactions. He has not posted these entries to ledger accounts. The ledger account numbers to be used are: Cash 1, Office Supplies 9, Land 20, Tennis Courts 22, Tennis Equipment 25, Notes Payable 30, Accounts Payable 31, and Jim Hand, Capital 50.

		General Journal			*Page 1*
July	1	Cash...		30,000	
		Jim Hand, Capital			30,000
		Investment in business by owner.			
	3	Land...		48,400	
		Tennis Courts		75,000	
		Cash....................................			20,000
		Notes Payable..........................			103,400
		Purchased land and tennis courts.			
	6	Tennis Equipment		1,680	
		Accounts Payable			1,680
		Bought equipment on credit from			
		Rackets, Inc.			
	7	Office Supplies...............................		315	
		Accounts Payable			315
		Bought supplies from Miller Supply.			
	12	Tennis Equipment		725	
		Accounts Payable			725
		Bought equipment from Rackets, Inc.			
	17	Accounts Payable		315	
		Cash....................................			315
		Made payment of liability to Miller Supply.			
	22	Accounts Payable		725	
		Cash....................................			725
		Made payment of liability to Rackets,			
		Inc., for purchase of July 12.			

INSTRUCTIONS   a   Post the journal entries to ledger accounts of the three-column running balance form.

b   Prepare a trial balance at July 31 from the ledger accounts completed in part **a.**

c   Prepare a balance sheet at July 31, 19___.

PROBLEM 2B-5
Preparing
Journal En-
tries, Posting,
and Preparing
a Trial Balance

Beach Property Management was started on November 1 by Rosa Garcia to provide management services for the owners of apartment buildings. The organizational period extended throughout November and included the transactions listed below.

Nov.   1   Garcia opened a bank account in the name of the business with a deposit of $25,000 cash.

Nov.   4   Purchased land and an office building for a price of $140,000, of which $75,000 was considered applicable to the land and $65,000 attributable to the building. A cash down payment of $20,000 was made and a note payable for $120,000 was issued for the balance of the purchase price.

Nov.   7   Purchased office equipment on credit from Harvard Office Equipment, $5,850.

Nov.   9   A typewriter (cost $490), which was part of the November 7 purchase of office equipment, proved defective and was returned for credit to Harvard Office Equipment.

Nov. 17   Sold one-third of the land acquired on November 4 to Ace Parking Lots at a price of $25,000. This price is equal to Beach Property's cost for this portion of the land, so there is no gain or loss on this transaction. Beach received a $5,000 cash down payment from Ace Parking Lots and a note receivable in the amount of $20,000, due in four monthly installments of $5,000 each, beginning on November 30 (ignore interest).

Nov. 28   Paid $1,600 in partial settlement of the liability to Harvard Office Equipment.

Nov. 30   Received cash of $5,000 as partial collection of the note receivable from Ace Parking Lots.

The account titles and account numbers to be used are

Cash	1	Office equipment	25
Notes receivable	5	Notes payable.......................	31
Land................................	21	Accounts payable	32
Building	23	Rosa Garcia, capital	51

INSTRUCTIONS   a   Prepare journal entries for the month of November.

b   Post to ledger accounts of the three-column running balance form.

c   Prepare a trial balance at November 30, 19___.

PROBLEM 2B-6
The Account-
ing Cycle: a
Comprehensive
Problem

Community TV was organized in February 1994 to operate as a local television station. The account titles and numbers used by the business are listed below:

Cash	11	Telecasting equipment...............	24
Accounts receivable	15	Film library	25
Supplies	19	Notes payable.......................	31
Land................................	21	Accounts payable	32
Building	22	James Ward, capital	51
Transmitter	23		

The transactions for February were as follows:

Feb. 1   James Ward deposited $400,000 cash in a bank checking account in the name of the business, Community TV.

Feb. 3   Community TV purchased the land, buildings, and telecasting equipment previously used by a local television station which had gone bankrupt. The total purchase price was $300,000, of which $100,000 was attributable to the land, $90,000 to the building, and the remainder to the telecasting equipment. The terms of the purchase required a cash payment of $200,000 and the issuance of a note payable for the balance.

Feb. 5   Purchased a transmitter at a cost of $225,000 from AC Manufacturing Company, making a cash down payment of $75,000. The balance, in the form of a note payable, was to be paid in monthly installments of $12,500, beginning February 15. (Interest expense is to be ignored.)

Feb. 9   Purchased a film library at a cost of $40,000 from Modern Film Productions, making a down payment of $15,000 cash, with the balance on account payable in 30 days.

Feb. 12   Bought supplies costing $3500, paying cash.

Feb. 15   Paid $12,500 to AC Manufacturing as the first monthly payment on the note payable created on February 5. (Interest expense to be ignored.)

Feb. 25   Sold part of the film library to City College; cost was $9,000 and the selling price also was $9,000. City College agreed to pay the full amount in 30 days.

INSTRUCTIONS   **a** Prepare journal entries for the month of February.

    b Post to ledger accounts of the three-column running balance form.

    c Prepare a trial balance at February 28, 1994.

    d Prepare a balance sheet at February 28, 1994.

CASES AND UNSTRUCTURED PROBLEMS

CASE 2-1 Computer-Based Accounting Systems   Bill Gates is planning to create a computer-based accounting system for small businesses. His system will be developed from a data base program and will be suitable for use on personal computers.

    The idea underlying data base software is that data needed for a variety of uses is entered into the data base only once. The computer is programmed to arrange this data into any number of desired formats. In the case of Gates's accounting system, the company's accounting personnel must enter the relevant information about each business transaction into the data base. The program which Gates plans to write will then enable the computer operator to have the information arranged by the computer into the formats of (1) journal entries (with written explanations), (2) three-column running balance form ledger accounts, (3) a trial balance, and (4) a balance sheet.

INSTRUCTIONS   **a** Identify the relevant information about each business transaction that the company's accounting personnel must enter into the data base to enable Gates's program to prepare the four types of accounting records and statements described above.

    b As described in this chapter, the accounting cycle includes the steps of (1) analyzing and recording business transactions, (2) posting the debit and credit amounts to ledger accounts, (3) preparing a trial balance, and (4) preparing financial statements (at this stage, only a balance sheet). Indicate which of these functions can be performed automatically by Gates's computer program and which must still be performed by the company's accounting personnel.

**CASE 2-2
Preparing Balance Sheets and an Introduction to Measuring Income**

Susan Lee, a college student with several summers' experience as a guide on canoe camping trips, decided to go into business for herself. On June 1, Lee organized Birchbark Canoe Trails by depositing $1,600 of personal savings in a bank account in the name of the business. Also on June 1, the business borrowed an additional $3,200 cash from John Lee (Susan's father) by issuing a three-year note payable. To help the business get started, John Lee agreed that no interest would be charged on the loan. The following transactions were also carried out by the business on June 1:

1 Bought a number of canoes at a total cost of $6,200; paid $2,000 cash and agreed to pay the balance within 60 days.

2 Bought camping equipment at a cost of $3,400 payable in 60 days.

3 Bought supplies for cash, $700.

After the close of the season on September 10, Lee asked another student, David Ray, who had taken a course in accounting, to help determine the financial position of the business.

The only record Lee had maintained was a checkbook with memorandum notes written on the check stubs. From this source Ray discovered that Lee had invested an additional $1,200 of savings in the business on July 1, and also that the accounts payable arising from the purchase of the canoes and camping equipment had been paid in full. A bank statement received from the bank on September 10 showed a balance on deposit of $2,790.

Lee informed Ray that all cash received by the business had been deposited in the bank and all bills had been paid by check immediately upon receipt; consequently, as of September 10 all bills for the season had been paid. However, nothing had been paid on the note payable.

The canoes and camping equipment were all in excellent condition at the end of the season and Lee planned to resume operations the following summer. In fact, she had already accepted reservations from many customers who wished to return.

Ray felt that some consideration should be given to the wear and tear on the canoes and equipment, but he agreed with Lee that for the present purpose the canoes and equipment should be listed in the balance sheet at the original cost. The supplies remaining on hand had cost $50, and Lee felt that these supplies could be used next summer.

Ray suggested that two balance sheets be prepared, one to show the condition of the business on June 1 and the other showing the condition on September 10. He also recommended to Lee that a complete set of accounting records be established.

INSTRUCTIONS

a Use the information in the first paragraph (including the three numbered transactions) as a basis for preparing a balance sheet dated June 1.

b Prepare a balance sheet at September 10. (Because of the incomplete information available, it is not possible to determine the amount of cash at September 10 by adding cash receipts and deducting cash payments throughout the season. The amount on deposit as reported by the bank at September 10 is to be regarded as the total cash belonging to the business at that date.)

c By comparing the two balance sheets, compute the change in owner's equity. Explain the sources of this change in owner's equity and state whether you consider the business to be successful. Also comment on the cash position at the beginning and end of the season. Has the cash position improved significantly? Explain.

ANSWERS TO SELF-TEST QUESTIONS

1 d   2 c   3 a   4 b   5 c

COMPREHENSIVE PROBLEM 1

LITTLE BEAR RAILROAD, INC.

A REVIEW OF CHAPTERS 1 AND 2

Note to students: This problem includes several issues that will be discussed later in the textbook. A basic purpose of the problem is to have you *think about situations which you have not seen illustrated and explained.* Use your best judgment in resolving any questionable issues, and be prepared to ask questions and to voice your opinion if the problem is discussed in class.

For many years Kim-Chung (K-C) Jones has owned and operated Little Bear Railroad, a narrow gauge railroad operating inside a national park. The Little Bear operates for only eight months each year—April 1 through November 30—offering park visitors a 22-mile scenic tour of the redwood forest. The train consists of a woodburning locomotive and three passenger cars. Until March 1994, the business had been organized as a sole proprietorship.

In March, prior to opening for the 1994 season, Jones decided to reorganize the business as Little Bear Railroad, Inc., a corporation. The following events occurred as the new corporation was being organized:

Mar. 1 Jones transferred into the new corporation all of the assets and liabilities of Little Bear Railroad, in exchange for which the corporation issued 50,000 shares of capital stock. The business assets and liabilities and their value at March 1 were as follows:

Cash	$ 48,000
Accounts receivable	8,600
Supplies	4,900
Spare parts	10,400
Buildings	170,000
Equipment & rolling stock	415,000
Roadbed, track, & ties..	250,000
Notes payable (due in 2001)	300,000
Accounts payable	6,900

In addition to the assets and liabilities listed above, Jones also transferred into the corporation a permanent "right-of-way" allowing the railroad to operate on specific portions of the national park's land. (Notice that the railroad owns no land; the land upon which it operates is part of the national park.) Jones acquired the right-of-way from the National Park Service many years ago at a cost of $100,000. However, this asset was considered to be worth $400,000 at the date that Jones transferred it into the new corporation.

Mar. 4 Jones sold 10% of her capital stock in the corporation to Adrian Wong-Boren, a relative, for $115,000 cash. Jones deposited this money in her personal bank account.

Mar. 10 The corporation borrowed $100,000 cash from Pine City Bank to provide capital for expanding its operations. A note payable was issued, due in 90 days. (Ignore interest charges.)

Mar. 12 Signed an agreement with Jay Gould Construction Company to build a three-mile extension of roadbed and track within company's right-of-way through the park. Work will begin on April 1 and is to be completed by August 15, 1994. The total cost will be $240,000, payable in thirds as each mile of track is completed.

Mar. 15 The corporation purchased a replica of an 1865 steam-driven locomotive and an original 1898 dining car from The Spud, a narrow-gauge railroad in Idaho that had gone bankrupt. The purchase price was $380,000; Little Bear, Inc., paid $90,000 in cash and issued a note payable for the balance. The note, payable to Silverado Savings, is due in one year.

INSTRUCTIONS

a Prepare all general journal entries necessary through March 15 to record these events in the accounting records of the new corporation. (Not all of these events require journal entries.) In your entry on March 1, enter in the accounts of the new corporation the assets invested by Jones, and ***also the liabilities*** (notes payable and accounts payable) which the corporation is assuming. Credit an account entitled ***Capital Stock*** for Jones's ownership equity in the new company.

b Post to ledger accounts of the three-column form. (You are to create the company's ledger by assigning names and numbers to an appropriate number of ledger accounts.)

c Prepare a trial balance at March 15, 1994.

d Prepare a balance sheet at March 15, 1994. Also, draft a note accompanying this balance sheet to disclose the company's contractual commitment to Jay Gould Construction Company. (Presentation of the stockholders' equity in the balance sheet of a corporation was illustrated in Chapter 1 on page 27. As this corporation has not yet begun operations, it has no retained earnings; the stockholders' equity consists only of the amount shown as capital stock.)

e Assume that you are a loan officer at Sequoia Savings Bank. Little Bear Railroad, Inc., wants to borrow from your bank the $240,000 to pay for the three-mile extension of its track. The corporation intends to repay this loan in one year. Based solely upon the available information, does the corporation appear to be a reasonably good credit risk? Explain the reasons for your conclusion.

3 Measuring Business Income

In Chapter 3 our coverage of the accounting cycle is expanded to include the measurement of business income. Attention is focused upon the nature of revenue, expenses, net income, and owner's equity. Several important accounting principles are introduced, including the realization principle and the matching principle. The continuing example of Roberts Real Estate Company is used to illustrate the recording of revenue and expense transactions and the preparation of an income statement and a statement of owner's equity. End-of-period *adjusting entries* and *closing procedures* also are explained and illustrated.

After studying this chapter you should be able to meet these Learning Objectives:

1 *Explain the nature of net income, revenue, and expenses.*

2 *Apply the realization and matching principles in recording revenue and expenses.*

3 *Apply the rules of debit and credit in recording revenue and expenses.*

4 *Define and record depreciation expense.*

5 *Describe and prepare an income statement and a statement of owner's equity. Explain how these statements relate to the balance sheet.*

6 *Explain the purposes served by closing entries; prepare these entries.*

7 *Describe the sequence of procedures in the accounting cycle.*

8 *Distinguish between the accrual basis and the cash basis of accounting.*

WHAT IS NET INCOME?

OBJECTIVE 1
Explain the
nature of
net income,
revenue,
and ex-
penses.

In Chapter 1, we stated that a basic objective of every business is to earn a profit, or net income. Why? The answer lies in the very definition of net income: ***an increase in owner's equity resulting from the profitable operation of the business.*** The opposite of net income, a ***decrease*** in owner's equity resulting from unprofitable operation of the business, is termed a ***net loss.***

If you were to organize a business of your own, you would do so with the hope and expectation that the business would operate at a profit, thereby increasing your ownership equity. Individuals who invest in the capital stock of a large corporation also expect the business to earn a profit which will increase the value of their investment.

Notice that net income does not consist of cash or any other specific asset. Rather, net income is a ***computation*** of the overall effects of many business transactions upon ***owner's equity.*** The increase in owner's equity resulting from profitable operations usually is accompanied by an increase in total assets, though not necessarily an increase in cash. In some cases, however, an increase in owner's equity is accompanied by a decrease in total liabilities.

Our point is that net income represents an ***increase in owner's equity*** and has no direct relationship to the types or amounts of assets on hand. Consequently even a business operating at a profit may run short of cash and become insolvent.

In the balance sheet, the changes in owner's equity resulting from profitable or unprofitable operations are reflected in the balance of the ***owner's capital account.*** The assets of the business organization appear in the ***assets*** section of the balance sheet.

Some of the largest corporations have become large by consistently retaining in the business most of the resources generated by profitable operations.

CASE IN POINT A recent annual report of Campbell Soup Company shows total owner's equity amounting to nearly $2 billion. The owners originally invested only about $71 million—less than 4% of the current equity—in exchange for capital stock. By operating profitably and retaining earnings, Campbell has added more than $1¾ billion to its ownership equity.

The Income Statement: A Preview

An income statement is a one-page financial statement which summarizes the profitability of the business entity over a specified period of time. In this statement, net income is determined by comparing for the time period: (1) the ***sales price*** of the goods sold and services rendered by the business with (2) the ***cost*** to the business of the goods and services used up in business operations. The technical accounting terms for these components of net income are ***revenue*** and ***expenses.*** Therefore, accountants say that net income is equal to ***revenue minus expenses,*** as shown in the following income statement.

ROBERTS REAL ESTATE COMPANY
Income Statement
For the Month Ended October 31, 19__

Income statement for October

Revenue:

Sales commissions earned $10,640

Expenses:

Advertising expense .... $ 630

Salaries expense.. 7,100

Telephone expense 144

Depreciation expense: building 150

Depreciation expense: office equipment......................... 45   8,069

Net income .... $ 2,571

When we measure the net income earned by a business we are measuring its economic performance—its success or failure as a business enterprise. The owner, managers, and major creditors are anxious to see the latest available income statement and thereby judge how well the company is doing. If the business is organized as a corporation, the stockholders and prospective investors also will be keenly interested in each successive income statement.

Later in this chapter we will show how this income statement is developed from the accounting records of Roberts Real Estate Company. For the moment, however, this illustration will assist us in discussing some of the basic concepts involved in measuring business income.

Income Must Be Related to a Specified Period of Time   Notice that our sample income statement covers a ***period*** of time—namely, the month of October. A balance sheet shows the financial position of a business at a ***particular date.*** An income statement, on the other hand, shows the results of business operations over a span of time. We cannot evaluate net income unless it is associated with a specific time period. For example, if an executive says, "My business earns a net income of $10,000," the profitability of the business is unclear. Does it earn $10,000 per week, per month, or per year?

CASE IN POINT   The late J. Paul Getty, one of the world's first billionaires, was once interviewed by a group of business students. One of the students asked Getty to estimate the amount of his income. As the student had not specified a time period, Getty decided to have some fun with his audience and responded, "About $11,000 . . . " He paused long enough to allow the group to express surprise over this seemingly low amount and then completed his sentence, " . . . an hour." Incidentally, $11,000 per hour (24 hours per day) amounts to about $100 million per year.

Accounting Periods   The period of time covered by an income statement is termed the company's ***accounting period.*** To provide the users of financial statements with timely information, net income is measured for relatively short accounting periods of equal length. This concept, called the *time period principle,* is one of the generally accepted accounting principles that guide the interpretation of financial events and the preparation of financial statements.

The length of a company's accounting period depends upon how frequently managers, investors, and other interested people require information about the company's performance. Every business prepares annual income statements, and most businesses prepare quarterly and monthly income statements as well. (Quarterly statements cover a three-month period and are prepared by all large corporations for distribution to their stockholders.)

The 12-month accounting period used by an entity is called its *fiscal year.* The fiscal year used by most companies coincides with the calendar year and ends on December 31. Some businesses, however, elect to use a fiscal year which ends on some other date. It may be convenient for a business to end its fiscal year during a slack season rather than during a time of peak activity.

CASE IN POINT Walt Disney Company ends its fiscal year on September 30. Why? One reason is that September and October are relatively slow months at Disney's theme parks; another is that September financial statements provide timely information about the preceding summer, which is the company's busiest season.

As another example, many department stores, including K mart, Neiman-Marcus, Nordstrom, and J. C. Penney, end their fiscal years on January 31—after the rush of the holiday season.

Let us now explore the meaning of the accounting terms *revenue* and *expenses.*

Revenue

Revenue is the price of goods sold and services rendered during a given accounting period. Earning revenue causes owner's equity to increase. When a business renders services or sells merchandise to its customers, it usually receives cash or acquires an account receivable from the customer. The inflow of cash and receivables from customers increases the total assets of the company. On the other side of the accounting equation, the liabilities do not change, but owner's equity increases to match the increase in total assets. Thus revenue is the gross *increase in owner's equity* resulting from operation of the business.

Various terms are used to describe different types of revenue; for example, the revenue earned by a real estate broker might be called *Sales Commissions Earned,* or alternatively, *Commissions Revenue.* In the professional practice of lawyers, physicians, dentists, and CPAs, the revenue is called *Fees Earned.* A business which sells merchandise rather than services (General Motors, for example) will use the term *Sales* to describe the revenue earned. Another type of revenue is *Interest Earned,* which means the amount received as interest on notes receivable, bank deposits, government bonds, or other securities.

When to Record Revenue: The Realization Principle   When is revenue recorded in the accounting records? For example, assume that on May 24, a real estate company signs a contract to represent a client in selling the client's personal residence. The contract entitles the real estate company to a commission equal to 5% of the selling price, due 30 days after the date of sale. On June 10, the real estate company sells the house at a price of $120,000, thereby earning a $6,000 commission ($120,000 × 5%), to be received on July 10. When should the company record this $6,000 commission revenue—in May, June, or July?

The company should record this revenue on June 10—the day it ***rendered the service*** of selling the client's house. As the company will not collect this commission until July, it must also record an account receivable on June 10. In July, when this receivable is collected, the company must not record revenue a second time. Collecting an account receivable increases one asset, Cash, and decreases another asset, Accounts Receivable. Thus, collecting an account receivable ***does not increase owner's equity*** and does not represent revenue.

Our answer illustrates a generally accepted accounting principle called the ***realization principle.*** The realization principle states that a business should record revenue at the time ***services are rendered to customers*** or ***goods sold are delivered to customers.*** In short, revenue is recorded when it is ***earned,*** without regard as to when the cash is received.

Expenses

Expenses are the costs of the goods and services used up in the process of earning revenue. Examples include the cost of employees' salaries, advertising, rent, utilities, and the gradual wearing-out (depreciation) of such assets as buildings, automobiles, and office equipment. All these costs are necessary to attract and serve customers and thereby earn revenue. Expenses are often called the "costs of doing business," that is, the cost of the various activities necessary to carry on a business.

An expense always causes a ***decrease in owner's equity.*** The related changes in the accounting equation can be either (1) a decrease in assets or (2) an increase in liabilities. An expense reduces assets if payment occurs at the time that the expense is incurred (or if payment has been made in advance). If the expense will not be paid until later, as, for example, the purchase of advertising services on account, the recording of the expense will be accompanied by an increase in liabilities.

When to Record Expenses: The Matching Principle   A significant relationship exists between revenue and expenses. Expenses are incurred for the ***purpose of producing revenue.*** In measuring net income for a period, revenue should be offset by ***all the expenses incurred in producing that revenue.*** This concept of offsetting expenses against revenue on a basis of "cause and effect" is called the ***matching principle***

Timing is an important factor in matching (offsetting) revenue with the related expenses. For example, in preparing monthly income statements, it is important to offset this month's expenses against this month's revenue.

We should not offset this month's expenses against last month's revenue, because there is no cause and effect relationship between the two.

To illustrate the matching principle, assume that the salaries earned by sales personnel waiting on customers during July are not paid until early August. In which month should these salaries be regarded as an expense? The answer is *July,* because this is the month in which the sales personnel's services *helped to produce revenue.*

We previously explained that revenue and cash receipts are not one and the same thing. Similarly, expenses and cash payments are not identical. The cash payment for an expense may occur before, after, or in the same period that an expense helps to produce revenue. In deciding when to record an expense, the critical question is *"In what period will this expenditure help to produce revenue?"* not "When will the cash payment occur?"

Expenditures Benefiting More Than One Accounting Period   Many expenditures made by a business benefit two or more accounting periods. Fire insurance policies, for example, usually cover a period of 12 months. If a company prepares monthly income statements, a portion of the cost of such a policy should be allocated to insurance expense each month that the policy is in force. In this case, apportionment of the cost of the policy by months is an easy matter. If the 12-month policy costs $2,400 for example, the insurance expense for each month amounts to $200 ($2,400 ÷ 12 months).

Not all transactions can be so precisely divided by accounting periods. The purchase of a building, furniture and fixtures, machinery, a typewriter, or an automobile provides benefits to the business over all the years in which such an asset is used. No one can determine in advance exactly how many years of service will be received from such long-lived assets. Nevertheless, in measuring the net income of a business for a period of one year or less, the accountant must *estimate* what portion of the cost of the building and other long-lived assets is applicable to the current year. Since the allocations of these costs are estimates rather than precise measurements, it follows that income statements should be regarded as useful *approximations* of net income rather than as absolutely exact measurements.

For some expenditures, such as those for advertising or employee training programs, it is not possible to estimate objectively the number of accounting periods over which revenue is likely to be produced. In such cases, generally accepted accounting principles require that the expenditure be charged *immediately to expense.* This treatment is based upon the accounting principle of *objectivity* and the concept of *conservatism.* Accountants require *objective evidence* that an expenditure will produce revenue in future periods before they will view the expenditure as creating an asset. When this objective evidence does not exist, they follow the conservative practice of recording the expenditure as an expense. *Conservatism,* in this context, means applying the accounting treatment which results in the *lowest* (most conservative) estimate of net income for the current period.

Debit and Credit Rules for Revenue and Expense

OBJECTIVE 3
Apply the
rules of
debit and
credit in
recording
revenue and
expenses.

We have stressed that revenue increases owner's equity and that expenses decrease owner's equity. The debit and credit rules for recording revenue and expenses in the ledger accounts are a natural extension of the rules for recording changes in owner's equity. The rules previously stated for recording increases and decreases in owner's equity were as follows:

- ■ **Increases** in owner's equity are recorded by **credits.**
- ■ **Decreases** in owner's equity are recorded by **debits.**

This rule is now extended to cover revenue and expense accounts:

- ■ Revenue **increases** owner's equity; therefore revenue is recorded by a **credit.**
- ■ Expenses **decrease** owner's equity; therefore expenses are recorded by **debits.**

Ledger Accounts for Revenue and Expenses

During the course of an accounting period, a great many revenue and expense transactions occur in the average business. To classify and summarize these numerous transactions, a separate ledger account is maintained for each major type of revenue and expense. For example, almost every business maintains accounts for advertising expense, telephone expense, and salaries expense. At the end of the period, all the advertising expenses appear as debits in the Advertising Expense account. The debit balance of this account represents the total advertising expense of the period and is listed as one of the expense items in the income statement.

Revenue accounts are usually much less numerous than expense accounts. A small business such as Roberts Real Estate Company in our continuing illustration may have only one or two types of revenue, such as commissions earned from arranging sales of real estate, and fees earned from managing properties on behalf of clients. In a business of this type, the revenue accounts might be called Sales Commissions Earned and Management Fees Earned.

Investments and Withdrawals by the Owner

The owner of an unincorporated business may at any time invest assets or withdraw assets from the business. These "investment transactions" cause changes in the amount of owner's equity, but they are **not** considered revenue or expenses of the business.

Investments of assets by the owner are recorded by debiting the asset accounts and crediting the owner's capital account. This transaction is not viewed as revenue, because the business has not sold any merchandise or rendered any service in exchange for the assets received.

The income statement of a sole proprietorship does not include any salary expense representing the managerial services rendered by the owner. One reason for not including a salary to the owner-manager is that individuals in such positions are able to set their salaries at any amount they choose. The use of an unrealistic salary to the proprietor would tend to destroy the usefulness of the income statement for measuring the profitability of the business. Thus, accountants regard the owner-manager as working to earn the *entire net income* of the business, rather than as working for a salary.

Even though the owner does not technically receive a salary, he or she usually makes withdrawals of cash from time to time for personal use. These withdrawals reduce the assets and owner's equity of the business, but they are *not* expenses. Expenses are incurred for the purpose of *generating revenue,* and withdrawals by the owner do not have this purpose.

Withdrawals could be recorded by debiting the owner's capital account. However, a clearer record is created if a separate Drawing account is debited. (In our Roberts Real Estate Company example, we will use an account entitled *James Roberts, Drawing* to record withdrawals by the owner.)

Debits to the owner's drawing account result from such transactions as:

1 Withdrawals of cash.
2 Withdrawals of other assets. The owner of a clothing store, for example, may withdraw merchandise for his or her personal use. The amount of the debit to the drawing account would be for the cost of the goods which were withdrawn.
3 Payment of the owner's personal bills out of company funds.

As investments and withdrawals by the owner are not classified as revenue and expenses, they are not included in the income statement. Instead, they are summarized in the statement of owner's equity, which will be discussed later in this chapter.

Recording Revenue and Expense Transactions: An Illustration

The organization of Roberts Real Estate Company during September has already been described. The illustration is now continued for October, during which the company earned commissions by selling several residences for its clients. Bear in mind that the company does not own any residential property; it merely acts as a broker or an agent for clients wishing to sell their houses. A commission of 6% of the sales price of the house is charged for this service. During October the company not only earned commissions but also incurred a number of expenses.

Note that each illustrated transaction which affects an income statement account also affects a balance sheet account. This pattern is consistent with our previous discussion of revenue and expenses. In recording revenue transactions, we debit the assets received and credit a revenue account. In recording expense transactions, we debit an expense account and credit the asset Cash, or a liability account if payment is to be made later. The transactions for October were as follows:

Oct. 1 Paid $360 for publication of newspaper advertising describing various houses offered for sale.

	Analysis	Rule	Entry
Advertising expense incurred and paid	The cost of advertising is an expense	Expenses decrease the owner's equity and are recorded by debits	Debit: Advertising Expense, $360
	The asset Cash was decreased	Decreases in assets are recorded by credits	Credit: Cash, $360

Oct. 6 Earned and collected a commission of $2,250 by selling a residence previously listed by a client.

	Analysis	Rule	Entry
Revenue earned and collected	The asset Cash was increased	Increases in assets are recorded by debits	Debit: Cash, $2,250
	Revenue was earned	Revenue increases the owner's equity and is recorded by a credit	Credit: Sales Commissions Earned, $2,250

Oct. 16 Newspaper advertising was purchased at a price of $270, payment to be made within 30 days.

	Analysis	Rule	Entry
Advertising expense incurred; to be paid later	The cost of advertising is an expense	Expenses decrease the owner's equity and are recorded by debits	Debit: Advertising Expense, $270
	An account payable, a liability, was incurred	Increases in liabilities are recorded by credits	Credit: Accounts Payable, $270

Oct. 20 A commission of $8,390 was earned by selling a client's residence. The sales agreement provided that the commission would be received in 60 days.

	Analysis	Rule	Entry
Revenue earned; to be collected later	An asset in the form of an account receivable was acquired	Increases in assets are recorded by debits	Debit: Accounts Receivable, $8,390
	Revenue was earned	Revenue increases the owner's equity and is recorded by a credit	Credit: Sales Commissions Earned, $8,390

Oct. 25 Roberts withdrew $2,800 for personal use.

	Analysis	Rule	Entry
Withdrawal of cash by the owner	*Withdrawal of assets by the owner decreases the owner's equity*	*Decreases in owner's equity are recorded by debits*	*Debit: James Roberts, Drawing, $2,800*
	The asset Cash was decreased	*Decreases in assets are recorded by credits*	*Credit: Cash, $2,800*

Oct. 30 Roberts found that he did not need all of the $2,800 withdrawn on October 25, and he redeposited $1,000 of this amount in the company's bank account.

	Analysis	Rule	Entry
Additional investment by the owner	*The asset Cash was increased*	*Increases in assets are recorded by debits*	*Debit: Cash, $1,000*
	The owner's equity was increased	*Increases in owner's equity are recorded by credits*	*Credit: James Roberts, Capital, $1,000*

Oct. 31 Paid salaries of $7,100 to employees for services rendered during October.

	Analysis	Rule	Entry
Salaries expense incurred and paid	*Salaries of employees are an expense*	*Expenses decrease the owner's equity and are recorded by debits*	*Debit: Salaries Expense, $7,100*
	The asset Cash was decreased	*Decreases in assets are recorded by credits*	*Credit: Cash, $7,100*

Oct. 31 A telephone bill for October amounting to $144 was received. Payment was required by November 10.

	Analysis	Rule	Entry
Telephone expense incurred; to be paid later	*The cost of telephone service is an expense*	*Expenses decrease the owner's equity and are recorded by debits*	*Debit: Telephone Expense, $144*
	An account payable, a liability, was incurred	*Increases in liabilities are recorded by credits*	*Credit: Accounts Payable, $144*

The journal entries to record the October transactions are as follows:

October journal entries for Roberts Real Estate Company

	Date		Account Titles and Explanation	LP	Debit	Credit
			General Journal		*Page 2*	
	19__ Oct	1	Advertising Expense .... Cash .... Paid for newspaper advertising.	70 1	360	360
		6	Cash .... Sales Commissions Earned .... Earned and collected commission by selling residence for client.	1 60	2,250	2,250
		16	Advertising Expense .... Accounts Payable................. Purchased newspaper advertising; payable in 30 days.	70 32	270	270
		20	Accounts Receivable .... Sales Commissions Earned .... Earned commission by selling residence for client; commission to be received in 60 days.	4 60	8,390	8,390
		25	James Roberts, Drawing................. Cash .... Withdrawal of cash by owner.	51 1	2,800	2,800
		30	Cash .... James Roberts, Capital............ Additional investment by owner.	1 50	1,000	1,000
		31	Salaries Expense....................... Cash .... Paid salaries for October.	72 1	7,100	7,100
		31	Telephone Expense .... Accounts Payable................. To record liability for October telephone service.	74 32	144	144

The column headings at the top of the illustrated journal page (*Date, Account Titles and Explanation, LP, Debit,* and *Credit*) are seldom used in practice. They are included here as an instructional guide but will be omitted from some of the later illustrations of journal entries.

The Ledger

The ledger of Roberts Real Estate Company after the October transactions have been posted is now illustrated. To conserve space in this illustration, several ledger accounts appear on a single page; in actual practice, however, each account occupies a separate page in the ledger.

Cash — Account No. 1

Date		Explanation	Ref	Debit	Credit	Balance
19 —						
Sept	1		1	180000		180000
	3		1		141000	39000
	5		1		15000	24000
	20		1	1500		25500
	30		1		3000	22500
Oct	1		2		360	22140
	6		2	2250		24390
	25		2		2800	21590
	30		2	1000		22590
	31		2		7100	15490

Accounts Receivable — Account No. 4

Date		Explanation	Ref	Debit	Credit	Balance
19 —						
Sept	10		1	11000		11000
	20		1		1500	9500
Oct	20		2	8390		17890

Land — Account No. 20

Date		Explanation	Ref	Debit	Credit	Balance
19 —						
Sept	3		1	141000		141000
	10		1		11000	130000

Building — Account No. 22

Date		Explanation	Ref	Debit	Credit	Balance
19 —						
Sept	5		1	36000		36000

	Office Equipment				Account No. 25	
Date	Explanation	Ref	Debit	Credit	Balance	
19 —						
Sept. 14		1	5400		5400	

	Accounts Payable				Account No 32	
Date	Explanation	Ref	Debit	Credit	Balance	
19 —						
Sept. 5		1		21000	21000	
14		1		5400	26400	
30		1	3000		23400	
Oct 16		2		270	23670	
31		2		144	23814	

	James Roberts, Capital				Account No. 50	
Date	Explanation	Ref	Debit	Credit	Balance	
19 —						
Sept. 1		1		180000	180000	
Oct 30		2		1000	181000	

	James Roberts, Drawing				Account No. 51	
Date	Explanation	Ref	Debit	Credit	Balance	
19 —						
Oct 25		2	2800		2800	

Sales Commissions Earned					Account No. *60*
Date	Explanation	Ref	Debit	Credit	Balance
19 —					
Oct 6		2		2 2 5 0	2 2 5 0
20		2		8 3 9 0	10 6 4 0

Advertising Expense					Account No. *70*
Date	Explanation	Ref	Debit	Credit	Balance
19 —					
Oct 1		2	3 6 0		3 6 0
16		2	2 7 0		6 3 0

Salaries Expense					Account No. *72*
Date	Explanation	Ref	Debit	Credit	Balance
19 —					
Oct 31		2	7 1 0 0		7 1 0 0

Telephone Expense					Account No. *74*
Date	Explanation	Ref	Debit	Credit	Balance
19 —					
Oct 31		2	1 4 4		1 4 4

The accounts in this illustration are listed in ***financial statement order***—that is, balance sheet accounts first (assets, liabilities, and owner's equity), followed by income statement accounts. The sequence of accounts within the balance sheet categories was discussed in Chapter 2. Within the categories of revenue and expense, accounts may be listed in any order.

The Trial Balance

A trial balance prepared from the ledger accounts of Roberts Real Estate Company is shown below:

Proving the equality of debits and credits

ROBERTS REAL ESTATE COMPANY
Trial Balance
October 31, 19__

Cash	$ 15,490	
Accounts receivable	17,890	
Land	130,000	
Building	36,000	
Office equipment	5,400	
Accounts payable		$ 23,814
James Roberts, capital		181,000
James Roberts, drawing	2,800	
Sales commissions earned		10,540
Advertising expense	630	
Salaries expense	7,100	
Telephone expense	144	
	$215,454	$215,454

This trial balance proves the equality of the debit and credit entries in the company's ledger. Notice that the trial balance contains income statement accounts as well as balance sheet accounts.

ADJUSTING ENTRIES: THE NEXT STEP IN THE ACCOUNTING CYCLE

Many transactions affect the revenue or expenses of two or more accounting periods. For example, a business may purchase equipment that will last for many years, insurance policies that cover 12 months, or enough office supplies to last for several months. Each of these assets is gradually used up—that is, becomes expense. How do accountants allocate the cost of these assets to expense over a span of several accounting periods? The answer is *adjusting entries.*

Adjusting entries are made at the end of each accounting period. There are several different types of adjusting entries; in fact, many businesses make a dozen or more adjusting entries at the end of every accounting period. In this chapter, we introduce the concept of end-of-period adjustments with the entry to record *depreciation expense.* This is the most common of all adjusting entries; every business that owns a building or equipment must record depreciation expense at the end of each accounting period.

Depreciation Expense Our definition of expense is the cost of goods and services used up in the process of earning revenue. Buildings and equipment are examples of goods that are purchased in advance but which are

OBJECTIVE 4
Define and
record de-
preciation
expense.

used up gradually over many accounting periods. Each year a portion of the usefulness of these assets expires, and a portion of their total cost should be recognized as **depreciation expense.** The term **depreciation** means the **systematic allocation of the cost of an asset to expense** over the accounting periods making up the asset's useful life.

Although depreciation expense occurs each month, it does not involve monthly transactions. In effect, depreciation expense is paid in advance when the related asset is originally acquired. Thus, adjusting entries are needed at the end of each accounting period to record the appropriate amount of depreciation expense. Failure to make these adjusting entries would result in understating the expenses of the period and consequently overstating net income.

Building The office building purchased by Roberts Real Estate Company at a cost of $36,000 is estimated to have a useful life of 20 years. The purpose of the $36,000 expenditure was to provide a place in which to carry on the business and thereby to obtain revenue. After 20 years of use the building is expected to be worthless and the original cost of $36,000 will have been entirely consumed. In effect, the company has purchased 20 years of "housing services" at a total cost of $36,000. A portion of this cost expires during each year of use of the building. If we assume that each year's operations should bear an equal share of the total cost (straight-line depreciation), the annual depreciation expense will amount to $\frac{1}{20}$ of $36,000, or $1,800. On a monthly basis, depreciation expense is $150 ($36,000 cost ÷ 240 months). There are alternative methods of spreading the cost of a depreciable asset over its useful life, some of which will be considered in Chapter 10.

The journal entry to record depreciation of the building during October follows:

General Journal   *Page 2*

Date		Account Titles and Explanation	LP	Debit	Credit
19__ Oct	31	Depreciation Expense: Building	76	150	
		Accumulated Depreciation:			
		Building	23		150
		To record depreciation for October. Cost of $36,000 ÷ 240 months = $150 a month.			

Recording de-
preciation of
the building

The depreciation expense account will appear in the income statement for October along with the other expenses of salaries, advertising, and telephone. The Accumulated Depreciation: Building account will appear in the balance sheet as a deduction from the Building account, as shown by the following illustration of a partial balance sheet:

ROBERTS REAL ESTATE COMPANY
Partial Balance Sheet
October 31, 19__

Showing accu-
mulated depre-
ciation in the
balance sheet

Building (at cost)	$36,000	
Less: Accumulated depreciation	150	$35,850

The end result of crediting the Accumulated Depreciation: Building account is much the same as if the credit had been made to the Building account; that is, the net amount shown on the balance sheet for the building is reduced from $36,000 to $35,850. Although the credit side of a depreciation entry **could** be made directly to the asset account, it is customary and more efficient to record such credits in a separate account entitled Accumulated Depreciation. The original cost of the asset and the total amount of depreciation recorded over the years can more easily be determined from the ledger when separate accounts are maintained for the asset and for the accumulated depreciation.

Accumulated Depreciation: Building is an example of a **contra-asset account,** because it has a credit balance and is offset against an asset account (Building) to produce the proper balance sheet amount for the asset.

Office Equipment Depreciation on the office equipment of Roberts Real Estate Company must also be recorded at the end of October. This equipment cost $5,400 and is assumed to have a useful life of 10 years. Monthly depreciation expense on the straight-line basis is, therefore, $45, computed by dividing the cost of $5,400 by the useful life of 120 months. The journal entry is as follows:

Recording depreciation of office equipment

		General Journal			Page 2
Date		Account Titles and Explanation	LP	Debit	Credit
19__ Oct	31	Depreciation Expense: Office Equipment	78	45	
		Accumulated Depreciation: Office			
		Equipment.........................	26		45
		To record depreciation for October. Cost of $5,400 ÷ 120 months = $45 a month.			

No depreciation was recorded on the building and office equipment for September, the month in which these assets were acquired, because regular operations did not begin until October. Generally, depreciation is not recognized until the business begins active operation and the assets are **placed in use.**

The journal entry by which depreciation is recorded at the end of the month is called an **adjusting entry.** The adjustment of certain asset accounts and related expense accounts is a necessary step at the end of each accounting period so that the information presented in the financial statements will be as accurate and complete as possible. In the next chapter, adjusting entries will be shown for some other items in addition to depreciation.

The Adjusted Trial Balance

After all the necessary adjusting entries have been journalized and posted, an **adjusted trial balance** is prepared to prove that the ledger is still in balance. It also provides a complete listing of the account balances to be used in preparing the financial statements. The following adjusted trial balance differs from the trial balance shown on page 118 because it includes accounts for depreciation expense and accumulated depreciation.

Adjusted trial balance

ROBERTS REAL ESTATE COMPANY
Adjusted Trial Balance
October 31, 19__

Cash	$ 15,490	
Accounts receivable	17,890	
Land	130,000	
Building	36,000	
Accumulated depreciation: building..........		$ 150
Office equipment	5,400	
Accumulated depreciation: office equipment		45
Accounts payable..........		23,814
James Roberts, capital		181,000
James Roberts, drawing..........	2,800	
Sales commissions earned		10,640
Advertising expense	630	
Salaries expense..........	7,100	
Telephone expense	144	
Depreciation expense: building	150	
Depreciation expense: office equipment..........	45	
	$215,649	$215,649

PREPARING A "SET" OF FINANCIAL STATEMENTS

Now that Roberts Real Estate Company has been operating for a month, managers and outside parties will want to know more about the company than just its financial position. They will want to know the results of operations—whether the month's activities have been profitable or unprofitable. To provide this additional information, we will prepare a more complete set of financial statements, consisting of an income statement, a statement of owner's equity, and a balance sheet.[1] These statements are illustrated on page 122.

The Income Statement

OBJECTIVE 5
Describe and prepare an income statement and a statement of owner's equity. Explain how these statements relate to the balance sheet.

The revenue and expenses shown in the income statement are taken directly from the company's adjusted trial balance. The income statement of Roberts Real Estate Company shows that revenue earned in October exceeded the expenses of the month, thus producing a net income of $2,571. Bear in mind, however, that our measurement of net income is not absolutely accurate or precise, because of the assumptions and estimates in the accounting process.

An income statement has certain limitations. Remember that the amounts shown for depreciation expense are based upon ***estimates*** of the useful lives of the company's building and office equipment. Also, the income statement includes only those events which have been ***evidenced by business transactions.*** Perhaps during October, Roberts Real Estate

---

[1]   A complete set of financial statements also includes a ***statement of cash flows,*** which will be discussed in Chapter 19.

ROBERTS REAL ESTATE COMPANY
Income Statement
For the Month Ended October 31, 19__

Revenue:

Sales commissions earned		$10,640
Expenses:		
Advertising expense	$ 630	
Office salaries expense	7,100	
Telephone expense	144	
Depreciation expense: building	150	
Depreciation expense: office equipment..........................	45	8,069
Net income		$ 2,571

Net income is an increase in owner's equity

ROBERTS REAL ESTATE COMPANY
Statement of Owner's Equity
For the Month Ended October 31, 19__

James Roberts, capital, Sept. 30, 19__	$180,000
Add: Net income for October	2,571
Additional investment by owner	1,000
Subtotal	$183,571
Less: Withdrawals by owner..	2,800
James Roberts, capital, Oct. 31, 19__	$180,771

The ending balance of owner's equity appears in the balance sheet

ROBERTS REAL ESTATE COMPANY
Balance Sheet
October 31, 19__

Assets

Cash		$ 15,490
Accounts receivable		17,890
Land		130,000
Building	$36,000	
Less: Accumulated depreciation	150	35,850
Office equipment	$ 5,400	
Less: Accumulated depreciation	45	5,355
Total assets		$204,585

Liabilities & Owner's Equity

Liabilities

Accounts payable...	$ 23,814
Owner's equity:	
James Roberts, capital, Oct. 31, 19__	180,771
Total liabilities & owner's equity	$204,585

Company has made contact with many people who are right on the verge of buying or selling homes. Good business contacts are an important step toward profitable operations. However, such contacts are not reflected in the income statement because their value cannot be measured *objectively* until actual transactions take place. Despite these limitations, the income statement is of vital importance and indicates that the new business has been profitable during its first month of operation.

Alternative titles for the income statement include *earnings statement, statement of operations,* and *profit and loss statement.* However, *income statement* is by far the most popular term for this important financial statement. In summary, we can say that an income statement is used to summarize the *operating results* of a business by matching the revenue earned during a given time period with the expenses incurred in obtaining that revenue.

The Statement of Owner's Equity

This financial statement summarizes the increases and decreases during the accounting period in the amount of owner's equity. Increases result from earning net income and from additional investments by the owner; decreases result from net losses and from withdrawals of assets by the owner.

The owner's equity at the beginning of the period ($180,000) may be obtained from the ledger or from the balance sheet of the preceding period. As we have just illustrated, the amount of net income or net loss for the period is determined in the company's *income statement.* Additional investments by the owner may be determined by reviewing the credit column of the owner's capital account in the ledger. Withdrawals during the period are indicated by the balance in the owner's drawing account. By adjusting the beginning amount of owner's equity for the increases and decreases occurring during the period, we are able to determine the owner's equity at the end of the period. This amount, *$180,771* in our example, will also appear in the company's October 31 balance sheet.

The Balance Sheet

The balance sheet lists the amounts of the company's assets, liabilities, and owner's equity at the *end* of the accounting period. The balances of the asset and liability accounts are taken directly from the adjusted trial balance on page 121. The amount of owner's equity at the end of the period, $180,771, was determined in the *statement of owner's equity.*

Previous illustrations of balance sheets have been arranged in *account form*—that is, with assets on the left and liabilities and owner's equity on the right. The illustration on page 122 is arranged in *report form,* with the liabilities and owner's equity sections listed below rather than to the right of the asset section. Both the account form and the report form of balance sheet are widely used.

Relationship among the Financial Statements

A set of financial statements becomes easier to understand if we recognize that the income statement, statement of owner's equity, and balance sheet all are related to one another. These relationships are emphasized by the arrows in the right-hand margin of our illustration on page 122.

The balance sheet prepared at the end of the preceding period and the one prepared at the end of the current period each show the amount of owner's equity at the respective balance sheet dates. The statement of owner's equity summarizes the changes in owner's equity occurring between these two balance sheet dates. The income statement provides a detailed explanation of the most important change in owner's equity—the amount of net income or net loss for the accounting period. Thus, the income statement and the statement of owner's equity explain the change in the amount of owner's equity shown in successive balance sheets.

CLOSING THE TEMPORARY ACCOUNTS

OBJECTIVE 6
Explain the purposes served by closing entries; prepare these entries.

As previously stated, revenue increases owner's equity, and expenses and withdrawals by the owner decrease owner's equity. If the only financial statement that we needed was a balance sheet, these changes in owner's equity could be recorded directly in the owner's capital account. However, owners, managers, investors, and others need to know amounts of specific revenues and expenses, and the amount of net income earned in the period. Therefore, we maintain separate ledger accounts to measure each type of revenue and expense, and the owner's drawings.

These revenue, expense, and drawing accounts are called ***temporary*** accounts, or ***nominal*** accounts, because they accumulate the transactions of ***only one accounting period.*** At the end of this accounting period, the changes in owner's equity accumulated in these temporary accounts are transferred into the owner's capital account. This process serves two purposes. First, it ***updates the balance of the owner's capital account*** for changes in owner's equity occurring during the accounting period. Second, it ***returns the balances of the temporary accounts to zero,*** so that they are ready for measuring the revenue, expenses, and drawings of the next accounting period.

The owner's capital account and other balance sheet accounts are called ***permanent*** or ***real*** accounts, because their balances continue to exist beyond the current accounting period. The process of transferring the balances of the temporary accounts into the owner's permanent capital account is called ***closing*** the accounts. The journal entries made for the purpose of closing the temporary accounts are called ***closing entries.***

It is common practice to close the accounts only once a year, but for illustration, we will now demonstrate the closing of the accounts of Roberts Real Estate Company at October 31 after one month's operation.

Closing Entries for Revenue Accounts   Revenue accounts have credit balances. Closing a revenue account, therefore, means transferring its credit balance to the Income Summary account. This transfer is accomplished by a journal entry debiting the revenue account in an amount equal to its credit balance, with an offsetting credit to the Income Summary account. The debit portion of this closing entry returns the balance of the revenue account to zero; the credit portion transfers the former balance of the revenue account into the Income Summary account. The only revenue account of Roberts Real Estate Company is Sales Commissions Earned, which had a credit balance of $10,640 at October 31. The closing entry is as follows:

General Journal					Page 3
Date		Account Titles and Explanation	LP	Debit	Credit
19__ Oct	31	Sales Commissions Earned..............	60	10,640	
		Income Summary	53		10,640
		To close the Sales Commissions Earned account.			

Closing a revenue account

After this closing entry has been posted, the two accounts affected will appear as follows. A few details of account structure have been omitted to simplify the illustration; a directional arrow has been added to show the transfer of the $10,640 balance of the revenue account into the Income Summary account.

Sales Commissions Earned					80	Income Summary					53
Date	Exp.	Ref	Debit	Credit	Balance	Date	Exp.	Ref	Debit	Credit	Balance
Oct 6		2		2,250	2,250	Oct 31		3		10,640	10,640
20		2		8,390	10,640						
31	To close	3	10,640		–0–						

Closing Entries for Expense Accounts

Expense accounts have debit balances. Closing an expense account means transferring its debit balance to the Income Summary account. The journal entry to close an expense account, therefore, consists of a credit to the expense account in an amount equal to its debit balance, with an offsetting debit to the Income Summary account.

There are five expense accounts in the ledger of Roberts Real Estate Company. Five separate journal entries could be made to close these five expense accounts, but the use of one ***compound journal entry*** is an easier, time-saving method of closing all five expense accounts. A compound journal entry is an entry that includes debits to more than one account or credits to more than one account.

General Journal					Page 3
Date		Account Titles and Explanation	LP	Debit	Credit
19__ Oct	31	Income Summary	53	8,069	
		Advertising Expense	70		630
		Salaries Expense	72		7,100
		Telephone Expense	74		144
		Depreciation Expense: Building.....	76		150
		Depreciation Expense: Office Equipment........................	78		45
		To close the expense accounts.			

Closing the various expense accounts by use of a compound journal entry

After this closing entry has been posted, the Income Summary account has a credit balance of $2,571, and the five expense accounts have zero balances, as shown on the following page.

Closing the Income Summary Account

The five expense accounts have now been closed and the total amount of $8,069 formerly contained in these accounts appears in the debit column of the Income Summary account. The commissions of $10,640 earned during October appear in the credit column of the Income Summary account. Since the credit entry of $10,640 representing October revenue is larger than the debit of $8,069 representing October expenses, the account has a credit balance of $2,571—the net income for October.

The net income of $2,571 earned during October causes the owner's equity to increase. The **credit** balance of the Income Summary account is, therefore, transferred to the owner's capital account by the following closing entry.

Net income increases the owner's equity

	General Journal				Page 3
Date	Account Titles and Explanation	LP	Debit	Credit
19__ Oct 31	Income Summary .... James Roberts, Capital............. To close the Income Summary account for October by transferring the net income to the owner's capital account.	53 50	2,571	2,571

After this closing entry has been posted, the Income Summary account has a zero balance, and the net income for October will appear as an increase (or credit entry) in the owner's capital account as shown below.

Income Summary account is closed into the owner's capital account

	Income Summary				Account No. 53
Date	Explanation	Ref	Debit	Credit	Balance
19__ Oct 31	Revenue	3		10,640	10,640
31	Expenses	3	8,069		2,571
31	To close	3	2,571		–0–

	James Roberts, Capital				Account No. 50
Date	Explanation	Ref	Debit	Credit	Balance
19__ Sept 1	Investment by owner	1		180,000	180,000
Oct 30	Additional investment by owner	2		1,000	181,000
31	Net income for October	3		2,571	183,571

In our illustration the business has operated profitably with revenue in excess of expenses. Not every business is so fortunate: if the expenses of a business are larger than its revenue, the Income Summary account will

Advertising Expense   Account No. 70

Date		Explanation	Ref	Debit	Credit	Balance
19__						
Oct	2		2	360		360
	16		2	270		630
	31	To close	3		630	–0–

Salaries Expense   Account No. 72

Date		Explanation	Ref	Debit	Credit	Balance
19__						
Oct	31		2	7,100		7,100
	31	To close	3		7,100	–0–

Telephone Expense   Account No. 74

Date		Explanation	Ref	Debit	Credit	Balance
19__						
Oct	31		2	144		144
	31	To close	3		144	–0–

Depreciation Expense: Building   Account No. 76

Date		Explanation	Ref	Debit	Credit	Balance
19__						
Oct	31		2	150		150
	31	To close	3		150	–0–

Depreciation Expense: Office Equipment   Account No. 78

Date		Explanation	Ref	Debit	Credit	Balance
19__						
Oct	31		2	45		45
	31	To close	3		45	–0–

Income Summary   Account No. 53

Date		Explanation	Ref	Debit	Credit	Balance
19__						
Oct	31		3		10,640	10,640
	31		3	8,069		2,571

have a debit balance, representing a ***net loss*** for the accounting period. In that case, the closing of the Income Summary account requires a debit to the owner's capital account and an offsetting credit to the Income Summary account. The owner's equity will, or course, be reduced by the amount of the loss debited to the capital account.

Note that the Income Summary account is used only at the end of the period when the accounts are being closed. The Income Summary account has no entries and no balance except during the process of closing the accounts at the end of the accounting period.

Closing the Owner's Drawing Account

As explained earlier in this chapter, withdrawals of cash or other assets by the owner are not considered as an expense of the business and, therefore, are not a factor in determining the net income for the period. Since drawings by the owner do not constitute an expense, the owner's drawing account is closed not into the Income Summary account but directly to the owner's capital account. The following journal entry serves to close the drawing account in the ledger of Roberts Real Estate Company at October 31.

Drawing account is closed into the owner's capital account

General Journal					Page 3
Date		**Account Titles and Explanation**	**LP**	**Debit**	**Credit**
19__ Oct	31	James Roberts, Capital	50	2,800	
		James Roberts, Drawing	51		2,800
		To close the owner's drawing account.			

After this closing entry has been posted, the drawing account will have a zero balance, and the amount withdrawn by Roberts during October will appear as a deduction or debit entry in the capital account.

James Roberts, Drawing						Account No. 51
Date		**Explanation**	**Ref**	**Debit**	**Credit**	**Balance**
19__ Oct	31	Withdrawal	2	2,800		2,800
	31	To close	3		2,800	–0–

One account now shows the total equity of the owner

James Roberts, Capital						Account No. 50
Date		**Explanation**	**Ref**	**Debit**	**Credit**	**Balance**
19__ Sept	1	Investment by owner	1		180,000	180,000
Oct	30	Additional investment by owner	2		1,000	181,000
	31	Net income for October	3		2,571	183,571
	31	From owner's drawing account	3	2,800		180,771

Summary of the Closing Process

Let us now summarize the process of closing the accounts.

1 Close the various *revenue* accounts by transferring their balances into the Income Summary account.

2 Close the various *expense* accounts by transferring their balances into the Income Summary account.

3 Close the *Income Summary account* by transferring its balance into the owner's capital account.

4 Close the owner's *drawing* account into the owner's capital account. (The balance of the owner's capital account in the ledger will now be the same as the amount of owner's equity appearing in the balance sheet.)

The closing of the accounts may be illustrated graphically by use of T accounts as follows:

Flowchart of the closing process

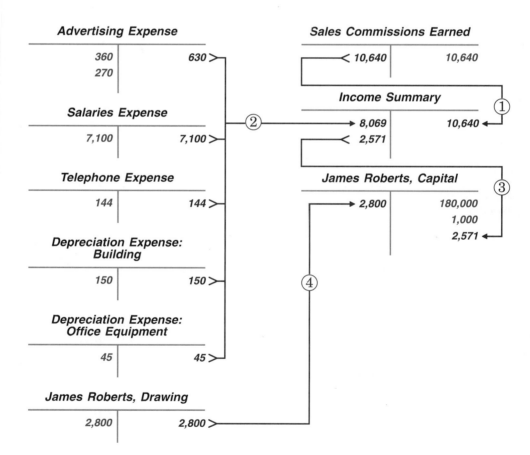

After-Closing Trial Balance

After the revenue and expense accounts have been closed, it is desirable to prepare an *after-closing trial balance,* which will consist of balance sheet accounts *only.* There is always the possibility that an error in posting the closing entries may have upset the equality of debits and credits in the ledger. The after-closing trial balance is prepared from the ledger. It gives assurance that the accounts are in balance and ready for the recording of the transactions of the new accounting period. The after-closing trial balance of Roberts Real Estate Company follows:

ROBERTS REAL ESTATE COMPANY
After-Closing Trial Balance
October 31, 19__

Cash	$ 15,490	
Accounts receivable	17,890	
Land	130,000	
Building	36,000	
Accumulated depreciation: building		$ 150
Office equipment	5,400	
Accumulated depreciation: office equipment		45
Accounts payable		23,814
James Roberts, capital		180,771
	$204,780	$204,780

SEQUENCE OF PROCEDURES IN THE ACCOUNTING CYCLE

The accounting procedures described to this point may be summarized in eight steps, as follows:

OBJECTIVE 7
Describe the sequence of procedures in the accounting cycle.

1 **Journalize transactions.**   Enter all transactions in the general journal, thus creating a chronological record of events.

2 **Post to ledger accounts.**   Post debits and credits from the general journal to the proper ledger accounts, thus creating a record classified by accounts.

3 **Prepare a trial balance.**   Prove the equality of debits and credits in the ledger.

4 **Make end-of-period adjustments.**   Draft adjusting entries in the general journal, and post to ledger accounts. Thus far we have illustrated only one type of adjustment: the recording of depreciation at the end of the period.

5 **Prepare an adjusted trial balance.**   Prove again the equality of debits and credits in the ledger.

6 **Prepare financial statements and appropriate disclosures.**   An income statement shows the results of operations for the period. A statement of owner's equity shows the changes in owner's equity during the period and the ending balance. A balance sheet shows the financial position of the business at the end of the period. Financial statements should be accompanied by ***notes*** disclosing any facts necessary for the ***proper interpretation*** of those statements.

7 **Journalize and post closing entries.**   The closing entries clear the revenue, expense, and drawing accounts, making them ready for recording the events of the next accounting period. The closing entries also

transfer the net income or loss of the completed period to the owner's capital account.

8 **Prepare an after-closing trial balance.** This step ensures that the ledger remains in balance after posting of the closing entries.

These eight procedures represent a complete accounting cycle. In Chapter 4, however, we shall see that the preparation of a **work sheet** will enable us to consolidate several of these procedures.

Accounting Procedures in a Computer-Based System

The sequence of procedures performed in computer-based systems is essentially the same as in manual systems. Of course, the computer is programmed to perform a number of these steps automatically. In the preceding list, procedures **1** and **4** both involve the analysis of business transactions and judgmental decisions as to accounts to be debited and credited and the dollar amounts. These two steps in the accounting cycle require human judgment, regardless of whether the data is processed manually or by computer. As mentioned in Chapter 2, a computer-based system may call for recording transactions first in a data base, rather than in a journal. The computer then arranges the data into the format of journal entries, ledger accounts, trial balances, and financial statements.

Procedures such as posting and the preparation of trial balances and financial statements merely involve the **rearrangement** of recorded data and may easily be performed by computer. Of course, drafting the appropriate **disclosures** that accompany financial statements requires human judgment.

The preparation and posting of closing entries are mechanical tasks, involving the transfer of recorded data from one ledger account to another. Thus, closing entries **may be performed automatically** in a computer-based system.

The Accrual Basis of Accounting

OBJECTIVE 8 Distinguish between the accrual basis and the cash basis of accounting.

The policy of recognizing revenue in the accounting records when it is **earned** and recognizing expenses when the related goods or services are **used** is called the **accrual basis** of accounting. The purpose of accrual accounting is to measure the profitability of the **economic activities conducted** during the accounting period.

The most important concept involved in accrual accounting is the **matching principle.** Revenue is offset with all of the expenses incurred in generating that revenue, thus providing a measure of the overall profitability of the economic activity.

An alternative to the accrual basis is something called **cash basis** accounting. Under cash basis accounting, revenue is recognized when cash is collected from the customer, rather than when the company sells goods or renders services. Expenses are recognized when payment is made, rather than when the related goods or services are used in business operations.

The cash basis of accounting measures the amounts of cash received and paid out during the period, but it does **not** provide a good measure of the **profitability of activities** undertaken during the period.

CASE IN POINT   Airlines sell many tickets weeks or even months **in advance** of scheduled flights. Yet many expenses relating to a flight—such as salaries of the flight crew and the cost of fuel used—may not be paid until **after** the flight has occurred. Thus, the cash basis often would fail to "match" in one accounting period both the revenue and all expenses relating to specific flights.

Generally accepted accounting principles usually **require** use of the accrual basis in measuring revenue, expenses, and net income. However the cash basis is acceptable for use in individuals' income tax returns. (Remember that income tax rules often differ from financial reporting requirements.) For this reason some small businesses—especially sole proprietorships—use the cash basis in their accounting records.

In this textbook, we will emphasize the **accrual basis** of accounting. Accrual basis accounting is used by virtually all businesses that distribute their financial statements to investors, stockholders, creditors, and other decision makers outside the business.

The Usefulness of Revenue and Expense Data to Managers

The revenue and expense data used by managers in planning and controlling business operations differ significantly from the income statements used by outsiders. Outsiders usually receive income statements on either a quarterly or an annual basis. Managers, on the other hand, need information about daily, weekly, and monthly performance. Also, the income statements distributed to investors and creditors describe the profitability of the business **viewed as a whole.** Managers need to know the revenue and expenses relating to **specific departments** within the organization.

In summary, the revenue and expense information used by managers generally covers much shorter time periods and is more detailed than the information contained in a formal income statement. For example, the manager of a large department store might receive a sales report every morning, showing separately the revenue earned by each sales department in the store on the preceding day.

The revenue and expense reports prepared daily or weekly for use by managers show only **selected** revenue and expenses—usually those items which are under the **direct control** of individual managers. Thus, revenue and expense reports usually do not contain all of the information necessary to determine net income.

Managers may compare the revenue and expenses of individual departments with such standards as past performance, budgeted performance for the current and future periods, and the performance of other departments. Their basic goal is to see that resources are being **used efficiently** throughout the organization.

END-OF-CHAPTER REVIEW

SUMMARY OF CHAPTER LEARNING OBJECTIVES

1 Explain the nature of net income, revenue, and expenses.
Net income is an increase in owner's equity that results from the profitable operation of a business during an accounting period. Net income also may be defined as revenue minus expenses. Revenue is the price of goods sold and services rendered to customers during the period, and expenses are the costs of the goods and services used up in the process of earning revenue.

2 Apply the realization and matching principles in recording revenue and expenses.
The realization principle indicates that revenue should be recorded in the accounting records when it is *earned*—that is, when goods are sold or services are rendered to customers. The matching principle indicates that expenses should be offset against revenue on a basis of *cause and effect*. Thus, an expense should be recorded in the period in which the related good or service is consumed in the process of earning revenue.

3 Apply the rules of debit and credit in recording revenue and expenses.
Revenue increases owner's equity; therefore, revenue is recorded by a credit. Expenses decrease owner's equity; therefore, expenses are recorded by debits.

4 Define and record depreciation expense.
The term *depreciation* refers to the systematic allocation of the cost of a long-lived asset (such as equipment or a building) to expense over the asset's useful life. Depreciation is recorded by an entry debiting *Depreciation Expense* and crediting the contra-asset account, *Accumulated Depreciation.*

5 Describe and prepare an income statement and a statement of owner's equity. Explain how these statements relate to the balance sheet.
An income statement shows the revenue and expenses of a business during a specified accounting period. Expenses are offset (matched) against revenue to measure net income for the period. Net income is then listed in the statement of owner's equity as an addition to the beginning balance of owner's equity. Withdrawals by the owner are shown as a deduction. Thus, the statement of owner's equity shows the increases and decreases in owner's equity from one balance sheet date to the next.

6 Explain the purposes served by closing entries; prepare these entries.
Closing entries serve two basic purposes. The first is to return the balances of the temporary owner's equity accounts (revenue, expenses, and drawing accounts) to zero so that these accounts may be used to measure the activities of the next accounting period. The second purpose of closing entries is to update the balance of the owner's capital account. Four closing entries generally are needed: (1) close the revenue ac-

counts into the Income Summary account, (2) close the expense accounts into the Income Summary account, (3) close the balance of the Income Summary account (representing net income or net loss) into the owner's capital account, and (4) close the drawing account into the owner's capital account.

7 **Describe the sequence of procedures in the accounting cycle.**
The accounting procedures in the accounting cycle may be summarized as follows: (1) journalize transactions, (2) post to ledger accounts, (3) prepare a trial balance, (4) make end-of-period adjustments, (5) prepare an adjusted trial balance, (6) prepare financial statements, (7) journalize and post closing entries, and (8) prepare an after-closing trial balance.

8 **Distinguish between the accrual basis and the cash basis of accounting.**
Under accrual accounting, revenue is recognized when it is earned and expenses are recognized in the period in which they contribute to the generation of revenue. Under the cash basis, on the other hand, revenue is recognized when cash is received and expenses are recognized when cash payments are made. The accrual basis gives a better measurement of profitability than does the cash basis, because the accrual basis associates the determination of income with the underlying earning process.

In Chapter 2, we introduced the double-entry system of accounting but illustrated this system using only balance sheet accounts. In this third chapter, we have seen that the double-entry system also allows us to measure revenue and expenses as we record changes in assets and liabilities. In fact, it is this double-entry system that makes possible the measurement of revenue and expenses.

We have now illustrated the complete accounting cycle for a service-type business. In Chapter 4, we will look more closely at one important element of this cycle—end-of-period adjusting entries—and will also see how a work sheet can be used to consolidate several steps in the cycle. Accounting for merchandising activities will be discussed in Chapter 5.

KEY TERMS INTRODUCED OR EMPHASIZED IN CHAPTER 3

Accounting period The span of time covered by an income statement. One year is a standard accounting period, but many companies also prepare monthly and quarterly financial statements.

Accrual basis of accounting Calls for recording revenue in the period in which it is earned and recording expenses in the period in which they are incurred. The effect of events on the business is recognized as services are rendered or consumed rather than when cash is received or paid.

Accumulated depreciation account A contra-asset account shown as a deduction from the related asset account in the balance sheet. Depreciation taken throughout the useful life of an asset is accumulated in this account.

Adjusted trial balance A listing of all ledger account balances after the amounts have been changed to include the adjusting entries made at the end of the period.

Adjusting entries Entries required at the end of the period to update the accounts before financial statements are prepared. Adjusting entries serve to apportion transactions properly between the accounting periods affected and to record any revenue earned or expenses incurred which have not been recorded prior to the end of the period.

After-closing trial balance   A trial balance prepared after all closing entries have been made. Consists only of accounts for assets, liabilities, and owner's equity.

Closing entries   Journal entries made at the end of the period for the purpose of closing temporary accounts (revenue, expense, and drawing accounts) and transferring balances to the owner's equity account.

Conservatism   The traditional accounting practice of resolving uncertainty by choosing the solution which leads to the lower (more conservative) amount of income being recognized in the current accounting period. This concept is designed to avoid overstatement of financial strength or earnings.

Contra-asset account   An account with a credit balance which is offset against or deducted from an asset account to produce the proper balance sheet valuation for the asset.

Depreciation   The systematic allocation of the cost of an asset to expense during the periods of its useful life.

Drawing account   The account used to record the withdrawals of cash or other assets by the owner. Closed at the end of the period by transferring its balance to the owner's capital account.

Expenses   The costs of the goods and services used up in the process of obtaining revenue.

Fiscal year   Any 12-month accounting period adopted by a business.

Income statement   A financial statement summarizing the results of operations of a business by matching its revenue and related expenses for a particular accounting period. Shows the net income or net loss.

Income Summary account   The summary account in the ledger to which revenue and expense accounts are closed at the end of the period. The balance (credit balance for a net income, debit balance for a net loss) is transferred to the owner's capital account.

Matching principle   The revenue earned during an accounting period is matched (offset) with the expenses incurred in generating this revenue.

Net income   An increase in owner's equity resulting from profitable operations. Also, the excess of revenue earned over the related expenses for a given period.

Realization principle   The generally accepted accounting principle that determines when revenue should be recorded in the accounting records. Revenue is realized when services are rendered to customers or when goods sold are delivered to customers.

Revenue   The price of goods sold and services rendered by a business.

Statement of owner's equity   A financial statement summarizing the increases and decreases in owner's equity during an accounting period.

Time period principle   To provide the users of financial statements with timely information, net income is measured for relatively short accounting periods of equal length. The period of time covered by an income statement is termed the company's accounting period.

DEMONSTRATION PROBLEM FOR YOUR REVIEW

Key Insurance Agency was organized on September 1, 19___. Assume that the accounts are closed and financial statements prepared each month. The company occupies rented office space but owns office equipment estimated to have a useful life of 10 years from date of acquisition, September 1. The unadjusted trial balance for Key Insurance Agency at November 30 is shown below.

Cash	$ 3,750	
Accounts receivable	1,210	
Office equipment	4,800	
Accumulated depreciation: office equipment		$ 80
Accounts payable		1,640
Jane Carl, capital		7,490
Jane Carl, drawing	500	
Commissions earned		6,220
Advertising expense	800	
Salaries expense	3,600	
Rent expense	770	
	$15,430	$15,430

INSTRUCTIONS

a Prepare the adjusting journal entry to record depreciation of the office equipment for the month of November.

b Prepare an adjusted trial balance at November 30, 19__.

c Prepare an income statement and a statement of owner's equity for the month ended November 30, 19__, and a balance sheet in report form at November 30, 19__.

SOLUTION TO DEMONSTRATION PROBLEM

a Adjusting journal entry:

Depreciation Expense: Office Equipment	40	
Accumulated Depreciation: Office Equipment		40
To record depreciation for November ($4,800 ÷ 120 months).		

b

KEY INSURANCE AGENCY
Adjusted Trial Balance
November 30, 19__

Cash	$ 3,750	
Accounts receivable	1,210	
Office equipment	4,800	
Accumulated depreciation: office equipment		$ 120
Accounts payable		1,640
Jane Carl, capital		7,490
Jane Carl, drawing	500	
Commissions earned		6,220
Advertising expense	800	
Salaries expense	3,600	
Rent expense	770	
Depreciation expense: office equipment	40	
Totals	$15,470	$15,470

c

KEY INSURANCE AGENCY
Income Statement
For the Month Ended November 30, 19__

Commissions earned		$6,220
Expenses:		
Advertising expense..	$ 800	
Salaries expense	3,600	
Rent expense	770	
Depreciation expense: office equipment	40	5,210
Net income...		$1,010

KEY INSURANCE AGENCY
Statement of Owner's Equity
For the Month Ended November 30, 19__

Jane Carl, capital, Oct. 31, 19__	$7,490
Net income for the month...	1,010
Subtotal...	$8,500
Less: Withdrawals by owner	500
Jane Carl, capital, Nov. 31, 19__..	$8,000

KEY INSURANCE AGENCY
Balance Sheet
November 30, 19__

Assets

Cash...		$3,750
Accounts receivable		1,210
Office equipment	$4,800	
Less: Accumulated depreciation	120	4,680
Total assets		$9,640

Liabilities & Owner's Equity

Liabilities:		
Accounts payable		$1,640
Owner's equity:		
Jane Carl, capital...		8,000
Total liabilities & owner's equity		$9,640

SELF-TEST QUESTIONS

Answers to these questions appear on page 157.

1 Identify any of the following statements that correctly describe net income. (Indicate all correct answers.) Net income:

a Is computed in the income statement, appears in the statement of owner's equity, and increases owner's equity in the balance sheet.

b Is equal to revenue minus expenses.

c Is computed in the income statement, appears in the statement of owner's equity, and increases the amount of cash shown in the balance sheet.

d Can be determined using the account balances appearing in an adjusted trial balance.

2 Which of the following are based upon the realization principle and the matching principle? (Indicate all correct answers.)

  a Adjusting entries.

  b Closing entries.

  c The accrual basis of accounting.

  d The measurement of net income under generally accepted accounting principles.

3 Which of the following explains the debit and credit rules relating to the recording of revenue and expenses?

  a Expenses appear on the left side of the balance sheet and are recorded by debits; revenue appears on the right side of the balance sheet and is recorded by credits.

  b Expenses appear on the left side of the income statement and are recorded by debits; revenue appears on the right side of the income statement and is recorded by credits.

  c The effects of revenue and expenses upon owner's equity.

  d The realization principle and the matching principle.

4 The entry to recognize **depreciation expense:** (Indicate all correct answers.)

  a Is an application of the matching principle.

  b Is a closing entry.

  c Usually includes an offsetting credit either to Cash or to Accounts Payable.

  d Is an adjusting entry.

5 In the accounting cycle: (Indicate all correct answers.)

  a Closing entries are made before adjusting entries.

  b Financial statements may be prepared as soon as an adjusted trial balance is complete.

  c The owner's equity account is not up-to-date until closing entries have been posted.

  d Adjusting entries are made before financial statements are prepared.

6 The balance in the owner's capital account of Dayton Company at the beginning of the year was $65,000. During the year, the company earned revenue at $430,000 and incurred expenses of $360,000, the owner withdrew $50,000 in assets, and the balance of the Cash account increased by $10,000. At year-end, the company's net income and the year-end balance in the owner's capital account were, respectively:

  a $20,000 and $95,000   c $60,000 and $75,000

  b $70,000 and $95,000   d $70,000 and $85,000

Use the following information in questions **7** and **8**.

Accounts appearing in the trial balance of Westside Plumbing at May 31 are listed below in alphabetical order:

Accounts payable	$2,450	Equipment	$16,200
Accounts receivable	3,100	J. T. Golden, capital	11,900
Accumulated depreciation:		J. T. Golden, drawing	2,100
equipment	8,100	Other expenses	900
Advertising expense	150	Service revenue	4,300
Cash	2,900	Supplies expense	1,000

No adjusting entry has yet been made to record depreciation expense of $270 for the month of May.

7 The balance of J. T. Golden's capital account appearing in the May 31 balance sheet should be:
   a $11,650   b $8,630   c $11,380   d Some other amount

8 In an *after-closing* trial balance prepared at May 31, the total of the credit column will be:
   a $26,620   b $22,200   c $13,830   d Some other amount

ASSIGNMENT MATERIAL

DISCUSSION QUESTIONS

1 Explain the effect of operating profitably upon the balance sheet of a business entity.

2 Does net income represent a supply of cash that can be withdrawn by the owner of a business? Explain.

3 What is the meaning of the term *revenue?* Does the receipt of cash by a business indicate that revenue has been earned? Explain.

4 What is the meaning of the term *expenses?* Does the payment of cash by a business indicate that an expense has been incurred? Explain.

5 A service enterprise performs services in the amount of $500 for a customer in May and receives payment in June. In which month is the $500 of revenue recognized? What is the journal entry to be made in May and the entry to be made in June?

6 When do accountants consider revenue to be realized? What basic question about recording revenue in accounting records is answered by the *realization principle?*

7 Late in March, Classic Auto Painters purchased paint on account, with payment due in 60 days. The company used the paint to paint customers' cars during the first three weeks of April. Late in May, the company paid the paint store from which the paint had been purchased. In which month should Classic Auto Painters recognize the cost of this paint as expense? What generally accepted accounting principle determines the answer to this question?

8 In what accounting period does the *matching principle* indicate that an expense should be recognized?

9 Explain the rules of debit and credit with respect to transactions recorded in revenue and expense accounts.

10 Supply the appropriate term (debit or credit) to complete the following statements.

   a The owner's equity account and revenue accounts are increased by _____ entries.

   b Asset accounts and expense accounts are increased by _____ entries.

   c Liability accounts and owner's equity accounts are decreased by _____ entries.

11 Why does any company that owns equipment or buildings need to make adjusting entries at the end of every accounting period?

12 Does a well-prepared income statement provide an exact measurement of net income for the period, or does it represent merely an approximation of net income? Explain.

13 How does depreciation expense differ from other operating expenses?

14 All ledger accounts belong in one of the following five groups: asset, liability, owner's equity, revenue, and expense. For each of the following accounts, state the group in which it belongs. Also indicate whether the normal balance would be a debit or a credit.

  a Fees Earned

  b Notes Payable

  c Telephone Expense

  d John Jones, Capital

  e Building

  f Depreciation Expense

  g Accumulated Depreciation: Building

15 For each of the following financial statements, indicate whether the statement relates to a single date or to a period of time:

  a Balance sheet

  b Income statement

  c Statement of owner's equity

16 Briefly describe the content and format of an income statement and of a statement of owner's equity.

17 Explain the relationships among the three financial statements discussed in this chapter—that is, the income statement, the statement of owner's equity, and the balance sheet.

18 Which of the following accounts are closed at the end of the accounting period?

Cash	*Donna Jackson, drawing*
Fees earned	*Donna Jackson, capital*
Income summary	*Accumulated depreciation*
Accounts payable	*Accounts receivable*
Telephone expense	*Depreciation expense*

19 Supply the appropriate term (debit or credit) to complete the following statements.

  a When a business is operating ***profitably,*** the journal entry to close the Income Summary account will consist of a _____ to that account and a _____ to the owner's capital account.

  b When a business is operating at a ***loss,*** the journal entry to close the Income Summary account will consist of a _____ to that account and a _____ to the owner's capital account.

  c The journal entry to close the owner's drawing account consists of a _____ to that account and a _____ to the owner's capital account.

20 How does the accrual basis of accounting differ from the cash basis of accounting? Which gives a more accurate picture of the profitability of a business? Explain.

EXERCISES

**EXERCISE 3-1
Accounting
Terminology**

Listed below are 12 technical accounting terms introduced in this chapter:

Accounting period	Depreciation	Net income
Accrual basis of accounting	Expenses	Realization
Cash basis of accounting	Income statement	Revenue
Closing entries	Matching	Conservatism

Each of the following statements may (or may not) describe one of these technical terms. For each statement, indicate the accounting term described, or answer "None" if the statement does not correctly describe any of the terms.

a The span of time covered by an income statement.

b An increase in owner's equity as a result of earning revenue and incurring expenses.

c An accounting concept intended to avoid overstatement of financial strength or earnings.

d The generally accepted accounting principle used in determining when expenses should be offset against revenue.

e The generally accepted accounting principle used in determining when to recognize revenue.

f Recognizing revenue when it is earned and expenses when the related goods or services are used in the effort to obtain revenue.

g The systematic allocation of the cost of a long-lived asset, such as a building or equipment, to expense over the useful life of the asset.

h The procedures for transferring the balances of the revenue, expense, Income Summary, and owner's drawing accounts into the owner's capital account.

i The cost of goods and services used up in the process of earning revenue.

**EXERCISE 3-2
Effects of
Transactions;
the Accounting
Equation**

Tri-State Trucking Company closes its accounts at the end of each month. Among the events occurring in **November** were the following:

a Hauled freight for a credit customer; payment due December 10.

b Paid Truck Service Center for repairs to trucks performed in October.

c Collected in full the amount due from a credit customer for hauling done in October.

d Received a bill from Apex Truck Stops for fuel used in November. Payment due December 15.

e Prepared an adjusting entry to record depreciation on trucks in November.

f Purchased two new trucks on November 30, paying part cash and issuing a note payable for the balance. The trucks are first scheduled for use on December 3.

INSTRUCTIONS Indicate the effects that each of these transactions will have upon the following six **total amounts** in the company's financial statements for the month of **November.** Organize your answer in tabular form, using the column headings shown below, and use the code letters **I** for increase, **D** for decrease, and **NE** for no effect. The answer to transaction **a** is provided as an example.

	Income Statement			Balance Sheet		
Transaction	Revenue −	Expenses =	Net Income	Assets =	Liabilities +	Owner's Equity
a	I	NE	I	I	NE	I

EXERCISE 3-3
Effects of Transactions

A number of transactions of PanAm Steamship Lines, Inc., are described below in terms of the accounts debited and credited:

1 Debit Wages Expense, credit Cash.
2 Debit Accounts Receivable, credit Freight Revenue.
3 Debit Depreciation Expense: Ships; credit Accumulated Depreciation: Ships.
4 Debit Repairs Expense, credit Accounts Payable.
5 Debit Cash, credit Accounts Receivable.
6 Debit Accounts Payable, credit Cash.

INSTRUCTIONS
a Indicate the effects of each transaction upon the elements of the income statement and the balance sheet. Use the code letters **I** for increase, **D** for decrease, and **NE** for no effect. Organize your answer in tabular form using the column headings shown below. The answer for transaction **1** is provided as an example.

	Income Statement			Balance Sheet		
Transaction	Revenue −	Expenses =	Net Income	Assets =	Liabilities +	Owners' Equity
1	NE	I	D	D	NE	D

b Write a one-sentence description of each transaction.

EXERCISE 3-4
Relationship between Net Income and Owner's Equity

Total assets and total liabilities of Yato Talent Agency as shown by the balance sheets at the beginning and end of the year were as follows:

	Beginning of Year	End of Year
Assets	$230,000	$290,000
Liabilities	110,000	140,000

INSTRUCTIONS
Compute the net income or net loss from operations for the year in each of the following independent cases:

a Yato made no withdrawals during the year and no additional investments.
b Yato made no withdrawals during the year but made an additional capital investment of $50,000.
c Yato made withdrawals of $20,000 during the year but made no additional investments.
d Yato made withdrawals of $80,000 during the year and made an additional capital investment of $25,000.

EXERCISE 3-5
Relationship between Net Income and Owner's Equity

Supply the missing figure in the following independent cases:

a Owner's equity at beginning of year $130,000
  Net income for the year .... −?−
  Owner's drawings during the year 32,000
  Owner's equity at end of year 145,500

b Owner's equity at beginning of year 91,200
  Net income for the year 28,500
  Owner's drawings during the year .... −?−
  Owner's equity at end of year 99,700

c Owner's equity at beginning of year .... −?−
   Net income for the year 189,400
   Owner's drawings during the year 106,000
   Owner's equity at end of year 532,900

d Owner's equity at beginning of year 74,000
   Additional investment by owner during the year........................... 10,000
   Net income for the year 17,500
   Owner's drawing during the year 12,000
   Owner's equity at end of year .... −?−

e Owner's equity at beginning of year 362,500
   Additional investment by owner during the year........................... 85,000
   Net income for the year .... −?−
   Owner's drawings during the year 30,000
   Owner's equity at end of year 469,100

**EXERCISE 3-6
Financial
Statement
Relationships**

Shown below is a list of abbreviated terms, each representing an element of financial statements.

Term	Explanation
REV	Revenue of the period
EXP	Expenses of the period
NI	Net Income for the period
DRW	Drawings by the owner during the period
OE_{BEG}	Owner's equity, beginning of the period
OE_{END}	Owner's equity, end of the period

INSTRUCTIONS

Shown below are five incomplete formulas describing interrelationships among the elements of financial statements. You are to complete the right-hand side of each formula by adding or subtracting the appropriate terms from the list provided above. (The number of question marks indicates the number of terms needed to complete each formula.)

a $NI = REV$ (+ or − ?)

b $EXP = REV$ (+ or − ?)

c $REV = EXP$ (+ or − ?)

d $OE_{END} = OE_{BEG}$ (+ or − ? and ?)

e $OE_{BEG} = OE_{END}$ (+ or − ? and ?)

**EXERCISE 3-7
Heading of an
Income State-
ment**

On January 14, the accountant for Sunray Appliance Company prepared an income statement for the year ended December 31, 1994. The accountant used the following heading on this financial statement:

**SUNRAY CO.
Profit and Loss Statement
January 14, 1995**

INSTRUCTIONS

a Identify any errors in this heading.

b Prepare a corrected heading.

**EXERCISE 3-8
When Is
Revenue
Realized?**

The following transactions were carried out during the month of June by K. Davis and Company, a firm of real estate brokers. For each of the five transactions, you are to state whether the transaction represented revenue to the firm during the month of June. Give reasons for your decision in each case.

a Davis invested an additional $6,400 cash in the business.

b Borrowed $12,800 from Century Bank to be repaid in three months.

c Earned $63 interest on a company bank account during the month of June. No withdrawals were made from this account in June.

d Collected cash of $2,400 from an account receivable. The receivable originated in May from services rendered to a client.

e Arranged a sale of an apartment building owned by a client. The commission for making the sale was $14,400, but this amount will not be received until August 20.

EXERCISE 3-9
When Are Expenses Incurred?

Evergreen Landscaping carried out the following transactions during May. Which of these transactions represented expenses in May? Explain.

a Paid an attorney $560 for legal services rendered in April.

b The owner withdrew $1,600 from the business for personal use.

c Purchased a copying machine for $2,750 cash.

d Paid $192 for gasoline purchases for a delivery truck during May.

e Paid $1,280 salary to an employee for time worked during May.

EXERCISE 3-10
Preparing Journal Entries to Record Revenue, Expense, and Drawings Transactions

Shown below are selected transactions of the law firm of Emmons & Associates. You are to prepare journal entries to record the transactions in the firm's accounting records. The firm closes its accounts at the end of each calendar year.

Mar. 19 Drafted a prenuptial agreement for C. J. McCall. Sent McCall an invoice for $750, requesting payment within 30 days. (The appropriate revenue account is entitled Legal Fees Earned.)

May 31 Received a bill from Lawyers' Delivery Service for process service during the month of May, $1,150. Payment due by June 10. (The appropriate expense account is entitled Process Service Expense.)

Aug. 7 Ralph Emmons, owner of the law firm, withdrew $15,000 cash for personal purposes.

Dec. 31 Made a year-end adjusting entry to record depreciation expense on the firm's law library, $2,700.

EXERCISE 3-11
Adjusting Entry for Depreciation

Ahmed Pharmacy acquired a delivery truck at a cost of $9,600. Estimated life of the truck is four years. State the amount of depreciation expense per year and per month. Give the adjusting entry to record depreciation on the truck at the end of the first month, and explain where the accounts involved would appear in the financial statements.

EXERCISE 3-12
Preparing an Income Statement and Statement of Owner's Equity

From the following account balances, prepare first an income statement and then a statement of owner's equity for Ross Painting Contractors for the year ended December 31, 1994. Include the proper headings on both financial statements.

T. Ross, capital, Dec. 31, 1993	$ 27,200	Rent expense	$9,600
T. Ross, drawing	18,000	Advertising expense	3,200
Painting fees earned	140,000	Depreciation expense: painting	
Paint & supplies expense	27,500	equipment	1,200
Salaries expense	66,800		

EXERCISE 3-13
Preparing Closing Entries

Prepare the year-end closing entries for Ross Painting Contractors, using the data given in Exercise 3-12. Use four separate entries, as illustrated on pages 125–129. Indicate the balance in the owner's capital account that should appear in the balance sheet dated December 31, 1994.

EXERCISE 3-14
Closing Entries

During the absence of the regular accountant of Lawn Care Company, a new employee, Ralph Jones, prepared the closing entries for the year ended December 31, 19___. Jones had very little understanding of accounting and the closing entries he prepared were not satisfactory in several respects. The entries by Jones were:

Entry 1

Lawn Service Revenue	78,000	
Accumulated Depreciation	8,000	
Accounts Payable	27,000	
Income Summary...		113,000
To close the revenue accounts.		

Entry 2

Income Summary	73,000	
Salaries...		56,000
J. Mallory, Drawing		11,000
Advertising..		4,000
Depreciation Expense		2,000
To close the expense accounts.		

Entry 3

J. Mallory, Capital	28,000	
Income Summary...		28,000
To close the owner's capital account.		

INSTRUCTIONS

a Identify any errors which Jones made.

b Prepare four correct closing entries, following the pattern illustrated on pages 125–128.

EXERCISE 3-15
The Accounting cycle

Listed below in random order are the eight steps comprising a complete accounting cycle.

a Prepare a trial balance.

b Journalize and post the closing entries.

c Prepare financial statements and appropriate disclosures.

d Post transaction data to the ledger.

e Prepare an adjusted trial balance.

f Make end-of-period adjusting entries.

g Journalize transactions.

h Prepare an after-closing trial balance.

INSTRUCTIONS

a List these eight steps in the logical sequence in which they would be performed.

b Indicate which of these steps are mechanical functions that can be performed by machine in a computerized accounting system and which require the judgment of people familiar with accounting principles and concepts.

PROBLEMS

Group A

PROBLEM 3A-1
Preparing Journal Entries

Bay Plumbers performs repair work on both a cash and credit basis. Credit customers are required to pay within 30 days from date of billing. The ledger accounts used by the company include:

Cash	David Cohen, drawing
Accounts receivable	Repair service revenue
Tools	Advertising expense
Notes payable	Rent expense
Accounts payable	Salaries expense

Among the September transactions were the following:

Sept. 1   Performed repair work for Arden Hardware, a credit customer. Sent bill for $1,322.

Sept. 2   Paid rent for September, $750.

Sept. 3   Purchased tools with estimated life of 10 years for $1,275 cash.

Sept. 10   Performed repairs for Harris Drugs and collected in full the charge of $565.

Sept. 15   Newspaper advertising to appear on September 18 was arranged at a cost of $275. Received bill from *Tribune* requiring payment within 30 days.

Sept. 18   Received payment in full of the $1,322 account receivable from Arden Hardware for our services on September 1.

Sept. 20   David Cohen, owner of Bay Plumbers, withdrew $1,100 cash from the business for personal use.

Sept. 30   Paid salaries of $3,425 to employees for services rendered during September.

INSTRUCTIONS   Prepare a journal entry (including explanation) for each of the above transactions.

PROBLEM 3A-2
Analyzing Transactions and Preparing Journal Entries

The July transactions of Auto Haus, an automobile repair shop, included the following:

1   On July 1, paid rent for the month of July, $2,400.

2   On July 3, at request of National Insurance, Inc., made repairs on car of Stanley West. Sent bill for $610 for services rendered to National Insurance, Inc. (Credit Repair Service Revenue.)

3   On July 9, made repairs to car of H. F. Smith and collected in full the charge of $430.

4   On July 14, placed advertisement in *Daily Star* to be published in issue on July 16 at cost of $150, payment to be made within 30 days.

5   On July 25, received a check for $610 from National Insurance, Inc., representing collection of the receivable of July 3.

6   On July 31, the owner, Hans Klauder, withdrew $3,600 cash for personal use.

7   On July 31, obtained a loan from bank. Received $15,000 cash and signed a note payable for that amount.

INSTRUCTIONS   a   Write an analysis of each transaction. An example of the type of analysis desired is as follows for transaction 1 above:

1 (a) Rent is an operating expense. Expenses are recorded by debits. Debit Rent Expense, $2,400.

(b) The asset Cash was decreased. Decreases in assets are recorded by credits. Credit Cash, $2,400.

b   Prepare a journal entry (including explanation) for each of the above transactions.

**PROBLEM 3A-3
Preparing
Journal En-
tries, Posting,
and Preparing
a Trial Balance**

In June 1994, Chris Scott organized a crop-dusting business. The company, a sole proprietorship, called Scott Crop Dusting, began operations immediately. Transactions during the month of June were as follows:

June 1   Scott deposited $60,000 cash in a bank account in the name of the business.

June 2   Purchased a crop-dusting aircraft from Utility Aircraft for $225,000. Made a $45,000 cash down payment and issued a note payable for $180,000.

June 4   Paid Woodrow Airport $2,500 to rent office and hangar space for the month.

June 15   Billed customers $8,320 for crop-dusting services rendered during the first half of June.

June 15   Paid $5,880 salaries to employees for services rendered during the first half of June.

June 18   Paid Hannigan's Hangar $1,890 for maintenance and repair services.

June 25   Collected $4,910 of the amounts billed to customers on June 15.

June 30   Billed customers $16,450 for crop-dusting services rendered during the second half of the month.

June 30   Paid $6,000 salaries to employees for services rendered during the second half of June.

June 30   Received a fuel bill from Henry's Feed & Fuel for $2,510 of aircraft fuel purchased during June. This amount is due by July 10.

June 30   Scott withdrew $2,000 cash from the business for personal use.

The account titles and numbers used by Scott Crop Dusting were:

Cash	*1*	*Chris Scott, drawing*	*43*
Accounts receivable	*5*	*Crop-dusting revenue*	*51*
Aircraft	*15*	*Maintenance expense*	*61*
Notes payable	*31*	*Fuel expense*	*62*
Accounts payable	*32*	*Salaries expense*	*63*
Chris Scott, capital	*41*	*Rent expenses*	*64*

INSTRUCTIONS   Based on the foregoing transactions:

a   Prepare journal entries. (Number journal pages to permit cross-reference to ledger.)

b   Post to ledger accounts. (Number ledger accounts to permit cross-reference to journal.) Enter ledger account numbers in the LP column of the journal as the posting work is done.

c   Prepare a trial balance at June 30, 1994.

**PROBLEM 3A-4
Assembling
Financial State-
ments from an
Adjusted Trial
Balance**

Playland operates a miniature golf course on rented land within a city park. Following is the company's adjusted trial balance at December 31, 1994. The company closes its accounts at the end of each calendar year.

PLAYLAND
Adjusted Trial Balance
December 31, 1994

Cash...	$ 13,500	
Accounts receivable	2,800	
Buildings	60,000	
Accumulated depreciation: buildings		$ 12,000
Golf course structures..	90,000	
Accumulated depreciation: golf course structures		30,000
Accounts payable		7,700
Salaries payable...		2,300
Lynn George, capital		109,000
Lynn George, drawing	25,000	
Admissions revenue..		192,000
Advertising expense..	15,000	
Rent expense	36,000	
Repairs expense	5,200	
Salaries expense	79,000	
Light & power expense	4,500	
Depreciation expense: buildings...................................	6,000	
Depreciation expense: golf course structures.......................	15,000	
	$352,000	$352,000

INSTRUCTIONS a Prepare an income statement and a statement of owner's equity for the year ended December 31, 1994.

b Prepare a balance sheet (in report form) as of December 31, 1994.

PROBLEM 3A-5
Preparing
Closing Entries

Using the adjusted trial balance presented in Problem 3A-4:

a Prepare journal entries to close the accounts. Use four entries: (1) to close the revenue account, (2) to close the expense accounts, (3) to close the Income Summary account, and (4) to close the owner's drawing account.

b Assume that in the following year Playland again had $192,000 of admissions revenue but expenses increased to **$200,000.** Assuming that the revenue account and all the expense accounts had been closed into the Income Summary account at December 31, prepare a journal entry to close the Income Summary account.

PROBLEM 3A-6
End-of-Period
Adjusting and
Closing Proce-
dures; Prepar-
ing Financial
Statements

The operations of Sunset Realty consist of obtaining listings of houses being offered for sale by owners, advertising these houses, and showing them to prospective buyers. The company earns revenue in the form of commissions. The building and office equipment used in the business were acquired on January 1 of the current year and were immediately placed in use. Useful life of the building was estimated to be 30 years and that of the office equipment 5 years. The company closes its accounts monthly; on March 31 of the current year, the trial balance is as follows:

SUNSET REALTY
Trial Balance
March 31, 19__

	Debit	Credit
Cash	$ 6,500	
Accounts receivable	5,000	
Land	25,000	
Building	72,000	
Accumulated depreciation: building		$ 400
Office equipment	24,000	
Accumulated depreciation: office equipment		800
Notes payable		81,000
Accounts payable		10,000
Ellen Norton, capital		37,800
Ellen Norton, drawing	2,000	
Commissions earned		20,000
Advertising expense	900	
Automobile rental expense	700	
Salaries expense	13,300	
Telephone expense	600	
	$150,000	$150,000

INSTRUCTIONS From the trial balance and supplementary data given, prepare the following as of March 31, 19__.

a Adjusting entries for depreciation during March of building and of office equipment

(Building: $72,000 cost ÷ 30 years × $\frac{1}{12}$ = one month's depreciation)
(Office equipment: $24,000 cost ÷ 5 years × $\frac{1}{12}$ = one month's depreciation)

b Adjusted trial balance
c Income statement and a statement of owner's equity for the month of March, and a balance sheet at March 31 in report form
d Closing entries
e After-closing trial balance

PROBLEM 3A-7
Complete Accounting Cycle

April Stein, M.D., after completing her medical education, established her own practice on May 1. The following transactions occurred during the first month.

May 1 Stein opened a bank account in the name of the practice, April Stein, M.D., by making a deposit of $12,000.

May 1 Paid office rent for May, $1,700.

May 2 Purchased office equipment for cash, $7,200.

May 3 Purchased medical instruments from Niles Instruments, Inc., at a cost of $9,000. A cash down payment of $1,000 was made and a note payable was issued for the remaining $8,000.

May 4 Retained by Brandon Construction to be on call for emergency service at a monthly fee of $400. The fee for May was collected in cash.

May 15 Excluding the retainer of May 4, fees earned during the first 15 days of the month amounted to $1,600, of which $600 was in cash and $1,000 was in accounts receivable.

May 15 Paid Mary Hester, R.N., her salary for the first half of May, $1,000.

May 16 Dr. Stein withdrew $975 for personal use.

May 19 Treated Michael Tracy for minor injuries received in an accident during employment at Brandon Construction. No charge was made as these services were covered by Brandon's payment on May 4.

May 27 Treated Cynthia Knight, who paid $25 cash for an office visit and who agreed to pay $35 on June 1 for laboratory medical tests completed May 27.

May 31 Excluding the treatment of Cynthia Knight on May 27, fees earned during the last half of month amounted to $4,000, of which $2,100 was in cash and $1,900 was in accounts receivable.

May 31 Paid Mary Hester, R.N., $1,000 salary for the second half of month.

May 31 Received a bill from McGraw Medical Supplies in the amount of $640 representing the amount of medical supplies used during May.

May 31 Paid utilities for the month, $300.

OTHER INFORMATION

Dr. Stein estimated the useful life of medical instruments at three years and of office equipment at five years. The account titles to be used and the account numbers are as follows:

Cash	10	*April Stein, drawing*	41
Accounts receivable	13	*Income summary*	45
Medical instruments	20	*Fees earned*	49
Accumulated depreciation:		*Medical supplies expense*	50
medical instruments	21	*Rent expense*	51
Office equipment	22	*Salaries expense*	52
Accumulated depreciation:		*Utilities expense*	53
office equipment	23	*Depreciation expense:*	
Notes payable	30	*medical instruments*	54
Accounts payable	31	*Depreciation expense:*	
April Stein, capital	40	*office equipment*	55

INSTRUCTIONS

a Journalize the above transactions. (Number journal pages to permit cross-reference to ledger.)

b Post to ledger accounts. (Use running balance form of ledger account. Number ledger accounts to permit cross-reference to journal.)

c Prepare a trial balance at May 31, 19__.

d Prepare adjusting entries to record depreciation for the month of May and post to ledger accounts. (For medical instruments, cost $9,000 ÷ 3 years × $\frac{1}{12}$. For office equipment, cost $7,200 ÷ 5 years × $\frac{1}{12}$.)

e Prepare an adjusted trial balance.

f Prepare an income statement and a statement of owner's equity for the month of May, and a balance sheet in report form at May 31. (As this is a new business, the first line in the statement of owner's equity should be: "Initial investment by owner, May 1, 19__, $12,000.")

g Prepare closing entries and post to ledger accounts.

h Prepare an after-closing trial balance.

Group B

PROBLEM 3B-1
Preparing
Journal Entries

Air Wolfe provides transportation by helicopter for skiers, backpackers, and others to remote mountainous areas. Among the ledger accounts used by the company are the following:

Cash	Advertising expense
Accounts payable	Fuel expense
Amy Wolfe, capital	Rent expense
Amy Wolfe, drawing	Repair & maintenance expense
Passenger fare revenue	Salaries expense

Some of the January transactions of Air Wolfe are listed below:

Jan. 3   Paid $1,600 rent for the building for January.

Jan. 4   Placed advertising in local newspapers for publication during January. The agreed price of $520 was payable within 10 days after the end of the month.

Jan. 15   Cash receipts from passengers for the first half of January amounted to $9,470.

Jan. 16   Amy Wolfe, the owner, withdrew $3,000 cash for personal use.

Jan. 16   Paid salaries to employees for services rendered in first half of January, $5,265.

Jan. 29   Received a bill for fuel used from Western Oil Company, amounting to $1,930, and payable by February 10.

Jan. 31   Paid $1,642 to Stevens Aircraft for repair and maintenance work during January.

INSTRUCTIONS Prepare a journal entry (including an explanation) for each of the above transactions.

PROBLEM 3B-2
Analyzing
Transactions
and Preparing
Journal Entries

Garwood Marine is a boat repair yard. During August its transactions included the following:

1   On August 1, paid rent for the month of August, $4,000.

2   On August 3, at request of Kiwi Insurance, Inc., made repairs on boat of Michael Fay. Sent bill for $4,680 for services rendered to Kiwi Insurance, Inc. (Credit Repair Service Revenue.)

3   On August 9, made repairs to boat of Dennis Conner and collected in full the charge of $1,575.

4   On August 14, placed advertisement in **Yachting World** to be published in issue of August 20 at cost of $95, payment to be made within 30 days.

5   On August 25, received a check for $4,680 from Kiwi Insurance, Inc., representing collection of the receivable of August 3.

6   On August 30, sent check to **Yachting World** in payment of the liability incurred on August 14.

7   On August 31, Barbara Garwood, owner of Garwood Marine, withdrew $3,500 from the business for personal use.

INSTRUCTIONS

a Write an analysis of each transaction. An example of the type of analysis desired is as follows for transaction **1** above:

   1 (a) Rent is an operating expense. Expenses are recorded by debits. Debit Rent Expense, $4,000.

     (b) The asset Cash was decreased. Decreases in assets are recorded by credits. Credit Cash, $4,000.

b Prepare a journal entry (including explanation) for each of the above transactions.

PROBLEM 3B-3
Preparing Journal Entries, Posting, and Preparing a Trial Balance

Metro Park was organized on March 1 for the purpose of operating an automobile parking lot. Included in the company's ledger are the following ledger accounts and their identification numbers.

Cash................................	11	Tony Poletti, drawing	42
Land................................	21	Parking fees earned	51
Notes payable......................	31	Advertising expense................	61
Accounts payable	32	Utilities expense....................	63
Tony Poletti, capital	41	Salaries expense	65

The business was organized and operations were begun during the month of March. Transactions during March were as follows:

Mar. 1   Tony Poletti deposited $50,000 cash in a bank account in the name of the business.

Mar. 5   Purchased land for $160,000, of which $40,000 was paid in cash. A short-term note payable was issued for the balance of $120,000.

Mar. 6   An arrangement was made with the Century Club to provide parking privileges for its customers. Century Club agreed to pay $1,200 monthly, payable in advance. Cash was collected for the month of March.

Mar. 7   Arranged with Times Printing Company for a regular advertisement in the *Times* at a monthly cost of $390. Paid for advertising during March by check, $390.

Mar. 15   Parking receipts for the first half of the month were $1,836, exclusive of the monthly fee from Century Club.

Mar. 31   Received bill for light and power from Pacific Power Company in the amount of $78, to be paid by April 10.

Mar. 31   Paid $2,720 to employees for services rendered during the month. (Payroll taxes are to be ignored.)

Mar. 31   Parking receipts for the second half of the month amounted to $5,338.

Mar. 31   Poletti withdrew $2,000 for personal use.

Mar. 31   Paid $5,000 cash on the note payable incurred with the purchase of land. (You are to ignore any interest on the note.)

INSTRUCTIONS

a Journalize the March transactions.

b Post to ledger accounts. Enter ledger account numbers in the LP column of the journal as the posting work is done.

c Prepare a trial balance at March 31.

PROBLEM 3B-4
Preparing Closing Entries

An adjusted trial balance for Okoye Insurance Agency at December 31 appears as follows.

OKOYE INSURANCE AGENCY
Adjusted Trial Balance
December 31, 19__

Cash..	$ 10,200	
Accounts receivable	20,000	
Office equipment	15,000	
Accumulated depreciation: office equipment........................		$ 3,000
Accounts payable		6,000
Christian Okoye, capital		19,700
Christian Okoye, drawing	18,000	
Sales commissions earned		185,000
Advertising expense..	36,500	
Rent expense	32,000	
Salaries expense	64,500	
Utilities expense...	16,000	
Depreciation expense: office equipment	1,500	
	$213,700	$213,700

INSTRUCTIONS

a Prepare journal entries to close the accounts. Use four entries: (1) to close the revenue account, (2) to close the expense accounts, (3) to close the Income Summary account, and (4) to close the owner's drawing account.

b Does the amount of net income or net loss appear in the closing entries? Explain fully.

**PROBLEM 3B-5
Preparing Financial Statements and Closing Entries**

Celebrity Caterers closes its accounts and prepares financial statements at the end of each calendar year. The following adjusted trial balance was prepared at December 31 of the most recent year.

CELEBRITY CATERERS
Adjusted Trial Balance
December 31, 19__

Cash..	$ 7,300	
Notes receivable	6,000	
Accounts receivable	12,800	
Land..	140,000	
Building...	90,000	
Accumulated depreciation: building		$ 12,000
Office equipment	4,000	
Accumulated depreciation: office equipment........................		1,600
Notes payable...		100,000
Accounts payable		16,200
Halley St. James, capital..		132,300
Halley St. James, drawing	24,000	
Catering revenue		89,500
Advertising expense..	12,500	
Insurance expense	2,800	
Utilities expense...	2,600	
Salaries expense	46,200	
Depreciation expense: building	3,000	
Depreciation expense: office equipment	400	
	$351,600	$351,600

INSTRUCTIONS

a Prepare an income statement and a statement of owner's equity for the year ended December 31, and a balance sheet in report form as of December 31.

b Prepare closing entries at December 31. Use four entries as illustrated on pages 125–128.

PROBLEM 3B-6
End-of-Period
Adjusting and
Closing Proce-
dures; Prepar-
ing Financial
Statements

Home Repair Club is a new business which began operations on July 1. The company follows a policy of closing its accounts and preparing financial statements at the end of each month. A trial balance at September 30 appears below.

HOME REPAIR CLUB
Trial Balance
September 30, 19__

Cash..	$ 2,500	
Accounts receivable	1,500	
Land..	29,400	
Building..	50,400	
Accumulated depreciation: building		$ 336
Repair equipment	7,500	
Accumulated depreciation: repair equipment.......................		250
Notes payable...		28,000
Accounts payable		1,594
Paul Morgan, capital..		58,800
Paul Morgan, drawing	1,400	
Repair service revenue		8,520
Advertising expense..	150	
Repair parts expense	700	
Utilities expense..	170	
Wages expense	3,780	
	$97,500	$97,500

Note that the trial balance includes two assets subject to depreciation: the building and the repair equipment. The accumulated depreciation accounts in the trial balance show the total depreciation for July and August; depreciation has not yet been recorded for September.

INSTRUCTIONS

a Prepare adjusting entries at September 30 to record depreciation. Use one entry to record depreciation on the building and a second entry to record depreciation on the repair equipment. The amounts of depreciation for September are $168 on the building and $125 on the repair equipment.

b Prepare an *adjusted* trial balance at September 30. (This will differ from the trial balance only by inclusion of the depreciation recorded in part **a.**)

c Prepare an income statement and a statement of owner's equity for the month ended September 30, and a balance sheet in report form.

d Prepare journal entries to close the accounts. Use four entries: (1) to close the revenue account, (2) to close the expense accounts, (3) to close the Income Summary account, and (4) to close the owner's drawing account.

e Prepare an after-closing trial balance.

**PROBLEM 3B-7
The Account-
ing Cycle; a
Comprehensive
Problem**

On November 1, 19___, Ken Ryan organized Continental Moving Company. The transactions occurring during the first month of operations were as follows:

Nov. 1   Ryan deposited $400,000 cash in a bank account in the name of the business.

Nov. 2   Purchased land for $170,000 and building for $360,000, paying $130,000 cash and signing a $400,000 note payable to Secure Mortgage Company bearing interest at 9%.

Nov. 3   Purchased six trucks from Willis Motors at a total cost of $432,000. A cash down payment of $200,000 was made, and a note payable was issued for the balance of the purchase price. (This note is due in 60 days and does not call for the payment of interest.)

Nov. 6   Purchased office equipment for cash, $24,000.

Nov. 6   Moved furniture for Mr. and Mrs. Don Fitch from New York to Los Angeles for $8,650. Collected $4,850 in cash, balance to be paid within 30 days (credit Moving Service Revenue).

Nov. 9   Moved furniture for various clients for $32,350. Collected $18,350 in cash, balance to be paid within 30 days.

Nov. 15   Paid salaries to employees for the first half of the month, $17,400.

Nov. 25   Moved furniture for various clients for a total of $27,000. Cash collected in full.

Nov. 30   Salaries paid for the second half of November amounted to $13,250.

Nov. 30   Received a gasoline bill for the month of November from Lucier Oil Company in the amount of $17,500, to be paid by December 10.

Nov. 30   Received bill of $1,250 for repair work on trucks during November by Newport Repair Company. Payment is due within 30 days.

Nov. 30   Paid $5,000 to Secure Mortgage Company. This $5,000 payment included $3,000 interest expense for November and a $2,000 reduction in the balance of the note payable issued on November 2.

Nov. 30   Ryan withdrew $4,000 cash from the business for his personal use.

Estimated useful life of the building is 20 years, trucks 4 years, and office equipment 10 years. The account titles to be used and the account numbers are as follows:

Cash	1	Ken Ryan, capital	40
Accounts receivable	3	Ken Ryan, drawing	41
Land	11	Income summary	50
Building	12	Moving service revenue	60
Accumulated depreciation: building	13	Salaries expense	70
		Gasoline expense	71
Trucks	15	Repairs & maintenance expense	72
Accumulated depreciation: trucks	16	Interest expense	73
Office equipment	18	Depreciation expense: building	74
Accumulated depreciation: office equipment	19	Depreciation expense: trucks	75
Notes payable	30	Depreciation expense: office equipment	76
Accounts payable	31		

INSTRUCTIONS

a   Prepare journal entries. (Number journal pages to permit cross-reference to ledger.)

b   Post to ledger accounts. (Number ledger accounts to permit cross-reference to journal.)

c Prepare a trial balance at November 30, 19__.

d Prepare adjusting entries and post to ledger accounts.

e Prepare an adjusted trial balance at November 30.

f Prepare an income statement and a statement of owner's equity for the month of November, and a balance sheet in report form at November 30. (As this is a new business, the first line in the statement of owner's equity should be: "Initial investment by owner, November 1, 19__, $400,000.")

g Prepare closing entries at November 30 and post to ledger accounts.

h Prepare an after-closing trial balance at November 30, 19__.

CASES AND UNSTRUCTURED PROBLEMS

**CASE 3-1
Revenue
Recognition**

The realization principle determines when a business should recognize revenue. Listed below are three common business situations involving revenue. After each situation, we give two alternatives as to the accounting period (or periods) in which the business might recognize this revenue. Select the appropriate alternative by applying the realization principle, and explain your reasoning.

a Airline ticket revenue: Most airlines sell tickets well before the scheduled date of the flight. (Period ticket sold, period of flight)

b Sales on account: In June 1992, a San Diego based furniture store had a big sale featuring "no payments until 1993." (Period furniture sold; periods that payments are received from customers)

c Magazine subscriptions revenue: Most magazine publishers sell subscriptions for future delivery of the magazine. (Period subscription sold; periods that magazines are mailed to customers)

**CASE 3-2
Expense
Recognition**

As a basis for deciding when to recognize expense, we have discussed the **matching principle,** the need for **objective evidence** to recognize the existence of an asset, and the concept of **conservatism.** Shown below are three costs that ultimately become expenses. Each situation is followed by two alternatives as to when the business might record this expense. Select the appropriate alternative based upon the principles described above, and explain your answer.

a Computers: Most businesses own them, and they are expensive. Due to the rapid advances in technology, it is very difficult to estimate in advance how long the business will keep them. (Period computers purchased; periods of an estimated useful life)

b Advertising: **Apple Computer** launched the Macintosh with an expensive television advertising campaign. The Macintosh line has been a major source of revenue for Apple ever since. (Period in which advertising was done; periods in estimated production life of the original model Macintosh)

c Interest expense: On some loans, the borrower does not pay any interest until the end of the loan. This practice is very common on short-term loans, such as 60 or 90 days, but may also occur in some special types of long-term borrowing. (Periods comprising the life of the loan; period in which interest is paid)

**CASE 3-3
Accrual Accounting; Relationship of Depreciation Expense to Cash Outlays**

The Dark Room is a business that develops film within one hour, using a large and expensive developing machine. The business is organized as a sole proprietorship and operates in rented quarters in a large shopping center. Sharon Douglas, owner of The Dark Room, plans to retire and has offered the business for sale. A typical monthly income statement for The Dark Room appears below:

Revenue:		
Fees earned...		*$8,900*
Operating expenses:		
Wages	*$1,600*	
Rent	*1,850*	
Supplies	*920*	
Depreciation: developing machine......................................	*1,510*	
Miscellaneous	*460*	*6,340*
Net income..		*$2,560*

Revenue is received in cash at the time that film is developed. The wages, rent, supplies, and miscellaneous expenses are all paid in cash on a monthly basis. Douglas explains that the developing machine, which is 12 months old and is fully paid for, is being depreciated over a period of 5 years. She is using this estimated useful life because she believes that faster and more efficient machines will probably be available at that time. However, if the business does not purchase a new machine, the existing machine should last for 10 years or more.

Dave Berg, a friend of yours, is negotiating with Douglas to buy The Dark Room. Berg does not have enough money to pay the entire purchase price in cash. However, Douglas has offered to accept a note payable from Berg for a substantial portion of the purchase price. The note would call for 18 monthly payments in the amount of $2,500, which would pay off the remainder of the purchase price as well as the interest charges on the note. Douglas points out that these monthly payments can be made "out of the monthly earnings of the business."

Berg comes to you for advice. He feels that the sales price asked by Douglas is very reasonable and that the owner-financing makes this an excellent opportunity. However, he is worried about turning over $2,500 of the business's earnings to Douglas each month. Berg states, "This arrangement will only leave me with about $60 each month. I figure that my family and I need to take about $1,200 out of this business each month just to meet our living expenses." Also, Berg is concerned about the depreciation expense. He does not understand when or to whom the depreciation expense must be paid, or how long this expense will continue.

INSTRUCTIONS

a Explain to Berg the nature of depreciation expense, including when this expense is paid and what effect, if any, it has upon monthly cash expenditures.

b Advise Berg as to how much cash the business will generate each month. Will this amount enable Berg to pay $2,500 per month to the former owner and still withdraw $1,200 per month to meet his personal living expenses?

c Caution Berg about the need to replace the developing machine. Briefly discuss when this expenditure might occur and how much control, if any, Berg has over the timing and dollar amount of this expenditure.

ANSWERS TO SELF-TEST QUESTIONS

1 a, b, d   2 a, c, d   3 c   4 a, d   5 b, c, d   6 d   7 c   8 b

Completion of the Accounting Cycle

In Chapter 4 we complete our coverage of the accounting cycle for a service-type business. The chapter consists of two major sections. In the first, we take a closer look at the various types of *adjusting entries* needed to measure the net income of a specific time period. An important new accounting principle—materiality—is introduced and explained. In the second section of the chapter, we introduce the *work sheet,* an informal accounting schedule illustrating the "flow" of financial information from a trial balance into financial statements.

Reversing entries—an optional step in the accounting cycle—are discussed in a Supplemental Topic section.

After studying this chapter you should be able to meet these learning objectives:

1 *State the purpose of adjusting entries and explain how these entries relate to the concepts of accrual accounting.*
2 *Describe the four basic types of adjusting entries; prepare these entries.*
3 *Explain the concept of materiality.*
4 *Prepare a work sheet and explain its usefulness.*
5 *Describe the sequence of steps in the accounting cycle when a work sheet is prepared.*
*6 *Explain when and why reversing entries may be used.*

---

*   *Supplemental Topic, "Reversing Entries"*

Accounting Periods and Financial Statements

For the purpose of measuring net income and preparing financial statements, the life of a business is divided into accounting periods of equal length. Because accounting periods are equal in length, we can compare the income of the current period with that of prior periods to see if operating results are improving or declining.

As explained in Chapter 3, the ***accounting period*** means the span of time covered by an income statement. The usual accounting period for which complete financial statements are prepared and distributed to investors, bankers, and governmental agencies is one year. However, most businesses also prepare quarterly and monthly financial statements so that management will be informed on the profitability of the business from month to month.

Transactions Affecting More Than One Accounting Period

Dividing the life of a business into relatively short accounting periods requires the use of ***adjusting entries*** at the end of each period. Adjusting entries are required for those transactions which affect the revenue or the expenses of ***more than one accounting period***. For example, assume that a company which prepares monthly financial statements purchases a one-year insurance policy at a cost of $1,200. Clearly, the entire $1,200 does not represent the insurance expense of the current month. Rather, it is the insurance expense for **12** months; only $\frac{1}{12}$ of this cost, or $100, should be recognized as expense in each month covered by the policy. The allocation of this cost to expense in 12 separate accounting periods is accomplished by making an ***adjusting entry*** at the end of each period.

Some transactions affect the revenue or expense of only one period. An example is the payment of a monthly salary to an employee on the last day of each month. Adjusting entries are not required for transactions of this type.

ADJUSTING ENTRIES: A CLOSER LOOK

OBJECTIVE 1
State the purpose of adjusting entries and explain how these entries relate to the concepts of accrual accounting.

The ***realization principle,*** as explained in Chapter 3, requires that revenue be recognized and recorded in the period it is earned. The ***matching principle*** stresses that expenses are incurred in order to produce revenue. To measure net income for an accounting period, we must "match" or compare the revenue earned during the period with the expenses incurred to produce that revenue. At the end of an accounting period, adjusting entries are needed so that all revenue ***earned*** is reflected in the accounts regardless of whether it has been collected. Adjusting entries are also needed for expenses to assure that all expenses ***incurred*** are matched against the revenue of the current period, regardless of when cash payment of the expense occurs.

Thus, adjusting entries help in achieving the goals of accrual accounting—recording revenue when it is ***earned*** and recording expenses when the related goods and services are ***used.*** The realization principle and the matching principle are key elements of accrual accounting. Adjusting entries are a technique of applying these principles to transactions which affect two or more accounting periods.

In Chapter 3, the concept of adjusting entries was introduced when Roberts Real Estate Company recorded depreciation for the month of October. Adjusting entries are necessary to record depreciation expense, because buildings and equipment are purchased in a single accounting period but are used over many periods. Some portion of the cost of these assets should be allocated to expense in each period of the asset's estimated life. In this chapter, we will see that the use of adjusting entries is not limited to recording depreciation expense. Adjusting entries are needed *whenever transactions affect the revenue or expense of more than one accounting period.*

Types of Adjusting Entries

OBJECTIVE 2 Describe the four basic types of adjusting entries; prepare these entries.

A business may need to make a dozen or more adjusting entries at the end of each accounting period. The exact number of adjustments will depend upon the nature of the company's business activities. However, all adjusting entries fall into one of four general categories:[1]

1 **Entries to apportion recorded costs.** A cost that will benefit more than one accounting period usually is recorded by debiting an asset account. In each period that benefits from the use of this asset, an adjusting entry is made to allocate a portion of the asset's cost to expense.

2 **Entries to apportion unearned revenue.** A business may collect in advance for services to be rendered to customers in future accounting periods. In the period in which services are rendered, an adjusting entry is made to record the portion of the revenue earned during the period.

3 **Entries to record unrecorded expenses.** An expense may be incurred in the current accounting period even though no bill has yet been received and payment will not occur until a future period. Such unrecorded expenses are recorded by an adjusting entry made at the end of the accounting period.

4 **Entries to record unrecorded revenue.** Revenue may be earned during the current period, but not yet billed to customers or recorded in the accounting records. Such unrecorded revenue is recorded by making an adjusting entry at the end of the period.

Characteristics of Adjusting Entries

It will be helpful to keep in mind two important characteristics of all adjusting entries. First, every adjusting entry *involves the recognition of either revenue or expense.* Revenue and expenses represent changes in owner's equity. However, owner's equity cannot change by itself; there also must be a corresponding change in either assets or liabilities. *Thus, every adjusting entry affects both an income statement account* (revenue or expense) *and a balance sheet account* (asset or liability).

---

[1]   A fifth category of adjusting entries consists of adjustments to the balance sheet valuation of certain assets, such as marketable securities and accounts receivable. Valuation adjustments will be explained and illustrated in later chapters.

Second, adjusting entries are based upon the concepts of accrual accounting, ***not upon monthly bills or month-end transactions.*** No one sends us a bill saying, "Depreciation expense on your building amounts to $500 this month." Yet, we must be aware of the need to estimate and record depreciation expense if we are to measure net income properly for the period. Making adjusting entries requires a greater understanding of accrual accounting concepts than does the recording of routine business transactions. In many businesses, the adjusting entries are made by the company's controller or by a professional accountant, rather than by the regular accounting staff.

To demonstrate the various types of adjusting entries, the illustration of Roberts Real Estate Company will be continued for November. We shall consider in detail only those November transactions which require adjusting entries at the end of the month.

In the next few pages we illustrate several ***transactions*** as well as the related ***adjusting entries.*** To help clarify the distinction between transactions and adjusting entries, journal entries recording regular transactions are shown in ***blue,*** and adjusting entries are printed in ***red.***

Apportioning Recorded Costs

When a business makes an expenditure that will benefit more than one accounting period, the amount usually is debited to an asset account. At the end of each period benefiting from this expenditure, an adjusting entry is made to transfer an appropriate portion of the cost from the asset account to an expense account. This adjusting entry reflects the fact that part of the asset has been used up—that is, become expense—during the current accounting period.

An adjusting entry to apportion a recorded cost consists of a debit to an expense account and a credit to an asset account (or a contra-asset account). Examples of these adjustments include the entries to record depreciation expense and to apportion the costs of ***prepaid expenses.***

Prepaid Expenses   Payments in advance are often made for such items as insurance, rent, and office supplies. If the advance payment (or prepayment) will benefit more than just the current accounting period, the cost ***represents an asset*** rather than an expense. The cost of this asset will be allocated to expense in the accounting periods in which the services or the supplies are used. In summary, ***prepaid expenses are assets;*** they become expenses only as the goods or services are used up.

Insurance   To illustrate these concepts, assume that on November 1, Roberts Real Estate Company paid $600 for a one-year fire insurance policy covering the building. This expenditure was debited to an asset account by the following journal entry:

Expenditure for insurance policy recorded as asset	*Unexpired Insurance*	*600*
	Cash	*600*
	Purchased a one-year fire insurance policy.	

Since this expenditure of $600 will protect the company against fire loss for one year, the insurance expense applicable to each month's operations is $\frac{1}{12}$ of the annual expense, or $50. In order that the accounting records for November show insurance expense of $50, the following ***adjusting entry*** is required at November 30:

<table>
<tr><td>**Adjusting entry. Portion of asset expires (becomes expense)**</td><td>*Insurance Expense* ....</td><td align="right">*50*</td><td></td></tr>
<tr><td></td><td>   *Unexpired Insurance* ....</td><td></td><td align="right">*50*</td></tr>
<tr><td></td><td>*To record insurance expense for November.*</td><td></td><td></td></tr>
</table>

This adjusting entry serves two purposes: (1) it apportions the proper amount of insurance expense to November operations, and (2) it reduces the asset account to $550 so that the correct amount of unexpired insurance will appear in the balance sheet at November 30.

What would be the effect on the income statement for November if the above adjustment were not made? The expenses would be understated by $50 and consequently the net income would be overstated by $50. The balance sheet also would be affected by failure to make the adjustment: the assets would be overstated by $50 and so would the owner's equity. The overstatement of the owner's equity would result from the overstated amount of net income transferred to the owner's equity account when the accounts were closed at November 30.

Office Supplies   On November 2, Roberts Real Estate Company purchased enough stationery and other office supplies to last for several months. The cost of the supplies was $720, and this amount was debited to an asset account by the following journal entry:

<table>
<tr><td>**Expenditure for office supplies recorded as asset**</td><td>*Office Supplies* ....</td><td align="right">*720*</td><td></td></tr>
<tr><td></td><td>   *Cash* ....</td><td></td><td align="right">*720*</td></tr>
<tr><td></td><td>*Purchased office supplies.*</td><td></td><td></td></tr>
</table>

No entries were made during November to record the day-to-day usage of office supplies, but on November 30 the office manager estimated that supplies costing about $500 were still on hand. Thus, supplies costing about $220 were used during November. On the basis of this month-end estimate, an adjusting entry is made debiting an expense account $220 (the cost of supplies consumed during November) and reducing the asset account by $220. The ***adjusting entry*** follows:

<table>
<tr><td>**Adjusting entry. Portion of supplies used represents expense**</td><td>*Office Supplies Expense* ....</td><td align="right">*220*</td><td></td></tr>
<tr><td></td><td>   *Office Supplies* ....</td><td></td><td align="right">*220*</td></tr>
<tr><td></td><td>*To record consumption of office supplies in November.*</td><td></td><td></td></tr>
</table>

After this entry is posted, the asset account Office Supplies will have a balance of $500, representing the estimated cost of office supplies on hand at November 30. The Office Supplies account will appear in the balance sheet as an asset; the Office Supplies Expense account will be shown in the income statement.

How would failure to make this adjustment affect the financial statements? In the income statement for November, the expenses would be understated by $220 and the net income overstated by the same amount. Since the overstated amount for net income in November would be transferred into the owner's equity account in the process of closing the accounts, the owner's equity section of the balance sheet would be overstated by $220. Assets also would be overstated because Office Supplies would be listed at $220 too much.

Recording Prepayments Directly in the Expense Accounts In our illustration, payments for insurance and office supplies which are expected to provide benefits for more than one accounting period are recorded by debiting an asset account, such as Unexpired Insurance or Office Supplies. However, some companies follow an alternative practice of debiting these prepayments directly to an expense account such as Insurance Expense. At the end of the period, the adjusting entry would then consist of a debit to Unexpired Insurance and a credit to Insurance Expense for the portion of the insurance cost ***which has not yet expired.***

This alternative method leads to the same results in the balance sheet and income statement as does the method used in our illustration. Under both procedures, the cost of benefits consumed in the current period is treated as an expense, and the cost of benefits applicable to future periods is carried forward in the balance sheet as an asset.

In this text and in the end-of-chapter problem material, we will follow the practice of recording prepayments in ***asset accounts*** and then making adjusting entries to transfer these costs to expense accounts as the assets expire. This approach correctly describes the ***conceptual flow of costs*** through the elements of financial statements. That is, a prepayment ***is*** an asset that later becomes an expense. The alternative approach is used widely in practice only because it is an efficient short-cut, which standardizes the recording of transactions and may reduce the number of adjusting entries needed at the end of the period. Remember, our goal in this course is to develop your ability to ***understand and use*** accounting information, not to train you in the most efficient bookkeeping procedures.

Depreciation of Building The recording of depreciation expense at the end of an accounting period provides another example of an adjusting entry which ***apportions a recorded cost.*** The November 30 adjusting entry to record depreciation of the building used by Roberts Real Estate Company is exactly the same as the October 31 ***adjusting entry*** explained in Chapter 3.

Adjusting entry. Cost of building is gradually converted to expense	*Depreciation Expense: Building* *150*	
	Accumulated Depreciation: Building..........................	*150*
	To record depreciation for November.	

This allocation of depreciation expense to November operations is based on the following facts: the building cost $36,000 and is estimated to have a useful life of 20 years (240 months). Using the straight-line method of depreciation, the portion of the original cost which expires each month is ¹⁄₂₄₀ of $36,000, or $150.

The Accumulated Depreciation: Building account now has a credit balance of $300 as a result of the October and November credits of $150 each. The book value of the building is $35,700; that is, the original cost of $36,000 minus the accumulated depreciation of $300. The term **book value** means the net amount at which an asset is shown in the accounting records, as distinguished from its market value. **Carrying value** is an alternative term, with the same meaning as book value.

Depreciation of Office Equipment The November 30 adjusting entry to record depreciation of the office equipment is the same as the **adjusting entry** for depreciation a month earlier, as shown in Chapter 3.

<table><tr><td>Adjusting entry. Cost of office equipment gradually converted to expense</td><td>Depreciation Expense: Office Equipment 45
    Accumulated Depreciation: Office Equipment 45
To record depreciation for November.</td></tr></table>

The original cost of the office equipment was $5,400, and the estimated useful life was 10 years (120 months). Depreciation each month under the straight-line method is therefore ¹⁄₁₂₀ of $5,400, or $45.

What is the book value of the office equipment at this point? The original cost of $5,400 minus accumulated depreciation of $90 for two months leaves a book value of $5,310.

Apportioning Unearned Revenue

In some instances, a business may **collect in advance** for services to be rendered to customers in later accounting periods. For example, a football team collects much of its revenue in advance through the sale of season tickets. Health clubs collect in advance by selling long-term membership contracts. Airlines sell many of their tickets well in advance of a scheduled flight.

For accounting purposes, amounts collected in advance **do not represent revenue,** because these amounts have **not yet been earned.** Amounts collected from customers in advance are recorded by debiting the Cash account and crediting an **unearned revenue** account. Unearned revenue also may be called **deferred revenue.**

When a company collects money in advance from its customers, it has an **obligation** to render services in the future. Therefore, the balance of an unearned revenue account is considered to be a liability; **it appears in the liability section of the balance sheet, not in the income statement.** Unearned revenue differs from other liabilities because it usually will be settled by rendering services, rather than by making payment in cash. In short, it will be **worked off** rather than **paid off.** Of course if the business is unable to render the service, it must discharge this liability by refunding money to its customers.

CASE IN POINT One of the largest liabilities in the balance sheet of UAL, Inc., (United Air Lines) is "Advance ticket sales and customer deposits." This account, with a balance of approximately $500 million, represents unearned revenue resulting from the sale of tickets for future flights. Most of this unearned revenue will be earned as the future flights occur. Some customers, however, will change their plans and will return their tickets to United Airlines for a cash refund.

When the company renders the services for which customers have paid in advance, it is working off its liability to these customers and is earning the revenue. At the end of the accounting period in which the revenue is earned, an ***adjusting entry*** is made to transfer an appropriate amount from the unearned revenue account to a revenue account. This adjusting entry consists of a debit to a liability account (unearned revenue) and a credit to a revenue account.

To illustrate these concepts, assume that on November 1, Roberts Real Estate Company agreed to act as manager of some rental properties for a monthly fee of $300. The owner of the properties, Frank Day, was leaving the country on an extended trip and therefore paid the company for six months' service in advance. The journal entry by Roberts Real Estate Company to record the transaction on November 1 was:

Management fee collected but not yet earned	*Cash*... *1,800*	
	Unearned Management Fees.............................	*1,800*
	Collected in advance six months' fees for management of properties owned by Frank Day.	

Remember that Unearned Management Fees is a ***liability*** account, not a revenue account. This management fee will be earned gradually over a period of six months as Roberts Real Estate Company performs the required services. At the end of each monthly accounting period, the company will make an adjusting entry transferring $\frac{1}{6}$ of this management fee, or $300, from the unearned revenue account to a revenue account. The first in this series of monthly transfers will be made on November 30 by the following ***adjusting entry:***

Adjusting entry to recognize earning of a part of management fee	*Unearned Management Fees*..................................... *300*	
	Management Fees Earned.................................	*300*
	Fee earned by managing Frank Day property during November.	

After this entry has been posted, the Unearned Management Fees account will have a $1,500 credit balance. This balance represents the company's obligation to render $1,500 worth of services over the next five months and will appear in the liability section of the company's balance sheet. The Management Fees Earned account will be shown as revenue in the November income statement.

Recording Advance Collections Directly in the Revenue Accounts We have stressed that amounts collected from customers in advance represent liabilities, not revenue. However, some companies prefer to follow an accounting practice of crediting these advance collections directly to revenue accounts. Under this practice, the adjusting entry required at the end of the period would consist of a debit to the revenue account and a credit to the unearned revenue account for the portion of the advance payment *not yet earned.* This alternative accounting practice leads to the same results in the financial statements as does the method used in our Roberts Real Estate Company illustration.

Throughout this book, we will follow the originally described practice of crediting advance payments from customers to an unearned revenue account.

Recording Unrecorded Expenses

This type of adjusting entry recognizes expenses that will be paid in *future* transactions; thus, no cost has yet been recorded in the accounting records. Salaries of employees and interest on borrowed money are common examples of expenses which accumulate from day to day but which usually are not recorded until they are paid. These expenses are said to *accrue* over time, that is, to grow or to accumulate. At the end of the accounting period, an adjusting entry should be made to record any expenses which have accrued but which have not yet been recorded. Since these expenses will be paid at a future date, the adjusting entry consists of a debit to an expense account and a credit to a liability account. We shall now use the example of Roberts Real Estate Company to illustrate this type of adjusting entry.

Accrual of Interest On November 1, Roberts Real Estate Company borrowed the sum of $3,000 from a bank for a period of three months. Banks require every borrower to sign a *promissory note,* that is, a formal, written promise to repay the amount borrowed plus interest at an agreed future date. (Various forms of notes in common use and the accounting problems involved will be discussed more fully in Chapter 11.) The note signed by Roberts, with certain details omitted, is shown below:

Note payable issued to bank

$3,000	Los Angeles, California	November 1, 19__

Three months _____ after date _____ I _____ promise to pay

to the order of _____ American National Bank _____ .

_____ ---Three thousand and no/100--- _____ dollars

for value received, with interest at _____ 12 percent per year _____

Roberts Real Estate Company

By _____ *James Roberts*

The note payable is a liability of Roberts Real Estate Company, similar to an account payable but different in that a formal written promise to pay is required and interest is charged on the amount borrowed. A Notes Payable account is credited when the note is issued; the Notes Payable account will be debited three months later when the note is paid. Interest accrues throughout the life of the note payable, but it is not payable until the note matures on February 1. To the bank making the loan, the note signed by Roberts is an asset, a note receivable.

The journal entry made on November 1 by Roberts Real Estate Company to record the borrowing of $3,000 from the bank was as follows:

Entry when bank loan is obtained

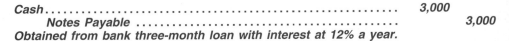

Cash.. **3,000**
    Notes Payable **3,000**
Obtained from bank three-month loan with interest at 12% a year.

Three months later, Roberts Real Estate Company must pay the bank $3,090, representing repayment of the $3,000 note payable plus $90 interest ($3,000 $\times$ .12 $\times$ $\frac{3}{12}$). The $90 is the total interest expense for the three months. Although no payment will be made for three months, one-third of the interest expense ($30) is ***incurred*** each month, as shown in the chart below.

Accrual of interest

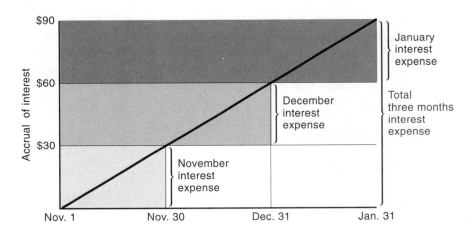

The following ***adjusting entry*** is made at November 30 to charge November operations with one month's interest expense and also to record the amount of interest owed to the bank at the end of November.

Adjusting entry for interest expense incurred in November

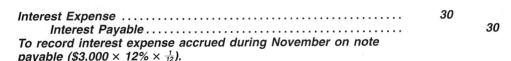

Interest Expense **30**
    Interest Payable... **30**
To record interest expense accrued during November on note payable ($3,000 $\times$ 12% $\times$ $\frac{1}{12}$).

The debit balance in the Interest Expense account will appear in the November income statement; the credit balances in the Interest Payable and Notes Payable accounts will be shown in the balance sheet as liabilities. These two liability accounts will remain in the records until the maturity date of the loan, at which time a cash payment to the bank will wipe out both the Notes Payable account and the Interest Payable account.

Accrual of Salary On November 20, Roberts hired Carl Nelson as a part-time salesperson whose job was to work evenings calling on property owners to secure listings of property for sale or rent. The agreed salary was $225 for a five-evening week, payable each Friday; payment for the first week was made on Friday, November 24. Personal income taxes and other taxes relating to payroll are ignored in this illustration.

Assume that the last day of the accounting period, November 30, fell on Thursday. Nelson had worked four evenings since being paid the preceding Friday and therefore had earned $180 ($\frac{4}{5} \times \$225$). In order that this $180 of November salary expense be reflected in the accounts before the financial statements are prepared, an ***adjusting entry*** is necessary at November 30.

Adjusting entry for salaries expense incurred but unpaid at November 30	*Salaries Expense* *180*	
	Salaries Payable	*180*
	To record salary expense and related liability to salesperson for last four evenings' work in November.	

The debit balance in the Salaries Expense account will appear as an expense in the November income statement; the credit balance of $180 in the Salaries Payable account is the amount owing to the salesperson for work performed during the last four days of November and will appear among the liabilities in the balance sheet at November 30.

The next regular payday for Nelson will be Friday, December 1, which is the first day of the new accounting period. Since the accounts were adjusted and closed on November 30, all the revenue and expense accounts have zero balances at the beginning of business on December 1. The payment of a week's salary to Nelson will be recorded by the following entry on December 1:

Payment of salary overlapping two accounting periods	*Salaries Payable*.. *180*	
	Salaries Expense *45*	
	Cash	*225*
	Paid weekly salary to salesperson.	

Note that the net result of the November 30 accrual entry has been to split the salesperson's weekly salary expense between November and December. Four days of the work week fell in November, so four days' pay, or $180, was recognized as November expense. One day of the work week fell in December, so $45 was recorded as December expense.

No accrual entry is necessary for other salaries in Roberts Real Estate Company because everyone except Nelson is paid regularly on the last working day of the month.

Recording Unrecorded Revenue

A business may earn revenue during the current accounting period but might not bill the customer until a future accounting period. This situation is likely to occur if additional services will be performed for the same customer, in which case the bill might not be prepared until all services are completed. Any revenue which has been ***earned but not recorded*** during the current accounting period should be recorded at the end of the period by means of an adjusting entry. This adjusting entry consists of a debit to an account receivable and a credit to the appropriate revenue account. The term *accrued revenue* often is used to describe revenue which has been earned during the period but which has *not been recorded* prior to the making of adjusting entries.

To illustrate this type of adjusting entry, assume that on November 16, Roberts Real Estate Company entered into a management agreement with Angela Clayton, the owner of a small office building. The company agreed to manage the Clayton property for a fee of $240 a month, payable on the fifteenth of each month. No entry is made in the accounting records at the time of signing a contract, because no services have yet been rendered and no change has occurred in assets or liabilities. The managerial duties are to begin immediately, but the first monthly fee will not be received until December 15. The following *adjusting entry* is therefore necessary at November 30:

Adjusting entry for fees earned but not yet billed	*Management Fees Receivable*	*120*
	Management Fees Earned	120
	To record accrued revenue from services rendered to Angela Clayton during November.	

The debit balance in the Management Fees Receivable account will be shown in the balance sheet as an asset. The credit balance of the Management Fees Earned account, including earnings from both the Frank Day and the Angela Clayton contracts, will appear in the November income statement.

The collection of the first monthly fee from Clayton will occur in the next accounting period (December 15, to be exact). Of this $240 cash receipt, half represents collection of the asset account, Management Fees Receivable, created at November 30 by the adjusting entry. The other half of the $240 cash receipt represents revenue earned during December; this should be credited to the December revenue account for Management Fees Earned. The entry on December 15 is as follows:

Management fee applicable to two accounting periods	*Cash*	*240*
	Management Fees Receivable	120
	Management Fees Earned	120
	Collected management fee from Angela Clayton for month ended December 15.	

The net result of the November 30 accrual entry has been to divide the revenue from managing the Clayton properties between November and December in accordance with the timing of the services rendered.

Adjusting Entries and the Accrual Basis of Accounting

Adjusting entries help make accrual basis accounting work successfully. By preparing adjusting entries, we can recognize revenue in the accounting period in which it is *earned* and also recognize any unrecorded expenses which helped to *produce that revenue.* For example, the adjusting entry to record revenue which has been earned but not yet recorded helps achieve our goal of including in the income statement all the revenue *real-*

ized during the accounting period. The adjusting entries which recognize expenses help to achieve the ***matching principle***—that is, offsetting revenues with all the expenses incurred in generating that revenue.

The Concept of Materiality

OBJECTIVE 3
Explain the
concept of
materiality.

The term ***materiality*** refers to the ***relative importance*** of an item or an event. An item is "material" if knowledge of the item might reasonably ***influence the decisions*** of users of financial statements. Accountants must be sure that all material items are properly reported in financial statements.

However, the financial reporting process should be ***cost effective***—that is, the value of the information should exceed the cost of its preparation. By definition, the accounting treatment accorded to ***immaterial*** items is of ***little or no consequence to decision makers.*** Therefore, accountants do not waste time accounting for immaterial items; these items may be handled in the ***easiest and most convenient manner.***

In summary, the concept of materiality allows accountants to use estimated amounts and even to ignore other accounting principles if the results of these actions ***do not have a "material effect"*** upon the financial statements. Materiality is one of the most important generally accepted accounting principles; we will encounter applications of this concept throughout the study of accounting.

Materiality and Adjusting Entries   The concept of materiality enables accountants to shorten and simplify the process of making adjusting entries in several ways. For example:

1 Businesses purchase many "assets" which have a very low cost, or which will be consumed quickly in business operations. Examples include wastebaskets, lightbulbs, and janitorial supplies. The materiality concept permits charging such purchases ***directly to expense accounts,*** rather than to asset accounts. This treatment conveniently eliminates the need for an adjusting entry at the end of the period to transfer a portion of these costs from an asset account to expense. This accounting short-cut is acceptable as long as the cost of the ***unused*** items on hand at the end of the period is "immaterial."

2 Some expenses, such as telephone bills and utility bills, may be charged to expense as the bills are ***paid,*** rather than as the services are used. Technically this treatment violates the ***matching principle.*** However, accounting for utility bills on a cash basis is very convenient, as the monthly cost of utility service is not even known until the utility bill is received. Under this "cash basis" approach, one month's utility bill is charged to expense each month. Although the bill charged to expense is actually the ***prior*** month's bill, the resulting "error" in the financial statements is not likely to be material.

3 Adjusting entries to accrue unrecorded expenses or unrecorded revenue may be ignored if the dollar amounts are immaterial.

4 If the amount of error is not likely to be material, adjusting entries may be based on ***estimates.*** For example, on page 162 we illustrate an adjusting entry allocating part of the $720 balance in the Office Supplies

account to expense. The amount of supplies used during the period ($220) was based upon an ***estimate*** of the supplies still on hand ($500). This $500 estimate is an educated guess; no one actually counted every pen, pencil, and pad of paper on hand at month-end.

Materiality Is a Matter of Professional Judgment   Whether or not a specific item or event is "material" is a matter of ***professional judgment.*** In making these judgments, accountants consider several factors.

First, what constitutes a "material amount" varies with the size of the organization. For example, a $1,000 expenditure may be material in relation to the financial statements of a small business but not to the statements of a large corporation such as General Motors.[2] There are no official rules as to what constitutes a "material amount," but most accountants would consider amounts of less than 2 or 3% of net income to be ***immaterial.***

Next, accountants must consider the ***cumulative effect*** of numerous "immaterial" events. Each of a dozen items may be immaterial when considered by itself. When viewed together, however, the ***combined effect*** of all twelve items may be material.

Finally, materiality depends upon the ***nature*** of the item, as well as its dollar amount. Assume, for example, that several managers systematically have been stealing money from the company that they manage. Stockholders probably would consider this fact important even if the dollar amounts were but a small percentage of the company's total resources.

Note to students: In the assignment material accompanying this textbook, you are to consider all dollar amounts to be material, unless the problem specifically states otherwise.

THE WORK SHEET

OBJECTIVE 4
Prepare a
work sheet
and explain
its useful-
ness.

The work necessary at the end of an accounting period includes construction of a trial balance, journalizing and posting of adjusting entries, preparation of financial statements, and journalizing and posting of closing entries. So many details are involved in these end-of-period procedures that it is easy to make errors. If these errors are recorded in the journal and in the ledger accounts, considerable time and effort can be wasted in correcting them. Both the journal and the ledger are formal, permanent records. They may be prepared manually in ink or printed by a computer. One way of avoiding errors in the permanent accounting records and also of simplifying the work to be done at the end of the period is to use a ***work sheet.***

In a manual accounting system, a work sheet is a large columnar sheet of paper, specially designed to arrange in a convenient systematic form all the accounting data required at the end of the period. The work sheet is not a part of the permanent accounting records; it is prepared in pencil by accountants for their own convenience. (The use of a computer to prepare a work sheet is discussed later in this chapter.) If an error is made on the

---

2   This point is emphasized by the fact that GM rounds the dollar amounts shown in its financial statements to the nearest $100,000. This rounding of financial statement amounts is, in itself, an application of the materiality concept.

work sheet, it may be erased and corrected much more easily than an error in the formal accounting records. Furthermore, the work sheet is designed to reduce errors by automatically bringing to light many types of discrepancies which otherwise might be entered in the journal and posted to the ledger accounts. Dollar signs, decimal points, and commas are not used with the amounts entered on work sheets, although commas are shown in this example. A work sheet for Roberts Real Estate Company appears on page 173.

The work sheet may be thought of as a testing ground on which the ledger accounts are adjusted, balanced, and arranged in the general form of financial statements. The satisfactory completion of a work sheet provides considerable assurance that all the details of the end-of-period accounting procedures have been properly brought together. After this point has been established, the work sheet then serves as the source from which the formal financial statements are prepared and the adjusting and closing entries are made in the journal.

Preparing the Work Sheet

Notice that the heading of the work sheet illustrated for Roberts Real Estate Company consists of three parts: (1) the name of the business, (2) the title **Work Sheet,** and (3) the period of time covered. The body of the work sheet contains five pairs of money columns, each pair consisting of a debit and a credit column. The procedures to be followed in preparing a work sheet will now be illustrated in five simple steps.

1 **Enter the ledger account balances in the Trial Balance columns.** The titles and balances of the ledger accounts at November 30 are copied into the Trial Balance columns of the work sheet, as illustrated on page 173. In practice these amounts may be taken directly from the ledger. It would be a duplication of work to prepare a trial balance as a separate schedule and then to copy this information into the work sheet. As soon as the account balances have been listed on the work sheet, these two columns should be added and the totals entered.

Notice that in our work sheet we have inserted captions indicating which ledger accounts relate to the **balance sheet** and which relate to the **income statement.**[3] The sequence of accounts in the ledger lends itself to these captions, because ledger accounts are arranged in financial statement order—that is, the balance sheet accounts appear first.

Including these "Balance sheet" and "Income statement" captions in a trial balance is an optional procedure, but the technique is widely used in practice. We strongly favor the use of these captions for **educational purposes.** They help emphasize, for example, that every adjusting entry affects **both the balance sheet and the income statement.** Also these captions help to clarify one of the final steps in completing a work sheet—extending the amounts shown in the adjusted trial balance to the appropriate financial statement columns.

---

[3] The Drawing account is included among the balance sheet accounts because withdrawals affect the amount of owner's equity, but they do ***not*** appear in the income statement.

Step 1: Prepare a trial balance

ROBERTS REAL ESTATE COMPANY
Work Sheet
For the Month Ended November 30, 19__

	Trial Balance Dr	Trial Balance Cr	Adjustments Dr	Adjustments Cr	Adjusted Trial Balance Dr	Adjusted Trial Balance Cr	Income Statement Dr	Income Statement Cr	Balance Sheet Dr	Balance Sheet Cr
Balance sheet accounts:										
Cash	21,740									
Accounts receivable	16,990									
Unexpired insurance	600									
Office supplies	720									
Land	130,000									
Building	36,000									
Accumulated depreciation: building		150								
Office equipment	5,400									
Accumulated depreciation: office equipment		45								
Notes payable		3,000								
Accounts payable		23,595								
Unearned management fees		1,800								
James Roberts, capital		180,771								
James Roberts, drawing	1,500									
Income statement accounts:										
Sales commissions earned		15,484								
Advertising expense	1,275									
Salaries expense	9,425									
Telephone expense	1,195									
	224,845	224,845								

If the work sheet is prepared manually, the accountant should leave a few **blank lines** after the last "balance sheet" account.[4] If additional balance sheet accounts are needed during the preparation of adjusting entries, they can be added on these lines. Additional income statement accounts needed during the adjustment process may be added below the trial balance totals.

2 Enter the adjustments in the Adjustments columns. The required adjustments for Roberts Real Estate Company were explained earlier in this chapter; these same adjustments are now entered in the Adjustments columns of the work sheet. (See the following page.)

As a cross-reference, the debit and credit parts of each adjustment are keyed together by placing a key letter to the left of each amount. For example, the adjustment debiting Insurance Expense and crediting Unexpired Insurance is identified by the key letter (a). The use of the key letters makes it easy to match a debit entry in the Adjustments columns with its related credit. The identifying letters also key the debit and credit entries in the Adjustments columns to the brief explanations which appear at the bottom of the work sheet.

In some cases, adjusting entries may require the use of accounts that were not included in the original trial balance. These accounts must be added to the work sheet. Balance sheet accounts—assets and liabilities—are added in the lines which had been left blank following the last balance sheet account in the trial balance. Income statement accounts—revenue and expenses—can be added on lines below the totals for the trial balance columns. After all the adjustment debits and credits have been entered in the Adjustments columns, this pair of columns must be totaled. Proving the equality of debit and credit totals helps to detect any arithmetical errors and to prevent them from being carried over into other columns of the work sheet.

3 Enter the account balances as adjusted in the Adjusted Trial Balance columns. The work sheet as it appears after completion of the Adjusted Trial Balance columns is illustrated on page 176. Each account balance in the first pair of columns is combined with the adjustment, if any, in the second pair of columns, and the combined amount is entered in the Adjusted Trial Balance columns. This process of combining the items on each line throughout the first four columns of the work sheet requires horizontal addition or subtraction. It is called **cross footing,** in contrast to the addition of items in a vertical column, which is called **footing** the column.

For example, the Office Supplies account has a debit balance of $720 in the Trial Balance columns. This $720 debit amount is combined with the $220 credit appearing on the same line in the Adjustments column; the combination of a $720 **debit** with a $220 **credit** produces an adjusted debit amount of **$500** in the Adjusted Trial Balance debit column. As another example, consider the Office Supplies Expense account. This account had no balance in the Trial Balance columns but shows a $220 debit in the Adjustments debit column. The combination of a zero start-

---

[4]   In a computer-based system, it is not necessary to leave any blank lines; additional lines may be inserted at any point.

Step 2: Prepare adjusting entries in "columnar form"

ROBERTS REAL ESTATE COMPANY
Work Sheet
For the Month Ended November 30, 19___

Account	Trial Balance Dr	Trial Balance Cr	Adjustments* Dr	Adjustments* Cr	Adjusted Trial Balance Dr	Adjusted Trial Balance Cr	Income Statement Dr	Income Statement Cr	Balance Sheet Dr	Balance Sheet Cr
Balance sheet accounts:										
Cash	21,740									
Accounts receivable	16,990									
Unexpired insurance	600			(a) 50						
Office supplies	720			(b) 220						
Land	130,000									
Building	36,000									
Accumulated depreciation: building		150		(c) 150						
Office equipment	5,400									
Accumulated depreciation: office equipment		45		(d) 45						
Notes payable		3,000								
Accounts payable		23,595								
Unearned management fees		1,800	(e) 300							
James Roberts, capital		180,771								
James Roberts, drawing	1,500									
Interest payable				(f) 30						
Salaries payable				(g) 180						
Management fees receivable			(h) 120							
Income statement accounts:										
Sales commissions earned		15,484								
Advertising expense	1,275									
Salaries expense	9,425		(g) 180							
Telephone expense	1,195									
	224,845	224,845								
Insurance expense			(a) 50							
Office supplies expense			(b) 220							
Depreciation expense: building			(c) 150							
Depreciation expense: office equipment			(d) 45							
Management fees earned				(e) 300 (h) 120						
Interest expense			(f) 30							
			1,095	1,095						

Explanatory footnotes keyed to adjustments
* Adjustments:
(a) Portion of insurance cost which expired during November.
(b) Office supplies used during November.
(c) Depreciation of building during November.
(d) Depreciation of office equipment during November.
(e) Earned one-sixth of the fee collected in advance on the Day properties.
(f) Interest expense accrued during November on note payable ($3,000 × 12% × 1/12).
(g) Salesperson's salary for last four days of November.
(h) Management fee accrued on Clayton contract in November.

Step 3: Determine the adjusted balances and enter them in Adjusted Trial Balance columns

ROBERTS REAL ESTATE COMPANY
Work Sheet
For the Month Ended November 30, 19__

	Trial Balance Dr	Trial Balance Cr	Adjustments* Dr	Adjustments* Cr	Adjusted Trial Balance Dr	Adjusted Trial Balance Cr	Income Statement Dr	Income Statement Cr	Balance Sheet Dr	Balance Sheet Cr
Balance sheet accounts:										
Cash	21,740				21,740					
Accounts receivable	16,990				16,990					
Unexpired insurance	600			(a) 50	550					
Office supplies	720			(b) 220	500					
Land	130,000				130,000					
Building	36,000				36,000					
Accumulated depreciation: building		150		(c) 150		300				
Office equipment	5,400				5,400					
Accumulated depreciation: office equipment		45		(d) 45		90				
Notes payable		3,000				3,000				
Accounts payable		23,595				23,595				
Unearned management fees		1,800	(e) 300			1,500				
James Roberts, capital		180,771				180,771				
James Roberts, drawing	1,500				1,500					
Interest payable				(f) 30		30				
Salaries payable				(g) 180		180				
Management fees receivable			(h) 120		120					
Income statement accounts:										
Sales commissions earned		15,484				15,484				
Advertising expense	1,275				1,275					
Sales salaries expense	9,425		(g) 180		9,605					
Telephone expense	1,195				1,195					
	224,845	224,845								
Insurance expense			(a) 50		50					
Office supplies expense			(b) 220		220					
Depreciation expense: building			(c) 150		150					
Depreciation expense: office equipment			(d) 45		45					
Management fees earned				(e) 300 (h) 120		420				
Interest expense			(f) 30		30					
			1,095	1,095	225,370	225,370				

* Explanatory notes relating to adjustments are the same as on page 175.

ing balance and $220 debit adjustment produces a $220 debit amount in the Adjusted Trial Balance.

Many of the accounts in the trial balance are not affected by the adjustments made at the end of the month; the balances of these accounts (such as Cash, Land, Building, or Notes Payable in the illustrated work sheet) are entered in the Adjusted Trial Balance columns in exactly the **same amounts** as shown in the Trial Balance columns. After all the accounts have been extended into the Adjusted Trial Balance columns, this pair of columns is totaled to prove that no arithmetical errors have been made up to this point.

4 **Extend each amount in the Adjusted Trial Balance columns into the Income Statement columns or into the Balance Sheet columns.** Assets, liabilities, and the owner's capital and drawing accounts are extended to the Balance Sheet columns; revenue and expense accounts are extended to the Income Statement columns.

The process of extending amounts horizontally across the work sheet should begin with the account at the top of the work sheet, which is usually Cash. The cash figure is extended to the Balance Sheet debit column. Then the accountant goes down the work sheet line by line, extending each account balance to the appropriate Income Statement or Balance Sheet column. The likelihood of error is much less when each account is extended in the order of its appearance on the work sheet, than if accounts are extended in random order. The work sheet as it appears after completion of this sorting process is illustrated on page 178. Note that each amount in the Adjusted Trial Balance columns is extended to one **and only one** of the four remaining columns.

5 **Total the Income Statement columns and the Balance Sheet columns. Enter the net income or net loss as a balancing figure in both pairs of columns, and again compute column totals.** The work sheet as it appears after this final step is shown on page 179.

The net income or net loss for the period is determined by computing the difference between the totals of the two Income Statement columns. In the illustrated work sheet, the credit column total is the larger and the excess represents net income:

Income Statement credit column total (revenue)............................	*$15,904*
Income Statement debit column total (expenses)............................	*12,570*
Difference: net income for period...	*$ 3,334*

Note on the work sheet that the net income of $3,334 is entered in the Income Statement **debit** column as a balancing figure and also on the same line as a balancing figure in the Balance Sheet **credit** column. The caption **Net Income** is written in the space for account titles to identify and explain this item. New totals are then computed for both the Income Statement columns and the Balance Sheet columns. Each pair of columns is now in balance.

The reason for entering the net income of $3,334 in the Balance Sheet credit column is that the net income accumulated during the period in the revenue and expense accounts causes an increase in the owner's equity. If the balance sheet columns did not have equal totals after the net income had been recorded in the credit column, the lack of

Step 4: Extend each adjusted amount to the appropriate financial statement columns

ROBERTS REAL ESTATE COMPANY
Work Sheet
For the Month Ended November 30, 19__

	Trial Balance Dr	Trial Balance Cr	Adjustments* Dr	Adjustments* Cr	Adjusted Trial Balance Dr	Adjusted Trial Balance Cr	Income Statement Dr	Income Statement Cr	Balance Sheet Dr	Balance Sheet Cr
Balance sheet accounts:										
Cash	21,740				21,740				21,740	
Accounts receivable	16,990				16,990				16,990	
Unexpired insurance	600			(a) 50	550				550	
Office supplies	720			(b) 220	500				500	
Land	130,000				130,000				130,000	
Building	36,000				36,000				36,000	
Accumulated depreciation: building		150		(c) 150		300				300
Office equipment	5,400				5,400				5,400	
Accumulated depreciation: office equipment		45		(d) 45		90				90
Notes payable		3,000				3,000				3,000
Accounts payable		23,595				23,595				23,595
Unearned management fees		1,800	(e) 300			1,500				1,500
James Roberts, capital		180,771				180,771				180,771
James Roberts, drawing	1,500				1,500				1,500	
Interest payable				(f) 30		30				30
Salaries payable				(g) 180		180				180
Management fees receivable			(h) 120		120				120	
Income statement accounts:										
Sales commissions earned		15,484				15,484		15,484		
Advertising expense	1,275				1,275		1,275			
Salaries expense	9,425		(g) 180		9,605		9,605			
Telephone expense	1,195				1,195		1,195			
	224,845	224,845								
Insurance expense			(a) 50		50		50			
Office supplies expense			(b) 220		220		220			
Depreciation expense: building			(c) 150		150		150			
Depreciation expense: office equipment			(d) 45		45		45			
Management fees earned				(e) 300 (h) 120		420		420		
Interest expense			(f) 30		30		30			
			1,095	1,095	225,370	225,370				

* Explanatory notes relating to adjustments are the same as on page 175.

Step 5: Total both sets of financial statement columns; then enter net income as the "balancing figure"

ROBERTS REAL ESTATE COMPANY
Work Sheet
For the Month Ended November 30, 19___

	Trial Balance Dr	Trial Balance Cr	Adjustments* Dr	Adjustments* Cr	Adjusted Trial Balance Dr	Adjusted Trial Balance Cr	Income Statement Dr	Income Statement Cr	Balance Sheet Dr	Balance Sheet Cr
Balance sheet accounts:										
Cash	21,740				21,740				21,740	
Accounts receivable	16,990				16,990				16,990	
Unexpired insurance	600			(a) 50	550				550	
Office supplies	720			(b) 220	500				500	
Land	130,000				130,000				130,000	
Building	36,000				36,000				36,000	
Accumulated depreciation: building		150		(c) 150		300				300
Office equipment	5,400				5,400				5,400	
Accumulated depreciation: office equipment		45		(d) 45		90				90
Notes payable		3,000				3,000				3,000
Accounts payable		23,595				23,595				23,595
Unearned management fees		1,800	(e) 300			1,500				1,500
James Roberts, capital		180,771				180,771				180,771
James Roberts, drawing	1,500				1,500				1,500	
Interest payable				(f) 30		30				30
Salaries payable				(g) 180		180				180
Management fees receivable			(h) 120		120				120	
	224,845	224,845								
Income statement accounts:										
Sales commissions earned		15,484				15,484		15,484		
Advertising expense	1,275				1,275		1,275			
Salaries expense	9,425		(g) 180		9,605		9,605			
Telephone expense	1,195				1,195		1,195			
Insurance expense			(a) 50		50		50			
Office supplies expense			(b) 220		220		220			
Depreciation expense: building			(c) 150		150		150			
Depreciation expense: office equipment			(d) 45		45		45			
Management fees earned				(e) 300 (h) 120		420		420		
Interest expense			(f) 30		30		30			
			1,095	1,095	225,370	225,370	12,570	15,904	212,800	209,466
Net income							3,334			3,334
							15,904	15,904	212,800	212,800

Enter net income to balance the Income Statement columns

Extend net income to bring Balance Sheet columns into balance

* Explanatory notes relating to adjustments are the same as on page 175.

agreement would indicate that an error had been made in the work sheet.

Let us assume for a moment that the month's operations had produced a *loss* rather than a profit. In that case the Income Statement debit column would exceed the credit column. The excess of the debits (expenses) over the credits (revenue) would have to be entered in the **credit column** in order to bring the two Income Statement columns into balance. The incurring of a loss would decrease the owner's equity; therefore, the loss would be entered as a balancing figure in the Balance Sheet **debit column.** The Balance Sheet columns would then have equal totals.

Self-Balancing Nature of the Work Sheet   Why does the entering of the net income or net loss in one of the Balance Sheet columns bring this pair of columns into balance? The answer is short and simple. All the accounts in the Balance Sheet columns have November 30 balances with the exception of the owner's capital account, which still shows the October 31 balance. By bringing in the current month's net income as an addition to the October 31 capital, the capital account is brought up to date as of November 30 (except for the drawing account which is later closed to the capital account). The Balance Sheet columns now prove the familiar proposition that assets are equal to the total of liabilities and owner's equity.

Uses for the Work Sheet

Preparing Financial Statements   Preparing the formal financial statements from the work sheet is an easy step. All the information needed for both the income statement and the balance sheet has already been sorted and arranged in convenient form in the work sheet. For example, compare the amounts in the following income statement with the amounts listed in the Income Statement columns of the completed work sheet.

Data taken
from income
statement
columns of
work sheet

ROBERTS REAL ESTATE COMPANY
Income Statement
For the Month Ended November 30, 19__

Revenue:		
Sales commissions earned		$15,484
Management fees earned		420
Total revenue		$15,904
Expenses:		
Advertising	$1,275	
Salaries	9,605	
Telephone	1,195	
Insurance..	50	
Office supplies	220	
Depreciation: building..	150	
Depreciation: office equipment	45	
Interest	30	
Total expenses		12,570
Net income		3,334

Notice that in our November 30 work sheet, the owner's capital account still contains its November 1 balance of $180,771. This is because all the changes in owner's equity occurring in the month were recorded in the **temporary** proprietorship accounts (the revenue, expense, and drawing accounts), rather than in the owner's capital account. In the ledger, the owner's capital account will be brought up-to-date when the November closing entries are recorded and posted.

The work sheet provides us with all the information we need to compute the amount of owner's equity at November 30. During November, owner's equity was increased by the earning of net income ($3,334) and decreased by the withdrawal of assets by the owner ($1,500).

The November statement of owner's equity for Roberts Real Estate Company is shown below:

<table>
<tr><td rowspan="6" style="vertical-align:top">**Net income exceeded withdrawals by owner**</td><td colspan="2" style="text-align:center">**ROBERTS REAL ESTATE COMPANY**
Statement of Owner's Equity
For the Month Ended November 30, 19__</td></tr>
<tr><td>James Roberts, capital, Nov. 1, 19__</td><td>$180,771</td></tr>
<tr><td>Add: Net income</td><td>3,334</td></tr>
<tr><td>Subtotal</td><td>$184,105</td></tr>
<tr><td>Less: Withdrawals</td><td>1,500</td></tr>
<tr><td>James Roberts, capital, Nov. 30, 19__</td><td>$182,605</td></tr>
</table>

Finally, the November 30 balance sheet for Roberts Real Estate Company contains the amounts for assets and liabilities listed in the Balance Sheet columns of the work sheet, along with the new balance of owner's equity.

<table>
<tr><td rowspan="13" style="vertical-align:top">**Compare these amounts with figures in balance sheet columns of work sheet**</td><td colspan="3" style="text-align:center">**ROBERTS REAL ESTATE COMPANY**
Balance Sheet
November 30, 19__</td></tr>
<tr><td colspan="3" style="text-align:center">**Assets**</td></tr>
<tr><td>Cash</td><td></td><td>$ 21,740</td></tr>
<tr><td>Accounts receivable</td><td></td><td>16,990</td></tr>
<tr><td>Management fees receivable</td><td></td><td>120</td></tr>
<tr><td>Unexpired insurance</td><td></td><td>550</td></tr>
<tr><td>Office supplies</td><td></td><td>500</td></tr>
<tr><td>Land</td><td></td><td>130,000</td></tr>
<tr><td>Building</td><td>$36,000</td><td></td></tr>
<tr><td>Less: Accumulated depreciation</td><td>300</td><td>35,700</td></tr>
<tr><td>Office equipment</td><td>$ 5,400</td><td></td></tr>
<tr><td>Less: Accumulated depreciation</td><td>90</td><td>5,310</td></tr>
<tr><td>Total assets</td><td></td><td>$210,910</td></tr>
</table>

Liabilities & Owner's Equity	
Liabilities:	
Notes payable	$ 3,000
Accounts payable..	23,595
Interest payable...	30
Salaries payable	180
Unearned management fees	1,500
Total liabilities	$ 28,305
Owner's equity:	
James Roberts, capital..	182,605
Total liabilities & owner's equity	$210,910

Recording Adjusting Entries in the Accounting Records After the financial statements have been prepared from the work sheet at the end of the period, adjusting journal entries are prepared to bring the ledger accounts into agreement with the financial statements. This is an easy step because the adjustments have already been computed on the work sheet. The amounts appearing in the Adjustments columns of the work sheet and the related explanations at the bottom of the work sheet provide all the necessary information for the adjusting entries, as shown below. These adjusting entries are first entered in the journal and then posted to the ledger accounts.

Adjustments on work sheet are entered in general journal

General Journal					Page 5
Date		Account Titles and Explanation	LP	Debit	Credit
19__ Nov	30	Insurance Expense....................... Unexpired Insurance................ Insurance expense for November.		50	50
	30	Office Supplies Expense .... Office Supplies .... Office supplies used during November.		220	220
	30	Depreciation Expense: Building.......... Accumulated Depreciation: Building Depreciation for November ($36,000 ÷ 240 = $150).		150	150
	30	Depreciation Expense: Office Equipment . Accumulated Depreciation: Office Equipment........................ Depreciation for November ($5,400 ÷ 120 = $45).		45	45
	30	Unearned Management Fees.............. Management Fees Earned.......... Earned one-sixth of fee collected in advance for management of the properties owned by Frank Day.		300	300

General Journal					Page 5
Date		**Account Titles and Explanation**	**LP**	**Debit**	**Credit**
19___ Nov	30	Interest Expense.......................... Interest Payable.................... *Interest expense accrued during November on note payable ($3,000 × 12% × $\frac{1}{12}$).*		30	30
	30	Salaries Expense........................ Salaries Payable.................... *To record expense and related liability to salesperson for last four evenings' work in November.*		180	180
	30	Management Fees Receivable........... Management Fees Earned.......... *To record the receivable and related revenue earned for managing properties owned by Angela Clayton.*		120	120

Recording Closing Entries   When the financial statements have been prepared, the revenue and expense accounts have served their purpose for the current period and should be closed. These accounts then will have *zero balances* and will be ready for the recording of revenue and expenses during the next fiscal period. The completed work sheet provides in convenient form all the information needed to make the closing entries. The preparation of closing entries from the work sheet may be summarized as follows:

1   To close the accounts listed in the Income Statement credit column, debit the revenue accounts and credit Income Summary.

2   To close the accounts listed in the Income Statement debit column, debit Income Summary and credit the expense accounts.

3   To close the Income Summary account, transfer the balancing figure in the Income Statement columns of the work sheet ($3,334 in the illustration) to the owner's capital account. A profit is transferred by debiting Income Summary and crediting the capital account; a loss is transferred by debiting the capital account and crediting Income Summary.

4   To close the owner's drawing account, debit the capital account and credit the drawing account. Notice on the work sheet that the account, James Roberts, Drawing, is extended from the Adjusted Trial Balance debit column to the Balance Sheet debit column. It does not appear in the Income Statement columns because a withdrawal of cash by the owner is not regarded as an expense of the business.

The closing entries at November 30 are shown as follows:

Closing entries derived from work sheet

General Journal					Page 6
Date		**Account Titles and Explanation**	**LP**	**Debit**	**Credit**
19__ Nov	30	Sales Commissions Earned		15,484	
		Management Fees Earned		420	
		Income Summary			15,904
		To close the revenue accounts.			
	30	Income Summary		12,570	
		Advertising Expense.			1,275
		Salaries Expense			9,605
		Telephone Expense.			1,195
		Insurance Expense			50
		Office Supplies Expense			220
		Depreciation Expense: Building . . .			150
		Depreciation Expense: Office			
		Equipment.			45
		Interest Expense			30
		To close the expense accounts.			
	30	Income Summary		3,334	
		James Roberts, Capital			3,334
		To close the Income Summary account.			
	30	James Roberts, Capital		1,500	
		James Roberts, Drawing			1,500
		To close the owner's drawing account.			

Work Sheets in Computer-Based Systems The "work sheet" in a computer-based accounting system usually consists of one or more displays on the monitor screen rather than a sheet of columnar paper. Spreadsheet programs, such as Lotus 1-2-3 and VP Planner, are ideally suited to preparing a work sheet in a computerized accounting system.

Most of the steps involved in preparing a work sheet are mechanical and can be performed automatically in a computer-based system. Thus, the work sheet can be prepared faster and more easily than in a manual system. A trial balance, for example, is merely a listing of the ledger account balances and can be prepared instantly by computer. Entering the adjustments, on the other hand, requires human judgment and analysis. Someone familiar with generally accepted accounting principles and with the unrecorded business activities of the company must decide what adjustments are necessary and must enter the adjustment data. Once the adjustments have been entered, the computer can instantly complete the work sheet. When the accountant is satisfied that the adjustments shown in the work sheet are correct, the adjusting and closing entries can be entered in the formal accounting records with the touch of a button.

The Accounting Cycle

As stated at the beginning of this chapter, the life of a business is divided into accounting periods of equal length. In each period we repeat a standard sequence of accounting procedures beginning with the journalizing of transactions and concluding with an after-closing trial balance.

Because the work sheet includes the trial balance, the adjusting entries in preliminary form, and an adjusted trial balance, the use of a work sheet will modify the sequence of procedures given in Chapter 3, as follows:

1 **Journalize transactions.**   Analyze business transactions as they occur and record them promptly in a journal.

2 **Post to ledger accounts.**   Transfer debits and credits from journal entries to ledger accounts.

3 **Prepare a work sheet.**   Begin with a trial balance of the ledger, enter all necessary adjustments, sort the adjusted account balances between income statement accounts and balance sheet accounts, and determine the net income or net loss.

4 **Prepare financial statements and appropriate notes.**   Utilize the information in the work sheet to prepare an income statement, a statement of owner's equity, and a balance sheet. (The appropriate notes come from a variety of other sources.)

5 **Journalize and post the adjusting and closing entries.**   Using the information in the work sheet as a guide, enter the adjusting entries in the journal. Post these entries to ledger accounts. Prepare and post journal entries to close the revenue and expense accounts into the Income Summary account and to transfer the net income or net loss to the owner's capital account. Also prepare and post a journal entry to close the owner's drawing account into the owner's capital account.

6 **Prepare an after-closing trial balance.**   Prove that equality of debit and credit balances in the ledger has not been upset by the adjusting and closing procedures.

The above sequence of accounting procedures constitutes a complete accounting process. The regular repetition of this standardized set of procedures in each accounting period is often referred to as the ***accounting cycle.*** The procedures of a complete accounting cycle are illustrated in the flowchart on the following page. The white symbols indicate the accounting procedures; the shaded symbols represent accounting records, schedules, and statements.

Note that the preparing of financial statements (Step 4) comes before entering adjusting and closing entries in the journal and posting these entries to the ledger (Step 5). This sequence reflects the fact that ***management wants the financial statements as soon as possible.*** Once the work sheet is complete, all information required for the financial statements is available. Top priority then goes to preparation of the financial statements.

In most business concerns the accounts are closed only once a year; for these companies the accounting cycle is one year in length. For purposes of illustration in a textbook, however, it is often convenient to assume that the entire accounting cycle is performed within the time period of one month. The completion of the accounting cycle is the occasion for preparing financial statements and closing the revenue and expense accounts.

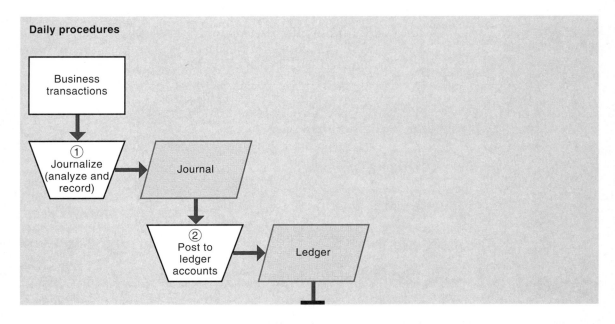

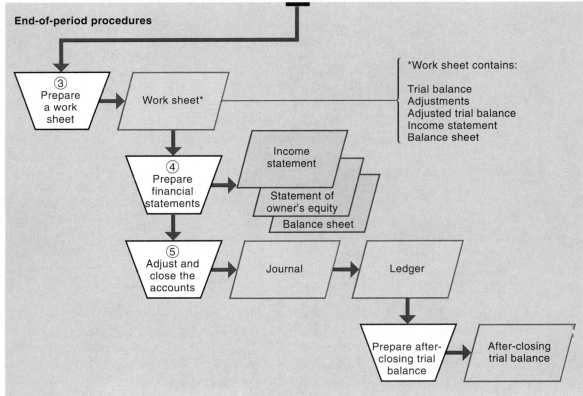

Preparing Monthly Financial Statements without Closing the Accounts

Many companies which close their accounts only once a year nevertheless prepare **monthly** financial statements for managerial use. These monthly statements are prepared from work sheets, but the adjustments indicated on the work sheets are not entered in the accounting records and no closing entries are made. Under this plan, the time-consuming operation of journalizing and posting adjustments and closing entries is performed only at the end of the fiscal year, but the company has the advantage of monthly financial statements. Monthly and quarterly financial statements are often referred to as **interim statements,** because they are in between the year-end statements. The annual or year-end statements are usually audited by a firm of certified public accountants; interim statements are usually unaudited.

■ ■ ■ *** Supplemental Topic**
Reversing Entries

OBJECTIVE 6
*Explain
when and
why revers-
ing entries
may be used.*

Reversing entries are an optional procedure which may be carried out at year-end to simplify the recording of certain routine cash receipts and payments in the following period. As the name suggests, a **reversing entry** is the exact reverse of an adjusting entry. It contains the same account titles and dollar amounts as the related adjusting entry, but the debits and credits are the reverse of those in the adjusting entry and the date is the first day of the next accounting period.

Let us use as an example a small company on a five-day work week which pays its employees each Friday. Assume that the payroll is $600 per day or $3,000 for a five-day week. Throughout the year, a company employee makes a journal entry each Friday as follows:

Regular weekly entry for payroll

Salaries Expense	*3,000*	
Cash		*3,000*
To record payment of salaries for the week.		

Next, let us assume that December 31, the last working day of Year 1, falls on Wednesday. All expenses of the year must be recorded before the accounts are closed and financial statements prepared at December 31. Therefore, an adjusting entry must be made to record the salaries expense and the related liability to employees for the three days they have worked since the last payday. The adjusting entry for $1,800 (computed as 3 × $600 daily salary expense) is shown below:

Adjusting entry at end of year

Dec. 31 Salaries Expense	*1,800*	
Salaries Payable		*1,800*
To record salaries expense and the related liability to		
employees for last three days worked in December.		

The closing of the accounts on December 31 will reduce the Salaries Expense account to zero, but the liability account, Salaries Payable, will remain open with its $1,800 credit balance at the beginning of the new year. On the next regular payday, Friday, January 2, an employee can record the $3,000 payroll by a debit of $1,800 to Salaries Payable, a debit of $1,200 to Salaries Expense, and a credit of $3,000 to Cash. However, splitting the debit side of the entry in this manner ($1,800 to the liability account and $1,200 to expense) requires more understanding and alertness from company personnel than if the entry were identical with the other 51 payroll entries made during the year.

By making a ***reversing entry*** as of the first day of the new accounting period, we can simplify the recording of routine transactions and avoid the need for the company's accounting staff to refer to prior adjusting entries for guidance. The reversing entry for the $1,800 year-end accrual of salaries would be dated January 1, Year 2, and would probably be made under the direction of the accountant responsible for the year-end closing of the accounts and preparation of financial statements. The entry would be as follows:

Reversing entry makes possible . . .

Jan. 1 Salaries Payable *1,800*
        Salaries Expense *1,800*
        To reverse the accrual of salaries made on Dec. 31, Year 1.

This reversing entry closes the Salaries Payable account by transferring the $1,800 liability to the credit side of the Salaries Expense account. Thus, the Salaries Expense account begins the new year with an abnormal credit balance of $1,800. On Friday, January 2, the normal payroll entry for $3,000 will be made to the same accounts as on every other Friday during the year.

. . . regular payroll entry for first payday of new year

Jan. 2 Salaries Expense *3,000*
        Cash *3,000*
        Paid salaries for week ended Jan. 2, Year 2.

After this January 2 entry has been posted, the ledger account for Salaries Expense will show a debit balance of $1,200, the result of this $3,000 debit and the $1,800 credit from the reversing entry on January 1. The amount of $1,200 is the correct expense for the two workdays of the new year at $600 a day. The results, of course, are ***exactly the same*** as if no reversing entry had been used and the company's accounting personnel had split the debit side of the January 2 payroll entry between Salaries Payable and Salaries Expense.

The ledger accounts for Salaries Expense and for Salaries Payable illustrate the effects of posting the adjusting entry and the reversing entry.

Salaries Expense			Debit	Credit	Balance
Year 1					
Various	*(51 weekly entries*				
	of $3,000)				153000
Dec. 31	*Adjusting entry*				
	(3 days @$600)		1800		154800
31	*To close at year-*				
	end			154800	— 0 —
Year 2					
Jan. 1	*Reversing entry*			1800	1800 cr
2	*Weekly payroll*		3000		1200

Salaries Payable			Debit	Credit	Balance
Year 1					
Dec. 31	Adjusting entry				
	(3 days @ $600)			1800	1800
Year 2					
Jan. 1	Reversing entry		1800		-0-

Which Adjusting Entries Should Be Reversed? Even when a company follows a policy of making reversing entries, *not all adjusting entries should be reversed.* Only those adjustments which *create an account receivable or a short-term liability* should be reversed. These adjustments will be followed by cash receipts or cash payments within the near future. Reversing these adjusting entries will enable the company's personnel to record the upcoming cash transactions in a routine manner.

An adjusting entry which apportions an amount recorded in the past *should not be reversed.* Thus we do *not* reverse the adjusting entries which apportion recorded costs (such as depreciation) or which record the earning of revenue collected in advance.

In summary, reversing entries may be made for those adjusting entries which record *unrecorded expenses* or *unrecorded revenue.* Reversing entries are *not* made for adjustments which apportion recorded costs or recorded revenue.

Reversing Entries in a Computer-Based System Reversing entries do not require any analysis of transactions. Rather, they merely involve reversing the debit and credit amounts of specific adjusting entries. The adjusting entries to be reversed can be identified by a simple rule—namely, reverse those adjustments which increase accounts receivable or short-term liabilities. Thus, a computer may be programmed to prepare reversing entries automatically.

Finally, remember that reversing entries are *optional.* They are intended to simplify the accounting process, but they are *not essential* in the application of generally accepted accounting principles or in the preparation of financial statements.

END-OF-CHAPTER REVIEW

SUMMARY OF CHAPTER LEARNING OBJECTIVES

1 **State the purpose of adjusting entries and explain how these entries relate to the concepts of accrual accounting.**
The purpose of adjusting entries is to record certain revenue and expenses that are not properly measured in the course of recording daily business transactions. Adjusting entries help to achieve the basic goals of accrual accounting—recognizing revenue when it is earned and recognizing expenses when the goods or services are used.

2 Describe the four basic types of adjusting entries; prepare these entries.

The four basic types of adjusting entries are entries to: (1) apportion recorded costs (debit expense, credit either an asset or contra-asset account); (2) apportion unearned revenue (debit unearned revenue, which is a liability account, and credit revenue); (3) record unrecorded expenses (debit expense, credit a liability); and (4) record unrecorded revenue (debit a receivable, credit revenue).

3 Explain the concept of materiality.

The concept of materiality allows accountants to use estimated amounts and even to ignore other accounting principles if these actions will not have a "material" effect upon financial statements. A "material" effect is one that might reasonably be expected to influence the decisions made by users of financial statements. Thus, accountants may account for *immaterial* items and events in the easiest and most convenient manner.

4 Prepare a work sheet and explain its usefulness.

A work sheet is a "testing ground" on which the ledger accounts are adjusted, balanced, and arranged in the format of financial statements. A work sheet consists of a trial balance, the end-of-period adjusting entries, an adjusted trial balance, and columns showing the ledger accounts arranged as an income statement and as a balance sheet. The completed work sheet is used as the basis for preparing financial statements and for recording adjusting and closing entries in the formal accounting records.

5 Describe the sequence of steps in the accounting cycle when a work sheet is prepared.

When a work sheet is prepared, the steps in the accounting cycle may be summarized as follows: (1) journalize transactions, (2) post to ledger accounts, (3) prepare a work sheet, (4) prepare financial statements, (5) adjust and close the accounts, and (6) prepare an after-closing trial balance.

*6 Explain when and why reversing entries may be used.

Reversing entries are an optional procedure which may be applied at the beginning of a new accounting period to simplify the recording of routine cash receipts and payments. When reversing entries are used, they should be made to "reverse" any adjusting entry that created an account receivable or a short-term liability. In short, for any adjusting entry that accrues either revenue or expense.

In Chapter 4 we have completed our study of the accounting cycle for a service-type business and have completed our continuing illustrated example of Roberts Real Estate Company. In Chapter 5 we will extend these concepts by focusing on some additional steps needed to account for the *inventories* which fill the sales counters and storerooms of a wholesale or retail merchandising business.

---

*   *Supplemental Topic, "Reversing Entries"*

KEY TERMS INTRODUCED OR EMPHASIZED IN CHAPTER 4

Accounting cycle   The sequence of accounting procedures performed during an accounting period. The procedures include journalizing transactions, posting, preparation of a work sheet and financial statements, adjusting and closing the accounts, and preparation of an after-closing trial balance.

Accrued expenses   Expenses such as salaries of employees and interest on notes payable which have been accumulating day-by-day but are unrecorded and unpaid at the end of the period. Also called *unrecorded expenses.*

Accrued revenue   Revenue which has been earned during the accounting period but has not been recorded or collected prior to the closing date. Also called *unrecorded revenue.*

Adjusting entries   Entries required at the end of the period to update the accounts before financial statements are prepared. Adjusting entries serve to apportion transactions properly between the accounting periods affected and to record any revenue earned or expenses incurred which have not been recorded prior to the end of the period.

Book value   The net amount at which an asset is shown in accounting records. For depreciable assets, book value equals cost minus accumulated depreciation. Also called *carrying value.*

Carrying value   See book value.

Deferred revenue   See unearned revenue.

Interim statements   Financial statements prepared at intervals of less than one year. Usually quarterly and monthly statements.

Materiality   The relative importance of an amount or item. An item which is not significant enough to influence the decisions of users of financial statements is considered *immaterial.* The accounting treatment of immaterial items may be guided by convenience rather than by theoretical principles.

Prepaid expenses   Advance payments for such expenses as rent and insurance. The portion which has not been used up at the end of the accounting period is included in the balance sheet as an asset.

Promissory note   A formal written promise to repay an amount borrowed plus interest at a future date.

Reversing entries   An optional year-end procedure consisting of the reversal on the first day of the new accounting period of those year-end adjusting entries which accrue expenses or revenue and thus will be followed by later cash payments or receipts. Purpose is to permit company personnel to record routine transactions in a standard manner without referring to prior adjusting entries.

Unearned revenue   An obligation to render services or deliver goods in the future because of receipt of advance payment. Also called *deferred revenue.*

Unrecorded expenses   See accrued expenses.

Unrecorded revenue   See accrued revenue.

Work sheet   A large columnar sheet designed to arrange in convenient form all the accounting data required at the end of the period. Facilitates preparation of financial statements and the work of adjusting and closing the accounts.

DEMONSTRATION PROBLEM FOR YOUR REVIEW

Reed Geophysical Company adjusts and closes its accounts at the end of the calendar year. At December 31, 19__, the balances in the ledger accounts **prior to making adjusting entries** were as follows:

REED GEOPHYSICAL COMPANY
Trial Balance
December 31, 19__

Cash...	$ 12,540	
Prepaid office rent...................................	3,300	
Prepaid dues and subscriptions.......................	960	
Supplies	1,300	
Equipment	20,000	
Accumulated depreciation: equipment.................		$ 1,200
Notes payable..		5,000
Unearned consulting fees.............................		35,650
Glen Reed, capital...................................		17,040
Glen Reed, drawing	27,000	
Consulting fees earned...............................		90,860
Salaries expense.....................................	66,900	
Telephone expense...................................	2,550	
Rent expense	11,000	
Miscellaneous expenses..............................	4,200	
	$149,750	$149,750

OTHER DATA

a For the first 11 months of the year, office rent had been charged to the Rent Expense account at a rate of $1,000 per month. On December 1, however, the company signed a new rental agreement and paid three months' rent in advance at a rate of $1,100 per month. This advance payment was debited to the Prepaid Rent account.

b Dues and subscriptions expired during the year in the total amount of $710.

c An estimate of supplies on hand was made at December 31; the estimated cost of the unused supplies was $450.

d The useful life of the equipment has been estimated at 10 years from date of acquisition. No depreciation expense has been recorded for the current year.

e Accrued interest on notes payable amounted to $100 at year-end. (Set up accounts for Interest Expense and for Interest Payable.)

f Consulting services valued at $32,550 were rendered during the year for clients who had made payment in advance.

g It is the custom of the firm to bill clients only when consulting work is completed or, in the case of prolonged engagements, at six-month intervals. At December 31, engineering services valued at $3,000 had been rendered to clients but not yet billed. No advance payments had been received from these clients.

h Salaries earned by employees but not yet paid amounted to $2,200 at December 31.

INSTRUCTIONS   Prepare a work sheet for the year ended December 31, 19__.

SOLUTION TO DEMONSTRATION PROBLEM

REED GEOPHYSICAL COMPANY
Work Sheet
For the Year Ended December 31, 19___

	Trial Balance Dr	Trial Balance Cr	Adjustments* Dr	Adjustments* Cr	Adjusted Trial Balance Dr	Adjusted Trial Balance Cr	Income Statement Dr	Income Statement Cr	Balance Sheet Dr	Balance Sheet Cr
Balance sheet accounts:										
Cash	12,540				12,540				12,540	
Prepaid office rent	3,300			(a) 1,100	2,200				2,200	
Prepaid dues and subscriptions	960			(b) 710	250				250	
Supplies	1,300			(c) 850	450				450	
Equipment	20,000				20,000				20,000	
Accumulated depreciation: equipment		1,200		(d) 2,000		3,200				3,200
Notes payable		5,000				5,000				5,000
Unearned consulting fees		35,650	(f) 32,550			3,100				3,100
Glen Reed, capital		17,040				17,040				17,040
Glen Reed, drawing	27,000				27,000				27,000	
Interest payable				(e) 100		100				100
Consulting fees receivable			(g) 3,000		3,000				3,000	
Salaries payable				(h) 2,200		2,200				2,200
Income statement accounts:										
Consulting fees earned		90,860		(f) 32,550 / (g) 3,000		126,410		126,410		
Salaries expense	66,900		(h) 2,200		69,100		69,100			
Telephone expense	2,550				2,550		2,550			
Rent expense	11,000		(a) 1,100		12,100		12,100			
Miscellaneous expense	4,200				4,200		4,200			
	149,750	149,750								
Dues and subscriptions expense			(b) 710		710		710			
Supplies expense			(c) 850		850		850			
Depreciation expense: equipment			(d) 2,000		2,000		2,000			
Interest expense			(e) 100		100		100			
			42,510	42,510	157,050	157,050	91,610	126,410	65,440	30,640
Net income							34,800			34,800
							126,410	126,410	65,440	65,440

* Adjustments:
(a) Rent expense for December.
(b) Dues and subscriptions expense for year.
(c) Supplies used for year ($1,300 − $450 = $850).
(d) Depreciation expense for year ($20,000 ÷ 10 = $2,000).
(e) Accrued interest on notes payable.
(f) Consulting services performed for clients who paid in advance.
(g) Services rendered but not billed.
(h) Salaries earned but not paid.

SELF-TEST QUESTIONS

Answers to these questions appear on page 215.

1 The purpose of adjusting entries is to:

   a Adjust the owner's capital account for the revenue, expense, and withdrawal transactions which occurred during the year.

   b Adjust daily the balances in asset, liability, revenue, and expense accounts for the effects of business transactions.

   c Apply the realization principle and the matching principle to transactions affecting two or more accounting periods.

   d Prepare revenue and expense accounts for recording the transactions of the next accounting period.

2 Before month-end adjustments are made, the January 31 trial balance of Rover Excursions contains revenue of $9,300 and expenses of $5,780. Adjustments are necessary for the following items:
   —portion of prepaid rent applicable to January, $900
   —depreciation for January, $480
   —portion of fees collected in advance earned in January, $1,100
   —fees earned in January not yet billed to customers, $650

   Net income in Rover Excursions' January income statement is:

   a $3,520   b $5,690   c $2,590   d Some other amount

3 The CPA firm auditing Tucker's Studio found that owner's equity was understated and liabilities were overstated. Which of the following errors could have been the cause?

   a Making the adjustment entry for depreciation expense twice.

   b Failure to record interest accrued on a note payable.

   c Failure to make the adjusting entry to record revenue which had been earned but not yet billed to customers.

   d Failure to record the earned portion of fees received in advance.

4 The concept of **materiality:** (Indicate all correct answers)

   a Requires that financial statements are accurate to the nearest dollar but need not show cents.

   b Is based upon what users of financial statements are thought to consider important.

   c Permits accountants to ignore other generally accepted accounting principles in certain situations.

   d Permits accountants to use the easiest and most convenient means of accounting for events that are **immaterial.**

5 When a work sheet is prepared at year-end:

   a Revenue and expense accounts do not have to be closed to the Income Summary account because the income statement is prepared from the work sheet and net income is already computed.

   b Adjusting entries must be journalized and posted, even though the Adjustments column is properly completed.

   c The amount of net income appears as a credit in the Income Statement column of the worksheet when revenue exceeds total expenses.

   d The Income Statement columns and Balance Sheet columns of the work sheet eliminate the need to prepare formal financial statements.

*6 On December 31, Elite Property Management made an adjusting entry to record $300 management fees earned but not yet billed to Marge Carson, a client. This entry was reversed on January 1. On January 15, Carson paid Elite $1,200, of which $900 was applicable to the period January 1 through January 15. The journal entry made by Elite to record receipt of the $1,200 on January 15 includes:

   a A credit to Management Fees Earned of $1,200.

   b A credit to Accounts Receivable of $300.

   c A debit to Management Fees Earned of $300.

   d A credit to Management Fees Earned of $900.

ASSIGNMENT MATERIAL

DISCUSSION QUESTIONS

1 What is the purpose of making adjusting entries? Your answer should relate adjusting entries to the goals of accrual accounting.

2 Do all transactions involving revenue or expenses require adjusting entries at the end of the accounting period? If not, what is the distinguishing characteristic of those transactions which do require adjusting entries?

3 Do adjusting entries affect income statement accounts, balance sheet accounts, or both? Explain.

4 Why does the recording of adjusting entries require a better understanding of the concepts of accrual accounting than does the recording of routine revenue and expense transactions occurring throughout the period?

5 Why does the purchase of a one-year insurance policy four months ago give rise to insurance expense in the current month?

6 If services have been rendered to customers during the current accounting period but no revenue has been recorded and no bill has been sent to the customers, why is an adjusting entry needed? What types of accounts should be debited and credited by this entry?

7 What is meant by the term **unearned revenue?** Where should an unearned revenue account appear in the financial statements? As the work is done, what happens to the balance of an unearned revenue account?

8 The weekly payroll for employees of Ryan Company, who work a five-day week, amounts to $20,000. All employees are paid up-to-date at the close of business each Friday. If December 31 falls on Thursday, what year-end adjusting entry is needed

9 The Marvin Company purchased a one-year fire insurance policy on August 1 and debited the entire cost of $3,600 to Unexpired Insurance. The accounts were not adjusted or closed until the end of the year. Give the adjusting entry at December 31.

10 At year-end the adjusting entry to reduce the Unexpired Insurance account by the amount of insurance premium applicable to the current period was accidentally omitted. Which items in the income statement will be in error? Will these

---

* *Supplemental Topic, "Reversing Entries"*

items be overstated or understated? Which items in the balance sheet will be in error? Will they be overstated or understated?

11 Briefly explain the concept of **materiality.** If an item is not material, how is the item treated for financial reporting purposes?

12 In Chapter 1, assets were defined as economic resources owned by a business and expected to benefit future business operations. By this definition, the gasoline in the tank of a business automobile, unused typewriter ribbons, and even ballpoint pens are actually "assets." Why, then, are purchases of such items routinely charged directly to expense?

13 What is the purpose of a work sheet?

14 In performing the regular end-of-period accounting procedures, does the preparation of the work sheet precede or follow the posting of adjusting entries to ledger accounts? Why?

15 Assume that when the Income Statement columns of a work sheet are first totaled, the total of the debit column exceeds the total of the credit column by $60,000. Explain how the amount of net income (or net loss) should be entered in the work sheet columns.

16 Does the ending balance of the owner's capital account appear in the work sheet? Explain.

17 Can each step in the preparation of a work sheet be performed automatically in a computer-based accounting system? Explain.

18 List in order the procedures comprising the accounting cycle when a work sheet is used.

19 Is a work sheet ever prepared when there is no intention of closing the accounts?

*20 The weekly payroll of Stevens Company, which has a five-day work week, amounts to $15,000 and employees are paid up to date every Friday. On January 1 of the current year, the Salaries Expense account showed a credit balance of $9,000. Explain the nature of the accounting entry or entries which probably led to this balance.

*21 Four general types of adjusting entries were discussed in this chapter. If reversing entries are made, which of these types of adjusting entries should be reversed? Why?

EXERCISES

EXERCISE 4-1
Accounting
Terminology

Listed below are nine technical accounting terms used in this chapter:

Unrecorded revenue	*Adjusting entries*	*Accrued expenses*
Work sheet	**Reversing entries*	*Book value*
Unearned revenue	*Materiality*	*Prepaid expenses*

Each of the following statements may (or may not) describe one of these technical terms. For each statement, indicate the accounting term described, or answer "None" if the statement does not correctly describe any of the terms.

a   The net amount at which an asset is carried in the accounting records as distinguished from its market value.

_____

*   *Supplemental Topic, "Reversing Entries"*

b An accounting concept that may justify departure from other accounting principles for purposes of convenience and economy.

c A device for organizing all the data needed at the end of the period to prepare financial statements and to make entries to adjust and close the accounts.

d Revenue earned during the current accounting period but not yet recorded or billed, which requires an adjusting entry at the end of the period.

e Entries made at the end of the period to achieve the goals of accrual accounting by recording revenue when it is earned and by recording expenses when the related goods and services are used.

f A type of account credited when customers pay in advance for services to be rendered in the future.

g A balance sheet category used for reporting advance payments of such items as insurance, rent, and office supplies.

h Entries made during the accounting period to correct errors in the original recording of complex transactions.

EXERCISE 4-2
Effects of Adjusting Entries

Security Service Company adjusts and closes its accounts at the end of the month. On November 30, adjusting entries are prepared to record:

a Depreciation expense for November.

b Interest expense that has accrued during November.

c Revenue earned during November which has not yet been billed to customers.

d Salaries payable to company employees which have accrued since the last pay-day in November.

e The portion of the company's prepaid insurance which has expired during November.

f Earning a portion of the amount collected in advance from a customer, Harbor Restaurant.

INSTRUCTIONS

Indicate the effect of each of these adjusting entries upon the major elements of the company's financial statements—that is, upon revenue, expenses, net income, assets, liabilities, and owner's equity. Organize your answer in tabular form, using the column headings shown below and the symbols **I** for increase, **D** for decrease, and **NE** for no effect. The answer for adjusting entry **a** is provided as an example.

	Income Statement			Balance Sheet		
Adjusting Entry	Revenue	− Expenses	= Net Income	Assets	= Liabilities +	Owner's Equity
a	NE	I	D	D	NE	D

EXERCISE 4-3
Preparing Adjusting Entries for Recorded Costs and Recorded Revenue

The Outlaws, a professional football team, prepare financial statements on a monthly basis. Football season begins in August, but in July the team engaged in the following transactions:

a Paid $1,500,000 to Dodge City as advance rent for use of Dodge City Stadium for the five-month period from August 1 through December 31. This payment was debited to the asset account, Prepaid Rent.

b Collected $2,560,000 cash from sales of season tickets for the team's eight home games. This amount was credited to Unearned Ticket Revenue.

During the month of August, The Outlaws played one home game and two games on the road. Their record was two wins, one loss.

INSTRUCTIONS

Prepare the two adjusting entries required at August 31 to apportion this recorded cost and recorded revenue.

EXERCISE 4-4
Preparing Adjusting Entries for Unrecorded Revenue and Expenses

The law firm of Dale & Clark prepares its financial statements on an annual basis at December 31. Among the situations requiring year-end adjusting entries were the following:

a   Salaries to staff attorneys are paid on the fifteenth day of each month. Salaries accrued since December 15 amount to $17,800 and have not yet been recorded.

b   The firm is defending J. R. Stone in a civil lawsuit. The agreed-upon legal fees are $2,100 per day while the trial is in progress. The trial has been in progress for nine days during December and is not expected to end until late January. No legal fees have yet been billed to Stone. (Legal fees are recorded in an account entitled Legal Fees Earned.)

INSTRUCTIONS   Prepare the two adjusting entries required at December 31 to record the accrued salaries expense and the accrued legal fees revenue.

EXERCISE 4-5
Get Your Tickets Early

When **TransWorld Airlines (TWA)** sells tickets for future flights, it debits cash and credits an account entitled Advance Ticket Sales. With respect to this Advance Ticket Sales account:

a   What does the balance of the account represent? Where should the account appear in TWA's financial statements?

b   Explain the activity that normally **reduces** the balance of this account. Can you think of any **other** transaction that would reduce this account?

EXERCISE 4-6
Preparing Various Adjusting Entries

Hill Corporation adjusts and closes its accounts at the end of the calendar year. Prepare the adjusting entries required at December 31 based on the following information. (Not all of these items may require adjusting entries.)

a   A bank loan had been obtained on September 1. Accrued interest on the loan at December 31 amounts to $4,800. No interest expense has yet been recorded.

b   Depreciation of office equipment is based on an estimated life of five years. The balance in the Office Equipment account is $25,000; no change has occurred in the account during the year.

c   Interest receivable on United States government bonds owned at December 31 amounts to $2,300. This accrued interest revenue has not been recorded.

d   On December 31, an agreement was signed to lease a truck for 12 months beginning January 1 at a rate of 35 cents a mile. Usage is expected to be 2,000 miles per month and the contract specifies a minimum payment equivalent to 18,000 miles a year.

e   The company's policy is to pay all employees up-to-date each Friday. Since December 31 fell on Monday, there was a liability to employees at December 31 for one day's pay amounting to $2,800.

EXERCISE 4-7
Adjusting Entry and Subsequent Business Transaction

On Friday of each week, Regis Products, Inc., pays its sales personnel weekly salaries amounting to $60,000 for a five-day work week.

a   Draft the necessary adjusting entry at year-end, assuming that December 31 falls on Wednesday.

b   Also draft the journal entry for the payment by Regis Company of a week's salaries to its sales personnel on Friday, January 2, the first payday of the new year. (Assume that the company does not use reversing entries.)

EXERCISE 4-8
Notes Payable and Interest

Venture Company adjusts and closes its accounts on December 31. On November 30, 1994, Venture Company signed a note payable and borrowed $12,000 from a bank for a period of six months at an annual interest rate of 10%.

a   How much is the total interest expense over the life of the note? How much is the monthly interest expense? (Assume equal amounts of interest expense each month.)

b In the company's annual balance sheet at December 31, 1994, what is the amount of the liability to the bank?

c Prepare the journal entry to record issuance of the note payable on November 30, 1994.

d Prepare the adjusting entry to accrue interest on the note at December 31, 1994.

e Assume the company prepared a balance sheet at March 31, 1995. State the amount of the liability to the bank at this date.

EXERCISE 4-9
Relationship of Adjusting Entries to Business Transactions

Among the ledger accounts used by Glenwood Speedway are the following: Prepaid Rent, Rent Expense, Unearned Admissions Revenue, Admissions Revenue, Prepaid Printing, Printing Expense, Concessions Receivable, and Concessions Revenue. For each of the following items, write first the journal entry (if one is needed) to record the external transaction and second the adjusting entry, if any, required on May 31, the end of the fiscal year.

a On May 1, borrowed $300,000 cash from National Bank by issuing a 12% note payable due in three months.

b On May 1, paid rent for six months beginning May 1 at $30,000 per month.

c On May 2, sold season tickets for a total of $910,000 cash. The season includes 70 racing days: 20 in May, 25 in June, and 25 in July.

d On May 4, an agreement was reached with Snack-Bars, Inc., allowing that company to sell refreshments at the track in return for 10% of the gross receipts from refreshment sales.

e On May 6, schedules for the 20 racing days in May and the first 10 racing days in June were printed and paid for at a cost of $12,000.

f On May 31, Snack-Bars, Inc., reported that the gross receipts from refreshment sales in May had been $165,000 and that the 10% owed to Glenwood Speedway would be remitted on June 10.

EXERCISE 4-10
Concept of Materiality

The concept of materiality is a generally accepted accounting principle.

a Briefly explain the concept of materiality.

b Is $2,500 a "material" dollar amount? Explain.

c Describe two ways in which the concept of materiality may save accountants' time and effort in making adjusting entries.

EXERCISE 4-11
Materiality: a Specific Application at Year-End

The income statement of **Southwest Airlines Company** for a recent year is reproduced below. Assume you learn that $100,000 of the fuel and oil charged to expense in 1989 actually had been on hand in the company's storage tanks at year-end. Would you consider this to be a "material" error in the company's financial statements? Explain fully.

SOUTHWEST AIRLINES COMPANY
Consolidated Statement of Income
For the Year Ended December 31, 1989
(In thousands)

Operating revenues:	
Passenger	$ 973,568
Freight	18,771
Other	22,713
Total operating revenues	$1,015,052
Operating expenses:	
Salaries, wages, and benefits	$ 301,066
Fuel and oil	163,579
Maintenance and repairs	73,842
Agency commissions	61,362
Aircraft rentals	21,636
Landing fees and other rentals	51,902
Depreciation	72,343
Other operating expenses	164,696
Total operating expenses	$ 917,426
Operating income	$ 97,626
Other expenses (income):	
Interest expense (net of amounts capitalized)	$ 23,269
Interest income	(16,637)
Nonoperating gains, net	(19,988)
Total other expenses (income)	$ (13,356)
Income before income taxes	$ 110,982
Provision for income taxes	39,424
Net income	$ 71,558

EXERCISE 4-12
Adjusting Entries—A Working Backwards Exercise

Shown below are the Trial Balance and Adjusted Trial Balance columns of the work sheet prepared for Fisher Insurance Agency for the month ended November 30, 1994.

	Trial Balance Dr	Trial Balance Cr	Adjusted Trial Balance Dr	Adjusted Trial Balance Cr
Balance sheet accounts:				
Cash...	$ 4,980		$ 4,980	
Commissions receivable..........................	3,000		3,850	
Office supplies	600		240	
Office equipment	6,600		6,600	
Accumulated depreciation: office equipment.........		$2,420		$ 2,530
Accounts payable		1,660		1,660
Salaries payable.................................				550
Unearned commissions...........................		400		190
Pat Fisher, capital		12,300		12,300
Pat Fisher, drawing.............................	1,000		1,000	
Income statement accounts:				
Commissions earned		6,900		7,960
Salaries expense	6,000		6,550	
Rent expense	1,500		1,500	
Office supplies expense			360	
Depreciation expense: office equipment			110	
	$23,680	$23,680	$25,190	$25,190

INSTRUCTIONS

By comparing the two trial balances shown above, it is possible to determine which accounts have been adjusted. You are to prepare the adjusting journal entries which must have been made to cause these changes in account balances. Include an explanation as part of each adjusting entry.

EXERCISE 4-13
Preparing Financial Statements from a Work Sheet

From the adjusted trial balance columns of the work sheet shown in Exercise 4-12, prepare an income statement and a statement of owner's equity for Fisher Insurance Agency for the month ended November 30, 1994, and also a balance sheet (in report form) at November 30.

EXERCISE 4-14
The Accounting Cycle with a Work Sheet

Listed below in random order are the steps comprising the accounting cycle when a work sheet is prepared:

a Prepare the work sheet.

b Prepare an after-closing trial balance.

c Journalize and post the adjusting and closing entries.

d Prepare financial statements and appropriate disclosures.

e Post transaction data to the ledger.

f Journalize transactions.

INSTRUCTIONS

a List these six steps in the logical sequence in which they would be performed.

b Indicate which of these steps are mechanical functions that can be performed by machine in a computerized accounting system and which require the judgment of people familiar with accounting principles and concepts. (In some cases, human judgment may be required to complete only a *portion* of the step. If so, explain.)

*EXERCISE 4-15
Preparing
Reversing
Entries

Blue Company closes its accounts at the end of each calendar year. The company operates on a five-day work week and pays its employees up to date each Friday. The weekly payroll is regularly $10,000. On Thursday, December 31, 1994, an adjusting entry was made to accrue $8,000 salaries expense for the four days worked since the last payday. The company *did not* make a reversing entry. On Friday, January 1, 1995, the regular weekly payroll of $10,000 was paid and recorded by the usual entry debiting Salaries Expense $10,000 and crediting Cash $10,000.

Were Blue Company's accounting records correct for the year 1994? For 1995? Explain two alternatives the company might have followed with respect to payroll at year-end. One of the alternatives should include a reversing entry.

EXERCISE 4-16
Accounting
Principles

For each of the situations described below, indicate the generally accepted accounting principle that is being *violated.* Choose from the following principles:

Matching   *Materiality*

Cost   *Realization*

Objectivity   *Adequate disclosure*

If you do not believe that the practice violates any of these principles, answer "None," and explain.

a The financial statements include no mention of a large lawsuit filed against the company, because the suit has not been settled as of year-end.

b The bookkeeper of a large metropolitan auto dealership depreciates the $7.20 cost of metal wastebaskets over a period of 10 years.

c A small commuter airline recognizes no depreciation expense on its aircraft because the planes are maintained in "as good as new" condition.

d Palm Beach Hotel recognizes room rental revenue on the date that a reservation is received. For the winter season, many guests make reservations as much as a year in advance.

PROBLEMS

Group A

PROBLEM 4A-1
Preparing
Adjusting
Entries

Alta Sequoia Resort adjusts and closes its accounts *once a year* on December 31. Most guests of the resort pay at the time they check out, and the amounts collected are credited to Rental Revenue. A few guests pay in advance for rooms, and these amounts are credited to Unearned Rental Revenue at the time of receipt. The following information is available as a source for preparing adjusting entries at December 31.

a Salaries earned by employees but not yet recorded or paid amount to $7,900.

b As of December 31, Alta Sequioa has earned $11,075 rental revenue from current guests who will not be billed until they are ready to check out. (Debit Rent Receivable.)

c On November 1, a suite of rooms was rented to a corporation for six months at a monthly rental of $3,200. The entire six months' rent of $19,200 was collected

---

*   *Supplemental Topic, "Reversing Entries"*

in advance and credited to Unearned Rental Revenue. At December 31, two months' rent is considered to be earned; the remainder is for the first four months of the following year.

d A limousine to carry guests to and from the airport had been rented beginning December 19 from Transport Rentals, Inc., at a daily rate of $120. No rental payment has yet been made. (The limousine has been rented for 13 days in December.)

e A six-month loan in the amount of $30,000 had been obtained on December 1. Interest is to be computed at a rate of 15% per year and is payable when the loan is due. No interest has been paid and no interest expense has been recorded.

f Depreciation on the resort's buildings is based upon an estimated useful life of 30 years. The original cost of the buildings was $1,755,000.

g In December, Alta Sequioa Resort entered into an agreement to host the annual symposium of ACE (Americans for a Clean Environment) in April of next year. The resort expects to earn rental revenue of at least $45,000.

h A one-year fire insurance policy had been purchased on September 1. The premium of $7,200 for the entire life of the policy had been paid on September 1 and recorded as Unexpired Insurance.

INSTRUCTIONS For each of the above lettered paragraphs, draft a separate adjusting journal entry (including explanation) if the information indicates that an adjusting entry is needed. One or more of the above paragraphs may not require any adjusting entry.

**PROBLEM 4A-2
Preparing Adjusting Entries from a Trial Balance** On April 1, 1994, Pat Hamilton, an attorney, opened her own legal practice, to be known as the Law Office of Pat Hamilton. The business adjusts and closes its accounts at the end of each month. The following trial balance was prepared at April 30, 1994, *after one month* of operations:

**LAW OFFICE OF PAT HAMILTON
Trial Balance
April 30, 1994**

Cash	$10,060	
Legal fees receivable	—0—	
Unexpired insurance	3,000	
Prepaid office rent	4,800	
Office supplies	1,460	
Office equipment	26,400	
Accumulated depreciation: office equipment		$—0—
Notes payable		16,000
Interest payable		—0—
Salaries payable		—0—
Unearned retainer fees		15,020
Pat Hamilton, capital		20,000
Pat Hamilton, drawing	3,000	
Legal fees earned		1,580
Salaries expense	2,680	
Miscellaneous expense	1,200	
Office rent expense	—0—	
Office supplies expense	—0—	
Depreciation expense: office equipment	—0—	
Interest expense	—0—	
Insurance expense	—0—	
	$52,600	$52,600

OTHER DATA

a No interest has yet been paid on the note payable. Accrued interest at April 30 amounts to $200.

b Salaries earned by the office staff but not yet recorded or paid amounted tc $970 at April 30.

c Many clients are asked to make an advance payment for the legal services to be rendered in future months. These advance payments are credited to the Un-earned Retainer Fees account. During April, $4,700 of these advances were earned by the business.

d Some clients are not billed until all services relating to their matter have been rendered. As of April 30, services priced at $2,780 had been rendered to these clients but had not yet been recorded in the accounting records.

e A professional liability insurance policy was purchased on April 1. The pre-mium of $3,000 for the first six months was paid and recorded as Unexpired Insurance.

f The business rents an office at a monthly rate of $1,600. On April 1, three months' rent was paid in advance and charged to the Prepaid Rent account.

g Office supplies on hand at April 30 amounted to $800.

h The office equipment was purchased on April 1 and is being depreciated over an estimated useful life of 10 years.

INSTRUCTIONS

a Prepare the adjusting entries required at April 30.

b Determine the amount of **revenue** that should appear in the company's income statement for the month ended April 30.

**PROBLEM 4A-3
Analysis of
Adjusted Data;
Preparing Ad-
justing Entries**

Sea Cat, Inc., operates a large catamaran which takes tourists at several island resorts on diving and sailing excursions. The company adjusts and closes its ac-counts at the end of each month. Selected account balances appearing on the June 30 **adjusted** trial balance are as follows:

Prepaid rent..	$ 6,000	
Unexpired insurance...	1,400	
Catamaran	46,200	
Accumulated depreciation: catamaran		$9,240
Unearned passenger revenue		825

OTHER DATA

a Six months' rent had been prepaid on June 1.

b The unexpired insurance is a 12-month fire insurance policy purchased on March 1.

c The catamaran is being depreciated over a 10-year estimated useful life, wizh no residual value.

d The unearned passenger revenue represents tickets good for future rides sold zo a resort hotel for $15 per ticket on June 1. During June, 145 of the tickets were used.

INSTRUCTIONS

a Determine

1 The monthly rent expense

2 The original cost of the 12-month fire insurance policy

3 The age of the catamaran in months

4 How many $15 tickets for future rides were sold to the resort hotel on June 1

b Prepare the adjusting entries which were made on June 30.

PROBLEM 4A-4
Format of a
Work Sheet

Shown below are the first 4 columns of the 10-column work sheet to be prepared for Geotechnical Testing Services for the month ended April 30, 1994.

GEOTECHNICAL TESTING SERVICES
Work Sheet
For the Month Ended April 30, 1994

	Trial Balance		Adjustments*	
	Dr	Cr	Dr	Cr
Balance sheet accounts:				
Cash....................................	3,700			
Accounts receivable	2,900			
Unexpired insurance......................	490			(a) 70
Supplies	1,460			(b) 560
Equipment	18,600			
Accumulated depreciation: equipment.......		2,480		(c) 310
Notes payable...........................		10,000		
Unearned revenue		1,200	(e) 400	
Max Benton, capital		14,190		
Max Benton, drawing	1,500			
Interest payable				(d) 80
Salaries payable..........................				(f) 500
Income statement accounts:				
Revenue from services		5,130		(e) 400
Rent expense	2,450			
Salaries expense	1,900		(f) 500	
	33,000	33,000		
Insurance expense			(a) 70	
Supplies expense			(b) 560	
Depreciation expense: equipment			(c) 310	
Interest expense..........................			(d) 80	
			1,920	1,920

* Adjustments
(a) Insurance expired for the month.
(b) Cost of supplies used, based on estimate of supplies at April 30.
(c) Depreciation expense on equipment.
(d) Interest accrued on notes payable at April 30.
(e) Advance payments by customers earned during April.
(f) Salaries earned by employees but not yet recorded or paid.

INSTRUCTIONS Prepare a 10-column work sheet utilizing the trial balance and adjustments shown above in the first 4 columns.

**PROBLEM 4A-5
Preparing a
Work Sheet**

Village Theater closes its accounts ***each month.*** At July 31, the trial balance and other information given below were available for adjusting and closing the accounts.

VILLAGE THEATER
Trial Balance
July 31, 19—

Cash..	$ 20,000	
Prepaid film rental...	31,200	
Land...	80,000	
Building...	168,000	
Accumulated depreciation: building		$ 10,500
Projection equipment	36,000	
Accumulated depreciation: projection equipment		3,000
Notes payable...		190,000
Accounts payable		4,400
Unearned admissions revenue (YMCA)		1,000
Li Trong, capital...		103,400
Li Trong, drawing	3,500	
Admissions revenue..		36,900
Salaries expense	8,700	
Light and power expense	1,800	
	$349,200	$349,200

OTHER DATA

a Film rental expense for July amounts to $21,050. However, the film rental expense for several months had been paid in advance.

b The building is being depreciated over a period of 20 years (240 months).

c The projection equipment is being depreciated over 5 years (60 months).

d At July 31, accrued interest payable on the note payable amounts to $1,650. No entry has yet been made to record interest expense for the month of July.

e Village Theater allows the local YMCA to bring children attending summer camp to the movies on any weekday afternoon for a fixed fee of $500 per month. On May 28, the YMCA made a $1,500 advance payment covering the months of June, July, and August.

f Village Theater receives a percentage of the revenue earned by Tastie Corporation, the concessionaire operating the snack bar. For snack bar sales in July, Tastie owes Village Theater $2,250, payable on August 10. No entry has yet been made to record this revenue. (Credit Concessions Revenue.)

g Salaries earned by employees but not recorded or paid as of July 31 amount to $1,500. No entry has yet been made to record this liability and expense.

INSTRUCTIONS

Prepare a 10-column work sheet utilizing the trial balance and adjusting data provided. Include at the bottom of the work sheet a brief explanation keyed to each adjusting entry.

PROBLEM 4A-6
Preparing a
Work Sheet,
Financial State-
ments, and
Adjusting and
Closing Entries

Island Hopper is an airline providing passenger and freight service among some Pacific islands. The accounts are adjusted and closed each month. At June 30 the trial balance shown below was prepared from the ledger.

ISLAND HOPPER
Trial Balance
June 30, 1994

Cash...	$ 23,600	
Accounts receivable	7,200	
Prepaid rent..	9,600	
Unexpired insurance..	21,000	
Aircraft	1,200,000	
Accumulated depreciation: aircraft		$ 380,000
Notes payable..		600,000
Unearned passenger revenue		60,000
Mary Earhart, capital		230,850
Mary Earhart, drawing	7,000	
Freight revenue		130,950
Fuel expense...	53,800	
Salaries expense	66,700	
Maintenance expense..	12,900	
	$1,401,800	$1,401,800

OTHER DATA

a The aircraft is being depreciated over a period of 10 years (120 months).

b The amount shown as unearned passenger revenue represents tickets sold to customers in advance of flights. During June, $38,650 of this amount was earned by the airline. (Credit Passenger Revenue.)

c Salaries earned by employees but not yet paid amount to $3,300 at June 30.

d Accrued interest on notes payable amounts to $5,000 at June 30 and has not yet been recorded.

e One of Island Hopper's regular customers is Pacific Trading Company. The airline keeps track of the weight of shipments carried for the trading company during the month and sends a bill shortly after month-end. No entry has yet been made to record $4,600 earned in June carrying freight for Pacific Trading Company.

f Three months' rent ($14,400) had been prepaid on May 1.

g On April 1, a 12-month insurance policy had been purchased for $25,200.

INSTRUCTIONS

a Prepare a work sheet for the month ended June 30, 1994.

b Prepare an income statement, a statement of owner's equity, and a balance sheet. Follow the format illustrated on pages 180 and 182.

c Prepare adjusting and closing journal entries.

*PROBLEM 4A-7
Reversing
Entries

Investor's Journal adjusts and closes its accounts at the end of each calendar year. The company works a five-day week and pays its employees up-to-date each Friday. The weekly salaries are $10,000 ($2,000 per day). Near year-end, the following events occurred relating to salaries:

---

*   *Supplemental Topic, "Reversing Entries"*

Dec. 26   (Friday) Recorded payment of regular weekly salaries of $10,000.

Dec. 31   (Wednesday) Prepared an adjusting entry for accrued salaries of $6,000.

Jan. 1   (Thursday) Made a reversing entry for accrued salaries.

Jan. 2   (Friday) Recorded payment of regular weekly salaries of $10,000.

INSTRUCTIONS   a   Prepare journal entries (with explanations) for the four events relating to salaries.

b   How much of the $10,000 in salaries paid on January 2 represents a January expense? Explain.

c   Assume that no reversing entry was made by the company; prepare the journal entry required to record the payment of salaries on January 2.

Group B

PROBLEM 4B-1
Preparing Adjusting Entries

Silver Spur Ranch, a dude ranch and resort, adjusts and closes its accounts ***once a year*** on December 31. Most guests of the ranch pay at the time they check out, and the amounts collected are credited to Rental Revenue. The following information is available as a source for preparing adjusting entries at December 31.

a   Among the assets owned by Silver Spur is an investment in government bonds in the face amount of $75,000. Accrued interest receivable on the bonds at December 31 was computed to be $2,250. None of the interest has yet been received. (Debit Interest Receivable.)

b   A 12-month bank loan in the amount of $90,000 had been obtained on November 1. Interest is to be computed at an annual rate of 12% and is payable when the loan becomes due. No interest has been paid and no interest expense has yet been recorded.

c   Depreciation on a station wagon owned by the ranch was based on a four-year life. The vehicle had been purchased new on September 1 of the current year at a cost of $25,200. Depreciation for 4 months should be recorded at December 31.

d   Management of the ranch signed an agreement on December 28 to lease a truck from Ace Motors for a period of 6 months beginning January 1 at a rate of 20 cents per mile, with a clause providing for a minimum monthly charge of $400.

e   Salaries earned by employees but not yet paid amounted to $9,900 at the end of the year.

f   As of December 31, Silver Spur has earned $12,500 rental revenue from current guests who will not be billed until they are ready to check out. (Debit Rent Receivable.)

g   A portion of land owned by Silver Spur had been leased on August 1 of the current year to a service station operator at a yearly rental rate of $18,000. Six months' rent was collected in advance at the date of the lease and credited to Unearned Rental Revenue.

h   A bus to carry guests to and from town and the airport had been rented early on December 10 at a daily rate of $50. No rental payment has been made, although Silver Spur has had use of the bus for 22 days in December.

INSTRUCTIONS   For each of the above lettered paragraphs, draft a separate adjusting journal entry (including explanation) if the information indicates that an adjusting entry is needed. One or more of the above paragraphs may not require any adjusting entry.

PROBLEM 4B-2
Preparing Adjusting Entries from a Trial Balance

Nick Charles operates a private investigating business called Nick Charles Investigations. Some clients are required to pay in advance for the company's services, while others are billed after the services have been rendered. Advance payments are credited to an account entitled Unearned Retainer Fees, which represents unearned revenue. The business adjusts and closes its accounts each month. At May 31, the trial balance appeared as follows:

NICK CHARLES INVESTIGATIONS
Trial Balance
May 31, 19__

Cash...	$ 17,150	
Fees receivable	37,800	
Unexpired insurance...................................	2,000	
Prepaid rent..	5,400	
Office supplies	1,050	
Office equipment	17,100	
Accumulated depreciation: office equipment........................		$ 5,700
Accounts payable		3,900
Unearned retainer fees		24,000
Nick Charles, capital..................................		48,600
Nick Charles, drawing	2,400	
Fees earned..		24,800
Telephone expense.....................................	1,200	
Travel expense	3,400	
Salaries expense	19,500	
	$107,000	$107,000

OTHER DATA

a The useful life of the office equipment was estimated at five years.

b Fees of $6,400 were earned during the month by performing services for clients who had paid in advance.

c Salaries earned by employees during the month but not yet recorded or paid amounted to $1,700.

d On May 1, the business moved into a new office and paid the first three months' rent in advance.

e Investigative services rendered during the month but not yet collected or billed to clients amounted to $2,900.

f Office supplies on hand May 31 amounted to $600.

g On April 1, $2,400 was paid as the premium for six months' liability insurance.

INSTRUCTIONS

a Prepare the adjusting entries required at May 31.

b Determine the amount of revenue that should appear in the company's income statement for the month ended May 31.

PROBLEM 4B-3
Making Use of a Completed Work Sheet

A 10-column work sheet for Reed Geophysical Company is illustrated on page 193.

INSTRUCTIONS
Using the information contained in that work sheet, prepare in journal entry form the adjusting and closing entries for Reed Geophysical Company at December 31, 19__.

PROBLEM 4B-4
Format of a
Work Sheet

Shown below are the first 4 columns of a 10-column work sheet to be prepared for Lakeside Executive Golf Course for the month ended October 31, 1994. The golf course operates on land rented from the city.

LAKESIDE EXECUTIVE GOLF COURSE
Work Sheet
For the Month Ended October 31, 1994

	Trial Balance		Adjustments*	
	Dr	Cr	Dr	Cr
Balance sheet accounts:				
Cash...........................	20,900			
Unexpired insurance.........................	7,200			(a) 800
Prepaid rent...............................	18,000			(b) 6,000
Equipment	24,000			
Accumulated depreciation: equipment.......		7,600		(c) 400
Notes payable.............................		10,000		
Unearned greens' fees revenue		6,400	(d) 2,200	
Walter Nelson, capital		38,200		
Walter Nelson, drawing	5,900			
Salaries payable............................				(e) 1,900
Interest payable				(f) 100
Income statement accounts:				
Greens' fees revenue........................		26,400		(d) 2,200
Salaries expense	8,600		(e) 1,900	
Water expense	1,200			
Advertising expense.........................	600			
Repairs and maintenance expense	1,500			
Miscellaneous expense	700			
	88,600	88,600		
Insurance expense			(a) 800	
Rent expense			(b) 6,000	
Depreciation expense: equipment			(c) 400	
Interest expense............................			(f) 100	
			11,400	11,400

* Adjustments
(a) Insurance expiring during October.
(b) Prepaid rent applicable to October.
(c) Depreciation for the month.
(d) Portion of revenue collected in advance but earned during October.
(e) Salaries owed to employees but unpaid as of month-end.
(f) Accrued interest on notes payable at October 31.

INSTRUCTIONS Prepare a 10-column work sheet utilizing the trial balance and adjustments shown above in the first 4 columns.

PROBLEM 4B-5
Preparing a
Work Sheet

O'Connell's Air Service operates several small airplanes providing passenger and freight service to small towns, oil fields, fishing lodges, and other remote locations in Alaska. The company adjusts and closes its accounts at the end of *each month.* At April 30, the following trial balance was prepared from the ledger:

O'CONNELL'S AIR SERVICE
Trial Balance
April 30, 19—

Cash	$ 22,750	
Accounts receivable	28,300	
Prepaid rent	8,100	
Unexpired insurance	36,900	
Airplanes	855,000	
Accumulated depreciation: airplanes		$ 232,750
Notes payable		450,000
Unearned passenger revenue		175,250
Maggie O'Connell, capital		171,750
Maggie O'Connell, drawing	7,750	
Freight revenue		54,250
Fuel expense	47,600	
Salaries expense	70,900	
Maintenance expense	6,700	
	$1,084,000	$1,084,000

OTHER DATA

a One of O'Connell's regular customers is Yukon Oil Company. The airline keeps track of the number of trips carrying freight for the oil company and sends a bill shortly after month-end. No entry has yet been made in the airline's accounting records to record $11,750 freight revenue earned in April from Yukon Oil Company.

b Three months' rent ($8,100) had been prepaid on April 1.

c On January 1, a 12-month insurance policy had been purchased for $49,200.

d O'Connell's depreciates its airplanes over a period of 15 years (180 months).

e Accrued interest on notes payable amounts to $4,500 at April 30 and has not yet been recorded.

f The amount shown as unearned passenger revenue represents the price of tickets sold to customers in advance of flights. During April, $94,750 of this amount was earned by the airline. (Credit Passenger Revenue.)

g Salaries earned by airline employees but not yet recorded or paid amount to $1,625 at April 30.

INSTRUCTIONS

Prepare a 10-column work sheet using the trial balance and adjusting data provided. Include at the bottom of the work sheet a brief explanation keyed to each adjusting entry.

PROBLEM 4B-6
A Comprehensive Work Sheet Problem

A trial balance and supplementary information needed for adjustments at September 30 are shown on the following page for Cinemax Stage & Theater. The company follows a policy of adjusting and closing its accounts at the *end of each month.*

CINEMAX STAGE & THEATER
Trial Balance
September 30, 1994

Cash..	$ 17,500	
Prepaid film rental...	65,000	
Land...	75,000	
Building...	210,000	
Accumulated depreciation: building		$ 6,125
Projection equipment	90,000	
Accumulated depreciation: projection equipment		7,500
Notes payable..		200,000
Accounts payable		8,500
Unearned admissions revenue		5,200
Helen James, capital		200,925
Helen James, drawing	10,500	
Admissions revenue..		63,750
Salaries expenses	21,250	
Light and power expense	7,750	
	$497,000	$497,000

OTHER DATA

a Film rental expense for the month is $42,275, all of which had been paid in advance.

b The building is being depreciated over a period of 20 years (240 months).

c The projection equipment is being depreciated over a period of 5 years (60 months).

d No entry has yet been made to record interest payable accrued during September. At September 30, accrued interest totals $1,800.

e When tickets are sold to future performances, Cinemax credits its Unearned Admissions Revenue account. No entry has yet been made recording that $3,650 of these advance ticket sales were for performances given during September.

f Cinemax receives a percentage of the revenue earned by Variety Corp., the concessionaire operating the snack bar. For snack bar sales in September, Variety Corp. owes Cinemax $6,200, payable on October 10. No entry has yet been made to record this revenue. (Credit Concessions Revenue.)

g Salaries earned by employees, but unpaid as of September 30, amount to $3,750. No entry has yet been made to record this liability and expense.

INSTRUCTIONS Prepare

a A work sheet for the month ended September 30, 1994.

b An income statement for the month.

c A statement of owner's equity for the month.

d A balance sheet as of September 30.

e The adjusting and closing entries required at month's end.

*PROBLEM 4B-7
Reversing
Entries

Lawton Industries holds a note receivable in the amount of $300,000, dated March 10, 1994, due in 24 months. Interest of $3,000 is received monthly on the tenth of each month, computed at an annual rate of 12%. Lawton maintains its accounts on

* *Supplemental Topic, "Reversing Entries"*

the basis of a fiscal year ending June 30. During June and July, the following events occurred relating to this note receivable.

June 10 Received regular monthly interest check of $3,000 for the preceding month ending June 10. (Credit Interest Revenue.)

June 30 Prepared an adjusting entry to record interest revenue for the last 20 days of June.

July 1 Prepared a reversing entry for accrued interest revenue.

July 10 Received regular monthly interest check of $3,000 for the month ending July 10.

INSTRUCTIONS

a Prepare journal entries (with explanations) for the four above items relating to interest.

b How much of the $3,000 in interest received on July 10 represents July revenue?

c Assume that no reversing entry had been made by Lawton. Prepare the journal entry for receipt of interest on July 10.

CASES AND UNSTRUCTURED PROBLEMS

CASE 4-1
Alaska Airlines

Alaska Air Group, Inc. (Alaska Airlines), credits the proceeds from advance ticket sales to an account entitled Air Traffic Liability. The company's 1989 annual report shows the following trend in the balance of this account over a three-year period:

	1987	1988	1989
Air traffic liability (in millions)	*$41.6*	*$46.8*	*$58.3*

INSTRUCTIONS

a What does the balance in the Air Traffic Liability account represent?

b How does the airline normally discharge this liability?

c Explain the most probable reason for the increases in the amount of this liability from year-to-year.

d Based solely upon the trend in the amount of this liability, would you expect the annual amounts of passenger revenue earned by the airlines to be increasing or decreasing over this three-year period? Explain.

CASE 4-2
Adjusting Entries: An Unstructured Problem

The purpose of this problem is to help you understand the need for adjusting entries in a specific business situation. You are to prepare examples of "typical" adjusting entries which might be made at the end of an accounting period by a company that owns and operates a *large hotel.* You are to decide upon the types of assets, liabilities, revenue, and expenses that might be involved in these entries. Prepare two examples of *each of the four basic types of adjusting entries.* Thus, you will prepare a total of eight adjusting entries.

You need not include dollar amounts—simply enter *"xxx"* in the debit and credit columns. However, your written explanations of each entry should describe specific facts that make the adjustment necessary. For example, one adjusting entry that a hotel might make to apportion unearned revenue is shown below.

a Examples of adjusting entries to apportion recorded revenue:

(1) Unearned Banquet Revenue .... *xxx*
    Banquet Revenue .... *xxx*
    To recognize revenue earned this period from catering the National Football League awards banquet in the hotel. The League had paid for this banquet in an earlier accounting period.

CASE 4-3
Adjusting Entries: An Alternative Case

This problem is an alternative to Case 4-2. You are to follow the same instructions as in Case 4-2, but use a large *law firm* as the business entity. Also, you are to prepare only *one* example of each of the four basic types of adjusting entries.

CASE 4-4
Should This Be Adjusted?

Property Management Professionals provides building management services to owners of office buildings and shopping centers. The company closes its accounts at the *end of the calendar year.* The manner in which the company has recorded several transactions occurring during 1994 is described below:

a On September 1, received advance payment from a shopping center for property management services to be performed over the three-month period beginning September 1. The entire amount received was credited directly to a *revenue* account.

b On December 1, received advance payment from the same customer described in part **a** for services to be rendered over the three-month period beginning December 1. This time, the entire amount received was credited to an *unearned revenue* account.

c Rendered management services for many customers in December. Normal procedure is to record revenue on the date the customer is billed, which is early in the month after the services have been rendered.

d On December 15, made full payment for a one-year insurance policy which goes into effect on January 1, 1995. The cost of the policy was debited to Unexpired Insurance.

e Numerous purchases of equipment were debited to asset accounts, rather than to expense accounts.

f Payroll expense is recorded when employees are paid. Payday for the last two weeks of December falls on January 2, 1995.

INSTRUCTIONS

For each transaction, explain whether an adjusting entry is needed at *December 31, 1994,* and state the reasons for your answer. If you recommend an adjusting entry, explain the effects this entry would have upon assets, liabilities, owner's equity, revenue, and expense in the 1994 financial statements.

CASE 4-5
The Concept of Materiality

The concept of materiality is one of the most basic generally accepted accounting principles.

a Answer the following questions:

1 Why is the materiality of a transaction or an event a matter of professional judgment?

2 What criteria should accountants consider in determining whether a transaction or an event is "material"?

3 Does the concept of materiality mean that financial statements are not precise, down to the last dollar? Does this concept make financial statements less useful to most users?

b **Avis Rent-a-Car** purchases a large number of cars each year for its rental fleet. The cost of any individual automobile is immaterial to Avis, which is a very large corporation. Would it be acceptable for Avis to charge the purchase of automobiles for its rental fleet directly to expense, rather than to an asset account? Explain.

CASE 4-6
Materiality in Practice

During the current year, East-West Airlines earned net income of $50 million from total revenue of $350 million. The company services primarily cities in the United States but also has service to several foreign countries. Three events are described below, along with the treatment accorded to these events in the company's financial statements.

This case focuses upon the question of "materiality." Therefore, some items described below may be viewed as *immaterial.*

a During the year, the company purchased $5 million in spare parts to be used in aircraft maintenance. All of these purchases were charged immediately to Maintenance Expense. No adjusting entry was made at year-end to reflect approximately $50,000 in spare parts remaining on hand, because the amount was considered immaterial.

b The company's internal auditors discovered that the vice president of in-flight services had embezzled $100,000 from the airlines by authorizing payments to a fictitious supplier of in-flight meals. The vice president was fired, and criminal charges currently are pending against her, as is a civil lawsuit to recover the embezzled funds. In the income statement, this $100,000 loss was deducted from revenue as part of the Flight Operations Expenses, which totaled more than $200 million. No special disclosures were made, because the amount of the embezzlement was considered immaterial.

c Shortly after year-end, the company suspended all flight operations to a particular foreign country as a result of political unrest. These flights provided approximately 2% of the company's revenue and net income during the current year. Cancellation of service to this country was not disclosed in notes to the current year's financial statements, because operations of the current year were not affected.

INSTRUCTIONS Explain whether in your own judgment you concur or disagree with the treatment accorded to these events by East-West in its current financial statements. If you recommend a different financial statement presentation, explain why you do. In each case, indicate whether or not you consider the item "material," and explain your reasons. Consider each of these three situations **_independently_** of the others.

CASE 4-7 Computer-Based Accounting System

In Case 2-1, Bill Gates used data base software to design a simple accounting system for use on personal computers. Gates's first system prepared only a balance sheet; he is now ready to design an enhanced system which will perform all of the steps in the accounting cycle and will produce a complete set of financial statements. This enhanced system also will utilize data base software.

The idea underlying data base software is that data intended for a variety of different uses must be entered into the data base only once. The computer can then arrange these data into any number of desired formats. It can also combine data and perform mathematical computations using data in the data base.

In Gates's new accounting system, the computer will arrange the data into the following formats: (1) journal entries (with explanations) for all transactions, (2) three-column running balance ledger accounts, (3) a 10-column work sheet, (4) a complete set of financial statements, (5) journal entries for all adjusting and closing entries, (6) an after-closing trial balance, and (7) reversing entries. As each of these records and statements is prepared, any totals or subtotals in the record are included automatically in the data base. For example, when ledger accounts are updated, the new account balances become part of the data base.

INSTRUCTIONS In Chapter 4, the steps of the accounting cycle were described as follows: (a) journalize transactions, (b) post to ledger accounts, (c) prepare a work sheet, (d) prepare financial statements, (e) adjust and close the accounts, (f) prepare an after-closing trial balance, and (g) prepare reversing entries. For each step in this cycle, briefly describe the types of data used in performing the step. Indicate whether the data are already contained in the data base, or whether the computer operator must enter data to enable the computer to perform the step.

ANSWERS TO SELF-TEST QUESTIONS

1 c   **2** d $3,890   **3** d   **4** b, c, d   **5** b   ***6** a

---

*   _Supplemental Topic, "Reversing Entries"_

COMPREHENSIVE PROBLEM 2

FRIEND WITH A TRUCK

A SHORT PRACTICE SET, BASED UPON A SERVICE BUSINESS

On June 1, 19__, Anthony Ferrara organized a business called Friend With A Truck for the purpose of operating an equipment rental yard. The new business was able to begin operations immediately by purchasing the assets and taking over the location of Rent-All, an equipment rental company that was going out of business.

Friend With A Truck uses the following chart of accounts:

Cash................................	1	Anthony Ferrara, Capital	30
Accounts Receivable	4	Anthony Ferrara, Drawing	35
Prepaid Rent	6	Income Summary	40
Office Supplies.....................	8	Rental Fees Earned	50
Rental Equipment	10	Salaries Expense	60
Accumulated Depreciation:		Maintenance Expense..............	61
Rental Equipment	12	Utilities Expense...................	62
Notes Payable......................	20	Rent Expense......................	63
Accounts Payable	22	Office Supplies Expense	64
Interest Payable	25	Depreciation Expense..............	65
Salaries Payable....................	26	Interest Expense...................	66
Unearned Rental Fees	29		

The company closes its accounts and prepares financial statements at the end of each month. During June, the company entered into the following transactions:

June 1   Anthony Ferrara deposited $150,000 cash in a bank account in the name of the business, Friend With A Truck.

June 1   Purchased for $240,000 all the equipment formerly owned by Rent-All. Paid $100,000 cash and issued a one-year note payable for $140,000, plus interest at the annual rate of 9%.

June 1   Paid $10,000 to Morrison Realty as four months' advance rent on the rental yard and office formerly occupied by Rent-All.

June 3   Received $12,000 cash as advance payment on equipment rental from McBryan Construction Company. (Credit Unearned Rental Fees.)

June 5   Purchased office supplies on account from Newport Office Company, $1,850. Payment due in 30 days. (These supplies are expected to last for several months; debit the Office Supplies asset account.)

June 9   Purchased on account from Foley Parts Distributor $290 in parts needed to repair a rental tractor. (Debit an expense account.) Payment is due in 10 days.

June 12   Paid salaries for the first two weeks in June, $3,200.

June 15   Excluding the advance payment from the McBryan Construction Company, equipment rental fees earned during the first 15 days of June amounted to $8,900, of which $7,200 was received in cash.

June 18   Paid the account payable to Foley Parts Distributor, $290.

June 19   Collected $800 of the accounts receivable recorded on June 15.

June 23   Rented a backhoe to Mission Landscaping at a price of $110 per day, to be paid when the backhoe is returned. Mission Landscaping expects to keep the backhoe for about two or three weeks.

June 26   Paid biweekly salaries, $3,200.

June 29   Anthony Ferrara withdrew $3,000 cash from the business to make a mortgage payment for his personal residence.

June 30   Equipment rental fees earned during the second half of June and received in cash amounted to $7,850.

June 30   Received a bill from Western Utilities for the month of June, $340. Payment is due in 30 days.

OTHER DATA

a   During June, the company earned $3,210 of the rental fees paid in advance by McBryan Construction Company on June 3.

b   Office supplies on hand at June 30 are estimated at $1,160.

c   The rental equipment is being depreciated over a period of 10 years.

d   The advance payment of rent on June 1 covered a period of four months.

e   As of June 30, Friend With A Truck has earned seven days' rent on the backhoe rented to Mission Landscaping on June 23.

f   Interest accrued on the note payable to Rent-All amounted to $1,050 at June 30.

g   Salaries earned by employees since the last payroll date (June 26) amounted to $960 at month-end.

INSTRUCTIONS

a   Journalize the above transactions.

b   Post to ledger accounts. (Use running balance form of ledger accounts. Enter numbers of journal pages and ledger accounts to complete the cross-referencing between the journal and ledger.)

c   Prepare a 10-column work sheet for the month ended June 30, 19__.

d   Prepare an income statement and a statement of owner's equity for the month of June, and a balance sheet (in report form) as of June 30.

e   Prepare adjusting and closing entries and post to ledger accounts.

f   Prepare an after-closing trial balance as of June 30.

*g   Prepare appropriate reversing entries (dated July 1) and post to ledger accounts.

---

*   *Supplemental Topic, "Reversing Entries"*

2 Merchandising Concerns and the Design of Accounting Systems

*T*his part contains two chapters. In the first, we explain the accounting concepts relating to merchandising activities—that is, to the sale of products rather than services. In the second chapter, we explore several characteristics of the accounting systems used in large organizations. These characteristics include the ability to process a large volume of transactions, the need for internal control, and financial and operational audits.

5   Accounting for Merchandising Activities; Classified Financial Statements

6   Accounting Systems, Internal Control, and Audits

CHAPTER

5 Accounting for Merchandising Activities; Classified Financial Statements

In this chapter our discussion of the accounting cycle is expanded to include merchandising companies—businesses that sell goods rather than services. Basic merchandising transactions, such as purchases and sales of merchandise, are discussed in the first half of the chapter. More specialized merchandising transactions are discussed at the end of the chapter in a Supplemental Topic section.

Our second major topic in this chapter is the preparation and use of classified financial statements. We illustrate and explain how creditors and investors use key financial statement relationships in evaluating the solvency, profitability, and future prospects of a business enterprise.

After studying this chapter you should be able to meet these Learning Objectives:

1 *Describe the operating cycle of a merchandising company.*

2 *Explain the need for various subsidiary ledgers in accounting for merchandising transactions.*

3 *Account for purchases and sales of merchandise using a perpetual inventory system.*

4 *Distinguish between the perpetual and periodic inventory systems.*

5 *Prepare a classified balance sheet. Compute the current ratio and amount of working capital.*

6 *Identify two standards for comparison widely used in evaluating financial ratios.*

7 *Analyze an income statement and evaluate the adequacy of net income.*

*8 *Account for cash discounts, merchandise returns, transportation costs, and sales taxes.*

---

* *Supplemental Topic, "Additional Merchandising Transactions"*

ACCOUNTING FOR MERCHANDISING ACTIVITIES

Merchandising Companies

In the preceding four chapters we have illustrated the accounting cycle for businesses which render **services** to their customers. Merchandising companies, in contrast to service-type businesses, earn revenue by selling **goods** rather than services.

The goods that a merchandising company sells to its customers are called **inventory** (or merchandise), regardless of the type of products that the company sells. Thus, the inventory of an automobile dealership consists of automobiles offered for sale, whereas the inventory of a grocery store consists of a wide variety of food items.

Merchandising companies often have large amounts of money invested in their inventories. In fact, inventory is one of the most costly assets appearing in the balance sheets of most merchandising companies. Fortunately, inventory is a relatively "liquid" asset—that is, it usually will be sold within a few weeks or months, thereby generating accounts receivable and cash receipts. For this reason, the asset inventory appears near the top of the balance sheet, immediately below accounts receivable.

The "Operating Cycle" of a Merchandising Company　The series of transactions through which a business generates its revenue and its cash receipts from customers is called the **operating cycle.** The operating cycle of a merchandising company consists of the following basic transactions: (1) purchases of merchandise; (2) sales of the merchandise, often on account; and (3) collection of the accounts receivable from customers. As the word **cycle** suggests, this sequence of transactions is repeated continuously. Some of the cash collected from the customer is used to purchase more merchandise, and the cycle begins anew.

This continuous sequence of merchandising transactions is illustrated in the following diagram:

OBJECTIVE 1
Describe the operating cycle of a merchandising company.

The operating cycle repeats continuously

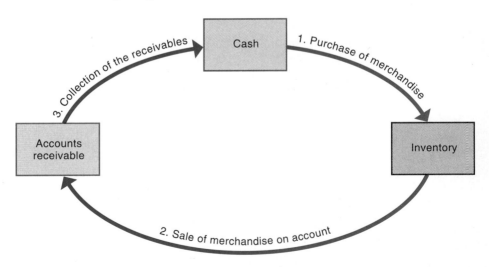

Merchandising Activities Compared with Manufacturing　Most merchandising companies purchase their inventories from other business organizations in a ***ready-to-sell*** condition. Companies that ***manufacture*** their inventories, such as General Motors, Apple Computer, and Boeing Aircraft, are called ***manufacturers,*** rather than merchandisers. The operating cycle of a manufacturing company is longer and more complex than that of a merchandising company, because the first transaction—purchasing merchandise—is replaced by the many transactions involved in manufacturing the merchandise.

The concepts discussed in this chapter apply equally to merchandising businesses and to manufacturers. However, accounting for manufacturing activities also involves many additional concepts which are addressed in later chapters. For this reason, our examples and illustrations in this chapter are limited to companies that purchase their inventory in a ready-to-sell condition.

Retailers and Wholesalers Merchandising companies include both retailers and wholesalers. A ***retailer*** is a business that sells merchandise directly to the public. Retailers may be large or small; they vary in size from giant department store chains, such as Sears and Wal-Mart, to small neighborhood businesses, such as gas stations and gift shops. In fact, more businesses engage in retail sales than in any other type of business activity.

The other major type of merchandising company is the ***wholesaler.*** Wholesalers buy large quantities of merchandise from several different manufacturers and then resell this merchandise to many different retailers. As wholesalers do not sell directly to the public, even the largest wholesalers are not well known to most consumers. Nonetheless, wholesaling is a major type of merchandising activity.

CASE IN POINT The nation's largest wholesale distributor of food products is Fleming Companies, Inc., which sells to more than 5,000 grocery stores and convenience stores in 36 states. Fleming's annual sales amount to more than \$12 billion—and that measurement is in "wholesale" prices.

The concepts discussed in the remainder of this chapter apply equally to retailers and to wholesalers.

Income Statement of a Merchandising Company

Selling merchandise introduces a new and major cost of doing business: the ***cost*** to the merchandising company of the goods which it resells to its customers. This cost is termed the ***cost of goods sold.*** In essence, the cost of goods sold ***is an expense;*** however, this item is of such importance to a merchandising company that it is shown separate from other expenses in the income statement.

A ***highly condensed*** income statement for a merchandising business is shown on the following page. In comparison with the income statement of a service-type business, the new features of this statement are the inclusion of the ***cost of goods sold*** and a subtotal called ***gross profit.***

Condensed income statement for a merchandising company

COMPUTER BARN Income Statement For the Year Ended December 31, 1994	
Revenue from sales	*$900,000*
Less: Cost of goods sold	*540,000*
Gross profit	*$360,000*
Less: Expenses	*270,000*
Net income	*$ 90,000*

Revenue from sales represents the **sales price** of merchandise sold to customers during the period. The cost of goods sold, on the other hand, represents the **cost** incurred by the merchandising company in purchasing these goods from the company's suppliers. The difference between revenue from sales and the cost of goods sold is called **gross profit** (or gross margin).

Gross profit is a useful means of measuring the profitability of sales transactions, but it does **not** represent the overall profitability of the business. A merchandising company has many expenses **other than** the cost of goods sold. Examples include salaries, rent, advertising, and depreciation. The company only earns a net income if its gross profit exceeds the sum of these other expenses.

What Accounting Information Does a Merchandising Company Need?

Before we illustrate how a merchandising company accounts for the transactions in its operating cycle, let us consider the basic **types of information** which the company's accounting system should develop. The company needs accounting information that will (1) meet its financial reporting requirements, (2) serve the needs of company personnel in conducting daily business operations, and (3) meet any special reporting requirements, such as information required by income tax authorities.

To meet its financial reporting requirements, a merchandising company must measure and record its revenue from sales transactions, and also the cost of goods sold. (Other types of revenue and expenses must also be recorded, but this is done in the same manner as in a service-type business.) In addition, the accounting system must provide a complete record of the company's assets and liabilities.

The information appearing in financial statements is highly summarized. For example, the amount shown as accounts receivable in a balance sheet represents the **total** accounts receivable at the balance sheet date. Managers and other company employees need **much more detailed** accounting information than that provided in financial statements. In billing customers, for example, the company's billing clerks need to know the amount receivable from **each credit customer.** In addition, the accounting system must provide the billing clerks with the dates and amounts of all charges and payments affecting each customer's account.

Businesses which are organized as corporations must file corporate income tax returns.[1] In many respects, the information needed for income tax purposes parallels that used in the financial statements. Differences between income tax rules and financial reporting requirements will be discussed in later chapters.

Let us now see how the accounting system of a merchandising company meets the company's needs for financial information.

General Ledger Accounts

Up to now, we have been recording transactions only in *general ledger* accounts. These general ledger accounts are used in preparing financial statements and other accounting reports which *summarize* the financial position of a business and the results of its operations.

Although general ledger accounts provide a useful *overview* of a company's financial activities, they do not provide much of the detailed information needed by managers and other company employees in daily business operations. This detailed information is found in accounting records called *subsidiary ledgers.*

Subsidiary Ledgers: A Source of More Detail

A subsidiary ledger shows separately the individual items which comprise the balance of a general ledger account. For example, an *accounts receivable subsidiary ledger* (or customers ledger) contains a *separate account for each credit customer.* If the company has 500 credit customers, there will be 500 separate accounts in the accounts receivable subsidiary ledger. The balances of these 500 subsidiary ledger accounts add up to the balance in the Accounts Receivable account in the general ledger.

*OBJECTIVE 2
Explain the need for various subsidiary ledgers in accounting for merchandising transactions.*

An accounts receivable subsidiary ledger includes all of the information needed to bill specific customers, including the amounts due, the dates and amounts of credit sales and past payments, the dates that payments are due, and the customers' billing addresses. In fact, each subsidiary account provides a complete history of the credit transactions between the company and a particular credit customer.

Most businesses maintain several different subsidiary ledgers, each providing details about the composition of a different general ledger account. A general ledger account which summarizes the content of a subsidiary ledger is called a *controlling account* (or control account).

For convenience, the word *subsidiary* often is omitted in describing a specific subsidiary ledger. Thus, an accounts receivable subsidiary ledger might simply be called the accounts receivable ledger (or customers ledger).

Subsidiary Ledgers Needed for Merchandising Transactions   In addition to a subsidiary ledger for accounts receivable, every merchandising company

---

[1]   The taxable income of a *sole proprietorship* is included in the personal income tax return of the *business owner,* rather than in a tax return filed by the business entity.

also maintains an **accounts payable subsidiary ledger,** showing the amount owned to each creditor. Most merchandising companies also maintain an **inventory subsidiary ledger,** with a separate account for each type of merchandise that the company sells. Thus, the inventory ledger of a large department store contains thousands of accounts. Each of these accounts shows for **one type of product** the quantities, per-unit costs, and total costs of all units purchased, sold, and currently "in inventory."

The following diagram shows the relationship between several subsidiary ledgers and the related controlling accounts in the general ledger:

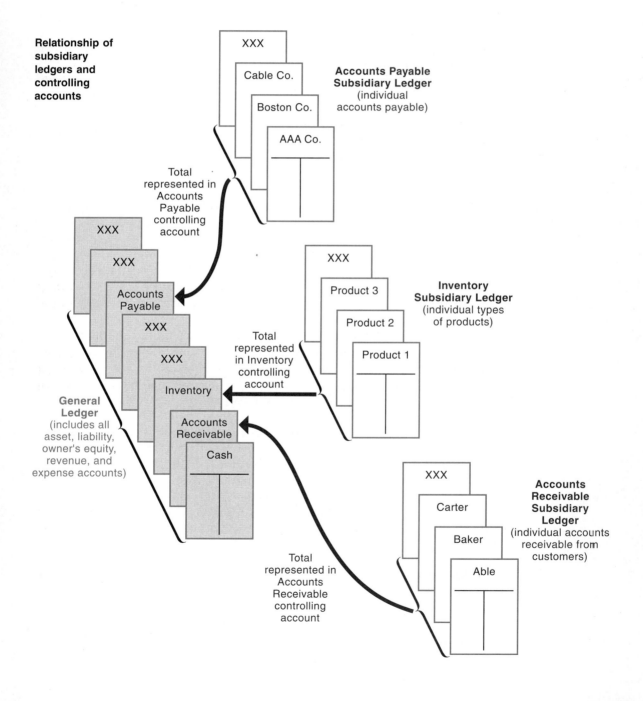

Other Types of Subsidiary Ledgers In this chapter, we discuss the subsidiary ledgers for inventory, accounts payable, and accounts receivable. However, subsidiary ledgers also are maintained for many other general ledger accounts. The following schedule lists some of the general ledger accounts usually supported by a subsidiary ledger:

Controlling Account in the General Ledger	Unit of Organization within the Subsidiary Ledger
Cash	Each bank account
Notes receivable	Each note receivable
Accounts receivable	Individual credit customers
Inventory	Each type of product offered for sale
Plant assets	Each asset (group of similar assets)
Notes payable	Each note payable
Accounts payable	Each creditor
Capital stock (only in a business organized as a corporation)	Each stockholder (this ledger shows each stockholder's name, address, and the number of shares owned)
Sales (or any revenue account)	Each department, branch location, or product line
Cost of goods sold	Same organization as the sales ledger
Any expense account	Each department incurring this type of expense

Subsidiary ledgers are intended to meet the information needs of the company's ***managers and employees.*** These accounting records are ***not*** used in the preparation of financial statements, nor are they usually made available to persons outside of the business organization.

Posting to Subsidiary Ledger Accounts Any entry which affects the balance of a subsidiary ledger account ***also*** affects the balance of the related controlling account. Thus, entries affecting subsidiary ledger accounts must be ***posted twice***—once to the subsidiary ledger account and once to the controlling account in the general ledger.

To illustrate, assume that on July 12 Hillside Company collects a $1,000 account receivable from L. Brown, a credit customer. This transaction is illustrated below in the form of a general journal entry:

Date		Account Titles and Explanation	LP	Debit	Credit
July	12	Cash		1,000	
		Accounts Receivable (L. Brown)....			1,000
		Collected an account receivable.			

Assume that in the general ledger the account number for the Cash account is ***101*** and the account number of the Accounts Receivable controlling account is ***120.*** Hillside also maintains an accounts receivable subsidiary ledger, in which customers' accounts are arranged alphabetically. We will assume that the company has only one bank account and, therefore, does not maintain a subsidiary ledger for cash.

Our original journal entry is repeated below, along with the appropriate posting references included in the LP (Ledger Page) column:

	Date		Account Titles and Explanation	LP	Debit	Credit
	July	12	Cash	101	1,000	
			Accounts Receivable (L. Brown) ...	✔/120		1,000
			Collected an account receivable.			

Notice the "double posting" of the credit entry

The account numbers **101** and **120** entered in this column indicate that the entry has been posted to both the Cash account and the Accounts Receivable controlling account in the general ledger. The check mark (✔) indicates that the credit portion of the entry also has been posted to the account for L. Brown in the accounts receivable subsidiary ledger.

(In working homework assignments in this text, you often are asked to describe the effects of business transactions in the form of general journal entries. You should **not** include posting references in these entries **unless you actually have posted the data** to ledger accounts.)

Reconciling Subsidiary Ledgers with the Controlling Account As previously mentioned, the balance in a general ledger controlling account should be equal to the **sum** of the balances of all of the accounts in the related subsidiary ledger. Periodically, accountants **reconcile** a subsidiary ledger with the controlling account—that is, they determine that the sum of the subsidiary ledger account balances **does,** in fact, equal that of the controlling account.

Reconciling a subsidiary ledger is an **internal control procedure** that may bring to light certain types of errors. For example, this procedure should detect a failure to post a transaction to the subsidiary ledger or a mechanical error in computing an account balance. Unfortunately, it does **not** provide assurance that all transactions were posted to the **correct account** within the subsidiary ledger. If a debit or credit entry is posted to the **wrong account** in the subsidiary ledger, the subsidiary ledger and controlling account will **remain "in balance."** These types of posting errors are difficult to detect and are one reason why individuals and businesses that purchase merchandise on account should review carefully the monthly billings which they receive from their suppliers.

Subsidiary Ledgers in Computer-Based Systems At first, it may seem that maintaining subsidiary ledgers with hundreds or thousands of separate accounts would involve a great deal of work. However, business organizations that are large enough to require large subsidiary ledgers use computer-based accounting systems. In a computer-based accounting system, subsidiary ledger accounts and general ledger accounts all are posted **automatically** as transactions are recorded. In addition, the computer automatically reconciles the subsidiary ledgers with the controlling accounts. Thus, no significant effort is required of accounting personnel to maintain subsidiary ledgers in a computer-based system.[2]

Two Approaches Widely Used in Accounting for Merchandising Transactions

Either of two approaches may be used in accounting for merchandising transactions: (1) a ***perpetual inventory system*** or (2) a ***periodic inventory system.*** In past decades, both systems were in widespread use. Today, however, virtually all large businesses (and many smaller ones) use perpetual systems. Periodic systems are used primarily in very small businesses which do not have significant financial reporting requirements.

Perpetual Inventory Systems

OBJECTIVE 3
Account for purchases and sales of merchandise using a perpetual inventory system.

In a perpetual inventory system, merchandising transactions are recorded ***as they occur.*** The system draws its name from the fact that the accounting records are kept perpetually up-to-date. Purchases of merchandise are recorded by debiting an asset account entitled Inventory. When merchandise is sold, two entries are necessary: one to recognize the ***revenue earned*** and the second to recognize the related ***cost of goods sold.*** This second entry also reduces the balance of the Inventory account to reflect the sale of some of the company's inventory.

A perpetual inventory system usually includes an ***inventory subsidiary ledger.*** This ledger provides company personnel with up-to-date information about every type of product that the company sells, including the cost and the number of units purchased, sold, and currently on hand.

To illustrate the perpetual inventory system, we will follow specific items of merchandise through the operating cycle of Computer Barn, a retail store. The transactions comprising this illustration are as follows:

Sept. 1   Purchased 10 Regent CX-21 computer monitors on account from Okawa Wholesale Company. The monitors cost $600 each, for a total of $6,000; payment is due in 30 days.

Sept. 7   Sold 2 monitors on account to RJ Travel Agency at a retail sales price of $1,000 each, for a total of $2,000. Payment is due in 30 days.

Oct.   1   Paid the $6,000 account payable to Okawa Wholesale Company.

Oct.   7   Collected the $2,000 account receivable from RJ Travel Agency.

In addition to a general ledger, Computer Barn maintains separate subsidiary ledgers for accounts receivable, inventory, and accounts payable.

Purchases of Merchandise   Purchases of inventory are recorded at cost. Thus, Computer Barn records its purchase of the 10 computer monitors on September 1 as follows:

---

[2]   The maintenance of subsidiary ledgers was one of the earliest applications of computers in the business world. For a large organization, the time savings in this area alone may justify the cost of a computer-based accounting system. Prior to the use of computers, large business organizations employed many clerical workers for the sole purpose of posting transactions to subsidiary ledger accounts.

```
Inventory.................................................  6,000
        Accounts Payable (Okawa Wholesale Co.)................      6,000
Purchased 10 Regent CX-21 computer monitors for $600 each;
payment due in 30 days.
```

The data contained in this entry is posted to the general ledger and also to the subsidiary ledgers. First, the entry is posted to the Inventory and Accounts Payable controlling accounts in the general ledger. The debit to Inventory also is posted to the Regent CX-21 Monitors account in the inventory subsidiary ledger.[3] The quantity of monitors purchased (10) and the per-unit cost ($600) also are recorded in this subsidiary ledger account. (This subsidiary ledger account is illustrated on page 231.)

The credit to Accounts Payable also is posted to the account for Okawa Wholesale Company in Computer Barn's accounts payable subsidiary ledger.

Sales of Merchandise   The revenue earned in a sales transaction is equal to the **sales price** of the merchandise and is credited to a revenue account entitled **Sales.** Except in rare circumstances, sales revenue is considered "realized" when the merchandise is **delivered to the customer,** even if the sale is made on account. Therefore, Computer Barn will recognize the revenue from the sale to RJ Travel Agency on September 7, as shown below:

Entries to record a sale . . .

```
Accounts Receivable (RJ Travel Agency) .......................  2,000
        Sales .................................................      2,000
Sold 2 Regent CX-21 monitors for $1,000 each; payment due in
30 days.
```

The **matching principle** requires that revenue be matched (offset) with all of the costs and expenses incurred in producing that revenue. Therefore, a **second journal entry** is required at the date of sale to record the cost of goods sold.

. . . and the related cost of goods sold

```
Cost of Goods Sold .............................................  1,200
        Inventory ..............................................      1,200
To transfer the cost of 2 Regent CX-21 monitors ($600 apiece)
from Inventory to the Cost of Goods Sold account.
```

Notice that this second entry is based upon the **cost** of the merchandise to Computer Barn, not upon its retail sales price. The per-unit cost of the Regent monitors ($600) was determined from the inventory subsidiary ledger (see page 231).

Both of the journal entries relating to this sales transaction are posted to Computer Barn's general ledger. In addition, the $2,000 debit to Accounts Receivable (first entry) is posted to the account for RJ Travel Agency in the accounts receivable ledger. The credit to Inventory (second

---

[3]   In journal entries, it is common practice to indicate specific suppliers and customers using a parenthetic note following the account title "Accounts Payable" or "Accounts Receivable." Similar notations usually are **not** used with the Inventory account, because **many different types of products** may be purchased in a single transaction. The detailed product information used in posting to the inventory ledger is found in the **invoice** (bill) which the seller sends to the buyer.

entry) also is posted to the Regent CX-21 Monitors account in the inventory subsidiary ledger.

Payment of Accounts Payable to Suppliers The payment to Okawa Wholesale Company on October 1 is recorded as follows:

Accounts Payable (Okawa Wholesale Co.) **6,000**
   Cash **6,000**
Paid account payable.

Both portions of this entry are posted to the general ledger. In addition, payment of the account payable is entered in the Okawa Wholesale Company account in the Computer Barn's accounts payable subsidiary ledger.

Collection of Accounts Receivable from Customers On October 7, collection of the account receivable from RJ Travel Agency is recorded as follows:

Cash **2,000**
      Accounts Receivable (RJ Travel Agency) **2,000**
Collected an account receivable from a credit customer.

Both portions of this entry are posted to the general ledger; the credit to Accounts Receivable also is posted to the RJ Travel Agency account in the accounts receivable ledger.

   Collection of the cash from RJ Travel Agency completes Computer Barn's operating cycle with respect to these two units of merchandise.

The Inventory Subsidiary Ledger An inventory subsidiary ledger includes a separate account (or "inventory card") for each type of product in the company's inventory. Computer Barn's subsidiary inventory record for Regent monitors is illustrated below:

Inventory sub-sidiary ledger account

Item Regent CX-21				Primary supplier Okawa Wholesale Company					
Description 21 Gray scale monitor				Second supplier Forbes Importers, Inc.					
Location Storeroom 2				Inventory level: Min: 2 Max: 10					

	PURCHASED			SOLD			BALANCE		
Date	Units	Unit Cost	Total	Units	Unit Cost	Cost of Goods Sold	Units	Unit Cost	Total
Sept. 1	10	$600	$6,000				10	$600	$6,000
7				2	$600	$1,200	8	$600	$4,800

   When Regent CX-21 monitors are purchased, the quantity, unit cost, and total cost are entered in this subsidiary ledger account. When any of these monitors are sold, the number of units, unit cost, and total cost of the units sold also are recorded in this subsidiary ledger account. After each purchase or sales transaction, the "Balance" columns are updated to show the quantity, unit cost, and total cost of the monitors still on hand.[4]

An inventory ledger provides useful information to a variety of company personnel. A few examples of the company personnel who utilize this information on a daily basis are listed below:

- ■ *Sales managers* use the inventory ledger to see at a glance which products are selling quickly and which are not.
- ■ *Accounting personnel* use these records to determine the unit costs of merchandise sold.
- ■ *Sales personnel* use this subsidiary ledger to determine the quantities of specific products currently on hand and the physical location of this merchandise.
- ■ *Employees responsible for ordering merchandise* refer to the inventory ledger to determine when specific products should be reordered, the quantities to order, and the names of major suppliers.

When a *physical inventory* is taken, management uses the inventory ledger to determine on a product-by-product basis whether *inventory shrinkage* has been reasonable or excessive.

Taking a Physical Inventory

The basic characteristic of the perpetual inventory system is that the Inventory account is *continuously updated* for all purchases and sales of merchandise. Over time, however, normal inventory shrinkage usually causes some discrepancies between the quantities of merchandise shown in the inventory records and the quantities actually on hand. *Inventory shrinkage* refers to unrecorded decreases in inventory resulting from such factors as breakage, spoilage, employee theft, and shoplifting.

In order to ensure the accuracy of their perpetual inventory records, most businesses take a *complete physical count* of the merchandise on hand at least once a year. This procedure is called *taking a physical inventory,* and it usually is performed near year-end.

Once the quantity of merchandise on hand has been determined by a physical count, the per-unit costs in the inventory ledger accounts are used to determine the total cost of the inventory. The Inventory controlling account and also the accounts in the inventory subsidiary ledger then are *adjusted* to the quantities and dollar amounts indicated by the physical inventory.

To illustrate, assume that at year-end the Inventory controlling account and inventory subsidiary ledger of Computer Barn both show an inventory with a cost of *$72,200.* A physical count, however, reveals that some of the merchandise listed in the accounting records is missing; the items actually on hand have a total cost of *$70,000.* Computer Barn would make the following adjusting entry to correct its Inventory controlling account:

---

[4]   In our illustration, all of the Regent monitors were purchased on the same date and have the same unit cost. Often a company's inventory of a given product includes units acquired at several *different* per-unit costs. This situation is addressed in Chapter 9.

Adjusting for inventory shrinkage	*Cost of Goods Sold* 2,200	
	Inventory	2,200

To adjust the perpetual inventory records to reflect the results of the year-end physical count.

Computer Barn also will adjust the appropriate accounts in its inventory subsidiary ledger to reflect the quantities indicated by the physical count.

Reasonable amounts of inventory shrinkage are viewed as a normal cost of doing business and simply are debited to the Cost of Goods Sold account, as illustrated above.[5]

Closing Entries in a Perpetual Inventory System

As explained and illustrated in Chapter 3, revenue and expense accounts are **closed** at the end of each accounting period. A merchandising business with a perpetual inventory system makes closing entries which parallel those of a service-type business. The Sales account is a revenue account and is closed into the Income Summary along with other revenue accounts. The Cost of Goods Sold account is closed into the Income Summary in the same manner as the other expense accounts.

Periodic Inventory Systems

OBJECTIVE 4
Distinguish between the perpetual and periodic inventory systems.

The alternative to the perpetual inventory system is called the **periodic inventory system.** In a periodic inventory system, no effort is made either to update the Inventory account or to record the cost of goods sold as transactions occur throughout the year. Rather, the accounting records are updated only "periodically"—usually at year-end.

The fact that the accounting records are not updated until year-end explains why this system is **not satisfactory** for a business which makes use of accounting information throughout the year. However, a periodic system is easy and inexpensive to operate and may meet the needs of a very small business.

A traditional periodic system operates as follows. When merchandise is purchased, its cost is debited to an account entitled **Purchases,** rather than to the Inventory account. When merchandise is sold, an entry is made to recognize the sales revenue earned, but **no entry is made to record the cost of goods sold.**

The foundation of the periodic inventory system is the taking of a **complete physical inventory** at year-end. This year-end count determines the amount of inventory to appear in the balance sheet and also is used as the basis for computing the cost of goods sold.

Under the periodic inventory system, the cost of goods sold for the entire year is determined at year-end by a short computation, as follows:

---

[5] If a large inventory shortage is caused by an event such as a fire or theft, the cost of the missing or damaged merchandise may be debited to a special loss account, such as Fire Loss. In the income statement, a loss is deducted from revenue in the same manner as an expense.

Computing the cost of goods sold in a periodic system	*Inventory, beginning of the year*	$ 12,000
	Add: Purchases	130,000
	Cost of goods available for sale	$142,000
	Less: Inventory, end of the year	8,000
	Cost of goods sold	$134,000

In this example, the business had merchandise costing **$12,000** on hand at the beginning of the year. During the year, it purchased additional merchandise at a cost of **$130,000.** Therefore, merchandise with a total cost of **$142,000** was available for sale during the year.

At year-end, merchandise with a cost of **$8,000** remains on hand. Thus, merchandise which had cost **$134,000** is no longer on hand, and is presumed to have been sold.[6]

Three amounts are used in computing the cost of goods sold: (1) the inventory at the beginning of the year, (2) purchases made during the year, and (3) the inventory at the end of the year. The amounts of inventory on hand at the beginning and end of each year are determined by taking a complete physical inventory at year-end. (Only one physical inventory is taken each year; the ending inventory of one year represents the beginning inventory of the following year.) The cost of all merchandise purchased during the year is indicated by the year-end balance in the Purchases account.

In a periodic inventory system, the closing entries are somewhat more complex than in a perpetual inventory system. These entries are explained and illustrated in Appendix A of this textbook.

Comparison of Perpetual and Periodic Inventory Systems

Both the perpetual and periodic inventory systems produce the **same results** in **annual** financial statements. Throughout the year, however, the perpetual inventory system provides a company with a great deal of useful information which simply is **not available** in a periodic system.

A perpetual inventory system provides up-to-date information about the quantity and cost of the inventory on hand and also about the cost of goods sold. This enables the company to prepare monthly or quarterly financial statements directly from the accounting records. In a periodic system, however, the amounts of inventory on hand and the cost of goods sold are **not known** until a physical inventory is taken at year-end. If interim financial statements are prepared, the amounts of inventory on hand and the cost of goods sold can only be estimated.

Also, a perpetual inventory system usually includes an inventory subsidiary ledger, showing for each type of product the cost and quantities of units purchased, sold, and currently on hand. A periodic system does **not** provide management with an inventory subsidiary ledger.

If a perpetual inventory system provides so much more useful information, why would any company use a periodic system? The periodic system

---

[6]   In a periodic inventory system, inventory shrinkage losses are included in the amount identified as "cost of goods sold."

has only one advantage: it is not necessary to record the cost of goods sold as sales transactions occur. Prior to the invention of electronic ***point-of-sale terminals,*** businesses which sold many different products had ***no choice*** but to use periodic inventory systems. A supermarket, for example, may sell between 5,000 and 10,000 different items ***per hour.*** Imagine the difficulty of determining and recording the cost of each item sold if the accounting records were maintained by hand.

With modern point-of-sale terminals, however, even supermarkets are now able to use perpetual inventory systems.

CASE IN POINT   Supermarkets, department stores, and many other retailers use electronic cash registers called "point-of-sale terminals." Through an optical scanner, these devices are able to read "product codes" (a pattern of thick and thin vertical bars) which are printed on each item of merchandise. These product codes identify the product to the computer, which then looks up both the cost and the retail sales price of the product in a computer-based inventory ledger. The computer then automatically records the sale and the cost of goods sold and also updates the inventory ledger.

Notice that no accounting personnel are involved in recording or posting these sales transactions. Transactions are recorded automatically as the cashier passes the magnetically coded merchandise over an optical scanner.

In summary, technology has made the periodic inventory system all but obsolete. All large merchandising companies and manufacturing firms use perpetual inventory systems for every significant component of their inventory. Throughout this textbook, you may assume that a perpetual inventory system is in use unless we specifically state otherwise.

Periodic systems are used only by some small businesses with manual accounting systems and by some larger companies to account for relatively minor components of their total inventory. When a periodic system is in use, it usually is modified along the lines described below.

A Short-Cut System for Small Inventories

Some businesses maintain very little inventory, yet still sell substantial amounts of merchandise. This situation is especially likely to arise if the inventory is highly perishable. For example, restaurants, flower shops, and fish markets maintain very little inventory. In any given month, these businesses usually purchase about the same quantity of merchandise as they sell.

Such businesses often follow a policy of immediately debiting the Cost of Goods Sold account for the cost of all merchandise purchased. This approach enables a company to prepare monthly income statements without taking a physical inventory ***or*** recording separately the cost of each sales transaction. If the amount of inventory on hand at year-end is ***material in dollar amount,*** a physical inventory is taken. The Inventory account then is adjusted to reflect the amount indicated by the physical count, with the offsetting debit or credit posted to the Cost of Goods Sold account. If the inventory on hand is *immaterial,* it may be omitted from the balance sheet altogether or shown at a small, estimated dollar amount.

This "short-cut" approach appeals to small businesses with manual accounting systems because very little record keeping is required. However, this approach does *not* produce satisfactory results if the size of the company's inventory *fluctuates* significantly from month to month. Also, this short-cut system does not provide management with the benefits of an inventory subsidiary ledger.

Despite these limitations, this system works well in some small businesses. Also, some large businesses use this system in accounting for insignificant components of their inventory. A department store, for example, may use this system in its candy department, in its cafeteria, and in accounting for low-cost products such as shoelaces and novelty items.

Our objective in describing this modified periodic system is not to illustrate the accounting practices of fish markets and flower shops. Rather, it is intended to make an important point. Accounting systems are designed to meet the company's needs for accounting information *as efficiently as possible.* It is neither necessary, nor desirable, to develop more accounting information than is needed or wanted.

Specialized Types of Merchandising Transactions

In addition to the basic transactions comprising the operating cycle, merchandising companies must account for a number of more specialized merchandising transactions. Examples include discounts offered to credit customers for prompt payment, returns of merchandise by dissatisfied customers, and the handling of sales taxes.

In most merchandising companies, these types of transactions do not have a *material* affect upon the financial position of the business. Nonetheless, these transactions must be recorded properly if the business is to keep track of the amounts owed to each creditor and the amount due from each customer. We discuss many of these transactions in the Supplemental Topic section at the end of this chapter.

CLASSIFIED FINANCIAL STATEMENTS

Most business organizations prepare *classified* financial statements, meaning that items with certain characteristics are placed together in a group, or "classification." The purpose of these classifications is to *develop useful subtotals* which will assist users of the statements in evaluating the company's solvency, profitability, and future prospects. These classifications and subtotals are standardized throughout most of U.S. business, thus assisting decision makers in comparing the financial statements of different companies.

A Classified Balance Sheet

In a classified balance sheet, assets usually are presented in three groups: (1) current assets, (2) plant and equipment, and (3) other assets. Liabilities

OBJECTIVE 5
Prepare a
classified
balance
sheet . . .

are classified into two categories: (1) current liabilities and (2) long-term debt. A classified balance sheet for Computer Barn is illustrated below:

A classified balance sheet

COMPUTER BARN
Balance Sheet
December 31, 1994

Assets

Current assets:			
Cash			$ 30,000
Marketable securities			11,000
Notes receivable			5,000
Accounts receivable			60,000
Inventory			70,000
Prepaid expenses			4,000
Total current assets			$180,000
Plant and equipment:			
Land		$151,000	
Building	$120,000		
Less: Accumulated depreciation	9,000	111,000	
Sales fixtures & equipment	$ 45,000		
Less: Accumulated depreciation	27,000	18,000	
Total plant and equipment			280,000
Other assets: Land held as a future building site			170,000
Total assets			$630,000

Liabilities & Owner's Equity

Current liabilities:	
Notes payable (due in 6 months)	$ 20,000
Accounts payable	65,000
Sales taxes payable	3,000
Accrued expenses payable	8,000
Unearned revenue and customer deposits	4,000
Total current liabilities	$100,000
Long-term liabilities:	
Mortgage payable (due in 20 years)	210,000
Total liabilities	$310,000
Owner's equity:	
Pat O'Brien, capital	320,000
Total liabilities & owner's equity	$630,000

Using a Classified Balance Sheet in Evaluating Solvency

The classifications *current assets* and *current liabilities* are especially useful to short-term creditors in evaluating the immediate debt-paying ability, or *solvency,* of the business entity.

Current Assets   Current assets are relatively "liquid" resources; this category includes cash, investments in marketable securities, receivables, inventories, and prepaid expenses. To qualify as a current asset, an asset must be capable of ***being converted into cash*** within a relatively short period of time without interfering with normal business operations.[7]

The time period in which current assets are expected to be converted into cash is usually one year. If a company requires more than a year to complete its normal operating cycle, however, the ***length of the operating cycle*** is used as the time period defining current assets. Thus, ***inventory*** and ***accounts receivable from customers*** normally are classified as current assets, even if the conversion of these assets into cash will not be completed within one year.[8]

In a balance sheet, current assets are listed in order of liquidity (the closer an asset is to becoming cash, the greater its liquidity). Thus, cash always is listed first among the current assets, followed by marketable securities, receivables, inventory, and prepaid expenses.

Current Liabilities Current liabilities are ***existing debts*** which must be paid within the ***same time period*** used in defining current assets. Among the most common current liabilities are notes payable (due within one year), accounts payable, unearned revenue, and accrued expenses, such as salaries payable and interest payable. In the balance sheet, notes payable usually are listed first, followed by accounts payable; other types of current liabilities may be listed in any sequence.

The ***relationship*** between current assets and current liabilities is more important than the total dollar amount in either category. Current liabilities must be paid in the near future, and the money to pay these liabilities usually comes—in large part—from the conversion of current assets into cash. Thus, decision makers evaluating the solvency of a business often compare the amounts of current assets and current liabilities.

The Current Ratio

The most widely used measure of short-term debt-paying ability is the current ratio. The reader of a balance sheet may compute this ratio by ***dividing*** total current assets by total current liabilities.

OBJECTIVE 5 . . . Compute the current ratio and amount of working capital.

In the balance sheet of Computer Barn illustrated previously, current assets amount to $180,000 and current liabilities total $100,000, indicating a current ratio of ***1.8 to 1*** ($180,000 ÷ $100,000 = 1.8). A current ratio of 1.8 to 1 means that the company's current assets are 1.8 times as large as its current liabilities.

The higher the current ratio, the more solvent the company appears to be. Many bankers and other short-term creditors traditionally have believed that a retailer should have a current ratio of at least 2 to 1 to qualify as a good credit risk. By this standard, Computer Barn comes up

---

[7] Prepaid expenses are not actually "converted" into cash, but they ***substitute*** for cash by eliminating the need to make certain future cash payments.

[8] The time period used in defining current assets is one year or the length of the operating cycle, whichever is ***longer.*** Most businesses have operating cycles far shorter than one year. However, companies that sell merchandise on long-term installment contracts or that manufacture products such as ships may have operating cycles requiring several years to complete. The user of financial statements should recognize that the current assets of such companies are converted into cash ***much more slowly*** than are the current assets of most businesses.

a little short; the company probably would *not* receive a top credit rating from a bank or other short-term creditor which applied this criteria.

Evaluating Financial Ratios

We caution users of financial statements *against* placing much confidence in "rules of thumb," such as "a current ratio should be at least 2 to 1." To interpret any financial ratio properly, the decision maker must first understand the unique characteristics of the company and of the industry in which it operates.

Retailers, for example, tend to have higher current ratios than do wholesalers or manufacturing companies. Service-type businesses—which have no inventory—generally have lower current ratios than do merchandising or manufacturing companies. Large businesses with highly reliable sources of revenue and cash receipts are able to operate with lower current ratios than are smaller companies with less stable earnings.

CASE IN POINT   Large telephone companies are regarded within the business community as "pillars of financial strength." Yet these companies usually do not have high current ratios. Such financially sound companies as Bell Atlantic, BellSouth, NYNEX, and Pacific Telesis often maintain current ratios of less than 1 to 1.

Although a high current ratio is one indication of strong debt-paying ability, an extremely high ratio—say, 4 or 5 to 1—may indicate that *too much* of the company's resources are "tied up" in current assets. In maintaining such a highly liquid position, the company may be passing up opportunities for growth.

Standards for Comparison   We have seen that Computer Barn has a current ratio of 1.8 to 1. What standards for comparison are commonly used in evaluating such a statistic?

*OBJECTIVE 6
Identify two
standards
for compari-
son widely
used in eval-
uating
financial
ratios.*

Users of financial information generally use two criteria in evaluating the reasonableness of a financial ratio. One criterion is the *trend* in the ratio over a period of years. By reviewing this trend, the analyst is able to determine whether a company's performance or financial strength is improving or deteriorating. Second, an analyst compares a company's financial ratios with the ratios of *similar companies* and also with *industry-wide averages.* These comparisons assist the analyst in evaluating a particular ratio in light of the company's current business environment.

In summary, ratios are useful tools; but they can be interpreted properly only by individuals who understand the characteristics of the company and its environment.

Publicly owned corporations issue *annual reports* providing a great deal of information about the company, including comparative financial data for several years, and a discussion and analysis by management of the company's financial condition and the results of its recent operations. Financial information about *entire industries* is available through a number of financial publications and on-line computer data bases.

CASE IN POINT   Dun & Bradstreet, Inc., annually publishes *Key Business Ratios and Industry Norms* for many industries. Recent editions of this publication cover more than 800 different lines of business.

As an example of this "industry data," the average current ratios of several industry groups are shown below for a recent year:

Industry Group	Average Current Ratio
Air transport (major carriers)	1 to 1
Retail—general merchandise	2.1 to 1
Retail—women's specialty clothing	3.3 to 1
Wholesale—hardware	1.7 to 1
Manufacturing—computers	1.5 to 1
Telephone (regional)	.9 to 1*

*   Telephone company data were accumulated directly from annual reports.

Usefulness and Limitations of Ratios Analysis   A financial ratio expresses the relationship of one quantity or amount relative to another. Most users of financial statements find that certain ratios assist them in quickly evaluating the financial position, profitability, and future prospects of a business. A comparison of key ratios for several successive years may indicate whether the business is becoming stronger or weaker. Ratios also provide a means of comparing quickly the financial strength and profitability of different companies.

Users of financial statements should recognize, however, that ratios have several limitations. For example, management may enter into year-end transactions which temporarily improve key ratios. To illustrate, the balance sheet of Computer Barn includes current assets of $180,000 and current liabilities of $100,000, resulting in a current ratio of *1.8 to 1.* What would happen if shortly before year-end, management were to use $20,000 of the company's cash to pay off accounts payable? This transaction would reduce current assets to $160,000 and current liabilities to $80,000. However, it would also increase the company's year-end current ratio to a more impressive *2 to 1* ($160,000 ÷ $80,000 = 2).

Financial statement ratios contain the same limitations as do the dollar amounts used in financial statements. For example, assets usually are valued at historical cost rather than at current market value. Also, financial statement ratios express only *financial* relationships. They give no indication of a company's progress in achieving nonfinancial goals, such as creating new jobs or protecting the environment. A thorough analysis of the future prospects of any business involves more than merely computing and comparing financial ratios.

Working Capital

Working capital is another measurement often used to express the relationship between current assets and current liabilities. Working capital is the *excess* of current assets over current liabilities.[9] Our illustrated balance sheet indicates that at the end of 1994, Computer Barn has working capital of *$80,000* ($180,000 − $100,000).

The amount of working capital that a company needs to remain solvent varies with the size of the organization and the nature of its business activities. An analyst familiar with the nature of a company's operations usually can determine from the amount of working capital whether the company is in a sound financial position or is soon likely to encounter financial difficulties.

The Owner's Responsibility for Debts of the Business

Accountants view a business entity as separate from the other economic activities of the business owner (or owners). The law, however, draws an important distinction between corporations and unincorporated business organizations.

Under the law, the owners of *unincorporated* businesses (sole proprietorships and partnerships) are *personally liable* for any and all debts of the business organization. Therefore, creditors of unincorporated businesses often base their lending decisions upon the solvency of the business *owners* rather than upon the financial position of the business itself.

If a business is organized as a *corporation,* however, the owners (stockholders) are *not* personally responsible for the debts of the business. Creditors may look *only to the business entity* in seeking payment of their claims. Thus, the solvency of the business entity becomes much more important if the business is organized as a corporation.

Small Corporations and Loan "Guarantees"   Often small corporations do not have sufficient financial resources to qualify for credit. In such cases, creditors may require that one or more of the company's stockholders personally guarantee (or "co-sign") specific debts of the business entity. By co-signing debts of the corporation, individual stockholders become personally liable for the debt if the corporation fails to make payment.

CASE IN POINT   A small, family-owned wholesale business was organized as a corporation. To operate efficiently, the business needed to purchase merchandise on account. However, the corporation had so few liquid assets that suppliers were unwilling to extend credit. To obtain credit for the business, a major stockholder pledged his vacation home—a condominium on the Hawaiian island of Maui—to secure the company's debt to a particular supplier. With this additional security, the supplier allowed the business to purchase large quantities of merchandise on account.

Unfortunately, however, the small wholesale business became insolvent and was forced into bankruptcy. Not only did the owners' equity in this business become worthless, but one stockholder also lost his vacation home to the company's creditors.

---

[9]   A company with current liabilities in excess of its current assets has a *negative* amount of working capital. Negative working capital does *not* necessarily mean that a company is insolvent. Any company with a current ratio of less than 1 to 1 has a negative amount of working capital. As stated in the Case in Point on page 239, many major telephone companies fall into this category.

Classifications in an Income Statement

An income statement may be prepared in either the **multiple-step** or the **single-step** format. The multiple-step income statement is more useful in illustrating accounting concepts and has been used in all of our illustrations thus far. A multiple-step income statement for Computer Barn is illustrated below:

A multiple-step income statement

COMPUTER BARN
Income Statement
For the Year Ended December 31, 1994

Net sales		$900,000
Less: Cost of goods sold (including transportation-in)		540,000
Gross profit		$360,000
Less: Operating expenses:		
Selling expenses:		
Sales salaries and commissions	$78,800	
Advertising	42,000	
Delivery service	14,200	
Depreciation: store equipment	9,000	
Other selling expenses	6,000	
Total selling expenses	$150,000	
General & administrative expenses:		
Administrative & office salaries	$73,000	
Utilities	6,500	
Depreciation: building	8,500	
Other general & administrative expenses	11,000	
Total general & administrative expenses	99,000	
Total operating expense		249,000
Operating income		$111,000
Less (add): Nonoperating items:		
Interest expense	$23,000	
Purchase discounts lost	1,200	
Interest revenue	(3,200)	21,000
Net income		$ 90,000

This income statement also is **classified,** meaning that revenue and expenses have been classified into several categories. (For comparative purposes, this income statement is illustrated in single-step format on page 245.)

Multiple-Step Income Statements

The multiple-step income statement is so named because of a **series of steps** in which costs and expenses are deducted from revenue. As a first step, the cost of goods sold is deducted from sales revenue to determine the subtotal **gross profit.** As a second step, operating expenses are deducted to obtain a subtotal called **operating income** (or income from operations).

As a final step, "nonoperating" items are taken into consideration to arrive at *net income.*

Notice that the income statement is divided into four major sections: (1) revenue, (2) cost of goods sold, (3) operating expenses, and (4) nonoperating items. Multiple-step income statements are noted for their numerous sections and the development of significant subtotals.

The Revenue Section   The revenue section of an income statement usually contains only one line, entitled *Net sales.* Net sales represents the balance in the sales revenue account, less some minor adjustments for transactions such as refunds made to customers. These adjustments to sales revenue usually are not material in dollar amount and seldom are shown as separate items in the body of the income statement. (We illustrate and explain these transactions in the Supplemental Topic section at the end of this chapter.)

The *trend* in net sales from period to period is considered by many users of financial statements to be a key indicator of a company's future prospects. Increasing sales suggest the probability of larger profits in future periods. Declining sales, on the other hand, may provide advance warning of financial difficulties.

In our economy, most prices increase over time. The *average* increase in prices during the year is called the *rate of inflation.* Because of inflation, a company's total dollar sales may increase somewhat from year-to-year without any increase in the quantity of merchandise sold. If a company is selling more merchandise each year, its net sales usually increase *faster* than the rate of inflation.

The Cost of Goods Sold Section   The *matching principle* requires that revenue be offset by the costs and expenses incurred in generating that revenue. Therefore, revenue from sales must be offset by the cost to the merchandising business of acquiring the goods which it sells. The cost of goods sold usually is shown as a single amount in the income statement.

Gross Profit: A Key Subtotal   Gross profit is the *difference* between the sales revenue earned during the period and the *cost* to the business of the merchandise it has sold. In evaluating the performance of a merchandising company, many analysts find it useful to express the gross profit as a *percentage* of net sales. This percentage is called the *gross profit rate.* In 1994, Computer Barn has an average gross profit rate of *40%* (gross profit, $360,000, divided by net sales, $900,000, equals 40%).

By computing the gross profit rate earned in successive accounting periods, users of financial statements may gain insight into the strength of the company's products in the marketplace. A rising gross profit rate usually means that demand for the company's products is strong enough that the company has been able to increase its sales prices.[10] A declining gross profit rate, on the other hand, generally indicates a weakness in demand for the company's products.

---

[10]   An alternative explanation could be that the company is reducing its cost of goods sold relative to its selling prices. Reductions in the cost of goods sold are more likely to occur in companies that *manufacture* their inventories than in merchandising companies.

In evaluating the rate of gross profit earned by a particular company, the users of the financial statements should consider the rate earned by the company in prior periods and also the gross profit rates earned by other companies in the same industry. In most merchandising companies, the gross profit rate remains reasonably consistent from one period to the next.

Gross profit rates usually lie between 30% and 50% of net sales, depending upon the type of merchandise sold. The gross profit rate usually is lowest on fast-moving merchandise, such as groceries, and highest on low-volume goods, such as fine jewelry.

The Operating Expense Section   Operating expenses are incurred for the purpose of ***producing revenue.*** These expenses often are subdivided into functional classifications, such as ***selling expenses*** and ***general and administrative expenses.*** Subdividing operating expenses into functional classifications aids management and other users of the statements in evaluating different aspects of the company's operations separately.

The classification of operating expenses into subcategories is a common practice, but it is ***not required*** under generally accepted accounting principles. Also, the categories into which operating expenses are classified often vary from one company to the next.

Operating Income: Another Key Subtotal   Operating income (or income from operations) shows the relationship between revenue ***earned from customers*** and expenses incurred in ***producing this revenue.*** In effect, operating income measures the profitability of a company's ***basic business operations*** and "leaves out" other types of revenue and expenses.

Nonoperating Items   Revenue and expenses which are not directly related to the company's primary business activities are listed in a final section of the income statement following the determination of operating income.

Two significant "nonoperating items" are interest expense and corporate income taxes expense. Interest expense stems from the manner in which assets are ***financed,*** not the manner in which these assets are ***used*** in business operations. Corporate income taxes are not viewed as operating expenses because paying income taxes does not help produce revenue.[11]

Any nonoperating revenue, such as interest revenue earned on investments, also is listed in this section of the income statement.

Net Income   Most equity investors—that is, the owners—consider net income (or net loss) to be the most important figure in the income statement. This amount represents the overall increase (or decrease) in owners' equity resulting from business operations during the period.

Single-Step Income Statements

With its several classifications and subtotals, a multiple-step income statement highlights significant relationships. For this reason, it is widely used

---

[11]   Only those businesses organized as corporations are subject to corporate income taxes. Because Computer Barn (the company used in our example) is organized as a sole proprietorship, no income taxes expense appears in the company's income statement.

in accounting textbooks and in classroom illustrations. However, many large corporations use a ***single-step*** format in the income statements appearing in their annual reports.

The single-step format income statement takes its name from the fact that all costs and expenses are deducted from total revenue in a single step. No subtotals are shown for gross profit or for operating income, although the statement provides investors with enough information to compute these subtotals on their own. The 1994 income statement of Computer Barn, previously illustrated in the multiple-step format, is rearranged below in the single-step format:

A single-step income statement

COMPUTER BARN		
Income Statement		
For the Year Ended December 31, 1994		
Revenue:		
Net sales		$900,000
Interest earned		3,200
Total revenue		$903,200
Costs and expenses:		
Cost of goods sold	$540,000	
Selling expenses..	150,000	
General & administrative expenses	99,000	
Interest expense	23,000	
Purchase discounts lost....................................	1,200	
Total costs and expenses		813,200
Net income		$ 90,000

Evaluating the Adequacy of Net Income

OBJECTIVE 7
Analyze an income statement and evaluate the adequacy of net income.

Should the $90,000 net income of Computer Barn be viewed as excellent, fair, or poor performance for a business of this size? First, notice that Computer Barn is organized as a ***sole proprietorship.*** In an unincorporated business, no "salary expense" is deducted for the value of the personal services rendered to the business by the owner.[12] Any amounts paid to the owner are recorded as "withdrawals." Thus, the net income of a sole proprietorship represents, in part, compensation to the owner for any time and effort devoted to running the business.

The owner of a business also may have a substantial amount of money invested in the business in the form of owner's equity. Thus, the net income of the business also represents the owner's "return" on this financial investment.

Finally, the net income of a business should be adequate to compensate the owner for taking significant ***risks.*** Some studies show that more than half of all new businesses fail in their first year. Remember, in an unincor-

---

[12] The reason for omitting the owner's "salary" from the expenses is that the owner could set this salary at any desired level. An unrealistic salary to the owner, whether too high or too low, would lessen the usefulness of the income statement as a measure of the earning power of the business.

porated business, the owners are ***personally liable*** for the debts of the business. Therefore, if an unincorporated business sustains large losses, the owners can lose more than the amount of their equity investment. In fact, they can lose almost everything they own.

In summary, the net income of an unincorporated business should be sufficient to compensate the owner for three factors: (1) personal services rendered to the business, (2) a return on capital invested, and (3) the degree of financial risk which the owner is taking. Using these criteria, let us now appraise the adequacy of the $90,000 net income of Computer Barn.

Assume that Pat O'Brien, the owner of Computer Barn, works full time in the business. Also assume that if he were not running his own business, he could earn a salary of $50,000 per year managing a similar store.

Also notice that O'Brien has $320,000 invested in Computer Barn as of the end of the year. Let us assume that this also was the average amount of his ownership equity throughout the year. If this money had been invested in savings bonds, or in an interest-bearing bank account, O'Brien might have earned investment income of, say, $25,000.

Thus, the two factors of the owner's personal services and financial investment indicate a need for the company to earn at least $75,000 per year to be considered successful. As the business actually earned $90,000, it has provided a $15,000 "cushion" to compensate O'Brien for the risk involved in owning this type of business.

Whether or not $15,000 is adequate compensation for these risks depends upon the degree of risk involved in this type of business activity and upon O'Brien's personal attitude toward risk taking.

Remember, Computer Barn's profitability in the current year is no guarantee that the business will remain profitable in future years. By looking at the ***trend*** in net income over a period of several years, a user of the financial statements can see whether the business is becoming more or less profitable.

Evaluating the Net Income of a Corporation   If Computer Barn were organized as a corporation, both the amount of net income for the year and our evaluation of this net income would have been somewhat different. First, profitable corporations incur the expense of corporate income taxes, whereas unincorporated businesses do not. Also, corporations record as expenses all salaries paid to employees, even if these employees are owners (stockholders) of the business. Thus, if Computer Barn were organized as a corporation, its net income would have been lower by the amount of O'Brien's salary and the income taxes expense for the period. On the other hand, we then could ignore the value of O'Brien's personal services in evaluating the adequacy of the company's net income.

Stockholders tend to evaluate the net income of a corporation only in terms of (1) the amount of their financial investment and (2) the degree of risk which they are taking. Remember, however, that stockholders usually are exposed to ***less*** financial risk than are the owners of an unincorporated business, as they are ***not personally liable*** for the debts of the business entity.

We will discuss specific techniques for evaluating the adequacy of a corporation's earnings in later chapters.

■ ■ ■ **** Supplemental Topic***
Additional Merchandising Transactions

OBJECTIVE 8
Account for cash discounts, merchandise returns, transportation costs, and sales taxes.

In addition to the basic transactions illustrated and explained in this chapter, merchandising companies must account for a variety of additional transactions relating to purchases and sales of merchandise. Examples include discounts offered to credit customers for prompt payment, merchandise returns and refunds, transportation costs, and collecting and remitting sales taxes.

TRANSACTIONS RELATING TO PURCHASES

Purchases of merchandise are recorded at cost. However, this cost may be affected by such factors as cash discounts and transportation charges.

Credit Terms and Cash Discounts

Manufacturers and wholesalers normally sell merchandise **on account.** The credit terms are stated in the seller's bill, or **invoice.** One common example of credit terms is "net 30 days," or "n/30," meaning full payment is due in 30 days. Another common form of credit terms is "10 eom," meaning payment is due 10 days after the end of the month in which the purchase occurred.

Manufacturers and wholesalers usually allow their customers 30 or 60 days in which to pay for credit purchases. Frequently, however, sellers offer their customers a small discount to encourage earlier payment.

Perhaps the most common credit terms offered by manufacturers and wholesalers are **"2/10, n/30."** This expression is read "2, 10, net 30," and it means that full payment is due in 30 days, but that the buyer may take a **2% discount** if payment is made within 10 days. The period during which the discount is available is termed the **discount period.** Because the discount provides an incentive for the customer to make an early cash payment, it is called a **cash discount.** Buyers, however, often refer to these discounts as **purchase discounts,** while sellers frequently call them **sales discounts.**

Most well-managed companies have a policy of taking advantage of all cash discounts available on purchases of merchandise.[13] These companies initially record purchases of merchandise at the **net cost**—that is, the invoice price **minus** any available discount. After all, this is the amount that the company expects to pay.

To illustrate, assume that on November 3 Computer Barn purchases 100 spreadsheet programs from PC Products. The cost of these programs is $100 each, for a total of $10,000. However, PC Products offers credit terms of 2/10, n/30. If Computer Barn pays for this purchase within the discount period, it will have to pay only **$9,800,** or 98% of the full invoice price. Therefore, Computer Barn will record this purchase as follows:

[13] The terms 2/10, n/30 offer the buyer a 2% discount for sending payment 20 days before it is otherwise due. Saving 2% over only 20 days is equivalent to earning an annual rate of return of more than 36% ($2\% \times 365/20 = 36.5\%$). Thus, taking cash discounts represents an excellent investment opportunity. Most companies take advantage of all cash discounts, even if they must borrow from a bank the cash necessary to make payment within the discount period.

Purchase recorded at net cost

Inventory..	*9,800*	
Accounts Payable (PC Products).........................		*9,800*
To record purchase of 100 spreadsheet programs at net cost		
($100 × 98% × 50 units).		

If the invoice is paid within the discount period, Computer Barn simply records payment of a $9,800 account payable.

Through oversight or carelessness, Computer Barn might fail to make payment within the discount period. In this event, Computer Barn must pay PC Products the entire invoice price of **$10,000,** rather than the recorded liability of $9,800. The journal entry to record payment **after the discount period**—on, say, December 3—is:

Recording the loss of a cash discount

Accounts Payable (PC Products)	*9,800*	
Purchase Discounts Lost	*200*	
Cash		*10,000*
To record payment of invoice after expiration of discount period.		

Notice that the additional $200 paid because the discount period has expired is debited to an account entitled Purchase Discounts Lost. Purchase Discounts Lost is an **expense account.** The only benefit to Computer Barn from this $200 expenditure was a **20-day delay** in paying an account payable. Thus, the lost purchase discount is basically a **finance charge,** similar to interest expense. In an income statement, finance charges usually are classified as nonoperating expenses.

The fact that purchase discounts **not taken** are recorded in a separate expense account is the primary reason why a company should record purchases of merchandise at **net cost.** The use of a Purchase Discounts Lost account immediately brings to management's attention any failure to take advantage of the cash discounts offered by suppliers.

Returns of Unsatisfactory Merchandise

On occasion, a purchaser may find the purchased merchandise unsatisfactory and want to return it to the seller for a refund. Most sellers permit such returns.

To illustrate, assume that on November 9 Computer Barn returns to PC Products five of the spreadsheet programs purchased on November 3, because these programs were not properly labeled. As Computer Barn has not yet paid for this merchandise, the return will reduce the amount that Computer Barn owes PC Products. The gross invoice price of the returned merchandise was $500 ($100 per program). Remember, however, that Computer Barn records purchases at **net cost.** Therefore, these spreadsheet programs are carried in Computer Barn's inventory subsidiary ledger at a per-unit cost of **$98,** or $490 for the five programs being returned. The entry to record this purchase return is:

Return is based upon recorded acquisition cost

Accounts Payable (PC Products)	*490*	
Inventory		*490*
Returned 5 defective spreadsheet programs to supplier. Net cost		
of the returned items, $490 ($100 × 98% × 5 units).		

The reduction in inventory must also be recorded in the subsidiary ledger accounts.

Transportation Costs on Purchases

The purchaser sometimes may pay the costs of having the purchased merchandise delivered to its premises. Transportation costs relating to the *acquisition* of inventory or any other asset are *not expenses* of the current period; rather, these charges are *part of the cost of the asset* being acquired.[14] If the purchaser is able to associate transportation costs with specific products, these costs should be debited directly to the Inventory account as part of the "cost" of the merchandise.

Often, many different products arrive in a single shipment. In such cases, it may be impractical for the purchaser to determine the amount of the total transportation cost which is applicable to each product. For this reason, many companies follow the convenient policy of debiting all transportation costs on inbound shipments of merchandise to an account entitled *Transportation-in.* The dollar amount of transportation-in usually is too small to show separately in the financial statements. Therefore, this amount is merely included in the amount reported in the income statement as cost of goods sold. At the end of the period, the Transportation-in account is closed into the Income Summary in the same manner as the Cost of Goods Sold account.

This treatment of transportation costs is not entirely consistent with the matching principle. Some of the transportation costs may apply to merchandise still in inventory rather than to goods sold during the current period. We have mentioned, however, that transportation costs are relatively small in dollar amount. The accounting principle of *materiality,* therefore, usually justifies accounting for these costs in the most convenient manner.

TRANSACTIONS RELATING TO SALES

Credit terms and merchandise returns also affect the amount of sales revenue earned by the seller. To the extent that credit customers take advantage of cash discounts or return merchandise for a refund, the seller's revenue is reduced. Thus, revenue shown in the income statement of a merchandising concern is often called *net sales.*

The term *net sales* means total sales revenue *minus* sales returns and allowances and *minus* sales discounts. The following partial income statement illustrates this relationship:

COMPUTER BARN
Partial Income Statement
For the Year Ended December 31, 1994

What is "net sales"?

Revenue:		
Sales		$912,000
Less: Sales returns and allowances	*$8,000*	
Sales discounts	*4,000*	*12,000*
Net sales..		*$900,000*

---

[14] The "cost" of an asset includes all reasonable and necessary costs of getting the asset to an appropriate location and putting it into usable condition.

As we stated earlier in the chapter, the details of this computation seldom are shown in an actual income statement. The normal practice is to begin the income statement with the amount of net sales.

Sales Returns and Allowances

Most merchandising companies allow customers to obtain a refund by returning any merchandise considered to be unsatisfactory. If the merchandise has only minor defects, customers sometimes agree to keep the merchandise if an **allowance** (reduction) is made in the sales price.

Under the perpetual inventory system, two entries are needed to record the sale of merchandise: one to recognize the revenue earned and the other to transfer the cost of the merchandise from the Inventory account to Cost of Goods Sold. If some of the merchandise is returned, both of these entries are partially reversed.

First, let us consider the effects upon revenue of granting either a refund or an allowance. Both refunds and allowances have the effect of nullifying previously recorded sales and reducing the amount of revenue earned by the business. The journal entry to reduce sales revenue as the result of a sales return (or allowance) is shown below:

Sales Returns and Allowances *200*
        Accounts Receivable (or Cash) *200*
Customer returned merchandise purchased on account for $200.
Allowed customer full credit for returned merchandise.

Sales Returns and Allowances is a **contra-revenue** account—that is, it is deducted from gross sales revenue as a step in determining net sales.

Why use a separate Sales Returns and Allowances account rather than merely debiting the Sales account? The answer is that using a separate contra-revenue account enables management to see both the total amount of sales **and also** the amount of sales returns. The relationship between these amounts gives management an indication of customer satisfaction with the merchandise.

If merchandise is returned by the customer, a second entry is made to remove the cost of this merchandise from the Cost of Goods Sold account and restore it to the inventory records. This entry is:

Inventory. *160*
        Cost of Goods Sold *160*
To restore in the Inventory account the cost of merchandise returned by a customer.

Notice that this entry is based upon the **cost** of the returned merchandise to the seller, **not upon its sales price.** (This entry is not necessary when a sales **allowance** is granted to a customer who keeps the merchandise.)

Special accounts are maintained in the inventory subsidiary ledger for returned merchandise. Often this merchandise will be returned to the supplier or sold to a damaged-goods "liquidator" rather than again being offered for sale to the company's regular customers.[15]

---

[15] An inventory of returned merchandise should not be valued in the accounting records at a cost which exceeds its **net realizable value.** The possible need to write down the carrying value of inventory is discussed in Chapter 9.

Sales Discounts

We have explained that sellers frequently offer cash discounts, such as 2/10, n/30, to encourage their customers to make early payments for purchases on account.

Sellers and buyers account for cash discounts quite differently. To the seller, the "cost" associated with cash discounts is not the discounts *lost* when payments are delayed, but rather the discounts *taken* by customers that do pay within the discount period. Therefore, sellers design their accounting systems to measure the sales discounts *taken* by their customers. To achieve this goal, the seller records the sale and the related account receivable at the *gross* (full) invoice price.

To illustrate, assume that Computer Barn sells merchandise to Susan Hall for $1,000, offering terms of 2/10, n/30. The sales revenue is recorded at the full invoice price, as shown below:

Sales are recorded at the gross sales price	Accounts Receivable (Susan Hall) 1,000	
	Sales	1,000
	Sold merchandise on account. Invoice price, $1,000; terms, 2/10, n/30.	

If Hall makes payment after the discount period has expired, Computer Barn merely records the receipt of $1,000 cash in full payment of this account receivable. If Hall pays *within* the discount period, however, she will pay only **$980** to settle her account. In this case, Computer Barn will record the receipt of Hall's payment as follows:

Cash... 980	
Sales Discounts 20	
Accounts Receivable (Susan Hall).........................	1,000
Collected a $1,000 account receivable from a customer who took a 2% discount for early payment.	

Sales Discounts is a *contra-revenue* account. In computing net sales, sales discounts are deducted from gross sales along with any sales returns and allowances. (If the customer has returned part of the merchandise, a discount may be taken only on the gross amount owed *after* the return.)

Contra-revenue accounts have much in common with expense accounts; both are deducted from gross revenue in determining net, and both have debit balances. Thus, contra-revenue accounts (Sales Returns and Allowances and Sales Discounts) are closed into the Income Summary account in the same manner as expense accounts.

Delivery Expenses

If the seller incurs any costs in delivering merchandise to the customer, these costs are debited to an expense account entitled Delivery Expense. In an income statement, delivery expense is classified as a *selling expense,* not as part of the cost of goods sold.

Accounting for Sales Taxes

Sales taxes are levied by many states and cities on retail sales.[16] Sales taxes actually are imposed upon the consumer, not upon the seller. How-

---

[16] Sales taxes are applicable only when merchandise is sold to the *final consumer;* thus, no sales taxes are levied when manufacturers or wholesalers sell merchandise to retailers.

ever, the seller must collect the tax, file tax returns at times specified by law, and remit the taxes collected on all reported sales.

For cash sales, sales tax is collected from the customer at the time of the sales transaction. For credit sales, the sales tax is included in the amount charged to the customer's account. The liability to the governmental unit for sales taxes may be recorded at the time the sale is made as shown in the following journal entry:

Sales tax recorded at time of sale

Cash (or Accounts Receivable)	*1,050*	
Sales Tax Payable		*50*
Sales		*1,000*

To record sales of $1,000 subject to 5% sales tax.

This approach requires a separate credit entry to the Sales Tax Payable account for each sale. At first glance, this may seem to require an excessive amount of bookkeeping. However, today's electronic cash registers can be programmed to record automatically the sales tax liability at the time of each sale.

An Alternative Approach to Sales Taxes Instead of recording the sales tax liability at the time of sale, some businesses prefer to credit the Sales account with the entire amount collected, including the sales tax, and to make an adjustment at the end of each period to reflect sales tax payable. For example, suppose that the total recorded sales for the period under this method were $315,000. Since the Sales account includes both the sales price and the sales tax (say, 5%), it is apparent that $315,000 is **105%** of the actual sales figure. Actual sales are $300,000 (computed $315,000 ÷ 1.05) and the amount of sales tax due is $15,000. (Proof: 5% of $300,000 = $15,000.) The entry to record the liability for sales taxes would be

Sales tax recorded as adjustment of sales

Sales	*15,000*	
Sales Tax Payable		*15,000*

To remove sales taxes of 5% on $300,000 of sales from the Sales account, and record as a liability.

This second approach is widely used in businesses which do not use electronic devices for recording each sales transaction.

If some of the products being sold are not subject to sales tax (such as food), the business must keep separate records of taxable and nontaxable sales.

END-OF-CHAPTER REVIEW

SUMMARY OF CHAPTER LEARNING OBJECTIVES

1 **Describe the operating cycle of a merchandising company.**
The operating cycle is the repeating sequence of transactions by which a company generates revenue and cash receipts from customers. In a merchandising company, the operating cycle consists of the following transactions: (1) purchases of merchandise; (2) sale of the merchandise, often on account; and (3) collection of accounts receivable from customers.

2 Explain the need for various subsidiary ledgers in accounting for merchandising transactions.

Subsidiary ledgers provide a detailed record of the individual items comprising the balance of a general ledger controlling account. With respect to merchandising transactions, subsidiary ledgers are needed to keep track of the amounts receivable from individual customers, the amounts owed to specific suppliers, and the quantities of specific products in inventory.

3 Account for purchases and sales of merchandise using a perpetual inventory system.

In a perpetual inventory system, purchases are recorded by debiting the asset account Inventory. Two entries are required to record each sale: one to recognize sales revenue and the second to record the cost of goods sold. This second entry consists of a debit to the expense account Cost of Goods Sold and a credit to Inventory.

4 Distinguish between the perpetual and periodic inventory systems.

In a perpetual system, ledger accounts for Inventory and Cost of Goods Sold are kept ***perpetually up-to-date***—hence the name ***perpetual*** inventory system. The Inventory account is debited whenever goods are purchased. When sales occur, Cost of Goods Sold is debited and Inventory is credited for the cost of the merchandise sold. An inventory subsidiary ledger is maintained showing the cost and quantity of every type of product in the inventory.

In a periodic system, up-to-date records are ***not*** maintained either for inventory or for the cost of goods sold. The beginning and ending inventory are determined by a physical count. Purchases are recorded in a Purchases account, and no entries are made to record the cost of individual sales transactions. Rather, the cost of goods sold is determined by a computation made at the end of the year.

5 Prepare a classified balance sheet. Compute the current ratio and amount of working capital.

In a classified balance sheet, assets are subdivided into the categories of ***current assets, plant and equipment,*** and ***other assets.*** Liabilities are classified as ***current liabilities*** (those due within one year or an operating cycle, whichever is longer) or ***long-term liabilities.***

The current ratio is computed by dividing total current assets by total liabilities. Working capital is equal to the excess of current assets over current liabilities. The purpose of both computations is to provide users of the financial statements with a quick indication of the ***solvency*** of a business.

6 Identify two standards for comparison widely used in evaluating financial ratios.

Users of financial statements normally compare a company's financial ratios with the same ratios in (1) prior years and (2) similar companies and the industry viewed as a whole. The first comparison indicates whether the company's position is improving or deteriorating; the second assists the user in interpreting the ratios within the company's business environment.

7 Analyze an income statement and evaluate the adequacy of net income.

In an unincorporated business, the net income represents the owner's (1) compensation for personal services rendered to the business, (2) return on the equity capital invested in the business, and (3) return for taking significant financial risks. The "adequacy" of net income is determined by the value that the owner assigns to each of these factors.

*8 Account for cash discounts, merchandise returns, transportation costs, and sales taxes.

Buyers should record purchases at the ***net*** cost and record any cash discounts lost in an expense account. Sellers record sales at the gross sales price and record in a contra-revenue account all cash discounts ***taken*** by customers.

The buyer records a purchase return by crediting the Inventory account for the net cost of the returned merchandise. In recording a sales return, the seller makes two entries: one debiting Sales Returns and Allowances (a contra-revenue account) for the amount of the refund and the other transferring the cost of the returned merchandise from the Cost of Goods Sold account back into the Inventory account.

Buyers record transportation charges on purchased merchandise either as part of the cost of the merchandise or as part of the cost of goods sold. Sellers view the cost of delivering merchandise to customers as an operating expense.

Sales taxes are collected by retailers from their customers and are remitted to state government. The retailer may credit a liability account, Sales Taxes Payable, as each sale is made ***or*** may wait until the end of the period and compute the tax liability as a percentage of taxable sales.

In Chapter 5 your knowledge of accounting concepts and practices has been expanded to include the purchase and sale of merchandise. You have now seen how both service-type businesses and merchandising companies measure and report their financial position and the results of their business operations in conformity with generally accepted accounting principles. In addition, you have made some important first steps toward proficiency in analyzing and interpreting financial statements.

In the next chapter we will continue our discussion of merchandising transactions with emphasis on internal control and upon streamlining an accounting system to process efficiently a large volume of transactions.

KEY TERMS INTRODUCED IN CHAPTER 5

Classified financial statements Financial statements in which similar items are arranged in groups; subtotals are shown to assist users in analyzing the statements.

Controlling account A general ledger account which summarizes the content of a specific subsidiary ledger.

Cost of goods sold The cost to a merchandising company of the goods which it has sold to its customers during the period.

---

* *Supplemental Topic, "Additional Merchandising Transactions"*

Current assets　Cash and other assets which can be converted into cash within one year or the operating cycle (whichever is longer) without interfering with normal business operations.

Current liabilities　Existing liabilities which must be paid within one year or the operating cycle (whichever is longer).

Current ratio　Current assets divided by current liabilities. A measure of short-term debt-paying ability.

Gross profit　Sales revenue minus the cost of goods sold.

Gross profit rate　Gross profit expressed as a percentage of net sales. Provides a useful measure over time of the strength of a company's products in the marketplace.

Inventory shrinkage　The loss of merchandise through such causes as shoplifting, breakage, and spoilage.

Multiple-step income statement　An income statement in which the cost of goods sold and expenses are subtracted from revenue in a series of steps, thus producing a number of useful subtotals.

Net sales　Gross sales revenue less sales returns and allowances and minus sales discounts. Usually the first figure shown in an income statement.

Operating cycle　The repeating sequence of transactions by which a business generates its revenue and cash receipts from customers.

Operating income　A subtotal in an income statement representing the revenue earned from customers less only those expenses incurred for the purpose of generating that revenue.

Periodic inventory system　An alternative to the perpetual inventory system which eliminates the need for recording the cost of goods sold as sales occur. However, the amounts of inventory and the cost of goods sold are not known until a complete physical inventory is taken at year-end.

Perpetual inventory system　A system of accounting for merchandising transactions in which the Inventory and Cost of Goods Sold accounts are kept perpetually up-to-date.

Point-of-sale terminals　Electronic cash registers used for computer-based processing of sales transactions. Capable of recording sales and the cost of goods sold and also of updating accounts receivable and inventory subsidiary records. Permit the use of a perpetual inventory system even in a business selling a high volume of merchandise.

Single-step income statement　An income statement in which the cost of goods sold and all expenses are combined and deducted from total revenue in a single step.

Subsidiary ledger　A ledger containing separate accounts for each of the items comprising the balance of a controlling account in the general ledger. The total of the account balances in a subsidiary ledger is equal to the balance in the general ledger controlling account.

Working capital　Current assets minus current liabilities. A measure of short-run debt-paying ability.

DEMONSTRATION PROBLEM FOR YOUR REVIEW

Texas Wholesale Corporation sold 100 pairs of boots to Boot Hill, a chain of retail stores. The sales price was $5,000 ($50 per pair), with terms of 2/10, n/30. United Express charged $162 to deliver this merchandise to Boot Hill's stores; these charges were split evenly between the buyer and seller and were paid in cash.

Boot Hill returned 10 pairs of these boots to Texas Wholesale because they were the wrong style. Texas Wholesale agreed to accept this return and credit Boot Hill's account for the full invoice price. Boot Hill then paid the remaining balance within the discount period.

Both companies use perpetual inventory systems.

INSTRUCTIONS

a Record this sequence of transactions in the general journal of Texas Wholesale Corporation. The company records sales at the full invoice price; these boots had cost Texas Wholesale $32 per pair.

b Record this sequence of transactions in the general journal of Boot Hill. The company records purchases of merchandise at *net cost* and uses a Transportation-in account in recording transportation charges on inbound shipments.

SOLUTION TO DEMONSTRATION PROBLEM

General Journal

a Journal entries by Texas Wholesale Corporation:

Accounts Receivable (Boot Hill)	5,000	
Sales		5,000
Sold merchandise on account; terms, 2/10, n/30.		
Cost of Goods Sold	3,200	
Inventory		3,200
To record cost of merchandise sold ($32/pr. × 100 pr.).		
Delivery Expense	81	
Cash		81
Paid delivery charges on outbound shipment.		
Sales Returns and Allowances	500	
Accounts Receivable (Boot Hill)		500
Customer returned merchandise with a sales price of $500.		
Inventory	320	
Cost of Goods Sold		320
Reduce cost of goods sold for cost of returned merchandise ($32/pr. × 10 pr.).		
Cash	4,410	
Sales Discount	90	
Accounts Receivable (Boot Hill)		5,000
Collected amount due from credit sale to Boot Hill, less $500 return and less 2% cash discount on remaining $4,500 balance ($4,500 × 2% = $90).		

b Journal entries by Boot Hill:

Inventory	4,900	
Accounts Payable (Texas Wholesale Corp.)		4,500
Purchased 100 pairs of boots on account; terms, 2/10, n/30. Net cost, $49 cost, $49 per pair ($50, less 2%).		
Transportation-in	81	
Cash		81
Paid transportation charges in inbound shipment.		

Accounts Payable (Texas Wholesale Corp.)	490	
Inventory		490

Returned 10 pairs of boots to supplier. (Net cost, $49 per pair × 10 pairs = $490.)

Accounts Payable (Texas Wholesale Corp.)	4,410	
Cash		4,410

Paid within discount period balance owed to Texas Wholesale Corp. ($4,900 − $490 = $4,410).

SELF-TEST QUESTIONS

Answers to these questions appear on page 272.

1   Mark and Amanda Carter own an appliance store and a restaurant. The appliance store sells merchandise on a 12-month installment plan; the restaurant sells only for cash. (More than one answer may be correct.)

   a   The appliance store has a longer operating cycle than the restaurant.

   b   The appliance store probably uses a perpetual inventory system, whereas the restaurant probably uses a periodic system.

   c   Both businesses require subsidiary ledgers for accounts receivable and inventory.

   d   Both businesses probably have subsidiary ledgers for accounts payable.

2   Which of the following types of information are found in subsidiary ledges, but *not* in the general ledger? (More than one answer may be correct.)

   a   Total cost of goods sold for the period.

   b   The quantity of a particular product sold during the period.

   c   The dollar amount owed to a particular creditor.

   d   The portion of total current assets that consists of cash.

3   The two basic approaches to accounting for inventory and the cost of goods sold are the ***perpetual*** inventory system and the ***periodic*** inventory system. Indicate which of the following statements are correct. (More than one answer may be correct.)

   a   Most large merchandising companies and manufacturing businesses use periodic inventory systems.

   b   As a practical matter, a grocery store or a large department store could not maintain a perpetual inventory system without the use of point-of-sale terminals.

   c   In a periodic inventory system the cost of goods sold is not determined until a complete physical inventory is taken.

   d   In a perpetual inventory system, the Cost of Goods Sold account is debited promptly for the cost of merchandise sold.

4   Pisces Market presently has current assets totaling $300,000 and a current ratio of 2.5 to 1. Compute the current ratio immediately ***after*** Pisces pays $30,000 of its accounts payable.

   a   3 to 1   b   3.33 to 1   c   2.2 to 1   d   2.25 to 1

5 Which of the following items are deducted as expense in the income statement of a merchandising business organized as a corporation, but **not** in the income statement of an unincorporated business? (More than one answer may be correct.)

a Cost of goods sold.

b Income taxes expense.

c Sales taxes expense.

d Amounts paid to the owner for services rendered to the business.

*6 Big Brother, a retail store, purchased 100 television sets from Krueger Electronics on account at a cost of $200 each. Krueger offers credit terms of 2/10, n/30. Big Brother uses a perpetual inventory system and records purchases at **net cost.** Big Brother determines that 10 of these television sets are defective and returns them to Krueger for full credit. In recording this return, Big Brother will:

a Debit Sales Returns and Allowances.

b Debit Accounts Payable, $1,960.

c Debit Cost of Goods Sold, $1,960.

d Credit Inventory, $2,000.

ASSIGNMENT MATERIAL

DISCUSSION QUESTIONS

1 Describe the operating cycle of a merchandising company.

2 Compare and contrast the merchandising activities of a wholesaler and a retailer.

3 The income statement of a merchandising company includes a major type of cost which does not appear in the income statement of a service-type business. Identify this cost and explain what it represents.

4 During the current year, Green Bay Company earned a gross profit of $350,000, whereas New England Company earned a gross profit of only $280,000. Does this mean that Green Bay is more profitable than New England? Explain.

5 Thornhill Company's income statement shows gross profit of $432,000, cost of goods sold of $638,000, and other expenses totaling $390,000. Compute the amounts of (a) revenue from sales (net sales) and (b) net income.

6 Explain the need for subsidiary ledgers in accounting for merchandising activities.

7 All Night Auto Parts, Inc., maintains subsidiary ledgers for accounts receivable, inventory, and accounts payable. Explain in detail what information from the following journal entry should be posted, and to which subsidiary and general ledger accounts.

Inventory *420*
        Accounts Payable (Boss Automotive) *420*
Purchased 12 Boss LoadMaster II shock absorbers. Cost,
$35 per unit.

---

*   *Supplemental Topic, "Additional Merchandising Transactions"*

8 What is meant by the phrase "reconciling a subsidiary ledger"? In general terms, what is the purpose of this procedure?

9 Define the term *inventory shrinkage.* How is the amount of inventory shrinkage determined in a business using a perpetual inventory system, and how is this shrinkage recorded in the accounting records?

10 Briefly contrast the accounting procedures in *perpetual* and *periodic* inventory systems.

11 Miracle Home Cleanser uses a *periodic* inventory system. During the current year the company purchased merchandise with a cost of $55,000. State the cost of goods sold for the year under each of the following alternative assumptions:

    a No beginning inventory; ending inventory $3,500.

    b Beginning inventory $10,000; no ending inventory.

    c Beginning inventory $2,000; ending inventory $7,200.

    d Beginning inventory $8,000; ending inventory $1,400.

12 Evaluate the following statement: "Without electronic point-of-sale terminals, it simply would not be possible to use perpetual inventory systems in businesses which sell large quantities of many different products."

13 Some companies use a modified version of the periodic inventory system in which purchases are charged directly to the Cost of Goods Sold account. Under what circumstances will such a system produce satisfactory results?

14 How does interest expense differ from normal operating expenses such as advertising and salaries? How is interest expense presented in a multiple-step income statement?

15 What is the basic purpose of *classifications* in financial statements?

16 What is the basic characteristic of *current assets?* Many retail stores regularly sell merchandise on "installment plans," calling for payments over a period of 24 or 36 months. Do such receivables qualify as current assets? Explain.

17 Madison Corporation has current assets of $570,000 and current liabilities of $300,000. Compute the current ratio and the amount of working capital.

18 Identify two criteria which users of financial statements often use in evaluating the reasonableness of the financial ratios of a particular company.

19 Briefly describe the extent of a business owner's personal liability for the debts of (a) an unincorporated business and (b) a corporation.

20 Describe the format of a multiple-step income statement and that of a single-step income statement.

21 Define the term *gross profit rate.* Explain two factors which may cause a company's gross profit rate to increase.

22 Distinguish between *operating income* and *net income.*

23 Identify the three basic factors for which the net income of a sole proprietorship compensates the owner.

*24 How does a balance arise in the Purchase Discounts Lost account? Why does management pay careful attention to the balance (if any) in this account?

---

*   *Supplemental Topic, "Additional Merchandising Transactions"*

*25 European Imports pay substantial freight charges to obtain inbound shipments of purchased merchandise. Should these freight charges be debited to the company's Delivery Expense account? Explain.

*26 Outback Sporting Goods purchases merchandise on terms of 4/10, n/60. The company has a "line of credit" which enables it to borrow money as needed from Northern Bank at an annual interest rate of 13%. Should Outback pay its suppliers within the 10 day discount period if it must draw on its line of credit (borrow from Northern Bank) to make these early payments? Explain.

*27 TireCo is a retail store in a state that imposes a 6% sales tax. Would you expect to find sales tax expense and sales tax payable in TireCo's financial statements? Explain.

*28 A seller generally records sales at the full invoice price, but the buyer usually records purchases at **net cost.** Explain the logic of the buyer and seller recording the transaction at different amounts.

EXERCISES

EXERCISE 5-1
Accounting
Terminology

Listed below are nine technical accounting terms introduced in this chapter.

Perpetual inventory system	*Periodic inventory system*	*Classified financial statements*
Gross profit	*Current ratio*	*Subsidiary ledger*
Cost of goods sold	*Working capital*	*Operating income*

Each of the following statements may (or may not) describe one of these technical terms. For each statement, indicate the term described, or answer "None" if the statement does not correctly describe any of the terms.

a Current assets plus current liabilities.

b An item deducted from revenue in the income statement of a merchandising company which **does not appear** in the income statement of a service-type business.

c Revenue earned from customers, less expenses relating directly to the production of this revenue.

d An approach to accounting for inventory and determining the cost of goods sold which is based upon complete annual physical counts of the inventory.

e An accounting record providing detail about the individual items comprising the balance of a controlling account.

f The difference between the sales price and the cost of all merchandise sold during the period.

g An approach to accounting for inventory and the cost of goods sold which produces up-to-date accounting records, including an inventory subsidiary ledger.

EXERCISE 5-2
Effects of
Basic Merchan-
dising Transac-
tions

Shown below are selected transactions of Marston's, a retail store which uses a perpetual inventory system:

a Purchased merchandise on account.

b Recognized the revenue from a sale of merchandise on account. (Ignore the related cost of goods sold.)

c Recognized the cost of goods sold relating to the sale in transaction **b.**

---

*   *Supplemental Topic, "Additional Merchandising Transactions"*

d Collected in cash the account receivable from the customer in transaction **b.**

e Following the taking of a physical inventory at year-end, made an adjusting entry to record a normal amount of inventory shrinkage.

Indicate the effects of each of these transactions upon the elements of the company's financial statements shown below. Organize your answer in tabular form, using the column headings shown below. (Notice that the cost of goods sold is shown separately from all other expenses.) Use the code letters *I* for increase, *D* for decrease, and *NE* for no effect.

	Income Statement				Balance Sheet		
Transaction	*Net Sales* −	*Cost of Goods Sold* −	*All Other Expenses* =	*Net Income*	*Assets* =	*Liabilities* +	*Owners'* Equity*
a							

EXERCISE 5-3
Subsidiary Ledgers

Listed below are eight typical merchandising transactions of Everyday Auto Parts, a retail auto supply store.

a Purchased merchandise from Acme Wholesale on account.

b Paid an account payable to a supplier.

c Sold merchandise for cash.

d Sold merchandise on account.

e Collected an account receivable from a customer.

*f Returned merchandise to a supplier, receiving credit against the amount owed.

*g Gave a cash refund to a customer who returned merchandise.

*h Reduced the account receivable from a credit customer who returned merchandise.

Among the account records of Everyday Auto Parts are subsidiary ledgers for inventory, accounts receivable, and accounts payable. For each of the eight transactions, you are to indicate any subsidiary ledger (or ledgers) to which the transaction would be posted. Use the codes below:

Inv = Inventory subsidiary ledger

AR = Accounts receivable subsidiary ledger

AP = Accounts payable subsidiary ledger

Also indicate whether each posting causes the balance in the subsidiary ledger account to *increase* or *decrease.* Organize your answer in tabular form as illustrated below. The answer for transaction **a** is provided as an example.

Transaction	*Subsidiary Ledger*	*Effect upon Subsidiary Account Balance*
a	*Inv*	*Increase*
	AP	*Increase*

EXERCISE 5-4
Posting to Subsidiary Ledgers

In addition to a general ledger, LeatherWorks maintains subsidiary ledgers for accounts receivable, inventory, and accounts payable (the company does not maintain a subsidiary ledger for cash). Two entries appearing in the company's journal are illustrated on the following page, along with the posting references which have been entered in the LP column:

---
*   *Supplemental Topic, "Additional Merchandising Transactions"*

General Journal

Accounts Titles and Explanation	LP	Debit	Credit
Inventory..	✓/130	2,500	
Accounts Payable (Pucci, Inc.)	✓		2,500
Purchased 50 shoulder bags from Pucci, Inc., @ $50; payment due in 30 days.			
Cash...	101	6,000	
Accounts Receivable (The Bag Man)	105		6,000
Collected an account receivable.			

INSTRUCTIONS

a Based upon the posting references shown, explain in detail the accounts to which the debit and credit portions of each journal entry apparently have been posted.

b Does it appear that the posting of each entry has been completed properly? Explain. (Assume that illustrated account numbers are correct.)

**EXERCISE 5-5
Perpetual
Inventory
System**

Caliente Products uses a perpetual inventory system. On January 1 the Inventory account had a balance of $93,500. During the first few days of January the following transactions occurred:

Jan. 2 Purchased merchandise on credit from Bell Company for $12,500.

Jan. 3 Sold merchandise for cash, $9,000. The cost of this merchandise was $6,300.

INSTRUCTIONS

a Prepare entries in general journal form to record the above transactions.

b What was the balance of the Inventory account at the close of business January 3?

**EXERCISE 5-6
Taking a Physi-
cal Inventory**

Electronics Warehouse uses a perpetual inventory system. At year-end, the Inventory account has a balance of $314,000, but a physical count shows that the merchandise on hand has a cost of only $307,500.

INSTRUCTIONS

a Explain the probable reason(s) for this discrepancy.

b Prepare the journal entry required in this situation.

c Indicate all the accounting records to which your journal entry in part **b** should be posted.

**EXERCISE 5-7
Periodic
Inventory
System**

Hanson's Gift Shop uses a periodic inventory system. At the end of 1994, the accounting records include the following information:

Inventory, December 31, 1993	$ 6,700
Inventory, December 31, 1994	4,400
Net sales...	160,400
Purchases	81,500

INSTRUCTIONS

a How were the amounts of beginning and ending inventory determined?

b Compute the amount of the cost of goods sold in 1994.

c Prepare a partial income statement showing the shop's gross profit in the year.

EXERCISE 5-8
A Quick Look at IBM's Current Position

A balance sheet of **IBM** contained the following items among others. (Dollar amounts are stated in millions.)

Cash	$ 770
Investment in marketable securities (current asset)	6,197
Notes & accounts receivable (net)	12,757
Other current receivables	1,092
Inventories	8,645
Prepaid expenses and other current assets	1,559
Plant & other property (net of depreciation)	20,082
Accounts payable	2,627
Loans payable (short term)	1,629
Taxes payable	2,534
Other current liabilities	6,587
Long-term debt	3,858
Stockholders' equity	38,263

INSTRUCTIONS

a From the above information, compute the amount of IBM's current assets and the amount of its current liabilities.

b How much working capital does IBM have?

c Compute the current ratio to the nearest tenth of a percent.

EXERCISE 5-9
Recognition of Industry Characteristics

Reebok is a manufacturer of popular athletic footware. **Bell Atlantic** is the largest telephone company in the northeastern United States. Both companies are solvent and profitable. Which company would you expect to have the higher current ratio? Which company do you believe has the greater debt-paying ability? Explain fully the reasons for your answers.

EXERCISE 5-10
Logical Gross Profit Relationships

Several factors must be considered in interpreting a company's gross profit rate.

a Companies such as **Lotus Development** and **Microsoft** usually enjoy a higher gross profit rate on sales of a particular software product when it is first introduced than they do in later years. Why?

b For each of the following pairs of businesses, indicate which you would expect to have the highest gross profit rate. Briefly explain the reasons for your answer.

   1 A grocery store, or a retail furniture store.

   2 **Neiman-Marcus** (a chain of high-fashion department stores), or **Wal-Mart** (a rapidly growing chain of discount stores).

EXERCISE 5-11
Classifications Within an Income Statement

Coast Hardware and Fashion Center are sole proprietorships of similar size. Also, both businesses earn similar amounts of revenue, incur similar amounts of operating expenses, and earn similar net incomes. However, Coast has a higher cost of goods sold, while Fashion Center has higher interest expense.

Indicate which of these companies has the higher (a) gross profit rate and (b) operating income. In each case, explain the reasons for your answer.

*EXERCISE 5-12
Cash Discounts

Key Imports sold merchandise to Marine Systems for $7,500, offering terms of 2/10, n/30. Marine Systems paid for the merchandise within the discount period. Both companies use perpetual inventory systems.

---

*   *Supplemental Topic, "Additional Merchandising Transactions"*

INSTRUCTIONS   a   Prepare journal entries in the accounting records of Key Imports to account for this sale and the subsequent collection. Assume the original cost of the merchandise to Key Imports had been $4,100.

b   Prepare journal entries in the accounting records of Marine Systems to account for the purchase and subsequent payment. Marine Systems records purchases of merchandise at **net cost.**

c   Assume that because of a change in personnel, Marine Systems failed to pay for this merchandise within the discount period. Prepare the journal entry in the accounting records of Marine Systems to record payment **after** the discount period.

*EXERCISE 5-13
Net Sales and
Gross Profit

Glamour, Inc., is a retail store. In 1993, the company had gross sales revenue of $2,490,000, cost of goods sold of $1,248,000, sales returns and allowances of $59,000, and allowed sales discounts of $31,000.

Compute for the year (a) net sales, (b) gross profit, and (c) gross profit rate. Show supporting computations.

*EXERCISE 5-14
Returned
Merchandise

College Bookstore returned certain merchandise which it had purchased from McGraw-Hill. McGraw-Hill allowed the bookstore full credit for this return against the account receivable from the bookstore.

The returned merchandise had been purchased by College Bookstore for $5,000, terms 2/10, n/30. College Bookstore records purchases of merchandise **net** of any available cash discounts.

INSTRUCTIONS   Prepare journal entries to record the return of this merchandise in the accounting records of (a) College Bookstore and (b) McGraw-Hill. (Assume that the cost of the merchandise to McGraw-Hill had been $3,900.)

*EXERCISE 5-15
Accounting for
Sales Taxes

Trophy Shop operates in an area in which a 5% sales tax is levied on all products handled by the store. On cash sales, the salesclerks include the sales tax in the amount collected from the customer and ring up the entire amount on the cash register without recording separately the tax liability. On credit sales, the customer is charged for the list price of the merchandise plus 5%, and the entire amount is debited to Accounts Receivable and credited to the Sales account. On sales of less than one dollar, the tax collected is rounded to the nearest cent.

Sales tax must be remitted to the government quarterly. At March 31 the Sales account showed a balance of $326,025 for the three-month period ended March 31.

INSTRUCTIONS   a   What amount of sales tax is owed at March 31?

b   Give the journal entry to record the sales tax liability in the accounting records.

PROBLEMS

Note: This chapter contains an unusually wide variety of problem assignments. In order to make all of these problems readily available to all users of the text, we present them in **one consecutive series,** rather than splitting them into A and B groups. This series is supported in **both** the Group A and Group B packages of accounting work sheets.

PROBLEM 5-1
The Only Lum-
beryard in
Beaumont

Indian Lake Lumber Company is the only lumberyard in Beaumont, a remote mountain town and popular ski resort. Some of Indian Lake's transactions during 1994 are as follows:

---

*   *Supplemental Topic, "Additional Merchandising Transactions"*

Nov. 5   Sold lumber on account to Dally Construction Company, $38,400. The inventory subsidiary ledger shows the cost of this merchandise to Indian Lake was $22,950.

Nov. 9   Purchased lumber on account from Pine Valley Mill, $104,000.

Dec. 5   Collected in cash the $38,400 account receivable from Dally Construction Company.

Dec. 9   Paid the $104,000 owed to Pine Valley Mill.

Dec. 31   Company personnel counted the inventory on hand and determined its cost to be $964,360. The accounting records, however, indicate inventory of $975,130 and a cost of goods sold of $3,217,130. The physical count of the inventory was observed by the company's auditors and is considered correct.

INSTRUCTIONS   a   Prepare journal entries to record these transactions and events in the accounting records of Indian Lake Lumber Company. (The company uses a perpetual inventory system.)

b   Prepare a partial income statement showing the company's gross profit for the year. (Net sales for the year amount to $4,966,000.)

c   Indian Lake purchases lumber at the same wholesale prices as other lumber companies. Due to its remote mountain location, however, the company must pay between $90,000 and $100,000 per year in extra transportation charges to receive delivery of its purchased lumber. (These additional charges are included in the amount shown as cost of goods sold.)

  Assume that an index of key business ratios in your library shows retail lumberyards of Indian Lake's approximate size (in total assets) average net sales of $5,000,000 per year and a gross profit rate of **27%**.

  Is Indian Lake Lumber Company able to pass its extra transportation costs on to its customers? Does the company appear to suffer or benefit financially from its remote location? Explain your reasoning and support your conclusions with specific accounting data comparing the operations of Indian Lake Lumber Company with the industry averages.

**PROBLEM 5-2
Perpetual Inventory System and an Inventory Subsidiary Ledger**   Facts-by-FAX sells facsimile machines, copiers, and other types of office equipment. On May 10, the company purchased for the first time a new "plain-paper" fax manufactured by Mitsui Corporation. Transactions relating to this product during May and June were as follows:

May 10   Purchased five P-500 facsimile machines on account from Mitsui Corporation, at a cost of $540 each. Payment due in 30 days.

May 23   Sold four P-500 facsimile machines on account to Foster & Cole, stockbrokers; sales price, $900 per machine. Payment due in 30 days.

May 24   Purchased an additional nine P-500 facsimile machines on account from Mitsui. Cost, $540 per machine; payment due in 30 days.

June 9   Paid $2,700 cash to Mitsui Corporation for the facsimile machines purchased on May 5.

June 19   Sold two P-500 facsimile machines to Tri-State Realty for cash. Sales price, $950 per machine.

June 22   Collected $3,600 from Foster & Cole in full settlement of the credit sale on May 23.

INSTRUCTIONS   a   Prepare journal entries to record these transactions in the accounting records of Facts-by-FAX. (The company uses a perpetual inventory system.)

b Post the appropriate information from these journal entries to an inventory subsidiary ledger account like the one illustrated on page 231.)

c How many Mitsui P-500 facsimile machines were in inventory on May 31? From what accounting record did you obtain the answer to this question?

d Describe the types of information contained in any inventory subsidiary ledger account and explain how this information may be useful to various company personnel in conducting daily business operations.

PROBLEM 5-3
The Periodic Inventory System

Mountain Mabel's is a small general store located just outside of Yellowstone National Park. The store uses a periodic inventory system. Every January 1, Mabel and her husband close the store and take a complete physical inventory while watching the Rose Parade on television. Last year, the inventory amounted to $1,700; this year it totaled $2,800. During the current year, the business recorded sales of $105,000 and purchases of $31,000.

INSTRUCTIONS

a Compute the cost of goods sold for the current year.

b Explain why a small business such as this might use the periodic inventory system.

c Explain some of the **disadvantages** of the periodic system to a larger business, such as a Sears store.

PROBLEM 5-4
Comparison of Inventory Systems

Satellite Trackers sells satellite tracking systems for receiving television broadcasts from satellites in outer space. At December 31 last year, the company's inventory amounted to $22,000. During the first week of January this year, the company made only one purchase and one sale. These transactions were as follows:

Jan. 3 Sold one tracking system costing $11,200 to Mystery Mountain Resort for cash, $18,900.

Jan. 6 Purchased merchandise on account from Yamaha, $9,600. Terms, net 30 days.

INSTRUCTIONS

a Prepare journal entries to record these transactions assuming that Satellite Trackers uses the perpetual inventory system. Use separate entries to record the sales revenue and the cost of goods sold for the sale on January 2.

b Compute the balance of the Inventory account on January 7.

c Prepare journal entries to record the two transactions assuming that Satellite Trackers uses the periodic inventory system.

d Compute the cost of goods sold for the first week of January assuming use of a periodic inventory system. Use your answer to part **b** as the ending inventory.

e Which inventory system do you believe that a company such as Satellite Trackers would probably use? Explain your reasoning.

PROBLEM 5-5
Alternate to Problem 5-4

Halley's Space Scope sells state-of-the-art telescopes to individuals and organizations interested in studying the solar system. At December 31 last year, the company's inventory amounted to $90,000. During the first week of January this year, the company made only one purchase and one sale. These transactions were as follows:

Jan. 2 Sold one telescope costing $28,000 to Eastern State University for cash, $40,000.

Jan. 5 Purchased merchandise on account from Solar Optics, $18,500. Terms, net 30 days.

INSTRUCTIONS

a Prepare journal entries to record these transactions assuming that Halley's Space Scope uses the perpetual inventory system. Use separate entries to record the sales revenue and the cost of goods sold for the sale on January 2.

b Compute the balance of the Inventory account on January 7.

c Prepare journal entries to record the two transactions assuming that Halley's Space Scope uses the periodic inventory system.

d Compute the cost of goods sold for the first week of January assuming use of a periodic inventory system. Use your answer to part **b** as the ending inventory.

e Which inventory system do you believe that a company such as Halley's Space Scope would probably use? Explain your reasoning.

PROBLEM 5-6 Computing Current Ratio and Working Capital; Evaluating Solvency

Some of the accounts appearing in the year-end financial statements of Diet Frozen Dinners (a corporation) appear below. This list includes all of the company's current assets and current liabilities.

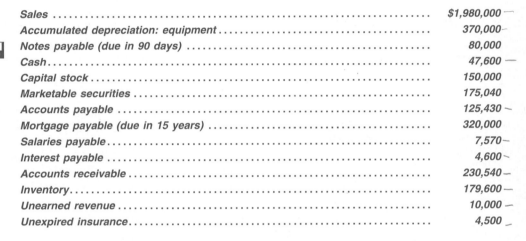

Sales	$1,980,000
Accumulated depreciation: equipment	370,000
Notes payable (due in 90 days)	80,000
Cash...	47,600
Capital stock	150,000
Marketable securities	175,040
Accounts payable	125,430
Mortgage payable (due in 15 years)	320,000
Salaries payable..	7,570
Interest payable	4,600
Accounts receivable	230,540
Inventory...	179,600
Unearned revenue	10,000
Unexpired insurance...	4,500

INSTRUCTIONS

a Prepare a partial balance sheet for Diet Frozen Dinners consisting of the current asset section and the current liability section *only.* Select the appropriate items from the above list.

b Compute the current ratio and the amount of working capital. Explain how each of these measurements is computed. State with reasons whether you consider the company to be in a strong or weak current position.

PROBLEM 5-7 Classified Financial Statements and Financial Ratios

Westport Department Store has advertised for an accounting student to work in its accounting department during the summer, and you have applied for the job. To determine whether you are familiar with the content of classified financial statements, the controller of Westport has developed the following problem based upon the store's operations in the year ended December 31, 1994:

Available information (dollar amounts in thousands):

Net sales	$10,000
Net income	?
Current liabilities	2,000
Selling expenses	1,000
Long-term liabilities	1,600
Total assets (and Total liabilities & stockholder's equity)	6,800
Stockholders' equity	?
Gross profit	?
Cost of goods sold	7,000
Current assets	4,000
Income taxes expense and other nonoperating items	220
Operating income	?
General and administrative expenses	980
Plant and equipment	2,600
Other assets	?

INSTRUCTIONS **a** Using the captions given above, prepare for Westport Department Store a condensed:

   1 Classified balance sheet at December 31, 1994.

   2 Multiple-step income statement for the year ended December 31, 1994. Show supporting computations used in determining any missing amounts. (***Note:*** Your financial statements should include only as much detail as these captions permit. For example, the first asset listed in your balance sheet will be "Current assets . . . $4,000." Notice also that this company is a corporation and that "stockholders' equity" is to be summarized in the balance sheet as a single dollar amount.)

b Using the classified financial statements developed in part **a,** compute the following:

   1 Current ratio

   2 Working capital

   3 Gross profit rate for 1994

*PROBLEM 5-8
Effects of Merchandising Transactions

Southeast Medical Supply, Inc., sells medical supplies to other businesses, such as drugstores and hospitals. Selected merchandising transactions are listed below:

a Paid air freight charges in order to receive overnight delivery of purchased merchandise needed immediately.

b Paid transportation charges to deliver merchandise to a customer.

c Returned defective merchandise to a supplier, receiving full credit against amounts currently owed.

d Paid an account payable to a merchandise supplier within the discount period.

e Paid an account payable to a merchandise supplier after the discount period had expired.

f A credit customer returned merchandise because its customer had canceled the order. Gave the customer full credit on its account receivable. [Show the effects of this transaction on two lines: (1) to record crediting the account receivable and (2) to record replacement of the returned merchandise into inventory.]

---

* *Supplemental Topic, "Additional Merchandising Transactions"*

g Collected an account receivable from a customer making payment within the discount period.

h Collected an account receivable from a customer making payment after the discount period had expired.

To interpret properly the effects of these transactions upon Southeast's financial statements, you first must be familiar with some of the company's accounting policies:

■ Southeast uses a perpetual inventory system.

■ All purchases are recorded **net** of available cash discounts.

■ Transportation costs on inbound shipments of merchandise are debited to a Transportation-in account, which in the income statement is combined with the cost of goods sold.

■ All credit sales are made on terms 2/10, n/30 and are recorded at the full invoice price.

■ The liability for sales taxes payable is recorded at the time of sale.

INSTRUCTIONS Indicate the effects of each of these transactions upon the following elements of the company's financial statements. Organize your answer in tabular form, using the column headings shown below. (Notice that the cost of goods sold is shown separately from all other expenses.) Use the code letters *I* for increase, *D* for decrease, and *NE* for no effect.

	Income Statement				Balance Sheet		
Transaction	Net Sales –	Cost of Goods Sold –	All Other Expenses =	Net Income	Assets =	Liabilities +	Owners'* Equity
a							

* The word *owners* is in plural form because this company is organized as a corporation.

*PROBLEM 5-9 Cash Discounts and Merchandise Returns

21st Century Sound purchased 50 compact disc players from Advance Technology at a price of $200 apiece. The terms of the sale were 2/10, n/30. 21st Century found two of the disc players to be defective and returned them immediately to the seller. 21st then paid for the remaining 48 disc players within the discount period.

INSTRUCTIONS **a** Record this sequence of transactions in the general journal of 21st Century. The company uses a perpetual inventory system and records purchases of merchandise at net cost.

b Record this sequence of transactions in the general journal of Advance Technology. Advance uses a perpetual inventory system and records sales transactions at the full invoice price. (Assume the cost of the disc players to Advance was $105 each.)

* *Supplemental Topic, "Additional Merchandising Transactions"*

*PROBLEM 5-10
Merchandising Transactions— A Short Comprehensive Problem

Riviera Fashions, a wholesaler, regularly sells merchandise on account to Caroline's, a chain of retail stores. Among the transactions between these companies are the following:

Mar. 3   Sold 1,000 cashmere sweaters to Caroline's on account, terms, 2/10, n/30. These sweaters had cost Riviera Fashions $32 each; the sales price to Caroline's was $50 per sweater.

Mar. 5   Caroline's returned 100 of the sweaters because they were the wrong color. Riviera Fashions always allows such returns.

Mar. 13   Caroline's paid within the discount period the remaining amount owed to Riviera Fashions, after allowing for the purchase return on Mar. 5.

Both companies use perpetual inventory systems. Caroline's records purchases of merchandise at *net cost.*

INSTRUCTIONS

a Prepare journal entries to record these transactions in the accounting records of Riviera Fashions.

b Prepare journal entries to record these transactions in the accounting records of Caroline's.

c Assume that Caroline's had not paid the remaining balance of its account payable to Riviera Fashions until April 2. Record this payment after the discount period in:

1 The accounting records of Riviera Fashions.

2 The accounting records of Caroline's.

CASES AND UNSTRUCTURED PROBLEMS

CASE 5-1
What Information Is Really Needed?

Always Fresh is a fish market operating on the pier in Santa Teresa Harbor; it sells fresh fish by the pound, and also fish sandwiches. All sales are made for cash. Every day, the market buys for cash a few hundred pounds of "whatever looks best" directly from incoming fishing boats. At closing time, it sells any leftover inventory to Best Friend, a cannery that makes pet food.

a Would Always Fresh benefit from using a perpetual inventory system? Explain.

b Briefly discuss the company's needs (if any) for subsidiary ledgers for inventory, accounts receivable, and accounts payable.

c Describe accounting procedures for recording purchases and sales which you believe will efficiently meet this company's needs.

---

*   *Supplemental Topic, "Additional Merchandising Transactions"*

**CASE 5-2
Evaluating
Debt-Paying
Ability**

You are a loan officer with First Kansas Bank. Dan Scott owns two successful restaurants, each of which has applied to your bank for a $250,000 one-year loan for the purpose of opening a second location. Condensed balance sheets for the two business entities are shown below:

KANSAS STEAK RANCH
Balance Sheet
December 31, 1994

Assets		*Liabilities & Stockholders' Equity*	
Current assets	$ 75,000	Current liabilities	$ 30,000
Plant and equipment	300,000	Long-term liabilities	200,000
		Capital stock	100,000
		Retained earnings	45,000
Total assets	$375,000	Total liabilities & stockholders' equity	$375,000

THE STOCKYARDS
Balance Sheet
December 31, 1994

Assets		*Liabilities & Owner's Equity*	
Current assets	$ 24,000	Current liabilities	$ 30,000
Plant and equipment	301,000	Long-term liabilities	200,000
		Capital, Dan Scott	95,000
Total assets	$325,000	Total liabilities & owner's equity	$325,000

Both restaurants are popular and have been successful over the last several years. Kansas Steak Ranch has been slightly more profitable, but the operating results for the two businesses have been quite similar. You think that either restaurant's second location should be successful. On the other hand, you know that restaurants are a very "faddish" type of business, and that their popularity and profitability can change very quickly.

Dan Scott is one of the wealthiest people in Kansas. He made a fortune—estimated at more than $2 billion—as the founder of Micro Time, a highly successful manufacturer of computer software. Scott now is retired and spends most of his time at Second Life, his 50,000 acre cattle ranch. Both of his restaurants are run by experienced professional managers.

INSTRUCTIONS
a Compute the current ratio and working capital of each business entity.

b Based upon the information provided in this case, which of these businesses do you consider to be the better credit risk? Explain fully.

c What simple measure might you insist upon which would make the other business as good a credit risk as the one you identified in part **b**? Explain.

**CASE 5-3
Hey, You! Put
That Back!**

Village Hardware is a retail store selling hardware, small appliances, and sporting goods. The business follows a policy of selling all merchandise at exactly twice the amount of its cost to the store and uses a *periodic* inventory system.

At year-end, the following information is taken from the accounting records:

Net sales..	$400,000
Inventory, January 1...	40,000
Purchases	205,000

A physical count indicates merchandise costing $34,000 is on hand at December 31.

INSTRUCTIONS

a Prepare a partial income statement showing computation of the gross profit for the year.

b Upon seeing your income statement, the owner of the store makes the following comment: "Inventory shrinkage losses are really costing me. If it weren't for shrinkage losses, the store's gross profit would be 50% of net sales. I'm going to hire a security guard and put an end to shoplifting once and for all."

   Determine the amount of loss from inventory "shrinkage" stated (1) at cost, and (2) at retail sales value. (Hint: Without any shrinkage losses, the cost of goods sold and the amount of gross profit would each amount to 50% of net sales.)

c Assume that Village Hardware could virtually eliminate shoplifting by hiring a security guard at a cost of $1,500 per month. Would this strategy be profitable? Explain your reasoning.

**CASE 5-4
Strategies to
Improve the
Current Ratio**

Home Improvement Centers owns a chain of nine retail stores which sell building materials, hardware, and garden supplies. In early October, the company's current ratio is 1.7 to 1. This is about normal for the company but is lower than the current ratios of several large competitors. Management feels that to qualify for the best credit terms from its suppliers, the company's year-end balance sheet should indicate a current ratio of at least 2 to 1.

INSTRUCTIONS

a Indicate whether taking each of the following actions would increase or decrease the company's current ratio. Explain your reasoning.

   1 Pay some of the company's current liabilities.

   2 Purchase large amounts of inventory on account.

   3 Offer credit customers a special discount if they pay their account balance prior to year-end.

b Propose several other *legitimate* steps which management might take to increase the company's current ratio prior to year-end.

ANSWERS TO SELF-TEST QUESTIONS

1 a, b, d   2 b, c   3 b, c, d   4 a   5 b, d   *6 b

---

* *Supplemental Topic, "Additional Merchandising Transactions"*

6 Accounting Systems, Internal Control, and Audits

In the first part of this chapter we discuss various techniques for speeding up the operation of an accounting system to meet the needs of a sizable business organization. Emphasis is placed upon such concepts as special journals, data bases, and on-line systems. In the second section of the chapter, we explore the topic of internal control. After explaining the relationship between internal control and accounting, we discuss several methods of achieving strong internal control. The chapter concludes with a discussion of the nature and purposes of both financial and operational audits.

After studying this chapter you should be able to meet these Learning Objectives:

1 *Explain why the structure of the accounting system varies from one organization to the next.*

2 *Define special journals and explain the reasons for their use.*

3 *Describe a data base and explain its usefulness.*

4 *Code transaction data so that they may be classified using alternative criteria.*

5 *Describe the objectives of internal controls.*

6 *Identify several specific measures useful in achieving strong internal control.*

7 *Explain the role of purchase orders and receiving reports in verifying a purchase invoice.*

8 *Distinguish between employee fraud and management fraud.*

9 *Explain the nature and purposes of financial audits, reviews, and operational audits.*

ACCOUNTING SYSTEMS

OBJECTIVE 1
Explain why the struc-ture of the accounting system var-ies from one organiza-tion to the next.

As defined in Chapter 1, an accounting system consists of the personnel, procedures, devices, and records used by an entity to develop accounting information and to communicate this information to decision makers. The structure and capabilities of these systems vary greatly from one organiza-tion the next. Accounting systems in common use range from simple man-ual systems which are operated entirely by the business owner, to highly sophisticated systems which make use of computers, communication satel-lites, and a large staff of professional accountants. In every case, however, the basic purpose of the accounting system remains the same: ***to meet the organization's needs for accounting information as efficiently as possible.***

Many factors affect the structure of the accounting system within a particular organization. Among the most important are (1) the company's needs for accounting information and (2) the resources available for opera-tion of the system.

Determining a Company's Information Needs

The types of accounting information which a company must generate vary with such factors as the size of the organization, whether it is publicly owned, and the philosophy of management. The need for some types of accounting information may be prescribed by law. For example, income tax regulations require every corporation to have an accounting system which can measure the company's taxable income and explain the nature and source of every item in the company's income tax return. Federal securities laws require publicly owned companies to prepare financial statements in conformity with generally accepted accounting principles. These state-ments must be filed with the Securities and Exchange Commission, dis-tributed to stockholders, and made available to the public.

Other types of accounting information are required as matters of practi-cal necessity. For example, every business needs to know the amounts re-ceivable from each customer and the amounts owed to each creditor.

Although much accounting information clearly is essential to business operations, management still has many choices as to the types and amount of accounting information to be developed. For example, should the ac-counting system of a department store measure separately the sales of each department and of each line of merchandise? The answer to such questions depends upon how ***useful*** management considers this informa-tion to be and upon the ***cost*** of developing this information.

The Cost of Producing Accounting Information

Accounting systems should be ***cost-effective***—that is, the value of the in-formation produced should ***exceed the cost*** of producing it. Management has little choice but to produce the types of accounting reports required by law. In other cases, however, management may use cost-effectiveness as the criterion for deciding whether or not to produce the information.[1]

---

[1]　The FASB considers cost-effectiveness as one criterion in the formulation of new accounting principles. The Board also has eliminated some reporting requirements for which it considered the cost of compliance to exceed the benefits.

In recent years, the development and installation of computer-based accounting systems have increased greatly the types and amounts of accounting information which can be produced in a cost-effective manner. In many cases, the installation of a computer-based system increases the amount of accounting information available to management and also *reduces* the cost of operating the accounting system.

Basic Functions of an Accounting System

In developing information about the financial position of a business and the results of its operations, every accounting system performs the following basic functions:

1 **Record** the effects of business transactions.
2 **Classify** the effects of similar transactions in a manner that permits development of the various totals and subtotals needed in business operations and for external reporting purposes.
3 **Summarize and communicate** the data contained in the system in a manner useful to decision makers.

The differences in accounting systems arise primarily in the manner, speed, and extent of detail with which these functions are performed.

In most of our textbook illustrations, we assume the use of a manual accounting system. In this system, transactions are recorded in a general journal, classified in both general and subsidiary ledger accounts, and summarized in the financial statements and various other schedules and reports. While such a system is useful in illustrating basic accounting concepts, it is too slow and cumbersome to meet the needs of a large business organization.

In a large business, transactions may occur at a rate of several hundred or several thousand per hour. To keep pace with such a rapid flow of accounting information, these companies must use computer-based accounting systems. Many small businesses continue to use manual accounting systems. However, these companies usually modify their accounting systems to process accounting information as quickly and efficiently as possible.

Design of Accounting Systems

The design of accounting systems is an area of specialization within the field of accounting. Large businesses have a staff of systems analysts, internal auditors, and other professionals who work full time in designing and improving the accounting system. Medium-size companies often hire a CPA firm to design or update their systems. Small businesses with limited resources usually purchase one of the many "packaged" accounting systems specially designed for small companies in a particular line of business. These packaged systems are available through many office supply stores, computer stores, and bookkeeping services.

We will now address the challenge of speeding up an accounting system to process information quickly and efficiently. We also will discuss how the system may be expanded to provide management with useful and detailed information about business operations.

Recording Business Transactions: The Need for Special Journals

A journal is sometimes called a "book of original entry," because the journal is the accounting record in which the effects of transactions are first recorded within the accounting system. In our preceding chapters, we have been using a general journal to illustrate the recording of transactions. Journals, however, come in many different forms. In fact, many journals are **machines** rather than paper accounting records.

OBJECTIVE 2
Define special journals and explain the reasons for their use.

Characteristics of a General Journal   The general journal is unique among journals, because it may be used to record **any type** of business transaction. The flexibility of a general journal makes it ideal for use in textbook illustrations. However, this flexibility also makes a general journal a relatively inefficient device for recording large numbers of routine transactions.

Recording all transactions in a general journal simply is not cost-effective. First, every entry in a general journal involves quite a bit of writing—at least two account titles, two dollar amounts, and a written explanation. Also, if all types of business transactions are recorded in a single journal, the person maintaining this journal must be a highly skilled accountant. For an accounting system to be cost-effective, routine transactions must be recorded by clerical personnel or by machines—not by professional accountants.

Special Journals   Most businesses are able to speed up and simplify the recording process by designing various **special journals.** Each special journal is an accounting record or device designed for recording **a particular type of transaction** quickly and efficiently. As only one type of transaction is recorded in each special journal, the person maintaining this journal need not be an expert in accounting.

Two concepts enter into the design of an efficient special journal. First, the person recording the transaction should have to enter **as little data as possible.** Second, the recording of transactions should be **combined with other essential business activities** in a manner which minimizes the time and effort involved in accounting functions.

"RRRrrrring!" It's a Special Journal   The old-fashioned mechanical cash register provides a familiar example of a special journal. As the salesclerk or cashier "rings up" each cash sale, the dollar amount is printed on a tape within the cash register. This tape provides a record of each cash sale.

Let us now identify some of the ways in which a cash register reduces the time and cost of recording transactions. First, notice that **no accounting personnel** are involved in recording the numerous cash sales—these transactions are recorded by the company's salesclerks as they accept payment and make change. Also notice how quickly the transactions are recorded. The only data which the salesclerk records on the cash register is the dollar amount of the sale. Ledger account titles and written explanations are not necessary, because **every** transaction recorded on the register is a cash sale.

The use of a cash register also saves time in posting the effects of transactions to the ledger. At the end of each day, only the **total** appearing at the end of the register tape is posted to the ledger (as a debit to Cash and a credit to Sales). This total amount may represent the overall effects of hundreds—perhaps thousands—of individual transactions.[2]

Point-of-Sale Terminals: A More Efficient Special Journal Modern ***point-of-sale*** terminals (cash registers tied into computer systems) are even more efficient special journals than the old-fashioned cash registers. With a point-of-sale terminal, data entry is reduced to a minimum and the need for manual posting is eliminated entirely. The salesclerk passes the merchandise over an optical scanner; this scanner reads a "product code" attached to the merchandise and enters the code into the computer system. Using this product code, the computer determines the cost and sales price of the merchandise from computer-based files, records the sale and the cost of goods sold, and updates the related general ledger accounts and also the inventory subsidiary ledger.

When sales are made on account, the salesclerk also enters the customer's credit card number into the terminal. This number identifies the customer to the computer, and the computer automatically updates the accounts receivable subsidiary ledger.

On-Line, Real-Time Systems In an on-line, real-time ***(OLRT)*** computer system, the accounting records are updated instantly for the effects of certain business transactions. The OLRT concept requires that transactions be recorded through an ***on-line*** input device ***as the transactions occur.*** An input device is "on-line" when it has direct and immediate access to the computer-based accounting records.

Point-of-sale terminals are on-line. When sales are recorded on these terminals, the general ledger and subsidiary ledger accounts are updated immediately.

An OLRT system allows managers and other company personnel to view through computer terminals accounting information which is ***absolutely current.*** For example, a salesperson may determine at any time how many units of a particular product are currently on hand. Department managers can review the daily sales of their departments at the end of each working day—or, for that matter, as of any point within the day.

Notice that point-of-sale terminals are located on the sales floor, not in the accounting department. As these input devices are used only in recording sales transactions, they may be located ***where the transactions occur.*** Placing on-line recording devices where transactions occur is essential to the concept of an OLRT system. In addition, this practice may facilitate recording transactions in conjunction with performing related business functions.

Even in a sophisticated accounting system, not all of the accounting records can be kept continuously up-to-date. Depreciation expense, for example, is recorded only at the end of each accounting period. Among the

---

[2] Most cash registers also permit the recording of sales on account. Credit sales are accumulated separately on the register tape, and the daily total is posted as a debit to Accounts Receivable and a credit to Sales. In recording a credit sale, the salesclerk must record the customer's account number as well as the dollar amount of the sale. The customer's account number is needed for updating the accounts receivable subsidiary ledger.

accounts which **can** be kept continuously up-to-date are the general and subsidiary ledger accounts for cash, accounts receivable, inventory, accounts payable, sales revenue, and the cost of goods sold.

Other Types of Automated Special Journals   Many special journals are machines. We have emphasized the point-of-sale terminals often used in retail stores; however, many other businesses also record their routine transactions in a highly automated manner. On-line terminals are widely used by banks (for recording deposits and withdrawals) and by airlines (for recording ticket sales). The gas meters, electric meters, and water meters located on most buildings also are types of special journals. These meters automatically record the utility companies' credit sales to individual customers.

Manual Special Journals   Not all special journals are automated devices. There are many **manual** special journals, in which transactions can be recorded far faster and more efficiently than in a general journal. Perhaps the most common manual special journal is the **check register** found in every checkbook. A check register can be used for efficiently recording every cash disbursement as the check is being issued. If the check register is maintained properly, it should contain all of the data necessary to post these cash transactions to the company's general and subsidiary ledger accounts. Other common examples of manual special journals include sales journals, cash receipts journals, purchases journals, voucher registers, and payroll registers.

In Appendix B (at the end of this textbook) we illustrate a "typical" set of manual special journals for a merchandising business. These journals illustrate many of the basic concepts widely used to increase the efficiency of manual accounting systems. Bear in mind, however, that the number and format of special journals vary significantly from one business to the next.

This textbook is accompanied by a number of supplemental **Accounting Applications** demonstrating the operation of either manual or computer-based accounting systems. Several of these applications make use of special journals similar to those illustrated in Appendix B. Therefore, if you intend to use these applications, you should first study Appendix B.

Recording Budgeted Amounts

Up to this point, we have discussed recording in the accounting system only the results of **actual** business transactions. Many businesses also enter into their accounting system **advance forecasts** (or budgets) of the levels of activity **expected in future periods.** As the actual results are recorded in the system, reports are generated showing the **differences** between the forecasts and the actual results. These reports aid managers in identifying those areas of the business which are performing above or below expectation.

Classifying and Storing Data in an Accounting System

Two methods of classifying and storing data within an accounting system are in widespread use: ledger accounts and computerized data bases.

Ledger Accounts

In both manual and computer-based accounting systems, the effects of business transactions are classified in terms of the company's chart of ledger accounts. The phrase *chart of accounts* refers to the number and titles of the ledger accounts used by the business.

In designing the ledger of any given business, questions always arise as to the *extent of detail* needed in the chart of accounts. For example, should one ledger account be used for advertising expense, or should separate accounts be maintained for newspaper advertising, direct mail advertising, and television advertising?

The extent of detail included in the chart of accounts depends primarily upon the types of information which management considers appropriate. The information appearing in financial statements and income tax returns is classified into broad general categories. Therefore, the preparation of these types of reports *does not* require a highly detailed chart of accounts. Management, however, usually finds more detailed accounting information useful in planning and controlling business operations. For example, management may want information about departmental revenue and expenses.

The chart of revenue and expense accounts often is designed along lines of *managerial responsibility.* Separate accounts are used for recording the revenue and expenses attributable to each department (or other area of managerial responsibility) within the organization. This *responsibility accounting system* provides top management with information useful in evaluating the performance of individual departments and department managers. (Responsibility accounting systems are discussed further in Chapter 24.)

A general ledger with a great many accounts would be unwieldy and difficult to use. Therefore, the accounts showing the detailed composition of specific assets, liabilities, revenue, and expenses usually are placed in *subsidiary ledgers.* Only the related *controlling accounts* appear in the general ledger.

Data Base Systems

OBJECTIVE 3 Describe a data base and explain its usefulness.

A data base provides greater flexibility in the classification of data than does even a highly detailed chart of ledger accounts. When transaction data are stored in a data base, they may be sorted into many *different* categories, according to a variety of classification criteria. A data base consists of *unclassified* data, which have not yet been grouped into categories. However, the data are accompanied by various classification *codes.* Each of these codes enables the computer to classify (or *sort*) the data according to different criteria.

An Illustration of a Data Base We will use the sales transactions of a department store to illustrate the concepts of a data base and of "coded" transaction data. Assume that our store has several different sales departments, such as appliances, furniture, men's clothing, shoes, women's cloth-

OBJECTIVE 4
Code trans-
action data
so that they
may be clas-
sified using
alternative
criteria.

ing, etc. Sales transactions are recorded at on-line point-of-sale terminals located in each sales department.

The first step in designing a data base is to determine the alternative ways in which the transaction data will be used. Assume that the management of our department store intends to use the data about sales transactions in the following ways:

1 General ledger accounts for Cash, Accounts Receivable, Inventory, Sales, and Cost of Goods Sold will be kept continuously up-to-date.
2 Subsidiary ledgers will be maintained for inventory and accounts receivable.
3 Daily sales reports will be developed for the store manager showing the total dollar sales within each of the store's sales departments.
4 Weekly sales reports will be developed for the store's merchandise buyers showing the **number of units** of each product which have been sold during the week.

To provide these types of information, the accounting system must be able to classify sales transaction data by (1) general ledger accounts, (2) customer account number, (3) sales department, and (4) product sold.

In recording each transaction, the salesperson enters into the computer terminal a **product code** identifying each item sold. If the merchandise is sold on account, the salesperson also must enter the number designating the customer's account in the accounts receivable subsidiary ledger.

Very little time is required for the salesperson to enter these codes. The computer automatically reads the product codes as the salesperson passes the merchandise over an optical scanner. To record customers' account numbers, the salesperson may either pass the customer's credit card over the scanner or enter the customer's account number on a keyboard. (If no customer number is entered, the computer accounts for the transaction as a cash sale.) Thus, each sales transaction can be recorded in a few seconds.

"Fields" of Information   The computer places each of the codes entered through the terminal in a separate space called a **data field.** All of the data fields relating to a given sales transaction are linked together in the data base. The data entered through the terminal enables the computer to complete the three data fields shown below. These fields may appear in any sequence.

1 Product Code	2* Customer Account No.	3 Quantity Sold
— — —	— — —	— —

*   For cash sales, zeros automatically are entered in the second field.

In addition, the date of the transaction is entered in a fourth data field. We have omitted the date field in order to conserve space later in our illustration.

The size of each data field depends upon the length of the required code. For example, a one-digit field can accept any of ten numeric code symbols

(*0* through *9*). A three-digit field can accept one thousand combinations of numeric codes (*000* through *999*).[3]

Recording the Classification Codes   To illustrate this coding system, assume that a salesperson in the appliance department sells two Zenith television sets on account to Dave Stewart. This particular model of television set has a product code of *218,* and Stewart's account number in the customer ledger is *830.* As the salesperson passes the scanner over the merchandise and the customer's credit card, the following information is entered in the data base:

Product Code	Customer Account No.	Quantity Sold
2 1 8	8 3 0	0 2

The computer then uses the product code to determine the unit sales price and unit cost of the television sets from computer-based files. In addition, the computer records the cost number identifying the *department* in which the sale is made. (Assume that the appliance department is dept. no. 1.) Thus, the computer automatically fills in three more data fields, as shown below:

Data Fields for One Sales Transaction

Data Entered at Terminal			Fields Completed by the Computer		
1 Product Code	2 Customer Account No.	3 Quantity Sold	4 Unit Sales Price	5 Unit Cost	6 Sales Dept.
2 1 8	8 3 0	0 2	$ 3 0 0.0 0	$ 1 8 0.0 0	1

These six data fields are stored together in the data base. (The dollar signs and decimal points in fields 4 and 5 are shown only for illustrative purposes and would not occupy space in the data base.)

Using Coded Data   To continue our illustration, assume that the following ten coded transactions have been entered in the data base during a given day. (The transactions are lettered **a** through **j** merely for reference. These identification letters are not entered in the data base.)

Data Fields							Data Fields					
1	2	3	4	5	6		1	2	3	4	5	6
a 218	- 830	- 02	- $300.00	- $180.00	- 1		f 218	- 000	- 01	- $300.00	- $180.00	- 1
b 130	- 000	- 01	- $110.00	- $065.50	- 6		g 080	- 716	- 02	- $124.00	- $072.50	- 3
c 301	- 830	- 05	- $025.00	- $015.00	- 2		h 067	- 000	- 03	- $012.00	- $008.00	- 4
d 206	- 110	- 04	- $120.00	- $085.00	- 1		i 201	- 425	- 01	- $600.00	- $460.00	- 1
e 420	- 000	- 01	- $035.90	- $023.10	- 3		j 075	- 122	- 01	- $099.00	- $056.50	- 5

Note: Field 2 represents the account number of credit customers. Three zeros in this field indicate a cash sale.

---

[3]   In terms of the number of required digits, alphabetic codes are more efficient than numeric codes, as any of 26 letters may be placed in each space. Thus, a three-digit field can accept 17,576 possible combinations (26^3). Despite the apparent space savings of alphabetic coding, most computer systems process numerically coded data more efficiently. We will use numeric coding in our illustrations and problem material.

Let us now see how this coded data can be classified in different ways to meet the four objectives specified by management:

1 **Updating the general ledger accounts.** Using the data in fields 3 and 4 (quantity sold and unit sales price), the computer is able to compute the total sales price. This amount immediately is debited to the Accounts Receivable controlling account (or Cash account) and credited to the Sales account in the general ledger. The cost of goods sold (field 3 × field 5) is debited to the Cost of Goods Sold account and credited to the Inventory controlling account.

2 **Updating the subsidiary ledgers.** Field 1 informs the computer of the products sold and field 2 identifies credit customers' account numbers. This information enables the computer to update the inventory and accounts receivable subsidiary ledgers for each sales transaction.

3 **Daily reports of departmental sales.** The special reports for various managers are prepared by computer routines which sort the transaction data according to a particular data field. For example, the store manager is to receive a daily report in which sales are classified by sales department. This report is prepared by sorting the transaction data by department (field 6) and then computing the total sales of each department.

4 **Weekly reports of unit sales, sorted by product.** These reports are prepared by first sorting the transaction data according to product code (field 1) and then totaling the unit sales for each product (field 3).

Comparison of Ledgers and Data Bases In a ledger-based system, the effects of transactions are classified in terms of specific ledger accounts *at the time transactions are recorded.* Thus, transaction data are classified in terms of the company's chart of accounts. In a data base, the effects of transactions are stored in an *unclassified format.* The computer has the capability of arranging the data in different ways at different times, depending upon the needs of decision makers.

A data base is not a substitute for a ledger; rather, it is intended to provide additional information about certain types of transactions. In order for the accounting system to supply financial statements quickly and efficiently, the effects of all business transactions must be classified within the company's ledger accounts. Only those transactions that management wants to see classified according to several different criteria are entered into the data base. Transactions entered into a data base often include departmental revenue, departmental expense, cash receipts, and cash payments.

Summarizing and Communicating Information

In general terms, the usefulness of accounting information to decision makers depends upon (1) the *relevance* of the information to the decisions at hand, (2) the *timeliness* of the information, and (3) its *reliability.* At this point, we will discuss only the first two factors—the relevance and timeliness of accounting information. The third factor—reliability—is closely related to the topics of internal control and audits of financial statements. These topics are discussed in the following sections of this chapter.

Both the relevance and timeliness of accounting information have been enhanced greatly by recent advancements in the technologies of computers and communications. Computer-based charts of ledger accounts and data base systems permit the preparation of accounting reports ***tailored to the needs*** of specific decision makers. Computers can arrange the data in the accounting system into the formats of accounting reports almost instantly. Through computer networks, electronic mail, facsimile machines, and communications satellites these reports can be transmitted quickly anywhere in the world. In OLRT systems, decision makers may use computer terminals to access information which is ***completely current.*** Thus, advances in technology are rapidly increasing the usefulness of accounting information.

Differences between Manual and Computer-Based Accounting Systems: A Summary

In the following table, we summarize the differences between a simple manual accounting system (such as the one used in our textbook illustrations) and the computer-based systems in use in most large organizations. Notice that both types of systems perform the same basic functions. The

Basic Functions of an Accounting System	Means of Performing These Functions		
	The manual system in our illustrations	A computer-based system in a modern business	Comments on the computer-based systems
Recording effects of transactions	General journal (all transactions)	Special journals (routine transactions) General journal (unusual transactions) Some transactions recorded using on-line input devices	Special journals may be on-line and located at transaction sites Budgeted data may be entered for comparative purposes
Classifying and storing effects of transactions	Simple chart of ledger accounts Some use of subsidiary ledgers	Detailed chart of ledger accounts and a data base Extensive use of subsidiary ledger	Data base allows classification in many different ways Revenue and expenses often classified along lines of managerial responsibility
Summarizing and communicating accounting information	Periodic printed reports	Printed reports, and computer displays Some information up-to-date and accessible on-line	On-line data may be completely current

differences between these systems lie in the methods and devices used in performing these functions.

In years ahead, readers may expect accounting systems to continue performing the functions shown in the left-hand column. The means of performing these functions are likely to change, however, as technological innovations occur in the fields of computers and communications.

INTERNAL CONTROL

OBJECTIVE 5
Describe the
objectives of
internal
controls.

Internal controls are all measures taken by an organization for the purposes of (1) protecting its resources against waste, fraud, or inefficient use; (2) ensuring the reliability of accounting data; (3) securing compliance with management's policies; and (4) evaluating the performance of all employees, managers, and departments within the organization. Thus, all measures and procedures intended to assure management that the entire business is operating according to management's plans and policies may be described as internal controls. Collectively, the internal controls in force throughout the organization are called the *internal control structure* (or the system of internal control).

Relationship between the Accounting System and the Internal Control Structure

The primary objective of an accounting system is to provide useful financial information to decision makers. The objective of the internal control structure is to keep the business "on track," operating in accordance with the policies and plans of management. These two systems are closely related; in fact, each depends greatly upon the other.

The accounting system depends upon internal control procedures to ensure the *reliability* of accounting data. Many internal control procedures, on the other hand, make use of accounting data in keeping track of assets and monitoring the performance of departments. The need for adequate internal control explains the nature and the very existence of many accounting records, reports, documents, and procedures. Thus, the topic of internal control and the study of accounting go hand-in-hand.

Accounting Controls and Administrative Controls

Internal controls fall into two broad categories: accounting controls and administrative controls. *Accounting controls* are measures that relate directly to the protection of assets or to the reliability of accounting information. An example is the use of cash registers to create an immediate record of cash receipts. Another example is the policy of making an annual physical count of inventory even when a perpetual inventory system is in use.

Administrative controls are measures designed to increase operational efficiency; they have *no direct bearing* upon the reliability of the accounting records. An example of an administrative control is a requirement that traveling salespeople submit reports showing the names of customers called upon each day. Another example is the requirement that airline pilots have annual medical examinations.

In this textbook, we will emphasize ***internal accounting controls***—those controls that have a ***direct bearing*** upon the reliability of accounting records, financial statements, and other accounting reports. Bear in mind, however, that sound administrative controls also play a vital role in the successful operation of a business.

Guidelines to Achieving Strong Internal Control

Establish Clear Lines of Responsibility Every organization should indicate clearly the persons or departments responsible for such functions as sales, purchasing, receiving incoming shipments, paying bills, and maintaining accounting records. The lines of authority and responsibility can be shown in an organization chart. (A partial organization chart is illustrated on the next page.) The organization chart should be supported by written job descriptions and by procedures manuals that explain in detail the authority and responsibilities of each person or department appearing in the chart.

OBJECTIVE 6
Identify several specific measures useful in achieving strong internal control.

Establish Routine Procedures for Processing Each Type of Transaction If management is to direct the activities of a business according to plan, every transaction should go through four separate steps; it should be authorized, approved, executed, and recorded. For example, consider the sale of merchandise on credit. Top management has the authority and responsibility to authorize credit sales to categories of customers who meet certain standards. The credit department is responsible for approving a credit sale of a given dollar amount to a particular customer. The transaction is executed by the shipping department which ships or delivers the merchandise to the customer. Finally, the transaction is recorded in the accounting department by an entry debiting Accounts Receivable and crediting Sales.

Subdivision of Duties Perhaps the most important concept in achieving internal control is an appropriate subdivision—or separation—of duties. Responsibilities should be assigned so that ***no one person or department handles a transaction completely from beginning to end.*** When duties are divided in this manner, the work of one employee serves to verify that of another and any errors which occur tend to be detected promptly.

To illustrate this concept, let us review the typical procedures followed by a wholesaler in processing a credit sale. The sales department of the company is responsible for securing the order from the customer; the credit department must approve the customer's credit before the order is filled; the stock room assembles the goods ordered; the shipping department packs and ships the goods; the billing department prepares the sales invoice; and the accounting department records the transaction.

Each department receives written evidence of the action by the other departments and reviews the documents describing the transaction to see that the actions taken correspond in all details. The shipping department, for instance, does not release the merchandise until after the credit department has approved the customer as a credit risk. The accounting department does not record the sale until it has received documentary evidence that (1) an order was received from a customer, (2) the extension of credit

PORTION OF AN ORGANIZATION CHART

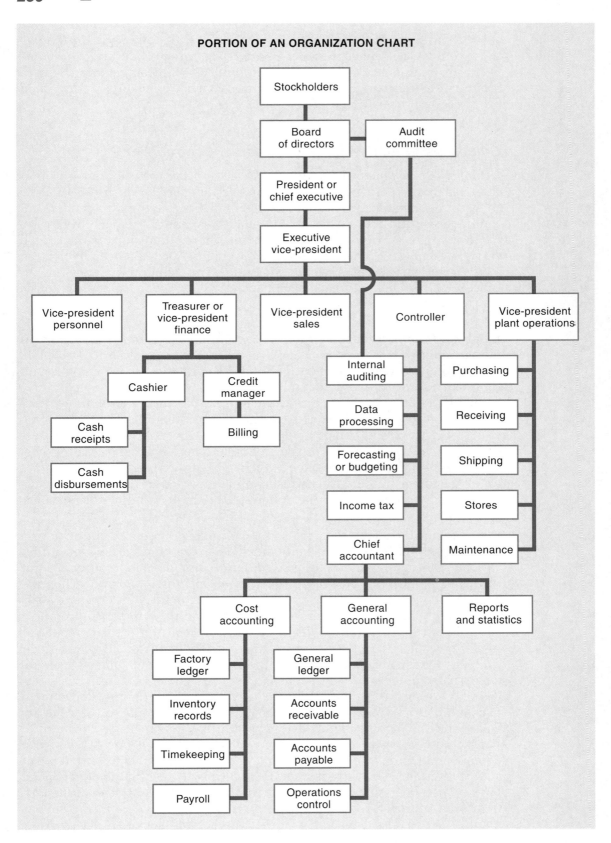

was approved, (3) the merchandise was shipped to the customer, and (4) a sales invoice was prepared and mailed to the customer.

Accounting Function Separate from Custody of Assets Basic to the separation of duties is the concept that an employee who has custody of an asset (or access to an asset) should not maintain the accounting record for that asset. If one person has custody of assets and also maintains the accounting records, there is both opportunity and incentive to falsify the records to conceal a shortage. However, the person with custody of the asset will not be inclined to waste it, steal it, or give it away if he or she is aware that another employee is maintaining a record of the asset.

The following diagram illustrates how this separation of duties contributes to strong internal control.

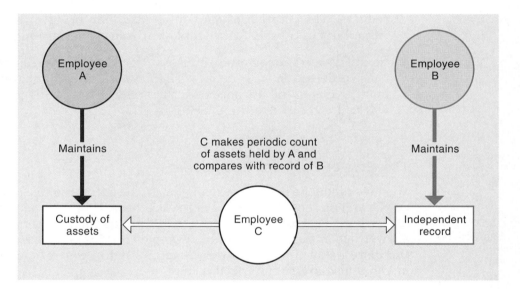

In this diagram Employee A has custody of assets and Employee B maintains an accounting record of the assets. Employee C periodically counts the assets and compares the count with the record maintained by B. This comparison should reveal any errors made by either A or B unless the two have collaborated to conceal an error or irregularity.

Other Steps Toward Achieving Internal Control Other important internal control measures include the following:

1 **Internal auditing.** Virtually every *large* organization has an internal auditing staff. The objectives of the internal auditors are to monitor and improve the system of internal control. Internal auditors test and evaluate both accounting controls and administrative controls in all areas of the organization and prepare reports to top management on their findings and recommendations. Much of the work of internal auditors may be described as *operational auditing.* Operational audits are discussed later in this chapter.

2 **Financial forecasts.** A plan of operations is prepared each year setting goals for each division of the business, as, for example, the expected

volume of sales, amounts of expenses, and future cash balances. ***Actual*** results are compared with ***forecast*** amounts month by month. This comparison strengthens control because variations from planned results are investigated promptly.

3 **Competent personnel.**   Even the best-designed system of internal control will not work well unless the people using it are competent. Competence and integrity of employees are in part developed through training programs, but they also are related to the policies for selection of personnel and to the adequacy of supervision.

4 **Rotation of employees.**   The rotation of employees from one job assignment to another may strengthen internal control. When employees know that another person will soon be taking over their duties, they are more likely to maintain records with care and to follow established procedures. The rotation of employees also may bring to light errors or irregularities caused by the employee formerly performing a given task.

5 **Serially numbered documents.**   Documents such as checks, purchase orders, and sales invoices should be serially numbered. If a document is misplaced or concealed, the break in the sequence of numbers will call attention to the missing item.

The Role of Business Documents

OBJECTIVE 7
Explain the role of purchase orders and receiving reports in verifying a purchase invoice.

We have made the point that strong internal control requires subdivision of duties among the departments of the business. How does each department know that the other departments have fulfilled their responsibilities? The answer lies in the use of carefully designed ***business documents.*** Some of the more important business documents used in controlling purchases of merchandise are summarized below:

Business Document	Initiated by	Sent to
Purchase requisition		
Issued when quantity of goods on hand falls below established reorder point	Departmental sales managers or stores department	Original to purchasing department, copy to accounting department
Purchase order		
Issued when order is placed; indicates type, quantities, and prices of merchandise ordered	Purchasing department	Original to selling company (vendor, supplier), copies to department requisitioning goods and the accounting department
Invoice		
Confirms that goods have been shipped and requests payment	Seller (supplier)	Accounting department of buying company

Business Document	Initiated by	Sent to
Receiving report Based on count and inspection of goods received	Receiving department of buying company	Original to accounting department, copies to purchasing department and to department requisitioning goods
Invoice approval form Based upon the documents listed above; authorizes payment of the purchase invoice	Accounting department of buying company	Finance department, to support issuance of check Returned to accounting department with a copy of the check

Purchase Requisition   A purchase requisition is a request from the sales department or stores department (warehousing) for the purchasing department to order merchandise. Thus, the purchasing department is not authorized to order goods ***unless it has first received a purchase requisition.*** A copy of the purchase requisition is sent to the accounting department.

Purchase Orders   Once a purchase requisition has been received, the purchasing department determines the lowest-cost supplier of the merchandise and places an order. This order is documented in a ***purchase order.*** A purchase order issued by Fairway Pro Shop to Adams Manufacturing Company is illustrated below:

A serially numbered purchase order

<table>
<tr><td colspan="4">PURCHASE ORDER   Order no. 999</td></tr>
<tr><td colspan="4">FAIRWAY PRO SHOP
10 Fairway Avenue, San Francisco, California</td></tr>
<tr><td colspan="4">To: Adams Manufacturing Company   Date: November 10, 19—
19 Union Street   Ship via Jones Truck Co.
Kansas City, Missouri   Terms: 2/10, n/30</td></tr>
<tr><td colspan="4">Please enter our order for the following:</td></tr>
<tr><th>Quantity</th><th>Description</th><th>Price</th><th>Total</th></tr>
<tr><td>15 sets</td><td>Model S irons</td><td>$ 120.00</td><td>$ 1,800.00</td></tr>
<tr><td>50 dozen</td><td>X3Y Shur-Par golf balls</td><td>14.00</td><td>700.00</td></tr>
<tr><td></td><td></td><td></td><td>$2,500.00</td></tr>
<tr><td colspan="4" align="center">Fairway Pro Shop
By DD McCarthy</td></tr>
</table>

Several copies of a purchase order are usually prepared. The original is sent to the supplier; it constitutes an authorization to deliver the merchandise and to submit a bill based on the prices listed. A second copy is sent to the department that initiated the purchase requisition to show that the requisition has been acted upon. Another copy is sent to the accounting department of the buying company.

The issuance of a purchase order does not call for any entries in the accounting records of either the prospective buyer or seller. The company which receives an order does not consider that a sale has been made *until the merchandise is delivered.* At that point ownership of the goods changes, and both buyer and seller should make accounting entries to record the transaction.

Invoices　When a manufacturer or wholesaler receives an order for its products, it takes two actions. One is to ship the goods to the customer and the other is to send the customer an invoice. By the act of shipping the merchandise, the seller is giving up ownership of one type of asset, inventory; by issuing the invoice, the seller is recording ownership of another form of asset, an account receivable.

An invoice contains a description of the goods being sold, the quantities, prices, credit terms, and method of shipment. The illustration below shows an invoice issued by Adams Manufacturing Company in response to the previously illustrated purchase order from Fairway Pro Shop.

INVOICE　　　　　　　　　　　　　　　　Invoice no. *782*
ADAMS MANUFACTURING COMPANY
19 Union Street
Kansas City, Missouri

Sold to: Fairway Pro Shop　　　　　　　Invoice date November 15, 19—

10 Fairway Avenue　　　　　　　Your purchase order no. 999

San Francisco, Calif.　　　　　　Date shipped November 15, 19—

Shipped to: Same　　　　　　　　　Shipped via Jones Truck Co.

Terms 2/10, n/30

Quantity	Description	Price	Total
15 sets	Model S irons	$ 120.00	$ 1,800.00
50 dozen	X3Y Shur-Par golf balls	14.00	700.00
			$2,500.00

From the viewpoint of the seller, an invoice is a ***sales invoice;*** from the buyer's viewpoint it is a ***purchase invoice.*** The invoice is the basis for an entry in the accounting records of ***both*** the seller and the buyer because it evidences the ***transfer of ownership of goods.*** At the time of issuing the invoice, the selling company makes an entry debiting Accounts Receivable and crediting Sales. The buying company, however, does not record the invoice as a liability until the invoice has been approved for payment.

Receiving Report   Evidence that the merchandise has been received in good condition is obtained from the receiving department. The receiving department receives all incoming goods, inspects them as to quality and condition, and determines the quantities received by counting, measuring, or weighing. The receiving department then prepares a serially numbered report for each shipment received; one copy of this ***receiving report*** is sent to the accounting department for use in approving the invoice for payment.

Invoice Approval Form   The approval of the invoice in the accounting department is accomplished by comparing the purchase requisition, the purchase order, the invoice, and the receiving report. Comparison of these documents establishes that the merchandise described in the invoice was actually ordered, has been received in good condition, and was billed at the prices specified in the purchase order.

The person who performs these comparisons then records the liability (debit Inventory, credit Accounts Payable) and signs an ***invoice approval form*** authorizing payment of the invoice by the finance department. (One type of invoice approval form, called a ***voucher,*** is discussed further in the following chapter.)

As explained in Chapter 5, most well-managed companies follow a policy of recording purchases at ***net cost***—that is, the invoice price less any available cash discount. This internal control policy requires the use of a Purchase Discounts Lost account which will call management's attention to any failures to take advantage of available cash discount.

Debit and Credit Memoranda (Debit Memos, Credit Memos)   If merchandise purchased on account is unsatisfactory and is to be returned to the supplier (or if a price reduction is agreed upon), a ***debit memorandum*** may be prepared by the purchasing company and sent to the supplier. The debit memorandum informs the supplier that the buyer has debited (reduced) its liability to the supplier and explains the circumstances.

Upon being informed of the return of damaged merchandise (or having agreed to a reduction in price), the seller will send the buyer a ***credit memorandum*** indicating that the account receivable from the buyer has been credited (reduced).

Notice that issuing a credit memorandum has the same effect upon a customer's account as does receiving payment from the customer—that is, the account receivable is credited (reduced). Thus, an employee with authority to issue credit memoranda ***should not be allowed to handle cash receipts from customers.*** If both of these duties were assigned to the same employee, that person could abstract some of the cash collected from customers and conceal this theft by issuing fictitious credit memoranda.

Internal Control in Computer-Based Systems

Computers do not eliminate the need for internal control. In fact, most recent cases of large-scale fraud have occurred in companies with computer-based accounting systems.

CASE IN POINT   An outside computer consultant for a major bank once used the bank's computer system to transfer $10 million of the bank's money into his personal account at another bank. The consultant's knowledge of the bank's computer system enabled him to commit this fraud. He had observed how bank employees used the computer to make legitimate transfers of funds. In addition, he had noticed that the "secret" computer codes used in these transfers were posted on the wall next to the computer terminal.

Despite the preceding case in point, computer-based accounting systems lend themselves well to the implementation of internal control procedures. One such procedure is the use of ***access codes*** or passwords, which limit access to the system to authorized users and also identify the user responsible for each entry. (Obviously these access codes should not be posted on the wall.)

In fact, computer-based accounting systems create many opportunities for implementing internal control procedures which might not be practicable in a manual accounting system.

CASE IN POINT   When on-line terminals are used in recording credit sales, the salesperson enters the customer's credit card number into the system. The computer then determines whether the proposed sales transaction will cause the customer's account balance to exceed any predetermined credit limit. Also, the computer compares the customer's card number with a list of credit cards reported lost or stolen. If either of these procedures indicates that credit should not be extended to this customer, the computer immediately notifies the salesperson not to make the sale.

We have mentioned that in computer-based accounting systems, company personnel may be able to view accounting information on a computer monitor. For internal control purposes, these monitors should have ***read-only access*** to the accounting system. Read-only means that the computer user may view the information but ***may not change it*** in any way.

Limitations and Cost of Internal Control

Although internal control is highly effective in increasing the reliability of accounting data and in safeguarding assets, no system of internal control provides complete protection against fraud, theft, or errors. For example, controls based upon a subdivision of duties may be defeated—at least temporarily—by ***collusion*** among two or more employees. Carelessness on the part of employees also may cause a breakdown in internal control.

In designing an internal control structure, the question of cost cannot be ignored. The internal control structure **should be cost-effective.** Too elaborate a control structure may entail greater expense than is justified by the protection gained.

Internal control is more difficult to achieve in a small business than in a large one because, with only a few employees, it is not possible to arrange an extensive subdivision of duties. Also, such internal controls as an internal audit staff usually are not cost-effective in a small business. An essential element of maintaining a reasonable degree of internal control in a small business is active participation by the owner-manager in strategic control procedures. In summary, an internal control structure must be tailored to meet the needs of the individual business.

Prevention of Fraud

Perhaps the most highly publicized objective of internal control is the prevention of fraud. **Fraud** may be defined as the deliberate misrepresentation of facts with the intent of deceiving someone. If the purpose of this deception is personal gain or causing harm to another, fraud may be a criminal act. In discussing the role of internal control in preventing acts of fraud, it is useful to distinguish between **errors** in the accounting records and **irregularities.**

Accountants use the term **errors** in reference to unintentional mistakes. **Irregularities,** on the other hand, refer to **intentional** mistakes, entered into accounting records or accounting reports for some fraudulent purpose. Irregularities may be further subdivided into the classifications of **employee fraud** and **management fraud.**

Employee Fraud

OBJECTIVE 8
Distinguish between employee fraud and management fraud.

Employee fraud refers to dishonest acts performed by the employees of a company **despite management's efforts to prevent these actions.** Examples of employee fraud include theft of assets, charging lower sales prices to favored customers, receiving kickbacks from suppliers, overstating hours worked, padding expense accounts, and embezzlement. (**Embezzlement** is a theft of assets which is concealed by falsification of the accounting records.)

If one employee handles all aspects of a transaction, the danger of irregularities increases. Studies of fraud cases suggest that individuals may be tempted into dishonest acts if given complete control of company property. Most of these persons, however, would not engage in fraud if doing so required collaboration with other employees. Thus, subdivision of duties is believed to substantially reduce the risk of employee fraud.

In addition to subdivision of duties, the risk of employee fraud is reduced by such control procedures as investigating the backgrounds of job applicants, periodic rotation of employees to different job assignments, and frequent comparisons of assets actually on hand with the quantities shown in the accounting records.

Fidelity Bonds No internal control structure can provide absolute protection against losses from dishonest employees. Therefore, many companies require that employees who handle cash or other negotiable assets be *bonded.* A *fidelity bond* is a type of insurance contract in which the bonding company agrees to reimburse an employer up to agreed dollar limits for losses caused by fraud or embezzlement by bonded employees.

Management Fraud

Management fraud refers to deliberate misrepresentation made by the *top management* of a business to persons *outside* the business organization. This type of fraud often involves the issuance of fraudulent financial statements intended to mislead investors and creditors.

CASE IN POINT   Some years ago, the bankruptcy of Allied Crude Vegetable Oil Corporation stunned the financial world. Allied had borrowed money from 51 different companies and banks, using as collateral its inventory of nearly 2 billion gallons of salad oil. After the company's bankruptcy, investigators learned that much of Allied's "inventory" consisted of nothing more than forged warehouse receipts. Inventory listed at $175 million in Allied's balance sheet simply did not exist.

Misuse of Company Assets   Another form of management fraud involves the misuse of company assets for the personal benefit of top management. The misuse of company assets may take many forms. Examples include excessive salaries to top managers and/or their relatives, and allowing managers to make extensive personal use of such company-owned assets as homes, yachts, and aircraft. Another area of possible abuse is fraudulently structured business transactions between the company and its top management.

The Impact of Management Fraud   In cases of management fraud, top management is a *willing participant* in the fraudulent acts. One characteristic of such fraud is that management uses its position of trust and authority to *override the internal control structure* and to enrich itself at the expense of the company and/or outsiders. The persons most often injured by management fraud are investors and creditors. However, the company's employees and customers and the general public also may be harmed severely.

The basic purpose of accounting is to *aid decision makers in allocating and using economic resources efficiently.* Cases of management fraud are far more destructive to this basic purpose than are most cases of employee fraud. The damage caused by employee fraud usually is limited to relatively small losses incurred by a specific company. Seldom, however, does employee fraud force a business into bankruptcy or affect the efficient allocation of resources throughout the economy.

When the financial statements of large companies are altered to mislead investors and creditors, however, the resulting losses may be enormous. In addition, the misallocation of economic resources may be so great as to affect the national economy.

CASE IN POINT Management fraud played a major role in the savings and loan crisis. Some S&Ls falsified their accounting records and financial statements to conceal from investors and government regulators their deteriorating financial positions and managements' misuse of company assets.

Ultimately, the S&L crisis may cost the American taxpayer—who insures deposits in these institutions—more than $500 billion. In addition, this crisis has contributed to an economic recession, federal income tax increases, and the loss of many jobs.

Management fraud is **not** commonplace in our society. The managers and directors of most large business organizations are people of integrity. However, even a few isolated instances of management fraud can severely damage the economy. Whenever the management of a large publicly owned company engages in fraud, investors, creditors, and the public tend to lose confidence in the business community and the financial reporting process. This loss of confidence may create doubts and reservations which impede the efficient allocation of investment capital for many years.

Protecting Society from Management Fraud To a limited extent systems of internal control protect outside decision makers against the possibility of a large-scale management fraud. Internal accounting controls are designed primarily to assure **management** that the company's accounting information is reliable. However, top management may be able to override these controls when it comes to reporting to people outside the organization.

The limited protection which internal control does provide against management fraud arises from the subdivision of duties within the organization. Many people in management and in the company's accounting department would be aware of a large-scale management fraud. Presumably, some of these people would refuse to participate in the fraud and would "blow the whistle" on a dishonest management.

Financial audits are more oriented toward providing outside decision makers with assurance as to the reliability of financial statements than is the internal control structure.

AUDITS

Audits of Financial Statements

OBJECTIVE 9
Explain the nature and purposes of financial audits, reviews, and operational audits.

A financial audit is an examination of a company's financial statements performed by a firm of certified public accountants (CPAs). The basic purpose of this audit is to provide decision makers outside the business organization with an independent expert's **opinion** as to the **fairness** of the financial statements. Auditors use the term "fair" in describing financial statements which are complete, unbiased, reliable, and presented in conformity with generally accepted accounting principles.

The Nature of a Financial Audit The financial statements of a business are prepared by the company's management. An audit of these financial statements is intended to bridge the "credibility gap" which otherwise might exist between the company's management and the users of these statements. For the auditors' opinion to have credibility, however, the auditors must (1) be *independent* of the company issuing the statements and of its management and (2) have a sound basis for their opinion. The term *audit* describes the *investigation* which the auditors undertake to provide the basis for their opinion.

As part of a financial audit, the CPAs study and evaluate the internal control structure within the company issuing the financial statements. This study gives them a "feel" for the accuracy and reliability of the information in the company's accounting system.

Next, the auditors gather evidence to substantiate every material item shown in the company's financial statements. For example, the CPAs count portions of the company's inventory and compare these test counts with the company's inventory records. They *confirm* some of the accounts receivable by contacting the debtor. In those areas in which internal control is weak, the auditors must gather more evidence from outside the organization, as they have less reason to rely upon the information contained in the company's accounting system.

In addition to substantiating the items shown in a company's financial statements, auditors perform procedures to determine that these statements and the accompanying notes are complete. For example, auditors apply procedures which are designed to bring to light any unrecorded liabilities.

Auditors' Reports   Upon concluding their investigation, the auditors issue an auditors' report, expressing their opinion as to the fairness of the financial statements. This report accompanies the financial statements whenever they are issued to persons outside the business organization.

Auditors also issue a report to the company's management—often called a *management letter*—detailing the auditors' recommendations for improving the company's internal control structure. Auditors have considerable expertise in the area of internal control, as they are continually studying and evaluating the control structures of many different organizations.

Audits and the Detection of Fraud   The primary purpose of financial audits is to determine the overall fairness of a set of financial statements, *not* to detect any and all acts of fraud. Users of financial statements should recognize that auditors cannot guarantee that financial statements are completely free of errors and irregularities. Most audit procedures are based upon samples; it simply is not possible for the auditors to verify all of the transactions of a large organization. Therefore, there is always the possibility that errors or irregularities may exist among the transactions which were not examined by the auditors.

Auditors design their investigation to detect those errors and irregularities which are *material* in relation to the financial statements.[4] We have

---

4   AICPA, *Statement on Auditing Standards No. 53,* "The Auditor's Reponsibility to Detect and Report Errors and Irregularities" (New York, 1988).

explained the concept of materiality in earlier chapters. With respect to financial statements, an item is "material" if knowledge of the item might reasonably be expected to *influence the decisions of users of the statements.*

Some cases of employee fraud, such as the theft of a few items from inventory, involve such small dollar amounts that they do not affect the overall fairness of the financial statements. An audit should not be expected to detect every such irregularity.

Any fraud of a scale which causes the financial statements to become misleading, however, *is* material. Such situations *should* be brought to light in the normal course of an audit. The principal purpose of an audit is to provide outsiders with assurance that the financial statements are a fair presentation. If these audited statements are misleading, the audit has failed to serve its purpose.

As explained in Chapter 1, audits are not the only factor contributing to the reliability of financial statements. Other factors include the company's internal control structure, the Securities and Exchange Commission, and federal securities laws. A most important element of reliable financial reporting is the personal commitment of professional accountants to *ethical conduct.* If these individuals do not conduct themselves with integrity, the financial reporting process may be rendered ineffective.

The importance of ethical conduct—that is, honorable behavior—has long been understood by members of the accounting profession. The major associations of professional accountants have developed codes of ethics to provide their members with guidelines for conducting themselves in a manner consistent with their responsibilities to society. (Two of these codes of professional ethics are discussed in some detail in Chapter 13.)

Auditors' Liability to the Users of Financial Statements   If auditors perform an audit with *due professional care,* they are *not responsible* for damages stemming from errors or irregularities that go undetected. On the other hand, if the audit is performed in a *negligent* manner, the auditors may be held financially liable for losses sustained by users of these statements.[5]

Although audits do not provide an absolute guarantee of reliability, audited financial statements have established an impressive track record of reliability in comparison with unaudited accounting information. The financial statements of Allied Crude Vegetable Oil, for example, were *unaudited.* Had creditors insisted upon receiving financial statements that have been either audited or *reviewed* prior to extending credit, the inventory shortages would have been discovered long before reaching such large amounts.

Federal laws require all publicly owned companies to have their annual financial statements audited. In dealing with nonpublic companies, creditors and investors often insist upon receiving financial statements that

---

[5]   In the context of auditing, *negligence* is a legal term which means failure to exercise due professional care.

have been either audited or *reviewed* before making substantial investments.

Reviews of Financial Statements   An audit is both time-consuming and expensive. (The cost of the audit normally is paid by the company issuing the financial statements.) All accounting information, including audited financial statements, should be cost-effective. For this reason, many nonpublic companies have their financial statements *reviewed* by a firm of CPAs, rather than having these statements audited.

"Reviews" of financial statements are intended to provide outsiders with *limited assurance* as to the fairness of the statements. A review is similar to a financial audit, except that the investigation is *substantially less thorough.* Thus, a review can be performed much more quickly than an audit and at a substantially lower cost.

Special-Purpose Audits

When CPAs perform a financial audit, the auditors' findings usually are made available to all users of the company's financial statements. Tax authorities and some regulatory agencies, however, frequently perform special-purpose audits to determine whether a company is in compliance with the agencies' rules and regulations. For example, each year the Internal Revenue Service audits the income tax returns of several million taxpayers. The results of special-purpose audits generally are *not* made available to the public or to other outside decision makers.

Operational Auditing

Financial audits focus primarily upon the verification of financial measurements. An operational audit, in contrast, focuses upon the *efficiency* and *effectiveness* of an operating unit within an organization.

An operational audit involves studying, testing, and evaluating the operating procedures and internal controls relating to a specific unit within an organization. The subject of the operational audit might be the accounting department, the purchasing department, a branch office, or any other subunit within the company. The purpose of the audit is to make recommendations to management for *improving the operational efficiency* of the department under study. The results normally are not communicated to decision makers outside the business organization.

Operational auditing is a rapidly growing field of specialization within accounting. Current economic pressures are forcing private companies, not-for-profit organizations, and all levels of government to reduce costs and to increase the efficiency of their operations. Within large organizations, operational auditing is a function of the internal audit staff. Smaller organizations may engage CPA firms to perform operational audits. The federal government has several agencies, such as the General Accounting Office (GAO) and the Naval Audit Service, which perform operational audits of various governmental agencies and programs.

END-OF-CHAPTER REVIEW

SUMMARY OF CHAPTER LEARNING OBJECTIVES

1 Explain why the structure of the accounting system varies from one organization to the next.

The basic purpose of an accounting system is to meet an organization's needs for accounting information as efficiently as possible. Therefore, the structure of a particular accounting system depends upon the specific company's needs for accounting information and the resources available for the operation of the system.

2 Define special journals and explain the reasons for their use.

Special journals are accounting records or devices designed to record a specific type of transaction in a highly efficient manner. Because a special journal is used to record only specific types of transaction, the journal may be located at the transaction site and maintained by employees other than accounting personnel. Thus, special journals reduce the time, effort, and cost of recording routine business transactions.

3 Describe a data base and explain its usefulness.

A data base is a "warehouse" within a computer-based accounting system in which data concerning certain transactions are stored. These transaction data are accompanied by classification codes which enable a computer to classify the data according to various criteria. A data base enables management to classify the data in accounting reports in the manner which best suits the decision makers' needs.

4 Code transaction data so that they may be classified using alternative criteria.

Coded transaction data include a separate *data field* for each general criterion by which the data are to be sorted or classified. The codes entered in these data fields identify the specific subunits within the broader classification category.

5 Describe the objectives of internal controls.

Internal controls include all measures taken by an organization for the purposes of (1) protecting its resources against waste, fraud, or inefficient use; (2) ensuring the reliability of accounting data; (3) securing compliance with management's policies; and (4) evaluating the performance of all employees, managers, and departments within the organization.

6 Identify several specific measures useful in achieving strong internal control.

Among the internal control measures emphasized in this chapter were: establishing clear lines of responsibility, establishing routine procedures for processing each type of transaction, appropriate subdivision of duties, separation of the accounting function from custody of assets, and the use of business documents.

Other internal control measures discussed include internal auditing, the use of financial forecasts, the need for competent employees, rotation of employees, serially numbered documents, separating responsibility for handling cash from authority to issue credit memoranda, and limiting access to computer programs and files to authorized personnel.

7 Explain the role of purchase orders and receiving reports in verifying a purchase invoice.

A purchase invoice is a bill for purchased merchandise. The purchase order is prepared by the buyer's purchasing department when the order is placed, and the receiving report is prepared by the receiving department when the goods are received. The buyer's accounting department compares these documents before recording the purchase or approving payment of the invoice.

Comparing the purchase invoice to the purchase order verifies (a) the type and quantity of goods ordered and (b) the prices that the buyer had agreed to pay. Comparing the invoice to the receiving report indicates that the merchandise was received in good condition.

8 Distinguish between employee fraud and management fraud.

Employee fraud refers to dishonest acts performed by the employees of a company despite management's efforts to prevent these actions. Management fraud, in contrast, refers to acts of fraud *perpetrated by management,* usually against persons outside the business organization. In essence, the distinction lies in whether top management tries to prevent the fraudulent actions or is a willing participant.

9 Explain the nature and purpose of financial audits, reviews, and operational audits.

A financial audit is a thorough investigation of a company's financial statements by an independent CPA firm. The primary purpose of this investigation is to provide decision makers outside the organization with an independent expert's opinion as to the fairness of the financial statements. A review is similar to an audit, but is less thorough and provides the outsiders with less assurance. However, a review may be performed more quickly than an audit and at a significantly lower cost.

An operational audit is a study of the efficiency of a department or subunit within a larger organization. The purpose of this investigation is to make recommendations to management for improving the operational efficiency of the department under study.

Our objective in these first six chapters has been to introduce you to financial accounting—what financial accounting information is, and how and why it is developed and used. In the next several chapters, we will explore in greater depth such topics as the valuation of assets and the recognition of revenue and expenses. As we do, you will add to your understanding of accounting and of business operations. You also will see many specific applications of the concepts introduced in these early chapters.

KEY TERMS INTRODUCED OR EMPHASIZED IN CHAPTER 6

Accounting system The personnel, procedures, devices, and records used by an entity to develop accounting information and to communicate this information to decision makers.

Auditors' report The expert opinion expressed by auditors as to the fairness of financial statements.

Cost-effective Having economic value in excess of its cost.

Credit memorandum A document issued by a seller to a buyer indicating that the seller is reducing (crediting) its account receivable from the buyer as the result of a sales return or allowance.

Data base A "warehouse" within a computer system in which unclassified coded data are stored. Data in the data base may be sorted and classified in any manner permitted by the classification codes attached to the data.

Debit memorandum A document issued by the buyer to the seller indicating that the buyer is reducing (debiting) its account payable to the seller in connection with a purchase return or allowance.

Embezzlement A theft of assets which is concealed by falsification of the accounting records.

Employee fraud Fraud perpetrated against a company by one or more of its employees.

Errors Unintentional mistakes; one source of erroneous accounting information. A distinction is drawn between errors and *irregularities.*

Fair presentation A term used by auditors and accountants in describing financial statements which are unbiased, complete, in conformity with generally accepted accounting principles, and not misleading.

Fidelity bond A type of insurance which reimburses an employer for losses caused by fraud or embezzlement by bonded employees.

Financial audit A thorough investigation of a company's financial statements by an independent CPA firm, conducted for the purpose of expressing an expert opinion as to the reliability and completeness (or "fairness") of the financial statements.

Fraud Misrepresentation with the intent to deceive. An illegal act if the purpose is financial gain or to cause loss to another.

Internal auditors Professional accountants employed by an organization to continually test and evaluate internal control structure and to report their findings and recommendations to top management.

Internal control All measures used by a business to guard against errors, waste, or fraud and to assure the reliability of accounting data. Designed to aid in the efficient operation of a business and to encourage compliance with company policies.

Invoice An itemized statement of goods being bought or sold. Shows quantities, prices, and credit terms. Serves as the basis for an entry in the accounting records of both seller and buyer because it evidences the transfer of ownership of goods.

Invoice approval form A business document prepared by a purchasing company's accounting department prior to recording or approving payment of a purchase invoice. Preliminary steps include comparing the purchase order and receiving report with the purchase invoice.

Irregularities Intentional "mistakes" introduced into accounting information for some fraudulent purpose.

Management fraud Fraud perpetrated by a company against outsiders. Usually involves the issuance of misleading financial statements.

On-line, real-time A computer system in which certain accounting records are kept completely up-to-date by recording transactions as they occur.

Operational auditing Studying, testing, and evaluating the efficiency and effectiveness of an operating unit within a larger organization. The purpose of an operational audit is to make recommendations to management for improving the operational efficiency of the unit.

Purchase order   A serially numbered document sent by the purchasing department of a business to a supplier or vendor for the purpose of ordering materials or services.

Receiving report   An internal form prepared by the receiving department for each incoming shipment showing the quantity and condition of goods received.

Review (of financial statements)   An investigation of financial statements for the purpose of providing outsiders with *limited assurance* that the statements are complete and reliable. A review is substantially less thorough than an audit but also is less costly.

Special journal   An accounting record or device designed for recording a particular type of transaction quickly and efficiently. A business may use many different types of special journals.

SELF-TEST QUESTIONS

The answers to these questions appear on page 312.

1   Which of the following factors is *not* a significant consideration in designing an accounting system for a business?

   a   The types of accounting information which the business is required by law to report to agencies or persons outside the organization.

   b   The cost of developing various types of accounting information.

   c   The need for subsidiary ledgers and other detailed information in conducting daily business operations.

   d   None of the above answers is correct.

2   Identify all answers which describe characteristics of special journals.

   a   Less familiarity with accounting principles is required of an employee maintaining a special journal than of an employee maintaining a general journal.

   b   The transactions best suited to special journals are routine transactions which occur frequently.

   c   For purposes of strong internal control, all special journals are located in the accounting department.

   d   Special journals are essential in an on-line, real-time accounting system.

3   In comparison with a manual accounting system, a computer-based system with point-of-sale terminals and a data base should reduce greatly which of the following? (More than one answer may be correct.)

   a   The time and effort spent in recording transactions.

   b   The need for internal control.

   c   The time and effort involved in maintaining subsidiary ledger accounts.

   d   The number of ways in which transaction data may be classified in special reports to management.

4   One means of achieving internal control is an appropriate subdivision of duties. Identify all answers consistent with this concept.

   a   No one employee should handle all aspects of a transaction.

   b   Each employee's area of responsibility should be carefully defined.

   c   To the extent practicable, employees should be rotated periodically to different job assignments.

   d   Employees with custody of assets should not maintain the accounting records relating to those assets.

5 Which of the following statements concerning the internal control structure is **not** correct?

   a One purpose of operational audits is to improve internal control.

   b It is easier to achieve strong internal control in a small business than in a large one.

   c The internal control structure is more effective in preventing large-scale employee fraud than large-scale management fraud.

   d No internal control structure provides complete protection against errors and irregularities.

6 Parker Corporation has recently issued capital stock to the public and now must be audited annually by an independent firm of CPAs. These annual audits should eliminate the need for:

   a Internal control.

   b Operational audits by the company's internal auditors.

   c Fidelity bonds on employees who handle negotiable assets.

   d None of the above.

7 Assume that audited financial statements turn out to be misleading and investors relying upon these statements sustain losses. Which of the following best describes the auditors' potential liability for these losses?

   a The auditors may be liable, because they have guaranteed the reliability of the statements.

   b The auditors are not liable, as they have only issued an opinion as to the reliability of the statements.

   c The auditors may be liable if they performed their audit in a negligent manner.

   d The auditors may be liable, but only if the statements were misleading because of management fraud.

ASSIGNMENT MATERIAL

DISCUSSION QUESTIONS

1 What are the basic factors affecting the design and structure of a company's accounting system?

2 Identify the sources from which an organization's accounting system may come. In other words, who designs it?

3 An accounting system should meet the specific needs of a business organization. Identify several examples of (a) information needs which are common to all publicly owned corporations and (b) accounting information which management may want developed for its own use in managing the business.

4 With respect to accounting information, define the term **cost-effective.** How does this concept affect the design and output of an accounting system?

5 Explain the unique characteristics of (a) a general journal and (b) a special journal.

6 How is it possible for cashiers using point-of-sale terminals to record cash sales by entering only a "product code" into the terminal? Why is it not necessary to enter the dollar amount of the sale and to instruct the computer to debit the Cash account and credit the Sales account?

7 Define an *on-line, real-time* accounting system. Identify several business situations in which on-line, real-time information would be useful to company personnel.

8 What is meant by the term *responsibility accounting system?* What are the implications of a responsibility accounting system with respect to a company's chart of ledger accounts?

9 Briefly explain the usefulness of a data base.

10 Identify two general criteria (other than reliability) which affect the usefulness of an accounting report to a decision maker. How has technology affected these criteria in recent years?

11 List four specific objectives of internal control structure.

12 The internal control structure includes *accounting controls* and *administrative controls.* Describe each group and give an example of each.

13 Briefly explain the concept of *subdivision of duties.* How does this concept reduce the risk of errors and irregularities?

14 Suggest a control device to protect against the loss of nondelivery of invoices or other documents which are routed from one department to another.

15 Name three business documents which are needed by the accounting department to verify that a purchase of merchandise has occurred and that payment of the invoice should be made.

16 Radio House received a shipment of 30 cellular car phones from Yamaha Corporation. The receiving report showed that 3 of these phones were defective and are being returned to Yamaha. Should Radio House issue Yamaha a debit memorandum or a credit memorandum when it returns this merchandise?

17 Briefly explain why a person who handles cash receipts from customers should not also have authority to issue credit memoranda for sales returns and allowances.

18 Is internal control necessary in a company with a highly reliable computer system? Explain.

19 Explain several reasons why an internal control structure may *fail* to prevent certain errors or irregularities.

20 Is it usually easier to achieve strong internal control in a large business or in a very small one? Explain the reasons for your answer.

21 Distinguish between *employee fraud* and *management fraud.* Provide an example of each.

22 Describe the nature and purpose of a financial audit. Who performs these audits?

23 Do auditors guarantee the reliability of audited financial statements? If the statements should turn out to be highly misleading, can the auditors be held financially liable for the losses sustained by decision makers relying upon the statements? Explain.

24 Distinguish between a *financial audit* and a *review* of financial statements. Who performs these services? Why pays for them?

25 Describe the nature and purpose of an operational audit. Who performs these audits?

EXERCISES

**EXERCISE 6-1
Accounting
Terminology**

Listed below are nine technical terms related to accounting systems and/or internal control structures:

Internal control structure	*Responsibility accounting system*	*On-line, real-time system*
Special journal	*Data base*	*Purchase order*
General journal	*Debit memorandum*	*Receiving report*

Each of the following statements may (or may not) describe one of these technical terms. For each statement, indicate the term described, or answer "None" if the statement does not correctly describe any of the terms.

a A chart of accounts which permits separate measurement of departmental revenue and expense.

b A document used in verifying the unit prices in a purchase invoice.

c A journal used in recording unusual types of transactions.

d An element of a computer-based accounting system which enables information to be classified according to various criteria.

e Measures intended to make all aspects of a business operate according to management's plans and policies.

f A system in which certain accounting records are kept continuously up-to-date.

g A business document which might be issued to conceal the theft of cash collected from a credit customer.

**EXERCISE 6-2
Accounting
Terminology—
Fraud and
Auditing**

Listed below are nine technical terms relating to fraud and/or auditing:

Management fraud	*Financial audit*	*Embezzlement*
Employee fraud	*Operational audit*	*Errors*
Fidelity bond	*Review*	*Irregularities*

Each of the following statements may (or may not) describe one of these technical terms. For each statement, indicate the term described, or answer "None" if the statement does not correctly describe any of the terms.

a An investigation conducted by a company's internal auditors for the purpose of providing outsiders with an independent opinion upon the fairness of the company's financial statements.

b A theft of assets which is concealed by falsification of the accounting records.

c An investigation intended to provide outside decision makers with a *limited* degree of assurance as to the reliability of financial statements.

d Intentional misstatements within financial statements which may result from employee fraud or may represent management fraud.

e A form of insurance policy which compensates users of financial statements for losses sustained as a result of management fraud.

f An investigation conducted for the purpose of evaluating the efficiency and effectiveness of a department or other subunit within an organization.

g An effort to deceive outsiders through the issuance of misleading financial statements.

**EXERCISE 6-3
Special
Journals**

In every accounting system, transactions initially are recorded in some type of journal.

a Compare and contrast basic characteristics of a *general journal* and a *special journal.*

b Is more knowledge of accounting required to maintain a general journal or a special journal? Explain.

c Provide several examples of special journals which you have observed in operation. Explain the nature of the transactions recorded in these journals.

d Does a business with highly efficient special journals also need a general journal? Explain.

EXERCISE 6-4
Ledgers and Data Bases

In computer-based accounting systems, data relating to certain types of transactions may be stored in a ***data base*** as well as in ledger accounts.

a Briefly distinguish between ***ledger accounts*** and a ***data base*** as a means of storing and classifying data.

b Is a data base more useful in preparing financial statements or reports to management? Explain.

EXERCISE 6-5
Coding Transaction Data

The Software Center program stores data relating to sales transactions in a data base. Department no. 7 has just sold 3 units of product no. 310 to a credit customer. The sales price of this product is $79.50 per unit, and its cost to Home Improvement Center was $40.00 per unit. The customer's account number in the accounts receivable ledger is 1004. In the data base, this transaction is coded as follows:

1004 - 310 - 3 - 79.50 - 40.00 - 7

a Show how the following transaction would be coded in the data base: Department no. 2 sells on account 5 units of product no. 132. The customer's account number is 4699; product no. 132 has a per-unit cost of $10.40 and a per-unit sales price of $19.95.

b Prepare a brief written description of the following coded transaction. (Your description should be similar to that appearing in part **a**.)

2102 - 218 - 2 - 46.50 - 29.80 - 4

EXERCISE 6-6
Internal Control and Business Documents

In each of the following independent cases, indicate the internal control which appears to be missing in the purchaser's invoice approval procedures.

a Baxter Construction Company, a builder of tract homes, ordered 100 mahogany front doors from Anderson Door Company at the agreed-upon price of $79 each. In the sales invoice, Anderson erroneously listed the price of these doors at $97 each. Baxter paid the invoice total of $9,700 without detecting the error.

b Jet Auto Parts ordered 50 Sure-Start auto batteries from Allied Battery at a price of $20 each. Allied sent Jet a sales invoice for 50 batteries at $20 but delivered only 20 batteries. Jet's accounting personnel recorded the transaction directly from the invoice, debiting Inventory and crediting Accounts Payable for $1,000.

EXERCISE 6-7
Internal Control and Fidelity Bonds

Strong internal control protects a company's assets against waste, fraud, and inefficient use. Fidelity bonds provide a means by which a company may recover losses caused by dishonest acts of employees. Would it be reasonable for a company to maintain strong internal control and also pay for a fidelity bond? Explain. Would you regard fidelity bonds as a satisfactory substitute for an internal control structure? Explain.

EXERCISE 6-8
Internal Control and Fraud Prevention

Golden Valley Farm Supply retained a firm of certified public accountants to design internal controls especially for its operations. Assuming that the CPA firm has finished its work and the newly designed internal control structure is in use, answer fully the following:

a Will it be possible for any type of fraud to occur without immediate detection once the new internal control structure is in full operation?

b Describe two limitations inherent in an internal control structure that prevent it from providing absolute assurance against inefficiency and fraud.

**EXERCISE 6-9
Types of
Audits**

Briefly distinguish among the following types of audits: (a) a financial audit, (b) an Internal Revenue Service audit of a taxpayer's income tax return, and (c) the ongoing operational audits in a large business organization. You should address such issues as the basic purpose of each audit, who performs the audit, and who makes use of the auditors' findings.

PROBLEMS

Note: Due to the nature of the problem material in this chapter, two sets of problems would result in substantial repetition. For this reason, we present the problems in one series, rather than our usual A and B groups. Both the A and B sets of accounting work sheets contain working papers for all of these problems. However, many of these problems also can be answered either on ordinary notebook paper or by using a word processor.

**PROBLEM 6-1
Accounting
Systems**

Evaluate each of the following statements, indicating any areas of agreement and disagreement.

a Transactions can be recorded more efficiently in special journals than in a general journal. Therefore, a well-designed accounting system should use only special journals.

b The transaction data stored in a data base can be arranged in the format of ledger accounts. Therefore, a business with a computer-based accounting system does not need a ledger. Whenever the balance of any ledger account is needed for any purpose, the computer can sort through the data base and determine this amount.

c In an on-line, real-time accounting system, a manager may view the up-to-the-moment balance of any ledger account from a computer terminal.

d Advances in the technologies of computers and communications have increased the usefulness of accounting information to decision makers.

e In recording cash sales, a cashier using a point-of-sale terminal may record a cash sale by entering only a product code which identifies the merchandise sold. This is single-entry accounting, not double-entry accounting.

**PROBLEM 6-2
Operation of a
Data Base**

Video Outlet operates two stores which rent and sell video tapes. (Tapes offered for sale are all new and are stored separately from the rental tapes.) The company sells annual memberships to most of its customers. Members are entitled to lower prices on tape rentals than are nonmembers.

Rental and sales transactions are recorded using point-of-sale terminals located in each store. Each tape has a label which can be read by an optical scanner. This label indicates the title of the tape and whether the tape is a rental or a product offered for sale. The data from these revenue transactions are stored in a data base and are coded as follows:

Field 1   Nature of the revenue; *0* indicates a rental, *1* indicates a sale.

Field 2   Store in which the transaction originates. Stores are coded *1* and *2.*

Field 3   Member number; three zeros in this field indicates a transaction with a nonmember. (Member numbers are recorded because members who have rented 20 tapes during the year receive an additional discount on future rentals.)

Field 4   Title of tape rented or sold. Each title is identified by a three-digit code number.

Field 5   Revenue earned. For rental transactions, this is the rental price; for sales transactions, the sales price is stored in this field. No sales price exceeds $99.99.

Field 6   Cost of goods sold. This field is completed only for sales transactions; zeros are entered whenever a *0* appears in Field 1.

INSTRUCTIONS

a   Identify the various ways in which this system enables Video Outlet to classify its revenue.

b   In recording both rental and sales transactions, the salesperson passes the tape over the optical scanner, enabling the computer to read the label on the tape. Indicate for each of the six data fields whether this action provides the computer with enough information to complete the field, or whether additional action is required of the terminal operator. In each case, explain the source of the data entered into each field.

c   To test your understanding of this data base, 10 coded transactions are shown below. [The numbers (1) through (10) are provided for reference only and are not part of the transaction coding.]

(1) 1 - 2 - 122 - 096 - 29.95 - 10.20	(6) 1 - 1 - 147 - 110 - 49.95 - 35.00
(2) 0 - 1 - 318 - 110 - 02.50 - 00.00	(7) 1 - 2 - 000 - 157 - 79.95 - 32.48
(3) 0 - 2 - 000 - 096 - 03.50 - 00.00	(8) 0 - 1 - 000 - 123 - 03.50 - 00.00
(4) 1 - 2 - 449 - 110 - 49.95 - 35.00	(9) 1 - 1 - 303 - 110 - 49.95 - 35.00
(5) 1 - 1 - 000 - 096 - 29.95 - 10.20	(10) 0 - 1 - 012 - 062 - 02.50 - 00.00

Although this function normally is performed automatically by the computer, you are to sort this transaction data to determine:

1 Total rental revenue earned from store no. 1.

2 Total revenue from sales of tape no. 110 (combine both stores).

3 Total gross profit earned from sales transactions at store no. 2.

4 Total rental revenue earned from nonmembers (combine both stores).

d   Show how the following transactions would be coded in this data base:

1 Store no. 1 sells tape no. 143 to member no. 702 for $39.95. The cost of this tape to Video Outlet was $19.30.

2 Store no. 2 rents tape no. 110 for $3.50 to a nonmember.

PROBLEM 6-3
Purpose of an Internal Control Structure

Three executives of Jetlab, a small electronics firm, disagree as to their company's need for an internal control structure. Jones argues as follows: "If we are going to spend money on fidelity bonds, it is a complete waste to duplicate that kind of protection by maintaining our own internal control structure." Smith disagrees and expresses the following view: "The benefits we would receive from a strong internal control structure would go way beyond protection against fraud." Adams says: "The best internal control structure in my opinion is to maintain two complete but separate sets of accounting records. If all our transactions are recorded twice by different employees, the two independent sets of records and financial statements can be compared and any discrepancies investigated."

Evaluate the views expressed by each of the three executives.

PROBLEM 6-4
Internal Control Measures

The lettered paragraphs that follow describe seven errors or problems which might occur in a merchandising business. Also listed are five internal control measures. List the letter (**a** through **g**) designating each of these errors or problems. Beside each letter, place the number indicating the internal control measure that would prevent this type of error or problem from occurring. If none of the specified control measures would effectively prevent the error or problem, place "0" after the letter.

Possible Errors or Problems

a Paid an invoice in which the supplier had accidentally doubled the price of the merchandise.

b Paid a supplier for goods that were delivered but that were never ordered.

c Purchased merchandise which turned out not to be popular with customers.

d Several sales invoices were misplaced and the accounts receivable department is therefore unaware of the unrecorded credit sales.

e Paid a supplier for goods that were never received.

f The purchasing department ordered goods from one supplier when a better price could have been obtained by ordering from another supplier.

g The cashier conceals the embezzlement of cash by reducing the balance of the Cash account.

Internal Control Measures

1 Comparison of purchase invoice with the receiving report

2 Comparison of purchase invoice with the purchase order

3 Separation of the accounting function from custody of assets

4 Separation of the responsibilities for approving and recording transactions

5 Use of serially numbered documents

0 None of the above control procedures can effectively prevent this error from occurring.

PROBLEM 6-5 Internal Control Measures—Emphasis upon Computer-Based Systems

The lettered paragraphs below describe seven possible errors or problems which might occur in a retail business. Also listed are five internal control measures. List the letter (**a** through **g**) designating the errors or problems. Beside each letter, place the number indicating the internal control measure that should prevent this type of error or problem from occurring. If none of the specified internal control measures would effectively prevent the error or problem, place a "0" opposite the letter. Assume that a computer-based accounting system is in use.

Possible Errors or Problems

a A salesclerk unknowingly makes a credit sale to a customer whose account has already reached the customer's prearranged credit limit.

b The cashier of a business conceals a theft of cash by adjusting the balance of the Cash account in the company's computer-based accounting records.

c Certain merchandise proves to be so unpopular with customers that it cannot be sold except at a price well below its original cost.

d A salesclerk rings up a sale at an incorrect price.

e A salesclerk uses a point-of-sale terminal to improperly reduce the balance of a friend's account in the company's accounts receivable records.

f One of the salesclerks is quite lazy and leaves most of the work of serving customers to the other salesclerks in the department.

g A shoplifter steals merchandise while the salesclerk is busy with another customer.

Internal Control Measures

1 Limiting the types of transactions which can be processed from point-of-sale terminals to cash sales and credit sales.

2 All merchandise has a magnetically coded label which can be read automatically by an optical scanner on a point-of-sale terminal. This code identifies to the computer the merchandise being sold.

3 Credit cards issued by the store have magnetic codes which can be read automatically by a device attached to the electronic cash register. Credit approval and posting to customers accounts are handled by the computer.

4 The computer prepares a report with separate daily sales totals for each salesperson.

5 Employees with custody of assets do not have access to accounting records.

0 None of the above control measures effectively prevents this type of error from occurring.

PROBLEM 6-6
Types of Fraud

Cases of fraud often are described either as *employee fraud* or *management fraud.*

a Briefly distinguish between employee fraud and management fraud.

b Identify three types of actions which constitute employee fraud.

c Identify three types of actions which constitute management fraud.

d Which type of fraud is likely to have the greatest impact upon the national economy? Explain the reasons for your answer.

PROBLEM 6-7
An Overview of Financial Audits

Answer each of the following questions concerning an audit of the financial statements of a publicly owned company.

a What is the basic purpose of this type of audit?

b Who performs the audit?

c Why is the concept of independence important in a financial audit?

d What consideration do these auditors give to the company's system of internal control?

e To whom are the auditors' findings made available?

f Do the auditors guarantee the reliability of the audited financial statements? If the audited statements are misleading, are the auditors held financially liable for losses incurred by people relying upon these statements? Explain.

g Who pays for the audit?

h Briefly distinguish between a financial audit and a review of financial statements by an auditing firm.

PROBLEM 6-8
Characteristics of Financial Audits and of Operational Audits

Listed below are nine statements about auditing. Indicate whether each statement applies to *financial audits, operational audits, both,* or *neither.* Explain your reasons for each answer.

a As part of their investigation, the auditors study and evaluate the internal control structure maintained by the company.

b The auditors guarantee the reliability of the financial statements to outside decision makers.

c The auditors' findings are communicated only to management and to the Internal Revenue Service.

d One major purpose of the audit is to determine compliance with generally accepted accounting principles.

e The audit usually focuses upon a department or subunit within the organization.

f In a large organization, these audits may be conducted continuously as part of the professional responsibilities of certain company employees.

g If the auditors are negligent, they may be held financially liable for losses incurred by decision makers outside the organization.

h The auditors are independent of the company and its management.

i The basic purpose of the audit is the detection of fraud.

CASES AND UNSTRUCTURED PROBLEMS

CASE 6-1
The Baker Street Diversion

Printing Made Easy sells a variety of printers for use with personal computers. Last April, Arthur Doyle, the company's purchasing agent, discovered a weakness in internal control and engaged in a scheme to steal printers. Doyle issued a purchase order for 20 printers to one of the company's regular suppliers, but he included a typewritten note on company letterhead stationery requesting that the printers be delivered to 221B Baker Street, a warehouse in which Doyle had rented space.

The supplier shipped the printers to Baker Street and sent a sales invoice to Printing Made Easy. When the invoice arrived, an accounting clerk carefully complied with company policy and compared the invoice with a copy of the purchase order. After noting agreement between these documents as to quantities, prices, and model numbers, the clerk recorded the transaction in the accounting records and authorized payment of the invoice.

INSTRUCTIONS

What is the weakness in internal control discovered by the purchasing agent to enable him to commit this theft? What changes would you recommend in the company's internal documentation and invoice approval procedures to prevent such problems in the future?

CASE 6-2
Internal Control in a Computer-Based System

Mission Stores uses point-of-sale terminals to record its sales transactions. All merchandise bears a magnetic code number which can be read by an optical scanner. When merchandise is sold, the salesclerk passes each item over the scanner. The computer reads the code number, determines the price of the item from a master price list, and displays the price on a screen for the customer to see. After each item has been passed over the scanner, the computer displays the total amount of the sale and records the transaction in the company's accounting records.

If the transaction is a credit sale, the salesclerk enters the customer's credit card number into the register. The computer checks the customer's credit status and updates the accounts receivable subsidiary ledger.

INSTRUCTIONS

Statements **a** through **d** describe problems which may arise in a retailing business which uses manual cash registers and accounting records. Explain how the point-of-sale terminals used by Mission Stores will help reduce or eliminate these problems. If the point-of-sale terminals will not help to eliminate the problems, explain why not.

a A salesclerk is unaware of a recent change in the price of a particular item.

b Merchandise is stolen by a shoplifter.

c A salesclerk fails to record a cash sale and keeps the cash received from the customer.

d A customer buys merchandise on account using a stolen Mission Stores credit card.

**CASE 6-3
Internal Control in a Typical Restaurant**

Alice's Restaurant has an internal control structure which is similar to most restaurants. A waiter or waitress (food server) writes each customer's order on a serially numbered sales ticket. The servers give these sales tickets to the kitchen staff, which prepares the meals. While the customer is eating, the server fills in the prices on the sales ticket and leaves it at the customer's table.

When the customers are ready to leave, they present the completed sales ticket, along with the payment due, to the cashier. The cashier verifies the prices listed on the sales ticket, rings up the sale on a cash register, and gives the customer an appropriate amount of change.

A manager is always on hand observing operations throughout the restaurant. At the end of each shift, the manager determines that all of the sales tickets issued by the food servers have been collected by the cashier and computes the total dollar amount of these tickets. Next, the manager counts the cash receipts and compares this amount with the total shown on the register tape and the total developed from the serially numbered sales tickets.

INSTRUCTIONS

Identify the control procedures (if any) which prevent:

a Food servers from providing free meals to family and friends simply by not preparing a sales ticket.

b Food servers from undercharging favored customers.

c Food servers from collecting the amount due from the customer and keeping the cash for themselves.

d The cashier from pocketing some of the customers' payment and concealing this theft by ringing up lower amounts on the cash register.

**CASE 6-4
Internal Control: Another Short Case**

At the Uptown Theater, the cashier is located in a box office at the front of the building. The cashier receives cash from customers and operates a ticket machine which ejects serially numbered tickets. The serial number appears on each end of the ticket. The tickets come from the printer in large rolls which fit into the ticket machine and are removed at the end of each cashier's working period.

After purchasing a ticket from the cashier, in order to be admitted to the theater a customer must hand the ticket to a doorman stationed some 50 feet from the box office at the entrance to the theater lobby. The doorman tears the ticket in half and returns the ticket stub to the customer. The other half of the ticket is dropped by the doorman into a locked box.

INSTRUCTIONS

a Describe the internal controls present in Uptown Theater's method of handling cash receipts.

b What steps should be taken regularly by the theater manager or other supervisor to make these and other internal controls work most effectively?

c Assume that the cashier and the doorman decided to collaborate in an effort to abstract cash receipts. What action might they take?

d On the assumption made in part c of collaboration between the cashier and the doorman, what features of the control procedures would be most likely to disclose this employee fraud?

ANSWERS TO SELF-TEST QUESTIONS

1 d   2 a, b, d   3 a, c   4 a, b, c, d   5 b   6 d   7 c

PART

3 Accounting for Assets

*T*he manner in which a business records and values its assets affects both the balance sheet and the income statement. By studying the accounting principles involved in asset valuation, we will learn much about the content and limitations of financial statements.

   This part concludes with a Comprehensive Problem in which we review various methods of asset valuation and the resulting effects upon net income.

7 The Control of Cash Transactions

As our chapter title suggests, this chapter focuses in large part upon internal control. The need for internal control over cash transactions should be apparent, as cash is the asset most susceptible to theft and embezzlement. Also, cash transactions affect every element of the financial statements—assets, liabilities, owner's equity, revenue, and expenses. If cash transactions are not recorded properly, none of a company's accounting data should be considered reliable.

After studying this chapter you should be able to meet these Learning Objectives:

1 *State the basic objectives of "cash management."*
2 *Explain the major steps in achieving internal control over cash transactions.*
3 *Describe how a voucher system contributes to internal control over cash disbursements.*
4 *Prepare a bank reconciliation and explain its purpose.*
5 *Describe the operation of a petty cash fund.*

What Do Accountants Mean by "Cash"?

Accountants define *cash* as money on deposit in banks and any items that a bank will accept for deposit. These items include not only coins and paper money but also checks, money orders, travelers' checks, and the charge slips signed by customers using bank credit cards, such as Visa and MasterCard.

Most companies maintain several bank accounts and also may keep small amounts of cash on hand. Therefore, the Cash account in the general ledger is a *controlling account.* A cash subsidiary ledger includes a separate account corresponding to each of the company's bank accounts and also to each petty cash fund or change fund within the organization.

Reporting Cash in the Balance Sheet

Cash is listed first in the balance sheet because it represents a resource that can be used immediately to pay any type of obligation. The term *liquid assets* is used to describe assets that can be converted quickly into cash. In the current asset section of the balance sheet, assets are listed in the order of their liquidity. Thus cash—being the ultimate in liquidity—is listed first.

For purposes of balance sheet presentation, however, the balance in the Cash controlling account generally is combined with the controlling account for Cash Equivalents.

Cash Equivalents Some short-term investments are so liquid that they are termed *cash equivalents.* Examples include money market funds, U.S. Treasury bills, certificates of deposit (CDs), and high-grade commercial paper. These items are considered so similar to cash that they often are combined with the amount of cash in the balance sheet. Therefore, many businesses call the first asset shown in the balance sheet *"Cash and cash equivalents."*

Not all short-term investments are viewed as cash equivalents. Investments in stocks and bonds, for example, are *not* considered cash equivalents. Such investments appear in the balance sheet as "marketable securities," which usually are listed *second* among the current assets. (Marketable securities are discussed further in Chapter 17.)

Evaluating Solvency Bankers, credit managers, and other creditors who study a balance sheet always are interested in the amount of cash and cash equivalents as compared to other balance sheet items, such as accounts payable. These users of a company's financial statements are interested in evaluating the company's *solvency*—that is, its ability to pay its debts as they come due. Creditors need to know the amount of liquid resources available to the business, but not such details as the number of separate bank accounts or the amount of cash on hand as compared to cash in banks.

Lines of Credit Many businesses have arranged lines of credit with their banks. A line of credit means that the bank has agreed in advance to lend the company any amount of money up to a specified limit. The company can borrow this money at any time, by drawing checks upon a special bank account. A liability to the bank arises as soon as any of the money is borrowed—that is, as soon as a portion of the line of credit is used.

The **unused** portion of a line of credit is neither an asset nor a liability; it represents only the **ability** to borrow money quickly and easily. Although an unused line of credit does not appear as an asset or a liability in the balance sheet, it does affect the company's solvency. For this reason, unused lines of credit are **disclosed** in notes accompanying the financial statements.

CASE IN POINT   A recent annual report of J.C. Penney, the giant retailer, included the following note to the financial statements:

> Confirmed lines of credit available to J.C. Penney amounted to $1.2 billion. None was in use at the balance sheet date.

"Restricted" Cash   Some bank accounts are restricted as to their use, so that they are not available to meet normal operating needs of the business. For example, a bank account may contain cash specifically earmarked for the acquisition of plant assets. Bank accounts in some foreign countries are restricted by laws which prohibit transferring the money to another country. Restricted bank accounts are not regarded as current assets if their balances are not available for use in paying current liabilities. Therefore, "restricted cash balances" may be listed just below the current asset section of the balance sheet in the section entitled **long-term investments.**

The Statement of Cash Flows

The balance sheet indicates the amount of cash owned by the business at a particular date. A separate financial statement, called the statement of cash flows, summarizes all of the cash **activity** (receipts and disbursements) during the accounting period. Interpreting the statement of cash flows requires an understanding of many types of business transactions, including the operating, investing, and financing activities of large corporations. Therefore, we will defer discussion of this financial statement to Chapter 18.

Management Responsibilities Relating to Cash

OBJECTIVE 1 State the basic objectives of "cash management."

The term **cash management** refers to planning, controlling, and accounting for cash transactions and cash balances. Efficient cash management is essential to the success—even to the survival—of every business organization. The basic objectives of cash management are:

■ **Provide accurate accounting for cash receipts, cash disbursements, and cash balances.** A large portion of the total transactions of a business involve the receipt or disbursement of cash. Also, cash transactions affect every classification within the financial statements—assets, liabilities, owner's equity, revenue, and expenses. If financial statements are to be reliable, it is **absolutely essential** that cash transactions be recorded correctly.

◼ *Prevent or minimize losses from theft or fraud.* Cash is more susceptible to theft than any other asset and, therefore, requires physical protection.

◼ *Anticipate the need for borrowing and assure the availability of adequate amounts of cash for conducting business operations.* Every business organization must have sufficient cash to meet its financial obligations as they come due. Otherwise, its creditors may force the business into bankruptcy.

◼ *Prevent unnecessarily large amounts of cash from sitting idle in bank accounts which produce no revenue.* Federal banking regulations prohibit banks from paying interest on corporate checking accounts. Therefore, well-managed corporations frequently review their bank balances for the purpose of transferring any excess cash into cash equivalents or other investments that generate revenue.

How Much Cash Is "Enough?"   Every business needs sufficient cash, cash equivalents, or lines of credit to meet the company's obligations on a timely basis. However, maintaining larger amounts of cash than necessary is *not* an efficient use of resources.

A large cash balance is a relatively nonproductive asset. Corporate checking accounts do not even earn interest. Because cash equivalents are such safe and highly liquid investments, they earn very modest rates of return. Such investments are an efficient way of investing *temporary* surpluses of cash which soon will be needed for other purposes. However, if a business has large amounts of cash which can be invested on a long-term basis, it should try to earn a substantially *higher* rate of return than is available from cash equivalents.

Efficient uses of cash balances which are available on a long-term basis often include financing the growth and expansion of the business, taking advantage of unusual investment opportunities, and repaying interest-bearing liabilities. Simply holding large amounts of cash and cash equivalents increases a company's solvency but adds little to its profitability.

The amount of cash needed to keep a company operating smoothly varies greatly from one business to the next. Most businesses, however, have no more than 5 or 10% of their total assets in the form of cash and cash equivalents, unless they are accumulating the money for some specific purpose. Cash which cannot be utilized efficiently within a particular business should be distributed to the company's owners, so that they may invest it elsewhere.

Cash Balances and Corporate Dividends

In the early chapters of this textbook, most of our illustrations have involved businesses organized as sole proprietorships. In these organizations, the owner may withdraw excess cash balances from the business at will. In a corporation, however, the decision of whether to distribute company-owned cash to the owners (stockholders) rests with the company's *board of directors.*[1]

---
[1]   The board of directors is the highest level of corporate management.

A distribution of cash by a corporation to its stockholders is called a **dividend.**[2] The timing and dollar amounts of dividend payments are determined by the corporation's directors and top management. (Limits upon dividend payments also may be imposed by state laws and by contractual agreements with creditors.) Among the factors that most influence the amount of dividends that a corporation pays are the:

- Company's profitability in recent periods.
- Amount of cash on hand which is not needed in business operations.
- Goals and philosophy of the company's top management.

By studying financial statements, investors easily can determine for recent periods a company's net income, the amount of cash on hand, and the amounts of dividends paid to the stockholders. The relationships among these factors can shed much light upon management's attitude toward the payment of dividends and can assist investors in evaluating the prospects of receiving future dividend distributions.

Internal Control over Cash

Internal control over cash is sometimes regarded merely as a means of preventing fraud and theft. A good system of internal control, however, will also aid in achieving the other objectives of efficient cash management, including accurate accounting for cash transactions, anticipating the need for borrowing, and the maintenance of adequate but not excessive cash balances.

OBJECTIVE 2 Explain the major steps in achieving internal control over cash transactions.

1 Separate the function of handling cash from the maintenance of accounting records. Employees who handle cash **should not have access to the accounting records,** and accounting personnel should not have access to cash.

2 Prepare for each department within the organization a **cash budget** (or forecast) of planned cash receipts, cash payments, and cash balances, scheduled month-by-month for the coming year. (Departmental budgets assume the use of a **responsibility accounting system.**[3])

3 Prepare a **control listing** of cash receipts at the time and place the money is received. For cash sales, this listing may be a cash register tape, created by ringing up each sale on a cash register. For checks received through the mail, a control listing of incoming checks should be prepared by the employee assigned to open the mail.

4 Require that all cash receipts be **deposited daily** in the bank.

5 Make all payments **by check.** The only exception should be for small payments to be made in cash from a **petty cash fund.** (Petty cash funds are discussed later in this chapter.)

---

[2] Accounting for dividends is explained and illustrated in later chapters.

[3] A **responsibility accounting system** includes a chart of accounts sufficiently detailed to measure separately the activities of each department (or area of managerial responsibility) within the organization. These systems were described in Chapter 6.

6 Require that the validity and amount of every expenditure be verified *before* a check is issued in payment. Separate the function of approving expenditures from the function of signing checks.

7 Promptly reconcile bank statements with the accounting records.

The application of these principles in building an adequate system of internal control over cash can best be illustrated by considering separately the topics of cash receipts and cash disbursements. A company may supplement its system of internal control by obtaining a fidelity bond from an insurance company. Under a fidelity bond, the insurance company agrees to reimburse an employer for *proven* losses resulting from fraud or embezzlement by bonded employees.

Cash Receipts

Cash receipts consist primarily of two types: cash received through the mail as collections of accounts receivable, and cash received over the counter from cash sales.

Cash Received Through the Mail   Cash received through the mail should be in the form of checks made payable to the company. When the mail is first opened, an employee should stamp the back of each check with a restrictive endorsement stamp, indicating that the check is *"For Deposit Only"* into the company's bank account. This *restrictive endorsement* prevents anyone else from being able to cash the check or deposit it into another bank account.

Next, the employee should prepare a *control listing* of the checks received each day. This list shows each customer's name (or account number) and the amount received. One copy of this list is sent with the customers' checks to the cashier, who deposits the money in the bank. Another copy is sent to the accounting department, to be recorded in the accounting records. Daily comparisons of this control listing with the amounts deposited by the cashier and with the receipts recorded by the accounting department should bring to light any cash shortages or recording errors.

Cash Received over the Counter   Cash sales should be rung up on a cash register located so that the customer can see the amount recorded. The register has a locked-in tape, which serves as a control listing for cash sales. When the salesperson ends a workday, he or she will count the cash in the register and turn it over to the cashier. A representative of the accounting department will remove the tape from the cash register, compare the total shown on the tape with the amount turned in to the cashier, and record the cash sales in the accounting records.

As explained in earlier chapters, most larger stores now use on-line *point-of-sale terminals.* When these terminals are in use, sales transactions are recorded instantly in the accounting records as the salesclerk passes the merchandise over an optical scanner. At first glance, it may appear that the salesclerk both handles cash and has access to the accounting records. Actually, the salesclerks do *not* have direct access to the accounting records; all entries in the accounting records are made automatically by the point-of-sale terminal.

Use of Prenumbered Sales Tickets Another means of establishing internal control over cash sales is by writing out a prenumbered sales ticket in duplicate at the time of each sale. The original is given to the customer and the carbon copy is retained. Prenumbered sales tickets are often used in businesses such as restaurants in which one central cashier rings up the sales made by all salespeople.

At the end of the day, an employee computes the total sales figure from these sales tickets and also makes sure that no tickets are missing from the series. This total sales figure is then compared with the cash register tape and the total cash receipts.

Cash Over and Short In handling over-the-counter cash receipts, a few errors in making change inevitably will occur. These errors will cause a cash shortage or overage at the end of the day, when the cash is counted and compared with the reading on the cash register.

For example, assume that total cash sales recorded on the point-of-sale terminals during the day amount to $4,500.00. However, the cash receipts in the register drawers total only $4,487.30. The following entry would be made to adjust the accounting records for this $12.70 shortage in the cash receipts:

Cash Over and Short	*12.70*	
Cash		*12.70*

To record a $12.70 shortage in cash receipts for the day
($4,500.00 − $4,487.30).

The account entitled Cash Over and Short is debited with shortages and credited with overages. If the cash shortages during an entire accounting period are in excess of the cash overages, the Cash Over and Short account will have a debit balance and will be shown as miscellaneous ***expense*** in the income statement. On the other hand, if the overages exceed the shortages, the Cash Over and Short account will show a credit balance at the end of the period and should be treated as an item of miscellaneous ***revenue.*** Management should review the daily entries to this account so as to be aware of any material cash shortages or consistent pattern of small shortages.

Subdivision of Duties Employees who handle cash receipts should ***not have access to the accounting records.*** This combination of duties might enable the employee to alter the accounting records and thereby conceal a cash shortage.

Employees who handle cash receipts also should ***not have authority to issue credit memoranda for sales returns.*** This combination of duties might enable the employee to conceal cash shortages by issuing fictitious credit memoranda. Assume, for example, that an employee with these responsibilities collects $500 cash from a customer as payment of the customer's account. The employee might remove this cash and issue a $500 credit memorandum, indicating that the customer had returned the merchandise instead of paying the account. The credit memoranda would cause the account receivable from this customer to be credited. However, the offsetting debit would be to the Sales Returns & Allowances account, not to the Cash account. Thus, the books would remain in balance, the customer would receive credit for the abstracted payment, and there would be no record of cash having been received.

Using Departmental Cash Budgets   Departmental cash budgets provide estimates of the cash receipts *expected* within each department during the accounting period. Management should investigate to determine *why* a department falls significantly short of the budgeted amounts. Perhaps this investigation will show that the budgeted amounts were overly optimistic; in this case, management will change the budget estimates for future months. On the other hand, the investigation may reveal weak departmental performance or fraud on the part of certain personnel. In either of these situations, management will want to initiate corrective action.

Cash Disbursements

To achieve adequate internal control over cash payments, all disbursements of significant dollar amount should be *made by check*. Checks should be prenumbered. Any spoiled checks should be marked "Void" and filed in sequence so that all numbers in the series can be accounted for.

Every transaction requiring a cash disbursement should be verified and approved before payment is made. The official designated to *sign* checks should not be given authority to *approve* invoices for payment or to make entries in the accounting records. When a check is presented to a company official for signature, it should be accompanied by the approved invoice and voucher showing that the transaction has been fully verified and that payment is justified. When the check is signed, the supporting invoices and vouchers should be perforated or stamped "Paid" to eliminate any possibility of their being presented later in support of another check. If these rules are followed, it is almost impossible for a fraudulent cash disbursement to be concealed without the collusion of two or more persons.

The Voucher System

OBJECTIVE 3 Describe how a voucher system contributes to internal control over cash disbursements.

One widely used method of establishing control over cash disbursements is the voucher system. The basic idea of this system is that every transaction which will result in a cash disbursement must be verified, approved in writing, and recorded before a check is issued. A written authorization called a *voucher* is prepared for every transaction that will require a cash payment, regardless of whether the transaction is for payment of an expense, purchase of inventory or a plant asset, or for payment of a liability.[4] Notice that *every purchase is treated as an independent transaction* even though many purchases may be made from the same supplier. Vouchers are serially numbered so that the loss or misplacement of a voucher would be immediately apparent.

To demonstrate the internal control inherent in a voucher system, consider the way a voucher is used in verifying an invoice received from a supplier. A serially numbered voucher is attached to each incoming in-

---

[4]   Other names for a *"voucher"* include *"invoice approval form"* and *"check authorization."*

Use of voucher ensures verification of invoice

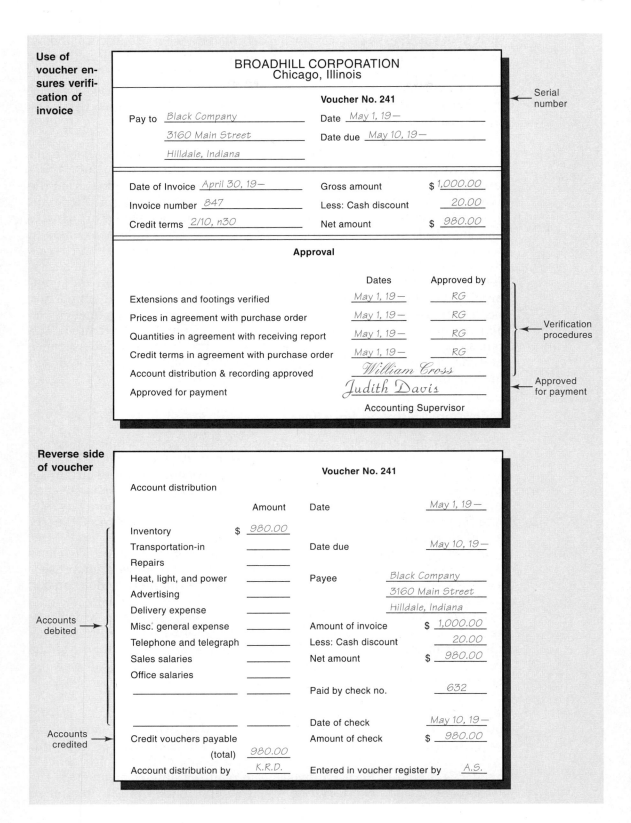

BROADHILL CORPORATION
Chicago, Illinois

Voucher No. 241

Serial number

Pay to *Black Company*   Date *May 1, 19—*
3160 Main Street   Date due *May 10, 19—*
Hilldale, Indiana

Date of Invoice *April 30, 19—*   Gross amount $ *1,000.00*
Invoice number *847*   Less: Cash discount   *20.00*
Credit terms *2/10, n30*   Net amount $ *980.00*

Approval

	Dates	Approved by
Extensions and footings verified	*May 1, 19—*	*RG*
Prices in agreement with purchase order	*May 1, 19—*	*RG*
Quantities in agreement with receiving report	*May 1, 19—*	*RG*
Credit terms in agreement with purchase order	*May 1, 19—*	*RG*
Account distribution & recording approved	*William Cross*	
Approved for payment	*Judith Davis*	

Verification procedures

Approved for payment

Accounting Supervisor

Reverse side of voucher

Voucher No. 241

Account distribution

	Amount		
		Date	*May 1, 19—*
Inventory	$ *980.00*		
Transportation-in	————	Date due	*May 10, 19—*
Repairs	————		
Heat, light, and power	————	Payee	*Black Company*
Advertising	————		*3160 Main Street*
Delivery expense	————		*Hilldale, Indiana*
Misc. general expense	————	Amount of invoice	$ *1,000.00*
Telephone and telegraph	————	Less: Cash discount	*20.00*
Sales salaries	————	Net amount	$ *980.00*
Office salaries	————		
———————	————	Paid by check no.	*632*
———————	————	Date of check	*May 10, 19—*
Credit vouchers payable		Amount of check	$ *980.00*
(total)	*980.00*		
Account distribution by	*K.R.D.*	Entered in voucher register by	*A.S.*

Accounts debited

Accounts credited

voice. The voucher has spaces for listing the data from the invoice and for showing the ledger accounts to be debited and credited in recording the transaction. Space is also provided for approval signatures for each step in the verification and approval process. A completed voucher provides a description of the transaction and also of the work performed in verifying the liability and approving the cash disbursement.

Preparing a Voucher   To illustrate the functioning of a voucher system, let us begin with the receipt of an invoice from a supplier. A voucher is prepared by filling in the appropriate blanks with information taken from the invoice, such as the invoice date, invoice number, amount, and the creditor's name and address. The voucher with the supplier's invoice attached is then sent to the employees responsible for verifying the extensions and footings on the invoice and for comparing prices, quantities, and terms with those specified in the purchase order and receiving report. When completion of the verification process has been evidenced by approval signatures of the persons performing these steps, the voucher and supporting documents are sent to an employee of the accounting department, who indicates on the voucher the accounts to be debited and credited. The voucher is then reviewed by an accounting official to provide assurance that the verification procedures have been satisfactorily completed and that the liability is a proper one.

Recording Approved Vouchers

After receiving the supervisory approval explained above, the voucher is entered in a special journal called a ***voucher register.*** Entries in the voucher register indicate the nature of the expenditure by debiting the appropriate asset, expense, or liability accounts. The credit portion of each entry is always to a short-term liability account entitled Vouchers Payable. Note that the entry in the voucher register is not made ***until the liability has been verified and approved.***

In a company using the voucher system, the ledger account, Vouchers Payable, replaces Accounts Payable. For purposes of balance sheet presentation, however, most companies continue to use the more widely understood term Accounts Payable.

Voucher systems are used principally by larger companies which process transactions by computer. Because our interest in voucher systems is in their internal control features and because manual voucher systems are rare, our discussion does not include illustration of a hand-operated voucher register.

Paying the Voucher within the Discount Period   After the voucher has been entered in the voucher register, it is placed (with the supporting documents attached) in a tickler file according to the date of required payment. Cash discount periods generally run from the date of the invoice. Since a voucher is prepared for each invoice, the required date of payment is the last day on which a check can be prepared and mailed to the creditor in time to qualify for the discount.

When the payment date arrives, an employee in the accounting department removes the voucher from the unpaid file, draws a check for signature by the treasurer, and records payment of the voucher in a special journal called a *check register.* Since checks are issued only in payment of approved vouchers, every entry in the check register represents a debit to Vouchers Payable and a credit to Cash.

An important factor in achieving internal control is that the employee in the accounting department who prepares the check *is not authorized to sign it.* The unsigned check and the supporting voucher are now sent to the treasurer or other designated official in the finance department. The treasurer reviews the voucher, especially the approval signatures, and signs the check. Thus, the invoice is *approved for payment* in the accounting department, but the actual cash disbursement is made by the finance department. *No one person or department is in a position both to approve invoices for payment and to issue signed checks.*

Once the check has been signed, the treasurer should mail it directly to the creditor. The voucher and all supporting documents are then perforated with a PAID stamp and are forwarded to the accounting department, which will note payment of the voucher in the voucher register and will file the paid voucher. The operation of a voucher system is illustrated in the flowchart on the following page. Notes have been made on the illustration identifying the most important internal control features in the system.

Establishing Control over the Issuance of Checks   In a small business, the officer authorized to sign checks is held responsible for signing only those checks which have been properly authorized. In a large company which issues hundreds or thousands of checks daily, it is not practicable for a company official to sign each check manually. Instead, check-signing machines with various built-in control devices are used. This automation of the check-signing function does not weaken the system of internal control if attention is given to proper use of the machine and to control of the checks both before and after they pass through the check-signing machine.

CASE IN POINT   A large Boston-based construction company issued a great many checks every day but paid little attention to internal controls over its cash payments. Stacks of unissued checks were kept in an unlocked supply closet along with Styrofoam coffee cups. Because the number of checks issued was too great for the treasurer to sign them manually, a check-signing machine was used. This machine, after signing the checks, ejected them into a box equipped with a lock. In spite of warnings from the company's CPA firm, company officials found that it was "too inconvenient" to keep the box locked. The company also failed to make any use of the check-counting device built into the check-signing machine. Although the company maintained very large amounts on deposit in checking accounts, it did not bother to reconcile bank statements for weeks or months at a time.

These weaknesses in internal control led to a crisis when an employee was given a three-week-old bank statement and a bundle of paid checks and told to prepare a bank reconciliation. The employee found that the bundle of paid checks accompanying the bank statement was incomplete. No paid checks were on hand to support over $700,000 of charges deducted on the bank statement. Further investigation revealed that over $1 million

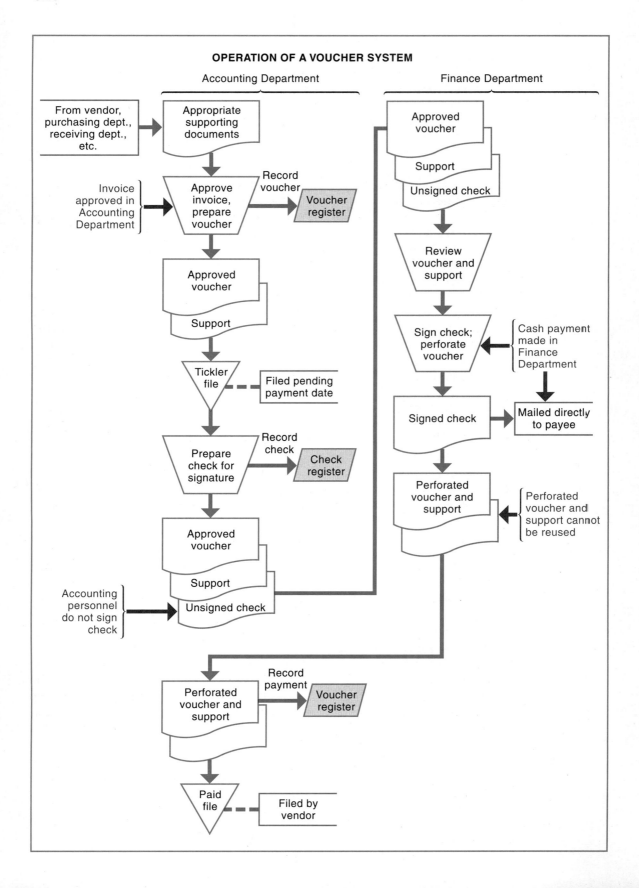

OPERATION OF A VOUCHER SYSTEM

in unauthorized and unrecorded checks had been paid from the corporation's bank accounts. These checks had been issued out of serial number sequence and had been run through the company check-signing machine. It was never determined who had carried out the theft and the money was not recovered.

Checking Accounts

Virtually every business organization maintains one or more checking accounts, which are opened and maintained in much the same way as a personal checking account. The use of checking accounts contributes to strong internal control in many ways. For example:

1 Checking accounts eliminate the need for keeping large amounts of currency on hand.
2 The owner of the business must notify the bank of the names of all persons authorized to sign checks. Thus, access to cash is limited to those company officers and employees designated by the business owner (or, for a corporation, by the board of directors).
3 The person responsible for each cash disbursement is readily identified by the signature on the check.
4 The bank returns to the depositor all checks which it has paid from the account. Thus, the depositor has documentary evidence showing the date and amount of each cash payment, and the identity of the person receiving the money.
5 Comparison of the monthly **bank statement** with the depositor's accounting records can bring to light many types of errors made either by the bank or by the depositor in accounting for cash transactions.

Bank Statements

Every month, banks provide each depositor with a bank statement summarizing the activity in the depositor's account.[5] The bank statement is accompanied by all of the checks which the bank has paid from the account and also by documents indicating the nature and amount of any other changes in the account balance. As illustrated on the next page, a bank statement shows the balance on deposit at the beginning of the month, the deposits, the checks paid, any other debits and credits during the month, and the new balance at the end of the month. (To keep the illustration short, we have shown a limited number of deposits rather than one for each business day in the month.)

Reconciling the Bank Statement

A **bank reconciliation** is a schedule **explaining any differences** between the balance shown in the bank statement and the balance shown in

---

[5] Large businesses usually receive bank statements on a weekly basis.

A bank statement provides an independent record of cash transactions.

WESTERN NATIONAL BANK
100 Olympic Boulevard
Los Angeles, California

Customer account no. 501390
Parkview Company
109 Parkview Road
Los Angeles, California

BANK STATEMENT
for the Month Ended July 31, 1994

Date	Deposits and Credits	Checks and Debits		Balance
June 30				5,029.30
July 1	300.00			5,329.30
July 2	1,250.00	1,100.00		5,479.30
July 3		415.20	10.00	5,054.10
July 8	993.60			6,047.70
July 10		96.00	400.00	5,551.70
July 12	1,023.77	1,376.57		5,198.90
July 15		425.00		4,773.90
July 18	1,300.00	2,095.75		3,978.15
July 22	500.00 CM	85.00	5.00 DM	4,388.15
July 24	1,083.25	1,145.27		4,326.13
July 30	711.55	50.25 NSF		4,987.43
July 31	24.74 INT	12.00 SC		5,000.17

Explanation of symbols

CM	Credit Memoranda	*INT*	Interest on average balance
DM	Debit Memoranda	*NSF*	Not Sufficient Funds
E	Error correction	*SC*	Service Charge

Summary of activity:

Previous statement balance, June 30, 1994	$ 5,029.30
Deposits and credit memoranda (9 items)	7,186.91
Checks and debit memoranda (13 items)	(7,216.04)
Current statement balance, July 31, 1994	$ 5,000.17

OBJECTIVE 4
Prepare a bank reconciliation and explain its purpose.

the depositor's accounting records. Remember that both the bank and the depositor are maintaining independent records of the deposits, the checks, and the current balance of the bank account. Each month, the depositor should prepare a bank reconciliation to verify that these independent sets of records are in agreement. This reconciliation may disclose internal control failures, such as unauthorized cash disbursements or failures to deposit cash receipts, as well as errors in either the bank statement or the depositor's accounting records. In addition, the reconciliation identifies certain transactions which must be recorded in the depositor's accounting records, and helps to determine the "actual" amount of cash on deposit.

For strong internal control, the employee who reconciles the bank statement should not have any other responsibilities for cash.

Normal Differences between Bank Statements and Accounting Records

The balance shown in a monthly bank statement seldom equals the balance appearing in the depositor's accounting records. Certain transactions recorded by the depositor may not have been recorded by the bank. The most common examples are:

1 **Outstanding checks.** Checks issued and recorded by the company but not yet presented to the bank for payment.

2 **Deposits in transit.** Cash receipts recorded by the depositor but which reached the bank too late to be included in the bank statement for the current month.

In addition, certain transactions appearing in the bank statement may not have been recorded by the depositor. For example:

1 **Service charges.** Banks often charge a fee for handling small accounts. The amount of this charge usually depends upon both the average balance of the account and the number of checks paid during the month.

2 **Charges for depositing NSF checks.** NSF stands for "Not Sufficient Funds." When checks are deposited, the bank increases (credits) the depositor's account. On occasion, one of these checks may prove to be uncollectible, because the maker of the check does not have sufficient funds in his or her account. In such cases, the bank will reduce the depositor's account by the amount of this uncollectible item and return the check to the depositor marked "NSF."

   The depositor should view an NSF check as an account receivable from the maker of the check, not as cash. The accounting entry required consists of a debit to the account receivable from the customer and credit to cash.

3 **Credits for interest earned.** Most banks offer some checking accounts which earn interest. At month-end, this interest is credited to the depositor's account and reported on the bank statement. (As previously mentioned, current laws prohibit interest on corporate checking accounts.)

4 **Miscellaneous bank charges and credits.** Banks charge for services—such as printing checks, handling collections of notes receivable, and processing NSF checks. The bank deducts these charges from the depositor's account and notifies the depositor by including a debit memorandum in the monthly bank statement.[6] If the bank collects a note receivable on behalf of the depositor, it adds the money to the depositor's account and issues a credit memorandum describing the collection.

In a bank reconciliation, the balances shown in the bank statement and in the accounting records both are adjusted for any unrecorded transactions. Additional adjustment may be required to correct any errors discovered in the bank statement or in the accounting records.

---

[6] Banks view each depositor's account as a liability. Debit memoranda are issued for transactions that ***reduce*** this liability, such as bank service charges. Credit memoranda are issued to recognize an ***increase*** in this liability, as results, for example, from interest earned by the depositor.

Steps in Preparing a Bank Reconciliation To prepare a bank reconciliation, we determine those items which make up the difference between the ending **balance per the bank statement and the balance of cash according to the depositor's records.** By listing and studying these reconciling items we can determine the correct figure for cash owned. This is the amount which should appear in the balance sheet. The specific steps to be taken in preparing a bank reconciliation are:

1 Compare the deposits listed on the bank statement with the deposits shown in the company's records. Any deposits not yet recorded by the bank are deposits in transit and should be added to the balance shown in the bank statement. If there were any deposits in transit listed in the prior month's bank reconciliation, these amounts should appear as deposits in the current month's bank statement. If they do not appear, immediate investigation is necessary.

2 Arrange the paid checks in sequence by serial numbers and compare each check with the corresponding entry in the check register. Any checks issued but not yet paid by the bank should be listed as outstanding checks to be deducted from the balance reported in the bank statement. Determine whether the checks listed as outstanding in the bank reconciliation for the preceding month have cleared the bank this month. If not, such checks should be listed as outstanding in the current reconciliation.

3 Add to the balance per the depositor's accounting records any credit memoranda issued by the bank which have not been recorded by the depositor. Examples in the illustrated bank reconciliation on page 331 are the $500 credit from collection of a note receivable and the $24.74 credit for interest earned.

4 Deduct from the balance per the depositor's records any debit memoranda issued by the bank which have not been recorded by the depositor. Examples in the illustrated bank statement on page 328 are the $5 collection fee, the $50.25 NSF check, and the $12 service charge.

5 Make appropriate additions or deductions to correct any errors in the balance per bank statement or the balance per depositor's records. An example in the illustrated bank reconciliation on page 331 is the $27 error by the company in recording check no. 875.

6 Determine that the adjusted balance of the bank statement is equal to the adjusted balance in the depositor's records.

7 Prepare journal entries to record any items in the bank reconciliation listed as adjustments to the balance per depositor's records.

Illustration of a Bank Reconciliation The July bank statement sent by the bank to Parkview Company was illustrated on page 328. This statement shows a balance of cash on deposit at July 31 of $5,000.17. Assume that on July 31, Parkview's ledger shows a bank balance of $4,262.83. The employee preparing the bank reconciliation has identified the following reconciling items:

1 A deposit of $410.90 made after banking hours on July 31 does not appear in the bank statement.

2 Four checks issued in July have not yet been paid by the bank. These checks are:

Check No.	Date	Amount
801	June 15	$100.00
888	July 24	10.25
890	July 27	402.50
891	July 30	205.00

3 Two credit memoranda were included in the bank statement:

Date	Amount	Explanation
July 22	$500.00	Proceeds from collection of a non-interest-bearing note receivable from J. David. Parkview Company had left this note with the bank's collection department.
July 31	24.74	Interest earned on average account balance during July. (Parkview is an unincorporated business.)

4 Three debit memoranda accompanied the bank statement:

Date	Amount	Explanation
July 22	$ 5.00	Fee charged by bank for handling collection of note receivable.
July 30	50.25	Check from customer J. B. Ball deposited by Parkview Company charged back as NSF.
July 31	12.00	Service charge by bank for the month of July.

5 Check no. 875 was issued July 20 in the amount of $85 but was erroneously recorded in the cash payments journal as $58. The check, in payment of telephone expense, was paid by the bank and correctly listed at $85 in the bank statement. In Parkview's ledger, the Cash account is **overstated** by $27 because of this error ($85 − $58 = $27).

The July 31 bank reconciliation for Parkview Company is shown below. (The numbered arrows coincide both with the steps in preparing a bank reconciliation listed on page 330 and with the reconciling items listed above.)

PARKVIEW COMPANY
Bank Reconciliation
July 31, 1994

Balance per bank statement, July 31, 1994		$5,000.17
(1) Add: Deposit of July 31 not recorded by bank		410.90
		$5,411.07
(2) Deduct: Outstanding checks:		
No. 801	$100.00	
No. 888	10.25	
No. 890	402.50	
No. 891	205.00	717.75
Adjusted cash balance		$4,693.32
Balance per depositor's records, July 31, 1994		$4,262.83
(3) Add: Note receivable collected for us by bank	$500.00	
Interest earned during July	24.74	524.74
		$4,787.57
(4) Deduct: Collection fee	$ 5.00	
NSF check of J. B. Ball	50.25	
Service charge	12.00	
(5) Error on check stub no. 875	27.00	94.25
Adjusted cash balance (as above)		$4,693.32

(6)

Updating the Accounting Records The last step in reconciling a bank statement is to update the depositor's accounting records for any unrecorded cash transactions brought to light. In the bank reconciliation, every adjustment to the **balance per depositor's records** is a cash receipt or a cash payment that has not been recorded in the depositor's accounts. Therefore, **each of these items should be recorded.**

In this illustration and in our assignment material, we will follow a policy of making one journal entry to record the unrecorded cash receipts and another to record the unrecorded cash reductions. (Acceptable alternatives would be to make separate journal entries for each item or to make one compound entry for all items.) Based on our recording policy, the entries to update the accounting records of Parkview Company are:

Per bank credit memoranda . . .	Cash.. 524.74	
	Notes Receivable..	500.00
	Interest Revenue	24.74
	To record collection of note receivable from J. David collected by bank and interest earned on bank account in July.	
. . . per bank debit memoranda (and correction of an error)	Bank Service Charges 17.00	
	Accounts Receivable, J. B. Ball 50.25	
	Telephone Expense... 27.00	
	Cash	94.25
	To record bank charges (service charge, $12; collection fee, $5), to reclassify NSF check from customer J. B. Ball as an account receivable, and to correct understatement of cash payment for telephone expense.	

Electronic Funds Transfer Systems

Banks today allow depositors to use a wide variety of electronic funds transfer systems. These systems enable depositors to transfer money in and out of their checking accounts without actually bringing deposits to the bank or writing checks. Common examples of these systems include automatic teller machines, automatic bill payment plans, transfers authorized by telephone, and the use of "debit cards."

Many businesses now use electronic funds transfers in meeting their payrolls. Every "payday," the business provides the bank with data indicating the amounts owed to specific employees. The bank electronically transfers these amounts from the company's checking account to the employees' personal checking accounts. Thus, employees receive their money immediately, and the employer is spared the nuisance of issuing and distributing paychecks.

Banks take many precautions to ensure that all electronic funds transfers are properly authorized by the depositor. Also, these transactions are fully documented in the monthly bank statements.

Petty Cash Funds

We have emphasized the importance of making all significant cash disbursements by check. However, every business finds it convenient to have a small amount of cash on hand with which to make some minor expendi-

OBJECTIVE 5
Describe the
operation of
a petty cash
fund.

tures. Examples of these expenditures include such things as small purchases of office supplies, taxi fares, and doughnuts for an office meeting.

Establishing a Petty Cash Fund To create a petty cash fund, a check is written payable to Petty Cash for a round amount such as $100 or $200, which will cover the small expenditures to be paid in cash for a period of two or three weeks. This check is cashed and the money kept on hand in a locked petty cash box or drawer in the office. One employee is designated as the **custodian** of the fund.

The entry for the issuance of the check creating a petty cash fund is:

Creating the
petty cash
fund

Petty Cash	200	
Cash		200
To establish a petty cash fund.		

Making Disbursements from a Petty Cash Fund As cash payments are made from the petty cash box, the custodian of the fund is required to fill out a **petty cash voucher** for each expenditure. A petty cash voucher shows the date, the amount paid, the purpose of the expenditure, and the signature of the person receiving the money. A petty cash voucher should be prepared for every payment made from the fund. The petty cash box should, therefore, always contain cash and/or vouchers **totaling the exact amount of the fund.**

The petty cash custodian should be informed that occasional surprise counts of the fund will be made and that he or she is personally responsible for the fund being intact at all times.

Replenishing a Petty Cash Fund Assume that a petty cash fund of $200 was established on June 1. On June 18, the custodian of the fund reports that the cash remaining in the fund is down to $20. Since the $200 originally placed in the fund is nearly exhausted, the fund should be replenished. To replenish a petty cash fund means to restore the fund to its original balance. Thus, a check is drawn for $180. This check is cashed and the money placed in the petty cash box.

The journal entry to record the issuance of the check includes debits to the expense accounts indicated by inspection of the vouchers, as follows:

Replenishing a
petty cash
fund

Office Supplies Expense	80.60	
Postage Expense	29.00	
Travel & Entertainment Expense................................	70.40	
Cash		180.00
To replenish the petty cash fund.		

The petty cash vouchers are perforated to prevent their being resubmitted and are filed in support of the replenishment check.

Note that **expense accounts** are debited each time the fund is replenished. The Petty Cash account is debited only when the fund is first established. There ordinarily will be no further entries in the Petty Cash account after the fund is established, unless the fund is discontinued or a decision is made to change its size from the original $200 amount.

The petty cash fund is usually replenished at the end of an accounting period, even though the fund is not running low, so that all vouchers in the fund are charged to expense accounts before these accounts are closed and financial statements prepared.

Employee Fraud Involving Petty Cash   There is a tendency to believe that internal control over petty cash funds is not important because the size of these funds is relatively small. However, these funds may be replenished frequently. Hence, a pattern of recurring irregularities may accumulate to significant dollar amounts.

To ensure the propriety of petty cash expenditures, **one person** (the custodian) should be responsible for approving and documenting all disbursements from the fund. When the fund is replenished, the accounting department should review the vouchers prepared by the fund custodian to determine the reasonableness of the expenditures and the adequacy of the documentation.

It is not uncommon for small errors to be made in petty cash transactions. Therefore, small discrepancies may arise between the amount of cash needed to replenish a petty cash fund and the sum of the vouchers documenting disbursements. Any discrepancies should be recorded in a Cash Over and Short account. The use of such an account helps bring to management's attention a pattern of recurring shortages.

The Cash Budget as a Control over Departmental Expenditures

Many businesses prepare detailed cash budgets which include forecasts of the monthly cash expenditures of each department within the organization. Management (or the internal auditors) will investigate any expenditures which are substantially in excess of the budgeted amounts. Thus, each department manager is held accountable for the monthly cash outlays occurring within his or her department.

Frequent comparisons of actual results with budgeted levels of performance greatly reduce the risks of fraud and waste. Of course, such comparisons require the use of a ***responsibility accounting system,*** that is, a chart of accounts which is sufficiently detailed to measure separately the activities of each department.

END-OF-CHAPTER REVIEW

SUMMARY OF CHAPTER LEARNING OBJECTIVES

1 **State the basic objectives of "cash management."**
The objectives of cash management are accurate accounting for all cash transactions, the prevention of cash fraud or loss, and the maintenance of adequate but not excessive balances.

2 **Explain the major steps in achieving internal control over cash transactions.**
The major steps in achieving internal control over cash transactions are as follows: (1) separate cash handling from the accounting function, (2) prepare departmental cash budgets, (3) prepare a control listing of all cash received through the mail and from over-the-counter cash sales,

(4) deposit all cash receipts in the bank daily, (5) make all payments by check, (6) verify every expenditure before issuing a check in payment, and (7) promptly reconcile bank statements.

3 Describe how a voucher system contributes to internal control over cash disbursements.

A voucher system provides assurance that every proposed cash disbursement is reviewed and approved before a check is issued. As part of the approval process, appropriate documentation is assembled justifying the expenditure, and specific employees must initial the voucher, thus taking responsibility for authorizing payment. Also, the system separates the function of approving payments from the function of signing checks.

4 Prepare a bank reconciliation and explain its purpose.

The balance of cash shown on the month-end bank statement usually will differ from the amount of cash shown in the depositor's ledger. The difference is caused by items which have been recorded by either the depositor or the bank, but not recorded by both. Examples are outstanding checks and deposits in transit. The bank reconciliation adjusts the cash balance per the books and the cash balance per the bank statement for any unrecorded items, and thus produces the correct amount of cash to be included in the balance sheet at the end of the month.

The purpose of a bank reconciliation is to achieve the control inherent in the maintenance of two independent records of cash transactions; one record maintained by the depositor and the other by the bank. When these two records are reconciled (brought into agreement), we gain assurance of a correct accounting for cash transactions.

5 Describe the operation of a petty cash fund.

A petty cash fund is a small amount of cash kept on hand for the purpose of making small incidental expenditures for which issuing a check would not be practical. A petty cash fund is established by writing and cashing a check payable to Petty Cash. The money is given to a designated custodian, who is responsible for making disbursements from the fund.

For each cash payment from the fund, a petty cash voucher is prepared and placed in the fund. When the fund runs low, it is replenished by a check for the amount of the vouchers in the fund. The entry to record replenishing the fund includes debits to various expense accounts for the amounts indicated by the vouchers and a credit to Cash. Discrepencies between the sum of the petty cash vouchers and the amount needed to replenish the fund should be recorded in a Cash Over and Short account.

This is the first of four chapters in which we explore accounting for assets. Our central theme in these chapters is the appropriate *valuation* of various types of assets.

The valuation of cash poses little problem, as this asset is shown in financial statements at its "face value." Still, it is necessary to determine the amount of cash actually on hand at the balance sheet date. The crucial issues in asset valuation change, however, from one type of asset to the next. For accounts receivable, the central issue is collectibility. For plant assets, in contrast, the key factor is the asset's estimated useful life.

You will find that the concepts of asset valuation affect not only the balance sheet but also the measurement of net income. Also, you will see that many accounting measurements involve estimates and judgment.

KEY TERMS INTRODUCED OR EMPHASIZED IN CHAPTER 7

Bank reconciliation   An analysis that explains the difference between the balance of cash shown on the bank statement and the balance of cash shown in the depositor's records.

Board of directors   The highest level of management within a business organized as a corporation.

Cash   Currency, coins, checks, bank credit card charge slips, and any other media which a bank will accept for deposit.

Cash equivalent   Very short-term investments which are so liquid they are considered "equivalent" to cash. Examples include deposits in money market funds, U.S. Treasury bills, certificates of deposit, and commercial paper.

Cash management   Planning, controlling, and accounting for cash transactions and cash balances.

Deposits in transit   Cash receipts which have been entered in the depositor's accounting records and mailed to the bank or left in the bank's night depository but reached the bank too late to be included in the current monthly bank statement.

Electronic funds transfer   The process of transferring money in or out of a bank account electronically, without the need for the depositor to physically bring in a deposit or write a check.

Line of credit   A prearranged loan agreement in which a bank stands ready to lend the borrower any amount up to the specified credit limit, without delay. The "unused" portion of a line of credit represents the ability to borrow cash immediately.

NSF check   A customer's check which was deposited but returned because of a lack of funds (Not Sufficient Funds) in the account on which the check was drawn.

Outstanding checks   Checks issued by a business to suppliers, employees, or other payees but not yet presented to the bank for payment.

Petty cash fund   A small amount of cash set aside for making minor cash payments for which writing of checks is not practicable.

Voucher   A written authorization used in approving a transaction for recording and payment.

Voucher register   A special journal used in a voucher system for the purpose of recording liabilities to pay approved vouchers, and the nature of the expenditures

Voucher system   An accounting system designed to provide strong internal control over cash disbursements. Requires that every transaction which will result in a cash payment be verified, approved, and recorded before a check is prepared.

DEMONSTRATION PROBLEM FOR YOUR REVIEW

The information listed below is available in reconciling the bank balance for the White River Company on November 30, 19___.

1   The bank statement at November 30 indicated a balance of $10,034.70. The ledger account for Cash showed a balance at November 30 of $12,761.94.

2   The November 30 cash receipts of $5,846.20 had been mailed to the bank on that date and did not appear among the deposits on the November bank statement.

3 Of the checks issued in November, the following were not included among the paid checks returned by the bank:

Check No.	Amount	Check No.	Amount
924	$136.25	944	$ 95.00
940	105.00	945	716.15
941	11.46	946	60.00
943	826.70		

4 A service charge for $40 by the bank had been made in error against the White River Company account.

5 The paid checks returned with the November bank statement disclosed two errors in the company's cash records. Check no. 936 for $504.00 had been erroneously recorded as $50.40 in the cash payments journal, and check no. 942 for $245.50 had been recorded as $254.50. Check no. 936 was issued in payment of advertising expense and check no. 942 was for the acquisition of office equipment.

6 Included with the November bank statement was an NSF check for $220 signed by a customer, J. Wilson. This amount had been charged against the bank account on November 30.

7 A non-interest-bearing note receivable for $1,890 owned by the White River Company had been left with the bank for collection. On November 30 the company received a memorandum from the bank indicating that the note had been collected and credited to the company's account after deduction of a $5 collection charge. No entry has been made by the company to record collection of the note.

8 A debit memorandum for $12 was enclosed with the paid checks at November 30. This charge covered the printing of checkbooks bearing the White River Company name and address.

INSTRUCTIONS

a Prepare a bank reconciliation at November 30.

b Prepare journal entries required at November 30 to bring the company's records up-to-date.

SOLUTION TO DEMONSTRATION PROBLEM

a

WHITE RIVER COMPANY
Bank Reconciliation
November 30, 19__

Balance per bank statement, Nov. 30		$10,034.70
Add: Deposit of Nov. 30 not recorded by bank	$5,846.20	
Service charge made by bank in error	40.00	5,886.20
Subtotal		$15,920.90
Less: Outstanding checks on Nov. 30:		
No. 924	$ 136.25	
No. 940	105.00	
No. 941	11.46	
No. 943	826.70	
No. 944	95.00	
No. 945	716.15	
No. 946	60.00	1,950.56
Adjusted cash balance		$13,970.34

Balance per depositor's records, Nov. 30 .... $12,761.94
Add: Error in recording check no. 942 for office equipment:
      Recorded as............................ $254.50
      Correct amount........................ $245.50 $ 9.00
      Note receivable collected by bank......................   1,890.00   1,899.00
                                                       $14,660.94

Less: Error in recording check no. 936 for advertising expense:
      Correct amount $504.00
      Recorded as ....   50.40 $ 453.60
      NSF check (J. Wilson).................................   220.00
      Collection fee............................... $ 5.00
      Printing checks 12.00   17.00   690.60
Adjusted cash balance (as above) $13,970.34

b Journal entries required at November 30 to bring the company's records up-to-date.

19__
Nov. 30 Cash 1,899.00
        Office Equipment...................................   9.00
        Notes Receivable..................................   1,890.00
        To record increase in Cash account as indicated by
        bank reconciliation.

Nov. 30 Advertising Expense 453.60
        Bank Service Charges....................................   17.00
        Accounts Receivable (J. Wilson) 220.00
        Cash 690.60
        To record decreases in Cash account as indicated by
        bank reconciliation.

SELF-TEST QUESTIONS

The answers to these questions appear on page 356.

1 Which of the following practices contributes to efficient cash management?

  a Never borrow money—maintain a cash balance sufficient to make all necessary payments.

  b Record all cash receipts and cash payments at the end of the month when reconciling the bank statements.

  c Prepare monthly forecasts of planned cash receipts, payments, and anticipated cash balances up to a year in advance.

  d Pay each bill as soon as the invoice arrives.

2 Each of the following measures strengthens internal control over cash receipts *except:*

  a The use of a voucher system.

  b Preparation of a daily listing of all checks received through the mail.

  c The deposit of cash receipts intact in the bank on a daily basis.

  d The use of cash registers.

3 When a voucher system is in use:

  a The voucher and supporting documents are perforated when the check is prepared for signature.

b The finance department signs the check and perforates the voucher and supporting documents.

c The accounting department does not have access to the perforated vouchers and support.

d The finance department signs the check and returns the signed check to the accounting department to be mailed.

Use the following data for questions 4 and 5.

Quinn Company's bank statement at January 31 shows a balance of $13,360, while the ledger account for Cash in Quinn's ledger shows a balance of $12,890 at the same date. The only reconciling items are the following:

■ Deposit in transit, $890.

■ Bank service charge, $24.

■ NSF check from customer Greg Denton in the amount of $426.

■ Error in recording check no. 389 for rent: check was written in the amount of $1,320, but was recorded in the bank statement as $1,230.

■ Outstanding checks, $?????

4 What is the total amount of outstanding checks at January 31?
  a $1,048   b $868   c $1,900   d $1,720

5 Assuming a single journal entry is made to adjust Quinn Company's accounting records at January 31, the journal entry includes:

a A debit to Rent Expense for $90.

b A credit to Accounts Receivable, G. Denton, for $426.

c A credit to Cash for $450.

d A credit to Cash for $1,720.

ASSIGNMENT MATERIAL

DISCUSSION QUESTIONS

1 If a company has checking accounts in three banks, should it maintain a separate ledger account for each? Should the company's balance sheet show as three separate items the amounts on deposit in the three banks? Explain.

2 What are *cash equivalents?* Provide two examples. Why are these items often combined with cash for the purpose of balance sheet presentation?

3 Does the expression "efficient management of cash" mean anything more than procedures to prevent losses from fraud or theft? Explain.

4 Why are cash balances *in excess* of those needed to finance business operations sometimes viewed as relatively nonproductive assets?

5 Suggest several ways in which a corporation might efficiently utilize cash balances in excess of the amounts needed for current operations.

6 Among the various assets owned by a business, cash is probably the one for which strong internal control is most urgently needed. What specific attributes of cash cause this special need for internal control?

7 Mention some principles to be observed by a business in establishing strong internal control over cash receipts.

8 Explain how internal control over cash transactions is strengthened by compliance with the following rule: "Deposit each day's cash receipts intact in the bank, and make all disbursements by check."

9 Ringo Store sells only for cash and records all sales on cash registers before delivering merchandise to the customers. On a given day the cash count at the close of business indicated $10.25 less cash than was shown by the totals on the cash register tapes. In what account would this cash shortage be recorded? Would the account be debited or credited?

10 With respect to a *voucher system,* what is meant by the terms *voucher, voucher register,* and *check register?*

11 Randall Company uses a voucher system to control its cash disbursements. With respect to a purchase of merchandise, what three documents would need to be examined to verify that the voucher should be approved?

12 Suggest an internal control procedure to prevent the documents supporting a paid voucher from being resubmitted later in support of another cash disbursement.

13 What information usually appears on a bank statement?

14 It is standard accounting practice to treat as cash all checks received from customers. When a customer's check is received, recorded, and deposited, but later returned by the bank marked "NSF," what accounting entry or entries would be appropriate?

15 List two items often encountered in reconciling a bank account which may cause cash per the bank statement to be *larger* than the balance of cash shown in the accounts.

16 In the reconciliation of a bank account, what reconciling items necessitate a journal entry in the depositor's accounting records?

17 Briefly describe how an employer may use *electronic funds transfers* in meeting its payroll obligations. Describe the advantages of this system to (1) the employees and (2) the employer.

18 A basic concept of internal control is that all cash disbursements of substantial dollar amount should be made by check. What then is the purpose of a *petty cash fund?* Also, identify three types of expenditures which are likely to be made from such a fund.

19 Pico Stationery Shop has for years maintained a petty cash fund of $75, which is replenished twice a month.

   a How many debit entries would you expect to find in the Petty Cash account each year?

   b When would expenditures from the petty cash fund be entered in the ledger accounts?

20 Describe the nature and usefulness of a *cash budget.*

EXERCISES

**EXERCISE 7-1
Accounting
Terminology—
Cash**

Listed below are nine technical accounting terms introduced in this chapter.

Cash equivalents	Cash budget	Marketable securities
Cash management	Voucher system	Bank reconciliation
Petty cash fund	NSF checks	Cash Over and Short

Each of the following statements may (or may not) describe one of these technical terms. For each statement, indicate the term described, or answer "None" if the statement does not correctly describe any of the terms.

a Short-term and highly liquid investments which often are combined with cash for the purpose of balance sheet presentation.

b A sequence of procedures for assuring that every potential expenditure has been reviewed and approved before a check is issued.

c A control procedure that should bring to light any unrecorded cash disbursements.

d The account in which errors in making change for cash customers are recorded.

e Checks issued by a business which have not yet been presented for payment.

f A document used in determining whether a department's cash receipts and cash expenditures are consistent with management's prior expectations.

g Includes measures to prevent the maintenance of excessively large balances in non-interest-bearing bank accounts.

h A means of conveniently making small, incidental disbursements of cash.

**EXERCISE 7-2
Effects of
Errors and
Irregularities**

DodgeTown, Inc., is an automobile dealership. The company uses a voucher system and has several bank accounts. Shown below are a series of situations which may (or may not) represent errors or irregularities that affect the reliability of the company's accounting records.

a Collection of an account receivable is recorded by debiting Sales Returns and Allowances and crediting Accounts Receivable.

b A check was issued in payment of voucher no. 4600, but no entry was made in the check register. Voucher no. 4600 was for property taxes expense.

c No entry was made to record the investment of cash in U.S. Treasury bills, which are considered cash equivalents.

d No entry was made to record the investment of cash in the stock of **Chrysler Corporation,** which is *not* considered a cash equivalent.

e No entry was made to record the failure to earn any interest revenue on the large cash balances in the corporation's checking account.

f No entry is made to adjust the company's accounting records for the amount of a deposit in transit listed in the year-end bank reconciliation.

g No entry was made to adjust the company's accounting records for customers' checks returned by the bank at year-end with the designation "NSF."

h Last month, a particular supplier was paid in full for services classified as an expense. This month, the same supporting documents were recirculated through the voucher system, and a second voucher was recorded authorizing a duplicate payment. (No check has yet been issued for this second payment.)

i The custodian "borrowed" $250 from the petty cash fund but replaced the money before the fund was counted or replenished.

j As the petty cash fund contained almost half of its original balance at year-end, the fund was not replenished and no entries were made in the accounting records.

INSTRUCTIONS Indicate the effects (if any) of each of these situations upon the elements of the company's financial statements listed below. (Notice that Cash & Cash Equivalents is listed separately from other assets.) Use the code letters *O* to indicate overstatement, *U* to indicate understatement, and *NE* to indicate no effect. Organize your answer in tabular form, using the following column headings:

Trans-action	Income Statement			Balance Sheet			
	Net Sales	− *Expenses*	= *Net Income*	*Cash & Cash Equivalents*	+ *All Other Assets*	= *Liabilities*	+ *Owners' Equity*
a							

EXERCISE 7-3
Internal Control: Identifying Strength and Weakness

Some of the following practices are suggestive of strength in internal controls; others are suggestive of weakness. Identify each of the eight practices with the term **Strength** or **Weakness.** Give reasons for your answers.

a Vouchers and all supporting documents are stamped "PAID" before being sent to the finance department for review and signing of checks.

b Personnel in the accounting department are not authorized to handle cash receipts. Therefore, accounts receivable records are maintained by the credit manager, who handles all collections from customers.

c Accounting department personnel are not authorized to prepare bank reconciliations. This procedure is performed in the finance department and the accounting department is notified of any required adjustments to the accounts.

d Checks received through the mail are recorded daily by the person maintaining accounts receivable records.

e All cash receipts are deposited daily.

f Any difference between a day's over-the-counter cash receipts and the day's total shown by the cash register is added to or removed from petty cash.

g After the monthly bank reconciliation has been prepared, any difference between the adjusted balance per the depositor's records and the adjusted balance per the bank statement is entered in the Cash Over and Short account.

h Employees who handle cash receipts are not authorized to issue credit memoranda or to write off accounts receivable as uncollectible.

EXERCISE 7-4
Subdivision of Duties

Certain subdivisions of duties are highly desirable for the purpose of achieving a reasonable degree of internal control. For each of the following six responsibilities, explain whether or not assigning the duty to an employee who also handles cash receipts would represent a significant weakness in internal control. Briefly explain your reasoning.

a Responsibility for executing both cash and credit sales transactions.

b Responsibility for maintaining the general ledger.

c Responsibility for maintaining the accounts receivable subsidiary ledger.

d Responsibility for issuing credit memoranda for sales returns.

e Responsibility for preparing a control listing of all cash collections.

f Responsibility for preparing monthly bank reconciliations.

EXERCISE 7-5
Voucher System

Laser Optic, Inc., uses a voucher system. The following transactions occurred early this month:

a Voucher no. 100 prepared to purchase office equipment at cost of $4,000 from Coast Furniture Co.

b Check no. 114 issued in payment of voucher no. 100.

c Voucher no. 101 prepared to establish a petty cash fund of $150.

d Check no. 115 issued in payment of voucher no. 101.

e Voucher no. 102 prepared to replenish the petty cash fund which contained $40 cash, and receipts for postage $38, miscellaneous expense $54, and delivery service $18.

f Check no. 116 issued in payment of voucher no. 102. Check cashed and proceeds placed in petty cash fund.

INSTRUCTIONS   You are to record the transactions in general journal form (without explanations). Also indicate after each entry the journal (or book of original entry) in which in actual practice the transaction would be recorded. For example, your treatment of transaction **a** should be as follows:

(a) Office Equipment *4,000*
        Vouchers Payable *4,000*
        (Voucher register)

EXERCISE 7-6
Short Bank
Reconciliation

The following information relating to the bank checking account is available for Music Hall at July 31:

Balance per bank statement at July 31	*$19,893.25*
Balance per depositor's records	*18,681.35*
Outstanding checks	*2,102.50*
Deposits in transit	*872.60*
Service charge by bank	*18.00*

INSTRUCTIONS   Prepare a bank reconciliation for Music Hall at July 31.

EXERCISE 7-7
Another Short
Bank Reconcil-
iation

The following information relating to the bank checking account is available for Wild Bill's Texas Barbeque at May 31.

Balance per bank statement at May 31	*$9,740.15*
Outstanding checks	*3,352.70*
Deposit in transit	*1,106.30*
Service charge by bank	*10.00*
Interest credited by the bank	*43.10*
Balance per depositor's accounting records at May 31	*7,460.65*

INSTRUCTIONS   Prepare a bank reconciliation at May 31.

EXERCISE 7-8
Bank Reconcil-
iation and En-
tries to Update
the Accounting
Records

Shown below is the information needed to prepare a bank reconciliation for Data Flow, Inc., at December 31.

1 At December 31, cash per the bank statement was $15,981; cash per the company's records was $17,445.

2 Two debit memoranda accompanied the bank statement: service charges for December of $24, and a $600 check drawn by Jane Jones marked "NSF."

3 Cash receipts of $4,353 on December 31 were not deposited until January.

4 The following checks had been issued in December but were not included among the paid checks returned by the bank: no. 620 for $978, no. 630 for $2,052, and no. 641 for $483.

INSTRUCTIONS   **a** Prepare a bank reconciliation at December 31.

b Prepare the necessary journal entry or entries to update the accounting records of Data Flow, Inc.

EXERCISE 7-9
Analysis of Reconciling Items

At September 30, the Cash account of Canvasback, a sole proprietorship, showed a balance of $72,900. The bank statement, however, showed a balance of $87,400 at the same date. The only reconciling items consisted of a $4,800 deposit in transit, a credit for interest earned of $200, and 30 outstanding checks.

INSTRUCTIONS

a Compute the amount of cash which should appear in the company's balance sheet at September 30.

b Compute the total amount of the outstanding checks.

EXERCISE 7-10
Adjustments to the Cash Account

In this exercise we focus on some of the basic computations required in almost all bank reconciliations. At the end of November, Glacier Lodge received a bank statement showing a balance of $105,000. The balance included interest earned during November of $450. All checks issued by Glacier Lodge were returned with the November bank statement except for 10 checks totaling $16,000 issued on November 30. Also, a deposit of $8,000 mailed to the bank by Glacier Lodge on November 30 did not appear on the bank statement.

INSTRUCTIONS

a Compute the amount of cash to appear on the November 30 balance sheet of Glacier Lodge. Show all computations.

b Compute the amount of cash shown by Glacier Lodge's records *before* any month-end entries were made to update the company's records.

EXERCISE 7-11
Reconciling Items

In reconciling the bank account of Lane Company, the accountant had to deal with the following six items.

1 Outstanding checks.

2 Bank service charges.

3 Check no. 502 was issued in the correct amount of $350 and paid by the bank in that amount, but had been incorrectly recorded in Lane Company's accounting records as $530.

4 Collection by bank of note receivable left with bank by Lane Company for collection and credit to Lane Company's account.

5 Customers' checks deposited by Lane Company but returned by bank marked "NSF."

6 Deposit in transit.

INSTRUCTIONS

You are to classify each of the above six items under one of the following headings: (a) an addition to the balance per the bank statement; (b) a deduction from the balance per the bank statement; (c) an addition to the balance per the depositor's records; (d) a deduction from the balance per the depositor's records.

EXERCISE 7-12
Petty Cash

Sunset Plaza established a petty cash fund of $200 on June 1. On June 20 the fund was replenished for the payments made to date as shown by the following petty cash vouchers: postage, $46; telephone expense, $17.50; repairs, $34.70; miscellaneous expense, $27. Prepare journal entries in *general journal form* to record the establishment of the fund on June 1 and its replenishment on June 20.

EXERCISE 7-13
More Petty Cash

On February 3, Executive Golf Course established a petty cash fund in the amount of $150. At February 28, the fund contained $9.20 in cash. The vouchers in the fund are summarized below:

Postage due	$ 0.36
Beer	20.60
Office supplies	82.14

Gas money for John..	*5.00*
Mark's lunch	*8.00*
Flowers for Linda's birthday.......................................	*12.35*
Doughnuts	*6.30*

The company replenishes this fund at the end of each month. All types of expenditures which amount to less than $50 during the month are charged to Miscellaneous Expense in one debit entry. Any type of expenditure exceeding $50 is debited to an expense account that describes the nature of the expenditure. Any cash shortage or excess is debited or credited to a Cash Over and Short account, regardless of the dollar amount.

INSTRUCTIONS   Prepare all journal entries relating to the operation of this petty cash fund during the month.

PROBLEMS

Group A

PROBLEM 7A-1
Internal Control Procedures
Listed below are nine errors or problems which might occur in the processing of cash transactions. Also shown is a separate list of internal control procedures.

Possible Errors or Problems

a   In serving customers who do not appear to be attentive, a salesclerk often rings up a sale at less than the actual sales amount and then removes the additional cash collected from the customer.

b   John Davis, who has prepared bank reconciliations for Marlo Corporation for several years has noticed that some checks issued by the company are never presented for payment. Davis, therefore, has formed the habit of dropping any checks outstanding for more than six months from the outstanding checklist and removing a corresponding amount of cash from the cash receipts. These actions taken together have left the ledger account for cash in agreement with the adjusted bank balance and have enriched Davis substantially.

c   A voucher was circulated through the system twice, causing the supplier to be paid twice for the same invoice.

d   Lisa Miller, an employee of Plaza Home Repairs, frequently has trouble in getting the bank reconciliation to balance. If the book balance is more than the bank balance, she writes a check payable to Cash and cashes it. If the book balance is less than the bank balance, she makes an accounting entry debiting Cash and crediting Cash Over and Short.

e   Without fear of detection, the cashier sometimes abstracts cash forwarded to him from the mailroom or the sales department instead of depositing these receipts in the company's bank account.

f   The monthly bank reconciliation continually shows a difference between the adjusted bank balance and the adjusted book balance because the cashier regularly deposits actual cash receipts, but the debits to the Cash account reflect cash register readings which differ by the amount of errors in making change in cash sales transactions.

g   All cash received from Monday through Thursday was lost in a burglary on Thursday night.

h   A salesclerk occasionally makes an error in the amount of change given to a customer.

    i The official designated to sign checks is able to steal blank checks and issue them for unauthorized purposes without fear of detection.

Internal Control Procedures

1 Periodic reconciliation of bank statements to accounting records.

2 Use of a Cash Over and Short account.

3 Adequate subdivision of duties.

4 Use of prenumbered sales tickets.

5 Depositing each day's cash receipts intact in the bank.

6 Use of electronic cash registers equipped with optical scanners to read magnetically coded labels on merchandise.

7 Immediate preparation of a control listing when cash is received, and the comparison of this listing to bank deposits.

8 Cancellation of paid vouchers.

9 Requirement that a voucher be prepared as advance authorization of every cash disbursement.

0 None of the above control procedures can effectively prevent this type of error from occurring.

INSTRUCTIONS List the letters (**a** through **i**) designating each possible error or problem. Beside this letter, place the number indicating the internal control procedure that should prevent this type of error or problem from occurring. If none of the specified internal control procedures would effectively prevent the error, place a **0** opposite the letter.

PROBLEM 7A-2
Preparing a
Bank Reconcil-
iation

At November 30, One Day Cleaners has available the following data concerning its bank checking account:

1 At November 30, cash per the bank statement was $37,758; per the accounting records, $42,500.

2 The cash receipts of $6,244 on November 30 were deposited on December 1.

3 Included on the bank statement was a credit for $167 interest earned on this checking account during November.

4 Two checks were outstanding at November 30: no. 921 for $964 and no. 925 for $1,085.

5 Enclosed with the bank statement were two debit memoranda for the following items: service charge for November, $14; and a $700 check of customer Tanya Miller, marked "NSF."

INSTRUCTIONS

a Prepare a bank reconciliation at November 30.

b Prepare adjusting entries (in general journal form) based on the bank reconciliation.

PROBLEM 7A-3
A More Com-
prehensive
Bank Reconcil-
iation

The cash transactions and cash balances of Norfleet Farm for July were as follows:

1 The ledger account for Cash showed a balance at July 31 of $16,766.95.

2 The July bank statement showed a closing balance of $18,928.12.

3 The cash received on July 31 amounted to $4,017.15. It was left at the bank in the night depository chute after banking hours on July 31 and was therefore not recorded by the bank on the July statement.

4   Also included with the July bank statement was a debit memorandum from the bank for $7.65 representing service charges for July.

5   A credit memorandum enclosed with the July bank statement indicated that a non-interest-bearing note receivable for $4,545 from Rene Manes, left with the bank for collection, had been collected and the proceeds credited to the account of Norfleet Farm.

6   Comparison of the paid checks returned by the bank with the entries in the accounting records revealed that check no. 821 for *$835.02,* issued July 15 in payment for office equipment, had been erroneously entered in Norfleet's records as *$853.02.*

7   Examination of the paid checks also revealed that three checks, all issued in July, had not yet been paid by the bank: no. 811 for $861.12; no. 814 for $640.80; no. 823 for $301.05.

8   Included with the July bank statement was a $180 check drawn by Howard Williams, a customer of Norfleet Farm. This check was marked "NSF." It had been included in the deposit of July 27 but had been charged back against the company's account on July 31.

INSTRUCTIONS   a   Prepare a bank reconciliation for Norfleet Farm at July 31.

b   Prepare journal entries (in general journal form) to adjust the accounts at July 31. Assume that the accounts have not been closed.

c   State the amount of cash which should be included in the balance sheet at July 31.

**PROBLEM 7A-4
Another Comprehensive
Bank Reconciliation**   Daytona Recycling Center reports the following information concerning cash balances and cash transactions for the month of September:

1   Cash balance per bank statement as of September 30 was $20,893.25.

2   Two debit memoranda accompanied the bank statement: one for $10 was for service charges for the month; the other for $64.60 was attached to an NSF check from A. Smith.

3   Included with the bank statement was $69 credit memorandum for interest earned on the bank account in September.

4   The paid checks returned with the September bank statement disclosed an error in Daytona's cash records. Check no. 851 for $77.44 for telephone expense had erroneously been listed in the cash payments journal as $44.77.

5   A collection charge for $26.00 (not applicable to Daytona) was erroneously deducted from the account by the bank. Notice that this was the *bank's* error.

6   Cash receipts of September 30 amounting to $585.25 were mailed to the bank too late to be included in the September bank statement.

7   Checks outstanding as of September 30 were as follows: no. 860 for $151.93, no. 867 for $82.46, and no. 869 for $123.61.

8   The Cash account showed the following entries during September:

		Cash					
Sept	1	*Balance*	18,341.82	Sept	30	*Month's payments*	11,598.63
	30	*Month's receipts*	14,441.58				

INSTRUCTIONS   a   Prepare a bank reconciliation at September 30.

b   Prepare the necessary adjusting entries in general journal form.

**PROBLEM 7A-5
Operating a
Petty Cash
Fund**

In order to handle small cash disbursements in an efficient manner, Off Broadway established a petty cash fund on July 10. The following events relating to petty cash occurred in July.

July 10   A check for $300 drawn payable to Petty Cash was issued and cashed to establish the fund.

July 31   At month-end, a count of the fund disclosed the following:

Office supplies expense	$50.40
Postage expense	69.00
Travel expense	49.38
Miscellaneous expense	50.62
Currency and coin remaining in the fund	78.60

July 31   A check was issued to replenish the petty cash fund.

INSTRUCTIONS

a   Prepare an entry in general journal form to record the establishment of the petty cash fund on July 10.

b   Prepare an entry to record the replenishment of the petty cash fund on July 31.

c   Net income for Off Broadway in July was $6,785.20. What amount of net income would have been reported in the July income statement if the company had *not* replenished the petty cash fund on July 31?

**PROBLEM 7A-6
"Charmed . . ."**

Equipment Rental Company had poor internal control over its cash transactions. Facts about the company's cash position at November 30, 1994, were as described below.

The accounting records showed a cash balance of $29,959.00, which included a deposit in transit of $3,420.60. The balance indicated in the bank statement was $18,299.40. Included in the bank statement were the following debit and credit memoranda:

Debit Memoranda:

Check from customer G. Davis, deposited by Equipment Rental Co., but charged back as NSF	$1,500.00
Bank service charges for November	25.00

Credit Memorandum:

Proceeds from collection of a note receivable from Regal Farms which Equipment Rental Co. had left with the bank's collection department	3,000.00

Outstanding checks as of November 30 were as follows:

Check No.	Amount
8231	$ 340.30
8263	800.50
8288	145.20
8294	2,100.00

Melanie Charm, the company's cashier, has been abstracting portions of the company's cash receipts for several months. Each month, Charm prepares the company's bank reconciliation in a manner that conceals her thefts. Her bank reconciliation for November is illustrated as follows:

Balance per bank statement, Nov. 30		$18,299.40
Add: Deposits in transit	$4,320.60	
Collection of note from Regal Farms	3,000.00	7,320.60
Subtotal		$26,620.00
Less: Outstanding checks:		
No. 8231	$ 340.30	
8263	800.50	
8288	145.20	1,186.00
Adjusted cash balance per bank statement		$25,434.00
Balance per accounting records, Nov. 30		$29,959.00
Add: Credit memorandum from bank		3,000.00
Subtotal		$26,959.00
Less: Debit memoranda from bank:		
NSF check of G. Davis	$1,500.00	
Bank service charges	25.00	1,525.00
Adjusted cash balance per accounting records		$25,434.00

INSTRUCTIONS

a Determine the amount of the cash shortage which has been concealed by Charm in her bank reconciliation. (As a format, we suggest that you prepare the bank reconciliation correctly. The amount of the shortage then will be the difference between the adjusted balances per the bank statement and per the accounting records. You can then list this unrecorded cash shortage as the final adjustment necessary to complete your reconciliation.)

b Carefully review Charm's bank reconciliation and explain in detail how she concealed the amount of the shortage. Include a listing of the dollar amounts that were concealed in various ways. This listing should total the amount of the shortage determined in part **a**.

c Suggest some specific internal control measures which appear to be necessary for Equipment Rental Company.

Group B

**PROBLEM 7B-1
Internal Control Procedures**

Listed below are nine errors or problems which might occur in the processing of cash transactions. Also shown is a separate list of internal control procedures.

Possible Errors or Problems

a Joy Hart, an employee of Center Hardware, frequently has trouble in getting the bank reconciliation to balance. If the book balance is more than the bank balance, she writes a check payable to Cash and cashes it. If the book balance is less than the bank balance, she makes an accounting entry debiting Cash and crediting Cash Over and Short.

b Without fear of detection, the cashier sometimes abstracts cash forwarded to him from the mailroom or the sales department instead of depositing these receipts in the company's bank account.

c The monthly bank reconciliation continually shows a difference between the adjusted bank balance and the adjusted book balance because the cashier regularly deposits actual cash receipts, but the debits to the Cash account reflect cash register readings which differ by the amount of errors in making change in cash sales transactions.

d All cash received from Monday through Thursday was lost in a burglary on Thursday night.

e A salesclerk occasionally makes an error in the amount of change given to a customer.

f The official designated to sign checks is able to steal blank checks and issue them for unauthorized purposes without fear of detection.

g In serving customers who do not appear to be attentive, a salesclerk often rings up a sale at less than the actual sales amount and then removes the additional cash collected from the customer.

h Teresa Hill, who has prepared bank reconciliations for Ross Stewart, Inc., for several years has noticed that some checks issued by the company are never presented for payment. Hill, therefore, has formed the habit of dropping any checks outstanding for more than six months from the outstanding checklist and removing a corresponding amount of cash from the cash receipts. These actions taken together have left the ledger account for cash in agreement with the adjusted bank balance and have enriched Hill substantially.

i A voucher was circulated through the system twice, causing the supplier to be paid twice for the same invoice.

Internal Control Procedures

1 Periodic reconciliation of bank statements to accounting records.

2 Use of a Cash Over and Short account.

3 Adequate subdivision of duties.

4 Use of prenumbered sales tickets.

5 Depositing each day's cash receipts intact in the bank.

6 Use of electronic cash registers equipped with optical scanners to read magnetically coded labels on merchandise.

7 Immediate preparation of a control listing when cash is received, and the comparison of this listing to bank deposits.

8 Cancellation of paid vouchers.

9 Requirement that a voucher be prepared as advance authorization of every cash disbursement.

0 None of the above control procedures can effectively prevent this type of error from occurring.

INSTRUCTIONS List the letters (**a** through **i**) designating each possible error or problem. Beside this letter, place the number indicating the internal control procedure that should prevent this type of error or problem from occurring. If none of the specified internal control procedures would effectively prevent the error, place a **0** opposite the letter.

PROBLEM 7B-2
Preparing a Bank Reconciliation Bluegrass Tonight is a nightclub in Nashville. The information necessary for preparing a bank reconciliation for the company at November 30 appears below:

1 As of November 30, cash per the bank statement is $41,631, per the accounting records, $48,609.

2 Cash receipts of $9,366 on November 30 were not deposited until December 1.

3 Among the paid checks returned by the bank was a stolen check for $1,512 paid in error after Bluegrass Tonight had officially notified the bank not to make payment. Thus, payment of this check was a bank error and should not have been charged against Bluegrass Tonight's bank account.

4 The following memoranda accompanied the bank statement:

a A debit memo for service charges, $21

    b A debit memo attached to an $1,167 check which Bluegrass had accepted from a customer and deposited in its account, but which the bank had returned with the marking "NSF"

    c A credit memo for interest earned on the account during November, $135

5 The following checks had been issued by the nightclub but had not been paid by the bank as of November 30: no. 921 for $2,346; no. 924 for $1,446; and no. 925 for $1,161.

INSTRUCTIONS Prepare the November 30 bank reconciliation.

PROBLEM 7B-3
A More Comprehensive Bank Reconciliation

During July the cash transactions and cash balances of Rapid Harvest were as follows:

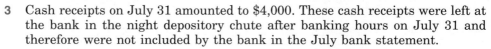

1 The cash balance per the bank statement at July 31 was $28,945.27.

2 The ledger account for Cash had a balance at July 31 of $26,686.95.

3 Cash receipts on July 31 amounted to $4,000. These cash receipts were left at the bank in the night depository chute after banking hours on July 31 and therefore were not included by the bank in the July bank statement.

4 Included with the July bank statement was a credit memorandum showing interest earned by the depositor on this account in the amount of $80.

5 Another credit memorandum enclosed with the July bank statement showed that a non-interest-bearing note for $3,663 from Ralph Warde, left with the bank for collection, had been collected and the proceeds credited to the account of Rapid Harvest.

6 Also included with the July bank statement was a debit memorandum from the bank for $19.45 representing service charges for July.

7 Comparison of the paid checks returned by the bank with the entries in the accounting records revealed that check no. 922 for $4,521.50 issued July 15 in payment for salaries expense had been erroneously entered in the accounting records as $5,421.50.

8 Examination of the paid checks also revealed that three checks, all issued in July, had not yet been paid by the bank: no. 921 for $944.32; no. 924 for $320.50; no. 935 for $538.15.

9 Included with the July bank statement was a $168.20 check drawn by Edward Jones, a customer of Rapid Harvest. This check was marked "NSF." It had been included in the deposit of July 27 but had been charged back against the company's account on July 31.

INSTRUCTIONS **a** Prepare a bank reconciliation for Rapid Harvest at July 31.

    b Prepare journal entries (in general journal form) to adjust the accounts at July 31. Assume that the accounts have not been closed.

    c State the amount of cash which should be included in the balance sheet at July 31.

PROBLEM 7B-4
Another Comprehensive Bank Reconciliation

The information needed to prepare a bank reconciliation and the related adjusting entries for Wicked Pony at March 31 is listed below.

1 Cash balance per the accounting records of Wicked Pony, $18,106.69.

2 The bank statement showed a balance of $22,134.27 at March 31.

3 Accompanying the bank statement was a debit memorandum relating to a check for $186 from a customer, D. Otay. The check was returned by the bank and stamped "NSF."

4   Checks outstanding as of March 31 were as follows: no. 84 for $1,841.02; no. 88 for $1,323.00; no. 89 for $16.26.

5   Also accompanying the bank statement was a debit memorandum for $44.80 for safe deposit box rent; the bank had erroneously charged this item to the account of Wicked Pony.

6   On March 29, the bank collected a non-interest-bearing note for Wicked Pony. The note was for $2,963; the bank charged a collection fee of $8.40.

7   A deposit of $2,008.50 was in transit; it had been mailed to the bank on March 31.

8   In recording a $160 check received on account from a customer, Ross Company, the accountant for Wicked Pony erroneously recorded the amount collected as $16. The check appeared correctly among the deposits on the March bank statement.

9   The bank service charge for March amounted to $20.40; a debit memo in this amount was returned with the bank statement.

INSTRUCTIONS

a   Prepare a bank reconciliation at March 31.

b   Prepare the necessary journal entries.

c   What amount of cash should be included in the company's March 31 balance sheet?

PROBLEM 7B-5
Operating a Petty Cash Fund

Santa Rosa Winery maintains a petty cash fund to control small cash payments. The company does not use a voucher system. Shown below are the transactions involving the establishment of the fund and its replenishment at September 30, the end of the company's fiscal year:

Sept. 12   A check for $500 was issued and cashed to establish a petty cash fund.

Sept. 30   A count of the fund showed currency and coin of $104.10 remaining on hand. Petty cash receipts in the fund were as follows:

Office supplies expense	$100.43
Postage expense	43.92
Travel & entertainment expense	183.10
Miscellaneous expense	66.44

Sept. 30   Although the fund had not been used fully, management wished to replenish the fund before the accounts were closed for the fiscal year. A check was therefore issued and cashed on this date in the amount necessary to restore the fund to its $500 balance.

INSTRUCTIONS

a   Prepare journal entries in general journal form to record the establishment of the fund on September 12 and its replenishment on September 30.

b   What would have been the effect, if any, on net income for the fiscal year ended September 30 if the company had forgotten to replenish the fund on September 30? Explain.

PROBLEM 7B-6
The Honorable Mr. Chan

Carriage Towne, a successful small business, had never given much consideration to the need for internal control, and the internal controls over cash transactions were inadequate. Thom Chan, the cashier-bookkeeper, handled cash receipts, made small disbursements from these cash receipts, maintained the accounting records, and prepared the monthly reconciliations of the bank account. Recognizing the weaknesses in internal control over cash transactions, Chan began pocketing some of the company's cash receipts.

At the end of April, the bank statement indicated a balance on deposit of $37,350.90. The following checks were outstanding: no. 7552 for $612.30, no. 7573 for $1,219.00, no. 7574 for $468.30, no. 7611 for $1,321.10, no. 7613 for $402.20, and no. 7622 for $3,211.00. All cash receipts for April (except those stolen by Chan) had been deposited in the bank, and the deposits all were listed correctly in the April 30 bank statement. The cash balance shown in the company's accounting records at April 30 was $38,467.00, including $200.00 in cash on hand. This information was known to Chan; however, he concealed the amount of his theft by preparing the bank "reconciliation" improperly, as shown below:

Balance per bank statement, April 30		$37,350.90
Less: Outstanding checks:		
No. 7611	$1,321.10	
No. 7613	402.20	
No. 7622	2,311.00	3,034.30
		$34,316.60
Add: Deposit in transit (April 30 receipts)	$3,650.40	
Cash on hand	500.00	4,150.40
Balance per accounting records, April 30		$38,467.00

INSTRUCTIONS

a Determine the amount of the cash shortage concealed by Chan in his November bank reconciliation. (As a format, we suggest that you prepare the bank reconciliation correctly. The amount of the shortage then will be the difference between the adjusted balances per the bank statement and per the accounting records.)

b Carefully review Chan's bank reconciliation and explain in detail how he concealed the amount of the shortage. Include a listing of the dollar amounts that were concealed in various ways. This listing should total the amount of the shortage as determined in part a.

c Suggest some specific internal control measures which appear to be necessary for Carriage Towne.

CASES AND UNSTRUCTURED PROBLEMS

**CASE 7-1
Money to Burn**

St. Jude Medical, Inc., is a large corporation engaged in the manufacture of heart valves and other medical products. In recent years, the company has accumulated large amounts of cash and cash equivalents as a result of profitable operations. A recent annual report shows cash and cash equivalents amounting to more than 50% of the company's total assets. As these large holdings of cash and cash equivalents have been accumulated, the company has paid no dividends.

INSTRUCTIONS Evaluate St. Jude's policies of accumulating liquid resources instead of paying dividends from the perspectives of:

a The company's creditors.

b The company's stockholders.

**CASE 7-2
Embezzlement,
She Wrote**

D. J. Fletcher, a trusted employee of Bluestem Products, found herself in personal financial difficulties and decided to "borrow" (steal) $3,000 from the company and to conceal her theft.

As a first step, Fletcher removed $3,000 in currency from the cash register. This amount represented the bulk of the cash received in over-the-counter sales during the three business days since the last bank deposit. Fletcher then removed a $3,000 check from the day's incoming mail; this check had been mailed in by a customer, Michael Adams, in full payment of his account. Fletcher made no journal entry to record the $3,000 collection from Adams but deposited the check in Bluestem Products' bank account in place of the $3,000 over-the-counter cash receipts she had stolen.

In order to keep Adams from protesting when his month-end statement reached him, Fletcher made a journal entry debiting Sales Returns and Allowances and crediting Accounts Receivable—Michael Adams. Fletcher posted this entry to the two general ledger accounts affected and also to Adams's account in the subsidiary ledger for accounts receivable.

INSTRUCTIONS

a Did these actions by Fletcher cause the general ledger to be out of balance or the subsidiary ledger to disagree with the controlling account? Explain.

b Assume that Bluestem Products prepares financial statements at the end of the month without discovering the theft. Would any items in the balance sheet or the income statement be in error? Explain.

c Several weaknesses in internal control apparently exist in Bluestem Products. Indicate three specific changes needed to strengthen internal control over cash receipts.

**CASE 7-3
Another Day,
Another Dollar**

Tom Pharro owns Pharro Concrete & Masonry, a small contracting business. On April 1, the company established a petty cash fund in the amount of $5,000, which was expected to last about three months. The cash was kept in a locked box in the desk of the company's receptionist. (The company has two part-time receptionists, who were designated the office custodians of the fund. The only other people with access to the petty cash box were Tom Pharro and his personal secretary, Chris Greer.) Vouchers were to be prepared for all disbursements from the fund, and these vouchers were to be placed in the petty cash box.

Unfortunately, the money in the petty cash fund did not last three months. On April 30, the receptionists reported that the vouchers in the fund totaled $4,390.90 but that the fund contained only $2.00 in cash. The vouchers were sent to the accounting department, reviewed, and canceled. All of the vouchers included adequate documentation. Replenishment of the fund then was recorded by the following entry:

Office Supplies Expense	160.20	
Travel & Entertainment Expense	1,501.00	
Office Equipment	804.70	
Repairs Expense (Roof)	925.00	
Drawing, Tom Pharro	1,000.00	
Miscellaneous Expense	607.10	
Cash		4,998.00
To replenish the petty cash fund.		

INSTRUCTIONS

Identify any control weaknesses relating to this fund. Explain your reasons for regarding any aspect of the fund's operations as a weakness, and make specific recommendations for improvement.

**CASE 7-4
Internal Control—A Challenging Case Study**

June Davis inherited a highly successful business, Solano, Inc., shortly after her twenty-second birthday and took over the active management of the business. A portion of the company's business consisted of over-the-counter sales for cash, but most sales were on credit and were shipped by truck. Davis had no knowledge of internal control practices and relied implicitly upon the bookkeeper-cashier, John Adams, in all matters relating to cash and accounting records. Adams, who had been with the company for many years, maintained the accounting records and prepared all financial statements with the help of two assistants, made bank deposits, signed checks, and prepared bank reconciliations.

The monthly income statements submitted to Davis by Adams showed a very satisfactory rate of net income; however, the amount of cash in the bank declined steadily during the first 18 months after Davis took over the business. To meet the company's weakening cash position, a bank loan was obtained and a few months later when the cash position again grew critical, the loan was increased.

On April 1, two years after Davis assumed the management of the company, Adams suddenly left town, leaving no forwarding address. Davis was immediately deluged with claims of creditors who stated their accounts were several months past due and that Adams had promised all debts would be paid by April 1. The bank telephoned to notify Davis that the company's account was overdrawn and that a number of checks had just been presented for payment.

In an effort to get together some cash to meet this emergency, Davis called on two of the largest customers of the company, to whom substantial sales on account had recently been made, and asked if they could pay their accounts at once. Both customers informed her that their accounts were paid in full. They produced paid checks to substantiate their payments and explained that Adams had offered them reduced prices on merchandise if they would pay within 24 hours after delivery.

To keep the business from insolvency, Davis agreed to sell at a bargain price a half interest in the company. The sale was made to Helen Smith, who had had considerable experience in the industry. One condition for the sale was that Smith should become the general manager of the business. The cash investment by Smith for her half interest was sufficient for the company to meet the demands on it and continue operations.

Immediately after Smith entered the business, she launched an investigation of Adams's activities. During the course of this investigation the following irregularities were disclosed:

1   During the last few months of Adams's employment with the company, bank deposits were much smaller than the cash receipts. Adams had abstracted most of the receipts and substituted for them a number of worthless checks bearing fictitious signatures. These checks had been accumulated in an envelope marked "Cash Receipts—For Deposit Only."

2   Numerous legitimate sales of merchandise on account had been charged to fictitious customers. When the actual customer later made payment for the goods, Adams abstracted the check or cash and made no entry. The account receivable with the fictitious customer remained in the records.

3   When checks were received from customers in payment of their accounts, Adams had frequently recorded the transaction by debiting an expense account and crediting Accounts Receivable. In such cases Adams had removed from the cash receipts an equivalent amount of currency, thus substituting the check for the currency and causing the bank deposit to agree with the recorded cash receipts.

4   More than $3,000 a month had been stolen from petty cash. Fraudulent petty cash vouchers, mostly charged to the Inventory account, had been created to conceal these thefts and to support the checks cashed to replenish the petty cash fund.

5   For many sales made over the counter, Adams had recorded lesser amounts on the cash register or had not rung up any amount. He had abstracted the funds received but not recorded.

6   To produce income statements that showed profitable operations, Adams had recorded many fictitious sales. The recorded accounts receivable included many from nonexistent customers.

7 In preparing bank reconciliations, Adams had omitted many outstanding checks, thus concealing the fact that the cash in the bank was less than the amount shown by the ledger.

8 Inventory had been recorded at inflated amounts in order to increase reported profits from the business.

INSTRUCTIONS

a For each of the numbered paragraphs, describe one or more internal control procedures you would recommend to prevent the occurrence of such fraud.

b Apart from specific internal controls over cash and other accounts, what general precaution could June Davis have taken to assure herself that the accounting records were properly maintained and the company's financial statements complete and dependable? Explain fully.

ANSWERS TO SELF-TEST QUESTIONS

1 c   2 a   3 b   4 d   5 c

8 Accounts Receivable and Notes Receivable

When a business sells goods or services on credit, it does so in the belief that the customer will make payment in accordance with the terms of sale. This confidence in the collectibility of receivables is the basis for showing accounts receivable and notes receivable as assets in the balance sheet and for including credit sales as revenue in the income statement. Along with our overall confidence in receivables, however, is a recognition that a few customers will fail to pay as agreed. Making sales on credit inevitably leads to some credit losses. In this chapter, we explore methods of measuring the expense of uncollectible accounts receivable and of reflecting this expense in the financial statements. We also consider various forms of notes receivable and the calculation of interest. In the final pages of the chapter, we show how the concept of present value is applied to long-term notes receivable.

After studying this chapter you should be able to meet these Learning Objectives:

1 *Prepare estimates of uncollectible accounts receivable, write off any accounts known to be uncollectible, and record any later recoveries.*

2 *Compare the allowance method and the direct write-off method of accounting for uncollectible accounts.*

3 *Explain why accounts receivable may be viewed as "nonproductive" assets. Identify several ways of converting receivables quickly into cash.*

4 *Account for sales to customers using credit cards.*

5 *Explain promissory notes and the nature of interest.*

6 *Compute the accounts receivable turnover rate. Explain why this ratio is of interest to short-term creditors.*

*7 *Account for notes receivable with the interest charges included in the face amount.*

*8 *Discuss the concept of present value in accounting for long-term notes receivable.*

---

* *Supplemental Topic, "Notes Receivable with Interest Charges Included in the Face Amount"*

ACCOUNTS RECEIVABLE

One of the key factors underlying the growth of the American economy is the trend toward selling goods and services on credit. Accounts receivable are liquid assets, usually being converted into cash within a period of 30 to 60 days. Therefore, accounts receivable from customers are classified as current assets, appearing in the balance sheet immediately after cash and marketable securities.

Sometimes companies sell merchandise on longer-term installment plans, requiring 12, 24, or even 48 months to collect the entire amount receivable from the customer. By definition, the normal period of time required to collect accounts receivable is part of a company's *operating cycle.* Therefore, accounts receivable arising from "normal" sales transactions usually are classified as current assets, even if the credit terms extend beyond one year.[1]

Uncollectible Accounts

No business wants to sell on credit to a customer who will prove unable or unwilling to pay his or her account. Therefore, most businesses have a credit department that investigates the creditworthiness of each prospective customer. This investigation usually includes obtaining a credit report from a national credit-rating agency such as *Dun & Bradstreet, Inc.* If the prospective customer is a business concern, its financial statements will be obtained and analyzed to determine its financial strength and the trend of its operating results.

A business that sells its goods or services on credit will inevitably find that some of its accounts receivable are uncollectible. Regardless of how thoroughly the credit department investigates prospective customers, some uncollectible accounts will arise as a result of errors in judgment or because of unexpected developments. In fact, a limited amount of uncollectible accounts is evidence of a sound credit policy. If the credit department should become too cautious and conservative in rating customers, it might avoid all credit losses but, in so doing, lose profitable business by rejecting many acceptable customers.

Reflecting Uncollectible Accounts in the Financial Statements An account receivable that has been determined to be uncollectible is no longer an asset. The loss of this asset represents an *expense,* termed *uncollectible accounts expense.*

In measuring business income, one of the most fundamental principles of accounting is that revenue should be *matched* with (offset by) the expenses incurred in generating that revenue. Uncollectible accounts expense is *caused by selling goods* on credit to customers who fail to pay their bills. Therefore, this expense is incurred in the month in which the *related sales* are made, even though specific accounts receivable may not

---

[1] As explained in Chapter 5, the period used to define current assets and current liabilities is one year or the company's operating cycle, whichever is longer. The *operating cycle* is the period of time needed to convert cash into inventory, the inventory into accounts receivable, and the accounts receivable back into cash.

OBJECTIVE 1
Prepare esti-
mates of
uncollectible
accounts
receivable,
write off any
accounts
known to be
uncollectible,
and record
any later
recoveries.

be determined to be uncollectible until a later accounting period. Thus, an account receivable that originates from a sale on credit in January and is determined to be uncollectible in August represents an expense in ***January.*** Unless each month's uncollectible accounts expense is ***estimated*** and reflected in the month-end income statement and balance sheet, these financial statements may show overstated earnings and overvalued assets.

To illustrate, assume that World Famous Toy Co. begins business on January 1, 1994, and makes most of its sales on account. At January 31, accounts receivable amount to $250,000. On this date, the credit manager reviews the accounts receivable and estimates that approximately $10,000 of these accounts will prove to be uncollectible. The following adjusting entry should be made at January 31:

Provision for
uncollectible
accounts

Uncollectible Accounts Expense	10,000	
Allowance for Doubtful Accounts		10,000

To record the portion of total accounts receivable estimated to be uncollectible.

The ***Uncollectible Accounts Expense*** account created by the debit part of this entry is closed into the Income Summary account in the same manner as any other expense account. The ***Allowance for Doubtful Accounts*** which was credited in the above journal entry will appear in the balance sheet as a deduction from the face amount of the accounts receivable. It serves to reduce the accounts receivable to their ***net realizable value*** in the balance sheet, as shown by the following illustration:

WORLD FAMOUS TOY CO.
Partial Balance Sheet
January 31, 1994

How much is
the estimated
net realizable
value of the
accounts re-
ceivable?

Current assets:		
Cash and cash equivalents		$ 75,000
Marketable securities		25,000
Accounts receivable	$250,000	
Less: Allowance for doubtful accounts	10,000	240,000
Inventory		300,000
Total current assets		$640,000

The Allowance for Doubtful Accounts

There is no way of telling in advance ***which*** accounts receivable will prove to be uncollectible. It is therefore not possible to credit the accounts of specific customers for our estimate of probable uncollectible accounts. Neither should we credit the Accounts Receivable controlling account in the general ledger. If the Accounts Receivable controlling account were to be credited with the estimated amount of doubtful accounts, this controlling account would no longer be in balance with the total of the numerous customers' accounts in the subsidiary ledger. The only practical alternative, therefore, is to credit a separate account called ***Allowance for Doubtful Accounts*** with the amount estimated to be uncollectible.

The Allowance for Doubtful Accounts often is described as a **contra-asset** account or a **valuation** account. Both of these terms indicate that the Allowance for Doubtful Accounts has a credit balance, which is offset against the asset Accounts Receivable to produce the proper balance sheet value for this asset.

Estimating the Amount of Uncollectible Accounts Before financial statements are prepared at the end of the accounting period, an estimate of the expected amount of uncollectible accounts receivables should be made. This estimate is based upon past experience and modified in accordance with current business conditions. Losses from uncollectible receivables tend to be greater during periods of recession than in periods of growth and prosperity. Because the allowance for doubtful accounts is necessarily an estimate and not a precise calculation, the factor of personal judgment may play a considerable part in determining the size of this valuation account.

Conservatism as a Factor in Valuing Accounts Receivable The larger the allowance established for doubtful accounts, the lower the net valuation of accounts receivable will be. Some accountants and some business executives tend to favor the most conservative valuation of assets that logically can be supported. **Conservatism** in the preparation of a balance sheet implies a tendency to resolve uncertainties in the valuation of assets by reporting assets at the lower end of the range of reasonable values rather than by establishing values in a purely objective manner.

The valuation of assets at conservative amounts is a long-standing tradition in accounting, stemming from the days when creditors were the major users of financial statements. From the viewpoint of bankers and others who use financial statements as a basis for granting loans, conservatism in valuing assets has long been regarded as a desirable policy.

Assume that the balance sheet of a company presents optimistic, exaggerated values for the assets owned. Assume also that this "unconservative" balance sheet is submitted to a banker in support of an application for a loan. The banker studies the balance sheet and grants the loan, relying upon the values listed. Later the banker finds it impossible to collect the loan and also finds that the assets upon which the loan was based had been greatly overstated in the balance sheet. The banker will undoubtedly consider the overly optimistic character of the balance sheet as partially responsible for the loss incurred by the bank. Experiences of this type have led creditors as a group to stress the desirability of conservatism in the valuation of assets.

In considering the argument for balance sheet conservatism, it is important to recognize that the income statement also is affected by the estimate made of uncollectible accounts. The act of providing a relatively large allowance for doubtful accounts involves a correspondingly heavy charge to expense. Setting asset values at a minimum in the balance sheet has the related effect of minimizing the amount of net income reported in the current period.

Monthly Adjustments of the Allowance Account In the adjusting entry made by World Famous Toy Co. at January 31, the amount of the adjustment ($10,000) was equal to the estimated amount of uncollectible accounts. This is true because January was the first month of operations and this was the company's first estimate of its uncollectible accounts. In future months, the amount of the adjusting entry will depend upon two factors: (1) the **estimate** of uncollectible accounts and (2) the **current balance** in the Allowance for Doubtful Accounts. Before we illustrate the adjusting entry for a future month, let us first see why the balance in the allowance account may change during the accounting period.

Writing Off an Uncollectible Account Receivable

Whenever an account receivable from a specific customer is determined to be uncollectible, it no longer qualifies as an asset and should be written off. To **write off** an account receivable is to reduce the balance of the customer's account to zero. The journal entry to accomplish this consists of a credit to the Accounts Receivable controlling account in the general ledger (and to the customer's account in the subsidiary ledger) and an offsetting debit to the **Allowance for Doubtful Accounts.**

To illustrate, assume that on February 15, World Famous Toy Co. learns that a customer, Discount Stores, has gone out of business and that the $4,000 account receivable from this customer is now worthless. The entry to write off this uncollectible account receivable is:

Writing off a receivable "against the allowance"	Allowance for Doubtful Accounts.................................	4,000
	Accounts Receivable (Discount Stores)	4,000
	To write off the receivable from Discount Stores as uncollectible.	

The important thing to note in this entry is that the debit is made to the **Allowance for Doubtful Accounts** and **not** to the Uncollectible Accounts Expense account. The estimated expense of credit losses is charged to the Uncollectible Accounts Expense account at the end of each accounting period. When a particular account receivable is later determined to be worthless and is written off, this action does not represent an additional expense but merely confirms our previous estimate of the expense. If the Uncollectible Accounts Expense account were first charged with **estimated** credit losses and then later charged with **proven** credit losses, we would be double counting the actual uncollectible accounts expense.

After the entry writing off the receivable from Discount Stores has been posted, the Accounts Receivable controlling account and the Allowance for Doubtful Accounts appear as follows:

Both accounts reduced by write-off of worthless receivable

Accounts Receivable

1994		1994	
Jan. 31	250,000	Feb. 15 (write-off)	4,000

Allowance for Doubtful Accounts

1994		1994	
Feb. 15 (write-off)	4,000	Jan. 31	10,000

Notice also that the entry to write off an uncollectible account receivable reduces both the asset account and the contra-asset account by the same amount. Thus, writing off an uncollectible account ***does not change*** the net realizable value of accounts receivable in the balance sheet. The following illustration shows the net realizable value of World Famous Toy Co.'s accounts receivable before and after the write-off of the account receivable from Discount Stores:

	Before the Write-Off		After the Write-Off	
Net value of receivables unchanged by write-off	Accounts receivable	$250,000	Accounts receivable	$246,000
	Less: Allowance for doubtful accounts	10,000	Less: Allowance for doubtful accounts	6,000
	Net value of receivables	$240,000	Net value of receivables	$240,000

The fact that writing off a worthless receivable against the Allowance for Doubtful Accounts does not change the net carrying value of accounts receivable shows that no expense is entered in the accounting records when an account receivable is written off. This example bears out the point stressed earlier in the chapter. ***Credit losses belong in the period in which the sale is made, not in a later period in which the account receivable is discovered to be uncollectible.*** This is another example of the use of the ***matching principle*** in determining net income.

Write-Offs Seldom Agree with Previous Estimates The total amount of accounts receivable actually written off will seldom, if ever, be exactly equal to the estimated amount previously credited to the Allowance for Doubtful Accounts.

If the amounts written off as uncollectible turn out to be less than the estimated amount, the Allowance for Doubtful Accounts will continue to show a credit balance. If the amounts written off as uncollectible are greater than the estimated amount, the Allowance for Doubtful Accounts will acquire a ***temporary debit balance,*** which will be eliminated by the adjustment at the end of the period.

Recovery of an Account Receivable Previously Written Off

Occasionally a receivable which has been written off as worthless will later be collected in full or in part. Such collections are often referred to as ***recoveries*** of bad debts. Collection of an account receivable previously written off is evidence that the write-off was an error; the receivable should therefore be reinstated as an asset.

Let us assume, for example, that a past-due account receivable in the amount of $200 from J. B. Barker was written off on February 16 by the following entry:

Barker account considered uncollectible

Allowance for Doubtful Accounts. 200
    Accounts Receivable (J. B. Barker) 200
To write off the receivable from J. B. Barker as uncollectible.

On February 27, the customer, J. B. Barker, pays the account in full. The entry to restore Barker's account will be:

Barker account reinstated	*Accounts Receivable (J. B. Barker)*................................	*200*
	Allowance for Doubtful Accounts	*200*
	To reinstate as an asset an account receivable previously written off.	

Notice that this entry is ***exactly the opposite*** of the entry made when the account was written off as uncollectible. A separate entry will be made in the cash receipts journal to record the collection from Barker. This entry will debit Cash and credit Accounts Receivable (J. B. Barker).

Monthly Estimates of Credit Losses

At the end of each month, management should again estimate the probable amount of uncollectible accounts ***and adjust the Allowance for Doubtful Accounts to this new estimate.***

To illustrate, assume that at the end of February the credit manager of World Famous Toy Company analyzes the accounts receivable and estimates that approximately ***$11,000*** of these accounts will prove uncollectible. Currently, the Allowance for Doubtful Accounts has a credit balance of only ***$6,000,*** determined as follows:

Current balance in the allowance account	*Balance at January 31 (credit)*		*$10,000*
	Less: Write-offs of accounts considered worthless:		
	Discount Stores	*$4,000*	
	J. B. Barker	*200*	*4,200*
	Subtotal...		*$ 5,800*
	Add: Recoveries of accounts previously written off: J. B. Barker		*200*
	Balance at end of February (prior to adjusting entry)...........................		*$ 6,000*

To increase the balance in the allowance account to $11,000 at February 28, the month-end adjusting entry must add $5,000 to the allowance. The entry will be:

Increasing the allowance for doubtful accounts	*Uncollectible Accounts Expense*		*5,000*
	Allowance for Doubtful Accounts		*5,000*
	To increase the Allowance for Doubtful Accounts to $11,000, computed as follows:		
	Required allowance at Feb. 28	*$11,000*	
	Credit balance prior to adjustment	*6,000*	
	Required adjustment.................................	*$ 5,000*	

Estimating Credit Losses—The "Balance Sheet" Approach The most widely used method of estimating the probable amount of uncollectible accounts is based upon an ***aging*** of the accounts receivable. This method is sometimes called the ***balance sheet*** approach, because the method emphasizes the proper balance sheet valuation of accounts receivable.

"Aging" accounts receivable means classifying each receivable according to its age. An aging schedule for the accounts receivable of Valley Ranch Supply is illustrated below:

Analysis of Accounts Receivable by Age
December 31, 1994

	Total	Not Yet Due	1–30 Days Past Due	31–60 Days Past Due	61–90 Days Past Due	Over 90 Days Past Due
Animal Care Center	$ 9,000	$ 9,000				
Butterfield, John D.	2,400			$ 2,400		
Citrus Groves, Inc.	4,000	3,000	$ 1,000			
Dairy Fresh Farms	1,600				$ 600	$1,000
Eastlake Stables	13,000	7,000	6,000			
(Other customers)	70,000	32,000	22,000	9,600	2,400	4,000
Totals	$100,000	$51,000	$29,000	$12,000	$3,000	$5,000

An aging schedule is useful to management in reviewing the status of individual accounts receivable and in evaluating the overall effectiveness of credit and collection policies. In addition, the schedule is used as the basis for estimating the amount of uncollectible accounts.

The longer an account is past due, the greater the likelihood that it will not be collected in full. Based upon past experience, the credit manager estimates the percentage of credit losses likely to occur in each age group of accounts receivable. This percentage, when applied to the total dollar amount in the age group, gives the estimated uncollectible portion for that group. By adding together the estimated uncollectible portions for all age groups, the ***required balance*** in the Allowance for Doubtful Accounts is determined. The following schedule lists the group totals from the aging schedule and shows how the estimated total amount of uncollectible accounts is computed:

Estimated Uncollectible Accounts Receivable
December 31, 1994

	Age Group Total	Percentage Considered Uncollectible*	Estimated Uncollectible Accounts
Not yet due	$ 51,000	1	$ 510
1–30 days past due	29,000	3	870
31–60 days past due	12,000	10	1,200
61–90 days past due	3,000	20	600
Over 90 days past due......	5,000	50	2,500
Totals...................	$100,000		$5,680

* These percentages are estimated each month by the credit manager, based upon recent experience and current economic conditions.

At December 31, Valley Ranch Supply has total accounts receivable of $100,000, of which $5,680 are estimated to be uncollectible. Thus, an adjusting entry is needed to increase the Allowance for Doubtful Accounts from its present level to $5,680. If the allowance account currently has a credit balance of, say, $4,000, the month-end adjusting entry should be in the amount of **$1,680.**[2]

An Alternative Approach to Estimating Credit Losses The procedures above describe the **balance sheet** approach to estimating and recording credit losses. This approach is based upon an aging schedule, and the Allowance for Doubtful Accounts is **adjusted to a required balance.** An alternative method, called the **income statement** approach, focuses upon estimating the uncollectible accounts **expense** for the period. Based upon past experience, the uncollectible accounts expense is estimated at some percentage of net credit sales. The adjusting entry is made in the **full amount of the estimated expense,** without regard for the current balance in the Allowance for Doubtful Accounts.

To illustrate, assume that a company's past experience indicates that about 2% of its credit sales prove to be uncollectible. If credit sales for September amount to $150,000, the month-end adjusting entry to record uncollectible accounts expense is:

The "income statement" approach

Uncollectible Accounts Expense	3,000	
Allowance for Doubtful Accounts		3,000

To record uncollectible accounts expense, estimated at 2% of credit sales ($150,000 × 2% = $3,000).

This approach is fast and simple—no aging schedule is required and no consideration is given to the existing balance in the Allowance for Doubtful Accounts. The aging of accounts receivable, however, provides a more reliable estimate of uncollectible accounts because of the consideration given to the age and collectibility of specific accounts receivable at the balance sheet date.

In past years, many small companies used the income statement approach as a shortcut in preparing monthly financial statements but used the balance sheet method in preparing annual financial statements. Today, however, most businesses have computer software that quickly and easily prepares monthly aging schedules of accounts receivable. Thus, most businesses today use the **balance sheet approach** in their monthly as well as annual financial statements.

---

[2] If accounts receivable written off during the period **exceed** the Allowance for Doubtful Accounts at the last adjustment date, the allowance account temporarily acquires a **debit balance.** This situation seldom occurs if the allowance is adjusted each month but often occurs if adjusting entries are made only at year-end.

    If Valley Ranch Supply makes only an annual adjustment for uncollectible accounts, the allowance account might have a debit balance of, say, $10,000. In this case, the year-end adjusting entry should be for **$15,680** in order to bring the allowance to the required credit balance of $5,680.

    Regardless of how often adjusting entries are made, the balance in the allowance account of Valley Ranch Supply should be **$5,680 at year-end.** Uncollectible accounts expense will be the same for the year regardless of whether adjusting entries are made annually or monthly. The only difference is in whether this expense is recognized in one annual adjusting entry or in 12 monthly adjusting entries, each for a smaller amount.

Direct Write-Off Method

OBJECTIVE 2
Compare the
allowance
method and
the direct
write-off
method of
accounting
for uncol-
lectible ac-
counts.

Some companies do not use any valuation allowance for accounts receivable. Instead of making end-of-period adjusting entries to record uncollectible accounts expense on the basis of estimates, these companies recognize no uncollectible accounts expense until specific receivables are determined to be worthless. This method makes no attempt to match revenue and related expenses. Uncollectible accounts expense is recorded in the period in which individual accounts receivable are determined to be worthless rather than in the period in which the sales were made.

When a particular customer's account is determined to be uncollectible, it is written off directly to Uncollectible Accounts Expense, as follows:

Uncollectible Accounts Expense 250
    Accounts Receivable (Bell Products) 250
To write off the receivable from Bell Products as uncollectible.

When the direct write-off method is in use, the accounts receivable will be listed in the balance sheet at their gross amount, and **no valuation allowance** will be used. The receivables, therefore, are not stated at estimated net realizable value.

In some situations, use of the direct write-off method is acceptable. If a company makes most of its sales for cash, the amount of its accounts receivable will be small in relation to other assets. The expense from uncollectible accounts should also be small. Consequently, the direct write-off method is acceptable because its use does not have a **material** effect on the reported net income. Another situation in which the direct write-off method works satisfactorily is in a company which sells all or most of its output to a few large companies which are financially strong. In this setting there may be no basis for making advance estimates of any credit losses.

Income Tax Regulations and Financial Reporting

In Chapter 1, we made the point that companies often use different accounting methods in preparing their income tax returns and their financial statements. The accounting treatments accorded to uncollectible accounts receivable provide an excellent example of this concept.

Current income tax regulations **require** taxpayers to use the direct write-off method in determining the uncollectible accounts expense used in computing **taxable income.** From a standpoint of accounting theory, the allowance method is better, because it enables expenses to be **matched** with the related revenue and thus provides a more logical measurement of net income. Therefore, most companies use the allowance method in their financial statements.[3]

---

[3] An annual survey of accounting practices of 600 publicly owned corporations consistently shows more than 500 of these companies using the allowance method in their financial statements. All of these companies, however, use the direct write-off method in their income tax returns.

Internal Controls for Receivables

One of the most important principles of internal control is that employees who have custody of cash or other negotiable assets must not maintain accounting records. In a small business, unfortunately, it is not uncommon to find that one employee has responsibility for handling cash receipts from customers, maintaining the accounts receivable records, issuing credit memos for goods returned by customers, and writing off receivables judged to be uncollectible. Such a combination of duties is an invitation to fraud. The employee in this situation is able to remove the cash collected from a customer without making any record of the collection. The next step is to dispose of the balance in the customer's account. This can be done by issuing a credit memo indicating that the customer has returned merchandise, or by writing off the customer's account as uncollectible. Thus, the employee has the cash, the customer's account shows a zero balance due, and the books are in balance.

To avoid fraud in the handling of receivables, some of the most important rules are that employees who maintain the accounts receivable subsidiary ledger must **not have access** to cash receipts, and employees who handle cash receipts must not have access to the records of receivables. Furthermore, **neither** the employees who maintain records of receivables **nor** those who handle cash receipts should have authority to issue credit memoranda or to authorize the write-off of receivables as uncollectible. These are classic examples of incompatible duties.

Management of Accounts Receivable

Management has two conflicting objectives with respect to the accounts receivable. On the one hand, management wants to generate as much sales revenue as possible. Offering customers lengthy credit terms, with little or no interest, has proven to be an effective means of generating sales revenue.

OBJECTIVE 3 Explain why accounts receivable may be viewed as "nonproductive" assets. Identify several ways of converting receivables quickly into cash.

Every business, however, would rather sell for cash than on account. Unless they earn interest, accounts receivable are a nonproductive asset which produce no revenue as they await collection. Therefore, another objective of management is to minimize the amount of money "tied up" in the form of accounts receivable.

Several tools are available to a management which must offer credit terms to its customers yet wants to minimize the company's investment in accounts receivable. We have already discussed offering credit customers cash discounts (such as 2/10, n/30) to encourage early payment. Other tools include factoring accounts receivable and selling to customers who use national credit cards.

Factoring Accounts Receivable

The term *factoring* describes transactions in which a business either sells its accounts receivable to a financial institution (often called a *factor*) or borrows money by pledging its accounts receivable as collateral (security) for the loan. In either case, the business obtains cash immediately instead of having to wait until the receivables can be collected.

The factoring of accounts receivable may create a potential liability to reimburse the factor for any losses sustained if some of the factored accounts are uncollectible. This "potential" liability is an example of *off-balance-sheet risk* which must be disclosed in notes to the financial statements. The disclosure of off-balance-sheet risk is discussed in Chapter 11.

Factoring accounts receivable is a practice limited primarily to small business organizations which do not have well-established credit. Large and solvent organizations usually are able to borrow money using unsecured lines of credit, so they need not factor their accounts receivable.

Credit Card Sales

*OBJECTIVE 4
Account for
sales to cus-
tomers using
credit cards.*

Many retailing businesses maximize sales opportunities while minimizing their investment in accounts receivable by making credit sales to customers who use well-known credit cards such as American Express, Visa, and MasterCard. A customer who makes a purchase using one of these cards must sign a multiple-copy form, which includes a *credit card draft*. A credit card draft is similar to a check which is drawn upon the funds of the credit card company rather than upon the personal bank account of the customer. The credit card company promptly pays cash to the merchant to redeem these drafts. At the end of each month, the credit card company bills the credit card holder for all the drafts it has redeemed during the month. If the credit card holder fails to pay the amount owed, it is the credit card company which sustains the loss.

By making sales through credit card companies, merchants receive cash more quickly from credit sales and avoid uncollectible accounts expense. Also, the merchant avoids the expenses of investigating customers' credit, maintaining an accounts receivable subsidiary ledger, and making collections from customers.

Bank Credit Cards   Some widely used credit cards (such as Visa and MasterCard) are issued by banks. When the credit card company is a bank, the retailing business may deposit the signed credit card drafts directly in its bank account, along with the currency and personal checks received from customers. Since banks accept these credit card drafts for immediate deposit, sales to customers using bank credit cards are recorded as *cash sales.*

In exchange for handling the credit card drafts, the bank makes a monthly service charge which usually runs between $1\frac{1}{4}$ and $3\frac{1}{2}\%$ of the amount of the drafts deposited by the merchant during the month. This monthly service charge is deducted from the merchant's bank account and appears with other bank service charges in the merchant's monthly bank statement.

Other Credit Cards   When customers use nonbank credit cards (such as American Express, Discover, and Carte Blanche), the retailing business cannot deposit the credit card drafts directly in its bank account. Instead of debiting Cash, the merchant records an account receivable from the credit card company. Periodically, the credit card drafts are mailed (or transmitted electronically) to the credit card company, which then sends a check to the merchant. Credit card companies, however, do not redeem the drafts at the full sales price. The agreement between the credit card company and the merchant usually allows the credit card company to take a discount of between $3\frac{1}{2}\%$ and 5% when redeeming the drafts.

To illustrate the procedures in accounting for these credit card sales, assume that Bradshaw Camera Shop sells a camera for $200 to a customer who uses a Quick Charge credit card. The entry would be:

This receivable is from the credit card company

Accounts Receivable (Quick Charge Co.) 200
     Sales 200
To record sale to customer using Quick Charge credit card.

At the end of the week, Bradshaw Camera Shop mails credit card drafts totaling $1,200 to Quick Charge Company, which redeems the drafts after deducting a 5% discount. When payment is received by Bradshaw, the entry is

Cash.. 1,140
Credit Card Discount Expense 60
    Accounts Receivable (Quick Charge Co.).................... 1,200
To record collection of account receivable from Quick Charge Co., less 5% discount.

The expense account, Credit Card Discount Expense, should be included among the selling expenses in the income statement of Bradshaw Camera Shop.

NOTES RECEIVABLE

OBJECTIVE 5
Explain
promissory
notes and
the nature
of interest.

A promissory note is an unconditional promise in writing to pay on demand or at a future date a definite sum of money.

The person who signs the note and thereby promises to pay is called the **maker** of the note. The person to whom payment is to be made is called the **payee** of the note. In the illustration below, G. L. Smith is the maker of the note and A. B. Davis is the payee.

Simplified form of promissory note

$100,000 Los Angeles, California	July 10, 19__

    One year   after date   I   promise to pay
to the order of   A. B. Davis
       ---One hundred thousand and no/100---   dollars
payable to   First National Bank of Los Angeles
for value received, with interest at   12% per annum
                          G. L. Smith

From the viewpoint of the maker, G. L. Smith, the illustrated note is a liability and is recorded by crediting the Notes Payable account. However, from the viewpoint of the payee, A. B. Davis, this same note is an asset and is recorded by debiting the Notes Receivable account. The maker of a note expects to pay cash at the **maturity date** (or due date); the payee expects to receive cash at that date.

Nature of Interest

Interest is a charge made for the use of money. A borrower incurs interest expense. A lender earns interest revenue. When you encounter notes payable in a company's financial statements, you know that the company is borrowing and you should expect to find interest expense. When you encounter notes receivable, you should expect interest revenue.

Computing Interest   A formula used in computing interest is as follows:

Principal × Rate of Interest × Time = Interest

(Often expressed as $P \times R \times T = I$)

Interest rates usually are stated on an **annual basis.** For example, the total interest charge on a $100,000 one-year, 12% note receivable is computed as follows:

$100,000 × 0.12 × 1 = $12,000

If the term of the note were only **four months** instead of one year, the total interest revenue earned in the life of the note would be $4,000, computed as shown below:

$100,000 × 0.12 × $\frac{4}{12}$ = $4,000

In making interest computations, it is convenient to assume that each month has **30** days, and a year has **360** days. Thus, each month represents $\frac{1}{12}$ of the year. As these assumptions greatly simplify the computation of interest and assist students in focusing upon the underlying concepts, we will use them in our illustrations and assignment material.[4]

If the term of a note is expressed in days, the exact number of days in each month must be considered in determining the maturity date of the note. The day on which a note is dated is not counted, but the date upon which it matures is. Thus, a two-day note dated today matures the day **after** tomorrow.

To illustrate these concepts, assume that a 60-day, 12% note for $100,000 is drawn on June 10. The **total** interest charge on this note will be $2,000, computed as follows:

$100,000 × 0.12 × $\frac{60}{360}$ = $2,000

---

[4]   Prior to the widespread use of computers, these assumptions were widely used in the business community. Today, however, most financial institutions compute interest using a 365-day year and the actual number of days in each month. The differences between these assumptions are **not material** in dollar amount.

The $102,000 maturity value of the note ($100,000 principal, plus $2,000 interest) will be payable on *August 9.* The maturity date is determined as follows:

Days remaining in June (30 − 10)	20
Days in July	31
Subtotal	51
Days in August needed to complete the term of the note (including maturity date)	9
Specified term of note (in days)	60

Accounting for Notes Receivable

In some fields of business, notes receivable are seldom encountered; in other fields they occur frequently and may constitute an important part of total assets. Business concerns that sell high-priced durable goods such as automobiles and farm machinery often accept notes receivable from their customers. Many companies obtain notes receivable in settlement of past-due accounts receivable.

All notes receivable are usually posted to a single account in the general ledger. A subsidiary ledger is not essential because the notes themselves, when filed by due dates, are the equivalent of a subsidiary ledger and provide any necessary information as to maturity, interest rates, collateral pledged, and other details. The amount debited to Notes Receivable is always the *face amount* of the note, regardless of whether or not the note bears interest. When an interest-bearing note is collected, the amount of cash received may be larger than the face amount of the note. The interest collected is credited to an Interest Revenue account, and only the face amount of the note is credited to the Notes Receivable account.

Illustrative Entries Assume that on December 1 a 90-day, 12% note receivable is acquired from a customer, Marvin White, in settlement of an existing account receivable of $30,000. The entry for acquisition of the note is as follows:

Note received to replace account receivable

Notes Receivable	30,000	
Accounts Receivable (Marvin White)		30,000
Accepted 90-day, 12% note in settlement of account receivable.		

At December 31, the end of the company's fiscal year, the interest earned to date on notes receivable should be accrued by an adjusting entry as follows:

Adjusting entry for interest revenue earned in December

Interest Receivable	300	
Interest Revenue		300
To accrue interest for the month of December on Marvin White note ($30,000 × 12% × $\frac{1}{12}$ = $300).		

On March 1 (90 days after the date of the note) the note matures. The entry to record collection of the note will be:

Collection of principal and interest

Cash	*30,900*	
Notes Receivable		*30,000*
Interest Receivable		*300*
Interest Revenue		*600*

Collected 90-day, 12% note from Marvin White ($30,000 × 12% × $\frac{3}{12}$ = $900 interest of which $600 was earned in current year).

The preceding three entries show that interest is being earned throughout the life of the note and that the interest should be apportioned between years on a time basis. The revenue of each year will then include the interest actually earned in that year.

If the Maker of a Note Defaults A note receivable which cannot be collected at maturity is said to have been ***defaulted*** by the maker. Immediately after the default of a note, an entry should be made by the holder to transfer the amount due from the Notes Receivable account to an account receivable from the debtor.

To illustrate, assume that on March 1, our customer, Marvin White, had defaulted on the note used in the preceding example. In this case, the entry on March 1 would have been:

Accounts Receivable (Marvin White)	*30,900*	
Notes Receivable		*30,000*
Interest Receivable		*300*
Interest Revenue		*600*

To record default by Marvin White on 90-day, 12% note.

Notice that the interest earned on the note is recorded through the maturity date and is included in the account receivable from the maker. The interest receivable on a defaulted note is just as valid a claim against the maker as is the principal amount of the note.

If the account receivable from White cannot be collected, it ultimately will be written off against the Allowance for Doubtful Accounts. Therefore, the balance in the Allowance for Doubtful Accounts should provide for estimated uncollectible ***notes*** receivable as well as uncollectible ***accounts*** receivable.

CASE IN POINT For many companies, the provision for doubtful accounts is small and does not have a material effect upon net income for the period. Notes receivable, however, are the largest and most important asset for nearly every bank. Interest on these notes is a bank's largest and most important type of revenue. Thus, the collectibility of notes owned by a bank is a key factor in determining the success or failure of that bank.

Citicorp, the nation's largest bank, recently added a staggering $3 billion to its allowance for doubtful loans to developing countries. The related debit to expense caused Citicorp to report one of the largest net losses for a single quarter (three-month period) in the history of American business. Citicorp is not alone in having problems with uncollectible loans. In recent years, uncollectible loans have been the largest expense in the income statements of many American banks and savings and loan associations.

Renewal of a Note Receivable Sometimes the two parties to a note agree that the note shall be renewed rather than paid at the maturity date. In this situation a new note should be prepared and the old one canceled. If the old note does not bear interest, the entry could be made as follows:

Renewal of note should be recorded

Notes Receivable	*10,000*	
Notes Receivable		*10,000*

A 60-day, non-interest-bearing note from Bell Company renewed today with new 60-day, 14% note.

Since the above entry causes no change in the balance of the Notes Receivable account, a question may arise as to whether the entry is necessary. The renewal of a note is an important transaction requiring managerial attention; a general journal entry is needed to record the action taken by management and to provide a permanent record of the transaction. If journal entries were not made to record the renewal of notes, confusion might arise as to whether some of the notes included in the balance of the Notes Receivable account were current or defaulted.

Discounting Notes Receivable In past years, some companies sold their notes receivable to banks in order to obtain cash prior to the maturity dates of these notes. As the banks purchased these notes at a "discount" from their maturity values, this practice became known as ***discounting*** notes receivable.

Discounting notes receivable is not a widespread practice today, because most banks no longer purchase notes receivable from their customers. Interestingly, the discounting of notes receivable remains a common practice among banks themselves. Many banks sell large "packages" of notes receivable (loans) to agencies of the federal government or to other financial institutions.

If a business organization wants to convert its receivables into cash prior to their maturity dates, it usually enters into some type of factoring arrangement. Accounting for the factoring of receivables varies with the terms and conditions of the contract between the company and the factor. Various factoring arrangements will be discussed in more advanced accounting courses.

Evaluating the Quality of Notes and Accounts Receivable

In the annual audit of a company by a CPA firm, the independent auditors will verify receivables by communicating directly with the customers of the company and with the makers of notes receivable. This ***confirmation*** process is designed to provide evidence that the customers and other debtors actually exist, and that they acknowledge the indebtedness. The CPA firm may also verify the credit rating of debtors.

Any company with large amounts of receivables needs the assurance of an annual audit to guard against the possibility that worthless notes and accounts receivable from bankrupt firms or fictitious customers may have been disguised as genuine assets. The quality of receivables may also be appraised by an internal auditing staff which will study the adequacy of the internal controls over such activities as the granting of credit, accounting for receivables, and the prompt recognition of credit losses.

OBJECTIVE 6
Compute the
accounts
receivable
turnover
rate. Ex-
plain why
this ratio is
of interest to
short-term
creditors.

Accounts Receivable Turnover Collecting accounts receivable ***on time*** is important; it spells the success or failure of a company's credit and collection policies. A past-due receivable is a candidate for write-off as a credit loss. To help us judge how good a job a company is doing in granting credit and collecting its receivables, we compute the ratio of net sales to average receivables. This ***accounts receivable turnover rate*** tells us how many times the receivables were converted into cash during the year.[5] The ratio is computed by dividing annual net sales by average accounts receivable.

For example, recent financial statements of 3M (Minnesota Mining and Manufacturing Company) show net sales of $9.4 billion. Receivables were $1.6 billion at the beginning of the year and $1.4 billion at the end of the year. Adding these two amounts and dividing the total by 2 gives us average receivables of $1.5 billion. Now we divide the year's net sales by the average receivables ($9.4 ÷ $1.5 = 6.3); the result indicates an accounts receivable turnover rate of 6.3 times per year for 3M. The higher the turnover rate the more liquid the company's receivables.

Another step that will help us judge the liquidity of a company's accounts receivable is to convert the accounts receivable turnover rate to the number of days (on average) required for the company to collect its accounts receivable. This is a simple calculation: divide the number of days in the year by the turnover rate. Continuing our 3M example, divide 365 days by turnover of 6.3 (365 ÷ 6.3 = 57.9). This calculation tells us that on average, 3M waited approximately 58 days to make collection of a sale on credit.

The data described above for computing the accounts receivable turnover rate and the average number of days to collect accounts receivable can be concisely stated as shown in the following equations:

Accounts Receivable Turnover

$$\frac{\text{Net Sales}}{\text{Average Accounts Receivable}} = \frac{\$9.4}{(\$1.6 + \$1.4) \div 2} = \frac{\$9.4}{\$1.5} = 6.3 \text{ times}$$

Average Number of Days to Collect Accounts Receivable

$$\frac{\text{Days in Year}}{\text{Accounts Receivable Turnover}} = \frac{365}{6.3} = 58 \text{ days}$$

Management closely monitors these ratios in evaluating the company's policies for extending credit to customers and the effectiveness of its collection procedures. Short-term creditors, such as factors, banks, and merchandise suppliers, also use these ratios in evaluating a company's ability to generate the cash necessary to pay it short-term liabilities.

Concentrations of Credit Risk Assume that a business operates a single retail store in a town in which the major employer is a steel mill. What would happen to the collectibility of the store's accounts receivable if the steel mill were to close, leaving most of the store's customers unemployed? This situation illustrates what accountants call a ***concentration of credit***

---

[5] From a conceptual point of view, net ***credit*** sales should be used in computing the accounts receivable turnover rate. It is common practice, however, to use the net sales figure, as the portion of net sales made on account usually is not disclosed in financial statements.

risk, because many of the store's credit customers can be affected *in a similar manner* by certain changes in economic conditions. Concentrations of credit risk occur if a significant portion of a company's receivables are due from a few major customers or from customers operating in the same industry or geographic region.

The FASB requires companies to disclose all *significant* concentrations of credit risk in the notes accompanying their financial statements. The disclosure includes (1) the economic characteristics defining each "concentration," (2) the amount of receivables within each concentration, and (3) the company's policies for requiring collateral (if any).[6] The basic purpose of these disclosures is to assist users of the financial statements in evaluating the extent of the company's vulnerability to credit losses stemming from changes in economic conditions.

■ ■ ■   * *Supplemental Topic*
Notes Receivable with Interest Charges Included in the Face Amount

*OBJECTIVE 7
Account for notes receivable with the interest charges included in the face amount.*

In our discussion to this point, we have used notes receivable with the interest rate *stated separately.* We now want to compare this form of note with an alternative form in which the interest charge is *included in the face amount* of the note. For example, assume that Genetic Services has a $10,000 account receivable from a customer, Biolab. The customer is short of cash and wants to postpone payment, so Genetic Services agrees to accept a six-month promissory note from Biolab with interest at the rate of 12% a year to replace the $10,000 account receivable. The interest for six months will amount to $600 and the total amount to be received at maturity will be $10,000 principal plus $600 interest, or $10,600 altogether.

If the note is drawn with interest stated separately, as in the illustration below, the wording will be ". . . Biolab promises to pay to Genetic Services the sum of $10,000 with interest at the rate of 12% per year."

This note is for the principal amount with interest stated separately

Miami, Florida   November 1, 19___

_____ Six months _____ after this date _____ Biolab _____

promises to pay to Genetic Services the sum of $ _____ 10,000 _____

with interest at the rate of _____ 12% per year _____

Signed _____ *George Harr* _____

Title _____ Treasurer, Biolab _____

---

[6]   FASB, *Statement No. 105,* "Disclosure about Financial Instruments with Off-Balance-Sheet Risk and Financial Instruments with Concentrations of Credit Risk" (Norwalk, Conn.: 1990), para. 20.

If the alternative form of note is used, the $600 interest will be included in the face amount and the note will appear as shown below:

Interest is included in face amount of this note

```
Miami, Florida                                    November 1, 19__

       Six months          after this date        Biolab

promises to pay to Genetic Services the sum of $ _____ 10,600 _____


                                      Signed    George Harr

                                      Title    Treasurer, Biolab
```

Notice that the face amount of the note ($10,600) is **greater** than the $10,000 account receivable which it replaces. However, the value of the note receivable at November 1 is only $10,000; the other $600 included in the face amount of the note represents **unearned interest revenue.** As this interest revenue is earned over the life of the note, the value of the note will rise to $10,600 at maturity.

The journal entry by Genetic Services at November 1 to record the acquisition of the note will be as follows:

Interest included in face of note

Notes Receivable	*10,600*	
Discount on Notes Receivable		*600*
Accounts Receivable		*10,000*
Obtained from Biolab a six-month note with a $600 interest		
charge included in the face amount.		

The asset account, Notes Receivable, was debited with the full face amount of the note ($10,600). It is, therefore, necessary to credit a contra-asset, Discount on Notes Receivable, for the $600 of future interest revenue included in the face amount of the note. The Discount on Notes Receivable will appear in the balance sheet as a deduction from Notes Receivable. In our illustration, the amounts in the balance sheet will be Notes Receivable, $10,600 **minus** Discount on Notes Receivable, $600, or a **net** asset value of $10,000 on November 1.

Discount on Notes Receivable   The $600 balance of the account Discount on Notes Receivable at November 1 represents **unearned interest revenue.** As this interest revenue is earned over the life of the note, the amount in the discount account will be gradually transferred into Interest Revenue. Thus, at the maturity date of the note, Discount on Notes Receivable will have a zero balance and the value of the note receivable will have increased to $10,600. The process of transferring the amount in the Discount on Notes Receivable account into the Interest Revenue account is called **amortization** of the discount.

Amortization of the Discount The discount on ***short-term*** notes receivable usually is amortized by the straight-line method, which allocates the ***same amount*** of discount to interest revenue for each month of the note's life.[7] Thus, the $600 discount on the Biolab note will be transferred from Discount on Notes Receivable into Interest Revenue at the rate of ***$100 per month*** ($600 ÷ 6 months).

Adjusting entries should be made to amortize the discount at the end of each accounting period and at the date the note matures. At December 31, Genetic Services will make the following adjusting entry to recognize the two months' interest revenue earned since November 1:

Amortization of discount

Discount on Notes Receivable	200	
Interest Revenue		200
To record interest revenue earned to end-of-year on six-month note dated Nov. 1 ($600 discount × $\frac{2}{6}$).		

At December 31, the net valuation of the note receivable will appear in the balance sheet of Genetic Services as shown below:

Asset shown net of discount

Current assets:		
Notes receivable	$10,600	
Less: Discount on notes receivable	400	$10,200

The net asset valuation of $10,200 consists of the $10,000 principal amount receivable from Biolab plus the $200 interest which has been earned since November 1.

When the note matures on May 1 of the following year, Genetic Services will recognize the $400 interest revenue earned since December 31 and will collect $10,600 from Biolab. The entry is:

Two-thirds of interest applicable to second year

Cash...	10,600	
Discount on Notes Receivable	400	
Interest Revenue		400
Notes Receivable..		10,600
To record collection of six-month note due today and to recognize four months' interest revenue earned since year-end ($600 discount × $\frac{4}{6}$ = $400).		

Comparison of the Two Forms of Notes Receivable

We have illustrated two alternative methods which Genetic Services could use in accounting for its $10,000 receivable, depending upon the form of the note. Journal entries for both methods, along with the resulting balance sheet presentations of the asset at November 1 and December 31, are summarized on the next page. Notice that both methods result in Genetic Services recognizing the ***same amount of interest revenue*** and the ***same overall asset valuation*** in the balance sheet. The form of the note does ***not change the economic substance*** of the transaction.

---

[7] When an interest charge is included in the face amount of a ***long-term*** note, the effective interest method of amortizing the discount is often used instead of the straight-line method. The effective interest method of amortization is explained and illustrated in Chapter 11.

Comparison of the Two Forms of Notes Receivable

	Note Written for $10,000 Plus 12% Interest	Note Written with Interest Included in Face Amount

Entry to record acquisition of note on Nov. 1	Notes Receivable 10,000
	  Accounts Receivable 10,000
		Notes Receivable 10,600
		  Discount on Notes Receivable 600
		  Accounts Receivable 10,000

Partial balance sheet at Nov. 1	Current assets: Notes receivable $10,000	Current assets: Notes receivable .... $10,600 Less: Discount on notes receivable 600 $10,000

Adjusting entry at Dec. 31	Interest Receivable 200
	  Interest Revenue 200
		Discount on Notes Receivable 200
		  Interest Revenue 200

Partial balance sheet at Dec. 31	Current assets: Notes receivable .... $10,000 Interest receivable 200 $10,200	Current assets: Notes receivable .... $10,600 Less: Discount on notes receivable 400 $10,200

Entry to record collection of note on May 1	Cash 10,600
	  Notes Receivable 10,000
	  Interest Receivable 200
	  Interest Revenue 400
		Cash 10,600
		Discount on Notes Receivable 400
		  Interest Revenue 400
		  Notes Receivable 10,600

THE CONCEPT OF PRESENT VALUE

OBJECTIVE 8 Discuss the concept of present value in accounting for long-term notes receivable.

Consider again the note receivable from Biolab in which interest is included in the face amount. The only dollar amount which appears in this note is **$10,600**—the maturity value. Yet this note appears in Genetic Services' November 1 balance sheet at a net valuation of only **$10,000.** Where did this $10,000 amount come from, and what does it represent?

At November 1, $10,000 is the **present value** to Genetic Services of the right to collect $10,600 at a date six months in the future. The term **present value** means the economic value **today** of a cash flow which will occur at some future date.

It is helpful to think of present value as the **amount that a knowledgeable investor would pay today for the right to receive the future cash amount.** Because an investor expects to earn a profit (or interest) on an investment, the present value is **always less** than the full amount of the future cash flow.

The **difference** between the present value and the actual future amount is viewed as an **interest charge** included in the future amount. Often the present value of a note receivable is apparent from the current market values of the assets or services which are **given in exchange** for the note. In our current illustration, for example, Genetic Services accepts the note from Biolab at November 1 in full settlement of a $10,000 account receivable. This provides evidence that the current economic value (present value) of the note receivable on this date is $10,000.

In the assignment material for this chapter, the present value of notes receivable will be apparent from the value of the assets given in exchange. In practice, however, this is not always the case. When the present value of future cash flows is not apparent from the other values in a transaction, it must be computed by mathematical techniques.[8]

An Illustration of Notes Recorded at Present Value

To illustrate the use of present value in transactions involving long-term notes receivable, let us assume that on September 1, Tru-Tool, Inc., sells equipment to Everts Company and accepts as payment a one-year note in the face amount of $218,000 with no mention of an interest rate. It is not logical to assume that Tru-Tool, Inc., would extend credit for one year without charging any interest. Therefore, some portion of the $218,000 face amount of the note **should be regarded as a charge for interest.**

Let us assume that the regular sales price of the equipment sold in this transaction is $200,000. In this case the **present value** of the note is apparently **$200,000,** and the remaining $18,000 of the face amount represents a charge for interest. (The rate of interest which will cause the $200,000 present value of the note to increase to the $218,000 maturity value in one year is 9%. Thus, the face amount of the note actually includes an interest charge computed at the effective annual interest rate of 9%.)

The selling company, Tru-Tool, Inc., should use the **present value** of the note in determining the amount of revenue to be recognized from the sale. The $18,000 interest charge included in the face amount of the note receivable from Everts Company represents **unearned interest revenue** to

---

[8] The mathematical computation of present values is discussed in Chapter 25 and in Appendix D, which is intended for use following Chapter 16.

Tru-Tool, Inc., and is **not part of the sales price of the equipment.** If Tru-Tool, Inc., were to treat the entire face amount of the note receivable as the sales price of the equipment, the result would be to overstate sales revenue and notes receivable by $18,000, and also to understate interest revenue by this amount over the life of the note.

At September 1, the date of sale, Tru-Tool, Inc., should record as sales revenue only an amount equal to the **present value** of the note receivable. The portion of the note which is regarded as unearned interest revenue ($18,000) should be credited to the contra-asset account, Discount on Notes Receivable. Thus, the entry to record the sale of equipment to Everts Company at September 1 is as follows:

Present value of the note begins at $200,000—the sales price	*Notes Receivable* *218,000*	
	Discount on Notes Receivable	*18,000*
	Sales	*200,000*
	Sold equipment to Everts Company and received a one-year note with an $18,000 interest charge included in the face amount.	

As the $18,000 interest is earned over the life of the note, this amount gradually will be transferred into Interest Revenue. At December 31, Tru-Tool, Inc., will have earned four months' interest revenue and will make the following entry:

Present value has increased $6,000 by Dec. 31	*Discount on Notes Receivable* *6,000*	
	Interest Revenue	*6,000*
	To record interest earned from Sept. 1 through Dec. 31 on Everts Company note ($18,000 discount × $\frac{4}{12}$).	

On September 1 of the following year, when the note receivable is collected from Everts Company, the required entry will be:

Present value has risen to $218,000 by maturity date	*Cash* *218,000*	
	Discount on Notes Receivable *12,000*	
	Interest Revenue	*12,000*
	Notes Receivable	*218,000*
	To record collection of Everts Company note and to recognize eight months' interest earned since year-end.	

In an earlier era of accounting practice, failure to use the concept of present value in recording transactions involving long-term notes sometimes resulted in large overstatements of assets and sales revenue, especially by real estate development companies. In recognition of this problem, the Financial Accounting Standards Board now requires the use of present value in recording transactions involving **long-term** notes receivable or payable which do not bear reasonable stated rates of interest.

If prevailing interest rates change, the present value (or **fair value**) of a company's long-term notes receivable also may change. Such changes in present value are **not** recorded in the company's accounting records. However, the company may need to **disclose** the fair value of its long-term notes receivables at the balance sheet date in the notes to its financial statements.[9] Disclosure of the fair value of notes receivable and other financial instruments will be discussed further in Chapter 16.

When a note is issued for a short period of time, any interest charge included in its face amount is likely to be relatively small. Therefore, the use of present value is not required in recording normal transactions with customers or suppliers involving notes due in less than one year. Notes given or received in such transactions which do not specify an interest rate may be considered non-interest-bearing.

Installment Receivables

Another application of present value is found in the recording of *installment sales.* Many retailing businesses sell merchandise on installment sales plans, which permit customers to pay for their credit purchases through a series of monthly payments. The importance of installment sales is emphasized by a recent balance sheet of Sears, Roebuck, and Company, which shows about $17 billion of receivables, nearly all of which call for collection in monthly installments.

When merchandise is sold on an installment plan, substantial interest charges are usually added to the "cash selling price" of the product in determining the total dollar amount to be collected in the series of installment payments. The amount of sales revenue recognized at the time of sale, however, is limited to the *present value* of these installment payments. In most cases, the present value of these future payments is equal to the regular sales price of the merchandise. The portion of the installment account receivable which represents unearned finance charges is credited to the contra-asset account, Discount on Installment Receivables. Thus, the entry to recognize the revenue on an installment sale consists of a debit to Installment Contracts Receivable, offset by a credit to Discount on Installment Receivables for the unearned finance charges and a credit to Sales for the regular sales price of the merchandise. The balance of the contra-asset account, Discount on Installment Receivables, is then amortized into Interest Revenue over the length of the collection period.

Although the collection period for an installment receivable often runs as long as 24 to 36 months, such receivables are regarded as current assets if they correspond to customary credit terms of the industry. In published balance sheets, the Discount on Installment Receivables is often called *Deferred Interest Income* or *Unearned Finance Charges.* A typical balance sheet presentation of installment accounts receivable is illustrated below:

Trade accounts receivable:	
Accounts receivable	$ 75,040,000
Installment contracts receivable, including $31,000,000 due after one year.	52,640,000
	$127,680,000
Less: Deferred interest income ($8,070,000) and allowance for doubtful	
accounts ($1,872,000)..	9,942,000
Total trade accounts and notes receivable	$117,738,000

---

[9] FASB, *Statement No. 107,* "Disclosure about Fair Value of Financial Instruments" (Norwalk, Conn.: 1991), para. 10-11

Income Tax Aspects of Installment Sales Current provisions of the federal income tax law permit sellers to spread the recognition of the gross profit from installment sales over the years in which collections are received. The result of this treatment is to postpone the recognition of taxable income and the payment of income tax. In financial statements, however, the entire gross profit from installment sales is recognized ***in the period in which the sale occurs.*** The method of recognizing gross profit from installment sales for income tax purposes will be illustrated in Chapter 13. There are a number of other more complex issues relating to installment sales; these are covered in advanced accounting courses.

END-OF-CHAPTER REVIEW

SUMMARY OF CHAPTER LEARNING OBJECTIVES

1 **Prepare estimates of uncollectible accounts receivable, write off any accounts known to be uncollectible, and record any later recoveries.**
To accomplish the objective of matching revenue with all related expenses, the portion of each period's credit sales that will prove to be uncollectible must be estimated. This estimated amount is recorded by a debit to Uncollectible Accounts Expense and a credit to the contra-asset account, Allowance for Doubtful Accounts. When specific accounts are determined to be uncollectible, they are written off by debiting Allowance for Doubtful Accounts and crediting Accounts Receivable.

Occasionally a receivable which has been written off as worthless will later be collected. Such collections are called recoveries of bad debts. Two accounting entries are needed: (1) to reinstate the receivable by debiting Accounts Receivable and crediting the Allowance for Doubtful Accounts and (2) to record the collection by debiting Cash and crediting Accounts Receivable.

2 **Compare the allowance method and the direct write-off method of accounting for uncollectible accounts.**
The allowance method is theoretically preferable because it applies the matching principle to revenue and to the expenses incurred in producing that revenue. Thus, bad debts associated with the year's sales are recognized as expenses of the period in which the sales were made. However, some companies (for which bad debts are not material) use the direct write-off method. Under this method, no uncollectible accounts expense is recognized until specific receivables are determined to be worthless. (Only the direct write-off method may be used in income tax returns.)

3 **Explain why accounts receivable may be viewed as "nonproductive" assets. Identify several ways of converting receivables quickly into cash.**
While awaiting collection, an account receivable generates no revenue unless it earns interest. Thus, accounts receivable which do not earn interest may be viewed as "nonproductive" assets.

Management can convert accounts receivable into cash quickly by: (1) offering discounts to customers that pay early, (2) selling to customers who use national credit cards, (3) borrowing against the receivables, or (4) selling (or discounting) the receivables to a factor or to a bank.

4 Account for sales to customers using credit cards.

Many retailing businesses avoid the risk of credit losses and the work of maintaining accounts receivable records by limiting sales on credit to those customers who present well-known credit cards such as Visa or American Express.

For credit cards issued by **banks**, the retailing business can deposit the signed credit card drafts in its bank account just as it would currency and customers' checks. For **nonbank** credit cards, such as American Express and Discover, the merchant collects directly from the credit card company, which deducts a service charge.

5 Explain promissory notes and the nature of interest.

A promissory note is an unconditional promise to pay on demand or at a future date a fixed sum of money. Companies that sell high-priced durable goods, such as farm machinery, regularly accept notes receivable from their customers. Sales of all types of merchandise on the installment plan also usually involve the use of notes. In addition, notes receivable are obtained by many companies in settlement of past-due accounts receivable.

Notes receivable usually bear interest, computed at an annual rate by the formula "Principal × Rate × Time = Interest." Interest is a charge for the use of money. Annual rates have varied widely in recent years with the prime rate rising to about 20% and then declining to its present level of about 8%.

6 Compute the accounts receivable turnover rate. Explain why this ratio is of interest to short-term creditors.

The accounts receivable turnover rate is computed by dividing annual net sales by the average amount of accounts receivable throughout the year. This rate indicates the number of **times** during the year that the average amount of accounts receivable is collected. Thus, dividing 365 days by the accounts receivable turnover rate indicates the number of **days** required (on average) for the company to collect its accounts receivable.

These computations are of interest to short-term creditors because they indicate the **liquidity** of the company's accounts receivable—that is, how quickly these assets convert into cash.

*7 Account for notes receivable with the interest charges included in the face amount.

A note may be drawn with the interest included in the face amount, as an alternative to stating the interest separately. Such notes are recorded at the face amount and the future interest is credited to Discount on Notes Receivable. The discount represents unearned interest and is amortized to Interest Revenue over the life of the note.

---

* *Supplemental Topic, "Notes Receivable with Interest Charges Included in the Face Amount"*

*8 Discuss the concept of present value in accounting for long-term notes receivable.

An amount of money to be received at a future date is equivalent to a smaller amount available today. If a long-term note receivable does not include a reasonable stated rate of interest, the present value of the note is less than its face amount. The entry to record the note will include a debit to Notes Receivable for the face amount and a credit to Discount on Notes Receivable for the difference between the face amount and the present value. The discount is earned over the life of the note and transferred to Interest Revenue. The carrying value of the note rises gradually to reach the face amount by the maturity date.

In this chapter we have explored the valuation of accounts receivable and notes receivable in financial statements. The current threat of large-scale insolvencies of many banks and savings and loan associations is dramatic evidence that the valuation of notes receivable can be of critical importance. In the following chapter, we will again explore the issue of asset valuation—this time in the area of inventories.

KEY TERMS INTRODUCED OR EMPHASIZED IN CHAPTER 8

Accounts receivable turnover A ratio used to measure the liquidity of accounts receivable and the reasonableness of the accounts receivable balance. Computed by dividing net sales by average receivables.

Aging the accounts receivable The process of classifying accounts receivable by age groups such as current, past due 1–30 days, past due 31–60 days, etc. A step in estimating the uncollectible portion of the accounts receivable.

Allowance for Doubtful Accounts A valuation account or contra account relating to accounts receivable and showing the portion of the receivables estimated to be uncollectible.

Collateral (for a loan) Assets pledged to secure a borrower's promise to repay a loan. In the event that the borrower fails to repay the loan, the creditor may foreclose against (take title to) the collateral.

Concentration of credit risk A significant portion of receivables due from one customer or from a group of customers likely to be affected in a similar manner by changes in economic conditions.

Conservatism A traditional practice of resolving uncertainties by choosing an asset valuation at the lower point of the range of reasonableness. Also refers to the policy of postponing recognition of revenue to a later date when a range of reasonable choice exists. Designed to avoid overstatement of financial strength and earnings.

Contingent liability A potential liability which either will develop into a full-fledged liability or will be eliminated entirely by a future event.

Contra-asset account A ledger account which is deducted from or offset against a related account in the financial statements—for example, Allowance for Doubtful Accounts and Discount on Notes Receivable.

Default Failure to pay interest or principal of a promissory note at the due date.

Direct write-off method A method of accounting for uncollectible receivables in which no expense is recognized until individual accounts are determined to be

---

* *Supplemental Topic, "Notes Receivable with Interest Charges Included in the Face Amount"*

worthless. At that point the account receivable is written off with an offsetting debit to uncollectible accounts expense. Fails to match revenue and related expenses.

Discount on Notes Receivable A contra-asset account representing any unearned interest included in the face amount of a note receivable. Over the life of the note, the balance of the Discount on Notes Receivable account is amortized into Interest Revenue.

Discounting notes receivable Selling a note receivable prior to its maturity date.

Effective interest rate The rate of interest which will cause the present value of a note to increase to the maturity value by the maturity date.

Factoring accounts receivable Transactions in which a business either sells its accounts receivable to a financial institution (often called a ***factor***) or borrows money by pledging its accounts receivable as collateral.

Interest A charge made for the use of money. The formula for computing interest is Principal × Rate of interest × Time = Interest ($P \times R \times T = I$).

Maker (of a note) A person or an entity who issues a promissory note.

Maturity date The date on which a note becomes due and payable.

Maturity value The value of a note at its maturity date, consisting of principal plus interest.

Payee The person named in a promissory note to whom payment is to be made (the creditor).

Present value of a future cash receipt The amount of money which an informed investor would pay today for the right to receive that future cash receipt. The present value is always less than the future amount, because money available today can be invested to earn interest and thereby become equivalent to a larger amount in the future.

Proceeds The amount received from selling a note receivable prior to its maturity. Maturity value minus discount equals proceeds.

DEMONSTRATION PROBLEM FOR YOUR REVIEW

Shown below are selected transactions of Gulf Corporation during the month of June:

June 1 Accepted a one-year promissory note from Target Company in settlement of a $30,000 account receivable due today. The note is drawn in the face amount of $32,700, with no mention of interest.

June 10 An account receivable from S. Willis in the amount of $700 is determined to be uncollectible and is written off against Allowance for Doubtful Accounts.

June 15 Made a loan of $120,000 to a supplier, Casa Blanca, Inc., in exchange for a three-year, 8% note. The note is drawn in the face amount of $120,000, with interest and principal due at maturity date.

June 22 Unexpectedly received $200 from F. Hill in full payment of her account. The $200 account receivable from Hill had previously been written off as uncollectible.

DATA FOR ADJUSTING ENTRIES

1 An aging of accounts receivable indicates probable uncollectible accounts totaling $9,000. At the end of May, the Allowance for Doubtful Accounts had a credit balance of $5,710.

2 In addition to the notes from Target Company and from Casa Blanca, Inc., Gulf Corporation held other notes receivable totaling $33,000 throughout the month of June. All these other notes bear interest at an annual rate of 10%. (Assume 360 days in a year.)

INSTRUCTIONS   a Prepare entries in general journal form for the June transactions.

b Prepare the month-end adjustments indicated by the two numbered paragraphs, as well as any additional adjustments for the notes received on June 1 and June 15.

SOLUTION TO DEMONSTRATION PROBLEM

a
General Journal

June 1	Notes Receivable	32,700	
	Discount on Notes Receivable		2,700
	Accounts Receivable (Target Co.)		30,000
	Received a one-year note receivable with interest included in the face amount.		
10	Allowance for Doubtful Accounts	700	
	Accounts Receivable (S. Willis)		700
	To write off receivable from S. Willis as uncollectible.		
15	Notes Receivable	120,000	
	Cash		120,000
	Made loan to Casa Blanca, Inc., in exchange for a three-year, 8% note receivable.		
22	Accounts Receivable (F. Hill)	200	
	Allowance for Doubtful Accounts		200
	To reinstate account receivable previously written off as uncollectible.		
22	Cash	200	
	Accounts Receivable (F. Hill)		200
	To record collection of account receivable.		

b
Adjusting Entries

June 30	Uncollectible Accounts Expense	3,790	
	Allowance for Doubtful Accounts		3,790
	To increase Allowance for Doubtful Accounts to $9,000 ($9,000 − [$5,710 − $700 + $200] = $3,790).		
30	Discount on Notes Receivable	225	
	Interest Revenue		225
	To record interest revenue earned during June on one-year note dated June 1 ($2,700 discount $\times \frac{1}{12}$).		
30	Interest Receivable	675	
	Interest Revenue		675
	To accrue interest on notes receivable for June (Casa Blanca note: $120,000 \times 8\% \times \frac{15}{360} = $400; other notes: $33,000 \times 10\% \times \frac{1}{12} = $275).		

SELF-TEST QUESTIONS

The answers to these questions appear on page 404.

1 Which of the following best describes the application of generally accepted accounting principles to the valuation of accounts receivable?

a Realization principle—Accounts receivable are shown at their net realizable value in the balance sheet.

b   Matching principle—The loss due to an uncollectible account is recognized in the period in which the sale is made, not in the period in which the account receivable is determined to be worthless.

c   Cost principle—Accounts receivable are shown at the initial cost of the merchandise to customers, less the cost the seller must pay to cover uncollectible accounts.

d   Principle of conservatism—Accountants favor using the lowest reasonable estimate for the amount of uncollectible accounts shown in the balance sheet.

2   On January 1, Dillon Company had a $3,100 balance in the Allowance for Doubtful Accounts. During the year, sales totaled $780,000 and $6,900 of accounts receivable were written off as uncollectible. A December 31 aging of accounts receivable indicated the amount probably uncollectible to be $5,300. (No recoveries of accounts previously written off were made during the year.) Dillon's financial statements for the current year should include:

a   Uncollectible accounts expense of $9,100.

b   Uncollectible accounts expense of $5,300.

c   Allowance for Doubtful Accounts with a credit balance of $1,500.

d   Allowance for Doubtful Accounts with a credit balance of $8,400.

3   Under the ***direct write-off*** method of accounting for uncollectible accounts:

a   The current year uncollectible accounts expense is less than the expense would be under the income statement approach.

b   The relationship between the current period net sales and current period uncollectible accounts expense illustrates the matching principle.

c   The Allowance for Doubtful Accounts is debited when specific accounts receivable are determined to be worthless.

d   Accounts receivable are not stated in the balance sheet at net realizable value, but at the balance of the Accounts Receivable ledger account.

4   On October 1, Blaine Company sold a parcel of land in exchange for a nine-month, 12% note receivable in the amount of $300,000. Interest is not included in the face amount of this note and the proper adjusting entry was made with respect to this note at December 31. Blaine's journal entry to record collection of this note at July 1 of the following year (maturity date) includes:

a   A debit to Cash for $318,000.

b   A credit to Interest Revenue of $18,000.

c   A debit to Interest Receivable of $9,000.

d   A credit to Notes Receivable of $327,000.

5   On September 1, 1994, Vickers Industries sold machinery in exchange for a six-month note receivable. An interest charge, computed at an annual rate of 12%, was included in the face amount of the note. In its December 31, 1994, balance sheet, Vickers correctly presented the note receivable as follows:

Note Receivable, due March 1, 1995	*$143,100*	
Less: Discount on note receivable	*(2,700)*	*$140,400*

What was the total amount of interest charge included in the face amount of the note on ***September 1, 1994?***

a $2,700   b $5,400   c $8,100   d $8,586

ASSIGNMENT MATERIAL

DISCUSSION QUESTIONS

1 Wolf Brothers, a retailer, makes most of its sales on credit. In the first 10 years of operation, the company incurred some bad debts or uncollectible accounts expense each year. Does this record indicate that the company's credit policies are in need of change? Explain.

2 Company A and Company B are virtually identical in size and nature of operations, but Company A is more conservative in valuing accounts receivable. Will this greater emphasis on conservatism cause A to report higher or lower net income than Company B? Assume that you are a banker considering identical loan applications from A and B and you know of the more conservative policy followed by A. In which set of financial statements would you have more confidence? Explain.

3 Explain the relationship between the **matching principle** and the need to estimate uncollectible accounts receivable.

4 Mako Company determines at year-end that its Allowance for Doubtful Accounts should be increased by $5,200. Give the adjusting entry to carry out this decision.

5 Clinton, Inc., which has accounts receivable of $371,520 and an allowance for doubtful accounts of $4,320, decides to write off as worthless a past-due account receivable for $1,800 from Cass Company. What effect will the write-off have upon total current assets? Upon net income for the period? Explain.

6 In making the annual adjusting entry for uncollectible accounts, a company may utilize a **balance sheet approach** to make the estimate or it may use an **income statement approach.** Explain these two alternative approaches.

7 At the end of its first year in business, Arthur Yokotake, Inc., had accounts receivable totaling $148,500. After careful analysis of the individual accounts, the credit manager estimated that $146,100 would ultimately be collected. Give the journal entry required to reflect this estimate in the accounts.

8 In February of its second year of operations, World Travel Network learned of the failure of a customer, Dale Corporation, which owed $800. Nothing could be collected. Give the journal entry to recognize the uncollectibility of the receivable from Dale Corporation, assuming World uses an allowance method.

9 Posner Company, which uses the allowance method of accounting for uncollectible accounts, wrote off as uncollectible a $1,500 receivable from Webb Company. Several months later, Webb Company obtained new long-term financing and promptly paid all its old debts in full. Give the journal entry or entries (in general journal form) which Posner Company should make to record this recovery of $1,500.

10 What is the direct write-off method of handling credit losses as opposed to the allowance method? What is its principal shortcoming?

11 Caballeros, Inc., had decided to write off its account receivable from Leisure Now because the latter has entered bankruptcy. What general ledger accounts should be debited and credited, assuming that the allowance method is in use? What general ledger accounts should be debited and credited if the direct write-off method is in use?

12 Must companies use the same method of accounting for uncollectible accounts receivable in their financial statements and in their income tax returns? Explain.

13 What are the advantages to a retailer of making credit sales only to customers who use nationally recognized credit cards?

14 Alta Mine Company, a restaurant that had always made cash sales only, adopted a new policy of honoring several nationally known credit cards. Sales did not increase, but many of Alta Mine's regular customers began charging dinner bills on the credit cards. Has the new policy been beneficial to Alta Mine Company? Explain.

15 Determine the maturity date of each of the following:

a   A three-month note dated March 10.

b   A 30-day note dated August 15.

c   A 90-day note dated July 2.

16 On April 10, Hilltop Growers receives a 60-day, 9% note receivable from Jane Stream, a customer, in settlement of a $6,000 account receivable due today. Give the journal entries to record (1) the receipt of this note and (2) its collection at the maturity date.

17 How is the accounts receivable turnover rate computed? Why is this rate significant to short-term creditors?

18 How does an annual audit by a CPA firm provide assurance that a company's accounts receivable and notes receivable are fairly presented in the company's financial statements?

*19 Define the ***present value*** of a future amount. Is the present value larger or smaller than the face amount of the future cash flow? Why?

*20 Williams Gear sold merchandise to Dayco in exchange for a one-year note receivable. The note was drawn with a face amount of $13,310, ***including*** a 10% interest charge. Compute the amount of sales revenue to be recognized by Williams Gear.

*21 Maxline Stores sells merchandise with a sales price of $1,260 on an installment plan requiring 12 monthly payments of $120 each. How much revenue will this sale ultimately generate for Maxline Stores? Explain the nature of this revenue and when it should be recognized in the accounting records.

*22 With reference to Question **21** above, make the journal entries required in the accounting records of Maxline Stores to record:

a   Recognition of revenue from sale of merchandise on installment contract.

b   Collection of the first monthly installment payment. (Assume that an equal portion of the discount is amortized at the time that each installment payment is received.)

EXERCISES

**EXERCISE 8-1
Accounting
Terminology**

Listed below are nine technical accounting terms introduced in this chapter.

Uncollectible accounts expense	Allowance for Doubtful Accounts	Accounts receivable turnover
Aging schedule	Conservatism	Direct write-off method
Factoring	Default	Maturity value

*   *Supplemental Topic, "Notes Receivable with Interest Charges Included in the Face Amount"*

Each of the following statements may (or may not) describe one of these technical terms. For each statement, indicate the term described, or answer "None" if the statement does not correctly describe any of the terms.

a   The principal amount of an interest-bearing note.

b   Resolving uncertainties in the valuation of assets by reporting assets at the lower end of the range of reasonable values rather than by estimating values in a purely objective manner.

c   The account indicating the portion of the year-end accounts receivable that are expected to prove uncollectible.

d   The account indicating the amount of accounts receivable originating during the year that are expected to prove uncollectible.

e   Failure to make payment of the principal or interest per the terms of a promissory note.

f   A computation useful in determining how quickly a company is able to collect its accounts receivable.

g   Recognition of credit losses when specific accounts receivable are determined to be uncollectible.

EXERCISE 8-2
Accounting for Uncollectible Accounts—The "Balance Sheet" Method

At May 31, the accounts receivable of Biway Central amounted in total to $705,600. The company uses the balance sheet approach to estimate bad debts and has prepared an aging schedule of accounts receivable at May 31 which indicates an expected loss of $17,568. You are to prepare as of May 31 the adjusting entry required under each of the following independent assumptions. The explanation portion of each entry should include appropriate supporting computations, and amounts should be rounded to the nearest dollar.

a   The Allowance for Doubtful Accounts has a credit balance of $12,672.

b   The Allowance for Doubtful Accounts has a debit balance of $4,262.

EXERCISE 8-3
Accounting for Uncollectible Accounts—The "Income Statement" Method

The income statement approach to estimating uncollectible accounts expense is used by Burgess Wholesale. On March 31 the firm had accounts receivable in the amount of $630,000. The Allowance for Doubtful Accounts had a credit balance of $3,950. The controller estimated that uncollectible accounts expense would amount to one-half of 1% of the $5,200,000 of net sales made during March. This estimate was entered in the accounts by an adjusting entry on March 31.

On April 12, an account receivable from Conrad Stern of $3,110 was determined to be worthless and was written off. However, on April 24, Stern won several thousand dollars on a TV game show and immediately paid the $3,110 past-due account.

INSTRUCTIONS   Prepare four journal entries in general journal form to record the above events.

EXERCISE 8-4
Uncollectible Accounts Expense— Allowance Methods and Direct Write-Off

The credit manager of Olympic Sporting Goods has gathered the following information about the company's accounts receivable and credit losses during the current year:

Net credit sales for the year		$3,000,000
Accounts receivable at year-end		360,000
Uncollectible accounts receivable:		
Actually written off during the year..............................	$43,650	
Estimated portion of year-end receivables expected to prove uncollectible (per aging schedule)..............................	18,000	61,650

INSTRUCTIONS Prepare one journal entry summarizing the recognition of uncollectible accounts expense for the entire year under each of the following independent assumptions:

a Uncollectible accounts expense is estimated at an amount equal to 1½% of net credit sales.

b Uncollectible accounts expense is recognized by adjusting the balance in the Allowance for Doubtful Accounts to the amount indicated in the year-end aging schedule. The balance in the allowance account at the beginning of the current year was $15,000. (Consider the effect of the write-offs during the year upon the balance in the Allowance for Doubtful Accounts.)

c The company uses the direct write-off method of accounting for uncollectible accounts.

EXERCISE 8-5
Write-Offs and
Recoveries

The balance sheet of Omni, Inc., at the end of last year included the following items:

Notes receivable from customers	$ 540,000
Accrued interest on notes receivable	10,800
Accounts receivable	2,268,000
Less: Allowance for doubtful accounts	54,000

INSTRUCTIONS You are to record the following events of the current year in general journal entries:

a Accounts receivable of $51,840 are written off as uncollectible.

b A customer's note for $14,850, on which interest of $810 has been accrued in the accounts, is deemed uncollectible, and both balances are written off against the Allowance for Doubtful Accounts.

c An account receivable for $7,020 previously written off is collected.

d Aging of accounts receivable at the end of the current year indicates a need for an $81,000 allowance to cover possible failure to collect accounts currently outstanding. (Consider the effect of entries for **a, b,** and **c** on the amount of the Allowance for Doubtful Accounts.)

EXERCISE 8-6
How Fast Are
Accounts Re-
ceivable Col-
lected?

In your analysis of the financial statements of Rayscan, Inc., you note that net sales for the year were $17,000,000; accounts receivable were $1,500,000 at the beginning of the year and $1,900,000 at the end of the year.

INSTRUCTIONS

a Compute the accounts receivable turnover rate for the year.

b Compute the number of days (on average) required to collect accounts receivable.

c Assume that during the following year sales increase and the accounts receivable turnover rate also increases. Would you regard this as a favorable development? Explain.

EXERCISE 8-7
Notes and
Interest

On September 1, a six-month, 15% note receivable is acquired from Shaun Young, a customer, in settlement of his $12,000 account receivable.

INSTRUCTIONS Prepare journal entries to record:

a The receipt of the note on September 1.

b The adjustment to record accrued interest revenue on December 31.

c Collection of the principal and interest on February 28.

*EXERCISE 8-8
Two Forms of
Notes Receiva-
ble

On October 1, Blackwood Company made a loan of $300,000 to a supplier, Niagara Mills. The loan agreement provided for repayment of the $300,000 in 12 months plus interest at an annual rate of 10%.

INSTRUCTIONS

You are to prepare two different presentations of the note receivable from Niagara Mills on Blackwood Company's balance sheet at December 31, assuming that the note was drawn as follows:

a For $300,000 with interest stated separately and payable at maturity.

b With the total interest charge included in the face amount of the note.

*EXERCISE 8-9
Interest In-
cluded in Face
Amount of
Note

West Motors, a truck dealer, sold three trucks to Day & Night Truck Lines on July 1, for a total price of $78,600. Under the terms of the sale, West Motors received $21,000 cash and a promissory note due in full in 24 months. The face amount of the note was $67,968, which included interest on the note for the 24 months.

West Motors uses a perpetual inventory system. The trucks sold to Day & Night Truck Lines were carried in West's inventory at an aggregate cost of $69,000.

INSTRUCTIONS

Prepare entries in general journal form for West Motors relating to this transaction and to the note for the year ended December 31. Include the adjusting entry needed to record interest earned to December 31. (Adjusting entries are made only at year-end. Assume the discount is amortized by the straight-line method—that is, an equal amount of interest revenue is considered earned in each month)

PROBLEMS

Group A

PROBLEM 8A-1
Hey, Pal . . .
When You
Gonna Pay for
This Beer?

Shown below are the net sales and the average amounts of accounts receivable of two beverage companies in a recent year:

	(Dollars in Millions)	
	Average Accounts Receivable	*Net Sales*
Adolph Coors	$ 95	$1,315
Anheuser-Busch Cos., Inc.	337	7,677

INSTRUCTIONS

a For each of these companies, compute:

1 The number of times that the average balance of accounts receivable turned over during this fiscal year. (Round to the nearest tenth.)

2 The number of days (on average) that each company must wait to collect its accounts receivable. (Round to the nearest day.)

b Based upon your computations in part **a,** which company's accounts receivable appear to be the more "liquid" asset? Explain briefly.

PROBLEM 8A-2
Aging Ac-
counts Receiv-
able; Write-Offs

Chandler Associates Inc., uses the balance sheet approach to estimate bad debts and maintains an allowance account to reduce accounts receivable to realizable value. An analysis of the accounts receivable at year-end produced the following age groups:

---

*   *Supplemental Topic, "Notes Receivable with Interest Charges Included in the Face Amount"*

Not yet due	*$348,000*
1–30 days past due	*180,000*
31–60 days past due	*78,000*
61–90 days past due	*18,000*
Over 90 days past due...	*30,000*
Total accounts receivable	*$654,000*

In reliance upon its past experience with collections, the company estimated the percentages probably uncollectible for the above five age groups to be as follows: Group 1, 1%; Group 2, 4%; Group 3, 10%; Group 4, 30%; and Group 5, 50%.

Prior to adjustment at December 31, the Allowance for Doubtful Accounts showed a credit balance of $12,600.

INSTRUCTIONS

a Compute the estimated amount of uncollectible accounts based on the above classification by age groups.

b Prepare the adjusting entry needed to bring the Allowance for Doubtful Accounts to the proper amount.

c Assume that on February 2 of the following year, Chandler Associates learned that an account receivable which had originated on October 6 in the amount of $7,200 was worthless because of the bankruptcy of the customer, Weaver Company. Prepare the journal entry required on February 2 to write off this account receivable.

PROBLEM 8A-3
Estimating Bad Debts: "Income Statement" Approach and "Balance Sheet" Approach

KilnKraft, Inc., owned by Abby Powers, had for the past five years been engaged in selling a line of ceramic merchandise to retail stores. Sales are made on credit and each month the company has estimated its uncollectible accounts expense as a percentage of net sales. The percentage used has been $\frac{1}{2}$ of 1% of net sales. However, it appears that this provision has been inadequate because the Allowance for Doubtful Accounts has a debit balance of $6,200 at May 31 prior to making the monthly provision. Powers has therefore decided to change the method of estimating uncollectible accounts expense and to rely upon an analysis of the age and character of the accounts receivable at the end of each month.

At May 31, the accounts receivable totaled $380,000. This total amount included past-due accounts in the amount of $86,000. None of these past-due accounts was considered hopeless; all accounts regarded as worthless had been written off as rapidly as they were determined to be uncollectible. After careful investigation of the past-due accounts at May 31, Abby Powers decided that the probable loss contained therein was 10%, and that in addition she should anticipate a loss of 1% of the current amounts receivable.

INSTRUCTIONS

a Compute the probable amount of uncollectible accounts included in the accounts receivable at May 31, based on the analysis by the owner.

b Prepare the journal entry necessary to carry out the change in company policy with respect to providing for uncollectible accounts expense.

PROBLEM 8A-4
Accounts Receivable: A Comprehensive Problem

Nagano International has 420 accounts receivable in its subsidiary ledger. All accounts are due in 30 days. On December 31, an aging schedule was prepared. The results are summarized below:

Customer	*Total*	*Not Yet Due*	*1–30 Days Past Due*	*31–60 Days Past Due*	*61–90 Days Past Due*	*Over 90 Days Past Due*
(418 names)						
Subtotals	*$863,125*	*$458,975*	*$236,700*	*$108,350*	*$22,500*	*$36,600*

Two accounts receivable were accidentally omitted from this schedule. The following data is available regarding these accounts:

1 J. Ardis owes $10,625 from two invoices; invoice no. 218, dated Sept. 14, in the amount of $7,450; and invoice no. 568, dated Nov. 9, in the amount of $3,175.

2 N. Selstad owes $9,400 from two invoices; invoice no. 574, dated Nov. 19, in the amount of $3,375; and invoice no. 641, dated Dec. 5, in the amount of $6,025.

INSTRUCTIONS

a Complete the aging schedule as of Dec. 31 by adding to the column subtotals an aging of the accounts of Ardis and Selstad.

b Prepare a schedule to compute the estimated portion of each age group that will prove uncollectible and the required balance in the Allowance for Doubtful Accounts. Arrange your schedule in the format illustrated on page 361. The following percentages of each age group are estimated to be uncollectible: Not yet due, 1%; 1–30 days, 4%; 31–60 days, 10%; 61–90 days, 30%; over 90 days, 50%.

c Prepare the journal entry to bring the Allowance for Doubtful Accounts up to its required balance at Dec. 31. Prior to making this adjustment, the account has a credit balance of $34,500.

d Show how accounts receivable would appear in the company's balance sheet at Dec. 31.

e On Jan. 7 of the following year, the credit manager of Nagano International learns that the $10,625 account receivable from J. Ardis is uncollectible because Ardis has declared bankruptcy. Prepare the journal entry to write off this account.

PROBLEM 8A-5
Note Receivable: Entries for Collection and for Default

Far Corners Imports sells a variety of merchandise to retail stores on open account, but it insists that any customer who fails to pay an invoice when due must replace it with an interest-bearing note. The company adjusts and closes its accounts at December 31. Among the transactions relating to notes receivable were the following:

Sept. 1 Received from a customer (Party Plus) a nine-month, 9% note for $42,000 in settlement of an account receivable due today.

June 1 Collected in full the nine-month, 9% note receivable from Party Plus, including interest.

INSTRUCTIONS

a Prepare journal entries (in general journal form) to record: (1) the receipt of the note on September 1; (2) the adjustment for interest on December 31; and (3) collection of principal and interest on June 1. Assume that the company does not use reversing entries.

b Assume that instead of paying the note on June 1, the customer (Party Plus) had defaulted. Give the journal entry by Far Corners Imports to record the default. Assume that Party Plus has sufficient resources that the note eventually will be collected.

*PROBLEM 8A-6
Notes Receivable: A Comprehensive Problem

Following are selected receivables of Clinton Agricultural Supply Company at December 1, 1994. The company adjusts and closes its accounts only at year-end. All interest computations are based upon a 360-day year.

---

* *Supplemental Topic, "Notes Receivable with Interest Charges Included in the Face Amount"*

Notes receivable:

Flag-Is-Up; 90-day, 10% note dated Sept. 10	*$10,000*
Trust-House Co-op; 60-day, 9% note dated Nov. 1	*20,000*
Applegate Farm; 45-day, 10% note dated Nov. 4	*28,800*
W. B. McCoy; 90-day, 12% note dated Dec. 1	*32,000*

Accounts receivable:

Morgan-Hill Farms	*$ 8,000*
T. J. Peppercorn	*12,700*

Installment contracts receivable:

M. Twain (19 monthly payments of $900)	*$17,100*

Unearned finance charges on installment contracts:

Applicable to M. Twain contract	*$ 2,280*

During December, transactions affecting these receivables were as follows:

Dec. 7 T. J. Peppercorn paid $700 on account and gave a 30-day, 10% note to cover the $12,000 balance of his account.

Dec. 9 Collected in full the maturity value of the Flag-Is-Up 90-day note.

Dec. 11 Received a 60-day note receivable from Morgan-Hill Farms in full settlement of its account receivable. The face amount of this note was $8,120, which included an interest charge.

Dec. 19 Tom Applegate wrote that Applegate Farm would be unable to pay the note due today. However, he enclosed a check for the interest due, along with a new 30-day, 10% note replacing the old note. Clinton Agricultural decided to accept this renewal of the Applegate note.

Dec. 31 Received notice from Trust-House Co-op that it was unable to pay its note due today. The defaulted note was not renewed, but Clinton expects that the amount due will eventually be collected.

Dec. 31 Received the $900 payment from M. Twain on her installment contract. The payment included $120 interest for the month of December. The interest charges included in the face amount of the installment contract originally had been credited to the contra-asset account, Unearned Finance Charges on Installment Contracts.

INSTRUCTIONS
a Prepare journal entries for the six December transactions listed above.

b Prepare the adjusting entries necessary at December 31 to recognize interest accrued on notes receivable through year-end. Remember, base your interest computations on the assumption of a 360-day year.)

Use one adjusting entry to accrue interest receivable on the three notes in which interest is stated separately (the Applegate, Peppercorn, and McCoy notes). Use a separate adjusting entry to recognize interest revenue earned on the note with interest included in the face amount (the Morgan-Hill note).

c Prepare the current asset section of Clinton Agricultural Supply Company's balance sheet at Dec. 31, 1994. In addition to the receivables described above, include the following items:

Cash & cash equivalents	*$ 42,500*
Accounts receivable (other than described above)	*120,000*
Allowance for doubtful receivables (all types)	*10,000*
Inventory	*105,000*

In listing the company's receivables, include captions indicating any unamortized discount, unearned finance charges, and accrued interest. Do **not**, however, identify the individual debtors. (Combine all four notes under the caption "Notes receivable.")

***PROBLEM 8A-7
Long-Term
Note Receiva-
ble with Inter-
est Included in
Face Amount**

On June 1, 1993, Monitor Corporation sold merchandise to Potomac Shipping in exchange for a note receivable due in ***one year.*** The note was drawn in the face amount of $325,500, which included the principal amount and an interest charge. In its December 31, 1993, balance sheet, Monitor Corporation correctly presented the note receivable as follows:

Note receivable, due May 31, 1994	$325,500	
Less: Discount on note receivable	10,625	$314,875

INSTRUCTIONS

a Determine the monthly interest revenue earned by Monitor Corporation from this note receivable. (Hint: The balance in the discount account represents unearned interest as of December 31, 1993.)

b Compute the amount of interest revenue recognized by Monitor Corporation from the note during 1993.

c Compute the amount of sales revenue recognized by Monitor Corporation on June 1, 1993 when this note was received.

d Compute the effective annual rate of interest (stated as a percentage) represented by the interest charge originally included in the face amount of the note.

e Prepare all journal entries relating to this note in the accounting records of Monitor Corporation for 1993 and 1994. Assume that adjusting entries are made only at December 31, and that the note was collected on the maturity date.

Group B

**PROBLEM 8B-1
Turnover of
Accounts Re-
ceivable**

Shown below are the net sales and the average amounts of accounts receivable of two computer makers in a recent year:

	(Dollars in Millions)	
	Average Accounts Receivable	Net Sales
Hewlett-Packard Company	$1,297	$7,102
Digital Equipment Corporation..........................	2,108	9,390

INSTRUCTIONS

a For each of these companies, compute:

   1 The number of times that the average balance of accounts receivable turned over during this fiscal year. (Round to the nearest tenth.)

   2 The number of days (on average) that each company must wait to collect its accounts receivable. (Round to the nearest day.)

b Based upon your computations in part **a,** which company's accounts receivable appear to be the more "liquid" asset? Explain briefly.

**PROBLEM 8B-2
Aging Ac-
counts Receiv-
able; Write-Offs**

Public Image, a firm specializing in marketing and publicity services, uses the balance sheet approach to estimate uncollectible accounts expense. At year-end an aging of the accounts receivable produced the following classification:

---

* *Supplemental Topic, "Notes Receivable with Interest Charges Included in the Face Amount"*

Not yet due	*$333,000*
1–30 days past due	*135,000*
31–60 days past due	*58,500*
61–90 days past due	*13,500*
Over 90 days past due..	*22,500*
Total	*$562,500*

On the basis of past experience, the company estimated the percentages probably uncollectible for the above five age groups to be as follows: Group 1, 1%; Group 2, 3%; Group 3, 10%; Group 4, 20%; and Group 5, 50%.

The Allowance for Doubtful Accounts before adjustment at December 31 showed a credit balance of $8,100.

INSTRUCTIONS

a Compute the estimated amount of uncollectible accounts based on the above classification by age groups.

b Prepare the adjusting entry needed to bring the Allowance for Doubtful Accounts to the proper amount.

c Assume that on January 10 of the following year, Public Image learned that an account receivable which had originated on September 1 in the amount of $8,550 was worthless because of the bankruptcy of the customer, Cranston Manufacturing. Prepare the journal entry required on January 10 to write off this account.

PROBLEM 8B-3
Estimating Bad Debts: "Balance Sheet" Approach

At December 31 last year, the balance sheet prepared by Luis Montoyo included $504,000 in accounts receivable and an allowance for doubtful accounts of $26,400. During January of the current year selected transactions are summarized as follows:

(1) Sales on account	*$360,640*
(2) Cash collections from customers (no cash discounts)	*364,800*
(3) Account receivable from Acme Company written off as worthless	*9,280*

After a careful aging and analysis of all customers' accounts at January 31, it was decided that the allowance for doubtful accounts should be adjusted to a balance of $29,280 in order to reflect accounts receivable at net realizable value in the January 31 balance sheet.

INSTRUCTIONS

a Prepare entries in general journal form summarizing for the entire month of January the activity described in the three numbered items. Also show the adjusting entry at January 31 to provide for uncollectible accounts.

b Show the amounts of accounts receivable and the allowance for doubtful accounts as they would appear in a partial balance sheet at January 31.

c Assume that three months after the receivable from Acme Company had been written off as worthless, Acme Company won a large award in the settlement of patent litigation and immediately paid the $9,280 debt to Luis Montoyo. Give the journal entry or entries (in general journal form) to reflect this recovery of a receivable previously written off.

PROBLEM 8B-4
Estimating Bad Debts: "Income Statement" Approach and "Balance Sheet" Approach

Rivero Graphics, owned by Maria Rivero, sells paper novelty goods to retail stores. All sales are made on credit and the company has regularly estimated its uncollectible accounts expense as a percentage of net sales. The percentage used has been ½ of 1% of net sales. However, it appears that this provision has been inadequate because the Allowance for Doubtful Accounts has a debit balance of $3,900 at May 31 prior to making the monthly provision. Rivero has therefore decided to change the method of estimating uncollectible accounts expense and to rely upon an analysis of the age and character of the accounts receivable at the end of each month.

At May 31, the accounts receivable totaled $260,000. This total amount included past-due accounts in the amount of $46,000. None of these past-due accounts was considered worthless; all accounts regarded as worthless had been written off as rapidly as they were determined to be uncollectible. After careful investigation of the $46,000 of past-due accounts at May 31, Rivero decided that the probable loss contained therein was 10%. In addition she decided to provide for a loss of 1% of the current accounts receivable.

INSTRUCTIONS

a Compute the probable amount of uncollectible accounts included in the $260,000 of accounts receivable at May 31, based on the analysis by the owner.

b Prepare the journal entry necessary to carry out the change in company policy with respect to providing for uncollectible accounts expense.

PROBLEM 8B-5
Note Receivable: Entries for Collection and for Default

Hanover Mills sells merchandise to retail stores on 30-day credit, but insists that any customer who fails to pay an invoice when due must replace it with an interest-bearing note. The company adjusts and closes its accounts at December 31. Among the transactions relating to notes receivable were the following.

Nov. 1   Received from a customer (Jones Brothers) a six-month, 9% note for $30,000 in settlement of an account receivable due today.

May 1   Collected in full the six-month, 9% note receivable from Jones Brothers, including interest.

INSTRUCTIONS

a Prepare journal entries in general journal form to record: (1) the receipt of the note on November 1, (2) the adjustment for interest on December 31, and (3) collection of principal and interest on the following May 1. Assume that the company does not use reversing entries.

b Assume that instead of paying the note on the following May 1, the customer (Jones Brothers) had defaulted. Give the journal entry by Hanover Mills to record the default. Assume that Jones Brothers has sufficient resources that the note will eventually be collected.

*PROBLEM 8B-6
Notes Receivable: A Comprehensive Problem

Selected receivables of Hartford Building Supply at December 1, 1994, are shown below. Hartford adjusts and closes its accounts only at December 31. All interest computations are based upon the assumption of a 360-day year.

Notes receivable:

Weiss Construction Co.; 90-day, 12% note dated Oct. 2	$25,000
Mr. Remodel; 60-day, 10% note dated Oct. 15	18,000
Tillamook Homes; 45-day, 10% note dated Nov. 4	16,000
J. D. Walters; 60-day, 9% note dated Dec. 1	30,000

Accounts receivable:

Regal Construction	$12,000
Dexter Dalton	8,200

Installment contracts receivable:

Jesse Cole (14 monthly payments of $600)	$ 8,400

Unearned finance charges on installment contracts:

Applicable to Jesse Cole contract	$ 728

---

*   *Supplemental Topic, "Notes Receivable with Interest Charges Included in the Face Amount"*

During the month of December, transactions affecting these receivables were as follows:

Dec. 1 Received a 90-day note receivable from Regal Construction in full settlement of its account receivable. The face amount of this note was $12,360, which included an interest charge.

Dec. 11 Dexter Dalton paid $2,200 on his account and gave a 30-day, 12% note to cover the $6,000 balance of his account.

Dec. 14 Collected in full the maturity value of the Mr. Remodel 60-day note.

Dec. 19 Tillamook Homes paid in cash the interest due on its $16,000 note but renewed the note for the $16,000 principal amount for another 30 days. The interest rate in the new note is 12%.

Dec. 31 Received the $600 payment from Jesse Cole on his installment contract. The payment included $52 interest for the month of December. The interest charges included in the face amount of the installment contract originally had been credited to the contra-asset account, Unearned Finance Charges on Installment Contracts.

Dec. 31 Received notice from Weiss Construction Company that it was unable to pay its note due today. The defaulted note was not renewed, but Hartford expects that the amount due will eventually be collectible.

INSTRUCTIONS **a** Prepare journal entries for the six December transactions listed above.

b Prepare the adjusting entries necessary at December 31 to recognize interest accrued on notes receivable through year-end. (Remember, base your interest computations on a 360-day year.)

Use one adjusting entry to accrue interest receivable on the three notes in which interest is stated separately (the Tillamook Homes, J. D. Walters, and Dexter Dalton notes). Use a separate adjusting entry to recognize interest revenue earned on the note with interest included in the face amount (the Regal Construction note).

c Prepare the current asset section of Hartford Building Supply's balance sheet at Dec. 31, 1994. In addition to the receivables described above, include the following items:

Cash & cash equivalents	$ 67,900
Accounts receivable (other than described above)	250,000
Allowance for doubtful receivables (all types)	24,000
Inventory	350,000

In listing the company's receivables, include captions indicating any unamortized discount, unearned finance charges, and accrued interest. Do **not,** however, identify the individual debtors. (Combine all four notes under the caption "Notes receivable.")

*PROBLEM 8B-7 Long-Term Note Receivable with Interest Included in Face Amount On April 1, 1993, Merrimac Corporation sold merchandise to Jefferson Davis Company in exchange for a note receivable due in **one year.** The note was drawn in the face amount of $189,200, which included the principal amount and an interest charge. In its December 31, 1993, balance sheet, Merrimac Corporation correctly presented the note receivable as follows:

Note receivable, due Mar. 31, 1994	$189,200	
Less: Discount on note receivable	3,300	$185,900

---

* *Supplemental Topic, "Notes Receivable with Interest Charges Included in the Face Amount"*

INSTRUCTIONS

a Determine the monthly interest revenue earned by Merrimac Corporation from this note receivable. (Hint: The balance in the discount account represents unearned interest as of December 31, 1993.)

b Compute the amount of interest revenue recognized by Merrimac Corporation from the note during 1993.

c Compute the amount of sales revenue recognized by Merrimac Corporation on April 1, 1993, when this note was received.

d Compute the effective annual rate of interest (stated as a percentage) represented by the interest charge originally included in the face amount of the note.

e Prepare all journal entries relating to this note in the accounting records of Merrimac Corporation for 1993 and 1994. Assume that adjusting entries are made only at December 31 and that reversing entries are not used. Assume also that the note was collected on the maturity date.

CASES AND UNSTRUCTURED PROBLEMS

**CASE 8-1
Accounting
Principles:
Cash and Re-
ceivables**

In each of the situations described below, indicate the accounting principles or concepts, if any, that have been violated and explain briefly the nature of the violation. If you believe the practice is *in accord* with generally accepted accounting principles, state this as your position and defend it.

a A small business in which credit sales fluctuate greatly from year to year uses the direct write-off method both for income tax purposes and in its financial statements.

b A manufacturing company charges all of its petty cash expenditures to Miscellaneous Expense rather than to the various expense accounts which reflect the nature of each expenditure.

c Computer Systems often sells merchandise in exchange for interest-bearing notes receivable, maturing in 6, 12, or 24 months. The company records these sales transactions by debiting Notes Receivable for the maturity value of the notes, crediting Sales for the sales price of the merchandise, and crediting Interest Revenue for the balance of the maturity value of the note. The cost of goods sold also is recorded.

d A company has $400,000 in unrestricted cash, $1 million in a bank account specifically earmarked for the construction of a new factory, and $2 million in cash equivalents. In the balance sheet, these amounts are combined and shown as "Cash and cash equivalents . . . $3.4 million."

e The credit manager of Audio Products estimates that between $1 million and $1.6 million of the company's accounts receivable will prove uncollectible. In its financial statements, Audio Products establishes an allowance for doubtful accounts of $1 million.

**CASE 8-2
How Did He
Do It?**

Allan Carter was a long-time employee in the accounting department of Marston Company. Carter's responsibilities included the following:

1 Maintain the accounts receivable subsidiary ledger.

2 Prepare vouchers for cash disbursements. The voucher and supporting documents were forwarded to John Marston, owner of the company.

3 Compute depreciation on all plant assets.

4 Authorize all sales returns and allowances given to credit customers and prepare the related credit memoranda. The credit memoranda were forwarded to Howard Smith, who maintains the company's journals and general ledger.

John Marston personally performs the following procedures in an effort to achieve strong internal control:

1 Prepare monthly bank reconciliations.

2 Prepare monthly trial balances from the general ledger and reconcile the accounts receivable controlling account with the subsidiary ledger.

3 Prepare from the subsidiary ledger all monthly bills sent to customers and investigate any complaints from customers about inaccuracies in these bills.

4 Review all vouchers and supporting documents before signing checks for cash disbursements.

Carter became terminally ill and retired. Shortly thereafter, he died. However, he left a letter confessing that over a period of years he had embezzled over $300,000 from Marston Company. As part of his scheme, he had managed to obtain both a bank account and a post office box in the name of Marston Company. He had then contacted customers whose accounts were overdue and offered them a 20% discount if they would make payment within five days. He instructed them to send their payments to the post office box. When the payments arrived, he deposited them in his "Marston Company" bank account. Carter stated in his letter that he had acted alone, and that no other company employees knew of his dishonest actions.

Marston cannot believe that Carter committed this theft without the knowledge and assistance of Howard Smith, who maintained the journals and the general ledger. Marston reasoned that Carter must have credited the customers' accounts in the accounts receivable subsidiary ledger, because no customers had complained about not receiving credit for their payments. Smith must also have recorded these credits in the general ledger, or Marston would have discovered the problem by reconciling the subsidiary ledger with the controlling account. Finally, Smith must have debited some other account in the general ledger to keep the ledger in balance. Thus, Marston is about to bring criminal charges against Smith.

INSTRUCTIONS
a Explain how Carter might have committed this theft without Smith's knowledge and without being detected by Marston's control procedures. (Assume that Carter had no personal access to the journals or general ledger.)

b Which of the duties assigned to Carter should not have been assigned to an employee responsible for maintaining accounts receivable? Would internal control be strengthened if this duty were assigned to the company's cashier? Explain.

*CASE 8-3
Installment
Sales, Timing
of Interest Revenue, and
Credit Policy

Record House and Concert Sound are two companies engaged in selling stereo equipment to the public. Both companies sell equipment at a price 50% greater than cost. Customers may pay cash, purchase on 30-day accounts, or make installment payments over a 36-month period. The installment receivables include a three-year interest charge (which amounts to 30% of the sales price) in the face amount of the contract. Condensed income statements prepared by the companies for their first year of operations are shown below:

	Record House	Concert Sound
Sales	$387,000	$288,000
Cost of goods sold	210,000	192,000
Gross profit on sales	$177,000	$ 96,000
Operating expenses	63,000	60,000
Operating income	$114,000	$ 36,000
Interest revenue	–0–	$ 10,800
Net income..	$114,000	$ 46,800

---

*   *Supplemental Topic, "Notes Receivable with Interest Charges Included in the Face Amount"*

When Record House makes a sale of stereo equipment on the installment plan it immediately credits the Sales account with the face amount of the installment receivable. In other words, the interest charges are included in sales revenue at the time of the sale. The interest charges included in Record House's installment receivables originating in the first year amount to $72,000, of which $59,100 is unearned at the end of the first year. Record House uses the direct write-off method to recognize uncollectible accounts expense. During the year, accounts receivable of $2,100 were written off as uncollectible, but no entry was made for $37,200 of accounts estimated to be uncollectible at year-end.

Concert Sound records sales revenue equal to the present value of its installment receivables and recognizes the interest *earned during the year* as interest revenue. Concert Sound provides for uncollectible accounts by the allowance method. The company recognized uncollectible accounts expense of $11,100 during the year and this amount appeared to be adequate.

INSTRUCTIONS

a Prepare a condensed income statement for Record House for the year, using the same methods of accounting for installment sales and uncollectible accounts as were used by Concert Sound. The income statement you prepare should contain the same seven items shown in the illustrated income statements. Provide footnotes showing the computations you made in revising the amount of sales and any other figures you decide to change.

b Compare the income statement you have prepared in part **a** to the one originally prepared by Record House. Which income statement do you believe better reflects the results of the company's operations during the year? Explain.

c What do you believe to be the key factor responsible for making one of these companies more profitable than the other? What corrective action would you recommend be taken by the less profitable company to improve future performance?

CASE 8-4
If Things Get Any Better, We'll Be Broke

Loud Max, Inc., sells stereo equipment. Traditionally, the company's sales have fallen into the following categories: cash sales, 25%; customers using national credit cards, 35%; sales on account (due in 30 days), 40%. With these policies, the company earned a modest profit, and monthly cash receipts exceeded monthly cash payments by a comfortable margin. Uncollectible accounts expense was approximately 1% of net sales. (The company uses the direct write-off method in accounting for uncollectible accounts receivable.)

Two months ago, the company initiated a new credit policy which it calls "Double Zero." Customers may purchase merchandise on account, with no down payment and no interest charges. The accounts are collected in 12 monthly installments of equal amounts.

The plan has proven quite popular with customers, and monthly sales have increased dramatically. Despite the increase in sales, however, Loud Max is experiencing cash flow problems—it hasn't been generating enough cash to pay its suppliers, most of which require payment within 30 days.

The company's bookkeeper has prepared the following analysis of monthly operating results:

	Before Double Zero	Last Month
Sales:		
Cash...	$12,500	$ 5,000
National credit card	17,500	10,000
30-day accounts...	20,000	–0–
Double Zero accounts	–0–	75,000
Total monthly sales.......................................	$50,000	$ 90,000
Cost of goods sold and expenses..............................	40,000	65,000
Net income..	$10,000	$ 25,000
Cash receipts:		
Cash sales	$12,500	$ 5,000
National credit card companies	17,500	10,000
30-day accounts...	19,500	–0–
Double Zero accounts	–0–	11,250
Total monthly cash receipts..............................	$49,500	$ 26,250
Accounts written off as uncollectible..........................	$ 500	$ –0–
Accounts receivable at month-end	$20,000	$135,000

The bookkeeper offers the following assessment: "Double Zero is killing us. Since we started that plan, our accounts receivable have increased nearly seven-fold, and they're still growing. We can't afford to carry such a large nonproductive asset on our books. Our cash receipts are down to nearly half of what they used to be. If we don't go back to more cash sales and receivables which can be collected more quickly, we'll become insolvent."

Maxwell "Loud Max" Swartz, founder and chief executive officer, shouts back: "Why do you say that our accounts receivable are nonproductive? They're the most productive asset we have! Since we started Double Zero, our sales have nearly doubled, our profits have more than doubled, and our bad debt expense has dropped to nothing!"

INSTRUCTIONS

a Is it logical that the Double Zero plan is causing sales and profits to increase while also causing a decline in cash receipts? Explain.

b Why has the uncollectible accounts expense dropped to zero? What would you expect to happen to the company's uncollectible accounts expense in the future—say, next year? Why?

c Do you think that the reduction in monthly cash receipts is permanent or temporary? Explain.

d In what sense are the company's accounts receivable a "nonproductive" asset?

e Suggest several ways that Loud Max (the company) may be able to generate the cash it needs to pay its bills without terminating the Double Zero plan.

f Would you recommend that the company continue offering Double Zero financing, or should it return to the use of 30-day accounts? Explain the reasons for your answer and identify any unresolved factors which might cause you to change this opinion in the future.

CASE 8-5
". . . Thinkin'
About Califor-
nia . . ."

The principal asset of **Wells Fargo & Company** is loans receivable. In its 1990 financial statements, Wells Fargo disclosed that approximately 24% of its loans are long-term mortgages secured by commercial real estate. The bank has made commercial mortgage loans in 38 states. However, 78% (in dollar amount) of these commercial mortgages are secured by real estate located in California.

INSTRUCTIONS

a What is the basic purpose disclosing to users of financial statements such details about the composition of loans receivable?

b Listed below are five highly publicized events transpiring in 1991. Explain whether each event is likely to increase or decrease the quality (collectibility) of Wells Fargo's California-based commercial mortgage loans. Explain your reasoning and consider each event independently.

1 On a nationwide basis, interest rates declined to their lowest levels in several decades.

2 California substantially increased its state sales tax in an effort to reduce a growing state budget deficit.

3 Due to the dissolution of the Soviet Union, the U.S. government is reducing its level of spending on defense projects. Defense contractors are among southern California's largest employers.

4 **The Walt Disney Company** announced its plans to greatly expand Disney-land, which is located in southern California. This expansion is expected to create more than 50,000 permanent jobs and attract millions of out-of-state tourists each year.

5 California's drought continued for the fifth consecutive year.

ANSWERS TO SELF-TEST QUESTIONS

1 b   2 a   3 d   4 b   5 c [($2,700 ÷ 2 months) × 6 months]

CHAPTER

9 Inventories and the Cost of Goods Sold

Our primary goal in this chapter is to explain and illustrate the different methods of allocating the costs of purchased merchandise between inventory and the cost of goods sold. Generally accepted accounting principles permit the use of several alternative methods—each having unique characteristics and producing different financial results.

Later in the chapter, we discuss other issues relating to the valuation of inventory, including the taking of physical inventory, periodic inventory systems, and techniques for estimating the cost of goods sold. The chapter concludes with a Supplemental Topic section discussing the nature and implications of LIFO reserves.

After studying this chapter you should be able to meet these Learning Objectives:

1   *Using a perpetual inventory system, determine the cost of goods sold using (a) specific identification, (b) average cost, (c) FIFO, and (d) LIFO. Discuss the advantages and shortcomings of each method.*

2   *Explain the need for taking a physical inventory.*

3   *Record shrinkage losses and other year-end adjustments to inventory.*

4   *In a periodic inventory system, determine the ending inventory and the cost of goods sold using (a) average cost, (b) FIFO, and (c) LIFO.*

5   *Explain the effects of an inventory error on the income statement of the current year and the following year.*

6   *Estimate the cost of goods sold and ending inventory by the gross profit method and by the retail method.*

7   *Identify several factors that management should consider in determining the optimal size of the company's inventory.*

8   *Compute the inventory turnover rate. Explain why this ratio is of interest to short-term creditors.*

*9   *Define a "LIFO reserve" and explain its implications to users of financial statements.*

---

*   *Supplemental Topic, "LIFO Reserves"*

Inventory Defined

One of the largest current assets of a retail store or of a wholesale business is the ***inventory*** of merchandise. The sale of this merchandise is the major source of revenue. In a merchandising company, the inventory consists of all goods owned and held for sale to customers. Inventory is converted into cash within the company's ***operating cycle*** and, therefore, is regarded as a current asset.[1] In the balance sheet, inventory is listed immediately after accounts receivable, because it is just one step further removed from conversion into cash than are the accounts receivable.

In a merchandising company, all of the inventory is purchased in a ready-to-sell condition. A manufacturing company, however, has three types of inventory: (1) ***finished goods,*** which are ready to sell; (2) ***work in process,*** which are goods in the process of being manufactured; and (3) ***materials,*** which are the raw materials and component parts used in the manufacture of finished products. All three classes of inventory are included in the current asset section of the balance sheet.[2]

THE FLOW OF INVENTORY COSTS

Inventory is an asset and—like most other assets—usually is shown in the balance sheet at its cost.[3] As items are sold from this inventory, their costs are removed from the balance sheet and transferred into the cost of goods sold, which is offset against sales revenue in the income statement. This "flow of costs" is illustrated in the following diagram:

"Flow" of costs through financial statements

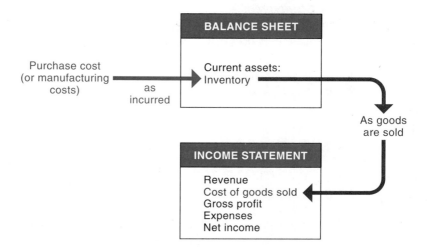

---

[1]   As explained in Chapter 5, the ***operating cycle*** of a merchandising business is the period of time required to convert cash into inventory, inventory into accounts receivable, and these accounts receivable into cash. Assets expected to be converted into cash within one year or the operating cycle, whichever is longer, are regarded as current assets.

[2]   In a manufacturing company, the manufacturing process is part of the operating cycle. Therefore, raw materials and work in process are considered current assets even if completion of the manufacturing process requires more than one year.

[3]   Some companies deal in inventories which can be sold in a worldwide market at quoted market prices. Examples include mutual funds, stock brokerages, and companies that deal in commodities such as agricultural crops or precious metals. Often these companies value their inventories at market price, rather than at cost. Our discussions in this chapter are directed to the far more common situation in which inventories are valued at cost.

In a perpetual inventory system, entries in the accounting records parallel this flow of costs. When merchandise is purchased, its cost (net of allowable cash discounts) is debited to the asset account Inventory. As the merchandise is sold, its cost is removed from the Inventory account and debited to the Cost of Goods Sold account.

The valuation of inventory and of the cost of goods sold are of critical importance to managers and to users of financial statements. In most cases, inventory is a company's largest current asset, and the cost of goods sold is its largest expense. These two accounts have a significant effect upon the financial statement subtotals and ratios used in evaluating the solvency and profitability of the business.

Several different methods of "pricing" inventory and of measuring the cost of goods sold are acceptable under generally accepted accounting principles. These different methods may produce significantly different results, both in a company's financial statements and in its income tax returns. Therefore, managers and investors alike should understand the usual effects of the different inventory valuation methods.

Which Unit Did We Sell? Does It Really Matter?

Purchases of merchandise are recorded in the same manner under all of the inventory valuation methods. The differences in these methods lie in determining **which costs** should be removed from the Inventory account when merchandise is sold.

We illustrated the basic entries relating to purchases and sales of merchandise in Chapter 5. In that introductory discussion, however, we made a simplifying assumption: all of the units in inventory had been acquired at the same unit costs. In practice, a company often has in its inventory units of a given product which were acquired at **different costs.** Acquisition costs may vary because the units were purchased at different dates, or from different suppliers.

When identical units of inventory have different unit costs, a question naturally arises as to **which of these costs** should be used in recording sales transactions.

Data for an Illustration

To illustrate the alternative methods of measuring the cost of goods sold, assume that Lake Mead Electric Company sells electrical equipment and supplies. Included in the company's inventory are five Elco AC-40 generators. These generators are identical; however, two were purchased on January 5 at a per-unit cost of **$1,000,** and the other three were purchased a month later, shortly after Elco had announced a price increase, at a per-unit cost of **$1,200.** These purchases are reflected in Mead's inventory subsidiary ledger as shown on the following page.

Notice that on February 5, the balance columns contain two "layers" of unit cost information, representing the units purchased at the two different unit costs. A new cost layer is created whenever units are acquired at a different per-unit cost. (As the units comprising a cost layer are sold, the layer is eliminated from the inventory. Therefore, a business is unlikely to have more than three or four cost layers in its inventory at any given time.)

Inventory subsidiary ledger record

Item	Elco AC-40			Primary supplier	Elco Manufacturing		
Description	Portable generator			Secondary supplier	Vegas Wholesale Co.		
Location	Daily St. warehouse			Inventory level: Min: 2 Max: 5			

	PURCHASED			SOLD			BALANCE		
Date	Units	Unit Cost	Total	Units	Unit Cost	Cost of Goods Sold	Units	Unit Cost	Total
Jan. 5	2	$1,000	$2,000				2	$1,000	$2,000
Feb. 5	3	1,200	3,600				2	1,000	
							3	1,200	5,600

Now assume that on March 1, Mead sells one of these Elco generators to Boulder Construction Company for $1,800, cash. What cost should be removed from the Inventory account and recognized as the cost of goods sold—$1,000 or $1,200?

In answering such questions, accountants may use an approach called *specific identification,* or they may adopt a *cost flow assumption.* Either of these approaches is acceptable. Once an approach has been selected, however, it should be *applied consistently* in accounting for all sales of this particular type of merchandise.

Specific Identification

OBJECTIVE 1 Using a perpetual inventory system, determine the cost of goods sold using (a) specific identification, (b) average cost, (c) FIFO, and (d) LIFO. Discuss the advantages and shortcomings of each method.

The specific identification method can be used only when the actual costs of individual units of merchandise can be determined from the accounting records. For example, each of the generators in Mead's inventory may have an identification number, and these numbers may appear on the purchase invoices. With this identification number, Mead's accounting department can determine whether the generator sold to Boulder Construction had cost $1,000 or $1,200. The *actual cost* of this particular unit then is used in recording the cost of goods sold.

Cost Flow Assumptions

If the items in inventory are *similar in terms of cost, function, and sales value, it is not necessary for the seller to use the specific identification method* in determining the cost of goods sold. Rather, the seller may follow the more convenient practice of using a *cost flow assumption.* (In practice, the phrase "cost flow assumption" often is shortened to "flow assumption.")

When a flow assumption is in use, the seller simply makes an *assumption* as to the *sequence in which units are withdrawn from inven-*

tory. For example, the seller might assume that the oldest merchandise always is sold first, or that the most recently purchased items are the first to be sold.

Three flow assumptions are in widespread use:

1 ***Average cost.*** This assumption values all merchandise—units sold and units remaining in inventory—at the ***average*** per-unit cost. (In effect, the average-cost method assumes that units are withdrawn from the inventory in random order.)

2 ***First-in, first-out (FIFO).*** As the name implies, FIFO involves the assumption that goods sold are the ***first*** units that were purchased—that is, the ***oldest*** goods on hand. Thus, the remaining inventory is comprised of the most recent purchases.

3 ***Last-in, first-out (LIFO).*** Under LIFO, the units sold are assumed to be those ***most recently*** acquired. The remaining inventory, therefore, is assumed to consist of the earliest purchases.

The cost flow assumption selected by a company ***need not correspond to the actual physical movement of the company's merchandise.*** When the units of merchandise are identical (or nearly identical), it ***does not matter*** which units are delivered to the customer in a particular sales transaction. Therefore, in measuring the income of a business that sells units of identical merchandise, accountants consider the flow of ***costs*** to be more important than the physical flow of the merchandise.

The use of a flow assumption ***eliminates the need for separately identifying each unit sold and looking up its actual cost.*** Experience has shown that these flow assumptions provide useful and reliable measurements of the cost of goods sold, as long as they are applied consistently to all sales of the particular type of merchandise.

Average-Cost Method

When the average-cost method is in use, the ***average cost*** of all units in the inventory is computed after every purchase. This average cost is computed by dividing the total cost of goods available for sale by the number of units in inventory. As the average cost may change following each purchase, this method also is called ***moving average.***

As of January 5, Mead has only two Elco generators in its inventory, each acquired at a purchase cost of $1,000. Therefore, the average cost is $1,000 per unit. After the purchase on February 5, Mead has five Elco generators in inventory, acquired at a total cost of $5,600 (2 units @ $1,000, plus 3 units @ $1,200 = $5,600). Therefore, the ***average*** per-unit cost now is ***$1,120*** ($5,600 ÷ 5 units = 1,120).

On March 1, two entries are made to record the sale of one of these generators to Boulder Construction Company. The first recognizes the revenue from this sale, and the second recognizes the cost of the goods sold. These entries follow, with the cost of goods sold measured by the average-cost method:

```
Cash............................................................     1,800
        Sales .....................................................            1,800
To·record the sale of one Elco AC-40 generator sold on account.

Cost of Goods Sold .........................................     1,120
        Inventory ...............................................            1,120
To record the cost of one Elco AC-40 generator sold to Boulder
Construction Co. Cost determined by the average-cost method.
```

(The entry to recognize the $1,800 in sales revenue remains the same, regardless of the inventory method in use. Therefore, we will not repeat this entry in our illustrations of the other cost flow assumptions.)

When the average-cost method is in use, the inventory subsidiary ledger is modified slightly from the format illustrated on page 408. Following the sale on March 1, Mead's subsidiary ledger card for Elco generators will appear as follows, modified to show the average unit cost.

Inventory subsidiary record— average cost basis

	PURCHASED			SOLD			BALANCE		
Date	Units	Unit Cost	Total	Units	Average Unit Cost	Cost of Goods Sold	Units	Average Unit Cost	Total
Jan. 5	2	$1,000	$2,000				2	$1,000	$2,000
Feb. 5	3	1,200	3,600				5	1,120*	5,600
Mar. 1				1	$1,120	$1,120	4	1,120	4,480

* $5,600 total cost ÷ 5 units = $1,120.

Notice that the unit cost column for purchases still shows actual unit costs— $1,000 and $1,200. The unit cost columns relating to sales and to the remaining inventory, however, show the ***average unit cost*** ($5,600 total ÷ 5 units = $1,120). As all units are valued at this same average cost, the inventory has only one cost layer.

Under the average-cost assumption, all items in inventory are assigned the ***same*** per-unit cost (the average cost). Hence, it does not matter which units are sold; the cost of goods sold always is based upon the current average unit cost. When one generator is sold on March 1, the cost of goods sold is $1,120; if four generators were sold on this date, the cost of goods sold would be $4,480 (4 units × $1,120 per unit).

First-In, First-Out Method

The first-in, first-out method, often called ***FIFO,*** is based upon the assumption that the ***first merchandise purchased is the first merchandise sold.*** Thus, the accountant for Mead Electric would assume that the generator sold on March 1 was one of those purchased on ***January 5.*** The entry to record the cost of goods sold would be:

> *Cost of Goods Sold* 1,000
>   *Inventory*   1,000
> *To record the cost of one Elco AC-40 generator sold to Boulder*
> *Construction Co. Cost determined by the FIFO flow assumption.*

Following this sale, Mead's inventory ledger would appear as follows:

Inventory subsidiary record—FIFO basis

	PURCHASED			SOLD			BALANCE		
Date	Units	Unit Cost	Total	Units	Unit Cost	Cost of Goods Sold	Units	Unit Cost	Total
Jan. 5	2	$1,000	$2,000				2	$1,000	$2,000
Feb. 5	3	1,200	3,600				2	1,000	
							3	1,200	5,600
Mar. 1				1	$1,000	$1,000	1	1,000	
							3	1,200	4,600

Notice that FIFO uses actual purchase costs, rather than an average cost. Thus, if merchandise has been purchased at several different costs, the inventory will include several different cost layers. The cost of goods sold for a given sales transaction also may involve several different cost layers. To illustrate, assume that Mead had sold *four* generators to Boulder Construction, instead of only one. Under the FIFO flow assumption, Mead would assume that it first sold the two generators purchased on January 5, and then two of those purchased on February 5. Thus, the total cost of goods sold ($4,400) would include items at *two different unit costs,* as shown below:

2 generators from January 5 purchase @ $1,000................................. $2,000
2 generators from February 5 purchase @ $1,200.............................. 2,400
Total cost of goods sold (4 units) $4,400

As the cost of goods sold always is recorded at the oldest available purchase costs, the units remaining in inventory are valued at the more recent acquisition costs.

Last-In, First-Out Method

The last-in, first-out method, commonly known as **LIFO,** is the most widely used method of determining the cost of goods sold and valuing inventory. As the name suggests, the **most recently** purchased merchandise (the "last-in") is assumed to be sold first. If Mead were using the LIFO method, it would assume that the generator sold on March 1 was one of those acquired on **February 5,** the most recent purchase date. Thus, the cost transferred from inventory to the cost of goods sold would be **$1,200.**

The journal entry to record the cost of goods sold is illustrated below, along with the inventory subsidiary ledger record after this entry has been posted:

Cost of Goods Sold   1,200
     Inventory   1,200
To record the cost of one Elco AC-40 generator sold to Boulder
Construction Co. Cost determined by the LIFO flow assumption.

Inventory
subsidiary
record—LIFO
basis

	PURCHASED			SOLD			BALANCE		
Date	Units	Unit Cost	Total	Units	Unit Cost	Cost of Goods Sold	Units	Unit Cost	Total
Jan. 5	2	$1,000	$2,000				2	$1,000	$2,000
Feb. 5	3	1,200	3,600				2	1,000	
							3	1,200	5,600
Mar. 1				1	$1,200	$1,200	2	1,000	
							2	1,200	4,400

The LIFO method uses actual purchase costs, rather than an average cost. Thus, the inventory may have several different cost layers. If a sale includes more units than are included in the most recent cost layer, some of the goods sold are assumed to come from the next most recent layer. For example, if Mead had sold four generators (instead of one) on March 1, the cost of goods sold determined under the LIFO assumption would be $4,600, as shown below:

3 generators from February 5 purchase @ $1,200 .... $3,600
1 generator from January 5 purchase @ $1,000   1,000
Total cost of goods sold (4 units) $4,600

As LIFO transfers the most recent purchase costs to the cost of goods sold, the goods remaining in inventory are valued at the oldest acquisition costs.

Evaluation of the Methods

All three of the cost flow assumptions described above are acceptable for use in financial statements and in income tax returns. As we have explained, it is not necessary that the physical flow of merchandise correspond to the cost flow assumption. Different flow assumptions may be used for different types of inventory, or for inventories in different geographical locations.

The only requirement for using a flow assumption is that the units to which the assumption is applied should be *homogeneous* in nature—that is, very similar in function, cost, and sales price. If each unit is unique, the specific identification method is needed in order to achieve a proper matching of sales revenue with the cost of goods sold.

As discussed below, each inventory valuation method has certain advantages and shortcomings. In the final analysis, the selection of inventory valuation methods is a managerial decision. However, the method (or methods) used in financial statements always should be disclosed in notes accompanying the statements.

Specific Identification The specific identification method is best suited to inventories of high-priced, low-volume items. This is the only method which exactly parallels the physical flow of the merchandise. If each item in the inventory is unique, as in the case of valuable paintings, custom jewelry, and most real estate, specific identification is clearly the logical choice.

The specific identification method has an intuitive appeal, because it assigns actual purchase costs to the specific units of merchandise sold or in inventory. However, when the units in inventory are identical (or nearly identical), the specific identification method may produce ***misleading results*** by implying differences in value which—under current market conditions—do not exist.

As an example, assume that a coal dealer has purchased 100 tons of coal at a cost of $60 per ton. A short time later, the company purchases another 100 tons of the ***same grade*** of coal—but this time, the cost is $80 per ton. The two purchases are in separate piles; thus, it would be possible for the company to use the specific identification method in accounting for sales.

Assume now that the company has an opportunity to sell 10 tons of coal at a retail price of $120 per ton. Does it really matter from which pile this coal is removed? The answer is ***no;*** the coal is a homogeneous product. Under current market conditions, the coal in each pile is equally valuable. To imply that it is more profitable to sell coal from one pile rather than the other is an argument of questionable logic.

Let us try to make this point in a more personal way: Would you be willing to shovel the more recently purchased coal out of the way so that the customer can get its truck back to the lower-cost coal pile?

Average Cost Identical items will have the same accounting values only under the average-cost method. Assume for example that a hardware store sells a given size nail for 65 cents per pound. The hardware store buys the nails in 100-pound quantities at different times at prices ranging from 40 to 50 cents per pound. Several hundred pounds of nails are always on hand, stored in a large bin. The average-cost method properly recognizes that when a customer buys a pound of nails it is not necessary to know exactly which nails the customer happened to select from the bin in order to measure the cost of goods sold. Therefore, the average-cost method avoids the shortcomings of the specific identification method. It is not necessary to keep track of the specific items sold and of those still in inventory. Also, it is not possible to manipulate income merely by selecting the specific items to be delivered to customers.

A shortcoming in the average-cost method is that changes in current replacement costs of inventory are concealed because these costs are averaged with older costs. Thus, neither the valuation of ending inventory nor the cost of goods sold will quickly reflect changes in the current replace-ment cost of merchandise.

First-In, First-Out   The distinguishing characteristic of the FIFO method is that the oldest purchase costs are transferred to the cost of goods sold, while the most recent costs remain in inventory.

Over the last 50 years, we have lived in an inflationary economy, which means that most prices tend to rise over time. When purchase costs are rising, the FIFO method assigns *lower* (older) costs to the cost of goods sold and the higher (more recent) costs to the goods remaining in inven-tory.

By assigning lower costs to the cost of goods sold, FIFO usually causes a business to report somewhat *higher profits* than would be reported under the other inventory valuation methods. Some companies favor the FIFO method for financial reporting purposes, because their goal is to report the highest net income possible. For income tax purposes, however, reporting more income than necessary results in paying more income taxes than necessary.

Some accountants and decision makers believe that FIFO tends to *overstate* a company's profitability. Revenue is based upon current mar-ket conditions. By offsetting this revenue with a cost of goods sold based upon older (and lower) prices, gross profits may be overstated consistently.

A conceptual advantage of the FIFO method is that inventory is valued at recent purchase costs. Therefore, this asset appears in the balance sheet at an amount closely approximating its current replacement cost.

Last-In, First-Out   The LIFO method is one of the most interesting and controversial flow assumptions. The basic assumption in the LIFO method is that the most recently purchased units are sold first and that the older units remain in inventory. This assumption is *not* in accord with the physi-cal flow of merchandise in most businesses. Yet, there are strong logical arguments in support of the LIFO method, in addition to income tax con-siderations.

For the purpose of measuring income, most accountants consider the *flow of costs* more important than the physical flow of merchandise. Sup-porters of the LIFO method contend that the measurement of income should be based upon *current market conditions.* Therefore, current sales revenue should be offset by the *current* cost of the merchandise sold. Under the LIFO method, the costs assigned to the cost of goods sold are relatively current, because they stem from the most recent purchases. Under the FIFO method, on the other hand, the cost of goods sold is based upon "older" costs.

Income tax considerations, however, provide the principal reason for the popularity of the LIFO method. Remember that the LIFO method as-signs the most recent inventory purchase costs to the cost of goods sold. In the common situation of rising prices, these "most recent" costs are also the highest costs. By reporting a higher cost of goods sold than results from the other inventory valuation methods, the LIFO method usually results in *lower taxable income.* In short, if inventory costs are rising, a company can reduce the amount of its income tax obligation by using the LIFO method in its income tax returns.

For the reason stated above, most companies use LIFO in their income tax returns. However, income tax regulations allow a corporation to use LIFO in its income tax return *only if the company also uses LIFO in its financial statements.* Thus, income tax considerations often provide an important reason for selecting the LIFO method.

There is one significant shortcoming to the LIFO method. The valuation of the asset inventory is based upon the company's "oldest" inventory acquisition costs. After the company has been in business for many years, these "oldest" costs may greatly understate the current replacement cost of the inventory. Thus, when an inventory is valued by the LIFO method, the company also should disclose the current replacement cost of the inventory in a note to the financial statements.

During periods of rising inventory replacement costs, the LIFO method results in the lowest valuation of inventory and measurement of net income. Therefore, LIFO is regarded as the most *"conservative"* of the inventory pricing methods. FIFO, on the other hand, is the "least conservative" method.[4]

The Principle of Consistency

The principle of *consistency* is one of the basic concepts underlying reliable financial statements. This principle means that once a company has adopted a particular accounting method, it should *follow that method consistently,* rather than switch methods from one year to the next. Thus, once a company has adopted a particular inventory flow assumption (or the specific identification method), it should continue to apply that assumption to all sales of that type of merchandise.

The principle of consistency does *not* prohibit a company from *ever* changing its accounting methods. If a change is made, however, the reasons for the change must be explained, and the effects of the change upon the company's net income must be fully disclosed.[5]

Just-in-Time (JIT) Inventory Systems

In recent years, much attention has been paid to the *just-in-time* inventory concept in manufacturing operations. The phrase "just-in-time" usually means that purchases of raw materials and component parts arrive just in time for use in the manufacturing process—often within a few hours of when the materials are scheduled for use. A second application of the just-in-time concept is completing the manufacturing process just in time to ship the finished goods to customers.

The principal advantage of a just-in-time system lies in reducing the amount of money "tied-up" in inventories of raw materials and finished goods. Also, the manufacturing company does not need to maintain large inventory storage facilities. The disadvantage of a just-in-time system is that a delay in the arrival of essential materials may bring manufacturing operations to a halt. Therefore, the just-in-time concept is feasible only

---

[4] During a prolonged period of *declining* inventory replacement costs, this situation reverses: FIFO becomes the most conservative method, and LIFO the least conservative.

[5] Disclosure of the effects of such "accounting changes" is discussed in Chapter 15. A change in the method of pricing inventory requires the approval of the Internal Revenue Service.

when the suppliers of materials (and the transportation systems) are highly reliable.

CASE IN POINT   One of the pioneers of just-in-time manufacturing is Toyota, the Japanese automaker. Toyota's main plant is located in an area of Japan called "Toyota City." Many of the company's suppliers of direct materials also are located in Toyota City and produce materials primarily for Toyota. Thus, the suppliers' economic survival depends upon their meeting their delivery schedules at the Toyota plant.

As a practical matter, a just-in-time system greatly reduces the size of the raw materials and finished goods inventories, but it usually does not eliminate these inventories entirely. (Just-in-time manufacturing systems are discussed further in Chapter 22.)

TAKING A PHYSICAL INVENTORY

*OBJECTIVE 2
Explain the
need for taking a physical inventory.*

In Chapter 5, we explained the need for businesses to make a complete physical count of the merchandise on hand at least once a year. The primary reason for this procedure of "taking inventory" is to adjust the perpetual inventory records for unrecorded ***shrinkage losses,*** such as theft, spoilage, or breakage.

The physical inventory usually is taken at (or near) the end of the company's fiscal year.[6] Often a business selects a fiscal year ending in a season of low activity. For example, most large retailers use a fiscal year ending in January.

Recording Shrinkage Losses

*OBJECTIVE 3
Record
shrinkage
losses and
other yearend adjustments to
inventory.*

In most cases, the year-end physical count of the inventory reveals some shortages or damaged merchandise. The costs of missing or damaged units are removed from the inventory records using the same flow assumption as is used in recording the costs of goods sold.

To illustrate, assume that a company's inventory subsidiary ledger shows the following 158 units of a particular product in inventory at year-end:

8 units purchased November 2 @ $100	$ 800
150 units purchased December 10 @ $115	17,250
Total (158 units)	$18,050

A year-end physical count, however, discloses that only ***148*** of these units actually are on hand. Based upon this physical count, the company should adjust its inventory records to reflect the loss of 10 units.

---

[6]   The reason for taking a physical inventory near year-end is to ensure that any shrinkage losses are reflected in the annual financial statements. The stronger the company's system of internal control over inventories, the further this procedure may be moved away from the balance sheet date. Obviously, no one wants to count inventory on New Year's Eve.

If the company uses **FIFO,** the missing units will be valued at the oldest purchase costs shown in the inventory records. Thus, 8 of the missing units will be assumed to have cost $100 per-unit and the other 2, $115 per-unit. Under FIFO, the shrinkage loss amounts to **$1,030** (8 units @ $100 + 2 units @ $115). If the company uses **LIFO,** on the other hand, the missing units all will be assumed to have come from the most recent purchase (on December 10). Therefore, the shrinkage loss amounts to **$1,150** (10 units @ $115).

If shrinkage losses are small, the costs removed from inventory may be charged (debited) directly to the Cost of Goods Sold account. If these losses are **material** in amount, the offsetting debit should be entered in a special loss account, such as Inventory Shrinkage Losses. In the income statement, a loss account is deducted from revenue in the same manner as an expense account.

LCM and Other Write-Downs of Inventory

In addition to shrinkage losses, the value of inventory may decline because the merchandise has become obsolete or is unsalable for other reasons.

CASE IN POINT   Several years ago, a deranged individual inserted a deadly poison into a few packages of Tylenol, a widely used medication. This criminal act of "product tampering" resulted in several tragic deaths. In response, Johnson & Johnson, the maker of Tylenol, promptly recalled all packages of this product and destroyed the entire inventory. The company later reintroduced Tylenol—this time in tablet form (rather than capsules) and in a tamperproof container. Other drug manufacturers quickly followed Johnson & Johnson's lead and changed the form and the packaging of their over-the-counter products.

The Tylenol tragedy often is studied by business managers and business students alike. The company's response is considered a classic example of fast, responsible, and effective action in a time of crisis.

If inventory has become obsolete or is otherwise unsalable, its carrying value in the accounting records should be **written down** to zero (or to its "scrap value," if any). A write-down of inventory reduces both the carrying value of the inventory and also the net income of the current period. The reduction in income is handled in the same manner as a shrinkage loss. If the write-down is relatively small, the loss is debited directly to the Cost of Goods Sold account. If the write-down is **material in amount,** however, it is charged to a special loss account, perhaps entitled Loss from Write-down of Inventory.

The Lower-of-Cost-or-Market (LCM) Rule   An asset is an economic resource. It may be argued that no economic resource is worth more than it would cost to **replace** that resource in the open market. For this reason, accountants traditionally have valued inventory in the balance sheet at the lower of its (1) cost or (2) market value. In this context, "market value" means *current replacement cost.* Thus, the inventory is valued at the lower of its historical cost or its current replacement cost.

The lower-of-cost-or-market rule may be applied in conjunction with any flow assumption and also with the specific identification method. If the current replacement cost of the ending inventory is substantially *below* the cost shown in the accounting records, the inventory is written down to this replacement cost. The offsetting debit is charged to either the Cost of Goods Sold account or the Loss from Write-down of Inventory account, depending upon the materiality of the dollar amount.

In their financial statements, most companies state that inventory is valued at the lower-of-cost-or-market. In our inflationary economy, however, the lower of these two amounts usually is cost, especially for companies using LIFO.[7]

The Year-End Cutoff of Transactions

Making a proper *cutoff* of transactions is an essential step in the preparation of reliable financial statements. A "proper cutoff" simply means that the transactions occurring near year-end are *recorded in the right accounting period.*

One aspect of a proper cutoff is determining that all purchases of merchandise through the end of the period are recorded in the inventory records and included in the physical count of merchandise on hand at year-end. Of equal importance is determining that the cost of all merchandise sold through the end of the period has been removed from the inventory accounts and charged to the Cost of Goods Sold. This merchandise should *not* be included in the year-end physical count.

If some sales transactions have not been recorded as of year-end, the quantities of merchandise shown in the inventory records will exceed the quantities actually on hand. When the results of the physical count are compared with the inventory records, these unrecorded sales easily could be mistaken for inventory shortages.

Making a proper cutoff may be difficult if sales transactions are occurring while the merchandise is being counted. For this reason, most businesses count their physical inventory during nonbusiness hours, even if they must shut down their sales operations for a day.

Matching Revenue and the Cost of Goods Sold   Accountants must determine that both the sales revenue and the cost of goods sold relating to sales transactions occurring near year-end are recorded in the *same* accounting period. Otherwise, the revenue and expense from these transactions will not be properly "matched" in the company's income statements.

Goods in Transit   A sale should be recorded *when title to the merchandise passes to the buyer.* In making a year-end cutoff of transactions, questions may arise when goods are in transit between the seller and the buyer as to which company owns the merchandise. The answer to such

---

[7]   A notable exception is the petroleum industry, in which the replacement cost of inventory can fluctuate very quickly and in either direction. Large oil companies occasionally report LCM adjustments of several hundred million dollars in a single year.

questions lies in the terms of shipment. If these terms are **F.O.B.** (free on board) **shipping point,** title passes at the point of shipment and the goods are the property of the buyer while in transit. If the terms of the shipment are **F.O.B. destination,** title does not pass until the shipment reaches its destination and the goods belong to the seller while in transit.

Many companies ignore these distinctions, because goods in transit always arrive within a day or two. In such cases, the amount of merchandise in transit usually is **not material** in dollar amount, and the company may follow the **most convenient** accounting procedures. It usually is most convenient to record all purchases when the inbound shipments arrive and all sales when the merchandise is shipped to the customer.

In some industries, however, goods in transit may be very material. Oil companies, for example, often have millions of dollars of inventory in transit in pipelines and supertankers. In these situations, the company must consider the terms of each shipment in recording its purchases and sales.

Periodic Inventory Systems

In our preceding discussions, we have emphasized the perpetual inventory system—that is, inventory records which are kept continuously up-to-date. Virtually all large business organizations use perpetual inventory systems.

OBJECTIVE 4
In a periodic inventory system, determine the ending inventory and the cost of goods sold using (a) average cost, (b) FIFO, and (c) LIFO.

Some small businesses, however, use **periodic** inventory systems. In a periodic inventory system, the cost of merchandise purchased during the year is debited to a **Purchases** account, rather than to the Inventory account. When merchandise is sold to a customer, an entry is made recognizing the sales revenue, but no entry is made to reduce the inventory account or to recognize the cost of goods sold.

The inventory on hand and the cost of goods sold for the year are not determined until year-end. At the end of the year, all goods on hand are counted and priced at cost. The cost assigned to this ending inventory is then used in computing the cost of goods sold, as shown below. (The dollar amounts are assumed for the purpose of completing the illustration.)

Inventory at the beginning of the year	*$10,000*
Add: Purchases during the year	*80,000*
Cost of goods available for sale during the year	*$90,000*
Less: Inventory at the end of the year	*7,000*
Cost of goods sold	*$83,000*

The only item in this computation that is kept continuously up-to-date in the accounting records is the Purchases account. The amounts of inventory at the beginning and end of the year are determined by annual physical counts.

Determining the cost of the year-end inventory involves two distinct steps: counting the merchandise and pricing the inventory, that is, determining the cost of the units on hand. Together, these procedures determine the proper valuation of inventory and also the cost of goods sold.

Applying Flow Assumptions in a Periodic System In our discussion of perpetual inventory systems, we have emphasized the costs which are transferred from inventory **to the cost of goods sold.** In a periodic system, the emphasis shifts to determining the costs which should be assigned *to inventory* at the end of the period.

To illustrate, assume that Cooks' Corner uses a periodic inventory system. The year-end physical inventory indicates that 12 units of a particular model food processor are on hand. Purchases of these food processors during the year are shown below:

	Number of Units	Cost Per Unit	Total Cost
Beginning inventory	10	$ 80	$ 800
First purchase (Mar. 1)	5	90	450
Second purchase (July 1)	5	100	500
Third purchase (Oct. 1)	5	120	600
Fourth purchase (Dec. 1)	5	130	650
Available for sale	30		$3,000
Units sold	18		
Units in ending inventory	12		

This schedule shows that 30 food processors were available for sale in the course of the year, of which 12 are still on hand. Thus, 18 of these food processors apparently were sold.[8] We will now use this data to determine the cost of the year-end inventory and the cost of goods sold using the specific identification method, and the average-cost, FIFO, and LIFO flow assumptions.

Specific Identification If specific identification is used, the company must identify the 12 food processors on hand at year-end and determine their actual costs from purchase invoices. Assume that these 12 units have an actual total cost of $1,240. The cost of goods sold then is determined by subtracting this ending inventory from the cost of goods available for sale:

Cost of goods available for sale	$3,000
Less: Ending inventory (specific identification)	1,240
Cost of goods sold	$1,760

Average Cost The average cost is determined by dividing the total cost of goods available for sale during the year by the total number of units available for sale. Thus, the average per-unit cost is *$100* ($3,000 ÷ 30 units). Under the average-cost method, the ending inventory would be priced at $1,200 (12 units × $100 per unit), and the cost of goods sold would be *$1,800* ($3,000 cost of goods available for sale, less $1,200 in costs assigned to the ending inventory).

FIFO Under the FIFO flow assumption, the oldest units are assumed to be the first sold. The ending inventory therefore is assumed to consist of the *most recently* acquired goods. (Remember, we are now talking about

---

[8]   The periodic inventory method does not distinguish between merchandise sold and shrinkage losses. Shrinkage losses are included automatically within the cost of goods sold.

the goods *in inventory,* not the goods sold.) Thus, the inventory of 12 food processors would be valued at the following costs:

5 units from the December 1 purchase @ $130	$ 650
5 units from the October 1 purchase @ $120	600
2 units from the July 1 purchase @ $100	200
Ending inventory, 12 units at FIFO cost	$1,450

The cost of goods sold would be *$1,550* ($3,000 − $1,450).

Notice that the FIFO method results in an inventory valued at relatively recent purchase costs. The cost of goods sold, however, is based upon the older acquisition costs.

LIFO   Under LIFO, the last units purchased are considered to be the first goods sold. Therefore, the ending inventory is assumed to contain the *earliest* purchases. The 12 food processors in inventory would be priced as follows:

10 units from the beginning inventory @ $80	$800
2 units from the March 1 purchase @ $90	180
Ending inventory, 12 units at LIFO cost	$980

The cost of goods sold under the LIFO method is *$2,020* ($3,000 − $980).

Notice that the cost of goods sold under LIFO is *higher* than that determined by the FIFO method ($2,020 under LIFO, as compared with $1,550 under FIFO). *LIFO always results in a higher cost of goods sold when purchase costs are rising.* Thus, LIFO tends to minimize net income and income taxes during periods of rising prices.

Notice also that the LIFO method may result in an ending inventory that is priced *well below its current replacement cost.*

Receiving the Maximum Tax Benefit from the LIFO Method   Many companies that use LIFO in a perpetual inventory system *restate* their year-end inventory at the costs indicated by the *periodic* LIFO costing procedures illustrated above. This "restatement" is accomplished by either debiting or crediting the Inventory account and making an offsetting entry to the Cost of Goods Sold account.

Often, restating the ending inventory at the unit costs indicated by periodic costing procedures results in pricing the ending inventory at older (and lower) costs than those indicated in the perpetual inventory records. If we assign less cost to the ending inventory, it follows that we will assign more of these merchandise costs to the cost of goods sold. A higher cost of goods sold, in turn, means less taxable income.

Let us briefly explain why applying LIFO at year-end may result in a lower valuation of inventory than does applying LIFO on a perpetual basis. Consider the last purchase in our example. This purchase of 5 food processors was made on December 31, at the relatively high unit cost of $130. Assuming these units were not sold prior to year-end, they would be included in the year-end inventory in perpetual inventory records, even if these records were maintained on a LIFO basis. When the ending inventory is priced using "periodic LIFO," however, this last-minute purchase is *not* included in inventory, but rather in the cost of goods sold.

Both the LIFO and average-cost methods produce somewhat different valuations of inventory under perpetual and periodic costing procedures. Only companies using LIFO, however, usually adjust their perpetual records to indicate the unit costs determined by periodic costing procedures.[9] When FIFO is in use, the perpetual and periodic costing procedures result in exactly the same valuation of inventory.

Pricing the Year-End Inventory by Computer   If purchase records are maintained by computer, the computer can compute the value of the ending inventory automatically using any of the flow assumptions discussed above. The computer operator must only enter the number of units on hand at year-end. A computer also can apply the specific identification method, but the computer operator then must enter an identification number for each unit in the ending inventory. This is one reason why the specific identification method usually is not used for inventories consisting of a large number of low-cost items.

Importance of an Accurate Valuation of Inventory

The most important current assets in the balance sheets of most companies are cash, accounts receivable, and inventory. Of these three, the inventory of merchandise is usually by far the largest. Because of the relatively large size of the inventory, an error in the valuation of this asset may not be readily apparent. However, a large error in inventory can cause a material misstatement of financial position and of net income. An error of 20% in valuing the inventory may have as much effect on the financial statements as would the complete omission of the asset cash. Therefore, care must be taken in counting and pricing the inventory at year-end.

An error in valuing the year-end inventory will of course lead to other erroneous figures in the balance sheet, such as the total current assets, total assets, and owner's equity.

The error will also affect key figures in the *income statement,* such as the cost of goods sold, the gross profit on sales, and the net income for the period. Finally, it is important to recognize that *the ending inventory of one year is also the beginning inventory of the following year.* Consequently, the income statement of the second year will also be in error by the full amount of the original error in inventory valuation.

Effects of an Error in Valuing Ending Inventory   To illustrate, assume that some items of merchandise in a company's inventory are overlooked during the year-end physical count. As a result of this error, the ending inventory will be ***understated.*** The costs of the uncounted merchandise erroneously will be transferred out of the Inventory account and included in the cost of

---

9   Income tax regulations permit a company to apply the LIFO concept in many different ways. However, these regulations require companies to use the *same* LIFO procedures in their financial statements and in their income tax returns.

OBJECTIVE 5
Explain the
effects of an
inventory
error on the
income
statement of
the current
year and the
following
year.

goods sold. This overstatement of the cost of goods sold, in turn, results in an understatement of gross profit and net income.[10]

Inventory Errors Affect Two Years An error in the valuation of ending inventory affects not only the financial statements of the current year, but also the income statement for the ***following*** year.

Assume that the ending inventory in ***1993*** is ***understated*** by $10,000. As we have described above, the cost of goods sold in 1993 will be overstated by this amount, and both gross profit and net income will be ***understated.***

The ending inventory in 1993, however, becomes the ***beginning inventory*** in ***1994.*** An understatement of the beginning inventory results in an understatement of the cost of goods sold and, therefore, an ***overstatement*** of gross profit and net income in 1994.

Notice that the original error has exactly the ***opposite effects*** upon the net incomes of the two successive years. Net income was ***understated*** by the amount of the error of 1993, and ***overstated*** by the same amount in 1994. For this reason inventory errors are said to be "counterbalancing" or "self-correcting" over a two-year period.

The fact that offsetting errors occur in the financial statements of two successive years does not lessen the consequences of errors in inventory valuation. Rather, this ***exaggerates*** the misleading effects of the error upon ***trends*** in the company's performance from one year to the next.

CASE IN POINT Some small businesses purposely have understated ending inventory in their income tax returns as an easy—though fraudulent—means of understating taxable income. In the following year, however, the effects of this error will reverse, and taxable income will be overstated. To avoid paying income taxes on this overstated income, the business may again understate its ending inventory, this time by an even greater amount. If this type of tax fraud continues for very long, the inventory becomes so understated that the situation becomes obvious.

When the Internal Revenue Service audits the income tax return of a small business, the auditors invariably try to determine whether inventory has been understated. If such an understatement exists, they will try to determine the taxpayer's intent. If the understatement has been allowed to reverse itself in the following year, the auditors probably will view the incident as an honest mistake. If they find a consistent pattern of understated inventories, however, they may decide to prosecute the taxpayer for income tax evasion—a criminal offense.

Effects of Errors in Inventory Valuation: A Summary The following table summarizes the effects of an error in the valuation of ending inventory over two successive years. In this table we indicate the effects of the error on various financial statement measurements using the code letters ***U***

---

[10] If income tax effects are ignored, the amount of the error is exactly the same in inventory, gross profit, and net income. If tax effects are considered, the amount of the error may be lessened in the net income figure.

(Understated), **O** (Overstated), and **NE** (No Effect). The effects of errors in the valuation of inventory are the same regardless of whether the company uses a perpetual or a periodic inventory system.

Original Error: Ending Inventory Understated

	Year of the Error	Following Year
Beginning inventory	NE	U
Cost of goods available for sale	NE	U
Ending inventory	U	NE
Cost of goods sold	O	U
Gross profit	U	O
Net income	U	O
Owner's equity at year-end	U	NE

Original Error: Ending Inventory Overstated

	Year of the Error	Following Year
Beginning inventory	NE	O
Cost of goods available for sale	NE	O
Ending inventory	O	NE
Cost of goods sold	U	O
Gross profit	O	U
Net income	O	U
Owner's equity at year-end	O	NE

Techniques for Estimating the Cost of Goods Sold and the Ending Inventory

OBJECTIVE 6
Estimate the cost of goods sold and ending inventory by the gross profit method and by the retail method.

Taking a physical inventory every month would be very expensive and time-consuming. Therefore, if a business using a periodic inventory system is to prepare monthly or quarterly financial statements, it usually *estimates* the amounts of its inventory and cost of goods sold. One approach to making these estimates is called the ***gross profit method;*** another—used primarily by retail stores—is the ***retail method.***

The Gross Profit Method

The gross profit method is a quick, simple technique for estimating the cost of goods sold and the amount of inventory on hand. In using this method, it is assumed that the rate of gross profit earned in the preceding year will remain the same for the current year. When we know the rate of gross profit, we can divide the dollar amount of net sales into two elements: (1) the gross profit and (2) the cost of goods sold. We view net sales as 100%. If the gross profit rate, for example, is 40% of net sales, the cost of goods sold must be 60%. In other words, the cost of goods sold percentage (or ***cost ratio***) is determined by deducting the gross profit rate from 100%.

When the gross profit rate is known, the ending inventory can be estimated by the following procedures:

1 Determine the ***cost of goods available for sale*** from the general ledger records of beginning inventory and net purchases.

2 Estimate the ***cost of goods sold*** by multiplying the net sales by the cost ratio.

3 Deduct the ***cost of goods sold*** from the ***cost of goods available for sale*** to find the estimated ending inventory.

To illustrate, assume that Metro Hardware has a beginning inventory of $50,000 on January 1. During the month of January, net purchases amount to $20,000 and net sales total $30,000. Assume that the company's normal gross profit rate is 40% of net sales; it follows that the cost ratio is **60%.** Using these facts, the inventory on January 31 may be estimated as follows:

Goods available for sale:			
Beginning inventory, Jan. 1			*$50,000*
Purchases			*20,000*
Step 1 . . .	*Cost of goods available for sale*		*$70,000*
	Deduct: Estimated cost of goods sold:		
	Net sales	*$30,000*	
	Cost ratio (100% − 40%)	*60%*	
Step 2 . . .	*Estimated cost of goods sold ($30,000 × 60%)*		*18,000*
Step 3 . . .	*Estimated ending inventory, Jan. 31*		*$52,000*

The gross profit method of estimating inventory has several uses apart from the preparation of monthly financial statements. For example, if an inventory is destroyed by fire, the company must determine the amount of the inventory on hand at the date of the fire in order to file an insurance claim. The most convenient way to determine this inventory amount is often the gross profit method.

The gross profit method is also used at year-end after the taking of a physical inventory to confirm the overall reasonableness of the amount determined by the counting and pricing process.

The Retail Method

The retail method of estimating inventory and the cost of goods sold is quite similar to the gross profit method. The basic difference is that the retail method is based upon the cost ratio of the ***current period,*** rather than that of the prior year.

To determine the cost ratio of the current period, the business must keep track of both the cost of all goods purchased during the period and the ***retail sales prices*** which were assigned to these goods. To illustrate, assume that during June the cost of goods available for sale in Tennis Gallery totaled $45,000. The store had offered this merchandise for sale to its customers at retail prices totaling $100,000. The cost ratio in June was **45%** ($45,000 ÷ $100,000). This cost ratio is used to estimate the monthly cost of goods sold and the month-end inventory by the same procedures as are applied under the gross profit method.

Many retail stores also use their current cost ratio as a quick method of pricing the inventory counted at year-end. In a retail store, the retail sales price is clearly marked on the merchandise. Therefore, employees quickly can determine the retail price of the ending inventory. This retail price may be reduced to a close approximation of cost simply by multiplying by the cost ratio.

Assume, for example, that the annual physical inventory at Tennis Gallery indicates the merchandise on hand at year-end has a retail sales price of $120,000. If the cost ratio for the year has been 44%, the cost of this inventory is approximately $52,800 ($120,000 × 44%). This version of the retail method approximates valuation of the inventory at average cost. A variation of this method approximates a LIFO valuation of the ending inventory.

Inventory Management

*OBJECTIVE 7
Identify several factors that management should consider in determining the optimal size of the company's inventory.*

How much inventory should a business keep on hand? The answer to this question is based upon many factors, including the nature of a company's business operations, the reliability and proximity of its suppliers, the physical characteristics of the inventory, marketing strategies, and management's willingness to risk the consequences of running out of merchandise or materials.

Inventory stored in a warehouse is an idle asset. Not only does this asset produce no revenue, it may require substantial storage costs.

Today, many manufacturing companies are implementing just-in-time inventory systems, designed to minimize their inventories of raw materials and finished goods. Although these systems can reduce the costs associated with carrying substantial inventories, they also involve considerable risk. As stated earlier, even a temporary delay in the arrival of key raw materials may bring the company's manufacturing operations to a halt.

Many retailing companies deliberately maintain large inventories to offer their customers a wide selection of merchandise. Such advertising slogans as "Largest selection in town," and "Available for immediate delivery" reflect marketing strategies that involve a large inventory.

In contrast, retailers that sell merchandise tailored to customers' specifications often maintain little or no inventory. These companies do not purchase their merchandise until *after* they have an order (and usually a deposit) from their customer. In essence, these businesses have just-in-time inventory systems.

Among the advantages of maintaining a *minimum*-size inventory are:

- Less money is tied up in an asset which generates little or no revenue while it is stored in a warehouse or on a shelf. (Many companies, such as automobile dealerships, finance their purchases of inventory. Thus, a smaller inventory reduces the company's interest expense.)

- Storage costs are minimized (including the need for maintaining storage facilities).

- The risk of loss from merchandise becoming obsolete, out-of-fashion, or otherwise unsalable is held to a minimum.

On the other hand, the following considerations favor maintaining a *larger* inventory:

- A large selection of merchandise may attract more customers. For retailers, fewer sales opportunities are lost because items are temporarily "out of stock." In most cases, a large inventory is required to generate a high volume of sales in a retail business.

- Suppliers may offer substantial discounts if merchandise is purchased in large quantities. (Automobile manufacturers, for example, offer larger discounts to dealerships that purchase more cars.)
- For manufacturers, larger inventories of raw materials reduce the risk that manufacturing operations will be interrupted by shortages of key materials.

In summary, the decision as to the appropriate size of an inventory involves not only financial considerations, but also management's marketing strategy and its willingness to take risks. These issues, and the related topic of determining the optimal reorder quantity, are discussed further in later accounting courses.

Evaluating the Liquidity of Inventory

OBJECTIVE 8 Compute the inventory turnover rate. Explain why this ratio is of interest to short-term creditors.

Inventory often is the largest of a company's current assets. But how liquid is this asset? How quickly will it be converted into cash? As a step toward answering these questions, short-term creditors often compute the ***inventory turnover rate.***

Inventory Turnover Rate   The inventory turnover rate is equal to the cost of goods sold divided by the average amount of inventory (beginning inventory plus ending inventory, divided by 2). This ratio indicates how many ***times*** in the course of a year the company is able to sell the amount of its average inventory. The higher this rate, the more quickly the company sells its inventory.

To illustrate, a recent annual report of J.C. Penney shows a cost of goods sold of $10,492 million and average inventory of $2,407 million. The inventory turnover rate for Penney's, therefore, is ***4.36 to 1*** ($10,492 million ÷ $2,407 million). We may compute the number of ***days*** required for the company to sell its inventory by dividing 365 days by the turnover rate. Thus, J.C. Penney requires ***84 days*** to turn over (sell) the amount of its average inventory (365 days ÷ 4.36).

Users of financial statements find the inventory turnover rate useful in evaluating the liquidity of the company's inventory. In addition, managers and independent auditors use this computation to help identify inventory which is not selling well and which may have become obsolete. A declining turnover rate indicates that merchandise is not selling as quickly as it used to.

Converting the Inventory into Cash   Most businesses sell merchandise on account. Therefore, inventory often is not converted into cash as soon as it is sold. To determine how quickly inventory is converted into cash, we must combine the number of days required to ***sell the inventory*** with the number of days required to ***collect the accounts receivable.***

Computation of the number of days required to collect accounts receivable was illustrated and explained in the preceding chapter. To review, the ***accounts receivable turnover rate*** is computed by dividing net sales by the average accounts receivable. The number of days required to collect these receivables then is determined by dividing 365 days by this turnover rate. Data for the J.C. Penney annual report indicate that the company needed ***97 days*** (on average) to collect its accounts receivable.

Length of the Operating Cycle   The **operating cycle** of a merchandising company is the average time period between the purchase of merchandise and the conversion of this merchandise back into cash.[11] In other words, the merchandise acquired as inventory gradually is converted into accounts receivable by selling the goods on account, and these receivables are converted into cash through the process of collection.

The operating cycle of J.C. Penney was approximately **181 days,** computed by adding the average 84 days required to sell its inventory and the 97 days required to collect its accounts receivable from customers. From the viewpoint of short-term creditors, the shorter the operating cycle, the higher the quality of the company's current assets.

Accounting Methods Can Affect Financial Statement Subtotals and Analytical Ratios

The accounting methods selected by a company may affect the ratios and financial statement subtotals used in evaluating the company's financial position and the results of its operations. To illustrate, let us consider the effects of inventory valuation methods upon inventory turnover rates.

Assume that during a period of rising prices Alpha Company uses LIFO, whereas Beta Company uses FIFO. In all other respects, the two companies **are identical;** they have the same size inventories, and they purchase and sell the same quantities of merchandise at the same prices and on the same dates. Thus, each company **physically** "turns over" its inventory at **exactly the same rate.**

Because Alpha uses the LIFO method, however, its inventory is valued at older (and lower) costs than is the inventory of Beta Company. Also, Alpha's cost of goods sold includes more recent (and higher) costs than does Beta's. When these amounts are used in computing the inventory turnover rate (cost of goods sold divided by average inventory), Alpha **appears** to have the higher turnover rate.

We already have stated that the inventories of these two companies are turning over at exactly the same rate. Therefore, the differences in the turnover rates computed from the companies' financial statements are caused **solely by the different accounting methods used in the valuation of the companies' inventories.**

Inventory turnover is not the only ratio which will be affected. Alpha will report lower current assets than Beta and, therefore, a lower current ratio and less working capital. In addition, using LIFO will cause Alpha to report less gross profit and lower net income than Beta.

Users of financial statements must understand the typical effects of different accounting methods. Also, a financial analyst should be able to restate on a **comparable basis** the financial statements of companies that use different accounting methods. Notes accompanying the financial statements usually provide the information necessary for comparing the operating results of companies using LIFO with those of companies using the FIFO method.

---

[11]   In a **manufacturing** business, the operating cycle also includes the time period involved in manufacturing the inventory.

CASE IN POINT Oshkosh B'Gosh, Inc. (a publicly owned maker of children's clothing) uses LIFO. However, a note accompanying the financial statements reads in part:

> Although the LIFO method results in a better matching of costs and revenue, information relating to the first-in, first-out (FIFO) method may be useful in comparing operating results to those companies not on LIFO. Had earnings been reported on a FIFO basis the results would have been: . . . .

In the remainder of the note, the company discloses the ending inventory, cost of goods sold, and net income that would have resulted from use of the FIFO method.

■ ■ ■ *** Supplemental Topic**
LIFO Reserves

OBJECTIVE 9
Define a "LIFO reserve" and explain its implications to users of financial statements.

We have stated that the significant shortcoming in the LIFO method is that the asset inventory is valued at the company's "oldest" inventory acquisition costs. After a period of years, these outdated costs may significantly understate the current replacement cost of the inventory. The difference between the LIFO cost of an inventory and its current replacement cost often is called a **LIFO reserve**.[12]

CASE IN POINT In a recent balance sheet, General Motors reported inventories of approximately $8 billion, valued by the LIFO method. A note accompanying the balance sheet, however, explained that the current replacement cost of these inventories exceeded $10.4 billion. Therefore, GM had a "LIFO reserve" of more than $2.4 billion.

THE SIGNIFICANCE OF A LIFO RESERVE

Users of financial statements should understand the implications of a large LIFO reserve.

Comparing LIFO and FIFO Inventories A LIFO reserve indicates that the company's inventory is ***undervalued*** in terms of its current replacement cost and in terms of the valuation that would have resulted from use of the FIFO method. Thus, the inventories of companies using LIFO are not directly comparable to those of companies using FIFO. Fortunately, this problem is solved in the notes to the financial statements: companies using

---

[12] The phrase "LIFO reserve" is used by accountants, investors, and business managers in conversation and many types of financial literature. The FASB, however, discourages use of the word "reserve" in formal financial statements, as this word has several different meanings. Therefore, in financial statements a LIFO reserve is likely to be described as "the difference between the LIFO cost and current (replacement) cost of inventory."

LIFO disclose the current replacement cost (or FIFO cost) of their inventories.

Liquidation of a LIFO Reserve The existence of a LIFO reserve may cause a company's profits to rise dramatically if inventory falls to an abnormally low level at year-end. As the company reduces its inventories, the costs transferred to the cost of goods sold will come from older—and lower—cost layers. The inclusion of these old and low costs in the cost of goods sold can cause the company's gross profit rate to soar. This situation is called a "liquidation" of the LIFO reserve.[13]

Many factors may cause the liquidation of a LIFO reserve. For example, the company may be unable to make the purchases necessary to replenish its inventory because of shortages or strikes. Often a company discontinues a particular product line and sells its entire inventory of this merchandise. Also, management deliberately may delay making normal year-end purchases in order to liquidate a portion of the company's LIFO reserve.

The user of financial statements should recognize that the abnormal profits which result from the liquidation of a LIFO reserve **do not** represent an improvement in financial performance. Rather, these profits are a one-time occurrence, resulting from old and relatively low unit costs temporarily being used in measuring the cost of goods sold. Users of financial statements easily can determine whether a company's reported earnings are affected by the liquidation of a LIFO reserve. This "liquidation" occurs whenever a company using LIFO ends its fiscal year with its inventory at a substantially lower level than at the beginning of the year. The dollar effect of this liquidation can be determined from notes accompanying the financial statements.

Assessing the Income Tax Benefits of Using LIFO A LIFO reserve represents the amount by which a company has reduced its taxable income over the years through use of the LIFO method. Referring to our Case in Point, General Motors has reduced its taxable income (over a long span of years) by more than $2.4 billion. If we assume that GM pays income taxes at a rate of, say, 33%, using LIFO has saved the company about $800 million in income taxes.

END-OF-CHAPTER REVIEW

SUMMARY OF CHAPTER LEARNING OBJECTIVES

1 **Using a perpetual inventory system, determine the cost of goods sold using (a) specific identification, (b) average cost, (c) FIFO, and (d) LIFO. Discuss the advantages and shortcomings of each method.**
Under the *specific identification method,* the actual costs of the specific units sold are transferred from inventory to the cost of goods sold. (Debit Cost of Goods Sold, credit Inventory.) This method achieves the

---

[13] In formal financial statements, the liquidation of a LIFO reserve simply is called a "LIFO liquidation."

proper matching of sales revenue and cost of goods sold when the individual units in the inventory are unique. However, the method becomes cumbersome and may produce misleading results if the inventory consists of homogeneous items.

The remaining three methods are *flow assumptions,* which should be applied only to an inventory of homogeneous items.

Under the *average-cost method,* the average cost of all units in the inventory is computed and used in recording the cost of goods sold. This is the only method in which all units are assigned the same (average) per-unit cost.

FIFO (first-in, first-out) is the assumption that the first units purchased are the first units sold. Thus, inventory is assumed to consist of the most recently purchased units. FIFO assigns current costs to inventory, but older (and often lower) costs to the cost of goods sold.

LIFO (last-in, first-out) is the assumption that the most recently acquired goods are sold first. This matches sales revenue with relatively current costs. In a period of inflation, LIFO results in lower reported profits and lower income taxes than the other methods. However, the "oldest" purchase costs are assigned to inventory, which may result in inventory becoming grossly understated in terms of current replacement costs.

2 Explain the need for taking a physical inventory.

In a perpetual inventory system, a physical inventory is taken to adjust the inventory records for shrinkage losses. In a periodic inventory system, the physical inventory is the basis for determining the cost of the ending inventory and for computing cost of goods sold.

3 Record shrinkage losses and other year-end adjustments to inventory.

Shrinkage losses are recorded by removing from the Inventory account the cost of the missing or damaged units. The offsetting debit may be to Cost of Goods Sold, if the shrinkage is normal in amount, or to a special loss account. If inventory is found to be obsolete or unsalable, it is written down to zero (or its scrap value, if any). If inventory is valued at the lower-of-cost-or-market, it is written down to its current replacement cost, if at year-end this amount is substantially below the cost shown in the inventory records.

4 In a periodic inventory system, determine the ending inventory and the cost of goods sold using (a) average cost, (b) FIFO, and (c) LIFO.

The cost of goods sold is determined by combining the beginning inventory with the purchases during the period, and subtracting the cost of the ending inventory. Thus, the cost assigned to ending inventory also determines the cost of goods sold.

Under the average-cost method, the ending inventory is determined by multiplying the number of units on hand by the average cost of the units available for sale during the year. Under FIFO, the units in inventory are priced using the unit costs from the *most recent* cost layers. Under the LIFO method, inventory is priced using the unit costs in the oldest cost layers.

5 Explain the effects of an inventory error on the income statement of the current year and the following year.

In the current year, an error in the costs assigned to *ending* inventory will cause an opposite error in the cost of goods sold and, therefore, a repetition of the original error in the amount of gross profit. For example, understating ending inventory results in an overstatement of the cost of goods sold, and an understatement of gross profit.

The error has exactly the opposite effects upon the cost of goods sold and the gross profit of the following year, because the error is now in the cost assigned to *beginning* inventory.

6 Estimate the costs of goods sold and ending inventory by the gross profit method and by the retail method.

Both the gross profit and retail methods use a *cost ratio* in estimating the cost of goods sold and ending inventory. The cost of goods sold is estimated by multiplying net sales by this cost ratio; ending inventory then is estimated by subtracting this cost of goods sold from the cost of goods available for sale.

In the gross profit method, the cost ratio is 100% minus the company's historical gross profit rate. In the retail method, the cost ratio for the current period is computed by keeping track of both the cost and the retail prices of merchandise available for sale.

7 Identify several factors that management should consider in determining the optimal size of the company's inventory.

Among the factors to be considered are (a) the amount of money invested in the inventory, (b) storage and insurance costs, (c) the risk of the inventory becoming obsolete, (d) the consequences of temporarily running out of a specific product or raw material, (e) the reliability of suppliers in meeting delivery schedules, (f) the availability of discounts on large purchases, and (g) marketing strategies, such as offering customers a wide selection of merchandise.

8 Compute the inventory turnover rate. Explain why this ratio is of interest to short-term creditors.

The inventory turnover rate is equal to the cost of goods sold divided by the average inventory. This computation is of interest to short-term creditors because it indicates the relative liquidity of the company's inventory—that is, how quickly this asset can be sold.

*9 Define a "LIFO reserve" and explain its implications to users of financial statements.

A LIFO reserve is the amount by which the current replacement cost of inventory exceeds the LIFO cost shown in the accounting records.

If a company has a large LIFO reserve, neither its inventory nor its cost of goods sold are comparable to those of a company using FIFO. Also, a LIFO reserve may cause earnings to increase dramatically if inventory falls below normal levels. Notes accompanying the financial statements provide the statement users with information useful in evaluating the implications of a LIFO reserve.

---

* *Supplemental Topic, "LIFO Reserves"*

In this chapter we have seen that different inventory valuation methods can have significant effects on net income as reported in financial statements, and on income tax returns as well. In the following chapter, we will see that a similar situation exists with respect to the alternative methods used in depreciating plant and equipment.

KEY TERMS INTRODUCED OR EMPHASIZED IN CHAPTER 9

Average-cost method A method of valuing all units in the inventory at the same average per-unit cost, which is recomputed after every purchase.

Consistency in inventory valuation An accounting standard that calls for the use of the same method of inventory pricing from year to year, with full disclosure of the effects of any change in method. Intended to make financial statements comparable.

Cost flow assumptions Assumptions as to the sequence in which units are removed from inventory for the purpose of sale. Need not parallel the physical movement of merchandise if the units are homogeneous.

Cost layer Units of merchandise acquired at the same unit cost. An inventory comprised of several cost layers is characteristic of all inventory valuation methods except *average cost.*

Cost ratio The cost of merchandise expressed as a percentage of its retail selling price. Used in inventory estimating techniques, such as the *gross profit method* and the *retail method.*

First-in, first-out (FIFO) method A method of computing the cost of inventory and the cost of goods sold based on the assumption that the first merchandise acquired is the first merchandise sold, and that the ending inventory consists of the most recently acquired goods.

F.O.B. destination A term meaning the seller bears the cost of shipping goods to the buyer's location. Title to the goods remains with the seller while the goods are in transit.

F.O.B. shipping point The buyer of goods bears the cost of transportation from the seller's location to the buyer's location. Title to the goods passes at the point of shipment and the goods are the property of the buyer while in transit.

Gross profit method A method of estimating the cost of the ending inventory based upon the assumption that the rate of gross profit remains approximately the same from year to year.

Inventory turnover rate The cost of goods sold divided by the average amount of inventory. Indicates how many times the average inventory is sold during the course of the year.

Just-in-time (JIT) inventory system A technique designed to minimize a company's investment in inventory. In a manufacturing company, this means receiving purchases of raw materials just in time for use in the manufacturing process, and completing the manufacture of finished goods just in time to fill existing sales orders.

Last-in, first-out (LIFO) method A method of computing the cost of goods sold by use of the prices paid for the most recently acquired units. Ending inventory is valued on the basis of prices paid for the units first acquired.

LIFO reserve The difference between the current replacement cost of a company's inventory and the LIFO cost shown in the accounting records. The fact that a LIFO reserve can become very large is the principal shortcoming of the LIFO method.

Liquidation of a LIFO reserve Selling merchandise from a LIFO inventory to the point at which the inventory falls below the traditional level. As a result, the costs passing into the cost of goods sold cease to become the costs of recent purchases and may, in fact, become very "old" costs. Tends to inflate reported profits.

Lower-of-cost-or-market (LCM) method A method of inventory pricing in which goods are valued at original cost or replacement cost (market), whichever is lower.

Operating cycle The sequence of steps (and length of time) by which a business converts cash into inventory, inventory into accounts receivable, and accounts receivable into cash. All assets expected to be converted into cash in the course of this cycle are viewed as current assets.

Physical inventory A systematic count of all goods on hand, followed by the application of unit prices to the quantities counted and development of a dollar valuation of the ending inventory.

Retail method A method of estimating the cost of goods sold and ending inventory. Similar to the gross profit method, except that the cost ratio is based upon current cost-to-retail price relationships rather than upon those of the prior year.

Shrinkage losses Losses of inventory resulting from theft, spoilage, or breakage.

Specific identification method Recording as the cost of goods sold the actual costs of the specific units sold. Required when each unit in inventory is unique, but not when the inventory consists of homogeneous products.

Write-down (of an asset) A reduction in the carrying value of an asset because it has become obsolete or its usefulness has otherwise been impaired. Involves a credit to the asset account, with an offsetting debit to a loss account.

DEMONSTRATION PROBLEM FOR YOUR REVIEW

The Audiophile sells high-performance stereo equipment. Massachusetts Acoustic recently introduced the Carnegie-440, a state-of-the-art speaker system. During the current year, The Audiophile purchased 9 of these speaker systems at the following dates and acquisition costs:

Date	Units Purchased	Unit Cost	Total Cost
Oct. 1	2	$3,000	$ 6,000
Nov. 17	3	3,200	9,600
Dec. 1	4	3,250	13,000
Available for sale during the year	9		$28,600

On **November 21,** The Audiophile sold 4 of these speaker systems to the Boston Symphony. The other 5 Carnegie-440s remained in inventory at December 31.

INSTRUCTIONS Assume that The Audiophile uses a **perpetual inventory system.** Compute (1) the cost of goods sold relating to the sale of Carnegie-440 speakers to the Boston Symphony, and (2) the ending inventory of these speakers at December 31, using each of the following flow assumptions:

a Average cost

b First-in, first-out (FIFO)

c Last-in, first-out (LIFO)

Show the number of units and the unit costs of the cost layers comprising the cost of goods sold and the ending inventory.

SOLUTION TO DEMONSTRATION PROBLEM

a *(1) Cost of goods sold (at average cost):*

Average unit cost at Nov. 21 [($6,000 + $9,600) ÷ 5 units] ...... $ 3,120

Cost of goods sold (4 units × $3,120 per unit) $12,480

(2) Inventory at Dec. 31 (at average cost):

Average unit cost at Dec. 31:

Units remaining after sale of November 21 (1 unit @ $3,120) .	$ 3,120
Units purchased on Dec. 1 (4 units @ $3,250)	13,000
Total cost of 5 units in inventory...........................	$16,120
Average unit cost at Dec. 31	$ 3,224
Inventory at Dec. 31 (5 units × $3,224 per unit)	$16,120

b *(1) Cost of goods sold (FIFO basis): (2 units @ $3,000 + 2 units @ $3,200)...* $12,400

(2) Inventory at Dec. 31 (4 units @ $3,250 + 1 units @ $3,200) $16,200

c *(1) Cost of goods sold (LIFO basis): (3 units @ $3,200 + 1 unit @ $3,000)...* $12,600

(2) Inventory at Dec. 31 (4 units @ $3,250 + 1 unit @ $3,000) $16,000

SELF-TEST QUESTIONS

The answers to these questions appear on page 453.

1 The primary purpose for using an inventory flow *assumption* is to:

  a Parallel the physical flow of units of merchandise.

  b Offset against revenue an appropriate cost of goods sold.

  c Minimize income taxes.

  d Maximize the reported amount of net income.

2 Ace Auto Supply uses a perpetual inventory record. On March 10, the company sells 2 Shelby four-barrel carburetors. Immediately prior to this sale, the perpetual inventory records indicate 3 of these carburetors on hand, as shown below:

Date	Quantity Purchased	Unit Cost	Units on Hand	Total Cost
Feb. 4	1	$220	1	$220
Mar. 2	2	235	3	690

With respect to this sale on March 10: (More than one of the following answers may be correct.)

  a If the average-cost method is used, the cost of goods sold is $460.

  b If these carburetors have identification numbers, Ace must use the specific identification method in determining the cost of goods sold.

  c If the company uses LIFO, the cost of goods sold will be $15 higher than if it were using FIFO.

  d If the company uses LIFO, the carburetor *remaining* in inventory after the sales will be assumed to have cost $220.

3 T-Shirt City uses a *periodic* inventory system. During the first year of operations, the company made four purchases of a particular product. Each purchase was for 500 units and the prices paid were: $9 per unit in the first purchase, $10 per unit in the second purchase, $12 per unit in the third purchase, and $13 per unit in the fourth purchase. At year-end, 650 of these units remained unsold. Compute the cost of goods sold under the FIFO method and LIFO method, respectively.

  a $13,700 (FIFO) and $16,000 (LIFO)

  b $8,300 (FIFO) and $6,000 (LIFO)

  c $16,000 (FIFO) and $13,700 (LIFO)

  d $6,000 (FIFO) and $8,300 (LIFO)

4 Trent Department Store uses a perpetual inventory system but adjusts its inventory records at year-end to reflect the results of a complete physical inventory. In the physical inventory taken at the ends of 1993 and 1994, Trent's employees failed to count the merchandise in the store's window displays. The cost of this merchandise amounted to $13,000 at the end of 1993 and $19,000 at the end of 1994. As a result of these errors, the cost of goods sold for 1994 will be:

  a Understated by $19,000.

  b Overstated by $6,000.

  c Understated by $6,000.

  d None of the above.

5 In July, 1994, the accountant for LBJ Imports is in the process of preparing financial statements for the quarter ended June 30, 1994. The physical inventory, however, was last taken on June 5 and the accountant must establish the approximate cost at June 30 from the following data:

Physical inventory, June 5, 1994	$900,000
Transactions for the period June 5–June 30:	
Sales..	700,000
Purchases...	400,000

    The gross profit on sales has consistently averaged 40% of sales. Using the gross profit method, compute the approximate inventory cost at June 30, 1994.

  a $420,000   b $880,000   c $480,000   d $1,360,000

6 Allied Products maintains a large inventory. The company has used the LIFO inventory method for many years, during which the purchase costs of its products have risen substantially. (More than one of the following answers may be correct.)

  a Allied would have reported a *higher* net income in past years if it had been using the average-cost method.

  b Allied's financial statements imply a *higher* inventory turnover rate than they would if the company were using FIFO.

  c If Allied were to let its inventory fall far below normal levels, the company's gross profit rate would *rise.*

  d Allied's current ratio is *lower* than it would be if the company were using FIFO.

ASSIGNMENT MATERIAL

DISCUSSION QUESTIONS

1 Is the cost of merchandise acquired during the period classified as an asset or an expense? Explain.

2 Why is it necessary to use either specific identification or a flow assumption in recording the cost of goods sold?

3 Briefly describe the advantages of using a flow assumption, rather than the specific identification method.

4 Under what circumstances do generally accepted accounting principles permit the use of an inventory cost flow assumption? Must a flow assumption closely parallel the physical movement of the company's merchandise?

5 Assume that a company has in its inventory units of a particular product which were purchased at several different per-unit costs. when some of these units were sold, explain how the cost of goods sold is measured under each of the following flow assumptions:

   a Average cost

   b FIFO

   c LIFO

6 A large art gallery has in inventory more than one hundred paintings. No two are alike. The least expensive is priced at more than $1,000 and the higher-priced items carry prices of $100,000 or more. Which of the four methods of inventory valuation discussed in this chapter would you consider to be most appropriate for this business? Give reasons for your answer.

7 During a period of steadily increasing purchase costs, which inventory flow assumption results in the highest reported profits? The lowest taxable income? The valuation of inventory which is closest to current replacement cost? Briefly explain your answers.

8 Assume that during the first year of Hatton Corporation's operation, there were numerous purchases of identical items of merchandise. However, there was no change during the year in the prices paid for this merchandise. Under these special circumstances how would the financial statements be affected by the choice between the FIFO and LIFO methods of inventory valuation?

9 Apex Corporation operates in two locations: New York and Oregon. The LIFO method is used in accounting for inventories at the New York facility and the specific identification method for inventories at the Oregon location. Does this concurrent use of two inventory methods indicate that Apex is violating the accounting principle of consistency? Explain.

10 What are the characteristics of a *just-in-time* inventory system? Briefly explain the advantages and risks of this type of system.

11 Why do most companies that use perpetual inventory systems also take an annual *physical inventory?* When is this physical inventory usually taken? Why?

12 Under what circumstances might a company write down its inventory to carrying value below cost?

13 What is meant by the year-end *cutoff* of transactions? If merchandise in transit at year-end is material in dollar amount, what determines whether these goods should be included in the inventory of the buyer or the seller? Explain.

14 Briefly explain the operation of a *periodic* inventory system. Include an explanation of how the cost of goods sold is determined.

15 Assume that a *periodic* inventory system is in use. Explain which per-unit acquisition costs are assigned to the year-end inventory under each of the following inventory costing procedures:
   a   The average-cost method
   b   FIFO
   c   LIFO

16 Why do companies using LIFO in a perpetual inventory system often restate their ending inventory at the per-unit costs that result from applying *periodic* LIFO costing procedures?

17 Explain why errors in the valuation of inventory at the end of the year are sometimes called "counterbalancing" or "self-correcting."

18 Briefly explain the *gross profit method* of estimating inventories. In what types of situations in this technique likely to be useful?

19 Estimate the ending inventory by the gross profit method, given the following data: beginning inventory $40,000, net purchases $100,000, net sales $112,000, average gross profit rate of 25% of net sales.

20 A store using the *retail inventory method* takes its physical inventory by applying current retail prices as marked on the merchandise to the quantities counted. Does this procedure indicate that the inventory will appear in the financial statements at retail selling price? Explain.

21 Briefly explain the benefits to a company of minimizing the amount of inventory on hand. Also indicate the benefits that may result from maintaining a larger inventory.

22 How is the *inventory turnover rate* computed? Why is this measurement of interest to short-term creditors?

23 Baxter Corporation has been using FIFO during a period of rising costs. Explain whether you would expect each of the following measurements to be higher or lower if the company had been using LIFO.
   a   Net income   c   Current ratio
   b   Inventory turnover rate   d   Income taxes expense

*24 What is a *LIFO reserve?* What is likely to happen to the gross profit rate of a company with a large LIFO reserve if it sells most of its inventory?

EXERCISES

Listed below are nine technical accounting terms introduced in this chapter.

Retail method	FIFO method	Average-cost method
Gross profit method	LIFO method	Lower-of-cost-or-market
Flow assumption	*LIFO reserve	Specific identification

---

*   *Supplemental Topic, "LIFO Reserves"*

Each of the following statements may (or may not) describe one of these technical terms. For each statement, indicate the term described, or answer "None" if the statement does not correctly describe any of the terms.

a A pattern of transferring unit costs from the Inventory account to the cost of goods sold which may (or may not) parallel the physical flow of merchandise.

b The excess of the current replacement cost of any inventory of merchandise over the cost of the inventory determined by the LIFO assumption.

c The only flow assumption in which all units of merchandise are assigned the same per-unit cost.

d The method used in recording the cost of goods sold when each unit in the inventory is unique.

e The most conservative of the flow assumptions during a period of sustained inflation.

f The flow assumption which provides the most current valuation of inventory in the balance sheet.

g A technique for estimating the cost of goods sold and the ending inventory which is based upon the relationships between cost and sales price during the *current* accounting period.

EXERCISE 9-2
"Flow" of Inventory Costs

Micro Measurements uses a perpetual inventory system. On January 1, the Inventory account had a balance of $124,600. During the first few days of January the following transactions occurred.

Jan. 4   Purchased merchandise on credit from Laser Pen, Inc., for $23,900.

Jan. 9   Sold merchandise on account to Soho Graphics for a retail price of $36,800. This merchandise had cost Micro Measurements $27,200.

INSTRUCTIONS

a Prepare entries in general journal form to record the above transactions.

b What was the balance of the Inventory account at the close of business January 9?

c Why is the purchase of merchandise intended for resale not charged directly to an expense account, as is—say—the purchase of a tankful of gasoline in a delivery truck?

EXERCISE 9-3
Flow Assumptions

On May 10, Merlin Computers sold 70 Portex lap-top computers to College Text Publishers. At the date of this sale, Merlin's perpetual inventory records included the following cost layers for the Portex lap-tops:

Purchase Date	Quantity	Unit Cost	Total Cost
April 9	60	$800	$48,000
May 1	40	850	34,000
Total on Hand	100		$82,000

INSTRUCTIONS

Prepare journal entries to record the cost of the 70 Portex lap-tops sold on May 10, assuming that Merlin Computers uses the:

a Specific identification method (50 of the units sold were purchased on April 9, and the remaining 20 units were purchased on May 1).

b Average-cost method.

c FIFO method.

d LIFO method.

EXERCISE 9-4
Evaluating Alternative Inventory Methods

Notes to the financial statements of two well-known clothing manufacturers are shown below:

J. P. Stevens & Co., Inc.

Inventories: The inventories are stated at the lower of cost, determined principally by the LIFO method, or market.

Bobbie Brooks, Incorporated

Inventories: Inventories are stated at the lower of cost (first-in, first-out method) or market value.

INSTRUCTIONS

Assuming a period of rising prices:

a Which company is using the more "conservative" method of pricing its inventories? Explain.

b Based upon the inventory methods in use in their financial statements, which company is in the better position to minimize the amount of income taxes that it must pay? Explain.

Exercises 9-5 and 9-6 are based upon the following data: Late in 1994, Software City began carrying WordCrafter, a new word processing software program. At December 31, Software City's perpetual inventory records included the following cost layers in its inventory of WordCrafter programs:

Purchase Date	Quantity	Unit Cost	Total Cost
Nov. 14	6	$400	$2,400
Dec. 12	20	310	6,200
Total available for sale at Dec. 31	26		$8,600

EXERCISE 9-5
Recording Shrinkage Losses

(This exercise is based upon the data presented above.) At December 31, Software City takes a complete physical inventory and finds only 23 WordCrafter programs on hand. Prepare the journal entry to record the shrinkage loss assuming that Software City uses (a) FIFO and (b) LIFO. Any write-down in excess of $1,000 is considered "material" in dollar amount.

EXERCISE 9-6
Lower-of-Cost-or-Market

(This exercise is based upon the data presented above Exercise *9-5*.) Assume that at December 31, all 26 units of WordCrafter are on hand, but that the current replacement cost (wholesale price) of this product is $250 per unit.

Prepare journal entries to record (a) the write-down of the inventory of WordCrafter programs to the lower-of-cost-or-market at December 31 and (b) the cash sale of 10 WordCrafter programs on January 9 at a retail price of $350 each. Assume that Software City uses the FIFO flow assumption. (Company policy is to change LCM adjustments of less than $2,000 to Cost of Goods Sold and larger amounts to a separate loss account.)

EXERCISE 9-7
F.O.B. Shipping Point and F.O.B. Destination

Fraser Company had two large shipments in transit at December 31. One was a $90,000 inbound shipment of merchandise (shipped December 28, F.O.B. shipping point) which arrived at the Fraser receiving dock on January 2. The other shipment was a $55,000 outbound shipment of merchandise to a customer which was shipped and billed by Fraser on December 30 (terms F.O.B. shipping point) and reached the customer on January 3.

In taking a physical inventory on December 31, Fraser counted all goods on hand and priced the inventory on the basis of average cost. The total amount was $480,000. No goods in transit were included in this figure.

What amount should appear as inventory on the company's balance sheet at December 31? Explain. If you indicate an amount other than $480,000, state which asset or liability other than inventory also would be changed in amount.

**EXERCISE 9-8
Costing Inventory in a Periodic System**

Herbor Company uses a *periodic* inventory system. The company's records show the beginning inventory of product no. T12 on January 1 and the purchases of this item during the current year to be as follows:

Jan. 1 Beginning inventory........................	900 units @ $10.00	$ 9,000
Feb. 23 Purchase	1,200 units @ $11.00	13,200
Apr. 20 Purchase	3,000 units @ $11.20	33,600
May 4 Purchase	4,000 units @ $11.60	46,400
Nov. 30 Purchase	900 units @ $13.00	11,700
Totals	10,000 units	$113,900

INSTRUCTIONS

A physical count indicates 1,500 units in inventory at year-end.

Determine the cost of the ending inventory, based upon each of the following methods of inventory valuation. (Remember to use *periodic* inventory costing procedures.)

a Average cost
b FIFO
c LIFO

**EXERCISE 9-9
Periodic Inventory Costing Methods**

Pacific Plumbing uses a *periodic* inventory system. One of the company's products is a ¾-inch brass gate valve. The company purchases these valves several times a year and makes sales of the item daily. Shown below are the inventory quantities, purchases, and sales for the year.

	Number of Units	Cost Per Unit	Total Cost
Beginning inventory (Jan. 1)	9,100	$4.00	$ 36,400
First purchase (Feb. 20)	20,000	4.10	82,000
Second purchase (May 10)............................	30,000	4.25	127,500
Third purchase (Aug. 24)	50,000	4.60	230,000
Fourth purchase (Nov. 30)	10,900	5.00	54,500
Goods available for sale	120,000		$530,400
Units sold during the year	106,000		
Ending inventory (Dec. 31)............................	14,000		

INSTRUCTIONS

Compute the cost of the ending inventory of gate valves, using the following *periodic* inventory valuation methods:

a FIFO
b LIFO
c Average cost

**EXERCISE 9-10
Adjusting to
Periodic LIFO**

Marston Products uses a perpetual inventory system and a LIFO flow assumption. At year-end, the perpetual inventory records indicate the following units of Product RB-21 are in inventory:

Purchase Date	Quantity	Unit Cost	Total Cost
Beginning inventory	50	$40	$ 2,000
June 18	300	45	13,500
Nov. 7	150	50	7,500
Total available for sale at Dec. 31	500		$23,000

A physical count of the merchandise indicates that only 490 units of Product RB-21 are on hand. Applying **periodic LIFO** costing procedures, these 490 units would be assigned the following unit costs:

Purchase Date	Quantity	Unit Cost	Total Cost
Beginning inventory	220	$40	$ 8,800
June 18	270	45	12,150
Total available for sale at Dec. 31	490		$20,950

INSTRUCTIONS

a Prepare a journal entry to record the shrinkage loss of 10 units in the LIFO-based perpetual inventory records. (In recording this loss, ignore the periodic pricing procedures. Charge any loss of less than $1,000 directly to Cost of Goods Sold.)

b Prepare a journal entry to restate the 490 units on hand at December 31 to the unit costs indicated by periodic LIFO costing procedures.

c Explain **why** a company using a perpetual inventory system might make a practice of restating its year-end inventory to the unit costs indicated by periodic LIFO costing procedures.

**EXERCISE 9-11
Effects of Er-
rors in Inven-
tory Valuation**

Norfleet Company prepared the following condensed income statements for two successive years:

	1994	1993
Sales	$1,500,000	$1,440,000
Cost of goods sold	879,600	914,400
Gross profit on sales	$ 620,400	$ 525,600
Operating expenses	460,500	447,000
Net income..	$ 159,900	$ 78,600

At the end of 1993 (right-hand column above) the inventory was understated by $50,400, but the error was not discovered until after the accounts had been closed and financial statements prepared at the end of **1994**. The balance sheets for the two years showed owner's equity of $414,200 at the end of 1993 and $460,400 at the end of 1994. (Norfleet is organized as a sole proprietorship and does not incur income taxes expense.)

INSTRUCTIONS

a Compute the corrected net income figures for 1993 and 1994.

b Compute the gross profit amounts and the gross profit percentages for each year based upon corrected data.

c What correction, if any, should be made in the amounts of the company's owner's equity at the end of 1993 and at the end of 1994?

EXERCISE 9-12
Estimating Inventory by the Gross Profit Method

When Anne Blair arrived at her store on the morning of January 29, she found empty shelves and display racks; thieves had broken in during the night and stolen the entire inventory. Blair's accounting records showed that she had had $55,000 inventory on January 1 (cost value). From January 1 to January 29, she had made net sales of $200,000 and net purchases of $141,800. The gross profit during the last several years had consistently averaged 30% of net sales. Blair wishes to file an insurance claim for the theft loss. You are to use the ***gross profit method*** to estimate the cost of her inventory at the time of the theft. Show computations.

EXERCISE 9-13
Estimating Inventory by the Retail Method

Westlake Accessories needs to determine the approximate amount of inventory at the end of each month without taking a physical inventory of merchandise in the shop. From the following information, you are to estimate the cost of goods sold and the cost of the July 31 inventory by the ***retail method*** of inventory valuation.

	Cost Price	Retail Selling Price
Inventory of merchandise, June 30	$264,800	$400,000
Purchases during July	170,400	240,000
Goods available for sale during July	$435,200	$640,000
Net sales during July		$275,200

EXERCISE 9-14
Inventory Turnover Rates

In your analysis of the financial statements of Retail Outlet, you note that the cost of goods sold for the year was $13,200,000; inventory was $2,000,000 at the beginning of the year and $2,400,000 at year-end.

INSTRUCTIONS

a Compute the inventory turnover rate for the year.

b Using the assumption of 365 days in a year, compute the number of days required for the company to sell the amount of its average inventory (round to the nearest day).

c Assume that an average of 45 days is required for Retail Outlet to collect its accounts receivable. What is the length of the company's operating cycle?

PROBLEMS

Note: This chapter contains an unusually wide variety of problem assignments. In order to make these assignments readily available to all users of the text, we present them in one consecutive series, rather than splitting them into A and B groups. This series is supported in both the Group A and Group B packages of accounting work sheets.

PROBLEM 9-1
Evaluating Different Inventory Methods

A note to the recent financial statements of **The Quaker Oats Company** includes the following information:

Inventories   Inventories are valued at the lower-of-cost-or-market, using various cost methods. The percentage of year-end inventories valued using each of the methods is as follows:

June 30 (fiscal year-end)

Average cost	54%
Last-in, first-out (LIFO)	29%
First-in, first-out (FIFO)	17%

INSTRUCTIONS

a Does the company's use of three different inventory methods violate the accounting principle of consistency?

b Assuming that the replacement cost of inventories has been steadily rising, would the company's reported net income be higher or lower if all inventories were valued by the FIFO method?

c Assume that management's primary objective is to minimize income taxes. Which inventory valuation method would you recommend using in the income tax returns? Would this recommendation influence your choice of inventory valuation methods used in the financial statements? Explain your answers.

**PROBLEM 9-2
Perpetual Inventory Records**

A perpetual inventory system is used by Black Hawk, Inc., and an inventory record card is maintained for each type of product in stock. The following transactions show beginning inventory, purchases, and sales of product KR9 for the month of May:

May 1	Balance on hand, 20 units, cost $40 each	$800
May 5	Sale, 8 units, sales price $60 each	480
May 6	Purchase, 20 units, cost $45 each	900
May 21	Sale, 10 units, sales price $60 each	600
May 31	Sale, 15 units, sales price $65 each	975

INSTRUCTIONS

a Record the beginning inventory, the purchases, the cost of goods sold, and the running balance on an inventory record card like the one illustrated on page 412. Use the *last-in, first-out* (LIFO) method.

b Prepare general journal entries to record the purchases and sales in May. Assume that all transactions were on account.

**PROBLEM 9-3
Perpetual Inventory Records in a Small Business**

Executive Suites, Inc., uses a perpetual inventory system. This system includes a perpetual inventory record card for each of the 60 types of products the company keeps in stock. The following transactions show the purchases and sales of a particular desk chair (product code DC-SB2) during September.

Sept. 1	Balance on hand, 50 units, cost $60 each	$3,000
Sept. 4	Purchase, 20 units, cost $65 each	1,300
Sept. 8	Sale, 35 units, sales price $100 each	3,500
Sept. 9	Purchase, 40 units, cost $65 each	2,500
Sept. 20	Sale, 60 units, sales price $100 each	6,000
Sept. 25	Purchase, 40 units, cost $70 each	2,800
Sept. 30	Sale, 5 units, sales price $110 each	550

INSTRUCTIONS

a Record the beginning inventory, the purchases, the cost of goods sold, and the running balance on an inventory record card like the one illustrated on page 411. Use the *first-in, first-out* (FIFO) method.

b Prepare general journal entries to record these purchases and sales in September. Assume that all transactions were on account.

**PROBLEM 9-4
Four Methods of Inventory Valuation**

On January 15, 1994, California Irrigation sold 2,000 RainMaster-30 oscillating sprinkler heads to Rancho Landscaping. Immediately prior to this sale, California's perpetual inventory records for this sprinkler head included the following cost layers:

Purchase Date	Quantity	Unit Cost	Total Cost
December 12, 1993	1,200	$18.50	$22,200
January 9, 1994	1,800	19.00	34,200
Total on hand	3,000		$56,400

INSTRUCTIONS   (*Note:* We present this problem in the normal sequence of the accounting cycle— that is, journal entries before ledger entries. However, you may find it helpful to work part **b** first.)

a Prepare a separate journal entry to record the cost of goods sold relating to the January 15 sale of 2,000 RainMaster-30 sprinkler heads, assuming that California Irrigation uses:

    1 Specific identification (1,000 of the units sold were purchased on December 12, and the remaining 1,000 were purchased on January 9).

    2 Average cost.

    3 FIFO.

    4 LIFO.

b Complete a subsidiary ledger record for RainMaster-30 sprinkler heads using each of the four inventory valuation methods listed above. Your inventory records should show both purchases of this product, the sale on January 15, and the balance on hand at December 12, January 9, and January 15. Use the formats for inventory subsidiary records illustrated on pages 408–412 of this chapter.

Problems 9-5 and 9-6 are based upon the following data: SK Marine sells high-performance marine equipment to power boat owners. Apollo Outboard recently introduced the world's first 400 horsepower outboard motor—the Apollo 400. During the current year, SK purchased 8 of these motors—all intended for resale to customers—at the following dates and acquisition costs:

Purchase Date	Units Purchased	Unit Cost	Total Cost
July 1...	2	$4,450	$ 8,900
July 22..	3	4,600	13,800
Aug. 3	3	4,700	14,100
Available for sale during the year	8		$36,800

On ***July 28,*** SK sold 4 of these motors to Mr. G Racing Associates. The other 4 motors remained in inventory at September 30, the end of SK's fiscal year.

PROBLEM 9-5
Alternative Flow Assumptions

Assume that SK Marine uses a ***perpetual inventory system.***

INSTRUCTIONS

a Compute (a) the cost of goods sold relating to the sale on July 28 and (b) the ending inventory of Apollo outboard motors at September 30, using each of the following flow assumptions:

    1 Average cost

    2 FIFO

    3 LIFO

Show the number of units and the unit costs of each cost layer comprising the cost of goods sold and the ending inventory.

b In part **a,** you have determined SK's cost of Apollo motors sold using three different inventory flow assumptions.

    1 Which of these methods will result in SK Marine reporting the ***highest net income*** for the current year? Would this always be the case? Explain.

    2 Which of these methods will ***minimize the income taxes owed*** by SK for the year? Would you expect this usually to be the case? Explain.

    3 May SK use the method resulting in the highest net income in its financial statements, and one which minimizes taxable income in its income tax returns? Explain.

PROBLEM 9-6
Periodic Cost-
ing Procedures

Assume that SK Marine uses a ***periodic inventory system.***

INSTRUCTIONS
Compute the ending inventory of Apollo motors at September 30 and the cost of goods sold through this date under each of the following periodic costing procedures:

a Average cost

b FIFO

c LIFO

Show the number of units and the unit costs in each cost layer of the ***ending inventory.*** (You may determine the cost of goods sold by deducting ending inventory from the cost of goods available for sale.)

PROBLEM 9-7
Year-End Ad-
justments;
Shrinkage
Losses and
LCM

Bunyon's Trees & Shrubs uses a perpetual inventory system. At December 31, 1994, the perpetual inventory records indicate the following quantities of a particular 5-gallon tree:

	Quantity	Unit Cost	Total Cost
First purchase (oldest)...............................	230	$18	$ 4,140
Second purchase.....................................	200	19	3,800
Third purchase	170	20	3,400
Total	600		$11,340

A year-end physical inventory, however, shows only 570 of these trees on hand and alive.

    In its financial statements, Bunyon's values its inventories at the lower-of-cost-or-market. At year-end, the per-unit replacement cost of this tree is $21. (Use $2,000 as the "level of materiality" in deciding whether to debit losses to Cost of Goods Sold or to a separate loss account.)

INSTRUCTIONS

Prepare the journal entries required to adjust the inventory records at year-end, assuming that:

a Bunyon's uses:

    1 Average cost.

    2 Last-in, first-out.

b Bunyon's uses the first-in, first-out method. However, the replacement cost of the trees at year-end is ***$15*** apiece, rather than the $21 stated originally. [Make separate journal entries to record (1) the shrinkage losses, and (2) the restatement of the inventory at a "market" value lower than cost. Record the shrinkage losses first.]

PROBLEM 9-8
Periodic Inventory Costing Procedures

Audio Shop uses a periodic inventory system. One of the most popular items carried in stock by Audio Shop is an 8-inch speaker unit. The inventory quantities, purchases, and sales of this unit for the most recent year are shown below.

	Number of Units	Cost Per Unit	Total Cost
Inventory, Jan. 1	2,700	$30.00	$ 81,000
First purchase (May 12)	3,540	30.60	108,324
Second purchase (July 9)	2,400	31.05	74,520
Third purchase (Oct. 4)	1,860	32.10	59,706
Fourth purchase (Dec. 18)	3,000	32.55	97,650
Goods available for sale	13,500		$421,200
Units sold during the year	9,600		
Inventory, Dec. 31	3,900		

INSTRUCTIONS

a Using *periodic* costing procedures, compute the cost of the December 31 inventory and the cost of goods sold for the 8-inch speaker units during the year under each of the following:

1 First-in, first-out

2 Last-in, first-out

3 Average-cost

b Which of the three inventory pricing methods provides the most realistic balance sheet valuation of inventory in light of the current replacement cost of the speaker units? Does this same method also produce the most realistic measure of income in light of the costs being incurred by Audio Shop to replace the speakers when they are sold? Explain.

PROBLEM 9-9
Comparisons of Perpetual and Periodic Inventory Systems

During 1994, Playground Specialists purchased 6 BigGym redwood playground sets at the following dates and acquisition costs:

Date	Units Purchased	Unit Cost	Total Cost
Aug. 4	2	$2,100	$ 4,200
Sep. 23	2	2,300	4,600
Oct. 2	2	2,560	5,120
Available for sale during the year	6		$13,920

On *September 25,* the company sold 3 of these BigGym sets to the Department of Parks and Recreation. The other 3 sets remained in inventory at December 31.

INSTRUCTIONS

a Assume that Playground Specialists uses a *perpetual inventory system.* Using each of the flow assumptions listed below, compute (a) the cost of goods sold relating to the sale of BigGym playground sets on September 25 and (b) the cost of the BigGym sets in inventory at December 31.

1 Average cost

2 FIFO

3 LIFO

Show the number of units and the unit costs of each cost layer comprising the cost of goods sold and the ending inventory.

b Assume that Playground Specialists uses a ***periodic inventory system.*** Compute the ending inventory of BigGym playground sets at December 31 and the related cost of goods sold under each of the following year-end costing procedures:

1 Average cost

2 FIFO

3 LIFO

Show the number of units and the unit costs in each cost layer of the ending inventory. (You may determine the cost of goods sold by deducting ending inventory from the cost of goods available for sale.)

c Now assume that Playground Specialists maintains perpetual inventory records and uses the LIFO flow assumption. At year-end, however, the company ***adjusts its inventory records*** to reflect the costs indicated by applying ***periodic*** LIFO costing procedures (as in part **b**).

1 Prepare a journal entry to adjust the Inventory account for the revaluation of the BigGym playground sets in the year-end inventory.

2 Briefly explain ***why*** the company might apply the LIFO method in this manner.

d Explain why a company using a perpetual inventory system would restate its year-end inventory to the unit costs indicated by periodic LIFO costing procedures.

PROBLEM 9-10
Inventory Errors: Effects on Earnings

The owners of Night & Day Window Coverings are offering the business for sale as a going concern. The income statements of the business for the three years of its existence are summarized below:

	1994	1993	1992
Net sales	$860,000	$850,000	$800,000
Cost of goods sold	481,600	486,000	480,000
Gross profit on sales	$378,400	$364,000	$320,000
Gross profit percentage	44%	43%*	40%

* Rounded to nearest full percentage point.

In negotiations with prospective buyers of the business, the owners of Night & Day are calling attention to the rising trends of the gross profit and of the gross profit percentage as very favorable elements.

Assume that you are retained by a prospective purchaser of the business to make an investigation of the fairness and reliability of Night & Day's accounting records and financial statements. You find everything in order except for the following: (1) An arithmetical error in the computation of inventory at the end of 1992 had caused a $24,000 understatement in that inventory and (2) a duplication of figures in the computation of inventory at the end of 1994 had caused an overstatement of $43,000 in that inventory. The company uses the periodic inventory system and these errors had not been brought to light prior to your investigation.

INSTRUCTIONS

a Prepare a revised three-year schedule similar to the one illustrated above.

b Comment on the trend of gross profit and gross profit percentage before and after the revision.

PROBLEM 9-11
Retail Method

Cherry Vanilla is called a "record" store, but its sales consist almost entirely of tapes and CDs. The company uses a periodic inventory system but also uses the retail method to estimate its monthly, quarterly, and annual cost of goods sold and ending inventory.

During the current year, Cherry Vanilla offered for sale merchandise which had cost a total of **$392,000.** As required by the retail method, the company also kept track of the retail sales values of this merchandise, which amounted to **$700,000.** The store's net sales for the year were **$610,000.**

INSTRUCTIONS

a Using the retail method, estimate (1) the cost of goods sold during the year and (2) the inventory at the end of the year.

b At year-end, Cherry Vanilla takes a physical inventory. The manager walks through the store counting each type of product and reading its retail price into a tape recorder. From this tape recording, an employee prepares a schedule listing the entire ending inventory at retail sales prices. The inventory on hand at year-end had a retail sales value of **$82,400.**

1 Use the cost ratio determined in part **a** to reduce the inventory counted by the manager from its retail value to an estimate of its cost.

2 Determine the estimated shrinkage losses (measured at cost) incurred by Cherry Vanilla during the year.

3 Compute the store's gross profit for the year. (Include shrinkage losses in the cost of goods sold.)

**PROBLEM 9-12
What If They'd
Used FIFO?**

Oshkosh B'Gosh, Inc., uses LIFO. Recent financial statements included the following data (dollars in thousands):

Average inventory (throughout the year)	$ 81,554
Current assets (at year-end)	115,852
Current liabilities (at year-end)	27,175
Net sales	315,076
Cost of goods sold	209,006
Gross profit	106,070

A note accompanying these statements indicated that had the company used the **FIFO** inventory method (dollars in thousands):

1 Average inventory would have been $88,474 ($6,920 **higher** than the LIFO amount).

2 Ending inventory would have been valued at a cost of $96,115 ($6,781 **higher** than the LIFO cost).

3 The cost of goods sold would have been $209,284 ($278 **higher** than that reported in the company's income statement).*

* **Note to student:** Notice that the cost of goods sold is **higher** under FIFO than LIFO. This is a somewhat unusual situation, indicating that the company has encountered **declining** replacement costs for its merchandise during the year.

INSTRUCTIONS

a Using the data contained in the company's financial statements (based upon the LIFO method), compute the following analytical measurements. (Round to the nearest tenth.)

1 Inventory turnover rate

2 Current ratio

3 Gross profit rate

b **Recompute** the three ratios required in part **a** in a manner that will be **directly comparable** to those of a company using the FIFO method in its financial statements. (Round to the nearest tenth.)

CASES AND UNSTRUCTURED PROBLEMS

CASE 9-1
Have I Got a Deal for You!

You are the sales manager of Continental Motors, an automobile dealership specializing in European imports. Among the automobiles in Continental Motors' showroom are two Italian sports cars, which are identical in every respect except for color: one is red and the other white. The red car had been ordered last February, at a cost of $48,300 American dollars. The white car had been ordered early last March, but because of a revaluation of the Italian lira relative to the dollar, the white car had cost only $47,000 American dollars. Both cars arrived in the United States on the same boat and had just been delivered to your showroom. Since the cars were identical except for color and both colors were equally popular, you had listed both cars at the same suggested retail price, $58,000. This price is about $2,000 less than competing dealerships are asking for this particular model.

Smiley Miles, one of your best salesmen, comes into your office with a proposal. He has a customer in the showroom who wants to buy the red car for $58,000. However, when Miles pulled the inventory card on the red car to see what options were included, he happened to notice the inventory card of the white car. Continental Motors, like most automobile dealerships, uses the specific identification method to value inventory. Consequently, Miles noticed that the red car had cost $48,300, while the white one had cost Continental Motors only $47,000. This gave Miles the idea for the following proposal.

"Have I got a deal for you! If I sell the red car for $58,000, Continental Motors makes a gross profit of $9,700. But if you'll let me discount that white car $500, I think I can get my customer to buy that one instead. If I sell the white car for $57,500, the gross profit will be $10,500, so Continental Motors is $800 better off than if I sell the red car for $58,000. Since I came up with this plan, I feel I should get part of the benefit, so Continental Motors should split the extra $800 with me. That way, I'll get an extra $400 commission, and the company still makes $400 more than if I sell the red car."

INSTRUCTIONS

Would you accept Miles's proposal? Explain your reasoning.

CASE 9-2
Just-in-Time or NQIT (Not-Quite-in-Time)

Fargo Manufacturing is located in Buffalo, New York. In the past, the company has rented several warehouses to store its inventories of raw materials and finished goods. Recently, management has been working to implement the principles of a just-in-time inventory system. At present, almost 70% of the company's raw materials arrive on a just-in-time basis, and all finished goods are shipped to customers immediately upon completion of the production process.

INSTRUCTIONS

a   Explain what is meant by "just-in-time," with respect to both raw materials and finished goods.

b   What are the advantages to Fargo of just-in-time manufacturing? What is the biggest risk?

CASE 9-3
Inventory Management

In this chapter, we discussed several factors which management should consider in deciding upon the size of inventory to be kept on hand. In each of the following cases, you are to indicate what you consider to be the most important factor (or factors) favoring (1) increasing the size of the company's inventory and (2) **not** increasing the size of the inventory.

a   Morgan Chevrolet is an automobile dealership in a large metropolitan area. It currently has an opportunity to buy several acres of land adjacent to the dealership which it could use to store additional inventory. The cost of this land would be approximately $200,000. General Motors—Morgan Chevrolet's supplier—allows substantial discounts to dealers that purchase a large volume of cars. Like most auto dealers, Morgan Chevrolet finances purchases of inventory through a bank and repays the bank as individual automobiles are sold.

b Marc's Furniture sells name-brand furniture to homeowners at discount prices. The company is located in a small rented office. At present, the company's inventory consists of five or six different pieces of furniture which are kept on hand primarily for purposes of display. Customers place their orders from catalogues and wait six to eight weeks for delivery. The manager has noticed that customers most frequently order those items that the company has on display.

c Captain's Choice is a fish market located near the waterfront. All of the fish is purchased fresh each day from the local fishing fleet. Captain's Choice sells the fish at a retail price of approximately five times its cost.

CASE 9-4
Comparison of LIFO and FIFO

You are making a detailed analysis of the financial statements of two companies in the same industry: APM and BFC. Both businesses are organized as corporations and, therefore, must pay income taxes on their earnings. Both companies maintain large inventories, and the replacement costs of their products have been rising steadily for several years. A note to APM's financial statements discloses that the company's inventory is shown at a cost that is *far below* current replacement cost. BFC's inventory, in contrast, is presented at a cost which is *very close* to its current replacement cost.

INSTRUCTIONS

Answer the following questions. Explain the reasoning behind your answers.

a What method of inventory valuation is probably used by APM? By BFC?

b If we assume that the two companies are identical except for the method used in valuing inventory:

1 Which company probably has been reporting the higher net income in recent years?

2 Which company's financial statements probably imply the higher inventory turnover rate?

3 Which company's financial statements probably imply the higher current ratio?

4 Comment upon your answers to parts **2** and **3** above. If the only difference between these companies is their method of inventory valuation, is one company actually more solvent than the other?

c If both companies sold their entire inventory at the same sales prices, which company would you expect to report the larger amount of gross profit?

CASE 9-5
"Hello. I'm from the IRS."

Carla Fontana is an auditor with the Internal Revenue Service. She has been assigned to audit the income tax return of Square Deal Lumber Company (a corporation). Selected figures from the company's income tax return are shown below.

Sales	$12,000,000
Beginning inventory	360,000
Purchases of merchandise	9,600,000
Ending inventory	260,000
Cost of goods sold	9,700,000
Gross profit	2,300,000

As Fontana examined these figures, she became suspicious that Square Deal had understated its taxable income by a significant amount and may have been engaging in this practice for several years.

Fontana looked up several ratios for the retail lumber industry in a recent publication of industry averages. She found that retail lumberyards, on average, had annual sales of $10 million, an inventory turnover rate of 10, and a gross profit rate of 20%. Fontana also noticed a newspaper advertisement by Square Deal, which read, "Many unique products in our huge yard. We carry what the other yards don't. This week's special: roofing materials—15% discount on shake, shingle, and composition. Large selection in stock." Fontana then sent a letter to Square Deal to arrange a date for visiting the company and performing an audit of its latest income tax return.

When Fontana arrived at Square Deal Lumber, she was met in the parking lot by Sam "Square Deal" Delano, president and owner of the business. Fontana noticed that Square Deal looked like most other retail lumberyards. There was one main building, containing offices and displays of such merchandise as power tools and electrical supplies. Behind this building was a large fenced yard, with many stacks of lumber, and several storage sheds. These sheds contained plywood, fiberglass insulation, and other products that required protection from the weather.

Fontana asked to see the company's perpetual inventory records. Delano told her that Square Deal uses a periodic inventory system, as it is not a publicly owned company and does not have to issue quarterly financial statements to stockholders or other outsiders. He pointed out that he and the general manager were on hand every day, and they both knew exactly what was in stock—down to the very last board.

By examining various accounting records, Fontana concluded that the amounts of sales revenues and merchandise purchases were correctly stated in Square Deal's income tax return. She noticed, however, that most types of merchandise were reordered at intervals of about five weeks.

INSTRUCTIONS

a What was it about the figures in Square Deal Lumber Company's income tax return that originally made Fontana suspect that the company might be understating its taxable income?

b What happened to confirm Fontana's suspicions? Identify all of the factors which have come to her attention and yours.

c Does it appear that Square Deal is engaging in a deliberate scheme to evade income taxes, or that the company has simply made an "honest mistake?" Explain.

d Assume that the industry averages correctly approximate the financial position and operating results of the Square Deal. Estimate for the current year the correct amounts of the company's (1) cost of goods sold, (2) gross profit, (3) average amount of inventory. (Show supporting computations.)

e Estimate the amount by which Square Deal appears to have understated its taxable income over a period of years. Explain the basis for your conclusion.

*CASE 9-6
Call Up the
(LIFO)
Reserves!

Steel Specialties has been in business for 52 years. The company maintains a perpetual inventory system, uses a LIFO flow assumption, and ends its fiscal year at December 31. At year-end, the cost of goods sold and inventory are adjusted to reflect periodic LIFO costing procedures.

A railroad strike has delayed the arrival of purchases ordered during the last several months of 1994, and Steel Specialties has not been able to replenish its inventories as merchandise is sold. At December 22, one product appears in the company's perpetual inventory records at the following unit costs:

Purchase Date	Quantity	Unit Cost	Total Cost
Nov. 14, 1954	3,000	$6	$18,000
Apr. 12, 1955...	2,000	8	16,000
Available for sale at Dec. 22, 1994.....................	5,000		$34,000

---

* *Supplemental Topic, "LIFO Reserves"*

Steel Specialties has another 8,000 units of this product on order at the current wholesale cost of $30 per unit. Because of the railroad strike, however, these units have not yet arrived (the terms of purchase are F.O.B. destination). Steel Specialties also has an order from a customer that wants to purchase 4,000 units of this product at the retail sales price of $45 per unit. Steel Specialties intends to make this sale on December 30, regardless of whether or not the 8,000 units on order arrive by this date. (The 4,000 unit sale will be shipped by truck, F.O.B. shipping point.)

INSTRUCTIONS

a Are the units in inventory really almost 40 years old? Explain.

b Prepare a schedule showing the sales revenue, cost of goods sold, and gross profit that will result from this sale on December 30, assuming that the 8,000 units currently on order (1) arrive before year-end and (2) do not arrive until sometime in the following year. (In each computation, show the number of units comprising the cost of goods sold and their related per-unit costs.)

c Comment upon these results.

d Might management be wise to delay this sale by a few days? Explain.

ANSWERS TO SELF-TEST QUESTIONS

1 b   **2** a, c, d   **3** a   **4** b   **5** b   **6** a, b, c, d

CHAPTER

10 Plant and Equipment, Depreciation, and Intangible Assets

Our primary goal in this chapter is to illustrate and explain the accounting concepts relating to the acquisition, use, and disposal of plant assets. An important element of this discussion is our coverage of alternative depreciation methods, including the straight-line, units-of-output, double-declining-balance, and sum-of-the-years'-digits methods. In the final portions of the chapter, we address the special topics of accounting for intangible assets and for natural resources.

A Supplemental Topic section addresses the special depreciation methods used in federal income tax returns.

After studying this chapter you should be able to meet these Learning Objectives:

1   *Determine the cost of plant assets.*
2   *Distinguish between capital expenditures and revenue expenditures.*
3   *Explain the relationship between depreciation and the matching principle.*
4   *Compute depreciation by the straight-line, units-of-output, declining-balance, and sum-of-the-years'-digits methods.*
5   *Record the disposal of a plant asset.*
6   *Explain the nature of goodwill and indicate when this asset should appear in the accounting records.*
7   *Account for the depletion of natural resources.*
8   *Identify some problems that may arise in accounting for the impairment of long-lived assets.*
*9   *Compute depreciation for income tax purposes using the MACRS guidelines.*

---

*   *Supplemental Topic, "Depreciation for Income Tax Purposes"*

PLANT AND EQUIPMENT

The term *plant and equipment* is used to describe long-lived assets acquired for use in the operation of the business and not intended for resale to customers. Among the more common examples are land, buildings, machinery, furniture and fixtures, office equipment, and automobiles. A cargo van in the showroom of an automobile dealer is inventory; when this same vehicle is sold to a furniture store for use in making deliveries to customers, it becomes a unit of plant and equipment.

The term *fixed assets* has long been used in accounting literature to describe all types of plant and equipment. This term, however, has virtually disappeared from the published financial statements of large corporations. *Plant and equipment* appears to be a more descriptive term. Another alternative title used on many corporation balance sheets is *property, plant, and equipment.*

Plant and Equipment—A Stream of Services

It is convenient to think of a plant asset as a stream of services to be received by the owner over a period of years. Ownership of a delivery truck, for example, may provide about 100,000 miles of transportation. The cost of the delivery truck is customarily entered in a plant and equipment account entitled Delivery Truck, which in essence represents the advance purchase of many years of transportation service. Similarly, a building may be regarded as advance purchase of many years' supply of housing services. As the years go by, these services are utilized by the business and the cost of the plant asset gradually is transferred into depreciation expense.

An awareness of the similarity between plant assets and prepaid expenses is essential to an understanding of the accounting process by which the cost of plant assets is allocated to the accounting periods in which the benefits of ownership are received.

Major Categories of Plant and Equipment

Plant and equipment items are often classified into the following groups:

1 **Tangible plant assets.** The term "tangible" denotes physical substance, as exemplified by land, a building, or a machine. This category may be subdivided into two distinct classifications:

   a Plant property subject to depreciation; included are plant assets of limited useful life such as buildings and office equipment.

   b Land. The only plant asset not subject to depreciation is land, which has an unlimited term of existence.

2 **Intangible assets.** The term "intangible assets" is used to describe assets which are used in the operation of the business but have no physical substance and are noncurrent. Examples include patents, copyrights, trademarks, franchises, and goodwill. Current assets such as accounts receivable or prepaid rent are not included in the intangible classification, even though they are lacking in physical substance.

3 Natural resources. A site acquired for the purpose of extracting or removing some valuable resource such as oil, minerals, or timber is classified as a ***natural resource,*** not as land. This type of plant asset is gradually converted into inventory as the natural resource is extracted from the site.

Determining the Cost of Plant and Equipment

OBJECTIVE 1
Determine
the cost of
plant assets.

The cost of plant and equipment includes all expenditures reasonable and necessary in acquiring the asset and placing it in a position and condition for use in the operations of the business. Only ***reasonable*** and ***necessary*** expenditures should be included. For example, if the company's truck driver receives a traffic ticket while hauling a new machine to the plant, the traffic fine is ***not*** part of the cost of the new machine. If the machine is dropped and damaged while being unloaded, the cost of repairing the damage should be recognized as expense in the current period and should ***not*** be added to the cost of the machine.

Cost is most easily determined when an asset is purchased for cash. The cost of the asset is then equal to the cash outlay necessary to acquire the asset plus any expenditures for freight, insurance while in transit, installation, trial runs, and any other costs necessary to make ***the asset ready for use.*** If plant assets are ***purchased*** on the installment plan or by issuance of notes payable, the interest element or carrying charge should be recorded as interest expense and ***not*** as part of the cost of the plant assets. However, if a company ***constructs*** a plant asset for its own use, interest costs incurred ***during the construction period*** are viewed as part of the cost of the asset.[1]

This principle of including in the cost of a plant asset all the incidental charges necessary to put the asset in use is illustrated by the following example. A factory in Minneapolis orders a machine from a San Francisco tool manufacturer at a list price of $10,000, with terms of 2/10, n/30. Sales tax of $588 must be paid, as well as freight charges of $1,250. Transportation from the railroad station to the factory costs $150, and installation labor amounts to $400. The cost of the machine to be entered in the Machinery account is computed as follows:

Items included in cost of machine

List price of machine	$10,000
Less: Cash discount (2% × $10,000)	200
Net cash price	$ 9,800
Sales tax	588
Freight	1,250
Transportation from railroad station to factory	150
Installation labor	400
Cost of machine	$12,188

Why should all the incidental charges relating to the acquisition of a machine be included in its cost? Why not treat these incidental charges as expenses of the period in which the machine is acquired?

---

[1] FASB, *Statement No. 34,* "Capitalization of Interest Costs" (Norwalk, Conn.: 1979).

The answer is to be found in the basic accounting principle of *matching costs and revenue.* The benefits of owning the machine will be received over a span of years, for example, 10 years. During those 10 years the operation of the machine will contribute to revenue. Consequently, the total costs of the machine should be recorded in the accounts as an asset and allocated against the revenue of the 10 years. All costs incurred in acquiring the machine are costs of the services to be received from using the machine.

Land When land is purchased, various incidental costs are generally incurred, in addition to the purchase price. These additional costs may include commissions to real estate brokers, escrow fees, legal fees for examining and insuring the title, delinquent taxes paid by the purchaser, and fees for surveying, draining, clearing, and grading the property. All these expenditures become part of the cost of the land.

Apportionment of a Lump-Sum Purchase Separate ledger accounts are necessary for land and buildings, because buildings are subject to depreciation and land is not. The treatment of land as a nondepreciable asset is based on the premise that land used as a building site has an unlimited life. When land and building are purchased for a lump sum, the purchase price must be apportioned between the land and the building. An appraisal may be necessary for this purpose. Assume, for example, that land and a building are purchased for a bargain price of $400,000. The apportionment of this cost on the basis of an appraisal may be made as follows:

	Value per Appraisal	Percentage of Total	Apportionment of Cost
Land..	$200,000	40%	$160,000
Building....................................	300,000	60%	240,000
Total.......................................	$500,000	100%	$400,000

Apportioning cost between land and building

Sometimes a tract of land purchased as a building site has on it an old building which is not suitable for the buyer's use. The Land account should be charged with the entire purchase price *plus any costs incurred in tearing down or removing the building.* Proceeds received from sale of the materials salvaged from the old building are recorded as a credit in the Land account.

Land Improvements Improvements to real estate such as driveways, fences, parking lots, and sprinkler systems have a limited life and are therefore subject to depreciation. For this reason they should be recorded in a separate account entitled Land Improvements.

Buildings Old buildings are sometimes purchased with the intention of repairing them prior to placing them in use. Repairs made under these circumstances are charged to the Buildings account. After the building has been placed in use, ordinary repairs are considered as maintenance expense when incurred.

Capital Expenditures and Revenue Expenditures

OBJECTIVE 2
Distinguish
between cap-
ital expendi-
tures and
revenue ex-
penditures.

Expenditures for the purchase or expansion of plant assets are called ***capital expenditures*** and are recorded in asset accounts. Expenditures for ordinary repairs, maintenance, fuel, and other items necessary to the ownership and use of plant and equipment are called ***revenue expenditures*** and are recorded by debiting expense accounts. The charge to an expense account is based on the assumption that the benefits from the expenditure will be used up in the current period, and the cost should therefore be deducted from the revenue of the period in determining the net income.

A business may purchase many small items which will benefit several accounting periods but which have a relatively low cost. Examples of such items include auto batteries, wastebaskets, and pencil sharpeners. Such items are theoretically capital expenditures, but if they are recorded as assets in the accounting records it will be necessary to compute and record the related depreciation expense in future periods. We have previously mentioned the idea that the extra work involved in developing more precise accounting information should be weighed against the benefits that result. Thus, for reasons of convenience and economy, expenditures which are ***not material*** in dollar amount are treated in the accounting records as expenses of the current period. In brief, ***any material expenditure that will benefit several accounting periods is considered a capital expenditure. Any expenditure that will benefit only the current period or that is not material in amount is treated as a revenue expenditure.***

Many companies develop formal policy statements defining capital and revenue expenditures as a guide toward consistent accounting practice from year to year. These policy statements often set a minimum dollar limit for a capital expenditure (such as $500).

Effect of Errors in Distinguishing between Capital and Revenue Expenditures Because a capital expenditure is recorded by debiting an asset account, the transaction has no immediate effect upon net income. However, the depreciation of the amount entered in the asset account will be reflected as an expense in future periods. A revenue expenditure, on the other hand, is recorded by debiting an expense account and therefore represents an immediate deduction from earnings in the current period.

Assume that the cost of a new delivery truck is erroneously debited to the Repairs Expense account. The result will be to overstate repairs expense, thereby understating the current year's net income. If the error is not corrected, the net income of subsequent years will be overstated because no depreciation expense will be recognized during the years in which the truck is used.

On the other hand, assume that ordinary truck repairs are erroneously debited to the asset account, Delivery Truck. The result will be to understate repairs expense, thereby overstating the current year's net income. If the error is not corrected, the net income of future years will be understated because of excessive depreciation charges based upon the inflated balance of the Delivery Truck account.

These examples indicate that a careful distinction between capital and revenue expenditures is essential to attainment of one of the most fundamental objectives of accounting—the determination of net income for each year of operation of a business.

Capital Budgeting

The process of planning and evaluating proposals for capital expenditures is called *capital budgeting.* Capital budgeting includes such decisions as whether to build new factories or automate old ones, buy competing businesses, and develop new products.

Decisions regarding the acquisition of plant assets may be among management's most significant responsibilities. These acquisitions often involve large dollar amounts, perhaps hundreds of millions—even billions—of dollars. If the company has the plant assets designed and constructed, the cash outlays to acquire these assets may continue over a period of years. In addition, acquisitions of plant assets may affect the nature and profitability of the company's operations for many years to come.

A major factor in most capital budgeting decisions is management's estimates of the *future cash flows* relating to the project—that is, the cash outlays needed to acquire the new assets, and the annual net cash receipts which these assets are expected to generate.

One approach widely used in the evaluation of capital budgeting proposals is *discounting* the expected future cash flows to their *present value.* Another approach is to compute the return on investment (ROI) expected from each proposed expenditure. These and other capital budgeting techniques are discussed in depth in Chapter 26. Our objective at this time is simply to emphasize the following points:

1 Decisions concerning the acquisition of plant assets are of considerable importance, as they may affect business operations for many years.

2 Accounting information—especially estimates of future cash flows and earnings—plays a vital role in these decisions.

Capital Expenditures Budget In Chapter 7, we explained that most well-managed companies prepare *cash budgets*—forecasts of expected cash receipts and cash payments for the coming year. In addition, these companies often prepare *capital expenditures budgets,* which forecast the company's capital expenditures over a period of several years.

The long-term capital expenditures budget and the annual cash budgets are interrelated. Both budgets should agree as to the amount of cash to be spent on capital expenditures during the current year.

DEPRECIATION

Allocating the Cost of Plant and Equipment over the Years of Use

Tangible plant assets, with the exception of land, are of use to a company for only a limited number of years. *Depreciation,* as the term is used in accounting, is the *allocation of the cost of a tangible plant asset to expense in the periods in which services are received from the asset.*

OBJECTIVE 3
Explain the
relationship
between de-
preciation
and the
matching
principle.

In short, the basic purpose of depreciation is to achieve the ***matching principle***—that is, to offset the revenue of an accounting period with the costs of the goods and services being consumed in the effort to generate that revenue.

Earlier in this chapter, we described a delivery truck as a "stream of transportation services" to be received over the years that the truck is owned and used. The cost of the truck initially is debited to an asset account, because this purchase of these "transportation services" will benefit many future accounting periods. As these services are received, however, the cost of the truck gradually is removed from the balance sheet and allocated to expense, through the process called "depreciation."

Depreciation: a
process of
allocating the
cost of an
asset to
expense

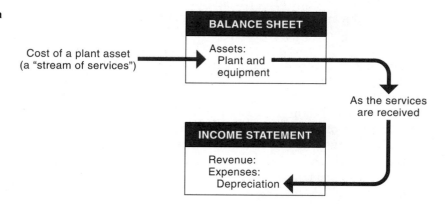

The journal entry to record depreciation expense consists of a debit to Depreciation Expense and a credit to Accumulated Depreciation. The credit portion of the entry removes from the balance sheet that portion of the asset's cost estimated to have been used up during the current period. The debit portion of the entry allocates this expired cost to expense.

Separate Depreciation Expense and Accumulated Depreciation accounts are maintained for different types of depreciable assets, such as factory buildings, delivery equipment, and office equipment. These separate accounts help accountants to measure separately the costs of different business activities, such as manufacturing, sales, and administration.

Depreciation Is Not a Process of Valuation Depreciation is a process of ***cost allocation,*** not a process of valuation. Accounting records do not attempt to show the current market values of plant assets. The market value of a building, for example, may increase during some accounting periods within the building's useful life. The recognition of depreciation expense continues, however, without regard to such temporary increases in market value. Accountants recognize that the building will render useful services only for a limited number of years, and that the full cost of the building should be ***systematically allocated to expense*** during these years.

Book Value Plant assets are shown in the balance sheet at their book values (or ***carrying values***). The ***book value*** of a plant asset is its ***cost minus the related accumulated depreciation.*** Accumulated depreciation is a contra-asset account, representing that portion of the asset's cost that has **already** been allocated to expense. Thus, book value represents the portion of the asset's cost that remains to be allocated to expense in future periods.

Depreciation and Cash Flows   Depreciation differs from most expenses in that it does not depend upon a cash payment at or near the time the expense is recorded. For this reason, depreciation sometimes is called a "non-cash" expense. Bear in mind, however, that "payment" of many years' depreciation expense is made in advance, when the plant asset is purchased. Also, when the asset eventually wears out, an even larger cash payment may be required to replace it.

Some people mistakenly believe that accumulated depreciation represents a fund of cash being accumulated for the purpose of replacing the plant assets when they wear out. This is a misconception. Accumulated depreciation is **not** an asset—it is the portion of the asset's cost that **already has been allocated to expense.** The amount of cash owned by a company is shown in the asset account, Cash and Cash Equivalents.

Causes of Depreciation

The two major causes of depreciation are physical deterioration and obsolescence.

Physical Deterioration   Physical deterioration of a plant asset results from use, as well as from exposure to sun, wind, and other climatic factors. When a plant asset has been carefully maintained, it is not uncommon for the owner to claim that the asset is as "good as new." Such statements are not literally true. Although a good repair policy may greatly lengthen the useful life of a machine, every machine eventually reaches the point at which it must be discarded. In brief, the making of repairs does not lessen the need for recognition of depreciation.

Obsolescence   The term **obsolescence** means the process of becoming out of date or obsolete. An airplane, for example, may become obsolete even though it is in excellent physical condition; it becomes obsolete because better planes of superior design and performance have become available.

The usefulness of plant assets may also be reduced because the rapid growth of a company renders such assets inadequate. **Inadequacy** of a plant asset may necessitate replacement with a larger unit even though the asset is in good physical condition. Obsolescence and inadequacy are often closely associated; both relate to the opportunity for economical and efficient use of an asset rather than to its physical condition.

Methods of Computing Depreciation

There are several alternative methods of computing depreciation. A business need not use the same method of depreciation for all its various assets. For example, a company may use straight-line depreciation on some assets and a declining-balance method for other assets. Furthermore, the

OBJECTIVE 4 *Compute depreciation by the straight-line, units-of-output, declining-balance, and sum-of-the-years'-digits methods.*

methods used for computing depreciation expense in financial statements **may differ** from the methods used in the preparation of the company's income tax return.

Data for Our Illustrations Our illustrations of the most widely used depreciation methods will be based upon the following data: On January 2, S&G Wholesale Grocery acquires a new delivery truck. The data and estimates needed for the computation of the annual depreciation expense are:

Cost	$17,000
Estimated residual value	$ 2,000
Estimated useful life	5 years (or 100,000 miles)*

* The estimated life stated in miles will be used only in the **units-of-output** depreciation method.

Straight-Line Method The simplest and most widely used method of computing depreciation is the straight-line method. Under this method an **equal portion** of the asset's cost is recognized as depreciation expense in each period of the asset's useful life. (The straight-line method was described in Chapter 3 and has been used in all of our illustrations and problems involving depreciation up to this point.)

Annual depreciation expense is computed by deducting the estimated **residual value** (or salvage value) from the cost of the asset and dividing the remaining **depreciable cost** by the years of estimated useful life. Using the data in our example, the annual straight-line depreciation is computed as follows:

$$\frac{\text{Cost} - \text{Residual Value}}{\text{Years of Useful Life}} = \frac{\$17,000 - \$2,000}{5} = \$3,000$$

This same depreciation computation is shown below in tabular form.

Computing depreciation by straight-line method

Cost of the depreciable asset	$17,000
Less: Estimated residual value (amount to be realized by sale of asset when it is retired from use)	2,000
Total amount to be depreciated (depreciable cost)	$15,000
Estimated useful life	5 years
Depreciation expense each year ($15,000 ÷ 5)	$ 3,000

The following schedule summarizes the effects of straight-line depreciation over the entire life of the asset:

Depreciation Schedule: Straight-Line Method

Constant annual depreciation expense

Year	Computation	Depreciation Expense	Accumulated Depreciation	Book Value
				$17,000
First	($15,000 × $\frac{1}{5}$)	$ 3,000	$ 3,000	14,000
Second	($15,000 × $\frac{1}{5}$)	3,000	6,000	11,000
Third........................	($15,000 × $\frac{1}{5}$)	3,000	9,000	8,000
Fourth	($15,000 × $\frac{1}{5}$)	3,000	12,000	5,000
Fifth	($15,000 × $\frac{1}{5}$)	3,000	15,000	2,000
Total		$15,000		

(We present similar depreciation schedules for most of the depreciation methods illustrated in this chapter. In these schedules, we highlight in red what we consider to be the most distinctive feature of each depreciation method.)

Notice that the depreciation expense over the life of the truck totals **$15,000**—the cost of the truck *minus the estimated residual value.* The residual value is *not* part of the cost "used up" in business operations. Instead, the residual value is expected to be recovered in cash upon disposal of the asset.

In practice, residual values are ignored if they are not expected to be *material* in amount. Traditionally, buildings, office equipment, furniture, fixtures, and special-purpose equipment seldom are considered to have significant residual values. Assets such as vehicles, aircraft, and computer systems, in contrast, often do have residual values which are material in amount.

In our example, S&G acquired the delivery truck on January 2. Therefore, we computed a "full year's" depreciation for the year of acquisition. Assume, however, that the truck had been acquired later in the year, say, on *October 1.* Thus, the truck would have been in use for only 3 months (or $\frac{3}{12}$) of the first year. In this case, depreciation expense for the first year would be limited to only *$750,* or $\frac{3}{12}$ of a "full year's" depreciation ($3,000 × $\frac{3}{12}$ = $750). (An alternative method of computing depreciation for fractional periods is explained later in this chapter.)

It often is convenient to state the portion of an asset's depreciable cost which will be written off during the year as a percentage, called the *depreciation rate.* When straight-line depreciation is in use, the depreciation rate is simply *1* divided by the *life* (in years) of the asset. The delivery truck in our example has an estimated life of 5 years, so the depreciation expense each year is $\frac{1}{5}$, or *20%,* of the depreciable amount. Similarly, an asset with a 10-year life has a depreciation rate of $\frac{1}{10}$, or *10%;* and an asset with an 8-year life, a depreciation rate of $\frac{1}{8}$, or *12$\frac{1}{2}$%.*

Units-of-Output Method   For certain kinds of assets, more equitable allocation of the cost can be obtained by dividing the cost (minus salvage value, if significant) by the estimated units of output rather than by the estimated years of useful life. A car rental company, for example, might compute depreciation on its vehicles by a mileage basis.

If we assume that the delivery truck in our example has an estimated useful life of 100,000 miles, the depreciation rate *per mile of operation* is *15 cents* ($15,000 ÷ 100,000 miles). This calculation of the depreciation rate may be stated as follows:

$$\frac{\text{Cost} - \text{Residual Value}}{\text{Estimated Units of Output (Miles)}} = \frac{\text{Depreciation per}}{\text{Unit of Output (Mile)}}$$

$$\frac{\$17,000 - \$2,000}{100,000 \text{ miles}} = \$.15 \text{ depreciation per mile}$$

At the end of each year, the amount of depreciation to be recorded would be determined by multiplying the 15-cent rate by the number of miles the truck had been driven during the year. After the truck has gone 100,000 miles, it is fully depreciated, and the depreciation program is stopped. This method is suitable only when the total units of output of the asset over its entire useful life can be estimated with reasonable accuracy.

Accelerated Depreciation Methods The term ***accelerated depreciation*** means recognition of relatively large amounts of depreciation in the early years of use and reduced amounts in the later years. Many types of plant and equipment are most efficient when new and therefore provide more and better services in the early years of useful life. If we assume that the benefits derived from owning an asset are greatest in the early years when the asset is relatively new, then the amount of the asset's cost which we allocate as depreciation expense should be greatest in these same early years. This is consistent with the basic accounting concept of matching costs with related revenue. Accelerated depreciation methods have been widely used in income tax returns because they reduce the current year's tax burden by recognizing a relatively large amount of depreciation expense.

Fixed-Percentage-of-Declining-Balance Method The most widely used form of accelerated depreciation is the fixed-percentage-of-declining-balance method. This method involves computing an ***accelerated depreciation rate*** which is a ***specified percentage of the straight-line depreciation rate.*** Depreciation expense is computed each year by applying this accelerated depreciation rate ***to the remaining book value*** (undepreciated cost) of the asset. This computation may be summarized as follows:

$$\text{Depreciation Expense} = \text{Remaining Book Value} \times \text{Accelerated Depreciation Rate}$$

The accelerated depreciation rate ***remains constant*** throughout the life of the asset. Hence, this rate represents the "fixed-percentage" described in the name of this depreciation method. The book value (cost minus accumulated depreciation) ***decreases every year,*** and represents the "declining-balance."

Thus far, we have described the accelerated depreciation rate as a "specified percentage" of the straight-line rate. Most often, this specified percentage is ***200%,*** meaning that the accelerated rate is exactly twice the straight-line rate. As a result, the declining-balance method of depreciation often is called ***double-declining-balance*** (or 200%-declining-balance). Tax rules, however, often specify a ***lower*** percentage, such as 150% of the straight-line rate. This version of the declining-balance method may be described as "150%-declining-balance."[2] In this text, we will limit our illustrations and problems to the most widely used version of the declining-balance method, in which the accelerated depreciation rate is ***double*** the straight-line rate.

To illustrate double-declining-balance, consider our example of the $17,000 delivery truck. The estimated useful life is 5 years; therefore, the

---

[2] The higher the specified percentage of the straight-line rate, the "more accelerated" this depreciation method becomes. Experience and tradition have established 200% of the straight-line rate as the maximum level. Tax rules often specify lower percentages in order to "slow down" the rates at which taxpayers may depreciate specific types of assets in their income tax returns.

straight-line depreciation rate is **20%** (1 ÷ 5 years). Doubling this straight-line rate indicates an accelerated depreciation rate of **40%.**[3] Each year, we will recognize as depreciation expense 40% of the truck's current book value, as shown below:

Depreciation Schedule: Declining-Balance Method

Year	Computation	Depreciation Expense	Accumulated Depreciation	Book Value
				$17,000
First	($17,000 × 40%)	$6,800	$ 6,800	10,200
Second	($10,200 × 40%)	4,080	10,800	6,120
Third	($6,120 × 40%)	2,448	13,328	3,672
Fourth	($3,672 × 40%)	1,469	14,797	2,203
Fifth	($2,203 × 40%) = ~~881~~	203	15,000	2,000
Total		$15,000		

Accelerated depreciation: declining-balance

Notice that the estimated residual value of the delivery truck **does not** enter into the computation of depreciation expense until the very end. This is because the declining-balance method provides an **"automatic"** residual value. As long as each year's depreciation expense is equal to only a portion of the undepreciated cost of the asset, the asset **will never be entirely written off.** However, if the asset has a significant residual value, depreciation should **stop at this point.** Since our delivery truck has an estimated residual value of **$2,000,** the depreciation expense for the fifth year should be **limited to $203,** rather than the $881 indicated by taking 40% of the remaining book value. By limiting the last year's depreciation expense in this manner, the book value of the truck at the end of the fifth year will be equal to its $2,000 estimated residual value.

If the asset in the above illustration had been acquired on October 1 rather than on January 1, depreciation for only 3 months would be recorded in the first year. The computation would be $17,000 × 40% × $\frac{3}{12}$, or $1,700. For the next calendar year the calculation would be ($17,000 − $1,700) × 40%, or $6,120.

Sum-of-the-Years'-Digits Method Another form of accelerated depreciation is the sum-of-the-years'-digits method, sometimes called SYD. In this method, the depreciation rate is stated as a **fraction,** which gets smaller each year. These "shrinking fractions" determine the percentage of the asset's **depreciable amount** (cost minus residual value) charged to depreciation expense each year.

The key to the sum-of-the-years'-digits method is computing the series of fractions used as depreciation rates. The method draws its name from the **denominator** of these fractions, which is the **sum** of the numbers which designate the years of the asset's useful life. To illustrate, consider our example of the delivery truck with a 5-year life. The sum of the numbers 1 through 5 is **15,** as shown below:

$$1 + 2 + 3 + 4 + 5 = 15$$

[3] Under the 150%-declining-balance method, the accelerated depreciation rate would be **30%** (20% straight-line rate × 150% = 30%).

Thus, the ***denominator*** of the depreciation rates for an asset with a 5-year useful life is 15. Notice that the denominator ***varies substantially*** with the estimated useful life of the asset. An asset with a 4-year life will have a denominator of 10 (1 + 2 + 3 + 4 = 10), whereas the denominator for assets with a 6-year life is 21 (1 + 2 + 3 + 4 + 5 + 6 = 21).[4]

The ***numerator*** of each depreciation rate fraction is the number of years ***remaining*** in the asset's useful life as of the ***beginning*** of the current year. Thus, the numerator becomes smaller each year.

In the example involving S&G's delivery truck, the amount to be depreciated is **$15,000** ($17,000 cost − $2,000 residual value). At the beginning of the first year, all 5 years of useful life remain; therefore, the depreciation rate is $\frac{5}{15}$, and depreciation expense for the year amounts to **$5,000** ($15,000 depreciable amount × $\frac{5}{15}$). In the second year, only 4 years of useful life remain; the depreciation rate is lowered to $\frac{4}{15}$, and depreciation expense is **$4,000** ($15,000 × $\frac{4}{15}$). This pattern continues over the asset's entire useful life; the depreciation rates are $\frac{3}{15}$ in the third year, $\frac{2}{15}$ in the fourth year, and $\frac{1}{15}$ in the fifth and final year. The depreciation program is summarized below:

Depreciation Schedule: Sum-of-the-Years'-Digits Method

	Year	Computation	Depreciation Expense	Accumulated Depreciation	Book Value
					$17,000
	First	($15,000 × $\frac{5}{15}$)	$ 5,000	$ 5,000	12,000
	Second	($15,000 × $\frac{4}{15}$)	4,000	9,000	8,000
	Third......................	($15,000 × $\frac{3}{15}$)	3,000	12,000	5,000
	Fourth	($15,000 × $\frac{2}{15}$)	2,000	14,000	3,000
	Fifth	($15,000 × $\frac{1}{15}$)	1,000	15,000	2,000
	Total		$15,000		

Accelerated depreciation: sum-of-the-years'-digits

Assume that the asset being depreciated by the sum-of-the-years'-digits method was acquired on October 1 and the company maintains its accounts on a calendar-year basis. Since the asset was in use for only 3 months during the first accounting period, the depreciation to be recorded in this first period will be for only $\frac{3}{12}$ of a full year, that is, $\frac{3}{12}$ × $5,000, or $1,250. For the second accounting period the depreciation computation will be:

$\frac{9}{12}$ × ($\frac{5}{15}$ × $15,000) $3,750

$\frac{3}{12}$ × ($\frac{4}{15}$ × $15,000) 1,000

Depreciation expense, second period... $4,750

A similar pattern of allocation will be followed for each accounting period of the asset's life.

---

[4] Alternatively, the denominator may be computed by using the formula $n\left(\dfrac{n+1}{2}\right)$, where n is the useful life of the asset. According to this formula, the sum of the years' digits for an asset with a 5-year life is computed as follows: $5\left(\dfrac{5+1}{2}\right) = 5(3) = 15$. Similarly, the sum of the years' digits for an asset with a 10-year life would be computed as follows: $10\left(\dfrac{10+1}{2}\right) = 10(5.5) = 55$.

Depreciation for Fractional Periods When an asset is acquired in the middle of an accounting period, it is not necessary to compute depreciation expense to the nearest day or week. In fact, such a computation would give a misleading impression of great precision. Since depreciation is based upon an estimated useful life of many years, the depreciation applicable to any one year is ***only an approximation.***

One widely used method of computing depreciation for part of a year is to round the calculation to the nearest whole month. Thus, if an asset is acquired on July 12, depreciation is computed for the six months beginning July 1. If an asset is acquired on July 16 (or any date in the latter half of July), depreciation is recorded for only five months (August through December) in the current calendar year.

Another acceptable approach, called the ***half-year convention,*** is to record six months' depreciation on all assets acquired during the year. This approach is based upon the assumption that the actual purchase dates will "average out" to approximately midyear. The half-year convention is widely used for assets such as office equipment, automobiles, and machinery. For buildings, however, income tax rules require that depreciation be computed for the actual number of months that the building is owned.

The half-year convention enables us to treat similar assets acquired at different dates during the year as a single group. For example, assume that an insurance company purchases hundreds of desk-top computers throughout the current year at a total cost of $600,000. The company depreciates these computers by the straight-line method, assuming a 5-year life and no residual value. Using the half-year convention, the depreciation expense on all of the computers purchased during the year may be computed as follows: $600,000 \div 5$ years $\times \frac{6}{12} = \$60,000$. If we did not use the half-year convention, depreciation would have to be computed separately for computers purchased in different months.

Management's Responsibility for Depreciation Methods and Related Estimates

Management is responsible for selecting the methods to be used in depreciating company assets. For purposes of financial reporting, management usually elects to use the straight-line method, because this method allows the company to report higher earnings. In fact, a recent survey of 600 large corporations shows that more than 90% of these companies used straight-line depreciation in their financial statements for at least some of their plant assets. In contrast, only about 21% of the companies surveyed used an accelerated method in depreciating some or all of their plant assets.[5]

The Principle of Consistency The ***consistent*** application of accounting methods is a generally accepted accounting principle. With respect to depreciation methods, this principle means that a company should ***not change*** from year to year the method used in computing the depreciation expense for a given plant asset. However, management ***may*** use different methods in computing depreciation for different assets. Also, management

---

[5]   AICPA, "Accounting Trends & Techniques" (New York: 1990), p. 261.

may use different depreciation methods in the company's financial statements and in its income tax returns.

Financial Statement Disclosures A company should ***disclose*** in notes to its financial statements the methods used to depreciate plant assets. Readers of these statements should recognize that accelerated depreciation methods transfer the costs of plant assets to expense more quickly than does the straight-line method. Thus, accelerated methods result in more ***conservative*** (lower) balance sheet valuations of plant assets and measurements of net income.

Estimates of Useful Life and Residual Value Estimating the useful lives and residual values of plant assets also is a responsibility of management. These estimates usually are based upon the company's past experience with similar assets, but they also reflect the company's current circumstances and management's future plans. Thus, the estimated lives of similar assets may vary from one company to another.

The estimated lives of plant assets affect the amount of net income reported each period. The longer the estimated useful life, the smaller the amount of cost transferred each period to depreciation expense, and the larger the amount of reported net income. Bear in mind, however, that all large corporations are ***audited*** annually by a firm of independent public accountants. One of the responsibilities of these auditors is to determine that management's estimates of the useful lives of plant assets are reasonable under the circumstances.

Automobiles typically are depreciated over relatively short estimated lives—say, from 3 to 5 years. Most other types of equipment are depreciated over a period of from 5 to 15 years. Buildings are depreciated over much longer lives—perhaps 30 to 50 years for a new building, and 15 years or more for a building acquired used.

Revision of Estimated Useful Lives What should be done if, after a few years of using a plant asset, management decides that the asset actually is going to last for a considerably longer or shorter period than was originally estimated? When this situation arises, a ***revised estimate*** of useful life should be made and the periodic depreciation expense decreased or increased accordingly.

The procedure for correcting the depreciation program is to spread the remaining undepreciated cost of the asset ***over the years of remaining useful life.*** This correction affects only the amount of depreciation expense that will be recorded in the current and future periods. The financial statements of past periods are ***not*** revised to reflect changes in the estimated useful lives of depreciable assets.

To illustrate, assume that a company acquires a $10,000 asset which is estimated to have a 10-year useful life and no residual value. Under the straight-line method, the annual depreciation expense is $1,000. At the end of the sixth year, accumulated depreciation amounts to $6,000, and the asset has an undepreciated cost (or book value) of $4,000.

At the beginning of the seventh year, it is decided that the asset will last for 8 more years. The revised estimate of useful life is, therefore, a total of

14 years. The depreciation expense to be recognized for the seventh year and for each of the remaining years is $500, computed as follows:

Revision of depreciation program

Undepreciated cost at end of sixth year ($10,000 − $6,000)	**$4,000**
Revised estimate of remaining years of useful life	**8 years**
Revised amount of annual depreciation expense ($4,000 ÷ 8)	**$ 500**

Depreciation and Federal Income Taxes

The depreciation methods used in preparing federal income tax returns usually differ from the methods used in financial statements. Many companies use straight-line depreciation in their financial statements because this permits reporting higher earnings. In preparing tax returns, however, most companies use *accelerated depreciation methods.* Accelerated depreciation methods result in larger amounts of depreciation expense, which reduces taxable income and the amount of income taxes due in the near future.[6]

Income tax rules are changed frequently by Congress, and the rules relating to depreciation seem especially subject to change. For assets acquired prior to 1981, taxpayers were permitted to choose among straight-line depreciation and accelerated methods such as double-declining-balance and sum-of-the-years'-digits. For assets acquired after 1980, taxpayers were required to use either straight-line depreciation or a special new accelerated depreciation method called the Accelerated Cost Recovery System, or *ACRS* (pronounced "acres").

ACRS replaced the traditional concept of making reasonable estimates of useful lives with shorter, arbitrary "recovery periods" for allocating the cost of depreciable assets to expense. Automobiles, for example, were to be written off in only 3 years, and buildings in only 15 years. The Internal Revenue Service publishes schedules indicating the appropriate recovery period for every type of asset, and also the percentage of the asset's cost which may be written off during each year of the recovery period.

In 1986, Congress adopted the Modified Accelerated Cost Recovery System, called *MACRS* (pronounced "makers"). MACRS lengthened the recovery periods for most types of assets and required taxpayers to apply different depreciation rates. When Congress changes the tax rules for depreciation, the new rules apply only to assets acquired *after* a specified date (usually December 31 of the year in which Congress passes the new tax law). Assets placed in service before that date remain subject to the tax rules that were in effect *when those assets were acquired.* Thus, *both* ACRS and MACRS are now in effect: ACRS is used in depreciating assets acquired from 1981 through 1986, and MACRS is used for assets acquired *after* 1986. (Depreciation computations under MACRS are illustrated in the Supplemental Topic section at the end of this chapter.)

Such "tax methods" as ACRS and MACRS are used *only in income tax returns.* These systems generally are not used in financial statements

---

[6] We have made the point that only businesses organized as corporations file income tax returns for the business entity. However, the taxable income of unincorporated businesses is computed and reported in the *personal* income tax returns of the owners of these companies.

because they are frequently altered and modified by Congress and because the recovery periods often differ substantially from realistic estimates of the assets' useful lives.

Inflation and Depreciation

We have illustrated that depreciation expense is based upon **historical costs,** that is, the costs actually incurred when the asset was acquired. For long-lived assets such as buildings, these costs may have been incurred 20, 30, perhaps even 50 years ago.

We live in an inflationary economy, which is characterized by rising prices. Sometimes inflation is severe, while at other times it is quite moderate. Still, prices have risen significantly over the long term. According to the Consumers' Price Index (CPI), prices today are about four times their levels of 40 years ago.

Many accountants, business executives, and economists believe that the "old" historical costs used in financial reporting should be **adjusted** to reflect the changes in prices over time. Without such an adjustment, they argue, expenses such as depreciation substantially **understate** the "current economic values" of the resources being consumed in business operations, thereby causing an overstatement of net income.

A Past Effort at "Inflation Accounting"   In the late 1970s, the FASB conducted a five-year experiment in which it required large corporations to **disclose** in their financial statements the **current replacement costs** of their plant assets, and also depreciation expense based upon these current costs. Eventually, however, the FASB **discontinued** these disclosure requirements. The Board concluded that these disclosures were not **cost-effective**—that is, the cost to businesses of developing this information each year **exceeded** the value of the information to decision makers. A basic concept of financial reporting is that all accounting information should be **cost-effective** when viewed from the perspective of our society as a whole.

Today, the FASB, the SEC, and many other organizations and individuals are showing renewed interest in the use of current market values in the valuation of various types of assets. The fact that the FASB has discontinued one experiment in the use of current costs does not mean that financial statements will remain based upon historical costs forever. It does suggest, however, that a shift away from historical cost is not likely to occur quickly, or without considerable public discussion and debate.

DISPOSAL OF PLANT AND EQUIPMENT

*OBJECTIVE 5
Record the
disposal of a
plant asset.*

When depreciable assets are disposed of at any date other than the end of the year, an entry should be made to record depreciation for the **fraction of the year** ending with the date of disposal. If the half-year convention is in use, six months' depreciation should be recorded on all assets disposed of during the year. In the following illustrations of the disposal of items of plant and equipment, it is assumed that any necessary entries for fractional-period depreciation already have been recorded.

As units of plant and equipment wear out or become obsolete, they must be scrapped, sold, or traded in on new equipment. Upon the disposal or retirement of a depreciable asset, the cost of the property is removed from the asset account, and the accumulated depreciation is removed from the related contra-asset account. Assume, for example, that office equipment purchased 10 years ago at a cost of $20,000 has been fully depreciated and is no longer useful. The entry to record the scrapping of the worthless equipment is as follows:

Scrapping fully depreciated asset

Accumulated Depreciation: Office Equipment	*20,000*	
Office Equipment..		*20,000*

To remove from the accounts the cost and the accumulated depreciation on fully depreciated office equipment now being scrapped. No salvage value.

Once an asset has been fully depreciated, no more depreciation should be recorded on it, even though the property is in good condition and is still in use. The objective of depreciation is to spread the **cost** of an asset over the periods of its usefulness; in no case can depreciation expense be greater than the amount paid for the asset. When a fully depreciated asset remains in use beyond the original estimate of useful life, the asset account and the Accumulated Depreciation account should remain in the accounting records without further entries until the asset is retired.

Gains and Losses on Disposals of Plant and Equipment

Since the residual value and useful life of plant assets are only estimates, it is not uncommon for plant assets to be sold at a price which differs from their book value at the date of disposal. When plant assets are sold, any gain or loss on the disposal is computed by comparing the **book value with the amount received from the sale.** A sales price in excess of the book value produces a gain; a sales price below the book value produces a loss. These gains or losses, if material in amount, should be shown separately in the income statement in computing the income from operations.

Disposal at a Price Above Book Value   Assume that a machine which cost $10,000 and has a book value of $2,000 is sold for $3,000. The journal entry to record this disposal is as follows:

Gain on disposal of plant asset

Cash...	*3,000*	
Accumulated Depreciation: Machinery	*8,000*	
Machinery		*10,000*
Gain on Disposal of Plant Assets		*1,000*

To record sale of machinery at a price above book value.

Disposal at a Price Below Book Value   Now assume that the same machine is sold for $500. The journal entry in this case would be as follows:

Loss on disposal of plant asset

Cash...	*500*	
Accumulated Depreciation: Machinery	*8,000*	
Loss on Disposal of Plant Assets	*1,500*	
Machinery		*10,000*

To record sale of machinery at a price below book value.

The disposal of a depreciable asset at a price equal to book value would result in neither a gain nor a loss. The entry for such a transaction would consist of a debit to Cash for the amount received, a debit to Accumulated Depreciation for the balance accumulated, and a credit to the asset account for the original cost.

Gains and Losses for Income Tax Purposes

Keep in mind that a business may use one depreciation method in its financial statements and *another method* for income tax purposes. As a result of using different depreciation methods, the asset's book value for income tax purposes (called *basis*) may differ from its book value in the financial statements. Since the gain or loss on disposal is determined by comparing the disposal price to the asset's book value, the amount of gain or loss computed for income tax purposes *may differ* from that reported in the company's financial statements. (The computation of gains and losses for tax purposes is illustrated in the Supplemental Topic section at the end of this chapter.)

Trading in Used Assets on New

Certain types of depreciable assets, such as automobiles and trucks, sometimes are traded in on new assets of the same kind. In most instances, a trade-in is viewed as both a *sale* of the old asset and a purchase of a new one.

To illustrate, assume that Rancho Landscape has an old pickup truck which originally cost $10,000 but which now has a book value of $2,000. Rancho trades in this old truck on a new one with a fair market value of $15,000. The truck dealership grants Rancho a "trade-in allowance" of $3,500 for the old truck, and Rancho pays the remaining $11,500 cost of the new truck in cash. Rancho Landscape should record this transaction as follows:

Entry to record a typical trade-in

Vehicles (new truck)	*15,000*	
Accumulated Depreciation: Trucks (old truck)	*8,000*	
Vehicles (old truck).......................................		*10,000*
Gain on Disposal of Plant Assets		*1,500*
Cash		*11,500*

Traded-in old truck on a new one costing $15,000. Received $3,500 trade-in allowance on the old truck, which had a book value of $2,000.

Notice that Rancho views the $3,500 trade-in allowance granted by the truck dealership as the *sales price* of the old truck. Thus, Rancho recognizes a ***$1,500 gain*** on the disposal (trade-in) of this asset ($3,500 trade-in allowance − $2,000 book value = $1,500 gain).

For financial reporting purposes, gains and losses on routine trade-ins are recorded in the accounting records whenever the transaction also involves the payment of a significant amount of cash (or the creation of debt).[7]

Income Tax Rules Require Special Treatment of "Like-Kind" Exchanges

Income tax rules do **not** permit recognition of gains or losses on exchanges of "like-kind" assets—that is, assets which are used for similar purposes. Thus, the $1,500 gain recorded in our example is not regarded as taxable income.[8] Also, the tax basis of the new truck is only **$13,500,** not the $15,000 recorded in the accounting records. For income tax purposes, the basis of a "like-kind" asset acquired in an exchange is equal to the **book value** of the asset traded in, plus any "boot" (additional amount paid or owed).

Small businesses which have no financial reporting requirements other than income tax returns **usually use this "tax method"** in accounting for trade-ins. If Rancho had used the "tax method," the cost debited to the Vehicles account would have been $13,500, and no gain on disposal of plant assets would have been recorded. Some large businesses also record trade-ins by the tax method as a matter of convenience, as gains or losses on trade-ins usually are immaterial in amount.

A Concluding Comment . . .

The accounting rules applicable to trade-ins are more complex for the entity receiving boot than for the entity which pays it. Also, special rules may apply whenever the amount of boot included in a like-kind exchange is unusually small (less than 25% of the transaction amount). As these special accounting rules do not affect normal trade-ins of used equipment for new, we will defer the discussion of such transactions to the intermediate accounting course.

INTANGIBLE ASSETS

Characteristics

As the word **intangible** suggests, assets in this classification have no physical substance. Leading examples are goodwill, patents, and trademarks. Intangible assets are classified in the balance sheet as a subgroup of plant assets. However, not all assets which lack physical substance are regarded as intangible assets. An account receivable, for example, or a short-term prepayment is of nonphysical nature but is classified as a current asset and is not regarded as an intangible. In brief, **intangible assets are assets which are used in the operation of the business but which have no physical substance and are noncurrent.**

The basis of valuation for intangible assets is cost. In some companies,

---

[7]   The FASB Emerging Issues Task Force takes the position that when 25% or more of the transaction value is comprised of cash or monetary obligations, the transaction should be viewed as **monetary,** rather than nonmonetary. Thus, gains on most routine trade-ins should be **recognized in full,** rather than "deferred" as they are for income tax purposes. See *EITF Abstract Nos. 84-29, 86-29, and 87-29.*

[8]   Had the trade-in allowance been less than book value, the resulting loss would **not be deductible** in the determination of taxable income.

certain intangible assets such as trademarks may be of great importance but may have been acquired without the incurring of any cost. An intangible asset should appear in the balance sheet *only* if a cost of acquisition or development has been incurred.

Operating Expenses versus Intangible Assets

For an expenditure to qualify as an intangible asset, there must be reasonable evidence of future benefits. Many expenditures offer some prospects of yielding benefits in subsequent years, but the existence and life-span of these benefits is so uncertain that most companies treat these expenditures as operating expenses. Examples are the expenditures for intensive advertising campaigns to introduce new products and the expense of training employees to work with new types of machinery or office equipment. There is little doubt that some benefits from these outlays continue beyond the current period, but because of the uncertain duration of the benefits, it is almost universal practice to treat expenditures of this nature as expense of the current period.

Amortization

The term *amortization* is used to describe the systematic write-off to expense of the cost of an intangible asset over its useful life. The usual accounting entry for amortization consists of a debit to Amortization Expense and a credit to the intangible asset account. There is no theoretical objection to crediting an accumulated amortization account rather than the intangible asset account, but this method is seldom encountered in practice.

Although it is difficult to estimate the useful life of an intangible such as a trademark, it is highly probable that such an asset will not contribute to future earnings on a permanent basis. The cost of the intangible asset should, therefore, be deducted from revenue during the years in which it may be expected to aid in producing revenue. Under the current rules of the Financial Accounting Standards Board, the maximum period for amortization of an intangible asset cannot exceed *40 years.*[9] The straight-line method normally is used for amortizing intangible assets.

Goodwill

Business executives used the term *goodwill* in a variety of meanings before it became part of accounting terminology. One of the most common meanings of goodwill in a nonaccounting sense concerns the benefits derived from a favorable reputation among customers. To accountants, however, goodwill has a very specific meaning not necessarily limited to customer relations. It means the *present value of future earnings in excess of the normal return on net identifiable assets.* Above-average earnings may arise not only from favorable customer relations but also from such factors as superior management, manufacturing efficiency, and weak competition.

The present value of future cash flows is the amount that a knowledgeable investor would pay today for the right to receive those future cash

OBJECTIVE 6
Explain the nature of goodwill and indicate when this asset should appear in the accounting records.

---

[9]   *APB Opinion No. 17,* "Intangible Assets," AICPA (New York: 1970), par. 29.

flows. (The present value concept is discussed further in later chapters and in Appendix D.)

The phrase **normal return on net identifiable assets** also requires explanation. **Net assets** means the owner's equity in a business, or assets minus liabilities. Goodwill, however, is not an **identifiable** asset. The existence of goodwill is implied by the ability of a business to earn an above-average return; however, the cause and precise dollar value of goodwill are largely matters of personal opinion. Therefore, **net identifiable assets** mean all assets **except goodwill,** minus liabilities. A **normal return** on net identifiable assets is the rate of return which investors demand in a particular industry to justify their buying a business at the **fair market value** of its net identifiable assets. A business has goodwill when investors will pay a higher price because the business earns more than the normal rate of return.

Assume that two similar restaurants are offered for sale and that the normal return on the fair market value of the net identifiable assets of restaurants of this type is 15% a year. The relative earning power of the two restaurants during the past five years is shown below:

	Mandarin Coast	Golden Dragon
Fair market value of net identifiable assets	$1,000,000	$1,000,000
Normal rate of return on net assets	15%	15%
Normal earnings, computed as 15% of net identifiable assets	150,000	150,000
Average net income for past five years.........................	$ 150,000	$ 190,000
Earnings in excess of normal	$ —0—	$ 40,000

An investor presumably would be willing to pay $1,000,000 to buy Mandarin Coast, because this restaurant earns the normal 15% return which justifies the fair market value of its net identifiable assets. Although Golden Dragon has the same amount of net identifiable assets, an investor would be willing to pay **more** for Golden Dragon than for Mandarin Coast, because Golden Dragon has a record of superior earnings which will presumably continue for some time in the future. The **extra amount** that a buyer would pay to purchase Golden Dragon represents the value of this business's **goodwill.**

Estimating Goodwill How much will an investor pay for goodwill? Above-average earnings in past years are of significance to prospective purchasers only if they believe that these earnings **will continue** after they acquire the business. Investors' appraisals of goodwill, therefore, will vary with their estimates of the future earning power of the business. Very few businesses, however, are able to maintain above-average earnings for more than a few years. Consequently, the purchaser of a business will usually limit any amount paid for goodwill to not more than four or five times the amount by which annual earnings exceed normal earnings.

Arriving at a fair value for the goodwill of an ongoing business is a difficult and subjective process. Any estimate of goodwill is in large part a matter of personal opinion. The following are several methods which a prospective purchaser might use in estimating a value for goodwill:

1 Agreement on the amount of goodwill may be reached through negotiation between buyer and seller. For example, it might be agreed that the fair market value of net identifiable assets is $1,000,000 and that the total purchase price for the business will be $1,180,000. This negotiated price implies a $180,000 payment for goodwill.

2 Goodwill may be determined as a multiple of the amount by which average annual earnings exceed normal earnings. Referring to our example involving Golden Dragon, a prospective buyer might be willing to pay four times the amount by which average earnings exceed normal earnings, indicating a value of $160,000 (4 × $40,000) for goodwill. The purchase price of the business, therefore, would be $1,160,000.

The multiple applied to the excess annual earnings will vary widely from perhaps 1 to 10. An investor who pays four times the excess earnings for goodwill must, of course, expect these earnings to continue for **at least** four years.

3 Goodwill may be estimated by **capitalizing** the amount by which average earnings exceed normal earnings. Capitalizing an earnings stream means dividing those earnings by the investor's required rate of return. The result is the maximum amount which the investor could pay for the excess earnings in order to achieve the required rate of return on the investment. To illustrate, assume that the prospective buyer decides to capitalize the $40,000 annual excess earnings of Golden Dragon at a rate of 20%. This approach results in a $200,000 estimate ($40,000 ÷ .20 = $200,000) for the value of goodwill. (Note that $40,000 per year represents a 20% return on a $200,000 investment.)

A weakness in the capitalization method is that **no provision is made for the recovery** of the investment. If the prospective buyer is to earn a 20% return on the $200,000 investment in goodwill, either the excess earnings must continue **forever** (an unlikely assumption) or the buyer must be able to recover the $200,000 investment at a later date by selling the business at a price above the fair market value of net identifiable assets.

Recording Goodwill in the Accounting Records   Goodwill is recorded in the accounting records **only when it is purchased;** this situation usually occurs only when a going business is purchased in its entirety. After the fair market values of all identifiable assets have been recorded in the accounting records of the new owners, any additional amount paid for the business may properly be debited to an asset account entitled Goodwill.

Generally accepted accounting principles require that any recorded goodwill be amortized to expense over a period not to exceed 40 years, although a much shorter amortization period often is appropriate. Current income tax rules, however, do **not** permit taxpayers to amortize goodwill in their computations of taxable income. (The tax treatment accorded to goodwill is somewhat unusual. Tax rules **do** permit amortization of most other types of intangible assets.)

Many businesses have never purchased goodwill but have generated it internally through developing good customer relations, superior management, or other factors which result in above-average earnings. Because there is no objective means of determining the dollar value of goodwill unless the business is sold, internally developed goodwill is ***not recorded*** in the accounting records. Thus, goodwill may be a very important asset of a successful business but may not even appear in the company's balance sheet.

Patents

A patent is an exclusive right granted by the federal government for manufacture, use, and sale of a particular product. The purpose of this exclusive grant is to encourage the invention of new machines and processes. When a company acquires a patent by purchase from the inventor or other holder, the purchase price should be recorded by debiting the intangible asset account Patents.

Patents are granted for a period of 17 years, and the period of amortization must not exceed that period. However, if the patent is likely to lose its usefulness in less than 17 years, amortization should be based on the shorter period of estimated useful life. Assume that a patent is purchased from the inventor at a cost of $100,000, after 5 years of the legal life have expired. The remaining ***legal*** life is, therefore, 12 years, but if the estimated ***useful*** life is only 4 years, amortization should be based on this shorter period. The entry to be made to record the annual amortization expense would be:

Entry for amortization of patent	*Amortization Expense: Patents* *25,000*	
	Patents	*25,000*
	To amortize cost of patent on a straight-line basis over an estimated life of 4 years.	

Trademarks and Trade Names

Coca-Cola's distinctive bottle was for years the classic example of a trademark known around the world. A trademark is a word, symbol, or design that identifies a product or group of products. A permanent exclusive right to the use of a trademark, brand name, or commercial symbol may be obtained by registering it with the federal government. The costs of developing a trademark or brand name often consist of advertising campaigns which should be treated as expense when incurred. If a trademark or brand name is ***purchased,*** however, the cost may be substantial. Such cost should be capitalized and amortized to expense over a period of not more than 40 years. If the use of the trademark is discontinued or its contribution to earnings becomes doubtful, any unamortized cost should be written off immediately.

Franchises

A franchise is a right granted by a company or a governmental unit to conduct a certain type of business in a specific geographical area. An example of a franchise is the right to operate a McDonald's restaurant in a specific neighborhood. The cost of franchises varies greatly and often may be quite substantial. When the cost of a franchise is small, it may be charged immediately to expense or amortized over a short period such as 5 years. When the cost is material, amortization should be based upon the life of the franchise (if limited); the amortization period, however, may not exceed 40 years.

Copyrights

A copyright is an exclusive right granted by the federal government to protect the production and sale of literary or artistic materials for the life of the creator plus 50 years. The cost of obtaining a copyright in some cases is minor and therefore is chargeable to expense when paid. Only when a copyright is **purchased** will the expenditure be **material enough** to warrant its being capitalized and spread over the useful life. The revenue from copyrights is usually limited to only a few years, and the purchase cost should, of course, be amortized over the years in which the revenue is expected.

Other Intangibles and Deferred Charges

Among the other intangibles found in the published balance sheets of large corporations are moving costs, plant rearrangement costs, organization costs, formulas, processes, name lists, and film rights. Some companies group items of this type under the title of Deferred Charges, meaning expenditures that will provide benefits beyond the current year and will be written off to expense over their useful economic lives. It is also common practice to combine these items under the heading of Other Assets, which is listed at the bottom of the balance sheet.

Research and Development (R&D) Costs

The spending of billions of dollars a year on research and development leading to all kinds of new products is a striking characteristic of U.S. industry. In the past, some companies treated all research and development costs as expense in the year incurred; other companies in the same industry recorded these costs as intangible assets to be amortized over future years. This diversity of practice prevented the financial statements of different companies from being comparable.

The lack of uniformity in accounting for R&D was ended when the Financial Accounting Standards Board ruled that all research and development expenditures should be charged to expense **when incurred.**[10] This action by the FASB had the beneficial effect of reducing the number of alternative accounting practices and helping to make financial statements of different companies more comparable.

NATURAL RESOURCES

Accounting for Natural Resources

Mining properties, oil and gas reserves, and tracts of standing timber are leading examples of natural resources. The distinguishing characteristics of these assets are that they are physically removed from their natural

---

[10] FASB, *Statement No. 2,* "Accounting for Research and Development Costs" (Norwalk, Conn.: 1974), par. 12.

OBJECTIVE 7
Account for the depletion of natural resources.

environment and are converted into inventory. Theoretically, a coal mine might be regarded as an underground "inventory" of coal; however, such as "inventory" is certainly not a current asset. In the balance sheet, mining property and other natural resources are classified as property, plant, and equipment. Once the coal is removed from the ground, however, this coal *does* represent inventory.

We have explained that plant assets such as buildings and equipment depreciate because of physical deterioration or obsolescence. A mine or an oil reserve does not "depreciate" for these reasons, but it is gradually *depleted* as the natural resource is removed from the ground. Once all of the coal has been removed from a coal mine, for example, the mine is "fully depleted" and will be abandoned or sold for its residual value.

To illustrate the depletion of a natural resource, assume that Rainbow Minerals pays $45 million to acquire the Red Valley Mine, which is believed to contain 10 million tons of coal. The residual value of the mine after all of the coal is removed is estimated to be $5 million. The depletion that will occur over the life of the mine is the original cost minus the residual value, or $40 million. This depletion will occur at the rate of *$4 per ton* ($40 million ÷ 10 million tons) as the coal is removed from the mine. If we assume that 2 million tons are mined during the first year of operations, the entry to record the depletion of the mine would be as follows:

Recording depletion

Inventory...................................	8,000,000	
Accumulated Depletion: Red Valley Mine		8,000,000

To record depletion of the Red Valley Mine for the year; 2,000,000 tons mined @ $4 per ton.

Once removed from the mine, coal becomes merchandise available for sale. Therefore, the estimated costs to this coal are debited to the Inventory account. As the coal is sold, these costs are transferred from the Inventory account to the Cost of Goods Sold account.

Accumulated Depletion is a *contra-asset account* similar to the Accumulated Depreciation account; it represents the portion of the mine which has been used up (depleted) to date. In Rainbow Mineral's balance sheet, the Red Valley Mine now appears as follows:

Property, Plant & Equipment:		
Mining properties: Red Valley Mine........................	$45,000,000	
Less: Accumulated depletion	8,000,000	$37,000,000

Depreciation of Buildings and Equipment Closely Related to Natural Resources Buildings and equipment installed at a mine or drilling site may be useful only at that particular location. Consequently, such assets should be depreciated over their normal useful lives, or over the life of the natural resource, *whichever is shorter.* Often depreciation on such assets is computed using the units-of-output method, thus relating the depreciation expense to the rate at which units of natural resource are removed.

Depreciation, Amortization, and Depletion—A Common Goal

The processes of depreciation, amortization, and depletion discussed in this chapter all have a common goal. That goal is to *allocate the acquisition cost of a long-lived asset to expense over the years in which the asset contributes to revenue.* By allocating the acquisition cost of long-lived assets over the years which benefit from the use of these assets, we stress again the importance of the **matching principle.** The determination of income requires the matching of revenue with the expenses incurred to produce that revenue.

Impairment of Long-Lived Assets

*OBJECTIVE 8
Identify some
problems that
may arise in
accounting
for the im-
pairment
of long-lived
assets.*

On occasion, it may become apparent that a company cannot reasonably expect to recover the cost of certain plant assets, either through use or through sale. For example, an oil company may pay a high price for land that it hopes contains large deposits of oil. If the company finds no oil, however, it may become apparent that the land is worth far less than its cost.

If the cost of an asset cannot be recovered through future use or sale, the asset should be **written down** to its net realizable value.[11] The offsetting debit is to a loss account.

This idea is a simple one—an asset should not be carried in the accounting records at an amount which clearly exceeds its economic worth. In practice, however, this concept may be very difficult to apply. What criteria should be used in determining when an asset has become "impaired"? Is the impairment likely to be permanent, or only temporary? How should the "net realizable value" of such an asset be estimated?

The FASB currently is studying these issues, but it has not yet taken an official position.[12] Therefore, accounting for the possible impairment of long-lived assets is an area in which management, professional accountants, and auditors must exercise professional judgment on a case-by-case basis.

In summary, the possible impairment of long-lived assets may involve such uncertainty that the amount of the company's loss cannot be determined with any objectivity. Regardless of whether or not potentially impaired assets are written down, the circumstances should be fully disclosed in notes accompanying the financial statements.

The possible impairment of long-lived assets is one type of **loss contingency.** Loss contingencies are discussed in the following chapter.

■ ■ ■ * *Supplemental Topic*
Depreciation for Income Tax Purposes

THE MODIFIED ACCELERATED COST RECOVERY SYSTEM (MACRS)

MACRS is the only accelerated depreciation method allowed for federal income tax purposes for assets acquired after December 31, 1986.

Under MACRS, all depreciable assets are classified into one of eight recovery periods: 3, 5, 7, 10, 15, 20, $29\frac{1}{2}$, or $31\frac{1}{2}$ years. For example, many

---

[11] In this context, the term **net realizable value** means the net amount estimated to be recoverable either through future use of the asset or through its sale.

[12] In December 1990, the FASB issued a *Discussion Memorandum,* entitled "Accounting for the Impairment of Long-Lived Assets and Identifiable Intangibles." A discussion memorandum is intended to solicit the comments and viewpoints of interested parties and does not represent an authoritative statement of generally accepted accounting principles. An official statement, however, probably will be forthcoming.

*OBJECTIVE 9
Compute
depreciation
for income
tax purposes
using the
MACRS
guidelines.*

special manufacturing tools are classified as "3-year property," meaning that they are assigned a 3-year recovery period. Automobiles, light trucks, and computers are "5-year property." Any depreciable asset which is not assigned a specific recovery period is treated as "7-year property."

Assets assigned a recovery period of 10 years or less are depreciated by the double-declining-balance method; assets in the 15- and 20-year recovery periods are depreciated by the 150%-declining-balance method. The half-year convention normally is used in all recovery periods of 20 years or less.[13]

The $29\frac{1}{2}$- and $31\frac{1}{2}$-year recovery periods apply to residential rental property and nonresidential real property, respectively. These recovery periods require the use of straight-line depreciation, with computations for partial years rounded to the middle of the month in which the asset is acquired.

Rate Tables Taxpayers may either compute MACRS depreciation according to the methods and conventions described above or simply refer to **depreciation rate tables** published by the Internal Revenue Service. These tables show the percentage of an asset's cost which may be written off in each year of the recovery period. Shown below are the rate tables for all recovery periods up to 20 years:[14]

MACRS Depreciation Rates*

Recovery Periods

Year	3 Years	5 Years	7 Years	10 Years	15 Years	20 Years
1	33.33%	20.00%	14.29%	10.00%	5.00%	3.750%
2	44.45	32.00	24.49	18.00	9.50	7.219
3	14.81	19.20	17.49	14.40	8.55	6.677
4	7.41	11.52	12.49	11.52	7.70	6.177
5		11.52	8.93	9.22	6.93	5.713
6		5.76	8.92	7.37	6.23	5.285
7			8.93	6.55	5.90	4.888
8			4.46	6.55	5.90	4.522
9				6.56	5.91	4.462
10				6.55	5.90	4.461
11				3.28	5.91	4.462
12					5.90	4.461
13					5.91	4.462
14					5.90	4.461
15					5.91	4.462
16					2.95	4.461
17						4.462
18						4.461
19						4.462
20						4.461
21						2.231
Total	**100.00%**	**100.00%**	**100.00%**	**100.00%**	**100.00%**	**100.000%**

*   **Caution:** This table is intended for **demonstration purposes only.** Congress may change the depreciation rates permitted for income tax purposes at any time. Therefore, this table should **not** be used in the preparation of actual income tax returns. Complete and up-to-date depreciation tables are available without charge from the Internal Revenue Service.

---

[13] **Mid-quarter convention** must be used for all assets purchased in a specific year if more than 40% of these assets (based upon cost) are acquired during the last three months. To apply mid-quarter convention, the taxpayer groups asset acquisitions by quarter and applies different depreciation rates to each group. Mid-quarter depreciation rates appear in tables published by the Internal Revenue Service.

[14] The illustrated tables reflect the half-year convention. Four separate sets of tables are needed to apply mid-quarter convention within any recovery period.

Notice that the depreciation rates listed under each recovery period **add up to 100%.** Current tax rules make **no provision** for residual values; 100% of the cost of the depreciable asset is written off over the designated recovery period.

Computing Depreciation for Tax Purposes: An Illustration   To illustrate the use of the rate table, let us consider our example of S&G Grocery's delivery truck, which cost $17,000. (For tax purposes, we will disregard the $2,000 residual value.) Under current tax rules, light-duty trucks are considered "5-year property."[15] The depreciation expense that may be deducted in the federal income tax return each year is determined as follows:

Depreciation Schedule: MACRS Income Tax Method

Year	Computation (Rate from IRS Table × Cost)	Depreciation Expense	Accumulated Depreciation	Basis (Book Value)
1	($17,000 × 20%)	$ 3,400	$ 3,400	$13,600
2	($17,000 × 32%)	5,440	8,840	8,160
3	($17,000 × 19.20%)	3,264	12,104	4,896
4	($17,000 × 11.52%)	1,958	14,062	2,938
5	($17,000 × 11.52%)	1,958	16,020	980
6	($17,000 × 5.76%)	980	17,000	–0–
Total		$17,000		

Notice that "5-year property" actually is depreciated over **6** years. The extra year results from application of the half-year convention. Also, notice that in tax schedules the term **basis** replaces **book value.** The concepts of basis and book value are quite similar. Both terms represent the **undepreciated cost** of the asset; that is, cost less accumulated depreciation. **Book value** represents the cost of the asset less the accumulated depreciation **recognized in financial statements. Basis,** in contrast, represents the cost of the asset less the accumulated depreciation **claimed in income tax returns.** Stated another way, **basis** means "book value for tax purposes."

GAINS AND LOSSES FOR INCOME TAX PURPOSES

As a result of using different depreciation methods, an asset's basis for tax purposes may differ significantly from its book value in the accounting records. When an asset is retired, any gain or loss is determined by comparing its disposal price with its undepreciated cost. The "undepreciated cost," however, is **book value** for purposes of financial reporting, and **basis** for income tax purposes. If the asset's basis differs from its book value, it follows that the gain or loss computed for income tax purposes will **differ** from that reported in the company's financial statements.

To illustrate, let us again refer to the example of S&G's delivery truck. Assume that this truck is depreciated by the **straight-line method** in S&G's financial statements and is depreciated by **MACRS** in the company's

[15]   The fact that the estimated useful life of this asset also is 5 years is a mere coincidence. In some cases, recovery periods differ substantially from the estimated useful life. Depreciation for tax purposes is based upon the recovery periods designated by Congress, **without regard** to the useful lives estimated by the company's management.

income tax returns. In both cases, the company applies the half-year convention. The depreciation to be recognized for both purposes over the life of the asset is summarized below:[16]

Summary of Depreciation for
Financial Statements and Income Tax Purposes
(Half-Year Convention)

End of Year	In Financial Statements			In Federal Income Tax Returns		
	Depreciation	Accumulated Depreciation	Book Value	Depreciation	Accumulated Depreciation	Basis
1	$ 1,500	$ 1,500	$15,500	$ 3,400	$ 3,400	$13,600
2	3,000	4,500	12,500	5,440	8,840	8,160
3	3,000	7,500	9,500	3,264	12,104	4,896
4	3,000	10,500	6,500 *8000*	1,958	14,062	2,938 *3917*
5	3,000	13,500	3,500	1,958	16,020	980
6	1,500	15,000	2,000	980	17, 000	–0–
Totals	$15,000			$17,000		

Notice that the basis of this truck for tax purposes is always *lower* than its book value in the financial statements. This is because the truck is being depreciated by an *accelerated* method for tax purposes, but by the straight-line method in S&G's financial statements.

Now assume that on April 10, Year 4, S&G sells this delivery truck for **$7,000** cash. The gain or loss for financial statement purposes is determined by comparing this $7,000 disposal price with the *book value* at the date of disposal. The gain or loss for tax purposes, on the other hand, is determined by comparing the $7,000 disposal price with the *tax basis* of the truck at the disposal date.

Depreciation in the Year of Disposal   Prior to computing the gain or loss on disposal, we must recognize depreciation for the fraction of Year 4 during which the truck was owned and determine both the book value and the tax basis of the asset at the disposal date. As the half-year convention is in use, it does not matter when during Year 4 the asset is sold; in Year 4, we will recognize *one-half* of the depreciation which had been scheduled for the full year.

The following schedule indicates the book value and the tax basis of this delivery truck at any disposal date in Year 4:

	In Financial Statements	For Tax Purposes
Undepreciated cost at the end of Year 3:		
Book value in financial statements	$9,500	
Basis in income tax returns.................................		$4,896
Less: Depreciation in year of disposal:		
For financial statements ($3,000 × $\frac{1}{2}$)	1,500	
For tax purposes ($1,958 × $\frac{1}{2}$)		979
Book value at date of disposal...............................	$8,000	
Tax basis at date of disposal		$3,917

---

[16]   The schedule for straight-line depreciation differs from that illustrated on page 462 because of the use of the half-year convention.

Computing the Gain or Loss   The gain or loss to be recognized in the company's financial statements and income tax returns now may be determined as follows:

	In Financial Statements	For Tax Purposes
Disposal price	$7,000	$7,000
Less: Undepreciated cost:		
Book value at date of disposal	8,000	
Tax basis at date of disposal		3,917
Loss on disposal (in financial statements)	$1,000	
Gain on disposal (for tax purposes)		$3,083

WHICH AMOUNTS ARE RECORDED IN THE ACCOUNTING RECORDS?

A primary purpose of the general ledger is to enable a company to prepare financial statements. Therefore, only those transactions which affect **financial statements** are recorded in the general ledger. Data regarding plant assets which are used exclusively in income tax returns may be accumulated in special work sheets or computer files, or in the company's plant and equipment **subsidiary** ledger.

At April 10, Year 4, S&G will make two journal entries to record the sale of its delivery truck. The first entry will update the Accumulated Depreciation account for the depreciation recognized **for financial statement purposes** in Year 4. This entry is:

Journal entries reflect financial statement amounts

Depreciation Expense: Delivery Truck	1,500	
Accumulated Depreciation: Delivery Truck		1,500

To record a half year's depreciation on delivery truck in the year of disposal ($3,000 \times \frac{1}{2}$).

The $979 in depreciation which will be claimed in the company's Year 4 income tax return is **not** recorded in the journals or general ledger.

The second entry required at April 10, Year 4, records the sale of the truck for $7,000 and the loss to be recognized **for financial statement purposes**:

Cash	7,000	
Loss on Disposal of Plant Assets	1,000	
Accumulated Depreciation	9,000	
Delivery Truck		17,000

To record sale of delivery truck for $7,000 cash and loss on disposal. (Accumulated depreciation: $7,500 at the end of Year 3 + $1,500 recorded in Year 4 = $9,000.)

The $3,083 gain which will be reported in the company's Year 4 income tax return may be recorded in special income tax records, but **not** in the company's general ledger accounts.

OTHER INCOME TAX REPORTING OBLIGATIONS

In the preceding discussions of depreciation for income tax purposes, we have focused upon the current MACRS rules. MACRS applies to all depreciable assets acquired after December 31, 1986. Assets acquired from 1981 through 1986, however, are subject to the ***ACRS*** tax rules. 'From a conceptual point of view, ACRS is applied in the same manner as MACRS. However, ACRS assigns different recovery periods to most assets and also requires the use of different depreciation rate tables. For tax purposes, assets acquired prior to 1981 should continue to be depreciated by the methods adopted when those assets were acquired.

MACRS is used in ***federal*** income tax returns. Most ***states,*** however, also levy an income tax upon business income. A company which operates in several states may have to file a state income tax return in every state in which it does business. International corporations often have to file income tax returns in several different countries. The tax rules of individual states and of foreign countries frequently differ from those of the federal government of the United States. Thus, a business may have to compute depreciation on its assets in perhaps half a dozen different ways in order to meet all of its financial reporting and income tax reporting requirements.

Large businesses usually have an income tax department within their accounting departments. Smaller businesses, on the other hand, often delegate most of their "tax accounting" to a firm of certified public accountants.

END-OF-CHAPTER REVIEW

SUMMARY OF CHAPTER LEARNING OBJECTIVES

1 Determine the cost of plant assets.
Plant assets are long-lived assets acquired for use in the business and not for resale to customers. The matching principle of accounting requires that we include in the plant and equipment accounts those costs which will provide services over a period of years. During these years, the use of the plant assets contributes to the earning of revenue. The cost of a plant asset includes all expenditures reasonable and necessary in acquiring the asset and placing it in a position and condition for use in the operations of the business.

2 Distinguish between capital expenditures and revenue expenditures.
Capital expenditures include any material expenditure that will benefit several accounting periods. Revenue expenditures are expenditures that benefit only the current period or that are not material in amount.

3 Explain the relationship between depreciation and the matching principle.
Depreciation is the allocation of the cost of a plant asset to expense in the periods in which services are received from the asset. Plant assets enable a business to earn revenue; therefore, the cost of the asset becomes expense over the years in which the asset generates revenue.

4 Compute depreciation by the straight-line, units-of-output, declining-balance, and sum-of-the-years'-digits methods.
The straight-line method is a simple and widely used method of computing depreciation. It allocates an equal portion of the cost of an asset to

each period of use. Very similar is the units-of-output method under which an equal portion of the cost is allocated to each unit produced. Accelerated methods of depreciation mean recognizing relatively large amounts of depreciation in the early years of use and reduced amounts in later years. The accelerated methods are based in part upon the assumption that plant and equipment provide greater economic benefits in the early years. Declining-balance and sum-of-the-year's-digits are accelerated depreciation methods.

5 Record the disposal of a plant asset.

When plant assets are disposed of, depreciation should be recorded to the date of disposal. The cost is then removed from the asset account and the total recorded depreciation is removed from the accumulated depreciation account. The sale of a plant asset at a price above or below book value results in a gain or loss to be reported in the income statement.

6 Explain the nature of goodwill and indicate when this asset should appear in the accounting records.

Goodwill is the present value of future earnings in excess of the normal return on net identifiable assets. A business has goodwill only if it earns more than the normal rate of return for the industry. Goodwill is recorded in the accounts only when an investor buys an entire company and pays a price higher than the fair market value of the net identifiable assets.

7 Account for the depletion of natural resources.

Natural resources (or wasting assets) include mines, oil fields, and standing timber. Their cost is converted into inventory as the resource is mined, pumped, or cut. This allocation of the cost of a natural resource to inventories is called depletion. The depletion rate per unit extracted equals the cost of the resource divided by the estimated number of units it contains.

8 Identify some problems that may arise in accounting for the impairment of long-lived assets.

Problems that may arise in accounting for the possible impairment of long-lived assets include (1) determining when an asset has become "permanently impaired" and (2) estimating the net realizable value of an impaired asset—that is, the amount that can be recovered either through future use or sale of the asset.

* 9 Compute depreciation for income tax purposes using the MACRS guidelines.

Under MACRS, a specific recovery period is designated for every type of depreciable asset, and the allowable depreciation method is specified for each recovery period. The IRS publishes tables showing the percentage of an asset's cost which may be recognized as expense during each year of the recovery period. In general, the depreciation rates used in MACRS are based either upon 200%- or 150%-declining-balance, with the half-year convention applied in the year of acquisition and of retirement.

---

*   *Supplemental Topic, "Depreciation for Income Tax Purposes"*

This chapter completes our discussion of the valuation of the major types of business assets. To review, we have seen that cash is reported in the financial statements at its face amount, receivables at their net realizable value, inventories at the lower-of-cost-or-market, and plant assets at cost less accumulated depreciation. Two ideas that are consistently reflected in each of these valuation bases are the matching principle and the concept of conservatism. In the next chapter, we will turn our attention to the measurement of liabilities.

KEY TERMS INTRODUCED OR EMPHASIZED IN CHAPTER 10

Accelerated depreciation Methods of depreciation that call for recognition of relatively large amounts of depreciation in the early years of an asset's useful life and relatively small amounts in the later years.

ACRS The Accelerated Cost Recovery System. The only accelerated depreciation method permitted in federal income tax returns for assets acquired from 1981 through 1986.

Amortization The systematic write-off to expense of the cost of an intangible asset over the periods of its economic usefulness.

Basis The book value or undepreciated cost of an asset for income tax purposes. Cost less the accumulated depreciation claimed in prior years' income tax returns.

Book value The cost of a plant asset minus the total recorded depreciation, as shown by the Accumulated Depreciation account. The remaining undepreciated cost is also known as *carrying value.*

Capital budgeting The process of planning and evaluating proposals for making capital expenditures.

Capital expenditure A cost incurred to acquire a long-lived asset. An expenditure that will benefit several accounting periods.

Deferred charge An expenditure expected to yield benefits for several accounting periods and therefore capitalized and written off during the periods benefited.

Depletion Allocating the cost of a natural resource to the units removed as the resource is mined, pumped, cut, or otherwise consumed.

Depreciation The systematic allocation of the cost of an asset to expense over the years of its estimated useful life.

Fixed-percentage-of-declining-balance depreciation An accelerated method of depreciation in which the rate is a multiple of the straight-line rate, which is applied each year to the *undepreciated cost* of the asset. Most commonly used is double the straight-line rate.

Goodwill The present value of expected future earnings of a business in excess of the earnings normally realized in the industry. Recorded when a business entity is purchased at a price in excess of the fair value of its net identifiable assets (excluding goodwill) less liabilities.

Half-year convention The practice of taking six months' depreciation in the year of acquisition and the year of disposition, rather than computing depreciation for partial periods to the nearest month. This method is widely used and is acceptable for both income tax reporting and financial reports, as long as it is applied to *all* assets of a particular type acquired during the year. The half-year convention generally is *not* used for buildings.

Impairment (of an asset) A change in economic conditions which reduces the economic usefulness of an asset. May necessitate writing down the carrying value of the asset.

Intangible assets Those assets which are used in the operation of a business but which have no physical substance and are noncurrent.

MACRS The Modified Accelerated Cost Recovery System. The only accelerated depreciation method permitted in federal income tax returns for assets acquired after December 31, 1986. Depreciation is based upon prescribed recovery periods and depreciation rates.

Natural resources Mines, oil fields, standing timber, and similar assets which are physically consumed and converted into inventory.

Net identifiable assets Total of all assets *except goodwill* minus liabilities.

Present value The amount that a knowledgeable investor would pay today for the right to receive future cash flows. The present value is always less than the sum of the future cash flows because the investor requires a return on the investment.

Replacement cost The estimated cost of replacing an asset at the current balance sheet date.

Residual (salvage) value The portion of an asset's cost expected to be recovered through sale or trade-in of the asset at the end of its useful life.

Revenue expenditure Any expenditure that will benefit only the current accounting period.

Straight-line depreciation A method of depreciation which allocates the cost of an asset (minus any residual value) equally to each year of its useful life.

Sum-of-the-years'-digits depreciation An accelerated method of depreciation. The depreciable cost is multiplied each year by a fraction of which the numerator is the remaining years of useful life (as of the beginning of the current year) and the denominator is the sum of the years of useful life.

Units-of-output depreciation A depreciation method in which cost (minus residual value) is divided by the estimated units of lifetime output. The unit depreciation cost is multiplied by the actual units of output each year to compute the annual depreciation expense.

DEMONSTRATION PROBLEM FOR YOUR REVIEW

On April 1, 1993, Argo Industries purchased new equipment at a cost of $325,000. Useful life of this equipment was estimated at 5 years, with a residual value of $25,000. For income tax purposes, however, this equipment is classified as "3-year property."

INSTRUCTIONS Compute the annual depreciation expense for each year until this equipment becomes fully depreciated under each depreciation method listed below. (Because you will record depreciation for only a fraction of a year in 1993, depreciation will extend through 1998 in all methods except MACRS.) Show supporting computations.

a Straight-line, with depreciation for fractional years rounded to the nearest whole month.

b 200%-declining-balance, with the half-year convention. Limit depreciation in 1998 to an amount which reduces the undepreciated cost to the estimated residual value.

c Sum-of-the-years'-digits, with the half-year convention.

d MACRS accelerated rates for "3-year property."

SOLUTION TO DEMONSTRATION PROBLEM

	Method of Depreciation			
Year	*a* Straight-Line	*b* 200%-Declining-Balance	*c* Sum-of-the-Years'-Digits	*d* MACRS
1993	$ 45,000	$ 65,000	$ 50,000	$108,322.50
1994	60,000	104,000	90,000	144,462.50
1995	60,000	62,400	70,000	48,132.50
1996	60,000	37,440	50,000	24,082.50
1997	60,000	22,464	30,000	–0–
1998	15,000	8,696	10,000	–0–
Totals	$300,000	$300,000	$300,000	$325,000.00

Supporting computations:

a

1993: $(\$325,000 - \$25,000) \times \frac{1}{5} \times \frac{9}{12} = \$45,000$

1994–1997: $\$300,000 \times \frac{1}{5} = \$60,000$

1998: $\$300,000 \times \frac{1}{5} \times \frac{3}{12} = \$15,000$

b

	Unde-preciated Cost	Rate	Depreciation Expense
1993:	$\$325,000 \times 40\% \times \frac{1}{2} =$		$65,000
1994:	260,000 ×	40% =	104,000
1995:	156,000 ×	40% =	62,400
1996:	93,600 ×	40% =	37,440
1997:	56,160 ×	40% =	22,464
1998:	33,696 − $25,000 =		8,696

c

1993: $\$300,000 \times \frac{5}{15} \times \frac{1}{2} =$ $50,000

1994: $\$300,000 \times \frac{5}{15} \times \frac{1}{2} = \$50,000$
    $+300,000 \times \frac{4}{15} \times \frac{1}{2} =$ 40,000 $90,000

1995: $\$300,000 \times \frac{4}{15} \times \frac{1}{2} = \$40,000$
    $+300,000 \times \frac{3}{15} \times \frac{1}{2} =$ 30,000 $70,000

1996: $\$300,000 \times \frac{3}{15} \times \frac{1}{2} = \$30,000$
    $+300,000 \times \frac{2}{15} \times \frac{1}{2} =$ 20,000 $50,000

1997: $\$300,000 \times \frac{2}{15} \times \frac{1}{2} = \$20,000$
    $+300,000 \times \frac{1}{15} \times \frac{1}{2} =$ 10,000 $30,000

1998: $\$300,000 \times \frac{1}{15} \times \frac{1}{2} =$ $10,000

d

1993: $\$325,000 \times 33.33\% = \$108,322.50$

1994: $325,000 \times 44.45\% =$ 144,462.50

1995: $325,000 \times 14.81\% =$ 48,132.50

1996: $325,000 \times 7.41\% =$ 24,082.50

SELF-TEST QUESTIONS

The answers to these questions appear on page 506.

1 In which of the following situations should the named company **not** record any depreciation expense on the asset described?

   a Commuter Airline is required by law to maintain its aircraft in "as good as new" condition.

b   Metro Advertising owns an office building that has been increasing in value each year since it was purchased.

c   Computer Sales Company has in inventory a new type of computer designed "never to become obsolete."

d   None of the above answers is correct—in each case, the named company should record depreciation on the asset described.

2   Which of the following statements is (are) correct?

a   Accumulated depreciation represents a fund being accumulated for the replacement of plant assets.

b   The cost of a machine includes the cost of repairing damage to the machine during the installation process.

c   A company may use different depreciation methods in its financial statements and its income tax return.

d   The use of an accelerated depreciation method causes an asset to wear out more quickly than does use of the straight-line method.

3   On April 1, 1993, Sanders Construction paid $10,000 for equipment with an estimated useful life of 10 years and a residual value of $2,000. The company uses the double-declining-balance method of depreciation and applies the half-year convention to fractional periods. In **1994,** the amount of depreciation expense to be recognized on this equipment is:

a $1,600   **b** $1,440   **c** $1,280   **d**   Some other amount

4   Delta Company sold a plant asset that originally had cost $50,000 for $22,000 cash. If Delta correctly reports a $5,000 gain on this sale, the ***accumulated depreciation*** on the asset at the date of sale must have been:

a $33,000   **b** $28,000   **c** $23,000   **d**   Some other amount

5   In which of the following situations would Burton Industries include goodwill in its balance sheet?

a   The fair market value of Burton's net identifiable assets amounts to $2,000,000. Normal earnings for this industry is 15% of net identifiable assets. Burton's net income for the past five years has averaged $390,000.

b   Burton spent $800,000 during the current year for research and development for a new product which promises to generate substantial revenue for at least 10 years.

c   Burton acquired Baxter Electronics at a price in excess of the fair market value of Baxter's net identifiable assets.

d   A buyer wishing to purchase Burton's entire operation has offered a price in excess of the fair market value of Burton's net identifiable assets.

ASSIGNMENT MATERIAL

DISCUSSION QUESTIONS

1   Which of the following characteristics would prevent an item from being included in the classification of plant and equipment? (a) Intangible, (b) limited life, (c) unlimited life, (d) held for sale in the regular course of business, (e) not capable of rendering benefits to the business in the future.

2   The following expenditures were incurred in connection with a large new machine acquired by a metals manufacturing company. Identify those which

should be included in the cost of the asset. (a) Freight charges, (b) sales tax on the machine, (c) payment to a passing motorist whose car was damaged by the equipment used in unloading the machine, (d) wages of employees for time spent in installing and testing the machine before it was placed in service, (e) wages of employees assigned to lubrication and minor adjustments of machine one year after it was placed in service.

3 What is the distinction between a ***capital expenditure*** and a ***revenue expenditure?***

4 If a capital expenditure is erroneously treated as a revenue expenditure, will the net income of the current year be overstated or understated? Will this error have any effect upon the net income reported in future years? Explain.

5 Which of the following statements best describes the nature of depreciation?

  a Regular reduction of asset value to correspond to the decline in market value as the asset ages.

  b A process of correlating the book value of an asset with its gradual decline in physical efficiency.

  c Allocation of cost in a manner that will ensure that plant and equipment items are not carried on the balance sheet at amounts in excess of net realizable value.

  d Allocation of the cost of a plant asset to the periods in which services are received from the asset.

6 Should depreciation continue to be recorded on a building when ample evidence exists that the current market value is greater than original cost and that the rising trend of market values is continuing? Explain.

7 What connection exists between the choice of a depreciation method used to depreciate expensive new machinery for income tax reporting and the amount of income taxes payable in the near future?

8 Criticize the following quotation:
"We shall have no difficulty in paying for new plant assets needed during the coming year because our estimated outlays for new equipment amount to only $80,000, and we have more than twice that amount in our accumulated depreciation account at present."

9 A factory machine acquired at a cost of $94,200 was to be depreciated by the sum-of-the-years'-digits method over an estimated life of 8 years. Residual salvage value was estimated to be $15,000. State the amount of depreciation during the ***first*** year and during the ***eighth*** year.

10 Explain two approaches to computing depreciation for a fractional period in the year in which an asset is purchased. (Neither of your approaches should require the computation of depreciation to the nearest day or week.)

11 a Does the accounting principle of consistency require a company to use the same method of depreciation for all of its plant assets?

  b Is it acceptable for a corporation to use different depreciation methods in its financial statements and its income tax returns?

12 After 4 years of using a machine acquired at a cost of $15,000, Ohio Construction Company determined that the original estimated life of 10 years had been too short and that a total useful life of 12 years was a more reasonable estimate. Explain briefly the method that should be used to revise the depreciation program, assuming that straight-line depreciation has been used. Assume that the

revision is made after recording depreciation and closing the accounts at the end of four years of use of the machine.

13 "The terms **ACRS** and **MACRS** refer to accelerated cost recovery systems established by the IRS for use in computing depreciation on income tax returns. Such endorsement of a depreciation system by the IRS automatically makes it acceptable for use in the published financial statements of major corporations." Do you agree with these two statements? Explain.

14 Explain what is meant by the following quotation: "In periods of rising prices companies do not recognize adequate depreciation expense, and reported corporate profits are overstated in terms of current market values."

15 Newton Products purchased for $2 million a franchise making it the exclusive distributor of Gold Creek Beer in three western states. This franchise has an unlimited legal life and may be sold by Newton Products to any buyer who meets with Gold Creek Beer's approval. The accountant at Newton Products believes that this franchise is a permanent asset, which should appear in the company's balance sheet indefinitely at $2 million, unless it is sold. Is this treatment in conformity with generally accepted accounting principles, as prescribed by the FASB?

16 Define **intangible assets.** Would an account receivable arising from a sale of merchandise under terms of 2/10, n/30 qualify as an intangible asset under your definition?

17 Over what period of time should the cost of various types of intangible assets be amortized by regular charges against revenue? (Your answer should be in the form of a principle or guideline rather than a specific number of years.) What method of amortization is generally used?

18 Several years ago March Metals purchased for $120,000 a well-known trademark for padlocks and other security products. After using the trademark for three years, March Metals discontinued it altogether when the company withdrew from the lock business and concentrated on the manufacture of aircraft parts. Amortization of the trademark at the rate of $3,000 a year is being continued on the basis of a 40-year life, which the owner of March Metals says is required by accounting standards. Do you agree? Explain.

19 Under what circumstances should **goodwill** be recorded in the accounts?

20 In reviewing the financial statements of Digital Products Company with a view to investing in the company's stock, you notice that net tangible assets total $1 million, that goodwill is listed at $400,000, and that average earnings for the past five years have been $50,000 a year. How would these relationships influence your thinking about the company?

21 Mineral King recognizes $20 depletion for each ton of ore mined. During the current year the company mined 600,000 tons but sold only 500,000 tons, as it was attempting to build up inventories in anticipation of a possible strike by employees. How much depletion should be deducted from revenue of the current year?

22 Identify two problems that may arise in attempting to account for the possible impairment of long-lived assets.

EXERCISES

**EXERCISE 10-1
Accounting
Terminology**

Listed below are nine technical accounting terms introduced or emphasized in this chapter:

Intangible asset	*Revenue expenditure*	*Amortization*
Book value	*Depletion*	*Declining-balance*
Goodwill	*Impairment*	*ACRS or MACRS*

Each of the following statements may (or may not) describe one of these technical terms. For each statement, indicate the accounting term described, or answer "None" if the statement does not correctly describe any of the terms.

a A type of asset usually found only in the financial statements of a company which has purchased another going business in its entirety.

b Noncurrent assets lacking in physical substance.

c A depreciation method which often consists of doubling the straight-line rate and applying this doubled rate to the undepreciated cost of the asset.

d A depreciation method designed for use in income tax returns but not in conformity with generally accepted accounting principles.

e The cost of a plant asset minus the total recorded depreciation on the asset.

f A material expenditure that will benefit several accounting periods.

g The systematic allocation to expense of the cost of an intangible asset.

h A sudden reduction in the usefulness of an asset which may necessitate writing down the carrying value in the accounting records.

**EXERCISE 10-2
Identifying
Costs to Be
Capitalized**

New machinery was purchased by HydroTech at a list price of $40,000; the credit terms were 2/10, n/30. Payment of the invoice was made within the discount period. The payment included 6% sales tax on the ***net price.*** HydroTech also paid transportation charges of $610 on the new machinery as well as $760 for installing the machinery in the appropriate locations. During the unloading and installation work, some of the machines fell from a forklift and were damaged. Repair of the damaged parts cost $2,170. After the machinery had been in use for 3 months, it was thoroughly cleaned and lubricated at a cost of $260. Prepare a list of the items which should be capitalized by a debit to the Machinery account and state the total cost of the new machinery.

**EXERCISE 10-3
Distinguishing
Capital Expenditures from
Revenue Expenditures**

Identify the following expenditures as capital expenditures or revenue expenditures:

a Immediately after acquiring a new delivery truck at a cost of $15,500, paid $225 to have the name of the store and other advertising material painted on the truck.

b Painted delivery truck at a cost of $250 after 2 years of use.

c Purchased new battery at a cost of $40 for 2-year-old delivery truck.

d Installed an escalator at a cost of $12,500 in a three-story building which had previously been used for some years without elevators or escalators.

e Purchased a pencil sharpener at a cost of $8.50.

f Original life of the delivery truck had been estimated at 4 years and straight-line depreciation of 25% yearly had been recognized. After 3 years' use, however, it was decided to recondition the truck thoroughly, including a new engine and transmission, at a cost of $4,000. By making this expenditure it was believed that the useful life of the truck would be extended from the original estimate of 4 years to a total of 6 years.

EXERCISE 10-4
Units-of-Output Method

During the current year, Airport Auto Rentals purchased 60 new automobiles at a cost of $13,000 per car. The cars will be sold to a wholesaler at an estimated $4,000 each as soon as they have been driven 50,000 miles. Airport Auto Rentals computes depreciation expense on its automobiles by the units-of-output method, based upon mileage.

INSTRUCTIONS

a Compute the amount of depreciation to be recognized for each mile that a rental automobile is driven.

b Assuming that the 60 rental cars are driven a total of 1,650,000 miles during the current year, compute the total amount of depreciation expense that Airport Auto Rentals should recognize on this fleet of cars for the year.

EXERCISE 10-5
Double-Declining-Balance Method

Machinery with an estimated useful life of 5 years was acquired by VPI Industries at a cost of $55,000 at the beginning of the year. The estimated residual value of the machinery is $6,000. Compute the annual depreciation on this machinery for each of the 5 years using the double-declining-balance method. Compute one full year's depreciation in each year. Limit the depreciation recognized in the fifth year to an amount that will cause the book value of the machinery to equal the estimated $6,000 residual value at year-end.

EXERCISE 10-6
Sum-of-the-Years'-Digits Method

On January 2, Bartel Company acquired a machine at a cost of $14,000. The machine is expected to have a useful life of 5 years with a residual value of $2,000. You are to compute the annual depreciation on the machine in each of the 5 years of its useful life using the sum-of-the-years'-digits method. (One full year's depreciation will be taken each year.)

EXERCISE 10-7
Three Depreciation Methods

Delta Company acquired new equipment with an estimated useful life of 5 years. Cost of the equipment was $50,000 and the residual salvage value was estimated to be $5,000. Compute the annual depreciation expense for each of the first 2 years under each of the following methods of depreciation. (Compute on full year's depreciation in each year.)

a Straight-line

b Sum-of-the-years'-digits

c Double-declining-balance

*EXERCISE 10-8
Depreciation for Fractional Years

On November 2, Glass Recycling Company purchased special-purpose equipment at a cost of $600,000. Useful life of the equipment was estimated to be 5 years and the residual value $90,000. Compute the depreciation expense to be recognized in each calendar year during the life of the equipment under each of the following methods:

a Straight-line (round computations for a partial year to the nearest full month).

b Straight-line (use the half-year convention).

c The Modified Accelerated Cost Recovery System (MACRS). Use the table on page 481, and assume that the equipment qualifies as "*3-year* property."

---

* *Supplemental Topic, "Depreciation for Income Tax Purposes"*

**EXERCISE 10-9
Revision of
Depreciation
Rates**

Grain Products uses straight-line depreciation on all its depreciable assets. The accounts are adjusted and closed at the end of each calendar year. On January 4, 1992, the corporation purchased machinery for cash at a cost of $80,000. Useful life was estimated to be 10 years and residual value $12,000. Depreciation for partial years is recorded to the nearest full month.

In 1994, after almost 3 years of experience with the equipment, management decided that the estimated life of the equipment should be revised from 10 years to 6 years. No change was made in the estimate of residual value. The revised estimate of useful life was decided upon *prior* to recording depreciation for the period ended December 31, 1994.

INSTRUCTIONS

Prepare journal entries in chronological order for the above events, beginning with the purchase of the machinery on January 4, 1992. Show separately the depreciation for 1992, 1993, and 1994.

**EXERCISE 10-10
Trade-in and
Cost Basis**

Ogilvie Construction traded in a used crane on a similar new one. The original cost of the old crane was $60,000 and the accumulated depreciation was $48,000. The new crane carried a list price of $75,000 and the trade-in allowance was $18,000. What amount of cash must Ogilvie pay? Compute the indicated gain or loss on disposal of the old crane. Compute the cost basis of the new crane to be used in figuring depreciation for determination of income subject to federal income tax.

**EXERCISE 10-11
Disposal of
Equipment by
Sale, Trade-in,
or as Scrap**

A tractor which cost $30,000 had an estimated useful life of 5 years and an estimated salvage value of $10,000. Straight-line depreciation was used. Give the entry (in general journal form) required by each of the following alternative assumptions:

a The tractor was sold for cash of $19,500 after 2 years' use.

b The tractor was traded in after 3 years on another tractor with a fair market value of $37,000. Trade-in allowance was $21,000. (Record any implied gain or loss.)

c The tractor was scrapped after 7 years' use. Since scrap dealers were unwilling to pay anything for the tractor, it was given to a scrap dealer for his services in removing it.

**EXERCISE 10-12
Estimating
Goodwill**

During the past several years the annual net income of Goldtone Appliance Company has averaged $540,000. At the present time the company is being offered for sale. Its accounting records show the book value of net assets (total assets minus all liabilities) to be $2,800,000. The fair market value of Goldtone's net identifiable assets, however, is $3,000,000.

An investor negotiating to buy the company offers to pay an amount equal to the fair market value for the net identifiable assets and to assume all liabilities. In addition, the investor is willing to pay for goodwill an amount equal to net earnings in excess of 15% on the fair market value of net identifiable assets, capitalized at a rate of 25%.

On the basis of this agreement, what price should the investor offer for Goldtone Appliance?

**EXERCISE 10-13
Depletion: Re-
cording and
Reporting**

King Mining Company purchased the Lost Creek Mine for $15,000,000 cash. The mine was estimated to contain 2 million tons of ore and to have a residual value of $3,000,000.

During the first year of mining operations at the Lost Creek Mine, 400,000 tons of ore were mined, of which 300,000 tons were sold.

INSTRUCTIONS

a Prepare a journal entry to record depletion of the Lost Creek Mine during the year.

b Show how the mine and the accumulated depletion would appear in King Mining Company's balance sheet after the first year of operations.

c Will the entire amount of depletion computed in part **a** be deducted from revenue in determining the income for the year? Explain.

*EXERCISE 10-14
Depreciation
for Income Tax
Purposes

Precision Corporation uses straight-line depreciation with a half-year convention in its financial statements, and MACRS accelerated rates (from page 481) in its income tax returns. Shown below are data concerning two assets acquired in 1992:

Cargo van   Acquired March 7 at a cost of $17,000. Estimated useful life is 4 years, with a residual value of $7,000. Classified under MACRS as "5-year property.'

Special-purpose equipment   Acquired August 1 at a cost of $30,000. Estimated useful life is 5 years, with a $10,000 residual value. Classified as "3-year property" under MACRS.

INSTRUCTIONS

Compute for each of these assets the depreciation expense to be recognized in *1993* (the year *after* acquisition) in Precision's (a) income statement, and (b) income tax return. Show supporting computations.

*EXERCISE 10-15
Tax Basis;
Gains and
Losses

On July 2, 1992, Financial Consultants, Inc., purchased a computer system for $10,000. For tax purposes, this system is classified as "5-year property" and is depreciated by the MACRS accelerated rates (as illustrated on page 481). On September 19, 1994, Financial Consultants sold this computer system for $5,000.

INSTRUCTIONS

Compute (a) the income tax basis of the computer system at the date of sale and (b) the gain or loss on disposal to be reported for income tax purposes.

EXERCISE 10-16
Evaluation of
Disclosures in
Annual Re-
ports

A recent annual report of **H. J. Heinz Company** includes the following note:

Depreciation: For financial reporting purposes, depreciation is provided on the straight-line method over the estimated useful lives of the assets. Accelerated depreciation methods generally are used for income tax purposes.

INSTRUCTIONS

a Identify four "accelerated depreciation" methods that the company might be using in its income tax returns. (Note: Because tax laws change from year-to-year, the company is using different accelerated methods on assets acquired in different years.)

b Is the company violating the accounting principle of consistency by using different depreciation methods in its financial statements and in its income tax returns? Explain.

c Why do you think that the company uses accelerated depreciation methods in its income tax returns?

d Would the use of accelerated depreciation methods in the financial statements be more "conservative," or less "conservative," than the current practice of using the straight-line method? Explain.

---

*   *Supplemental Topic, "Depreciation for Income Tax Purposes"*

PROBLEMS

Group A

**PROBLEM 10A-1
Determining
the Cost of
Plant Assets**

Early this summer, Crystal Car Wash purchased new "brushless" car washing equipment for all 10 of its car washes. The following information refers to the purchase and installation of this equipment.

1 The list price of the brushless equipment was $7,200 for the equipment needed at each car wash. Because Crystal Car Wash purchased 10 sets of equipment at one time, it was given a special "package price" of $63,000 for all of the equipment. Crystal paid $23,000 of this amount in cash (no cash discount was allowed) and issued a 90-day, 8% note payable for the remaining $40,000. Crystal paid this note promptly at its maturity date, along with $800 in accrued interest charges.

2 In addition to the amounts described above, Crystal paid sales taxes of $3,780 at the date of purchase.

3 Freight charges for delivery of the equipment totaled $3,320.

4 Crystal paid a contractor $2,250 per location to install the equipment at six of Crystal's car washes. Management was able to find a less expensive contractor who installed the equipment in the remaining four car washes at a cost of $1,900 per location.

5 During installation, one of the new machines was accidentally damaged by an employee of Crystal Car Wash. The cost to repair this damage, $914, was paid by Crystal.

6 As soon as the machines were installed, Crystal Car Wash paid $5,700 for a series of radio commercials advertising the fact that it now uses brushless equipment in all of its car washes.

INSTRUCTIONS

a In one sentence, make a general statement summarizing the nature of the expenditures properly included in the cost of plant and equipment.

b For each of the six numbered paragraphs, indicate which items should be included by Crystal Car Wash in the cost debited to the Equipment account. Also briefly indicate the accounting treatment that should be accorded to any items that you ***do not*** regard as part of the cost of the equipment.

c Prepare a list of the expenditures that should be included in the cost of the equipment. (Determine the total cost of the equipment at all 10 locations; do not attempt to separate costs by location.)

d Prepare a journal entry at the end of the current year to record depreciation on this equipment. Crystal depreciates this equipment by the straight-line method over an estimated useful life of 10 years, assumes zero salvage value, and applies the half-year convention.

**PROBLEM 10A-2
Basic Depreci-
ation Methods
—No Frac-
tional Years**

Integrated Waste Management purchased new equipment on January 3, 1993, at a cost of $240,000. The equipment had an estimated useful life of 8 years, with an estimated residual value of $24,000.

INSTRUCTIONS

Compute the annual depreciation expense throughout the 8-year life of this equipment under the three depreciation methods listed below. Company policy is to round depreciation for fractional periods to the nearest month. As the equipment was acquired in early January, one full year's depreciation will be taken each year.

a Straight-line.

b Sum-of-the-years'-digits.

c Double-declining-balance. (Limit depreciation in the eighth year to an amount that will cause the book value of the equipment at year-end to equal the estimated residual value.)

***PROBLEM 10A-3
Alternative
Depreciation
Methods—
Including Fractional Periods
and MACRS**

On March 29, 1993, Global Manufacturing purchased new equipment with a cost of $100,000, an estimated useful life of 5 years, and an estimated residual value of $10,000. For income purposes, this equipment is classified as "5-year property."

INSTRUCTIONS

a Compute the annual depreciation expense for each year until this equipment becomes fully depreciated under each of the depreciation methods listed below. (Because you will record depreciation for only a fraction of a year in 1993, depreciation will extend through 1998.) Show supporting computations.

1 Straight-line, with depreciation for fractional years rounded to the nearest whole month.

2 200%-declining-balance, with the half-year convention. (Limit depreciation in 1998 to an amount which reduces the undepreciated cost to the estimated residual value.)

3 Sum-of-the-years'-digits, with the half-year convention.

*4 MACRS accelerated rates for "5-year property."

b Global has two conflicting objectives. Management wants to report the highest possible earnings to stockholders in the near future, yet also wants to minimize the taxable income reported to the IRS. Indicate the depreciation method which the company will probably use in (1) its financial statements and (2) its federal income tax return. Explain the reasons for your answers.

c Explain the similarities and differences between the 200%-declining-balance method and the depreciation allowed under MACRS.

**PROBLEM 10A-4
Depreciation: A
Comprehensive
Problem**

In the first few years of business, Midwest Agricultural Cooperative acquired several expensive pieces of machinery. Because there was no set policy on depreciation methods, the various machines are being depreciated according to a variety of methods. Information concerning four of the machines appears below:

Machine	Date Acquired	Cost	Estimated Useful Life, Years	Estimated Residual Value	Method of Depreciation
A	Aug. 25, 1992	$308,000	6	10%	Straight-line
B	Apr. 3, 1992	160,000	8	None	Double-declining-balance
C	Jan. 8, 1993	250,000	6	$40,000	Sum-of-the-years'-digits
D	Sept. 5, 1994	204,000	10	$25,000	Double-declining-balance

INSTRUCTIONS

a Compute the amount of accumulated depreciation, if any, on each machine at December 31, 1993. In the year of acquisition, assume that depreciation was computed to the nearest month.

b Prepare a depreciation schedule for use in the computation of the depreciation expense. Use the following column headings:

Machine	Method of Depreciation	Date of Acquisition	Cost	Estimated Residual Value	Amount to Be Depreciated	Useful Life, Years	Accumulated Depreciation, Dec. 31, 1993	Depreciation Expense, 1994

* *Supplemental Topic, "Depreciation for Income Tax Purposes"*

*c   Using the MACRS rate table on page 481, compute the amount of depreciation (cost recovery) that would be allowed on each machine for income tax reporting in 1994. Assume that all the machines qualify as "5-year property."

d   Prepare a journal entry to record depreciation expense for 1994 in the general ledger accounts.

PROBLEM 10A-5
Disposal of
Plant Assets

During 19___, Cabrillo Moving and Storage disposed of plant assets in the following transactions:

Mar. 12   Cabrillo traded in an old moving van for a new one. The old moving van had cost $27,000 and accumulated depreciation amounted to $19,000. The list price of the new moving van was $38,000. Cabrillo received a $12,000 trade-in allowance for the old moving van and paid the $26,000 balance in cash. (Moving vans are included in the Vehicles account.)

May 23   Cabrillo sold land and an unused storage facility to Self-Store, Inc., for $850,000, receiving $300,000 in cash and a 5-year, 10% note receivable for $550,000. Cabrillo's accounting records showed the following amounts: Land, $120,000; Building, $570,000; Accumulated Depreciation: Building (as of May 23), $230,000.

Sept. 20   Cabrillo traded in its old computer system as part of the purchase of a new system. The old computer had cost $126,000 and, as of September 20, accumulated depreciation amounted to $98,000. The new computer had a list price of $95,000. Cabrillo was granted a $10,000 trade-in allowance for the old computer system, paid $35,000 in cash, and issued a $50,000, 2-year, 12% note payable to Business Systems for the balance. (Computers are included in the Office Equipment account.)

Nov. 8   Office equipment costing $11,000 was given to a scrap dealer. No proceeds were received from the scrap dealer. At the date of disposal, accumulated depreciation on the office equipment amounted to $8,900.

INSTRUCTIONS   Prepare journal entries to record each of these transactions. Assume that depreciation expense on each asset already has been recorded up to the date of disposal. Thus, you need not update the accumulated depreciation figures stated in the problem.

PROBLEM 10A-6
Intangible Assets or Operating Expense:
GAAP

During the current year Magnum Industries incurred the following five expenditures which should be recorded either as operating expenses of the current year or as intangible assets.

a   Expenditure to acquire a franchise as one of four American distributors of an Italian automobile. The franchise expires in 49 years.

b   Incurred research and development costs in an effort to produce a 100,000-mile tire. At year-end, the project looks promising. If successful, the product will be patented for 17 years, but it should contribute to revenue for at least 20 years.

c   Purchased a patent on a fuel-saving device. The patent has a remaining legal life of 13 years, but Magnum Industries expects to produce and sell the device for a period of 5 years.

d   Expenditures to advertise a new product. The product is patented and is expected to contribute to company revenue for the entire 17-year life of the patent.

---

*   *Supplemental Topic, "Depreciation for Income Tax Purposes"*

e Expenditures for management training programs. The average manager stays with the company for a period of $9\frac{1}{2}$ years but attends a management training program every 2 years.

INSTRUCTIONS Explain whether each of the above expenditures should be recorded as an operating expense of the current year or as an intangible asset. If you view the expenditure as creating an intangible asset, indicate the number of years over which the asset should be amortized. Explain your reasoning.

***PROBLEM 10A-7
Depreciation in
Financial State-
ments and in
Income Tax
Returns**

On October 12, 1992, Speedy Print purchased a color photocopy machine at a cost of $20,000. Management estimated that the machine would have a useful life of 8 years and a residual value of $4,000. Speedy Print uses straight-line depreciation in its financial statements, rounding depreciation for partial periods to the nearest full month. In income tax returns, the company uses the MACRS accelerated rates (from the table on page 481). Copiers are classified as "5-year property."

Speedy Print found that not many of its customers used the color copier. Therefore, on March 19, 1994, Speedy Print sold this machine to Commercial Graphics Company for $10,000 cash.

INSTRUCTIONS **a** Prepare a schedule showing side by side the annual amounts of depreciation expense that management originally expects to recognize over the 8-year life of this asset in (1) the company's financial statements and (2) its income tax returns.

b For financial statement purposes, compute (1) the book value of the copier at the date of disposal and (2) the gain or loss on the sale.

c For income tax purposes, compute (1) the **basis** of the copier at the date of disposal and (2) the taxable gain or loss on the sale.

d Prepare journal entries to record in Speedy Print's accounting records (1) depreciation on the copier for 1994 (through the date of disposal) and (2) the sale of the color copier. (Prepare both entries in general journal form and date them March 19, 1994.)

Group B

**PROBLEM 10B-1
Determining
Cost of Plant
Assets**

Brenner Graphics, a newly organized St. Louis corporation, purchased typesetting equipment having a list price of $204,000 from a manufacturer in the New England area. Credit terms for the transaction were 2/10, n/30. Brenner Graphics paid the invoice within the discount period, as well as an additional 7% sales tax on the **net price.** Other payments relating to the acquisition of the equipment were a freight bill of $2,596 and a labor cost for installing the equipment of $4,210. During the installation process, an accident caused damage to the equipment, which was repaired at a cost of $5,900. As soon as the equipment was in place, the company obtained insurance on it for a premium of $1,800. All the items described above were charged to the Typesetting Equipment account. No entry for depreciation has yet been made and the accounts have not yet been closed.

INSTRUCTIONS **a** Prepare a list of the expenditures which should have been capitalized by debiting the Typesetting Equipment (round amounts to the nearest dollar). Show the correct total cost for this asset.

b Prepare one compound journal entry to **correct** the error or errors by the company in recording these transactions.

---

* *Supplemental Topic, "Depreciation for Income Tax Purposes"*

c Prepare a journal entry at the end of the current year to record depreciation on this equipment. Brenner Graphics depreciates typesetting equipment by the straight-line method over an estimated useful life of 10 years, assumes no residual value, and applies the half-year convention.

d In one sentence state the accounting principle or concept which indicates the nature of expenditures properly included in the cost of equipment. (Do not list individual types of expenditure.)

PROBLEM 10B-2
Basic Depreciation Methods —No Fractional Years

On January 2, 1993, Atlantic Iron Works acquired new machinery at a cost of $270,000. The useful life of the machinery was estimated at 5 years, with a residual value of $24,000.

INSTRUCTIONS

Compute the annual depreciation expense throughout the 5-year life of this equipment under each of the following depreciation methods. As the equipment was acquired early in January, one full year's depreciation will be taken in each year.

a Straight-line.

b Sum-of-the-years'-digits.

c Double-declining-balance. (Limit depreciation in the fifth year to an amount that will cause the book value of the equipment at year-end to equal the estimated residual value.)

*PROBLEM 10B-3
Alternative Depreciation Methods— Including Fractional Periods and MACRS

Micro Circuit Company purchased new equipment on September 4, 1993, at a cost of $80,000. Useful life of this equipment was estimated at 4 years, with an estimated residual value of $5,000. For income tax purposes, this equipment is classified as "3-year property."

INSTRUCTIONS

Compute the annual depreciation expense for each year until this equipment becomes fully depreciated under each of the depreciation methods listed below. (Because you will record depreciation for only a fraction of a year in 1993, depreciation will extend through 1997 in all methods except MACRS.) Show supporting computations.

a Straight-line, with depreciation for fractional years rounded to the nearest whole month.

b Sum-of-the-years'-digits, with the half-year convention.

c 200%-declining-balance, with the half-year convention. (Limit depreciation in 1997 to an amount which reduces the undepreciated cost to the estimated residual value.)

*d MACRS accelerated rates for "3-year property."

---

*   *Supplemental Topic, "Depreciation for Income Tax Purposes"*

**PROBLEM 10B-4
Depreciation: A
Comprehensive
Problem**

During the last few years, Sunhill Corporation has acquired four costly machines but has given little consideration to depreciation policies. At the time of acquisition of each machine, a different accountant was employed; consequently, various methods of depreciation have been adopted for the several machines. For machines A and D, assume that the depreciation rate was double the rate under the straight-line method. Information concerning the four machines appears below.

Machine	Date Acquired	Cost	Estimated Useful Life, Years	Estimated Residual Value	Method of Depreciation
A	Jan. 1, 1992	$150,000	5	None	Declining-balance
B	June 30, 1992	360,000	8	10%	Straight-line
C	Jan. 1, 1993	221,600	10	$23,600	Sum-of-the-years-digits
D	May 27, 1994	237,000	10	None	Declining-balance

INSTRUCTIONS

a Compute the amount of accumulated depreciation, if any, on each machine at December 31, 1993. In the year of acquisition, assume that depreciation was computed to the nearest month.

b Prepare a depreciation schedule for use in the computation of the depreciation expense. Use the following column headings:

Machine	Method of Depreciation	Date of Acquisition	Cost	Estimated Residual Value	Amount to Be Depreciated	Useful Life, Years	Accumulated Depreciation, Dec. 31, 1993	Depreciation Expense, 1994

*c Using the MACRS rate table on page 481, compute the amount of depreciation that would be allowed on each machine for income tax reporting in 1994. Assume that all the machines qualify as "5-year property."

d Prepare a journal entry to record the total depreciation expense relating to these machines for 1994 in Sunhill's general ledger accounts.

**PROBLEM 10B-5
Disposal of
Plant Assets**

During 19__, Crown Developers disposed of plant assets in the following transactions:

Feb. 10 Office equipment costing $14,000 was given to a scrap dealer. No proceeds were received from the scrap dealer. At the date of disposal, accumulated depreciation on the office equipment amounted to $11,900.

Apr. 1 Crown sold land and a building to Villa Associates for $630,000, receiving $200,000 in cash and a 5-year, 10% note receivable for $430,000. Crown's accounting records showed the following amounts: Land, $120,000; Building, $350,000; Accumulated Depreciation: Building (as of April 1), $115,000.

Aug. 15 Crown traded in an old truck for a new one. The old truck had cost $11,000, and accumulated depreciation amounted to $7,000. The list price of the new truck was $17,000; Crown received a $5,000 trade-in allowance for the old truck and paid the $12,000 balance in cash. (Trucks are included in the Vehicles account.)

Oct. 1 Crown traded in its old computer system as part of the purchase of a new system. The old computer had cost $150,000 and, as of October 1, accumulated depreciation amounted to $110,000. The new computer had a list price of $90,000. Crown was granted a $10,000 trade-in al-

---

*   *Supplemental Topic, "Depreciation for Income Tax Purposes"*

lowance for the old computer system, paid $30,000 in cash, and issued a $50,000, 2-year, 9% note payable to Action Computers for the balance. (Computers are included in the Office Equipment account.)

INSTRUCTIONS Prepare journal entries to record each of these transactions. Assume that depreciation expense on each asset already has been recorded up to the date of disposal. Thus, you need not update the accumulated depreciation figures stated in the problem.

PROBLEM 10B-6 Intangible Assets or Operating Expenses: GAAP During the current year, Home Sales Corporation incurred the following expenditures which should be recorded either as operating expenses of the current year or as intangible assets:

a Expenditures for the training of new employees. The average employee remains with the company for 7 years, but is retrained for a new position every 3 years.

b Purchased from another company the trademark to a household product. The trademark has an unlimited legal life, and the product is expected to contribute to revenue indefinitely.

c Incurred significant research and development costs to develop a dirt-resistant fiber. The company expects that the fiber will be patented and that sales of the resulting products will contribute to revenue for at least 50 years. The legal life of the patent, however, will be 17 years.

d An expenditure to acquire the patent on a popular video game. The patent has a remaining life of 14 years, but Home Sales expects to produce and sell the game for only 3 years.

e Spent a large amount to sponsor a television mini-series about the French Revolution. The purpose in sponsoring the program was to make television viewers more aware of the company's name and its product lines.

INSTRUCTIONS Explain whether each of the above expenditures should be recorded as an operating expense or an intangible asset. If you view the expenditure as an intangible asset, indicate the number of years over which the asset should be amortized. Explain your reasoning.

*PROBLEM 10B-7 Depreciation and Gains and Losses in Income Tax Returns On March 2, 1992, Gourmet Market purchased a delivery truck for $10,000. For financial statement purposes, this asset was depreciated by the straight-line method, using an estimated useful life of 5 years, a residual value of $2,000, and the half-year convention. For income tax purposes, the truck was depreciated by the MACRS accelerated rates (in the table on page 481) as "5-year property." On September 4, 1994, Gourmet Market sells the truck for $5,200 cash.

INSTRUCTIONS a Prepare a schedule showing side by side the annual amounts of depreciation expense that management will recognize in (1) the company's financial statements and (2) its income tax returns. Continue this schedule until the asset is fully depreciated for both purposes.

b For *financial statement purposes,* compute (1) the book value of the truck at the date of disposal and (2) the amount of gain or loss on the sale.

c For *income tax purposes,* compute (1) the **basis** of this asset at the date of disposal and (2) the amount of gain or loss on the sale.

d Prepare journal entries (in general journal form) to record in Gourmet Market's accounting records (1) depreciation on the truck for the year of disposal and (2) the sale of the truck. Date both entries September 4, 1994.

---

* *Supplemental Topic, "Depreciation for Income Tax Purposes"*

CASES AND UNSTRUCTURED PROBLEMS

CASE 10-1
Depreciation Policies in Annual Reports

Shown below is a note accompanying a recent financial statement of **International Paper Company:**

Plant, Properties, and Equipment

Plant, properties, and equipment are stated at cost less accumulated depreciation.

For financial reporting purposes, the company uses the units-of-production method of depreciating its major pulp and paper mills and certain wood products facilities, and the straight-line method for other plants and equipment.

Annual straight-line depreciation rates for financial reporting purposes are as follows: buildings $2\frac{1}{2}$% to 8%; machinery and equipment 5% to 33%; woods equipment 10% to 16%. For tax purposes, depreciation is computed utilizing accelerated methods.

INSTRUCTIONS

a Are the depreciation methods used in the company's financial statements determined by current income tax laws? If not, who is responsible for selecting these methods? Explain.

b Does the company violate the consistency principle by using different depreciation methods for its paper mills and wood products facilities than it uses for its other plant and equipment? If not, what does the principle of consistency mean? Explain.

c What is the estimated useful life of the machinery and equipment being depreciated with a straight-line depreciation rate of:

1 5%.

2 33% (round to the nearest year).
Who determines the useful lives over which specific assets are to be depreciated?

d Why do you think the company uses accelerated depreciation methods for income tax purposes, rather than using the straight-line method? Explain.

CASE 10-2
Effects of Depreciation Policies upon Earnings

Two independent cases are described below. You are to comment separately on each case.

Case A Assume that Adams Company and Barnes Company are in the same line of business, have similar plant assets, and report the same amount of net income. In their financial statements, Adams Company uses straight-line depreciation and Barnes Company uses an accelerated method.

INSTRUCTIONS

Do you have any reason for considering one of these companies to be more profitable than the other? Explain.

Case B The income statement of Morris Foods includes depreciation expense of $200,000 and net income of $100,000. A note accompanying the financial statements discloses the following information about the company's depreciation policies:

Depreciation. For financial statement purposes, depreciation is computed by the straight-line method using the following estimated useful lives:

Automobiles	*12 years*
Furniture and equipment	*25 to 30 years*
Buildings	*60 to 90 years*

For tax purposes, depreciation is computed using the designated recovery periods and accelerated MACRS depreciation rates.

INSTRUCTIONS　In general terms, evaluate the effects of these depreciation policies upon the net income reported by the company in its income statement.

CASE 10-3
Did I Do This
Right?

Protein Plus is a processor and distributor of frozen foods. The company's management is anxious to report the maximum amount of net income allowable under generally accepted accounting principles and, therefore, uses the longest acceptable lives in depreciating or amortizing the company's plant assets. Depreciation and amortization computations are rounded to the nearest full month.

Near year-end the company's regular accountant was in an automobile accident, so a clerk with limited accounting experience prepared the company's financial statements. The income statement prepared by the clerk indicated a net loss of $45,000. However, the clerk was unsure that he had properly accounted for the following items:

1　On April 4, the company purchased a small food processing business at a cost $80,000 above the value of that business's net identifiable assets. The clerk classified this $80,000 as goodwill on Protein Plus's balance sheet and recorded no amortization expense because the food processor's superior earnings are expected to continue indefinitely.

2　During the year the company spent $32,000 on a research project to develop a method of freezing avocados. The clerk classified these expenditures as an intangible asset on the company's balance sheet and recorded no amortization expense because it was not yet known whether the project would be successful.

3　Two gains from the disposal of plant assets were included in the income statement. One gain, in the amount of $4,300, resulted from the sale of a plant asset at a price above its book value. The other gain, in the amount of $2,700 on December 31, was based on receiving an offer for equipment which has not yet been sold.

4　A CPA firm had determined that the company's depreciation expense for income tax purposes was $51,400, using accelerated methods such as ACRS and MACRS. The clerk used this figure as depreciation expense in the income statement, although in prior years the company had used the straight-line method of depreciation in its financial statements. Depreciation for the current year amounts to $35,600 when computed by the straight-line method over realistic estimates of useful lives.

5　On January 4, the company paid $90,000 to purchase a 10-year franchise to become the exclusive distributor in three eastern states for a brand of Mexican frozen dinners. The clerk charged this $90,000 to expense in the current year because the entire amount had been paid in cash.

6　During the year, the company incurred advertising costs of $22,000 to promote the newly acquired line of frozen dinners. The clerk did not know how many periods would be benefited from these expenditures, so he included the entire amount in the selling expenses of the current year.

INSTRUCTIONS　**a**　For each of the numbered paragraphs, explain whether the clerk's treatment of the item is in conformity with generally accepted accounting principles.

　　b　Prepare a schedule determining the correct net income (or net loss) for the year. Begin with "Net loss originally reported . . . $45,000," and indicate any adjustments that you consider appropriate. If you indicate adjustments for the amortization of intangible assets acquired during the year, round the amortization to the nearest month.

CASE 10-4
Any Word from
Kuwait?

It is early 1991 and you are a CPA auditing the 1990 financial statements of Norco, a multinational corporation. One of Norco's assets is a large plant located in the country of Kuwait; this facility currently is carried in Norco's accounting records at a book value of $140 million. In August of 1990, Kuwait was invaded by neighboring Iraq, and currently is under Iraqi control.

Early in 1991 (but before the issuance of Norco's 1990 financial statements), a U.S.-led coalition initiated military action to "liberate Kuwait." Most military experts expect the coalition forces ultimately to prevail, although the extent of physical damage that may be caused within Kuwait cannot be predicted. (Losses caused by acts of war are not covered by insurance.)

Norco has received no communication from its Kuwait facility since last August. The company has no way of knowing the current physical condition of this facility, nor what may happen to it in the coming months.

INSTRUCTIONS

Summarize briefly the arguments for and against Norco immediately writing down the carrying value of its Kuwait plant. What actions would you require Norco to take before you would consider that the company's 1990 financial statements provide a "fair presentation" of this situation?

ANSWERS TO SELF-TEST QUESTIONS

1 c (Depreciation is not recorded on inventory.)   **2** c   **3** d [$1,800, computed as 20% of ($10,000 $-\frac{1}{2}$ of 20% of $10,000)]   **4** a (Book value = $22,000 $-$ $5,000 = $17,000; accumulated depreciation = $50,000 cost $-$ $17,000 book value = $33,000)   **5** c

COMPREHENSIVE PROBLEM 3

ALPINE VILLAGE AND NORDIC SPORTS

CONCEPTS OF ASSET VALUATION AND EFFECTS UPON NET INCOME

Chris Scott, a former Olympic skier, wants to purchase an established ski equipment and clothing shop in Aspen, Colorado. Two such businesses currently are available for sale: Alpine Village and Nordic Sports. Both businesses are organized as sole proprietorships and have been in business for three years. Summaries of the current balance sheet data of both shops are shown below:

Assets	Alpine Village	Nordic Sports
Cash	$ 31,200	$ 37,800
Accounts receivable	169,300	188,500
Inventory	141,700	150,400
Plant and equipment:		
Land	33,000	42,000
Building (net of accumulated depreciation)	87,480	99,900
Equipment (net of accumulated depreciation)	8,200	7,600
Goodwill		22,200
Total assets	$470,880	$548,400

Liabilities & Owner's Equity		
Total liabilities	$194,400	$176,200
Owner's equity	276,480	372,200
Total liabilities & owner's equity	$470,880	$548,400

Income statements for the last three years show that Alpine Village has reported total net income of $201,480 since the business was started. The income statements of Nordic Sports show total net income of $256,200 for the same three-year period.

With the permission of the owners of the two businesses, Scott arranges for a certified public accountant to review the accounting records of both companies. This investigation discloses the following information:

Accounts Receivable Nordic Sports uses the direct write-off method of recording uncollectible accounts expense. The accountant believes that the $188,500 of accounts receivable appearing in the company's balance sheet includes about $18,000 in uncollectible accounts. Alpine Village makes monthly estimates of its uncollectible accounts and shows accounts receivable in its balance sheet at estimated net realizable value.

Inventories Nordic Sports uses the first-in, first-out *(FIFO)* method of pricing its inventory. Had the company used the last-in, first-out *(LIFO)* method, the balance sheet valuation of inventory would be about $12,000 lower. Alpine Village uses the LIFO method to value inventory; if it had used FIFO, the balance sheet valuation of inventory would be about $10,000 greater.

Buildings Nordic Sports depreciates its building over an estimated life of 40 years using the straight-line method. Alpine Village depreciates its building over 20 years using the double-declining-balance method. Alpine has owned its building for 3 years, and the accumulated depreciation on the building now amounts to $32,520.

Goodwill   Three years ago, each business provided $24,000 in prize money for ski races held in the area. Nordic Sports charged this expenditure to goodwill, which it is amortizing over a period of 40 years. Alpine Village charged its $24,000 prize money expenditure directly to advertising expense.

INSTRUCTIONS

a Prepare a revised summary of the balance sheet data in a manner that makes the information about the two companies more comparable. You will adjust the asset values of one company or the other so that the balance sheet data for both companies meet the following standards:

1 Accounts receivable are valued at estimated net realizable value.

2 Inventories are valued by the method that will minimize income taxes during a period of rising prices.

3 Depreciation on the buildings is based upon the straight-line method and an estimated useful life of 40 years.

4 The cost of the $24,000 payment of prize money is treated in the manner required by generally accepted accounting principles.

After making the indicated adjustments to the valuation of certain assets, show "owner's equity" at the residual amount needed to bring total liabilities & owner's equity into agreement with total assets.

When you revalue an asset of either company, show supporting computations.

b Revise the cumulative amount of net income reported by each company during the last three years, taking into consideration the changes in accounting methods and policies called for in part **a.**

c Assume that after revision of asset values as described in part **a,** the revised book value of net identifiable assets is not materially different from aggregate fair market value of net identifiable assets. Therefore, Scott is willing to buy either company at a price equal to the revised amount of owner's equity as determined in part **a,** plus an amount for goodwill. For goodwill, Scott is willing to pay four times the amount by which average annual net income exceeds a 20% return on this revised owner's equity.

Determine the price that Scott is willing to pay for each of the two companies. Base your computations on the revised data about owner's equity and net income that you developed in parts **a** and **b.** (Hint: Remember that the cumulative net income in part **b** was earned over a three-year period. To find average *annual* net income, divide this amount by 3.)

PART

4 Liabilities, Partnerships, and Accounting Principles

*P*art 4 consists of three chapters. In Chapter 11 we discuss the types of liabilities commonly found in most business organizations; in Chapter 12, we explore the specialized field of accounting for partnerships.

Chapter 13 is intended as a "capstone" chapter for the first semester course. It includes a review of many accounting principles introduced in earlier chapters, and also a discussion of the professional ethics relating to the practice of accounting.

CHAPTER

11 Liabilities Common to Most Business Organizations

Our primary coverage of liabilities is split between this chapter and Chapter 16. In this chapter, we address the types of liabilities likely to arise in almost any type or size of business organization, and also the accounting and disclosure requirements relating to loss contingencies and commitments. Accounting for payrolls is discussed in a Supplemental Topic section at the end of the chapter.

In Chapter 16, we will address the special types of liabilities which appear primarily in the balance sheets of large, publicly owned corporations.

After studying this chapter you should be able to meet these Learning Objectives:

1 *Define* liabilities; *distinguish between liabilities and owner's equity.*

2 *Distinguish between current and long-term liabilities.*

3 *Account for notes payable and the accrual of interest.*

4 *Account for notes payable with the interest included in the face amount.*

5 *Prepare an amortization table allocating payments on an install-ment loan between interest and repayment of principal.*

6 *Compute the quick ratio, debt ratio, and interest coverage ratio, and explain their usefulness.*

7 *Define* loss contingencies. *Explain the criteria determining their presentation in financial statements.*

*8 *Describe the basic separation of duties in a payroll system, and explain how this plan contributes to strong internal control.*

*9 *Account for a payroll, including computation of amounts withheld and payroll taxes on the employer.*

---

* *Supplemental Topic, "Accounting for Payrolls"*

*C*ompanies that cannot pay their liabilities eventually will be forced out of business—and, perhaps, into bankruptcy. In evaluating the solvency of a business, or its ability to finance future growth, users of financial statements should consider carefully the nature and amount of the company's liabilities.

The Nature of Liabilities

OBJECTIVE 1
Define lia-
bilities; dis-
tinguish
between
liabilities
and owner's
equity.

Liabilities may be defined as *debts or obligations arising from past transactions or events and requiring settlement at a future date.* Thus, liabilities represent *existing obligations* for the business to part with resources in the future. All liabilities have certain characteristics in common; however, the terms of different liabilities vary greatly, as do the rights of the specific creditors.

Distinctions between Debt and Equity   Businesses have two basic sources of financing: debt (liabilities) and equity. Liabilities differ from owner's equity in several respects. The feature which most clearly distinguishes the claims of creditors from owner's equity is that all liabilities eventually *mature*—that is, they come due. Owner's equity *does not* mature. The date upon which a liability comes due is called the *maturity date.*[1]

Although all liabilities mature, their maturity dates vary. Some liabilities are so short in term that they are paid before the financial statements reach the user's desk. Long-term liabilities, in contrast, may not mature for many years. The maturity dates of key liabilities may be a critical factor in the solvency of a business.

The providers of borrowed capital are *creditors* of the business, not owners. As creditors, they have financial claims against the business, but they usually do *not* have the right to control business operations. The traditional roles of owners, managers, and creditors may be modified, however, in an *indenture contract.* Creditors sometimes insist upon being granted some control over business operations as a condition of making a loan, particularly if the business is in poor financial condition. Indenture contracts may impose such restrictions as limits upon management salaries and upon dividends, and may require the creditor's approval for additional borrowing or for large capital expenditures.

The claims of creditors have *legal priority* over the claims of owners. If a business ceases operations and liquidates, creditors must be *paid in full* before any distributions are made to the owners. The relative security of creditors' claims, however, can vary among the creditors. Sometimes the borrower pledges title to specific assets as *collateral* for a loan. If the borrower defaults on a secured loan, the creditor may foreclose upon the pledged assets. Assets which have been pledged as security for loans should be identified in notes accompanying the borrower's financial statements.

---

[1]   Some liabilities are *due on demand,* which means that the liability is payable upon the creditor's request. From a bank's point of view, customers' checking accounts are "demand liabilities." Liabilities due on demand may come due at any time and in a classified balance sheet are shown as current liabilities.

Liabilities which are not secured by specific assets are termed **general credit obligations.** The priorities of general credit obligations vary with the nature of the liability, and the terms of indenture contracts.

Most long-term liabilities, and some short-term ones, require the borrower to pay interest. In some companies, the requirements to pay future interest charges are so large that they threaten the very survival of the business. Obligations to pay interest **stem only from liabilities;** a company does **not** pay interest upon its owner's equity.

Estimated Liabilities   Most liabilities are for a definite dollar amount, clearly stated by contract. Examples include notes payable, accounts payable, and accrued expenses, such as interest payable and salaries payable. In some cases, however, the dollar amount of a liability must be **estimated** at the balance sheet date.

Estimated liabilities have two basic characteristics: The liability is **known to exist,** but the precise dollar amount cannot be determined until a later date. For instance, the automobiles sold by most auto makers are accompanied by a warranty obligating the auto maker to replace defective parts for a period of several years. As each car is sold, the auto maker **incurs a liability** to perform any work which can be required under the warranty. The dollar amount of this liability, however, can only be estimated.

CURRENT LIABILITIES

Current liabilities are obligations that must be paid within one year or within the operating cycle, whichever is longer. Another requirement for classification as a current liability is the expectation that the debt will be paid from current assets (or through the rendering of services). Liabilities that do not meet these conditions are classified as long-term liabilities.

OBJECTIVE 2 Distinguish between current and long-term liabilities.

The time period used in defining current liabilities parallels that used in defining current assets. As explained in Chapter 5, the amount of **working capital** (current assets less current liabilities) and the **current ratio** (current assets divided by current liabilities) are valuable indicators of a company's ability to pay its debts in the near future.

Among the most common examples of current liabilities are accounts payable, short-term notes payable, the current portion of long-term debt, accrued liabilities (such as interest payable, income taxes payable, and payroll liabilities), and unearned revenue.

Accounts Payable

Accounts payable often are subdivided into the categories of trade accounts payable and other accounts payable. Trade accounts payable are short-term obligations to suppliers for purchases or merchandise. Other accounts payable include liabilities for any goods and services other than merchandise.

Accounts payable usually are recorded at an amount **net** of any available cash discounts. If payment is not made until after the discount period has lapsed, the additional amount paid is charged to an expense account entitled Purchase Discounts Lost.

Technically, the date at which a trade account payable comes into existence depends upon whether goods are purchased F.O.B. shipping point or F.O.B. destination. However, unless **material** amounts of merchandise are purchased on terms of F.O.B. shipping point, most companies follow the convenient practice of recording the transaction when the merchandise is received.

Notes Payable

*OBJECTIVE 3
Account for
notes paya-
ble and the
accrual of
interest.*

Notes payable are issued whenever bank loans are obtained. Other transactions which may give rise to notes payable include the purchase of real estate or costly equipment, the purchase of merchandise, and the substitution of a note for a past-due account payable.

Notes payable generally require the borrower to pay an interest charge. Accounting for interest charges is easiest if the interest rate is stated separately from the **principal** amount of the note. To illustrate, assume that on November 1 Porter Company borrows $10,000 from its bank for a period of six months at an annual interest rate of 12%. Six months later, on May 1, Porter Company will have to pay the bank the **principal** amount of $10,000, plus $600 interest ($10,000 $\times \frac{6}{12} \times$ .12). The owners of Porter Company have authorized John Caldwell, the company's treasurer, to sign notes payable issued by the company. The note issued by Porter Company is shown below with the interest rate stated separately from the principal amount.

**This note is for
the principal
amount with
interest stated
separately**

Miami, Florida	November 1, 19_
Six months after this date	Porter Company
promises to pay to Security National Bank the sum of $	$10,000
with interest at the rate of 12% per annum.	
	Signed *John Caldwell*
	Title Treasurer

The journal entry in Porter Company's accounting records for this November 1 borrowing is:

**Face amount
of note**

Cash	*10,000*	
Notes Payable		*10,000*
Borrowed $10,000 for six months at 12% interest per year.		

Notice that no liability is recorded for the interest charges when the note is issued. At the date that money is borrowed, the borrower has a liability **only for the principal amount of the loan;** the liability for interest accrues day by day over the life of the loan. At December 31, two months' interest expense has been incurred, and the following year-end adjusting entry is made:

A liability for interest accrues day by day

Interest Expense 200
       Interest Payable   200
To record interest expense incurred through year-end on
six-month, 12% note dated Nov. 1 ($10,000 × $\frac{2}{12}$ × 12% = $200).

If we assume that the company does not use reversing entries, the entry on May 1 when the note is paid will be:

Payment of principal and interest

Notes Payable.. 10,000
Interest Payable 200
Interest Expense 400
      Cash   10,600
To record payment of six-month, 12% note on maturity date
and to recognize interest expense incurred since year-end
($10,000 × $\frac{4}{12}$ × .12 = $400).

Notes Payable with Interest Charges Included in the Face Amount

Instead of stating the interest rate separately as in the preceding illustration, the note payable issued by Porter Company could have been drawn to **include the interest charge in the face amount of the note,** as shown below:

This note shows interest included in face amount

Miami, Florida   November 1, 19_
___Six months___   after this date   Porter Company
promises to pay to Security National Bank the sum of $ _____ $10,600 _____
Signed _John Caldwell_
Title _____ Treasurer

OBJECTIVE 4
Account for notes payable with the interest included in the face amount.

    Notice that the face amount of this note ($10,600) is greater than the $10,000 amount borrowed. Porter Company's liability at November 1 is only $10,000—the **present value** of the note.[2] The other $600 included in the face amount of the note represents **future interest charges.** As interest expense is incurred over the life of the note, Porter Company's liability will grow to $10,600, just as in the preceding illustration.

---

[2] The concept of present value was introduced in Chapter 8. The mechanics of computing present values is explained in Appendix C.

The entry to record Porter Company's $10,000 borrowing from the bank at November 1 will be as follows for this type of note payable:

Interest included in face of note

```
Cash.......................................................  10,000
Discount on Notes Payable .................................     600
    Notes Payable ........................................          10,600
Issued to bank a six-month, 12% note payable with interest
charge included in the face amount of note.
```

The liability account, Notes Payable, was credited with the full face amount of the note ($10,600). It is therefore necessary to debit a ***contra-liability*** account, ***Discount on Notes Payable,*** for the future interest charges included in the face amount of the note. Discount on Notes Payable is shown in the balance sheet as a deduction from Notes Payable. In our illustration, the amounts in the balance sheet would be Notes Payable, $10,600, minus Discount on Notes Payable, $600, or a net liability of $10,000 at November 1.

Discount on Notes Payable The balance of the account Discount on Notes Payable represents ***interest charges applicable to future periods***. As this interest expense is incurred, the balance of the discount account gradually is transferred into the Interest Expense account. Thus, at the maturity date of the note, Discount on Notes Payable will have a zero balance, and the net liability will have increased to $10,600. The process of transferring the amount in the Discount on Notes Payable account into the Interest Expense account is called ***amortization*** of the discount.

Amortization of the Discount The discount on ***short-term*** notes payable usually is amortized by the straight-line method, which allocates the same amount of discount to interest expense for each month the note is outstanding. Thus, the $600 discount on the Porter Company note payable will be transferred from Discount on Notes Payable into Interest Expense at the rate of $100 per month ($600 ÷ 6 months).

Adjusting entries should be made to amortize the discount at the end of each accounting period and at the date the note matures. At December 31, Porter Company will make the following adjusting entry to recognize the two months' interest expense incurred since November 1:

Amortization of discount

```
Interest Expense .............................................  200
    Discount on Notes Payable ..............................          200
To record interest expense incurred to end of year on
six-month, 12% note dated Nov. 1 ($600 discount × 2/6).
```

Notice that the liability for accrued interest is recorded by crediting Discount on Notes Payable rather than Interest Payable. The credit to Discount on Notes Payable reduces the debit balance in this contra-liability account from $600 to $400, thereby increasing the ***net liability*** for notes payable by $200.

At December 31, Porter Company's net liability for the bank loan will appear in the balance sheet as shown below:

Liability shown net of discount

```
Current liabilities:
    Note payable ..........................................  $10,600
    Less: Discount on notes payable.......................      400   $10,200
```

The net liability of $10,200 consists of the $10,000 principal amount of the debt plus the $200 interest which has accrued since November 1.

When the note matures on May 1, Porter Company will recognize the four months' interest expense incurred since year-end and will pay the bank $10,600. The entry is:

Two-thirds of interest applicable to second year

Notes Payable	*10,600*	
Interest Expense	*400*	
Discount on Notes Payable		*400*
Cash		*10,600*

To record payment of six-month, 12% note due today and recognize interest expense incurred since year-end ($10,000 × $\frac{4}{12}$ × 12% = $400).

Comparison of the Two Forms of Notes Payable

We have illustrated two alternative methods which Porter Company could use in accounting for its $10,000 bank loan, depending upon the form of the note payable. The journal entries for both methods, along with the resulting balance sheet presentations of the liability at November 1 and December 31, are summarized on the next page. Notice that both methods result in Porter Company recognizing the **same amount of interest expense** and the **same total liability** in its balance sheet. The form of the note does not change the economic substance of the transaction.

The Current Portion of Long-Term Debt

Notes payable usually are classified as current liabilities or as long-term liabilities based upon the maturity date. Thus, notes payable maturing in one year or less normally are classified as current liabilities, whereas notes maturing in the more distant future are classified as long-term liabilities.

As the maturity date of a long-term liability approaches, the obligation eventually becomes due within the current period. Long-term liabilities which become payable within the current year generally are **reclassified** in the balance sheet as current liabilities.[3]

Some long-term notes payable, such as mortgage loans, are payable in a series of monthly or quarterly **installments.** In these cases, the principal amount to be repaid within the coming year is classified as a current liability, and the remainder of the principal amount is classified as a long-term liability. (Notice that the current portion of an installment note payable includes only the **principal amount** to be repaid within one year, **not the interest payments** scheduled for the year.)

Accrued Liabilities

Accrued liabilities arise from the recognition of expenses for which payment will be made in future periods. Thus, accrued liabilities also may be

---

[3]   Exceptions are made to this rule if the maturing liability will be **refinanced** (that is, extended or renewed) on a long-term basis or if a special **sinking fund** has been accumulated for the purpose of repaying the liability. In these cases, the debt continues to be classified as a long-term liability, as it is not expected to be paid from current assets.

Comparison of the Two Forms of Notes Payable

	Note Written for $10,000 Plus 12% Interest	Note Written with Interest Included in Face Amount
Entry to record borrowing on Nov. 1	Cash.......... 10,000 　Notes Payable.......... 10,000	Cash.......... 10,000 Discount on Notes Payable.......... 600 　Notes Payable.......... 10,600
Partial balance sheet at Nov. 1	Current liabilities: Notes payable.......... $10,000	Current liabilities: Notes payable.......... $10,600 Less: Discount on notes payable.......... 600　$10,000
Adjusting entry at Dec. 31	Interest Expense.......... 200 　Interest Payable.......... 200	Interest Expense.......... 200 　Discount on Notes Payable.......... 200
Partial balance sheet at Dec. 31	Current liabilities: Notes payable.......... $10,000 Interest payable.......... 200　$10,200	Current liabilities: Notes payable.......... $10,600 Less: Discount on notes payable.......... 400　$10,200
Entry to record payment of note on May 1	Notes Payable.......... 10,000 Interest Payable.......... 200 Interest Expense.......... 400 　Cash.......... 10,600	Notes Payable.......... 10,600 Interest Expense.......... 400 　Discount on Notes Payable.......... 400 　Cash.......... 10,600

called *accrued expenses.* Examples of accrued liabilities include interest payable, income taxes payable, and payroll liabilities. As accrued liabilities stem from the recording of expenses, the timing and amounts of these liabilities are governed by the *matching principle.*

All companies incur accrued liabilities. In most cases, however, these liabilities are paid at frequent intervals—usually within a month or less. Therefore, accrued liabilities *usually do not accumulate to large dollar amounts.* In the balance sheet, accrued liabilities often are combined with accounts payable, rather than being listed separately.

Interest Payable Interest—the cost of borrowing—accrues with the passage of time. When companies enter into long-term borrowing agreements, they may become committed to paying large amounts of interest for many years to come. At any balance sheet date, however, only a *small portion* of this total interest obligation represents a "liability."

Remember, liabilities stem from *past transactions.* Therefore, the only interest obligation which represents a "liability" is the unpaid interest which has *already* accrued. (At the end of each period, any accrued interest payable is recorded by debiting Interest Expense and crediting Interest Payable.)

To illustrate this point, assume that HighTech Stores borrows $500,000 from its bank for a period of five years at an interest rate of 12%. Although the principal amount of this loan will not be due for five years, interest is to be paid monthly—on the first day of each month.

The interest expense on this loan amounts to *$60,000* per year ($500,000 × 12%). Over the life of the loan, HighTech will pay *$300,000* in interest charges. At the end of each month, however, HighTech will have a liability for only *one month's interest*—the interest which has accrued since the last interest payment date. Thus, HighTech's balance sheets normally will show accrued interest payable of only *$5,000* ($500,000 × $\frac{1}{12}$ × 12%).

If this loan had called for the accrued interest to be paid on the *last* day of each month, HighTech's balance sheets would include *no* liability for accrued interest payable.

A borrower's contractual obligation to pay interest in future periods is *not yet a liability* and *does not appear* in the borrower's balance sheet. However, this information may be of vital importance to investors and creditors evaluating the company's solvency and its ability to finance future growth. For this reason, accounting principles require businesses to *disclose* the terms of major borrowing arrangements in the notes which accompany their financial statements.

To determine the amount of a company's interest *expense* for the year, the reader of financial statements should look in the *income statement,* not the balance sheet. For information about the company's interest obligations in *future* years, this reader must study the *notes* which accompany the financial statements.

Income Taxes Payable Profitable corporations are required to pay income taxes equal to a portion of their taxable income. Income taxes expense accrues *as profits are earned.* At the end of each accounting period, income taxes expense is estimated and recorded in an adjusting entry, as shown below:[4]

Adjusting entry to accrue estimated income taxes

Income Taxes Expense	*72,750*	
Income Taxes Payable		*72,750*
To accrue estimated income taxes expense for the first quarter of the year (Jan. 1 through Mar. 31).		

The account debited in this entry, Income Taxes Expense, is an expense account and usually appears as the very last deduction in the income statement. For example, the income taxes expense recorded above would appear as follows in an income statement for the quarter ended March 31:

Income before income taxes	*$200,000*
Less: Income taxes expense	*72,750*
Net income	*127,250*

Only businesses organized as **corporations** incur income taxes expense. Unincorporated businesses—sole proprietorships and partnerships—do not pay income taxes. The incomes earned by unincorporated businesses are taxable directly to the **owners** of these businesses, not to the business entities themselves.

The liability account, Income Taxes Payable, ordinarily will be paid within a few months and, therefore, appears in the current liability section of the balance sheet.

Payroll Liabilities Every business incurs a number of accrued liabilities relating to its payroll. The largest of these liabilities is the obligation to pay employees for services rendered during the period. Payroll **expense** often is among the largest expenses of a business organization. Accrued payroll liabilities, however, seldom accumulate to large amounts because they are paid in full at frequent intervals.

Accounting for payrolls involves much more than merely recording the liability for accrued wages and salaries payable. Employers must compute numerous taxes which the government levies either upon employees or upon the employer. The employer then is responsible for withholding the taxes upon employees from the employees' paychecks and forwarding these amounts directly to the government. The employer also is responsible for maintaining records indicating for **each employee** the amounts earned during the year and the amounts of taxes withheld. All of this information must be computed separately for every pay period—usually every one or two weeks. Thus, payroll accounting is a specialized function within most accounting departments.

Every business student should have some familiarity with payrolls, including the purpose and relative size of the various payroll taxes, and whether these taxes are paid by the employees or by the employer. An introduction to accounting for payrolls is presented in the Supplemental Topic section at the end of this chapter.

---

[4] Actual income tax expense for the year cannot be determined until after year-end, when the company prepares its income tax return. Therefore, monthly or quarterly adjusting entries recognizing income taxes expense are based upon **estimated** amounts.

Unearned Revenue

A liability for unearned revenue arises when a customer pays in advance. Upon receipt of an advance payment from a customer, the company debits Cash and credits a liability account such as Unearned Revenue, or Customers' Deposits. As the services are rendered to the customer, an entry is made debiting the liability account and crediting a revenue account. Notice that the liability for unearned revenue normally is "paid" by rendering services to the creditor, rather than by making cash payments.

Unearned revenue ordinarily is classified as a current liability, as the activities involved in earning revenue are part of the business's normal operating cycle.

LONG-TERM LIABILITIES

Long-term obligations usually arise from major expenditures, such as acquisitions of plant assets, the purchase of another company, or refinancing an existing long-term obligation which is about to mature. Thus, transactions involving long-term liabilities are relatively few in number but often involve large dollar amounts. In contrast, current liabilities usually arise from routine operating transactions.

Many businesses regard long-term liabilities as an alternative to owners' equity as a source of "permanent" financing. Although long-term liabilities eventually mature, they often are *refinanced*—that is, the maturing obligation simply is replaced with a new long-term liability.

Maturing Obligations Intended to Be Refinanced

One special type of long-term liability is an obligation which will mature in the current period but which is expected to be refinanced on a long-term basis. For example, a company may have a bank loan which "comes due" each year but is routinely extended for the following year. Both the company and the bank may intend for this arrangement to continue on a long-term basis.

If management has both the *intent* and the *ability* to refinance soon-to-mature obligations on a long-term basis, these obligations are classified as long-term liabilities In this situation, the accountant looks to the *economic substance* of the situation, rather than to its legal form.

When the economic substance of a transaction differs from its legal form or its outward appearance, financial statements should reflect the *economic substance.* Accountants summarize this concept with the phrase, ***"Substance takes precedence over form."*** Today's business world is characterized by transactions of ever-increasing complexity. Recognizing those situations in which the substance of a transaction differs from its form is one of the greatest challenges confronting the professional accountant.

Installment Notes Payable

Purchases of real estate and certain types of equipment often are financed by the issuance of long-term notes which call for a series of installment payments. These payments (often called **debt service**) may be due monthly, quarterly, semiannually, or at any other interval. If these installments continue until the debt is completely repaid, the loan is said to be "fully amortizing." Often, however, installment notes contain a "due date" at which the remaining unpaid balance is to be repaid in a single "balloon" payment.

Some installment notes call for installment payments equal to the periodic interest charges (an "interest only" note). Under these terms, the principal amount of the loan is payable at a specified maturity date. More often, however, the installment payments are **greater** than the amount of interest accruing during the period. Thus, only a portion of each installment payment represents interest expense, and the remainder of the payment reduces the principal amount of the liability. As the amount owed is reduced by each payment, the portion of each successive payment representing interest expense will **decrease,** and the portion going toward repayment of principal will **increase.**

Allocating Installment Payments between Interest and Principal   In accounting for an installment note, the accountant must determine the portion of each payment that represents interest expense, and the portion that reduces the principal amount of the liability. This distinction is made in advance by preparing an **amortization table.**

OBJECTIVE 5
Prepare an amortization table allocating payments on an installment loan between interest and repayment of principal.

To illustrate, assume that on October 15, 1993, King's Inn purchases furnishings at a total cost of $16,398. In payment, the company issues an installment note payable for this amount, plus interest at 12% per annum (or 1% per month). This note will be paid in 18 monthly installments of $1,000 each, beginning on November 15. An amortization table for this installment note payable appears at the top of the following page. (Amounts of interest expense are **rounded to the nearest dollar.**)

Preparing an Amortization Table   Let us explore the content of this table. First, notice that the payments are made on a **monthly** basis. Therefore, the amounts of the payments (column A), interest expense (column B), and reduction in the unpaid balance (column C) are all **monthly amounts.**

The interest rate used in the table is of special importance; this rate must coincide with the period of time **between payment dates**—in this case, one month. Thus, if payments are made monthly, column B must be based upon the **monthly** rate of interest. If payments were made quarterly, this column would use the quarterly rate of interest.

An amortization table begins with the original amount of the liability ($16,398) listed at the top of the unpaid balance column. The amounts of the monthly payments, shown in column A, are specified by the installment contract. The monthly interest expense, shown in column B, is computed for each month by applying the monthly interest rate to the unpaid balance at the **beginning of that month.** The portion of each payment that reduces the amount of the liability (column C) is simply the remainder of the payment (column A minus column B). Finally, the unpaid balance of the liability (column D) is reduced each month by the amount indicated in column C.

Rather than continuing to make monthly payments, King's Inn could settle this liability at any time by paying the amount currently shown as the unpaid balance.

Amortization Table
(12% Note Payable for $16,398; Payable in 18 Monthly Installments of $1,000)

Interest Period	Payment Date	(A) Monthly Payment	(B) Interest Expense (1% of the Last Unpaid Balance)	(C) Reduction in Unpaid Balance (A) − (B)	(D) Unpaid Balance
Issue date	Oct. 15 1993	—	—	—	$16,398
1	Nov. 15	$1,000	$164	$836	15,562
2	Dec. 15	1,000	156	844	14,718
3	Jan. 15, 1994	1,000	147	853	13,865
4	Feb. 15	1,000	139	861	13,004
5	Mar. 15	1,000	130	870	12,134
6	Apr. 15	1,000	121	879	11,255
7	May 15	1,000	113	887	10,368
8	June 15	1,000	104	896	9,472
9	July 15	1,000	95	905	8,567
10	Aug. 15	1,000	86	914	7,653
11	Sept. 15	1,000	77	923	6,730
12	Oct. 15	1,000	67	933	5,797
13	Nov. 15	1,000	58	942	4,855
14	Dec. 15	1,000	49	951	3,904
15	Jan. 15, 1995	1,000	39	961	2,943
16	Feb. 15	1,000	29	971	1,972
17	Mar. 15	1,000	20	980	992
18	Apr. 15	1,000	8*	992	-0-

* In the last period, interest expense is equal to the amount of the final payment minus the remaining unpaid balance. This compensates for the cumulative effect of rounding interest amounts to the nearest dollar.

Notice that the amount of interest expense listed in column B *changes every month.* In our illustration, the interest expense is *decreasing* each month, because the unpaid balance is continually decreasing.[5]

Preparing each horizontal line in an amortization table involves making the same computations, based upon a new unpaid balance. Thus, an amortization table of any length can be easily and quickly prepared by computer. (Most "money management" software includes a program for preparing amortization tables.) The data which must be entered into the computer consist of only three items: (1) the original amount of the liability, (2) the amount of periodic payments, and (3) the interest rate (per payment period).

Using an Amortization Table Once an amortization table has been prepared, the entries to record each payment are taken directly from the amounts shown in the table. For example, the entry to record the first monthly payment (November 15, 1993) is:

---

[5] If the monthly payments were *less* than the amount of the monthly interest expense, the unpaid balance of the note would *increase* each month. This, in turn, would cause the interest expense to increase each month. This pattern, termed *negative amortization,* occurs temporarily in some "adjustable-rate" home mortgages.

Payment is allocated between interest and principal	*Interest Expense* 164	
	Installment Note Payable 836	
	Cash	*1,000*
	Made November payment on installment note payable.	

Similarly, the entry to record the **second** payment, made on **December 15, 1993,** is:

Notice that interest expense is less in December	*Interest Expense* 156	
	Installment Note Payable 844	
	Cash	1,000
	Made December payment on installment note payable.	

At December 31, 1993, King's Inn should make an adjusting entry to record one-half month's accrued interest on this liability. The amount of this adjusting entry is based upon the unpaid balance shown in the amortization table as of the last payment (December 15). This entry is:

Year-end adjusting entry	*Interest Expense* 74	
	Interest Payable	74
	Adjusting entry to record interest expense on installment note for the last half of December: $14,718 \times 1\% \times \frac{1}{2} = \$74$.	

The Current Portion of Long-Term Debt Notice that as of December 31, **1993,** the unpaid balance of this note is $14,718. As of December 31, **1994,** however, the unpaid balance will be only $3,904. Thus, the principal amount of this note will be reduced by **$10,814** during 1994 ($14,718 − $3,904 = $10,814). In the balance sheet prepared at December 31, 1993, the $10,814 portion of this debt which is scheduled for repayment within the **next 12 months** should be classified as a **current liability.** The remaining $3,904 should be classified as a long-term liability.

Disclosure Requirements for Long-Term Debt

A company should disclose in notes to its financial statements the interest rates and maturity dates of all long-term notes payable.[6] In addition, the company should disclose the total amounts of long-term debt maturing in each of the next five years. These disclosures are intended to assist users of the financial statements in evaluating the company's solvency—not just today, but over a period of several years.

The FASB requires businesses to disclose the **fair value** of long-term liabilities if this value differs significantly from the amount shown in the balance sheet.[7] The term **fair value** generally means the **present value** of the future cash payments (including both interest and principal) determined under **current** market conditions. This disclosure requirement will be discussed further in Chapter 16.

---

[6] If a company has many different notes payable, it is not practicable to disclose separately the terms of each note. In such cases, the notes are grouped into categories of similar liabilities, and the **range** of interest rates and maturity dates of each category is disclosed. Drafting disclosures which are informative, yet not excessively detailed, requires professional judgment.

[7] FASB, *Statement of Financial Accounting Standards No. 107,* "Disclosure About Fair Value of Financial Instruments" (Norwalk, Conn.: 1991), para. 10–13.

EVALUATING THE SAFETY OF CREDITORS' CLAIMS

OBJECTIVE 6
Compute the
quick ratio,
debt ratio,
and interest
coverage
ratio, and
explain their
usefulness.

In recent years, some companies with profitable business operations have incurred so much debt that they have been unable to make the required interest payments. If a company cannot pay its debts and is forced into bankruptcy, creditors and investors alike may sustain large losses. Management, too, is concerned with the company's debt-paying ability. Not only does management want the business to remain solvent, but it wants the company to maintain a high *credit rating* with agencies such as Dun & Bradstreet and Standard & Poor's. A high credit rating helps the company borrow money more easily and at lower interest rates.

Analysis by Short-Term Creditors

In evaluating debt-paying ability, short-term creditors and long-term creditors look at different financial relationships. Short-term creditors are interested in the company's immediate solvency and look toward such measures of liquidity as working capital and the current ratio. As explained in earlier chapters, they also may compute the turnover rates for receivables and for inventory, in order to evaluate the liquidity of these assets.

Quick Ratio   Although inventories and prepaid expenses are classified as current assets, they are further removed from conversion into cash than are other current assets. Therefore, short-term creditors often use a statistic called the *quick ratio,* rather than the current ratio, to provide a quick evaluation of a company's short-term solvency.

   The quick ratio is computed by dividing *quick assets* by current liabilities. Quick assets include only cash, investments in marketable securities,[8] and short-term receivables. Thus, the quick ratio provides a more rigid test of short-term solvency than does the current ratio.

   A quick ratio of 1.0 to 1 or better usually is considered satisfactory, and a quick ratio of over 1.5 to 1 indicates a high degree of liquidity. Of course, all ratios vary substantially among companies of different sizes or in different industries. However, an analyst familiar with the nature of a company's operations generally can determine from the quick ratio whether the company represents a good credit risk in the short run.

Analysis by Long-Term Creditors

Long-term creditors are less concerned than short-term creditors in the amount of liquid assets a business has on hand today. Rather, they are interested in the borrower's ability to meet its interest obligations *over a period of years,* and also its ability to repay or refinance large obligations years in the future.

Debt Ratio   One measurement often used in evaluating the overall safety of long-term creditors' investments is the debt ratio. This ratio is computed

---

[8]   Investments in marketable securities are investments which can be sold readily at quoted market prices. They include, for example, investments in government bonds and in the stocks and bonds issued by major corporations. Marketable securities are discussed in Chapter 17.

by dividing total liabilities by total assets. Basically, the debt ratio indicates the **percentage** of total assets which are financed with borrowed money (liabilities), in comparison with the percentage financed with equity capital.

Creditors prefer a **low** debt ratio, as this means that their claims amount to only a small percentage of total assets. This relationship increases the prospects that the creditors will be paid in full, even if the company ceases operations and liquidates its assets.

Of course, individual creditors should look beyond the overall debt ratio to determine the safety of their claims. Holders of subordinated debt, for example, should consider the priority of their claims relative to those of other creditors. The holders of secured debt should consider the value and salability of the specific assets which secure their claims.

Interest Coverage Ratio   Creditors, investors, and managers all feel more comfortable when a company has enough income to cover its interest payment obligations by a wide margin. One widely used measure of the relationship between earnings and interest expense is called the **interest coverage ratio.**

The interest coverage ratio is computed by dividing annual **operating income** by the annual interest expense. From the creditors' point of view, the higher this ratio, the better. In past years, most companies with high credit ratings had interest coverage ratios of, perhaps, 4 to 1 or more. With the spree of corporate borrowing which characterized the 1980s, many large corporations have let their interest coverage ratios decline below 2 to 1. In most cases, their credit ratings have dropped accordingly.

ESTIMATED LIABILITIES, LOSS CONTINGENCIES, AND COMMITMENTS

Estimated Liabilities

The term **estimated liabilities** refers to **liabilities which appear in financial statements at estimated dollar amounts.** Let us again consider the example of the auto maker's liability to honor its "new car warranties." A manufacturer's liability for warranty work is recorded by an entry debiting Warranty Expense and crediting Liability for Warranty Claims. The **matching principle** requires that the expense of performing warranty work be recognized in the period in which the products are **sold,** in order to offset this expense against the related sales revenue. As the warranty may extend several years into the future, the dollar amount of this liability (and expense) must be estimated. Rather than estimate when warranty work will be performed, accountants traditionally have classified the liability for warranty claims as a current liability.

By definition, estimated liabilities involve some degree of uncertainty. However, the liabilities are (1) known to exist, and (2) the uncertainty is **not so great** as to prevent the company from making a reasonable estimate and recording the liability.

Loss Contingencies

OBJECTIVE 7
Define loss contingencies. Explain the criteria for determining their presentation in financial statements.

Loss contingencies are similar to estimated liabilities, but may involve much more uncertainty. A **loss contingency** is a **possible loss** (or expense), stemming from **past events,** that will be resolved as to existence and amount by some future event.

Central to the definition of a loss contingency is the element of **uncertainty**—uncertainty to the amount of loss and, in some cases, uncertainty as to **whether or not any loss actually has been incurred.** A common example of a loss contingency is a lawsuit pending against a company. The lawsuit is based upon past events, but until the suit is resolved, uncertainty exists as to the amount (if any) of the company's liability.

Loss contingencies differ from estimated liabilities in two ways. First, a loss contingency involves a **greater degree of uncertainty.** Often the uncertainty extends to whether or not any loss or expense actually has been incurred. In contrast, the loss or expense relating to an estimated liability is **known to exist.**

Second, the concept of a loss contingency extends not only to possible liabilities but also to possible **impairments of assets.** Assume, for example, that a bank has made large loans to a foreign country which is now experiencing political instability. Uncertainty exists as to the amount of loss, if any, associated with this loan. From the bank's point of view, this loan is an **asset which may be impaired,** not a liability.

Loss Contingencies in Financial Statements The manner in which loss contingencies are presented in financial statements depends upon the **degree of uncertainty involved.**

Loss contingencies are **recorded** in the accounting records only when both of the following criteria are met: (1) it is **probable** that a loss has been incurred, and (2) the amount of loss can be **reasonably estimated.** An example of a loss contingency that usually meets these criteria and is recorded in the accounts is the estimated loss from doubtful accounts receivable.

When these criteria are **not** met, loss contingencies still are **disclosed** in financial statements if there is a **reasonable possibility** that a material loss has been incurred. Pending lawsuits, for example, usually are disclosed in notes accompanying the financial statements, but the loss, if any, is not recorded in the accounting records until the lawsuit is settled.

Companies generally need not disclose loss contingencies if the risk of a material loss is considered **remote.**

Notice the **judgmental nature** of the criteria used in accounting for loss contingencies. These criteria involved assessments as to whether the risk of material loss is "probable," "reasonably possible," or "remote." Thus, the **professional judgment** of the company's management, accountants, legal counsel, and auditors is the deciding factor in accounting for loss contingencies.

When loss contingencies are disclosed in footnotes to the financial statements, the footnote should describe the nature of the contingency and, if possible, provide an estimate of the amount of possible loss. If a reasonable estimate of the amount of possible loss cannot be made, the footnote should include the range of possible loss or a statement that an estimate cannot be made. The following footnote is typical of the disclosure of the loss contingency arising from pending litigation:

Footnote disclosure of a loss contingency

Note 8: Contingencies

In October of the current year, the Company was named as defendant in a lawsuit alleging patent infringement and claiming damages of $408 million. The Company denies all charges in this case and is preparing its defenses against them. The Company is advised by legal counsel that it is not possible at this time to determine the ultimate legal or financial responsibility with respect to this litigation.

Sometimes a ***portion*** of a loss contingency qualifies for immediate recognition, whereas the remainder only meets the criteria for disclosure. Assume, for example, that a company has been sued for $10 million. Legal counsel cannot predict the outcome of this litigation, but considers it "probable" that the company will lose at least $1 million. The company should recognize this $1 million expected loss and record it as a liability. In addition, the company should disclose the nature and amount of the litigation, stating that the loss ultimately may exceed the recorded amount.

CASE IN POINT The federal Food and Drug Administration (FDA) recently imposed an indefinite moratorium on the use of silicon breast implants, saying there wasn't enough evidence of the products' safety.

Dow Corning, the nation's largest manufacturer of silicon implants, promptly closed its production lines and accrued a $25 million liability for pending and future lawsuits and claims concerning these implants. Although the company cannot estimate with precision the outcome of current and future lawsuits, it apparently believes that losses of at least $25 million appear "probable."

Potential Significance of Loss Contingencies Users of financial statements should pay close attention to the notes disclosing loss contingencies. Even if no loss has yet been recorded in the accounting records, loss contingencies may be so material as to threaten the continued existence of the company.

CASE IN POINT In August 1982, Johns-Manville Corporation surprised the financial community by filing for bankruptcy. Johns-Manville, with its worldwide mining and manufacturing operations, had a long record of profitability and financial strength. In fact, the corporation was one of the 30 "blue chip" companies whose stock prices are used in the computation of the famous Dow-Jones Industrial Average. As late as 1981, the dollar amounts in the company's financial statements showed Johns-Manville to be both profitable and solvent.

A clue to the company's impending problems, however, could be found in the notes accompanying the statements. Beginning in 1979, the statements included a note disclosing that the company was a defendant in "numerous legal actions alleging damage to the health of persons exposed to dust from asbestos-containing products manufactured or sold by the Company. . . ." It was these pending lawsuits, which numbered over 50,000 by August of 1982, which caused the company to file for bankruptcy.

Notice that loss contingencies relate only to possible losses from **past events.** For Dow Corning, these "past events" were sales of silicon breast implants; for Johns-Manville, they were the manufacture and sale of asbestos.

The risk that losses may result from **future** events is **not** a loss contingency. The risk of future losses generally is **not** disclosed in financial statements for several reasons.[9] For one, any disclosure of future losses would be sheer speculation. For another, no one can foresee all of the events which might give rise to future losses.

Commitments

Contracts for future transactions are called **commitments.** They are not liabilities, but, if material, they are disclosed in footnotes to the financial statements. For example, a professional baseball club may issue a three-year contract to a player at an annual salary of, say, $1 million. This is a commitment to pay for services to be rendered in the future. There is no obligation to make payment until the services are received. As liabilities stem only from **past transactions,** this commitment has not yet created a liability.

Other examples of commitments include a corporation's long-term employment contract with a key officer, a contract for construction of a new plant, and a contract to buy or sell inventory at future dates. The common quality of all these commitments is an intent to enter into transactions **in the future.** Commitments that are material in amount should be disclosed in notes to the financial statements.

Losses on Commitments A basic concept of accounting is that losses should be recorded as soon as evidence exists that a loss has been incurred. Therefore, if a commitment existing at the balance sheet date appears to "lock the company into a loss," that loss should be recorded. The offsetting credit entry is to a liability account, which will be paid when the company honors its commitment.

To illustrate, assume that in December of 1990—just prior to the Persian Gulf War—an independent oil refinery entered into a firm contractual commitment to purchase 1 million barrels of oil in January 1991 at a price of **$30** per barrel. By December 31, 1990, however, the price of oil unexpectedly had declined to only **$20** per barrel.

The refinery's purchase commitment obligated it to buy 1 million barrels of oil at a per-barrel price **$10 above** current replacement cost. Thus, under the terms of this agreement, the refinery contractually was obli-

---

9   The risk of future losses **is** disclosed if this risk stems from **existing contracts.** Such situations are discussed in Chapter 16.

gated to sustain a $10 million economic loss. At December 31, 1990, the refinery recognized this loss by making the following adjusting entry:

Recognition of a "locked-in" loss

Loss on Purchase Commitment	*10,000,000*	
Liability for Loss on Purchase Commitment		*10,000,000*

To record loss from commitment to purchase 1 million barrels of oil at a price $10 per barrel in excess of market.

When the oil was received in January, the refinery recorded the purchase as shown below:

Purchases recorded at market value below cost

Inventory...	*20,000,000*	
Liability for Loss on Purchase Commitment	*10,000,000*	
Cash		*30,000,000*

To record purchase of 1 million barrels of oil at $30 per barrel under terms of an unfavorable purchase commitment.

Notice that when the inventory is received, it is recorded at its current replacement cost, not at the $30 per barrel price specified in the purchase commitment. This practice is consistent with the idea that inventories should be valued at the ***lower-of-cost-or-market*** value.

"Gains" on Commitments Are Not Recognized Assume for a moment that at the end of 1990, the price of oil has been **$40** per barrel—a price well in excess of the cost specified in the refinery's purchase commitment. The facts underlying a favorable purchase commitment may be disclosed in notes to the financial statements, but no "gain" is recorded in the accounting records. A gain is not ***realized*** merely because inventory is purchased on favorable terms; gains are realized only when that inventory is ***sold*** at a price above cost.

Topics Deferred to Chapter 16

In this chapter, we have discussed the types of liabilities which are common to almost every business organization. Our discussion, however, does not address some of the largest liabilities of many large, publicly owned corporations.

In a large corporation, such liabilities as bonds payable, pensions and other post-retirement benefits, and deferred income taxes often dwarf such obligations as accounts payable and installment debt. Liabilities which relate primarily to large corporations will be discussed in Chapter 16, after we have explored more fully the nature and characteristics of the corporate form of business entity.

■ ■ ■   **** Supplemental Topic***
Accounting for Payrolls

In most business organizations, the largest expense accruing on a daily basis is payroll. In the airlines industry, for example, labor costs usually represent 40% to 50% of total operating expenses.

The task of accounting for payroll costs would be an important one simply because of the large amounts involved; however, it is further complicated by the many federal and state laws which require employers to maintain certain specific information in their payroll records not only for the business as a whole but also for each individual employee. Frequent reports of wages paid and amounts withheld must be filed with government agencies. These reports are prepared by every employer and must be accompanied by **payment** to the government of the amounts withheld from employees and of the payroll taxes levied on the employer.

A basic rule in most business organizations is that every employee must be paid on time, and the payment must be accompanied by a detailed explanation of the computations used in determining the net amount received by the employee. The payroll system must therefore be capable of processing the input data (such as employee names, social security numbers, hours worked, pay rates, overtime, and taxes) and producing a prompt and accurate output of paychecks, payroll records, withholding statements, and reports to governmental agencies. In addition, the payroll system must have built-in safeguards against overpayments to employees, the issuance of duplicate paychecks, payments to fictitious employees, and the continuance on the payroll of persons who have been terminated as employees.

INTERNAL CONTROL OVER PAYROLLS

OBJECTIVE 8 Describe the basic separation of duties in a payroll system, and explain how this plan contributes to strong internal control.

Every business needs to establish adequate internal control over payrolls. Without such controls, a business has little assurance that employees will be paid the correct amounts, or that payroll-related taxes will be computed correctly and paid on time. Failure to pay employees promptly and in the proper amounts is certain to damage employee morale. Failures to remit payroll taxes to tax authorities on schedule may result in severe fines and penalties. Finally, payroll historically has been an area in which poor internal control has sometimes led to employee fraud.

Payroll fraud can take many forms. Small-scale payroll fraud may consist of employees overstating the number of hours (or days) which they have actually worked. "Padding" the payroll—adding fictitious employees to the payroll in order to generate extra paychecks—is a larger-scale payroll fraud.

A basic means of achieving adequate internal control over payrolls is an appropriate separation of duties. In most organizations, payroll activities include (1) employing workers, (2) timekeeping, (3) payroll preparation and record keeping, and (4) the distribution of pay to employees. Internal control is strengthened if each of these functions is handled by a separate department.

Employment (Personnel) Department The work of the employment or personnel department begins with interviewing and hiring job applicants. When a new employee is hired, the personnel department prepares records showing the date of employment, the authorized rate of pay, and payroll deductions. The personnel department sends a written notice to the payroll department to place the new employee on the payroll. The personnel department also is responsible for notifying the payroll department of changes in employees' rates of pay and of persons whose employment has been terminated.

Timekeeping For employees paid by the hour, the time of arrival and departure should be punched on time cards. A new time card should be placed in the rack by the time clock at the beginning of each week or other pay period. Control procedures should exist to ensure that each employee punches his or her own time card and no other. The timekeeping function should be lodged in a separate department which will control the time cards and transmit these source documents to the payroll department.

In a computer-based payroll system, record keeping is simplified if the time clocks are on-line devices—that is, if they are connected directly with the computer system. In this way, the hours worked by each employee are entered automatically into the payroll accounting system.

The Payroll Department The input of information to the payroll department consists of hours reported by the timekeeping department and authorized names, pay rates, and payroll deductions received from the personnel department. The output of the payroll department includes (1) payroll checks, (2) individual employee records of earnings and deductions, and (3) regular reports to the government showing employee earnings and taxes withheld.

Distribution of Paychecks The paychecks prepared in the payroll department are transmitted to the ***paymaster,*** who distributes them to the employees. The paymaster should ***not*** have responsibility for hiring or firing employees, timekeeping, or preparation of the payroll.

Paychecks for absent employees should never be turned over to other employees or to supervisors for delivery. Instead, the absent employee should later pick up the paycheck from the paymaster after presenting proper identification and signing a receipt. The distribution of paychecks by the paymaster provides assurance that paychecks will not continue to be issued to fictitious employees or employees who have been terminated.

CASE IN POINT A California-based manufacturing company suffered large losses in a payroll fraud because it vested in production supervisors too much responsibility for payroll activities. Production supervisors oversaw the use of time clocks, distributed paychecks to production workers, and were allowed to terminate employees.

This combination of duties enabled several supervisors to maintain more than 20 fictitious names on the payroll. The supervisors simply did not report to the payroll department the names of employees who quit or were fired. Instead, they continued to punch time cards in the names of these former employees and abstracted the paychecks issued in these names. One supervisor even had a company time clock in his home, which enabled him to keep phantom employees "at work" on night shifts and on holidays.

The Operation of a Payroll System: A Summary

The operation of a typical payroll system is illustrated in the following flowchart. Notes have been made indicating the major internal control points within the system.

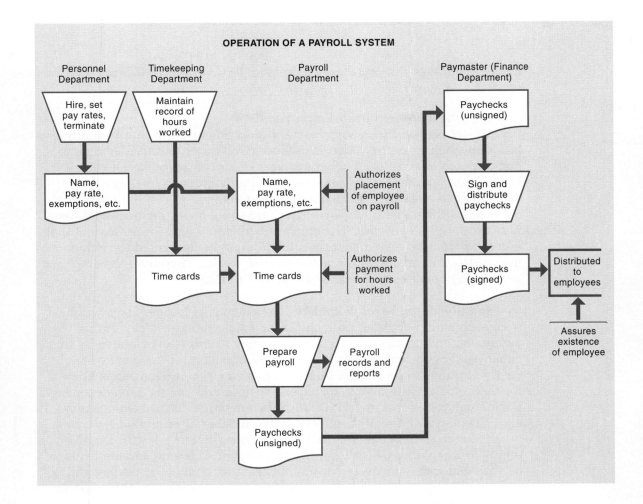

OPERATION OF A PAYROLL SYSTEM

Personnel Department — Hire, set pay rates, terminate → Name, pay rate, exemptions, etc.

Timekeeping Department — Maintain record of hours worked → Time cards

Payroll Department — Name, pay rate, exemptions, etc. (Authorizes placement of employee on payroll) → Time cards (Authorizes payment for hours worked) → Prepare payroll → Payroll records and reports → Paychecks (unsigned)

Paymaster (Finance Department) — Paychecks (unsigned) → Sign and distribute paychecks → Paychecks (signed) → Distributed to employees (Assures existence of employee)

THE COMPUTATION OF PAYROLL AMOUNTS

OBJECTIVE 9
Account for
a payroll,
including
computation
of amounts
withheld
and payroll
taxes on the
employer.

The actual preparation of a payroll, including the computation of dollar amounts, maintenance of payroll records, and printing of paychecks, is the responsibility of the payroll department. The dollar amounts associated with payrolls fall into three categories: (1) employees' gross pay, (2) amounts withheld from employees' gross pay, and (3) payroll taxes levied on the employer.

Gross Pay

Gross pay is the amount earned by the employees during the pay period. Except to the extent that employers **withhold** amounts for taxes or other purposes, all gross pay is payable directly to the employees.

Gross pay also includes compensation during sick days, holidays, and vacations. However, it does not include **fringe benefits,** such as health insurance paid by the employer or the use of a "company car." The distinction is that fringe benefits are not payable directly to the employees.

Gross pay must be computed separately for each employee. For employees paid an hourly wage, the payroll system must keep track of the **number of hours** that each employee works each day. In many cases, federal laws require that employees be paid at an overtime rate for hours worked in excess of 8 per day or 40 per week. For employees who receive sales commissions, the system must record separately the sales revenue attributable to each salesperson. The amount of an employee's gross pay affects the amounts of taxes that must be withheld and also the payroll taxes levied upon the employer.

Amounts Withheld from Employees' Pay

The **net pay** (or "take-home pay") of most employees is substantially less than their gross pay. This is because government authorities require employers to **withhold** specified amounts of income taxes, social security taxes, and medicare taxes from each employee's gross pay. (Employees often refer to amounts withheld as **deductions.**)

Taxes withheld from employees' pay are taxes levied **on the employees,** not taxes on the employer. The employer's role in withholding taxes is that of a tax **collector.** The amounts withheld must be forwarded to governmental tax authorities within a few days or weeks. Therefore, the employer records the amounts withheld as **current liabilities.**

Federal Income Taxes Withheld
The amount of income taxes withheld from each employee depends upon (1) the employee's gross pay during the pay period and (2) the number of withholding **exemptions** claimed by that employee. Each exemption causes a specified amount of the employee's yearly earnings to be exempt from income taxes. One exemption is allowed for the taxpayer, one for the taxpayer's spouse, and one for each dependent. Each employee is required to file with the employer a Withholding Allowance Certificate (Form W-4) indicating the number of exemptions claimed.

The Internal Revenue Service (IRS) provides employers with lengthy sets of "withholding tables" showing the amount of federal income taxes to be withheld from employees earning different amounts of gross pay and claiming different numbers of exemptions. The amounts of withholding indicated in these tables is intended to approximate the taxpayer's total income tax liability for the year.

Most states and a few cities also levy income taxes and require employers to withhold these taxes from employees' gross pay. The amounts withheld are computed in the same manner as federal income taxes withheld, but using different sets of tables. Because these situations involve a variety of rates, we will illustrate only the withholding of **federal** income taxes.

Social Security and Medicare Taxes
Under the terms of the Federal Insurance Contributions Act (or Social Security Act), qualified workers who retire after reaching a specified age are entitled to monthly retirement benefits (social security) and medicare benefits.[10] The taxes which fund these programs are called **FICA taxes.** Currently there are two FICA taxes: **social security tax** and a separate **medicare tax.**

FICA taxes are levied equally upon employees and upon their employers. Therefore, the social security and medicare programs are financed half through taxes paid by workers and half through taxes levied directly upon employers.

Employers are required by law to withhold from employees' paychecks the employees' share of FICA taxes and to forward the amounts withheld directly to the government. The employer also must pay FICA taxes of its own, equal to the total amount withheld from its employees.

---

[10] Survivors' benefits also are provided to the family of a worker who dies before or after reaching retirement age.

Two factors are involved in computing the amounts of social security and medicare taxes: the **base,** or amount of earnings subject to the tax; and the **rate** which is applied to earnings within the base. Different rates and bases are used in the computation of social security taxes and medicare taxes.

The rates used in computing FICA taxes have changed frequently in the past, and the bases change annually. In all of the examples and assignment material in this textbook, we will **assume** the following FICA tax rates and bases:

FICA rates assumed in examples and assignments

Assumed Rates and Bases for Computations of Social Security Taxes and Medicare Taxes

FICA Tax	Tax Rate	Base (Earnings Subject to Tax)
Social security	6.0%	The first $60,000 of gross pay earned during the year
Medicare	1.5%	The first $130,000 of gross pay earned during the year

These assumptions should approximate the actual rates and bases in effect during the next several years, and also have the advantage of producing relatively round dollar amounts.[11]

An example may clarify the concept of "earnings subject to FICA taxes."

Computing FICA Taxes: An Illustration   Assume that you earn a salary of $64,000. As you receive paychecks, 6% of your gross pay will be withheld as social security taxes until your total pay for the year reaches **$60,000.** Thus, a total of $3,600 in social security taxes will be withheld ($60,000 × 6%). No social security taxes will be withheld from the last $4,000 of salary that you receive, as your total earnings for the year now exceed the social security earnings base.

As the base for medicare taxes ($130,000) is **larger than your annual salary,** medicare taxes will be withheld from **all** of your gross pay. Over the year, $960 in medicare taxes will be withheld from your gross pay ($64,000 × 1.5% = $960).

Withholding for Items Other Than Taxes   The withholding of taxes is compulsory. Also, employers often are required by law to withhold amounts to satisfy legal claims against individual employees.

CASE IN POINT   Recent federal laws require employers to withhold court-ordered child support payments from the paychecks of all employees with such obligations. The amounts withheld are to be sent directly to the custodial parents. One automaker withholds child support from the paychecks of more than 6,000 of its employees. Every pay period, the automaker's payroll department must issue an additional 6,000 checks forwarding these support payments to the custodial parents.

In addition, employees **voluntarily** may authorize an employer to withhold additional amounts from their pay for a variety of purposes. Examples

---

[11]   The actual rates and bases in effect during any given year are enacted by Congress and appear in *Circular E,* "Employer's Tax Guide," published by the Internal Revenue Service.

include payments of union dues and insurance premiums, and contributions to savings plans, retirement plans, and charitable organizations.

Employer's Responsibility for Amounts Withheld   Amounts withheld must be forwarded promptly to the designated recipients, which include government tax authorities, custodial parents, insurance companies, and pension plans. From the employer's viewpoint, amounts withheld from employees' pay represent **current liabilities** until payment is sent.

Basic Payroll Records

The formats of payroll records vary greatly among different businesses, depending upon the number of employees and the extent of automation. However, there are two basic records common to the payroll system of every organization: the **payroll register** and the **employees' individual earnings records.**

Payroll Register   The payroll register is a special journal used for developing all of the information needed for processing and recording the payroll of a specific pay period. This journal includes a separate line of data about each employee. On this line, the employee's gross pay, various amounts withheld, and net pay are entered in separate columns. Thus, each line of the payroll register provides the data necessary for preparing one employee's paycheck, and also for updating the employee's individual earnings record. Totaling each column, on the other hand, provides information about the **entire** payroll, which is posted to the general ledger accounts.

To illustrate, assume that Data Management Co. has 40 salaried employees, who are paid monthly. A payroll register containing data relating to the March payroll is illustrated on the following page (along with the individual earnings record for one employee).

The illustrated payroll register includes separate columns for gross pay, four different types of withholding, and net pay.[12] The **totals** of these columns represent the expenses and liabilities associated with the issuance of paychecks to employees. (These totals do **not** reflect the payroll taxes on the employer for March.)

One common practice is to summarize the column totals of the payroll register in the form of a general journal entry, as follows:[13]

Journal entry summarizing the March payroll—except for taxes on the employer	*Salaries Expense*	*80,000*	
	Income Taxes Withheld		*12,200*
	Social Security Taxes Payable		*4,800*
	Medicare Taxes Payable		*1,200*
	Liability to Employees' Pension Plan		*2,320*
	Accrued Payroll		*59,480*
	To record the monthly payroll for March.		

---

[12]   The illustrated payroll register is highly simplified. An actual payroll register includes many more columns for such items as employees' social security numbers and several other types of withholding. For employees paid an hourly wage, additional columns would indicate pay rates and regular hours and overtime hours worked during the pay period. Actual payroll registers generally are a computer printout with, perhaps, 15 or more data columns.

[13]   A general journal entry is not actually necessary; the column totals could be posted directly from the payroll register to the general ledger accounts.

PAYROLL REGISTER

Payroll period ended: March 31, 19___

| Employee | Gross Pay | Amounts Withheld | | | | Net Pay | Check No. |
		Income Taxes	Soc. Sec.	Medicare	Pension Plan		
Abrams, H	$ 1,600	$ 227	$ 90	$ 24	$ 50	$ 1,209	841
Boice, C	2,000	232	120	30	100	1,518	842
Cato, Y	3,000	382	180	45	-0-	2,393	843
Zucco, R	2,400	184	144	36	240	1,796	880
Totals	$80,000	$12,200	$4,800	$1,200	$2,320	$59,480	_ _

EMPLOYEE EARNINGS RECORD

Name: Carol Boice   **Soc. Sec. #** 555-00-9999

Address: 900 Sea View Lane, Apt. D   **Date of Birth:** July 17, 1968

San Diego, CA 92101   **Date employed:** Aug. 3, 1992

Position: Commercial artist-grade 1   **Date of termination:**

Marital status: M   **Reason for termination:**

Withholding exemptions: 2   **Monthly salary:** $2,000

| Pay Period | Gross Pay | Year-to-Date | Amounts Withheld | | | | Net Pay | Check No. |
			Income Taxes	Soc. Sec.	Medicare	Pension Plan		
Jan.	$2,000	$2,000	$232	$120	$30	-0-	$1,618	762
Feb.	2,000	4,000	232	120	30	$100	1,518	802
Mar.	2,000	6,000	232	120	30	100	1,518	842
Total for quarter	$6,000	$6,000	$696	$360	$90	$200	$4,654	_ _
Apr.								
May.								

All of the accounts credited in this entry are current liabilities of the employer. Accrued payroll represents the net pay owed to employees; this liability will be discharged almost immediately through the issuance of paychecks. The liabilities for amounts withheld all will be discharged within a short period of time by remitting these amounts to the appropriate recipients.

Employees' Individual Earnings Records　An employer also must maintain an ***individual earnings record*** for each employee. These records contain basically the same information as does the payroll register: each employee's gross pay, amounts withheld, and net pay. The differences between a payroll register and the employees' individual earnings records are primarily in the manner in which the data are ***organized.***

A payroll register shows in one place all of the payroll data for ***one payroll period,*** including data for all employees. An earnings record shows in one place all of the payroll data ***for one employee,*** including data for every payroll period. The individual earnings record for one of Data Management's salaried employees is illustrated on page 537.

An employee's earnings record always includes a column showing the employee's ***cumulative*** gross pay earned thus far during the year. This year-to-date earnings figure determines when (and if) the employee's earnings exceed the bases subject to FICA taxes, and it also is used in computing payroll taxes levied upon employers. In addition, employers must report each employee's gross earnings for the year to the employee and to federal and state income tax authorities.

By January 31 of each year, employers must furnish each employee with a Wage and Tax Statement (Form W-2), showing the employee's gross earnings for the preceding calendar year and the amounts of all taxes withheld. The employer provides one copy of this form to the federal government, one copy to the state government, and three copies to the employee. When the employee files a federal income tax return, he or she must attach a copy of this form. A copy also must be attached to state income tax returns.

Payroll Taxes Levied upon the Employer

The discussion of payroll taxes up to this point has dealt with taxes levied on employees and withheld from their pay. From the viewpoint of the employing company, such withheld taxes are significant because they must be accounted for and remitted in a timely manner to the appropriate government agencies. However, ***payroll taxes are also levied on the employer.*** These taxes on the employer are expenses of the business and ***are recorded by debits to expense accounts,*** just as in the case of property taxes or license fees for doing business.

The Employer's Share of Social Security and Medicare　Employers are required to help finance the social security and medicare programs by paying taxes ***equal in amount*** to those withheld from their employees.

Federal Unemployment Insurance Tax　Unemployment taxes are levied upon employers for the purpose of funding programs that provide temporary assistance to unemployed persons. The ***FUTA*** (Federal Unemployment

Tax Act) *tax* is levied on *employers only* and is not deducted from the wages of employees. The rates of tax and the wage base subject to the tax are changed from time to time. For purposes of illustration in this textbook, we shall assume that employers are subject to federal unemployment tax at the rate of *6.2%* on the first $7,000 of each employee's earnings in each calendar year. However, the employer may take a credit against this tax (not in excess of 5.4% of the first $7,000 of each employee's wages) for amounts that are paid into *state* unemployment programs. As a result, an employer may be subject to a *federal* unemployment tax of only *0.8%* on wages up to $7,000 per employee.

State Unemployment Insurance Tax   All the states participate in the federal-state unemployment insurance program. The usual *state* unemployment tax rate is *5.4%* of the first $7,000 earned by each employee during the calendar year. Under this provision, the employer actually makes payment of the larger part of the FUTA tax directly to state governments which carry out the federal-state unemployment insurance program. This arrangement means that the FUTA tax is divided into two parts: the larger part, or 5.4%, of the first $7,000 of wages paid going to the state and the remainder (0.8%) to the federal government. The portion paid to the state is called *SUTA* (State Unemployment Tax Act) *tax.*

Entry Recording an Employer's Payroll Taxes   The entry to record the employer's payroll taxes is made at the end of each pay period, along with the entry recording the payroll. To illustrate, let us again consider the $80,000 March payroll of Data Management Co. The entry to record this payroll, including the taxes withheld from employees, appeared on page 537. Now, however, we are addressing the payroll taxes levied directly upon the *employer.*

The employer's liability for social security taxes and medicare taxes is exactly equal to the amounts withheld from employees—$4,800 and $1,200, respectively. By the end of March, we will assume that several of Data Management's employees have earned gross pay for the year in excess of the $7,000 base for unemployment taxes. Assume that a review of the employees' earnings records indicates that *$72,000* of the March payroll is subject to unemployment taxes. A general journal entry recording the payroll taxes levied upon Data Management in March appears below:

Journal entry to record payroll taxes on the employer	
Payroll Taxes Expense *10,464*	
Social Security Taxes Payable (equal to amount withheld from employees)	*4,800*
Medicare Taxes Payable (equal to amount withheld from employees)	*1,200*
FUTA Taxes Payable ($72,000 × 0.8%)	*576*
SUTA Taxes Payable ($72,000 × 5.4%)	*3,888*
To record employer's payroll taxes relating to the March payroll.	

All of the accounts credited represent current liabilities which must be paid within a short period of time.

"Hey—Can't We Do This by Computer?"

Because of the repetitious nature of payroll computations, payrolls are ideally suited to computer processing. In fact, accounting for payrolls was among the first applications of the computer in the business world. As an alternative to accounting for payrolls "in-house," small businesses often delegate this function to an outside agency. Many banks, for example, provide complete payroll accounting services for small business.

Given the complexities of payroll accounting, computer-based payroll systems are amazingly efficient. Often, the only input required for processing the entire payroll is the **number of hours** worked by each employee receiving an hourly wage. If time clocks are on-line devices, payrolls sometimes can be prepared without any manual input of data or manual computations. (Of course, the computer-based files must be updated for changes in pay rates, tax rates, or the personnel comprising the work force.)

In conclusion, it simply is **not cost-efficient** to account for payrolls manually in a business which has more than just a few employees.

Fringe Benefits

Many companies provide employees with various fringe benefits, such as group health insurance and a pension plan. The cost of fringe benefits usually is determined for the work force as a whole, rather than computed separately for each employee. Separate expense accounts and liability accounts are used in recording each type of fringe benefit.

To illustrate, assume that Data Management pays health insurance for its employees and also contributes an amount equal to 5% of their gross pay to an employees' pension plan. A general journal entry recording the cost of fringe benefits relating to the March 31 payroll is shown below:

Journal entry to record the cost of fringe benefits	*Health Insurance Expense*	*4,600*	
	Pension Expense	*4,000*	
	Insurance Premiums Payable		*4,600*
	Liability to Employees' Pension Plan		*4,000*
	To record the cost of fringe benefits provided to employees in March.		

The Total Cost of Employee Compensation

Our discussion of payrolls has been based upon the $80,000 March payroll of Data Management Company. Notice, however, that the company's **total** payroll cost in March actually amounts to **$99,064**—a figure substantially higher than the employees' gross pay. The "total payroll cost" includes the following elements:

Employees cost more than they're paid	*Gross pay earned by employees*	*$80,000*
	Payroll taxes levied upon employer	*10,464*
	Fringe benefits paid by employer	*8,600*
	Total employee compensation costs for the pay period	*$99,064*

These results are not at all unusual. An employer's total payroll cost generally exceeds employees' gross pay by 15% to 25%.

Distinction between Employees and Independent Contractors

Every business obtains personal services from **employees** and also from **independent contractors.** The employer-employee relationship exists when the company paying for the services has a right to direct and supervise the person rendering the services. Independent contractors, on the other hand, are retained to perform a specific task and exercise their own judgment as to the best methods for performing the work. Examples of independent contractors include CPAs engaged to perform an audit, attorneys retained to represent a company in a law suit, and a plumber called in to repair a broken pipe.

The **fees** paid to independent contractors are not included in payroll records and are **not subject to withholding or payroll taxes.** Also, independent contractors do not participate in the fringe benefits provided to employees.

END-OF-CHAPTER REVIEW

SUMMARY OF LEARNING OBJECTIVES

1 Define *liabilities;* distinguish between liabilities and owner's equity.

Liabilities are debts or obligations arising from **past transactions or events** and requiring payment (or the rendering of services) at some future date. Liabilities differ from owner's equity in several ways: liabilities mature, whereas owner's equity does not; liabilities are specific in amount, rather than being residual claims; liabilities have priority over owners' equity in the event of liquidation; and creditors usually do not have the right to control business operations.

2 Distinguish between current and long-term liabilities.

Current liabilities are those which mature within one year or the company's operating cycle (whichever is longer) **and** which are expected to be paid from current assets. Liabilities classified as long-term include obligations maturing more than one year in the future and also shorter-term obligations that will be refinanced, or paid from noncurrent assets.

3 Account for notes payable and the accrual of interest.

In this form of note, the face amount represents the principal amount of the liability—the amount upon which interest is computed. The notes payable account is credited with the face amount of the note upon issuance and debited with this amount when the note is paid at maturity. Interest is recorded whenever it is paid; in addition, interest which has accrued through the end of the accounting period is recognized in an adjusting entry.

4 Account for notes payable with the interest included in the face amount.

In this form of note, the face amount represents the principal amount of the liability plus the future interest charges for the life of the note. The entry to record issuance of the note includes a debit to the contra-liability account Discount on Notes Payable for the interest charges included in the face amount. The discount is amortized into interest expense over the life of the note. Amortizing the discount gradually increases the carrying value of the liability toward its face amount, which is the note's maturity value.

5 Prepare an amortization table allocating payments on an installment loan between interest and repayment of principal.
An amortization table includes four "money" columns, showing (1) the amount of each payment, (2) the portions of the payment representing interest expense, (3) the portion of the payment that reduces the principal amount of the loan, and (4) the remaining unpaid balance (or principal amount). The table begins with the original amount of the loan listed in the unpaid balance column. A separate line then is completed showing the allocation of each payment between interest and principal reduction, and indicating the new unpaid balance subsequent to the payment.

6 Compute the quick ratio, debt ratio, and interest coverage ratio, and explain their usefulness.
The quick ratio is quick assets divided by current assets; the debt ratio is total liabilities divided by total assets; and the interest coverage ratio is operating income divided by interest expense. All of these ratios measure the amount of "safety margin" in a debtor's ability to pay its liabilities and/or related interest charges. The quick ratio focuses upon short-term solvency, whereas the debt ratio and interest coverage ratios provide more insight into a debtor's ability to meet its obligations over the long term.

7 Define *loss contingencies*. Explain the criteria determining their presentation in financial statements.
A loss contingency is a possible loss (or expense) stemming from past events that will be resolved as to existence and amount by some future event. Loss contingencies are accrued (recorded) if (1) it is ***probable*** that a loss has been incurred, and (2) the amount of loss can be estimated reasonably. Even if these conditions are not met, loss contingencies should be disclosed if it is ***reasonably possible*** that a material loss has been incurred.

*8 Describe the basic separation of duties in a payroll system, and explain how this plan contributes to strong internal control.
The separation of duties needed to achieve strong internal control over payrolls includes placing in separate departments the functions of (a) employment (personnel), (b) timekeeping, (c) preparation of payroll checks, records, and reports, and (d) distribution of paychecks. With this separation of duties, payroll fraud such as placing fictitious names on the payroll, overstating employees' earnings, or retaining employees' names on the payroll after their termination would be next to impossible without collusion among departments.

*9 Account for a payroll, including computation of amounts withheld and payroll taxes on the employer.
Accounting for a payroll includes computing the gross earnings for each employee and making the proper deductions for FICA taxes withheld,

---

* *Supplemental Topic, "Accounting for Payrolls"*

income taxes withheld, and any other deductions authorized by employees. FICA taxes on the employer and FUTA and SUTA taxes must also be computed and recorded as expenses. The employer must maintain accounting records which will permit the filing of required reports and timely payment of both payroll taxes and amounts withheld from employees' checks.

We have now completed an overview of the manner in which businesses measure their financial position and profitability in conformity with generally accepted accounting principles. These principles apply equally to all forms of business organizations. In these early chapters, however, we have introduced many accounting concepts in the context of a sole proprietorship, which is the simplest and most common form of business organization.

In the next several chapters, we will apply our accumulated understanding of accounting to issues and situations which arise primarily in business entities organized as partnerships or as corporations.

KEY TERMS INTRODUCED OR EMPHASIZED IN CHAPTER 11

Accrued liabilities The liability to pay an expense which has accrued during the period. Also called *accrued expenses.*

Amortization of discount The process of systematically writing off to interest expense each period a portion of the discount on a note payable. Causes the carrying value of the liability to rise to the face value of the note by the maturity date.

Amortization table A schedule that indicates how installment payments are allocated between interest expense and repayments of principal.

Commitments Agreements to carry out future transactions. Not a liability because the transaction has not yet been performed, but may be disclosed in footnotes to the financial statements.

Contra-liability account A ledger account which is deducted from or offset against a related liability account in the balance sheet; for example, Discount on Notes Payable.

Debt ratio Total liabilities divided by total assets. Indicates the percentage of total assets financed by borrowing.

Discount on Notes Payable A contra-liability account representing any interest charges applicable to future periods included in the face amount of a note payable. Over the life of the note, the balance of the Discount on Notes Payable account is amortized into Interest Expense.

Estimated liabilities Liabilities known to exist but which must be recorded in the accounting records at estimated dollar amounts.

FICA taxes Payroll taxes imposed by the Federal Insurance Contributions Act (FICA) on both employees and employers for the purpose of funding the nation's social security program. There actually are two FICA taxes: social security and medicare.

Fringe benefits Portions of the compensation package offered to employees that are not paid directly to the employees. Paid health insurance is an example.

FUTA tax A tax imposed on the employer by the Federal Unemployment Tax Act (FUTA) based on amounts of payrolls. Designed to provide temporary payments to unemployed persons.

Gross pay   The total amount earned by an employee which is payable, at least in part, to that employee. Does not include fringe benefits.

Independent contractor   A person or firm providing services to a company for a fee or commission. Not controlled or supervised by the client company. Not subject to payroll taxes.

Interest coverage ratio   Operating income divided by interest expense. Indicates the number of times that the company was able to earn the amount of its interest charges.

Loss contingency   A situation involving uncertainty as to whether or not a loss has occurred. The uncertainty will be resolved by a future event. An example of a loss contingency is the possible loss relating to a lawsuit pending against a company. Although loss contingencies are sometimes recorded in the accounts, they are more frequently disclosed only in footnotes to the financial statements.

Maturity value   The value of a note at its maturity date, consisting of principal plus any interest payable at that date.

Medicare taxes   One of two FICA taxes. In this text, we assume these taxes are levied both upon employees and upon the employer at a rate of 1.5% upon the first $130,000 of each employee's gross pay. The actual tax rate and wage base may change from year to year.

Operating income   A subtotal in the income statement representing the revenue earned from customers less only operating expenses. Widely used in evaluating the relationship between earnings and interest expense, as operating income represents the earnings *before* deductions for interest expense and other "nonoperating" items.

Payroll register   A form of payroll record showing for each pay period all payroll information for employees individually and in total.

Principal amount   That portion of the maturity value of a note which is attributable to the amount borrowed or to the cost of the asset acquired when the note was issued, rather than being attributable to interest charges.

Quick ratio   Quick assets divided by current liabilities. A more stringent measure of immediate solvency than the current ratio.

Social security taxes   One of two FICA taxes. In this text, we assume these taxes are levied both upon employees and upon the employer at a rate of 6% upon the first $60,000 of each employee's gross pay. The actual rate and wage base may change from year to year.

State unemployment tax   A tax generally levied on employers only and based on payrolls. A part of the joint federal-state program to provide payments to unemployed persons. (In a few states a tax also is levied on employees.)

Wage and Tax Statement (Form W-2)   A form furnished by the employer to every employee showing the employee's gross earnings for the calendar year and the amounts withheld for FICA taxes and income taxes.

DEMONSTRATION PROBLEM FOR YOUR REVIEW

Listed below are selected items from the financial statements of G & H Pump Mfg. Company for the year ended December 31, 1994:

Note payable to Porterville Bank	*$100,000*
Discount on note payable (to Porterville Bank)	*1,000*
Income taxes payable	*63,000*
Loss contingency relating to lawsuit	*200,000*

Accounts payable	163,230
Mortgage note payable	240,864
Accrued interest payable (mortgage note)	1,606
Accrued payroll	18,700
Amounts withheld from employees' pay	2,940
Payroll taxes payable	1,260
Unearned revenue	25,300

OTHER INFORMATION

1 The note payable owed to Porterville Bank is due in 30 days. G & H has arranged with this bank to renew the note for an additional 2 years.

2 G & H has been sued for $200,000 by someone claiming the company's pumps are excessively noisy. It is reasonably possible, but not probable, that a loss has been sustained.

3 The mortgage note is payable at $8,000 per month over the next 3 years. During the next 12 months, the principal amount of this note will be reduced to $169,994.

INSTRUCTIONS

a Using this information, prepare the current liabilities and long-term liabilities sections of a classified balance sheet at December 31, 1994.

b Explain briefly how the information in each of the three numbered paragraphs affected your presentation of the company's liabilities.

SOLUTION TO DEMONSTRATION PROBLEM

a

G & H PUMP MFG. COMPANY
Partial Balance Sheet
December 31, 1994

Liabilities:

Current liabilities:

Accounts payable		$163,230
Income taxes payable		63,000
Accrued Interest payable (mortgage note)		1,606
Accrued payroll		18,700
Amounts withheld from employees' pay		2,940
Payroll taxes payable		1,260
Unearned revenue		25,300
Current portion of long-term debt (mortgage note)		70,870
Total current liabilities		$346,906

Long-term liabilities:

Note payable to Porterville Bank	100,000	
Less: Discount on note payable	1,000	$ 99,000
Mortgage note payable		169,994
Total long-term liabilities		$268,994
Total liabilities		$615,900

b 1 Although the note payable to Porterville Bank is due in 30 days, it is classified as a long-term liability as it will be refinanced on a long-term basis.

2 The pending lawsuit is a loss contingency requiring disclosure, but it is not listed in the liability section of the balance sheet.

3 The $70,870 of the mortgage note which will be repaid within the next 12 months ($240,864 − $169,994) is a current liability; the remaining balance, due after December 31, 1994, is long-term debt.

SELF-TEST QUESTIONS

The answers to these questions appear on page 561.

1   Which of the following is characteristic of liabilities, rather than of equity? (More than one answer may be correct.)

   a   The obligation matures.

   b   The capital providers frequently are entitled to receive interest payments.

   c   The capital providers' claims are *residual* in the event of liquidation of the business.

   d   The capital providers normally have the right to exercise control over business operations.

2   Which of the following situations require recording a liability in 1994? (More than one answer may be correct.)

   a   In 1994, a company manufactures and sells stereo equipment which carries a three-year warranty.

   b   In 1994, a theater group receives payments in advance from season ticket holders for productions to be performed in 1995.

   c   A company is a defendant in a legal action. At the end of 1994, the company's attorney feels it is possible the company will lose, and that the amount of the loss might be material.

   d   During 1994, a midwest agricultural co-operative is concerned about the risk of loss if inclement weather destroys the crops.

Use the following data for questions 3 and 4.

   On May 1, 1994, Thompkins Company borrowed $350,000 from the bank and agreed to repay that amount plus 12% interest at the end of one year.

3   Assume the note payable is drawn in the amount of $350,000 with interest stated separately. With respect to this note, Thompkins's financial statements for the year ended December 31, 1994 include:

   a   Interest expense of $42,000.

   b   An overall current liability for this loan of $392,000.

   c   An overall current liability for this loan of $378,000.

   d   Unamortized Discount on Notes Payable of $14,000.

4   Assume the note payable is drawn with interest included in the face of the note. Thompkins's adjusting entry on December 31, 1994 with regard to this note includes:

   a   A credit to Notes Payable of $14,000.

   b   A debit to Interest Expense of $14,000.

   c   A credit to Interest Payable of $28,000.

   d   A credit to Discount on Notes Payable of $28,000.

*5   Each of the following indicates a significant weakness in internal control over payrolls *except:*

   a   The paymaster is responsible for timekeeping and for distributing paychecks to employees.

   b   The personnel department is responsible for hiring and firing employees and for the distribution of paychecks.

---

*   *Supplemental Topic, "Accounting for Payrolls"*

   c The payroll department is responsible for preparing the payroll checks for signature by the paymaster, maintaining individual employees' earnings records of earnings and deductions, and filing required payroll reports with the government.

   d The payroll department prepares the payroll, the paymaster prepares and signs paychecks, and the paychecks are distributed by the timekeeping department.

*6 Hennesey receives a salary of $70,000 per year from Carling Company. Federal income taxes withheld amount to $9,000. The social security tax rate is 6.0% of the first $60,000, and medicare is 1.5% of the first $130,000. The state unemployment tax is 5.4% of earnings up to $7,000, and the federal unemployment tax is 0.8% of earnings to $7,000. Hennesey's take-home pay and the total cost to Carling Company of having Hennesey on the payroll (excluding fringe benefits) are, respectively:

   a $65,350 and $84,084   c $55,916 and $74,650
   b $61,000 and $75,084   d Some other combination

ASSIGNMENT MATERIAL

DISCUSSION QUESTIONS

1 Define *liabilities.* Identify several characteristics that distinguish liabilities from owner's equity.

2 Explain the relative priority of the claims of owners and of creditors to the assets of a business. Do all creditors have equal priority? Explain.

3 Define *estimated liabilities* and provide three examples. Are estimated liabilities recorded in accounting records?

4 Jonas Company issues a 90-day, 12% note payable to replace an account payable to Smith Supply Company in the amount of $8,000. Draft the journal entries (in general journal form) to record the issuance of the note payable and the payment of the note at the maturity date.

5 Howard Benson applied to the City Bank for a loan of $20,000 for a period of 3 months. The loan was granted at an annual interest rate of 12%. Write a sentence illustrating the wording of the note signed by Benson if

   a Interest is stated separately in the note.

   b Interest is included in the face amount of the note.

6 With reference to Question **5** above, give the journal entry required on the books of Howard Benson for issuance of each of the two types of notes.

7 What kind of account is Discount on Notes Payable? Where and how should it appear in the financial statements? What is the eventual disposition of amounts in Discount on Notes Payable?

8 Define *current liabilities* and *long-term liabilities.* Under what circumstances might a 5-year note payable be classified as a current liability? Under what circumstances might a note payable maturing 30 days after the balance sheet date be classified as a long-term liability?

---

* *Supplemental Topic, "Accounting for Payrolls"*

9 Is the failure to record an accrued liability likely to affect the income statement as well as the balance sheet? Explain.

10 Trong Corporation had a $300,000 note payable outstanding throughout the entire year. The note calls for interest to be computed at the annual rate of 9% and to be paid monthly on the last day of each month. How much accrued interest payable will appear in Trong's December 31 balance sheet? Explain.

11 Ace Garage has an unpaid mortgage loan of $63,210, payable at $1,200 per month. An amortization table indicates that $527 of the current monthly payment represents interest expense. What will be the amount of this mortgage obligation immediately **after** Ace makes this current payment?

12 A friend of yours has just purchased a house and has incurred a $50,000, 11% mortgage, payable at $476.17 per month. After making the first monthly payment, he received a receipt from the bank stating that only $17.84 of the $476.17 had been applied to reducing the principal amount of the loan. Your friend computes that at the rate of $17.84 per month, it will take over 233 years to pay off the $50,000 mortgage. Do you agree with your friend's analysis? Explain.

13 Among the long-term liabilities listed on Reese Corporation's balance sheet is "Long-term installment debt . . . $2,300,000." What **disclosures** should be made concerning this debt to assist users of the financial statements in evaluating the company's financial position?

14 Why is the **quick ratio** often considered a more useful measure of short-term solvency than the current ratio?

15 Would long-term creditors prefer that a corporation's **debt ratio** be high or low? How about its **interest coverage ratio?** Explain your answers.

16 What is the meaning of the term **loss contingency?** Give several examples. How are loss contingencies presented in financial statements? Explain.

17 What is the meaning of the term **commitment?** Give several examples. How are commitments usually presented in financial statements? Explain.

*18 MetroScape has 210 employees, but no liability for accrued payroll appears in the company's balance sheet. Assuming no error has been made, how can this be? Explain.

*19 The personnel department of Meadow Company failed to notify the payroll department that five hourly factory workers had been terminated at the end of the last pay period. Assuming a normal subdivision of duties regarding personnel, timekeeping, preparation of payroll, and distribution of paychecks, what control procedure will prevent the payroll department from preparing paychecks for these five employees in the current period?

*20 The type of payroll fraud known as "padding" a payroll is a more difficult maneuver under today's payroll accounting practices than it was a generation or more ago. What present-day factors make the padding of payrolls a complex and more difficult type of fraud?

---

* *Supplemental Topic, "Accounting for Payrolls"*

*21 Explain which of the following taxes relating to an employee's wages are borne by the employee and which by the employer:

  a FICA taxes

  b Federal unemployment compensation taxes

  c State unemployment compensation taxes

  d Federal income taxes

*22 Is the Salaries Expense account equal to take-home pay or to gross earnings? Why?

*23 Why is the cost to an employer of having an employee on the payroll greater than that person's gross pay?

*24 Distinguish between an employee and an independent contractor. Why is this distinction important with respect to payroll accounting?

EXERCISES

EXERCISE 11-1
Accounting
Terminology

Listed below are nine technical terms introduced or emphasized in this chapter:

Loss contingencies	*FICA taxes	Quick ratio
Amortization table	*FUTA taxes	Debt ratio
Maturity value of a note payable	Discount on notes payable	Interest coverage ratio

Each of the following statements may (or may not) describe one of these technical terms. For each statement, indicate the term described, or answer "None" if the statement does not correctly describe any of the terms.

  a Future interest charges included in the face amount of a note payable.

  b A tax levied upon employees but not upon employers.

  c A more stringent measure of short-term solvency than the current ratio.

  d A schedule allocating payments on an installment note payable between the portion representing interest expense of the current period and the portion reducing the principal amount of the debt.

  e Total liabilities divided by annual interest expense.

  f The risk that a loss may occur in a future period as a result of risks inherent in the nature of a company's business operations.

  g The amount owed on a note payable *excluding* any interest charges.

EXERCISE 11-2
Effects of
Transactions
on the
Accounting
Equation

Listed below are eight events or transactions of GemStar Corporation.

  a Made an adjusting entry to record interest on a short-term note payable which has the interest charge included in the face amount.

  b Made a monthly installment payment of a fully amortizing, 6-month, interest-bearing installment note payable.

  c Entered into a contractual commitment with a television network to purchase sixty 30-second commercials in each of the next 18 months. The cost is $75,000 per month, payable on the last day of the month in which the commercial is aired.

  d Came within 12 months of the maturity date of a note payable originally issued for a period of 3 years.

---

*   *Supplemental Topic, "Accounting for Payrolls"*

e Made an adjusting entry recognizing the accrued interest on a 30-year mortgage which is payable in 360 monthly installments.

f Estimated the income taxes expense relating to this month's business income.

*g Recorded a regular bi-weekly payroll, including the amounts withheld from employees, the issuance of paychecks, and payroll taxes upon the employer.

*h Remitted the amounts withheld from employees' paychecks to the designated recipients.

INSTRUCTIONS Indicate the effects of each of these transactions upon the financial statement categories shown below. Organize your answer in tabular form, using the illustrated column headings. Use the following code letters to indicate the effects of each transaction upon the accounting element listed in the column heading:

I = Increase   *D* = Decrease   *NE* = No Effect

	Income Statement			Balance Sheet			
Transaction	Revenue – Expenses =		Net Income	Assets =	Current Liab. +	Long-Term Liab. +	Owner's Equity
a							

EXERCISE 11-3
Financial Statement Presentation of Liabilities

Using the following information, prepare a listing and descriptions of the amounts which you would classify as (a) current liabilities and (b) long-term liabilities. If you do not list part or all of an item in either classification, briefly explain your reasoning.

Interest expense that will arise on interest bearing notes over the next 12 months	$134,000
Long-term mortgage note payable (of which $3,200 will be paid within the next 12 months)	800,000
Accrued interest payable on the mortgage note payable	2,600
Lawsuit pending against the company, claiming $500,000 in damages. Legal counsel can make no reasonable estimate of company's potential liability at this time	500,000
Note payable due in 60 days, but which will be extended for an additional 18 months	75,000
Three-year commitment to Charlene Doyle as chief financial officer at a salary of $140,000 per year	420,000
*Amounts withheld from employees' paychecks	6,100

EXERCISE 11-4
Two Forms for Notes Payable

On November 1, Metals Exchange, Inc., borrowed $250,000 from a bank, and promised to repay that amount plus 12% interest (per year) at the end of 6 months. (Remember that the interest is stated at an annual rate.) You are to prepare two different presentations of the liability to the bank on Metals Exchange's December 31 balance sheet, assuming that the note payable to the bank was drawn as follows:

a For $250,000, with interest stated separately and payable at maturity.

b With the total interest charge included in the face amount of the note.

---

*   *Supplemental Topic, "Accounting for Payrolls"*

EXERCISE 11-5
Interest In-cluded in Face Amount of Note Payable

On April 1, Tiger Truck Lines bought four trucks from Freeway Motors for a total price of $272,000. The transactions required Tiger Truck Lines to pay $80,000 cash and to issue a promissory note due in full 18 months later. The face amount of the note was $215,040, which included interest on the note for the 18 months.

Prepare all entries (in general journal form) for Tiger Truck Lines relating to the purchase of the trucks and the note for the current fiscal year ended December 31. Include the adjusting entries to record interest expense and depreciation expense to December 31. (The trucks are to be depreciated over an 8-year service life by the straight-line method. There is no estimated salvage value.)

EXERCISE 11-6
The Nature of an Accrued Liability

Late in 1992, Marco Construction borrowed $1 million, signing a 5-year, 7.2% note payable. The note calls for payment of interest charges monthly, on the sixteenth day of each month. Compute the following amounts relating to this note payable:

a Total interest that will be paid over the life of the note.

b Interest expense that will appear in Marco's income statement for **1994**.

c Accrued interest payable that will appear in Marco's balance sheet at **December 31, 1994**. (Compute interest payable based on a 360-day year.)

EXERCISE 11-7
Use of an Amortization Table

Blue Cays Marina has a $200,000 mortgage liability. This mortgage is payable in monthly installments of $2,057, which include interest computed at the rate of 12% per year (1% per month).

INSTRUCTIONS

a Prepare a partial amortization table showing the original balance of this loan and the allocation of the ***first two*** monthly payments between interest expense and reduction in the unpaid balance. (Round amounts to the nearest dollar.)

b Prepare the journal entry to record the ***second*** monthly payment.

EXERCISE 11-8
Safety of Cred-itors' Invest-ments

Shown below are data from the recent annual reports of two publicly owned toy makers. Amounts are stated in thousands.

	Mattel Inc.	Hasbro Inc.
Total assets	$830,273	$1,246,485
Total liabilities	554,103	444,161
Interest expense	50,029	24,288
Operating income	163,116	170,079

INSTRUCTIONS

a Compute for each company (1) the debt ratio and (2) the interest coverage ratio. (Round the debt ratio to one-tenth of 1%, and interest coverage to one decimal place.)

b In your opinion, which of these companies would a long-term creditor probably view as the safer investment? Explain.

EXERCISE 11-9
"He's Outta There!"

The Iron Dukes, a major league baseball team, signed a 2-year employment contract with Antonio Ramirez, a promising young catcher. The contract calls for Ramirez to receive an annual salary of $1.5 million, even if he is unable to play because of a "baseball-related" injury. Prepare the journal entry (if any is required) to record in the Dukes' accounting records each of the following events.

a Signing the contract with Ramirez.

b After one season, Ramirez sustains a "baseball-related" injury that terminates his major league baseball career.

If you do not consider a journal entry necessary for recording either of these events, explain.

*EXERCISE 11-10
Internal Control over Payroll

A supervisor in the factory of Barton Products, a large manufacturing company, discharged an employee but did not notify the personnel department of this action. The supervisor then began forging the employee's signature on time cards. When giving out paychecks, the supervisor diverted to his own use the paychecks drawn payable to the discharged worker. What internal control measure would be most effective in preventing this fraudulent activity?

*EXERCISE 11-11
Entries for Payroll and Payroll Taxes

For the week ended January 7, the payroll records of WHACK! Golf Products showed the following total salaries: sales employees $3,100; office employees, $1,900. Amounts withheld consisted of social security taxes of 6.0% and medicare taxes of 1.5% on all earnings for this period; federal income taxes, $680; and group insurance premiums, $410.

a After computing the amounts of FICA taxes withheld, prepare a general journal entry to record the payroll. (Do not include payroll taxes on the employer in this entry.)

b Prepare a general journal entry to record the payroll taxes expense to WHACK! Golf Products relating to this payroll. Assume that the federal unemployment tax rate is 6.2% of the first $7,000 paid each employee, and that 5.4% of this tax is payable to the state. No employee received more than $7,000 in this first pay period of the year.

*EXERCISE 11-12
Gross Pay, Net Pay, and Total Cost

In the current year, Del Mar Corporation had a total payroll of $1,450,000. Of this amount, $1,120,000 was subject to social security taxes; $1,355,000, to medicare taxes; and $510,000, to unemployment taxes. Income taxes of $165,000 were withheld, as were child support payments of $27,000. Fringe benefits were provided to employees during the year at a cost of $145,000.

Assume the social security tax rate is 6.0%, and the medicare rate is 1.5%. State unemployment taxes are levied at a 5.4% rate, and federal unemployment taxes at 0.8%. Compute for the year:

a The amount of payroll taxes levied upon Del Mar Corporation.

b Employees' total take-home pay.

c The total cost of employee compensation incurred by the employer.

d Express as a ***percentage*** the portion of the employer's total payroll costs that is paid in cash directly to the employees. (Round to the nearest full percent.)

PROBLEMS

Note: In this chapter, we provide an unusually wide variety of problem assignments. In order to make the full range of these assignments available to all users of the text, we present them in one consecutive series, rather than splitting them into A and B groups. This entire series is supported in both the Group A and Group B accounting work sheets.

PROBLEM 11-1
The Nature of Liabilities

Listed below are seven publicly owned corporations and a liability which regularly appears in each corporation's balance sheet:

a **Wells Fargo & Company** (banking): Deposits: interest bearing

b **The New York Times Company:** Unexpired subscriptions

c **The Hollywood Park Companies** (horse racing): Outstanding mutuel tickets

---

* *Supplemental Topic, "Accounting for Payrolls"*

    d American Greetings (greeting cards and gift wrap products manufacturer): Sales returns

    e Wausau Paper Mills Company: Current maturities of long-term debt

    f Club Med., Inc. (resorts): Amounts received for future vacations

    g Apple Computer, Inc.: Accrued marketing and distribution

INSTRUCTIONS Briefly explain what you believe to be the nature of each of these liabilities, including how the liability arose and the manner in which it is likely to be discharged.

PROBLEM 11-2
**Effects of
Transactions
on Financial
Statements**

Twelve transactions or events affecting Laptop Computer, Inc., are listed below:

a Made a year-end adjusting entry to accrue interest on a note payable which has the interest rate stated separately from the principal amount.

b Made a year-end adjusting entry to amortize the discount on a 120-day note payable with interest included in the face amount.

c A liability classified for several years as long-term becomes due within the next 12 months.

d Earned an amount previously recorded as unearned revenue.

e Made arrangements to extend for another 18 months a bank loan due in 60 days.

f Made a monthly payment on a fully amortizing installment note payable. (Assume this note is classified as a current liability.)

g Recorded income taxes expense for the fourth quarter in the year (October 1 through December 31). Payment will be made within 3 months.

h Recorded an estimated liability for future warranty claims on products sold during the current year.

i Entered into a 2-year commitment to buy all hard drives from a particular supplier at a price 10% below market.

j The company has a noncancellable commitment to purchase a specified number of semiconductors during each of the next 3 months at a fixed price. As of the balance sheet date, the current replacement cost of these semiconductors was well *below* this contractual purchase price.

k Received notice that a lawsuit has been filed against the company for $7 million. The amount of the company's liability, if any, cannot be reasonably estimated at this time.

*l Recorded the regular bi-weekly payroll, including amounts withheld from employees, the issuance of paychecks, and payroll taxes levied upon the employer.

INSTRUCTIONS Indicate the effects of each of these transactions upon the following elements of the company's financial statements. Organize your answer in tabular form, using the column headings shown below. Use the following code letters to indicate the effects of each transaction upon the accounting element listed in the column heading:

I = Increase   *D* = Decrease   *NE* = No Effect

	Income Statement			Balance Sheet			
Transaction	Revenue	− Expenses =	Net Income	Assets =	Current Liab. +	Long-Term Liab. +	Owner's Equity
a							

* *Supplemental Topic, "Accounting for Payrolls"*

**PROBLEM 11-3
Balance Sheet
Presentation of
Liabilities**

Listed below are selected items from the accounting records of GOOD 'N' LITE Candy Co. for the year ended December 31, 1994:

Note payable to Northwest Bank	$200,000
Discount on note payable to Northwest Bank	2,000
Income taxes payable	43,000
Accrued expenses and payroll taxes	53,800
Mortgage note payable	301,080
Accrued interest on mortgage note payable	2,508
Trade accounts payable	129,345
Unearned revenue	52,100
Potential liability in pending lawsuit	750,000

**OTHER INFOR-
MATION**

1 The note payable to Northwest Bank is due in 60 days. Arrangements have been made to renew this note for an additional 12 months.

2 The mortgage note payable requires payments of $10,000 per month for the next 36 months. An amortization table shows that as of December 31, *1995,* this note will be paid down to $212,430.

3 Accrued interest on the mortgage note payable is paid monthly.

4 GOOD 'N' LITE has been sued for $750,000 in a contract dispute. It is not possible at this time to make a reasonable estimate of the possible loss, if any, which the company may have sustained.

INSTRUCTIONS

a Using this information, prepare the current liabilities section and long-term liabilities section of a classified balance sheet at December 31, 1994. (Within each classification, items may be listed in any order.)

b Explain briefly how the information in each of the four numbered paragraphs affected your presentation of the company's liabilities.

**PROBLEM 11-4
Notes Payable;
Adjusting
Entries for
Interest**

In the fiscal year ended October 31, Harbor Corporation carried out several transactions involving notes payable. The company uses a 360-day year in making all interest calculations. Listed below are the transactions relating to notes payable.

June 1 Borrowed $20,000 from Holden Investments, by issuing a 60-day, 12% note payable to Holden as evidence of the indebtedness.

July 19 Bought office equipment from Western Office Supply. The invoice amount was $18,000 and Western Office Supply accepted as full payment a 3-month, 10% note for this amount.

July 31 Paid the Holden note for $20,000 plus interest.

Sept. 1 Borrowed $240,000 from Midwest Bank at an annual interest rate of 8%; signed a 90-day note with interest included in the face amount of the note.

Oct. 1 Purchased merchandise for $16,200 from Earthware Imports. Gave in settlement a 90-day note bearing interest at 10%. (Harbor Corporation uses a perpetual inventory system.)

Oct. 19 The $18,000 note payable to Western Office Supply matured today. Paid the interest accrued and issued a new 30-day, 12% note to replace the matured note.

INSTRUCTIONS

a Prepare journal entries (in general journal form) to record the above transactions.

b Prepare the adjusting entries needed at October 31, prior to closing the accounts. Use one adjusting entry to accrue interest on the two notes in which interest is stated separately (the Earthware Imports note and the Western Office Supply note). Use a separate adjusting entry to record interest expense accrued on the note with interest included in the face amount (the Midwest Bank note).

PROBLEM 11-5
Notes Payable Accruing Interest—An Alternate Problem

During the fiscal year ended December 31, Dunleer Corporation carried out the following transactions involving notes payable.

Aug. 6   Borrowed $11,200 from Tom Hutchins, issuing to him a 45-day, 12% note payable.

Sept. 16   Purchased office equipment from Harper Company. The invoice amount was $16,800 and Harper Company agreed to accept as full payment a 3-month, 12% note for the invoice amount.

Sept. 20   Paid the Hutchins note plus accrued interest.

Nov. 1   Borrowed $235,200 from Sun National Bank at an interest rate of 12% per annum; signed a 90-day note payable for $242,256, which included a $7,056 interest charge in the face amount.

Dec. 1   Purchased merchandise in the amount of $3,000 from Kramer Company. Gave in settlement a 90-day note bearing interest at 14%. (A perpetual inventory system is in use.)

Dec. 16   The $16,800 note payable to Harper Company matured today. Paid the interest accrued and issued a new 30-day, 12% note to replace the maturing note.

INSTRUCTIONS   **a** Prepare journal entries (in general journal form) to record the above transactions. Use a 360-day year in making the interest calculations.

b Prepare the adjusting entries needed at December 31, prior to closing the accounts. Use one entry for the two notes on which interest is stated separately and a separate entry for the Sun National Bank note in which interest is included in the face amount of the note.

PROBLEM 11-6
Notes Payable: A Comprehensive Problem

The following transactions relating to notes payable were completed by Desktop Graphics during the three months ended June 30.

Apr. 1   Bought office equipment for use in the business from Stylecraft, Inc., for $39,000, making a $5,400 cash down payment and issuing a 1-year note payable for the balance. The face amount of the note was $38,976, which included a 16% interest charge. Use one compound journal entry which includes Discount on Notes Payable.

Apr. 16   Paid $15,000 cash and issued a 90-day, 8%, $27,000 note to Hall Company in settlement of open account payable in the amount of $42,000.

Apr. 25   Purchased office equipment from ADM Company for $52,200, issuing a 60-day, 9% note payable in settlement.

May 11   Borrowed $216,000 from Manufacturers Bank, issuing a 90-day note payable as evidence of indebtedness. An interest charge computed at 17% per year was included in the face amount of the note.

June 15   Purchased merchandise on account from Texas Company, $54,000. (The company uses a perpetual inventory system.)

June 18   Issued a 60-day note bearing interest at 9% in settlement of the account payable to Texas Company.

June 24   Paid the 60-day, 9% note due to ADM Company, which matured today.

INSTRUCTIONS

a Prepare journal entries (in general journal form) to record the listed transactions for the 3 months ended June 30. (Use a 360-day year in computing interest.)

b Prepare adjusting entries to record the interest expense on notes payable through June 30. Prepare one adjusting entry to record the accrued interest payable on the two notes for which interest is stated separately (the Hall Company note and the Texas Company note). The other adjusting entry should record the amortization of discount on the two notes in which interest is included in the face amount (the Stylecraft, Inc., note and the Manufacturers Bank note).

c Prepare a partial balance sheet at June 30 reflecting the above transactions. Show "Notes Payable to Bank" (minus the discount) as one item and "Notes Payable: Other" (minus the discount) as a separate liability. Also include the interest payable in the current liability section of the balance sheet.

PROBLEM 11-7
Amortization Table and Installment Debt

On December 31, 1994, Kay Architectural Services purchased equipment at a cost of $20,215, paying $5,000 cash and issuing a 2-year installment note payable for $15,215. This note calls for four semiannual installments of $4,800, which include interest computed at the annual rate of 20% per year (10% per semiannual period). Payments are due on June 30 and December 31. The first payment is due June 30, 1995, and the note will be fully amortized at December 31, 1996.

Kay can retire this note at any interest payment date by paying the unpaid balance plus any accrued interest.

INSTRUCTIONS

a Prepare an amortization table showing the allocation of each of the four semiannual payments between interest expense and reductions in the principal amount of the note.

b Prepare journal entries to record the issuance of this note and each of the four semiannual payments in 1995 and 1996.

c Assume that on December 31, **1995,** Kay decided to pay the entire unpaid balance of this note. Prepare a journal entry to record the early retirement of this note. (Assume that the semiannual payment due on this date already has been paid.)

d Illustrate the presentation of this note in the company's balance sheet at December 31, **1994.** (Show separately the current and long-term portions of this debt.)

PROBLEM 11-8
Preparation and Use of an Amortization Table

On September 1, 1994, Kansas Steak House signed a 30-year, $540,000 mortgage note payable to Dodge City Savings and Loan in conjunction with the purchase of a restaurant. This mortgage note calls for interest at the rate of 12% per year (1% per month), and monthly payments of $5,555. The note is fully amortizing over a period of 360 months (30 years).

Dodge City Savings sent Kansas Steak House an amortization table showing the allocation of the monthly payments between interest and principal over the life of the loan. A small part of this amortization table is illustrated below. (For convenience, amounts have been rounded to the nearest dollar.)

Amortization Table
(12%, 30-Year Mortgage Note Payable for $540,000;
Payable in 360 Monthly Installments of $5,555)

Interest Period	Payment Date	Monthly Payment	Interest Expense	Reduction in Unpaid Balance	Unpaid Balance
Issue date	Sept. 1, 1994	—	—	—	$540,000
1	Oct. 1	$5,555	$5,400	$155	539,845
2	Nov. 1	$5,555	5,398	157	539,688

INSTRUCTIONS
a Explain whether the amounts of interest expense and the reductions in the unpaid balance are likely to change in any predictable pattern from month to month.

b Prepare journal entries to record the first two monthly payments on this mortgage.

c Complete this amortization table for two more monthly installments—those due on December 1, 1994, and January 1, 1995. (Round amounts to the nearest dollar.)

d Will any amounts relating to this 30-year mortgage be classified as **current** liabilities in the December 31, 1994, balance sheet of Kansas Steak House? Explain, but you need not compute any additional dollar amounts.

*PROBLEM 11-9
Payroll—A
Short Problem

For the one-week pay period ended January 6, the payroll records of Copper Kettle show that employees earned total salaries of $19,000.

Amounts withheld consisted of social security taxes computed at an assumed rate of 6.0%, medicare taxes computed at an assumed rate of 1.5%, federal income taxes of $2,120, child support payments of $1,250, and employees' voluntary contributions to their pension plans of $1,090.

State unemployment taxes are levied at a rate of 5.4%, and federal unemployment taxes at a rate of 0.8%. As this is the first pay period within a new year, no employee has yet earned more than the $7,000 base for unemployment taxes.

As a fringe benefit, Copper Kettle contributes an amount equal to 5% of employees' gross pay to an employee pension plan. (Payments to the pension plan are made at the end of each month.)

The weekly payroll is recorded on Friday, January 6, and paychecks will be issued to employees on Monday, January 9.

INSTRUCTIONS
a Prepare separate general journal entries to record the (1) salaries earned by employees, amounts withheld, and liability for net pay; (2) payroll taxes levied upon the employer; (3) cost of fringe benefits; and (4) issuance of paychecks.

b Compute the **total cost** to Copper Kettle of employee compensation for the first week of January.

c Assuming no change in pay rates, tax rates, or number of employees, would you expect the total cost of Copper Kettle's weekly payroll to increase or decrease as the year progresses? Explain.

*PROBLEM 11-10
Payroll—A
Comprehensive
Problem

The individual employees' earnings records of Surveillance Systems show the following cumulative earnings as of year-end.

Employee	Cumulative Earnings	Employee	Cumulative Earnings
Arthur, D. S.	$27,410	Hamilton, A. J.	$ 4,568
Barnett, S. T.	6,932	Maison, G. R.	19,720
Donahue, E. G.	167,010	Sanchez, K. U.	72,600
Gerdik, C. K.	43,790	Yamishire, L. T.............	57,380

Social security taxes were levied at the rate of 6.0% on the first $60,000 of gross earnings, and medicare taxes were levied at 1.5% of the first $130,000 earned. State and federal unemployment taxes were levied on the first $7,000 of each employee's earnings at a combined rate of 6.2% (5.4% state plus 0.8% federal).

During the year, the employer has withheld income taxes of $50,600 from employees' pay and has incurred costs of $54,100 relating to fringe benefits.

---

*   *Supplemental Topic, "Accounting for Payrolls"*

INSTRUCTIONS **a** Prepare a schedule with four data columns for each employee. In the first column, enter the employee's cumulative gross pay, as indicated above. In the remaining three columns, indicate the amounts of this gross pay which were subject to (1) social security taxes, (2) medicare taxes, and (3) unemployment taxes. Show totals for each column.

b Compute the following total amounts for the current year:

1 Total amount withheld from employees' pay (combine all types of withholdings).

2 Employees' net pay.

3 Payroll taxes levied upon the employer.

4 The employer's total payroll costs.

c Reconcile the total amount of employees' net pay [**b(2)**] with the total payroll costs incurred by the employer [**b(4)**].

***PROBLEM 11-11
Payroll—A
More Compre-
hensive Prob-
lem**

The Daily Chronicle is a large business organization, with perhaps 1,500 employees. For illustrative purposes, however, we will demonstrate certain payroll procedures using the earnings of *only three* of these employees in the month of October.

The monthly salaries of these three employees, and their cumulative gross pay for the year as of September 30, appear below:

Employee	Monthly Salary	Year-to-Date, Sept. 30
Adams...	$5,500	$49,500
Colbert...	2,000	6,500*
Henderson	6,300	56,700

* Colbert started work in mid-June.

This information is obtained from the employees' individual earnings records.

Assume that social security taxes are levied upon both employees and the employer at the rate 6.0% of the first $60,000 of each employee's gross earnings and that medicare taxes are levied at 1.5% of the first $130,000. Federal and state unemployment taxes are levied at the rates of 0.8% and 5.4%, respectively, upon the first $7,000 of an employee's pay.

The Daily Chronicle provides the following fringe benefits to all employees:

∎ Paid health insurance (cost: $110 per month for each employee)

∎ Contributions to an employees' retirement plan (at the rate of 5% of each employee's monthly salary)

Liabilities relating to fringe benefits are paid at the end of each calendar quarter.

INSTRUCTIONS **a** Prepare a four-column schedule showing payroll data for each employee. In the first column, enter each employee's gross pay for October. In the remaining columns, show the amount of this October's gross pay which is subject to (1) social security taxes, (2) medicare taxes, and (3) unemployment taxes. (If none of an employee's October salary is subject to a particular tax, explain why not. If only part of the employee's October salary is subject to a particular type of tax, show a supporting computation.)

Show totals in each of the four columns.

b Prepare three separate general journal entries, each dated **October 31,** summarizing for the month:

---

* *Supplemental Topic, "Accounting for Payrolls"*

1 The gross pay, amounts withheld, and net pay of these employees. In addition to the amounts withheld for FICA taxes, assume that a total of *$1,290* is withheld for federal income taxes, and *$300* is withheld for court-ordered child support. Paychecks will be issued on the next business day (November 3).

2 The payroll taxes *levied upon the employer.*

3 The cost of fringe benefits.

c Compute the *total cost* to The Daily Chronicle of having these three employees on the payroll during the month of October.

d List all of the current liabilities at October 31 resulting from this monthly payroll. Sequence this listing by dollar amount, from the largest liability to the smallest.

e The dollar amounts of some payroll liabilities arising each pay period follow a predictable pattern as the year progresses. Listed below are five current liabilities arising every pay period:

1 Social security taxes payable

2 Medicare taxes payable

3 Income taxes withheld

4 SUTA taxes payable

5 Accrued payroll (net pay)

For each of these obligations, explain whether you would expect the amount of liability arising every pay period to increase, decrease, or remain unchanged over the course of the year. If you expect the amount of a particular liability to change in later pay periods, explain *why.* Also indicate *when* during the year these changes should begin to occur.

For purposes of this discussion, assume the lowest-paid employee earns $9,000 per year, the highest-paid employee earns $250,000, and average annual pay amounts to $20,000. Also assume *no changes* during the year in pay rates, tax rates, personnel, or withholding exemptions claimed.

CASES AND UNSTRUCTURED PROBLEMS

**CASE 11-1
Liabilities: Recognition and Measurement**

The eight events listed below occurred at National Products on or near the end of the fiscal year, December 31, 1993:

a On October 12, the company was named as a defendant in a lawsuit alleging $20 million in damages caused by lead paint used on products manufactured by the company in the late 1970s. National's legal counsel cannot reasonably estimate the outcome of this litigation but believes that National probably has liability of at least $2 million. The suit is not expected to be settled for several years.

b On November 1, borrowed $900,000 from a bank, signing a 90-day note payable for $918,000 with interest included in the face amount.

c On December 15, signed a contract for the purchase of 50,000 barrels of oil per month in 1994 at a price of $18 per barrel, a price slightly below current market price.

d On December 31, purchased machinery at a price of $200,000 and signed a note payable due in 6 months with interest stated at the annual rate of 9%.

e On December 31, signed a 2-year contract with a labor union providing for a 6% increase in wage rates each year. The increase in wages for the first year is estimated at $540,000.

*f On December 31, processed the bi-weekly payroll. Paychecks totaling $289,000 were issued to employees. As these checks were issued after banking hours on December 31, no cash will be disbursed from National's payroll bank account until early in January 1994. The amounts withheld from employees' pay and payroll taxes on the employer, $51,000 and $27,000, respectively, were remitted to tax authorities on January 3, 1994.

g On December 31, estimated that warranty work costing $200,000 probably will need to be performed in future months on products which were sold in 1993 with a 12-month warranty.

h On January 5, 1994, a preliminary estimate was made of the company's income taxes expense for 1993. This expense was estimated at $2,800,000, of which $2,100,000 had already been paid in quarterly tax payments made during 1993. In March 1994 the company completed the preparation of its 1993 income tax return, and income taxes expense for 1993 was determined to be $2,779,806.

INSTRUCTIONS For each of these eight events, indicate the dollar amounts (if any) which should appear in either the current or long-term liability sections of National's 1993 year-end balance sheet. Also indicate any information that should be disclosed in the notes accompanying the 1993 financial statements. Briefly explain the reasons underlying your answers. (*Note:* As a practical matter, much of the task of preparing the 1993 financial statements must be performed in January 1994. Assume the financial statements are completed and issued on January 21.)

CASE 11-2
Loss Contin-
gencies?

Discuss each of the following situations, indicating whether the situation is a loss contingency which should be recorded or disclosed in the financial statements of Aztec Airlines. If the situation is not a loss contingency, explain how (if at all) it should be reported in the company's financial statements. (Assume that all dollar amounts are material.)

a Aztec estimates that $100,000 of its accounts receivable will prove to be uncollectible.

b The company's president is in poor health and has previously suffered two heart attacks.

c As with any airline, Aztec faces the risk that a future airplane crash could cause considerable loss.

d Aztec is being sued for $2 million for failing to adequately provide for passengers whose reservations were cancelled as a result of the airline overbooking certain flights. This suit will not be resolved for a year or more.

*CASE 11-3
"Hey—Can't
We Do This by
Computer?"

A W Clausen's is a large department store with a highly automated accounting system. The computer program used in processing payrolls includes all tax rates and withholding tables, employees' individual earnings records, and every employee's rate of compensation. Employees' gross pay is determined as follows:

Warehouse workers	*Hourly wages*
Office workers and management	*Monthly salaries*
Salespeople	*Monthly salary plus commissions*

Sales commissions are based upon the gross profit generated by the individual salesperson during the pay period.

---

* *Supplemental Topic, "Accounting for Payrolls"*

Employees are paid twice each month. Every payroll period, the computer program compiles a payroll register, updates the employees' earnings records, prints paychecks, and records in the general ledger both the payroll and the payroll taxes upon the employer.

INSTRUCTIONS

a Indicate the **additional information** which must be entered into this computerized system **each pay period** to enable the computer to perform the processing tasks described above. Suggest means by which each type of additional information might be entered into the computerized payroll system **automatically,** instead of manually.

b Describe a plan for distributing paychecks to the company's employees which is both efficient and contributes to strong internal control.

CASE 11-4
Are Rubbermaid's Checks Likely to Bounce?

The financial statements of **Rubbermaid Incorporated,** a publicly owned corporation, appear in Comprehensive Problem 5, which follows Chapter 20.

INSTRUCTIONS

a Compute Rubbermaid's (1) quick ratio, (2) debt ratio, and (3) interest coverage ratio at the ends of both 1989 and 1990. (Round each computation to one decimal place.)

b From the notes to the company's financial statements determine:

1 The amounts of long-term debt maturing in 1991 and in 1992.

2 Why the company classifies as current liabilities $8,500,000 in bonds (notes payable) which do not mature until 2009.

3 The interest rates and maturity dates applicable to the $39,191,000 shown by the company as long-term debt.

4 Whether the company appears to be confronting any significant loss contingencies.

c As of the end of 1990, evaluate the apparent safety of the claims of Rubbermaid's (1) short-term creditors and (2) long-term creditors. As part of your evaluation, indicate whether the safety of these claims appears to have increased or decreased since the end of 1989, and whether such change appears to be significant.

ANSWERS TO SELF-TEST QUESTIONS

1 a, b   2 a, b   3 c   4 d   *5 c   *6 d ($56,350 and $75,084; see below)

Computation for *6:

Take-home pay: $70,000 − $9,000 − $3,600 ($60,000 × .06) − $1,050 ($70,000 × .015) = $56,350

Total cost to Carling Company: $70,000 + $3,600 ($60,000 × .06) + $1,050 ($70,000 × .015) + $434 ($7,000 × .062) = $75,084

---

*   *Supplemental Topic, "Accounting for Payrolls"*

12 Partnerships

In prior chapters we have used the sole proprietorship as a model in our study of basic accounting concepts. In this chapter we focus on the partnership and the accounting issues related to this form of business organization. Among these topics are the maintenance of a separate capital account for each partner, the equitable division of partnership income or loss among the partners, the admission and the withdrawal of individual partners, and finally the liquidation of a partnership business.

After studying this chapter you should be able to meet these Learning Objectives:

1 *Describe the basic characteristics of a partnership.*
2 *Discuss the advantages and disadvantages of the partnership as a form of business organization.*
3 *Distinguish between a regular partnership and a limited partnership.*
4 *Account for the formation of a partnership.*
5 *Divide the net income of a partnership among the partners.*
6 *Account for the admission of a new partner and the withdrawal of a partner.*
7 *Account for the liquidation of a partnership.*

*T*hree types of business organization are common to American business: the sole proprietorship, the partnership, and the corporation. Partnerships are a popular form of organization because they provide a convenient, inexpensive means of combining the capital and the special abilities of two or more persons. The partnership form of organization is widely used in all types of small business and also in the professions. The Uniform Partnership Act, which has been adopted by most states, defines a partnership as "an association of two or more persons to carry on, as co-owners, a business for profit." A partnership is often referred to as a *firm;* the name of the firm often includes the word *company,* as, for example, "Adams, Barnes, and Company."

Significant Features of a Partnership

OBJECTIVE 1
Describe the
basic char-
acteristics of
a partner-
ship.

Before taking up the accounting problems peculiar to partnerships, it will be helpful to consider briefly some of the distinctive characteristics of the partnership form of organization. These characteristics (such as limited life and unlimited liability) all stem from the concept that a partnership is not a separate legal entity in itself but merely a voluntary association of individuals.

Ease of Formation   A partnership can be created without any legal formalities. When two or more persons agree to become partners, such agreement constitutes a contract and a partnership is automatically created. The contract should be in writing in order to lessen the chances for misunderstanding and future disagreement. The voluntary aspect of a partnership agreement means that no one can be forced into a partnership or forced to continue as a partner.

CASE IN POINT   Richard and Mike were friends and employees of the same large corporation. They became interested in forming a partnership to acquire a nearby small business being offered for sale for a down payment of $50,000. They felt that they could manage the business (which had two employees) in their spare time. Richard and Mike agreed that each would deposit $25,000 in a partnership bank account. There was no written agreement of partnership. Richard made his deposit from his personal savings; Mike had only $10,000 of his own but was able to obtain the other $15,000 from his brother-in-law, Joe, to whom he described the business with great enthusiasm. Mike then deposited $25,000 in the partnership bank account and the business was purchased. Richard had never met Joe and was not aware of his $15,000 investment.

A few months later, Joe became annoyed because he had received no return on his investment. He appeared suddenly at the business while Richard was there, stating that he was a partner and demanding to see the accounting records and the bank statements. Richard refused, and after an angry argument, Joe was forcibly ejected. The question of whether Joe was a "silent partner" caused bitter disagreement among all three of the principals. During this dispute, the business was forced to shut down because of lack of working capital. Richard, Mike, and Joe each retained an attorney to seek damages from the others.

Although a partnership may be at times a somewhat unstable form of organization, a written agreement of partnership might have avoided the problems encountered by Richard and Mike—and by Joe.

Limited Life A partnership may be ended at any time by the death or withdrawal of any member of the firm. Other factors which may bring an end to a partnership include the bankruptcy or incapacity of a partner, the expiration of the period specified in the partnership contract, or the completion of the project for which the partnership was formed. The admission of a new partner or the retirement of an existing member means an end to the old partnership, although the business may be continued by the formation of a new partnership.

Mutual Agency Each partner acts as an agent of the partnership, with authority to enter into contracts for the purchase and sale of goods and services. The partnership is bound by the acts of any partner as long as these acts are within the scope of normal operations. The factor of mutual agency suggests the need for exercising great caution in the selection of a partner. To be in partnership with an irresponsible person or one lacking in integrity is an intolerable situation.

Unlimited Liability Each partner is ***personally*** responsible for all the debts of the firm. The lack of any ceiling on the liability of a partner may deter a wealthy person from entering a partnership.

A new member joining an existing partnership may or may not assume liability for debts incurred by the firm prior to his or her admission. A partner withdrawing from membership must give adequate public notice of withdrawal; otherwise the former partner may be held liable for partnership debts incurred subsequent to his or her withdrawal. The retiring partner remains liable for partnership debts existing at the time of withdrawal unless the creditors agree to a release of this obligation.

Co-ownership of Partnership Property and Profits When a partner invests a building, inventory, or other property in a partnership, he or she does not retain any personal right to the assets contributed. The property becomes jointly owned by all partners. Each member of a partnership also has an ownership right in the profits.

Advantages and Disadvantages of a Partnership

OBJECTIVE 2 Discuss the advantages and disadvantages of the partnership as a form of business organization.

Perhaps the most important advantage of most partnerships is the opportunity to bring together sufficient capital to carry on a business. The opportunity to combine special skills, as, for example, the specialized talents of an engineer and an accountant, may also induce individuals to join forces in a partnership. To form a partnership is much easier and less expensive than to organize a corporation. Members of a partnership enjoy more freedom from government regulation and more flexibility of action than do the owners of a corporation. The partners may withdraw funds and make business decisions of all types without the necessity of formal meetings or legalistic procedures.

Operating as a partnership *may* in some cases produce income tax advantages as compared with doing business as a corporation. The partnership itself is neither a legal entity nor a taxable entity. A partnership does not actually pay income taxes. (However, it must *report* its annual net income to the Internal Revenue Service along with each partner's *share* of this net income. The partners then include their respective shares of the firm's net income in their *personal* income tax returns.)

Offsetting these advantages of a partnership are such serious disadvantages as limited life, unlimited liability, and mutual agency. Furthermore, if a business is to require a large amount of capital, the partnership is a less effective device for raising funds than is a corporation. Many persons who invest freely in common stocks of corporations are unwilling to enter a partnership because of the unlimited liability imposed on partners.

Limited Partnerships

OBJECTIVE 3 Distinguish between a regular partnership and a limited partnership.

In past years a number of businesses have been organized as "limited partnerships." This form of organization is widely used for businesses which provide tax-sheltered income to investors, such as real estate syndications and oil drilling ventures. However, limited partnerships are *not* appropriate for businesses in which the owners intend to be active managers. Recent tax legislation has also reduced greatly the income tax advantages formerly available to investors in limited partnerships.

A limited partnership must have at least one *general partner* as well as one or more *limited partners.* The general partners are partners in the traditional sense, with unlimited liability for the debts of the business and the right to make managerial decisions. The limited partners, however, are basically *investors* rather than traditional partners. They have the right to participate in profits of the business, but their liability for losses is limited to the amount of their investment. Also, limited partners do not actively participate in management of the business. Thus, the concepts of unlimited liability and mutual agency apply only to the general partners in a limited partnership.

In this chapter, we emphasize the characteristics and accounting practices of conventional partnerships rather than limited partnerships. Limited partnerships are discussed in depth in courses on business law and federal income taxes.

The Partnership Contract

Although a partnership can be formed by an oral agreement, it is highly desirable that a written partnership agreement be prepared, summarizing the partners' mutual understanding on such points as:

1 Names of the partners
2 The duties and rights of each partner, effective the specified date of formation of the partnership
3 Amount to be invested by each partner, including the procedure for valuing any noncash assets invested or withdrawn by partners
4 Methods of sharing profits and losses
5 Withdrawals to be allowed each partner

Partnership Accounting

As mentioned earlier in this chapter, a partnership **does not** constitute a **legal** entity with an identity separate from its owners. However, from a record-keeping and reporting point of view, a partnership does constitute a **separate and distinct accounting entity.**

An adequate accounting system and an accurate measurement of income are needed by every business, but they are especially important in a partnership because the net income is divided among two or more owners. Each partner needs current, accurate information on profits so that he or she can make intelligent decisions on such questions as additional investments, expansion of the business, or sale of an interest in the partnership.

CASE IN POINT   Rowe and Davis were partners in an automobile dealership and auto repair shop. Rowe was the active manager of the business, but Davis had supplied nearly all the capital. Aware that the firm was quite profitable, Rowe devised a scheme to become the sole owner by buying out his partner. In order to persuade Davis to sell his interest at a bargain price, Rowe deliberately began falsifying the accounting records and financial statements in a manner to understate the earnings of the business. Much of the revenue from auto repair work was not recorded at all, depreciation expense was overstated, ending inventories were understated, and the cost of new items of plant and equipment were charged to expense. The result was a series of monthly income statements which showed the business operating at a larger loss each month. Faced with these discouraging financial statements, Davis became pessimistic over the prospects for the business and was on the verge of selling his interest to Rowe at a price far below the balance in his capital account.

However, a friend suggested that before selling out, Davis should insist upon an audit of the business by a CPA firm. An audit was performed and revealed that the business was in fact highly profitable. When confronted by Davis with the auditors' findings, Rowe withdrew from the partnership and Davis became the sole owner.

Opening the Accounts of a New Partnership

OBJECTIVE 4 Account for the formation of a partnership.

When a partner contributes assets other than cash, a question always arises as to the value of such assets. The valuations assigned to noncash assets should be their **fair market values** at the date of transfer to the partnership. The valuations assigned must be agreed to by all partners.

To illustrate the opening entries for a newly formed partnership, assume that on January 1, Joan Blair and Richard Cross, who operate competing retail stores, decide to form a partnership by consolidating their two businesses. A capital account will be opened for each partner and credited with the agreed valuation of the **net assets** (total assets less total liabilities) that the partner contributes. The journal entries to open the accounts of the partnership of Blair and Cross are as follows:

Entries for formation of partnership.	Cash..	40,000	
	Accounts Receivable	60,000	
	Inventory..	90,000	
	Accounts Payable.....................................		30,000
	Joan Blair, Capital		160,000
	To record the investment by Joan Blair in the partnership of Blair and Cross.		

	Cash..	10,000	
	Inventory..	60,000	
	Land..	60,000	
	Building..	100,000	
	Accounts Payable.....................................		70,000
	Richard Cross, Capital		160,000
	To record the investment by Richard Cross in the partnership of Blair and Cross.		

Partnership accounting is similar to that in a sole proprietorship, except that separate capital and drawing accounts are maintained for each partner. These capital and drawing accounts show for each partner the amounts invested, the amounts withdrawn, and the appropriate share of partnership net income. In brief, each partner is provided with a history of his or her equity in the firm.

The values assigned to assets in the accounts of the new partnership may be quite different from the amounts at which these assets were carried in the accounts of their previous owners. For example, the land contributed by Cross and valued at $60,000 might have appeared in his accounting records at a cost of $20,000. The building which he contributed was valued at $100,000 by the partnership, but it might have cost Cross only $80,000 some years ago and might have been depreciated on his records to a net value of $60,000. Assuming that market values of land and buildings had risen sharply while Cross owned this property, it is only fair to recognize the ***current market value*** of these assets at the time he transfers them to the partnership and to credit his capital account accordingly. Depreciation of the building in the partnership accounts will be based on the assigned value of $100,000 at the date of acquisition by the partnership.

Additional Investments

Assume that after six months of operation the firm is in need of more cash, and the partners make an additional investment of $10,000 each on July 1. These additional investments are credited to the capital accounts as shown below:

Entry for additional investment	Cash..	20,000	
	Joan Blair, Capital		10,000
	Richard Cross, Capital		10,000
	To record additional investments.		

Drawing Accounts

The drawing account maintained for each partner serves the same purpose as the drawing account of the owner of a sole proprietorship. The transactions calling for debits to the drawing accounts of partners may be summarized as follows:

1 Cash or other assets withdrawn by a partner
2 Payments from partnership funds of the personal debts of a partner
3 Partnership cash collected on behalf of the firm by a partner but retained by the partner personally

Loans from Partners

Ordinarily any funds furnished to the firm by a partner are recorded by crediting that partner's capital account. Occasionally, however, a partnership may be in need of funds but the partners do not wish to increase their permanent capital investment in the business, or perhaps one partner is willing to advance funds when the others are not. Under these circumstances, the advance of funds may be designated as a loan from the partner and credited to a liability account. However, partnership liabilities to outsiders always take precedence over liabilities to partners.

Closing the Accounts of a Partnership at Year-End

At the end of the accounting period, the balance in the Income Summary account is closed into the partners' capital accounts. The profits or losses of a partnership may be divided among the partners in ***any manner agreed upon*** by the partners. However, this agreement should be carefully explained in the partnership contract. In the event that the partners ***do not*** have a formal profit-and-loss sharing agreement, the law requires all profits or losses to be ***divided equally*** among the partners.

In our illustration, let us assume that Blair and Cross have agreed to share profits equally. (We will discuss other profit-and-loss sharing arrangements later in this chapter.) Assuming that the partnership earns net income of $60,000 in the first year of operations, the entry to close the Income Summary account is as follows:

Closing income summary: profits shared equally

Income Summary	*60,000*	
Joan Blair, Capital		*30,000*
Richard Cross, Capital		*30,000*
To divide net income for the year in accordance with partnership agreement to share profits equally.		

The next step in closing the accounts is to transfer the balance of each partner's drawing account to his capital account. Assuming that withdrawals during the year amounted to $24,000 for Blair and $16,000 for Cross, the entry at December 31 to close the drawing accounts is as follows:

Closing the drawing accounts to capital accounts

Joan Blair, Capital	*24,000*	
Richard Cross, Capital	*16,000*	
Joan Blair, Drawing		*24,000*
Richard Cross, Drawing		*16,000*
To transfer debit balances in partners' drawing accounts to their respective capital accounts.		

Income Statement for a Partnership   The income statement for a partner-ship differs from that of a sole proprietorship in only one respect: a final section may be added to show the division of the net income between the partners, as illustrated below for the firm of Blair and Cross. The income statement of a partnership is consistent with that of a sole proprietorship in showing no income taxes expense and no salaries expense relating to services rendered by partners.

Note division of net income

BLAIR AND CROSS
Income Statement
For the Year Ended December 31, 19__

Sales		$600,000
Cost of goods sold:		
Inventory, Jan. 1	$150,000	
Purchases	460,000	
Cost of goods available for sale	$620,000	
Less: Inventory, Dec. 31	210,000	
Cost of goods sold		400,000
Gross profit on sales		$200,000
Operating expenses:		
Selling expenses	$100,000	
General & administrative expenses	40,000	140,000
Net income		$ 60,000
Division of net income:		
To Joan Blair (50%)	$ 30,000	
To Richard Cross (50%)	30,000	$ 60,000

Statement of Partners' Capital   The partners will usually want an explana-tion of the change in their capital accounts from one year-end to the next. A supplementary schedule called a ***statement of partners' capital*** is pre-pared to show this information. A statement of partners' capital for Blair and Cross appears below:

BLAIR AND CROSS
Statement of Partners' Capital
For the Year Ended December 31, 19__

Changes in capital ac-counts during the year

	Blair	Cross	Total
Balances, Jan. 1, 19__	$160,000	$160,000	$320,000
Add: Additional investments	10,000	10,000	20,000
Net income for the year	30,000	30,000	60,000
Subtotals	$200,000	$200,000	$400,000
Less: Drawings	24,000	16,000	40,000
Balances, Dec. 31, 19__	$176,000	$184,000	$360,000

The balance sheet of Blair and Cross would show the capital balance for each partner, as well as the total capital of $360,000.

Partnership Profits and Income Taxes

Partnerships Are Not Required to Pay Income Taxes   However, a partnership is required to file an information tax return showing the amount of the partnership net income and the share of each partner in the net income. Partners must include their shares of the partnership profit (after certain technical adjustments) on their individual income tax returns. Partnership net income is thus taxable to the partners individually in the year in which it is earned. The income tax rules applicable to investment in a partnership are quite complex; those complexities are appropriate to advanced accounting courses.

Note that partners report and pay tax on their respective shares of the net income earned by the partnership during the year and ***not*** on the amounts which they have drawn out of the business during the year. ***The net income of the partnership is taxable to the partners each year,*** even though there may have been no withdrawals. This treatment is consistent with that accorded a sole proprietorship.

The Nature of Partnership Profits

Profits earned by partnerships, like those earned by sole proprietorships, compensate the owners for (1) personal services rendered to the business. (2) capital invested in the business, and (3) "entrepreneurial risk"—that is, taking the risk that the investments of personal services and of capital may be lost if the business is unsuccessful. Recognition of these three factors is helpful in developing an equitable plan for the division of partnership profits.

If one partner devotes full time to the business while another devotes little or no time, the difference in the partners' contributions of time and effort should be reflected in the profit-sharing agreement. If one partner possesses special skills, the profit-sharing agreement should reward this partner's talent. Also, partners may each provide different amounts of capital to the business entity. Again, the differences in the value of the partners' contributions to the business should be reflected in the profit-and-loss sharing agreement.

To recognize the particular contributions of each partner to the business, partnership profit-and-loss sharing agreements often include "salary allowances" to partners and "interest" on the balances of partners' capital accounts. These "salaries" and "interest" are ***not expenses*** of the business; rather, they are ***steps in the computation made to divide partnership net income among the partners.***

In the preceding illustrations of the partnership of Blair and Cross, we assumed that the partners invested equal amounts of capital, rendered equal services, and divided net income equally. We are now ready to consider cases in which the partners invest ***unequal*** amounts of capital and services.

Dividing Partnership Net Income among the Partners

Partners can share net income or loss in any manner they decide upon; however, most profit-sharing agreements fall under one of the following types:

OBJECTIVE 5
Divide the
net income
of a partner-
ship among
the part-
ners.

1 A fixed ratio. The fixed ratio method has already been illustrated in the example of the Blair and Cross partnership in which profits were shared equally, that is, 50% and 50%. Partners may agree upon any fixed ratio such as 60% and 40%, or 70% and 30%.

2 Salary allowances to the partners, with remaining net income or loss divided in a fixed ratio.

3 Interest allowances on partners' capital balances, with remaining net income or loss divided in a fixed ratio.

4 Salary allowances to the partners, interest allowances on partners' capital balances, and remaining net income or loss divided in a fixed ratio.

All these methods of sharing partnership net income are intended to recognize differences in the personal services rendered by partners and in the amounts of capital invested in the firm.

In the illustrations which follow, it is assumed that beginning balances in the partners' capital accounts were Brooke Adams, $160,000, and Ben Barnes, $40,000. At year-end, the Income Summary account showed a credit balance of $96,000, representing the net income for the year before any partners' salaries or interest on capital account balances.

Salaries to Partners, with Remainder in a Fixed Ratio Because partners often contribute different amounts of personal services, partnership agreements often provide for partners' salaries as a factor in the division of profits.

For example, assume that Adams and Barnes agree to annual salary allowances of $24,000 for Adams and $48,000 for Barnes. These salaries, which total $72,000 per year, are agreed upon by the partners in advance. Of course, the net income of the business is not likely to be exactly $72,000 in a given year. Therefore, the profit-and-loss sharing agreement should also specify a fixed ratio for dividing any profit or loss remaining after giving consideration to the agreed-upon salary allowances. We will assume that Adams and Barnes agree to divide any remaining profit or loss equally.

The division of the $96,000 in partnership net income between Adams and Barnes is illustrated in the schedule shown below. The first step is to allocate to each partner his or her agreed-upon salary allowance. This step allocates $72,000 of the partnership net income. The remaining $24,000 is then divided in the agreed-upon fixed ratio (50-50 in this example).

Division of Partnership Net Income

	Adams	Barnes	Net income
Net income to be divided			$96,000
Salary allowances to partners	$24,000	$48,000	(72,000)
Remaining income after salary allowances			$24,000
Allocated in a fixed ratio:			
Adams (50%)	12,000		
Barnes (50%)		12,000	(24,000)
Total share to each partner	$36,000	$60,000	$ -0-

**Profit sharing;
salary allow-
ances and
remainder in a
fixed ratio**

Under this agreement, Adams's share of the $96,000 profit amounts to $36,000 and Barnes's share amounts to $60,000. The entry to close the Income Summary account would be:

Income Summary..	96,000	
Brooke Adams, Capital		36,000
Ben Barnes, Capital		60,000

To close the Income Summary account by crediting each partner with agreed-upon salary allowance and dividing the remaining profits equally.

The "salary allowances" used in dividing partnership net income are sometimes misinterpreted, even by the partners. These salary allowances are merely an agreed-upon device for dividing net income; they are ***not expenses*** of the business and are ***not recorded in any ledger account.*** A partner is considered an owner of the business, not an employee. Therefore, the services that a partner renders to the firm are assumed to be rendered in anticipation of earning a share of the profits, not a salary.

The amount of cash or other assets that a partner withdraws from the partnership may be greater than or less than the partner's salary allowance. Even if a partner decides to withdraw an amount of cash equal to his or her "salary allowance," the withdrawal should be recorded by debiting the partner's drawing account, ***not by debiting an expense account.*** Let us repeat the main point: ***"salary allowances" to partners should not be recorded as expenses of the business.***[1]

Because of this treatment of salary allowances, the net income reported by a partnership will differ from the net income that would be reported if the business were organized as a corporation. Corporations do record as expenses any salaries paid to owners.[2]

Interest Allowances on Partners' Capital, with Remainder in a Fixed Ratio
Next we shall assume a business situation in which the partners spend very little time in the business and net income depends primarily on the amount of money invested. The profit-sharing plan then might emphasize invested capital as a basis for the first step in allocating income.

For example, assume that Adams and Barnes agree that both partners are to be allowed interest at *15%* on their beginning capital balances, with any remaining profit or loss to be divided equally. Net income to be divided is $96,000, and the beginning capital balances are Adams, ***$160,000,*** and Barnes, ***$40,000.***

---

[1]   Some exceptions to this general rule will be discussed in advanced accounting courses.

[2]   The net income reported by a corporation also differs from that reported by an unincorporated business because the corporation is subject to income taxes on its earnings. Accounting practices of corporations are discussed in later chapters.

Division of Partnership Net Income

		Adams	Barnes	Net Income
Profit sharing; interest on capital and remainder in a fixed ratio	*Net income to be divided*			*$96,000*
	Interest allowances on beginning capital:			
	Adams ($160,000 × 15%)..........................	*$24,000*		
	Barnes ($40,000 × 15%)..........................		*$ 6,000*	
	Total allocated as interest allowances			*(30,000)*
	Remaining income after interest allowances			*$66,000*
	Allocated in a fixed ratio:			
	Adams (50%).......................................	*33,000*		
	Barnes (50%).......................................		*33,000*	*(66,000)*
	Total share to each partner	*$57,000*	*$39,000*	*$ –0–*

The entry to close the Income Summary account in this example would be:

Income Summary..	*96,000*	
Brooke Adams, Capital		*57,000*
Ben Barnes, Capital		*39,000*

To close the Income Summary account by crediting each partner with interest at 15% on beginning capital and dividing the remaining profits equally.

Interest allowances on partners' capital, like partners' salary allowances, are computational devices used in dividing partnership net income. This "interest" is not recorded as an expense of the business.

Salary Allowances, Interest on Capital, and Remainder in a Fixed Ratio The preceding example took into consideration the difference in amounts of capital provided by Adams and Barnes but ignored any difference in personal services performed. In the next example, we shall assume that the partners agree to a profit-sharing plan providing for salaries and for interest on beginning capitals. Salary allowances, as before, are authorized at $24,000 for Adams, $48,000 for Barnes. Beginning capital balances are $160,000 for Adams, $40,000 for Barnes. Partners are to be allowed interest at 10% on their beginning capital balances, and any profit or loss remaining after authorized salary and interest allowances is to be divided equally.

Division of Partnership Net Income

		Adams	Barnes	Net Income
Profit sharing; salaries, interest, and remainder in a fixed ratio	*Net income to be divided*			*$96,000*
	Salary allowances to partners........................	*$24,000*	*$48,000*	*(72,000)*
	Income after salary allowances.......................			*$24,000*
	Interest allowances on beginning capital:			
	Adams ($160,000 × 10%)..........................	*16,000*		
	Barnes ($40,000 × 10%)..........................		*4,000*	
	Total allocated as interest allowances			*(20,000)*
	Remaining income after salary and interest allowances			*$ 4,000*
	Allocated in a fixed ratio:			
	Adams (50%).......................................	*2,000*		
	Barnes (50%).......................................		*2,000*	*(4,000)*
	Total share to each partner	*$42,000*	*$54,000*	*$ –0–*

The journal entry to close the Income Summary account in this case will be:

Income Summary...	96,000	
Brooke Adams, Capital		42,000
Ben Barnes, Capital		54,000

To close the Income Summary account by crediting each partner with authorized salary, interest at 10% on beginning capital, and dividing the remaining profits equally.

Authorized Salary and Interest Allowance in Excess of Net Income   In the preceding example the total of the authorized salaries and interest was $92,000 and the net income to be divided was $96,000. Suppose that the net income had been only **$80,000;** how should the division have been made?

If the partnership contract provides for salaries and interest on invested capital, these provisions are to be followed even though the net income for the year is *less* than the total of the authorized salaries and interest. If the net income of the firm of Adams and Barnes amounted to only $80,000, this amount would be allocated as shown below:

Division of Partnership Net Income

	Adams	Barnes	Net Income
Net income to be divided			$ 80,000
Salary allowances to partners......................	$24,000	$48,000	(72,000)
Income after salary allowances.....................			$ 8,000
Interest allowances on beginning capital:			
Adams ($160,000 × 10%).........................	16,000		
Barnes ($40,000 × 10%)..........................		4,000	
Total allocated as interest allowances			(20,000)
Residual loss after salary and			
interest allowances			$(12,000)
Allocated in a fixed ratio:			
Adams (50%).....................................	(6,000)		
Barnes (50%).....................................		(6,000)	12,000
Total share to each partner	$34,000	$46,000	$ –0–

Left margin: Authorized salary and interest allowances in excess of net income

Notice that after deducting for the specified salary and interest allowances, there is a residual loss of $12,000 to be divided equally between Adams and Barnes. ***This does not mean that the partnership has generated a loss for the period.*** The partnership earned net income of $80,000. The residual loss allocation is simply a computational step in the process of dividing net income according to the partnership contract. The entry to close the Income Summary account will be as follows:

Income Summary...	80,000	
Brooke Adams, Capital		34,000
Ben Barnes, Capital		46,000

To close the Income Summary account by crediting each partner with authorized salary and with interest on invested capital and by dividing the residual loss equally.

Admission of a New Partner

An individual may gain admission to an existing partnership in either of two ways: (1) by buying an equity interest from one or more of the present partners or (2) by making an investment in the partnership. When an incoming partner purchases an equity interest from a present member of the firm, the payment goes personally to the old partner, and there is no change in the assets or liabilities of the partnership. On the other hand, if the incoming partner acquires an equity interest by making an investment in the partnership, the assets of the firm are increased by the amount paid in by the new partner.

OBJECTIVE 6
Account for the admission of a new partner and the withdrawal of a partner.

By Purchase of an Interest When a new partner buys an equity interest from a present member of a partnership, the only change in the accounts will be a transfer from the capital account of the selling partner to the capital account of the incoming partner.

Assume, for example, that Pam Lee has an $80,000 equity interest in the partnership of Lee, Martin, and Nash. Lee arranges to sell her entire interest to Paul Trent for $100,000 cash. Partners Martin and Nash agree to the admission of Trent, and the transaction is recorded in the partnership accounts by the following entry:

Incoming partner buys interest from present partner

Pam Lee, Capital	*80,000*	
Paul Trent, Capital		*80,000*
To record the transfer of Pam Lee's equity interest to the incoming partner, Paul Trent.		

Note that the entry in the partnership accounts is for **$80,000,** the balance of Lee's capital account. The entry does ***not*** indicate the price paid by Trent to the retiring partner. The payment of $100,000 by Trent to Lee was a ***personal transaction*** between these two individuals; it does not affect the assets or liabilities of the partnership and, therefore, is ***not*** entered in the partnership accounting records.

As a separate but related example, assume that Trent is to gain admission to the firm of Lee, Martin, and Nash by purchasing one-fourth of the equity interest of each partner. The present capital accounts are as follows: Lee $80,000; Martin, $60,000; Nash, $100,000. Assume also that Trent makes payment directly to the old partners, ***not to the partnership.*** The amount paid to each existing partner for one-fourth of his or her equity interest is a privately negotiated matter, and the amounts of these payments are ***not*** recorded in the partnership records. The only entry required in the partnership accounting records is the following:

Pam Lee, Capital	*20,000*	
Pat Martin, Capital	*15,000*	
Tom Nash, Capital	*25,000*	
Paul Trent, Capital		*60,000*
To record purchase of 25% of partner's equity by Paul Trent.		

This entry transfers to Paul Trent one-fourth of the balance formerly appearing in the capital accounts of each of the existing partners. The amounts actually paid to these partners by Trent are ***not recorded*** in the partnership accounts, because these payments did not flow into the partnership business entity. Thus, the transfer of ownership equity among the partners does not affect the assets, liabilities, or *total* partners' equity in the business.

By Investing in the Firm Now let us assume that an incoming partner acquires his or her equity interest by making an investment directly into the firm. In this case the payment by the new partner goes to the partnership and not to the partners as individuals; the investment therefore increases the partnership assets and also the total owners' equity of the firm. The portion of total equity granted to a new partner is based upon the terms negotiated by both existing and incoming partners. This equity interest (credited to the new partner's capital account) may be equal to, less than, or greater than the amount invested in the partnership by the incoming partner.

Assume that Ann Phillips and Judy Ryan are partners, each having a capital account of $100,000. They agree to admit Bart Smith and negotiate to grant him a one-half equity interest in the business upon his investment of $200,000 in cash. The recording of Smith's admission to the partnership is based on the following calculations:

Net assets (owners' equity) of old partnership	*$200,000*
Cash investment by Bart Smith	*200,000*
Net assets (owners' equity) of new partnership	*$400,000*
Smith's one-half interest	*$200,000*

To acquire an interest of $200,000 in the net assets of $400,000, Smith invested $200,000. In this situation, the amount of equity interest acquired is equal to the amount of Smith's investment. The entry to record the admission of Smith would be as follows:

Investment in business by new partner

Cash	*200,000*	
* Bart Smith, Capital*		*200,000*
To record the admission of Bart Smith to a one-half interest in the firm.		

Although Smith has a one-half equity interest in the net assets of the new firm of Phillips, Ryan, and Smith, he is not necessarily entitled to receive one-half of the profits. Profit sharing is a matter for agreement among the partners; if the new partnership contract contains no mention of profit sharing, the assumption is that the three partners intended to share profits and losses equally.

Allowing a Bonus to Former Partners If an existing partnership has exceptionally high earnings year after year, the present partners may demand a ***bonus*** as a condition of admission of a new partner. In other words, to acquire an equity interest of, say, $80,000, the incoming partner may be required to invest $120,000 in the partnership. The excess investment of $40,000 may be regarded as a bonus to the old partners and credited to their capital accounts in the established ratio for profit sharing.

To illustrate the recording of a bonus to the old partners, let us assume that Jane Rogers and Richard Steel are members of a highly successful partnership. Their partnership agreement calls for profits and losses to be divided 60% to Rogers and 40% to Steel. As a result of profitable operations, the partners' capital accounts have doubled within a few years and presently stand at $100,000 each. David Taylor desires to join the firm and offers to invest $100,000 for a one-third interest. Rogers and Steel refuse this offer but extend a counteroffer to Taylor of $120,000 for a one-fourth interest in the capital of the firm and a one-fourth interest in profits. Taylor accepts these terms because of his desire to share in the unusually large profits of the business. The recording of Taylor's admission to the partnership is based on the following calculations:

Calculation of bonus to old partners	

Net assets (owners' equity) of old partnership	*$200,000*
Cash investment by David Taylor	*120,000*
Net assets (owners' equity) of new partnership	*$320,000*
Taylor's one-fourth interest	*$ 80,000*

To acquire an interest of $80,000 in the net assets of $320,000, Taylor has invested $120,000. His ***excess investment,*** or ***bonus,*** of $40,000 will be allocated 60% to Rogers ($24,000) and 40% to Steel ($16,000), in accordance with the profit-sharing arrangement in effect prior to Taylor's admission.

The entry to record Taylor's admission to the partnership follows:

Recording bonus to old partners	*Cash*	*120,000*
	David Taylor, Capital	*80,000*
	Janet Rogers, Capital	*24,000*
	Richard Steel, Capital	*16,000*

To record admission of David Taylor as a partner with a one-fourth interest in capital and profits.

The total capital of the new partnership is now $320,000, in which Taylor has a one-fourth interest ($80,000). Rogers' capital account is $124,000 and Steel's capital account is $116,000 after admission of Taylor. Although in this case Taylor was also granted a one-fourth share of future partnership profits, ***the equity interest and the profit-sharing ratio of a partner are not necessarily the same.*** Old partners Rogers and Steel will set a new profit-sharing arrangement for the remaining 75% of profits to be divided between themselves.

Allowing a Bonus to New Partner An existing partnership may sometimes be very anxious to bring in a new partner who can bring needed cash to the firm. In other instances the new partner may possess special talents or may have advantageous business contacts that will add to the profitability of the partnership. Under either of these sets of circumstances, the present partners may offer the new member a bonus in the form of a capital account larger than the amount of the incoming partner's investment.

Assume, for example, that John Bryan and Merle Davis are partners in an existing partnership. Their partnership agreement calls for partnership profits and losses to be divided 70% to Bryan and 30% to Davis. Capital account balances are presently $120,000 for Bryan and $100,000 for Davis. Since the firm is in desperate need of cash, they offer to admit Kay Grant to a one-third equity interest in the firm upon her investment of only $80,000 in cash. The recording of Grant's admission to the partnership is based on the following calculations:

Net assets (owner's equity) of old partnership	$220,000
Cash invested by Kay Grant	80,000
Net assets (owners' equity) of new partnership	$300,000
Grant's one-third interest	$100,000

To acquire an equity interest of $100,000 in the new partnership's net assets of $300,000, Grant has invested only $80,000. The $20,000 excess allocated to Grant's capital account is a bonus to Grant from the existing partners, Bryan and Davis. A bonus granted to a new partner is charged to the existing partners' capital accounts according to the profit-sharing arrangement in effect **prior to** admission of the new partner.

The following journal entry records the admission of Grant to a one-third equity interest in the business, with allowance of the $20,000 bonus to Grant from the two old partners:

Entry for bonus to new partner

Cash	80,000	
John Bryan, Capital	14,000	
Merle Davis, Capital	6,000	
Kay Grant, Capital		100,000

To record admission of Grant to a one-third interest, and the allowance of a $20,000 bonus to Grant: 70% from Bryan and 30% from Davis.

Withdrawal of a Partner

To illustrate the withdrawal or retirement of a partner, assume the following data for the partnership of Acres, Bundy, and Coe:

	Capital Account	Share of Profits
Chris Acres	$ 75,000	20%
Brit Bundy	125,000	30%
John Coe	100,000	50%
Total partners' capital	$300,000	

We will use this data to illustrate the retirement of Coe and the treatment accorded the partners' capital accounts under several different assumptions.

Coe Sells His Interest to Someone Else The simplest case is when Coe, with the consent of Acres and Bundy, sells his equity in the business to a new partner. In this case, the payment by the incoming partner goes directly to Coe, and there is **no change** in the assets or liabilities of the partnership. Regardless of the price received by Coe, the only entry required in the partnership accounts is to transfer the $100,000 balance in Coe's capital account into the capital account of the new partner. This transaction is virtually the same as the one described on page 575 for the admission of a new partner by purchase of an interest.

Now let us change this situation slightly and assume that Coe sells equal amounts of his equity in the business to his fellow partners, Acres and Bundy. If Acres and Bundy pay Coe from their ***personal funds,*** the assets and liabilities of the partnership are again unchanged. Regardless of the price Acres and Bundy pay to Coe, the transaction is recorded in the partnership accounting records merely by transferring the $100,000 in Coe's capital account into the capital accounts of the remaining two partners, as follows:

Notice there is no change in total capital	*John Coe, Capital* *100,000*	
	Chris Acres, Capital	*50,000*
	Brit Bundy, Capital	*50,000*
	To record the sale of Coe's interest to Acres and Bundy.	

Coe's Interest Is Purchased by the Partnership Now let us assume that the partnership pays Coe in cash for his equity in the business. (The distribution of assets other than cash to a retiring partner will be discussed in advanced accounting courses.) If the partnership pays Coe exactly $100,000 cash for his equity—an amount equal to the balance in his capital account—the entry is simple: debit Coe's capital account $100,000 and credit Cash $100,000. However, the payment to Coe may be greater or less than the balance in his capital account.

Partnership Pays Coe More Than the Balance in His Capital Account A partner withdrawing from a partnership naturally expects to receive an amount for his or her equity that reflects the ***current market value*** of the partnership's net assets. Often, current market values exceed the book values appearing in the firm's balance sheet. For example, assets such as real estate may have appreciated greatly in value since they were acquired by the business. Also, if the business has been successful, it may have developed ***unrecorded goodwill.***[3] Thus, the settlement paid to a retiring partner often is greater than the balance in the partner's capital account.

An amount paid to a retiring partner in excess of the balance in his or her capital account is treated as a ***bonus to the withdrawing partner*** and comes out of the capital accounts of the continuing partners. This bonus is charged against (debited to) the continuing partners' capital accounts in proportion to their ***relative*** profit- and loss-sharing ratio.

The term ***relative profit-sharing ratio*** describes the relationship between the profit- and loss-sharing ratios of the continuing partners, excluding the share formerly received by the retiring partner. The relative profit- and loss-sharing ratio of each continuing partner is computed by the following formula:

$$\frac{\textbf{Percentage Formerly Received by This Partner}}{\textbf{Total Percentage Formerly Received by All Continuing Partners}}$$

Based upon this formula, the relative profit- and loss-sharing ratios of Acres and Bundy are as follows:

Acres (20% ÷ 50%)	*40%*
Bundy (30% ÷ 50%)	*60%*

---

[3]   As discussed in Chapter 10, goodwill is recorded only when it is purchased.

Assume now that Coe receives **$140,000** in cash from the partnership in full settlement of his equity in the firm. As Coe's capital account has a balance of only $100,000, he is receiving a **$40,000 bonus** from Acres and Bundy. This bonus is charged against the capital accounts of Acres and Bundy in relation to their relative profit- and loss-sharing ratios (Acres, 40%; Bundy, 60%). Thus, Coe's withdrawal from the firm is recorded as follows:

Bonus paid to withdrawing partner

John Coe, Capital (retiring partner)	100,000	
Chris Acres, Capital	16,000	
Brit Bundy, Capital	24,000	
Cash		140,000

To record the withdrawal of partner Coe, and payment of his capital account plus a bonus of $40,000. Bonus charged 40% to Acres, 60% to Bundy.

Partnership Pays Coe Less Than the Balance in His Capital Account Now assume that Coe is willing to accept a cash payment of **only $80,000** in full settlement of his $100,000 capital account. This situation might arise if, for example, Coe has a pressing need for cash or the future of the firm is jeopardized by loss contingencies not yet recorded in its balance sheet accounts. In our example, the continuing partners' equity in the firm will **increase** by a total of $20,000 as a result of Coe's withdrawal. Acres and Bundy should divide this **"bonus to the continuing partners"** in their relative profit- and loss-sharing ratios. The entry is:

Payment to withdrawing partner of less than book equity

John Coe, Capital	100,000	
Cash		80,000
Chris Acres		8,000
Brit Bundy		12,000

To record the withdrawal of Coe, and settlement in full for $20,000 less than the balance of his capital account. Bonus to continuing partners allocated 40% to Acres, 60% to Bundy.

Death of a Partner

A partnership is dissolved by the death of any member. To determine the amount owing to the estate of the deceased partner, it is usually necessary to close the accounts and prepare financial statements. This serves to credit all partners with their individual shares of the net income earned during the fractional accounting period ending with the date of **dissolution.**

The partnership agreement may prescribe procedures for making settlement with the estate of a deceased partner. Such procedures often include an audit by certified public accountants, appraisal of assets, and computation of goodwill. If payment to the estate must be delayed, the amount owed should be carried in a liability account replacing the deceased partner's capital account.

Insurance on Lives of Partners Members of a partnership often obtain life insurance policies which name the partnership as the beneficiary. Upon the death of a partner, the cash collected from the insurance company is used to pay the estate of the deceased partner. In the absence of insurance on the lives of partners, there might be insufficient cash available to pay the deceased partner's estate without disrupting the operation of the business.

Liquidation of a Partnership

OBJECTIVE 7
*Account for
the liquida-
tion of a
partnership.*

A partnership is terminated or dissolved whenever a new partner is added or an old partner withdraws. The termination or dissolution of a partnership, however, does not necessarily indicate that the business is to be discontinued. Often the business continues with scarcely any outward evidence of the change in membership of the firm. Termination of a partnership indicates a change in the membership of the firm, which may or may not be followed by liquidation.

The process of breaking up and discontinuing a partnership business is called **liquidation.** Liquidation of a partnership spells an end to the business. If the business is to be discontinued, the assets will be sold, the liabilities paid, and the remaining cash distributed to the partners.

Sale of the Business The partnership of Royal, Simms, and Tate sells its business to the North Corporation. The balance sheet appears as follows:

Partnership at
time of sale

ROYAL, SIMMS, AND TATE
Balance Sheet
December 31, 19__

Cash...........................	$ 50,000	Accounts payable	$100,000
Inventory.......................	200,000	Ann Royal, capital..............	140,000
Other assets	150,000	Ed Simms, capital	120,000
		Jon Tate, capital................	40,000
Total...........................	$400,000	Total............................	$400,000

The terms of sale provide that the inventory and other assets will be sold to the North Corporation for a consideration of $230,000, a price resulting in a loss of $120,000. The liabilities will not be transferred to North Corporation, but will be paid by the partnership out of existing cash plus the proceeds of the sale, prior to any distribution of cash to the partners. The entry to record the sale of the inventory and other assets to North Corporation is:

Entry to record
the sale of the
business

Cash...	230,000	
Loss on Sale of Business....................................	120,000	
Inventory		200,000
Other Assets...		150,000
To record the sale of all assets other than cash to North Corporation.		

Division of the Gain or Loss from Sale of the Business The gain or loss from the sale of the business must be divided among the partners in the agreed profit- and loss-sharing ratio *before* any cash is distributed to them. The amount of cash to which each partner is entitled in liquidation cannot be determined until each capital account has been increased or decreased by the proper share of the gain or loss on disposal of the assets. Assuming that Royal, Simms, and Tate share profits and losses equally, the entry to allocate the $120,000 loss on the sale of the business will be as follows:

Entry to divide loss on sale	*Ann Royal, Capital*..	*40,000*
	Ed Simms, Capital..	*40,000*
	Jon Tate, Capital	*40,000*
	Loss on Sale of Business	*120,000*
	To divide the loss on the sale of the business among the partners in the established ratio for sharing profits and losses.	

Distribution of Cash The balance sheet of Royal, Simms, and Tate appears as follows after the loss on the sale of the assets has been entered in the partners' capital accounts:

Balance sheet after sale of assets

ROYAL, SIMMS, AND TATE			
Balance Sheet			
(After the Sale of All Assets Except Cash)			
Cash.........................	*$280,000*	*Accounts payable*	*$100,000*
		Ann Royal, capital	*100,000*
		Ed Simms, capital	*80,000*
		Jon Tate, capital..............	*–0–*
Total	*$280,000*	*Total*	*$280,000*

The creditors must be paid in full before cash is distributed to the partners. The sequence of entries will be as follows:

(1) Pay creditors	*Accounts Payable*	*100,000*
	Cash	*100,000*
	To pay the creditors in full.	

(2) Pay partners	*Ann Royal, Capital*..	*100,000*
	Ed Simms, Capital...	*80,000*
	Cash	*180,000*
	To complete liquidation of the business by distributing the remaining cash to the partners according to the balances in their capital accounts.	

Note that the equal division of the $120,000 loss on the sale of the business reduced the capital account of Jon Tate to zero; therefore, Tate received nothing when the cash was distributed to the partners. This action is consistent with the original agreement of the partners to share profits and losses equally. In working partnership liquidation problems, accounting students sometimes make the error of dividing the cash among the partners in the profit- and loss-sharing ratio. A profit- and loss-sharing ratio means just what the name indicates; it is a ratio for sharing profits and losses, ***not a ratio for sharing cash or any other asset.*** The amount of cash which a partner should receive in liquidation will be indicated by the balance in his or her capital account ***after*** the gain or loss from the disposal of assets has been divided among the partners in the agreed ratio for sharing profits and losses.

Treatment of Debit Balance in a Capital Account To illustrate this situation, let us change our assumptions concerning the sale of the assets by the firm of Royal, Simms, and Tate, and say that the partnership assets (except cash) are sold to North Corporation for $206,000. The amount of cash received by the partnership is $24,000 less than in the prior example, and the loss incurred on the sale of assets is ***$144,000*** rather than the ***$120,000*** previously illustrated. Tate's one-third share of a $144,000 loss would be $48,000, which would wipe out the $40,000 credit balance in his capital account and create an ***$8,000 debit balance.*** After the liabilities are paid, a balance sheet for the partnership would appear as follows:

<table>
<tr><td colspan="4" align="center">**ROYAL, SIMMS, AND TATE**
Balance Sheet
(After the Sale of All Assets Except Cash)</td></tr>
<tr><td>*Cash*.........................</td><td>*$156,000*</td><td>*Ann Royal, capital*............</td><td>*$ 92,000*</td></tr>
<tr><td></td><td></td><td>*Ed Simms, capital*............</td><td>*72,000*</td></tr>
<tr><td></td><td></td><td>*Jon Tate, capital (deficiency)*..</td><td>*(8,000)*</td></tr>
<tr><td>*Total*.......................</td><td>*$156,000*</td><td>*Total*........................</td><td>*$156,000*</td></tr>
</table>

Tate now owes $8,000 to the partnership

To eliminate the debit balance in his capital account, Tate should pay $8,000 to the partnership. If Tate makes this payment, the balance in his capital account will become zero, and the cash on hand will be increased to $164,000, which is just enough to pay Royal and Simms the balances shown in their capital accounts.

If Tate is unable to pay the $8,000 due to the firm, how should the $156,000 of cash on hand be divided between Royal and Simms, whose capital accounts stand at $92,000 and $72,000, respectively? Failure of Tate to pay in the debit balance means an additional loss to Royal and Simms; according to the original partnership agreement, Royal and Simms have equal profit- and loss-sharing ratios. Therefore, each must absorb $4,000 additional loss resulting from Tate's inability to pay the $8,000 due to the partnership.[4] The $156,000 of cash on hand should be divided between Royal and Simms in such a manner that the capital account of each will be paid down to $4,000, their respective shares of the additional loss. The journal entry to record this distribution of cash to Royal and Simms is as follows:

---

[4]   If the profit- and loss-sharing ratios of Royal and Simms were not equal, the $8,000 loss would be absorbed by Royal and Simms according to their ***relative*** profit- and loss-sharing ratios. The computation of each partner's share of the additional loss would be similar to the allocation of the bonus paid by or received by remaining partners illustrated on page 580.

Entry to record distribution of cash on hand

Ann Royal, Capital...	88,000	
Ed Simms, Capital..	68,000	
Cash		156,000

To divide the remaining cash by paying down the capital accounts of Royal and Simms to a balance of $4,000 each, representing the division of Tate's loss between them.

After this entry has been posted, the only accounts still open in the partnership records will be the capital accounts of the three partners. A trial balance of the ledger will appear as follows:

ROYAL, SIMMS, AND TATE
Trial Balance
(After Distribution of Cash)

Trial balance after cash distribution

Ann Royal, capital		$4,000
Ed Simms, capital		4,000
Jon Tate, capital (deficiency)..	$8,000	
	$8,000	$3,000

If Tate is later able to pay in the $8,000 debit balance, Royal and Simms will then receive the additional $4,000 each indicated by the credit balances in their accounts. If Tate is not able to make good the debit balance, the distribution of cash to Royal and Simms will have been equitable under the circumstances.

END-OF-CHAPTER REVIEW

SUMMARY OF CHAPTER LEARNING OBJECTIVES

1 **Describe the basic characteristics of a partnership.**

A partnership is a voluntary association of two or more persons who agree to combine their efforts and resources to carry on as co-owners a business for profit. Among the basic characteristics is the ***ease of formation.*** A partnership can be created merely by the action of two persons in agreeing to become partners. This agreement should be in writing, however, and should specify the capital contributions of each partner, the plan for sharing profits, and other aspects of operation. Another characteristic is the ***limited life*** of a partnership. The admission of a new partner, as well as the withdrawal or death of a partner, dissolves a partnership. Each partner has the right to act as agent for the firm ***(mutual agency)*** and each partner is ***personally responsible*** for all debts of the firm.

2 **Discuss the advantages and disadvantages of the partnership as a form of business organization.**

The advantages include the combining of the capital and the special skills of two or more persons, the ease of formation, relative freedom from government regulation, and freedom from income taxes. The disadvantages are limited life, unlimited liability, and mutual agency.

3 Distinguish between a regular partnership and a limited partnership.

A limited partnership is made up of the following: (1) at least one general partner and (2) one or more limited partners. The general partner has the traditional role of a partner with unlimited liability for partnership debts and managerial responsibility. The limited partners are basically investors; their liability for losses is limited to the amount of their investments, and they do not participate in management. Limited partnerships are commonly used for ventures which offer tax-sheltered income to investors.

4 Account for the formation of a partnership.

When a partnership is formed by partners contributing cash and/or other assets to the firm, these investments are recorded by debiting asset accounts and crediting the partners' capital accounts. For noncash assets, the amount should be the **_fair market value_** at the date of transfer to the partnership. When two or more owners of going businesses become partners, the partnership usually assumes the liabilities. The capital accounts are credited with the value of the net assets (assets less total liabilities).

5 Divide the net income of a partnership among the partners.

The partnership agreement should specify how net income or loss is to be divided. If the agreement does not mention profit sharing, partners will share equally any amount of profit or loss. To recognize differences in the value and amount of personal services rendered by partners, it is common to provide salaries to partners as a step in sharing profits. To compensate for differences in the amounts of capital contributed, interest may be allowed on capital as a further step in sharing profits. Often both salaries and interest allowances are agreed upon, with any residual profit or loss to be divided in a fixed ratio.

6 Account for the admission of a new partner and the withdrawal of a partner.

A new member may be admitted to an existing partnership in either of two ways: (1) by purchase of an interest from a present partner or (2) by investing assets in the partnership. The purchase of an interest is a transaction between two individuals and is recorded by a transfer from the capital account of the selling partner to the capital account of the incoming partner. The alternative method, investment of assets in the firm by the incoming partner, increases total assets and owners' equity. It may involve a bonus to the old partners or to the new partner depending upon the terms of admitting the new partner.

To withdraw from a partnership, a partner may sell his or her interest. This is recorded by an entry transferring the capital account of the former partner to the new partner. As an alternative, the withdrawing partner may be paid from partnership assets.

7 Account for the liquidation of a partnership.

Liquidation of a partnership means ending the business by selling the assets, paying creditors, and distributing remaining assets to the partners. Any gains or losses on selling the assets are divided according to the agreed profit- and loss-sharing ratio. A debit balance in a partner's capital account represents an amount owed to the partnership by that partner. If a partner whose capital account has a debit balance is insolvent, the other partners must absorb an additional loss equal to the amount owed by the insolvent partner.

This chapter completes our discussion of accounting for unincorporated businesses—that is, sole proprietorships and partnerships. Beginning with Chapter 14, we will shift our emphasis to the special accounting problems of businesses organized as corporations. Now, however, you are probably approaching the end of the first semester in accounting. Therefore, in Chapter 13 we will pause and review the accounting concepts introduced in the first half of this textbook. These concepts also serve as the foundation for many topics that will be introduced in later chapters.

KEY TERMS INTRODUCED OR EMPHASIZED IN CHAPTER 12

Dissolution (of a partnership)   Termination of an existing partnership by any change in the personnel of the partners or by liquidating the business.

General partner   A partner in a limited partnership who has the traditional rights and responsibilities of a partner, including mutual agency and unlimited personal liability for the debts of the business.

Limited partner   A partner in a limited partnership who has the right to participate in profits, but whose liability for losses is limited to the amount he or she has invested and who does not have the right to participate in management of the business. A limited partner's role is that of an investor rather than that of a traditional partner.

Limited partnership   A partnership which has one or more *limited partners* as well as one or more *general partners.* Limited partnerships are used primarily to attract investment capital from the limited partners for such ventures as exploratory oil drilling and real estate development.

Liquidation of a partnership   The process of breaking up and discontinuing a partnership, including the sale of assets, payment of creditors, and distribution of remaining assets to the partners.

Mutual agency   Authority of each partner to act as agent for the partnership within its normal scope of operations and to enter into contracts which bind the partnership.

Partnership contract   An agreement among partners on the formation and operation of the partnership. Usually includes such points as a plan for sharing profits, amounts to be invested, and provision for dissolution.

Statement of partners' capital   A financial statement which shows for each partner and for the firm the amounts of beginning capitals, additional investments, net income, drawings, and ending capitals.

Uniform Partnership Act   Uniform legislation enacted by most states. Governs the formation, operation, and liquidation of partnerships.

SELF-TEST QUESTIONS

The answers to these questions appear on page 600.

1   When a partnership is formed,

    a   A written partnership agreement, signed by all partners, must be filed in the state in which the partnership is formed.

b Each partner may bind the business to contracts and may withdraw an unlimited amount of assets from the partnership, unless these rights are limited in the partnership contract.

c Each member of the partnership is entitled to participate equally in the earnings of and management of the partnership, unless the partnership is a limited partnership.

d The partnership must file an income tax return and pay income taxes on its net income.

2 Carter and Dixie have capital account balances of $80,000 and $100,000, respectively, at the beginning of 1994. Their partnership agreement provides for interest on beginning capital account balances, 10%; salaries to Carter, $30,000, and to Dixie, $24,000; residual profit or loss divided 60% to Carter and 40% to Dixie. Partnership net income for 1994 is $62,000. Neither partner made any additional investment in the partnership during 1992, but Carter withdrew $1,500 monthly and Dixie withdrew $1,000 monthly throughout 1994. The partnership balance sheet at December 31, 1994, should include:

a Capital, Carter, $94,000

b Capital, Carter, $112,000

c Capital, Dixie, $30,000

d Total partners' equity, $242,000

3 Quinn and Ryan are partners who divide profits and losses 30% to Quinn and 70% to Ryan. At the present time, Quinn's capital account balance is $80,000 and Ryan's capital account balance is $160,000. Stone is admitted to a one-third equity interest in the partnership for an investment of $60,000. Each of the following statements relating to the admission of Stone is true with the exception of:

a Quinn has a capital account balance of $68,000 after recording Stone's admission.

b Stone has a capital account balance of $60,000 upon his admission to the partnership.

c Stone received a "bonus" of $40,000 from Quinn and Ryan.

d Total capital (equity) of the new partnership is $300,000 after Stone's admission is recorded.

4 Link, Martin, and Nolan are partners dividing profits and losses 30% to Link, 40% to Martin, and 30% to Nolan. Their capital accounts are as follow: Link, $500,000; Martin, $100,000; Nolan, $400,000. Nolan decides to retire and receives $393,000 from the partnership in exchange for his equity interest. Recording Nolan's withdrawal involves:

a A debit to Nolan's capital account for $393,000.

b Debits to Link's and to Martin's capital accounts for $3,500 each.

c A credit to Link's capital account for $3,000 and a credit to Martin's capital account for $4,000.

d Credits to Link's and to Martin's capital accounts for $200,000 each.

5 When a partnership is liquidated:

a Any cash distribution to partners is allocated according to the profit- and loss-sharing ratios.

b Cash is distributed to each partner in an amount equal to his or her capital account balance prior to the sale of partnership assets.

c Any gain or loss on disposal of partnership assets is divided among the partners according to their relative capital account balances.

d A partner who maintained a credit balance in his or her capital account prior to liquidation may end up owing cash to the partnership if partnership assets are sold at a loss.

ASSIGNMENT MATERIAL

DISCUSSION QUESTIONS

1 Jane Miller is the proprietor of a small manufacturing business. She is considering the possibility of joining in partnership with Mary Bracken, whom she considers to be thoroughly competent and congenial. Prepare a brief statement outlining the advantages and disadvantages of the potential partnership to Miller.

2 Allen and Baker are considering forming a partnership. What do you think are the two most important factors for them to include in their partnership agreement?

3 What is meant by the term *mutual agency?*

4 A real estate development business is managed by two experienced developers and is financed by 50 investors from throughout the state. To allow maximum income tax benefits to the investors, the business is organized as a partnership. Explain why this type of business would probably be a limited partnership rather than a regular partnership.

5 What factors should be considered in drawing up an agreement as to the way in which income shall be shared by two or more partners?

6 Scott has land having a book value of $50,000 and a fair market value of $80,000 and a building having a book value of $70,000 and a fair market value of $60,000. The land and building become Scott's sole capital contribution to a partnership. Assuming no bonus to any partner, what is Scott's capital balance in the new partnership? Why?

7 Is it possible that a partnership agreement containing interest and salary allowances as a step toward dividing net income could cause a partnership net loss to be distributed so that one partner's capital account would be decreased by *more* than the amount of the entire partnership net loss?

8 Partner John Young has a choice to make. He has been offered by his partners a choice between no salary allowance and a one-third share in the partnership income or a salary of $16,000 per year and a one-quarter share of residual profits. Write a brief memorandum explaining the factors he should consider in reaching a decision.

9 Helen Lee withdraws $25,000 from a partnership during the year. When the financial statements are prepared at the end of the year, Lee's share of the partnership income is $45,000. Which amount must Lee report on her income tax return?

10 What factors should be considered when comparing the net income figure of a partnership to that of a corporation of similar size?

11 Explain the difference between being admitted to a partnership by buying an interest from an existing partner and by making an investment in the partnership.

12 If C is going to be admitted to the partnership of A and B, why is it first necessary to determine the current fair market value of the assets of the partnership of A and B?

13 Shirley Bray and Carl Carter are partners who share profits and losses equally. The current balances in their capital accounts are: Bray, $50,000; Carter, $35,000. If Carter sells his interest in the firm to Deacon for $70,000 and Bray consents to the sale, what entry should be made in the partnership accounting records?

14 Farley invests $80,000 cash in the partnership of Dale and Erskin, but is granted a capital interest of only $60,000 upon his admission to the partnership. What is the nature of the $20,000 difference between the amount invested by Farley and the equity interest he received? How is this $20,000 difference handled in the partnership accounting records?

15 Majors, who has a capital account balance of $90,000, received cash of $120,000 from the partnership of Linden, Majors, & Napp upon his retirement. Discuss the nature of the $30,000 paid to Majors in excess of his capital account balance and how this excess payment is handled in the partnership books upon Majors' withdrawal.

16 Describe how a ***dissolution*** of a partnership may differ from a ***liquidation*** of a partnership.

17 What measure can you suggest to prevent a partnership from having insufficient cash available to pay the estate of a deceased partner without disrupting the operation of the business?

18 Upon the death of Robert Bell, a partner in the firm of Bell, Cross, and Davis, Charles Bell, the son of Robert Bell, demanded that he replace his father as a member of the partnership. Can Charles Bell enforce this demand? Explain.

EXERCISES

EXERCISE 12-1
Accounting
Terminology

Listed below are nine technical terms introduced in this chapter:

Unlimited liability	*Partnership contract*	*Termination of partnership*
Liquidation	*Fair market value*	*Interest on partners' capital*
General partner	*Limited partner*	*Partnership net income*

Each of the following statements may (or may not) describe one of these technical terms. For each statement, indicate the accounting term described, or answer "None" if the statement does not correctly describe any of the terms.

a Serves to identify partners, specify capital contributions, and establish profit-sharing formula.

b The process of breaking up and discontinuing a partnership business.

c Amounts to be entered in asset accounts of a partnership to record the investment of noncash assets by partners.

d A method of dividing partnership net income to ensure that no partner's share of profits will be less than the prime rate of interest applied to his or her capital account.

e A characteristic of the partnership type of organization which causes many wealthy investors to choose investments in limited partnerships or corporations rather than in regular partnerships.

f Results from the retirement of a partner from the firm or the admission of a new partner.

g A partner whose financial responsibility does not exceed the amount of his or her investment and who does not actively participate in management.

h A profit-sharing provision designed to compensate for differences in dollar amounts invested by different partners.

EXERCISE 12-2
Formation of a Partnership

A business owned by Fern Douglas was short of cash and Douglas therefore decided to form a partnership with Andy McKuen, who was able to contribute cash to the new partnership. The assets contributed by Douglas appeared as follows in the balance sheet of her business: cash, $600; accounts receivable, $34,900, with an allowance for doubtful accounts of $960; inventory, $45,600; and store equipment, $21,600. Douglas had recorded depreciation of $1,800 during her use of the store equipment in her sole proprietorship.

Douglas and McKuen agreed that the allowance for doubtful accounts was inadequate and should be $1,800. They also agreed that a fair value for the inventory was its replacement cost of $54,000 and that the fair value of the store equipment was $19,000. You are to open the partnership accounts by making a general journal entry to record the investment by Douglas.

EXERCISE 12-3
Partners' Capital and Drawing Accounts

Explain briefly the effect of each of the transactions given below on a partner's capital and drawing accounts:

a Partner borrows funds from the business.

b Partner collects a partnership account receivable while on vacation and uses the funds for personal purposes.

c Partner receives in cash the salary allowance provided in the partnership agreement.

d Partner takes home merchandise (cost $80, selling price $120) for personal use.

e Partner has loaned money to the partnership. The principal together with interest at 15% is now repaid to the partner in cash.

EXERCISE 12-4
Dividing Partnership Income

Guenther and Firmin, both of whom are CPAs, form a partnership, with Guenther investing $100,000 and Firmin, $80,000. They agree to share net income as follows:

1 Salary allowances of $80,000 to Guenther and $60,000 to Firmin.

2 Interest allowances at 15% of beginning capital account balances.

3 Any partnership earnings in excess of the amount required to cover the interest and salary allowances to be divided 60% to Guenther and 40% to Firmin.

INSTRUCTIONS

The partnership net income for the first year of operations amounted to $247,000 before interest and salary allowances. Show how this $247,000 should be divided between the two partners. Use a three-column schedule of the type illustrated on page 573. List on separate lines the amounts of interest, salaries, and the residual amount divided.

EXERCISE 12-5
Admission of a New Partner; Bonus to Old Partners

Abrams and Boling are partners with capital account balances of $102,000 and $63,000. They divide profits and losses one-third to Abrams and two-thirds to Boling. The partnership has been quite profitable and has an excellent reputation. Abrams and Boling agree to admit Cato to a one-third equity interest in the partnership for an investment of $105,000. The assets of the business are **not** to be revalued. Explain how the bonus to the old partners is computed and prepare a general journal entry to record the admission of Cato.

**EXERCISE 12-6
Admission of a
New Partner;
Bonus to New
Partner**

Randall and Dirks are partners who divide profits and losses 60% to Randall and 40% to Dirks. At the present time, each partner's capital account balance is $140,000. Randall and Dirks agree to admit Foster to a one-fourth equity interest in the partnership for an investment of $80,000. Prepare a general journal entry to record the admission of Foster. Explain how any bonus (to existing partners *or* to the incoming partner) is computed.

**EXERCISE 12-7
Withdrawal of
a Partner**

The capital accounts of the Triple D partnership are as follows: Drake, $90,000; Dunlap, $210,000; Dyson, $180,000. Profits and losses are allocated 25% to Drake, 50% to Dunlap, and 25% to Dyson. Dyson is withdrawing from the partnership and it is agreed that he shall be paid $240,000 for his interest because the earnings of the business are high in relation to the assets of the firm. Assuming that the excess of the settlement over the amount of Dyson's capital account is to be recorded as a bonus to Dyson, prepare a general journal entry to record Dyson's retirement from the firm.

**EXERCISE 12-8
Liquidation of
a Partnership**

The CDE partnership is being liquidated. After all liabilities have been paid and all assets sold, the balances of the partners' capital accounts are as follows: Cooley, $42,000 credit balance; Dean, $16,000 *debit* balance; Emmett, $53,000 credit balance. The partners share profits and losses: Cooley, 10%; Dean, 60%; Emmet, 30%.

a How should the available cash (the only remaining asset) be distributed if it is impossible to determine at this date whether Dean will be able to pay the $16,000 he owes the firm? Draft the journal entry to record payment of all available cash at this time.

b Draft the journal entries to record a subsequent partial payment of $13,000 to the firm by Dean, and the distribution of this cash. Prepare a schedule (similar to the one prepared in part **a**) showing computation of amount to be distributed to each partner.

PROBLEMS

Group A

**PROBLEM 12A-1
Formation of a
Partnership;
Closing the
Income Sum-
mary Account**

The partnership of Barton and Liu was formed on July 1, when Tina Barton and Sam Liu agreed to invest equal amounts and to share profits and losses equally. The investment by Barton consists of $40,000 cash and an inventory of merchandise valued at $56,000.

Liu also is to contribute a total of $96,000. However, it is agreed that his contribution will consist of the following assets of his business along with the transfer to the partnership of his business liabilities. The agreed values of the various items as well as their carrying values on Liu's records are listed below. Liu also contributes enough cash to bring his capital account to $96,000.

	Investment by Liu	
	Balances on Liu's Records	*Agreed Value*
Accounts receivable	$89,600	$89,600
Allowance for doubtful accounts	3,840	8,000
Inventory..	9,600	12,800
Office equipment (net)	12,800	9,000
Accounts payable	28,800	28,800

INSTRUCTIONS **a** Draft entries (in general journal form) to record the investments of Barton and Liu in the new partnership.

b Prepare the beginning balance sheet of the partnership (in report form) at the close of business July 1, reflecting the above transfers to the firm.

c On the following June 30 after one year of operation, the Income Summary account showed a credit balance of $78,000 and the Drawing account for each partner showed a debit balance of $32,000. Prepare journal entries to close the Income Summary account and the drawing accounts at June 30.

**PROBLEM 12A-2
Dividing Partnership Income; Financial Statements**

The adjusted trial balance of B & G Distributors indicates the following account balances at the end of the current year:

	Debit	Credit
Cash..	$ 32,620	
Accounts receivable (net).................................	81,000	
Inventory..	28,200	
Prepaid expenses	3,900	
Equipment	90,000	
Accumulated depreciation		$ 18,000
Notes payable...		9,600
Accounts payable		38,520
Accrued expenses..		2,880
Bolton, capital (beginning of year)		70,000
Bolton, drawing	10,080	
Gorman, capital (beginning of year)		60,000
Gorman, drawing...	7,200	
Sales		648,960
Cost of goods sold...	390,960	
Selling expenses	112,380	
Administrative expenses..................................	91,620	
Totals..	$847,960	$847,960

There were no changes in partners' capital accounts during the year. A perpetual inventory system is used by the company. The partnership agreement provided that partners are to be allowed 10% interest on invested capital as of the beginning of the year and that the residual net income is to be divided equally.

INSTRUCTIONS

a Prepare an income statement for the current year, using the appropriate accounts from the above list. At the bottom of the income statement, prepare a schedule showing the division of net income.

b Prepare a statement of partners' capitals for the current year.

c Prepare a balance sheet at the end of the current year.

**PROBLEM 12A-3
Various Methods for Dividing Partnership Net Income**

Alicia Dunn and Roberto Pascal, both real estate appraisers, formed a partnership, with Dunn investing $40,000 and Pascal investing $60,000. During the first year, the net income of the partnership amounted to $45,000.

INSTRUCTIONS

a Determine how the $45,000 net income would be divided under each of the following four independent assumptions as to the agreement for sharing profits and losses. Using schedules of the types illustrated on pages 571–573, show all steps in the division of net income between the partners.

1 The partnership agreement does not mention profit sharing.

2 Interest at 15% to be allowed on beginning capital investments and balance to be divided equally.

3 Salaries of $24,000 to Dunn and $20,000 to Pascal; balance to be divided equally.

4 Salaries of $18,000 to Dunn and $26,000 to Pascal; interest at 15% to be allowed on beginning capital investments; balance to be divided equally.

b Prepare the journal entry to close the Income Summary account, using the division of net income developed in part **4** above.

PROBLEM 12A-4
Dividing Partnership Profit and Loss

Financial Planners has three partners—Reed, Stein, and Trump. During the current year their capital balances were: Reed, $140,000; Stein, $100,000; and Trump, $60,000. The partnership agreement provides that partners shall receive salary allowances as follows: Reed, none; Stein, $60,000; and Trump, $38,000. The partners shall also be allowed 12% interest annually on their capital balances. Residual profit or loss is to be divided: Reed, 50%; Stein, 30%; Trump, 20%.

INSTRUCTIONS

Prepare separate schedules showing how income or loss will be divided among the three partners in each of the following cases. The figure given in each case is the annual partnership net income or loss to be allocated among the partners.

a Income of $554,000

b Income of $83,000

c Loss of $19,000

PROBLEM 12A-5
Admission of a New Partner

Aspen Lodge is a partnership with a record of profitable operations. At the end of the current year the capital accounts of the three partners and the ratio for sharing profits and losses are as shown in the following schedule. At this date, it is agreed that a new partner, Wolfgang Ritter, is to be admitted to the firm.

	Capital	Profit-Sharing Ratio
Olga Svenson	*$300,000*	*60%*
Jill Kidd...	*240,000*	*30%*
Miles Kohl	*180,000*	*10%*

INSTRUCTIONS

For each of the following situations involving the admission of Ritter to the partnership, give the necessary journal entry to record his admission.

a Ritter purchases on-half of Kidd's interest in the firm, paying Kidd personally $150,000.

b Ritter buys a one-quarter interest in the firm for $200,000 by purchasing one-fourth of the present interest of each of the three partners. Ritter pays the three individuals directly.

c Ritter invests $200,000 in the firm and receives a one-fourth interest in the capital and profits of the business. In addition to the journal entry to record Ritter's admission, show computation of the equity interest received and bonus (if any) to either the old partners or to Ritter.

d Ritter invests $360,000 in the firm and receives a one-fourth interest in the capital and profits of the business. In addition to the journal entry to record Ritter's admission, show computation of the equity interest received and bonus (if any) to either the old partners or to Ritter.

PROBLEM 12A-6
Retirement of a Partner

In the partnership of World Travel Agency, the partners' capital accounts at the end of the current year were as follows: Roy Kim, $220,000; Susan John, $148.000; and Mark Ray, $60,000. The partnership agreement provides that profits will be shared 40% to Kim, 50% to John, and 10% to Ray. At this time Kim decides to retire from the firm.

INSTRUCTIONS

Described below are a number of independent situations involving the retirement of Kim. In each case prepare the journal entries necessary to reflect the withdrawal of Kim from the firm.

a Kim sells three-fourths of his interest to Ray for $208,000 and the other one-fourth to John for $64,000. The payments to Kim are made from the personal funds of Ray and John, not from the partnership.

b Kim accepts $90,000 in cash and a patent having a book value of $100,000 in full payment for his interest in the firm. This payment consists of a transfer of partnership assets to the retiring partner. As the fair value of the patent is approximately $100,000, the continuing partners agree that a revaluaticn of assets is not needed. The excess of Kim's capital account over the payment to him for withdrawal should be credited to the continuing partners (five-sixths to John and one-sixth to Ray).

c Kim receives $100,00 in cash and a 10-year, 12% note for $180,000 in full payment for his interest. Assets are not to be revalued. The bonus to Kim is to be charged against the capital accounts of the continuing partners (five-sixths and one-sixth).

PROBLEM 12A-7
Liquidation of a Partnership

The partnership of Talent Scouts has ended its operations and is in the process of liquidation. All assets except for cash and accounts receivable have already been sold. The task of collecting the accounts receivable is now to be carried out as rapidly as possible. The general ledger balances are as follows:

	Debit	Credit
Cash	$ 27,200	
Accounts receivable	116,800	
Allowance for doubtful accounts		$ 6,400
Liabilities		36,800
May, capital (profit-loss share 30%)		43,200
Nix, capital (profit-loss share 50%)		33,600
Peat, capital (profit-loss share 20%)		24,000

INSTRUCTIONS

For each of the two independent situations shown below, prepare journal entries to record the collection or sale of the receivables, the payment of liabilities, and the distribution of all remaining cash to the partners. Support all entries with adequate explanation; the entries for distribution of cash to the partners should have explanations showing how the amounts were determined.

a Collections of $66,400 are made on receivables, and the remainder are deemed uncollectible. Debit the uncollectible receivables in excess of the allowance to an account entitled Loss on Sale of Business.

b Receivables are sold to a collection agency; the partnership receives in cash as a final settlement 30% of the gross amount of its receivables. The personal financial status of the partners is uncertain, but all available cash is to be distributed at this time. (Nix's deficiency will be charged to May and Peat in a 30:20 ratio.)

Group B

**PROBLEM 12B-1
Formation of a
Partnership**

The partnership of Silver and Hawk was formed on January 1, when Anna Silver and John Hawk agreed to invest equal amounts and to share profits equally. The investment by Silver consists of $44,000 cash and an inventory of merchandise valued at $76,000. Hawk is also to contribute a total of $120,000. However, it is agreed that his contribution will consist of the following assets of his business along with the transfer to the partnership of his business liabilities. The agreed value of the various items as well as their carrying values on Hawk's records are listed below:

	Investment by Hawk	
	Balances on Hawk's Records	Agreed Value
Accounts receivable...	$117,600	$117,600
Allowance for doubtful accounts	5,040	8,500
Inventory...	16,600	20,800
Office equipment (net)......................................	16,800	19,500
Accounts payable	37,800	37,800

Hawk also contributed enough cash to bring his capital account to $120,000.

INSTRUCTIONS

a Draft general journal entries to record the investments of Silver and Hawk in the new partnership.

b Prepare the beginning balance sheet of the partnership (in report form) at the close of business January 1, reflecting the above transfers to the firm.

c On the following December 31 after one year of operations, the Income Summary account had a credit balance of $92,000 and the Drawing account for each partner showed a debit balance of $36,000. Prepare journal entries to close the Income Summary and the drawing accounts at December 31.

**PROBLEM 12B-2
Dividing In-
come; State-
ment of Part-
ners' Capitals**

The adjusted trial balance of Design for Living indicates the following account balances at the end of the current year:

	Debit	Credit
Cash...	$ 17,800	
Accounts receivable	105,200	
Allowance for doubtful accounts		$ 2,000
Inventory...	28,500	
Showroom fixtures	32,400	
Accumulated depreciation		6,400
Notes payable...		9,000
Accounts payable		38,000
Lloyd, capital...		70,000
Lloyd, drawing	32,000	
Johnson, capital...		60,000
Johnson, drawing	24,000	
Sales		648,000
Cost of goods sold..	391,000	
Selling expenses	110,000	
Administrative expenses...................................	92,500	
Totals...	$833,400	$833,400

There were no changes in partners' capital accounts during the year. Design for Living uses a perpetual inventory system. The partnership agreement provided that partners are to be allowed 15% interest on invested capital as of the beginning of the year and that the residual net income is to be divided equally.

INSTRUCTIONS

a Prepare an income statement for the current year, using the appropriate accounts from the above list. At the bottom of the income statement, prepare a schedule showing the distribution of net income.

b Prepare a statement of partners' capitals for the current year.

c Prepare a balance sheet at the end of the current year.

PROBLEM 12B-3
Sharing Partnership Net Income: Various Methods

A small nightclub called Comedy Tonight was organized as a partnership with Lewis investing $80,000 and Martin investing $120,000. During the first year, net income amounted to $110,000.

INSTRUCTIONS

a Determine how the $110,000 net income would be divided under each of the following three independent assumptions as to the agreement for sharing profits and losses. Use schedules of the type illustrated in this chapter to show all steps in the division of net income between the partners.

   1 Net income is to be divided in a fixed ratio: 40% to Lewis and 60% to Martin.

   2 Interest at 15% to be allowed on beginning capital investments and balance to be divided equally.

   3 Salaries of $36,000 to Lewis and $56,000 to Martin; interest at 15% to be allowed on beginning capital investments; balance to be divided equally.

b Prepare the journal entry to close the Income Summary account, using the division of net income developed in part **3** above.

PROBLEM 12B-4
Dividing Partnership Profit and Loss

Research Consultants has three partners—Axle, Brandt, and Conrad. During the current year their capital balances were: Axle, $180,000; Brandt, $140,000; and Conrad, $80,000. The partnership agreement provides that partners shall receive salary allowances as follows: Axle, $10,000; Brandt, $50,000; Conrad, $28,000. The partners shall also be allowed 12% interest annually on their capital balances. Residual profit or loss is to be divided: Axle, one-half; Brandt, one-third; Conrad, one-sixth.

INSTRUCTIONS

Prepare separate schedules showing how income will be divided among the three partners in each of the following cases. The figure given in each case is the annual partnership net income or loss to be allocated among the partners.

a Income of $526,000

b Income of $67,000

c Loss of $32,000

PROBLEM 12B-5
Admission of a New Partner

Art of Asia is a partnership organized by Howell and So. A condensed balance sheet for the gallery at September 30 is shown on the next page. On this date the two partners agreed to admit a new partner, Lee. Howell and So have been dividing profits in a ratio of 3:2 (that is, 60% and 40%). The new partnership will have a profit- and loss-sharing ratio of Lee, 50%; Howell, 25%; and So, 25%.

ART OF ASIA
Balance Sheet
September 30

Current assets	$180,000	Liabilities			$160,000
Plant & equipment (net).......	420,000	Partners' capitals:			
		Howell, capital ..	$280,000		
		So, capital	160,000		440,000
Total	$600,000	Total			$600,000

INSTRUCTIONS Described below are four different situations under which Lee might be admitted to partnership. Considering each independently, prepare the journal entries necessary to record the admission of Lee to the firm.

a Lee purchases a one-half interest (50% of the entire ownership equity) in the partnership from Howell for $260,000. Payment is made to Howell as an individual.

b Lee purchases one-half of Howell's interest and one-half of So's interest, paying Howell $168,000 and So $96,000.

c Lee invests $300,000 in the firm and receives a one-half interest in capital and income. In addition to the journal entry to record Lee's admission, show computation of the equity interest received and bonus (if any) to either the old partners or to Lee.

d Lee invests $560,000 in the firm and receives a one-half interest in the capital and profits of the business. In addition to the journal entry to record Lee's admission, show computation of the equity interest received and bonus (if any) to either the old partners or to Lee.

PROBLEM 12B-6
Withdrawal of a Partner

Terra Management is a partnership of three individuals which specializes in the management of professional office buildings. The partnership owns and maintains offices in one such professional center and provides management services for several other buildings owned by clients. At the end of the current year, the firm had the following balance sheet:

TERRA MANAGEMENT
Balance Sheet
December 31, 19__

Cash.........................	$175,000	Liabilities		$198,000
Receivables	67,000	Partners' capitals:		
Land.........................	210,000	Spence, capital.....	$264,000	
Building (net of accumulated		Carver, capital......	180,000	
depreciation)	260,000	Drake, capital	168,000	612,000
Furniture & fixtures (net of				
accumulated depreciation) ..	98,000			
Total	$810,000	Total		$810,000

The partners share profits and losses in the ratio of 50% to Spence, 30% to Carver, and 20% to Drake. It is agreed that Drake is to withdraw from the partnership on this date.

INSTRUCTIONS Following are a number of different assumptions involving the withdrawal of Drake from the firm. Considering each case independently, prepare the general journal entry or entries needed to record Drake's withdrawal.

a   Drake, with the permission of the other partners, gives his equity to his brother-in-law, Holmes, who is accepted as a partner in the firm.

b   Drake sells one-fourth of his interest to Carver for $48,000 cash and sells the other three-fourths to Spence for $104,000 cash. The payments are made by Carver and Spence personally and not by the partnership.

c   Drake retries and agrees to accept as full settlement of his partnership interest $120,000 cash and accounts receivable having a book value of $36,000. These assets come from the firm. The partners agree that no revaluation of assets will be made. (Ratio for sharing profits and losses between Spence and Carver is 5:3.)

d   The partners agree that land is worth $390,000 at present market prices. They do not wish to write up this asset in the accounts but believe that Drake is entitled to a settlement which includes his 20% interest in the increase in value. Drake is paid $96,000 in cash and given a 2-year, 12% note for $108,000. The bonus should be charged against Spence and Carver in the ratio of five-eighths and three-eighths.

PROBLEM 12B-7
Liquidation;
Insolvent Partners

The December 31 balance sheet of MRC Group a partnership specializing in market research and consulting, appears below. In order to focus attention on the principles involved in liquidating a partnership, the balance sheet has been shortened by combining all assets other than cash under the caption of "Other assets."

Merit, Rush, and Carroll share the profits in a ratio of 3:2:1, respectively. At the date of the balance sheet the partners decided to liquidate the business.

MRC GROUP
Balance Sheet
December 31, 19___

Cash.........................	$ 90,000	Liabilities	$160,000
Other assets	450,000	Partners' capitals:	
		Merit, capital $135,000	
		Rush, capital 120,000	
		Carroll, capital 105,000	360,000
Total	$540,000	Total	$540,000

INSTRUCTIONS   For each of the three independent situations shown below, prepare journal entries to record the sale of the "other assets," payment of liabilities, division of the loss on the sale of "other assets" among the partners, and distribution of the available cash to the partners. Support all entries with adequate explanation; the entries for distribution of cash to the partners should have explanations showing how the amounts were determined.

a   Other assets are sold for $378,000

b   Other assets are sold for $144,000. Each partner has personal assets and will contribute the amount necessary to cover any debit balance in his or her capital account that may arise in the liquidation process.

c   Other assets are sold for $117,000. Rush has personal assets and will contribute any necessary amount. Merit and Carroll are both personally bankrupt; any deficit in either capital account must be absorbed by remaining partners.

CASES AND UNSTRUCTURED PROBLEMS

CASE 12-1
Developing an Equitable Plan for Dividing Partnership Income

Juan Ramirez and Robert Cole are considering forming a partnership to engage in the business of aerial photography. Ramirez is a licensed pilot, is currently earning $48,000 a year, and has $50,000 to invest in the partnership. Cole is a professional photographer who is currently earning $30,000 a year. He has recently inherited $70,000 which he plans to invest in the partnership.

Both partners will work full-time in the business. After careful study, they have estimated that expenses are likely to exceed revenue by $10,000 during the first year of operations. In the second year, however, they expect the business to become profitable, with revenue exceeding expenses by an estimated $90,000. (Bear in mind that these estimates of expenses do not include any salaries or interest to the partners.) Under present market conditions, a fair rate of return on capital invested in this type of business is 20%.

INSTRUCTIONS

a On the basis of this information, prepare a brief description of the income-sharing agreement which you would recommend for Ramirez and Cole. Explain the basis for your proposal.

b Prepare a separate schedule for each of the next two years showing how the estimated amounts of net income would be divided between the two partners under your plan. (Assume that the original capital balances for both partners remain unchanged during the 2-year period. This simplifying assumption allows you to ignore the changes which would normally occur in capital accounts as a result of divisions of profits, or from drawings or additional investments.)

c Write a brief statement explaining the differences in allocation of income to the two partners and defending the results indicated by your income-sharing proposal.

CASE 12-2
An Offer of Partnership

Upon graduation from college, Ray Bradshaw began work as a staff assistant for a Big Six CPA firm. During the next few years, Bradshaw received his CPA certificate and was promoted to the level of senior on the firm's audit staff.

At this time, Bradshaw received an offer from a small local CPA firm, Ames and Bolt, to join that firm as a third partner. Both Ames and Bolt have been working much overtime and they would expect a similar workload from Bradshaw. Ames and Bolt draw salaries of $60,000 each and share residual profits equally. They offer Bradshaw a $60,000 salary plus one-third of residual profits. The offer provides for Bradshaw to receive a one-third equity in the firm and requires him to make a cash investment of $120,000. Balance sheet data for the firm of Ames and Bolt are as follows:

Current assets	$ 72,000	Current liabilities	$ 36,000
Property & equipment	288,000	Long-term liabilities	174,000
		Ames, capital	75,000
		Bolt, capital	75,000
Total	$360,000	Total	$360,000

Projected net income of the CPA firm for the next four years is estimated below. These estimated earnings are before partners' salaries and are based on the assumption that Bradshaw joins the firm and makes possible an increased volume of business.

1st year.....................	$192,000	3rd year.....................	$228,000
2nd year	$204,000	4th year.....................	$240,000

If Bradshaw decides to continue in his present position with the national CPA firm rather than join the local firm, he estimates that his salary over the next four years will be as follows:

1st year......................	$62,000	3rd year......................	$73,000
2nd year	$66,000	4th year......................	$80,000

INSTRUCTIONS

a Assuming that Bradshaw accepts the offer from Ames and Bolt, determine the amount of his beginning capital and prepare the entry in the partnership accounts to record Bradshaw's admission to the firm.

b Compute the yearly amounts of Bradshaw's income from the partnership for the next four years. Compare these amounts with the salary that he will receive if he continues in his present employment and write a memo explaining the factors Bradshaw should consider in deciding whether to accept or decline the offer from Ames and Bolt.

c Assuming that Bradshaw declines the offer, suggest some alternatives that he might propose if he decides to present a counteroffer to Ames and Bolt.

ANSWERS TO SELF-TEST QUESTIONS

1 b   2 a   3 b   4 c   5 d

13 Accounting Concepts, Professional Judgment, and Ethical Conduct

Throughout this text, we have tried to explain the theoretical rationale for each new accounting concept, practice, and procedure as it has first come under discussion. In this chapter, we look back and review some of the major ideas, concepts, and assumptions that comprise the theoretical framework of financial reporting. In addition, we discuss independent auditors' reports, the indispensible role of professional judgment in the financial reporting process, and some of the ethical considerations associated with careers in accounting.

After studying this chapter you should be able to meet these Learning Objectives:

1   *Explain the need for recognized accounting standards.*

2   *Discuss the nature and sources of generally accepted accounting principles.*

3   *Discuss the accounting principles and concepts presented on pages 604–613.*

4   *Explain the percentage-of-completion method of income recognition.*

5   *Define an independent audit and discuss the assurances provided by the auditors' report.*

6   *Describe the role of professional judgment in the financial reporting process.*

7   *Explain the basic purpose of a code of ethics within a profession.*

8   *Identify two professional associations that have issued codes of ethics for accountants, and indicate the areas of professional activity emphasized in each code.*

9   *Apply the basic concepts of ethical conduct to various situations likely to arise in accounting practice.*

The Need for Recognized Accounting Standards

OBJECTIVE 1
*Explain the
need for rec-
ognized ac-
counting
standards.*

The basic purpose of financial statements is to provide information about a business entity—information that will be **useful in making economic decisions.** Investors, managers, creditors, financial analysts, economists, and government policy makers all rely upon financial statements and other accounting reports in making the decisions which shape our economy. Therefore, it is of vital importance that the information contained in financial statements possess certain characteristics. The information should be:[1]

1 **Relevant** to the information needs of the decision makers.
2 As **reliable** as possible.
3 **Comparable** to the financial statements of prior accounting periods and also to the statements of other companies.
4 **Understandable** to the users of the financial statements.

We need a well-defined body of accounting principles or standards to guide accountants in preparing financial statements which possess these characteristics. The users of financial statements also must be familiar with these principles in order to interpret properly the information contained in these statements.

GENERALLY ACCEPTED ACCOUNTING PRINCIPLES (GAAP)

The principles which constitute the ground rules for financial reporting are called **generally accepted accounting principles.** Accounting principles may also be termed **standards, assumptions, conventions,** or **concepts.** The various terms used to describe accounting principles stem from the many efforts that have been made to develop a satisfactory framework of accounting theory.[2] For example, the word **standards** was chosen rather than **principles** when the Financial Accounting Standards Board (FASB) replaced the Accounting Principles Board (APB) as the top rule-making body in the accounting profession. The effort to construct a satisfactory body of accounting theory is an ongoing process, because accounting theory must continually change with changes in the business environment and changes in the needs of financial statement users.

Nature of Accounting Principles

Accounting principles do not exist in nature; rather, they are developed by humans in light of what we view as the most important objectives of financial reporting. In Chapter 1, we drew a parallel between generally accepted

---

[1] Adapted from *Statement of Financial Accounting Concept No. 2,* "Qualitative Characteristics of Accounting Information," FASB (Norwalk, Conn.: 1980).

[2] See, for example, *Accounting Research Study No. 3,* "A Tentative Set of Broad Accounting Principles for Business Enterprises," AICPA (New York: 1962), *APB Statement No. 4,* "Basic Concepts and Accounting Principles Underlying Financial Statements of Business Enterprises," AICPA (New York: 1970); and *Statements of Financial Accounting Concepts Nos. 1–6,* FASB (Norwalk, Conn.: 1978–1985).

OBJECTIVE 2
*Discuss the
nature and
sources of
generally
accepted
accounting
principles.*

accounting principles and the rules established for an organized sport, such as basketball or football. For example, both accounting principles and sports rules originate from a combination of experience, tradition, and official decree. Also, both may change over time as gaps or shortcomings in the existing rules come to light.

An important aspect of accounting principles is the ***need for consensus*** within the economic community. If these principles are to provide a useful framework for financial reporting, they must be understood and observed by the participants in the financial reporting process. Thus, the words ***generally accepted*** are an important part of the phrase "generally accepted accounting principles."

As accounting principles are closely related to the needs, objectives, and traditions of a society, they vary somewhat from one country to another. Our discussion is limited to accounting principles "generally accepted" within the United States. An effort is underway to create greater uniformity in accounting principles among nations, but this effort will be a long, slow process.

Authoritative Support for Accounting Principles

To qualify as generally accepted, an accounting principle must have substantial authoritative support. This support may come from official sources, such as the FASB or SEC, or from unofficial sources, such as common sense, tradition, and widespread use.

Official Sources of GAAP Over the years, the official sources of accounting principles in the United States have included (1) the American Institute of Certified Public Accountants, (2) the Financial Accounting Standards Board, and (3) the Securities and Exchange Commission. Also important in the development of accounting theory has been the American Accounting Association (AAA), an organization of accounting educators.

Unofficial Sources of GAAP Not all of what we call generally accepted accounting principles can be found in the "official pronouncements" of the standard-setting organizations. The business community is too complex and changes too quickly for every possible type of transaction to be covered by an official pronouncement. Thus, practicing accountants often must account for situations that have never been addressed by the FASB.

When the method of accounting for a particular situation is not explained in any official literature, generally accepted accounting principles are based upon such considerations as:

■ Accounting practices that are in widespread use.

■ Accounting practices recommended in authoritative, but "unofficial," accounting literature.[3]

■ Broad theoretical concepts that underlie most accounting practices.

---

[3] Authoritative, but unofficial, accounting literature includes the *Accounting Guides, Audit Guides,* and *Statements of Position* published by the AICPA; "unofficial" publications by the FASB and the SEC; research studies published by the American Accounting (AAA), other professional associations, trade associations, and individuals engaged in accounting research; and accounting textbooks.

Thus, an understanding of generally accepted accounting principles requires a familiarity with (1) authoritative accounting literature, (2) accounting practices in widespread use, and (3) the broad theoretical concepts that underlie accounting practices. We will discuss these "broad theoretical concepts" in the following sections of this chapter.

The Accounting Entity Concept

OBJECTIVE 3
Discuss the
accounting
principles
and con-
cepts pre-
sented on
pages 604–
613.

One of the basic principles of accounting is that information is compiled for a clearly defined accounting entity. An ***accounting entity*** is any economic unit which controls resources and engages in economic activities. An individual is an accounting entity. So is a business enterprise, whether organized as a proprietorship, partnership, or corporation. Governmental agencies are accounting entities, as are nonprofit clubs and organizations. An accounting entity may also be defined as an identifiable economic unit ***within a larger accounting entity.*** For example, the Chevrolet Division of General Motors Corporation may be viewed as an accounting entity separate from GM's other activities.

The basic accounting equation, Assets = Liabilities + Owner's Equity, reflects the accounting entity concept because the elements of the equation relate ***to the particular entity whose economic activity is being reported in the financial statements.*** Although we have considerable flexibility in defining our accounting entity, we must be careful to use the ***same definition*** in the measurement of assets, liabilities, owners' equity, revenue, and expense. An income statement would not make sense, for example, if it included all the revenue of General Motors Corporation but listed the expenses of only the Chevrolet Division.

Although the entity concept appears straightforward, it can pose some judgmental allocation problems for accountants. Assume, for example, that we want to prepare an income statement for only the Chevrolet Division of General Motors. Also assume that a given plant facility is used in the production of Chevrolets, Pontiacs, and school buses. How much of the depreciation on this factory building should be regarded as an expense of the Chevrolet Division? Such situations illustrate the importance of the entity concept in developing meaningful financial information.

The Going-Concern Assumption

An underlying assumption in accounting is that an accounting entity will continue in operation for a period of time sufficient to carry out its existing commitments. The assumption of continuity, especially in the case of corporations, is in accord with experience in our economic system. This assumption leads to the concept of the ***going concern.*** In general, the going-concern assumption justifies ignoring immediate liquidating values in presenting assets and liabilities in the balance sheet.

For example, suppose that a company has just purchased a three-year insurance policy for $5,000. If we assume that the business will continue in operation for three years or more, we will consider the $5,000 cost of the insurance as an asset which provides services (freedom from certain risks) to the business over a three-year period. On the other hand, if we assume that the business is likely to terminate in the near future, the insurance policy should be recorded at its cancellation value—the amount of cash which can be obtained from the insurance company as a refund on immediate cancellation of the policy, which may be, say $3,500.

Although the assumption of a going concern is justified in most normal situations, it should be dropped when it is not in accord with the facts. Accountants are sometimes asked to prepare a statement of financial position for an enterprise that is about to liquidate. In this case the assumption of continuity is no longer valid and the accountant drops the going-concern assumption and reports assets at their current liquidating value and liabilities at the amount required to settle the debts immediately.

The Time Period Principle

The users of financial statements need information that is reasonably current and that is comparable to the information relating to prior accounting periods. Therefore, for financial reporting purposes, the life of a business must be divided into a series of relatively short accounting periods of equal length. This concept is called the time period principle.

The need for periodic reporting creates many of the accountant's most challenging problems. Dividing the life of an enterprise into relatively short time segments, such as a year or a quarter of a year, requires numerous estimates and assumptions. For example, estimates must be made of the useful lives of depreciable assets and assumptions must be made as to appropriate depreciation methods. Thus periodic measurements of net income and financial position are at best only informed estimates. The tentative nature of periodic measurements should be understood by those who rely on periodic accounting information.

The Stable-Dollar Assumption

The stable-dollar assumption means that money is used as the basic measuring unit for financial reporting. The dollar, or any other monetary unit, is a measure of value—that is, it indicates the relative price (or value) of different goods and services.

When accountants add or subtract dollar values originating in different years, they imply that the dollar is a *stable unit of measure,* just as the gallon, the acre, and the mile are stable units of measure. Unfortunately, the dollar is *not* a stable measure of value.

To illustrate, assume that in 1970, you purchased land for $20,000. In 1990, you sell this land for $30,000. Under generally accepted accounting principles, which include the stable-dollar assumption, you have made a $10,000 "gain" on the sale. Economists would point out, however, that $30,000 in 1990 represents less "buying power" than did $20,000 in 1970. When the relative buying power of the dollar in 1970 and 1990 is taken into consideration, you came out behind on the purchase and the sale of this land.

To compensate for the shortcomings of the stable-dollar assumption, the FASB asks large corporations voluntarily to prepare *supplementary information* disclosing the effects of inflation upon their financial statements.[4]

---

[4]   FASB, *Statement No. 89,* "Financial Reporting and Changing Prices" (Norwalk, Conn.: 1986).

Let us stress, however, that despite its shortcomings, the stable-dollar assumption remains a generally accepted accounting principle. In periods of low inflation, this assumption does not cause serious problems. During periods of severe inflation, however, the assumption of a stable dollar may cause serious distortions in accounting information.

The Objectivity Principle

The term *objective* refers to measurements that are *unbiased* and subject to verification by independent experts. For example, the price established in an arm's-length transaction is an objective measure of exchange value at the time of the transaction. Exchange prices established in business transactions constitute much of the raw material from which accounting information is generated. Accountants rely on various kinds of evidence to support their financial measurements, but they seek always the most evidence available. Invoices, contracts, paid checks, and physical counts of inventory are examples of objective evidence.

If a measurement is objective, 10 competent investigators who make the same measurement will come up with substantially identical results. However, 10 competent accountants who set out independently to measure the net income of a given business would *not* arrive at an identical result. Despite the goal of objectivity, *it is not possible to insulate accounting information from opinion and personal judgment.* For example, the cost of a depreciable asset can be determined objectively but not the periodic depreciation expense. Depreciation expense is merely an estimate, based upon estimates of the useful life and the residual value of the asset, and a judgment as to which depreciation method is most appropriate. Such estimates and judgments can produce significant variations in the measurement of net income.

Objectivity in accounting has its roots in the quest for reliability. Accountants want to make their economic measurements reliable and, at the same time, as relevant to decision makers as possible. Where to draw the line in the trade-off between *reliability* and *relevance* is one of the crucial issues in accounting theory. Accountants are constantly faced with the necessity of compromising between what users of financial information would like to know and what it is possible to measure with a reasonable degree of reliability.

Asset Valuation: The Cost Principle

Both the balance sheet and the income statement are affected by the cost principle. Assets are initially recorded in the accounts at cost, and no adjustment is made to this valuation in later periods, except to allocate a portion of the original cost to expense as the assets expire. At the time an asset is originally acquired, cost represents the "fair market value" of the goods or services exchanged, as evidenced by an arm's-length transaction. With the passage of time, however, the fair market value of such assets as land and buildings may change greatly from their historical cost. These later changes in fair market value generally have been ignored in the accounts, and the assets have continued to be valued in the balance sheet at historical cost (less the portion of that cost which has been allocated to expense.)

Many accountants and users of financial statements believe that current market value, rather than historical cost, should be used as the basis for asset valuation. This group argues that the use of current values would result in a more meaningful balance sheet. Also, they claim that expenses shown in the income statement should reflect the current market values of the goods and services consumed in the effort to generate revenue.

The cost principle is derived, in large part, from the principle of objectivity. Those who support the cost principle argue that it is important that users have confidence in financial statements, and that this confidence can best be maintained if accountants recognize changes in assets and liabilities only on a basis of completed transactions. Objective evidence generally exists to support cost; current market values, however, may be largely a matter of personal opinion.

The question of whether to value assets at cost or estimated market value is a classic illustration of the "trade-off" between the relevance and the reliability of accounting information.

Revenue Recognition: The Realization Principle

When should revenue be recognized? Under the assumptions of accrual accounting, revenue should be recognized "when it is earned." However, the "earning" of revenue usually is an extended *economic process* and does not actually take place at a single point in time.

Some revenue, such as interest earned, is directly related to time periods. For this type of revenue, it is easy to determine how much revenue has been earned by computing how much of the earning process is complete. However, the earning process for sales revenue is related to *economic activity* rather than to a specific period of time. In a manufacturing business, for example, the earning process involves (1) acquisition of raw materials, (2) production of finished goods, (3) sale of the finished goods, and (4) collection of cash from credit customers.

In the manufacturing example, there is little objective evidence to indicate how much revenue has been earned during the first two stages of the earning process. Accountants therefore usually do not recognize revenue until the revenue has been *realized.* Revenue is realized when both of the following conditions are met: (1) the earning process is *essentially complete* and (2) *objective evidence* exists as to the amount of revenue earned.

In most cases, the realization principle indicates that revenue should be recognized *at the time goods are sold or services are rendered.* At this point the business has essentially completed the earning process and the sales value of the goods or services can be measured objectively. At any time prior to sale, the ultimate sales value of the goods or services sold can only be estimated. After the sale, the only step that remains is to collect from the customer, and this is usually a relatively certain event.

In Chapter 3, we described a *cash basis* of income measurement whereby revenue is recognized only when cash is collected from customers and expenses are recorded only when cash is actually paid out. Cash basis accounting *does not conform* to generally accepted accounting principles, but it is widely used by individuals in determining their ***taxable*** income. (Remember that the accounting methods used in income tax returns often differ from those used in financial statements.)

The Installment Method Companies selling goods on the installment plan sometimes use the installment method of accounting for income tax purposes. Under the installment method, the seller recognizes the gross profit on sales gradually over an extended time span as the cash is actually collected from customers. If the gross profit rate on installment sales is 30%, then out of every dollar collected on installment receivables, the sum of 30 cents represents gross profit.

To illustrate, assume that on December 15, 1992, a retailer sells for $400 a television set which cost $280, or 70% of the sales price. The terms of the sale call for a $100 cash down payment with the balance payable in 15 monthly installments of $20 each, beginning on January 1, 1993. (Interest charges are ignored in this illustration.) The collections of cash and recognition of profit under the installment method are summarized below:

Installment method illustrated

Year	Cash Collected −	Cost Recovery (70%) =	Profit Earned (30%)
1992	$100	$ 70	$ 30
1993	240	168	72
1994	60	42	18
Totals..............	$400	$280	$120

This method of profit recognition exists largely because it is allowed for income tax purposes; it postpones the payment of income taxes until cash is collected from customers. From an accounting viewpoint, there is little theoretical justification for delaying the recognition of profit beyond the point of sale. Therefore, the installment method is seldom used in financial statements.[5]

Percentage-of-Completion: An Exception to the Realization Principle
Under certain circumstances, accountants may depart from the realization principle and recognize income during the production process. An example arises in the case of long-term construction contracts, such as the building of a dam over a period of several years. Clearly the income statements of a company engaged in such a project would be of little use to managers or investors if no profit or loss were reported until the dam was finally completed. The accountant therefore estimates the portion of the project completed during each accounting period, and recognizes the gross profit on the project ***in proportion*** to the work completed. This is known as the percentage-of-completion method of accounting for long-term contracts.

The percentage-of-completion method works as follows:

OBJECTIVE 4
Explain the percentage-of-completion method of income recognition.

1 An estimate is made of the total costs to be incurred and the total profit to be earned over the life of the project.

---

[5] Under generally accepted accounting principles, use of the installment method is permissible only when the amounts likely to be collected on installment sales are ***so uncertain*** that no reasonable basis exists for estimating an allowance for doubtful accounts.

2 Each period, an estimate is made of the portion of the total project completed during the period. This estimate is usually made by expressing the costs incurred during the period as a percentage of the estimated total cost of the project.

3 The percentage figure determined in step **2** is applied to the estimated total profit on the contract to compute the amount of profit applicable to the current accounting period.

4 No estimate is made of the percentage of work during the final period. In the period in which the project is completed, any remaining profit is recognized.

To illustrate, assume that Reed Construction Company enters into a contract with the government to build an irrigation canal at a price of $50,000,000. The canal will be built over a three-year period at an estimated total cost of $40,000,000. Therefore, the estimated total profit on the project is $10,000,000. The following schedule shows the actual costs incurred and the amount of profit to be recognized in each of the three years using the percentage-of-completion method:

	(A) Actual Costs Incurred	(B) Percentage of Work Done in Year (Column A ÷ $40,000,000)	(C) Profit Considered Earned ($10,000,000 × Column B)
Year			
1	$ 6,000,000	15	$1,500,000
2	20,000,000	50	5,000,000
3	14,520,000	*	2,980,000 balance
Totals	$40,520,000		$9,480,000

Profit recognized as work progresses

* Balance required to complete the contract.

The percentage of the work completed during Year 1 was estimated by dividing the actual cost incurred in the year by the estimated total cost of the project ($6,000,000 ÷ $40,000,000 = 15%). Because 15% of the work was done in Year 1, 15% of the estimated total profit of $10,000,000 was considered earned in that year ($10,000,000 × 15% = $1,500,000). Costs incurred in Year 2 amounted to 50% of the estimated total costs ($20,000,000 ÷ $40,000,000 = 50%); thus, 50% of the estimated total profit was recognized in Year 2 ($10,000,000 × 50% = $5,000,000). Note that no percentage-of-work-completed figure was computed for Year 3. In Year 3, the total actual cost is known ($40,520,000), and the actual total profit on the contract is determined to be $9,480,000 ($50,000,000 − $40,520,000). Since profits of $6,500,000 were previously recognized in Years 1 and 2, the **remaining** profit ($9,480,000 − $6,500,000 = $2,980,000) is recognized in Year 3.

Although an expected ***profit*** on a long-term construction contract is recognized in proportion to the work completed, a different treatment is accorded to an expected ***loss.*** If at the end of any accounting period it appears that a loss will be incurred on a contract in progress, the ***entire loss should be recognized at once.***

The percentage-of-completion method should be used only when the total profit expected to be earned can be ***reasonably estimated in advance.*** If there are substantial uncertainties in the amount of profit which will ultimately be earned, no profit should be recognized until ***production***

is completed. This approach is often referred to as the ***completed-contract method.*** If the completed-contract method had been used in the preceding example, no profit would have been recognized in Years 1 and 2; the entire profit of $9,480,000 would have been recorded in Year 3 when the contract was completed and actual costs known.

Expense Recognition: The Matching Principle

The relationship between expenses and revenue is one of ***cause and effect.*** Expenses are ***causal factors*** in the earning of revenue. To measure the profitability of an economic activity, we must consider not only the revenue earned, but also all the expenses incurred in the effort to produce this revenue. Thus, accountants attempt to ***match*** (or ***offset***) the revenue appearing in an income statement with all the expenses incurred in generating that revenue. This concept, called the ***matching principle,*** governs the timing of expense recognition in financial statements.

To illustrate, assume that in June a painting contractor purchases paint on account. The contractor uses the paint on jobs completed in July but does not pay for the paint until August. In which month should the contractor recognize the cost of the paint as expense? The answer is ***July,*** because this is the month in which the paint was ***used in the process of earning revenue.***

Because of the matching principle, costs that are expected to benefit future accounting periods are debited to asset accounts. These costs are then allocated to expense in the periods that the costs contribute to the production of revenue. The matching principle underlies such accounting practices as depreciating plant assets, computing the cost of goods sold each period, and amortizing the cost of unexpired insurance policies. All end-of-the-period adjusting entries involving recognition of expense are applications of the matching principle.

Costs are matched with revenue in one of two ways:

1 **Direct association of costs with specific revenue transactions.** The ideal method of matching revenue with expenses is to determine the amount of expense associated with the specific revenue transactions occurring during the period. However, this approach works only for those costs and expenses that can be directly associated with specific revenue transactions. The cost of goods sold and commissions paid to salespeople are examples of costs and expenses that can be ***directly associated*** with the revenue of a specific accounting period.

2 **Systematic allocation of costs over the "useful life" of the expenditure.** Many expenditures contribute to the earning of revenue for a number of accounting periods but cannot be directly associated with specific revenue transactions. Examples include the costs of insurance policies, depreciable assets, and intangible assets such as goodwill. In these cases, accountants attempt to match revenue and expenses by ***systematically allocating the cost to expense*** over its useful life. Straight-line amortization and the various methods of depreciation are examples of the "systematic allocation" techniques used to match revenue with the related costs and expenses.

Unfortunately, it is not possible to apply the matching principle objectively to every type of expenditure. Many expenditures offer at least some hope of producing revenue in future periods; however, there may be little or no objective evidence to support these hopes. Accountants defer recognition of an expense to the future only when there is **reasonable evidence** that the expenditure will, in fact, benefit future operations. If this evidence is not available, or is not convincing, accountants do not attempt to apply the matching principle; rather, they charge the expenditure **immediately to expense.** Expenditures generally considered "too subjective" for accountants to apply the matching principle include advertising, research and development, and the cost of employee training programs.

CASE IN POINT   Large pharmaceutical companies such as Merck, Upjohn, and Marion Labs spend hundreds of millions of dollars each year in research and development (R&D). Ten or more years may be spent developing and testing a new product. During this time, no revenue is received from the product, but related R&D costs totaling hundreds of millions of dollars are charged to expense. Every now and then, these companies discover a "blockbuster" drug, which can bring in revenue of perhaps $1 billion per year for a decade or more. The costs of manufacturing pharmaceutical products are relatively small; the primary costs incurred in generating the companies' revenues are the R&D expenditures incurred in prior years.

As a result of accountants' inability to match R&D costs against the subsequent revenue, the income of pharmaceutical companies is understated during the years of product development and is overstated in the years that a successful product brings in revenue. Unfortunately, there is no simple solution to this problem. How are accountants to determine objectively whether or not today's research expenditures will result in a "blockbuster" product 10 years down the road?

The Consistency Principle

The principle of **consistency** implies that a particular accounting method, once adopted, will not be changed from period to period. This assumption is important because it assists users of financial statements in interpreting changes in financial position and changes in net income.

Consider the confusion which would result if a company ignored the principle of consistency and changed its method of depreciation every year. The company could cause its net income for any given year to increase or decrease merely by changing its depreciation method.

The principle of consistency does not mean that a company should **never** make a change in its accounting methods. In fact, a company **should** make a change if a proposed new accounting method will provide more useful information than does the method presently in use. But when a significant change in accounting methods does occur, the fact that a change has been made and the dollar effects of the change should be **fully disclosed** in the financial statements.

Consistency applies to a single accounting entity and increases the comparability of financial statements from period to period. Different companies, even those in the same industry, may follow different accounting methods. For this reason, it is important to determine the accounting methods used by companies whose financial statements are being compared.

The Disclosure Principle

Adequate disclosure means that all *material* and *relevant facts* concerning financial position and the results of operations *are communicated to users.* This can be accomplished either in the financial statements or in the notes accompanying the statements. Such disclosure should make the financial statements more useful and less subject to misinterpretation.

Adequate disclosure does not require that information be presented in great detail; it does require, however, that no important facts be withheld. For example, if a company has been named as a defendant in a large lawsuit, this information must be disclosed. Other examples of information which should be disclosed in financial statements include:

1 A summary of the *accounting methods* used in the preparation of the statements.
2 Dollar effects of any *changes* in these accounting methods during the current period.
3 Any *loss contingencies* that may have a material effect upon the financial position of the business.
4 Contractual provisions that will affect future cash flows, including the terms and conditions of borrowing agreements, employee pension plans, and commitments to buy or sell material amounts of assets.

Even significant events which occur *after* the end of the accounting period but before the financial statements are issued may need to be disclosed.

Naturally, there are practical limits to the amount of disclosure that can be made in financial statements and the accompanying notes. The key point to bear in mind is that the supplementary information should be *relevant to the interpretation* of the financial statements.

Materiality

The term *materiality* refers to the *relative importance* of an item or an event. An item is "material" if knowledge of the item might reasonably *influence the decisions* of users of financial statements. Accountants must be sure that all material items are properly reported in the financial statements.

However, the financial reporting process should be *cost-effective*—that is, the value of the information should exceed the cost of its preparation. By definition, the accounting treatment accorded to *immaterial* items is of little or no value to decision makers. Therefore, accountants should not waste time accounting for immaterial items; these items may be treated in the *easiest and most convenient manner.* In short, the concept of materiality allows accountants to *ignore other accounting principles* with respect to items that are not material.

An example of the materiality concept is found in the manner in which most companies account for low-cost plant assets, such as pencil sharpeners or wastebaskets. Although the matching principle calls for depreciating plant assets over their useful lives, these low-cost items usually are charged immediately to an expense account. The resulting "distortion" in the financial statement is too small to be of any importance.

If a large number of immaterial items occur in the same accounting period, accountants should consider the *cumulative effect* of these items. Numerous "immaterial" items may, in aggregate, *have a material effect upon the financial statements.* In these situations, the numerous immaterial events must be properly recorded to avoid a material distortion of the financial statements.

We must recognize that the materiality of an item is a relative matter; what is material in a small business organization may not be material in a larger one. The materiality of an item depends not only upon its dollar amount but also upon its nature. In a large corporation, for example, it may be immaterial whether a given $50,000 expenditure is classified as an asset or as an expense. However, if the $50,000 item is a misuse of corporate funds, such as an unauthorized payment of the personal living expense of the chief executive, the *nature* of the item may make it quite material to users of the financial statements.

Conservatism as a Guide in Resolving Uncertainties

We have previously referred to the use of *conservatism* in connection with the measurement of net income and the reporting of accounts receivable and inventories in the balance sheet. Although the concept of conservatism may not qualify as an accounting principle, it has long been a powerful influence upon asset valuation and income determination. Conservatism is most useful when matters of judgment or estimates are involved. Ideally, accountants should base their estimates on sound logic and select those accounting methods which neither overstate nor understate the facts. When some doubt exists about the valuation of an asset or the realization of a gain, however, accountants traditionally select the accounting option which produces a lower net income for the current period and a less favorable financial position.

An example of conservatism is the traditional practice of pricing inventory at the lower-of-cost-or-market (replacement cost). Decreases in the market value of the inventory are recognized as a part of the cost of goods sold in the current period, but increases in market value of inventory are ignored. Failure to apply conservatism when valuations are especially uncertain may produce misleading information and result in losses to creditors and stockholders.

Audited Financial Statements

The annual financial statements of large corporations are used by great numbers of stockholders, creditors, government regulators, and members of the general public. What assurance do these people have that the infor-

OBJECTIVE 5
Define an
independent
audit and
discuss the
assurances
provided by
the auditors'
report.

mation in these statements is reliable and is presented in conformity with generally accepted accounting principles? The answer is that the annual financial statements of large corporations are *audited* by independent certified public accountants (CPAs).

An audit is a thorough investigation of every item, dollar amount, and disclosure which appears in the financial statements. (Keep in mind that many ledger balances and other types of information are combined and condensed in preparing financial statements. Consequently, each caption appearing in financial statements usually is considered material.)

After completing the audit, the CPAs express their opinion as to the *fairness* of the financial statements. This opinion, called the *auditors' report,* is published with the financial statements in the company's annual report to its stockholders. A report by a CPA firm might read as follows:

To the Stockholders and Board of Directors of CD Technologies

We have audited the accompanying balance sheet of CD Technologies as of December 31, 19__, and the related statements of income, retained earnings, and cash flow for the year then ended. These financial statements are the responsibility of the Company's management. Our responsibility is to express an opinion on these financial statements based on our audit.

We conducted our audit in accordance with generally accepted auditing standards. Those standards require that we plan and perform the audit to obtain reasonable assurance about whether the financial statements are free of material misstatement. An audit includes examining, on a test basis evidence supporting the amounts and disclosures in the financial statements. An audit also includes assessing the accounting principles used and significant estimates made by management, as well as evaluating the overall financial statement presentation. We believe that our audit provides a reasonable basis for our opinion.

In our opinion, the financial statements referred to above present fairly in all material respects, the financial position of CD Technologies as of December 31, 19__, and the results of its operations and its cash flows for the year then ended in conformity with generally accepted accounting principles.

Springfield, MO
January 29, 19__

Blue, White & Company
Certified Public Accountants

Over many decades, audited financial statements have developed an excellent track record of reliability. Note, however, that the CPAs *do not guarantee* the accuracy of financial statements; rather, they render their *professional opinion* as to the overall *fairness* of the statements. "Fairness," in this context, means that the financial statements are *not misleading.* However, just as a physician may make an error in the diagnosis of a particular patient, there is always a possibility that an auditor's opinion may be in error. The primary responsibility for the reliability of financial statements rests with the management of the issuing company, not with the independent CPAs.

Setting New Accounting Standards

As stated earlier, accounting principles are not "laws of nature" that await discovery. Rather, these principles are developed and shaped by organizations and individuals, for the purpose of meeting the needs of economic decision makers. As the business environment changes, the need for new principles (or standards) often becomes apparent. In fact, the FASB typically issues several new standards each year.

In an effort to meet the needs of the entire economic community, the FASB invites all elements of the community to express their views during the standard-setting process. For example, the Board issues a **Discussion Memorandum** explaining the issue under consideration and encouraging all interested parties to comment and to express their views. After considering the responses to the Discussion Memorandum, the Board issues an **Exposure Draft** of the proposed new standard and again encourages public response. These responses also are considered carefully before the Board issues a formal new **Statement of Financial Accounting Standards.**

By inviting the public to participate in the standard-setting process, the FASB tries to develop the understanding and support which will cause the new standard to be "generally accepted."

The Conceptual Framework Project

In addition to responding to the needs of the economic community, the FASB tries to make each new accounting standard consistent with the general framework of accounting theory set forth by the Board in a series of **Statements of Financial Accounting Concepts.** These "concepts statements" explain the interrelationships among the following:

- Objectives of financial reporting
- Desired characteristics of accounting information (such as relevance, reliability, and understandability)
- Elements of financial statements (such as assets, liabilities, revenue, and expenses)
- Criteria for deciding what information to include in financial statements
- Valuation concepts relating to the determination of financial statement amounts

The primary purpose of the conceptual framework is to provide guidance to the FASB in developing future accounting standards.[6] By making each new standard consistent with this framework, the Board hopes that the standards will resolve accounting problems in a logical and consistent manner.

The concepts statements do not represent "official" generally accepted accounting principles, as do the FASB's *Statements of Financial Accounting Standards*. However, these concepts statements are very useful to practicing accountants in accounting for situations that are not specifically addressed by one of the FASB's standards.

---

[6] FASB, *Statement of Financial Accounting Concepts No. 1,* "Objectives of Financial Reporting by Business Enterprises" (Norwalk, Conn.: 1978), p. 4.

PROFESSIONAL JUDGMENT: AN ESSENTIAL ELEMENT IN FINANCIAL REPORTING

OBJECTIVE 6 Describe the role of professional judgment in the financial reporting process.

Judgment plays a major role in financial reporting. For those situations not specifically covered by an official pronouncement, accountants must exercise professional judgment in determining the treatment that is most consistent with generally accepted accounting principles. Judgment also is exercised in selecting appropriate accounting methods (as for example, deciding whether to use the FIFO or LIFO method of inventory valuation), in estimating the useful lives of depreciable assets, and in deciding what events are "material" to a given business entity.

Judgment is a personal matter; competent accountants often will make different judgments. This explains why the financial statements of different companies are not likely to be directly comparable in all respects.

ETHICAL CONDUCT IN THE ACCOUNTING PROFESSION

What Are "Ethics"?

Ethics are the moral principles that an individual uses in governing his or her behavior. In short, ethics are the personal criteria by which an individual distinguishes "right" from "wrong."

Every society has a strong interest in the ethical standards of its citizens. If people had no ethics, for example, they would see nothing "wrong" in cheating, stealing, or even committing murder as a means of achieving their goals. Obviously a society without ethics would be a chaotic and dangerous place in which to live. For this reason, governments, organized religions, and educators have long attempted to create or promote certain ethical standards among all members of society. Governments pass laws requiring or prohibiting certain types of behavior; organized religions attempt to define "right" and "wrong" through sermons and religious teachings. Throughout the educational process, educators attempt to teach students to distinguish between "right" and "wrong" using criteria (ethics) acceptable to the greater society.

Ethics Relating to Certain Types of Activities Some ethical concepts, such as a belief that it is wrong to steal, apply to almost all situations. Other ethical concepts, however, apply specifically to some particular type of activity. For example, many of us have ethical principles relating directly to sports. Assume that you are playing a competitive sport and the umpire or referee makes a "bad call" *in your favor.* Do you challenge the call? Your answer to this question will depend upon your *personal* ethical principles concerning participation in competitive sports.

Some ethical concepts relate specifically to doing business. For example, if a member of the royal family in a foreign country demands a secret cash payment before allowing you to do business in that country, is it "ethical" for you to make this payment? If you manufacture a product that is useful, legal, and profitable, but evidence shows that its use is harmful to the environment, should you continue to produce this product? These are ethical decisions unique to the field of business. There also are many ethical decisions that relate specifically to the practice of *professions,* such as medicine, law, and accounting.

To understand and appreciate the ethics applicable to a specialized type of activity, one must first understand the *nature of that activity.* Consider, for example, a painter who encounters a building badly in need of new paint. The painter has no "ethical obligation" to stop and paint this building. Now consider a physician encountering an accident victim who is unconscious and badly in need of immediate medical attention. The physician *does* have an ethical obligation to stop and render emergency medical care. The obligation to render immediate service simply because it is needed is an ethical concept somewhat unique to the medical profession, because that profession is devoted to the public's health and safety.[7]

Ethics Relating to the Practice of Accounting   Accountants, too, have unique ethical responsibilities. For example, CPAs auditing financial statements have an ethical obligation to be *independent* of the company issuing the statements. An accountant preparing an income tax return has an ethical obligation to prepare the return *honestly,* even though the taxpayer paying the accountant's fee may want the return prepared in a manner that understates taxable income. An accountant employed by a private company has the conflicting ethical obligations of respecting the *confidentiality* of information gained on the job and also making *appropriate disclosures* to people outside the organization.

The Concept of a "Profession"   Accountants are proud to consider themselves members of a recognized *profession.* Just what is a "profession"? Actually, there exists no single definition or criterion that distinguishes a profession from other fields of endeavor. Over time, however, some occupations have come to be regarded as professions, while others have not. Among the occupations most commonly regarded as professions are the practices of medicine, law, engineering, architecture, and theology. Accounting, too, is widely viewed as having achieved the status of a profession.

Although a profession is not easily defined, all professions do have certain characteristics in common. Perhaps the most important of these characteristics is the special responsibility of persons practicing a profession to *serve the public interest,* even at the sacrifice of personal gain.

Professional Codes of Ethics

OBJECTIVE 7
Explain the basic purpose of a code of ethics within a profession.

All recognized professions have developed *codes of professional ethics.* The basic purpose of these codes is to provide members of the profession with guidelines for conducting themselves *in a manner consistent with the responsibilities of the profession.* Codes of ethics relating to the practice of accounting have been developed by several professional associations of accountants. In addition to these codes, there are many laws, income tax regulations, and professional pronouncements that govern the conduct of practicing accountants.

---

[7]   Similar ethical responsibilities also exist for people working in a variety of "public safety" occupations.

Codes of ethics developed by professional associations generally hold the practicing professional to ***higher*** standards of conduct than do the laws regulating that profession. In part, this tendency evolves from the fact that professional associations have a vested interest in enhancing the public image of the profession. Also, these organizations have a better understanding than do lawmakers of the special problems confronting the professional. For these reasons, all professions are, to some extent, ***self-regulating.*** (The term ***self-regulating*** means that society expects the profession to establish its own rules of "professional conduct" for individuals practicing the profession, and also to develop methods of enforcing these rules.)

In this introductory discussion of ethical principles applicable to the accounting profession, we will explore briefly the ethical codes developed by two of the largest professional associations of accountants—the ***American Institute of Certified Public Accountants (AICPA)*** and the ***Institute of Management Accountants (IMA).***[8]

The AICPA Code of Professional Conduct

OBJECTIVE 8
Identify two
professional
associations
that have
issued codes
of ethics for
accountants,
and indicate
the areas of
professional
activity
emphasized
in each
code.

Most CPAs are members of the AICPA. The membership of this association has voted to adopt a code of professional conduct to provide members with guidelines in fulfilling their professional responsibilities. Most CPAs are engaged in ***public accounting***—that is, performing audits, income tax work, and accounting services for a variety of different clients. Thus, the AICPA's *Code of Professional Conduct* focuses upon ethical concepts specifically relating to the practice of public accounting.

The *Code* consists of two sections. The first section, entitled *Principles,* discusses in broad terms the profession's responsibilities to the public, to clients, and to fellow practitioners. The principles provide the framework for the second section of the *Code,* entitled *Rules.*

Quoted below are the preamble and the six Articles comprising the *Principles* section of the *Code.* Also quoted are portions of two of the eleven *Rules.*[9]

SECTION I—PRINCIPLES
Preamble

Membership in the American Institute of Certified Public Accountants is voluntary. By accepting membership, a certified public accountant assumes an obligation of self-discipline above and beyond the requirements of laws and regulations.

These Principles of the *Code of Professional Conduct* of the American Institute of Certified Public Accountants express the profession's recognition of its responsibilities to the public, to clients, and to colleagues. They guide members in the performance of their professional responsibilities and express the basic tenets of ethical and professional conduct. The Principles call for an unswerving commitment to honorable behavior, even at the sacrifice of personal advantage.

---

[8]   Formerly called the National Association of Accountants (NAA).
[9]   Copyright 1991 by the American Institute of Certified Public Accountants, Inc.

Article I
Responsibilities

In carrying out their responsibilities as professionals, members should exercise sensitive professional and moral judgments in all their activities.

Article II
The Public Interest

Members should accept the obligation to act in a way that will serve the public interest, honor the public trust, and demonstrate commitment to professionalism.

Article III
Integrity

To maintain and broaden public confidence, members should perform all professional responsibilities with the highest sense of integrity.

Article IV
Objectivity and Independence

A member should maintain objectivity and be *free of conflicts of interest* in discharging professional responsibilities. A member in public practice should be *independent in fact and appearance when providing auditing and other attestation services.* [Emphasis supplied.]

Article V
Due Care

A member should observe the profession's technical and ethical standards, strive continually to improve competence and the quality of services, and discharge professional responsibilities to the best of the member's ability.

Article VI
Scope and Nature of Services

A member in public practice should observe the Principles of the *Code of Professional Conduct* in determining the scope and nature of services to be provided.

Two of the AICPA "Rules"

In addition to the Articles cited above, the AICPA *Code of Professional Conduct* includes eleven specific rules. Quoted below is Rule 102, regarding *integrity and objectivity,* and a portion of Rule 301, which addresses the concept of *confidentiality.*

SECTION II—RULES
Integrity and Objectivity

Rule 102 In the performance of any professional service, a member shall maintain objectivity and integrity, shall be free of conflicts of interest, and shall *not knowingly misrepresent facts* or subordinate his or her judgment to others. [Emphasis supplied.]

Confidential Client Information

Rule 301   A member in public practice shall not disclose any confidential client information without the specific consent of the client.

This rule shall not be construed to . . . relieve a member of the member's professional obligations . . . (to comply with legal and professional reporting and disclosure requirements).

Applicability of the AICPA Code of Professional Conduct

Most of the principles and rules in the *Code* apply to **all aspects** of a CPA's professional practice. One rule, which states that "A member shall not commit an act discreditable to the profession," applies to the CPA's personal life as well as his or her professional practice. The concept of **independence** (which is both a principle and a rule) applies primarily to **auditing engagements,** not to income tax work or the rendering of other professional services.[10]

The AICPA *Code of Professional Conduct* is binding upon all CPAs who are members of the AICPA. Most large CPA firms **require** all their partners to be members of this organization. Thus, adherence to the *Code* is essential for anyone planning a career in public accounting. In addition, many states have adopted the *Code* into the laws governing the practice of public accounting and the licensing of CPAs within that state. Thus, a CPA found guilty of violating the *Code* could lose his or her license to practice, as well as being barred from membership in the AICPA.

To assist CPAs in applying the ethical concepts embodied in the *Code of Professional Conduct,* the AICPA publishes **interpretations** and **ethics rulings** on an ongoing basis.

A Closer Look at Some Key Concepts

Two ethical concepts of special importance in the practice of public accounting are **independence** and the **confidentiality** of information obtained in the course of a professional engagement.

Independence   When CPAs **audit** a company's financial statements, they express their **professional opinion** as to whether the financial statements represent a fair and complete presentation of the company's financial position and the results of its operations. Stockholders, creditors, and potential investors all rely upon these audited financial statements in deciding how to allocate their investment resources. Thus, if the auditors' report is to lend **credibility** to audited financial statements, users of the statements must view the auditor as being fair and impartial.

OBJECTIVE 9 Apply the basic concepts of ethical conduct to various situations likely to arise in an accounting practice.

For auditors to be viewed as impartial, the profession feels that they must be **independent** of the company issuing the financial statements. By "independent," we mean that the auditor must not be perceived as being under the company's influence or control or as having any **vested interest** in the results reported in the financial statements. Assume, for example, that an auditor owned a large investment in the common stock of an audit

---

[10]   The concept of independence also applies to **review** services and any engagements involving **attestation.**

client. Many users of the financial statements might assume that the auditor would be reluctant to insist upon the disclosure of facts that might lower the company's stock price. Thus, the auditor would not be regarded as impartial by these users of the statements.

CPAs take extensive measures to be independent in fact and also *to appear* independent of their audit clients. This concept of independence places a number of constraints upon the auditors' relationship with audit clients. CPAs must not have any financial interest in a client firm, must not accept expensive gifts from the client, and must not be employees of the client organization. Other restrictions require that close relatives of the CPAs not have major investments or hold key management positions with a client company. In terms of inspiring public confidence, the *appearance* of independence is just as important as being independent in fact.

CPAs need be independent only when they are expressing an opinion on the representations made by another party. Thus, the concept of independence applies primarily to the CPA's role as an *auditor.* In rendering income tax services, consulting services, and many types of accounting services, CPAs are *not* required to be independent of their clients.

Integrity and Objectivity One of the most important concepts in the AICPA *Code* is that in the performance of any professional engagement, a member shall *not knowingly misrepresent facts.* This concept goes to the very heart of the professional accountant's responsibility to the public interest.

Facts may be misrepresented even if the facts themselves are stated correctly. For example, facts are considered to be misrepresented if the accounting document does not contain *adequate disclosure* of relevant information that may reasonably influence the intended user's *interpretation* of the facts.

In summary, a CPA *must not be associated* with misleading financial statements, income tax returns, or other accounting reports. If a client insists upon preparing an accounting document in a misleading manner, the CPA must *resign from the engagement.*

Confidentiality If individuals are to discuss sensitive and private matters openly with professionals, they must trust that professional not to misuse the information provided. Thus, most professions have ethical requirements that information provided to the professional must be held in strict confidence. Physicians, attorneys, and clergy, for example, are ethically and legally prohibited from disclosing to others personal information obtained from persons who have sought their professional services.

By the nature of their work, accountants must have access to much financial information about their clients which the client regards as "confidential." If CPAs are to earn the trust and respect of their clients, they must respect the confidential nature of this information. Thus, CPAs should not disclose sensitive information about a client company to the company's competitors or to other outsiders, or use that information for the CPA's personal gain.[11]

---

[11] Federal laws prohibiting "insider trading" make it illegal for accountants or other "insiders" to use information not yet available to the general public in order to profit from trading in a publicly owned company's financial securities (stocks, bonds, and other financial instruments). Thus, the ethical concept of confidentiality is reinforced, to some extent, by federal law.

The idea that information obtained during a professional engagement is to be held in confidence differs somewhat between CPAs and other professionals. In all aspects of their work, CPAs have an ethical obligation **not to misrepresent facts.** CPAs may face a conflict between their professional obligation to correctly and fully disclose facts, and a client's desire that certain information be held in confidence.

Notice that *Rule 301* specifically states that the concept of confidentiality is **not** intended to "relieve a member of the member's professional obligations . . . (to comply with legal and professional reporting and disclosure requirements)." Thus, the CPA **always should insist** that the client make any and all disclosures consistent with applicable reporting standards. If the client refuses to make such disclosure, the CPA should **resign from the engagement.**

Once having resigned from a professional engagement, the CPA often no longer has professional or legal obligations to make disclosures. In this event, the CPA should still view the information obtained during the engagement as confidential, not to be disclosed without the client's express permission. On the other hand, the CPA must report any information that he or she still is **legally obligated** to disclose. Legal obligations to disclose information may arise from inquiries by the Securities and Exchange Commission (SEC), from court subpoenas, or from a citizen's general responsibility to disclose knowledge of illegal activities that might prove harmful to the public.[12]

CASE IN POINT   Emma Jones, CPA, was engaged to audit the financial statements of Stewart Industries, and also to prepare the company's income tax return. During the course of her work, Jones discovered that the "advertising expenses" Stewart was deducting in its income tax return included $75,000 in political campaign contributions that clearly were not deductible. Jones advised her client that these expenditures were not legally deductible. However, the client insisted on deducting these items anyway. The company's chief financial officer said, "The IRS audits our tax return almost every year. Let them find these items if they can—you don't need to do their work for them. If the IRS throws these deductions out, we'll pay any additional taxes that are assessed."

In the financial statements, the political expenditures were properly included within the broad caption, *Selling and Promotional Expenses.* In addition, the amounts of income taxes expense and income taxes payable shown in the financial statements were large enough to provide for any additional taxes that might be assessed if the IRS disallowed the improper deductions.

Jones is aware that the IRS pays a "finder's fee" to anyone who provides information enabling the Service to collect additional taxes due from another taxpayer.

What are Jones's ethical responsibilities with respect to (1) completing her professional engagements for Stewart and (2) disclosing Stewart's improper actions to the IRS?

---

[12]   When CPAs believe that they may have a legal obligation to disclose confidential information, they should consult with legal counsel to determine whether this legal obligation takes priority over the ethical concept of confidentiality.

Answer: (1) Jones may *not* prepare Stewart's income tax return, as she knows that certain deductions claimed in the return are not legally deductible. Unless Stewart will accord proper treatment to the political expenditures in its tax return, Jones must resign from this portion of her professional engagement. Jones may continue her audit engagement, however, as the facts *are presented fairly* in the financial statements.

Although Jones ethically may continue with the audit engagement, she should consider whether she wants to be associated with a client of Stewart's questionable character. If Stewart is willing to misrepresent facts to the IRS, perhaps it also is willing to misrepresent other facts to Jones and to users of its financial statements. Thus, Jones may elect to resign from both the tax and audit engagements.

(2) The information obtained while working on the Stewart engagement is confidential. Therefore, Jones may *not* inform the IRS of the situation without her client's express permission. However, Jones must respond to a subpoena or other legal requirement to disclose this information.

It would be highly unethical for Jones to disclose this confidential information to collect a "finder's fee" or for any form of personal gain.

IMA Standards of Ethical Conduct for Management Accountants

The IMA is an association consisting primarily of management accountants—that is, accountants working for one particular organization.[13] The members of the IMA have adopted a code of professional ethics designed to assist management accountants in executing their duties in an ethical and professional manner. The standards comprising this code are as follows:[14]

Competence

Management accountants have a responsibility to:

- Maintain an appropriate level of professional competence by ongoing development of their knowledge and skills.
- Perform their professional duties in accordance with relevant laws, regulations, and technical standards.
- Prepare complete and clear reports and recommendations after appropriate analysis of relevant and reliable information.

Confidentiality

Management accountants have a responsibility to:

- Refrain from disclosing confidential information acquired in the course of their work except when authorized, unless legally obligated to do so.

---

[13] The term *management accountants* describes accountants employed by private companies, nonprofit organizations, and by governmental agencies. These accountants may specialize in any number of fields, including systems design, internal auditing, financial reporting, income taxes, and assisting management in developing and using accounting information in planning and controlling the operations of the organization.

[14] Institute of Management Accountants, *Statement on Management Accounting: Standards of Ethical Conduct for Management Accountants,* Statement No. 1C, New York, 1983.

■ Inform subordinates as appropriate regarding the confidentiality of information acquired in the course of their work and monitor their activities to assure maintenance of that confidentiality.

■ Refrain from using or appearing to use confidential information acquired in the course of their work for unethical or illegal advantage either personally or through third parties.

Integrity

Management accountants have a responsibility to:

■ Avoid actual or apparent conflicts of interest and advise all appropriate parties of any potential conflict.

■ Refrain from engaging in any activity that would prejudice their ability to carry out their duties ethically.

■ Refuse any gift, favor, or hospitality that would influence or would appear to influence their actions.

■ Refrain from either actively or passively subverting the attainment of the organization's legitimate and ethical objectives.

■ Recognize and communicate professional limitations or other constraints that would preclude responsible judgment or successful performance of an activity.

■ Communicate unfavorable as well as favorable information and professional judgments or opinions.

■ Refrain from engaging in or supporting any activities that would discredit the profession.

Objectivity

Management accountants have a responsibility to:

■ Communicate information fairly and objectively.

■ Disclose fully all relevant information that could reasonably be expected to influence an intended user's understanding of the reports, comments, and recommendations presented.

Applicability of the IMA's Code of Ethics

The IMA's *Code* applies to all members of the organization in their role as management accountants. All CMAs (Certified Management Accountants) also agree to abide by this code. At present, compliance is primarily voluntary.

A Closer Look at Some Key Concepts

Confidentiality   Every organization views much of its internal accounting information as ***confidential***—that is, as information that should not be disclosed to people outside the organization, or even to many employees inside the organization. For example, a company might not want its advertising budget made known to competitors, or the salaries of its executives and managers made known to employees throughout the organization.

Thus, management accountants, just as CPAs, should respect the confidentiality of information obtained during professional engagements. This means that the accountant should not disclose confidential information except with the employer's (or client's) permission. Also, the accountant should never use this information for personal gain in a manner that is either unethical or illegal.

CASE IN POINT   Both management accountants and independent auditors often have advance knowledge that a company's earnings for the year will be higher or lower than most investors are expecting. It would be illegal and unethical for the accountants to use this "inside information" to profit from changes in the company's stock price, either personally or by passing this confidential information to third parties.

As in the case of public accountants, an exception to the confidentiality requirement exists when there is a *legal obligation* for the accountant to make disclosure. Also, the confidentiality concept does *not* justify withholding appropriate disclosures from an accounting document.

What about Independence?   Notice that the IMA's *Code* does not mention the concept of *independence.* Independence is an ethical concept pertaining only to public accountants engaged in auditing activities.

An important distinction between a management accountant and a public accountant is that the management accountant is an *employee* of the company for which he or she performs accounting services. The public accountant, on the other hand, is employed by a public accounting firm but provides accounting services for a variety of different clients. Employees are not regarded as independent of their employers. Thus, although management accountants perform many different types of accounting services, they cannot perform independent audits of their employer's financial statements.

Although management accountants are not independent of their employers, they still are expected to develop accounting information that is fair, honest, and free from bias. Guidelines helpful in achieving this goal are found in the code sections entitled *Integrity* and *Objectivity.*

Integrity   The Integrity section of the IMA's *Code* deals primarily with the management accountant's ethical obligations to his or her employer. For example, management accountants are to avoid conflicts of interest and to disclose to appropriate parties any potential conflicts that may arise. Also, they are to refuse gifts that would influence (or appear to influence) their actions. The purpose of these standards is to avoid situations which might compete with the accountant's professional obligations to his or her employer.

Objectivity   We have seen that the ethical standards of confidentiality and integrity deal primarily with management accountants' ethical obligations to their employers. Of even greater importance to the profession is the accountants' responsibilities to the *public* and to outside parties who rely upon accounting reports and disclosures. In the IMA's *Code,* these responsibilities are addressed in the ***Objectivity*** standard.

The statement that management accountants have a responsibility to "communicate information fairly and objectively" means, simply, that a professional accountant must ***not be associated*** with any financial statement, tax return, or other accounting report that the accountant ***believes to be misleading.***

Resolution of Ethical Conflicts

The IMA also makes suggestions to its members on how to resolve ethical conflicts. When faced with a significant ethical issue, the member should first follow any established policies within the employer organization for resolving such issues. If the issue cannot be resolved properly in this manner, the member should discuss the matter with his or her immediate supervisor, assuming that this supervisor is not involved. If this superior is involved in the situation, the problem should be submitted to the next higher level of management.

If the ethical conflict cannot be resolved after exhausting all levels of internal review, the management accountant may have no alternative other than to ***resign from the organization,*** and to submit a memorandum describing the situation to an appropriate level of management.

Even after an accountant resigns, the ethical concept of confidentiality continues to apply. The accountant may not discuss confidential information except with the former employer's permission, or when there exists a legal obligation to make disclosure.

The Challenge of Adhering to a Code of Ethics

In principle, a professional code of ethics is a good thing. Society benefits when professionals conduct themselves in an honorable and ethical manner. (Surely, no one would argue against professionals striving toward such goals as increased competence and integrity.) A professional code of ethics provides professionals with some general guidelines in conducting themselves in an ethical manner.

However, even an "honest" person may find it difficult to act in an ethical manner in some situations. Let us briefly consider a few of the "barriers" to ethical conduct.

The "Price" of Ethical Behavior   We would like to think that professionals will do the "right" (ethical) thing, regardless of the amount of personal sacrifice involved. This is an easier course of action to advocate than to follow. Management accountants, interestingly, may have to pay a far greater "price" for ethical conduct than the public accountants. Let us first consider the case of a public accountant.

Assume that a CPA has a client that intends to issue misleading financial statements or to understate taxable income in an income tax return. The CPA should not be associated with such misrepresentation and should resign from the engagement. This, of course, may mean that the CPA is unable to collect his or her fee from this engagement, but this is a relatively small price to pay.

First, this "unethical" client is but one of many clients for the typical CPA. Thus, the fee from this engagement probably represents only a small percentage of the CPA's total revenue. More importantly, CPAs simply *cannot afford* to be associated with misleading financial statements or fraudulent income tax returns. Such associations could leave the CPA personally liable to persons deceived by the misleading accounting documents, create adverse publicity that could destroy the CPA's practice, cause the CPA to lose his or her license to practice public accounting, and result in the CPA going to prison for committing fraud. Thus, the CPA's choice is relatively clear: it is far better to give up an unethical client than to continue the association.

Now consider the situation of the management accountant. If the management accountant's employer rejects the accountant's concerns over an ethical problem, the management accountant may have no further recourse other than to resign. This may mean giving up a high and steady income, losing future pension rights, and joining the ranks of the unemployed. Clearly, this management accountant is asked to pay a much higher price for choosing the "ethical path" than is the public accountant in the preceding example.

Incomplete Information A professional accountant may "suspect" that activities in which he or she is asked to participate are unethical, but not be sure.

CASE IN POINT Wilson, a management accountant for International Equipment Company, is asked to process the paper work to reimburse the Vice-President of International Operations for a $50,000 "advertising expenditure" claimed in the executive's expense account. Wilson considers it improbable that the Vice-President actually spent $50,000 in personal funds for company advertising. More likely, Wilson thinks, the funds were paid as a bribe to some foreign official. However, Wilson has no facts concerning the expenditure, other than that top management wants the vice-president reimbursed.

In most situations, accountants have neither the responsibility nor the right to investigate their employers or clients. If a further investigation of the facts is not directly related to the accountant's professional responsibilities, the accountant simply may never have enough information to reach an informed decision as to whether or not specific activities are "ethical."

Just What Is the "Ethical" Thing to Do? Codes of ethics consist of broad, general guidelines, intended to be useful to practitioners in identifying and resolving ethical problems. However, no code of ethics can address every situation that might arise. Every "ethical dilemma" is somewhat unique, having its own facts and circumstances.

CASE IN POINT Assume that Barnes, CPA, is performing income tax services for Regis Company: Regis insists that Barnes prepare the company's income tax return in a manner that understates the amount of taxes owed. What should Barnes do?

Answer: Barnes cannot ethically comply with the client's instructions. Therefore, Barnes should resign from the engagement.

In many situations, however, the ethical course of action *is not readily apparent.*

CASE IN POINT Assume that Riley, CPA, is auditing the 1994 financial statements of Quest Corporation. During this audit, Quest Corporation is acquired by Gordon Communications. Riley's brother is the Controller of Gordon Communications. Has Riley's independence been impaired with respect to the Quest audit? Must Riley resign from this engagement?

Answer: ???[15]

Codes of ethics, including the "official interpretations," typically do not address such specific questions. Therefore, it often is not possible to simply "look up" the solution to an ethical problem. In deciding when an ethical problem exists, and in determining what constitutes ethical behavior, the practitioner must often rely primarily upon his or her own *professional judgment.*

In addition to studying a code of ethics, professionals attempting to resolve an ethical dilemma might ask themselves the following questions: "Would the action that I am considering be fair to everyone involved?" and "If my friends and family knew all the facts, would they be proud of my actions?" "Ethical conduct" means more than abiding by a list of rules; it means an *"unswerving commitment to honorable behavior; even at the sacrifice of personal advantage."* [Emphasis supplied.][16]

END-OF-CHAPTER REVIEW

SUMMARY OF CHAPTER LEARNING OBJECTIVES

1 **Explain the need for recognized accounting standards.**
Recognized accounting standards guide companies in preparing financial statements which are reasonably comparable and which meet the needs of users. Recognized standards also assist users in interpreting the information within these statements.

---

[15] Our Case in Point involving Riley and his brother is intended to show that ethical dilemmas *do not always have clear-cut answers.* This case hinges upon personal judgments, including the closeness of the relationship between Riley and his brother, and what impairs the "appearance" of independence. Thus, even with all the facts in hand, experts are likely to disagree on the answer to this case.

[16] AICPA, *Code of Professional Conduct* (New York: 1988), Preamble.

2 **Discuss the nature and sources of generally accepted accounting principles.**

Generally accepted accounting principles stem both from official sources, such as the FASB and the SEC, and from unofficial sources, such as tradition and widespread use.

3 **Discuss the accounting principles and concepts presented on pages 604–613.**

The principles and concepts discussed in this chapter include the concept of an accounting entity, the going-concern assumption, the time period principle, the stable-dollar assumption, objectivity, the cost principle, the realization principle, matching, consistency, disclosure, materiality, and conservatism. This is neither a complete nor an official listing of generally accepted accounting principles, but these are some of the most important concepts which underlie current accounting practices.

4 **Explain the percentage-of-completion method of income recognition.**

The percentage-of-completion method is used in recognizing income on long-term construction projects in which the total profit can be *reasonably estimated* in advance. Under this method, the company recognizes gross profit *in proportion* to the work completed during the period, rather than waiting until the project is finished.

The percentage-of-completion method is an exception to the realization principle. This exception is justified because delaying profit recognition to the end of such projects would make the periodic financial statements less useful.

5 **Define an independent audit and discuss the assurances provided by the auditors' report.**

An *audit* is an investigation conducted by a firm of certified public accountants to verify the content of a company's financial statements. After performing this investigation, the CPA firm issues an *auditors' report* expressing the firm's professional opinion as to the fairness and completeness of these statements. Virtually all large corporations have their financial statements audited each year, and the auditors' report is made available both to investors and to the general public.

6 **Describe the role of professional judgment in the financial reporting process.**

Professional judgment is required in nearly every aspect of the financial reporting process. For example, accountants must use judgment in selecting appropriate accounting methods, making the many estimates inherent in financial statements, deciding which items are "material," and identifying those events requiring special disclosure.

7 **Explain the basic purpose of a code of ethics within a profession.**

The basic purpose of a code of ethics is to provide members of the profession with guidelines for conducting themselves in a manner consistent with the responsibilities of the profession.

8 Identify two professional associations that have issued codes of ethics for accountants, and indicate the areas of professional activity emphasized in each code.

The American Institute of Certified Public Accountants (AICPA) has issued a code of professional ethics relating to the practice of public accounting. The Institute of Management Accountants (IMA) has issued a code of professional ethics intended primarily for management accountants—that is, accountants working for one particular organization.

9 Apply the basic concepts of ethical conduct to various situations likely to arise in accounting practice.

Ethical conduct involves many concepts, including integrity, competence, confidentiality, and—in the case of audit and review services— independence. In summary, ethical conduct means an "unswerving commitment to honorable behavior, even at the sacrifice of personal advantage."[17]

The concepts discussed in this chapter form the theoretical framework of the financial reporting process. Thus, an understanding of these concepts will be useful throughout the study of accounting. In the preceding chapters, we have focused primarily upon unincorporated business—that is, sole proprietorships and partnerships. In the remaining chapters, we will emphasize the corporate form of business entity. You will find that generally accepted accounting principles are equally applicable to all three forms of business organizations.

KEY TERMS INTRODUCED OR EMPHASIZED IN CHAPTER 13

American Institute of Certified Public Accountants (AICPA) A professional organization of Certified Public Accountants (CPAs) that has long been influential in the development of accounting principles.

Auditors' report The report issued by a firm of certified public accountants after auditing the financial statements of a business. The auditors' report expresses an opinion on the fairness of the financial statements and indicates the nature and limits of the responsibility being assumed by the independent auditors.

Conservatism A traditional practice of resolving uncertainties by choosing an asset valuation at the lower point of the range of reasonableness. This term refers to the policy of postponing recognition of revenue to a later date when a range of reasonable choice exists. Conservatism is designed to avoid overstatement of financial strength and earnings.

Consistency An assumption that once a particular accounting method is adopted, it will not be changed from period to period. Consistency is intended to make financial statements of a given company comparable from year to year.

Disclosure principle Financial statements should include all material and relevant information about the financial position and operating results of the business. The notes accompanying financial statements are an important means of making the necessary disclosures.

Ethical conduct Doing "what is right," even at the sacrifice of personal advantage.

---

[17] Ibid.

Financial Accounting Standards Board (FASB) The organization with primary responsibility for formulating new accounting standards. The FASB is part of the private sector and is not a governmental agency.

Generally accepted accounting principles (GAAP) The "ground rules" for financial reporting. This concept includes principles, concepts, and methods that have received authoritative support (such as from the *FASB*) or that have become "generally accepted" through widespread use.

Going-concern assumption An assumption that a business entity will continue in operation indefinitely and thus will carry out its existing commitments.

Installment method An accounting method used principally in the determination of taxable income. It provides for recognition of realized profit on installment contracts in proportion to cash collected.

Institute of Management Accountants (IMA) A professional association consisting primarily of management accountants. (Formerly called the National Association of Accountants.)

Management accountant An accountant employed within a specific organization. Management accountants develop accounting information to meet the various needs of the organization and also assist management in the interpretation of this information.

Matching principle The accounting principle that governs the timing of expense recognition. This principle indicates that expenses should be offset against revenue on a basis of cause and effect. That is, the revenue of an accounting period should be offset by those costs and expenses that were causal factors in producing that revenue.

Materiality The relative importance of an amount or item. An item which is not significant enough to influence the decisions of users of financial statements is considered to be *not* material. The accounting treatment of immaterial items may be guided by convenience rather than by theoretical principles.

Objectivity (objective evidence) The valuation of assets and the measurement of income are to be based as much as possible on objective evidence, such as exchange prices in arm's-length transactions.

Percentage-of-completion method A method of accounting for long-term construction projects which recognizes revenue and profits in proportion to the work completed, based on an estimate of the portion of the project completed each accounting period.

Professional judgment Using one's professional knowledge, experience, and ethics to make decisions which have no prescribed or obvious answer.

Realization principle The principle of recognizing revenue in the accounts only when the earning process is virtually complete, which is usually at the time of sale of goods or rendering service to customers.

Securities and Exchange Commission (SEC) A governmental agency with the legal power to set accounting principles. However, the SEC traditionally has adopted the principles developed by the *FASB,* rather than developing its own set of principles. The SEC enforces accounting principles by giving the weight of law to standards developed by the FASB. The SEC reviews the financial statements of publicly owned corporations for compliance with the Commission's reporting requirements.

Stable-dollar assumption In using money as a measuring unit and preparing financial statements expressed in dollars, accountants make the assumption that the dollar is a stable unit of measurement. This assumption is faulty in an environment of continued inflation.

Time period principle The idea that to be useful, financial statements should be prepared for relatively short accounting periods of equal length. While this principle contributes to the timeliness of financial statements, it conflicts with the objectivity principle by forcing accountants to make many estimates, such as the useful lives of depreciable assets.

SELF-TEST QUESTIONS

The answers to these questions appear on page 645.

1   Generally accepted accounting principles (GAAP):

   a   Include only the official pronouncements of the standard-setting organizations, such as the AICPA, SEC, and FASB.

   b   May include customary accounting practices in widespread use even if not mentioned specifically in official pronouncements.

   c   Eliminate the need for professional judgment in the area in which an official pronouncement exists.

   d   Are laws issued by the FASB and the SEC, based upon a vote by the CPAs in the United States.

2   Which of the following situations best illustrates the application of the ***realization*** principle?

   a   A company sells merchandise on the installment method and recognizes gross profit as the cash is collected from customers.

   b   A construction company engaged in a three-year project determines the portion of profit to be recognized each year using the percentage-of-completion method.

   c   A construction company engaged in a three-month project recognizes no profit until the project is completed under the completed-contract method.

   d   A manufacturer that sells washing machines with a three-year warranty recognizes warranty expense related to current year sales, based upon the estimated future liability.

3   Which of the following concepts has the ***least*** influence in determining the depreciation expense reported in the income statement under current GAAP?

   a   Reliability—The price of a depreciable asset established in an exchange transaction can be supported by verifiable, objective evidence.

   b   Cost principle—Assets are initially recorded in the account at cost and no adjustment is made to this valuation in subsequent periods, except to allocate a portion of the original cost to expense as assets expire.

   c   Relevance—Amounts shown in the financial statements should reflect current market values, as these are the most relevant to decision makers.

   d   Matching principle—Accountants attempt to match revenue with the expenses incurred in generating that revenue by systematically allocating an asset's cost to expense over its useful life.

4   The existence of generally accepted accounting principles has eliminated the need for professional judgment in:

   a   Estimating the useful lives and residual values of depreciable plant assets.

   b   Selecting an appropriate inventory valuation method, such as LIFO, FIFO, average cost, or specific identification.

   c   Determining which events are "material" to a given entity.

    d None of the above is correct; each of the above situations requires the use of professional judgment.

5 The fact that a corporation's financial statements have been audited means that:

    a An independent firm of CPAs has expressed an opinion upon the fairness of the statements.

    b The IRS has examined the financial statements to investigate compliance with tax laws.

    c The financial statements are guaranteed to be accurate by the CPAs who prepared them.

    d The financial statements were prepared by a CPA firm, rather than by the company itself.

6 The concept of ethical conduct would ***prohibit*** a professional accountant from which of the following? (More than one answer may be correct.)

    a Resolving issues based upon professional judgment.

    b After resigning because of an ethical dispute with an employer, accepting employment elsewhere in the same industry.

    c Using for personal gain information which has not yet been released to the public about the financial position of a publicly owned employer or client.

    d Investing in the common stocks of any publicly owned companies.

7 Which of the following are ***not*** included among the IMA's suggestions as to how a management accountant might resolve an ethical conflict with his or her employer? (More than one answer may be correct.)

    a Discuss the matter with a management official ***above*** the position of the accountant's immediate supervisor.

    b In strict confidence, anonymously inform the SEC.

    c Resign from the organization.

    d Call a press conference and "go public" with the issue.

ASSIGNMENT MATERIAL

DISCUSSION QUESTIONS

1 Briefly explain the meaning of the term ***generally accepted accounting principles.***

2 Why is it important that the accounting principles be "generally accepted"?

3 Name the three groups in the United States that have been the most influential in developing generally accepted accounting principles.

4 To be "generally accepted," must an accounting method be set forth in the official pronouncements of an accounting rule-making organization? Explain.

5 Are generally accepted accounting principles in worldwide use? Explain.

6 What is the ***time period principle?*** Does this principle tend to increase or decrease the objectivity of accounting information? Explain.

7 What is meant by the term ***stable-dollar assumption?*** Is this assumption completely valid? Explain.

8 What is the meaning of the term *objectivity* as it is used by accountants? Is accounting information completely objective? Explain.

9 An argument has long existed as to whether assets should be valued in financial statements at cost or at estimated market value. Explain the implications of the *objectivity principle* in this controversy.

10 Explain what is meant by the expression "trade-off between *reliability* and *relevance*" in connection with the preparation of financial statements.

11 What two conditions should be met before accountants consider revenue to be *realized?*

12 Long-term construction projects often are accounted for by the percentage-of-completion method.
   a Is this method consistent with the realization principle? Explain.
   b What is the justification for the use of this method?

13 Briefly explain the *matching principle.* Indicate two approaches that accountants follow in attempting to "match" revenue with expense.

14 Does the concept of *consistency* mean that all companies should use the same accounting methods? Explain.

15 Briefly define the principle of *disclosure.* List four examples of information that should be disclosed in financial statements or in notes accompanying the statements.

16 Briefly explain the concept of *materiality.* If an item is not material, how is the item treated for financial reporting purposes?

17 Does *conservatism* mean that assets should be deliberately understated in accounting records? Explain fully.

18 Indicate how the concept of *conservatism* would apply to:
   a Estimating the allowance for doubtful accounts receivable.
   b Estimating the useful lives of depreciable assets.

19 What are *audited* financial statements? Is the auditing of financial statements made easier or more difficult by the principle of objectivity? Explain.

20 What organization is primarily responsible for the development of new accounting standards? Why does this organization encourage all elements of the economic community to express their views during the standard-setting process?

21 Professional judgment plays an important role in financial reporting. Explain at least three areas in which the accountant preparing financial statements must make professional judgments that will affect the content of the statements.

22 Briefly explain why society benefits from "ethical conduct" by all citizens. Next, explain why a society expects professionals to observe additional ethical standards, beyond those which pertain to all citizens.

23 Explain why all recognized professions have developed their own codes of professional ethics.

24 Identify two associations of professional accountants that have developed codes of professional ethics for their members. Also, indicate the types of accounting activity emphasized in each of these codes.

25 Identify an ethical concept that is unique to the auditing of financial statements. Explain why this ethical concept is important in the auditing function.

26 Briefly describe the ethical concept of **confidentiality.** Does this concept apply to public accountants, to management accountants, or to both? Does this concept prevent CPAs from insisting that their clients make "adequate disclosure" in financial statements intended for use by outsiders?

27 Briefly explain the steps that a management accountant should take to resolve an ethical problem existing at his or her place of employment.

28 Why may a management accountant have to "pay a higher price" in resolving an ethical conflict than the "price paid" by a public accountant?

29 Briefly explain several reasons why even an honest person may have difficulty in always following the "ethical" course of action.

EXERCISES

EXERCISE 13-1
**Accounting
Terminology**

Listed below are nine technical accounting terms introduced or emphasized in this chapter.

GAAP	Professional judgment	Realization
SEC	Materiality	Matching
Objectivity	Conservatism	Consistency

Each of the following statements may (or may not) describe one of these technical terms. For each statement, indicate the accounting term described, or answer "None" if the statement does not correctly describe any of the terms.

a The concept of associating expenses with revenue on a basis of cause and effect.

b An essential element for an accountant making estimates, selecting appropriate accounting methods, and resolving trade-offs between the goals of conflicting accounting principles.

c The organization which is primarily responsible for developing new accounting standards in the United States.

d The goal of having all companies use the same accounting methods.

e The list of acceptable accounting principles developed by the SEC as part of its conceptual framework project.

f The accounting principle used in determining when revenue should be recognized in financial statements.

g An accounting concept that may justify departure from other accounting principles for purposes of convenience and economy.

EXERCISE 13-2
**Asset
Valuation**

Milestone Manufacturing Company has just purchased expensive equipment that was custom-made to suit the firm's manufacturing operations. Because of the custom nature of this machinery, it would be of little value to any other company. Therefore, the controller of Milestone is considering writing these machines down to their estimated resale value in order to provide a conservative valuation of assets in the company's balance sheet. In the income statement, the write-down would appear as a "loss on revaluation of machinery."

Separately discuss the idea of writing down the carrying value of the machinery in light of each of the four following accounting concepts:

a The going-concern assumption

b The matching principle

c   Objectivity

d   Conservatism

EXERCISE 13-3
Revenue
Recognition

In deciding when to recognize revenue in financial statements, accountants normally apply the realization principle.

a   Revenue is considered realized when two conditions are met. What are these conditions?

b   Indicate when the conditions for recognition of revenue have been met in each of the following situations. (Assume that financial statements are prepared monthly.)

   1   An airline sells tickets several months in advance of its flights.

   2   An appliance dealer sells merchandise on 24-month payment plans.

   3   A professional sports team sells season tickets in July for eight home games to be played in the months of August through December.

   4   Interest revenue relating to a 2-year note receivable is all due at the maturity of the note.

EXERCISE 13-4
Expense
Recognition

Mystery Playhouse prepares monthly financial statements. At the beginning of its 3 month summer season, the company has programs printed for each of its 48 upcoming performances. Under certain circumstances, either of the following accounting treatments of the costs of printing these programs would be acceptable. Justify both of the accounting treatments using accounting principles discussed in this chapter.

a   The cost of printing the programs is recorded as an asset and is allocated to expense in the month in which the programs are distributed to patrons attending performances.

b   The entire cost of printing the programs is charged to expense when the invoice is received from the printer.

EXERCISE 13-5
Violations of
Accounting
Principles

For each situation described below, indicate the principle of accounting that is being violated. You may choose from the following:

Accounting entity	*Materiality*
Consistency	*Objectivity*
Disclosure	*Realization*
Matching	*Stable-dollar assumption*

a   The bookkeeper for a large metropolitan auto dealership depreciates metal wastebaskets over a period of 5 years.

b   Upon completion of the construction of a condominium project which will soon be offered for sale, Townhome Developers increased the balance sheet valuation of the condominiums to their sales value and recognized the expected profit on the project.

c   Plans to dispose of a major segment of the business are not communicated to readers of the financial statements.

d   The cost of expensive, custom-made machinery installed in an assembly line is charged to expense because it is doubtful that the machinery would have any resale value if the assembly line were shut down.

e   A small commuter airline recognizes no depreciation on its aircraft because the planes are maintained in "as good as new" condition.

EXERCISE 13-6
Profit Recognition: Installment Method

On September 15, 1993, Susan Moore sold a piece of property which cost her $56,000 for $80,000, net of commissions and other selling expenses. The terms of sale were as follows: down payment, $8,000; balance, $3,000 on the fifteenth day of each month for 24 months, starting October 15, 1993. Compute the gross profit to be recognized by Moore in 1993, 1994, and 1995 using the *accrual basis* of accounting and (b) the *installment basis* of accounting. Moore uses a fiscal year ending December 31.

EXERCISE 13-7
Profit Recognition: Percentage-of-Completion Method

The Clinton Corporation recognizes the profit on a long-term construction project as work progresses. From the information given below, compute the profit that should be recognized each year, assuming that the original cost estimate on the contract was $6,000,000 and that the contract price is $7,500,000.

Year	Costs Incurred	Profit Considered Realized
1992	$1,800,000	$?
1993	3,000,000	?
1994	1,171,000	?
Total	$5,971,000	$1,529,000

EXERCISE 13-8
Audits of Financial Statements

The annual financial statements of all large, publicly owned corporations are audited.

a What is an audit of financial statements?

b Who performs these audits?

c What is the basic purpose of an audit?

EXERCISE 13-9
Developing New Accounting Standards

Answer the following questions relating to the creation of new accounting standards:

a Why will a need for new standards always exist?

b What organization has primary responsibility for setting new accounting standards?

c What role is played by the SEC in the standard-setting process? (See pages 14 and 35 in Chapter 1.)

d Why are all elements of the economic community invited to comment and to express their views during the standard-setting process?

EXERCISE 13-10
The Conceptual Framework

The FASB recently issued a series of *Statements of Financial Accounting Concepts* intended to set forth a broad "conceptual framework" of accounting theory. Explain how an understanding of accounting theory is useful to:

a Members of the FASB.

b Accountants involved in the preparation of financial statements.

c Users of financial statements.

EXERCISE 13-11
Ethical Responsibilities of a CPA

Teresa Ortiz, CPA, was engaged to audit the financial statements of Meglo Corporation and also to prepare the company's income tax return. During the course of her work, Ortiz discovered that in its income tax return, Meglo had classified $75,000 in amortization of goodwill as "depreciation expense." (Depreciation is deductible in determining taxable income, but amortization of goodwill is not.) Ortiz discussed this problem with her client, but the client insisted on deducting the amortization under the caption "Depreciation expense." A representative of management stated: "This distinction makes no sense. If amortization of goodwill isn't deductible, it should be. After all, it's the same basic concept as depreciation expense."

Also during this engagement, Ortiz learned that Meglo has owed $36,000 to Martin Advertising Agency for a period of 17 months. Apparently, Martin had underbilled Meglo for services rendered 2 years ago and has made no request for the $36,000 additional payments due.

In the financial statements, Meglo included appropriate amounts of income taxes expense and income taxes payable. The company also properly included the $36,000 among its liabilities. However, management has told Ortiz that it has no intention of making payment of this amount unless it receives a bill from Martin.

Discuss Ortiz's ethical responsibilities with respect to (a) completing her professional engagements for Meglo, and (b) personally disclosing the facts directly to the affected third parties (the IRS and/or Martin).

EXERCISE 13-12
The Honorable Mr. Chan

Hong-Ching Chan, CMA, was hired this year as a management accountant for Drexel, Inc. While working for Drexel, Chan learns that in the preceding year the company understated its tax liability in its income tax return by more than $400,000. Chan also knows that the IRS pays a 10% finder's fee to people who provide information enabling the IRS to collect taxes due.

a Can Chan ethically report Drexel to the IRS and claim the finder's fee?

b Would your answer be different if Chan had been fired by Drexel?

c Would your answer be different if Chan were a CPA engaged by Drexel to conduct an audit of the company's financial statements?

PROBLEMS

Note: Due to the nature of the problem material in this chapter, two sets of problems would result in substantial repetition. For this reason, we present the problems in one series, rather than in our usual A and B groups. Both the A and B sets of accounting work sheets support this series of problems. However, most of the problems also can be answered either on ordinary notebook paper or by using a word processor.

PROBLEM 13-1
Rationale Behind Acceptable Practices

Paragraphs a through e describe accounting practices which *are in accord* with generally accepted accounting principles. From the following list of accounting principles, identify those principles which you believe justify or explain each described accounting practice. (Most of the described practices are explained by a single principle; however, more than one principle may relate to a given practice.) Briefly explain the relationship between the described accounting practice and the underlying accounting principle.

Accounting Principles

Consistency	*Accounting entity concept*
Materiality	*Matching revenue with expense*
Objectivity	*Going-concern assumption*
Realization	*Adequate disclosure*
Conservatism	*Stable-dollar assumption*

Accounting Practices

a If land costing $60,000 were sold for $65,000, a $5,000 gain would be reported regardless of inflation during the years that the land has been owned.

b When equipment is purchased an estimate is made of its useful life, and the equipment is then depreciated over this period.

c The personal assets of the owner of a sole proprietorship are not disclosed in the financial statements of the business, even when these personal assets are sufficient to assure payment of all the business's liabilities.

d In estimating the appropriate size of the allowance for doubtful accounts, most accountants would rather see this allowance be a little too large rather than a little too small.

e The methods used in the valuation of inventory and for the depreciation of plant assets are described in a footnote to the financial statements.

PROBLEM 13-2
Accounting
Principles

Paragraphs **a** through **e,** below, describe accounting practices which ***are in accord*** with generally accepted accounting principles. From the following list of accounting principles, identify those principles which you believe justify or explain each described accounting practice. (Most of the practices are explained by a single principle; however, more than one principle may relate to a particular practice.) Briefly explain the relationship between the described accounting practice and the underlying accounting principle.

Accounting Principles

Consistency	*Accounting entity concept*
Materiality	*Matching revenue with expense*
Objectivity	*Going-concern assumption*
Realization	*Adequate disclosure*
Conservatism	*Stable-dollar assumption*

Accounting Practices

a The purchase of a 2-year fire insurance policy is recorded by debiting an asset account even though no refund will be received if the policy is canceled.

b Hand tools with a small unit cost are charged to expense when purchased even though the individual tools have a useful life of several years.

c An airline records depreciation on its aircraft even though an excellent maintenance program keeps the planes in "as good as new" condition.

d A lawsuit filed against a company is described in footnotes to the company's financial statements even though the lawsuit was filed with the court shortly after the company's balance sheet date.

e A real estate developer carries an unsold inventory of condominiums in its accounting records at cost rather than at estimated sales value.

PROBLEM 13-3
Violations of
GAAP

Six independent situations are described below.

a Morris Construction, Inc., does not have sufficient current assets to qualify for a much needed loan. Therefore, the corporation included among its current assets the personal savings accounts of several major stockholders, as these stockholders have promised to invest more money in the corporation if necessary.

b First Bank incurred large losses on uncollectible agricultural loans. On average, these loans call for payments to be received over a period of 10 years. Therefore, First Bank is amortizing its losses from the uncollectible loans against the revenue that will be earned over this 10-year period.

c The Ghost of 42nd Street, a Broadway play, has sold out in advance for the next 2 years. These ticket sales were recognized as revenue at the time cash was received from the customers.

d Wall Street Advisory Service has been sued by clients for engaging in illegal securities transactions. No mention is made of this lawsuit in the company's financial statements, as the suit has not been settled and the company cannot objectively estimate the extent of its liability.

e   Carver Company sold for $200,000 land that had been purchased 10 years ago for $150,000. As the general price level had doubled during this period, Carver Company restated the cost of the land at $300,000 and recognized a $100,000 loss.

f   In recent years, many savings and loan associations have become bankrupt. Although Red River Savings Bank was in no danger of bankruptcy, it reduced the carrying value of its assets to liquidation value to make its financial statements more comparable to those of other companies in the industry.

INSTRUCTIONS   For each situation, identify the accounting principle that has been violated and explain the nature of the violation.

PROBLEM 13-4
Applying Ac-
counting Prin-
ciples

Six independent situations are described below.

a   Pearl Cove Hotel recognizes room rental revenue on the date that a reservation is received. For the summer season, many guests make reservations as much as a year in advance of their intended visit.

b   In prior years Regal Corporation had used the straight-line method of depreciation for both financial reporting purposes and for income tax purposes. In the current year, Regal continued to use straight-line depreciation on all assets for financial reporting purposes but began depreciating newly acquired assets by an accelerated method for income tax purposes.

c   The liabilities of Ellis Construction Company are substantially in excess of the company's assets. In order to present a more impressive balance sheet for the business, Roy Ellis, the owner of the company, included in the company's balance sheet such personal assets as his saving account, automobile, and real estate investments.

d   On January 9, 1994, Gable Company's only plant was badly damaged by a tornado and will be closed for much of the coming year. No mention was made of this event in the financial statements for the year ended December 31, 1993, as the tornado occurred after year-end.

e   Friday Production follows a policy of valuing its plant assets at liquidation values in the company's balance sheet. No depreciation is recorded on these assets. Instead, a loss is recognized if the liquidation values decline from one year to the next. If the liquidation values increase during the year, a gain is recognized.

INSTRUCTIONS   For each situation, indicate the accounting principle or concept, if any, that has been violated and explain briefly the nature of the violation. If you believe the treatment *is in accord with generally accepted principles,* state this as your position and briefly defend it.

PROBLEM 13-5
Evaluating
Applications of
Accounting
Principles

Assume that you are an independent CPA performing audits of financial statements. In the course of your work, you encounter the following situations:

a   Reliable Appliance Company sells appliances on long-term payment plans. The company uses the installment method of recognizing revenue in its income tax returns and in its financial statements. Uncollectible accounts consistently range between 1.5% and 2.0% of net sales.

b   Akron Labs has spent $700,000 during the year in a very imaginative advertising campaign. The controller is sure that the advertising will generate revenue in future periods, but he has no idea how much revenue will be produced or over what period of time it will be earned. Therefore, he has decided to follow the "conservative" policy of charging the advertising expenditures to expense in the current period.

c Taylor Corporation has purchased special-purpose equipment, designed to work with other machinery already in place in Taylor's assembly line. Due to the special nature of this machinery, it has virtually no resale value to any other company. Therefore, Taylor's accountant has charged the entire cost of this special-purpose machinery to expense in the current period.

d Architectural Associates charges all purchases of drafting supplies directly to expense. At year-end, the company makes no entry to record the fact that $100 to $200 of these supplies remain on hand.

e Newton Company prepares financial statements four times each year. For convenience, these statements are prepared when business is slow and the accounting staff is not busy with other matters. Last year, financial statements were prepared for the two-month period ended February 28, the five-month period ended July 31, the three-month period ended October 31, and the one-month period ended November 30.

INSTRUCTIONS Discuss each of the above situations. If you consider the treatment to be in conformity with generally accepted accounting principles, explain why. If you do not, explain which principle or principles have been violated, and also explain how the situation should have been reported.

PROBLEM 13-6
Alternative Methods of Income Recognition

Early in 1993 Roadbuilders, Inc., was notified that it was the successful bidder on the construction of a section of state highway. The bid price for the project was $24 million. Construction began in 1993 and will take about 27 months to complete; the deadline for completion is in April of 1995.

The contract calls for payments of $6 million per year to Roadbuilders, Inc., for 4 years, beginning in 1993. (After the project is complete, the state will also pay a reasonable interest charge on the unpaid balance of the contract.) The company estimates that construction costs will total $16 million, of which $6 million will be incurred in 1993, $8 million in 1994, and $2 million in 1995.

The controller of the company, Joe Morgan, recognizes that there are a number of ways he might account for this contract. He might recognize income at the time the contract is completed (completed-contract method), in April of 1995. Alternatively, he might recognize income during construction (percentage-of-completion method), in proportion to the percentage of the total cost incurred in each of the 3 years. Finally, he might recognize income in proportion to the percentage of the total contract price collected in installment receipts during the 4-year period (installment method).

INSTRUCTIONS a Prepare a schedule (in millions of dollars) showing the profit that would be recognized on this project in each of the 4 years (1993 through 1996) under each of the three accounting methods being considered by the controller. Assume that the timing and construction costs go according to plan. (Ignore the interest revenue relating to the unpaid balance of the contract.)

b Explain which accounting method you consider to be *most* appropriate in this situation. Also explain why you consider the other two methods less appropriate.

PROBLEM 13-7
Ethical Dilemmas

Below are five independent cases that may confront professional accountants. In each case, identify the specific article, rule, or standard from the AICPA or IMA code that should guide the accountant's conduct, and indicate the ethical course of action. If the situation does not create any ethical problem, briefly explain why not.

a Brewster, CMA, works for the Defense Department. Part of her job is to evaluate bids of various defense contractors for Defense Department business. In the course of her work, she has come to know many people in the defense industry quite well. Today John Helms, a vice-president with General Systems Corporation, a defense contractor, offered Brewster the use of a condominium at a nearby ski resort any time she wanted to use it. He explained, "I know you like to ski. Our company owns this condominium, but no one ever seems to use it. Here's the key; just consider the place yours."

b Bello, CPA, has been requested to audit the financial statements of Bello Corporation, a family business. The business is owned and operated entirely by Bello's parents, brothers, and sisters. Bello has no direct financial interest in the business and does not personally participate in its management.

c Ross, CMA, works for One Million Auto Parts. The vice-president of marketing has asked Ross to prepare a summary of the market value of the company's inventory, arranged by geographic sales territories. Ross does not know the intended use of this summary. He does know, of course, that generally accepted accounting principles do not permit the valuation of inventories at market value in financial statements.

d Jacobs, CPA, is a member of a CPA firm that audits four regional banks in the area. Jacobs is the firm's specialist in the banking industry. Yesterday, she received a request that her firm audit the financial statements of First Fidelity, the largest regional bank in the area.

e Two months ago, Arnold Chiou, CMA, worked as a cost accountant for Ewing Oil Company, but he is now employed by WestStar Oil. A manager at WestStar tells Chiou that WestStar is thinking of cutting its prices to win market share from Ewing. However, the manager needs to know Ewing Oil's per-gallon production cost in order to know which company is likely to win a price war.

**PROBLEM 13-8
More Ethical
Dilemmas**

Below are five independent cases that may confront professional accountants. In each case, identify the specific article, rule, or standard from the AICPA or IMA code that should guide the accountant's conduct, and indicate the ethical course of action. If the situation does not create any ethical problem, briefly explain why not.

a Brown, CPA, has been engaged by Marshal Corporation to help the company design a more efficient accounting system. In the course of this engagement, Brown learns that in the preceding year, Marshal prepared its income tax return in a manner that understated the amount of income taxes due. Brown was not involved in the preparation of this tax return. However, she knows that the IRS pays a 10% finder's fee to anyone providing information that assists the agency in collecting additional taxes owed by another taxpayer.

Brown is considering alerting the IRS to the additional taxes owed by Marshal.

b Huang, CMA, is asked by his employer to prepare financial statements in which depreciation expense is computed by the straight-line method. Huang knows that the company uses accelerated depreciation methods in its income tax return.

c Porter, CPA, considers Commuter Airlines to be a well-managed company with a good future. For years, Porter has been purchasing stock in Commuter Airlines as a means of saving for her children's college education. Recently, Porter has received a request from Commuter Airlines to assist them in the preparation of its income tax return.

d DMX Corporation does custom manufacturing and bills each of its customers on a "cost plus" basis. In advertising, DMX uses the slogan, "We'll treat you like our only customer."

DMX has just purchased for $300,000 special machinery that will be used on seven separate contracts. Swartz, a management accountant at DMX, is told by his supervisor to charge each of these contracts with the entire $300,000 cost. The supervisor explains, "We would have had to buy this machinery if we were working on just one contract, and in that case, the customer would be charged the entire $300,000. So we'll just treat each customer as if it were our only customer."

e Mandella, CPA, is engaged in the audit of Wells Medical Products. Wells is in financial difficulties and will be using the audited financial statements in its effort to raise much needed capital. The company hopes to issue 10-year bonds payable in the near future.

Mandella learns that Wells is a defendant in numerous lawsuits alleging that Microtain, a product produced by Wells in the early 1960s, caused birth defects. The lawsuits probably will not be resolved for perhaps 5, 10, or 15 years. If Wells should lose the suit, the damages awarded to the plaintiffs could bankrupt the company.

The chief financial officer for Wells tells Mandella, "Look, we aren't about to disclose this stuff in our financial statements. First, we're innocent; Microtain never hurt anyone. When it's all said and done, we won't owe a dime. Also, if we lose, we'll appeal. These suits won't even be settled until long after our 10-year bond issue has been repaid. If you insist on disclosing this mess in the financial statements, we'll never get our financing. We'll have to close up, and thousands of our employees will lose their jobs. In short, I can't allow disclosure of this information; you'll just have to regard it as 'confidential'."

CASES AND UNSTRUCTURED PROBLEMS

CASE 13-1
Gotta Match?

In determining when to recognize an expenditure as expense, accountants attempt to apply the matching principle. If there is insufficient evidence to apply this principle in a meaningful manner, the expenditure is charged immediately to expense.

INSTRUCTIONS Listed below are 10 types of costs frequently encountered by business organizations. Indicate in which period or periods these costs should be recognized as expense.

Types of Costs

1 The cost of merchandise purchased for resale.

2 The cost to an auto dealer of a training program for mechanics. On average, mechanics stay with the dealership for 4 years.

3 Sales commissions owed to employees for sales in the current period but payable in the next period.

4 The cost of a 2-year insurance policy.

5 The cost of accounts receivable estimated to be uncollectible.

6 The cost of expensive factory equipment with an estimated life of 10 years.

7 Research and development costs that may benefit the company for a decade or more if successful products are discovered and brought to market.

8 The cost of four wastebaskets with an estimated useful life of 10 years.

9 Interest on notes payable that has accrued during one period but is not payable until a future period.

10 The cost of an advertising campaign promoting the opening of a new store that is expected to remain in operation for 20 years.

CASE 13-2
"Trade-Offs" among Accounting Principles

It is not possible to be consistent with all accounting principles all the time. Sometimes trade-offs are necessary; accountants may need to compromise one accounting principle or goal in order to achieve another more fully.

INSTRUCTIONS

Describe a situation that requires a trade-off between the following sets of principles or goals:

a The relevance of accounting information to decision makers and the need for this information to be reliable.

b The comparability of information reported by different companies and the idea that a company should consistently apply the same accounting methods from year-to-year.

c The realization principle and the need for relatively timely information.

d The desire to match revenue with expenses and the quest for objectivity.

CASE 13-3
GAAP from an Auditor's Perspective

Assume that you are an independent CPA performing audits of financial statements. In the course of your work, you encounter the following situations:

a Gala Magazine receives most of its revenue in the form of 12-month subscriptions. Even though this subscription revenue has already been received in cash, the company's controller defers recognition in the income statement; the revenue is recognized on a monthly basis as the monthly issues of the magazine are mailed to subscribers.

b Due to the bankruptcy of a competitor, Regis Trucking was able to buy plant assets worth at least $400,000 for the "bargain price" of $300,000. In order to reflect the benefits of this bargain purchase in the financial statements, the company recorded the assets at a cost of $400,000 and reported a $100,000 "gain on purchase of plant assets."

c Metro Development Company built a 400-unit furnished apartment complex. All materials and furnishings used in this project that had a unit cost of less than $200 were charged immediately to expense. The total cost of these items amounted to $6 million.

d In January 1994, the main plant of Hillside Manufacturing Company was destroyed in a fire. As this event happened in 1994, no loss was shown in the income statement for 1993. However, the event was thoroughly disclosed in notes to the 1993 financial statements.

e In an effort to match revenue with all related expenses in an objective manner, Brentwood Company has established "useful life" standards for all types of expenditures. For example, expenditures for advertising are amortized over 12 months; the costs of employee training programs, 24 months; and research and development costs, 10 years.

INSTRUCTIONS

Discuss each of the above situations. If you consider the treatment to be in conformity with generally accepted accounting principles, explain why. If you do not, explain which principle or principles have been violated, and also explain how the situation should have been reported.

CASE 13-4
"What? Me? Fired?"

Christine Davis, a member of IMA, is a management accountant for CalTex Industries. Davis believes that she is being asked to accumulate inappropriate costs on a "cost plus" contract. All costs accumulated on the contract ultimately are billed to the customer (along with a markup representing CalTex's profit margin), an agency of the government.

a Does this situation represent an ethical problem for Davis? Explain.

b If you believe that an ethical problem exists, briefly explain the steps that Davis should take to resolve it.

c Assume that as a result of taking the steps that you suggested in part **b,** Davis is fired. Based on IMA standards, does Davis have an ethical obligation to inform the governmental agency of her suspicions that it is being overcharged? Explain.

CASE 13-5
Ethics in the
"Real World"

Bring into class a copy of a newspaper or magazine article describing a situation in which professional accountants probably faced an ethical dilemma. (Your article need not specifically mention the accountants' roles in the situation. Also, your article need not be current; you may select any article from any business publication.)

Describe the ethical problems that you believe confronted the accountants in this situation and the course of action they should have considered. Also, express your *personal opinion* as to whether or not the accountants acted in an ethical manner, including the reasons behind your opinion. Finally, discuss what *you* would have done in the accountants' place, identifying any factors that may have made your decision difficult.

ANSWERS TO SELF-TEST QUESTIONS

1 b   2 c   3 c   4 d   5 a   6 c (This practice also is illegal "insider trading.")   7 b, d

5 Corporations

*T*he next four chapters focus on accounting issues which primarily affect corporations. Although sole proprietorships are more numerous than corporations, it is the corporation that plays the dominant role in our economy. Corporations own more assets, earn more revenue, provide more jobs, and attract more capital than all other forms of business organizations combined.

Part 5 also contains Comprehensive Problem 4. This problem provides a review of much of the first half of this textbook, as well as of corporate accounting issues.

Corporations: Organization and Stockholders' Equity

This chapter begins our study of businesses organized as corporations. First, we describe the nature of a corporation, explain the concept of a "separate legal entity," and discuss the advantages and disadvantages of the corporate form of organization. Next, we focus attention upon the stockholders' equity section of a corporate balance sheet. Paid-in capital is distinguished from retained earnings, and preferred stock is contrasted with common stock. Distinctions are drawn among the concepts of par value, book value, and market value. Various stockholders' equity transactions are illustrated and explained, including the issuance of capital stock and the declaration and payment of cash dividends. Also covered are such topics as subscriptions to capital stock, accounting for donated capital, and the computation of book value per share.

After studying this chapter you should be able to meet these Learning Objectives:

1. *Discuss the advantages and disadvantages of organizing a business as a corporation.*
2. *Explain the rights of stockholders and the roles of corporate directors and officers.*
3. *Contrast the balance sheet presentation of the ownership equity in a corporation and in a sole proprietorship.*
4. *Account for the issuance of capital stock.*
5. *Contrast the features of common stock with those of preferred stock.*
6. *Discuss the factors affecting the market price of preferred stock and of common stock.*
7. *Explain the meaning and significance of book value, market value, and par value of capital stock.*

Who owns General Motors Corporation? The owners of a corporation are called ***stockholders.*** Stockholders in General Motors include over one million men and women, as well as many pension funds, mutual investment funds, labor unions, banks, universities, and other organizations. Because a corporation can be used to pool the savings of any number of investors, it is an ideal means of obtaining the capital necessary for large-scale business activities.

Nearly all large businesses and many small ones are organized as corporations. There are many more sole proprietorships and partnerships than corporations, but in dollar volume of business activity, corporations hold an impressive lead. Because of the dominant role of the corporation in our economy, it is important for everyone interested in business, economics, or politics to have an understanding of corporations and their accounting practices.

What Is a Corporation?

A corporation is a ***legal entity*** having an existence separate and distinct from that of its owners. In the eyes of the law a corporation is an "artificial person," having many of the rights and responsibilities of a real person.

A corporation, as a separate legal entity, may own property in its own name. Thus, the assets of a corporation belong to the corporation itself, ***not to the stockholders.*** A corporation has legal status in court—that is, it may sue and be sued as if it were a person. As a legal entity, a corporation may enter into contracts, is responsible for its own debts, and pays income taxes on its earnings.

Advantages of the Corporate Form of Organization

The corporation offers a number of advantages not available in other forms of organization. Among these advantages are the following:

OBJECTIVE 1 Discuss the advantages and disadvantages of organizing a business as a corporation.

1 **No personal liability for stockholders.**   Creditors of a corporation have a claim against the assets of the corporation, not against the personal property of the stockholders. Thus, the amount of money which stockholders risk by investing in a corporation is ***limited to the amount of their investment.*** To many investors, this is the most important advantage of the corporate form.

2 **Ease of accumulating capital.**   Ownership of a corporation is evidenced by transferable ***shares of stock.*** The sale of corporate ownership in units of one or more shares permits both large and small investors to participate in ownership of the business. Some corporations actually have more than a million individual stockholders. A corporation whose ownership shares are offered for sale to the general public is said to be ***publicly owned.*** Of course not all corporations are large. Many small businesses are organized as corporations and restrict ownership to a limited group of stockholders. Such corporations are said to be ***closely held.***

3 **Readily transferable ownership shares.**   Shares of stock may be sold by one investor to another without dissolving or disrupting the business organization. The shares of most large corporations may be

bought or sold by investors in organized markets, such as the **New York Stock Exchange.** Investments in these shares have the advantage of **liquidity,** because investors may easily convert their corporate ownership into cash by selling their stock.

4 **Continuous existence.** A corporation is a separate legal entity with a perpetual existence. The continuous life of the corporation, despite changes in ownership, is made possible by the issuance of transferable shares of stock. By way of contrast, a partnership is a relatively unstable form of organization which is dissolved by the death or retirement of any of its members. The continuity of the corporate entity is essential to most large-scale business activities.

5 **Professional management.** The stockholders own the corporation, but they do not manage it on a daily basis. To administer the affairs of the corporation, the stockholders elect a **board of directors.** The directors, in turn, hire a president and other corporate officers to manage the business. There is no mutual agency in a corporation; thus, an individual stockholder has no right to participate in the management of the business unless he or she has been hired as a corporate officer.

Disadvantages of the Corporate Form of Organization

Among the disadvantages of the corporation are:

1 **Heavy taxation.** The income of a partnership or a sole proprietorship is taxable only as personal income to the owners of the business. The income of a corporation, on the other hand, is subject to income taxes which must be paid by the corporation. The combination of federal and state corporate income taxes usually takes a substantial share of a corporation's before-tax income.

   If a corporation distributes its earnings to stockholders, the stockholders must pay personal income taxes on the amounts they receive. This practice of first taxing corporate income to the corporation and then taxing distributions of that income to the stockholders is sometimes called **double taxation.**

2 **Greater regulation.** A corporation comes into existence under the terms of state laws, and these same laws may provide for considerable regulation of the corporation's activities. For example, the withdrawal of funds from a corporation is subject to certain limits set by law. Federal laws administered by the Securities and Exchange Commission require publicly owned corporations to make extensive disclosure of their affairs.

3 **Separation of ownership and control.** The separation of the functions of ownership and management may be an advantage in some cases but a disadvantage in others. On the whole, the excellent record of growth and earnings in most large corporations indicates that the separation of ownership and control has benefited rather than injured stockholders. In a few instances, however, a management group has chosen to operate a corporation for the benefit of insiders. The stockholders may find it difficult in such cases to take the concerted action necessary to oust the officers.

Income Taxes in Corporate Financial Statements

As mentioned previously, a corporation is subject to income taxes on its earnings. Income taxes are levied as a percentage of **taxable income.** Taxable income is a subtotal developed in an income tax return, consisting of those revenues subject to income taxes, minus the expenses (deductions) allowed by income tax laws. Notice that taxable income is a net amount; it is **not** the corporation's total revenue.

As we pointed out in earlier chapters, there are a number of differences between income tax rules and generally accepted accounting principles. For example, depreciation expense is computed differently in income tax returns and in financial statements. Also, amortization of goodwill is not deductible in the computation of taxable income.

In summary, taxable income does not correspond precisely with any subtotal in an income statement. In most cases, however, it is reasonably close to the subtotal Income Before Taxes, which is determined by subtracting from revenue all expenses **other than** income taxes expense.

At the end of every accounting period, the estimated amount of a corporation's income taxes expense for the period is recorded in an adjusting entry. As illustrated in Chapter 11, this entry consists of a debit to **Income Taxes Expense** and a credit to the current liability **Income Taxes Payable.**[1]

Corporate income taxes expense cannot be determined with precision until several months after year-end, when the corporation completes the preparation of its annual income tax return. Thus, the end-of-period adjusting entries are based upon estimates. Corporate income taxes expense usually amounts to about one-third of a corporation's income before taxes.

The topic of corporate income taxes is discussed further in Chapters 16 and 26.

Formation of a Corporation

A corporation is created by obtaining a corporate **charter** from the state in which the company is to be incorporated. To obtain a corporate charter, an application called the **articles of incorporation** is submitted to the state corporations commissioner or other designated official. Once the charter is obtained, the stockholders in the new corporation hold a meeting to elect **directors** and to pass **bylaws** as a guide to the company's affairs. The directors in turn hold a meeting at which officers of the corporation are appointed.

Organization Costs   The formation of a corporation is a much more costly step than the organization of a partnership. The necessary costs include the payment of an incorporation fee to the state, the payment of fees to attorneys for their services in drawing up the articles of incorporation, payments to promotors, and a variety of other outlays necessary to bring the corporation into existence. These costs are charged to an asset account called Organization Costs. In the balance sheet, organization costs appear under the "Other assets" caption, as illustrated on page 672.

---

[1]   The recognition of income taxes expense may also involve "deferred" income taxes. This topic is addressed in Chapter 16.

The incurring of these organization costs leads to the existence of the corporate entity; consequently, the benefits derived from these costs may be regarded as extending over the entire life of the corporation. Since the life of a corporation may continue indefinitely, one might argue that organization costs are an asset with an unlimited life. However, income tax rules have permitted organization costs to be written off over a period of five years or more; consequently, most companies have elected to write off organization costs over a five-year period. Accountants have been willing to accept this practice, because organization costs are not material in dollar amount. The accounting principle of **materiality** permits departures from theoretical concepts on the grounds of convenience if the practice in question will not cause any material distortion of net income or financial position.

Rights of Stockholders The ownership of stock in a corporation usually carries the following basic rights:

OBJECTIVE 2
Explain the
rights of
stockholders
and the roles
of corporate
directors
and officers.

1 To vote for directors, and thereby to be represented in the management of the business. The approval of a majority of stockholders may also be required for such important corporate actions as mergers and acquisitions, the selection of independent auditors, the incurring of long-term debts, the establishment of stock option plans, or the splitting of capital stock into a larger number of shares.

   When a corporation issues both common stock and preferred stock, voting rights generally are granted only to the holders of common stock. These two different types of capital stock will be discussed in detail later in this chapter.

2 To share in profits by receiving **dividends** declared by the board of directors. Stockholders in a corporation may not make withdrawals of company assets, as may an owner of an unincorporated business. However, the earnings of a profitable corporation may be distributed to stockholders in the form of cash dividends. The payment of a dividend always requires formal authorization by the board of directors.

3 To share in the distribution of assets if the corporation is liquidated. When a corporation ends its existence, the creditors of the corporation must first be paid in full; any remaining assets are divided among stockholders in proportion to the number of shares owned.

Stockholders' meetings usually are held once a year. Each share of stock is entitled to one vote. In large corporations, these annual meetings are usually attended by relatively few persons, often by less than 1% of the stockholders. Prior to the meeting, the management group will request stockholders who do not plan to attend in person to send in **proxy statements** assigning their votes to the existing management. Through this use of the proxy system, management may secure the right to vote as much as, perhaps, 80% or more of the total outstanding shares.

Functions of the Board of Directors The primary functions of the board of directors are to manage the corporation and to protect the interests of the stockholders. At this level, management may consist principally of formulating policies and reviewing acts of the officers. Specific duties of the directors include declaring dividends, setting the salaries of officers, reviewing the system of internal control with the internal auditors and with the company's independent auditors, and authorizing important contracts of various kinds.

In recent years increasing importance has been attached to the inclusion of outside directors on the boards of large corporations. The term *outside directors* refers to individuals who are not officers of the company and who thus have a view independent of that of the corporate officers.

Functions of Corporate Officers   Corporate officers are the top level of the professional managers appointed by the board of directors to run the business. These officers usually include a president or chief executive officer (CEO), one or more vice presidents, a controller, a treasurer, and a secretary. A vice president is often made responsible for the sales function; other vice presidents may be given responsibility for such important functions as personnel, finance, and production.

The responsibilities of the controller, treasurer, and secretary are most directly related to the accounting phase of business operation. The ***controller,*** or chief accounting officer, is responsible for the maintenance of adequate internal control and for the preparation of accounting records and financial statements. Such specialized activities as budgeting, tax planning, and preparation of tax returns are usually placed under the controller's jurisdiction. The ***treasurer*** has custody of the company's funds and is generally responsible for planning and controlling the company's cash position. The ***secretary*** represents the corporation in many contractual and legal matters and maintains minutes of the meetings of directors and stockholders. Another responsibility of the secretary is to coordinate the preparation of the annual report, which includes the financial statements and other information relating to corporate activities. In small corporations, one officer frequently acts as both secretary and treasurer. The following organization chart indicates lines of authority extending from stockholders to the directors to the president and other officers.

Typical corporate organization

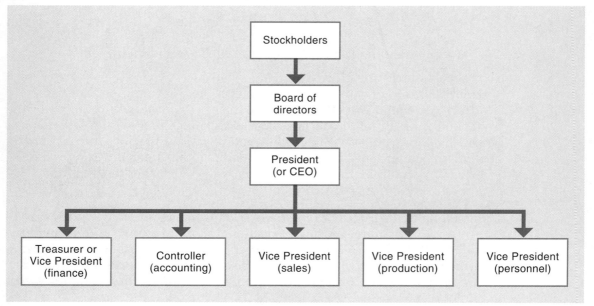

Stockholders' Equity

OBJECTIVE 3
Contrast the
balance
sheet pre-
sentation of
the owner-
ship equity
in a corpo-
ration and
in a sole
proprietor-
ship.

The sections of the balance sheet showing assets and liabilities are much the same for a corporation as for a sole proprietorship. The owner's equity section is the principal point of contrast. In the balance sheet of a corporation, the term **stockholders' equity** is used instead of owner's equity.

The owners' equity in a corporation, as in other types of business organizations, is equal to the assets of the business minus the liabilities. However, state laws require that the stockholders' equity section of a corporate balance sheet clearly indicate the **source** of the owners' equity. The two basic sources of owners' equity are (1) investment by the stockholders **(paid-in capital),** and (2) earnings from profitable operation of the business **(retained earnings).**

When stockholders invest cash or other assets in the business, the corporation issues to them in exchange shares of capital stock as evidence of their ownership. In the simplest case, capital invested by the stockholders is recorded in the corporation's accounting records by a credit to an account entitled **Capital Stock.** The capital paid in by stockholders is regarded as permanent capital not ordinarily subject to withdrawal.

The increase in stockholders' equity arising from profitable operations is called **retained earnings.** At the end of the year the balance of the Income Summary account is closed into the Retained Earnings account. For example, if net income for the year is $70,000, the closing entry will be as follows:

Income Summary *70,000*
     Retained Earnings *70,000*
*To close the Income Summary account by transferring the
year's net income into the Retained Earnings account.*

If the company operates at a loss of, say, $25,000, the Income Summary account will have a debit balance. The account must then be credited to close it. The closing entry will be:

Retained Earnings *25,000*
     Income Summary *25,000*
*To close the Income Summary account by transferring the
year's net loss into the Retained Earnings account.*

If a corporation has sufficient cash, a distribution of profits may be made to stockholders. Distributions of this nature are termed **dividends** and decrease both total assets and total stockholders' equity. Because dividends are regarded as distributions of earnings, the decrease in stockholders' equity is recorded in the Retained Earnings account. Thus, the amount of retained earnings at any balance sheet date represents the **accumulated earnings of the company since the date of incorporation, minus any losses, and minus all dividends.**

Some people mistakenly believe that retained earnings represents a fund of cash available to a corporation. **Retained earnings is not an asset; it is an element of stockholders' equity.** Although the amount of retained earnings indicates the portion of total assets which are **financed** by earning and retaining net income, it does **not** indicate the **form** in which these resources are currently held. The resources generated by retaining profits may have been invested in land, buildings, equipment, or any other kind of asset. The total amount of cash owned by a corporation is shown by the balance of the Cash account, which appears in the asset section of the balance sheet.

Stockholders' Equity in the Balance Sheet For a corporation with $1,000,000 of capital stock and $600,000 of retained earnings, the stockholders' equity section of the balance sheet (omitting certain details) will appear as follows:

Paid-in capital and retained earnings	*Stockholders' equity:*	
	Capital stock	*$1,000,000*
	Retained earnings	*600,000* *$1,600,000*

If this same company had been unprofitable and had incurred losses aggregating $300,000 since its organization, the stockholders' equity section of the balance sheet would be as follows:

Paid-in capital less losses incurred	*Stockholders' equity:*	
	Capital stock	*$1,000,000*
	Less: Deficit	*300,000* *$700,000*

This second illustration tells us that $300,000 of the original $1,000,000 invested by stockholders has been lost. Note that the capital stock in both illustrations remains at the fixed amount of $1,000,000, the stockholders' original investment. The accumulated profits or losses since the organization of the corporation are shown as ***retained earnings*** or as a ***deficit*** and are not intermingled with the paid-in capital. The term ***deficit*** indicates a negative amount of retained earnings.

Cash Dividends

The term ***dividend,*** when used by itself, is generally understood to mean a distribution of cash by a corporation to its stockholders. Dividends are stated as a specific amount per share of capital stock, as, for example, a dividend of $1 per share. The amount received by each stockholder is in proportion to the number of shares owned. Thus, a stockholder who owns 100 shares will receive a check for $100.

Dividends are paid only through action by the board of directors. The board has full discretion to declare a dividend or to refrain from doing so. Once the declaration of a dividend has been announced, the obligation to pay the dividend is a current liability of the corporation and cannot be rescinded.

Because a dividend is declared on one date by the board of directors and paid at a later date, two separate journal entries are necessary. To illustrate the entries for declaration and payment of a cash dividend, assume that a corporation declares a dividend of $1 per share on 100,000 shares of outstanding stock. The dividend is declared on December 15 and is payable on January 25. The two entries would be as follows:

Dividends are first declared . . .	*Dec. 15*	*Retained Earnings*	*100,000*	
		Dividends Payable..........................		*100,000*
		To record declaration by the board of directors of a cash dividend of $1 per share on the 100,000 shares of stock outstanding.		
. . . and then paid	*Jan. 25*	*Dividends Payable*	*100,000*	
		Cash.......................................		*100,000*
		To record payment of the $1 per share dividend declared Dec. 15 on the 100,000 shares of stock outstanding.		

The account **Dividends Payable,** which was credited at the date of declaring the dividend, is a current liability. If a company has more than one issue of capital stock (such as both common stock and preferred stock), it may use a separate Dividends Payable account for each issue.

Some companies in recording the declaration of a dividend will debit an account entitled Dividends instead of debiting the Retained Earnings account. Whenever a Dividends account is used, a closing entry will be required at the end of the year to transfer the debit balance in the Dividends account into the Retained Earnings account. Under either method the end result is a reduction in retained earnings for the amount of the dividends **declared.** (In our end-of-chapter material we will debit the Retained Earnings account, as illustrated above.)

What Is Capital Stock?

As previously mentioned, the caption **capital stock** in the balance sheet of a corporation represents the amount invested by the owners of the business. When the owners of a corporation invest cash or other assets in the business, the corporation issues capital stock as evidence of the investors' ownership equity.

The basic unit of capital stock is called a **share,** but a corporation may issue capital stock certificates in denominations of 1 share, 100 shares, or any other number. The total number of shares of capital stock outstanding at any given time represents 100% ownership of the corporation. **Outstanding** shares are those in the hands of stockholders. The number of shares owned by an individual investor determines the extent of his or her ownership of the corporation.

Assume, for example, that Star Corporation issues a total of 50,000 shares of capital stock to investors in exchange for cash. If you were to acquire 5,000 shares of the 50,000 shares, you would own a 10% interest in the corporation.

Authorization and Issuance of Capital Stock

The articles of incorporation specify the number of shares of capital stock which a corporation is authorized to issue and the **par value,** if any, per share. Large issues of capital stock to be offered for sale to the general public must be approved by the SEC as well as by state officials. The corporation may choose not to issue immediately all the authorized shares; in fact, it is customary to secure authorization for a larger number of shares than presently needed. In future years, if more capital is needed, the previously authorized shares will be readily available for issue; otherwise, the corporation would be forced to apply to the state for permission to increase the number of authorized shares.

Par Value   Par value (or stated value) represents the ***legal capital*** per share—the amount below which stockholders' equity cannot be reduced except by losses from business operations or special legal action. A dividend cannot be declared by a corporation if such action would cause the stockholders' equity to fall below the par value of the outstanding shares. Par value, therefore, may be regarded as a minimum cushion of equity capital existing for the protection of creditors.

Because of the legal restrictions associated with par value, state laws require corporations to show separately in the stockholders' equity section of the balance sheet the par value of shares issued. The special balance sheet presentation has led some people to believe that par value has some special significance. In most corporations, the par value of the shares issued is such a small portion of total stockholders' equity that it is ***insignificant.***

A corporation may set the par value of its stock at $1 per share, $5 per share, or any other amount that it chooses. Most large corporations set the par value of their common stocks at nominal amounts, such as 1 cent per share or $1 per share. The par value of the stock is ***no indication of its market value;*** the par value merely indicates the amount per share to be entered in the Capital Stock account. The common stocks of Ford, AT&T, and Coca-Cola all have par values of $1; COMPAQ Computer's stock has a par value of 1 cent, and Microsoft stock has a par value of one-tenth of a cent. The market value of all these securities is far above their par value. Microsoft's stock, for example, has recently traded at a market value in excess of $100 per share, or more than ***100,000 times*** its par value.

Issuance of Par Value Stock   Mere authorization of a stock issue does not bring an asset into existence, nor does it give the corporation any capital. The obtaining of authorization from the state for a stock issue merely affords a legal opportunity to obtain assets through the sale of stock.

When par value stock is ***issued,*** the Capital Stock account is credited with the par value of the shares issued, regardless of whether the issuance price is more or less than par. Assuming that 50,000 shares of $2 par value stock have been authorized and that 10,000 of these authorized shares are issued at a price of $2 each, Cash would be debited and Capital Stock would be credited for $20,000. When stock is sold for more than par value, the Capital Stock account is credited with the par value of the shares issued, and a separate account, ***Additional Paid-in Capital,*** is credited for the excess of selling price over par. If, for example, our 10,000 shares were issued at a price of $10 per share, the entry would be:

Stockholders' investment in excess of par value

Cash	*100,000*	
Capital Stock		*20,000*
Additional Paid-in Capital		*80,000*

Issued 10,000 shares of $2 par value stock at a price of $10 a share.

The additional paid-in capital does not represent a profit to the corporation. It is part of the invested capital and it will be added to the capital stock in the balance sheet to show the total paid-in capital. The stockholders' equity section of the balance sheet is illustrated below. (The existence of $150,000 in retained earnings is assumed in order to have a complete illustration.)

Corporation's capital classified by source

Stockholders' equity:

Capital stock, $2 par value, authorized 50,000 shares, issued and	
outstanding 10,000 shares	*$ 20,000*
Additional paid-in capital	*80,000*
Total paid-in capital	*$100,000*
Retained earnings	*150,000*
Total stockholders' equity	*$250,000*

If stock is issued by a corporation for less than par, the account Discount on Capital Stock should be debited for the difference between the issuance price and the par value. The issuance of stock at a discount is seldom encountered; it is illegal in many states.

No-Par Stock   Some states allow corporations to issue stock without designating a par or stated value. When this "no-par" stock is issued, the ***entire issue price*** is credited to the Capital Stock account and is viewed as legal capital not subject to withdrawal.

Common Stocks and Preferred Stocks

OBJECTIVE 5 Contrast the features of common stock with those of preferred stock.

The account title ***capital stock*** is widely used when a corporation has issued only ***one type*** of stock. In order to appeal to as many investors as possible, however, many corporations issue several types (or classes) of capital stock, each providing investors with different rights and opportunities.

The "basic" type of capital stock issued by every corporation often is called ***common stock.*** Common stock possesses the traditional rights of ownership—voting rights, participation in dividends, and a residual claim to assets in the event of liquidation. When any of these rights is modified, the term ***preferred stock*** (or sometimes Class B Common) is used to describe the resulting type of capital stock. A few corporations issue two or more classes of preferred stock, with each class having distinctive features designed to appeal to a particular type of investor. In summary, we may say that ***every*** corporation has common stock, and that some corporations also have one or more types of preferred stock.

The following stockholders' equity section illustrates the balance sheet presentation for a corporation having both preferred and common stock:

Balance sheet presentation

Stockholders' equity:

9% cumulative preferred stock, $100 par value, authorized 100,000 shares, issued 50,000 shares	$ 5,000,000
Common stock, $5 par value, authorized 3 million shares, issued 2 million shares	10,000,000
Additional paid-in capital:	
Preferred	200,000
Common	20,000,000
Total paid-in capital	$35,200,000
Retained earnings	13,500,000
Total stockholders' equity	$48,700,000

Notice that the par value and additional paid-in capital are shown separately for each type of stock. This implies that separate capital stock accounts and additional paid-in capital accounts are used in recording the issuance of each type of stock.

Characteristics of Preferred Stock

The characteristics of preferred stocks vary from one issue to the next. The term *preferred* stems from the fact that these stocks almost always have "preference"—or priority—over the common stock in receiving dividends and in the event of liquidation. However, preferred shares usually *lack* significant advantages found in common stock. For example, the dividends paid to preferred stockholders normally *do not increase* if the company prospers. Also, preferred stockholders usually do *not* have voting rights and, therefore, have little say in management.

Among the features usually associated with issues of preferred stock are the following:

1 Preferred as to dividends
2 Cumulative dividend rights
3 Preferred as to assets in event of the liquidation of the company
4 Callable at the option of the corporation
5 No voting power

Another very important but less common feature is a clause permitting the *conversion* of preferred stock into common at the option of the holder. Preferred stocks vary widely with respect to the special rights and privileges granted. Careful study of the terms of the individual preferred stock contract is a necessary step in the evaluation of any preferred stock.

Stock Preferred as to Dividends Stock preferred as to dividends is entitled to receive each year a dividend of specified amount before any dividend is paid on the common stock. The dividend is usually stated as a dollar amount per share. Some preferred stocks state the dividend preference as a *percentage of par value.* For example, a *9%* preferred stock with a par value of $100 per share would mean that $9 must be paid yearly on each share of preferred stock before any dividends are paid on the common.

CASE IN POINT Consolidated Edison has three issues of preferred stock which are publicly traded on the New York Stock Exchange. The first issue is a $5 preferred stock, which pays annual dividends of $5 per share. The other two issues include a 4.65% preferred and a 6% preferred. As both of these issues have $100 par values, they pay annual dividends of $4.65 and $6.00 per share, respectively.

Dividends on all three issues of preferred stock must be paid in full before Consolidated Edison pays any dividend on its common stock.

The holders of preferred stock have no assurance that they will always receive the indicated dividend. A corporation is obligated to pay dividends to stockholders only when the board of directors declares a dividend. Dividends must be paid on preferred stock before anything is paid to the common stockholders, but if the corporation is not prospering, it may decide not to pay dividends on either preferred or common stock. For a corporation to pay dividends, profits must be earned and cash must be available. However, preferred stocks in general offer ***more assurance*** of regular dividend payments than do common stocks.

Cumulative Preferred Stock The dividend preference carried by most preferred stocks is a ***cumulative*** one. If all or any part of the regular dividend on the preferred stock is omitted in a given year, the amount omitted is said to be ***in arrears*** and must be paid in a subsequent year before any dividend can be paid on the common stock. Assume that a corporation was organized January 1, 1992, with 10,000 shares of $8 cumulative preferred stock and 50,000 shares of common stock. Dividends paid in 1992 were at the rate of $8 per share of preferred stock and $2 per share of common. In 1993, earnings declined sharply and the only dividend paid was $2 per share on the preferred stock. No dividends were paid in 1994. What is the status of the preferred stock at December 31, 1994? Dividends are in arrears in the amount of $14 per share ($6 omitted during 1993 and $8 omitted in 1994). On the entire issue of 10,000 shares of preferred stock, the dividends in arrears amount to $140,000.

Dividends in arrears ***are not listed among the liabilities of a corporation, because no liability exists until a dividend is declared by the board of directors.*** Nevertheless, the amount of any dividends in arrears on preferred stock is an important factor to investors and should always be ***disclosed.*** This disclosure is usually made by a note accompanying the balance sheet such as the following:

Footnote disclosure of dividends in arrears

Note 6: Dividends in arrears

As of December 31, 1994, dividends on the $8 cumulative preferred stock were in arrears to the extent of $14 per share and amounted in total to $140,000.

In 1995, we shall assume that the company earned large profits and wished to pay dividends on both the preferred and common stocks. Before paying a dividend on the common, the corporation must pay the $140,000 in arrears on the cumulative preferred stock ***plus*** the regular $8 per share applicable to the current year. The preferred stockholders would, therefore, receive a total of $220,000 in dividends in 1995; the board of directors would then be free to declare dividends on the common stock.

For a **noncumulative** preferred stock, any unpaid or omitted dividend is lost forever. Because of this factor, investors view the noncumulative feature as an unfavorable element, and very few noncumulative preferred stocks are issued.

Stock Preferred as to Assets   Most preferred stocks carry a preference as to assets in the event of liquidation of the corporation. If the business is terminated, the preferred stock is entitled to payment in full of its par value or a higher stated liquidation value before any payment is made on the common stock. This priority also includes any dividends in arrears.

Callable Preferred Stock   Most preferred stocks include a **call provision.** This provision grants the issuing corporation the right to repurchase the stock from the stockholders at a stipulated **call price.** The call price is usually slightly higher than the par value of the stock. For example, $100 par value preferred stock may be callable at $105 or $110 per share. In addition to paying the call price, a corporation which redeems its preferred stock must pay any dividends in arrears. A call provision gives a corporation flexibility in adjusting its financial structure, for example, by eliminating a preferred stock and replacing it with other securities if future growth of the company makes such change advantageous.

Convertible Preferred Stock   In order to add to the attractiveness of preferred stock as an investment, corporations sometimes offer a **conversion privilege** which entitles the preferred stockholders to exchange their shares for common stock in a stipulated ratio. If the corporation prospers, its common stock will probably rise in market value, and dividends on the common stock will probably increase. The investor who buys a convertible preferred stock rather than common stock has greater assurance of regular dividends. In addition, through the conversion privilege, the investor is assured of sharing in any substantial increase in value of the company's common stock.

As an example, assume that Remington Corporation issued a 9%, $100 par, convertible preferred stock on January 1, at a price of $100 per share. Each share was convertible into four shares of the company's $10 par value common stock at any time. The common stock had a market price of $20 per share on January 1, and an annual dividend of $1 per share was being paid. During the next few years, Remington Corporation's earnings increased, the dividend on the common stock was raised to an annual rate of $3, and the market price of the common stock rose to $40 per share. At this point the preferred stock would have a market value of **at least $160,** since it could be converted at any time into four shares of common stock with a market value of $40 each. In other words, the market value of a convertible preferred stock will tend to move in accordance with the price of the common.

When the dividend rate is increased on the common stock, some holders of the preferred stock may convert their holdings into common stock in order to obtain a higher cash return on their investments. If the holder of

100 shares of the preferred stock presented these shares for conversion, Remington Corporation would make the following journal entry:

Conversion of preferred stock into common	*9% Convertible Preferred Stock* *10,000*	
	Common Stock	*4,000*
	Additional Paid-in Capital: Common Stock.................	*6,000*

To record the conversion of 100 shares of preferred stock, par $100, into 400 shares of $10 par value common stock.

Note that the issue price recorded for the 400 shares of common stock is based upon the ***carrying value*** of the preferred stock in the accounting records, not upon market prices at the date of conversion. (If the preferred stock originally had been issued at a price greater than par value, its carrying value would include a proportionate share of the related additional paid-in capital, as well as the par value.)

Participating Preferred Stock   On rare occasions, a corporation may issue a participating preferred stock. A ***participating*** preferred stock is one which, in addition to the regular specified dividend, is entitled to participate (or share) in some manner in additional dividends declared by the board of directors.

For example, assume a corporation has outstanding both common stock and 8%, ***fully participating,*** $100 par value preferred stock. Any dividends declared are first allocated (at $8 per share) to the preferred stockholders. After the common stockholders are allocated an equivalent dividend (8% of par value), the preferred and common stockholder groups share proportionally the residual amount, if any. ***Partially participating*** preferred stock is subject to limits on amounts received in excess of the stated preferred dividend.

It is important to remember that nearly all preferred stocks are ***not*** participating. Although common stock dividends may increase year after year if the corporation prospers, the dividends on most preferred stocks are fixed in amount. A $6 preferred stock, unless it is participating, ***will never pay an annual dividend in excess of $6.***

Market Price of Preferred Stock

Investors buy preferred stocks primarily to receive the dividends that these shares pay. Thus, the dividend rate is one important factor in determining the market price of a preferred stock.

OBJECTIVE 6 Discuss the factors affecting the market price of preferred stock and of common stock.

But what happens to the market price of an 8% preferred stock, originally issued at a par value of $100, if government policies and other factors cause long-term interest rates to rise to, say, 15% or 16%? If investments offering a return of 16% are readily available, investors will no longer pay $100 for a share of preferred stock which provides a dividend of only $8 per year. Thus, the market price of the preferred stock will fall to about half of its original issue price, or about $50 per share. At this market price, the stock offers a 16% return (called the ***dividend yield***) to an investor purchasing the stock ($8 per year ÷ $50 = 16%). However, if the prevailing long-term interest rates decline to the 8% range, the market price of this 8% preferred stock should rise quickly to approximately par value.

In conclusion, the market price of preferred stock ***varies inversely with interest rates.*** As interest rates rise, preferred stock prices decline; as interest rates fall, preferred stock prices rise.

CASE IN POINT The preceding point is illustrated by the performance of Philadelphia Electric's $9\frac{1}{2}\%$, $100 par value, preferred stock as interest rates have fluctuated over the years:

	Long-Term Interest Rates*	Stock Price
September 1978	$9\frac{1}{2}\%$	$99
August 1981	$15\frac{1}{4}\%$	60
March 1983	$12\frac{1}{2}\%$	76
April 1985	$13\frac{1}{2}\%$	68
August 1987	$9\frac{3}{4}\%$	102
January 1992	$8\frac{1}{2}\%$	105

* The long-term interest rates cited in this example are the market yields of federally insured 30-year fixed-rate mortgages.

Market Price of Common Stock

Interest rates also have a significant effect upon the market prices of common stocks. However, common stock dividends are not fixed in amount. If the company prospers, these dividends are likely to increase—perhaps every year. Therefore, ***investors' expectations*** as to the profitability of ***future operations*** greatly affect the market value of common shares.

In addition, many large corporations grow by acquiring smaller companies with excellent future prospects. This generally is accomplished by offering to buy all (or most) of the smaller company's common stock at a price that will induce the existing stockholders to sell. As preferred stockholders usually have no voting rights, an investor seeking control of a business entity need not acquire these shares.

Bear in mind that after shares have been issued they belong to the ***stockholders,*** not to the issuing corporation. Therefore, changes in the market price of the shares ***do not affect the financial statements of the corporation,*** and these changes are not recorded in the corporation's accounting records. The paid-in capital shown in a corporate balance sheet represents the amount ***received when the stock was issued,*** not the current market value of shares.

Issuing Capital Stock: The Role of an Underwriter

When a large amount of stock is to be issued, most corporations use the services of an investment banking firm, frequently referred to as an ***underwriter.*** The underwriter guarantees the issuing corporation a specific price for the stock and makes a profit by selling the shares to the investing public at a slightly higher price. The corporation records the issuance of the stock at the net amount received from the underwriter. The use of an underwriter assures the corporation that the entire stock issue will be sold without delay and that the entire amount of funds to be raised will be available on a specific date.

The price that a corporation will ask for a new issue of stock is based upon such factors as (1) expected future earnings and dividends, (2) the financial strength of the company, and (3) the current state of the investment markets. However, if the corporation asks too much, it simply will not find an underwriter or other buyers willing to purchase the shares.

Stock Issued for Assets Other Than Cash

Corporations generally sell their capital stock for cash and use the cash to buy the various types of assets needed in the business. Sometimes, however, a corporation may issue shares of its capital stock in a direct exchange for land, buildings, or other assets. Stock may also be issued in payment for services rendered by attorneys and promoters in the formation of the corporation.

When a corporation issues capital stock in exchange for services or for assets other than cash, the transaction should be recorded at the current *market value* of the goods or services received. For some types of assets such as land or buildings, the services of a firm of professional appraisers may be useful in establishing current market value. Often, the best evidence as to the market value of these goods or services is the market value of the shares issued in exchange. For example, assume that a company issues 10,000 shares of its $1 par value common stock in exchange for land. Competent appraisers may have differing opinions as to the market value of the land. But let us assume that the company's stock is currently selling on a stock exchange for $90 per share. It is logical to say that the cost of the land to the company is $900,000, the market value of the shares issued in exchange.

Once the valuation has been decided, the entry to record the issuance of the stock in exchange for the land is as follows:

Notice the use of current market values	Land	900,000
	Common Stock	10,000
	Additional Paid-in Capital: Common Stock	890,000

To record the issuance of 10,000 shares of $1 par value common stock in exchange for land. Current market value of stock ($90 per share) used as basis for valuing the land.

Subscriptions to Capital Stock

Small, newly formed corporations sometimes offer investors an opportunity to **subscribe** to shares of the company's capital stock. Under a subscription plan, the investors agree to purchase specified numbers of shares at a stated price *at a future date,* often by making a series of installment payments. The stock is issued after the entire subscription price has been collected.

In summary, selling stock through subscriptions is similar to selling merchandise on a "layaway" plan. One reason for this procedure is to attract small investors. Another reason is to appeal to investors who prefer

not to invest cash until the corporation is ready to start business operations.

When stock is subscribed, the company debits Stock Subscriptions Receivable for the subscription price, credits Capital Stock Subscribed for the
par value of the subscribed shares, and credits Additional Paid-in Capital
for any excess of the subscription price over par value. (These account titles
are modified if the subscribed shares are designated as common stock or
preferred stock.) Later, as installments are collected, the entry is a debit to
Cash and a credit to Stock Subscriptions Receivable. When the entire subscription price has been collected, the stock certificates are issued. The
issuance of the stock is recorded by debiting Capital Stock Subscribed and
crediting Capital Stock. The following illustration demonstrates the accounting procedures for stock subscriptions.

In this example, 10,000 shares of $1 par value common stock are sub-
scribed at a price of $15. Subscriptions for 6,000 of these shares are then
collected in full. A partial payment is received on the other 4,000 shares.

Subscription price above par	*Stock Subscriptions Receivable*	*150,000*
	Common Stock Subscribed	*10,000*
	Additional Paid-in Capital: Common Stock	*140,000*
	Received subscriptions for 10,000 shares of $1 par value stock at price of $15 a share.	

When the subscriptions for 6,000 shares are collected in full, certificates
for 6,000 shares will be issued. The following entries are made:

	Cash	*90,000*
	Stock Subscriptions Receivable	*90,000*
	Collected subscriptions in full for 6,000 shares at $15 each.	
Certificates issued for fully paid shares	*Capital Stock Subscribed*	*6,000*
	Common Stock	*6,000*
	Issued certificates for 6,000 fully paid $1 par value shares.	

The subscriber to the remaining 4,000 shares paid only half of the
amount of the subscription but promised to pay the remainder within a
month. Stock certificates will not be issued until the subscription is collected in full, but the partial collection is recorded by the following entry:

Partial collection of subscription	*Cash*	*30,000*
	Stock Subscriptions Receivable	*30,000*
	Collected partial payment on subscription for 4,000 shares.	

From the corporation's point of view, Stock Subscriptions Receivable is
a current asset, which ordinarily will be collected within a short time. If
financial statements are prepared between the date of obtaining subscriptions and the date of issuing the stock, the Capital Stock Subscribed
account is regarded as legal capital and will appear in the stockholders'
equity section of the balance sheet.

Donated Capital

On occasion, a corporation may receive assets as a gift. To increase local employment, for example, some cities have given corporations the land upon which to build factories. When a corporation receives such a gift, both total assets and total stockholders' equity increase by the market value of the assets received. ***No profit is recognized when a gift is received;*** the increase in stockholders' equity is regarded as paid-in capital. The receipt of a gift is recorded by debiting the appropriate asset accounts and crediting an account entitled ***Donated Capital.*** Donated capital appears in the stockholders' equity section of the balance sheet, as illustrated on page 672.

Stockholder Records in a Corporation

A large corporation with shares listed on the New York Stock Exchange usually has millions of shares outstanding and hundreds of thousands stockholders. Each day many stockholders sell their shares; the buyers of these shares become new members of the company's family of stockholders. An investor purchasing stock in a corporation receives a ***stock certificate*** from the company indicating the number of shares acquired. An illustration of a stock certificate appears on the following page. If the investor later sells these shares, this stock certificate must be surrendered to the corporation for cancellation before a new certificate is issued to the new owner of the shares.

A corporation must have an up-to-date record of the names and addresses of this constantly changing army of stockholders so that it can send dividend checks, financial statements, and voting forms to the right people. Also, the corporation must make sure that old stock certificates are canceled as new ones are issued so that no excess certificates become outstanding.

Stockholders Subsidiary Ledger   When there are numerous stockholders, it is not practical to include a separate account for each stockholder in the general ledger. Instead, a single controlling account entitled Capital Stock appears in the general ledger, and a ***stockholders subsidiary ledger*** is maintained. This ledger contains an account for each individual stockholder. Entries in the stockholders subsidiary ledger are made in number of shares rather than in dollars. Thus, each stockholder's account shows the number of shares owned and the dates of acquisitions and sales. This record enables the corporation to send each stockholder a single dividend check, even though the stockholder may have acquired several stock certificates at different dates.

A corporation which has one or more issues of preferred stock outstanding, as well as common stock, will maintain a separate set of stockholders subsidiary records for each issue.

Stock Transfer Agent and Stock Registrar   Large, publicly owned corporations use an independent stock transfer agent and a stock registrar to maintain their stockholder records and to establish strong internal control

over the issuance of stock certificates. These transfer agents and registrars usually are large banks or trust companies. When stock certificates are to be transferred from one owner to another, the old certificates are sent to the transfer agent, who cancels them, makes the necessary entries in the stockholders subsidiary ledger, and prepares a new certificate for the new owner of the shares. This new certificate then must be registered with the stock registrar before it represents valid and transferable ownership of stock in the corporation.

Small, closely held corporations generally do not use the services of independent registrars and transfer agents. In these companies, the stockholder records usually are maintained by a corporate officer. To prevent the accidental or fraudulent issuance of an excessive number of stock certificates, even a small corporation should require that each certificate be signed by at least two designated corporate officers.

Book Value per Share of Common Stock

Because the equity of each stockholder in a corporation is determined by the number of shares he or she owns, an accounting measurement of interest to many stockholders is book value per share of common stock. Book value per share is equal to the **net assets** represented by one share of stock. The term **net assets** means total assets minus total liabilities; in other words, net assets are equal to total stockholders' equity. Thus in a corporation which has issued common stock only, the book value per share is computed by dividing total stockholders' equity by the number of shares outstanding (or subscribed).

For example, assume that a corporation has 4,000 shares of capital stock outstanding and the stockholders' equity section of the balance sheet is as follows:

How much is book value per share?

Capital stock, $1 par value (4,000 shares outstanding)	$ 4,000
Additional paid-in capital	40,000
Retained earnings	76,000
Total stockholders' equity	$120,000

The book value per share is $30; it is computed by dividing the stockholders' equity of $120,000 by the 4,000 shares of outstanding stock. In computing book value, we are not concerned with the number of authorized shares but merely with the **outstanding** shares, because the total of the outstanding shares represents 100% of the stockholders' equity.

Book Value When a Company Has Both Preferred and Common Stock
Book value is usually computed only for common stock. If a company has both preferred and common stock outstanding, the computation of book value per share of common stock requires two steps. First, the redemption value or **call price** of the entire preferred stock issue and any dividends in arrears are deducted from total stockholders' equity. Second, the remaining amount of stockholders' equity is divided by the number of common shares outstanding to determine book value per common share. This proce-

dure reflects the fact that the common stockholders are the residual owners of the corporate entity.

To illustrate, assume that the stockholders' equity of Video Company at December 31 is as follows:

**Two classes
of stock**

8% preferred stock, $100 par, callable at $110	$1,000,000
Common stock, $10 stated value; authorized 100,000 shares, issued and	
outstanding 50,000 shares	500,000
Additional paid-in capital: common stock.	750,000
Retained earnings	130,000
Total stockholders' equity	$2,380,000

Because of a weak cash position, Video Company has paid no dividends during the current year. As of December 31, dividends in arrears on the cumulative preferred stock total **$80,000.**

All the equity belongs to the common stockholders, except the $1.1 million call price ($110 × 10,000 shares) applicable to the preferred stock and the $80,000 of dividends in arrears on preferred stock. The calculation of book value per share of common stock is shown below:

Total stockholders' equity		$2,380,000
Less: Equity of preferred stockholders:		
Call price of preferred stock	$1,100,000	
Dividends in arrears	80,000	1,180,000
Equity of common stockholders.		$1,200,000
Number of common shares outstanding		50,000
Book value per share of common stock		
($1,200,000 ÷ 50,000 shares)		$24

*OBJECTIVE 7
Explain the
meaning and
significance
of book value,
market value,
and par
value of capi-
tal stock.*

Book Value and Market Price   To some extent, book value is used in evaluating the reasonableness of the market price of a stock. However, it must be used with great caution; the fact that a stock is selling at less than book value does not necessarily indicate a bargain.

Book value is a historical concept, representing the amounts invested by stockholders plus the amounts earned and retained by the corporation. If a stock is selling at a price well ***above*** book value, investors believe that management has created a business worth substantially more than the historical cost of the resources entrusted to its care. This, in essence, is the sign of a successful corporation. If the excess of market price over book value becomes very great, however, investors should consider whether the company's prospects really justify a market price so much above the underlying book value of the company's resources.

On the other hand, if the market price of a stock is ***less than*** book value, investors believe that the company's resources are worth less than their cost while under the control of current management. Thus, the relationship between book value and market price is one measure of investors' confidence in a company's management.

CASE IN POINT Shortly after the introduction of its *Windows* software, the common stock of Microsoft Corp. rose to a market value of more than $100 per share, although its book value per share was only about $6.50. Investors believed that Microsoft's products—and its management—made the business worth far more than the historical amounts of capital that had been invested.

In contrast, the common stock of Tucson Electric Power recently sold at a market price of $12 per share, although its book value was more than $23 per share. This utility company had invested heavily in plant assets intended to generate more electrical power. Unfortunately, demand for this power did not develop, and the company found itself unable to sell its additional output. These new facilities produced very little revenue, but increased operating expenses substantially. Although these new facilities had a high book value, investors did not consider them to be worth the amounts invested.

Balance Sheet for a Corporation Illustrated

A fairly complete balance sheet for a corporation is illustrated on the following page. Note the inclusion in this balance sheet of liabilities for income taxes payable and dividends payable. These liabilities do not appear in the balance sheet of an unincorporated business. Note also that the caption for each capital stock account indicates the type of stock, the par value per share, and the number of shares authorized and issued. The caption for preferred stock also indicates the dividend rate, call price, and other important features.

Bear in mind that current practice includes many alternatives in the choice of terminology and the arrangement of items in financial statements.

END-OF-CHAPTER REVIEW

SUMMARY OF CHAPTER LEARNING OBJECTIVES

1 **Discuss the advantages and disadvantages of organizing a business as a corporation.**
The primary advantages are: no personal liability of stockholders for the debts of the business, the transferability of ownership shares, continuity of existence, ability to hire professional management, and the relative ease of accumulating large amounts of capital. The primary disadvantages are: "double taxation" of earnings and greater governmental regulation.

2 **Explain the rights of stockholders and the roles of corporate directors and officers.**
Stockholders in a corporation normally have the right to elect the board of directors, to share in dividends declared by the directors, to share in the distribution of assets if the corporation is liquidated, and to sub-

DEL MAR CORPORATION
Balance Sheet
December 31, 1994

Assets

Current assets:

Cash and cash equivalents	$ 305,600
Accounts receivable (net)	1,105,200
Stock subscriptions receivable	110,000
Inventories	1,300,800
Short-term prepayments	125,300
Total current assets	$2,947,500

Plant and equipment:

Land		900,000
Buildings and equipment	$5,283,000	
Less: Accumulated depreciation	1,250,000	4,033,000
Other assets: Organization costs		14,000
Total assets		$7,894,500

Liabilities & Stockholders' Equity

Current liabilities:

Accounts payable	$ 998,100
Income taxes payable	324,300
Dividends payable	109,700
Interest payable	20,000
Total current liabilities	$1,452,100
Long-term liabilities: Bonds payable, 12%, due Oct. 1, 1999	1,000,000
Total liabilities	$2,452,100

Stockholders' equity:

Cumulative 8% preferred stock, $100 par, callable at $104, authorized and issued 10,000 shares	$1,000,000
Common stock, $1 par, authorized 1,000,000 shares, issued 600,000 shares	600,000
Common stock subscribed, 20,000 shares	20,000
Additional paid-in capital: common	2,070,000
Donated capital	210,000
Total paid-in capital	$3,900,000
Retained earnings	1,542,400
Total stockholders' equity	$5,442,400
Total liabilities & stockholders' equity	$7,894,500

scribe to additional shares if the corporation decides to increase the number of shares outstanding.

The directors formulate company policies, review the actions of the corporate officers, and protect the interests of the company's stockholders. Corporate officers are professional managers appointed by the board of directors to manage the business on a daily basis.

3 Contrast the balance sheet presentation of the ownership equity in a corporation and in a sole proprietorship.

In the balance sheet of a sole proprietorship, the total amount of ownership equity appears in a single account, entitled, for example, J. Doe, Capital. In the balance sheet of a corporation, separate accounts are used to distinguish between paid-in capital and earned capital. In the simplest case, this may be accomplished with two accounts: Capital Stock and Retained Earnings. Additional accounts are needed if the corporation has issued more than one type of capital stock or if stock is issued at a price above par value.

4 Account for the issuance of capital stock.

When capital stock is issued, appropriate asset accounts are debited for the **market value** of the goods or services received in exchange for the stock. A capital stock account (which indicates the type of stock issued) is credited for the **par value** of the issued shares. **Any excess** of the market value received over the par value of the issued shares is credited to an additional paid-in capital account.

5 Contrast the features of common stock with those of preferred stock.

Common stock represents the true "residual ownership" of a corporation. These shares have voting rights and cannot be called. Also, the common stock dividend is not fixed in dollar amount—thus, it may increase or decrease based upon the company's performance.

Preferred stock has preference over common stock with respect to dividends and to distributions in the event of liquidation. This "preference" means that preferred stockholders must be paid in full before any payments are made to holders of common stock. The dividends on preferred stock usually are fixed in amount. In addition, the stock usually is callable at the option of the issuing corporation and often has no voting rights. Preferred stocks sometimes have special features, such as being convertible into shares of common stock.

6 Discuss the factors affecting the market price of preferred stock and of common stock.

The market price of preferred stock varies **inversely** with interest rates. As interest rates rise, preferred stock prices decline; as interest rates fall, preferred stock prices rise. If a company's ability to continue the preferred dividend is in doubt, the solvency of the company also affects preferred stock prices.

Interest rates also affect the market price of common stock. However, common stock dividends are not fixed in amount. Both the amount of the dividend and the market value of the stock may fluctuate, based upon the prosperity of the company. Therefore, the principal factor in the market price of common stock is **investors' expectations** as to the future profitability of the company.

7 Explain the meaning and significance of book value, market value, and par value of capital stock.

Book value is the amount of net assets represented by each share of common stock. Book value may be either higher or lower than the current market value; however, it may give an indication of the reasonableness of the current market price.

Market value is the current price at which shares of stock may be bought or sold. When a stock is traded on an organized stock exchange, the market price is quoted daily in the financial press. Market price is based upon a combination of factors, including investors' expectations of future earnings, dividend yield, interest rates, and alternative investment opportunities.

Par value is the amount of legal capital per share—that is, the amount below which stockholders' equity cannot be reduced except by losses or special legal action. Thus, par value is a minimum cushion of equity capital existing for the protection of creditors. Par value is not directly related either to market value or to book value.

We will continue our discussion of corporate accounting issues over the next three chapters, concluding with a discussion of corporate securities (stocks and bonds) from the viewpoint of the investor. Throughout the remainder of this textbook, and in later accounting courses, the corporation will be the form of organization used in most illustrations and assignment material.

KEY TERMS INTRODUCED OR EMPHASIZED IN CHAPTER 14

Additional paid-in capital   Amounts invested in a corporation by stockholders (or as donated capital) in excess of the par value or stated value of any shares issued in exchange. In short, *paid-in capital* in excess of *legal capital.*

Board of directors   Persons elected by common stockholders to direct the affairs of a corporation.

Book value per share   The stockholders' equity represented by each share of common stock, computed by dividing common stockholders' equity by the number of common shares outstanding.

Call price   The price to be paid by a corporation for each share of callable preferred stock if the corporation decides to call (redeem) the preferred stock.

Capital stock   Transferable units of ownership in a corporation. A broad term which may refer to common stock, preferred stock, or both.

Common stock   A type of capital stock which possesses the basic rights of ownership including the right to vote. Represents the residual element of ownership in a corporation.

Deficit   Accumulated losses incurred by a corporation. A negative amount of retained earnings.

Dividend   A distribution of cash by a corporation to its stockholders.

Legal capital   Equal to the *par value* or *stated value* of capital stock issued. This amount represents a "permanent commitment" of capital by the owners of a corporation and cannot be removed without special legal action. Of course, it may be eroded by losses.

Organization costs   Costs incurred to form a corporation.

Paid-in capital   The amounts invested in a corporation by its stockholders (also includes donated capital).

Par value or stated value   The *legal capital* of a corporation. Represents the minimum amount per share to be invested in the corporation by its owners and cannot be withdrawn except by special legal action.

Preferred stock A class of capital stock usually having preferences as to dividends and in the distribution of assets in event of liquidation.

Retained earnings That portion of stockholders' equity resulting from profits earned and retained in the business. Retained earnings is increased by the earning of net income and is decreased by the incurring of net losses and by the declaration of dividends.

Stock certificate A document issued by a corporation (or its transfer agent) as evidence of the ownership of the number of shares stated on the certificate.

Stock registrar An independent fiscal agent, usually a large bank, retained by a corporation to provide assurance against overissuance of stock certificates.

Stock transfer agent A bank or trust company retained by a corporation to maintain its records of capital stock ownership and to make transfers from one investor to another.

Stockholder Someone with an ownership interest in a corporation. The percentage of this ownership interest is determined by the percentage of the outstanding shares owned.

Stockholders subsidiary ledger A record showing the number of shares owned by each stockholder.

Underwriter An investment banking firm which handles the sale of a corporation's stock to the public.

DEMONSTRATION PROBLEM FOR YOUR REVIEW

At the close of the current year, the stockholders' equity section of Rockhurst Corporation's balance sheet was as follows:

Stockholders' equity:

$6 preferred stock, $100 par value, callable at $102, 200,000		
shares authorized		$12,000,000
Common stock, $5 par value, 5,000,000 shares authorized:		
Issued	$10,000,000	
Subscribed..	4,000,000	14,000,000
Additional paid-in capital:		
Preferred..	$ 360,000	
Common (including subscribed shares)	30,800,000	31,160,000
Retained earnings		2,680,000
Total stockholders' equity		$59,840,000

Assets of the corporation include *subscriptions receivable, $7,200,000.*

INSTRUCTIONS On the basis of this information, answer the following questions and show any necessary supporting computations.

a How many shares of preferred stock have been issued?

b What is the total annual dividend requirement on the outstanding preferred stock?

c How many shares of common stock have been issued or subscribed?

d What was the average price per share received by the corporation for its common stock, including shares subscribed?

e What is the average amount per share that subscribers to common stock have yet to pay on their subscriptions?

f What is the total amount of legal capital, including shares subscribed?

g   What is the total paid-in capital, including shares subscribed?

h   What is the book value per share of common stock? (Assume no dividends in arrears.)

SOLUTION TO DEMONSTRATION PROBLEM

a   <u>120,000 shares</u> ($12,000,000 total par value, divided by $100 par value per share)

b   <u>$720,000</u> (120,000 shares × $6 per share)

c   <u>2,800,000 shares</u> ($14,000,000 total par value, divided by $5 par value per share)

d
Par value of common shares issued and subscribed	*$14,000,000*
Additional paid-in capital on common shares	*30,800,000*
Total issue price of common shares (including subscribed)	*$44,800,000*
Shares issued and subscribed (part c)	*2,800,000*
Average issue price per share ($44,800,000 ÷ 2,800,000 shares)	*$16*

e
Subscriptions receivable	*$ 7,200,000*
Shares subscribed ($4,000,000 total par value, divided by $5 par value per share)	*800,000*
Average amount due per share ($7,200,000 ÷ 800,000 shares)	*$9*

f   <u>$26,000,000</u> ($12,000,000 preferred, $14,000,000 common)

g   <u>$57,160,000</u> ($26,000,000 legal capital, plus $31,160,000 additional paid-in capital)

h
Total stockholders' equity	*$59,840,000*
Less: Claims of preferred stockholders (120,000 shares × $102 call price)	*12,240,000*
Equity of common stockholders	*$47,600,000*
Common shares outstanding or subscribed (part c)	*2,800,000*
Book value per share ($47,600,000 ÷ 2,800,000 shares)	*$17*

SELF-TEST QUESTIONS

The answers to these questions appear on page 689.

1   When a business is organized as a corporation:

   a   Stockholders are liable for the debts of the business only in proportion to their percentage ownership of capital stock.

   b   Stockholders do **not** have to pay personal income taxes on dividends received, because the corporation is subject to income taxes on its earnings.

   c   Fluctuations in the market value of outstanding shares of capital stock do **not** affect the amount of stockholders' equity shown in the balance sheet.

   d   Each stockholder has the right to bind the corporation to contracts and to make other managerial decisions.

2   Great Plains Corporation was organized with authorization to issue 100,000 shares of $1 par value common stock. Forty thousand shares were issued to Tom Morgan, the company's founder, at a price of $5 per share. No other shares have yet been issued.

   a   Morgan owns **40%** of the stockholders' equity of the corporation.

    b The corporation should recognize a $160,000 gain on the issuance of these shares.

    c If the balance sheet includes retained earnings of $50,000, total ***paid-in*** capital amounts to $250,000.

    d In the balance sheet, the Additional Paid-in Capital account will have a $160,000 balance, regardless of the profits earned or losses incurred since the corporation was organized.

3 Which of the following is ***not*** a characteristic of the ***common stock*** of a large, publicly owned corporation?

    a The shares may be transferred from one investor to another without disrupting the continuity of business operations.

    b Voting rights in the election of the board of directors.

    c A cumulative right to receive dividends.

    d After issuance, the market value of the stock is unrelated to its par value.

4 Tri-State Electric is a profitable utility company that has increased its dividend to ***common*** stockholders every year for 62 consecutive years. Which of the following is ***least*** likely to affect the market price of the company's ***preferred*** stock?

    a The company's earnings are expected to increase significantly over the next several years.

    b An increase in long-term interest rates.

    c The annual dividend paid to preferred shareholders.

    d Whether or not the preferred stock carries a conversion privilege.

5 The following information is taken from the balance sheet and related disclosures of Blue Oyster Corporation:

Total paid-in capital	*$5,400,000*
Outstanding shares:	
Common stock, $5 par value	*100,000 shares*
6% preferred stock, $100 par value, callable at $108 per share	*10,000 shares*
Preferred dividends in arrears	*2 years*
Total stockholders' equity	*$4,700,000*

Which of the following statements is true? (More than one answer may be correct.)

    a The preferred dividends in arrears amount to $120,000 and should appear as a liability in the corporate balance sheet.

    b The book value per share of common stock is $35.

    c The stockholders' equity section of the balance sheet should include a deficit of $700,000.

    d The company has paid no dividend on its ***common*** stock during the past two years.

ASSIGNMENT MATERIAL

DISCUSSION QUESTIONS

1 Why are large corporations often said to be ***publicly owned?***

2 Distinguish between corporations and partnerships in terms of the following characteristics:

    a   Owners' liability for debts of the business

    b   Transferability of ownership interest

    c   Continuity of existence

    d   Federal taxation on income

3 What are the basic rights of the owner of a share of corporate stock? In what way are these basic rights commonly modified with respect to the owner of a share of preferred stock?

4 Explain the meaning of the term **double taxation** as it applies to corporate profits.

5 Distinguish between **paid-in capital** and **retained earnings** of a corporation. Why is such a distinction useful?

6 If the Retained Earnings account has a debit balance, how is it presented in the balance sheet and what is it called?

7 Explain the significance of **par value.** Does par value indicate the reasonable market price for a share of stock? Explain.

8 Describe the usual nature of the following features as they apply to a share of preferred stock: (a) cumulative, (b) convertible, and (c) callable.

9 Why is noncumulative preferred stock considered a very unattractive form of investment?

10 When stock is issued by a corporation in exchange for assets other than cash, accountants face the problem of determining the dollar amount at which to record the transaction. Discuss the factors to be considered and explain their significance.

11 State the classification (asset, liability, stockholders' equity, revenue, or expense) of each of the following accounts:

    a   Subscriptions receivable

    b   Organization costs

    c   Preferred stock

    d   Retained earnings

    e   Capital stock subscribed

    f   Additional paid-in capital

    g   Income taxes payable

12 A professional baseball team received as a gift from the city the land upon which to build a stadium. What effect, if any, will the receipt of this gift have upon the baseball team's balance sheet and income statement? Explain.

13 Explain the following terms:

    a   Stock transfer agent

    b   Stockholders subsidiary ledger

    c   Underwriter

    d   Stock registrar

14 What does **book value per share** of common stock represent? Does it represent the amount common stockholders would receive in the event of liquidation of the corporation? Explain briefly.

15 How is book value per share of common stock computed when a company has both preferred and common stock outstanding?

16 What would be the effect, if any, on book value per share of common stock as a result of each of the following independent events: (a) a corporation obtains a bank loan; (b) a dividend is declared (to be paid in the next accounting period).

17 In the great stock market crash of October 19, 1987, the market price of **IBM's** capital stock fell by over $31 per share. Explain the effects, if any, of this decline in share price on IBM's balance sheet.

EXERCISES

EXERCISE 14-1
Accounting Terminology

Listed below are nine technical accounting terms introduced or emphasized in this chapter:

Retained earnings	*Preferred stock*	*Par value*
Deficit	*Common stock*	*Book value*
Dividend in arrears	*Paid-in capital*	*Market value*

Each of the following statements may (or may not) describe one of these technical terms. For each statement, indicate the term described, or answer "None" if the statement does not correctly describe any of the terms.

a That portion of stockholders' equity arising from the issuance of capital stock.

b The type of capital stock most likely to increase in value as a corporation becomes increasingly profitable.

c The net assets represented by one share of common stock.

d A distribution of cash by a corporation to its owners.

e The type of capital stock for which the dividend usually is fixed in amount.

f Cash provided by profitable operations that is available for distribution to stockholders as dividends.

g The per-share value of common stock that reflects investors' expectations of future profitability.

h A dividend paid to common stockholders that is smaller than the dividend paid in the prior year.

EXERCISE 14-2
Computing Retained Earnings

Johnson Pump, Inc., began operations in 1993. In that year, the corporation earned net income of $195,000 and paid dividends of $2.25 per share on its 40,000 outstanding shares of capital stock. In 1994, the corporation incurred a net loss of $127,000 and paid no dividends.

INSTRUCTIONS

a Prepare the journal entry to close the Income Summary account at December 31, 1994 (the year of the $127,000 net loss).

b Compute the amount of retained earnings or deficit which will appear in the company's balance sheet at December 31, 1994.

EXERCISE 14-3
Recording Dividends

Westfall Corporation has outstanding 60,000 shares of $2 par value common stock, which were issued for $22 per share. The net income in the first year of operations was $235,000. On December 31, the board of directors declared a dividend of $1.50 per share, payable on January 31 of the following year.

INSTRUCTIONS

a Prepare the journal entries at December 31 of the first year (1) to close the Income Summary account and (2) to record declaration of the dividend.

b Prepare the journal entry to record payment of the dividend on January 31 of the second year.

c Compute the amount of retained earnings reported in Westfall's balance sheet at ***December 31,*** the end of the first year of operations.

d Assume that the board of directors of Westfall did not meet on December 31 as above but waited until January 15 of the second year because the chairman was on vacation. On January 15, they declared the dividend of $1.50 per share payable on February 15. Compute the amount of retained earnings that would have been reported in Westfall's balance sheet at ***December 31,*** the end of the first year of operations in this situation.

EXERCISE 14-4
Stockholders'
Equity Section
of a Balance
Sheet

When Enviro Systems, Inc., was formed, the company was authorized to issue 5,000 shares of $100 par value, 8% cumulative preferred stock, and 100,000 shares of $2 stated value common stock. The preferred stock is callable at $106.

Half of the preferred stock was issued at a price of $103 per share, and 70,000 shares of the common stock were sold for $13 per share. At the end of the current year, Enviro Systems, Inc., has retained earnings of $297,000. Prepare the stockholders' equity section of the company's balance sheet at the end of the current year.

EXERCISE 14-5
Dividends: Pre-
ferred and
Common

The stockholders' equity section from the December 31, 1994, balance sheet of Palermo Corporation appears below:

Stockholders' equity:

Preferred stock, 9% cumulative, $50 par, 40,000 shares authorized and issued	*$2,000,000*
Preferred stock, 12% noncumulative, $100 par, 8,000 shares authorized and issued	*800,000*
Common stock, $5 par, 400,000 shares authorized and issued	*2,000,000*
Additional paid-in capital: common	*2,800,000*
Retained earnings	*890,000*
Total stockholders' equity	*$8,490,000*

INSTRUCTIONS

Assume that all the stock was issued on January 1, 1992, and that no dividends were paid during the first two years of operations. During 1994 Palermo Corporation declared and paid total cash dividends of $736,000.

a Compute the amount of cash dividends paid during 1994 to each of the three classes of stock.

b Compute the dividends paid ***per share*** during 1994 for each of the three classes of stock.

c Palermo Corporation generated a net loss of $190,000 in 1992 and earned net income of $627,000 in 1993. Compute the amount of net income (or net loss) generated by Palermo during 1994.

EXERCISE 14-6
Computing
Retained
Earnings

Wolfe Company has outstanding two classes of $100 par value stock: 5,000 shares of 8% cumulative preferred and 25,000 shares of common. The company had a $50,000 deficit at the beginning of the current year, and preferred dividends had not been paid for two years. During the current year, the company earned $300,000. What will be the balance in retained earnings at the end of the current year, if the company pays a dividend of $2 per share on the common stock?

EXERCISE 14-7
Analyzing Stockholders' Equity

The year-end balance sheet of Maui Corporation includes the following stockholders' equity section (with certain details omitted):

Stockholders' equity:

$8.25 cumulative preferred stock, $100 par value, callable at $105	$ 12,000,000
Common stock, $5 par value, 5,000,000 shares authorized	20,000,000
Additional paid-in capital:	
Preferred..	240,000
Common	31,200,000
Retained earnings	57,160,000
Total stockholders' equity	$120,600,000

INSTRUCTIONS

From this information, compute answers to the following questions:

a How many shares of preferred stock have been issued?

b What is the total amount of the annual dividends paid to preferred stockholders?

c What was the average issuance price per share of common stock?

d What is the amount of legal capital and the amount of total paid-in capital?

e What is the book value per share of common stock?

EXERCISE 14-8
Issuing Stock for Assets Other Than Cash

Kato Manufacturing issued 45,000 shares of common stock in exchange for land with a fair market value of $790,000. Prepare the journal entry to record this transaction under each of the following independent assumptions:

a The stock has a $2 par value.

b The stock has a $10 par value.

c The stock has no par value or stated value.

EXERCISE 14-9
Stock Subscriptions

To raise capital for a new polo field, Santa Fe Polo Club offered shares of its common stock to club members on a subscription plan. Prepare journal entries in the club's accounting records to record the following transactions:

Sept. 15 Members subscribed to 30,000 shares of $2 par value common stock at a subscription price of $25 per share.

Dec. 20 Collected $300,000 cash in full payment of 12,000 of the subscribed shares. Issued stock certificates for these shares.

EXERCISE 14-10
Computing Book Value

Presented below is the information necessary to compute the net assets (stockholders' equity) and book value per share of common stock for Ahora Advertising, Inc.:

8% cumulative preferred stock, $100 par (callable at $110) .3000...............	$300,000
Common stock, $5 par, authorized 100,000 shares ..90,000.....................	450,000
Additional paid-in capital	679,200
Deficit	130,200
Dividends in arrears on preferred stock, 1 full year	24,000

INSTRUCTIONS

a Compute the amount of net assets (stockholders' equity).

b Compute the book value per share of common stock.

EXERCISE 14-11
Nature of Market, Par, and Book Values

International Business Machines Corporation (IBM), the world's largest manufacturer of computers, has had a long track record of growing sales and earnings. In December 1991, however, IBM announced projected revenue growth of only 6% for 1992, below the computer industry average. In addition, heavy competition would enable IBM to hold gross profit margins at just 51% to 53%, several points below what analysts had expected. According to company management, this lower-than-expected growth projection will not affect the company's ability or commitment to continue paying dividends at the current rate.

What would you expect the immediate effect of this announcement to be upon the following values of IBM's common stock? Explain.

a Par value

b Market value

c Book value

PROBLEMS

Group A

PROBLEM 14A-1
Journal Entries for Corporate Transactions

Shown below are five selected transactions of Reclamation Systems, Inc., for the year ended December 31, 1994:

Jan. 15 Paid a cash dividend totaling $45,000. This dividend was declared on December 15, 1993, payable on January 15, 1994.

June 19 Issued an additional 20,000 shares of $5 par value capital stock to Baldwin Development Corporation in exchange for an adjoining parcel of land needed for expansion. The stock of Reclamation Systems is not widely traded. Although Baldwin paid $385,000 for the land 5 years ago, two independent appraisals have estimated the value of the real estate to be $310,000 on this date.

Dec. 15 The board of directors declared a dividend of 30 cents per share, payable on January 15, 1995, to the owners of the corporation's 170,000 outstanding shares of capital stock.

Dec. 31 Recorded income tax expense for the three-month period ended December 31, 1994, $54,200. These taxes will be paid on January 15, 1995. (Income taxes for the first nine months of 1994, amounting to $184,600, have already been recorded and paid.)

Dec. 31 Closed the Income Summary account at the end of a profitable year. Net income, $472,000.

INSTRUCTIONS

a Prepare journal entries to record the above transactions.

b Assume the balance sheet of Reclamation Systems at December 31, 1993, reported retained earnings of $1,516,000. Compute the amount of retained earnings to be reported in the corporation's balance sheet at December 31, *1994.* Show computation.

PROBLEM 14A-2
Stockholders' Equity in the Balance Sheet

Bauman Pharmaceutics was organized early in 1989 with authorization to issue 50,000 shares of $100 par value preferred stock and 1 million shares of $1 par value common stock. All of the preferred stock was issued at par, and 600,000 shares of common stock were sold for $16 per share. The preferred stock pays a 9% cumulative dividend and is callable at $110.

During the first five years of operations (1989 through 1993), the corporation earned a total of $6,920,000 and paid dividends of 50 cents per share each year on the common stock. In 1994, however, the corporation reported a net loss of $2,400,000 and paid no dividends.

INSTRUCTIONS

a Prepare the stockholders' equity section of the balance sheet at December 31, 1994. Prepare a separate supporting schedule showing your computation of the amount of retained earnings or deficit.

b Draft a footnote to accompany the financial statements disclosing any dividends in arrears at the end of 1994.

PROBLEM 14A-3
Stockholders' Equity Section—A More Challenging Problem

Tomahawk Tools, Inc., was organized in January 1991. The corporation issued at $18 per share one-half of its 100,000 authorized shares of $2 par common stock. On January 2, *1992,* the company sold at par the entire 10,000 authorized shares of $50 par value, 8% cumulative preferred stock. On January 2, *1993,* the company again needed money and issued 5,000 shares of an authorized 20,000 shares of $11, no-par, cumulative preferred stock for a total of $518,000.

The company suffered losses and paid no dividends during 1991 and 1992, reporting a deficit of $200,000 at the end of 1992. During 1993 and 1994 combined, the company earned a total of $800,000. Dividends of $1.50 per share were paid on common stock in 1993 and $3.00 per share in 1994.

INSTRUCTIONS

Prepare the stockholders' equity section of the balance sheet at December 31, 1994. Include a separate supporting schedule showing your computation of retained earnings or deficit at this balance sheet date.

PROBLEM 14A-4
Stockholders' Equity: A Short, Comprehensive Problem

Pat Breeden has been working in the child care field for many years as both a child care provider and as a consultant. She and several associates recently formed a corporation, Wee Care, Inc., to provide organization and administration of on-site child care programs for large employers. The corporation is authorized to issue 100,000 shares of $100 par value, $8 cumulative preferred stock and 200,000 shares of $2 par value common stock. The following transactions (among others) occurred during the first year of operations:

Jan. 5   Issued for cash 20,000 shares of common stock at $14 per share. The shares were issued to Breeden and 10 other investors.

Jan. 8   Issued 4,500 shares of preferred stock for cash of $450,000. ۱ ٥٥

Feb. 10   Issued an additional 500 shares of common stock to Breeden in exchange for her services in organizing the corporation. The stockholders agreed that these services were worth $7,000.

Nov. 15   The board of directors declares the first annual dividend on the preferred stock, to be paid on December 15.

Nov. 27   Acquired land as a future building site in exchange for 15,000 shares of common stock. Wee Care's stock is not widely traded on any organized exchange, but the parcel of land has been appraised at approximately $225,000 by two different independent appraisers.

Dec. 15   Paid the cash dividend declared on November 15.

Dec. 31   After the revenue and expenses (except income taxes) were closed into the Income Summary account, that account showed a before-tax profit of $216,000. Income taxes were determined to be $59,440.

INSTRUCTIONS

a Prepare journal entries in general journal form to record the above transactions. Include entries at December 31 to (1) record the income tax liability, (2) close the Income Taxes Expense account into the Income Summary account, and (3) close the Income Summary account.

b Prepare the stockholders' equity section of the Wee Care, Inc., balance sheet at December 31.

PROBLEM 14A-5
Starting a New Corporation; Includes Stock Subscriptions

Pancho's Cantina is the best Mexican restaurant in town—maybe the best anywhere. For years, the restaurant was a sole proprietorship owned by Wayne Label. Many of Label's friends and customers had offered to invest in the business if he ever decided to open new locations. So, early this year, Label decided to expand the business. He formed a new corporation, called Pancho's Cantinas, Inc., which planned to issue stock and use the money received to open new restaurants in various locations.

The new corporation is authorized to issue 200,000 shares of $1 par value capital stock. In May the corporation entered into the following transactions:

May 1   Received subscriptions from various investors for 30,000 shares of capital stock to be issued at a price of $25 per share.

May 24   Received an invoice from an attorney for $7,100 for services relating to the formation of the new corporation. This invoice is due in 30 days.

May 28   Received $75,000 cash as full payment from Alan Richmond, an investor who had subscribed to 3,000 shares of capital stock. A stock certificate was immediately issued to Richmond for 3,000 shares. (No payments have been received from the subscribers to the other 27,000 shares.)

May 31   Issued 30,000 shares of capital stock to Label in exchange for the assets of the original Pancho's Cantina. These assets and their current market values on this date are listed below.

Inventory	$ 23,000
Land	325,000
Building	260,000
Equipment and fixtures	142,000

May 31   Issued 200 shares of capital stock to Label in exchange for $5,000 cash, thus assuring Label voting control of the corporation even after the other investors pay for their subscribed shares.

The new corporation will begin operation of the original Pancho's Cantina on June 1. Therefore, the corporation had no revenue or expenses relating to restaurant operations during May. No depreciation of plant assets or amortization of organization costs will be recognized until June, when operations get under way.

INSTRUCTIONS

a Prepare journal entries to record the May transactions in the accounting records of the new corporation.

b Prepare a classified balance sheet for the corporation as of May 31, 19___.

PROBLEM 14A-6
Analysis of an Equity Section of a Balance Sheet

The year-end balance sheet of DeskTop Products includes the following stockholders' equity section (with certain details omitted):

Stockholders' equity:

$7\frac{1}{2}$% cumulative preferred stock, $100 par value, callable at $105,	
100,000 shares authorized	$2,400,000
Common stock, $2 par value, 900,000 shares authorized	900,000
Additional paid-in capital: common stock	8,325,000
Donated capital	720,000
Retained earnings	2,595,000
Total stockholders' equity	$14,940,000

INSTRUCTIONS

From this information, compute answers to the following questions:

a How many shares of preferred stock have been issued?

b What is the total amount of the annual dividends paid to preferred stockholders?

c How many shares of common stock are outstanding?

d What was the average issuance price per share of common stock?

    e What is the amount of legal capital?

    f What is the total amount of paid-in capital?

    g What is the book value per share of common stock? (There are no dividends in arrears.)

    h Assume that retained earnings at the beginning of the year amounted to $717,500, and that net income for the year was $3,970,000. What was the dividend declared during the year on *each share* of common stock?

Group B

**PROBLEM 14B-1
Journal Entries
for Corporate
Transactions**

Shown below are selected transactions of St. Claire Vineyards for the year ended December 31, 1994:

Jan. 19   Issued capital stock to Martin DiBello in exchange for land. Two firms hired to appraise the land have differing opinions as to the fair market value of the real estate. DiBello, however, agrees to accept 10,000 shares of $1 par value capital stock as a fair exchange. St. Claire's stock is widely traded and is quoted at $19 per share on a national stock exchange on this date.

June 10   At their June meeting, the board of directors declared a dividend of 20 cents per share, payable on July 15, to owners of the corporation's 200,000 outstanding shares of capital stock.

July 15   Paid the dividend declared on June 10.

Dec. 10   At their December meeting, the board of directors declared a dividend of 25 cents per share, payable on January 15 of the following year. No capital stock has been issued since the January 19 transaction.

Dec. 31   Recorded income tax expense for the three months ended December 31, 1994, $34,900. These taxes will be paid on January 15, 1995. (Income taxes for the first nine months of 1994 have already been recorded and paid.)

Dec. 31   Closed the Income Summary account at the end of a profitable period. Net income, $365,000.

INSTRUCTIONS

    a Prepare journal entries to record the above transactions.

    b Assume the balance sheet of St. Claire Vineyards at December 31, 1993, reported retained earnings of $1,215,000. Compute the amount of retained earnings to be reported in the corporation's balance sheet at December 31, *1994*. Show computation.

**PROBLEM 14B-2
Stockholders'
Equity in a
Balance Sheet**

Early in 1990, Sinclair Press was organized with authorization to issue 100,000 shares of $100 par value preferred stock and 500,000 shares of $1 par value common stock. Ten thousand shares of the preferred stock were issued at par, and 170,000 shares of common stock were sold for $15 per share. The preferred stock pays an 8% cumulative dividend and is callable at $105.

    During the first four years of operations (1990 through 1993), the corporation earned a total of $1,025,000 and paid dividends of 75 cents per share each year on the common stock. In 1994, however, the corporation reported a net loss of $340,000 and paid no dividends.

INSTRUCTIONS

    a Prepare the stockholders' equity section of the balance sheet at December 31, 1994. Include a supporting schedule showing your computation of the amount of retained earnings or deficit.

    b Draft a footnote to accompany the financial statements disclosing any dividends in arrears at the end of 1994.

PROBLEM 14B-3
Stockholders' Equity Section—A More Challenging Problem

Maria Martinez organized Manhattan Transport Company in January 1991. The corporation immediately issued at $8 per share one-half of its 200,000 authorized shares of $2 par common stock. On January 2, *1992,* the corporation sold at par the entire 5,000 authorized shares of 8%, $100 par value, cumulative preferred stock. On January 2, *1993,* the company again needed money and issued 5,000 shares of an authorized 10,000 shares of $9, no-par, cumulative preferred stock for a total of $512,000.

The company suffered losses in its first two years reporting a deficit of $170,000 at the end of 1992. During 1993 and 1994 combined, the company earned a total of $890,000. Dividends of 50 cents per share were paid on common stock in 1993 and $1.60 per share in 1994.

INSTRUCTIONS

Prepare the stockholders' equity section of the balance sheet at December 31, 1994. Include a supporting schedule showing your computation of retained earnings or deficit at the balance sheet date.

PROBLEM 14B-4
Dividends, Closing Entries, and Stockholders' Equity

Hua Lai organized Pacific Rim Corporation early in 1993. On January 9, the corporation issued to Hua Lai and other investors 100,000 of its 500,000 authorized shares of $1 par value common stock at a price of $9 per share.

After the revenue and expense accounts (except income taxes expense) were closed into the Income Summary account at the end of the year, that account showed a before-tax profit of $288,000. Income taxes were determined to be $64,000. No dividends were paid during 1993.

On January 15, 1994, the board of directors declared a cash dividend of 75 cents per share, payable February 15.

INSTRUCTIONS

a Prepare the journal entries for 1993 to (1) record the issuance of the common stock, (2) record the income tax liability at December 31, (3) close the Income Taxes Expense account into the Income Summary account, and (4) close the Income Summary account.

b Prepare the journal entries in 1994 for the declaration of the dividend on January 15 and payment of the dividend on February 15.

c Operations in 1994 resulted in a $158,800 net loss. Prepare the journal entry to close the Income Summary account at December 31, 1994.

d Prepare the stockholders' equity section of the balance sheet at December 31, 1994. Include a separate supporting schedule showing your determination of retained earnings at that date. Disregard the possibility of an income tax refund.

PROBLEM 14B-5
Issuance of Capital Stock and Stock Subscriptions

For several years, Kathryn Mead has operated a successful business organized as a sole proprietorship. In order to raise the capital to operate on a larger scale, she decided to organize a new corporation to continue in the same line of business. In January, Mead organized Down Home, Inc., which was authorized to issue 500,000 shares of $2 par value common stock. During January, Down Home, Inc., completed the following transactions:

Jan. 9   Issued 8,000 shares of common stock to various investors for cash at $32 per share.

Jan. 12   Issued 27,000 shares of common stock to Mead in exchange for assets with a current market value as follows:

Inventory	$198,000
Land	235,000
Equipment	124,000
Building	307,000

Jan. 14 Received an invoice from an attorney for $8,950 for services relating to the formation of Down Home, Inc. The invoice will be paid in 30 days.

Jan. 15 Received subscriptions for 7,000 shares of common stock at $32 per share; 2,000 of the shares were subscribed by Mead and 5,000 were subscribed by other investors.

Jan. 31 Collected from Mead the full amount of her subscription to 2,000 shares of common stock and issued a stock certificate for these shares. (No collection has yet been made from the subscribers to the other 5,000 shares.)

The corporation will begin operations in February; no revenue was earned and no expenses were incurred during January. No depreciation of plant assets and no amortization of organization cost will be recognized until February, when operations get under way.

INSTRUCTIONS
a Prepare journal entries to record the transactions for January in the accounting records for Down Home, Inc.

b Prepare a classified balance sheet for the corporation at January 31.

PROBLEM 14B-6
Analysis of Stockholders' Equity

The year-end balance sheet of LaserTech, Inc., includes the following stockholders' equity section (with certain details omitted):

Stockholders' equity:

$8 cumulative preferred stock, $100 par value, callable at $103, 200,000 shares authorized		$ 6,000,000
Common stock, $2 par value, 5,000,000 shares authorized:		
Issued	$ 3,600,000	
Subscribed	1,400,000	5,000,000
Additional paid-in capital:		
Preferred	$ 240,000	
Common (including subscribed shares)	25,000,000	25,240,000
Retained earnings		3,690,000
Total stockholders' equity		$39,930,000

Assets of the corporation include *subscriptions receivable, $5,600,000.*

INSTRUCTIONS
On the basis of this information, answer the following questions and show any necessary supporting computations.

a How many shares of preferred stock have been issued?

b What is the total annual dividend requirement on the outstanding preferred stock?

c How many shares of common stock have been issued or subscribed?

d What was the average price per share received by the corporation for its common stock, including shares subscribed?

e What is the average amount per share that subscribers to common stock have yet to pay on their subscriptions?

f What is the total amount of legal capital, including shares subscribed?

g What is the total paid-in capital, including shares subscribed?

h What is the book value per share of common stock? (Assume no dividends in arrears.)

i Total dividends of $780,000 were declared on the preferred and common stock during the year, and the balance of retained earnings at the beginning of the year was $2,302,000. What was the amount of net income for the year?

CASES AND UNSTRUCTURED PROBLEMS

CASE 14-1
Par, Book, and Market Values. An Open-Ended Discussion

Microsoft Corp. is the producer of such software products as **Windows, Excel,** and **Word.** In mid-1990, an investment service published the following per-share amounts relating to Microsoft's only class of capital stock:

Par value	$ 0.001
Book value (estimated)	6.50
Market value	73.00

INSTRUCTIONS

a Without reference to dollar amounts, explain the nature and significance of *par value, book value,* and *market value.*

b Comment upon the *interrelationships,* if any, among the per-share amounts shown for Microsoft Corp. What do these amounts imply about the company and its operations? Also comment upon what these amounts imply about the security of *creditors'* claims against the company.

CASE 14-2
Issuing Stock for Assets Other Than Cash

The following independent cases involve the issuance of capital stock in exchange for assets other than cash.

1 DuPar Corporation, a successful, family-owned company, is in the process of acquiring a tract of land suitable for the construction of a factory. The DuPar Corporation has agreed to offer 26,000 shares of common stock in exchange for the land, which has an agreed fair market value of $650,000, based on two independent appraisals. DuPar Corporation stock is not traded on any stock exchange.

INSTRUCTIONS

Give the journal entry that should be made to record this transaction under each of the following assumptions:

a The stock has a $2 par value.

b The stock has a $20 par value.

c The stock has *no* par value.

2 Irwin Products, a well-established company, issued 3,800 shares of its $5 par value common stock in exchange for certain patents. The patents were entered in the accounts at $19,000. At this time, Irwin Products common stock was quoted on the over-the-counter market at "25 bid and 27 asked"; that is, sellers were offering stock at $27 per share, and buyers were offering to buy at $25 per share.

INSTRUCTIONS

a Comment on the company's treatment of this transaction. Write a brief statement explaining whether you agree or disagree, and why.

b What is the essential difference between the evidence available to the accountant as a basis for the record of DuPar Corporation and the evidence available for Irwin Products?

CASE 14-3
Factors Affecting the Market Prices of Preferred and Common Stocks

ADM Labs is a publicly owned company with several issues of capital stock outstanding. Over the past decade, the company has consistently earned modest profits and has increased its common stock dividend annually by 5 or 10 cents per share. Recently the company introduced several new products which you believe will cause future sales and profits to increase dramatically. You also expect a gradual increase in long-term interest rates from their present level of about 9% to, perhaps, 10% or 10½%. Based upon these forecasts, explain whether you would expect to see the market prices of the following issues of ADM capital stock increase or decrease. Explain your reasoning in each answer.

a 8%, $100 par value, preferred stock (currently selling at $90 per share)

b $1 par value common stock (currently paying an annual dividend of $1.20 and selling at $40 per share)

c 5%, $100 par value, convertible preferred stock (currently selling at $125 per share)

CASE 14-4
Whether or Not
To Incorporate

Mario Valenti owns Valenti Ford, a successful automobile dealership. For 25 years, Valenti has operated the business as a sole proprietorship and has acted as both owner and manager. Now, he is 70 years old and is planning on retiring from active management. However, he wants the dealership to stay in the family; his long-term goal is to leave the business to his two children and five grandchildren.

Valenti is wondering whether or not he should incorporate his business. If he were to reorganize Valenti Ford as a corporation, he could then leave an appropriate number of shares of stock to each of his heirs. Otherwise, he could leave the entire business to his heirs to be operated as a partnership. In selecting the appropriate form of business entity, Valenti has formulated the following objectives:

1 **Ownership:** Valenti wants each of his two children to own 25% of the business and each of his five grandchildren to own 10%.

2 **Continuity of existence:** Valenti wants the business to continue indefinitely, even if one or more of the heirs should die or should no longer want to participate in ownership.

3 **Management:** When Valenti retires, he plans to give Joe Heinz, a long-time employee, responsibility for managing the business. Although Valenti wants to keep the ownership of the business in the family, he does not believe that any of his family members have the time or experience to manage the business on a daily basis. In fact, Valenti believes that two of his grandchildren simply have no "business sense," and he does not want them to participate in management.

4 **Income taxes:** Valenti wants to organize the business in a manner which will minimize the income taxes to be paid by his heirs. He expects that all the earnings of the business normally will be distributed to its owners on an annual basis.

5 **Owners' liability:** Valenti recognizes that an automobile dealership might become liable for vast amounts of money, if, for example, improper repairs caused a customer's car to be involved in an accident. Although the business carries insurance, he wants to be sure that his heirs' equity in the business does not place their personal assets at risk in the event of business losses.

INSTRUCTIONS

a For each of the five numbered paragraphs above, explain how the choice of business organization (partnership or corporation) relates to Valenti's stated objective.

b In light of your analysis in part **a**, above, would you recommend that Valenti reorganize Valenti Ford as a corporation, or leave the business unincorporated so that his heirs may operate it as a partnership?

ANSWERS TO SELF-TEST QUESTIONS

1 c   2 d   3 c   4 a   5 b, c, d

15 Corporations: Operations and Additional Stockholders' Equity Transactions

In this chapter we explore special topics relating primarily to the financial statements of large corporations. The chapter is divided into two major parts. In the first part, we show how an income statement is organized to present certain "unusual" items separately from the income or loss from normal business activities. Also, we illustrate and explain the presentation of earnings per share, with emphasis upon the interpretation of the different per-share amounts. In the second part, we look at various stockholders' equity transactions, including cash dividends, stock dividends, stock splits, prior period adjustments, and treasury stock transactions.

After studying this chapter you should be able to meet these Learning Objectives:

1 *Describe how discontinued operations, extraordinary items, and accounting changes are presented in the income statement.*

2 *Compute earnings per share.*

3 *Distinguish between primary and fully diluted earnings per share.*

4 *Account for stock dividends and stock splits, and explain the probable effect of these transactions upon market price.*

5 *Describe and prepare a statement of retained earnings.*

6 *Define prior period adjustments and explain how they are presented in financial statements.*

7 *Account for treasury stock transactions.*

8 *Describe and prepare a statement of stockholders' equity.*

REPORTING THE RESULTS OF OPERATIONS

The most important aspect of corporate financial reporting, in the view of most stockholders, is the determination of periodic net income. Both the market price of common stock and the amount of cash dividends per share depend to a considerable extent on the current level of earnings (net income). Even more important than the absolute amount of net income is the ***trend*** of earnings over time.

Developing Predictive Information

An income statement tells us a great deal about the performance of a company over the past year. For example, study of the income statement makes clear the types and amounts of revenue earned and expenses incurred as well as the amounts of gross profit and net income. But can we expect the income statement for ***next year*** to indicate about the same level of performance? If the transactions summarized in the income statement for the year just completed were of a normal recurring nature, such as selling merchandise, paying employees, and incurring other normal expenses, we can reasonably assume that the operating results were typical and that somewhat similar results can be expected in the following year. However, in any business, unusual and nonrecurring events may occur which cause the current year's net income to be quite different from the income we should expect the company to earn in the future. For example, the company may have sustained large losses in the current year from an earthquake or some other event which is not likely to recur in the near future.

Ideally, the results of unusual and nonrecurring transactions should be shown in a separate section of the income statement ***after*** the income or loss from normal business activities has been determined. Income from ***normal and recurring*** activities presumably should be a more useful figure for ***predicting future earnings*** than is a net income figure which includes the results of nonrecurring events. The problem in creating such an income statement, however, is in determining which events are so unlikely to recur that they should be excluded from the results of "normal" operations. Three categories of events that require special treatment in the income statement are (1) the results of discontinued operations, (2) extraordinary items, and (3) the cumulative effects of changes in accounting principles.

Reporting Unusual Items—An Illustration

To illustrate the presentation of these items, assume that Ross Corporation operates both a small chain of retail stores and two motels. Near the end of the current year, the company sells both motels to a national hotel chain. In addition, Ross Corporation reports two "extraordinary items" and also changes the method used in computing depreciation expense. An income statement illustrating the correct format for reporting these events appears on the next page.

ROSS CORPORATION
Income Statement
For the Year Ended December 31, 1994

Net sales		$8,000,000
Cost and expenses:		
Cost of goods sold	$4,500,000	
Selling expenses..	1,500,000	
General and administrative expenses	920,000	
Loss on settlement of lawsuit	80,000	
Income taxes (on continuing operations)..................	300,000	7,300,000
Income from continuing operations		$ 700,000
Discontinued operations:		
Operating loss on motels (net of $90,000 income tax benefit)	$ (210,000)	
Gain on sale of motels (net of $195,000 income taxes)	455,000	245,000
Income before extraordinary items and cumulative effect of accounting change		$ 945,000
Extraordinary items:		
Gain on condemnation of land by State Highway Department (net of $45,000 income taxes)..............	$ 105,000	
Loss from earthquake damage to Los Angeles store (net of $75,000 income tax benefit)................	(175,000)	(70,000)
Cumulative effect of change in accounting principle:		
Effect on prior years' income of change in method of computing depreciation (net of $60,000 income taxes)..........................		140,000
Net income		$1,015,000

Notice the order in which the "special items" are reported

This income statement is designed to illustrate the presentation of various "unusual events." Rarely, if ever, will all these types of events appear in the income statement of one company within a single year.

Continuing Operations

The first section of the income statement contains only the results of *continuing business activities*—that is, the retail stores. Notice that the income taxes expense shown in this section relates *only to continuing operations.* The income taxes relating to the "special items" are shown separately in the income statement as adjustments to the amounts of these items.

Income from Continuing Operations The subtotal *income from continuing operations* measures the profitability of the ongoing operations. This subtotal should be helpful in making predictions of the company's future earnings. For example, if we predict no significant change in the profitability of its retail stores, we would expect Ross Corporation to earn a net income of approximately $700,000 next year.

Discontinued Operations

OBJECTIVE 1
Describe how
discontinued
operations,
extraordinary
items, and
accounting
changes are
presented in
the income
statement.

If management enters into a formal plan to sell or discontinue a *segment* of the business, the results of that segment's operations are shown separately in the income statement. This enables users of the financial statements to better evaluate the performance of the company's ongoing (continuing) operations.

Two items are included in the "discontinued operations" section of the income statement: (1) the income or loss from *operating* the segment prior to its disposal and (2) the gain or loss on *disposal* of the segment. Notice also that the income taxes relating to the discontinued operations are *shown separately* from the income taxes expense relating to continuing business operations.

Discontinued Operations Must Be a "Segment" of the Business   To qualify for separate presentation in the income statement, the discontinued operations must represent an *entire segment* of the business. A "segment" of a business is a separate line of business activity or an operation that services a distinct category of customers.

For example, Allstate Insurance Company is a segment of Sears, Roebuck & Company. From time to time, Sears closes individual Allstate offices. Such office closures do *not* qualify as "discontinued operations," because Sears remains in the insurance business. If, however, Sears were to sell the entire Allstate Insurance Company, insurance activities would be shown in Sears' income statement as discontinued operations.

Discontinued Operations Are Not Really "Unusual"   In recent years, a characteristic of the American economy has been the "restructuring" of many large corporations. As part of this restructuring, corporations often sell one or more segments of the business. Thus, the presence of "discontinued operations" is not uncommon in the income statements of large corporations.

CASE IN POINT   In one recent year, TWA sold Hilton International, a hotel chain, to Allegis (parent company of United Airlines). Later that year, Allegis disposed of several segments of its business, including Hilton hotels and Hertz rental cars. In the same year, Sears sold its savings bank segment, RJR Nabisco sold its Heublein (wine and spirits) segment, Owens-Illinois sold its forest products division, and Metromedia sold its cellular telephone operations. All in all, several hundred large corporations reported discontinued operations.

Extraordinary Items

The second category of events requiring disclosure in a separate section of the income statements is extraordinary items. An extraordinary item is a gain or loss that is *(1) material in amount, (2) unusual in nature, and (3) not expected to recur in the foreseeable future.* By definition, extraordinary items are extremely rare; hence, they seldom appear in financial statements. Examples of extraordinary items include the effects of unusual casualties such as earthquakes or tornadoes; expropriation or condemnation of assets by a governmental agency; and gains or losses that may result from a newly enacted law or from the early retirement of long-term debt.

When a gain or loss qualifies as an extraordinary item, it appears after the section on discontinued operations (if any), following the subtotal *Income before Extraordinary Items.* Since the extraordinary item is so unusual, this subtotal is considered necessary to show investors what the net income *would have been* if the unusual event had not occurred. Extraordinary items are shown net of any related income tax effects.

Other "Unusual" Gains and Losses   Some transactions are not typical of normal operations but also do not meet the criteria for separate presentation as extraordinary items. Among such events are losses incurred because of strikes and the gains or losses resulting from sales of plant assets. Such items, if material, should be individually listed as items of revenue or expense, rather than being combined with other items in broad categories such as sales revenue or general and administrative expenses.

In the illustrated income statement of Ross Corporation (page 692), the $80,000 loss resulting from the settlement of a lawsuit was disclosed separately in the income statement but was *not* listed as an extraordinary item. This loss was important enough to bring to the attention of readers of the financial statements, but most lawsuits are not so unusual or infrequent as to be considered extraordinary items.

Changes in Accounting Principle

The accounting principle of *consistency* means that a business should continue to use the same accounting principles and methods from one period to the next. However, this principle does not mean that a business can *never* make a change in its accounting methods. A change may be made if the need for the change can be justified and the effects of the change are *properly disclosed* in the financial statements.

The "Cumulative Effect" of an Accounting Change   In reporting most changes in accounting principle, the *cumulative effect* of the change upon the income of *prior* years is shown in the income statement of the year in which the change is made. To compute this one-time "catch up adjustment," we recompute the income of prior years *as if the new accounting method had always been in use.* The difference between this recomputed net income and the net income actually reported in those periods is the "cumulative effect" of the accounting change.

To illustrate, assume that Ross Corporation has been using the double-declining-balance method of depreciation but decides in the current year to change to the straight-line method. The company determines that if the straight-line method had always been in use, the total net income of prior years would have been $140,000 higher than was actually reported. This $140,000 is the *cumulative effect* of the change in accounting principle and is shown as a separate item in the current year's income statement (following discontinued operations and extraordinary items, if any). Depreciation expense in the current and future years' income statements is computed by the straight-line method, just as if this method had always been in use.

Changes in Principle versus Changes in Estimate   A change in accounting principle refers to a change in the *method* used to compute financial statement amounts, not to a change in the underlying estimates. For example, a switch from straight-line to another method of computing depreciation is regarded as a change in accounting principle. However, a change in the estimated useful life used in computing depreciation expense is a *change in estimate.* This distinction is an important one. When we change an accounting *principle* (method), the cumulative effect of the change upon the income of prior years usually is reported as a one-time adjustment to income in the year of the change. Changes in *estimate,* however, affect only the current year and future years; no effort is made to recompute the income of prior years.

Earnings per Share (EPS)

OBJECTIVE 2
Compute
earnings per
share.

Perhaps the most widely used of all accounting statistics is *earnings per share* of common stock. Everyone who buys or sells stock in a corporation needs to know the annual earnings per share. Stock market prices are quoted on a per-share basis. If you are considering investing in IBM stock at a price of, say, $120 per share, you need to know the earnings per share and the annual dividend per share in order to decide whether this price is reasonable. In other words, how much earning power and how much dividend income would you be getting for each share you buy?

To compute earnings per share, the annual net income applicable to the common stockholders is divided by the average number of common shares outstanding. The concept of earnings per share applies *only to common stock;* preferred stock has no claim to earnings beyond the stipulated preferred stock dividends.

Many financial analysts express the relationship between earnings per share and market price per share as a *price-earnings ratio* (p/e ratio). This ratio is computed by dividing the market price per share of common stock by the annual earnings per share.

Weighted-Average Number of Shares Outstanding   The simplest example of computing earnings per share is found when a company has issued only common stock and the number of shares outstanding has not changed during the year. In this situation, the net income for the year divided by the number of shares outstanding at year-end equals earnings per share.

In many companies, however, the number of shares of stock outstanding changes one or more times during the year. When additional shares are issued in exchange for assets during the year, the computation of earnings per share is based upon the *weighted-average* number of shares outstanding.[1]

---

[1]   When the number of shares outstanding changes as a result of a stock split or a stock dividend (discussed later in this chapter), the computation of the weighted-average number of shares outstanding should be adjusted *retroactively* rather than weighted for the period the new shares were outstanding. Earnings per share data for prior years thus will be consistently stated in terms of the current capital structure.

The weighted-average number of shares for the year is determined by multiplying the number of shares outstanding by the fraction of the year that said number of shares outstanding remained unchanged. For example, assume that 100,000 shares of common stock were outstanding during the first nine months of 1994 and 140,000 shares during the last three months. Assume also that the increase in shares outstanding resulted from the sale of 40,000 shares for cash. The weighted-average number of shares outstanding during 1994 would be *110,000* determined as follows:

100,000 shares × $\frac{9}{12}$ of a year	75,000
140,000 shares × $\frac{3}{12}$ of a year	35,000
Weighted-average number of common shares outstanding	110,000

This procedure gives more meaningful earnings per share data than if the total number of shares outstanding at the end of the year were used in the calculations. By using the weighted-average number of shares, we recognize that the proceeds from the sale of the 40,000 shares were available to generate earnings only during the last three months of the year. Although the weighted-average number of shares outstanding must be used in earnings-per-share computations, this figure does not appear in the stockholders' equity section of the balance sheet. A balance sheet prepared at year-end reports the *actual* number of shares outstanding at that date, regardless of when the shares were issued during the year.

Preferred Dividends and Earnings per Share   When a company has preferred stock outstanding, the preferred stockholders participate in net income to the extent of the preferred stock dividends. To determine the earnings *applicable to the common stock,* we first deduct from net income the amount of current year preferred stock dividends. The annual dividend on *cumulative* preferred stock is *always* deducted, even if not declared by the board of directors for the current year. Noncumulative preferred stock dividends are deducted only if declared.

To illustrate, let us assume that Tanner Corporation has 200,000 shares of common stock and 10,000 shares of $6 cumulative preferred stock outstanding throughout the year. Net income for the year totals $560,000. Earnings per share of common stock would be computed as follows:

Net income	$560,000
Less: Dividends on preferred stock (10,000 shares × $6)	60,000
Earnings applicable to common stock	$500,000
Weighted-average number of common shares outstanding	200,000
Earnings per share of common stock ($500,000 ÷ 200,000 shares)	$2.50

Even when there are dividends in arrears, only the **current year's** cumulative preferred stock dividend is deducted in the earnings per share computation. Dividends in arrears from previous years have already been deducted in the prior years' earnings per share computations.

Presentation of Earnings per Share in the Income Statement   All publicly owned corporations are *required* to present earnings per share data in their ***income statements.***[2] If an income statement includes subtotals for income from continuing operations, or for income before extraordinary items, per-share figures are shown for these amounts as well as for net income. These additional per-share amounts are computed by substituting the amount of the appropriate subtotal for the net income figure in the preceding calculation.

To illustrate all of the potential per-share computations, we will expand our Tanner Corporation example to include income from continuing operations and income before extraordinary items. We should point out, however, that all of these figures seldom appear in the same income statement. Very few companies have discontinued operations, an extraordinary item, and an accounting change to report in the same year. The following condensed income statement is intended to illustrate the proper format for presenting earnings per share figures and to provide a review of the calculations.

TANNER CORPORATION Condensed Income Statement For the Year Ended December 31, 1994		
Net sales		$9,000,000
Costs and expenses (including taxes on continuing operations)		8,310,000
Income from continuing operations		$ 690,000
Loss from discontinued operations (net of income tax benefits)...........		(90,000)
Income before extraordinary items and cumulative effect of account- ing change		$ 600,000
Extraordinary loss (net of income tax benefit)	$(120,000)	
Cumulative effect of accounting change (net of related income taxes)	80,000	(40,000)
Net income		$ 560,000
Earnings per share of common stock:		
Earnings from continuing operations		$3.15[a]
Loss from discontinued operations		(.45)
Earnings before extraordinary items and cumulative effect of accounting change...		$2.70[b]
Extraordinary loss		(.60)
Cumulative effect of accounting change		.40
Net earnings...		$2.50[c]

[a] ($690,000 − $60,000 preferred dividends) ÷ 200,000 shares
[b] ($600,000 − $60,000) ÷ 200,000 shares
[c] ($560,000 − $60,000) ÷ 200,000 shares

Earnings per share figures are required in the income statement

Interpreting the Different Per-Share Amounts To informed users of financial statements, each of these figures has a different significance. Earnings per share from continuing operations represents the results of continuing and ordinary business activity. This figure is the most useful one for pre-

---

[2]   The FASB has exempted closely held corporations (those not publicly owned) from the requirement of computing and reporting earnings per share. See *FASB Statement No. 23*, "Suspension of the Reporting of Earnings per Share and Segment Information by Nonpublic Enterprises" (Norwalk, Conn.: 1978).

dicting future operating results. ***Net earnings*** per share, on the other hand, shows the overall operating results of the current year, including any discontinued operations or extraordinary items.

Unfortunately the term ***earnings per share*** often is used without qualification in referring to various types of per-share data. When using per-share information, it is important to know exactly which per-share statistic is being presented. For example, the price-earnings ratios (market price divided by earnings per share) for common stocks listed on major stock exchanges are reported daily in ***The Wall Street Journal*** and many other newspapers. Which earnings per share figures are used in computing these ratios? If a company reports an extraordinary gain or loss, the price-earnings ratio is computed using the per-share ***earnings before the extraordinary item.*** Otherwise, the ratio is based upon ***net earnings*** per share.

Primary and Fully Diluted Earnings per Share

OBJECTIVE 3
Distinguish
between pri-
mary and
fully diluted
earnings per
share.

Let us assume that a company has an outstanding issue of preferred stock that is convertible into shares of common stock at a rate of, say, two shares of common for each share of preferred. The conversion of this preferred stock would increase the number of common shares outstanding and might ***dilute*** (reduce) earnings per share. Any common stockholder interested in the trend of earnings per share will want to know what effect the conversion of the preferred stock would have upon this statistic.

To inform investors of the potential dilution which might occur, two figures are presented for each earnings per share statistic. The first figure, called ***primary*** earnings per share, is based upon the weighted-average number of common shares actually outstanding during the year. Thus, this figure ignores the potential dilution represented by the convertible preferred stock.[3] The second figure, called ***fully diluted*** earnings per share, shows the impact that conversion of the preferred stock would have upon primary earnings per share.

Primary earnings per share are computed in the same manner illustrated in our preceding example of Tanner Corporation. Fully diluted earnings per share, on the other hand, are computed on the assumption that all the preferred stock ***had been converted into common stock at the beginning of the current year.***[4] (The mechanics of computing fully diluted earnings per share are covered in the intermediate accounting course.)

It is important to remember that fully diluted earnings per share represent a ***hypothetical case.*** This statistic is computed even though the preferred stock actually was ***not*** converted during the year. The purpose of showing fully diluted earnings per share is to warn common stockholders what ***could*** have happened. When the difference between primary and fully diluted earnings per share becomes significant, investors should rec-

---

[3]   If certain criteria are met, convertible securities qualify as ***common stock equivalents*** and enter into the computation of primary earnings per share. Common stock equivalents and other complex issues relating to earnings per share are discussed in intermediate accounting courses and in *APB Opinion No. 15,* "Earnings per Share," AICPA (New York: 1969).

[4]   If the preferred stock had been issued during the current year, we would assume that it was converted into common stock on the date it was issued.

ognize the *risk* that future earnings per share may be reduced by conversions of other securities into common stock.

When a company reports both primary and fully diluted earnings per share, the price-earnings ratio shown in newspapers is based upon the *primary* figure.

OTHER STOCKHOLDERS' EQUITY TRANSACTIONS

Cash Dividends

The prospect of receiving cash dividends is a principal reason for investing in the stocks of corporations. An increase or a decrease in the established rate of dividends will usually cause an immediate rise or fall in the market price of the company's stock. Stockholders are keenly interested in prospects for future dividends and as a group are strongly in favor of more generous dividend payments. The board of directors, on the other hand, is primarily concerned with the long-run growth and financial strength of the corporation; it may prefer to restrict dividends to a minimum in order to conserve cash for the purchase of plant and equipment or for other needs of the company. Many of the so-called "growth companies" plow back into the business most of their earnings and pay only very small cash dividends.

The preceding discussion suggests three requirements for the payment of a cash dividend. These are:

1 **Retained earnings.**   Since dividends represent a distribution of earnings to stockholders, the theoretical maximum for dividends is the total undistributed net income of the company, represented by the credit balance of the Retained Earnings account. As a practical matter, many corporations limit dividends to somewhere near 40% of annual net income, in the belief that a major portion of the net income must be retained in the business if the company is to grow and to keep pace with its competitors.

2 **An adequate cash position.**   The fact that the company reports large earnings does not mean that it has a large amount of cash on hand. Cash generated from earnings may have been invested in new plant and equipment, or in paying off debts, or in acquiring a larger inventory. There is no necessary relationship between the balance in the Retained Earnings account and the balance in the Cash account. The traditional expression of "paying dividends out of retained earnings" is misleading. Cash dividends can be paid only "out of" cash.

3 **Dividend action by the board of directors.**   Even though a company's net income is substantial and its cash position seemingly satisfactory, dividends are not paid automatically. A formal action by the board of directors is necessary to declare a dividend.

Dividend Dates

Four significant dates are involved in the distribution of a dividend. These dates are:

1 **Date of declaration.** On the day on which the dividend is declared by the board of directors, a liability to make the payment comes into existence.

2 **Date of record.** The date of record always follows the date of declaration, usually by a period of two or three weeks, and is always stated in the dividend declaration. In order to be eligible to receive the dividend, a person must be listed as the owner of the stock on the date of record.

3 **Ex-dividend date.** The ex-dividend date is significant for investors in companies with stocks traded on the stock exchanges. To permit the compilation of the list of stockholders as of the record date, it is customary for the stock to go *ex-dividend* three business days before the date of record. A stock is said to be selling ex-dividend on the day that it loses the right to receive the latest declared dividend. A person who buys the stock before the ex-dividend date is entitled to receive the dividend; conversely, a stockholder who sells shares before the ex-dividend date does not receive the dividend.

4 **Date of payment.** The declaration of a dividend always includes announcement of the date of payment as well as the date of record. Usually the date of payment comes from two to four weeks after the date of record.

The journal entries to record the declaration and payment of a cash dividend were illustrated in Chapter 14 but are repeated here with emphasis on the date of declaration and date of payment.

Entries made on declaration date and . . .	*June 1*	Retained Earnings................................ Dividends Payable .... *To record declaration of a cash dividend of $1 per share on the 100,000 shares of common stock outstanding. Payable July 10 to stockholders of record on June 20.*	*100,000* *100,000*
. . . on payment date	*July 10*	Dividends Payable .... Cash.. *To record payment of $1 per share dividend declared June 1 to stockholders of record on June 20.*	*100,000* *100,000*

As mentioned in Chapter 14, some companies record the declaration of a dividend by debiting a Dividends account instead of debiting Retained Earnings. In this case, a closing entry is required at the end of the year to transfer the debit balance of the Dividends account into the Retained Earnings account. Under either method, the balance of the Retained Earnings account ultimately is reduced by the amount of all dividends *declared* during the period.

Most dividends are paid in cash, but occasionally a dividend declaration calls for payment in assets other than cash. A large distillery once paid a dividend consisting of a bottle of whiskey for each share of stock. When a corporation goes out of existence (particularly a small corporation with only a few stockholders), it may choose to distribute noncash assets to its owners rather than to convert all its assets into cash.

Liquidating Dividends

A *liquidating dividend* occurs when a corporation pays a dividend that *exceeds the balance in the Retained Earnings account.* Thus, the dividend returns to stockholders all or part of their paid-in capital investment. Liquidating dividends usually are paid only when a corporation is going out of existence or is making a permanent reduction in the size of its operations. Normally dividends are paid as a result of profitable operations; stockholders may assume that a dividend represents a distribution of profits unless they are notified by the corporation that the dividend is a return of invested capital.

Stock Dividends

OBJECTIVE 4 Account for stock dividends and stock splits, and explain the probable effect of these transactions upon market price.

Stock dividend is a term used to describe a distribution of *additional shares of stock* to a company's stockholders in proportion to their present holdings. In brief, the dividend is payable in *additional shares of stock* rather than in cash. Most stock dividends consist of additional shares of common stock distributed to holders of common stock, and our discussion will be limited to this type of stock dividend.

An important distinction must be drawn between a cash dividend and a stock dividend. In a *cash dividend,* assets are distributed by the corporation to the stockholders. Thus, a cash dividend reduces both assets and stockholders' equity. In a *stock dividend,* however, *no assets are distributed.* Thus, a stock dividend causes *no change* in assets or in total stockholders' equity. Each stockholder receives additional shares, but his or her total ownership in the corporation is *no larger than before.*

To illustrate this point, assume that a corporation with 2,000 shares of stock is owned equally by James Davis and Susan Miller, each owning 1,000 shares of stock. The corporation declares a stock dividend of 10% and distributes 200 additional shares (10% of 2,000 shares), with 100 shares going to each of the two stockholders. Davis and Miller now hold 1,100 shares apiece, but each *still owns one-half of the business.* Furthermore, the corporation has not changed in size; its assets and liabilities and its total stockholders' equity are exactly the same as before the dividend.

Now let us consider the logical effect of this stock dividend upon the *market price* of the company's stock. Assume that before the stock dividend, the outstanding 2,000 shares in our example had a market price of $110 per share. This price indicates a total market value for the corporation of $220,000 (2,000 shares × $110 per share). As the stock dividend does not change total assets or total stockholders' equity, the total market value of the corporation *should remain $220,000* after the stock dividend. As 2,200 shares are now outstanding, the market price of each share *should fall* to $100 ($220,000 ÷ 2,200 shares). In short, the market value of the stock *should fall in proportion* to the number of new shares issued. Whether the market price per share *will* fall in proportion to a small increase in number of outstanding shares is another matter. The market prices of common stocks are influenced by many different factors.

Reasons for Issuing Stock Dividends Although stock dividends cause no change in total assets or total stockholders' equity, they are popular both with management and with stockholders. Management likes stock dividends because they do not cost anything (other than administrative costs)—the corporation does not have to surrender any assets. Stockholders enjoy stock dividends because often the market price of the stock *does not fall enough* to reflect fully the increased number of shares. While this failure of the stock price to fall proportionately is not logical, it is nonetheless a common phenomenon. In such cases, the stock dividend actually does increase the total market value of the corporation and of each stockholder's investment.

Entries to Record a Stock Dividend   In accounting for *small* stock dividends (say, less than 20%), the *market value* of the new shares is transferred from the Retained Earnings accounts to the paid-in capital accounts. This process sometimes is called *capitalizing* retained earnings. The overall effect is the same as if the dividend had been paid in cash, and the stockholders had immediately reinvested the cash in the business in exchange for additional shares of stock. Of course, no cash actually changes hands—the new shares of stock are sent directly to the stockholders.

To illustrate, Aspen Corporation, on June 1, has outstanding 100,000 shares of $5 par value common stock with a market value of $22 per share. On this date, the company declares a 10% stock dividend, distributable on July 15 to stockholders of record on June 20. The entry at June 1 to record the *declaration* of this dividend is:

Stock dividend declared; note use of market price of stock

Retained Earnings	*220,000*	
Stock Dividend to Be Distributed		*50,000*
Additional Paid-in Capital: Stock Dividends		*170,000*

Declared a 10% stock dividend consisting of 10,000 shares (100,000 shares × 10%) of $5 par value common stock, market price $22 per share. Distributable July 15 to stockholders' of record on June 20.

The Stock Dividend to Be Distributed account is *not a liability,* because there is no obligation to distribute cash or any other asset. If a balance sheet is prepared between the date of declaration of a stock dividend and the date of distribution of the shares, this account, as well as Additional Paid-in Capital: Stock Dividends, should be presented in the stockholders' equity section of the balance sheet.

Notice that the Retained Earnings account was debited for the *market value* of the shares to be issued (10,000 shares × $22 per share = $220,000). Notice also that *no change* occurs in the total amount of stockholders' equity. The amount removed from the Retained Earnings account was simply transferred into two other stockholders' equity accounts.

On July 15, the entry to record the *distribution* of the dividend shares is:

Stock dividend distributed

Stock Dividend to Be Distributed	*50,000*	
Common Stock		*50,000*

Distributed 10,000 share stock dividend declared June 1.

Large stock dividends (for example, those in excess of 20 to 25%) should be recorded by transferring *only the par or stated value* of the dividend shares from the Retained Earnings account to the Common Stock account. Large stock dividends generally have the effect of proportionately reducing the market price of the stock. For example, a 100% stock dividend would reduce the market price by about 50%, because twice as many shares would be outstanding. A 100% stock dividend is very similar to the 2-for-1 **stock split** discussed in the following section of this chapter.

Stock Splits

A corporation may split its stock by increasing the number of outstanding shares of common stock and reducing the par or stated value per share in proportion. The purpose of the split is to reduce substantially the market price of the common stock, with the intent of making the stock more attractive to investors.

For example, assume that Pelican Corporation has outstanding 1 million shares of $10 par value stock. The market price is $90 per share. The corporation now reduces the par value from $10 to $5 per share and increases the number of shares from 1 million to 2 million. This action would be called a 2-for-1 stock split. A stockholder who owned 100 shares of the stock before the split would own 200 shares after the split. Since the number of outstanding shares has been doubled without any change in total assets or total stockholders' equity, the market price of the stock should drop from $90 to approximately $45 a share.

A stock split does not change the balance of any ledger account; consequently, the transaction may be recorded merely by *a memorandum entry* in the general journal and in the Common Stock account. For Pelican Corporation, this memorandum entry might read:

Memorandum entry to record a stock split	*Sept. 30* *Memorandum: Issued additional 1 million shares of common stock in a 2-for-1 stock split. Par value reduced from $10 per share to $5 per share.*

The description of common stock also is changed in the balance sheet to reflect the lower par value and the greater number of shares outstanding.

Stock may be split in any desired ratio. Among the more common ratios are 2 for 1, 3 for 2, and 3 for 1. The determining factor is the number of shares needed to bring the price of the stock into the desired trading range. For example, assume that a $5 par value stock is selling at a price of $150 per share and that management wants to reduce the price to approximately $30 per share. This objective may be accomplished with a *5-for 1* stock split ($150 ÷ 5 = $30). Par value *after* the 5-for-1 stock split is $1 per share ($5 par value × $\frac{1}{5}$).

Distinction between Stock Splits and Large Stock Dividends   What is the difference between a 2-for-1 stock split and a 100% stock dividend? There is very little difference; both will double the number of outstanding shares without changing total stockholders' equity, and both should serve to cut the market price of the stock approximately in half. The stock dividend, however, will cause a transfer from the Retained Earnings account to the Common Stock account equal to the par or stated value of the dividend shares. A 2-for-1 stock split will reduce the par value per share by one-half, but it will not change the dollar balance of any account.

After an increase in the number of shares as a result of a stock split or stock dividend, earnings per share are computed in terms of the increased number of shares. In presenting 5- or 10-year summaries, the earnings per share for earlier years are **retroactively restated** to reflect the increased number of shares currently outstanding and thus make the trend of earnings per share from year to year a valid comparison.

CASE IN POINT   In 1980, Mylan Laboratories, Inc., reported earnings of 54 cents per share. Over the next six years, the company declared a 100% stock dividend and five separate stock splits. By 1986, each share outstanding in 1980 had been split into 27 shares. Thus, each share outstanding in 1986 represented only $\frac{1}{27}$ of an original 1980 share. In the 10-year summary appearing in the company's 1986 annual report, the 1980 earnings were restated at 2 cents per share ($\$0.54 \times \frac{1}{27} = \$0.02$).

Statement of Retained Earnings

OBJECTIVE 5
Describe
and prepare
a statement
of retained
earnings.

The term **retained earnings** refers to the portion of stockholders' equity derived from profitable operations. Retained earnings is increased by earning net income and is reduced by incurring net losses and by the declaration of dividends.

In addition to a balance sheet and an income statement, a complete set of financial statements includes a statement of retained earnings and a statement of cash flows. The statement of cash flows will be discussed in Chapter 19; a statement of retained earnings is illustrated below:

SHORE LINE CORPORATION
Statement of Retained Earnings
For the Year Ended December 31, 1994

Retained earnings, December 31, 1993		$600,000
Net income for 1994		180,000
Subtotal		$780,000
Less: Cash dividends:		
Preferred stock ($5 per share)	$ 17,500	
Common stock ($2 per share)	55,300	
10% stock dividend	140,000	212,800
Retained earnings, December 31, 1994		$567,200

Prior Period Adjustments

On occasion, a company may discover that a material error was made in the measurement of net income in a prior year. Since net income is closed into the Retained Earnings account, an error in reported net income will cause an error in the amount of retained earnings shown in all subsequent balance sheets. When such errors come to light, they should be corrected. The correction, called a **prior period adjustment,** is shown in the **state-**

OBJECTIVE 6
Define prior
period ad-
justments
and explain
how they are
presented in
financial
statements.

ment of retained earnings as an adjustment to the balance of retained earnings at the beginning of the current year. The amount of the adjustment is shown net of any related income tax effects.

To illustrate, assume that late in 1994 Shore Line Corporation discovers that it failed to record depreciation on certain assets in 1993. After considering the income tax effects of this error, the company finds that the net income reported in 1993 was overstated by $35,000. Thus, the current balance of retained earnings ($600,000 at December 31, 1993) also is overstated by $35,000. Correction of this error leads to a revised 1994 statement of retained earnings as follows:

Notice the adjustment to beginning retained earnings

SHORE LINE CORPORATION
Statement of Retained Earnings
For the Year Ended December 31, 1994

Retained earnings, December 31, 1993:		
As originally reported		$600,000
Less: Prior period adjustment for error in recording 1993 depreciation expense (net of $15,000 income taxes)		35,000
As restated		$565,000
Net Income for 1994		180,000
Subtotal		$745,000
Less: Cash dividends:		
Preferred stock ($5 per share)	$ 17,500	
Common stock ($2 per share)	55,300	
10% stock dividend	140,000	212,800
Retained earnings, December 31, 1994		$532,200

Prior period adjustments rarely appear in the financial statements of large, publicly owned corporations. The financial statements of these corporations are audited annually by certified public accountants and are not likely to contain material errors which subsequently will require correction by prior period adjustments. Such adjustments are much more likely to appear in the financial statements of closely held corporations that are not audited on an annual basis.

Restrictions of Retained Earnings   Some portion of retained earnings may be restricted because of various contractual agreements. A "restriction" of retained earnings prevents a company from declaring a dividend that would cause retained earnings to fall below a designated level. Most companies disclose restrictions of retained earnings in notes accompanying the financial statements. For example, a company with retained earnings of $10 million might include the following note in its financial statements:

Footnote disclosure of restrictions placed on retained earnings

Note 7: Restriction of retained earnings
As of December 31, 1994, certain long-term debt agreements prohibited the declaration of cash dividends that would reduce the amount of retained earnings below $5,200,000. Retained earnings not so restricted amounted to $4,800,000.

Treasury Stock

Corporations frequently reacquire shares of their own capital stock by purchase in the open market. Paying out cash to reacquire shares will reduce the assets of the corporation and reduce the stockholders' equity by the same amount. One reason for such purchases is to have stock available to reissue to officers and employees under stock option or bonus plans. Other reasons may include a desire to increase the reported earnings per share or to support the current market price of the stock.

Treasury stock may be defined as shares of a corporation's own capital stock that have been issued and later *reacquired by the issuing company,* but that have not been canceled or permanently retired. Treasury shares may be held indefinitely or may be issued again at any time. Shares of capital stock held in the treasury are not entitled to receive dividends, to vote, or to share in assets upon dissolution of the company. In the computation of earnings per share, shares held in the treasury are not regarded as outstanding shares.

Recording Purchases of Treasury Stock

OBJECTIVE 7
Account for treasury stock transactions.

Purchases of treasury stock should be recorded by debiting the Treasury Stock account with the cost of the stock.[5] For example, if Torrey Corporation reacquires 1,500 shares of its own $5 par stock at a price of $100 per share, the entry is as follows:

Treasury Stock	150,000	
Cash		150,000
Purchased 1,500 shares of $5 par treasury stock at $100 per share.		

Note that the Treasury Stock account is debited for the *cost* of the shares purchased, not their par value.

Treasury Stock Is Not an Asset   When treasury stock is purchased, the corporation is eliminating part of its stockholders' equity by a payment to one or more stockholders. The purchase of treasury stock should be regarded as a *reduction of stockholders' equity,* not as the acquisition of an asset. For this reason, the Treasury Stock account should appear in the balance sheet *as a deduction in the stockholders' equity section.*[6] The presentation of treasury stock in a corporate balance sheet is illustrated on page 710.

Reissuance of Treasury Stock

When treasury shares are reissued, the Treasury Stock account is credited for the cost of the shares reissued and Additional Paid-in Capital from

---

[5]   State laws may prescribe different methods of accounting for treasury stock transactions. In this text, we illustrate only the widely used "cost method."

[6]   Despite a lack of theoretical support, a few corporations do classify treasury stock as an asset, on the grounds that the shares could be sold for cash just as readily as shares owned in another corporation. The same argument could be made of treating unissued shares as assets. Treasury shares are basically the same as unissued shares, and an unissued share of stock is definitely not an asset.

Treasury Stock Transactions is debited or credited for any difference between *cost* and the reissue price. To illustrate, assume that 1,000 of the treasury shares acquired by Torrey Corporation at a cost of $100 per share are now reissued at a price of $115 per share. The entry to record the reissuance of these shares at a price above cost would be:

Treasury stock reissued at a price above cost	*Cash* *115,000*	
	Treasury Stock	*100,000*
	Additional Paid-in Capital: Treasury Stock Transactions	*15,000*
	Sold 1,000 shares of treasury stock, which cost $100,000, at a price of $115 per share.	

If treasury stock is reissued at a price below cost, additional paid-in capital from previous treasury stock transactions is reduced (debited) by the excess of cost over the reissue price. To illustrate, assume that Torrey Corporation reissues its remaining 500 shares of treasury stock (cost $100 per share) at a price of $90 per share. The entry would be:

Reissued at a price below cost	*Cash* *45,000*	
	Additional Paid-in Capital: Treasury Stock Transactions *5,000*	
	Treasury Stock	*50,000*
	Sold 500 shares of treasury stock, which cost $50,000, at a price of $90 each.	

If there is no additional paid-in capital from previous treasury stock transactions, the excess of the cost of the treasury shares over the reissue price may be recorded as a debit to Retained Earnings.

No Profit or Loss on Treasury Stock Transactions Notice that ***no gain or loss is recognized on treasury stock transactions,*** even when the shares are reissued at a price above or below cost. A corporation earns profits by selling goods and services to outsiders, not by issuing or reissuing shares of its own capital stock. When treasury shares are reissued at a price above cost the corporation receives from the new stockholder an amount of paid-in capital larger than the reduction in stockholders' equity when the corporation acquired the treasury shares. Conversely, if treasury shares are reissued at a price below cost, the corporation ends up with less paid-in capital as a result of the purchase and reissuance of the shares. Thus, any changes in stockholders' equity resulting from treasury stock transactions are regarded as changes in ***paid-in capital*** and are ***not*** included in the measurement of net income.

Restriction of Retained Earnings for Treasury Stock Owned Purchases of treasury stock, like cash dividends, are distributions of assets to the stockholders in the corporation. Many states have a legal requirement that distributions to stockholders (including purchases of treasury stock) cannot exceed the balance in the Retained Earnings account. Therefore, retained earnings usually are restricted by an amount equal to the ***cost*** of any shares held in the treasury.

Stock "Buyback" Programs

In past years, most treasury stock transactions involved relatively small dollar amounts. Hence, the topic was not of much importance to investors or other users of financial statements. Late in 1987, however, many corporations initiated large "buyback" programs, in which they repurchased huge amounts of their own common stock.[7] As a result of these programs, treasury stock has become a very material item in the balance sheets of many corporations.

CASE IN POINT Shown below is the cost of the treasury stock listed in the balance sheets of several publicly owned corporations at the end of a recent year.

	Treasury Stock	
Company	At Cost (in Thousands)	As a % of Other Elements of Stockholders' Equity*
Coca-Cola	$ 3,235,963	48
Exxon	16,224,000	35
Lotus	194,937	41
King World	159,587	72

* To place these holdings in perspective, we have shown the cost of the treasury stock as a percentage of total stockholders' equity **before** deducting the cost of the repurchased shares.

These large buyback programs serve several purposes. First, by creating demand for the company's stock in the marketplace, these programs tend to increase the market value of the shares. Also, reducing the number of shares outstanding usually increases earnings per share. When stock prices are low, some companies find that they can increase earnings per share by a greater amount through repurchasing shares than through expanding business operations.

Statement of Stockholders' Equity

OBJECTIVE 8 Describe and prepare a statement of stockholders' equity.

Many corporations expand their statement of retained earnings to show the changes during the year in all of the stockholders' equity accounts. This expanded statement, called a ***statement of stockholders' equity,*** is illustrated for Shore Line Corporation on the next page.

The top line of this statement shows the beginning balance in each stockholders' equity account. All of the transactions affecting these accounts during the year then are listed in summary form, along with the related changes in the balances of specific stockholders' equity accounts.

---

[7] On October 19, 1987, a date known as ***Black Monday,*** stock prices around the world suffered the largest one-day decline in history. Many economists and investors believed that this stock market "crash" would trigger a worldwide economic depression. Within hours of the market's close on Black Monday, many large corporations announced their intention to enter the market and spend hundreds of million of dollars repurchasing their own shares. In the opinions of the authors, the announcement of these buyback programs did much to stabilize the world's financial markets, restore investors' confidence, and possibly avoid a depression.

The bottom line of the statement shows the ending balance in each stockholders' equity account and should agree with the amounts shown in the year-end balance sheet.

A statement of stockholders' equity is not a required financial statement. However, it is widely used as a substitute for the ***statement of retained earnings*** because it presents a more complete description of the transactions affecting stockholders' equity. Notice that the Retained Earnings column of this statement contains the same items shown in the statement of retained earnings illustrated on page 705.

SHORE LINE CORPORATION
Statement of Stockholders' Equity
For the Year Ended December 31, 1994

	5% Convertible preferred stock ($100 par value)	Common stock ($10 par value)	Additional paid-in capital	Retained earnings	Treasury stock	Total stockholders' equity
Balances, Dec. 31, 1993	$400,000	$200,000	$300,000	$600,000	$ –0–	$1,500,000
Prior period adjustment (net of $15,000 taxes)				(35,000)		(35,000)
Issued 5,000 common shares @ $52		50,000	210,000			260,000
Conversion of 1,000 preferred into 3,000 common shares	(100,000)	30,000	70,000			
Distributed 10% stock dividend (2,800 shares at $50; market price)		28,000	112,000	(140,000)		
Purchased 1,000 shares of common stock for the treasury at $47 a share					(47,000)	(47,000)
Net income				180,000		180,000
Cash dividends:						
Preferred ($5 a share)				(17,500)		(17,500)
Common ($2 a share)				(55,300)		(55,300)
Balances, Dec. 31, 1994	$300,000	$308,000	$692,000	$532,200	$(47,000)	$1,785,200

Illustration of a Stockholders' Equity Section

The stockholders' equity section of a balance sheet illustrated on the following page includes some of the items discussed in this chapter. For illustrative purposes, we also show the computation of book value per share. (This computation is not shown in an actual balance sheet.) You should be able to explain the nature and origin of each account and disclosure printed in red.

The published financial statements of leading corporations indicate that there is no one standard arrangement for the various items making up the stockholders' equity section. Variations occur in the selection of titles, in the sequence of items, and in the extent of detailed classification. Many companies, in an effort to avoid excessive detail in the balance sheet, will combine several related ledger accounts into a single balance sheet item.

Stockholders' Equity

Capital stock:

8% Preferred stock, $100 par value, call price $110 per share,
authorized and issued 2,000 shares $200,000

Common stock, $5 par value, authorized 100,000 shares, issued
33,000 shares *(of which 3,000 are held in the treasury)*.................... 165,000

Additional paid-in capital:

From issuance of common stock............................... $250,000

From stock dividends 50,000

From treasury stock transactions 10,000   310,000

Total paid-in capital $675,000

Retained earnings (of which $87,000, an amount equal to the cost of
treasury stock owned, is not available for dividends) 232,000

Subtotal... $907,000

Less: Treasury stock (3,000 shares of common, at cost) 37,000

Total stockholders' equity $820,000

*   Book value per share: $820,000 − (2,000 preferred shares × $110) = $600,000 equity of common stockholders; $600,000 ÷ 30,000 outstanding common shares = $20 per share.

END-OF-CHAPTER REVIEW

SUMMARY OF CHAPTER LEARNING OBJECTIVES

1 **Describe how discontinued operations, extraordinary items, and accounting changes are presented in the income statement.** Each of these "unusual" items is shown in a separate section of the income statement, after determination of the income or loss from ordinary and continuing operations. Each special item is shown net of any related income tax effects.

2 **Compute earnings per share.** Net earnings per share is computed by dividing the income applicable to the common stock by the weighted average number of common shares outstanding. If the income statement includes subtotals for income from continuing operations, or for income before extraordinary items, per-share figures are shown for these amounts as well as for net income.

3 **Distinguish between primary and fully diluted earnings per share.** Fully diluted earnings per share must be computed only for companies that have outstanding securities convertible into shares of common stock. In such situations, the computation of primary earnings per share is based upon the number of common shares actually outstanding during the year. The computation of fully diluted earnings, however, is based upon the potential number of common shares outstanding if the various securities were converted into common shares. The purpose of showing fully diluted earnings is to warn investors of the extent to which conversions of securities could dilute primary earnings per share.

4 Account for stock dividends and stock splits, and explain the probable effect of these transactions upon market price.

Small stock dividends are recorded by transferring the market value of the additional shares to be issued from retained earnings to the appropriate paid-in capital accounts. (Large stock dividends—over 20 or 25%—are recorded at par value, rather than market value.) A stock split, on the other hand, is recorded only by a memorandum entry indicating that the number of outstanding shares has been increased and that the par value per share has been reduced proportionately. Both stock dividends and stock splits increase the number of shares outstanding, but neither transaction changes total stockholders' equity. Therefore, both stock dividends and stock splits should reduce the market price per share in proportion to the number of additional shares issued.

5 Describe and prepare a statement of retained earnings.

A statement of retained earnings shows the changes in the balance of the Retained Earnings account during the period. In its simplest form, this financial statement shows the beginning balance of retained earnings, adds the net income for the period, subtracts any dividends declared, and thus computes the ending balance of retained earnings. Any prior period adjustments also are shown in this financial statement.

6 Define prior period adjustments and explain how they are presented in financial statements.

A prior period adjustment is an entry to correct any error in the amount of net income reported in a *prior* year. As the income of the prior year has already been closed into retained earnings, the error is corrected by debiting or crediting the Retained Earnings account. Prior period adjustments appear in the statement of retained earnings as adjustments to beginning retained earnings. They are *not* reported in the income statement for the current period.

7 Account for treasury stock transactions.

Purchases of treasury stock are recorded by debiting a contra-equity account entitled Treasury Stock. No profit or loss is recorded when the treasury shares are reissued at a price above or below cost. Rather, any difference between the reissuance price and the cost of the shares is debited or credited to a paid-in capital account.

8 Describe and prepare a statement of stockholders' equity.

This expanded version of the statement of retained earnings explains the changes during the year in each stockholders' equity account. It is not a required financial statement, but is often prepared instead of a statement of retained earnings. The statement lists the beginning balance in each stockholders' equity account, explains the nature and the amount of each change, and thus computes the ending balance in each equity account.

This chapter—the second in our unit on corporate accounting—completes our discussion of capital stock and stockholders' equity. In our remaining chapters, we will continue to use the corporate entity as the basis for discussions and illustrations.

When a corporation needs to raise vast amounts of capital, it may elect to issue **bonds payable** as an alternative to issuing additional shares of capital stock. The next chapter addresses the topics of bonds payable and other liabilities of large corporations.

KEY TERMS INTRODUCED OR EMPHASIZED IN CHAPTER 15

Book value   The stockholders' equity represented by each share of common stock. Book value is computed by dividing the common stockholders' equity by the number of common shares outstanding.

Date of record   The date on which a person must be listed as a shareholder in order to be eligible to receive a dividend. Follows the date of declaration of a dividend by two or three weeks.

Discontinued operations   The net operating results (revenue and expenses) of a segment of a company which has been or is being sold.

Earnings per share   Net income applicable to the common stock divided by the weighted-average number of common shares outstanding during the year.

Ex-dividend date   A date three days prior to the date of record specified in a dividend declaration. A person buying a stock prior to the ex-dividend date also acquires the right to receive the dividend. The three-day interval permits the compilation of a list of stockholders as of the date of record.

Extraordinary items   Transactions and events that are material in dollar amount, unusual in nature, and occur infrequently—for example, a large earthquake loss. Such items are shown separately in the income statement after the determination of Income before Extraordinary Items.

Fully diluted earnings per share   Earnings per share computed under the assumption that all convertible securities had been converted into additional common shares at the beginning of the current year. The purpose of this hypothetical computation is to warn common stockholders of the risk that future earnings per share might be diluted by the conversion of other securities into common stock.

Price-earnings (p/e) ratio   Market price of a share of common stock divided by annual earnings per share.

Primary earnings per share   Net income applicable to the common stock divided by weighted-average number of common shares outstanding during the year.

Prior period adjustment   A correction of a material error in the earnings reported in the financial statements of a prior year. Prior period adjustments are recorded directly in the Retained Earnings account and are not included in the income statement of the current period.

Segment of a business   Those elements of a business that represent a separate and distinct line of business activity or that service a distinct category of customers.

Statement of retained earnings   A basic financial statement explaining the change during the year in the amount of retained earnings. May be expanded into a **statement of stockholders' equity.**

Statement of stockholders' equity   An expanded version of a **statement of retained earnings.** Summarizes the changes during the year in all stockholders' equity accounts. Not a required financial statement, but widely used as a substitute for the statement of retained earnings.

Stock dividend   A distribution of additional shares to common stockholders in proportion to their holdings.

Stock split   An increase in the number of shares outstanding with a corresponding decrease in par value per share. The additional shares are distributed proportionately to all common shareholders. Purpose is to reduce market price per share and encourage wider public ownership of the company's stock. A 2-for-1 stock split will give each stockholder twice as many shares as previously owned.

Treasury stock   Shares of a corporation's stock which have been issued and then reacquired, but not canceled.

DEMONSTRATION PROBLEM FOR YOUR REVIEW

The stockholders' equity of Sutton Corporation at December 31, 1993, is shown below:

Stockholders' equity:	
Common stock, $10 par, 100,000 shares authorized, 40,000 shares issued ...	$ 400,000
Additional paid-in capital: common stock....................................	200,000
Total paid-in capital	$ 600,000
Retained earnings	1,500,000
Total stockholders' equity	$2,100,000

Transactions affecting stockholders' equity during 1994 are as follows:

Mar. 31   A 5-for-4 stock split proposed by the board of directors was approved by vote of the stockholders. The 10,000 new shares were distributed to stockholders.

Apr. 1   The company purchased 2,000 shares of its common stock on the open market at $37 per share.

July 1   The company reissued 1,000 shares of treasury stock at $45 per share.

July 1   Issued for cash 20,000 shares of previously unissued $8 par value common stock at a price of $45 per share.

Dec. 1   A cash dividend of $1 per share was declared, payable on December 30, to stockholders of record at December 14.

Dec. 22   A 10% stock dividend was declared; the dividend shares are to be distributed on January 15 of the following year. The market price of the stock on December 22 was $48 per share.

The net income for the year ended December 31, 1994, amounted to $177,000, after an extraordinary loss of $35,400 (net of related income tax benefits).

INSTRUCTIONS   **a**   Prepare journal entries (in general journal form) to record the transactions relating to stockholders' equity that took place during the year.

b   Prepare the lower section of the income statement for 1994, beginning with the *income before extraordinary items* and showing the extraordinary loss and the net income. Also illustrate the presentation of earnings per share in the income statement, assuming that earnings per share is determined on the basis of the *weighted-average* number of shares outstanding during the year.

c Prepare a statement of retained earnings for the year ending December 31, 1994.

SOLUTION TO DEMONSTRATION PROBLEM

a

General Journal

Mar. 31	*Memorandum: Stockholders approved a 5-for-4 stock split. This action increased the number of shares of common stock outstanding from 40,000 to 50,000 and reduced the par value from $10 to $8 per share. The 10,000 new shares were distributed.*		
Apr. 1	Treasury Stock...	74,000	
	Cash...		74,000
	Acquired 2,000 shares of treasury stock at $37 per share.		
July 1	Cash..	45,000	
	Treasury Stock.......................................		37,000
	Additional Paid-in Capital: Treasury Stock Transactions		8,000
	Sold 1,000 shares of treasury stock at $45 per share.		
1	Cash..	900,000	
	Common Stock, $8 par		160,000
	Additional Paid-in Capital: Common Stock............		740,000
	Issued 20,000 shares of previously unissued $8 par value stock for cash of $45 per share.		
Dec. 1	Retained Earnings...	69,000	
	Dividends Payable....................................		69,000
	To record declaration of cash dividend of $1 per share on 69,000 shares of common stock outstanding (1,000 shares in treasury are not entitled to receive dividends).		

Note: Entry to record the payment of the cash dividend is not shown here since the action does not affect the stockholders' equity.

22	Retained Earnings...	331,200	
	Stock Dividends to Be Distributed		55,200
	Additional Paid-in Capital: Stock Dividends...........		276,000
	To record declaration of 10% stock dividend consisting of 6,900 shares of $8 par value common stock to be distributed on Jan. 15 of next year.		
31	Income Summary..	177,000	
	Retained Earnings....................................		177,000
	To close Income Summary account.		

b

SUTTON CORPORATION
Partial Income Statement
For Year Ended December 31, 1994

Income before extraordinary items	$212,400
Extraordinary loss (net of income tax benefits)	(35,400)
Net income..	$177,000

Earnings per share:*

Income before extraordinary items	*$3.60*
Extraordinary loss	*(0.60)*
Net income	*$3.00*

* On 59,000 weighted-average number of shares of common stock outstanding during 19___, determined as follows:

Jan. 1–Mar. 31: (40,000 + 10,000 shares issued pursuant to a 5 for 4 split) $\times \frac{1}{4}$ of year	12,500
Apr. 1–June 30: (50,000 − 2,000 shares of treasury stock) $\times \frac{1}{4}$ of year	12,000
July 1–Dec. 31: (50,000 + 20,000 shares of new stock − 1,000 shares of treasury stock) $\times \frac{1}{2}$ of year	34,500
Weighted-average number of shares outstanding	59,000

c

SUTTON CORPORATION
Statement of Retained Earnings
For Year Ended December 31, 1994

Retained earnings, December 31, 1993		*$1,500,000*
Net income for 1994		*177,000*
Subtotal		*$1,677,000*
Less: Cash dividends ($1 per share)	*$ 69,000*	
10% stock dividend	*331,200*	*400,200*
Retained earnings, December 31, 1994		*$1,276,800*

SELF-TEST QUESTIONS

The answers to these questions appear on page 732.

1 The primary purpose of showing special types of events separately in the income statement is to:

   a Increase earnings per share.

   b Assist users of the income statement in evaluating the profitability of normal, ongoing operations.

   c Minimize the income taxes paid on the results of ongoing operations.

   d Prevent unusual losses from recurring.

2 Which of the following situations would *not* be presented in a separate section of the current year's income statement of Marlow Corporation? During the current year:

   a Marlow's St. Louis headquarters are destroyed by a tornado.

   b Marlow sells its entire juvenile furniture operations and concentrates upon its remaining children's clothing segment.

   c Marlow changes from the straight-line method of depreciation to the double-declining-balance method.

   d Marlow's accountant discovers that the entire price paid several years ago to purchase company offices in Texas had been charged to a Land account; consequently, no depreciation has ever been taken on these buildings.

3 When a corporation has outstanding both common and preferred stock:

   a Primary and fully diluted earnings per share are reported only if the preferred stock is cumulative.

   b Earnings per share are reported for each type of stock outstanding.

   c Earnings per share may be computed without regard to the amount of dividends declared on common stock.

   d Earnings per share may be computed without regard to the amount of the annual preferred dividends.

4 The statement of retained earnings:
   a Need not be prepared if a separate statement of stockholders' equity accompanies the financial statements.
   b Indicates the amount of cash available for the payment of dividends.
   c Includes prior period adjustments and cash dividends, but not stock dividends.
   d Shows revenue, expenses, and dividends for the accounting period.

5 On December 10, 1993, Totem Corporation reacquired 2,000 of its own $5 par stock at a price of $60 per share. In 1994, 500 of the treasury shares are reissued at a price of $70 per share. Which of the following statements is correct?
   a The treasury stock purchased is recorded at cost and is shown in Totem's December 31, 1993, balance sheet as an asset.
   b The two treasury stock transactions result in an overall reduction in Totem's stockholders' equity of $85,000.
   c Totem recognizes a gain of $10 per share on the reissuance of the 500 treasury shares in 1994.
   d Totem's stockholders' equity was increased by $110,000 when the treasury stock was acquired.

ASSIGNMENT MATERIAL

DISCUSSION QUESTIONS

1 What is the purpose of arranging an income statement to show subtotals for *Income from Continuing Operations* and for *Income before Extraordinary Items?*

2 Pappa Joe's owns 30 pizza parlors and a minor league baseball team. During the current year, the company sold three of its pizza parlors and closed another when the lease on the building expired. Should any of these events be classified as "discontinued operations" in the company's income statement? Explain.

3 Define *extraordinary items.* Give three examples of losses which qualify as extraordinary items and three examples of losses which would *not* be classified as extraordinary.

4 In past years, the management of St. Thomas Medical Supply had consistently estimated the allowance for doubtful accounts at 2% of total accounts receivable. At the end of the current year, management estimated that uncollectible accounts would equal 4% of accounts receivable. Should the uncollectible accounts expense of prior years be recomputed in order to show in the income statement the cumulative effect of this change in accounting estimate?

5 Both the *cumulative effect of a change in accounting principle* and *prior period adjustment* affect the income of past accounting periods. Distinguish between these two items and explain how each is shown in the financial statements.

6 In the current year, Garden Products decided to switch from use of an accelerated method of depreciation to the straight-line method. Will the cumulative effect of this change in accounting principle increase or decrease the amount of net income reported in the current year? Explain.

7 *Earnings per share* and *book value per share* are statistics that relate to common stock. When both preferred and common stock are outstanding, explain the computation involved in determining the following:

a Earnings allocable to the common stockholders

b Aggregate book value allocable to the common stockholders

8 Assume a corporation has only common stock outstanding. Is the number of common shares used in the computation of earnings per share *always* the same as the number of common shares used in computing book value per share for this corporation? Is the number of common shares used in computing these two statistics *ever* the same? Explain.

9 Explain how each of the following is computed:

a Price-earnings ratio

b Primary earnings per share

c Fully diluted earnings per share

10 Throughout the year, Gold Seal Company had 4 million shares of common stock and 120,000 shares of convertible preferred stock outstanding. Each share of preferred is convertible into four shares of common. What number of shares should be used in the computation of (a) primary earnings per share and (b) fully diluted earnings per share?

11 A financial analyst notes that Baxter Corporation's earnings per share have been rising steadily for the last five years. The analyst expects the company's net income to continue to increase at the same rate as in the past. In forecasting future primary earnings per share, what special risk should the analyst consider if Baxter's primary earnings are significantly larger than its fully diluted earnings?

12 Explain the significance of the following dates relating to dividends: date of declaration, date of record, date of payment, ex-dividend date.

13 What is the purpose of a *stock split?*

14 Distinguish between a *stock split* and a *stock dividend.* Is there any reason for the difference in accounting treatment of these two events?

15 What are *prior period adjustments?* How are they presented in financial statements?

16 Identify three items that may appear in a statement of retained earnings as changes in the amount of retained earnings.

17 What is *treasury stock?* Why do corporations purchase their own shares? Is treasury stock an asset? How should it be reported in the balance sheet?

18 In many states, the corporation law requires that retained earnings be restricted for dividend purposes to the extent of the cost of treasury shares. What is the reason for this legal rule?

19 A *statement of stockholders' equity* sometimes is described as an "expanded" statement of retained earnings. Why?

EXERCISES

**EXERCISE 15-1
Accounting
Terminology**

Listed below are nine technical accounting terms introduced or emphasized in this chapter:

p/e ratio	*Treasury stock*	*Discontinued operations*
Stock dividend	*Extraordinary item*	*Prior period adjustment*
Primary earnings per share	*Cumulative effect of an accounting change*	*Fully diluted earnings per share*

Each of the following statements may (or may not) describe one of these technical terms. For each statement, indicate the term described, or answer "None" if the statement does not correctly describe any of the terms.

a A gain or loss that is material in amount, unusual in nature, and not expected to recur in the foreseeable future.

b The asset represented by shares of capital stock that have not yet been issued.

c A distribution of additional shares of stock that reduces retained earnings but causes no change in total stockholders' equity.

d The effect that retroactive application of a newly adopted accounting principle has upon the amount of net income reported in prior accounting periods.

e An adjustment to the beginning balance of retained earnings to correct an error previously made in the measurement of net income.

f A statistic expressing a relationship between the current market value of a share of common stock and the underlying earnings per share.

g A separate section sometimes included in an income statement as a step in helping investors to evaluate the profitability of ongoing business activities.

h A hypothetical figure indicating what earnings per share would have been if all securities convertible into common stock had been converted at the beginning of the current year.

**EXERCISE 15-2
Discontinued
Operations**

During the current year, SunSports, Inc., operated two business segments: a chain of surf and dive shops and a small chain of tennis shops. The tennis shops were not profitable and were sold near year-end to another corporation. SunSports' operations for the current year are summarized below. The first two captions, "Net sales" and "Costs and expenses," relate only to the company's continuing operations.

Net sales..	$9,800,000
Costs and expenses (including applicable income taxes)......................	8,600,000
Operating loss from tennis shops (net of income tax benefit).................	192,000
Loss on sale of tennis shops (net of income tax benefit).....................	348,000

The company had 150,000 shares of a single class of capital stock outstanding throughout the year.

INSTRUCTIONS

Prepare a condensed income statement for the year. At the bottom of the statement, show any appropriate earnings-per-share figures. (A **condensed** income statement is illustrated on page 697.)

**EXERCISE 15-3
Reporting an
Extraordinary
Item**

For the year ended December 31, Union Chemical had net sales of $8,000,000, costs and other expenses (including income taxes) of $7,060,000, and an extraordinary gain (net of income tax) of $400,000. Prepare a condensed income statement (including earnings per share), assuming that 500,000 shares of common stock were outstanding throughout the year.

EXERCISE 15-4
Computing Earnings Per Share: Changes in Number of Shares Outstanding

In the year just ended, Sunshine Citrus earned net income of $6,300,000. The company has issued only one class of $1 par value capital stock, of which 1 million shares were outstanding at January 1. Compute the company's earnings per share under each of the following *independent* assumptions:

a No change occurred during the year in the number of shares outstanding.

b On October 1, the company issued an additional 200,000 shares of capital stock in exchange for cash of $1,500,000.

c On July 1, the company distributed an additional 200,000 shares of capital stock as a 20% stock dividend. On July 1, Sunshine's stock had a market value of $7.25 per share.

EXERCISE 15-5
Computing Earnings Per Share: Effect of Preferred Stock

The net income of Carriage Trade Clothiers amounted to $2,550,000 for the current year. Compute the amount of earnings per share assuming that the shares of capital stock outstanding throughout the year consisted of:

a 300,000 shares of $10 par value common stock and no preferred stock.

b 200,000 shares of 9%, $100 par value preferred stock and 300,000 shares of $5 par value common stock.

EXERCISE 15-6
Restating Earnings per Share After a Stock Dividend

The 1989 annual report of **Microsoft Corp.** included the following comparative summary of earnings per share over the last three years:

	1989	*1988*	*1987*
Earnings per share	*$3.03*	*$2.22*	*$1.30*

Early in 1990, Microsoft Corp. declared and distributed a 100% stock dividend. Following this stock dividend, the company reported earnings per share of $2.35 for 1990.

INSTRUCTIONS

a Prepare a three-year schedule similar to the one above, but compare earnings per share during the years 1990, 1989, and 1988. (Hint: All per-share amounts in your schedule should be based on the number of shares outstanding after the stock dividend.)

b In preparing your schedule, which figure (or figures) did you have to restate? Why? Explain the logic behind your computation.

EXERCISE 15-7
Restating Earnings per Share After a Stock Split

The 1987 annual report of **Merck & Co., Inc.** included the following comparative summary of earnings per share over the last three years:

	1987	*1986*	*1985*
Earnings per share	*$6.69*	*$4.86*	*$3.78*

During 1988, Merck & Co., Inc., split its common stock 3 for 1. Following this stock split, the company reported earnings per share of $3.05 in 1988 and $3.78 in 1989.

INSTRUCTIONS

a Prepare a three-year schedule similar to the one above, but compare earnings per share during the years 1989, 1988, and 1987. (Hint: All per-share amounts in your schedule should be based on the number of shares outstanding after the stock split.)

b In preparing your schedule, which figure (or figures) did you have to restate? Why? Explain the logic behind your computation.

EXERCISE 15-8
Cash Dividends, Stock Dividends and Stock Splits

Global Technology Corporation has 500,000 shares of $10 par value capital stock outstanding on January 1. The following equity transactions occurred during the current year:

Apr. 30	Distributed additional shares of capital stock in a 2-for-1 stock split. Market price of stock was $35 per share.
June 1	Declared a cash dividend of 60 cents per share.
July 1	Paid the 60-cent cash dividend to stockholders.
Aug. 1	Declared a 5% stock dividend. Market price of stock was $19 per share.
Sept. 10	Issued shares pursuant to the 5% stock dividend declared on August 1.
Dec. 1	Declared a 50% stock dividend. Market price of stock was $23 per share.

INSTRUCTIONS

a Prepare journal entries to record the above transactions.

b Compute the number of shares of capital stock outstanding at year-end.

c What is the par value per share of Global Technology stock at the end of the year?

EXERCISE 15-9
Effect of Stock Dividends on Stock Price

Tarreytown Corporation has a total of 80,000 shares of common stock outstanding and no preferred stock. Total stockholders' equity at the end of the current year amounts to $5 million and the market value of the stock is $66 per share At year-end, the company declares a 10% stock dividend—one share for each ten shares held. If all parties concerned clearly recognize the nature of the stock dividend, what should you expect the market price per share of the common stock to be on the ex-dividend date?

EXERCISE 15-10
Recording Treasury Stock Transactions

Cachet, Inc., engaged in the following transactions involving treasury stock:

Feb. 10	Purchased for cash 14,500 shares of treasury stock at a price of $30 per share.
June 4	Reissued 6,000 shares of treasury stock at a price of $33 per share.
Dec. 22	Reissued 4,000 shares of treasury stock at a price of $28 per share.

INSTRUCTIONS

a Prepare general journal entries to record these transactions.

b Compute the amount of retained earnings that should be restricted because of the treasury stock still owned at December 31.

EXERCISE 15-11
Effects of Various Transactions upon Earnings per Share

Explain the immediate effects, if any, of each of the following transactions upon a company's net earnings per share:

a Split the common stock 3 for 1.

b Realized a gain from the sale of a discontinued operation.

c Switched from an accelerated method of depreciation to the straight-line method, resulting in a large debit to the Accumulated Depreciation account.

d Declared and paid a cash dividend on common stock.

e Declared and distributed a stock dividend on common stock.

f Acquired several thousand shares of treasury stock.

EXERCISE 15-12
Where to Find Financial Information

You have now been exposed to the following financial statements issued by corporations: balance sheet, income statement, statement of retained earnings, and statement of stockholders' equity. Listed below are various items frequently of interest to a corporation's owners, potential investors, and creditors, among others.

You are to specify which of the above corporate financial statements, if any, reports the desired information. If the listed item is not reported in any formal financial statement issued by a corporation, indicate an appropriate source for the desired information.

a Number of shares of stock outstanding as of year-end

b Total dollar amount of cash dividends declared during the current year

c Market value per share at balance sheet date

d Cumulative dollar effect of an accounting error made in a previous year

e Cumulative dollar effect of switching from one generally accepted accounting principle to another acceptable accounting method during the current year

f Explanation of why the number of shares of stock outstanding at the end of the current year is greater than the number outstanding at the end of the prior year

g Earnings per share of common stock

h Book value per share

i Price/earnings (p/e) ratio

j The total amount the corporation paid to buy back shares of its own stock which it now holds

PROBLEMS

Group A

PROBLEM 15A-1
Reporting Unusual Events; Using Predictive Subtotals

Gulf Coast Airlines operated both an airline and several motels located near airports. During the year just ended, all motel operations were discontinued and the following operating results were reported:

Continuing operations (airlines):	
Net sales..	*$51,120,000*
Costs and expenses (including income taxes on continuing operations) ...	*43,320,000*
Other data:	
Operating income from motels (net of income taxes)......................	*864,000*
Gain on sale of motels (net of income taxes)	*4,956,000*
Extraordinary loss (net of income tax benefit)	*3,360,000*

The extraordinary loss resulted from the destruction of an airliner by terrorists.
    Gulf Coast Airlines had 1,200,000 shares of capital stock outstanding throughout the year.

INSTRUCTIONS

a Prepare a condensed income statement including proper presentation of the discontinued motel operations and the extraordinary loss. Include all appropriate earnings per share figures.

b Assume that you expect the profitability of Gulf Coast's airlines operations to **decline by** 6% next year, and the profitability of the motels to decline by 10%. What is your estimate of the company's net earnings per share next year?

PROBLEM 15A-2
Format of an Income Statement and a Statement of Retained Earnings

Shown on the following page are data relating to the operations of Academic Testing Services, Inc., during 1994:

Continuing operations:

Net sales..	$15,750,000
Costs and expenses (including applicable income taxes).................	12,800,000

Other data:

Operating income during 1994 on segment of the business discontinued near year-end (net of income taxes)....................................	225,000
Loss on disposal of discontinued segment (net of income tax benefit).....	675,000
Extraordinary loss (net of income tax benefit)	780,000
Cumulative effect of change in accounting principle (increase in net income, net of related income taxes)....................................	135,000
Prior period adjustment (increase in 1991 depreciation expense, net of income tax benefit)..	150,000
Cash dividends declared...	925,000

INSTRUCTIONS

a Prepare a condensed income statement for 1994, including earnings per share statistics. Academic Testing Services, Inc., had 300,000 shares of $1 par value common stock and 40,000 shares of $6.25, $100 par value preferred stock outstanding throughout the year.

b Prepare a statement of retained earnings for the year ended December 31, 1994. As originally reported, retained earnings at December 31, 1993 amounted to $6,450,000.

c Compute the amount of cash dividend *per share* of *common stock* declared by the board of directors for 1994. Assume no dividends in arrears on the preferred stock.

PROBLEM 15A-3
Reporting Unusual Events: A Comprehensive Problem

The following income statement was prepared by a new and inexperienced employee in the accounting department of Keller Interiors, a business organized as a corporation.

KELLER INTERIORS
Income Statement
For the Year Ended December 31, 1994

Net sales		$10,800,000
Gain on sale of treasury stock..		54,000
Excess of issuance price over par value of capital stock		510,000
Prior period adjustment (net of income taxes)		60,000
Extraordinary gain (net of income taxes)		36,000
Total revenue		$11,460,000
Less:		
Cost of goods sold...	$6,000,000	
Selling expenses..	1,104,000	
General and administrative expenses	1,896,000	
Loss from settlement of litigation	24,000	
Income taxes on continuing operations	720,000	
Operating loss on discontinued operations (net of income tax benefit)	252,000	
Loss on disposal of discontinued operations (net of income tax benefit).......................................	420,000	
Cumulative effect of change in accounting principle (net of income tax benefit).......................................	84,000	
Dividends declared on capital stock	350,000	
Total costs and expenses		10,850,000
Net income		$ 610,000

INSTRUCTIONS

a Prepare a corrected income statement for the year ended December 31, 1994, using the format illustrated on page 692. Include at the bottom of your income statement all appropriate earnings per share figures. Assume that throughout the year, the company had outstanding a weighted average of 200,000 shares of a single class of capital stock.

b Prepare a statement of retained earnings for 1994. (As originally reported, retained earnings at December 31, 1993 amounted to $1,400,000.)

**PROBLEM 15A-4
Effects of
Stock Divi-
dends, Stock
Splits, and
Treasury Stock
Transactions**

At the beginning of the year, Recovery Sciences, Inc., has total stockholders' equity of $660,000 and 20,000 outstanding shares of a single class of capital stock. During the year, the corporation completes the following transactions affecting its stockholders' equity accounts:

Jan. 10   A 10% stock dividend is declared and distributed. (Market price, $40 per share.)

Mar. 15   The corporation acquires 1,000 shares of its own capital stock at a cost of $40.50 per share.

May 30   All 1,000 shares of the treasury stock are reissued at a price of $44.90 per share.

July 31   The capital stock is split 2 for 1.

Dec. 15   The board of directors declares a cash dividend of $1.10 per share, payable on January 15.

Dec. 31   Net income of $127,600 (equal to $2.90 per share) is reported for the year ended December 31.

INSTRUCTIONS

Compute the amount of total stockholders' equity, the number of shares of capital stock outstanding, and the book value per share following each successive transaction. Organize your solution as a three-column schedule with these separate column headings: (1) Total Stockholders' Equity, (2) Number of Shares Outstanding, and (3) Book Value per Share.

**PROBLEM 15A-5
Preparing a
Statement of
Stockholders'
Equity**

Shown below is a summary of the transactions affecting the stockholders' equity of Granite Hills Corporation during the current year:

Prior period adjustment (net of income tax benefit)	$(50,000)
Issuance of common stock: 10,000 shares of $10 par value	
capital stock at $62 per share...	620,000
Declaration and distribution of 5% stock dividend (6,000 shares, market price	
$60 per share)...	360,000
Purchased 1,000 shares of treasury stock at $58..............................	(58,000)
Reissued 500 shares of treasury stock at a price of $64 per share	32,000
Net income...	510,000
Cash dividends declared ($1 per share)	125,500

Brackets () indicate a debit change—a reduction—in stockholders' equity.

INSTRUCTIONS

Prepare a statement of stockholders' equity for the year. Use the column headings and beginning balances shown below. (Notice that all additional paid-in capital accounts are combined into a single column.)

	Capital Stock ($10 Par Value)	Additional Paid-in Capital	Retained Earnings	Treasury Stock	Total Stock- Holders' Equity
Balances, January 1, 19__	$1,100,000	$1,800,000	$900,000	$ –0–	$3,800,000

**PROBLEM 15A-6
Recording
Stock Divi-
dends and
Treasury Stock
Transactions**

At the beginning of 1994, OverNight Letter showed the following amounts in the stockholders' equity section of its balance sheet:

Stockholders' equity:

Capital stock, $1 par value, 500,000 shares authorized,	
382,000 issued	*$ 382,000*
Additional paid-in capital: capital stock.........................	*4,202,000*
Total paid-in capital	*$4,584,000*
Retained earnings	*2,704,600*
Total stockholders' equity	*$7,288,600*

The transactions relating to stockholders' equity accounts during the year are as follows:

Jan. 3 Declared a dividend of $1 per share to stockholders of record on January 31, payable on February 15.

Feb. 15 Paid the cash dividend declared on January 3.

Apr. 12 The corporation purchased 6,000 shares of its own capital stock at a price of $40 per share.

May 9 Reissued 4,000 shares of the treasury stock at a price of $44 per share.

June 1 Declared a 5% stock dividend to stockholders of record at June 15 to be distributed on June 30. The market price of the stock at June 1 was $42 per share. (The 2,000 shares remaining in the treasury do not participate in the stock dividend.)

June 30 Distributed the stock dividend declared on June 1.

Aug. 4 Reissued 600 of the 2,000 remaining shares of treasury stock at a price of $37 per share.

Dec. 31 The Income Summary account, showing net income for the year of $1,928,000 was closed into the Retained Earnings account.

INSTRUCTIONS **a** Prepare in general journal form the entries to record the above transactions.

b Prepare the stockholders' equity section of the balance sheet at December 31, 1994. Use the format illustrated on page 710. Include a supporting schedule showing your computation of retained earnings at that date.

c Compute the maximum cash dividend per share which legally could be declared at December 31, 1994 without impairing the paid-in capital of OverNight Letter. (Hint: The availability of retained earnings for dividends is restricted by the cost of treasury stock owned.)

**PROBLEM 15A-7
Preparing the
Stockholders'
Equity Section:
A Challenging
Case**

The Mandella family decided early in 1993 to incorporate their family-owned vineyards under the name Mandella Corporation. The corporation was authorized to issue 500,000 shares of a single class of $10 par value capital stock. Presented below is the information necessary to prepare the stockholders' equity section of the company's balance sheet at the end of 1993 and at the end of 1994.

1993. In January the corporation issued to members of the Mandella family 150,000 shares of capital stock in exchange for cash and other assets used in the operation of the vineyards. The fair market value of these assets indicated an issue price of $30 per share. In December, Joe Mandella died, and the corporation purchased 10,000 shares of its own capital stock from his estate at $34 per share. Because of the large cash outlay to acquire this treasury stock, the directors decided not to declare cash dividends in 1993 and instead declared a 10% stock dividend to be distributed in January of 1994. The stock price at the declaration date was $35 per share. (The treasury shares do not participate in the stock dividend.) Net income for 1993 was $940,000.

1994. In January the corporation distributed the stock dividend declared in 1993, and in February, the 10,000 treasury shares were sold to Maria Mandella at $39 per share. In June, the capital stock was split 2 for 1. (Approval was obtained to increase the authorized number of shares to 1 million.) On December 15, the directors declared a cash dividend of $2 per share, payable in January of 1995. Net income for 1994 was $1,080,000.

INSTRUCTIONS

Using the format illustrated on page 710, prepare the stockholders' equity section of the balance sheet at:

a December 31, 1993

b December 31, 1994

Show any necessary computations in supporting schedules.

Group B

PROBLEM 15B-1
Reporting Unusual Events; Using Predictive Subtotals

Sea Quest Corporation operated both a fleet of commercial fishing vessels and a chain of six seafood restaurants. The restaurants continuously lost money and were sold to a large restaurant chain near year-end. The operating results of Sea Quest Corporation for the year ended December 31, 1994, are shown below:

Continuing operations (fishing fleet):	
Net sales...	*$23,000,000*
Costs and expenses (including related income taxes)......................	*20,100,000*
Other data:	
Operating loss from restaurants (net of income tax benefit)...............	*1,540,000*
Gain on sale of restaurant properties (net of income taxes)..............	*460,000*
Extraordinary loss (net of income tax benefit).............................	*720,000*

The extraordinary loss resulted from the expropriation of a fishing vessel by a foreign government.

Sea Quest Corporation had 500,000 shares of capital stock outstanding throughout the year.

INSTRUCTIONS

a Prepare a condensed income statement including proper presentation of the discontinued restaurant operations and the extraordinary loss. Include all appropriate earnings per share figures.

b Assume that you expect the profitability of Sea Quest's fishing operations to *increase by 5%* in the next year and the profitability of the restaurants to remain unchanged. What is your estimate of the company's net earnings per share for 1995?

PROBLEM 15B-2
Format of an Income Statement and a Statement of Retained Earnings

Shown below are data relating to the operations of Synthetic Genetics, Inc., during 1994:

Continuing operations:
Net sales... $21,000,000
Costs and expenses (including applicable income taxes).................. 18,300,000
Other data:
Operating loss during 1994 on segment of the business discontinued near year-end (net of income tax benefit).............................. 300,000
Loss on disposal of discontinued segment (net of income tax benefit)..... 900,000
Extraordinary gain (net of income tax)..................................... 620,000
Cumulative effect of change in accounting principle (decrease in net income, net of related income tax benefit).............................. 140,000
Prior period adjustment (increase in 1993 research and development expense, net of income tax benefit).................................... 240,000
Cash dividends declared... 1,200,000

INSTRUCTIONS

a Prepare a condensed income statement for 1994, including earnings per share statistics. Synthetic Genetics had 400,000 shares of $2 par value common stock as well as 50,000 shares of 8%, $100 par value preferred stock outstanding throughout 1994.

b Prepare a statement of retained earnings for the year ended December 31, 1994. As originally reported, retained earnings at December 31, 1993, amounted to $7,400,000.

c What was the cash dividend *per share* of *common stock* declared by Synthetic Genetics' board of directors for 1994? Assume there were no dividends in arrears on the preferred stock.

PROBLEM 15B-3
Reporting the Results of Operations—A Comprehensive Problem

Katherine McCall, the accountant for Alternative Energy Systems, was injured in a skiing accident, and the following income statement was prepared by a temporary employee with little knowledge of accounting:

ALTERNATIVE ENERGY SYSTEMS
Income Statement
For the Year Ended December 31, 1994

Net sales... $5,400,000
Gain on sale of treasury stock... 30,000
Excess of issuance price over par value of capital stock..................... 120,000
Operating income from segment of business discontinued during the year (net of income taxes)... 200,000
Cumulative effect of change in accounting principle (net of income taxes)..... 75,000
Total revenue... $5,825,000
Less:
Prior period adjustment (net of income tax benefit)............ $ 250,000
Cost of goods sold... 2,480,000
Selling expenses... 1,160,000
General and administrative operations......................... 820,000
Income taxes on continuing operations........................ 270,000
Extraordinary loss (net of income tax benefit)................. 230,000
Loss on sale of discontinued segment (net of income tax benefit)... 450,000
Dividends declared on capital stock........................... 300,000   5,960,000
Net loss... $ 135,000

INSTRUCTIONS **a** Prepare a corrected income statement for the year ended December 31, 1994, using the format illustrated on page 692. Include at the bottom of your income statement all appropriate earnings per share figures. Assume that throughout the year the company had outstanding a weighted average of 50,000 shares of a single class of capital stock.

b Prepare a statement of retained earnings for 1994. Assume that retained earnings at December 31, 1993, were originally reported at $2,300,000.

PROBLEM 15B-4
Effects of Stock Dividends, Stock Splits, and Treasury Stock Transactions

On January 1, Alton Pump & Compressor Corporation has total stockholders' equity of $4,400,000 and 50,000 outstanding shares of a single class of capital stock. During the year, the corporation completes the following transactions affecting its stockholders' equity accounts:

Jan. 10	The board of directors declares a cash dividend of $4.20 per share, payable on February 15.
Apr. 30	The capital stock is split 2 for 1.
June 11	The corporation acquires 2,000 shares of its own capital stock at a cost of $56.60 per share.
July 21	All 2,000 shares of the treasury stock are reissued at a price of $61.60 per share.
Nov. 10	A 5% stock dividend is declared and distributed (market value $60 per share).
Dec. 31	Net income of $378,000 (equal to $3.60 per share) is reported for the year.

INSTRUCTIONS Compute the amount of total stockholders' equity, the number of shares of capital stock outstanding, and the book value per share following each successive transaction. Organize your solution as a three-column schedule with these separate column headings: (1) Total Stockholders' Equity, (2) Number of Shares Outstanding, and (3) Book Value per Share.

PROBLEM 15B-5
Preparing a Statement of Stockholders' Equity

Shown below is a summary of the transactions affecting the stockholders' equity of Watch Hill Resort, Inc., during 19__:

Prior period adjustment (net of income taxes)	$ (25,000)
Declaration and distribution of a 10% stock dividend (2,000 shares, market price $40 per share)	80,000
Issuance of 5,000 shares of $5 par value capital stock at $42 per share.........	210,000
Purchased 1,000 shares of treasury stock at $38 per share.....................	(38,000)
Reissued 500 shares of treasury stock at $43 per share........................	21,500
Net income...	164,600
Cash dividends declared ($2 per share)	(53,000)

Parentheses () indicate a debit change—a reduction in stockholders' equity.

INSTRUCTIONS Prepare a statement of stockholders' equity for the year ended December 31, 19__. Use the column headings and beginning balances shown below. (Notice that one column is used to combine the additional paid-in capital from all sources.)

	Capital Stock ($5 Par Value)	Additional Paid-In Capital	Retained Earnings	Treasury Stock	Total Stockholders' Equity
Balances, January 1, 19__	$100,000	$420,000	$340,000	$ –0–	$860,000

PROBLEM 15B-6
Recording Stock Dividends and Treasury Stock Transactions

The stockholders' equity of Cornish Productions, Inc., at January 1, 1994, is as follows:

Stockholders' equity:

Common stock, $5 par value, 500,000 shares authorized, 260,000 issued	$1,300,000
Additional paid-in capital: common stock.................................	4,065,000
Total paid-in capital	$5,365,000
Retained earnings	2,810,000
Total stockholders' equity	$8,175,000

During the year the following transactions relating to stockholders' equity occurred:

Jan. 15 Paid a $1.50 per share cash dividend declared in December of the preceding year. This dividend was properly recorded at the declaration date and was the only dividend declared during the preceding year.

June 10 Declared a 10% stock dividend to stockholders of record on June 30, to be distributed on July 15. At June 10, the market price of the stock was $35 per share.

July 15 Distributed the stock dividend declared on June 10.

Aug. 4 Purchased 10,000 shares of treasury stock at a price of $30 per share.

Oct. 15 Reissued 6,000 shares of treasury stock at a price of $32 per share.

Dec. 10 Reissued 2,000 shares of treasury stock at a price of $28.50 per share.

Dec. 15 Declared a cash dividend of $1.50 per share to be paid on January 15 to stockholders of record on December 31.

Dec. 31 The Income Summary account, showing net income of $1,620,000, was closed into the Retained Earnings account.

INSTRUCTIONS

a Prepare in general journal form the entries necessary to record these transactions.

b Prepare the stockholders' equity section of the balance sheet at December 31, 1994, following the format illustrated on page 710. Include a note following your stockholders' equity section indicating any portion of retained earnings which is not available for dividends. Also include a supporting schedule showing your computation of the balance of retained earnings at year-end.

c Comment on whether Cornish Productions, Inc., increased or decreased the total amount of cash dividends declared during the year in comparison with dividends declared in the preceding year.

PROBLEM 15B-7
Preparing the Stockholders' Equity Section of a Balance Sheet

David Klein was a free-lance engineer who developed and patented a highly efficient turbocharger for automotive engines. In 1993, Klein and Scott Harris organized Performance, Inc., to manufacture the turbocharger. The corporation was authorized to issue 150,000 shares of $10 par value capital stock. Presented below is the information necessary to prepare the stockholders' equity section of the company's balance sheet at the end of 1993 and at the end of 1994.

1993. On January 20, the corporation issued 80,000 shares of common stock to Harris and other investors for cash at $34 per share. In addition, 10,000 shares of common stock were issued on that date to Klein in exchange for his patents. In November, Klein was killed while auto racing in Europe. At the request of Klein's heirs, Performance, Inc., purchased the 10,000 shares of its stock from Klein's estate at $45 per share. Because of the unexpected cash outlay to acquire treasury stock, the directors decided against declaring any cash dividends in 1993. Instead, they declared a 5% stock dividend which was distributed on December 31. The stock price at the declaration date was $42 per share. (The treasury shares did not participate in the stock dividend.) Net income for the year was $415,000.

1994. In March, the 10,000 treasury shares were reissued at a price of $52 per share. In August, the stock was split 4 for 1, with a reduction in the par value to $2.50 per share and an increase in the number of shares authorized to 600,000. On December 20, the directors declared a cash dividend of 70 cents per share, payable in January of 1995. Net income for the year was $486,000.

INSTRUCTIONS   Prepare the stockholders' equity section of the balance sheet at:

a   December 31, 1993

b   December 31, 1994

Use the format illustrated on page 710 and show any necessary supporting computations.

CASES AND UNSTRUCTURED PROBLEMS

CASE 15-1
What's This?

The following events have been reported in the financial statements of large, publicly owned corporations.

a   **Atlantic Richfield Company (ARCO)** sold or abandoned the entire "noncoal minerals" segment of its operations. In the year of disposal, this segment had an operating loss. ARCO also incurred a loss of $514 million on disposal of its noncoal minerals segment of the business.

b   **American Airlines** increased the estimated useful life used in computing depreciation on its aircraft. If the new estimated life had always been in use, the net income reported in prior years would have been substantially higher.

c   **Union Carbide Corp.** sustained a large loss as a result of the explosion of a chemical plant.

d   **AT&T** changed the method used to depreciate certain assets. Had the new method always been in use, the net income of prior years would have been $175 million lower than was actually reported.

e   **Georgia Pacific Corporation** realized a $10 million gain as a result of condemnation proceedings in which a governmental agency purchased assets from the company in a "forced sale."

INSTRUCTIONS   Indicate whether each event should be classified as a discontinued operation, an extraordinary item, the cumulative effect of an accounting change, or included among the revenue and expenses of normal and recurring business operations. Briefly explain your reasons for each answer.

CASE 15-2
The Case of the Extraordinarily Ordinary Loss

In 1986 **Squibb Corporation** recognized a $68 million loss from the write-off of certain foreign-based assets due to "escalating war, social upheaval, the weakening economies of oil-producing nations, and growing political instability." (Squibb's operations in these foreign countries were not discontinued.) Squibb originally classified this loss as an extraordinary item. Upon reviewing the company's financial statements, however, the Securities and Exchange Commission requested that Squibb reclassify this item as a normal operating loss. In 1987, Squibb revised its 1986 income statement to comply with the SEC's request.

INSTRUCTIONS   Indicate the effect of the reclassification of this loss upon Squibb's:

  a   Net income for 1986.

  b   Income before extraordinary items for 1986.

  c   Income from continuing operations in 1986.

  d   Price-earnings ratio as shown in financial newspapers such as *The Wall Street Journal.*

  e   1987 financial statements.

  f   Ability to pay cash dividends.

Explain the reasoning behind your answers.

CASE 15-3
Is There Life without Baseball?

Midwestern Publishing, Inc., publishes two newspapers and until recently owned a professional baseball team. The baseball team had been losing money for several years and was sold at the end of 1993 to a group of investors who plan to move it to a larger city. Also in 1993, Midwestern suffered an extraordinary loss when its Raytown printing plant was damaged by a tornado. The damage has since been repaired. A condensed income statement is shown below:

MIDWESTERN PUBLISHING, INC.
Income Statement
For the Year Ended December 31, 1993

Net revenue		$41,000,000
Costs and expenses		36,500,000
Income from continuing operations		$ 4,500,000
Discontinued operations:		
Operating loss on baseball team	$(1,300,000)	
Gain on sale of baseball team	4,700,000	3,400,000
Income before extraordinary items		$ 7,900,000
Extraordinary loss:		
Tornado damage to Raytown printing plant		(600,000)
Net income		$ 7,300,000

INSTRUCTIONS   On the basis of this information, answer the following questions. Show any necessary computations and explain your reasoning.

  a   What would Midwestern's net income have been for 1993 if it **had not** sold the baseball team?

  b   Assume that for 1994, you expect a 7% increase in the profitability of Midwestern's newspaper business but had projected a $2,000,000 operating loss for the baseball team if Midwestern had continued to operate the team in 1994. What amount would you forecast as Midwestern's 1994 net income *if the company had continued to own and operate the baseball team?*

  c   Given your assumptions in part **b,** but given that Midwestern **did** sell the baseball team in 1993, what would you forecast as the company's estimated net income for 1994?

  d   Assume that the expenses of operating the baseball team in 1993 amounted to $32,200,000, net of any related income tax effects. What was the team's **net revenue** for the year?

CASE 15-4
Using Earnings per Share Statistics

For many years American Studios has produced television shows and operated several FM radio stations. Late in the current year, the radio stations were sold to Times Publishing, Inc. Also during the current year, American Studios sustained an extraordinary loss when one of its camera trucks caused an accident in an international grand prix auto race. Throughout the current year, the company had 3 million shares of common stock and a large quantity of convertible preferred stock outstanding. Earnings per share reported for the current year were as follows:

	Primary	Fully Diluted
Earnings from continuing operations	$8.20	$6.80
Earnings before extraordinary items	$6.90	$5.50
Net earnings	$3.80	$2.40

INSTRUCTIONS

a Briefly explain why American Studios reports fully diluted earnings per share amounts as well as earnings per share computed on a primary basis. What is the purpose of showing investors the fully diluted figures?

b What was the total dollar amount of the extraordinary loss sustained by American Studios during the current year?

c Assume that the price-earnings ratio shown in the morning newspaper for American Studios' common stock indicates that the stock is selling at a price equal to 10 times the reported earnings per share. What is the approximate market price of the stock?

d Assume that you expect both the revenue and expenses involved in producing television shows to increase by 10% during the coming year. What would you forecast as the company's net earnings per share (primary basis) for the coming year under each of the following independent assumptions? (Show your computations and explain your reasoning.)

1 *None* of the convertible preferred stock is converted into common stock during the coming year.

2 *All* of the convertible preferred stock is converted into common stock at the beginning of the coming year.

CASE 15-5
Interpreting a Statement of Stockholders' Equity

The following information is excerpted from the Statement of Common Stockholders' Equity included in a recent annual report of **The Quaker Oats Company and Subsidiaries.** (Dollar figures are in millions.)

	Common Stock		Additional Paid-in Capital	Retained Earnings	Treasury Stock	
	Shares	Amount			Shares	Amount
Balances, beginning of year	83,989,396	$420.0	$19.5	$ 998.4	4,593,664	$(132.9)
Net income				203.0		
Cash dividends declared on common stock				(95.2)		
Common stock issued for stock option plans			(1.4)		(601,383)	16.7
Repurchases of common stock					1,229,700	(68.6)
Balances, year-end	83,989,396	$420.0	$18.1	$1,106.2	5,221,981	$(184.8)

INSTRUCTIONS Use the information presented above to answer the following questions.

a How many shares of common stock are outstanding at the **beginning** of the year? At the **end** of the year?

b What was the total common stock dividend declared during the above year? Quaker's annual report disclosed that the common stock dividend during the above year was $1.20 per share (30 cents per quarter). Approximately how many shares of common stock were entitled to the $1.20 per share dividend during the year? Is this answer compatible with your answers to part **a**?

c The above statement indicates that common stock was both issued during the year and repurchased during the year, yet the number of common shares shown and the common stock amount (first and second columns) did not change from beginning to end of the year. Explain.

d What was the average price per share Quaker paid to acquire the treasury shares held at the **beginning** of the year?

e Was the aggregate issue price of the 601,383 treasury shares issued during the year for stock option plans higher or lower than the cost Quaker paid to acquire those treasury shares? (Hint: Analyze the impact upon Additional Paid-in Capital.)

f What was the average purchase price per share paid by Quaker to acquire treasury shares **during the current year?**

g In its annual report, Quaker disclosed that the (weighted) average number of common shares outstanding during the year was 79,307,000. In part **a,** above, you determined the number of common shares outstanding as of the end of the year. Which figure is used in computing **earnings per share?** Which is used in computing **book value per share?**

ANSWERS TO SELF-TEST QUESTIONS

1 b   2 d   3 c   4 a   5 b

16 Special Types of Liabilities

"Routine" types of business liabilities were discussed in Chapter 11. In this second chapter about liabilities we explore many special types of liabilities. We will consider such questions as: How can a corporation borrow a huge amount of money on a long-term basis from many small, short-term investors? Why are some long-term lease agreements viewed as liabilities, whereas others are not? How can the balance sheet of a large corporation that has promised millions of dollars of retirement benefits to its employees include no liability for this obligation? And just what are deferred taxes, anyway?

The liabilities discussed in this chapter appear primarily in the financial statements of large, publicly owned corporations. Some, however, also affect the financial statements of smaller organizations.

After studying this chapter you should be able to meet these Learning Objectives:

1 *Describe the typical characteristics of corporate bonds.*

2 *Explain the tax advantage of raising capital by issuing bonds instead of stock.*

3 *Account for the issuance of bonds, accrual and payment of interest, and retirement of bonds.*

4 *Describe the relationship between interest rates and bond prices.*

5 *Explain the effects of amortizing bond discount and premium upon bond interest expense.*

6 *Explain the accounting treatment of operating leases and of capital leases.*

7 *Account for the costs of pensions and other postretirement benefits.*

8 *Explain the nature of deferred income taxes.*

*9 *Amortize bond discount and premium by the effective interest method.*

---

* *Supplemental Topic A, "An Alternative Method of Amortizing Bond Discount and Premium"*

BONDS PAYABLE

Financially sound corporations may arrange limited amounts of long-term financing by issuing notes payable to banks or to insurance companies. But to finance a large project, such as developing an oil field or purchasing a controlling interest in the capital stock of another company, a corporation may need more capital than any single lender can supply. When a corporation needs to raise large amounts of long-term capital—perhaps 50, 100, or 500 million dollars (or more)—it generally sells additional shares of capital stock or issues **bonds payable.**

What Are Bonds?

OBJECTIVE 1
Describe the typical characteristics of corporate bonds.

The issuance of bonds payable is a technique for splitting a very large loan into a great many transferable units, called bonds. Each bond represents a **long-term, interest-bearing note payable,** usually in the face amount (or par value) of $1,000, or some multiple of $1,000. The bonds are sold to the investing public, enabling many different investors (bondholders) to participate in the loan.

Bonds usually are very long-term notes, maturing in perhaps 30 or 40 years. The bonds are transferable, however, so individual bondholders may sell their bonds to other investors at any time. Most bonds call for semiannual interest payments to the bondholders, with interest computed at a specified **contract rate** throughout the life of the bond. Thus, investors often describe bonds as "fixed income" investments.

An example of a corporate bond issue is the 8½% bonds of Pacific Bell (a Pacific Telesis company, known as PacBell), due August 15, 2031. Interest on these bonds is payable semiannually on February 15 and August 15. With this bond issue, PacBell borrowed $225 million by issuing 225,000 bonds of $1,000 each.

PacBell did not actually print and issue 225,000 separate notes payable. Each bondholder is issued a single **bond certificate** indicating the number of bonds purchased. An illustration of a bond certificate appears on the following page. This specimen certificate is in the face amount of $25,000 and, therefore, represents ownership of 25 bonds. Investors such as mutual funds, banks, and insurance companies often buy thousands of bonds at one time.

Bonds payable differ from capital stock in several ways. First, bonds payable are a liability; thus, bondholders are **creditors** of the corporation, not owners. Bondholders generally do not have voting rights and do not participate in the earnings of the corporation beyond receiving contractual interest payments. Next, bond interest payments are **contractual obligations** of the corporation. Dividends, on the other hand, do not become legal obligations of the corporation until they have been formally declared by the board of directors. Finally, bonds have a specified **maturity date,** upon which the corporation must redeem the bonds at their face amount. Capital stock, on the other hand, does not have a maturity date and may remain outstanding indefinitely.

Authorization of a Bond Issue   Formal approval of the board of directors and the stockholders usually is required before bonds can be issued. If the

bonds are to be sold to the general public, approval also must be obtained from the SEC, just as for an issue of capital stock which is offered to the public.

When bonds are issued, the corporation usually utilizes the services of an investment banking firm, called an **underwriter.** The underwriter guarantees the issuing corporation a specific price for the entire bond issue and makes a profit by selling the bonds to the investing public at a higher price. The corporation records the issuance of the bonds at the net amount received from the underwriter. The use of an underwriter assures the corporation that the entire bond issue will be sold without delay, and the entire amount of the proceeds will be available at a specific date.

Transferability of Bonds Corporate bonds, like capital stocks, are traded daily on organized securities exchanges, such as the **New York Bond Exchange.** The holders of a 25-year bond issue need not wait 25 years to convert their investments into cash. By placing a telephone call to a broker, an investor may sell bonds within a matter of minutes at the going market price. This quality of **liquidity** is one of the most attractive features of an investment in corporate bonds.

Quoted Market Prices Bond prices are quoted as a **percentage** of their face value or **maturity** value, which is usually $1,000. The maturity value is the amount the issuing company must pay to redeem the bond at the date it matures (becomes due). A $1,000 bond quoted at **102** would therefore have a market price of $1,020 (102% of $1,000). Bond prices are quoted at the nearest one-eighth of a percentage point. The following line from the financial page of a daily newspaper summarizes the previous day's trading in bonds of Sears, Roebuck and Company.

What is the market value of this bond?

Bonds	Sales	High	Low	Close	Net Change
Sears R $7\frac{7}{8}$'07	245	$97\frac{1}{2}$	$95\frac{1}{2}$	97	+1

This line of condensed information indicates that 245 of Sears, Roebuck and Company's $7\frac{7}{8}$%, $1,000 bonds maturing in 2007 were traded during the day. The highest price is reported as $97\frac{1}{2}$, or $975 for a bond of $1,000 face value. The lowest price was $95\frac{1}{2}$, or $955 for a $1,000 bond. The closing price (last sale of the day) was 97, or $970. This was one point above the closing price of the previous day, an increase of $10 in the price of a $1,000 bond.

The primary factors which determine the market value of a bond are (1) the relationship of the bond's interest rate to other investment opportunities, (2) the length of time until the bond matures, and (3) investors' confidence that the issuing company has the financial strength to make all future interest and principal payments promptly. Thus, a bond with a 10% interest rate will command a higher market price than an 8% bond with the same maturity date if the two companies issuing the bonds are of equal financial strength.

A bond selling at a market price greater than its maturity value is said to be selling at a **premium;** a bond selling at a price below its maturity value is selling at a **discount.** As a bond nears its maturity date, the market price of the bond moves toward the maturity value. At the maturity date the market value of the bond will be exactly equal to its maturity value, because the issuing corporation will redeem the bond for that amount.

Types of Bonds Bonds secured by the pledge of specific assets are called *mortgage bonds.* An unsecured bond is called a *debenture bond;* its value rests upon the general credit of the corporation. A debenture bond issued by a very large and strong corporation may have a higher investment rating than a secured bond issued by a corporation in less satisfactory financial condition. For example, the $500 million of debenture bonds recently issued by IBM are rated by Standard & Poor's Corp. as AAA, the highest possible rating.

Bond interest is paid semiannually by mailing to each bondholder a check for six months' interest on the bonds he or she owns.[1] Almost all bonds are *callable,* which means that the corporation has the right to redeem the bonds *in advance* of the maturity date by paying a specified *call price.* To compensate bondholders for being forced to give up their investments, the call price usually is somewhat higher than the face value of the bonds.

Corporations must maintain a *bondholders subsidiary ledger,* showing each bondholder's name and address and the face value of bonds owned. This record provides the information necessary for determining the amount of interest payable to each bondholder and for notifying bondholders if their bonds are called.

Traditionally, bonds have appealed to conservative investors, interested primarily in a reliable income stream and in the safety of the principal which they have invested. To make a bond issue more attractive to these investors, some corporations create a bond *sinking fund,* designated for repaying the bonds at maturity. At regular intervals, the corporation deposits cash into this sinking fund. A bond sinking fund is not classified as a current asset, because it is not available for the payment of current liabilities. Such funds are shown in the balance sheet under the caption "Long-term Investments," which appears just below the current asset section.

As an additional attraction to investors, corporations sometimes include a conversion privilege in the bond indenture. A *convertible bond* is one which may be exchanged at the option of the bondholder for a specified number of shares of common stock. Thus, the market value of a convertible bond tends to fluctuate with the market value of an equivalent number of shares of common stock.

"Junk Bonds" In recent years, some corporations have issued securities which have come to be known as *junk bonds.* This term describes a bond issue which involves a substantially greater risk of default than normal. A

---

[1] In recent years, corporations have issued only *registered* bonds, for which interest is paid by mailing a check to the registered owners of the bonds. In past decades, some companies issued *coupon bonds* or *bearer bonds,* which had a series of redeemable coupons attached. At each interest date, the bondholder was to "clip" the coupon and present it to a bank to collect the interest. These bonds posed a considerable hazard to investors—if the investor lost the coupon, or forgot about an interest date, he or she received no interest. In many states, issuing coupon bonds now is illegal.

company issuing junk bonds usually has so much long-term debt that its ability to meet interest and principal repayment obligations has become questionable. To compensate bondholders for this unusual level of risk, junk bonds promise a substantially higher rate of interest than do more "highly rated" bonds.

Tax Advantage of Bond Financing

OBJECTIVE 2 Explain the tax advantage of raising capital by issuing bonds instead of stock.

A principal advantage of raising money by issuing bonds instead of stock is that interest payments are **deductible** in determining income subject to corporate income taxes. Dividends paid to stockholders, however, are **not deductible** in computing taxable income.

To illustrate, assume that a corporation pays income taxes at a rate of **30**% on its taxable income. If this corporation issues $10 million of 10% bonds payable, it will incur interest expense of $1 million per year. This interest expense, however, will reduce taxable income by $1 million, thus reducing the corporation's annual income taxes by $300,000. As a result, the **after-tax** cost of borrowing the $10 million is only **$700,000,** as shown below:

Interest expense ($10,000,000 × 10%)	$1,000,000
Less: Income tax savings ($1,000,000 deduction × 30%)	300,000
After-tax cost of borrowing	$700,000

A short-cut approach to computing the after-tax cost of borrowing is simply multiplying the interest expense by **1 minus the company's tax rate,** as follows: $1,000,000 × (1 − .30) = $700,000.

Accounting for Bonds Payable

OBJECTIVE 3 Account for the issuance of bonds, accrual and payment of interest, and retirement of bonds.

Accounting for bonds payable closely parallels accounting for notes payable. The "accountable events" in the life of a bond issue usually are (1) issuance of the bonds, (2) semiannual interest payments, (3) accrual of interest payable at the end of each accounting period,[2] and (4) retirement of the bonds at maturity.

To illustrate these events, assume that on March 1, 1993, Wells Corporation issues $1 million of 12%, 20-year bonds payable.[3] These bonds are dated March 1, 1993, and interest is computed from this date. Interest on the bonds is payable semiannually, each September 1 and March 1. If all of the bonds are sold at par value (face amount), the issuance of the bonds on March 1 will be recorded by the following entry:

Cash	$1,000,000	
Bonds Payable		1,000,000
Issued 12% 20-year bonds payable at a price of 100.		

---

[2] To simplify our illustrations, we assume in all of our examples and assignment material that adjusting entries for accrued bond interest payable are made **only at year-end.** In practice, these adjustments usually are made on a monthly basis.

[3] The amount of $1 million is used only for purposes of illustration. As explained earlier, actual bond issues are for many millions of dollars.

Every September 1 during the life of the bond issue, Wells Corporation must pay $60,000 to the bondholders ($1,000,000 × .12 × ½ = $60,000). This semiannual interest payment will be recorded as shown below:

Bond Interest Expense...............................	*60,000*	
Cash		*60,000*
Semiannual payment of bond interest.		

Every December 31, Wells Corporation must make an adjusting entry to record the four months' interest which has accrued since September 1:

Bond Interest Expense...............................	*40,000*	
Bond Interest Payable		*40,000*
To accrue bond interest payable for four months ended		
Dec. 31 ($1,000,000 × .12 × $\frac{4}{12}$ = $40,000).		

The accrued liability for bond interest payable will be paid within a few months and, therefore, is classified as a current liability.

Two months later, on March 1, a semiannual interest payment is made to bondholders. This transaction represents payment of the four months' interest accrued at December 31, and of two months' interest which has accrued since year-end. If we assume that the company does not use reversing entries, the entry to record the semiannual payments every March 1 will be:

Bond Interest Expense...............................	*20,000*	
Bond Interest Payable	*40,000*	
Cash		*60,000*
To record semiannual interest payment to bondholders,		
and to recognize two months' interest expense accrued		
since year-end ($1,000,000 × .12 × $\frac{2}{12}$ = $20,000).		

When the bonds mature 20 years later on March 1, 2013, two entries are required: one entry to record the regular semiannual interest payment and a second entry to record the retirement of the bonds. The entry to record retirement of the bond issue is:

Bonds Payable	*1,000,000*	
Cash		*1,000,000*
Paid face amount of bonds at maturity.		

Bonds Issued between Interest Dates The semiannual interest dates (such as January 1 and July 1, or April 1 and October 1) are printed on the bond certificates. However, bonds are often issued between the specified interest dates. The *investor* is then required to pay the interest accrued to the date of issuance *in addition* to the stated price of the bond. This practice enables the corporation to pay a full six months' interest on all bonds outstanding at the semiannual interest payment date. The accrued interest collected from investors purchasing bonds between interest payment dates is thus returned to them on the next interest payment date.

To illustrate, let us modify our illustration to assume that Wells Corporation issues $1 million of 12% bonds at a price of 100 on **May 1**—two months **after** the date printed on the bonds. The amount received from the bond purchasers now will include two months' accrued interest, as follows:

Bonds issued between inter-est dates	Cash...	1,020,000	
	Bonds Payable......................................		1,000,000
	Bond Interest Payable.............................		20,000

Issued $1,000,000 face value of 12%, 20-year bonds at 100 plus accrued interest for two months ($1,000,000 × 12% × $\frac{2}{12}$ = $20,000).

Four months later on the regular semiannual interest payment date, a full six months' interest ($60 per each $1,000 bond) will be paid to all bondholders, ***regardless of when they purchased their bonds.*** The entry for the semiannual interest payment is illustrated below:

Notice only part of the in-terest payment is charged to expense	Bond Interest Payable	20,000	
	Bond Interest Expense................................	40,000	
	Cash		60,000

Paid semiannual interest on $1,000,000 face value of 12% bonds.

Now consider these interest transactions from the standpoint of the ***investors.*** They paid for two months' accrued interest at the time of purchasing the bonds, and then received checks for six months' interest after holding the bonds for only four months. They have, therefore, been reimbursed properly for the use of their money for four months.

When bonds are subsequently sold by one investor to another, they sell at the quoted market price ***plus accrued interest*** since the last interest payment date. This practice enables the issuing corporation to pay all the interest for an interest period to the investor owning the bond at the interest date. Otherwise, the corporation would have to make partial payments to every investor who bought or sold the bond during the interest period.

The amount which investors will pay for bonds is the ***present value*** of the principal and interest payments they will receive. Before going further in our discussion of bonds payable, it will be helpful to review the concepts of present value and effective interest rate.

The Concept of Present Value

The concept of present value is based upon the "time value" of money—the idea that receiving money today is preferable to receiving money at some later date. Assume, for example, that a bond will have a maturity value of $1,000 five years from today but will pay no interest in the meantime. Investors would not pay $1,000 for this bond today, because they would receive no return on their investment over the next five years. There are prices less than $1,000, however, at which investors would buy the bond. For example, if the bond could be purchased for $600, the investor could expect a return (interest) of $400 from the investment over the five-year period.

The ***present value*** of a future cash receipt is the amount that a knowledgeable investor will pay ***today*** for the right to receive that future payment. The exact amount of the present value depends upon (1) the amount of the future payment, (2) the length of time until the payment will be received, and (3) the rate of return required by the investor. However, the present value will always be ***less*** than the future amount. This is because money received today can be invested to earn interest and thereby becomes equivalent to a larger amount in the future.

The rate of interest which will cause a given present value to grow to a given future amount is called the ***discount rate*** or ***effective rate.*** The effective interest rate required by investors at any given time is regarded as the going ***market rate*** of interest. (The procedures for computing the present value of a future amount are illustrated in Appendix C at the end of this textbook.)

OBJECTIVE 4
Describe the
relationship
between in-
terest rates
and bond
prices.

The Present Value Concept and Bond Prices   The price at which bonds will sell is the present value to investors of the future principal and interest payments. If the bonds sell at par, the market rate is equal to the ***contract interest rate*** (or nominal rate) printed on the bonds. The ***higher*** the effective interest rate that investors require, the ***less*** they will pay for bonds with a given contract rate of interest. For example, if investors insist upon a 10% return, they will pay less than $1,000 for a 9%, $1,000 bond. Thus, if investors require an effective interest rate ***greater*** than the contract rate of interest for the bonds, the bonds will sell at a ***discount*** (price less than face value). On the other hand, if investors require an effective interest rate of ***less*** than the contract rate, the bonds will sell at a ***premium*** (price above face value).

A corporation wishing to borrow money by issuing bonds must pay the going market rate of interest. Since market rates of interest are fluctuating constantly, it must be expected that the contract rate of interest may vary somewhat from the market rate at the date the bonds are issued. Thus, bonds may be issued at either a discount or a premium.

Bonds Issued at a Discount

To illustrate the sale of bonds at a discount, assume that SCUBA TECH plans to issue $1 million face value of 9%, 10-year bonds. At the issuance date of January 1, the going market rate of interest is slightly above 9% and the bonds sell at a price of only **98** ($980 for each $1,000 bond). The issuance of the bonds will be recorded by the following entry:

Issuance of bonds at a discount

Cash..	980,000	
Discount on Bonds Payable............................	20,000	
Bonds Payable.......................................		1,000,000
Issued $1,000,000 face value of 9%, 10-year bonds at 98.		

If a balance sheet is prepared immediately after the issuance of the bonds, the liability for bonds payable will be shown as follows:

Reporting the net liability

Long-term liabilities:		
9% bonds payable, due in 10 years	*$1,000,000*	
Less: Discount on bonds payable	*20,000*	*$980,000*

The amount of the discount is deducted from the face value of the bonds payable to show the ***carrying value*** or book value of the liability. At the date of issuance, the carrying value of bonds payable is equal to the amount for which the bonds were sold. In other words, the amount of the company's liability at the date of issuing the bonds is equal to the ***amount of money borrowed.*** Over the life of the bonds, however, we shall see that this carrying value gradually increases until it reaches the face value of the bonds at the maturity date.

Bond Discount as Part of the Cost of Borrowing   In Chapter 11, we illustrated two ways in which interest charges can be specified in a note payable: the interest may be stated as an annual percentage rate of the face amount of the note, or it may be included in the face amount. Bonds issued at a discount include ***both*** types of interest charge. The $1 million bond issue in our SCUBA TECH example calls for cash interest payments of $90,000 per year ($1,000,000 × 9% contract interest rate), payable semiannually. In addition to making the semiannual interest payments, the corporation must redeem the bond issue for $1 million on the maturity date. This maturity value is ***$20,000 more*** than the $980,000 received when the bonds were issued. Thus, the $20,000 discount in the issue price may be regarded as an ***interest charge included in the maturity value of the bonds.***

OBJECTIVE 5
Explain the effects of amortizing bond discount and premium upon bond interest expense.

Although the interest charge represented by the discount will not be paid to bondholders until the bonds mature, SCUBA TECH benefits from this cost during the entire period that it has the use of the bondholders' money. Therefore, the cost represented by the discount should be allocated over the life of the bond issue. The process of allocating bond discount to interest expense is termed ***amortization*** of the discount.

Bonds are sometimes issued between interest dates. In this situation the bonds are outstanding for a shorter time; therefore, the amortization period is shorter. For example, if a 10-year bond issue dated January 1, 1994, is issued on March 1, 1994, the bonds will be outstanding for 9 years and 10 months, or a total of ***118 months.*** Under the straight-line method of amortization, the discount amortized per month will be $\frac{1}{118}$ of the total discount.

Whenever bonds are issued at a discount, the total interest cost over the life of the bonds is equal to the total of the regular cash interest payments ***plus the amount of the discount.*** For the $1 million bond issue in our example, the total interest cost over the 10-year life of the bonds is ***$920,000*** of which $900,000 represents the 20 semiannual cash interest payments and $20,000 represents the discount. The average annual interest expense, therefore, is ***$92,000*** ($920,000 ÷ 10 years), consisting of $90,000 paid in cash and $2,000 amortization of the bond discount. This analysis is illustrated below:

Total cash interest payments to bondholders		
($1,000,000 × 9% × 10 years)		*$900,000*
Add: Interest charge included in face amount of bonds:		
Maturity value of bonds	*$1,000,000*	
Amount borrowed	*980,000*	*20,000*
Total cost of borrowing over life of bond issue		*$920,000*
Average annual interest expense ($920,000 ÷ 10 years)		*$ 92,000*

Amortization of Bond Discount   The simplest method of amortizing bond discount is the ***straight-line method,*** which allocates an equal portion of the discount to Bond Interest Expense in each period.[4] In our example, the Discount on Bonds Payable account has a beginning debit balance of $20,000; each year $\frac{1}{10}$ of this amount, or $2,000, will be amortized into Bond Interest Expense. Assuming that the interest payment dates are June 30 and December 31, the entries to be made each six months to record bond interest expense are as follows:

Payment of bond interest and straight-line amortization of bond discount

Bond Interest Expense...	*45,000*	
Cash		*45,000*
Paid semiannual interest on $1,000,000 of 9%, 10-year bonds.		

Bond Interest Expense...	*1,000*	
Discount on Bonds Payable		*1,000*
Amortized discount for six months on 10-year bond issue ($20,000 discount × $\frac{1}{20}$).		

The two entries shown above to record the cash payment of bond interest and to record the amortization of bond discount can conveniently be combined into one compound entry, as follows:

Bond Interest Expense...	*46,000*	
Cash		*45,000*
Discount on Bonds Payable		*1,000*
To record payment of semiannual interest on $1,000,000 of 9%, 10-year bonds ($1,000,000 × 9% × $\frac{1}{2}$) and to amortize $\frac{1}{20}$ of the discount on the 10-year bond issue.		

Regardless of whether the cash payment of interest and the amortization of bond discount are recorded in separate entries or combined in one entry, the amount recognized as Bond Interest Expense is the same— $46,000 each six months, or a total of $92,000 a year. An alternative accounting procedure that will produce the same results is to amortize the bond discount only at year-end rather than at each interest-payment date.

Note that the additional interest expense resulting from amortization of the discount does not require any additional cash payment. The credit portion of the entry is to the contra-liability account, Discount on Bonds Payable, rather than to the Cash account. Crediting this contra-liability account increases the carrying value of bonds, which is a long-term liability. The original $20,000 discount will be completely amortized by the end of the tenth year, and the net liability (carrying value) will be the full face value of the bonds.

In this example, the bonds were outstanding for the full term of 10 years or 120 months. If the bonds had been issued between interest dates, say, March 1, rather than January 1, the amortization period would have been the shortened life of 118 months.

Zero Coupon Bonds Some companies have issued bonds which pay ***no interest*** over the life of the bond. Thus, the entire interest charge is included in the face amount of the bonds and is represented by a ***very large***

---

[4] An alternative method of amortization, called the ***effective interest method,*** is illustrated in Supplemental Topic A at the end of this chapter. Although the effective interest method is theoretically preferable to the straight-line method, the resulting differences generally are not material in dollar amount.

discount at the issuance date. Such bonds, called *zero coupon* (or *zeros*), usually are issued at a price of less than 20% of their maturity value.

The discount on zero coupon bonds is so material that the straight-line method of amortization produces misleading results. Therefore, generally accepted accounting principles require that the discount on such bonds be amortized by the *effective interest method,* which is discussed in Supplemental Topic A at the end of this chapter.

Further discussion of zero coupon bonds is deferred to the intermediate accounting course and to courses in corporate finance.

Bonds Issued at a Premium

Bonds will sell *above* par if the contract rate of interest specified on the bonds is *higher* than the current market rate for bonds of this grade. Let us now change our basic illustration by assuming that the $1 million issue of 9%, 10-year bonds is sold at a price of 102 ($1,020 for each $1,000 bond). The entry is shown below:

Issuance of bonds at a premium

Cash...	1,020,000	
Bonds Payable......................................		1,000,000
Premium on Bonds Payable		20,000
Issued $1,000,000 face value of 9%, 10-year bonds at price of 102.		

If a balance sheet is prepared immediately following the sale of the bonds, the liability will be shown as follows:

Reporting the carrying value of the liability

Long-term liabilities:		
9% bonds payable, due in 10 years	$1,000,000	
Add: Premium on bonds payable.............................	20,000	$1,020,000

The amount of any unamortized premium is *added* to the maturity value of the bonds payable to show the current carrying value of the liability. Over the life of the bond issue, this carrying value will be *reduced* toward the maturity value of $1 million.

Bond Premium as Reduction in the Cost of Borrowing   We have illustrated how issuing bonds at a discount increases the cost of borrowing above the amount of the regular cash interest payments. Issuing bonds at a premium, on the other hand, *reduces the cost of borrowing below the amount of the regular cash interest payments.*

The amount received from issuance of the bonds is $20,000 greater than the amount which must be repaid at maturity. This $20,000 premium is not a gain but is to be offset against the periodic interest payments in determining the net cost of borrowing.

Whenever bonds are issued at a premium, the total interest cost over the life of the bonds is equal to the regular cash interest payments *minus the amount of the premium.* In our example, the total interest cost over the life of the bonds is computed as $900,000 of cash interest payments, minus $20,000 of premium amortized, or a net borrowing cost of *$880,000.* The average annual interest expense will be *$88,000,* consisting of $90,000 paid in cash each year, less an offsetting $2,000 reduction in the net liability for bonds payable which results from amortization of the premium.

The semiannual entries on June 30 and December 31 to record the payment of bond interest and amortization of bond premium (by the straight-line method) are as follows:

Payment of bond interest and straight-line amortization of bond premium

Bond Interest Expense..	*45,000*	
Cash		*45,000*
Paid semiannual interest on $1,000,000 of 9%, 10-year bonds.		
Premium on Bonds Payable...................................	*1,000*	
Bond Interest Expense		*1,000*
Amortized premium for six months on 10-year bond issue ($20,000 premium × $\frac{1}{20}$).		

In our prior discussion of bond discount, we stated that if bonds are issued between interest dates, the amortization period will be shortened. This concept also applies to bonds issued at a premium. In brief, the period for amortization of either bond discount or premium is determined by the number of years and months the bonds are actually outstanding.

Year-End Adjustments for Bond Interest Expense

In the preceding illustration, it was assumed that one of the semiannual dates for payment of bond interest coincided with the end of the company's accounting year. In most cases, however, the semiannual interest payment dates will fall during an accounting period rather than on the last day of the year.

For purposes of illustration, assume that $1 million of 12%, 10-year bonds are issued at a price of 97 on **October 1,** 1994. Interest payment dates are April 1, and October 1. The total discount to be amortized amounts to $30,000, or $1,500 in each six-month interest period. (Notice that the discount is amortized at a rate of $250 per month.) Now also assume that the corporation closes its accounts at the end of each calendar year. At December 31, an **adjusting entry** will be needed to (1) record accrued interest at the 12% contract rate for the three months since October 1 and (2) amortize the bond discount for the three months since October 1. This adjusting entry will be:

Bond Interest Expense..	*30,750*	
Bond Interest Payable		*30,000*
Discount on Bonds Payable		*750*
To adjust for accrued interest on bonds and to amortize discount for period from Oct. 1 to Dec. 31. Accrued interest: $1,000,000 × .12 × $\frac{3}{12}$ = $30,000. Amortization: $30,000 × $\frac{3}{120}$ = $750.		

A similar adjusting entry will be required every December 31 throughout the life of the bond issue.

In the December 31, 1994 balance sheet, the accrued interest payable of $30,000 will appear as a current liability. The long-term liability for bonds payable will appear as follows:

Long-term liabilities:
12% Bonds payable, due Oct. 1, 2004 .... *$1,000,000*
Less: Discount on bonds payable .... <u>*29,250*</u>   *$970,750*

When the bonds were issued on October 1, the net liability for bonds payable was $970,000. Notice that the carrying value of the bonds has **increased** over the three months by the amount of discount amortized. When the entire discount has been amortized, the carrying value of the bonds will be $1 million, which is equal to their maturity value.

On April 1, we must record interest expense and discount amortization only for the **three-month period since year-end.** Of the semiannual $60,000 cash payment to bondholders, one-half, or $30,000, represents payment of the liability for bond interest payable recorded on December 31. The entry on April 1 is:

Bond Interest Expense *30,750*
Bond Interest Payable *30,000*
      Discount on Bonds Payable *750*
      Cash *60,000*
To record bond interest expense and amortization of discount
for three-month period since year-end and to record semiannual
payment to bondholders.

Bond Prices after Issuance

As stated earlier, many corporate bonds are traded daily on organized securities exchanges at quoted market prices. After bonds are issued, their market prices vary **inversely** with changes in market interest rates. As interest rates rise, investors will be willing to pay less money to own a bond that pays a given contract rate of interest. Conversely, as interest rates decline, the market prices of bonds rise.

CASE IN POINT   IBM sold to underwriters $500 million of $9\frac{3}{8}$%, 25-year debenture bonds. The underwriters planned to sell the bonds to the public at a price of $99\frac{5}{8}$. Just as the bonds were offered for sale, however, a change in Federal Reserve credit policy started an upward surge in interest rates. The underwriters encountered great difficulty selling the bonds. Within one week, the market price of the bonds had fallen to $94\frac{1}{2}$. The underwriters dumped their unsold inventory at this price and sustained one of the largest underwriting losses in Wall Street history.

During the months ahead, interest rates soared to record levels. Within five months, the price of the bonds had fallen to $76\frac{3}{8}$. Thus, nearly one-fourth of the market value of these bonds evaporated in less than half a year. The financial strength of IBM was never in question; this dramatic loss in market value was caused entirely by rising interest rates.

Changes in the current level of interest rates are not the only factors influencing the market prices of bonds. The length of time remaining until the bonds mature is another major force. As a bond nears its maturity date, its market price normally moves closer and closer to the maturity value.

This trend is dependable because the bonds are redeemed at par value on the maturity date.

CASE IN POINT Commonwealth Edison has outstanding two issues of $8\frac{1}{4}\%$ bonds, one issue maturing in 1993 and the other in 2007. Recently, the going market rate of interest was greater than $8\frac{1}{4}\%$ and both bonds were selling at a discount. The bonds maturing in 1993, however, were selling at a market price of 98, whereas the bonds maturing in 2007 were selling at a price of only 85. Both bonds pay the same amount of interest, were issued by the same company, and have identical credit ratings. Thus, the difference in the market prices is caused solely by the differences in the bonds' maturity dates.

Volatility of Short-Term and Long-Term Bond Prices When interest rates fluctuate, the market prices of long-term bonds are affected to a far greater extent than are the market prices of bonds due to mature in the near future. To illustrate, assume that market interest rates suddenly soar from 9% to 12%. A 9% bond scheduled to mature in but a few days will still have a market value of approximately $1,000—the amount to be collected in a few days from the issuing corporation. However, the market price of a 9% bond maturing in 10 years will drop significantly. Investors who must accept these "below market" interest payments for many years will buy the bonds only at a discounted price.

In summary, fluctuations in interest rates have a far greater effect upon the market prices of long-term bonds than upon the prices of short-term bonds.

Remember that after bonds have been issued, they belong to the bond-holder, *not to the issuing corporation.* Therefore, changes in the market price of bonds subsequent to their issuance *do not* affect the amounts shown in the financial statements of the issuing corporation, and these changes are not recorded in the company's accounting records.

Early Retirement of Bonds Payable

Bonds are sometimes retired before the maturity date. The principal reason for retiring bonds early is to relieve the issuing corporation of the obligation to make future interest payments. If interest rates decline to the point that a corporation can borrow at an interest rate below that being paid on a particular bond issue, the corporation may benefit from retiring those bonds and issuing new bonds at a lower interest rate.

Most bond issues contain a call provision, permitting the corporation to redeem the bonds by paying a specified price, usually a few points above par. Even without a call provision, the corporation may retire its bonds before maturity by purchasing them in the open market. If the bonds can be purchased by the issuing corporation at less than their carrying value, a **gain** is realized on the retirement of the debt. If the bonds are reacquired by the issuing corporation at a price in excess of their carrying value, a **loss** must be recognized. If material in dollar amount, any gain or loss from the early retirement of debt is classified in the income statement as an extraordinary item.

For example, assume that Briggs Corporation has outstanding a 13%, $10 million bond issue, callable on any interest date at a price of 104. Assume also that the bonds were issued at par and will not mature for nine years. Recently, however, market interest rates have declined to less than 10%, and the market price of Briggs' bonds has increased to 106.[5]

Regardless of the market price, Briggs can call these bonds at 104. If the company exercises this call provision for 10% of the bonds ($1 million face value), the entry will be:

Bonds called at a price above carrying value

Bonds Payable	1,000,000	
Loss on Early Retirement of Bonds (Extraordinary)	40,000	
Cash		1,040,000

To record the call of $1,000,000 in 13% bonds payable at a call price of 104.

Notice that Briggs *called* these bonds, rather than repurchasing them at market prices. Therefore, Briggs is able to retire these bonds at their call price of 104.

Classification of Bonds Payable in a Balance Sheet

Bonds payable generally are classified as *long-term* liabilities, even when the bonds are within one year of maturity. This is because the obligation for maturing bonds usually is paid either (1) by issuing new bonds and using the proceeds to retire the maturing bond issue or (2) from a bond *sinking fund.*

If new bonds are issued, the maturing bond liability has been *refinanced.* As explained in Chapter 11, maturing obligations that will be refinanced on a long-term basis are classified as long-term liabilities rather than current liabilities. Now consider maturing bonds that will be repaid from a sinking fund accumulated over the years specifically for this purpose. A sinking fund is not regarded as a current asset, because its contents *cannot be used* for paying operating expenses or the claims of most short-term creditors. The bonds payable, therefore, do not become a current liability, as they will be paid from the sinking fund *rather than from current assets.*

Accrued interest payable on long-term bonds *is* regarded as a current liability, because accrued interest normally is paid in cash within six months or less.

Commercial Paper

The term *commercial paper* describes *very short-term* notes payable issued by financially strong corporations. These notes mature generally in 30 days to 270 days and are issued in denominations of $25,000 or more.

---

[5] Falling interest rates cause bond prices to rise. On the other hand, falling interest rates also provide the issuing company with an incentive to call the bonds and, perhaps, replace them with bonds bearing a lower rate of interest. For this reason, call prices often serve as an approximate "ceiling" on market prices.

Commercial paper is similar to bonds payable in that it splits a large loan into small units, enabling many different investors to act as the lender. Also, an organized marketplace exists in which the holders of commercial paper may sell their investment immediately at a quoted market price.

Because commercial paper matures so quickly, it is regarded as a safer and more liquid investment than are stocks or bonds. The market price of commercial paper does not fluctuate significantly as a result of changes in interest rates. Rather, the market price tends to progress day by day toward maturity value.

Many investors purchase commercial paper as a means of earning interest revenue on idle cash balances for very short periods of time—perhaps over a weekend. For this reason, investors usually regard commercial paper as a ***cash equivalent***.[6] The issuing corporation, of course, views these notes as a current liability.

Commercial paper is issued at a discount; that is, with the interest charges included in the face amount. (Accounting for short-term notes payable with interest charges included in the face amount was discussed in Chapter 11.)

OTHER "CORPORATE" LIABILITIES

Bonds payable and commercial paper are issued only by large corporations. These debt instruments are attractive to investors only if the continued existence and solvency of the business enterprise can be taken for granted.

We now will discuss the liabilities arising from lease agreements, pension plans, and the deferral of income taxes. These liabilities appear primarily in the financial statements of large corporations, but they may also affect smaller business organizations. Many small businesses, however, do not have financial reporting obligations to investors and creditors. Therefore, these businesses sometimes use income tax rules, rather than accounting principles, in recording the liabilities and expenses relating to leases and pensions. Our discussion of these topics emphasizes generally accepted accounting principles—the accounting standards used in the financial statements of publicly owned companies.

Lease Payment Obligations

OBJECTIVE 6
Explain the accounting treatment of operating leases and of capital leases.

A company may purchase the assets needed in its business operations or, as an alternative, it may lease them. A ***lease*** is a contract in which the lessor gives the lessee the right to use an asset for a specified period of time in exchange for periodic rental payments. The ***lessor*** is the owner of the property; the ***lessee*** is a tenant or renter. Examples of assets frequently acquired by lease include automobiles, building space, computers, and equipment.

---

[6] To qualify as a cash equivalent, a short-term investment must mature within three months of acquisition and must involve very little risk. As discussed in Chapter 7, companies often combine cash equivalents with cash, showing these assets in the balance sheet as a single item.

Operating Leases

When the lessor gives the lessee the right to use leased property for a limited period of time but retains the usual risks and rewards of ownership, the contract is known as an *operating lease.* An example of an operating lease is a contract leasing office space in an office building. If the building increases in value, the *lessor* can receive the benefits of this increase by either selling the building or increasing the rental rate once the lease term has expired. On the other hand, if the building declines in value, it is the lessor who bears the loss.

In accounting for an operating lease, the lessor views the monthly lease payments received as rental revenue, and the lessee regards these payments as rental expense. No asset or liability (other than a short-term liability for accrued rent payable) relating to the lease appears in the lessee's balance sheet. Thus, operating leases are sometimes termed *off-balance-sheet financing.*

Capital Leases

Some lease contracts are intended to provide financing to the lessee for the eventual purchase of the property or to provide the lessee with use of the property over most of its useful life. These lease contracts are called *capital leases* (or financing leases). In contrast to an operating lease, a capital lease transfers most of the risks and rewards of ownership from the lessor to the *lessee.* Assume, for example, that City Realty leases a new automobile for a period of three years. Also assume that at the end of the lease, title to the automobile transfers to City Realty at no additional cost. Clearly, City Realty is not merely "renting" the use of the automobile; rather, it is using the lease agreement as a means of *financing the purchase* of the car.

From an accounting viewpoint, capital leases are regarded as *essentially equivalent to a sale* of the property by the lessor to the lessee, even though title to the leased property has not been transferred. Thus, a capital lease should be recorded by the *lessor as a sale* of property and by the *lessee as a purchase.* In such lease agreements, an appropriate interest charge usually is added to the regular sales price of the property in determining the amount of the lease payments.

Some companies use capital lease agreements as a means of financing the sale of their products to customers. In accounting for merchandise "sold" through a capital lease, the lessor debits *Lease Payments Receivable* and credits *Sales* for an amount equal to the *present value* of the future lease payments.[7] In most cases, the present value of these future payments is equal to the regular sales price of the merchandise. In addition, the lessor transfers the cost of the leased merchandise from the Inventory account to the Cost of Goods Sold account. When lease payments

---

[7]   We have elected to record the present value of the future lease payments by a single debit entry to Lease Payments Receivable. An alternative is to debit Lease Payments Receivable for the total amount of the future payments and to credit Discount on Lease Payments Receivable, a contra-asset account, for the unearned finance charges included in the contractual amount. Either approach results in the lessor recording a net receivable equal to the present value of the future lease payments.

are received, the lessor should recognize an appropriate portion of the payment as representing interest revenue and the remainder as a reduction in Lease Payments Receivable.

When equipment is acquired through a capital lease, the lessee should **debit an asset account,** Leased Equipment, and **credit a liability account,** Lease Payment Obligation, for the present value of the future lease payments. Lease payments made by the lessee are allocated between Interest Expense and a reduction in the liability, Lease Payment Obligation. The portion of the lease payment obligation that will be repaid within the next year is classified as a current liability, and the remainder is classified as long-term.

No rent expense is involved in a capital lease. The asset account, Leased Equipment, is depreciated over the life of the equipment rather than the life of the lease. (The journal entries used in accounting for a capital lease are illustrated in Appendix C at the end of this textbook.)

Distinguishing between Capital Leases and Operating Leases The FASB requires that a lease which meets any one of the following criteria be accounted for as a capital lease:

1 The lease transfers ownership of the property to the lessee at the end of the lease term.

2 The lease contains a "bargain purchase option."

3 The lease term is equal to 75% or more of the estimated economic life of the leased property.

4 The present value of the minimum lease payments amounts to 90% or more of the fair value of the lease property.

Only those leases which meet **none** of the above criteria may be accounted for as operating leases.

Liabilities for Pensions and Other Postretirement Benefits

Pensions Many employers agree to pay their employees a pension; that is, monthly cash payments for life, beginning upon retirement. Pensions are not an expense of the years in which cash payments are made to retired workers. Employees earn the right to receive the pension **while they are working for their employer.** Therefore, the employer's cost of future pension payments **accrues** over the years that each employee is "on the payroll."

OBJECTIVE 7 Account for the costs of pensions and other postretirement benefits.

Of course, the amounts of the retirement benefits that will be paid to today's workers after they retire is not known with certainty. Among other things, these amounts depend upon how long retired employees live. Therefore, the employer's obligation for future pension payments arising during the current year **can only be estimated.**

Employers do not usually pay retirement pensions directly to retired employees. Most employers meet their pension obligations by making periodic deposits in a **pension fund** (or pension plan) throughout the years of each worker's employment.

A pension fund is **not an asset** of the employer. Rather, it is an **independent entity** managed by a trustee (usually a bank or an insurance company). As the employer makes deposits in the pension fund, the trustee invests the money in securities such as stocks and bonds. Over time, the pension fund earns investment income and normally accumulates to a balance far in excess of the employer's deposits. It is the ***pension fund***—not the employer—that disburses monthly pension benefits to retired workers.

If the employer meets ***all*** of its estimated pension obligations by promptly depositing cash in a pension fund, the pension fund is said to be ***fully funded.*** The operation of a fully funded pension plan is summarized in the following illustration:

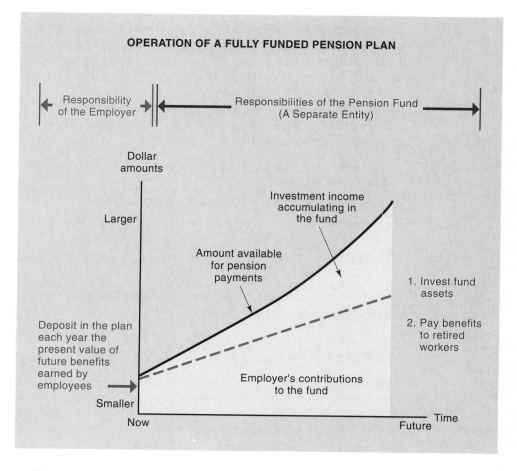

OPERATION OF A FULLY FUNDED PENSION PLAN

If a pension plan is fully funded, ***no liability*** for pension payments appears in the employer's balance sheet. The employer's obligation is discharged in the ***current period*** through the payments made to the pension fund. The employer records each payment to this fund by debiting Pension Expense and crediting Cash.

Most pension plans are fully funded; therefore, most corporations do ***not*** report any pension liability. However, an employer must credit a liability account, Unfunded Pension Liability, for any portion of its periodic pension expense which ***is not*** paid immediately to the pension fund.

Determining Pension Expense   From a conceptual point of view, the pension expense of a given period is the ***present value*** of the future pension rights granted to employees as a result of their services during the period. The computation of annual pension expense is complex and involves many assumptions. The amount of this expense is not computed by accountants, but rather by a professional **actuary.** Among the factors considered by the actuary are:

- Average age, retirement age, and life expectancy of employees.
- Employee turnover rates.
- Compensation levels and estimated rate of pay increases.
- Expected rate of return to be earned on pension fund assets.

As a step in determining the pension expense for the year, the actuary estimates the employer's total pension liability as of year-end. Thus, the estimates are updated annually, and estimating errors in prior years are "corrected" in the current year.

Postretirement Benefits Other Than Pensions   In addition to pension plans, many companies have promised their employees other types of postretirement benefits, such as health insurance. In most respects, these "nonpension" postretirement benefits are accounted for in the same manner as are pension benefits. Most companies, however, have not fully funded their obligations for nonpension postretirement benefits. Thus, recognition of the annual expense often involves a credit to an unfunded liability.

To illustrate, assume that at the end of 1994 Cable Company receives the following report from its actuaries:

CABLE COMPANY
Summary of Postretirement Benefits Expenses
For the Year Ended December 31, 1994
Prepared by Gibson & Holt, Professional Actuaries

Pension Plan:

Estimated liability at Dec. 31, 1994	$4,500,000
Estimated liability at Dec. 31, 1993	4,100,000
Pension expense for 1994	$ 400,000
Payments during the year to National Trust Co. (trustee for the pension plan)	400,000
Increase (decrease) in unfunded pension liability	$ -0-

Nonpension Postretirement Benefits:

Estimated liability at Dec. 31, 1994	$1,600,000
Estimated liability at Dec. 31, 1993	1,350,000
Nonpension postretirement benefits expense for 1994	$ 250,000
Payments during the year to National Trust Co. (trustee for the nonpension *postretirement benefits plan)*	140,000
Increase (decrease) in unfunded liability	$ 110,000

As the pension plan is fully funded, an entry summarizing Cable Company's pension expense for 1994 is shown at the top of the following page:[8]

---

[8]   This entry summarizes the pension expense and payments to the trustee for the ***entire year.*** In practice, payments to the trustee often are made on a monthly or quarterly basis.

| Pension Expense.. | 400,000 | |
| Cash .... | | 400,000 |

Pension expense for the year as determined by actuarial firm of Gibson & Holt. Fully funded by payments to National Trust Co.

The company's "nonpension" postretirement benefits expense was only partially paid in cash. The entry to summarize this expense for the year is:

Nonpension Postretirement Benefits Expense...............	250,000	
Cash		140,000
Unfunded Liability for Nonpension Postretirement Benefits...		110,000

To record nonpension postretirement benefits expense per report of Gibson & Holt, actuaries. Expense funded to the extent of $140,000.

Any portion of the unfunded liability which the company intends to fund during the next year is classified as a current liability; the remainder is classified as a long-term liability.

There are many complex issues involved in computing and reporting unfunded liabilities for postretirement benefits. These issues will be discussed in more advanced accounting courses.

Deferred Income Taxes

OBJECTIVE 8 Explain the nature of deferred income taxes.

We have seen in earlier chapters that differences sometimes exist between the dates certain types of revenue or expense are recognized in financial statements and the dates these items are reported in income tax returns. For example, sales revenue usually is recognized in an income statement in the period in which the sale occurs. Income tax rules, however, may permit use of the installment method, which delays recognition of the revenue in income tax returns until cash is collected from the customer.[9] In an income statement, depreciable assets are depreciated over their useful lives. In tax returns, however, they often are written off over "recovery periods" designated by law.

Because of such *timing differences* between accounting principles and tax rules, income may be reported in the income statement of one year but in the income tax return of a different year. Most timing differences result in *postponing* (deferring) the recognition of income for tax purposes.[10] The recognition of income in income tax returns is postponed by those tax rules that enable taxpayers either to (1) delay the recognition of revenue (such as the installment method) or (2) accelerate the recognition of expense (such as accelerated depreciation methods).

In summary, income appearing in the income statement today may not be subject to income taxes until future years. However, the *matching principle* requires that the income shown in an income statement be offset by all related income taxes expense, regardless of when these taxes will

---

[9] The installment method of revenue recognition was discussed in Chapter 13.

[10] In some situations, income may be subject to income taxes *prior* to recognition of the income for financial reporting purposes. In these instances, the taxpayer *prepays* its income taxes expense. Prepaid income taxes is an asset, similar to prepaid rent. In this chapter, we limit our discussion to the more common situation in which the payment of income taxes is *deferred* to later periods.

be paid. Thus, the entry to record a corporation's income taxes expense often appears as follows:

Payment of some taxes expense often can be deferred

Income Taxes Expense	*1,000,000*	
Income Taxes Payable		*800,000*
Deferred Income Taxes		*200,000*
To record corporate income taxes applicable to the income of the current year.		

Income Taxes Payable is a current liability representing the portion of the income taxes expense that must be paid when the company files its income tax return for the current year. That portion of the income taxes expense which is deferred to future tax returns is credited to a liability account entitled Deferred Income Taxes. Notice that deferred income taxes are tax obligations that have been ***postponed*** to future periods; the company has ***not eliminated*** its obligation to pay these taxes.

Growing businesses often are able to defer part of their income taxes expense every year. Of course, some of the income taxes deferred in prior years constantly are coming due. Nonetheless, the liability for deferred taxes usually continues to grow as the company grows—just as does the overall liability for accounts payable.

Deferred Income Taxes in the Balance Sheet Whether deferred income taxes are classified as current or long-term liabilities depends upon the classification of the assets and liabilities that ***caused*** the tax deferrals.[11] For example, installment receivables are classified as current assets. Therefore, if the methods used in accounting for installment receivables result in deferred taxes, the deferred taxes are classified as a current liability. Depreciable assets, however, are not viewed as current assets. Therefore, if deferred taxes result from the use of accelerated depreciation methods in income tax returns, the deferred tax liability is classified as long-term.

Accounting for deferred taxes involves a number of complex issues which will be addressed in the intermediate accounting course.

Disclosures about Financial Instruments

Except for deferred income taxes, all the liabilities discussed in this chapter are among the contracts regarded as financial instruments. The term ***financial instruments*** describes cash, equity investments in another business, and any contracts calling for the receipt or payment of cash. Notice that this term applies to certain assets, as well as to most liabilities.

Many financial instruments, such as bonds payable, investments in stocks and bonds, and long-term loans receivable or payable, have market values which can ***differ substantially*** from their carrying values in financial statements. In such cases, the Financial Accounting Standards Board requires companies to ***disclose*** the ***fair value*** of these instruments in notes accompanying the financial statements.[12]

---

[11] FASB, *Statement No. 109,* "Accounting for Income Taxes" (Norwalk, Conn.: 1992), para. 41.

[12] FASB, *Statement No. 107,* "Disclosure about Fair Value of Financial Instruments" (Norwalk, Conn.: 1991), para. 10.

Fair value generally means ***current market value.*** As the disclosures of fair value appear in ***notes*** to the financial statements, these disclosures do ***not*** affect the carrying values of the financial instruments in the company's balance sheet.

The FASB has two basic reasons for requiring disclosures of fair values. First, the fair value represents the current "economic" value of the financial instruments. Thus, it is the best indication of the ***value today*** of the resources owned or owed. Second, financial instruments often can be settled (sold or discharged) at their fair value. If these settlement prices differ from the book values of the financial instruments, the settlement transactions will result in the recognition of gains or losses. Disclosures of the fair values of these instruments may alert investors to the possibility—or probability—of such future gains or losses.

Measuring Fair Value   Bonds payable usually have quoted market prices. Thus, the fair value of an issue of bonds payable is determined by multiplying the quoted price by the number of bonds outstanding. Investments in stocks and bonds also are financial instruments which usually have readily determinable market values. For financial instruments that ***do not*** have quoted market prices, fair value often is considered to be the ***present value*** of the future cash flows, computed under current market conditions. (Computation of the present value of future cash flows is explained and illustrated in Appendix C, at the end of this textbook.)

The fair market value of financial instruments must be disclosed only if this value (1) is reasonably determinable and (2) is ***significantly different*** from the carrying value in the financial statements. These conditions greatly limit the types of financial instruments for which this disclosure is required. Cash, accounts receivables, accounts payable, and commercial paper, for example, normally have carrying values which ***closely approximate*** their fair values. (In addition, the FASB specifically exempts lease payment obligations and pension plans from the fair value disclosure requirement.)

Bonds payable, long-term notes payable or receivable, and investments in stocks and bonds, however, often ***do*** have fair values differing substantially from their carrying values. Thus, the requirement for disclosure of fair value applies primarily to these types of financial instruments.

Disclosure of Off-Balance-Sheet Risk   Some financial instruments do not create assets or liabilities that appear in financial statements but still create a risk of ***future losses.*** When a financial instrument does not appear in the balance sheet, the risk of loss created by the instrument is called an ***off-balance-sheet risk.***

The possibility of ***future losses*** ordinarily is ***not*** disclosed in financial statements, because all of the situations which may cause future losses cannot be identified. However, if the risk of a future loss ***is created by an existing contract*** (financial instrument), the FASB requires disclosure of the potential for loss.

As an example, large and financially strong corporations sometimes guarantee bank loans or other specific liabilities of less financially sound companies. In these situations, the guarantor promises to repay the loan if the original borrower is unable to do so. The basic purpose of a loan guarantee is to enable the weaker company to borrow money at more favorable terms than its own credit rating would justify.

Why would one company guarantee the debts of another? Often the borrower pays the guarantor a fee for this service. In other cases, the borrower may be an important customer or supplier of the guarantor.

A loan guarantee (also called an ***accommodation endorsement***) creates a loss contingency for the guarantor.[13] Unless a loss is considered ***probable,*** however, no liability appears in the guarantor's financial statements. Therefore, the guarantor's risk of loss—that is, the possibility of having to assume responsibility for the guaranteed loan—is an ***off-balance-sheet risk.***

The FASB requires companies to disclose any material off-balance-sheet risk created by financial instruments. The required disclosure is to include a written discussion of the nature and terms of the financial instrument, and the maximum amount of loss which might be sustained.

Mark to Market   The FASB may soon require that long-term financial instruments be shown in the balance sheet at their current fair value. (If adopted, this rule would eliminate the need to disclose these current fair values in notes to the financial statements.) Because fair values are intended to represent current "market values," the proposal which the FASB is considering often is called ***mark to market.***

Several complex conceptual issues arise in connection with the revaluation of financial instruments at every balance sheet date. For example, changes in the valuations of assets and liabilities also cause changes in the amount of owners' equity. Should these changes in owners' equity be recognized in the income statement, or should they be recorded directly in some type of special owners' equity account?

The FASB has not yet resolved the many controversial issues surrounding the mark to market valuation concept. Therefore, we will defer further discussion of this concept to future accounting courses.

Some Old Ratios Take on New Importance

In Chapter 11, we discussed two ratios widely used by long-term creditors in evaluating the safety of their investments: the ***debt ratio*** and the ***interest coverage ratio.***

The debt ratio, which is total liabilities divided by total assets, indicates the percentage of total assets financed with borrowed money. Creditors prefer a ***low*** debt ratio, as this indicates that their claims amount to only a small percentage of the company's total assets. The interest coverage ratio, which equals operating income divided by interest expense, indicates how many times the company's earnings for the period "covered" its interest obligations. Creditors prefer a high interest coverage ratio.

The ability of large corporations to meet their interest obligations has taken on new importance in recent years. During the 1980s, a number of well-known corporations borrowed startling amounts of money by issuing "junk bonds" bearing interest rates of 12, 14, and 16 percent—and sometimes even higher. As a result, the very existence of some of these corpo-

---

[13]   Accounting for loss contingencies is discussed in Chapter 11.

rations now is threatened by the size of the companies' annual interest obligations. Such long-established companies as TWA and Federated Department Stores already have declared bankruptcy, and others are sure to follow.

Bankruptcy affects much more than the claims of long-term creditors. Stockholders have only a residual claim to assets; therefore, capital stocks are the first securities to lose value. Top management often is replaced, and many employees usually lose their jobs. Perhaps most devastating in human terms, bankrupt companies may be unable to meet unfunded post-retirement obligations.

In conclusion, debt ratios and interest coverage ratios have become measurements of importance to **everyone** concerned with the long-run survival and health of a business organization.

■ ■ ■ * *Supplemental Topic A*
An Alternative Method of Amortizing Bond Discount and Premium

STRAIGHT-LINE AMORTIZATION: A THEORETICAL SHORTCOMING

Although the straight-line method of amortizing bond discount or premium recognizes the full cost of borrowing over the life of a bond issue, the method has one conceptual weakness: The same dollar amount of interest expense is recognized each year. Amortizing a discount, however, causes a gradual increase in the liability for bonds payable; amortizing a premium causes a gradual decrease in the liability. If the uniform annual interest expense is expressed as a **percentage** of either an increasing or a decreasing liability, it appears that the borrower's cost of capital is changing over the life of the bonds.

This problem can be avoided by using the **effective interest method** of amortizing bond discount or premium. The effective interest method recognizes annual interest expense equal to a **constant percentage of the carrying value of the related liability.** This percentage is the effective rate of interest incurred by the borrower. For this reason, the effective interest method of amortization is considered theoretically preferable to the straight-line method. Whenever the two methods would produce **materially different** annual results, the Financial Accounting Standards Board requires the use of the effective interest method.

Over the life of the bonds, both amortization methods recognize the **same total amount** of interest expense. Even on an annual basis, the results produced by the two methods are quite similar (unless the bonds were issued at an enormous discount, as are zero coupon bonds). Thus, both methods usually meet the requirements of the FASB.

EFFECTIVE INTEREST METHOD OF AMORTIZATION

When bonds are sold at a discount, the effective interest rate incurred by the issuing corporation is **higher** than the contract rate printed on the bonds. Conversely, when bonds are sold at a premium, the effective rate of interest is **lower** than the contract rate.

OBJECTIVE 9
Amortize
bond dis-
count and
premium by
the effective
interest
method.

When the effective interest method is used, bond interest expense is determined by multiplying the **carrying value of the bonds** at the beginning of the period by the **effective rate of interest** for the bond issue. The amount of discount or premium to be amortized is the **difference** between the interest expense computed in this manner and the amount of interest paid (or payable) to bondholders for the period. The computation of effective interest expense and the amount of discount or premium amortization for the life of the bond issue is made in advance in a specially designed **amortization table**.

Sale of Bonds at a Discount To illustrate the effective interest method, assume that on May 1 a corporation issues $1 million face value, 9%, 10-year bonds with interest dates of November 1 and May 1. The bonds sell for **$937,689,** a price resulting in an effective interest rate of 10%.[14] An amortization table for this bond issue is shown below. (Amounts of interest expense have been **rounded to the nearest dollar.**)

Amortization Table for Bonds Sold at a Discount
($1,000,000, 10-year bonds, 9% interest payable semiannually,
sold at $937,689 to yield 10% compounded semiannually)

Six-Month Interest Period	(A) Interest Paid Semiannually ($4\frac{1}{2}$% of Face Value)	(B) Effective Semiannual Interest Expense (5% of Bond Carrying Value)	(C) Discount Amorti- zation (B − A)	(D) Bond Discount Balance	(E) Carrying Value of Bonds, End of Period ($1,000,000 − D)
Issue date	—	—	—	$62,311	$937,689
1	$45,000	$46,884	$1,884	60,427	939,573
2	45,000	46,979	1,979	58,448	941,552
3	45,000	47,078	2,078	56,370	943,630
4	45,000	47,182	2,182	54,188	945,812
5	45,000	47,291	2,291	51,897	948,103
6	45,000	47,405	2,405	49,492	950,508
7	45,000	47,525	2,525	46,967	953,033
8	45,000	47,652	2,652	44,315	955,685
9	45,000	47,784	2,784	41,531	958,469
10	45,000	47,923	2,923	38,608	961,392
11	45,000	48,070	3,070	35,538	964,462
12	45,000	48,223	3,223	32,315	967,685
13	45,000	48,384	3,384	28,931	971,069
14	45,000	48,553	3,553	25,378	974,622
15	45,000	48,731	3,731	21,647	978,353
16	45,000	48,918	3,918	17,729	982,271
17	45,000	49,114	4,114	13,615	986,385
18	45,000	49,319	4,319	9,296	990,704
19	45,000	49,535	4,535	4,761	995,239
20	45,000	49,761*	4,761	-0-	1,000,000

* In the last period, interest expense is equal to interest paid to bondholders plus the remaining balance on the bond discount. This compensates for the accumulated effects of rounding amounts.

---

[14] Computation of the exact effective interest rate involves mathematical techniques beyond the scope of this discussion. A close approximation of the effective interest rate can be obtained by dividing the **average** annual interest expense by the **average** carrying value of the bonds.

This amortization table can be used to illustrate the concepts underlying the effective interest method of determining interest expense and discount amortization. Note that the "interest periods" in the table are the **semiannual** (six-month) interest periods. Thus, the interest payments (column A), interest expense (column B), and discount amortization (column C) are for six-month periods. Similarly, the balance of the Discount on Bonds Payable account (column D) and the carrying value of the liability (column E) are shown as of each semiannual interest payment date.

The original issuance price of the bonds ($937,689) is entered at the top of column E. This represents the carrying value of the liability throughout the first six-month interest period. The semiannual interest payment, shown in column A, is $4\frac{1}{2}\%$ (one-half of the original contract rate) of the $1 million face value of the bond issue. The semiannual cash interest payment does not change over the life of the bonds. The interest expense shown in column B, however, **changes every period.** This expense is always a **constant percentage** of the carrying value of the liability as of the end of the preceding period. The "constant percentage" is the effective interest rate of the bond issue. The bonds have an effective annual interest rate of 10%, indicating a semiannual rate of 5%. Thus, the effective interest expense for the first six-month period is $46,884 (5% of $937,689). The discount amortization for Period 1 is the difference between this effective interest expense and the contract rate of interest paid to bondholders.

After the discount is reduced by $1,884 at the end of Period 1, the carrying value of the bonds in column E **increases** by $1,884 (from $937,689 to $939,573). In Period 2, the effective interest expense is determined by multiplying the effective semiannual interest rate of 5% by this new carrying value of $939,573 (5% × $939,573 = $46,979).

Semiannual interest expense may be recorded every period directly from the data in the amortization table. For example, the entry to record bond interest expense at the end of the first six-month period is:

Bond Interest Expense *46,884*
        Discount on Bonds Payable *1,884*
        Cash *45,000*
*To record semiannual interest payment and amortize discount
for six months.*

Similarly, interest expense at the end of the **fifteenth** six-month period would be recorded by the following journal entry:

Bond Interest Expense *48,731*
        Discount on Bonds Payable *3,731*
        Cash *45,000*
*To record semiannual interest payment and amortize discount
for six months.*

When bond discount is amortized, the carrying value of the liability for bonds payable **increases** every period toward the maturity value. Since the effective interest expense in each period is a constant percentage of this increasing carrying value, the interest expense also increases from one period to the next. This is the basic difference between the effective interest method and straight-line amortization.

Sale of Bonds at a Premium Let us now change our illustration by assuming that the $1 million issue of 9%, 10-year bonds is sold on May 1 at a price of **$1,067,952**, resulting in an effective interest rate of 8% annually (4% per six-month interest period). An amortization table for this bond issue follows:

Amortization Table for Bonds Sold at a Premium
**($1,000,000, 10-year bonds, 9% interest payable semiannually,
sold at $1,067,952 to yield 8% compounded semiannually)**

Six-Month Interest Period	(A) Interest Paid Semiannually (4½% of Face Value)	(B) Effective Semiannual Interest Expense (4% of Bond Carrying Value)	(C) Premium Amortization (A − B)	(D) Bond Premium Balance	(E) Carrying Value of Bonds, End of Period ($1,000,000 + D)
Issue date	—	—	—	$67,952	$1,067,952
1	$45,000	$42,718	$2,282	65,670	1,065,670
2	45,000	42,627	2,373	63,297	1,063,297
3	45,000	42,532	2,468	60,829	1,060,829
4	45,000	42,433	2,567	58,262	1,058,262
5	45,000	42,330	2,670	55,592	1,055,592
6	45,000	42,224	2,776	52,816	1,052,816
7	45,000	42,113	2,887	49,929	1,049,929
8	45,000	41,997	3,003	46,926	1,046,926
9	45,000	41,877	3,123	43,803	1,043,803
10	45,000	41,752	3,248	40,555	1,040,555
11	45,000	41,622	3,378	37,177	1,037,177
12	45,000	41,487	3,513	33,664	1,033,664
13	45,000	41,347	3,653	30,011	1,030,011
14	45,000	41,200	3,800	26,211	1,026,211
15	45,000	41,048	3,952	22,259	1,022,259
16	45,000	40,890	4,110	18,149	1,018,149
17	45,000	40,726	4,274	13,875	1,013,875
18	45,000	40,555	4,445	9,430	1,009,430
19	45,000	40,377	4,623	4,807	1,004,807
20	45,000	40,193*	4,807	-0-	1,000,000

* In the last period, interest expense is equal to interest paid to bondholders minus the remaining balance of the bond premium. This compensates for the accumulated effects of rounding amounts.

In this amortization table, the interest expense for each six-month period is equal to **4%** of the carrying value of the liability at the beginning of that period. This amount of interest expense is **less** than the amount of cash being paid to bondholders, illustrating that the effective interest rate is less than the contract rate.

Based upon this amortization table, the entry to record the interest payment and amortization of the premium for the first six months of the bond issue is:

Amortization of premium decreases interest expense

Bond Interest Expense...	42,718	
Premium on Bonds Payable....................................	2,282	
Cash		45,000
To record semiannual interest payment and amortization of premium.		

As the carrying value of the liability declines, so does the amount recognized as bond interest expense.

Year-End Adjusting Entries Since the amounts recognized as interest expense change from one period to the next, we must refer to the appropriate interest period in the amortization table to obtain the dollar amounts for use in year-end adjusting entries. To illustrate, consider our example of the bonds sold at a premium on May 1. The entry shown above records interest and amortization of the premium through November 1. If the company keeps its accounts on a calendar-year basis, two months' interest has accrued as of December 31, and the following adjusting entry is made at year-end:

Year-end adjusting entry	*Bond Interest Expense*	*14,209*	
	Premium on Bonds Payable	*791*	
	Bond Interest Payable		*15,000*

To record two months' accrued interest and amortize one-third of the premium for the interest period.

This adjusting entry covers one-third (two months) of the second interest period. Consequently, the amounts shown as bond interest expense and amortization of premium are ***one-third*** of the amounts shown in the amortization table for the second interest period. Similar adjusting entries must be made at the end of every accounting period while the bonds are outstanding. The dollar amounts of these adjusting entries will vary, however, because the amounts of interest expense and premium amortization change in every interest period. The amounts applicable to any given adjusting entry will be the appropriate fraction of the amounts for the interest period then in progress.

Following the year-end adjusting entry illustrated above, the interest expense and premium amortization on May 1 of the second year, are recorded as follows:

Interest payment in the following year	*Bond Interest Expense*	*28,418*	
	Bond Interest Payable	*15,000*	
	Premium on Bonds Payable	*1,582*	
	Cash		*45,000*

To record semiannual interest payment, a portion of which had been accrued, and amortize remainder of premium applicable to interest period.

■ ■ ■ **** Supplemental Topic B***
Convertible Bonds Payable

Convertible bonds represent a popular form of financing, particularly during periods when common stock prices are rising. The conversion feature gives bondholders an opportunity to profit from a rise in the market price of the issuing company's common stock while still maintaining their status as creditors rather than stockholders. Because of this potential gain, convertible bonds generally carry lower interest rates than nonconvertible bonds.

The number of shares of common stock into which each bond may be converted is termed the ***conversion ratio.*** The market value of this number of shares represents the ***stock value*** of the bond. When the bond is originally issued, a conversion ratio is selected that sets the stock value well below the face value of the bond. In future periods, however, both the price of the stock and the stock value of the bond may increase without limit.

For example, assume that the current market rate of interest on long-term bonds is 9%, and that the common stock of Ling Corporation has a current market price of ***$27*** per share. Instead of issuing 9% bonds payable, the company might issue **7% *convertible bonds,*** with a conversion ratio of 20 to 1. At the issuance date, the stock value of each convertible bond would be only $540 (20 shares × $27). If the value of the common stock rises above ***$50*** per share, however, the stock value will rise above the $1,000 face value of the bond. (The per-share stock price that causes the stock value and maturity value of the bond to be equal—$50 in our example—is called the ***conversion price.***)

When the price of the common stock rises above the conversion price, the stock value of the bond becomes far more important than the current level of interest rates in establishing the market price of a convertible bond. (See, for example, the Case in Point on the following page.)

Ling Corporation benefits from issuing these convertible bonds because it is able to pay less than the going market rate of interest. The bondholders also may benefit from the conversion feature, ***but only if the price of the common stock rises above the conversion price*** ($50 per share) during the life of the bonds.

Let us assume that Ling Corporation issues $5 million of these convertible bonds at par. Some years later, when the price of the common stock has risen to $90 per share, holders of 100 bonds decide to convert their bonds into common stock (which has a par value of $1 per share). Ling Corporation will record this conversion as follows:

Conversion of bonds into common stock

Convertible Bonds Payable 100,000
    Common Stock, $1 par *2,000*
    Additional Paid-in Capital *98,000*
To record the conversion of 100 bonds payable into 2,000 shares of $1 par value common stock.

Notice that the current market price of the stock ($90 per share) ***does not*** affect this entry. The carrying value of the bonds is simply assigned to the common stock issued in exchange. Thus, the effect of the entry is to transfer the carrying value of the bonds from the liability section to the stockholders' equity section of the balance sheet. (If the bonds had been issued at a price above or below the face amount, any unamortized premium or discount relating to the converted bonds would be written off at the time of conversion in order to assign the ***net*** carrying value of the bonds to the common stock.)

CONVERSION OF BONDS FROM THE INVESTOR'S VIEWPOINT

Investors do not always convert their investment in convertible bonds into capital stock as soon as the market value of the capital stock they would receive rises above the $1,000 maturity value of their bonds. As the bonds easily can be converted into capital stock, their market value *rises right along* with that of the capital stock.

CASE IN POINT   Walgreen Company recently had an outstanding issue of bonds payable in which each bond was convertible into 247.98 shares of the company's capital stock. The company's capital stock was selling at $40 per share, indicating a market value for 247.98 shares of $9,919.20. The market value of the convertible bonds was quoted at 992, even though the bonds would mature at a price of only 100 in the near future.

In fact, there may be several good reasons for *not* converting an investment in bonds into capital stock. First, the periodic interest payments received from the investment in bonds may exceed the dividends that would be received from the shares of capital stock into which the bonds could be converted. Second, an investment in bonds has less *downside risk* than an investment in capital stock. (The term "downside risk" means the threat of possible loss to the investor from a drop in market price.) Bonds ultimately mature and are redeemed by the issuing corporation at their maturity value (usually $1,000 per bond). Capital stock, on the other hand, has no maturity value. The price of a company's capital stock may decline dramatically even though the company is not in such financial difficulty that it might default upon its obligations to bondholders.

In conclusion, *when are the owners of convertible bonds likely to exchange their bonds for shares of capital stock?* The exchange point is reached when the dividends that would be received from the capital stock *exceed the interest payments* currently being received from the investment in bonds. When the capital stock dividends increase to this level, the bondholders can *increase their cash receipts* by converting their bonds into shares of capital stock. Regardless of the relationship between interest and dividends, convertible bonds should be converted prior to their maturity date if the market price of the common stock exceeds the conversion price.

END-OF-CHAPTER REVIEW

SUMMARY OF CHAPTER LEARNING OBJECTIVES

1 **Describe the typical characteristics of corporate bonds.**
Corporate bonds are transferable long-term debt securities. Each bond usually has a face amount of $1,000 (or a multiple of $1,000), receives interest payments semiannually, and must be redeemed at its face amount at a specified maturity date. By issuing thousands of bonds at one time, the corporation is able to borrow millions of dollars from many different investors.

2 Explain the tax advantage of raising capital by issuing bonds instead of stock.

The principal advantage of issuing bonds rather than stock is that interest payments to bondholders are ***deductible for income tax purposes,*** whereas dividends to stockholders are not.

3 Account for the issuance of bonds, accrual and payment of interest, and retirement of bonds.

Accounting for bonds payable closely parallels accounting for notes payable. The basic "accountable events" are (1) issuance of the bonds, (2) semiannual interest payments, (3) accrual of interest payable at the end of the period, and (4) retirement of the bonds.

If bonds are issued between interest dates, the liability for accrued interest payable is recorded separately from the liability for the bonds payable. If bonds are retired prior to maturity, they may be retired at a price other than the carrying value of the liability, which results in either a gain or a loss.

4 Describe the relationship between interest rates and bond prices.

Prices of outstanding bonds vary inversely with interest rates. As interest rates rise, prices of existing bonds fall. Conversely, as interest rates fall, bond prices rise.

5 Explain the effects of amortizing bond discount and premium upon bond interest expense.

When bonds are issued at a discount, the maturity value of the bonds will exceed the amount originally borrowed. Thus, the discount may be viewed as an interest charge included in the maturity value of the bonds. Amortization of this discount over the life of the bond issue ***increases*** periodic interest expense. When bonds are issued at a premium, the maturity value of the bonds will be less than the amount originally borrowed. Thus, amortization of bond premium ***reduces*** the periodic interest expense.

6 Explain the accounting treatment of operating leases and of capital leases.

Operating leases are essentially rental agreements; the lessor recognizes rental revenue and the lessee recognizes rent expense. Capital leases, on the other hand, are treated by the lessor as a sale of the related asset and by the lessee as a purchase.

7 Account for the costs of pensions and other postretirement benefits.

The annual expense for pensions and other postretirement benefits is equal to the ***present value*** of the future benefits granted to employees as a result of their services during the year. This amount must be determined by a professional actuary. An employer shows a liability only for ***unfunded*** postretirement obligations.

8 Explain the nature of deferred income taxes.

Deferred income taxes are income taxes that will be levied in ***future years*** against pretax income which already has been reported as earned in the company's income statements. This postponement of income taxes, often for a period of years, arises because of differences between generally accepted accounting principles and income tax rules with respect to the *timing* of revenue and expense recognition.

*9 Amortize bond discount and premium by the effective interest method.

Under the effective interest method, bond interest is computed by multiplying the carrying value of the bonds by the *effective interest rate.* The amount of discount or premium amortized is the *difference* between the interest expense computed in this manner and the interest payable based upon the contract rate stated on the bonds. As a result, interest expense changes every period but remains a *constant percentage* of the carrying value of the bond liability.

This chapter completes our discussion of corporate securities (stocks and bonds) from the perspective of the issuing company. In the following chapter, we will discuss accounting for investments in these types of securities.

KEY TERMS INTRODUCED OR EMPHASIZED IN CHAPTER 16

Amortization of discount or premium on bonds payable The process of systematically writing off a portion of bond discount to increase interest expense or writing off a portion of bond premium to decrease interest expense each period the bonds are oustanding.

Capital lease A lease contract which, in essence, finances the eventual purchase by the lessee of leased property. The lessor accounts for a capital lease as a sale of property; the lessee records an asset and a liability equal to the present value of the future lease payments. Also called a *financing lease.*

Commercial paper Very short-term notes payable issued by financially strong corporations. Highly liquid from the investors' point of view.

Contract interest rate The contractual rate of interest printed on bonds. The contract interest rate, applied to the face value of the bonds, determines the amount of the annual cash interest payments to bondholders. Also called the *nominal interest rate.*

Convertible bond A bond which may be exchanged (at the bondholders' option) for a specified number of shares of the company's capital stock.

Deferred income taxes Income taxes upon income which already has been reported for financial reporting purposes but which will not be reported in income tax returns until future periods.

Discount on bonds payable Amount by which the face amount of the bond exceeds the price received by the corporation of the date of issuance. Indicates that the contractual rate of interest is lower than the market rate of interest.

Effective interest method of amortization A method of amortizing bond discount or premium which causes bond interest expense to be a constant percentage of the carrying value of the liability.

Effective interest rate The actual rate of interest expense to the borrowing corporation, taking into account the contractual cash interest payments and the discount or premium to be amortized.

---

*   *Supplemental Topic A, "An Alternative Method of Amortizing Bond Discount and Premium"*

Fair value   A measure of current economic value. Usually means current market value, if determinable.

Financial instrument   Cash, equity investments in another business, and contracts involving the receipt or payment of cash.

Junk bonds   Bonds payable which, when issued, were abnormally risky but also offered an abnormally high contract rate of interest.

Lessee   The tenant, user, or renter of leased property.

Lessor   The owner of property leased to a lessee.

Off-balance-sheet financing   An arrangement in which the use of resources is financed without the obligation for future payments appearing as a liability in the balance sheet. An operating lease is a common example of off-balance-sheet financing.

Off-balance-sheet risk   The risk of future losses resulting from an existing financial instrument which does not currently appear on the balance sheet. An example is the risk of loss from a loan guarantee.

Operating lease   A lease contract which is in essence a rental agreement. The lessee has the use of the leased property, but the lessor retains the usual risks and rewards of ownership. The periodic lease payments are accounted for as rent expense by the lessee and as rental revenue by the lessor.

Pension fund   A fund managed by an independent trustee into which an employer company makes periodic payments. The fund is used for the purpose of paying retirement benefits to company employees.

Premium on bonds payable   Amount by which the issuance price of a bond exceeds the face value. Indicates that the contractual rate of interest is higher than the market rate.

Present value of a future amount   The amount of money that an informed investor would pay today for the right to receive the future amount, based upon a specific rate of return required by the investor.

Zero coupon bonds   Bonds payable which do not provide for a periodic interest payments. Instead, the bonds are issued at a large discount, and all interest charges are included in the face amount.

SELF-TEST QUESTIONS

Answers to these questions appear on page 782.

1   Which of the following statements are correct? (More than one statement may be correct.)

   a   A bond issue is a technique for subdividing a very large loan into a great many small, transferable units.

   b   Bond interest payments are contractual obligations, whereas the board of directors determines whether or not dividends will be paid.

   c   As interest rates rise, the market prices of bonds fall; as interest rates fall, bond prices tend to rise.

   d   Bond interest payments are deductible in determining income subject to income taxes, whereas dividends paid to stockholders are not deductible.

2   A few years ago, Glasco issued 30-year, 9% bonds payable, callable at 105. At the issuance date, the market interest rate for such bonds was about $8\frac{1}{2}\%$; today, it is about 11%. Indicate statement(s) with which you agree. (More than one answer may be correct.)

   a   The bonds probably were issued at a discount.

b   Glasco's disclosure of current fair value probably shows these bonds trading at a discount.

c   The market price of these bonds probably has increased since the issuance date.

d   Glasco is unlikely to call these bonds in the near future even if it has the resources to do so.

3   Lawton International leases its manufacturing equipment from Atlas under an arrangement that qualifies as a capital lease. Lawton's financial statements should include which of the following? (More than one answer may be correct.)

a   Depreciation expense on the leased equipment.

b   Rent expense each period for the amount of the lease payment made.

c   A liability for the present value of all future lease payments.

d   A liability for the total amount of all future lease payments.

4   Silverado maintains a fully funded pension plan. During 1994, $1 million was paid to retired workers, and workers currently employed by the company earned the right to receive pension payments expected to total $3 million *over their lifetimes.* Silverado's pension *expense* for 1994 amounts to:

a $1

b $3 million

c $4 million

d   Some other amount

5   Deferred income taxes result from:

a   The fact that bond interest is deductible in the computation of taxable income.

b   Depositing income taxes due in future years in a special fund managed by an independent trustee.

c   Timing differences between when income is recognized in financial statements and in income tax returns.

d   The inability of a bankrupt company to pay its income tax liability on schedule.

*6   Waste Disposal Corporation issued 30-year bonds at a price very close to par value. The company uses the effective interest method of amortizing bond discount and premium. Indicate any of the following statements with which you *agree.* (More than one statement may be correct.).

a   If these bonds were issued at a discount, bond interest expense will *increase* from year to year.

b   If these bonds were issued at a premium, bond interest expense will *decrease* from year to year.

c   Total interest expense over the life of the bond issue will be the *same* as would result from use of the straight-line method of amortization.

d   The annual differences between interest expense computed by the effective interest method and the straight-line method will not be material in dollar amount.

---

*   *Supplemental Topic A, "An Alternative Method of Amortizing Bond Discount and Premium"*

ASSIGNMENT MATERIAL

DISCUSSION QUESTIONS

1 Distinguish between the two terms in each of the following pairs:
   a Bonds payable; commercial paper
   b Mortgage bond; debenture
   c Callable bond; convertible bond
   d Junk bond; zero coupon bond

2 *The Wall Street Journal* recently quoted a market price of *102* for an issue of 8% **Indiana Bell** (Telephone) bonds. What would be the market price for $25,000 face value of these bonds (ignoring accrued interest)? Is the market rate of interest for bonds of this quality higher or lower than 8%? Explain.

3 Briefly explain the income tax advantage of raising capital by issuing bonds rather than by capital stock.

4 Tampa Boat Company pays federal income taxes at a rate of 30% on taxable income. Compute the company's annual *after-tax* cost of borrowing on a 10%, $5 million bond issue. Express this after-tax cost as a percentage of the borrowed $5 million.

5 Why is the *present value* of a future amount always less than the future amount?

6 Does issuing bonds at a discount increase or decrease the issuing company's cost of borrowing? Explain.

7 Explain why the effective rate of interest differs from the contract rate when bonds are issued (a) at a discount and (b) at a premium.

8 Why do bond prices *vary inversely* with interest rates?

9 Some bonds now being bought and sold by investors on organized securities exchanges were issued when interest rates were much higher than they are today. Would you expect these bonds to be trading at prices above or below their face values? Explain.

10 The 6% bonds of Central Gas & Electric are selling at a market price of 72, whereas the 6% bonds of Interstate Power are selling at a price of 97. Does this mean that Interstate Power has a better credit rating than Central Gas & Electric? Explain. (Assume current long-term interest rates are in the 11% to 13% range.)

11 Discuss the advantages and disadvantages of a *call provision* in a bond contract from the viewpoint of (a) the bondholder and (b) the issuing corporation.

12 Explain how the lessee accounts for an operating lease and a capital lease. Why is an operating lease sometimes called *off-balance-sheet financing?*

13 Ortega Industries has a fully funded pension plan. Each year, pension expense runs in excess of $10 million. At the present time, employees are entitled to receive pension benefits with a present value of $125 million. Explain what liability, if any, Ortega Industries should include in its balance sheet as a result of this pension plan.

14 What is meant by the term *deferred income taxes?* Identify two measurement techniques often used in income tax returns which result in the deferral of income taxes.

15 Define *financial instruments.* What are the basic reasons for disclosing the fair value of these instruments when this value differs significantly from the carrying values shown in the balance sheet?

16 Why does the requirement for disclosure of fair value often apply to financial instruments such as bonds payable, long-term notes payable and receivable, and investments in stocks and bonds, but usually *not* to cash, accounts payable or receivable, or commercial paper?

17 What is meant by a financial instrument creating *off-balance-sheet risk?* Provide an example.

18 As a result of issuing 20-year bonds payable, Low-Cal Foods now has an interest coverage ratio of *.75 to 1.* Should this ratio be of greater concern to short-term creditors or to stockholders? Explain.

19 A $200 million bond issue of NDP Corporation (a solvent company) recently matured. The entire maturity value was paid from a bond sinking fund. What effect did this transaction have upon the company's current ratio? Upon its debt ratio? Explain.

*20 When the effective interest method is used to amortize bond discount or premium, the amount of bond interest expense will differ in each period from that of the preceding period. Explain how the amount of bond interest expense changes from one period to another when the bonds are issued (a) at a discount and (b) at a premium.

*21 Explain why the effective interest method of amortizing bond discount or premium is considered to be theoretically preferable to the straight-line method.

**22 What is a *convertible bond?* Discuss the advantages and disadvantages of convertible bonds from the standpoint of (a) the investor and (b) the issuing corporation.

**23 What situation or condition is most likely to cause the holders of convertible bonds to convert their bonds into shares of common stock? (Do not assume that the bonds have been called or that they are about to mature.)

EXERCISES

Listed below are nine technical accounting terms introduced or emphasized in this chapter.

Unfunded pension liability	*Deferred income taxes*	*Effective interest method (of amortization)*
Off-balance-sheet risk	*Present value of future amounts*	*Straight-line method (of amortization)*
Operating lease	*Bond premium*	*Commercial paper*

Each of the following statements may (or may not) describe one of these technical terms. For each statement, indicate the term described, or answer "None" if the statement does not correctly describe any of the terms.

---

*   *Supplemental Topic A, "An Alternative Method of Amortizing Bond Discount and Premium"*
**   *Supplemental Topic B, "Convertible Bonds Payable"*

a The measurement concept applied to the liabilities for capital lease obligations and to unfunded pension liabilities.

b Income taxes applicable to earnings which have already been included in the income statement but which appear in the income tax returns of a future year.

c Cash, equity investments in another business organization, or contracts calling for receipts or payments of cash.

d Amortizing bond discount or premium in a manner that results in the same amount of interest expense every period.

e Future interest charges included in the maturity value of bonds payable.

f A long-term liability appearing in the balance sheet of any company that offers a pension to retired workers.

g A lease agreement that results in the lessee recording ownership of an asset and a long-term liability to the lessor.

h Potential future losses which could result from existing financial instruments which are not listed either as assets or as liabilities.

EXERCISE 16-2
Effects of Bond Transactions upon the Accounting Equation

Listed below are seven events relating to debt instruments issued by Wizard Computer, Inc.:

a Issued 30-year bonds payable at a discount.

b Issued 90-day commercial paper at a discount.

c Made a semiannual interest payment and amortized discount on the bond issue described in part **a,** above.

d Made a semiannual interest payment and amortized premium on a 20-year bond issue that has been outstanding for nine years.

e Due to a decline in interest rates, the market value of the bond issues described in both parts **a** and **d** have increased in market value.

f Called bonds payable described in part **d,** above, at a price above carrying value but below current market value. (Assume all interest expense already has been properly recorded.)

g Redeemed at face value the commercial paper described in part **b,** above.

INSTRUCTIONS

Indicate the effects of each of these transactions upon the financial statement categories shown below. Organize your answer in tabular form, using the illustrated column headings. Use the following code letters to indicate the effects of each transaction upon the accounting element listed in the column heading:

I = Increase   *D* = Decrease   *NE* = No Effect

Trans-action	Income Statement			Balance Sheet			
	Revenue −	*Expenses and Losses* =	*Net Income*	*Assets* =	*Current Liab.* +	*Long-Term Liab.* +	*Owners' Equity*
a							

EXERCISE 16-3
Effects upon the Accounting Equation— Transactions Other Than Bonds

The following seven items are among the transactions of Commuter Train Corporation during the current year:

a Leased equipment, signing a five-year capital lease payable in monthly installments.

b Leased land to be used as a storage yard, signing a one-year lease payable in monthly installments.

c   Paid a monthly installment on a capital lease (assume all remaining payments on this particular lease are due within one year).

d   Made a monthly payment on an operating lease (assume all remaining payments on this particular lease are due within one year).

e   Recorded pension expense on a fully funded pension plan and remitted in cash the amount owed to the trustee.

f   Recorded expense relating to postretirement benefits other than pensions earned by employees during the current period. This liability is **partially** funded; no payments are made now, but 50% of the obligation arising this period will be funded within the next 12 months.

g   Made an adjusting entry recording income taxes expense for the period, including a considerable amount of deferred taxes.

INSTRUCTIONS   Indicate the effects of each of these transactions upon the financial statement categories shown below. Organize your answer in tabular form, using the illustrated column headings. Use the following code letters to indicate the effects of each transactions upon the accounting element listed in the column heading:

I = Increase   *D* = Decrease   *NE* = No Effect

Trans-action	Income Statement			Balance Sheet			
	Revenue	*− Expenses*	*= Net Income*	*Assets =*	*Current Liab. +*	*Long-Term Liab. +*	*Owners' Equity*
a							

EXERCISE 16-4
After-Tax Cost of Borrowing

NY Central, Inc., issued $20 million of 12% bonds payable at face value. The company pays income taxes at an average rate of 35% of its taxable income.

Compute the company's annual **after-tax** cost of borrowing on this bond issue, stated as (a) a total dollar amount and (b) a percentage of the amount borrowed.

EXERCISE 16-5
Bond Interest (Bonds Issued at Par)

On March 31, Bancor Corporation received authorization to issue $30 million of 12%, 30-year debenture bonds. Interest payment dates were March 31 and September 30. The bonds were all issued at par on April 30, one month after the interest date printed on the bonds.

INSTRUCTIONS   a   Prepare the journal entry at April 30, to record the sale of the bonds.

b   Prepare the journal entry at September 30, to record the semiannual bond interest payment.

c   Prepare the adjusting entry at December 31, to record bond interest accrued since September 30.

EXERCISE 16-6
Basic Entries for a Bond Issue: Issuance, Interest Payment, and Retirement

La Paloma Corporation issued $10 million of 15-year, $10\frac{1}{2}$% bonds on July 1, 1993, at $98\frac{1}{2}$. Interest is due on June 30 and December 31 of each year, and the bonds mature on June 30, 2008. The fiscal year ends on December 31; bond discount is amortized by the straight-line method. Prepare the following journal entries:

a   July 1, 1993, to record the issuance of the bonds

b   December 31, 1993, to pay interest and amortize the bond discount (make two entries)

c   June 30, 2008, to pay interest, amortize the bond discount, and retire the bonds at maturity (make three entries)

EXERCISE 16-7
Amortizing Bond Discount and Premium: Straight-line Method

North Company issued $80 million of 12%, 10-year bonds on January 1. Interest is payable semiannually on June 30 and December 31. The bonds were sold to an underwriting group at 105.

South Company issued $80 million of 11%, 10-year bonds on January 1. Interest is payable semiannually on June 30 and December 31. The bonds were sold to an underwriting group at 95.

Prepare journal entries to record all transactions during the year for (a) the North Company bond issue and (b) the South Company bond issue. Assume that both companies amortize bond discount or premium by the straight-line method at each interest payment date.

EXERCISE 16-8
Bond Prices and Accrued Interest

On August 1, 1994, Cellular Industries issued $10 million face value, 9%, 20-year bonds payable to an underwriter for total cash proceeds of $10,064,000. The bonds were dated April 1, 1994, and pay interest semiannually at October 1 and April 1.

a State the issue price of these bonds as a ***percentage*** of the face amount. (Round to the nearest $\frac{1}{10}$ of 1%.)

b Compute the amount of cash paid to bondholders at each semiannual interest date.

c Compute the company's semiannual bond interest expense (for a full six-month period), assuming that any discount or premium is amortized by the straight-line method.

EXERCISE 16-9
Accounting for Leases

On July 1, City Hospital leased equipment from MedTech Instruments for a period of five years. The lease calls for monthly payments of $2,000, payable in advance on the first day of each month, beginning July 1.

INSTRUCTIONS Prepare the journal entry needed to record this lease in the accounting records of City Hospital on July 1 under each of the following independent assumptions:

a The lease represents a simple rental arrangement.

b At the end of five years, title to this equipment will be transferred to City Hospital at no additional cost. The present value of the 60 monthly lease payments is $90,809, of which $2,000 is paid in cash on July 1.

EXERCISE 16-10
Pension Plans

During the current year, Deltron Corporation paid $3 million into a fully funded pension plan for the company's employees. At year-end, the plan has total assets of $42 million, and the present value of all future pension payments earned to date is estimated at $40 million. During the current year, the plan paid $5 million in pension benefits to retired Deltron employees.

INSTRUCTIONS a What is Deltron's pension expense for the year?

b Identify any assets or liabilities relating to this pension plan which will appear in Deltron's balance sheet, and indicate the appropriate dollar amount.

c If Deltron becomes insolvent in future years, what prospects, if any, do today's employees have of receiving the pension benefits which they have earned to date?

EXERCISE 16-11
Accounting for Retirement Benefits

At the end of the current year, Krepshaw Power Tools, Inc., received the following information from its actuary:

Pension expense *$1,790,000*
Nonpension postretirement benefits *316,000*

The pension plan is fully funded. Krepshaw has funded only $23,000 of the nonpension postretirement benefits this year.

Prepare a separate journal entry to summarize for the entire year (a) the pension expense and (b) the nonpension postretirement benefits expense.

**EXERCISE 16-12
Deferred Income Taxes**

The following journal entry summarizes for the current year the income taxes expense of American Coachworks:

Income Taxes Expense	14,000,000	
Cash		9,000,000
Income Taxes Payable		2,900,000
Deferred Income Taxes Payable		2,100,000

To record income taxes expense for the current year.

Of the deferred income taxes, only $240,000 is classified as a current liability.

INSTRUCTIONS

a Define *deferred income taxes payable.*

b What is the amount of income taxes which the company has paid or expects to pay in conjunction with its income tax return for the current year?

c Illustrate the allocation of the liabilities shown in the above journal entry between the classifications of *current liabilities* and *long-term liabilities.*

***EXERCISE 16-13
Effective Interest Method—
Bond Discount**

Three Flags Corporation issued on the authorization date $1 million of 10-year, 9% bonds payable and received proceeds of $937,689, resulting in an effective interest rate of 10%. The discount is amortized by the effective interest method; the amortization table for this bond issue is illustrated on page 759. Interest is payable semiannually.

INSTRUCTIONS

a Show how the liability for the bonds would appear on a balance sheet prepared immediately after issuance of the bonds.

b Show how the liability for the bonds would appear on a balance sheet prepared after *14* semiannual interest periods (three years prior to maturity).

c Show the necessary calculations to determine interest expense by the effective interest method for the *second* six-month period; the discount amortized at the end of that second period; and the cash payment of interest. Round all amounts to the nearest dollar.

***EXERCISE 16-14
Effective Interest Method—
Premium**

On April 1, Financial Publications issued $1 million of 10-year, 9% bonds payable and received proceeds of $1,067,952 resulting in an effective interest rate of 8%. Interest is payable on September 30 and March 31. The effective interest method is used to amortize bond premium; an amortization table for this bond issue is illustrated on page 761.

INSTRUCTIONS

Prepare the necessary journal entries (rounding all amounts to the nearest dollar) on:

a April 1, to record the issuance of the bonds

b September 30, to record the payment of interest and amortization of premium at the first semiannual interest payment date

c December 31, to accrue bond interest expense through year-end

d March 31, to record payment of interest and amortization of bond premium at the second semiannual interest payment date

---

* *Supplemental Topic A, "An Alternative Method of Amortizing Bond Discount and Premium"*

****EXERCISE 16-15
Convertible
Bonds**

A recent annual report of **McGraw-Hill, Inc.** shows that 406 of the company's $3\frac{7}{8}$%, $1,000 face amount, convertible bonds are still outstanding. These bonds mature in less than 3 years and have a conversion ratio of 32 to 1. The company's common stock has a par value of $1 per share, a current market price of $60 per share, and currently pays dividends of $1.68 per share.

INSTRUCTIONS

a Prepare the journal entry that would be made by McGraw-Hill to record the conversion of these outstanding convertible bonds into shares of common stock. (Assume the bonds originally were issued at par.)

b Under the circumstances described above, would it be advantageous for the bondholders to exchange the bonds for shares of McGraw-Hill's common stock? Explain.

PROBLEMS

Note: In this chapter, we provide an unusually wide variety of problem assignments. In order to make the full range of these assignments available to all users of the text, we present them in one consecutive series, rather than in the usual A and B groups. This entire series is supported in both the Group A and Group B accounting work sheets.

**PROBLEM 16-1
Bond Interest
(Bonds Issued
at Par)**

Bar Harbor Gas & Electric obtained authorization to issue $90 million face value of 10%, 20-year bonds, dated May 1, 1993. Interest payment dates were November 1 and May 1. Issuance of the bonds did not take place until August 1, 1993. On this date all the bonds were sold at a price of 100 plus three months' accrued interest.

INSTRUCTIONS

Prepare the necessary entries in general journal form on:

a August 1, 1993, to record the issuance of the bonds

b November 1, 1993, to record the first semiannual interest payment on the bond issue

c December 31, 1993, to accrue bond interest expense through year-end

d May 1, 1994, to record the second semiannual interest payment

**PROBLEM 16-2
Amortization of
Bond Dis-
count:
Straight-line
Method**

On May 1, 1994, Festival Cruise Ships, Inc., sold a $60 million face value, 11%, 10-year bond issue to an underwriter at a price of 98. Interest is payable semiannually on May 1 and November 1. Company policy is to amortize bond discount by the straight-line method at each interest payment date and at year-end. The company's fiscal year ends at December 31.

INSTRUCTIONS

a Prepare journal entries to record the issuance of these bonds, the payment of interest at November 1, 1994, and the bond interest expense through year-end.

b Show the proper balance sheet presentation of all liabilities relating to this bond issue at December 31, 1994. Include captions indicating whether the liabilities are classified as current or long-term.

c Why do you think that Festival was able to receive a price of only 98 for these bonds, rather than being able to issue them at par? What will issuing these bonds at a discount mean about the relationship between Festival's annual bond interest expense and the amount of cash paid annually to bondholders? Explain.

** *Supplemental Topic B, "Convertible Bonds Payable"*

PROBLEM 16-3
Amortizing Bond Discount and Premium: Straight-line Method

On September 1, 1993, American Farm Equipment issued $60 million in 10% debenture bonds. Interest is payable semiannually on March 1 and September 1, and the bonds mature in 20 years. Company policy is to amortize bond discount or premium by the straight-line method at each interest payment date and at year-end. The company's fiscal year ends at December 31.

INSTRUCTIONS

a Make the necessary adjusting entries at December 31, 1993, and the journal entry to record the payment of bond interest on March 1, 1994, under each of the following assumptions:

1 The bonds were issued at 98.

2 The bonds were issued at 101.

b Compute the net bond liability at December 31, 1994, under assumptions **1** and **2** above.

PROBLEM 16-4
Comprehensive Problem: Straight-line Amortization

Country Recording Studios obtained the necessary approvals to issue $30 million of 12%, 10-year bonds, dated March 1, 1993. Interest payment dates were September 1 and March 1. Issuance of the bonds did not occur until June 1, 1993. On this date, the entire bond issue was sold to an underwriter at a price which included three months' accrued interest. Country Recording Studios follows the policy of amortizing bond discount or premium by the straight-line method at each interest date as well as for year-end adjusting entries at December 31.

INSTRUCTIONS

a Prepare all journal entries necessary to record the issuance of the bonds and bond interest expense during 1993, assuming that the total proceeds from issuance of the bonds on June 1 amounted to **$30,315,000** including accrued interest. (Note that the bonds will be outstanding for a period of only **9 years and 9 months.**)

b Assume that the proceeds received from the underwriter on June 1 had amounted to **$31,180,800** including accrued interest. Prepare journal entries for 1993 parallel to those in part **a** above.

c Show the proper balance sheet presentation of the liability for bonds payable (including accrued interest) in the balance sheet prepared at December 31, **1998,** assuming that the total proceeds from issuance of the bonds (including accrued interest) had been:

1 $30,315,000, as described in part **a**

2 $31,180,800, as described in part **b**

PROBLEM 16-5
An Alternate to Problem 16-4

Liberty Broadcasting Corporation obtained authorization to issue $80 million of 12%, 10-year bonds, dated May 1, 1993. Interest payment dates were May 1 and November 1. Issuance of the bonds did not take place until July 1, 1993. On this date, the entire bond issue was sold to an underwriter at a price which included the two months' accrued interest. Liberty Broadcasting follows the policy of amortizing bond discount or premium by the straight-line method at each interest date as well as for year-end adjusting entries at December 31.

INSTRUCTIONS

a Prepare all journal entries necessary to record the issuance of the bonds and bond interest expense during 1993, assuming that the sales price of the bonds on July 1 was $83,960,000 **including accrued interest.** (Note that the bonds will be outstanding for a period of only 9 years and 10 months.)

b Assume that the total proceeds from issuance of the bonds on July 1 had been $79,830,000 including accrued interest. Prepare journal entries for 1993 parallel to those in part **a** above.

c Show the proper balance sheet presentation of the liability for bonds payable in the balance sheet prepared at December 31, *1999,* assuming that the total proceeds from issuance of the bonds (including accrued interest) had been:

1 $83,960,000, as described in part **a**

2 $79,830,000, as described in part **b**

PROBLEM 16-6
Factors Affecting Bond Prices

Shown below are three independent cases, each involving two bond issues of a publicly owned corporation. In each case, both bond issues have identical credit ratings.

a **Pacific Gas & Electric Company** has two bond issues maturing in the year 2020; one has a contract interest rate of $8\frac{1}{2}\%$, and the other, a contract rate of 10%.

b **Citicorp** has outstanding two issues of $10\frac{1}{2}\%$ bonds—one issue maturing in 1995 and the other in 2016.

c **COMPAQ Computer** has issued the following convertible bonds: (1) $5\frac{1}{4}\%$ bonds maturing in 2012, with a conversion ratio of 50.44 to 1, and (2) $6\frac{1}{2}\%$ bonds maturing in 2013, with a conversion ratio of 30.76 to 1. In March 1991, the market price of COMPAQ's common stock was $64 per share.

INSTRUCTIONS

For each case, explain which of the two bonds you would expect to have been selling at the higher market price in March *1991.* Also indicate whether each bond should have been selling at a premium or a discount at that time. Explain the reasoning behind your answers. Assume that in March 1991, market interest rates for bonds of this quality were as follows:

Maturity	*Market Interest Rate*
Years 1991–1996	*9%*
Years 1997–2002	*10%*
Year 2002 and beyond	*11%*

PROBLEM 16-7
Capital Leases: A Comprehensive Problem

Beach Equipment Company frequently uses long-term contracts as a means of financing the sale of its products. On November 1, 1994, Beach Equipment Company leased to Star Industries a machine carried in the perpetual inventory records at a cost of $18,120. The terms of the lease called for 48 monthly payments of $650 each, beginning November 30, 1994. The present value of these payments, after considering a built-in interest charge of 1% per month, is equal to $24,680, the regular sales price of the machine. At the end of the 48-month lease, title to the machine will transfer to Star Industries.

INSTRUCTIONS

a Prepare journal entries for 1994 in the accounts of Beach Equipment Company on:

1 November 1 to record the sale financed by the lease and the related cost of goods sold. (Debit Lease Payments Receivable for the $24,680 present value of the future lease payments.)

2 November 30, to record receipt of the first $650 monthly payment. (Prepare a compound journal entry which allocates the cash receipt between interest revenue and reduction of Lease Payments Receivable. The portion of each monthly payment recognized as interest revenue is equal to 1% of the balance of the account Lease Payments Receivable, at the beginning of that month. Round all interest computations to the nearest dollar.)

3 December 31, to record receipt of the second monthly payment.

b Prepare journal entries for 1994 in the accounts of Star Industries on:

   1 November 1, to record acquisition of the leased machine.

   2 November 30, to record the first monthly lease payment. (Determine the portion of the payment representing interest expense in a manner parallel to that described in part **a**.)

   3 December 31, to record the second monthly lease payment.

   4 December 31, to recognize depreciation on the leased machine through year-end. Compute the depreciation expense by the straight-line method, using a 10-year service life and an estimated salvage value of $6,680.

c Compute the net carrying value of the leased machine in the balance sheet of Star Industries at December 31, 1994.

d Compute the amount of Star Industries' lease payment obligation at December 31, 1994.

PROBLEM 16-8
Reporting Liabilities in a Balance Sheet

Listed below are selected items from the accounting records of Gulf Coast Telephone Company (GulfTel) for the year ended December 31, *1994* (dollar amounts in thousands):

Accounts payable	$ 65,600
Accrued expenses payable (other than interest)	11,347
6¾% Bonds payable, due Feb. 1, 1995	100,000
8½% Bonds payable, due June 1, 1995	250,000
Unamortized bond discount (8½% bonds of '95)	260
11% Bonds payable, due June 1, 2004	300,000
Unamortized bond premium (11% bonds of '04)	1,700
Accrued interest payable	7,333
Bond interest expense	61,000
Other interest expense	17,000
Commercial paper (net of unamortized discount)	110,000
Lease payment obligations—capital leases	23,600
Pensions obligation	410,000
Unfunded obligation for postretirement benefits other than pensions	72,000
Deferred income taxes	130,000
Income taxes expense	66,900
Income taxes payable	17,300
Accommodation endorsements (loan guarantees)	28,600
Operating income	280,800
Net income	134,700
Total assets	2,093,500

OTHER INFORMATION

1 The 6¾% bonds due in February 1995 will be refinanced in January 1995 through the issuance of $150,000 in 9%, 20-year general debentures.

2 The 8½% bonds due June 1, 1995, will be repaid entirely from a bond sinking fund.

3 GulfTel is committed to total lease payments of $14,400 in 1995. Of this amount, $7,479 is applicable to operating leases, and $6,921 to capital leases. Payments on capital leases will be applied as follows: $2,300 to interest expense and $4,621 to reduction in the capitalized lease payment obligation.

4 GulfTel's pension plan is fully funded with an independent trustee.

5 The obligation for postretirement benefits other than pensions consists of a commitment to maintain health insurance for retired workers. During 1995, GulfTel will fund $18,000 of this obligation.

6 The $17,300 in income taxes payable relates to income taxes levied in 1994 and must be paid on or before March 15, 1995. No portion of the deferred tax liability is regarded as a current liability.

7 The accommodation endorsements are guarantees of bank loans and other indebtedness of various suppliers of specialized telecommunications equipment. In the opinion of management, the risk of material losses arising from these loan guarantees is remote.

INSTRUCTIONS
a Using this information, prepare the current liabilities and long-term liabilities sections of a classified balance sheet as of December 31, 1994. (Within each classification, items may be listed in any order.)

b Explain briefly how the information in each of the seven numbered paragraphs affected your presentation of the company's liabilities.

c Compute as of December 31, 1994, the company's (1) debt ratio and (2) interest coverage ratio.

d Based solely upon information stated in this problem, indicate whether this company appears to be an outstanding, medium, or poor long-term credit risk. State specific reasons for your conclusion.

*PROBLEM 16-9
Effective Interest Method: Bonds Issued at Discount

Arcades R Fun maintains its accounts on a calendar-year basis. On June 30, 1994, the company issued $6 million face value of 7.6% bonds at a price of 97¼, resulting in an effective rate of interest of 8%. Semiannual interest payment dates are June 30 and December 31. Bond discount is amortized by the effective interest method. The bonds mature on June 30, 2004.

INSTRUCTIONS
a Prepare the required journal entries on:

1 June 30, 1994, to record the sale of the bonds.

2 December 31, 1994, to pay interest and amortize the discount using the effective interest method.

3 June 30, *2004,* to pay interest, amortize the discount, and retire the bonds. Assume that at the beginning of this last interest period, the carrying value of the bonds is *$5,988,462.* (Use a separate journal entry to show the retirement of the bonds.)

b Show how the accounts Bonds Payable and Discount on Bonds Payable should appear on the balance sheet at December 31, *1994.*

*PROBLEM 16-10
Effective Interest Method of Amortizing Bond Discount

On December 31, 1992, Glenview Hospital issued $10 million face value, 10%, 10-year bonds to an underwriter at a price of 94. This price results in an effective annual interest rate of 11%. Interest is payable semiannually on June 30 and December 31. Glenview Hospital amortizes bond discount by the effective interest method.

---

* *Supplemental Topic A, "An Alternative Method of Amortizing Bond Discount and Premium"*

INSTRUCTIONS   **a**   Prepare an amortization table for the first two years (four interest periods) of this bond issue. Round all amounts to the nearest dollar and use the following column headings for your table:

Six Month Interest Period	(A) Interest Paid Semi-annually ($10,000,000 × 5%)	(B) Effective Semi-annual Interest Expense (Carrying Value × $5\frac{1}{2}$%)	(C) Discount Amorti-zation (B − A)	(D) Bond Discount Balance	(E) Carrying Value of Bonds, End of Period ($10,000,000 − D)
Issue date	—	—	—	$600,000	$9,400,000

b Using the information from your amortization table, prepare all journal entries necessary to record issuance of the bonds in *1992,* and bond interest for *1993.* (Use a compound entry for interest payment and amortization of bond discount at each semiannual interest payment date.)

c Show the proper balance sheet presentation of Bonds Payable and Discount on Bonds Payable at December 31, *1994.*

*PROBLEM 16-11
Effective Interest Method: Bonds Issued at Premium

On December 31, 1993, Rocky Mountain Railroad sold a $10 million, $10\frac{1}{4}$%, 20-year bond issue to an underwriter at a price of 102. This price results in an effective annual interest rate of 10%. The bonds were dated December 31, and the interest payment dates were June 30 and December 31. Rocky Mountain Railroad follows a policy of amortizing the bond premium by the effective interest method at each semiannual payment date.

INSTRUCTIONS   **a**   Prepare an amortization table for the first two years (four interest periods) of the life of this bond issue. Round all amounts to the nearest dollar and use the following column headings:

Six-Month Interest Period	(A) Interest Paid Semi-annually ($10,000,000 × $5\frac{1}{8}$%)	(B) Effective Semi-annual Interest-Expense (Carrying Value × 5%)	(C) Premium Amortization (A − B)	(D) Bond Premium Balance	(E) Carrying Value of Bonds, End of Period ($10,000,000 + D)

b Using the information in your amortization table, prepare all journal entries necessary to record the issuance of the bonds in *1993,* and the bond interest expense during *1994.*

c Show the proper balance sheet presentation of the liability for bonds payable at December 31, *1995.*

*PROBLEM 16-12
Effective Interest Method: Discount and Premium

On September 1, 1993, Camelot Hotel & Casino issued $9 million par value, $8\frac{1}{2}$%, 10-year bonds payable with interest dates of March 1 and September 1. The company maintains its accounts on a calendar-year basis and follows the policy of amortizing bond discount and bond premium by the effective interest method at the semiannual interest payment dates as well as at the year-end adjusting of the accounts.

---

*   *Supplemental Topic A, "An Alternative Method of Amortizing Bond Discount and Premium"*

INSTRUCTIONS

a Prepare the necessary journal entries to record the following transactions, assuming that the bonds were sold for *$8,700,000,* a price resulting in an effective annual interest rate of *9%.*

1 Sale of the bonds on September 1, 1993

2 Adjustment of the accounts at December 31, 1993, for accrued interest and amortization of a discount

3 Payment of bond interest and amortization of discount on March 1, 1994

b Assume that the sales price of the bonds on September 1, 1993, had been *$9,300,000,* resulting in an effective annual interest rate of *8%.* Prepare journal entries parallel to those called for in **a** above at the dates of September 1, 1993; December 31, 1993; and March 1, 1994.

c State the amounts of bond interest expense for 1993 and the *net* amount of the liability for the bonds payable at December 31, 1993, under the independent assumptions set forth in both **a** and **b** above. Show your computations.

CASES AND UNSTRUCTURED PROBLEMS

CASE 16-1
Don't Call Us . . . We'll Call You

On December 31 of the current year, SYNEX Corporation has outstanding $200 million of $14\frac{1}{2}\%$ bonds payable that mature in 20 years. These bonds were issued at par and are callable at a price of 106. Because of a recent decline in market interest rates, the company today can issue $200 million of 20-year bonds with an interest rate of only 11% and use the proceeds to call the $14\frac{1}{2}\%$ bonds.

INSTRUCTIONS

a Compute the reduction in the company's annual bond interest expense that would result from issuing 11% bonds to replace the $14\frac{1}{2}\%$ bonds.

b Compute the gain or loss in the current year that will result from calling the $14\frac{1}{2}\%$ bond issue on December 31.

c In light of your answers to parts **a** and **b,** would you recommend that SYNEX replace the $14\frac{1}{2}\%$ bond issue, or leave it outstanding? Justify your recommendation.

d If the $14\frac{1}{2}\%$ bonds are called, how will the related gain or loss be classified in the company's financial statements?

e Assume that you are an investor willing to earn the current market rate of return of 11%. If you were to purchase the SYNEX $14\frac{1}{2}\%$ bonds at a price of 113 and hold these bonds until their maturity date, you would earn a return slightly greater than 12%. Does this investment sound attractive? Explain.

CASE 16-2
Accounting for Leases

At the beginning of the current year, Cable TV entered into the two long-term lease agreements described below:

Building Lease. Leased from Lamden Properties the use of an office building for a period of 5 years. The monthly lease payments are based upon the square footage of the building and increase by 5% each year. The estimated useful life of the building is 40 years.

Satellite Lease. Leased from SpaceNet, Inc., the use of a communications satellite for a period of 5 years. The monthly payments are intended to pay SpaceNet the current sales price of the satellite, plus a reasonable charge for interest. At the end of the lease, ownership of the satellite will transfer to Cable TV at no additional cost. The estimated useful life of the satellite is 15 years.

INSTRUCTIONS Answer each of the following questions as they relate to the building lease. After answering all four questions, answer them again as they relate to the satellite lease.

a Is this agreement an operating lease or a capital lease? Why?

b Will this lease result in any assets or liabilities being included in Cable TV's future balance sheets? If so, identify these assets and liabilities.

c Indicate the nature of any expenses that will appear in Cable TV's future income statements as a result of the lease, and indicate the number of years for which the expense will be incurred.

d Briefly explain how the *lessor* should account for this lease agreement, including the receipt of future lease payments. Indicate whether the lessor should recognize depreciation on the leased asset.

****CASE 16-3
Convertible
Bonds**

Dreyer's Grand Ice Cream, Inc., has outstanding $50 million face value of $6\frac{1}{2}\%$ convertible bonds payable, callable at $106\frac{1}{2}$, maturing in 2011. Each $1,000 bond is convertible into 31.25 shares of the company's $1 par value common stock. Today's newspaper indicates a market price for the company's common stock, which pays a dividend of 20 cents per share, of $36. On this date, the market rate of interest for bonds of similar quality and maturity date but *without* a conversion feature is approximately 10%.

INSTRUCTIONS

a Compute the conversion price and the stock value for one of these bonds.

b Prepare journal entries in the company's accounting records to record the following alternative possibilities:

1 Dreyer's calls the bonds (assume the bonds were originally issued at par).

2 Bondholders convert the entire bond issue into common stock.

c Given the circumstances described above, would you expect:

1 The bonds to be selling at a discount or a premium?

2 Dreyer's to call the bonds in the immediate future?

3 Bondholders to convert the bonds into common stock in the immediate future?

Explain the reasons for your answers to each question in part **c**.

ANSWERS TO SELF-TEST QUESTIONS

1 a, b, c, d   **2** b, d   **3** a, c   **4** d (The pension expense is equal to the *present value* of the $3 million in estimated future payments; this amount will be considerably less than $3 million.)   **5** c   ***6** a, b, c, d

---

**   *Supplemental Topic B, "Convertible Bonds Payable"*

COMPREHENSIVE PROBLEM 4

SHADOW MOUNTAIN HOTEL

A CORPORATE "PRACTICE SET."

Note to Students and Instructors: This problem **requires** use of the partially completed working papers which accompany this textbook.

Shadow Mountain Hotel is a profitable resort hotel and convention center that has been in operation for several years. Max Griffith, a motion picture producer, organized a new corporation called Shadow Mountain Corporation to purchase and operate the Shadow Mountain Hotel. The new corporation raised capital by issuing both capital stock and bonds payable, and on July 1, 1994, purchased the Shadow Mountain Hotel from the previous owners.

You have been hired as the corporation's controller. The hotel's accounting staff records and posts all the routine transactions, but you have instructed them **not** to record any transaction which they do not understand. Rather, they are to prepare a written description of these items for your review, and you will handle the recording of these transactions. You also perform the end-of-period procedures, including the preparation of a work sheet, adjusting and closing entries, and financial statements. The corporation adjusts and closes its accounting records at the end of each **calendar quarter** (three-month period).

It is now September 30, 1994, the end of the first calendar quarter after Shadow Mountain Corporation acquired the Shadow Mountain Hotel. Management has asked you to provide an income statement and statement of retained earnings for this three-month period, and also a balance sheet as of September 30. Almost all of the routine transactions have **already been recorded** in the accounting records and posted to ledger accounts by your staff. Per your instructions, they have prepared the following written description of each transaction or event **not yet recorded,** as well as information necessary for end-of-period adjustments.

Transactions or Events Not Recorded by Staff

Date 1993	Transaction or Event
June 2	Max Griffith organized Shadow Mountain Corporation, obtaining authorization from the State Commissioner of Corporations to issue 1 million shares of $1 par value common stock, and 25,000 shares of $100 par value, 6% convertible preferred stock (each convertible into six shares of common stock).
June 3	Griffith and other investors subscribed to 480,000 shares of the corporation's common stock at a price of $16 per share. Griffith states that he expects to have another 70,000 shares subscribed by the end of the month.
June 4	Issued to Dianna Trump all 25,000 authorized shares of the convertible preferred stock at par, receiving $2,500,000 cash.

June 6   Underwriters Milken & Burnham agreed to purchase $10 million of 15%, 20-year bonds payable to be issued by the corporation on July 1, 1994. The bonds will pay interest every December 31 and June 30. The exact issue price will be determined at the date of issuance, based upon an index of interest rates and bond prices.

June 25   Collected in cash all $7,680,000 receivable from subscribers to the common stock. Issued stock certificates for 480,000 shares.

June 29   Issued an additional 2,000 shares of common stock to Griffith for his services in organizing the corporation. The board of directors agrees that these services were worth the $32,000 market value of these shares.

July 1   Issued the $10 million of 15%, 20-year bonds payable, dated today, to underwriters Milken & Burnham. The issue price was 98, and the corporation received $9,800,000 in cash from the underwriters.

July 1   Purchased Shadow Mountain Hotel by assuming the liabilities of the hotel and paying an additional $19 million cash to National Resorts, Inc. Exhibit 1 (see July 14 transaction) indicates the current values of the specific assets purchased, and also the amounts of the liabilities assumed. The excess of our $19 million purchase price over the current value of the net *identifiable* assets is regarded as a purchase of unrecorded goodwill.

July 4   Isadora Duncan, a stockholder who owned 12,000 shares of common stock in Shadow Mountain Corporation, was killed in an automobile accident. Duncan was a personal friend of Max Griffith.

July 10   Shadow Mountain Corporation repurchased 12,000 shares of its common stock from the estate of Isadora Duncan at a price of $18 per share. These shares will be held temporarily as treasury stock and will be reissued in the near future.

July 11   Milken & Burnham, the underwriters of the bond issue, reported that they had resold all the bonds to investors at an average price of 101.

July 12   As part of the normal refurbishing of hotel rooms, older furniture was sold to Freight Liquidators for $119,900 cash. In the acquisition transaction on July 1, these furnishings had been assigned a cost of $200,000. (As these assets were sold less than one-half month after acquisition, there is no related accumulated depreciation, and no depreciation need be computed through the date of sale.)

July 14   Purchased new furnishings for $500,000 cash to replace those sold on July 12.

Exhibit 1
Shadow Mountain Hotel
Valuation of Assets Purchased and Liabilities Assumed
July 1, 1994

Assets acquired:

Accounts receivable	$ 50,800	
Allowance for doubtful accounts	(1,000)	*(credit)*
Inventory	36,200	
Supplies	44,000	
Land	10,570,000	
Buildings	14,000,000	
Furnishings & equipment	1,200,000	
Total identifiable assets	$25,900,000	

Liabilities assumed:

Accounts payable	$ 99,000
Interest payable	41,000
Unearned deposits	615,000
Income taxes payable	305,000
Mortgage note payable (10%)	9,840,000
Total liabilities..	$10,900,000
Current value of net identifiable assets purchased	$15,000,000
Purchase price	$19,000,000

Aug. 10 Dianna Trump converted 10,000 shares of her $100 par value convertible preferred stock into 60,000 shares of $1 par value common stock. In light of her increased voting rights, Trump was given a seat on the corporation's board of directors.

Aug. 18 The City of Shadow Mountain gave to Shadow Mountain Corporation several acres of land including the riverbed along the western boundary of the hotel parking lot. The land was given to the corporation at no cost, but with the understanding that the corporation would build a flood control channel in this riverbed to prevent land erosion. The corporation intends to build this flood control channel underground, and then to expand the parking lot on top of the riverbed and the donated land.

  The donated land currently is estimated to be worth $320,000 in its present condition.

Sept. 2 Received a $48,000 advance deposit from the American Accounting Association to reserve a block of 300 rooms for its national convention next August.

Sept. 10 The board of directors declared the regular quarterly dividend of $1.50 per share on the shares of 6% convertible preferred stock still outstanding. The dividend is payable on October 10 to stockholders of record on September 20.

Sept. 10 The board of directors declared a 2% stock dividend on currently outstanding shares of common stock. The current market price of the common stock is $20 per share. The dividend will be distributed on September 30 to stockholders of record on September 20.

  (Corporate laws in this state prohibit shares held in a corporation's treasury from participating in either cash or stock dividends.)

Sept. 20 Date of record for the stock dividend declared on September 10. The market value of the stock today is $21 per share.

Sept. 24 Reissued 10,400 shares of the common stock held in the treasury at a price of $21, receiving $218,400 in cash. (As these shares were held as treasury stock on September 20, the date of record, they will **not** participate in the stock dividend to be distributed on September 30.)

Sept. 26 The State Highway Department paid Shadow Mountain Corporation cash of $310,000 in compensation for land that was condemned and taken by the state to permit widening of a state highway. The cost of this land to the corporation, based upon the July 1 purchase transaction, was $200,000.

  The condemnation of land by a state agency is a transaction regarded as **unusual in nature** and **not expected to recur in the foreseeable future.** In this case, the transaction also is **material in dollar amount.**

Sept. 27 Max Griffith sold 100,000 shares of his common stock in Shadow Mountain Corporation to Dianna Trump at a price of $20 per share. On this date, Griffith resigned as the corporation's chief executive officer, and the board named Trump as his replacement.

You remain the company's controller.

Sept. 30 Distributed the 10,600 share stock dividend declared on September 10. The market price of the common stock today is $22 per share.

Sept. 30 Although paychecks have been prepared and distributed, no entries have yet been made in the accounting records to record the biweekly payroll occurring on this date. Your accounting staff has provided you with the following information:

The wages and salaries earned by employees in the two weeks ended September 30 amounted to $108,000. Amounts withheld from employees' checks consisted of $14,320 in income taxes, social security taxes at a rate of 6.0% of $104,000 in earnings subject to this tax, and Medicare taxes at a rate of 1.5% of $108,000 in earnings subject to Medicare taxes. SUTA taxes and FUTA taxes were computed at rates of 5.4%, and 0.8%, respectively. Only $40,000 of the payroll was subject to SUTA and FUTA taxes.

Company policy is to make two entries to record biweekly payrolls: one recording the payroll and amounts withheld and the other recording the payroll taxes upon the employer.

Sept. 30 Paid in cash all the liabilities at month-end for social security taxes, Medicare taxes, SUTA and FUTA taxes, as well as for income taxes withheld from employees. This payment included the liabilities arising from the September 30 payroll. (Make one compound journal entry to record payment of these five separate liabilities.)

Information for End-of-Period Adjustments

a Hotel guests normally are billed for their room rental when they check out. As of September 30, guests currently registered at the hotel owe $44,100 in room rental charges that have not yet been recorded or billed.

b The hotel's accounts receivable consist primarily of amounts owed by current guests who have not yet checked out. Based upon experience, the company's policy is to provide an allowance for uncollectible accounts equal to 2% of these receivables. The amount of the allowance determined in this manner is rounded to the nearest $100.

c The Unearned Deposits account represents advance deposits made by conventions and other groups to reserve large blocks of rooms for future dates. As of September 30, $402,300 of the amounts credited to this account have been earned, and $642,000 remains unearned.

d Supplies on hand at September 30 amount to $40,000.

e The insurance policies were purchased on July 1 for $300,000 and cover a period of 12 months. (Remember, your adjusting entries cover a period of 3 months.)

f Depreciation on the hotel building and other structures is computed by the *straight-line* method, assuming a 25-year life and no salvage value.

g Depreciation on furniture and equipment is computed by the *double-declining-balance* method, assuming a 5-year life. (Depreciation for fractional periods is rounded to the nearest full month. In this case, you are to take 3 full months' depreciation on all assets included in the Furniture & Equipment account at September 30.)

h Goodwill is amortized by the straight-line method over the longest allowable amortization period.

i For income tax purposes, organization costs are amortized by the straight-line method over the shortest period allowed by law. For convenience, the same policies are applied for financial statement purposes.

j Property taxes payable accrue at the rate of $30,000 per month, beginning on July 1. These taxes are payable within a year.

k Interest accrues on the mortgage note payable at the annual rate of 10%, and accrued interest is payable on the 15th of each month. Thus, at September 30, one-half month's interest expense has accrued. (The principal amount of this note is not due until April 30, 1997.)

l In recognizing interest expense on the 15% bonds payable, bond discount is amortized by the straight-line method.

m A CPA has determined that income taxes applicable to the quarter ended September 30 amount to $256,000, including $212,000 in taxes applicable to normal operations, and $44,000 in taxes resulting from the gain from the condemnation of land by the state government. The $44,000 in taxes relating to this extraordinary gain should be debited to **account no. 600,** Gains on Disposals of Plant Assets (Extraordinary), rather than to the Income Taxes Expense account.

All income tax obligations will be paid within 90 days.

INSTRUCTIONS a Prepare general journal entries to record any of the transactions and events listed above that should be recorded in the accounting records of Shadow Mountain, Inc. (**Note:** Not all of these events require journal entries.)

Next, post your journal entries to the general ledger accounts in the partially completed accounting work sheets booklet (a supplement to the text). You will find the company's chart of accounts in the work sheets booklet.

Remember, your accounting staff **already** has recorded and posted the routine transactions occurring during the quarter ended September 30. Entries summarizing the transactions recorded by your staff **already appear** in the general ledger accounts and are identified by the caption "Summary of entries posted by staff." After **you** post an entry to the ledger, enter the new balance of the ledger account.

b Prepare a 10-column work sheet for the **three months** ended September 30, 1994 using the information for end-of-period adjustments provided. (We have included in this work sheet a **correct and complete unadjusted trial balance** as of September 30, 1994. By comparing your September 30 account balances to the amounts shown, you may determine whether or not you have correctly completed the earlier portions of this problem.)

c Prepare the following financial statements:

1 An income statement for the three months ended September 30, 1994 using single-step format. A single-step format is illustrated on page 245 of the text. Your income statement should also include a separate section for an **extraordinary item,** following a subtotal **Income Before Extraordinary Items.**

Your income statement is to include the **earnings per share figures** normally found in the income statement of a publicly owned corporation. (Round per-share amounts to the nearest cent. Fully diluted amounts are not required.)

2 A statement of retained earnings for the three months ended September 30, 1994.

3 A classified balance sheet as of September 30, 1994. Include a separate classification in your balance sheet for Intangible Assets, immediately following the Plant and Equipment section. For retained earnings, show only the ending balance as of September 30.

d Journalize and post the adjusting and closing entries.

e Prepare an after-closing trial balance as of September 30, 1994.

CHAPTER

17 Investments in Corporate Securities

In this chapter, we discuss investments in corporate securities (stocks and bonds) from the viewpoint of the investor. We first focus upon short-term investments in marketable securities— that is, highly liquid investments made primarily for the purpose of earning dividend or interest revenue. Next, we discuss long-term investments in common stock made for the purpose of exercising influence or control over the issuing corporation. We illustrate the equity method of accounting for these investments and explain how a parent company and its subsidiaries function as one economic entity. The chapter concludes with a discussion of consolidated financial statements. The special accounting problems of multinational corporations are discussed in Appendix D at the end of the text.

After studying this chapter you should be able to meet these Learning Objectives:

1 *Account for short-term investments in stocks and bonds.*
2 *Account for an investment in common stock by the equity method.*
3 *Explain how a parent company "controls" its subsidiaries.*
4 *Describe the distinctive feature of consolidated financial statements.*
5 *Explain why intercompany transactions must be eliminated as a step in preparing consolidated financial statements.*
6 *Prepare a consolidated balance sheet.*

*T*he term *corporate securities* refers to the stocks and bonds issued by corporations. The securities issued by large, publicly owned corporations such as IBM or General Motors are owned by literally millions of different investors. On the other hand, all of the common stock issued by a small, closely held corporation may be owned by one individual or by a small group of investors, such as the members of a family. From the investor's point of view, most investments in corporate securities fall into one of two broad categories: (1) investments in *marketable securities* and (2) investments for purposes of *influence or control*.

INVESTMENTS IN MARKETABLE SECURITIES

Marketable securities consist primarily of U.S. government bonds and the bonds and stocks of large corporations. These securities are traded on organized securities exchanges, such as the New York Stock Exchange. Thus, they are easily purchased or sold at quoted market prices. Investments in marketable securities earn a return for the investor, yet are almost as liquid as cash itself. For this reason, marketable securities usually are listed in the balance sheet second among current assets, immediately after cash.

To qualify as a current asset, an investment in marketable securities must be readily marketable. *Readily marketable* means immediately salable at a quoted market price. In addition, management must be *willing* to use the invested funds to pay current liabilities. Investments which are not readily marketable, or which management intends to hold on a long-term basis, are *not* current assets. Such investments should be shown in the balance sheet just below the current asset section under the caption Long-Term Investments.

Quoted Market Prices   The current market prices of most marketable securities are quoted daily by securities exchanges, by brokerage houses, and in the financial pages of major newspapers. The market prices of stocks are quoted in terms of dollars per share. As illustrated in Chapter 16, bond prices are stated as a percentage of the bond's maturity value, which usually is $1,000. Thus, a bond with a quoted price of *87* has a market value of *$870* ($1,000 × 87%).

Accounting for Marketable Securities

OBJECTIVE 1
Account for
short-term
investments
in stocks
and bonds.

Accounting principles differ somewhat between investments in marketable *equity* securities (stocks) and in marketable *debt* securities (bonds). For this reason, separate controlling accounts are used in the general ledger for each type of investment. For each controlling account, a subsidiary ledger is maintained which shows for each security owned the acquisition date, total cost, number of shares (or bonds) owned, and the cost per share (or bond). This subsidiary ledger provides the information necessary to determine the amount of gain or loss when an investment in a particular stock or bond is sold.

The principal distinction in accounting for investments in stocks and in bonds is that *interest on bonds accrues* from day to day. An investor in bonds must account for this accrued interest when the bonds are purchased, at the end of each accounting period, and when the bonds are sold. Dividends on stock, however, *do not accrue.*

Marketable Debt Securities (Bonds)

The amount of interest paid annually to bondholders is equal to a stated percentage of the bond's maturity value. Thus, the owner of a 10% bond receives $100 interest ($1,000 × 10%) every year. Since bond interest usually is paid semiannually, the bondholder receives two semiannual interest payments of $50 each.

When bonds are purchased between interest dates, the purchaser pays the quoted market price for the bond *plus* the interest accrued since the last interest payment date. By this arrangement the new owner becomes entitled to receive in full the next semiannual interest payment. An account called Bond Interest Receivable should be debited for the amount of accrued interest purchased.

To illustrate the accounting entries for an investment in bonds, assume that on August 1 an investor purchases ten 9%, $1,000 bonds of Rider Co. which pay interest on June 1 and December 1. The investor buys the bonds on August 1 at a price of 99 (or $9,900), plus a brokerage commission of $50 and two months' accrued interest of $150 ($10,000 × 9% × $\frac{2}{12}$ = $150). The brokerage commission is viewed as part of the cost of the bonds. However, the accrued interest receivable at the time of purchase must be accounted for separately. Therefore, the journal entry made by the investor on August 1 is:

<table>
<tr><td>**Separate account for accrued bond interest purchased**</td><td>Marketable Debt Securities ....</td><td>9,950</td><td></td></tr>
<tr><td></td><td>Bond Interest Receivable ....</td><td>150</td><td></td></tr>
<tr><td></td><td>   Cash ....</td><td></td><td>10,100</td></tr>
<tr><td></td><td colspan="3">Purchased ten 9% bonds of Rider Co. for $9,900 plus a brokerage commission of $50 and two months' accrued interest.</td></tr>
</table>

On December 1, the semiannual interest payment date, the investor will receive an interest check for $450, which will be recorded as follows:

<table>
<tr><td>**Note portion of interest check earned**</td><td>Cash...</td><td>450</td><td></td></tr>
<tr><td></td><td>   Bond Interest Receivable ....</td><td></td><td>150</td></tr>
<tr><td></td><td>   Bond Interest Revenue ....</td><td></td><td>300</td></tr>
<tr><td></td><td colspan="3">Received semiannual interest on Rider Co. bonds.</td></tr>
</table>

The $300 credit to Bond Interest Revenue represents the amount actually earned during the four months the bonds were owned by the investor (9% × $10,000 × $\frac{4}{12}$ = $300).

If the investor's accounting records are maintained on a calendar-year basis, the following adjusting entry is required at December 31 to record bond interest earned since December 1:

<table>
<tr><td>Bond Interest Receivable ....</td><td>75</td><td></td></tr>
<tr><td>   Bond Interest Revenue ....</td><td></td><td>75</td></tr>
<tr><td colspan="3">To accrue one month's interest earned (Dec. 1–Dec. 31) on Rider Co. bonds ($10,000 × 9% × $\frac{1}{12}$ = $75).</td></tr>
</table>

Amortization of Bond Discount or Premium from the Investor's Viewpoint

We have discussed the need for the corporation issuing bonds payable to amortize any bond discount or premium to measure correctly the bond interest expense. But what about the **purchaser** of the bonds? Should an investor in bonds amortize any difference between the cost of the investment and its future maturity value in order to measure investment income correctly? The answer to this question depends upon whether the investor considers the bonds to be a current asset or a long-term investment.

When an investment in bonds is classified as a current asset, the investor usually **does not** amortize discount or premium. The justification for this practice is the accounting principle of **materiality.** Given that the investment may be held for but a short period of time, amortization of bond discount or premium probably will not have a material effect upon reported net income. When an investment in bonds will be held for the long term, however, the investor should amortize discount or premium. Amortization of a discount will increase the amount of interest revenue recognized by the investor; amortization of a premium will reduce the amount of interest revenue recognized.

Marketable Equity Securities (Stocks)

Since dividends on stock do not accrue, the **entire cost** of purchasing stock (including brokerage commissions) is debited to the Marketable Equity Securities account. Dividend revenue usually is recognized when the dividend check arrives; the entry consists of a debit to Cash and a credit to Dividend Revenue. No adjusting entries are needed to recognize dividend revenue at the end of an accounting period.

Additional shares of stock received in stock splits or stock dividends **are not income** to the stockholder, and only a **memorandum entry** is used to record the increase in the number of shares owned. The **cost basis per share** is decreased, however, because of the larger number of shares comprising the investment after receiving additional "free" shares from a stock split or a stock dividend.

As an example, assume that an investor purchases 100 shares of Delta Co. common stock at a total cost of $7,200, including commission. The investor's original cost basis is $72 per share ($7,200 ÷ 100 shares). Later the investor receives an additional 20 shares as the result of a 20% stock dividend. The investor's cost basis per share is thereby reduced to **$60** per share, computed by dividing the total cost of $7,200 by the **120** shares owned after the stock dividend. The memorandum entry to be made in the investor's general journal would be:

> July 10   *Memorandum: Received 20 additional shares of Delta Co. common stock as a result of 20% stock dividend. Now own 120 shares with a cost basis of $7,200, or $60 per share.*

Gains and Losses from Sales of Investments

The sale of an investment in **stocks** is recorded by debiting Cash for the amount received and crediting the Marketable Equity Securities account for the cost of the securities sold. Any difference between the proceeds of the sale and the cost of the investment is recorded by a debit to Loss on

Sale of Marketable Securities or by a credit to Gain on Sale of Marketable Securities.

At the day of sale of an investment in **bonds,** any interest which has accrued since the last interest payment date (or year-end) should be recognized as interest revenue. For example, assume that 10 bonds of the Elk Corporation carried in the accounts of an investor at $9,600 are sold at a price of **94,** plus accrued interest of **$90,** and less a brokerage commission of **$50.** The gain or loss may be computed as follows:

Proceeds from sale ($9,400 + $90 − $50)	$9,440
Less: Proceeds representing interest revenue	90
Sales price of investment in bonds...	$9,350
Cost of investment in bonds	9,600
Loss on sale	$ 250

This sale should be recorded by the following journal entry:

Investment in bonds sold at a loss

Cash...	9,440	
Loss on Sale of Marketable Securities	250	
Marketable Debt Securities		9,600
Bond Interest Revenue		90
Sold 10 bonds of Elk Corporation at 94 and accrued interest		
of $90, less broker's commission of $50.		

Balance Sheet Valuation of Marketable Securities

Although the market price of a bond may fluctuate from day to day, we can be reasonably certain that when the maturity date arrives the market price will be equal to the bond's maturity value. Stocks, on the other hand, do not have maturity values. When the market price of a stock declines, there is no way we can be certain whether the decline will be temporary or permanent. For this reason, different valuation standards are applied in accounting for investments in marketable **debt** securities (bonds) and investments in marketable **equity** securities (stocks).

Valuation of Marketable Debt Securities   A short-term investment in bonds is generally carried in the accounting records at **cost** and a gain or loss is recognized when the investment is sold. If bonds are held as a long-term investment and the difference between the cost of the investment and its maturity value is substantial, the valuation of the investment is adjusted each year by amortization of the discount or premium.

Valuation of Marketable Equity Securities   The market values of stocks may rise or fall dramatically during an accounting period.

CASE IN POINT   In a single day, the market price of IBM's capital stock dropped over $31 per share, falling from $135 to $103.25. Of course, this was not a "typical" day. The date—October 19, 1987—will long be remembered as "Black Monday." On this day, stock prices around the world suffered the greatest one-day decline in history. Those stocks listed on the

New York Stock Exchange lost about 20% of their total value in six hours. Given that annual dividends on these stocks amounted to about 2% of market value, this one-day "market loss" was approximately equal to the loss by investors of all dividend revenue for a period of 10 years.

An investor who sells an investment at a price above or below cost will recognize a gain or loss on the sale. But what if the investor continues to hold securities after a significant change in their market value? In this case, should any gain or loss be recognized in the financial statements? Should current market values of investments in marketable securities be disclosed in the financial statements?

Lower-of-Cost-or-Market

The FASB has stated that a portfolio[1] of marketable equity securities should be shown in the investor's balance sheet at the **lower of** the portfolio's total cost or current market value. If the market value of the portfolio **falls below cost,** the decline in value is **reported as a loss** in the investor's income statement. Recoveries in the market value of the portfolio are reported in the income statement as gains, but only as the market value rises back up to cost.[2] Increases in market value above cost are **not shown** in the income statement.

The lower-of-cost-or-market rule produces **conservative results** in both the balance sheet and the income statement. In the balance sheet, the portfolio of marketable equity securities is shown at the lowest justifiable amount—that is, the lower of its cost or its market value. In the income statement, declines in market value below cost immediately are recognized as losses. Increases in market value above cost, however, are not recognized until the securities are sold.

Accountants traditionally have applied different criteria in recognizing gains and losses. One of the basic principles in accounting is that gains shall not be recognized until they are **realized,** and the usual test of realization is the sale of the asset in question. Losses, on the other hand, are recognized as soon as **objective evidence** indicates that a loss has been incurred.

Applying the Lower-of-Cost-or-Market Rule: An Illustration

In applying the lower-of-cost-or-market rule, the total cost of the **portfolio** of marketable equity securities is compared with its current market value, and the **lower** of these two amounts is used as the balance sheet valuation. If the market value of the portfolio is below cost, an entry is made to reduce the carrying value of the portfolio to current market value and to recognize

---

[1] In this context, a "portfolio" of securities includes all investments that are accorded similar accounting treatment and similar balance sheet classification. Those marketable equity securities classified as current assets and those classified as long-term investments represent **two separate portfolios.** Other "portfolios" of investment securities include debt securities classified as current assets, and debt securities classified as long-term investments.

[2] Recognition of these gains and losses in the income statement assumes that the investor classifies the marketable equity securities as current assets. Treatment of these gains and losses on a portfolio classified as a long-term investment is discussed on page 797.

an *unrealized loss* for the amount of the market decline. The write-down of an investment in marketable equity securities to a market value below cost is an end-of-period adjusting entry and should be based upon market prices at the balance sheet date.

To illustrate the lower-of-cost-or-market adjustment, assume the following facts for the investment portfolio of Eagle Corporation at December 31, 1994:

	Cost	Market Value
Common stock of Adams Corporation.........................	$100,000	$106,000
Common stock of Barnes Company	60,000	52,000
Preferred stock of Parker Industries.........................	200,000	182,000
Other marketplace equity securities	25,000	25,000
Totals..	$385,000	$365,000

Because the total market value of the securities in our example is less than their cost to Eagle Corporation, the balance sheet valuation would be the lower amount of *$365,000.* This downward adjustment of $20,000 means that an *unrealized loss* of $20,000 will be included in the determination of the year's net income. The accounting entry would be as follows:

Dec. 31	Unrealized Loss on Marketable Equity Securities	20,000	
	Valuation Allowance for Marketable Equity Securities		20,000

To reduce the carrying value of the investment in marketable equity securities to the lower of cost or market.

The loss from the decline in the market value of securities owned is termed an *unrealized loss* to distinguish it from a loss which is realized by an actual sale of securities.

The Valuation Account   The Valuation Allowance for Marketable Equity Securities is a *contra-asset* account or *valuation* account. In the balance sheet, this valuation account is offset against the asset Marketable Equity Securities in the same manner as the Allowance for Doubtful Accounts is offset against Accounts Receivable. The following partial balance sheet illustrates the use of the Valuation Allowance for Marketable Equity Securities:

EAGLE CORPORATION
Partial Balance Sheet
December 31, 1994

Current assets:		
Cash...		$ 80,000
Marketable securities	$385,000	
Less: Valuation allowance for marketable equity securities	20,000	365,000
Accounts receivable	$573,000	
Less: Allowance for doubtful accounts	9,000	564,000

The Valuation Account Is Adjusted Every Period   At the end of every period, the balance of the valuation account is adjusted so that marketable equity securities will be shown in the balance sheet at the lower of cost or current market value. If the valuation allowance must be increased because of further declines in market value, the adjusting entry will recognize an additional unrealized loss. On the other hand, if market prices have gone up since the last balance sheet date, the adjusting entry will reduce or eliminate the valuation allowance and recognize an ***unrealized gain.***

To illustrate the adjustment of the valuation account, let us assume that by the end of 1995 the market value of Eagle Corporation's portfolio ***increases*** to an amount greater than cost. Since market value is no longer below cost, the valuation allowance, which has a credit balance of $20,000, is no longer needed. Thus, the following entry would be made to eliminate the balance of the valuation allowance:

Unrealized gain is limited to former balance of the valuation account

Dec. 31	*Valuation Allowance for Marketable Equity Securities* .	*20,000*	
	Unrealized Gain on Marketable Equity Securities		*20,000*
	To increase the carrying value of marketable equity securities to original cost following recovery of market value.		

Note that the amount of unrealized gain recognized is limited to the amount in the valuation account. ***Increases in market value above cost are not recognized in the accounting records.*** In brief, when marketable equity securities have been written down to the lower of cost or market, they can be written back up ***to original cost*** if the market prices recover. However, current rules of the FASB do not permit recognition of a market rise above the original cost of the portfolio.

Because the valuation allowance is based upon a comparison of total ***portfolio*** cost and market value, the allowance cannot be directly associated with individual investments. The valuation allowance reduces the carrying value of the total portfolio but does not affect the individual carrying values of the investments which comprise the portfolio. Lower-of-cost-or-market adjustments, therefore, have ***no effect*** upon the gain or loss recognized when an investment is sold. When specific securities are sold, the gain or loss realized from the sale is determined by comparing the ***cost*** of the securities (without regard to lower-of-cost-or-market adjustments) to their selling price.[3]

Income Tax Rule for Marketable Securities   The FASB rules described above are not acceptable in determining income subject to income tax. The only gains or losses recognized for income tax purposes are ***realized*** gains and losses resulting from sale of an investment.

Presentation of Marketable Securities in Financial Statements

Gains and losses on the sale of investments, as well as interest and dividend revenue, are types of nonoperating income. These items should be

---

[3]   The reader may notice that a decline in the market value of securities owned could be reported in the income statement on two separate occasions: first, as an unrealized loss in the period in which the price decline occurs; and second, as a realized loss in the period in which the securities are sold. However, after securities with market values below cost have been sold, the valuation allowance may be reduced or eliminated. The entry to reduce the valuation allowance involves the recognition of an unrealized gain, which offsets the unrealized losses reported in earlier periods.

specifically identified in the income statement and shown after the determination of operating income.

We have explained that different accounting principles are involved in accounting for marketable ***debt*** securities and marketable ***equity*** securities. In the balance sheet, however, these two types of investments generally are combined and shown under a single caption, such as ***Marketable Securities.***

Although marketable securities are usually classified as current assets in the balance sheet, they may alternatively be classified as long-term investments if management has a definite intention to hold the securities for more than one year. Regardless of how marketable ***equity*** securities are classified in the balance sheet, they are shown at the lower-of-cost-or-market value.

The unrealized gains and losses resulting from application of the lower-of-cost-or-market rule, however, are presented differently in the financial statements depending upon whether the securities portfolio is classified as a current asset or a long-term investment. When the portfolio is viewed as a ***current*** asset, the unrealized gains and losses are closed into the Income Summary account and shown in the income statement along with other types of investment income.

The FASB has ruled that unrealized gains and losses on ***long-term*** investments should ***not*** be included in the measurement of the current year's net income, because management does not intend to sell these securities in the near future. Therefore, any net unrealized loss relating to long-term investments is shown in the balance sheet as a ***reduction in stockholders' equity*** and is ***not*** included in the income statement.

Presentation of Investments That Are Not Readily Marketable Securities issued by small businesses may not be traded on securities exchanges and, therefore, may not have quoted market prices. These securities are not "readily marketable"; an investor owning such securities should classify the investment as long-term, rather than as a current asset. Also, such investments should be identified as "Other Long-Term Investments," rather than as marketable securities. As these securities do not have quoted market prices, the lower-of-cost-or-market rule is not applied. These investments normally are shown in the investor's balance sheet at ***cost.***[4]

Reporting the "Fair Value" of Financial Instruments

Investments in the stocks and bonds of other companies are types of ***financial instruments*** and are subject to special disclosure rules. Whenever the "fair value" of financial instruments at the balance sheet date ***differs substantially*** from the carrying value in the accounting records, the fair value ***must be disclosed.***[5]

---

[4]   As with any asset valued at cost, the asset should be written down to an estimated recoverable amount if it becomes apparent that the original cost cannot be recovered.

[5]   Quoted market prices, if available, are the best evidence of the fair value of financial instruments. If quoted market prices are not available, management's best estimate of fair value may be based on the quoted market price of similar securities, or upon other valuation techniques. See *FASB Statement No. 107,* "Disclosures about Fair Value of Financial Instruments" (Norwalk, Conn.: 1991).

At present, these disclosures appear only in **notes** to the financial statements and do not affect the carrying values of the financial instruments in the balance sheet. However, the FASB soon is expected to issue a new accounting standard—called **mark-to-market**—which will make fair value the basis for the valuation of financial instruments in the balance sheet itself.

As explained in Chapter 16, several complex issues arise in connection with the revaluation of financial instruments at every balance sheet date. Perhaps the most significant issue is whether the fluctuations in fair value during the accounting period will be recognized in the income statement as gains and losses. Have these changes in value been "realized"?

Because these issues have not yet been resolved, we will defer further discussion of the mark-to-market proposal to later accounting courses. However, readers should recognize that a significant change in accounting principles may be in the works. If adopted, the mark-to-market concept will affect the balance sheet valuation of numerous assets and liabilities and also may affect the measurement of periodic net income.

INVESTMENTS FOR PURPOSES OF INFLUENCE OR CONTROL

An investor may acquire enough of a company's common stock to **influence or control** that company's activities through the voting rights of the shares owned. Such large holdings of common stock create an important business relationship between the investor and the issuing company (called the **investee**). Since investments of this type cannot be sold without disrupting this relationship, they are not included in the portfolio of marketable securities. Such investments are shown in the investor's balance sheet under the caption Long-Term Investments and are accounted for quite differently from an investment in marketable equity securities.

If an investor is able to exercise **significant influence** over the investee's management, dividends paid by the investee may no longer be a good measure of the investor's income from the investment. This is because the investor may influence the investee's dividend policy. In such cases, dividends paid by the investee are likely to reflect the **investor's** cash needs and income tax considerations, rather than the profitability of the investment.

For example, assume that Sigma Company owns all the common stock of Davis Company. For three years Davis Company is very profitable but pays no dividends, because Sigma Company has no need for additional cash. In the fourth year, Davis Company pays a large cash dividend to Sigma Company despite operating at a loss for that year. Clearly, it would be misleading for Sigma Company to report no investment income while the company it owns is operating profitably, and then to show large investment income in a year when Davis Company incurred a net loss.

The investor does not have to own 100% of the common stock of the investee to exercise a significant degree of influence. An investor with much less than 50% of the voting stock may have influence or even effective control, since the remaining shares are not likely to vote as an organized block. In the absence of other evidence (such as another large stockholder), ownership of **20% or more** of the investee's common stock is viewed as giving the investor significant influence over the investee's policies and operations. In such cases, the investor should account for the investment by using the **equity method.**

The Equity Method

OBJECTIVE 2
Account for an investment in common stock by the equity method.

When the equity method is used, an investment in common stock is first recorded at cost but later is adjusted each year for changes in the stockholders' equity in the investee. As the investee earns net income, the stockholders' equity in the company increases. An investor using the equity method recognizes its **proportionate share of the investee's net income** as an increase in the carrying value of its investment. A proportionate share of a net loss reported by the investee is recognized as a decrease in the investment.

When the investee pays dividends, the stockholders' equity in the company is reduced. The investor, therefore, treats dividends received from the investee as a conversion of part of the investment into cash, thus reducing the carrying value of the investment. In effect, the equity method causes the carrying value of the investment (the amount reported in the balance sheet) to rise and fall with changes in the book value of the shares.

Investments accounted for by the equity method are **not** adjusted to the lower-of-cost-or-market value. When a quoted market price is available, the market value of the investment accounted for under the equity method must be disclosed in notes to the financial statements.

Illustration of the Equity Method Assume that Cove Corporation purchases 10,000 shares (25%) of the common stock of Bay Company for $200,000, which corresponds to 25% of the underlying book value of Bay Company. During the following year, Bay Company earns net income of $120,000 and pays dividends of $80,000. At the end of the year, the quoted market price of Bay Company stock is $22.75 per share. Cove Corporation would account for its investment as follows:

Investment in Bay Company	200,000	
Cash		200,000
To record acquisition of 25% of the common stock of Bay Company.		

Investment in Bay Company	30,000	
Investment Income		30,000
To increase the investment for 25% share of net income earned by Bay Company (25% × $120,000).		

Cash..	20,000	
Investment in Bay Company		20,000
To reduce investment for dividends received from Bay Company (25% × $80,000).		

The net result of these entries by Cove Corporation is to increase the carrying value of the Investment in Bay Company account by $10,000, to $210,000. This corresponds to 25% of the increase reported in Bay Company's retained earnings during the period [25% × ($120,000 − $80,000) = $10,000]. Cove Corporation **reports in its balance sheet** the investment in Bay Company at $210,000 under the caption Long-Term Investments. The market value of the investment, $227,500, is **disclosed in footnotes** to the financial statements.

In this illustration of the equity method, we have made several simplifying assumptions: (1) Cove Corporation purchased the stock of Bay Company at a price equal to the underlying book value; (2) Bay Company had issued common stock only and the number of shares outstanding did not change during the year; and (3) there were no intercompany transactions between Cove Corporation and Bay Company. If we were to change any of these assumptions, the computations in applying the equity method would become more complicated. Application of the equity method in more complex situations is discussed in advanced accounting courses.

Parent and Subsidiary Companies

OBJECTIVE 3
Explain how a parent company "controls" its subsidiaries.

A corporation which owns **all or a majority** of another corporation's outstanding voting stock is called a **parent** company, and the corporation which is wholly owned or majority-held is called a **subsidiary.**[6] Through the voting rights of the owned shares, the parent company can elect the board of directors of the subsidiary company and thereby control the subsidiary's resources and activities. In effect, the **affiliated companies** (the parent and its subsidiaries) function as a **single economic unit** controlled by the directors of the parent company. This relationship is illustrated in the diagram on the next page.

For simplicity, our illustration shows a parent company with only two subsidiaries. It is not unusual, however, for a parent company to own and control a dozen or more subsidiaries.

There are a number of economic, legal, and income tax advantages which encourage large business organizations to operate through subsidiaries rather than through a single legal entity. Although we think of Sears, General Electric, or IBM as single companies, each of these organizations is really a parent company with many subsidiaries. Since the parent company in each case controls the resources and activities of its subsidiaries, it is logical for us to consider an organization such as IBM as one **economic** entity.

Growth through the Acquisition of Subsidiaries

A parent company may acquire another corporation as a subsidiary by purchasing more than 50% of the other corporation's voting stock. The purchase of one corporation by another may be termed a **merger,** a **business combination,** an **acquisition,** or a **takeover.** The acquisition of new subsidiaries is a fast and effective way for a company to grow, to diversify into new product lines, and to acquire new technology. In one recent year, more than 2,500 existing corporations were acquired by other companies at a total cost of over $120 billion.

---

[6] Ownership of a majority of a company's voting stock means holding at least 50% plus one share.

PARENT COMPANY AND TWO SUBSIDIARIES

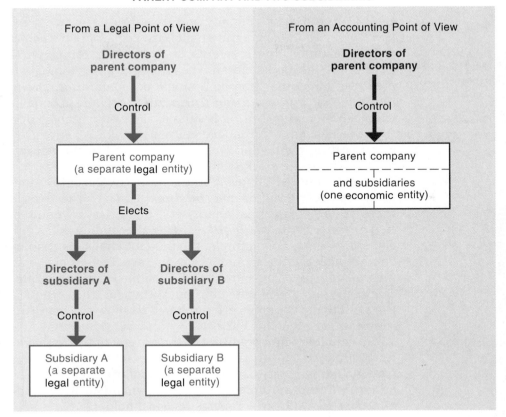

CASE IN POINT Here are just a few of the large business combinations in recent years: Chevron Corporation greatly increased the size of its oil reserves by acquiring as a subsidiary one of its largest competitors, Gulf Corporation. R. J. Reynolds, a tobacco company, expanded its product line by acquiring the well-known food company Nabisco Brands. Mobil Oil went into the department store business by acquiring the giant retailer Montgomery Ward. Eli Lilly, a manufacturer of pharmaceutical products, acquired a "high tech" medical research company called Hybritech, Inc., in hopes that Hybritech's research will lead to important new pharmaceutical products.

The acquisition of one corporation by another is, perhaps, the largest and most interesting of all business transactions. Such transactions may involve billions of dollars, bidding wars among prospective buyers, and dramatic increases in the value of a sought-after company's capital stock. Sometimes a company borrows vast amounts of money and acquires a corporation much larger than itself, thus doubling or tripling the size of the parent company overnight. For example, ABC, a major television network, recently was acquired by Capital Communications, Inc. Prior to the acquisition, Capital Communications was only about one-fourth the size of ABC.

Financial Statements for a Consolidated Economic Entity

OBJECTIVE 4
*Describe the
distinctive
feature of
consolidated
financial
statements.*

Because the parent company and its subsidiaries are separate legal entities, separate financial statements are prepared for each company. In the
separate financial statements of the parent company, the subsidiaries
appear only as assets classified as long-term investments. Since the affiliated companies function as a single economic unit, the parent company
also prepares *consolidated financial statements* which show the financial position and operating results of the *entire group of companies.*[7] It
is these consolidated financial statements which are of greatest interest to
the investing public and which are included in the parent company's annual report to its stockholders.

In consolidated financial statements, the parent company and its subsidiaries are viewed as *one business entity.* The distinctive feature of
these statements is that the assets, liabilities, revenue, and expenses of
two or more separate legal entities are combined in a single set of financial statements. For example, the amount shown as cash in a consolidated
balance sheet is the total of the cash owned by all of the affiliated companies. Liabilities of the parent and subsidiary companies also are combined.
Similarly, in a consolidated income statement, the revenue and expenses of
the affiliated companies are combined to show the operating results of the
consolidated economic entity.

Stockholders and creditors of the parent company have a vital interest
in the financial results of all operations under the parent company's control, including those conducted by subsidiaries. Therefore, it is the consolidated financial statements which are included in the parent company's
annual and quarterly reports to stockholders. (The separate financial
statements of certain major subsidiaries sometimes are presented in footnotes to the consolidated financial statements.)

There are many interesting accounting issues involved in the preparation of consolidated financial statements. A brief introduction to some of
these issues is provided in the following section of this chapter. However,
*no special problems are posed in reading a set of consolidated fi-
nancial statements.* The number of separate legal entities within the
consolidated organization is an unimportant detail. For most purposes,
consolidated financial statements may be interpreted as if the parent company and its subsidiaries *were just one organization.*

CONSOLIDATED FINANCIAL STATEMENTS: CONCEPTS AND MECHANICS

Methods of Consolidation

The purchase of an entire corporation usually is a very big investment. To
accumulate the money necessary to buy another corporation, the parent

---

[7] In the past, some subsidiaries were omitted from the consolidated financial statements for
such reasons as the subsidiaries being engaged in business activities substantially different from
those of the parent company. New rules, however, require every subsidiary controlled by the
parent company to be included in the consolidated statements unless this control will be temporary. In this case, the investment in the subsidiary is shown in the balance sheet at cost and is
classified as a long-term investment; dividends received are recorded as revenue.

company often needs to issue capital stock or bonds payable. If the parent company pays cash or issues debt securities to purchase the other corporation's capital stock, the business combination is accounted for by the ***purchase method.***

A second method of accounting for a business combination is called a ***pooling of interests.*** The pooling method may be appropriate if the stock of a subsidiary is acquired in direct exchange for shares of the parent company's capital stock.[8] A key aspect of such a transaction is that the former stockholders of the subsidiary ***become stockholders in the parent corporation.*** The vast majority of business combinations are viewed as purchases, rather than poolings. In this textbook, we shall illustrate only the purchase method of accounting for business combinations. The special case of a pooling of interests will be covered in more advanced accounting courses.

Consolidated financial statements are prepared by combining the amounts that appear in the separate financial statements of the parent and subsidiary companies. In the combining process, however, certain adjustments are made to ***eliminate the effects of intercompany transactions*** and thus to reflect the assets, liabilities, and stockholders' equity as those of a single economic entity.

Intercompany Transactions   The term ***intercompany transactions*** refers to transactions between affiliated companies. These transactions may include, for example, the sale of merchandise, the leasing of property, and the making of loans. When the affiliated companies are viewed separately, these transactions may create assets and liabilities for the individual companies. However, when the affiliated companies are viewed as a single business entity, these assets and liabilities are merely the result of internal transfers within the business organization and should ***not appear*** in the consolidated financial statements.

For example, if a subsidiary borrows money from the parent company, a note payable will appear as a liability in the balance sheet of the subsidiary company and a note receivable will appear as an asset in the separate balance sheet of the parent. When the two companies are viewed as a single consolidated entity, however, this "loan" is nothing more than a transfer of cash from one part of the business to another. Transferring assets between two parts of a single business entity does not create either a receivable or a payable for that entity. Therefore, the parent company's note receivable and the subsidiary's note payable should not appear in the consolidated financial statements.

Preparing Consolidated Financial Statements   Separate accounting records are maintained for each company in an affiliated group, but no accounting records are maintained for the consolidated entity. The amounts

---

[8]   In addition to the parent company issuing only common stock in exchange for the subsidiary's shares, other specific criteria must be met for the affiliation to qualify as a pooling of interests. For example, at least 90% of the subsidiary's stock must be acquired within one year following the beginning of negotiations. For a more complete discussion of the differences between a purchase and a pooling of interests, see *APB Opinion No. 16,* "Business Combinations," AICPA (New York: 1970).

OBJECTIVE 5 Explain why intercompany transactions must be eliminated as a step in preparing consolidated financial statements.

shown in consolidated financial statements *do not come from a ledger;* they are determined on a *working paper* by combining the amounts of like items on the financial statements of the affiliated companies. For example, the inventories of all the affiliated companies are combined into one amount for inventories. Entries to eliminate the effects of intercompany transactions are made *only* on this working paper. These elimination entries are *not recorded in the accounting records* of either the parent company or its subsidiaries.

Consolidation at the Date of Acquisition

OBJECTIVE 6
Prepare a consolidated balance sheet.

To illustrate the basic principles of consolidation, we will now prepare a consolidated balance sheet. Assume that on January 1 Post Corporation purchases for cash 100% of the capital stock of Sun Company at its book value of $3,000,000. (The shares are purchased from Sun Company's former stockholders.) Also on this date, Post Corporation lends $200,000 cash to Sun Company, receiving a note as evidence of the loan. Immediately after these two transactions, the separate balance sheet accounts of Post Corporation and Sun Company are as shown in the first two columns of the following working paper:

POST CORPORATION AND SUBSIDIARY
Working Paper—Consolidated Balance Sheet
January 1, 19— (Date of Acquisition)

	Post Corporation	Sun Company	Intercompany Eliminations Debit	Intercompany Eliminations Credit	Consolidated Balance Sheet
Cash & cash equivalents	500,000	350,000			850,000
Notes receivable	200,000			(b) 200,000	—
Accounts receivable (net).....	300,000	400,000			700,000
Inventories	1,100,000	950,000			2,050,000
Investment in Sun Company ..	3,000,000			(a) 3,000,000	—
Plant & equipment (net).......	2,800,000	1,800,000			4,600,000
Totals.....................	7,900,000	3,500,000			8,200,000
Notes payable...............		200,000	(b) 200,000		—
Accounts payable	425,000	300,000			725,000
Capital stock—					
Post Corporation	4,000,000				4,000,000
Sun Company		2,000,000	(a) 2,000,000		—
Retained earnings—					
Post Corporation	3,475,000				3,475,000
Sun Company		1,000,000	(a) 1,000,000		—
Totals.....................	7,900,000	3,500,000	3,200,000	3,200,000	8,200,000

Explanation of elimination:
(a) To eliminate the Investment in Sun Company against Sun Company's stockholders' equity.
(b) To eliminate intercompany note receivable against related note payable.

Intercompany Eliminations

Before the balance sheet amounts of Post Corporation and Sun Company are combined, entries are made in the working paper to eliminate the effects of intercompany transactions. Intercompany eliminations may be classified into three basic types:

1 Elimination of intercompany stock ownership
2 Elimination of intercompany debt
3 Elimination of intercompany revenue and expenses

The first two types of eliminations are illustrated in our example of Post Corporation and Sun Company. The elimination of intercompany revenue and expenses will be discussed later in this chapter.

To understand the need for elimination entries, we must adopt the viewpoint of the consolidated entity, in which Post Corporation and Sun Company are regarded as two departments within a single company.

Entry (a): Elimination of Intercompany Stock Ownership The purpose of entry (*a*) in the working paper on page 804 is to eliminate from the consolidated balance sheet both the asset account and the stockholders' equity accounts representing the parent company's ownership of the subsidiary.

Post Corporation's ownership interest in Sun Company appears in the *separate* balance sheets of both corporations. In the parent's balance sheet, this ownership interest is shown as the asset Investment in Sun Company. In the separate balance sheet of the subsidiary, the parent company's ownership interest is represented by the stockholders' equity accounts Capital Stock and Retained Earnings. In the *consolidated* balance sheet, however, this "ownership interest" is neither an asset nor a part of stockholders' equity.

From the viewpoint of the single consolidated entity, *there are no stockholders in Sun Company.* "Stockholders" are outside investors who have an ownership interest in the business. All of Sun Company's capital stock is "internally owned" by another part of the consolidated entity. A company's "ownership" of its own stock does not create either an asset or stockholders' equity. Therefore the asset account Investment in Sun Company and Sun Company's related stockholders' equity accounts must be eliminated from the consolidated balance sheet.

Entry (b): Elimination of Intercompany Debt When Post Corporation loaned $200,000 to Sun Company, the parent company recorded a note receivable and the subsidiary recorded a note payable. This "receivable" and "payable" exist only when Post Corporation and Sun Company are viewed as two separate entities. When both corporations are viewed as a single company, this "loan" is merely a transfer of cash from one part of the business to another. Such internal transfers of assets do not create either a receivable or a payable for the consolidated entity. Therefore, entry (*b*) is made to eliminate Post Corporation's note receivable and Sun Company's note payable from the consolidated balance sheet.

After the necessary eliminations have been entered in the working paper, the remaining balance sheet amounts of Post Corporation and Sun

Company are combined to determine the assets, liabilities, and stockholders' equity of the consolidated entity. The following consolidated balance sheet is then prepared from the last column of the working paper.

POST CORPORATION AND SUBSIDIARY
Consolidated Balance Sheet
January 1, 19___

Assets

Current assets:	
Cash & cash equivalents	$ 850,000
Accounts receivable (net)	700,000
Inventories	2,050,000
Total current assets	$3,600,000
Plant & equipment (net)	4,600,000
Total assets	$8,200,000

Liabilities & Stockholders' Equity

Current liabilities:		
Accounts payable		725,000
Stockholders' equity:		
Capital stock	$4,000,000	
Retained earnings	3,475,000	
Total stockholders' equity		7,475,000
Total liabilities & stockholders' equity		$8,200,000

Notice the stockholders' equity is that of the parent company

Acquisition of Subsidiary's Stock at a Price above Book Value

When a parent company purchases a controlling interest in a subsidiary, it usually pays a price for the shares *in excess of* their book value.[9] We cannot ignore a difference between the cost of the parent company's investment and the underlying book value of these shares. In consolidation, the parent's investment is offset against the stockholders' equity accounts of the subsidiary, and if the two amounts are not equal, we must determine what the difference between them represents.

To illustrate, let's use the preceding example with one significant change. Assume that on January 1 Post Corporation purchases all of the outstanding shares of Sun Company for $3,400,000 instead of $3,000,000. On this date, Sun Company's balance sheet shows total stockholders' equity of $3,000,000, consisting of capital stock of $2,000,000 and retained earnings of $1,000,000. In preparing the elimination entry on the working papers for a consolidated balance sheet, we must determine what to do with the $400,000 difference between the price paid, $3,400,000, and the stockholders' equity (book value) of Sun Company, $3,000,000.

Why would Post Corporation pay a price in excess of book value for Sun Company's stock? Post's management must believe that either (1) the fair market value of certain specific assets of Sun Company (such as land or

---

[9] The parent company also might acquire the shares of the subsidiary at a price below book value. This situation will be discussed in an advanced accounting course.

buildings) is in excess of book value or (2) Sun Company's future earnings prospects are so favorable as to justify paying $400,000 for Sun Company's unrecorded **goodwill.**

If we assume that the $400,000 represents unrecorded goodwill, entry (*a*) in the working papers to eliminate Post Corporation's investment account against the stockholders' equity accounts of Sun Company would be:

Note: This entry is made only in the working papers, not in the accounting records of either company

Capital Stock—Sun Company	*2,000,000*	
Retained Earnings—Sun Company	*1,000,000*	
Goodwill	*400,000*	
Investment in Sun Company (Post Corporation's asset account)		*3,400,000*

To eliminate the cost of Post Corporation's 100% interest in Sun Company against Sun's stockholders' equity accounts and to recognize Sun Company's unrecorded goodwill.

Although we have shown this entry in general journal form, it actually would be made **only** in the Intercompany Eliminations columns of the working paper for a consolidated balance sheet, as illustrated below:

POST CORPORATION AND SUBSIDIARY
Working Paper—Consolidated Balance Sheet
January 1, 19__ (Date of Acquisition)

	Post Corporation	*Sun Company*	*Intercompany Eliminations*		*Consolidated Balance Sheet*
			Debit	*Credit*	
Cash & cash equivalents	*100,000*	*350,000*			*450,000*
Notes receivable	*200,000*			*(b) 200,000*	—
Accounts receivable (net).....	*300,000*	*400,000*			*700,000*
Inventories	*1,100,000*	*950,000*			*2,050,000*
Investment in Sun Company ..	*3,400,000*			*(a) 3,400,000*	
Plant & equipment (net).......	*2,800,000*	*1,800,000*			*4,600,000*
Goodwill			*(a) 400,000*		*400,000*
Totals	*7,900,000*	*3,500,000*			*8,200,000*
Notes payable		*200,000*	*(b) 200,000*		—
Accounts payable	*425,000*	*300,000*			*725,000*
Capital stock—					
Post Corporation	*4,000,000*				*4,000,000*
Sun Company		*2,000,000*	*(a) 2,000,000*		
Retained earnings—					
Post Corporation	*3,475,000*				*3,475,000*
Sun Company		*1,000,000*	*(a) 1,000,000*		
Totals	*7,900,000*	*3,500,000*	*3,600,000*	*3,600,000*	*8,200,000*

Explanation of elimination:
(a) To eliminate the Investment in Sun Company against Sun Company's stockholders' equity, and to recognize goodwill.
(b) To eliminate intercompany note receivable against related note payable.

The following consolidated balance sheet is then prepared from the last column of the working paper. It is important to note that the $400,000 of goodwill will appear as an asset only in the ***consolidated*** balance sheet, ***not*** in the accounting records of Sun Company or Post Corporation.[10] This asset will be amortized to expense over its useful life.

POST CORPORATION AND SUBSIDIARY
Consolidated Balance Sheet
January 1, 19__

Assets

Current assets:	
Cash & cash equivalents	$ 450,000
Accounts receivable (net)	700,000
Inventories	2,050,000
Total current assets	$3,200,000
Plant & equipment (net)	4,600,000
Goodwill	400,000
Total assets	$8,200,000

Liabilities & Stockholders' Equity

Current liabilities:		
Accounts payable		725,000
Stockholders' equity:		
Capital stock	$4,000,000	
Retained earnings	3,475,000	
Total stockholders' equity		7,475,000
Total liabilities & stockholders' equity		$8,200,000

(Margin note: Notice that goodwill appears only in the consolidated balance sheet)

Less Than 100% Ownership in Subsidiary

If a parent company owns a majority interest in a subsidiary but less than 100% of the outstanding shares, a new kind of ownership equity known as the ***minority interest*** will appear in the consolidated balance sheet. This minority interest represents the ownership interest in the subsidiary held by stockholders other than the parent company.

When there are minority stockholders, only the portion of the subsidiary's stockholders' equity owned by the parent company is eliminated. The remainder of the stockholders' equity of the subsidiary is included in the consolidated balance sheet under the caption Minority Interest.

To illustrate, assume that on January 1 Park Company purchases 75% of the outstanding capital stock of Sims Company for $150,000 cash, an amount equal to 75% of the book value (stockholders' equity) of Sims Company. The working paper to prepare a consolidated balance sheet on the date that control of Sims Company is acquired appears as follows:

---

[10] If specific assets of Sun Company had been undervalued, the $400,000 would be allocated to increase the valuation of those assets in the consolidated working papers. The revaluation of specific assets is beyond the scope of our introductory discussion.

PARK COMPANY AND SUBSIDIARY
Working Paper—Consolidated Balance Sheet
January 1, 19__ (Date of Acquisition)

	Park Company	Sims Company	Intercompany Eliminations		Consolidated Balance Sheet
			Debit	Credit	
Cash........................	200,000	50,000			250,000
Other assets	500,000	210,000			710,000
Investment in Sims Company .	150,000			(a) 150,000	
Totals.....................	850,000	260,000			960,000
Liabilities	250,000	60,000			310,000
Capital stock—					
Park Company	500,000				500,000
Sims Company		120,000	(a) 90,000 (b) 30,000		
Retained earnings—					
Park Company	100,000				100,000
Sims Company		80,000	(a) 60,000 (b) 20,000		
Minority interest (25% of $200,000).................				(b) 50,000	50,000
Totals.....................	850,000	260,000	200,000	(b) 200,000	960,000

Explanation of elimination:
(a) To eliminate Park Company's investment in 75% of Sims Company's stockholders' equity.
(b) To classify the remaining 25% of Sims Company's stockholders' equity as a minority interest.

Entry (*a*) in this working paper offsets Park Company's asset, Investment in Sims Company, against 75% of Sims Company's capital stock and retained earnings. The purpose of this entry is to eliminate intercompany stock ownership from the assets and stockholders' equity shown in the consolidated balance sheet. Entry (*b*) reclassifies the remaining 25% of Sims Company's capital stock and retained earnings into a special stockholders' equity account entitled Minority Interest. The FASB recommends that the minority interest appear in the stockholders' equity section of the consolidated balance sheet as follows:[11]

Stockholders' equity:	
Capital stock	$500,000
Minority interest	50,000
Retained earnings	100,000
Total stockholders' equity	$650,000

---

[11] Some companies emphasize the limited ownership of the minority stockholders by showing the minority interest in a special section of the balance sheet between liabilities and stockholders' equity. However, the FASB supports the classification of minority interest as stockholders' equity. See *FASB Statement of Financial Accounting Concepts No. 3,* "Elements of Financial Statements of Business Enterprise" (Norwalk, Conn.: 1980), para. 179.

Minority Interest   Why is the minority interest shown separately in the consolidated balance sheet instead of being included in the amounts shown for capital stock and retained earnings? The reason for this separate presentation is to distinguish between the ownership equity of the controlling stockholders and the equity of the minority stockholders.

The stockholders in the parent company own the controlling interest in the consolidated entity. Because these stockholders elect the directors of the parent company, they control the entire group of affiliated companies. The minority interest, however, has ***no control*** over any of the affiliated companies. Because they own shares only in a subsidiary, they cannot vote for the directors of the parent company. Also, they can never outvote the majority stockholder (the parent company) in electing the directors or establishing the policies of the subsidiary.

The minority stockholders receive 25% of the dividends declared by Sims Company but do not participate in dividends declared by the parent company. The controlling stockholders, on the other hand, receive all the dividends declared by Park Company but do not receive directly dividends declared by the subsidiary.

Consolidated Income Statement

At date of acquisition of a controlling interest, the consolidated balance sheet is the only appropriate financial statement, as no revenue or expenses have yet occurred. Once operations begin, however, a complete set of four corporate financial statements is required: consolidated income statement, consolidated statement of retained earnings, consolidated balance sheet, and consolidated statement of cash flows. We shall discuss briefly some of the basic concepts involved in the preparation of a consolidated income statement.

A ***consolidated income statement*** is prepared simply by combining the revenue and expense accounts of the parent and subsidiary. Revenue or expenses that are the result of ***intercompany transactions*** are eliminated because they do not change the net assets from a consolidated viewpoint—they merely reflect transfers of assets from one affiliated company to another. Assume a subsidiary pays $12,000 to its parent company for rent of warehouse facilities during the year. The subsidiary's $12,000 rent expense as well as the parent's $12,000 rental income should be disregarded (eliminated) in reporting the results of operations for the consolidated entity. This rental transaction neither increased nor decreased the net assets ***of the consolidated entity.***

Elimination of Intercompany Revenue and Expenses   Some of the more common examples of intercompany items that should be eliminated in preparing a consolidated income statement are:

- Sales to affiliated companies
- Cost of goods sold resulting from sales to affiliated companies
- Interest expense on loans from affiliated companies
- Interest revenue on loans made to affiliated companies
- Rent or other revenue received for services rendered to affiliated companies

■ Rent or other expenses paid for services received from affiliated companies

Because of the complexity of the intercompany eliminations, the preparation of a consolidated income statement, a consolidated statement of retained earnings, and a consolidated statement of cash flows are topics appropriately deferred to an advanced accounting course.

Accounting for Investments in Corporate Securities: A Summary

In this chapter, we have discussed the accounting principles applied to investments in corporate securities under various circumstances. The accounting treatment accorded to investments in **bonds** depends upon whether the investment is viewed as a current asset or a long-term investment. The accounting treatment of an investment in **stock** depends primarily upon the **degree of control** which the investor is able to exercise over the issuing corporation. These relationships are summarized as follows:

Situation	Accounting Practice
Investments in bonds:	
Classified as current asset	Combined with current asset portfolio of stocks and shown as marketable securities. Interest revenue accrues each period. Difference between cost and maturity value (discount or premium) generally not amortized. Fair value is disclosed in notes to the financial statements.
Classified as a long-term investment	Combined with long-term portfolio of stocks and shown as marketable securities, under the classification Long-Term Investments. Interest revenue accrues each period. Difference between cost and maturity value is amortized. Fair value is disclosed in notes to the financial statements.
Investment in stocks:	
Noninfluential interest (ownership of less than 20% of the voting stock)	(Readily marketable) Shown as a marketable security (may be classified as a current asset or a long-term investment). Each portfolio valued at lower-of-cost-or-market. Dividends recorded as revenue when received. Fair value is disclosed in notes to the financial statements.
	(Not readily marketable) Shown as a long-term investment and carried at cost. Dividends recorded as revenue when received. Fair value is disclosed in notes to the financial statements.
Influential but noncontrolling interest (ownership from 20% to 50% of the voting stock)	Shown as a long-term investment, accounted for by the equity method. When quoted market price is available, aggregate market value is disclosed in notes to the financial statements.
Controlling interest (ownership of more than 50% of voting stock)	The assets, liabilities, revenue, and expenses of controlled subsidiary are combined with those of the parent corporation in consolidated financial statements.

END-OF-CHAPTER REVIEW

SUMMARY OF CHAPTER LEARNING OBJECTIVES

1   **Account for short-term investments in stocks and bonds.**
    Investments in stocks and bonds are initially recorded at cost, and gains or losses from changes in the market value of the investments are recognized when the investments are sold. Interest revenue from an investment in bonds is recognized as it accrues. Dividend revenue from stocks, however, does not accrue. Rather, it is recognized when the dividends are actually received. Short-term investments in debt securities (bonds) generally appear in the balance sheet at cost; a portfolio of short-term investments in marketable equity securities, on the other hand, is valued at the lower of total cost or market value. The fair value of investments in stocks and bonds of other companies must be disclosed in footnotes to the financial statements.

2   **Account for an investment in common stock by the equity method.**
    Under the equity method, the investor company recognizes as investment income its proportionate share of the investee's net income for the period. Dividends received from the investee are viewed as a conversion of the investment into cash. The equity method generally is used when the investor owns 20% or more of the investee's voting shares. When a quoted market price is available, the fair value of an investment in common stock accounted for by the equity method is disclosed in notes to the financial statements.

3   **Explain how a parent company "controls" its subsidiaries.**
    A parent company controls a subsidiary by electing the subsidiary's board of directors, who, in turn, appoint the subsidiary's management personnel. From a practical point of view, a subsidiary is similar to a department within the parent company.

4   **Describe the distinctive feature of consolidated financial statements.**
    Consolidated financial statements include the assets, liabilities, revenue, and expenses of two or more affiliated corporations, as if the affiliated companies were a single business entity.

5   **Explain why intercompany transactions must be eliminated as a step in preparing consolidated financial statements.**
    The term ***intercompany transactions*** refers to transactions between affiliated companies. When the affiliated companies are viewed as separate legal entities, these transactions may create assets (such as receivables) and liabilities (such as accounts payable) for the individual corporations. However, these "assets" and "liabilities" do not exist when the affiliated corporations are viewed as a single business entity.

6   **Prepare a consolidated balance sheet.**
    A consolidated balance sheet is prepared by combining on a working paper the assets and liabilities of a parent company and all of its subsidiaries which are to be consolidated. It also is necessary, however, to eliminate the effects of intercompany transactions.

This chapter concludes our four-chapter introduction to the corporate form of business organization. Because of the dominant role of corporations in our economy, this form of organization will be emphasized in the remainder of this textbook and in most following accounting courses.

KEY TERMS INTRODUCED OR EMPHASIZED IN CHAPTER 17

Business combination The combining of two or more companies into a single economic entity. Also called a *merger,* an *acquisition,* or a *takeover.*

Consolidated financial statements A set of statements presenting the combined financial position and operating results of a consolidated entity consisting of a parent company and one or more subsidiaries.

Equity method The method of accounting used when the investment by one corporation in another is large enough to influence the policies of the *investee.* The investor recognizes as investment income its proportionate share of the investee's net income, rather than considering dividends received as income.

Intercompany transactions Transactions between two affiliated companies. The effects of intercompany transactions, such as intercompany loans, are eliminated as a step in preparing consolidated financial statements.

Lower-of-cost-or-market (LCM) The conservative practice of valuing a portfolio of marketable equity securities in the balance sheet at the lower of total cost or current market value.

Marketable securities Investments in stocks (equity securities) and bonds (debt securities). These are highly liquid investments that may be sold at any time. Classified as a current asset second only to cash in liquidity.

Minority interest Shares of a subsidiary owned by investors other than the parent.

Parent company A corporation which owns a controlling interest in another company.

Portfolio A group of investment securities that receive similar accounting treatment and balance sheet classification. An investor's holdings of marketable *equity* securities and of marketable *debt* securities are considered two separate portfolios. In addition, the investor may have both a long-term and a short-term portfolio in each category.

Purchase method The method used in preparing consolidated financial statements when the parent company has purchased the shares of its subsidiary by paying cash or issuing debt securities. The purchase method is not used for those special transactions which qualify as a *pooling of interests.*

Subsidiary A corporation in which a controlling stock interest is held by another corporation (the parent).

Unrealized gains and losses Increases and decreases in the market value of an asset which have not yet been realized through sale of the asset. Unrealized losses and some unrealized gains on a portfolio of marketable equity securities are recognized in the accounting records.

SELF-TEST QUESTIONS

The answers to these questions appear on page 828.

1 During 1994, Bonner Company bought and sold a short-term investment in $200,000 face value, 9% bonds which pay interest each April 1 and October 1. Bonner purchased the bonds at 98 plus accrued interest on February 1, 1994,

and held the bonds until December 1, 1994, when the entire investment was sold for $200,000, including accrued interest. Each of the following is true, *except:*

a Bonner recognizes bond interest revenue of $15,000 for 1994.

b Bonner paid a total of $202,000 to acquire the investment on February 1, 1994.

c Bonner recognizes a gain of $1,000 on the sale of these marketable securities on December 1, 1994.

d Bonner received semiannual interest checks in the amounts of $3,000 on April 1 and $9,000 on October 1.

2 Early in 1992, Rodgers Corp. purchased for $1,000,000 a portfolio of several marketable equity securities as a short-term investment. The market value of this portfolio was $900,000 at the end of 1992, $990,000 at the end of 1993, and $1,180,000 at the end of 1994. Based on these facts (more than one answer may be correct):

a Rodgers will recognize in its income statement an unrealized loss of $100,000 in 1992, and unrealized gains of $90,000 in both 1993 and 1994.

b At the end of 1993, Rodgers' ledger account Valuation Allowance for Marketable Equity Securities should have a $10,000 credit balance.

c In 1994, Rodgers' income statement should include an unrealized gain of $10,000.

d If the entire portfolio is sold in 1995 for $1,200,000, Rodgers' income statement for 1995 will include a realized gain of $20,000.

3 Which of the following is *true* with regard to investments in corporate securities?

a When an investor acquires more than 20% of the common stock of a company, the investment is no longer classified as a marketable equity security even if it is traded on the stock exchanges.

b An investor who owns more than 20% of the outstanding bonds of a company should account for this investment by using the equity method.

c Whenever an investor owns less than 50% of the common stock of a corporation, the investment is valued at the lower-of-cost-or-market value.

d Regardless of percentage ownership, an investor in the common stock of another corporation records dividends as revenue when they are received.

4 On January 1, 1994, Stockdale Company purchased 30% (30,000 shares) of the common stock of Equus, Inc., for $600,000. At December 31, 1994, Equus reported net income of $200,000 and paid cash dividends of $80,000. At December 31, 1994, Equus' stock is trading at $19 per share. With regard to this investment, Stockdale's financial statements for 1994 should report:

a Dividend revenue of $24,000.

b Investment in Equus, Inc., of $636,000.

c Investment income of $36,000.

d Unrealized loss on marketable equity securities of $30,000.

5 When consolidated financial statements are issued by a parent and a subsidiary:

a The consolidated balance sheet includes the stockholders' equity accounts of both the parent and the subsidiary.

b Intercompany transactions are reported in separate sections of the income statement and the balance sheet.

c There is no need for the parent and the subsidiary to maintain separate accounting records or prepare separate financial statements.

d Minority interest appears in the consolidated balance sheet whenever the parent does not own 100% of the outstanding shares of the subsidiary.

ASSIGNMENT MATERIAL

DISCUSSION QUESTIONS

1 Why are investments in marketable securities usually regarded as current assets?

2 Why must an investor who owns numerous marketable securities maintain a marketable securities subsidiary ledger?

3 If an investor buys a bond between interest dates, he or she pays as a part of the purchase price the accrued interest since the last interest date. On the other hand, if the investor buys a share of common or preferred stock, no "accrued dividend" is added to the quoted price. Explain why this difference exists.

4 Should stock dividends received be considered revenue to an investor? Explain.

5 Because of a decline in market prices, National Corporation had to write down the carrying value of its investment in marketable securities by $70,000 in the current year. In the determination of net income for the current year, does it make any difference if National Corporation's investment portfolio is classified as a current asset or a long-term investment? Explain fully.

6 In the current asset section of its balance sheet at December 31, 1994, Delta Industries shows marketable equity securities at a market value of $3,000,000, which is $190,000 below cost. If the market value of these securities rises by $250,000 during 1995, how large an unrealized gain (if any) should Delta Industries include in its 1995 income statement? Explain fully.

7 Using the data presented in Discussion Question **6** above, compute the market value of Delta Industries' investment in marketable equity securities at December 31, 1995. Is this market value the amount reported in the current asset section of Delta's 12/31/95 balance sheet for its investment in marketable equity securities? If not, compute the amount that is to be reported for the investment in marketable equity securities and describe how the market value would be disclosed in the financial statements at December 31, 1995, if at all.

8 How does the financial reporting requirement of valuing marketable equity securities at the lower-of-cost-or-market value compare with income tax rules concerning marketable securities?

9 When should investors use the equity method to account for an investment in common stock?

10 Dividends on stock owned are usually recognized as income when they are received. Does an investor using the *equity method* to account for an investment in common stock follow this policy? Explain fully.

11 When the equity method is used to account for an investment in common stock that is traded on organized exchanges, is the investment adjusted to the lower-of-cost-or-market at the end of each accounting period? Is the fair value of such

an investment accounted for under the equity method disclosed at all in the financial statements? Explain your answer.

12 Alexander Corporation owns 80% of the outstanding stock of Benton Company. Explain the basis for the assumption that these two companies constitute a single economic entity operating under unified control.

13 What are consolidated financial statements? Explain briefly how these statements are prepared.

14 List the three basic types of intercompany eliminations which should be made as a step in the preparation of consolidated financial statements.

15 Explain why the price paid to acquire a controlling interest in a subsidiary company may be different from the book value of the equity acquired.

16 The following items appear on a consolidated balance sheet: "Minority interest in subsidiary . . . $620,000." Explain the nature of this item, and where you would expect to find it on the consolidated balance sheet.

17 Briefly explain when a business combination is viewed as a *purchase* and when it might be viewed as a *pooling of interests.*

18 As a general rule, when are consolidated financial statements appropriate?

19 What groups of investors are likely to be primarily interested in consolidated financial statements? Why?

EXERCISES

EXERCISE 17-1
Accounting
Terminology

Listed below are nine technical accounting terms emphasized in this chapter:

Consolidated financial statements	Lower-of-cost-or-market	Elimination of intercompany transactions
Parent company	Minority interest	Equity method
Goodwill	Subsidiary	Marketable debt securities

Each of the following statements may (or may not) describe one of these technical terms. For each statement, indicate the accounting term described, or answer "None" if the statement does not correctly describe any of the terms.

a A separate legal entity owned and controlled by another corporation.

b An accounting procedure which is a necessary step in preparing consolidated financial statements, but which does not involve making entries in the ledger accounts.

c A single set of financial statements showing the assets, liabilities, revenue, and expenses of all companies in a given industry.

d An investment in voting stock of a large corporation that is too small to give the investor significant influence within the issuing company and that is almost as liquid an asset as cash.

e Procedures used to account for an investment in which a corporate investor has significant influence over the policies of another corporation.

f An unrecorded asset that often explains why a parent company pays far more than book value to acquire the capital stock of a subsidiary.

g The equity in a subsidiary held by stockholders other than the parent company.

h Method used in the balance sheet valuation of a portfolio of marketable equity securities.

**EXERCISE 17-2
Investment in
Bonds**

Yamato Company purchased as a short-term investment $300,000 face value of the 7% bonds of Lorenzo, Inc., on May 31 of the current year, at a total cost of $305,750, including interest accrued since January 1. Interest is paid by Lorenzo, Inc., on June 30 and December 31. On October 31, five months after the purchase, Yamato Company sold the bonds and interest accrued since July 1 for a total price of $304,900.

INSTRUCTIONS

Prepare in general journal form all entries required in the accounting records of Yamato Company relating to the investment in Lorenzo, Inc., bonds. (Commissions are to be ignored.)

**EXERCISE 17-3
Investment in
Stocks**

During the current year, the following events occurred with respect to the Deutz Company's investments in stocks:

Jan. 17   Purchased as a temporary investment 5,000 shares of Cooper Industries common stock at a price of $83.50 per share, plus a brokerage commission of $2,500.   417,500 + 2500 = 420,000

Mar. 10   Received a cash dividend of $1.25 per share on the investment in Cooper Industries stock.

July 9   Received an additional 250 shares of Cooper Industries common stock as a result of a 5% stock dividend.

Sept. 11   Sold 2,500 shares of Cooper Industries common stock at a price of $85 per share, less a brokerage commission of $1,450.

INSTRUCTIONS

a Prepare the journal entries in the accounting records of the Deutz Company to record the above transactions. Include a memorandum entry on July 9 to show the change in the cost basis per share.

b Assume the stock of Cooper Industries is widely traded and has a quoted market price of $87 per share at the end of the current year. What is the amount reported in Deutz Company's year-end **balance sheet** for this investment? Describe any additional disclosure requirements for an investment of this nature.

**EXERCISE 17-4
Valuation at
Lower-of-Cost-
or-Market**

The cost and market value of Escobar Corporation's portfolio of marketable equity securities at the end of 1993 and 1994 are shown below. The marketable equity securities are viewed as a current asset.

	Cost	Market Value
1993	$395,000	$334,000
1994	435,000	458,000

INSTRUCTIONS

a Show how the portfolio would appear **in the balance sheet** at the end of 1993 and at the end of 1994. If appropriate, use a valuation account in your presentation.

b Other than amounts reported in the balance sheet, are there any additional required disclosures regarding Escobar's marketable equity securities in either 1993 or 1994? Explain fully.

**EXERCISE 17-5
The Equity
Method**

On January 1, 1993, Southern Transport purchases 40% of the common stock of Delta Shipping, Inc., for $900,000, which corresponds to the underlying book value. Delta Shipping, Inc., has issued common stock only. At December 31, 1993, Delta Shipping reported net income for the year of $400,000 and paid cash dividends of $130,000. Southern Transport uses the equity method to account for this investment.

INSTRUCTIONS a Prepare all journal entries in the accounting records of Southern Transport relating to the investment during 1993.

b During 1994, Delta Shipping, Inc., reports a net loss of $300,000 and pays no dividends. Compute the carrying value of Southern Transport's investment in Delta Shipping, Inc., at the end of 1993 (refer to your answer to part **a**) and at the end of 1994.

c Based upon quoted market prices, the fair market value of Southern Transport's investment in Delta Shipping, Inc. was $995,000 at the end of 1993 but has fallen to $850,000 at the end of 1994. Do these market values affect amounts reported *in the balance sheet* for this investment? Are these market values reflected *in any way* in the financial statements?

EXERCISE 17-6
Eliminating Intercompany Stock Ownership; Recording Goodwill

Merit Brands, Inc., has purchased all the outstanding shares of Eduardo Foods for $670,000. At the date of acquisition, Eduardo Foods' balance sheet showed total stockholders' equity of $600,000, consisting of $250,000 capital stock and $350,000 retained earnings. The excess of this purchase price over the book value of Eduardo Foods' shares is regarded as payment for Eduardo Foods' unrecorded goodwill.

In general journal entry form, prepare the eliminating entry necessary on the working paper to consolidate the balance sheets of these two companies.

EXERCISE 17-7
Computing Consolidated Amounts

Selected account balances from the separate balance sheets of Primis Corporation and its wholly owned subsidiary, Syntech, Inc., immediately after acquisition, are shown below:

	Primis Corporation	Syntech, Inc.	Consolidated
Accounts receivable	$ 300,000	$ 140,000	$ 416,000
Accrued rent receivable—Primis Corporation		7,000	0
Investment in Syntech, Inc.	1,475,000		
Accounts payable	390,000	120,000	486,000
Accrued expenses payable	29,000		22,000
Bonds payable	1,400,000	900,000	23,000
Capital stock................................	4,000,000	1,000,000	4,000
Retained earnings	2,934,000	475,000	

Primis Corporation owes Syntech, Inc., $7,000 in accrued rent payable and Syntech, Inc., owes Primis Corporation $24,000 on account for services rendered prior to acquisition.

INSTRUCTIONS Indicate the amount that should appear in the consolidated balance sheet for each of these selected accounts. If the account would not appear in the consolidated balance sheet, enter −0− as the consolidated account balance. Show supporting computations.

EXERCISE 17-8
Preparing a Consolidated Balance Sheet; Minority Interest

On June 30 Peabody, Inc., **purchased** 80% of the stock of Stern Co. for $1,200,000 in cash. The separate condensed balance sheets immediately after the purchase are shown at the top of the next page.

	Peabody, Inc.	Stern Co.
Cash	$ 350,000	$ 225,000
Investments in Stern Co.	1,200,000	
Other assets	5,450,000	1,775,000
	$7,000,000	$2,000,000
Liabilities	$1,500,000	$ 500,000
Capital stock	3,000,000	1,000,000
Retained earnings	2,500,000	500,000
	$7,000,000	$2,000,000

INSTRUCTIONS Prepare a consolidated balance sheet immediately after Peabody, Inc., acquired control of Stern Co.

PROBLEMS

Group A

**PROBLEM 17A-1
Investments in
Marketable
Debt Securities**

On April 1, 1993, Imperial Motors purchased $450,000 face value of the 8% bonds of Crest Theatres, Inc., at a price of 98 plus accrued interest. The bonds pay interest semiannually on March 1 and September 1. Imperial regards these bonds as a short-term investment.

INSTRUCTIONS

a In general journal form, prepare the entries required in 1993 to record:

1 Purchase of the bonds on April 1.

2 Receipt of the semiannual interest payment on September 1.

3 Adjustment of the accounts at December 31 for bond interest earned since September 1. (Imperial Motors adjusts and closes its accounts annually, using the calendar year.)

b Assume that on January 31, 1994, Imperial Motors sells the entire investment in Crest Theatres bonds for $444,700 plus accrued interest. Prepare the entries to:

1 Accrue bond interest earned from December 31, 1993 through the date of sale.

2 Record the sale of the bonds on January 31, 1994.

**PROBLEM 17A-2
Investments in
Marketable
Equity Securities**

During the current year, the following transactions occurred relating to Talley Manufacturing Company's investments in marketable equity securities:

Jan. 31 Purchased as a temporary investment 4,000 shares of Raleigh Corporation common stock at $64.75 per share, plus broker's commission of $1,400.

Mar. 31 Received a cash dividend of $1.25 per share from Raleigh Corporation. Raleigh declared the dividend on February 15, payable on March 31 to stockholders of record on March 15.

June 30 Raleigh Corporation distributed a 5% stock dividend.

July 31 Raleigh Corporation shares were split 2 for 1; Talley Manufacturing received additional shares pursuant to this stock split.

Sept. 30 Raleigh Corporation paid a cash dividend of 70 cents per share. Dividend was declared on August 25 payable on September 30 to stockholders of record on September 15.

Dec. 21   Talley Manufacturing sold 3,000 shares of Raleigh Corporation stock at $29 per share. Commission charges on the sale amounted to $600.

As of December 31, Raleigh Corporation common stock had a market value of $28.50 per share. Talley Manufacturing classifies its Raleigh Corporation stock as a current asset and owns no other marketable equity securities.

INSTRUCTIONS   Prepare journal entries to account for this investment in Talley Manufacturing's accounting records. Include memorandum entries when appropriate to show changes in the cost basis per share. Also include the year-end adjusting entry, if one is necessary, to reduce the investment to the lower-of-cost-or-market value. For journal entries involving computations, the explanation portion of the entry should include the computation.

PROBLEM 17A-3
Accounting for
Marketable
Securities: A
Comprehensive
Problem

The marketable securities owned by Freitag Development at the beginning of the current year are listed below. Management considers all investments in marketable securities to be current assets.

36,000

$300,000 maturity value of Micro Computer Co. 12% bonds due Apr. 30, 1999. Interest payable on Apr. 30 and Oct. 31 of each year. Cost basis $990 per bond	*$297,000*
4,000 shares of Ryan Corporation common stock. Cost basis $52.50 per share	*210,000*

Transactions relating to marketable securities during the current year were as follows:

Jan. 21   Received semiannual cash dividend of 90 cents per share on the 4,000 shares of Ryan Corporation common stock.

Feb. 8   Purchased 1,500 shares of Gramm Co. common stock at $39¾ per share. Brokerage commissions amounted to $375.

Mar. 15   Received an additional 1,500 shares of Gramm Co. common stock as a result of a 2-for-1 split.

Apr. 30   Received semiannual interest on Micro Computer Co. 12% bonds Accrued interest of $6,000 had been recorded on December 31 of last year in the Bond Interest Receivable account.

May 31   Sold $200,000 face value of Micro Computer Co. 12% bonds at a price of 103, plus one month's accrued interest, less a brokerage commission of $575.

July 21   Received cash dividend on 4,000 shares of Ryan Corporation common stock. Amount of dividend has increased to $1.05 per share.

Oct. 18   Received an additional 200 shares of Ryan Corporation common stock as a result of a 5% stock dividend.

Oct. 19   Sold 1,200 shares of Ryan Corporation common stock at $47 per share, less a brokerage commission of $250.

Oct. 31   Received semiannual interest payment on remaining $100,000 face value of Micro Computer Co. 12% bonds.

At December 31 of the current year, the quoted market prices of the marketable equity securities owned by Freitag Development were as follows: Ryan Corporation, $46 per share; Gramm Co., $21.50 per share. The Micro Computer Co. 12% bonds were quoted at 102.5 on this date.

INSTRUCTIONS

a Prepare journal entries to record the transactions listed above. Include an adjusting entry to record the accrued interest on the remaining Micro Computer Co. bonds through December 31. (Do not consider a lower-of-cost-or-market adjustment in part **a**.)

b Prepare a schedule showing the cost and market value of the marketable *equity* securities owned by Freitag Development at December 31. Prepare an adjusting entry, if one is required, to reduce the portfolio to the lower-of-cost-or-market. (At the beginning of the current year, the market value of the portfolio was above cost and the Valuation Allowance for Marketable Equity Securities account had a zero balance.)

c Compute the carrying value and the market value of Freitag Development's investment in marketable debt securities (the Micro Computer Co. bonds) at December 31. Explain how each of these amounts is reflected in the financial statements at December 31, if at all.

**PROBLEM 17A-4
Equity Method—
Financial Statement Effects**

On January 1, 1993, Minelli Foods purchased 30% (300,000 shares) of the widely traded common stock of Kansas Grain Products, Inc., for $5,100,000. (This price was equal to 30% of Kansas Products' book value at that date.) The following data is available regarding Kansas Grain Products, Inc., for 1993 and 1994:

	1993	1994
Net income (loss)	$2,500,000	$(900,000)
Dividends declared & paid	$1,300,000	$ 650,000
Quoted market price per share at December 31	$ 19	$ 14

INSTRUCTIONS

a Briefly describe how Minelli Foods should account for this investment (e.g., cost, lower-of-cost-or-market, equity method, consolidate, etc.). Identify the principal factors which determine the accounting treatment.

b Compute each of the following amounts relating only to Minelli's investment in Kansas Grain Products, Inc. (All items may not be applicable.)

1 Cash dividends received by Minelli in 1993 and in 1994.

2 Amounts (if any) reported in Minelli's *income statement* in 1993 and in 1994 for each of the following: Dividend Revenue; Investment Income (or Loss); Unrealized Gain (or Loss) on Marketable Equity Securities.

3 Carrying value of this investment reported in Minelli's *balance sheet* at December 31, 1993, and at December 31, 1994.

c Compute the *market value* of Minelli Foods' investment in Kansas Grain Products, Inc., at the end of 1993 and 1994. How are these market values reflected in Minelli Foods' financial statements, if at all?

**PROBLEM 17A-5
Basic Elements of a Consolidated Balance Sheet**

On December 31, 1994, the Home Club, Inc., purchased for cash 70% of the capital stock of Winston Paint Co. The separate year-end balance sheets of the two companies include the following items:

	Home Club, Inc.	Winston Paint Co.
Accounts receivable—Home Club, Inc.	–0–	315,000
Investments in Winston Paint Co.	1,050,000	–0–
Total assets	6,500,000	2,180,000
Accounts payable—Winston Paint Co.	315,000	–0–
Total liabilities	3,900,000	980,000
Total stockholders' equity	2,600,000	1,200,000

The excess of the $1,050,000 purchase price over the book value of the acquired shares in Winston Paint Co. is regarded as a purchase of Winston Paint's unrecorded goodwill.

INSTRUCTIONS Showing your computations, compute the amounts to appear in the year-end consolidated balance sheet for each of the following:

a Goodwill

b Minority interest

c Total assets

d Total liabilities

e Total stockholders' equity (including minority interest)

PROBLEM 17A-6
Preparing a Consolidated Balance Sheet

On January 1, 1994, Maxwell Entertainment purchased all the outstanding common stock of Video Scene, Inc., for $800,000. Immediately *before* the acquisition, the condensed separate balance sheets of the two companies were as shown below. (As these balance sheets were prepared just *before* the purchase, the current assets of Maxwell Entertainment still include the $800,000 in cash which was paid to acquire Video Scene, Inc.)

Assets	Maxwell Entertainment	Video Scene, Inc.
Current assets	$1,630,000	$240,000
Other assets	1,970,000	660,000
Total assets	$3,600,000	$900,000

Liabilities & Stockholders' Equity		
Current liabilities	$ 580,000	$120,000
Long-term debt...	900,000	208,000
Capital stock...	1,000,000	200,000
Retained earnings	1,120,000	372,000
Total liabilities & stockholders' equity	$3,600,000	$900,000

The excess, if any, of the purchase price over the book value of Video Scene's acquired shares is regarded as payment for Video Scene's unrecorded goodwill.

INSTRUCTIONS Prepare a consolidated balance sheet for Maxwell Entertainment and its newly acquired subsidiary (Video Scene, Inc.) on January 1, 1994, the date of acquisition.

PROBLEM 17A-7
Working Paper for a Consolidated Balance Sheet

On March 31, 1994, Connor Yacht Design purchased for $375,000 cash 90% of the capital stock of Wing Sails, Inc. The separate balance sheets of the two corporations immediately *after* this purchase are shown at the top of the next page.

Assets	Connor Yacht Design	Wing Sails, Inc.
Cash	$ 69,000	$ 40,000
Accounts receivable	150,000	60,000
Inventories	120,000	80,000
Investment in Wing Sails, Inc.	375,000	
Plant and equipment	500,000	360,000
Accumulated depreciation	(100,000)	(80,000)
Total assets	$1,114,000	$460,000

Liabilities & Stockholders' Equity		
Accounts payable	$ 80,000	$ 80,000
Accrued liabilities	50,000	20,000
Common stock	600,000	200,000
Retained earnings	384,000	160,000
Total liabilities & stockholders' equity	$1,114,000	$460,000

ADDITIONAL INFORMATION

1 Connor Yacht's asset account, Investment in Wing Sails, Inc., represents ownership of 90% of Wing Sails' stockholders' equity, which has a book value of $324,000 [90% × ($200,000 + $160,000) = $324,000]. The remainder of the Investment account balance represents the purchase of Wing Sails, Inc.'s unrecorded goodwill.

2 Wing Sails owes Connor Yacht Design $14,000 in accrued rent payable. This amount is included in the accrued liabilities of the subsidiary and the accounts receivable of the parent company.

3 Connor Yacht Design owes Wing Sales $32,000 for services rendered. This amount is included in the parent company's accounts payable and the subsidiary's accounts receivable.

INSTRUCTIONS   Prepare a working paper for a consolidated balance sheet at March 31, 1994—the date of this business combination. Include at the bottom of the working paper explanations of the elimination entries.

Group B

**PROBLEM 17B-1
Investments in
Marketable
Debt Securities**

On June 1, 1993, Allied Chemical purchased $600,000 face value of the 9% bonds of Tiger Trucking at a price of 102 plus accrued interest. The bonds pay interest semiannually on April 1 and October 1. Allied Chemical regards these bonds as a short-term investment.

INSTRUCTIONS   a In general journal form, prepare the entries required in 1993 to record:

   1 Purchase of the bonds on June 1.

   2 Receipt of the semiannual interest payment on October 1.

   3 Adjustment of the accounts at December 31 for bond interest earned since October 1. (Allied Chemical adjusts and closes its accounts annually, using the calendar year.)

b Assume that on February 28, 1994, Allied Chemical sells the entire investment in Tiger Trucking bonds for total proceeds of $628,900, which includes accrued interest. Prepare the entries to:

   1 Accrue bond interest earned from December 31, 1993, through the date of sale.

   2 Record the sale of the bonds on February 28, 1994.

**PROBLEM 17B-2
Investments in
Marketable
Equity Securities**

During the current year, Overnight Air Freight (OAF) engaged in the following transactions relating to marketable equity securities:

Feb. 28 Purchased 5,000 shares of National Products common stock for $88.50 per share plus a broker's commission of $1,500.

Mar. 15 National Products paid a cash dividend of 75 cents per share which had been declared on February 20 payable on March 15 to stockholders of record on March 6.

May 31 National Products distributed a 20% stock dividend.

Nov. 15 National Products distributed additional shares as the result of a 2-for-1 stock split.

Dec. 5 OAF sold 3,500 shares of its National Products stock at $39 per share, less a broker's commission of $450.

Dec. 10 National Products paid a cash dividend of 30 cents per share. Dividend was declared November 20 payable December 10 to stockholders of record on November 30.

As of December 31, National Products common stock had a market value of $35 per share. OAF classifies its National Products stock as a current asset and owns no other marketable equity securities.

INSTRUCTIONS

Prepare journal entries to account for this investment in OAF's accounting records. Include memorandum entries when appropriate to show changes in the cost basis per share. Also include the year-end adjusting entry, if one is necessary, to reduce the investment to the lower-of-cost-or-market value. For journal entries involving computations, the explanation portion of the entry should include the computation.

**PROBLEM 17B-3
Accounting for
Marketable
Securities: A
Comprehensive
Problem**

The portfolio of marketable securities owned by Bar Harbor Corporation at January 1 consisted of the three securities listed below. All marketable securities are classified as current assets.

$200,000 maturity value Copper Products Co. 9% bonds due Apr. 30, 2002.
Interest is payable on Apr. 30 and Oct. 31 of each year. Cost basis $990 per bond *$198,000*

3,000 shares of Aztec Corporation common stock. Cost basis $38.50 share *115,500*

1,500 shares of Donner-Pass, Inc., $7.00 cumulative preferred stock. Cost basis $55 per share *82,500*

Jan. 10 Acquired 1,000 shares of Rhodes Co. common stock at $65.50 per share. Brokerage commissions paid amounted to $500.

Jan. 21 Received quarterly dividend on $1.75 per share on 1,500 shares of Donner-Pass, Inc., preferred stock.

Mar. 5 Sold all 1,500 shares of Donner-Pass, Inc., preferred stock at $58 per share less a brokerage commission of $375.

Apr. 1 Received additional 2,000 shares of Rhodes Co. common stock as a result of a 3-for-1 split.

Apr. 30 Received semiannual interest on Copper Products Co. 9% bonds. Accrued interest of $3,000 had been recorded on December 31 of last year in the Bond Interest Receivable account.

June 30 Sold $100,000 face value of Copper Products Co. 9% bonds at 93, plus two months' accrued interest, less a commission of $125.

July 10 Received additional 300 shares of Aztec Corporation common stock as a result of 10% stock dividend.

Sept. 24 Sold 1,300 shares of Aztec Corporation common stock at $40 per share, less a brokerage commission of $250.

Oct. 31 Received semiannual interest payment on remaining $100,000 face value of Copper Products Co. 9% bonds.

At December 31, 19__, the quoted market prices of the marketable equity securities owned by Bar Harbor Corporation were as follows: Aztec Corporation common stock, $37; and Rhodes Co. common stock, $18. Copper Products Co. 9% bonds were quoted at 96 on this date.

INSTRUCTIONS

a Prepare journal entries to record the transactions listed above. Include an adjusting entry to record accrued interest on the remaining Copper Products Co. bonds through December 31. (Do not consider a lower-of-cost-or-market adjustment in part **a**.)

b Prepare a schedule showing the cost and market value of the marketable *equity* securities owned by Bar Harbor Corporation at December 31. Prepare an adjusting entry, if one is required, to reduce the portfolio to the lower-of-cost-or-market. (At the beginning of the current year, the market value of the portfolio was above cost and the Valuation Allowance for Marketable Equity Securities account had a zero balance.)

c Compute the carrying value and the market value of Bar Harbor Corporation's investment in marketable debt securities (Copper Products Co. 9% bonds) at December 31. Explain how each of these amounts is reflected in Bar Harbor Corporation's financial statements, if at all, on December 31.

PROBLEM 17B-4
Equity Method—Financial Statement Effects

On January 1, 1993, Bishop Industries purchased 60,000 shares of the widely traded common stock of Franklin-Parker Corporation for $1,500,000. On this date, Franklin-Parker had 150,000 shares of a single class of stock outstanding and total stockholders' equity of $3,750,000. The following data is available regarding Franklin-Parker Corporation for 1993 and 1994:

	1993	1994
Net income (loss)	$(300,000)	$1,500,000
Dividends declared & paid	$ 75,000	$ 600,000
Quoted market price per share at December 31	$ 22	$ 30

INSTRUCTIONS

a Briefly describe how Bishop Industries should account for this investment (e.g., cost, lower-of-cost-or-market, equity method, consolidate, etc.). Identify the principal factors which determine the accounting treatment.

b Compute each of the following amounts relating only to Bishop's investment in Franklin-Parker Corporation. (All items may not be applicable.)

1 Cash dividends received by Bishop in 1993 and in 1994.

2 Amounts (if any) reported in Bishop's *income statement* in 1993 and in 1994 for each of the following: Dividend Revenue; Investment Income (or Loss); Unrealized Gain (or Loss) on Marketable Equity Securities.

3 Carrying value of this investment reported on Bishop's *balance sheet* at December 31, 1993, and at December 31, 1994.

c Compute the *market value* of Bishop Industries' investment in Franklin-Parker at December 31, 1993, and December 31, 1994. How are these market values reflected in Bishop's financial statements, if at all?

PROBLEM 17B-5
Basic Elements of a Consolidated Balance Sheet

On December 31, 1994, Northwest Building Materials purchased for cash 80% of the capital stock of Corning Electrical Supply. The separate year-end balance sheets of the two companies include the following items:

	Northwest Building Materials	Corning Electrical Supply
Accounts receivable—Corning Electrical Supply	130,000	–0–
Investment in Corning Electrical Supply	1,600,000	–0–
Total assets	9,800,000	2,200,000
Accounts payable—Northwest Building Materials	–0–	130,000
Total liabilities...	3,600,000	700,000
Total stockholders' equity	6,200,000	1,500,000

The excess of the $1,600,000 purchase price over the book value of the acquired shares in Corning is regarded as a purchase of Corning's unrecorded goodwill.

INSTRUCTIONS Showing your computations, compute the amounts to appear in the year-end consolidated balance sheet for each of the following:

a Goodwill

b Minority interest

c Total assets

d Total liabilities

e Total stockholders' equity (including minority interest)

PROBLEM 17B-6
Preparing a Consolidated Balance Sheet

On June 30, 19__, American Sportswear paid $1,800,000 cash to acquire all the outstanding capital stock of Jeans by Jorge. Immediately *before* this acquisition, the condensed separate balance sheets of the two companies were as shown below. (As these balance sheets were prepared immediately *before* the acquisition, the current assets of American Sportswear still include the $1,800,000 in cash which will be paid to acquire Jeans by Jorge.)

Assets	American Sportswear	Jeans by Jorge
Current assets	$3,760,000	$ 640,000
Plant and equipment	3,040,000	1,800,000
Total assets	$6,800,000	$2,440,000

Liabilities & Stockholders' Equity	American Sportswear	Jeans by Jorge
Current liabilities	$1,080,000	$ 560,000
Long-term debt..	2,400,000	400,000
Capital stock	1,200,000	600,000
Retained earnings	2,120,000	880,000
Total liabilities & stockholders' equity	$6,800,000	$2,440,000

The excess, if any, of the purchase price over the book value of Jeans by Jorge shares acquired is regarded as payment for unrecorded goodwill.

INSTRUCTIONS Prepare a consolidated balance sheet for American Sportswear and its newly acquired subsidiary (Jeans by Jorge) on June 30, 19__, the date of acquisition.

PROBLEM 17B-7
Working Paper for a Consolidated Balance Sheet

On September 30, 1994, Morse Communications purchased 80% of the stock of Graham Cable for cash. The separate balance sheets of the two companies immediately after this purchase are shown at the top of the next page.

Assets	Morse Communications	Graham Cable
Cash...	$ 52,000	$ 45,000
Note receivable from Graham Cable......................	50,000	
Accounts receivable.....................................	108,000	60,000
Inventories...	120,000	174,000
Investment in Graham Cable.............................	570,000	
Plant and equipment	420,000	540,000
Accumulated depreciation	(168,000)	(100,000)
Total assets	$1,152,000	$719,000

Liabilities & Stockholders' Equity		
Notes payable..	$ 120,000	$ 50,000
Accounts payable.......................................	144,000	45,000
Accrued liabilities	36,000	24,000
Common stock..	500,000	350,000
Retained earnings.......................................	352,000	250,000
Total liabilities & stockholders' equity	$1,152,000	$719,000

ADDITIONAL INFORMATION

1 Morse Communications' asset account Investment in Graham Cable represents ownership of 80% of Graham Cable's stockholders' equity, which has a book value of $480,000 [80% × ($350,000 + $250,000) = $480,000]. The remainder of the investment account balance represents the purchase of Graham Cable's unrecorded goodwill.

2 Graham Cable's $50,000 note payable is owed to Morse Communications. (All interest has been paid through September 30.)

3 The accounts payable of Morse Communications include $15,000 owed to Graham Cable. This amount also is included in the accounts receivable of Graham Cable.

INSTRUCTIONS Prepare a working paper for a consolidated balance sheet at September 30, 1994—immediately after the purchase of Graham Cable. Include at the bottom of the working paper explanations of the elimination entries.

CASES AND UNSTRUCTURED PROBLEMS

**CASE 17-1
Apples and
Oranges**

Dane Electronics has the following investments in the securities of other corporations:

a 2,000 shares of the common stock of Apple Computer. Apple is a large publicly owned corporation and sells at a quoted market price in excess of Dane's cost. Dane's management stands ready to sell these shares at any time.

b $100,000 face amount of Central Telephone's $3\frac{5}{8}\%$ bonds maturing in 10 years. The bonds were acquired at a substantial discount. These bonds are readily marketable, and Dane's management stands ready to sell them to meet any current cash requirements.

c 5 million of the 15 million voting shares in Micro-Desk, Inc. Micro-Desk is a publicly owned corporation, and its quoted stock price recently has declined to a level below Dane's cost.

d $300,000 face value of Carver Stores $12\frac{1}{4}\%$ bonds maturing in 10 years. These bonds are readily marketable at a quoted price. However, Dane intends to hold these bonds until their maturity date. The bonds were acquired at a premium.

e 90% of the voting stock in Consumer Finance Corp. Consumer Finance is a profitable company, but it is not publicly owned. There is no quoted market price for Consumer's capital stock.

f 50,000 of the 1 million outstanding shares of SIMCO Products, a publicly owned corporation. The market price of SIMCO's shares has declined steadily since Dane purchased its shares. Dane's management, however, believes in the long-run prospects of SIMCO and intends to hold this investment for at least 10 years.

g 5,000 shares of voting stock of Orange Express. Orange Express operates profitably, but it is not publicly owned and has no quoted market value. This investment does not give Dane an influential interest in Orange Express. Dane's management stands ready to sell these shares at any time that an attractive offer is received.

INSTRUCTIONS Explain how Dane Electronics should account for each of these investments. Your explanations should include discussion of the three topics listed below. You may find the summary on page 811 helpful in preparing your answers to this case.

1 Whether the investment qualifies for consolidation and, if not, the appropriate balance sheet classification of the investment account.

2 The basis for balance sheet valuation (e.g., consolidation, equity method, cost, cost adjusted for amortization of bond discount or premium, or lower-of-cost-or-market).

3 The factors involved in the recognition of income (or loss) from the investment (e.g., Do lower-of-cost-or-market adjustments enter into the determination of net income? Is bond discount or premium amortized? Are dividends recorded as income when received? Is the equity method in use?).

ANSWERS TO SELF-TEST QUESTIONS

1 d   2 b, c   3 a   4 b   5 d

PART

6 Special Purpose Reports and Financial Statement Analysis

In the next three chapters we discuss several specialized uses of accounting information, including the determination of taxable income, the measurement of cash flows, and the analysis of financial statements by investors.

Part 6 also includes Comprehensive Problem 5, which provides an opportunity to analyze and evaluate the financial statements of a well-known corporation.

Income Taxes and Business Decisions

For many college students, this chapter may be their only academic exposure to the truly remarkable system known as federal income taxes. The early part of this chapter presents a brief history and rationale of the federal income tax structure. In this introduction we stress the pervasive influence of income taxes upon economic activity. The next section portrays the basic process of determining taxable income and tax liability for individual taxpayers. The income tax computations for a small corporation are also explained and illustrated. The final section of our discussion gives students an understanding of the important role that *tax planning* can play in the affairs of individuals and also in the decision-making of a business entity.

After studying this chapter you should be able to meet these Learning Objectives:

1 *Describe the federal income tax: its history and objectives.*

2 *Discuss the advantages of the cash basis of accounting for preparation of individual income tax returns.*

3 *State the formula for determining the taxable income of an individual.*

4 *Explain the recent changes in taxation of capital gains and losses.*

5 *Contrast the determination of taxable income for a corporation with that for an individual.*

6 *Describe the circumstances that create a liability for deferred income taxes.*

7 *Explain how tax planning is used in choosing the form of business organization and the capital structure.*

NOTE TO READERS: Congress makes minor changes in tax rates and regulations almost every year. On some occasions, it makes major changes. Therefore, the tax rates and regulations described in this chapter are intended only to illustrate basic concepts and to *approximate* current tax law. For the actual tax rates and regulations of a given year, we refer readers to the annual publications of the Internal Revenue Service.

The Federal Income Tax: Its History and Objectives

OBJECTIVE 1 Describe the federal income tax: its history and objectives.

The present federal income tax dates from the passage of the Sixteenth Amendment to the Constitution in 1913.[1] This amendment, only 30 words in length,[2] removed all questions of the constitutionality of income taxes and paved the way for the more than 50 revenue acts passed by Congress since that date. In 1939 these tax laws were first combined into what is known as the Internal Revenue Code. The administration and enforcement of the tax laws are duties of the Treasury Department, operating through a division known as the Internal Revenue Service (IRS). The Treasury Department publishes its interpretation of the tax laws in Treasury regulations; the final word in interpretation lies with the federal courts.

Originally the purpose of the federal income tax was simply to obtain revenue for the government. And at first, the tax rates were quite low—by today's standards. In 1913, a married person with taxable income of $15,000 would have been subject to a tax rate of 1%, resulting in a tax liability of $150. The maximum federal income tax rate in 1913 was 7%. By the 1970s, the maximum tax rate had risen to 70%; and for most of the 1980s the top rate was 50%. Then Congressional action lowered the top rate to 28% beginning with the year 1988. By 1991, however, the top rate had been raised to 31%.

The purpose of federal income tax now includes *several goals apart from raising revenue.* Examples of these other goals are: influencing the rate of economic growth, encouraging full employment, combatting inflation, favoring small businesses, and redistributing national income on a more equal basis.

Classes of Taxpayers

The income tax law recognizes four major classes of taxpayers: *individuals, corporations, estates,* and *trusts.* A business organized as a sole proprietorship or as a partnership is not taxed as a separate entity; its income is taxed directly to the individual proprietor or partners, *whether or not the income is withdrawn from the business.* However, a partnership must file an *information return* showing the computation of

---

[1]   A federal income tax was proposed as early as 1815, and an income tax law was actually passed and income taxes collected during the Civil War. This law was upheld by the Supreme Court, but it was repealed when the need for revenue subsided after the war. In 1894 a new income tax law was passed, but the Supreme Court declared this law invalid on constitutional grounds.

[2]   It reads "The Congress shall have power to lay and collect taxes on incomes, from whatever source derived, without apportionment among the several States, and without regard to any census or enumeration."

total partnership net income and the allocation of this income among the partners.

A sole proprietor reports his or her income from ownership of a business on an individual tax return (Form 1040); the members of a partnership include on their individual income tax returns their *respective shares* of the partnership net income. Of course, an individual's income tax return must include not only any business income from a proprietorship or partnership but also any interest, dividends, salary, or other forms of income received.

A corporation is a separate taxable entity; it must file a corporate income tax return (Form 1120) and pay a tax on its annual taxable income. In addition, individual stockholders must report dividends received from corporations as part of their personal taxable income. The taxing of corporate dividends has led to the charge that there is "double taxation" of corporate income—once to the corporation and again when it is distributed to stockholders. This double impact of tax is particularly apparent when a corporation is owned by one person or one family.

To illustrate, let us use the tax rates in effect during the early 1980s to consider the tax impact on one dollar of corporate earnings. The income before *taxes* earned by a corporation was (in general) subject to a federal corporate income tax rate of 46%. First, the corporation paid 46%, or 46 cents, out of the dollar to the Internal Revenue Service. That left 54 cents for the corporation. Next, assume that the 54 cents was distributed as dividends to individual stockholders. The dividend was taxable to the stockholders personally at rates varying from 12 to 50%, depending on their individual tax brackets. Thus, the 54 cents of after-tax income to the corporation could be reduced by 50%, or 27 cents of individual income tax, leaving 27 cents of the original dollar for the shareholder. In summary, *federal income taxes could take as much as 73 cents out of a dollar earned by a corporation and distributed as a dividend to a shareholder.* The remaining 27 cents could be reduced further by state income taxes. This example would, of course, appear less extreme if we used the lower rates effective today.

Special and complex rules apply to the determination of taxable income for estates and trusts. These rules will not be discussed in this chapter.

The Critical Importance of Income Taxes

Taxes levied by federal, state, and local governments are a significant part of the cost of operating a typical household, as well as a business enterprise. Every manager who makes business decisions, and every individual who makes personal investments, urgently needs some knowledge of income taxes. A general knowledge of income taxes will help any business manager or owner to benefit more fully from the advice of the professional tax accountant.

Some understanding of income taxes will also aid the individual citizen in voting intelligently, because a great many of the issues decided in every election have tax implications. Such issues as pollution, inflation, foreign policy, and employment are quite closely linked with income taxes. For example, the offering of special tax incentives to encourage businesses to reduce pollution is one approach to protection of the environment.

In terms of revenue generated, the four most important kinds of taxes in the United States are ***income taxes, sales taxes, property taxes,*** and ***excise taxes.*** Income taxes exceed all others in terms of the amounts involved, and they also exert a pervasive influence on all types of business decisions. For these reasons, we shall limit our discussion to the basic federal income tax rules applicable to individuals, partnerships, and corporations.

Income tax returns are based on accounting information. In many respects this information is consistent with the accounting concepts we have discussed in earlier chapters. However, the measurement of ***taxable income*** includes some unique principles and computations which differ from those used for published financial statements. An understanding of the unique aspects of taxable income can assist an individual or a business in minimizing the amount of income taxes owed.

Tax Planning versus Tax Evasion

Tax Planning   Taxpayers who manage their affairs in ways which ***legally*** minimize their income tax obligations are engaging in a practice called ***tax planning.*** Tax planning is both legal and ethical; in the words of the distinguished jurist, Judge Learned Hand:

> Over and over again courts have said that there is nothing sinister in so arranging one's affairs as to keep taxes as low as possible. Everybody does so, rich or poor, and all do right, for nobody owes any public duty to pay more than the law demands: taxes are enforced exactions, not voluntary contributions. To demand more in the name of morals is mere cant.

The goals of tax planning usually are either to minimize the total amount of taxes owed or to postpone into future years the dates at which the taxes become due. One major type of tax planning involves ***structuring transactions*** in a manner which provides tax advantages. For example, the tax deductions resulting from the use of an automobile in a business differ substantially depending upon whether the automobile is leased or owned. A second type of tax planning involves selecting for use in the income tax return those accounting methods that produce the most advantageous measurement of taxable income. For example, the taxpayer may elect to use LIFO rather than FIFO, or an accelerated depreciation method instead of straight-line. Some of these choices may significantly affect the amount and timing of the taxpayer's income tax obligations.

If tax planning is to be efficient, it should be undertaken ***before*** the taxpayer engages in the related transactions. Once a transaction is complete, it usually is ***too late*** to change its tax consequences. Every taxpayer, whether an individual or a corporation, can benefit from thoughtful tax planning. Tax planning is one of the major services which CPA firms offer their clients.

Tax Evasion   In contrast to tax planning, ***tax evasion*** refers to ***illegal*** efforts by taxpayers to avoid their tax obligations. Examples include failure to file an income tax return or fraudulently understating the amount of taxable income reported in the return.

By definition, tax evasion is a crime, punishable by fines, imprisonment, or both.

CASE IN POINT Al Capone, one of the most infamous gangsters in American history, was believed to have committed many crimes, including bootlegging, extortion, and murder. Capone was the subject of an intense criminal investigation conducted by federal law enforcement agents—including the legendary Elliot Ness and "The Untouchables."

The only crime for which the government was able to convict Capone was income tax evasion. The end result, however, was the same as if he had been convicted of murder and given a life sentence. He died in prison while serving his term.

Enforcement of Income Tax Laws

Our system of income taxes relies upon taxpayers measuring their own taxable income, computing the taxes which they owe, and filing an income tax return in which these amounts are reported to governmental income tax authorities. For this reason, our system of collecting income taxes often is described as a system of *self-assessment.*

However, income tax authorities have several means of enforcing this "self-assessment" system. To begin with, much of the taxable income earned by taxpayers is reported to the tax authorities by a third party. For example, employers must send *W-2* forms to the government indicating the total salary or wages paid to each employee during the year. Corporations and banks are required to send *1099* forms reporting to the government the dividends and interest earned by each investor and creditor. Through the use of its computers, the Internal Revenue Service traces many of these reported amounts directly into the recipient's income tax return.

Next, each year income tax authorities *audit* the tax returns filed by many taxpayers. Only a small percentage of the returns filed each year are audited; however, the IRS has considerable experience in identifying those returns in which taxable income may be understated. Many of the returns selected for audit are those which appear "suspicious" in some way, or in which taxpayers have claimed deductions to which they might not be entitled. Thus, by claiming certain deductions (such as expenses relating to a "home office" or a large casualty loss), a taxpayer may increase the chances that his or her return will be audited.

An interesting quirk in American law is that when a tax return is audited, *the burden of proof rests with the taxpayer.* Thus, taxpayers who do not maintain adequate records may lose deductions to which they otherwise would be entitled.

Finally, tax authorities may impose financial penalties upon taxpayers who have understated their taxable incomes. First, the taxpayer must pay interest on any additional taxes owed. In addition, substantial fines and penalties may be levied if the taxpayer has been careless or fraudulent. As previously stated, fraudulent tax evasion is a criminal offense and may be punishable by imprisonment, as well as by financial penalties.

INCOME TAXES: INDIVIDUALS

Cash Basis of Accounting for Income Tax Returns

Almost all ***individual*** income tax returns are prepared on the ***cash basis*** of accounting. Many small service-type business concerns and professional firms also choose to prepare their tax returns on the cash basis. Revenue is recognized when collected in cash; expenses (except depreciation) are recognized when a cash payment is made. The cash basis (as prescribed in IRS rules) does not permit expenditures for plant and equipment to be deducted in the year of purchase. These capital expenditures are ***capitalized and depreciated*** for tax purposes. Also, the income tax laws do not permit use of the cash basis by companies in which inventories and the sale of merchandise are significant factors.

Although the cash basis of accounting does not measure income in accordance with generally accepted accounting principles, it has much merit in the area of taxation. From the government's viewpoint, the logical time to collect tax on income is when the taxpayer receives the income in cash. At any earlier date, the taxpayer may not have the cash to pay income taxes; at any later date, the cash may have been used for other purposes.

The cash basis is advantageous for the individual taxpayer and for service-type businesses for several reasons. It is relatively simple and requires a minimum of records. The income of most individuals comes in the form of salaries, interest, and dividends. At the end of each year, an individual receives from his or her employer a W-2 form showing the salary earned and the income tax withheld during the year. This report is prepared on a cash basis without any accrual of unpaid wages. Persons receiving interest or dividends also receive from the paying companies Form 1099 showing amounts received for the year. Thus, most individuals are provided with ***reports prepared on a cash basis*** for use in preparing their individual tax returns.

The cash basis has other advantages for the individual taxpayer and for many professional firms and service-type businesses. It often permits tax savings by individuals who deliberately shift the timing of revenue and expense transactions from one year to another. For example, a dentist whose taxable income is higher than usual in the current year may decide in December to delay billing patients until January 1 and thus postpone the receipt of gross income to the next year. The timing of ***expense payments*** near year-end is also controllable by a taxpayer using the cash basis. A taxpayer who has received a bill for a deductible expense item in December may choose to pay it before or after December 31 and thereby influence the amount of taxable income in each year. However, a cash-basis taxpayer is not permitted to deduct rent paid in advance on business property. Such an advance payment must be treated as an asset and amortized over the rental period.

Any taxpayer who maintains a set of accounting records may elect to use the ***accrual basis*** in preparing a tax return, but very few taxpayers (individual or corporate) choose to do so if they are eligible to use the ***cash basis.***

Tax Rates

All taxes may be characterized as progressive, proportional, or regressive with respect to any given base. A *progressive* tax becomes a larger portion of the base as that base increases. Federal income taxes are *progressive* with respect to income, since a higher tax *rate* applies as the amount of taxable income increases. A *proportional* tax remains a constant percentage of the base no matter how that base changes. For example, a 6% sales tax remains a constant percentage of sales regardless of changes in the dollar amount of sales. A *regressive* tax becomes a smaller percentage of the base as the base increases. Regressive taxes, however, are extremely rare.

Keep in mind that tax rates have been changed many times in the past and no doubt will continue to be changed frequently in the future. To simplify the arithmetic in our illustrations, we have used tax rates of round amounts rather than the rates of any particular year. Also, we have rounded the dollar amount of tax brackets and of such items as the standard deduction and the personal exemption.

Our *assumed* tax structure for individuals consists of three brackets of 15%, 30%, and 32%. The 15% rate is applicable to all taxable income of single individuals up to $20,000. The 30% rate is applicable to income over $20,000 and up to $50,000. The top rate of 32% applies to income above $50,000.

For married couples filing joint returns, the 15% rate applies to taxable income up to $34,000. The 30% rate is applicable to income over $34,000 and up to $84,000. The top rate of 32% applies to income above $84,000.

These rates are summarized below.

Tax Rate Schedules

Taxable Income	Tax Rate
Single taxpayers:	
First $20,000	15%
Amount owed over $20,000 but not over $50,000	30%
Amount over $50,000	32%
Married taxpayers filing joint returns:	
First $34,000	15%
Amount owed over $34,000 but not over $84,000	30%
Amount over $84,000	32%

Example:	Compute the income tax for a single person with taxable income of $52,000.	
Answer:	Tax on first $20,000 at 15%	$ 3,000
	Tax on next $30,000 at 30%	9,000
	Tax on remaining $2,000 at 32%	640
	Total tax for a single person with $52,000 of taxable income	$12,640

Income Tax Formula for Individuals

The federal government supplies standard income tax forms on which taxpayers are guided to a proper computation of their taxable income and the

OBJECTIVE 3
State the
formula for
determining
the taxable
income of
an individ-
ual.

amount of the tax. It is helpful to visualize the computation in terms of an income tax formula as diagrammed on the next page. The sequence of items on actual income tax forms differs somewhat from the arrangement in this formula. However, it is easier to understand the structure and logic of the federal income tax by referring to the tax formula rather than to tax forms.

Total Income and Gross Income

Total income as defined for tax purposes is a very broad concept that includes all income from whatever source. Not all types of income, however, are subject to taxation; tax laws permit some types of income to be **excluded** in the computation of taxable income. **Gross income** is the total amount of income which must be **reported in an income tax return;** it consists of total income, less those items specifically excluded by law.

Exclusions   Items which may be excluded from gross income are called **exclusions.** Not many items qualify as exclusions; among those that do are:

- Interest on municipal bonds
- Gifts and inheritances
- Proceeds from life insurance policies
- Workers' compensation benefits and (within certain limits) social security benefits
- Pensions to veterans
- Certain types of scholarships
- Compensation received for damages

Only those items **identified by law** qualify as exclusions. Thus, types of income **not mentioned** in the tax code must be **included** in gross income. These include, for example, money found in the street, gambling winnings (in excess of losses), prizes won in contests, "high-performance awards" given by employers to employees, and income from illegal sources.

CASE IN POINT   A partially deaf 78-year-old woman once was a successful contestant on a television game show. Among the prizes she won was a replica of a 1950s jukebox. Having no use for this prize, she gave it to a neighbor who had several teenaged children.

At year-end, the "lucky contestant" was stunned to learn the tax consequence of these events. Winning the jukebox increased her taxable income by approximately $9,000, and her taxes for the year by nearly $3,000. (She could have avoided the additional taxes by declining the prize or by donating it to a recognized charity.)

Deductions to Arrive at Adjusted Gross Income

As steps in determining taxable income, taxpayers may deduct from gross income two broad categories of **deductions:** (1) deductions to arrive **at** adjusted gross income and (2) deductions **from** adjusted gross income.

General Federal Income Tax Formula for Individuals

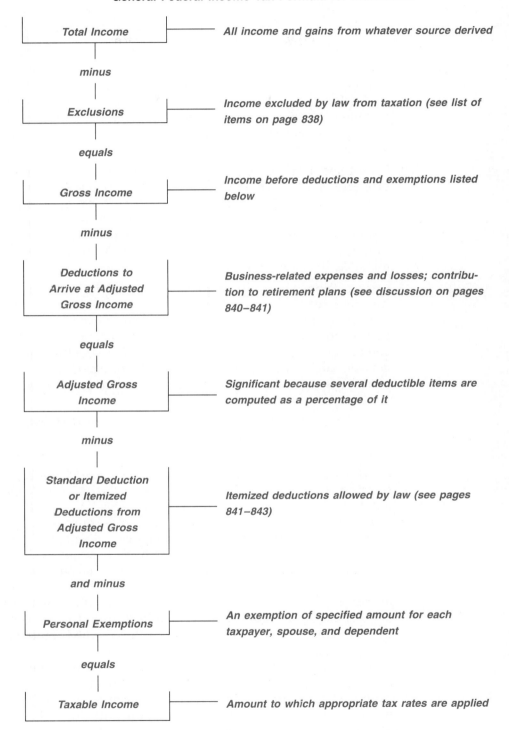

Use this formula to compute taxable income for individuals

Total Income	*All income and gains from whatever source derived*
minus	
Exclusions	*Income excluded by law from taxation (see list of items on page 838)*
equals	
Gross Income	*Income before deductions and exemptions listed below*
minus	
Deductions to Arrive at Adjusted Gross Income	*Business-related expenses and losses; contribution to retirement plans (see discussion on pages 840–841)*
equals	
Adjusted Gross Income	*Significant because several deductible items are computed as a percentage of it*
minus	
Standard Deduction or Itemized Deductions from Adjusted Gross Income	*Itemized deductions allowed by law (see pages 841–843)*
and minus	
Personal Exemptions	*An exemption of specified amount for each taxpayer, spouse, and dependent*
equals	
Taxable Income	*Amount to which appropriate tax rates are applied*

The first of these categories, deductions to arrive *at* adjusted gross income, consists in large part of the costs and expenses incurred *in efforts to generate income.* Among the more common deductions in this category are:

1 **Business expenses of a sole proprietorship.**   These include all ordinary and necessary expenses of carrying on a trade, business, or profession (other than as an employee). For the actual tax computation, business expenses are deducted from business revenue, and net business income is then included in adjusted gross income on the proprietor's tax return.

2 **Expenses attributable to rental properties.**   The owner of rental property, such as an apartment building, incurs a variety of operating expenses. Depreciation, property taxes, repairs, maintenance, interest on indebtedness related to property, and other expenses incurred in connection with the earning of rental income are allowed as deductions. This means that only the *net income* derived from rental property is included in adjusted gross income.

3 **Losses from the sale of property used in a trade or business.** Any loss resulting from the sale of business assets may be deducted from gross income. However, losses arising from the sale of *personal* assets, such as a home, a personal automobile, or furniture are *not* deductible. In general, tax laws *prohibit* deductions for personal expenses, such as rent, meals, clothing, transportation, and entertainment. The reduction over time in the value of personal assets is considered a type of "personal expense."

4 **Net capital losses.**   Up to $3,000 of *net capital losses* may be deducted in arriving at adjusted gross income. Capital losses are discussed further on pages 844–846.

5 **Contributions to retirement plans: IRA and Keogh plans.**   A retirement plan known as IRA (Individual Retirement Arrangement) is one that you set up and contribute to yourself, without any participation by your employer. The purpose is to encourage you to set money aside for your retirement in a personal savings plan. The incentive offered is that your contributions may be fully or partially deductible in computing your current taxable income—that is, not taxable until withdrawn upon your retirement. Moreover, the *income earned* on amounts in the IRA is not taxable until the time of withdrawal. Thus, an IRA may grow more rapidly than most investments because the entire current earnings go to increase the amount invested without any current taxation.

Until recently, almost everyone could receive a tax deduction by contributing up to $2,000 to an IRA plan. This deduction still is available to people who are *not covered* by an employer-sponsored pension plan at work. For taxpayers covered by such plans, the amount of the deduction allowed for contributions to an IRA is "phased-out" as the taxpayer's adjusted gross income rises. Thus, IRA deductions (and contributions) are not as commonplace as they were in the past. Many members of Congress, however, favor reinstating IRA deductions for most taxpayers.

If you are self-employed, a ***Keogh plan*** is a valuable device for reducing your income taxes and building assets for retirement. Individuals who are self-employed are permitted to deduct from gross income the amounts they contribute to a Keogh plan. The present limit on such contributions is the lower of $30,000 or 25% of the self-employment earnings. The amounts contributed, plus earnings on the fund assets, are not taxable until the taxpayer retires and begins making withdrawals from the fund. The Keogh plan is intended to provide self-employed persons with opportunities similar to those of persons employed by companies with pension plans.

6 **Other deductions to arrive at adjusted gross income.** Among other deductions are alimony paid and penalties paid on early withdrawals from long-term savings deposits.

Adjusted Gross Income By deducting from gross income the various items described in the preceding section, we arrive at a very significant total called ***adjusted gross income*** (AGI). This amount is significant because several deductible items such as medical expense and casualty losses are limited by their percentage relationship to adjusted gross income. For example, medical expenses are deductible only to the extent they ***exceed*** $7\frac{1}{2}\%$ of adjusted gross income.

Deductions from Adjusted Gross Income

Taxpayers have a choice with respect to deductions from adjusted gross income. They may choose to take a lump-sum ***standard deduction,*** or they may choose to ***itemize*** their deductions, in which case they can deduct a number of expenses specified in the tax law as itemized deductions.

Standard Deduction Most taxpayers choose to take the standard deduction from adjusted gross income rather than to itemize their deductions by listing such items as mortgage interest payments and state income taxes. In recent years the amounts of the standard deduction were increased substantially to approximately the following levels: $5,700 for married couples filing jointly and $3,400 for single taxpayers. As a matter of convenience, these round amounts are to be used in all exercises and problems in this book which involve the standard deduction. However, the law provides that the amounts of the standard deduction will continue to be adjusted annually for inflation.

Does It Pay to Itemize? Should you itemize your deductions or claim the standard deduction? To find out, add up your deductible expenses to see if the total exceeds the standard deduction. If it does, you will save taxes by itemizing. If the total is less than the standard deduction, you will benefit by claiming the standard deduction. If you itemize deductions, however, you may be asked to provide evidence supporting the nature and amount of the deductions.

Itemized Deductions The major types of itemized deductions allowable under current tax laws are described below.

1 **Mortgage interest.** Interest on mortgages on a first and a second home continues to be deductible. However, consumer interest charges, as on credit cards, auto loans, and boat loans, were phased out during the years from 1988 through 1990.

2 **State income taxes and property taxes.** State income taxes and taxes by local government on real estate and personal property continue to be deductible. Sales taxes and gasoline taxes no longer may be deducted. No *federal* taxes qualify as itemized deductions.

3 **Contributions.** Contributions by individuals to charitable, religious, educational, and certain nonprofit organizations are deductible within certain limits, but only for taxpayers who itemize deductions. In other words, a taxpayer who takes the standard deduction cannot also take deductions for charitable contributions. Gifts to friends, relatives, and other persons are not deductible.

4 **Medical expenses.** Medical and dental expenses may be deducted only to the extent that they exceed $7\frac{1}{2}\%$ of adjusted gross income.

5 **Casualty losses.** Losses in excess of $100 from any fire, storm, earthquake, theft, or other sudden, unexpected, or unusual causes are deductible only to the extent that they exceed 10% of adjusted gross income. For example, assume that a taxpayer with adjusted gross income of $45,000 sustains an uninsured fire loss of $10,100. First, we eliminate $100 of the loss, leaving the amount of $10,000. Next, we reduce the loss by 10% of the adjusted gross income of $45,000, a reduction of $4,500. This leaves $5,500 as the net deduction from adjusted gross income in arriving at the amount subject to tax.

6 **Miscellaneous deductions.** Such items as union dues, investment expenses, professional journals, and deductions for employee business expenses are allowable only to the extent that they exceed 2% of adjusted gross income.

Why Is Only Part of Some "Deductions" Deductible? Notice that some expenses, such as medical expenses and casualty losses, are deductible only to the extent that they *exceed* a specified percentage of adjusted gross income. These "percentage hurdles" are included in the tax law for several specific reasons. One reason is to prevent taxpayers from deducting small "personal" expenses, such as an annual physical examination, over-the-counter medicines, and, perhaps, the theft of a car radio. On the other hand, these rules still provide tax relief to individuals who sustain catastrophic losses.

These percentages also relate the concept of a "catastrophic loss" to the taxpayer's income. To illustrate, assume that a taxpayer incurs medical expenses during the year of $10,000. If this taxpayer has an adjusted gross income of $20,000, $8,500 of these expenses are deductible [$10,000 − ($20,000 × 7.5%) = $8,500]. For a taxpayer with an adjusted gross income of $200,000, none of this $10,000 expense is deductible. The percentage hurdles are one manner in which the tax structure is made more progressive.

Limitations on Deductions for High-Income Taxpayers Beginning in 1991, high-income taxpayers were allowed to deduct only a percentage of their itemized deductions. Up to 20% of a taxpayer's itemized deductions may become nondeductible, based upon the taxpayer's income and filing status. This is an additional means by which the tax structure is made more progressive.

What Qualifies as a Deduction?   Earlier in this chapter, we made the point that only those items specifically identified by law qualify as exclusions. The same concept applies to deductions—unless the tax law specifically states that a type of expense or loss qualifies as a deduction, the item is *not deductible.*

CASE IN POINT   An employee was convicted in court of embezzling $310,000 from his employer. In addition to sentencing the man to prison, the court ordered him to repay his employer. In his income tax return, the embezzler reported the embezzled money as income and deducted the amount returned to his employer as a "business expense."

Tax authorities concurred that the $310,000 in embezzled funds had to be shown as income, because no exclusion exists for illegal income. On the other hand, they disallowed the deduction, stating that the return of stolen funds did not conform to any category of allowable deduction. Thus, the embezzler owed more than $80,000 in income taxes on the embezzled funds which had been returned to the employer. (With the addition of interest and penalties, he owed the tax authorities slightly over $105,000.)

Personal Exemptions

A deduction from adjusted gross income is allowed for one or more **personal exemptions,** as well as for the standard deduction discussed above. An unmarried individual is entitled to one personal exemption, provided that he or she is not listed as a dependent on some other person's tax return. In addition, a taxpayer can claim a personal exemption for each dependent.

An "indexing" plan provides for an annual inflation adjustment of the amount of the personal exemption. As a matter of convenience in illustrations and problems in this book we assume the round amount of $2,000 for each personal exemption. High-income taxpayers are not permitted to take a personal exemption. This denial of personal exemptions to high-income taxpayers makes the tax system more progressive than indicated by the stated rates.

The term **dependent** means a person who (1) receives over one-half of his or her support from the taxpayer, (2) is closely related to the taxpayer or lives in the taxpayer's home, (3) has gross income during the year of less than the current exemption amount unless he or she is a child of the taxpayer and is under 19 years of age or is a full-time student, (4) meets a citizenship test, and (5) does not file a joint return. For any dependent 1 or more years of age, the taxpayer must list the dependent's social security number. To summarize the tax savings from personal exemptions, we assume that each personal exemption reduces taxable income by $2,000. With a tax rate of 30%, the tax saving is $600, computed as $2,000 × 30%.

Taxable Income—Individuals

We have now traced the steps required to determine the taxable income of an individual. In brief, this process includes:

1 Computation of total income
2 Exclusion of certain items specified by law to determine gross income
3 Deduction of business-related expenses to arrive at adjusted gross income
4 Deduction of the standard deduction (or itemized deductions) and personal exemptions to arrive at the key figure of taxable income

The concept of taxable income is important because it is the amount to which the appropriate tax rate is applied to determine the tax liability.

Capital Gains and Losses

As stated earlier, an individual may deduct up to $3,000 in net capital losses as a step in arriving at adjusted gross income. To understand this concept, we first need to understand the nature of capital gains and losses.

Certain kinds of property are defined under the tax laws as **capital assets.** For most individuals, investments in securities and in real estate (including a personal residence) are the most important capital assets. However, **almost everything** that an individual owns is a capital asset, including household furniture, an automobile, jewelry, clothing, artwork, and a stamp or coin collection. Capital assets actually include all assets **other than** those used in a trade or business.

Capital assets have a **basis** for income tax purposes, which is a concept similar to "book value." The **tax basis** of an asset is equal to the asset's cost, less any depreciation which has been allowed for income tax purposes.[3] If any capital asset is sold at a price in excess of its basis, the taxpayer has a capital gain. If a capital asset is sold at a price below its basis, the taxpayer has a capital loss.

All capital gains are included in income subject to income taxes. Two limitations apply, however, to the deductibility of capital losses. First, capital losses on **personal assets,** such as your car or your home, are not deductible at all. Second, the amount of capital losses which can be deducted from other types of income is **limited to $3,000** in any given year.

Tax Treatment of Capital Gains Taxpayers are required to report separately their **short-term** and **long-term** capital gains and losses. Capital gains and losses are classified as long-term when the investor has owned the asset for more than one year.

OBJECTIVE 4 Explain the recent changes in taxation of capital gains and losses.

Short-term capital gains traditionally have been taxed as ordinary income. Until 1986, however, long-term capital gains were given a special and highly favorable tax treatment. Under the "old law," investors were required to include only 40% of long-term capital gains in the computation of taxable income. Thus, 60% of a long-term capital gain was not subject to tax.

---

[3] Basis also may be adjusted for other events, such as casualty losses and "like-kind" exchanges.

The rationale underlying this favorable treatment of long-term capital gains was to encourage the flow of investment capital into new growth industries. In brief, a tax incentive was offered to encourage investors to take risks, rather than to invest in "risk-free" securities, such as government bonds. Almost all industrialized countries give favorable tax treatment to capital gains.

The Tax Reform Act of 1986 eliminated the "preference" accorded to long-term capital gains and called for taxing these gains as ordinary income. The treatment of long-term capital gains remains an area of controversy, and we will address this topic again in a few paragraphs.

Tax Treatment of Capital Losses   Capital losses, whether short-term or long-term, first are offset against any capital gains. A taxpayer whose total capital losses *exceed* total capital gains has a *net capital loss.* On an individual's income tax return, a net capital loss can be deducted only from other income up to a *maximum of $3,000 per year.* The remainder of the loss may be carried forward and offset against capital gains (if any) in future years, or offset against other income at the rate of $3,000 per year.

The limited deductibility of capital losses can pose a serious problem for taxpayers and illustrates the importance of tax planning. For example, assume that John Forbes, an investor, sells an investment late in 1991 and realizes a capital gain of $300,000. Early in 1992, Forbes sells another investment, this time incurring a $300,000 capital loss.

If Forbes had sold both investments in the same year, the gain and loss would have offset one another, and Forbes would owe no tax on these transactions. As it stands, however, Forbes must pay income taxes in 1991 on the entire $300,000 gain, which amounts to about *$90,000* in additional taxes. In his 1992 income tax return, Forbes will be able to deduct only $3,000 of his capital loss, thus reducing his taxes due in that year by only about *$900.* Unless Forbes is able to offset his 1992 loss against future capital gains, it will take him *100 years* to deduct the full amount of this loss in his income tax returns.

This example is intended to make two points. First, Forbes could have avoided this "tax trap" with a little tax planning; he should have sold both investments in the same year. Second, the popular idea that investors *like* to incur financial losses because they can "write them off" is pure fiction.

Business Plant and Equipment   Buildings, equipment, and other depreciable assets used in a trade or business *are not capital assets* under the tax law and are not subject to the $3,000 capital loss limitation. This means that losses realized on sales or disposals of *business* property are fully deductible.

The Changing Treatment of Long-Term Capital Gains

After the Tax Reform Act of 1986, debate continued as to whether or not long-term capital gains should be taxed in a preferential manner. President Bush expressed strong support for *reinstating* favorable treatment for these gains. In 1988, the House of Representatives voted for such reinstatement, but the bill was defeated in the Senate.

In 1991, a very small long-term capital gains preference was reinstated. The tax rate schedules for 1991 included three tax brackets, with progressive tax rates of 15%, 28%, and 31%. Long-term capital gains were taxed as ordinary income, except that the highest tax rate (31%) was not applied to these gains. In 1991, therefore, long-term capital gains were taxed at a maximum rate of 28%.

The present tax status of capital gains may be summarized as follows: (1) taxpayers must identify and report separately net short-term and net long-term capital gains and losses, which then are offset to determine the net capital gain or loss; (2) net capital gains are taxed as ordinary income, except that net long-term capital gains are not taxed at rates in excess of 28%; and (3) net capital losses can be deducted from an individual's other income only to the extent of $3,000 per year. (In our problem material, we will assume that long-term capital gains are taxed as ordinary income, using the tax rate schedules on page 837.)

Investors should watch future developments with respect to the taxation of long-term capital gains. In the event that a highly favorable treatment is reinstated, holding assets until gains become long-term will become a major element of tax planning. Also, investors will favor those assets which offer a good prospect of capital gains, such as stocks and real estate, over those investments with fixed maturity values.

Tax Strategy for Capital Gains and Losses   One widely used tax strategy is to "defer income and accelerate deductions." A first step in carrying out this strategy is to review one's security holdings as the year-end approaches. Identify any investments for which the current market price is less than the taxpayer's cost basis. Consider selling this investment before year-end in order to generate a capital loss which can be offset against any capital gains already realized in the current year or against other income (subject to the $3,000 limitation previously discussed). The sale of an investment in securities to generate a capital loss must not be accompanied by the purchase of the same security within 30 days or the IRS may disallow the loss on grounds that it was part of a "wash transaction."

Computing the Tax Liability

After determining the amount of taxable income, we are ready to compute the gross tax liability. For a single taxpayer, we apply the 15% rate to the first $20,000, the 30% rate to the next $30,000, and the 32% rate to any amount over $50,000. For example, assume that Joe Garcia is single and has taxable income of $60,000. The computation produces a tax (rounded to the nearest dollar) of $15,200, as shown below.

Taxable Income	Tax Rate	Tax
$20,000	15%	$ 3,000
30,000	30%	9,000
10,000	32%	3,200
$60,000		$15,200

For a married couple filing a joint return, first we apply the 15% rate to the first $34,000 of taxable income, next we apply the 30% rate to taxable income above $34,000 but not over $84,000, and finally we apply the 32% rate to any taxable income in excess of $84,000. For example, assume that Patrick and Cheryl Finnegan have taxable income of $100,000. The computation produces a tax (rounded to the nearest dollar) of $25,220, as shown below.

Taxable Income	Tax Rate	Tax
$ 34,000	15%	$ 5,100
50,000	30%	15,000
16,000	32%	5,120
$100,000		$25,220

Tax Credits   The gross tax liability as computed by the methods described above is reduced by subtracting any tax credits. Note that a tax credit is subtracted **directly from the tax owed,** whereas a deduction (as for charitable contributions) is subtracted from adjusted gross income and thus leads to a smaller amount of taxable income to which the tax rate is applied. For many years, tax credits were claimed by many individual taxpayers and by almost every business. However, in recent years, most tax credits have been eliminated. The few remaining tax credits include a credit for qualifying low-income taxpayers and a credit of up to several hundred dollars for child care expenses incurred by working parents.

Tax Prepayments   Taxpayers pay most of their tax liability well **in advance** of filing their income tax return. The most common example of these tax prepayments is the withholding of income taxes from a person's salary. Tax law requires persons with taxable income which is not subject to withholding to pay **estimated taxes** in advance quarterly installments.

The gross tax liability computed in the taxpayer's income tax return is reduced by subtracting all tax prepayments. The remaining amount is the **net tax liability**—the amount to be paid with the tax return. (If the tax prepayments exceed the gross tax liability for the year, the taxpayer is entitled to a **refund** of the difference.)

Tax Returns, Tax Refunds, and Payment of the Tax

The tax return must be filed within $3\frac{1}{2}$ months after the close of the taxable year. Most taxpayers are on a calendar-year basis; therefore, the deadline for filing is April 15. However, the taxpayer has the alternative of paying the tax due at April 15 and requesting an extension of time to August 15 for filing of the return.

Withholding Makes the System Work   Without the withholding feature, the present income tax system would probably be unworkable. The high rate of income taxes would pose an impossible collection problem if employees received their total earnings in cash and were later called upon at the end of the year to pay the government a major portion of a year's salary.

The amounts withheld from an employee's salary for income tax can be considered as payments on account. If the amount of income tax as computed by preparing a tax return at the end of the year is less than the amount withheld during the year, the taxpayer is entitled to a refund. On the other hand, if the tax as computed at year-end is more than the amount withheld, the taxpayer must pay the additional amount with the tax return.

The Deceptive Lure of a Tax Refund Check Most American taxpayers receive tax refunds each year. Apparently these 60 million or more persons so enjoy receiving a refund check that they are willing to have the government withhold excessive amounts of tax from their paychecks throughout the year. The IRS reports that millions of individual taxpayers declare fewer personal exemptions than they expect to claim at year-end. The result is over-withholding of billions of dollars on which the government pays no interest. It is interesting that even during periods of inflation and high interest rates, American taxpayers would choose to have the government hold their money throughout the year with no interest in order to be repaid at year-end in dollars worth less in purchasing power than when earned.

Computation of Individual Income Tax Illustrated

The computation of the federal income tax liability for Mary and John Reed is illustrated below:

MARY AND JOHN REED
Illustrative Federal Income Tax Computation

Gross income (excluding $700 interest on municipal bonds):		
Gross fees from John Reed's law practice..........................	$81,000	
Less: Expenses incurred in law practice.........................	32,000	
Net income from law practice		$ 49,000
Salary received by Mary Reed...		54,400
Dividends received		7,240
Interest received		1,120
Long-term capital gain...		1,000
Gross income		$112,760
Deductions to arrive at adjusted gross income:		
Contribution to Keogh retirement plan.......................................		3,000
Adjusted gross income		$109,760
Deductions from adjusted gross income:		
Itemized deductions	$12,920	
Personal exemptions (4 × $2,000)	8,000	20,920
Taxable income		$ 88,840
Computation of tax:		
Tax on first $34,000 at 15%	$ 5,100	
Tax on next $50,000 at 30%...	15,000	
Tax on remaining $4,840 at 32%....................................	1,549	
Total tax		$21,649
Less: Quarterly payments of estimated tax and amounts withheld:		
Quarterly payments of estimated tax	$ 9,000	
Tax withheld from salary..	11,000	20,000
Tax to be paid with return		$ 1,649

In this example it is assumed that the Reeds provide over one-half the support of their two children. John Reed is a practicing attorney who received $81,000 in gross fees from his law practice and incurred $32,000 of business expenses. Mary Reed earned $54,400 during the year as a CPA working for a national firm of accountants. During the year, $11,000 was withheld from her salary for federal income taxes. Just before the end of the year, John Reed contributed $3,000 to a Keogh retirement plan. The Reeds received $700 interest on municipal bonds and $1,120 interest on savings accounts. Dividends received on stock jointly owned amounted to $7,240. During the year, stock purchased several years ago by John Reed for $2,600 was sold for $3,600, net of brokerage fees, thus producing a $1,000 long-term capital gain.

The Reeds have total itemized deductions of $12,920, including contributions, mortgage interest expense, property taxes, etc. They paid a total of $9,000 on their declaration of estimated tax during the year. In this illustration, as in the assignment material at the end of this chapter, we have for convenience used the amount of $2,000 for each personal exemption.

On the basis of these facts, the taxable income for the Reeds is shown to be $88,840, and the total tax is $21,649. Taking withholdings and quarterly payments of estimated tax into account, the Reeds have already paid income taxes of $20,000 and thus owe $1,649 at the time of filing their tax return.

Alternative Minimum Tax

You may have read newspaper stories about a few high-income individuals who were able through extensive use of tax shelters and various loopholes in the tax law to avoid paying any income tax. Although such cases have been extremely rare, they create strong reaction by the public and by Congress. One goal of recent tax legislation has been to assure that every person with large income pays a significant amount of income tax. The approach taken was to strengthen the **Alternative Minimum Tax** (AMT). This minimum tax requires that you add back to adjusted gross income a long list of deductions (such as state income tax) and tax preferences (such as accelerated depreciation). The total resulting from these additions to adjusted gross income is your Alternative Minimum Tax income. You apply a 24% rate to this total. If your Alternative Minimum Tax is higher than your tax under the regular computation, you must pay the Alternative Minimum Tax.

Partnerships

Partnerships are not taxable entities. Although a partnership pays no income tax, the partnership must file an **information return** showing the computation of net income or loss and the share of net income or loss allocable to each partner. The partners must include in their individual tax returns their respective shares of the net income or loss of the partnership.

INCOME TAXES: CORPORATIONS

OBJECTIVE 5
Contrast the
determina-
tion of taxa-
ble income
for a corpo-
ration with
that for an
individual.

A corporation is a separate taxable entity. Our discussion is focused on the general business corporation and does not cover certain other types of corporations for which special tax treatment applies. Every corporation, unless specifically exempt from taxation, must file an income tax return whether or not it has taxable income or owes any tax.

The earning of taxable income inevitably creates a liability to pay income taxes. This liability and the related charge to expense must be entered in the accounting records before financial statements are prepared. For example:

Income Taxes Expense	60,000	
Income Taxes Payable....................................		60,000
To record corporate income taxes for the current period.		

Corporation Tax Rates

Tax law currently sets the top basic corporate tax rate at 34%, allows lower rates for small corporations, and levies a 5% surtax on a portion of earnings in excess of $100,000. These tax rates are shown in the following table. (These brackets may change in future years, but they will be used for all examples and assignment material in this text.)

Corporate Income Tax Rates

Taxable Income	Rates
First $50,000	15%
Amount over $50,000, but not over $75,000........................	25%
Amount over $75,000, but not over $100,000.......................	34%
Amount over $100,000, but not over $335,000 (includes 5% surtax)	39%
Amount over $335,000	34%

For corporations earning a taxable income in excess of $100,000, the benefit of having part of their income taxed at the lower 15% and 25% rates gradually is phased out. A 5% **surtax** is applied to taxable earnings between $100,000 and $335,000. After taxable income exceeds $335,000, this surtax is discontinued, as it has recouped the benefits which the company derived from the two lower tax brackets.

To illustrate, let us compute the tax for a corporation with taxable income of $1,000,000.

	Taxable Income	Tax Rate	Tax
First	$ 50,000	15%	$ 7,500
Next	25,000	25%	6,250
Next	25,000	34%	8,500
Next	235,000	39%*	91,650
Remaining	665,000	34%	226,100
Total........	$1,000,000		$340,000

*   Includes a 5% surtax designed to deny high-income corporations any benefit from the lower tax rates on the first $75,000 of corporate income.

Notice that the total tax of $340,000 is **exactly 34%** of the entire $1,000,000 of taxable income, indicating that the use of the 5% surtax has nullified the benefits of the 15% and 25% rates for this corporation. Any corporation with taxable income of $335,000 or more pays tax at a flat rate of 34%.

Taxable Income of Corporations

In many respects, the taxable income of corporations is computed by following the same concepts we employ in preparing an income statement. The starting point is total revenue. From this amount, we deduct ordinary and necessary business expenses. However, net income determined by generally accepted accounting principles usually differs from taxable income. The difference is caused by specific rules in the tax laws which prescribe for certain items of revenue and expense a treatment different from that called for by GAAP. Another difference is the fact that from time to time, Congress makes drastic changes in the rules for determining taxable income. Shown below are some of the special factors to be considered in preparing a corporation tax return.

1 **Dividends received.** Dividends received by a corporation on investments in stocks of other domestic corporations are included in gross income, but at least 70% of such dividends can be deducted from gross income.[4] As a result, only 30% or less of dividend income is taxable to the receiving corporation.

2 **Capital gains and losses.** The net capital gains of corporations are taxed as ordinary income. Thus, rates may vary from 15% to 34%. Capital gains are treated the same as any other form of income in determining the extent, if any, to which the 5% surtax is applied. Corporations may deduct capital losses only by offsetting them against capital gains.

3 **Other variations from taxation of individuals.** The concept of adjusted gross income is not applicable to a corporation. There is no standard deduction and no personal exemption. Gross income minus the deductions allowed to corporations equals **taxable income.**

4 **Alternative minimum tax.** The starting point in calculating the Alternative Minimum Tax is the corporation's regular taxable income. This amount is adjusted by recalculating various deductions and deferrals, such as deferred gain on installment sales and any excess of income reported to stockholders over reported taxable income. A 20% minimum tax (AMT) is applied to this recalculated base. The minimum tax must be paid if it is higher than the tax calculated by regular procedures.

Illustrative Tax Computation for Corporation

Shown on the following page is an income statement for Stone Corporation, along with a separate supporting schedule for the tax computation. In this

---

[4] The percentage of dividends received that may be deducted in arriving at taxable income increases to 80% if the investor corporation owns 20% or more of the other company's stock, and to 100% if the investor owns 80% or more of the stock. Thus, a parent company is not taxed upon dividends received from a wholly owned subsidiary.

supporting schedule, we compute the amount of income taxes to appear in the income statement and also show the payments of estimated tax, thus arriving at the amount of tax payable with the tax return.

STONE CORPORATION
Income Statement
For the Year Ended December 31, 19__.

Revenue:		
Sales		$800,000
Dividends received from domestic corporations		20,000
Total revenue		$820,000
Expenses:		
Cost of goods sold	$537,000	
Other expenses (includes capital loss of $13,000)	100,000	637,000
Income before income taxes		$183,000
Income taxes expense		54,230
Net income		$128,770

SCHEDULE A
Computation of Income Tax

Income before income taxes		$183,000
Add back: Items not deductible for tax purposes:		
Capital loss deducted as operating expense		13,000
Subtotal		$196,000
Deduct: Dividends received deduction ($20,000 × 70%)		14,000
Taxable income		$182,000
Income tax:		
15% of first $50,000	$ 7,500	
25% of next $25,000	6,250	
34% of next $25,000	8,500	
39% of $82,000 (includes 5% surtax)	31,980	
Total income tax		$ 54,230
Deduct: Quarterly payments of estimated tax		50,000
Balance of tax payable with tax return		$ 4,230

Deferred Income Taxes

OBJECTIVE 6
Describe the circum-
stances that
create a lia-
bility for
deferred in-
come taxes.

In the determination of pretax **accounting income,** the objective is to measure and report the results of business operations in conformity with generally accepted accounting principles. **Taxable income,** on the other hand, is a legal concept governed by tax law and subject to frequent change by Congress. In setting the rules for determining taxable income, Congress is interested not only in meeting the revenue needs of government, but in achieving a variety of social objectives.

Since accounting income and taxable income are determined with different objectives in mind, it is not surprising that pretax accounting income and taxable income may differ by a material amount. The items causing this difference fall into two broad categories: permanent differences and temporary timing differences.

Permanent differences are revenue or expenses that enter into the computation of one type of income, but never are considered in determining the other. Most permanent differences are the result of special tax law provisions unrelated to accounting principles. For example, interest earned from municipal bonds is included in the determination of accounting income but specifically is excluded from the computation of taxable income. As stated earlier, tax laws also permit corporations to omit from taxable income 70% of the dividends received from investments in stock.

Timing differences arise when the *same dollar amount* of revenue or expense is recognized for tax purposes and for accounting purposes, but the *timing* of the recognition under tax rules differs from that under accounting principles. For example, a company may use an accelerated method of depreciation in its income tax return but use the straight-line method in its income statement. Over the life of the depreciable asset, however, the total amount of depreciation claimed in the tax returns will be the same as that reported in the company's income statements.

As another example, most companies use an allowance method of recognizing uncollectible accounts expense, whereas tax law requires use of the direct write-off method. Over the long run, however, both methods produce the same cumulative results.

Most businesses have a policy of using in their income tax returns those accounting methods which will *accelerate as much as possible the recognition of expenses, and delay as long as possible the recognition of revenue.* As a result of using these methods, many businesses are able to defer the recognition of significant portions of their pretax accounting income into the tax returns of future years. Hence, they are able to defer payment of the related income taxes.

Accounting for Deferred Taxes: An Illustration

When differences between pretax accounting income and taxable income are caused by timing differences, a business bases its income tax expense for the period upon its pretax accounting income. This practice achieves a proper *matching* of income taxes expense with the related earnings. However, some of this income taxes expense will not be paid until later years, when the income is included in future tax returns. Through timing differences, payment of part of a company's income taxes expense may be deferred on a long-term basis.

To illustrate, let us consider a very simple case involving only one timing difference. Assume that Pryor Corporation has before-tax accounting income of $600,000 in both 1993 and 1994. However, the company takes as a tax deduction in 1993 an expense of $200,000 which is not deducted as expense in the income statement until 1994. The company's accounting income, taxable income, and the actual income taxes due (assuming an average tax rate of 34%) are shown below.

	1994	1993
Accounting income (before income taxes)	$600,000	$600,000
Taxable income	800,000	400,000
Actual income taxes due each year at 34% rate:		
1993: $600,000 − $200,000 = $400,000 taxable income × 34%		$136,000
1994: $600,000 + $200,000 = $800,000 taxable income × 34%	$272,000	

Let us assume the Pryor Corporation reports as an expense in its income statement each year the amount of income taxes due for that year. The effect on reported net income as shown in the company's financial statements would be as follows:

Company reports actual taxes

	1994	1993
Accounting income (before income taxes)	$600,000	$600,000
Income taxes expense (amount actually due)	272,000	136,000
Net income	$328,000	$464,000
Income taxes expense as a percentage of pretax accounting income	45%	23%

The readers of Pryor Corporation's income statement might well wonder why the same $600,000 accounting income before income taxes in the two years produced such widely varying amounts of tax expense and net income.

To deal with this distortion between pretax income and after-tax income, an accounting policy known as ***interperiod income tax allocation*** is required for financial reporting purposes.[5] Briefly, the objective of income tax allocation is to ***accrue income taxes expense*** in ***relation to accounting income,*** even if the items comprising accounting income will be taxable or deductible in a different period.

In the Pryor Corporation example, this means we would report in the 1993 income statement a tax expense based on $600,000 of accounting income even though a portion of this income ($200,000) will not be subject to income tax until the second year. The effect of this accounting procedure is demonstrated by the following journal entries to record the income tax expense in each of the two years:

Entries to record income tax allocations

1993	*Income Taxes Expense*	204,000	
	Income Taxes Payable		136,000
	Deferred Income Taxes		68,000
	To record current and deferred income taxes at 34% of accounting income of $600,000.		

Deferred income taxes is a liability. As explained in Chapter 16, classification as current or long-term depends upon the nature of the items causing the tax deferral.[6]

In 1994, the timing difference will "reverse," and Pryor will report taxable income of $200,000 in excess of its pretax accounting income. Thus, the income taxes deferred in 1993 are coming due. The entry to record income taxes expense in 1994 is:

1994	*Income Taxes Expense*	204,000	
	Deferred Income Taxes	68,000	
	Income Taxes Payable		272,000
	To record income taxes at 34% of accounting income of $600,000 and to record actual income taxes due.		

---

[5] For a more complete discussion of tax allocation procedures, see *FASB Statement of Financial Accounting Standards No. 109,* "Accounting for Income Taxes" (Norwalk, Conn.: 1992).

[6] Timing differences also may require a company to pay some income taxes ***before*** the related income appears in accounting income. This situation creates an asset, which might be called Prepaid Income Taxes. In this chapter, we illustrate only the more common situation in which the payment of taxes is deferred, thereby creating a liability.

Notice that as in 1993, income tax expense is based upon the pretax accounting income shown in the company's income statement.

Using these interperiod tax allocation procedures, Pryor Corporation's financial statements would report net income during the two-year period as follows:

	1994	*1993*
Accounting income (before income taxes)	*$600,000*	*$600,000*
Income taxes expense (tax allocation basis)	*204,000*	*204,000*
Net income	*$396,000*	*$396,000*
Income taxes expense as a percentage of pretax accounting income	*34%*	*34%*

Deferred Taxes: An Evaluation   In 1994, Pryor Corporation faces the unpleasant prospect of paying an amount of income taxes which is **greater** than its income taxes expense for the current year. Although this situation can arise, it does not usually happen as long as a company continues to grow.

A growing company usually defers more taxes each year than the previous deferrals which are coming due. Thus, a growing company may pay less in taxes each year than the amount of its current tax expense, and its liability for deferred income taxes continues to grow. The liability for deferred taxes is, in essence, an **interest-free loan**—capital made available to the business by selecting advantageous accounting methods for use in the company's income tax returns. Hence, deferring income taxes generally is viewed as a desirable business strategy.

TAX PLANNING

Federal income tax laws have become so complex that detailed tax planning is now a way of life for most business firms. Almost all companies today engage professional tax specialists to review the tax aspects of major business decisions and to develop plans for legally minimizing income taxes. We will now consider some areas in which tax planning may offer substantial benefits.

Form of Business Organization

OBJECTIVE 7
Explain how tax planning is used in choosing the form of business organization and the capital structure.

Tax factors should be considered at the time a business is organized. As a sole proprietor or partner, a business owner will pay taxes at individual rates (ranging under our assumptions from 15% to 32%) on income earned in any year **whether or not it is withdrawn from the business.** Corporations, on the other hand, are taxed on earnings at rates varying from 15 to 34% under our assumptions. In determining taxable income, corporations deduct salaries paid to owners for services but cannot deduct dividends paid to stockholders. Both **salaries and dividends** are taxable income to the persons receiving them.

These factors must be weighed in deciding in any given situation whether the corporate or noncorporate form of business organization is preferable. There is no simple rule of thumb, even considering only these basic differences. To illustrate, suppose that Able, **an unmarried man,** starts a business which he expects will produce, before any compensation to himself and before income taxes, an average annual income of $80,000. Able plans to withdraw $20,000 yearly from the business. The combined corporate and individual taxes under the corporate and sole proprietorship form of business organization are summarized below.

Form of Business Organization

	Corporation		Sole Proprietorship
Business income		$80,000	$80,000
Salary to Able		20,000	
Taxable income		$60,000	$80,000
Corporate tax:			
15% of first $50,000	$7,500		
25% of next $10,000	2,500	10,000	
Net income		$50,000	$80,000
Combined corporate and individual tax:			
Corporate tax on $60,000 income		$10,000	
Individual tax—single taxpayer*			
On Able's $20,000 salary		3,000	
On Able's $80,000 business income			$21,600
Total tax on business income		$13,000	$21,600

*   Able's personal exemptions and deductions have been ignored, on the assumption that his other income equals personal exemptions and deductions. We have rounded amounts to the nearest dollar.

Under these assumptions, the formation of a corporation is favorable from an income tax viewpoint. If the business is incorporated, the combined tax on the corporation and on Able personally will be $13,000. If the business is not incorporated, the tax will be $21,600, or over 50% more. The key to the advantage indicated for choosing the corporate form of organization is that Able did not take much of the earnings out of the corporation.

If Able decides to operate as a corporation, the $50,000 of net income retained in the corporation will be taxed to Able as ordinary income **when and if** it is distributed as dividends. In other words, Able cannot get the money out of the corporation without paying personal income tax on it. An advantage of the corporation as a form of business organization is that Able can **postpone** payment of a significant amount of tax as long as the earnings remain invested in the business.

If All Earnings of the Business Are to Be Withdrawn   Now let us change one of our basic assumptions and say that Able plans to **withdraw all net income** from the business each year. Under this assumption the sole proprietorship form of organization would be better than a corporation from an income tax standpoint. If the business is incorporated and Able again is to receive a $20,000 salary plus dividends equal to the $50,000 of corporate net income, the total tax will be much higher. The corporate tax of $10,000 plus personal tax of $18,400 (based on $20,000 salary and $50,000 in dividends) would amount to **$28,400.** This is considerably higher than the

$21,600 which we previously computed as the tax liability if the business operated as a proprietorship.

We have purposely kept our example as short as possible. You can imagine some variations which would produce different results. Perhaps Able might incorporate and set his salary at, say, $75,000 instead of $20,000. If this salary were considered reasonable by the IRS, the corporation's taxable income would drop to $5,000 rather than the $60,000 used in our illustration. Thus, the choice between a corporation and a sole proprietorship requires careful consideration of a number of factors in each individual case. Both the marginal rate of tax to which individual business owners are subject and the extent to which profits are to be withdrawn are always basic issues in studying the relative advantages of one form of business organization over another.

Under certain conditions, small, closely held corporations may elect to be **Subchapter S** corporations, in which case the corporation pays no tax but the individual shareholders are taxed directly on the corporation's earnings.

Tax Planning in the Choice of Financial Structure

In deciding upon the best means of raising capital to start or expand a business, consideration should be given to income taxes. Different forms of business financing produce different amounts of tax expense. Interest paid on debt, for example, if **fully deductible** in computing taxable income, but dividends paid on preferred or common stock are not. This factor operates as a strong incentive to finance expansion by borrowing.

The choice of financial structure should be considered from the viewpoint of investors, especially in the case of a small, closely held corporation.

CASE IN POINT   The owners of a small incorporated business decided to invest an additional $100,000 in the business to finance expanding operations. They were undecided whether to make a $100,000 loan to the corporation or to purchase $100,000 worth of additional capital stock. Finally, the owners turned to a CPA firm for advice. The CPAs suggested that the loan would be better because the $100,000 cash invested could be returned by the corporation at the maturity date of the loan without imposing any individual income tax on the owners. The loan could be arranged to mature in installments or at a single fixed date. Renewal of the note could be easily arranged if desired.

On the other hand, if the $100,000 investment were made by purchase of additional shares of capital stock, the return of these funds to the owners would be more difficult. If the $100,000 came back to the owners in the form of dividends, a considerable portion would be consumed by individual income taxes. If the corporation repurchased $100,000 worth of its stock from the owners, the retained earnings account would become restricted by this amount. In summary, the CPAs pointed out that it is easier for persons in control of a small corporation to get their money back if the investment takes the form of a loan rather than the purchase of additional capital stock.

Tax Shelters

A tax shelter is an investment which produces a loss for tax purposes in the near term but hopefully proves profitable in the long run. The reason for seeking a tax loss is to offset this loss against other income and, by so doing, lower both taxable income and the income tax owed for the current year. Near the close of each year, many newspaper advertisements offer an opportunity to invest in a program which promises to reduce the investor's present tax liability yet produce future profits. These programs have a particular appeal to persons in high tax brackets who face the prospect of paying much of a year's net income as taxes.

A limited partnership organization has often been used for tax shelter ventures, so that each investor may claim his or her share of the immediate losses. Typical of the types of ventures are oil and gas drilling programs and real estate investments offering high leverage and accelerated depreciation. The real estate limited partnership appears to have been virtually wiped out by the Tax Reform Act of 1986, but no doubt the promoters of tax shelters will find new loopholes to exploit. A principal appeal of real estate tax shelters has been their use of rapid depreciation to produce losses in early years of the partnership. The change in the law drastically curtails rapid depreciation. A major goal of the Tax Reform Act of 1986 was to curtail or eliminate tax shelters in general. Among the heaviest blows to tax shelters were (1) the elimination of favorable treatment of long-term capital gains, (2) the strengthening of the Alternative Minimum Tax to catch investors deeply involved in sheltering income, and (3) the change to less liberal depreciation. The depreciation of rental residential property is limited to the straight-line method over a period of 27.5 years and other real estate to 31.5 years.

Unfortunately, many so-called tax shelters have proved to be merely unprofitable investments, in which the investors saved taxes but lost larger amounts of capital. A sound approach to tax shelters should probably be based on the premise that if an investment does not appear ***worthwhile without the promised tax benefits, it should be avoided.***

Some tax shelters, on the other hand, are not of a high-risk nature. State and municipal bonds offer a modest rate of interest which is tax exempt. Investment in real estate with deductions for mortgage interest, property taxes, and depreciation will often show losses which offset other taxable income, yet eventually prove profitable because of rising market value, especially in periods of inflation.

END-OF-CHAPTER REVIEW

SUMMARY OF LEARNING OBJECTIVES

1 **Describe the federal income tax: its history and objectives.**
The federal income tax when established in 1913 called for very low rates and was intended only for the purpose of raising revenue for the government. Since then, tax rates have soared, reaching levels as high as 70% in some years. The purposes have broadened to include such objectives as stimulating the economy, protecting the environment, and

enforcing a more equal distribution of the national income. The Tax Reform Act of 1986 was the most drastic revision of the tax laws in many years. Its sweeping changes included relieving millions of low-income taxpayers from paying any income tax, the lowering of tax rates for individuals and corporations, the elimination of many types of deductions, and a shifting of the tax burden from individuals to corporations.

2 Discuss the advantages of the cash basis of accounting for preparation of individual income tax returns.

The cash basis of accounting means that revenue is recognized when received in cash and expenses (except depreciation) are recognized when paid. From the government's viewpoint, the use of the cash basis facilitates collection of taxes, because the taxpayer is required to pay the tax as cash from revenue becomes available. From the taxpayer's viewpoint, the cash basis requires a minimum of record keeping. Yearly amounts of income from salaries, interest, and dividends are reported to individual taxpayers on a cash basis by means of Forms W-2 and 1099. The cash basis also permits tax savings by individuals who deliberately shift the timing of revenue and expense transactions from one year to another. Thus, the taxpayer who will incur a deductible expense near the year-end can choose whether to pay it before or after December 31 and, by this choice, influence the amount of taxable income in each year. In general, the strategy is to accelerate expenses and delay receipt of revenue.

3 State the formula for determining the taxable income of an individual.

A formula for determining the taxable income for individual taxpayers consists of the following steps in gathering and organizing tax data.

a Compute ***total income.***	Consists of all income and gains from whatever source derived.
b Subtract ***exclusions.***	Items which the law says are not taxable, such as interest on municipal bonds.
c Compute ***gross income.***	A subtotal representing total income minus exclusions.
d Subtract ***deductions to arrive at adjusted gross income.***	Gross income is reduced by such items as business expenses, and contributions to retirement plans.
e Compute ***adjusted gross income.***	Consists of gross income minus deductions.
f Subtract ***standard deduction*** or ***itemized deductions.***	Itemized deductions include mortgage interest paid, property taxes, and charitable contributions.
g Subtract ***personal exemptions.***	An exemption of specified amount for each taxpayer, spouse, and dependent.
h Equals ***taxable income.***	Amount to which the tax rates are applied.

4 Explain the recent changes in the taxation of capital gains and losses.

For a great many years, government encouraged taxpayers to invest in capital assets such as securities and real estate. The encouragement was in the form of favorable tax treatment of long-term capital gains. This policy was ended by the Tax Reform Act of 1986, which provided that capital gains should be taxed as ordinary income. In 1991, a very small long-term capital gains preference was reinstated.

5 Contrast the determination of taxable income for a corporation with that for an individual.

Among the points of difference are (a) a separate tax schedule with different rates and brackets; (b) no concept of adjusted gross income, and no standard deduction or personal exemption; (c) only 30% of dividends received by a corporation treated as taxable; and (d) no deduction by a corporation of net capital losses.

6 Describe the circumstances that create a liability for deferred income taxes.

Accounting income measures the results of business operations in accordance with generally accepted accounting principles. Taxable income, on the other hand, measures the results of operations in accordance with the rules of tax law. Because accounting income and taxable income are determined under different rules, the dollar amount of accounting income often differs materially from the amount of taxable income. *Interperiod income tax allocation* is used to accrue income tax expense in the income statement in proportion to the *accounting income* shown in that statement.

Most businesses use in their income tax returns those accounting methods which accelerate the recognition of expenses and delay the recognition of revenue. This policy of deferring the payment of income taxes to future years creates a liability for deferred taxes, often of quite material amount.

7 Explain how tax planning is used in choosing the form of business organization and the capital structure.

An important decision in tax planning is whether a business will achieve tax benefits by incorporating rather than operating as a sole proprietorship or partnership. The decision will vary from case to case depending on such factors as the tax bracket of the owners as individual taxpayers, and the intent of the owners to withdraw earnings from the corporation in the form of dividends as opposed to retaining earnings in the corporation to facilitate growth of the business.

In deciding on a capital structure, the owners of a business should be aware that interest on debt such as bonds and notes payable is deductible in arriving at taxable income, but dividends paid on common or preferred stock are not.

KEY TERMS INTRODUCED OR EMPHASIZED IN CHAPTER 18

Adjusted gross income   A subtotal in an individual's tax return computed by deducting from gross income any business-related expenses and other deductions authorized by law. A key figure to which many measurements are linked.

Capital asset   Stocks, bonds, and real estate not used in a trade or business.

Capital gain or loss   The difference between the cost basis of a capital asset and the amount received from its sale.

Cash basis of accounting   Revenue is recorded when received in cash and expenses are recorded in the period in which payment is made. Widely used for individual tax returns and for tax returns of professional firms, farms, and service-type businesses. Gives taxpayers a degree of control over taxable income by deliberate timing of collections and payments. Not used in most financial statements because it fails to match revenue with related expenses.

Gross income   All income and gains from whatever source derived unless specifically excluded by law, such as interest on state and municipal bonds.

Interperiod tax allocation   Allocation of income tax expense among accounting periods because of timing differences between accounting income and taxable income. Causes income tax expense reported in financial statements to be in logical relationship to accounting income.

Itemized deductions   Personal expenses deductible from adjusted gross income, such as mortgage interest, property taxes, contributions, and medical expenses and casualty losses in excess of certain amounts.

Personal exemption   A deduction of specified amounts from adjusted gross income for the taxpayer, the taxpayer's spouse, and each dependent.

Standard deduction   A specified amount to be deducted from adjusted gross income. An alternative to listing itemized deductions, such as mortgage interest and property taxes.

Tax credit   An amount to be subtracted from the tax itself. Examples are the earned income credit and the credit for child care expenses.

Tax planning   A systematic process of minimizing income taxes by considering in advance the tax consequences of alternative business or investment actions. A major factor in choosing the form of business organization and capital structure, in lease-or-buy decisions, and in timing of transactions.

Tax shelters   Investment programs designed to show losses in the short term to be offset against other taxable income, but offering the hope of long-run profits.

Taxable income   The computed amount to which the appropriate tax rate is to be applied to arrive at the tax liability.

SELF-TEST QUESTIONS

Answers to these questions appear on page 874.

1   Which of the following statements is applicable to the federal income tax system in the United States? (More than one answer may be correct.)

   a   A taxpayer who structures a transaction so as to lower or avoid income taxes is guilty of tax evasion.

   b   The major classes of taxpayers are individuals, sole proprietorships, partnerships, and corporations.

   c   Individuals and corporations have numerous legal means of reducing their income tax obligations through tax planning.

   d   The original United States Constitution provided for a federal income tax system and authorized the Treasury Department to pass new tax legislation as necessary.

2   In preparing the income tax return for an individual taxpayer:

   a   Federal income taxes withheld from an individual's salary are deducted from taxable income before computing the tax liability.

    b A cash basis taxpayer may postpone paying an expense in order to receive a tax deduction in a subsequent year.

    c Individual taxpayers may choose to itemize their deductions or to deduct the personal exemptions, but they are not allowed to deduct both.

    d Receipt of a large refund each year indicates better tax planning than does receipt of a very small refund.

3 Following the Tax Reform Act of 1986, the status of capital gains and losses became as follows: (More than one answer may be correct.)

    a In computing adjusted gross income for individuals, only $3,000 of capital losses may be offset against capital gains.

    b Short-term capital gains are taxed at the same rate as other income.

    c An individual taxpayer who had a net capital gain of $10,000 in 1991 was taxed on the entire amount in 1991; a taxpayer who had a net capital loss of $10,000 in 1991 was permitted to deduct only $3,000 in 1991.

    d Capital assets include assets used in a trade or business but not items such as a personal residence or an automobile acquired for personal use.

4 When a business is organized as a corporation:

    a Income taxes expense recorded in the accounting records is based upon accounting income and may differ from the income tax liability shown in the corporate income tax return.

    b The treatment of capital gains and losses is the same as for individuals—capital gains are taxed at ordinary income rates; net capital losses of $3,000 may be deducted in computing taxable income.

    c The amount of the standard deduction is greater than the amount of standard deduction for individuals.

    d Taxable income is the same as net income before taxes in the income statement.

5 Which of the following are valid statements regarding tax planning and the choice of business organization? (More than one answer may be correct.)

    a When a business is organized as a corporation, no income tax is paid on earnings that remain invested in the business.

    b In computing a corporation's taxable income, the corporation may deduct salaries paid to owners, but may not deduct dividends.

    c When a business is organized as a sole proprietorship, the owner must pay taxes at individual rates on the entire amount of business income, regardless of amounts withdrawn by the owner.

    d An individual who organizes a business as a corporation must pay individual income taxes on any salary received from the corporation, as well as on any dividends received.

ASSIGNMENT MATERIAL

DISCUSSION QUESTIONS

1 What are the four major classes of taxpayers under the federal income tax law?

2 Explain the differences between *tax planning* and *tax evasion,* and give an example of each.

3 Why is the American income tax system described as one of **self-assessment?** What means do tax authorities have of enforcing this system?

4 State in equation form the federal income tax formula for individuals, beginning with total income and ending with taxable income.

5 Shirley Hill, M.D., files her income tax return on a cash basis. During the current year, she collected $18,900 from patients for medical services rendered in the prior year and billed patients for $115,500 for services rendered this year. At the end of the current year, she had $24,600 in accounts receivable relating to the current year's billings. What amount of gross income from her practice should Hill report on her tax return?

6 An individual with a yearly salary of $40,000 had a net capital loss of $60,000. To what extent, if any, can this capital loss be offset against salary in computing taxable income? Explain.

7 Explain the principal factors which should be considered by a taxpayer in determining **when** it would be most advantageous to sell an investment which will result in the recognition of a large capital loss.

8 What is meant by the phrase "preferential treatment for long-term capital gains"? Do long-term capital gains receive a preferential tax treatment today? Explain.

9 List some differences between the tax rules for corporations and the tax rules for individuals.

10 Explain the origin of a liability for deferred income taxes. What does an increase in this liability over the period imply about the relationship between the income tax expense reported in the income statement and the amount of cash payments for income taxes during the year?

11 Explain the advantages to the sole owner of a small corporation of supplying capital to this business in the form of a loan, rather than as an equity investment.

12 How did the income tax rates for individuals during the 1980s compare with the rates prevailing in the 1970s? Explain.

13 State two goals of tax planning.

14 "The increase in the standard deduction by the Tax Reform Act of 1986 was primarily of benefit to those individuals who usually did not itemize their deductions." Do you agree with this statement? Explain.

15 It has been claimed that corporate income is subject to "double taxation." Explain the meaning of this expression.

16 Taxes are characterized as **progressive, proportional,** or **regressive** with respect to any given base. Describe an income tax structure that would fit each of these characterizations.

17 Andrew Schmidt, a single man, files his income tax return on a cash basis. During 1992, $800 of interest was credited to him on his savings account; he withdrew his interest on January 18 of 1993. No other interest and no dividends were received by Schmidt. In December of 1992, Schmidt purchased some business equipment having an estimated service life of 10 years. He also paid a year's rent in advance on certain business property on December 29 of 1992. Explain how these items would be treated on Schmidt's income tax return for 1992.

18 Which of the following is not a capital asset according to the Internal Revenue Code?

  a An investment in General Motors stock

  b A personal residence

  c Equipment used in the operations of a business

  d An investment in Krugerrands (gold coins)

19 Even when a taxpayer uses the accrual method of accounting for tax purposes, taxable income may differ from accounting income. Give four examples of differences between the tax treatment and accounting treatment of items that are included in the determination of income.

20 Under what circumstances is the accounting procedure known as **income tax allocation** appropriate? Explain the purpose of this procedure.

21 List some tax factors to be considered in deciding whether to organize a new business as a corporation or as a partnership.

22 Explain how the corporate income tax makes debt financing in general more attractive than financing through the issuance of preferred stock.

23 Some of the decisions that business owners must make in organizing and operating a business will affect the amount of income taxes to be paid. List some of these decisions which affect the amount of income taxes legally payable.

EXERCISES

Listed below are nine technical accounting terms emphasized in this chapter:

Alternative Minimum Tax	*Itemized deductions*	*Tax credit*
Adjusted gross income	*Tax shelter*	*Personal exemption*
Deferred income taxes	*Standard deduction*	*Cash basis of accounting*

Each of the following statements may (or may not) describe one of these technical terms. For each statement, indicate the accounting term described, or answer "None" if the statement does not correctly describe any of the terms.

  a Important to individual taxpayers who pay large amounts of state income tax, have a home mortgage, or make large charitable contributions.

  b An amount subtracted from the gross tax liability.

  c Assures that profitable corporations and high-income individuals do not escape taxation altogether through any combination of tax shelters and tax preferences.

  d A subtotal in an individual's tax return, computed by deducting from gross income any business-related expenses, contributions to retirement plans, and other deductions authorized by law.

  e Revenue recorded when received in cash and expenses recorded in period payment is made.

  f Income tax recognized each period as a constant percentage of net sales.

  g An investment program designed to show losses in the short run to be offset against other taxable income, but offering the hope of long-run profits.

  h An option chosen by many individual taxpayers who do not own a home and whose payments of state income taxes are small.

  i A liability which comes into existence as the result of permanent differences between tax rules and accounting principles which benefit the taxpayer.

**EXERCISE 18-2
Cash Basis or
Accrual Basis**

Individual taxpayers have the choice of preparing their income tax returns on the cash basis of accounting or on the accrual basis. However, nearly all tax returns filed by individuals are prepared on the cash basis. Many small corporations in service-type businesses also file on the cash basis. How do you explain:

a The strong preference by taxpayers for the cash basis of accounting?

b The government's willingness to accept tax returns prepared on the cash basis in an era in which the accrual basis is the standard approach underlying generally accepted accounting principles?

**EXERCISE 18-3
Gross Income:
Items to Include
and Items
to Exclude**

You are to consider the income tax status of the items listed below. List the numbers 1 to 15 on your answer sheet. For each item state whether it is ***included in gross income*** or ***excluded from gross income*** for federal income tax on individuals. Add explanatory comments if needed.

1 Inheritance of ranch from estate of deceased uncle

2 Amount received as damages for injury in automobile accident

3 Tips received by waiter

4 Pension received by veteran from U.S. government for military service

5 Dividends received on investment in Ford Motor stock

6 Trip to London received by employee as award for outstanding performance

7 Rent received on personal residence while on an extended European tour

8 First prize of $14 million won in California state lottery

9 Gain on the sale of a 1953 Jaguar purchased 10 years ago

10 Proceeds of life insurance policy received on death of spouse

11 Share of income from partnership in excess of drawings

12 Gain on sale of Super Bowl tickets by season ticket holder

13 Interest received on bonds of state of Texas

14 Value of U.S. Savings Bonds received as a gift

15 Salary received from corporation by a stockholder who owns all of the corporation's capital stock

**EXERCISE 18-4
Is It
Deductible?**

You are to determine the deductibility status, for federal income tax purposes, of each of the items listed below. List the numbers 1 to 10 on your answer sheet. For each item state whether the item is ***deducted to arrive at adjusted gross income; deducted from adjusted gross income;*** or ***not deductible.***

1 Sales taxes

2 Medical expense of $2,000 incurred by a taxpayer with adjusted gross income of $50,000

3 State income tax paid

4 Property taxes paid on personal residence

5 Interest paid on mortgage on personal residence

6 Loss on sale of equipment used in a business

7 Capital loss on sale of an investment in securities

8 Contribution to a Keogh retirement plan

9 Depreciation on rental property

10 Damage by storm to motorboat used for pleasure

The Approach to Preparing a Statement of Cash Flows

The items listed in an income statement or a balance sheet represent the balances of specific general ledger accounts. Notice, however, that the captions used in the statement of cash flows *do not* correspond to specific ledger accounts. A statement of cash flows summarizes *cash transactions* during the accounting period. The general ledger, however, is maintained on the *accrual basis* of accounting, not the cash basis. Thus, an amount such as "Cash received from customers . . . $870,000" does not appear as the balance in a specific ledger account.

In a very small business, it may be practical to prepare a statement of cash flows directly from the special journals for cash receipts and cash payments. For most businesses, however, it is easier to prepare the statement of cash flows by examining the income statement and the *changes* during the period in all of the balance sheet accounts *except for* Cash. This approach is based upon the double-entry system of accounting; any transaction affecting cash must also affect some other asset, liability, or owners' equity account.[5] The change in these *other accounts* makes clear the nature of the cash transaction.

To illustrate this approach, assume that the Marketable Securities controlling account of Allison Corporation shows the following activity during the year:

Balance, January 1, 19___	$ 70,000
Debit entries during the year	65,000
Credit entries during the year	(44,000)
Balance, December 31, 19___	$ 91,000

Also assume that the company's income statement for the year includes a *$4,000 loss* on sales of marketable securities.

The *debit entries* in the Marketable Securities account represent the cost of securities *purchased* during the year. These debit entries provide the basis for the item *"Purchases of marketable securities . . . $(65,000)"* appearing in the investing activities section of the statement of cash flows (page 878). Thus, increases in the asset Marketable Securities correspond to an outflow of cash.

The credit entries of $44,000 represent the *cost* of securities sold during the year. Remember, however, that the income statement shows that these securities were sold at a *loss of $4,000.* The cash proceeds from these sales, which also appear in the statement of cash flows, may be computed as follows:

Cost of marketable securities sold	$44,000
Less: Loss on sales of marketable securities	4,000
Proceeds from sales of marketable securities	$40,000

By looking at the changes occurring in the Marketable Securities account and the related income statement account, we were able to determine quickly two items appearing in the company's statement of cash

---

[5] Accounts used to record revenue, expenses, and dividends are "owners' equity accounts," as they ultimately are closed into the Retained Earnings account.

flows. We could have assembled the same information from the company's cash journals, but we would have had to review the journals for the entire year and then added together the cash flows of numerous individual transactions. In summary, it usually is more efficient to prepare a statement of cash flows by analyzing the *changes in noncash accounts* than by locating and combining numerous entries in the company's journals.

PREPARING A STATEMENT OF CASH FLOWS: AN ILLUSTRATION

Earlier in this chapter we illustrated the statement of cash flows of Allison Corporation. We will now show how this statement was developed from the company's accrual-basis accounting records. Shown below are the company's income statement and the necessary information about changes in balance sheet accounts during the year.

ALLISON CORPORATION
Income Statement
For the Year Ended December 31, 19__

Revenue and gains:		
Net sales		$900,000
Dividends revenue		3,000
Interest revenue		6,000
Gain on sales of plant assets.............................		31,000
Total revenue and gains...............................		$940,000
Costs, expenses, and losses:		
Cost of goods sold	$500,000	
Operating expenses (including depreciation of $40,000)........	300,000	
Interest expense	35,000	
Income taxes expense	36,000	
Loss on sales of marketable securities	4,000	
Total costs, expenses, and losses		875,000
Net income		$ 65,000

Additional Information An analysis of changes in the balance sheet accounts of Allison Corporation provides the following information about the company's activities in the current year. To assist in the preparation of a statement of cash flows, we have classified this information into the categories of operating activities, investing activities, and financing activities.

Operating Activities

1 Accounts receivable increased by $30,000 during the year.

2 Dividend revenue is recognized on the cash basis, but interest revenue is recognized on the accrual basis. Accrued interest receivable decreased by $1,000 during the year.

3 Inventory increased by $10,000 and accounts payable increased by $15,000 during the year.

4 During the year, short-term prepaid expenses increased by $3,000 and accrued expenses payable (other than for interest or income taxes) decreased by $6,000. Depreciation for the year amounted to $40,000.

5 The accrued liability for interest payable increased by $7,000 during the year.

6 The accrued liability for income taxes payable decreased by $2,000 during the year.

Investing Activities

7 Analysis of the Marketable Securities account shows debit entries of $65,000, representing the cost of securities purchased, and credit entries of $44,000, representing the cost of securities sold. (None of the marketable securities is viewed as a cash equivalent.)

8 Analysis of the Notes Receivable account shows $17,000 in debit entries, representing cash lent to borrowers by Allison Corporation during the year, and $12,000 in credit entries, representing collections of notes receivable. (Collections of interest were recorded in the Interest Revenue account and are considered cash flows from operating activities.)

9 Allison Corporation purchased plant assets for $200,000 during the year, paying $160,000 cash and issuing a long-term note payable for the $40,000 balance. In addition, the company sold plant assets with a book value of $44,000.

Financing Activities

10 During the year, Allison Corporation borrowed $45,000 cash by issuing short-term notes payable to banks. Also, the company repaid $55,000 in principal amounts due on these loans and other notes payable. (Interest payments are classified as operating activities.)

11 The company issued bonds payable for $100,000 cash.

12 The company issued for cash 1,000 shares of $10 par value capital stock at a price of $50 per share.

13 Cash dividends declared and paid to stockholders amounted to $40,000 during the year.

Cash and Cash Equivalents

14 Cash and cash equivalents as shown in Allison Corporation's balance sheets amounted to $40,000 at the beginning of the year and $75,000 at year-end—a net increase of $35,000.

Using this information, we will now illustrate the steps in preparing Allison Corporation's statement of cash flows and also a supporting schedule disclosing the "noncash" investing and financing activities. In our discussion, we will often refer to these items of "Additional Information" by citing the paragraph numbers shown in the above list.

The distinction between accrual-basis measurements and cash flows is of fundamental importance in understanding financial statements and other accounting reports. To assist in making this distinction, we use two colors in our illustrated computations. We show in blue the accrual-based data from Allison Corporation's income statement and the preceding numbered paragraphs. The cash flows that we compute from this data are shown in black.

Cash Flows from Operating Activities

OBJECTIVE 3 Compute the major cash flows relating to operating activities.

As shown in our statement of cash flows on page 878, the net cash flow from operating activities is determined by combining certain cash inflows and subtracting certain cash outflows. The inflows are cash received from customers, and interest and dividends received; the outflows are cash paid to suppliers and employees, interest paid, and income taxes paid.

In computing each of these cash flows, our starting point is an income statement amount, such as net sales, the cost of goods sold, or interest expense. As you study each computation, be sure that you **understand why** the income statement amount must be increased or decreased to determine the related cash flow. You will find that an understanding of these computations will do more than show you how to compute cash flows: it will also strengthen your understanding of the income statement and the balance sheet.

Cash Received from Customers To the extent that sales are made for cash, there is no difference between the amount of cash received from customers and the amount recorded as sales revenue. Differences do arise, however, when sales are made on account. If accounts receivable have increased during the year, credit sales have exceeded collections of accounts receivable. Therefore, we must **deduct the increase** in accounts receivable over the year from net sales in order to determine the amount of cash received. If accounts receivable have decreased over the year, collections of these accounts must have exceeded credit sales. Therefore, we must **add the decrease** in accounts receivable to net sales to determine the amount of cash received. The relationship between cash received from customers and net sales is summarized below:

$$\begin{array}{c}\textbf{Cash Received}\\\textbf{from Customers}\end{array} = \begin{array}{c}\textbf{Net}\\\textbf{Sales}\end{array}\left\{\begin{array}{c}\textbf{+ Decrease in Accounts Receivable}\\\textbf{or}\\\textbf{- Increase in Accounts Receivable}\end{array}\right\}$$

The increase or decrease in accounts receivable is determined simply by comparing the year-end balance in the account to its balance at the beginning of the year.

In our Allison Corporation example, paragraph **1** of the Additional Information tells us that accounts receivable have **increased** by $30,000 during the year. The income statement shows net sales for the year of $900,000. Therefore, the amount of cash received from customers may be computed as follows:

Net sales (accrual basis)...	*$900,000*
Less: Increase in accounts receivable...	*30,000*
Cash received from customers...	**$870,000**

Interest and Dividends Received Our next objective is to determine the amounts of cash received during the year as dividends and interest. As explained in paragraph **2** of the Additional Information, dividend revenue is recorded on the cash basis. Therefore, the $3,000 shown in the income statement also represents the amount of cash received as dividends.

Interest revenue, on the other hand, is recognized on the accrual basis. We have already shown how to convert one type of revenue, net sales, from the accrual basis to the cash basis. We may use the same approach in converting interest revenue from the accrual basis to the cash basis. Our formula for converting net sales to the cash basis may be modified to convert interest revenue to the cash basis as follows:

$$\begin{array}{ccc} \textbf{Interest} \\ \textbf{Received} \end{array} = \begin{array}{c} \textbf{Interest} \\ \textbf{Revenue} \end{array} \left\{ \begin{array}{c} \textbf{+ Decrease in Interest Receivable} \\ \textbf{or} \\ \textbf{− Increase in Interest Receivable} \end{array} \right\}$$

The income statement for Allison Corporation shows interest revenue of $6,000, and paragraph **2** states that the amount of accrued interest receivable has **decreased** by $1,000 during the year. Thus, the amount of cash received as interest may be computed as follows:

Interest revenue (accrual basis)	$6,000
Add: Decrease in accrued interest receivable	1,000
Interest received (cash basis)	$7,000

The amounts of interest and dividends received in cash are combined for presentation in the statement of cash flows:

Interest received (cash basis)	$ 7,000
Dividends received (cash basis)	3,000
Interest and dividends received	$10,000

Cash Payments for Merchandise and for Expenses

The next item in the statement of cash flows, "Cash paid to suppliers and employees," includes all cash payments for purchases of merchandise and for operating expenses (all expenses other than interest and income taxes). Payments of interest and income taxes are listed as a separate item in the statement. The amounts of cash paid for purchases of merchandise and for operating expenses are computed separately.

Cash Paid for Purchases of Merchandise An accrual basis income statement reflects the **cost of goods sold** during the year, regardless of whether the merchandise was acquired or paid for in that period. The statement of cash flows, on the other hand, reports the **cash paid** for merchandise during the year, even if the merchandise was acquired in a previous period or remains unsold at year-end. The relationship between cash payments for merchandise and the cost of goods sold depends upon the changes during the period in **two** related balance sheet accounts: inventory and accounts payable to suppliers of merchandise. This relationship may be stated as follows:

$$\text{Cash Payments for Purchases} = \text{Cost of Goods Sold} \begin{Bmatrix} \textbf{+ Increase in} \\ \textbf{Inventory} \\ \text{or} \\ \textbf{−Decrease in} \\ \textbf{Inventory} \end{Bmatrix} \text{and} \begin{Bmatrix} \textbf{+ Decrease in} \\ \textbf{Accounts Payable} \\ \text{or} \\ \textbf{−Increase in} \\ \textbf{Accounts Payable} \end{Bmatrix}$$

Suppliers

Using information from the Allison Corporation income statement and paragraph **3,** the cash payments for purchases may be computed as follows:

Cost of goods sold	*$500,000*
Add: Increase in inventory	*10,000*
Net purchases (accrual basis)	*$510,000*
Less: Increase in accounts payable to suppliers	*15,000*
Cash payments for purchases of merchandise	***$495,000***

Let us review the logic behind this computation. If a company is increasing its inventory, it will be ***buying more merchandise than it sells*** during the period; furthermore, if the company is increasing its account payable to merchandise creditors, it is ***not paying cash*** for all of these purchases.

Cash Payments for Expense   Expenses, as shown in the income statement, represent the cost of goods and services used up during the period. However, the amounts shown as expenses may differ significantly from the cash payments made during the period. Consider, for example, depreciation expense. Recording depreciation expense ***requires no cash payment,*** but it does increase total expenses measured on the accrual basis. Thus, in converting accrual-basis expenses to the cash basis, we must deduct depreciation expense and any other "noncash" expenses from our accrual-basis operating expenses. The other "noncash" expenses—expenses not requiring cash outlays—include amortization of intangible assets and amortization of bond discount.

A second area of difference arises from short-term timing differences between the recognition of expenses and the actual cash payments. Expenses are recorded in accounting records when the related goods or services are used. However, the cash payments for these expenses might occur (1) in an earlier period, (2) in the same period, or (3) in a later period. Let us briefly consider each case.

1 If payment is made in advance, the payment creates an asset, termed a prepaid expense, or, in our formula, a "prepayment." Thus, to the extent that prepaid expenses increase over the year, cash payments ***exceed*** the amount recognized as expense.

2 If payment is made in the same period, no problem arises because the cash payment is equal to the amount of expense.

3 If payment is made in a later period, the payment reduces a liability for an accrued expense payable. Thus, to the extent that accrued expenses payable decrease over the year, cash payments exceed the amount recognized as expense.

The relationship between cash payments and accrual-basis expenses are summarized below:

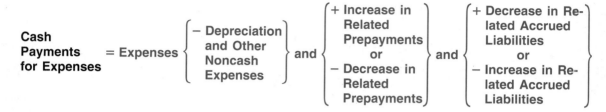

In a statement of cash flows, cash payments for interest and for income taxes are shown separately from cash payments for operating expenses. Using data from Allison Corporation's income statement and from paragraph **4,** we may compute the company's cash payments for operating expenses as follows:

Operating expenses (including depreciation).....................................		$300,000
Less: Noncash expenses (depreciation)		40,000
Subtotal...		$260,000
Add: Increase in short-term prepayments	$3,000	
Decrease in accrued liabilities.................................	6,000	9,000
Cash payments for operating expenses		**$269,000**

Cash Paid to Suppliers and Employees The caption used in our cash flow statement, "Cash paid to suppliers and employees," includes both cash payments for purchases of merchandise and for operating expenses. This cash outflow may now be computed as follows:

Cash payments for purchases of merchandise..................................	$495,000
Cash payments for operating expenses	269,000
Cash payments to suppliers and employees	**$764,000**

Cash Payments for Interest and Taxes Interest expense and income taxes expense may be converted to cash payments with the same formula we used to convert operating expenses. Allison Corporation's income statement shows interest expense of $35,000, and paragraph **5** states that the liability for interest payable increased by $7,000 during the year. The fact that the liability for unpaid interest *increased* over the year means that *not all of the interest expense shown in the income statement was paid in cash.* To determine the amount of interest actually paid, we must *subtract* from total interest expense the portion that has been financed through an increase in the liability for interest payable. This computation is shown below:

Interest expense...	$35,000
Less: Increase in related accrued liability.......................................	7,000
Interest paid	**$28,000**

Similar reasoning is used in determining the amount of income taxes paid by Allison Corporation during the year. The accrual-based income taxes expense, reported in the income statement, amounts to $36,000. However, paragraph **6** states that the company has reduced its liability for income taxes payable by $2,000 over the year. Incurring income taxes expense increases the tax liability; making cash payments to tax authorities reduces it. Thus, if the liability **decreases** over the year, cash payments to tax authorities **must have been greater** than the income taxes expense for the current year. The amount of the cash payments is determined as follows:

Income taxes expense	$36,000
Add: Decrease in related accrued liability ...~Income TAX PAYABLE~......	2,000
Income taxes paid	**$38,000**

A Quick Review We have now shown the computation of each cash flow relating to Allison Corporation's operating activities. Previously we illustrated a complete statement of cash flows for the company. For your convenience, we will again show the operating activities section of that statement, illustrating the information developed in the preceding paragraphs.

Cash flows from operating activities:		
Cash received from customers	$ 870,000	
Interest and dividends received	10,000	
Cash provided by operating activities		$ 880,000
Cash paid to suppliers and employees	$(764,000)	
Interest paid	(28,000)	
Income taxes paid	(38,000)	
Cash disbursed for operating activities		(830,000)
Net cash flow from operating activities		$ 50,000

Differences between Net Income and Net Cash Flow from Operating Activities

Allison Corporation reported net income of **$65,000,** but net cash flow from operating activities of only **$50,000.** What caused this $15,000 difference?

OBJECTIVE 4 Explain why net income differs from net cash flow from operating activities.

The answer, in short, is many things. First, **depreciation expense** reduces net income but does not affect net cash flow. Next, all the adjustments that we made to net sales, cost of goods sold, and expenses represented short-term **timing differences** between net income and the underlying net cash flow from operating activities. Finally, **nonoperating gains and losses** may cause substantial differences between net income and net cash flow from operations.

Nonoperating gains and losses may result from sales of plant assets, marketable securities, and other investments; or from the retirement of long-term debt. These gains and losses affect the cash flows relating to investing or financing activities, not the cash flows from operating activities.

Reporting Operating Cash Flow: The Direct and Indirect Methods

OBJECTIVE 5
Distinguish
between the
direct and
indirect
methods of
reporting
operating
cash flow.

In our illustration, we use the ***direct method*** of computing and reporting the net cash flow from operating activities. The direct method shows the ***specific cash inflows and outflows*** comprising the operating activities of the business. The FASB has expressed its preference for the direct method, but it also allows companies to use an alternative, called the ***indirect method.***

Computation of net cash flow from operating activities by the indirect method looks quite different from the direct method computation. However, both methods result in the ***same net cash flow*** from operating activities. Under the indirect method, the computation begins with accrual-based net income (as shown in the income statement) and then shows the various adjustments necessary to ***reconcile net income with net cash flow from operating activities.*** The general format of this computation is summarized below:

Net income
Add: ■ Expenses that do not require cash outlays in the period (such as depreciation expense)
■ Operating cash inflows not recorded as revenue in the period
■ "Nonoperating" losses deducted in the determination of net income
Less: ■ Revenue that does not result in cash inflows in the period
■ Operating cash outflows not recorded as expense in the period
■ "Nonoperating" gains included in the determination of net income
Net cash flow from operating activities

The above summary describes the differences between net income and net cash flow from operating activities in broad, general terms. In an actual statement of cash flows, a dozen or more specific items may appear in this reconciliation. (Supplementary Schedule A, on page 892, illustrates the application of the indirect method to the operating activities of Allison Corporation.)

In this chapter we emphasize the ***direct*** method, as we consider it to be the more informative approach and it is the method recommended by the FASB. Most of our assignment material is based upon the direct method. Further coverage of the indirect method is provided in the first Supplemental Topic section* at the end of the chapter.

Cash Flows from Investing Activities

OBJECTIVE 6
Compute the
cash flows
relating to
investing
and financ-
ing activi-
ties.

Paragraphs **7** through **9** in the Additional Information for our Allison Corporation example provide most of the information necessary to determine the cash flows from investing activities. In the following discussion, we will illustrate the presentation of these cash flows and also explain the sources of the information contained in the numbered paragraphs.

Much information about investing activities can be obtained simply by looking at the changes in the related asset accounts during the year. Debit entries in these accounts represent purchases of the assets, or cash out-

* *Supplemental Topic A, "The Indirect Method"*

lays. Credit entries represent sales of the assets, or cash receipts. However, credit entries in asset accounts represent only the *cost (or book value)* of the assets sold. To determine the cash proceeds from these sales transactions, we must adjust the amount of the credit entries for any gains or losses recognized on the sales.

Purchases and Sales of Securities   To illustrate, consider paragraph **7,** which summarizes the debit and credit entries to the Marketable Securities account. As explained earlier in this chapter, the $65,000 in debit entries represent purchases of marketable securities. The $44,000 in credit entries represent the *cost* of marketable securities sold during the period. However, the income statement shows that these securities were sold at a *$4,000 loss.* Thus, the cash proceeds from these sales amounted to only *$40,000* ($44,000 cost, minus $4,000 loss on sale). In the statement of cash flows, these investing activities are summarized as follows:

Purchases of marketable securities	**$(65,000)**
Proceeds from sales of marketable securities.................................	**$ 40,000**

Loans Made and Collected   Paragraph **8** provides all the information necessary to summarize the cash flows from making and collecting loans:

Loans made to borrowers..	**$(17,000)**
Collections on loans...	**$ 12,000**

This information comes directly from the Notes Receivable account. Debit entries in the account represent new loans made during the year; credit entries indicate collections of the *principal* amount on outstanding notes (loans). (Interest received is credited to the Interest Revenue account and is included among the cash receipts from operating activities.)

Cash Paid to Acquire Plant Assets   Paragraph **9** states that Allison Corporation purchased plant assets during the year for $200,000, paying $160,000 in cash and issuing a long-term note payable for the $40,000 balance. Notice that *only the $160,000 cash payment* appears in the statement of cash flows. However, one objective of this financial statement is to show all of the company's *investing and financing activities* during the year. Therefore, the *noncash aspects* of these transactions are shown in a supplementary schedule, as follows:

*OBJECTIVE 7
Explain why
and how
noncash in-
vesting and
financing
activities
are disclosed
in a state-
ment of cash
flows.*

Supplementary Schedule of Noncash Investing and Financing Activities

Purchases of plant assets	**$200,000**
Less: Portion financed through issuance of long-term debt	40,000
Cash paid to acquire plant assets	**$160,000**

This supplementary schedule accompanies the statement of cash flows.

Proceeds from Sales of Plant Assets   Assume that an analysis of the plant asset accounts shows net credit entries totaling $44,000 in the year. ("Net credit entries" means all credit entries, net of related debits to accumulated depreciation when assets were sold.) These "net credit entries" represent the **book value** of plant assets sold during the year. However, the income statement shows that these assets were sold at a **gain of $31,000.** Therefore, the **cash proceeds** from sales of plant assets amounted to $75,000, as shown below:

Book value of plant assets sold...	*$44,000*
Add: Gain on sales of plant assets...	*31,000*
Proceeds from sales of plant assets	*$75,000*

Cash Flows from Financing Activities

Cash flows from financing activities are determined by analyzing the debit and credit changes recorded during the period in the related liability and stockholders' equity accounts. In a sense, cash flows from financing activities are more easily determined than those relating to investing activities, because financing activities seldom involve gains or losses.[6] Thus, the debit or credit changes in the balance sheet accounts usually are equal to the amounts of the related cash flows.

Credit changes in such accounts as Notes Payable and the accounts for long-term debt and paid-in capital usually indicate cash receipts; debit changes indicate cash payments.

Short-Term Borrowing Transactions To illustrate, consider paragraph **10,** which provides the information supporting the following cash flows:

Proceeds from short-term borrowing	*$ 45,000*
Payments to settle short-term debts...	*$(55,000)*

Is it possible to determine the proceeds of short-term borrowing transactions throughout the year without carefully reviewing each cash receipt? The answer is **yes**—easily. The proceeds from short-term borrowing are equal to the **sum of the credit entries** in the short-term **Notes Payable** account. Payments to settle short-term debts are equal to the **sum of the debit entries** in this account.

Proceeds from Issuing Bonds Payable and Capital Stock Paragraph **11** states that Allison Corporation received cash of $100,000 by issuing bonds payable. This amount was determined by summing the credit entries in the Bonds Payable account. The Bonds Payable account included no debit entries during the year; thus, no bonds were retired.

Paragraph **12** states that during the year Allison Corporation issued capital stock for $50,000. The proceeds from issuing stock are equal to the sum of the credit entries made in the Capital Stock and Additional Paid-in Capital accounts.

---

[6]   An early retirement of debt is an example of a financing transaction that may result in a gain or a loss.

Cash Dividends Paid to Stockholders   Paragraph **13** states that Allison Corporation declared and paid cash dividends of $40,000 during the year. In practice, most corporations pay cash dividends in the same year in which these dividends are declared. In these situations, the cash payments are equal to the related debit entries in the Retained Earnings account.

If the balance sheet includes a liability for dividends payable, the amounts debited to Retained Earnings represent dividends **declared** during the period, which may differ from the amount of dividends **paid.** To determine cash dividends paid, we must adjust the amount of dividends declared by adding any decrease (or subtracting any increase) in the Dividends Payable account over the period.

Relationship between the Statement of Cash Flows and the Balance Sheet

As stated in Chapter 7, the first asset appearing in the balance sheet is Cash and cash equivalents. The statement of cash flows explains in some detail the change in this asset from one balance sheet date to the next. The last three lines in the cash flow statement illustrate this relationship, as shown in our Allison Corporation example:

Net increase (decrease) in cash and cash equivalents	$35,000
Cash and cash equivalents, beginning of year	40,000
Cash and cash equivalents, end of year	$75,000

The Statement of Cash Flows: A Second Look

Allison Corporation's statement of cash flows was illustrated earlier in this chapter. Now that we have explained the nature and computation of each cash flow in that statement, a second illustration is in order. We use this second illustration as an opportunity to illustrate the ***indirect method*** of reporting net cash flow from operating activities. (Our preceding illustration uses the ***direct method.***) Also, we illustrate two ***supplementary schedules*** that often accompany a statement of cash flows.

Supplementary Schedule A illustrates the determination of net cash flow from operating activities by the ***indirect method.*** The purpose of this schedule is to explain the differences between the reported net income and the net cash flow from operating activities. This supplementary schedule also is required of companies that use the direct method of reporting operating cash flows.

Supplementary Schedule B discloses any "noncash" aspects of the company's investing and financing activities. This type of supplementary schedule is required whenever some aspects of the company's investing and financing activities do not coincide with cash flows occurring within the current period.

ALLISON CORPORATION
Statement of Cash Flows
For the Year Ended December 31, 19

Cash flows from operating activities:

Net cash flows from operating activities (see supplementary schedule A) .... $ 50,000

Cash flows from investing activities:

Purchases of marketable securities	$ (65,000)	
Proceeds from sales of marketable securities	40,000	
Loans made to borrowers	(17,000)	
Collections on loans	12,000	
Cash paid to acquire plant assets (see supplementary schedule B)	(160,000)	
Proceeds from sales of plant assets	75,000	
Net cash used by investing activities		(115,000)

Cash flows from financing activities:

Proceeds from short-term borrowing	$ 45,000	
Payments to settle short-term debts	(55,000)	
Proceeds from issuing bonds payable	100,000	
Proceeds from issuing capital stock	50,000	
Dividends paid	(40,000)	
Net cash provided by financing activities		100,000
Net increase (decrease) in cash		$ 35,000
Cash and cash equivalents, beginning of year		40,000
Cash and cash equivalents, end of year		$ 75,000

Supplementary Schedule A   Net Cash Flow from Operating Activities

Net income		$ 65,000
Add: Depreciation expense		40,000
Decrease in accrued interest receivable		1,000
Increase in accounts payable		15,000
Increase in accrued liabilities		7,000
Nonoperating loss on sales of marketable securities		4,000
Subtotal		$ 132,000
Less: Increase in accounts receivable	$ 30,000	
Increase in inventory	10,000	
Increase in prepayments	3,000	
Decrease in accrued liabilities	8,000	
Nonoperating gain on sales of plant assets	31,000	82,000
Net cash flow from operating activities		$ 50,000

Supplementary Schedule B   Noncash Investing and Financing Activities

Purchases of plant assets	$ 200,000
Less: Portion financed through issuance of long-term debt	40,000
Cash paid to acquire plant assets	$ 160,000

Notice this supplementary schedule illustrating the indirect method of determining cash flow from operations

■ ■ ■ * *Supplemental Topic A*
The Indirect Method

In a statement of cash flows, the net cash flow from operating activities may be determined either by the ***direct method*** or the ***indirect method.*** We previously have illustrated both methods using the data in our Allison Corporation example. For your convenience, these illustrations are repeated below:

OBJECTIVE 8
Compute net cash flow from operating activities using the indirect method.

Direct Method

Cash flows from operating activities:		
Cash received from customers.	$ 870,000	
Interest and dividends received	10,000	
Cash provided by operating activities		$ 880,000
Cash paid to suppliers and employees	$(764,000)	
Interest paid	(28,000)	
Income taxes paid	(38,000)	
Cash disbursed for operating activities		(830,000)
Net cash flow from operating activities		$ 50,000

Indirect Method

Net income			$ 65,000
Add:	Depreciation expense		40,000
	Decrease in accrued interest receivable		1,000
	Increase in accounts payable		15,000
	Increase in accrued interest liabilities		7,000
	Nonoperating loss on sales of marketable securities		4,000
Subtotal			$ 132,000
Less:	Increase in accounts receivable	$ 30,000	
	Increase in inventory	10,000	
	Increase in prepaid expenses	3,000	
	Decrease in accrued operating expenses payable	6,000	
	Decrease in accrued income taxes payable	2,000	
	Nonoperating gain on sales of plant assets	31,000	82,000
Net cash flow from operating activities			$ 50,000

Comparison of the Direct and Indirect Methods

The two methods of computing net cash flow from operating activities are more similar than they appear at first glance. Both methods are based upon the same accounting data and both result in the ***same net cash flow.*** Also, the computations underlying both methods are quite similar. Both methods convert accrual-based income statement amounts into cash flows by adjusting for changes in related balance sheet accounts.

To illustrate the similarity in the computations, look briefly at the formulas for computing the cash inflows and outflows shown under the direct method (pages 883–886). Each formula begins with an income statement amount and then adds or subtracts the change during the period in related balance sheet accounts. Now look at our illustration of the indirect method.

Notice that this computation also focuses upon the net changes during the period in balance sheet accounts.

The differences between the two methods lie only in format. However, the two formats provide readers of the cash flow statement with different types of information. The direct method informs these readers of the nature and dollar amounts of the *specific cash inflows and outflows* comprising the operating activities of the business. The indirect method, in contrast, *explains why* the net cash flow from operating activities differs from another measurement of performance—net income.

Differences between Net Income and Net Cash Flow from Operating Activities

As previously stated, net cash flow from operating activities differs from net income for three major reasons. (Note: In the following discussions, we will assume that both net income and net cash flow are positive amounts.)

1 **"Noncash" expenses.** Some expenses, such as depreciation expense, reduce net income but do not require any cash outlay during the current period.

2 **Timing differences.** Revenue and expenses are measured using the concepts of accrual accounting. Net cash flow, on the other hand, reflects the effects of cash transactions. Thus, revenue and expenses may be recognized in a different accounting period from the related cash flows.

3 **"Nonoperating" gains and losses.** By definition, net cash flow from operating activities shows only the effects of those cash transactions classified as "operating activities." Net income, on the other hand, may include gains and losses relating to investing and financing activities.

Reconciling Net Income with Net Cash Flow

To acquaint you with the indirect method, we will now discuss some common types of adjustments needed in reconciling net income with net cash flow from operating activities. The nature and dollar amounts of these adjustments are determined by an accountant using a working paper or a computer program; they are *not* entered in the company's accounting records.

1. Adjustments for "Noncash" Expenses

Depreciation is an example of a "noncash" expense—that is, depreciation expense reduces net income but does not require any cash outlay during the period. Thus, expenses on the accrual basis exceed cash payments, and net income for the period is less than the net cash flow. To reconcile net income with net cash flow, we must add back to net income the amount of depreciation and any other "noncash" expenses. (Other "noncash" expenses include amortization of intangible assets, depletion of natural resources, and amortization of bond discount.)

2. Adjusting for Timing Differences

Timing differences between net income and net cash flow arise whenever revenue or expense is recognized by debiting or crediting an account *other than* cash. Changes over the period in the balances of these asset and liability accounts represent differences between the amount of revenue or expense recognized in the income statement and the net cash flow from operating activities. The balance sheet accounts that give rise to these timing differences include accounts receivable, inventories, prepaid expenses, accounts payable, and accrued expenses payable. Let us look separately at the effects of changes in each type of account.

Changes in Accounts Receivable

Receivables increase as revenue is earned and decrease as cash is collected from customers. A net increase in accounts receivable over the period indicates that the revenue from credit sales exceeds collections from customers. Thus, net income measured on the accrual basis is *greater than* net cash flow; in our reconciliation of these two amounts, the net increase in accounts receivable is *deducted* from net income.

On the other hand, a net decrease in accounts receivable indicates cash receipts in excess of revenue from credit sales and is added to the amount of net income.

Changes in Inventory

The balance in the Inventory account increases as merchandise is purchased and decreases as goods are sold. A net increase during the period in the Inventory account indicates that purchases during the period exceed the cost of goods sold. Thus, to reconcile net income with net cash flow, we deduct from net income the amount of these additional purchases (the net increase in the balance of the Inventory account).

A net decrease over the period in the balance of the Inventory account indicates that the cost of goods sold (reported in the income statement) exceeds purchases made during the period. To the extent that the cost of goods sold consists of a decrease in inventory, no cash payment is required in the current period. Therefore, we add to net income the amount of a net decrease in inventory.

Changes in Prepaid Expenses

Prepaid expenses appear in the financial statements as assets. Increases in these assets result from cash payments, and decreases result from expiring amounts being recognized as expenses of the period. Thus, a net increase over the period in the amount of prepaid expenses indicates that cash payments made for these items must exceed the amounts recognized as expense. Thus, in determining net cash flow from operating activities, we deduct from net income the net increase in a company's prepaid expenses.

A net decrease in prepaid expenses indicates that cash outlays during the period were less than the amounts deducted as expense in the computation of net income. Thus, a net decrease in prepaid expenses is added back to net income.

Changes in Accounts Payable

Accounts payable are increased by purchases on account and are reduced by cash payments to suppliers. A net increase in accounts payable indicates that the accrual-based figure for purchases, which is included in the cost of goods sold, is greater than the cash payments made to suppliers. Therefore, in converting net income to cash flow, we add back the amount of merchandise purchases financed by a net increase in accounts payable.

A net decrease in accounts payable indicates that cash payments to suppliers exceed the purchases made during the period. Thus, a net decrease in accounts payable is subtracted from net income in the computation of net cash flow.

Changes in Accrued Expenses Payable The liability for accrued expenses payable increases with the recognition of expenses that will be paid in the future and decreases as cash payments are made. A net increase in accrued expenses payable indicates that expenses in the period exceed the related cash payments. Thus, net income is less than net cash flow, and the increase in the accrued expenses payable accounts should be added to net income.

A net decrease in accrued expenses payable indicates that cash payments exceed the related amounts of expense. This decrease, therefore, is subtracted from net income.

The liability for deferred income taxes may be viewed as a long-term accrued expense payable. However, in the reconciliation of net income with net cash flow from operating activities, the change in the liability for deferred income taxes is shown separately from the net change in other accrued expenses payable. A net increase in this liability is added to net income; a net decrease is subtracted.

A Helpful Hint Based on Debits and Credits In our preceding discussion, we explain *why* increases and decreases in a number of asset and liability accounts represent differences between the net income and net cash flow for the period. We do not expect you to memorize the effects of all of these changes. Rather, we hope that you will identify the types of transactions that cause a given account balance to increase or decrease and will then evaluate the effects of these transactions upon net income and net cash flow. This type of analysis will enhance your understanding of the relationships between accrual accounting and cash transactions.

However, let us offer you a quick hint. Double-entry accounting provides a simple rule that will let you check your analysis. For those asset and liability accounts that explain timing differences between net income and net cash flow, *a net credit change in the account's balance is always added to net income; a net debit change is always subtracted.* (For practice, test this rule on the adjustments in the illustration of the indirect method on the facing page. It applies to every adjustment that describes an increase or a decrease in a balance sheet account.)

3. Adjusting for "Nonoperating" Gains and Losses

In a statement of cash flows, cash flows are classified as operating activities, investing activities, or financing activities. "Nonoperating" gains and losses, by definition, do not affect *operating activities.* However, these gains and losses do enter into the determination of net income. Therefore, in converting net income to net cash flow from operating activities, we *add back any nonoperating losses* and *deduct any nonoperating gains* included in net income.

Nonoperating gains and losses include gains and losses from sales of investments, plant assets, and discontinued operations (which relate to investing activities); and gains and losses on early retirement of debt (which relate to financing activities).

The Indirect Method: A Summary

The adjustments to net income explained in our preceding discussion are summarized in the following diagram:

Net income
Add: Depreciation, amortization of intangibles, and depletion
Decrease in accounts receivable
Decrease in inventories
Decrease in prepaid expenses
Increase in accounts payable
Increase in accrued expenses payable
Increase in deferred income taxes payable
"Nonoperating" losses deducted in computing net income
Deduct: Increase in accounts receivable
Increase in inventories
Increase in prepaid expenses
Decrease in accounts payable
Decrease in accrued expenses payable
"Nonoperating" gains included in net income
Net cash flow from operating activities

Indirect Method May Be Required in a Supplementary Schedule

The FASB recommends use of the **direct method** in presenting net cash flow from operating activities. As of 1989, however, the vast majority of companies were electing to use the indirect method. One reason for this trend is that the FASB saddled companies opting for the direct method with an additional reporting requirement.

Companies using the direct method are required to provide a **supplementary schedule** illustrating the computation of net cash flow from operating activities by the indirect method. However, no supplementary computations are required of companies that illustrate the indirect method computations in their cash flow statements. In the opinion of the authors, this reporting requirement severely undermines the FASB's efforts to encourage use of the direct method.

■ ■ ■ *** *Supplemental Topic B***
Annotated Statement of Cash Flows:
Lotus Development Corporation

Shown on the following page is the statement of cash flows of **Lotus Development Corporation**, adapted from the company's 1989 annual report.[7] We have added notations which highlight some of the concepts emphasized in our discussion.

---

[7] Lotus Development Corporation, *1989 Annual Report* (Cambridge, Mass.: 1990).

LOTUS DEVELOPMENT CORPORATION
Consolidated Statement of Cash Flows
Year Ended December 31, 1989
(in thousands)

Lotus uses ———→
the direct
method

Cash flow from operations:	
Cash received from customers	$ 545,997
Cash paid to suppliers and employees....................................	(429,245)
Interest received	18,153
Interest paid	(14,684)
Income taxes recovered (paid)...	9,270
Other, net	(3,856)
Net cash provided by operations	$ 125,435

Notice
investing is
a net use
of cash ———→

Cash flow from investments:	
Payments for purchases of property and equipment......................	$ (68,906)
Payments for investments	(24,513)
Payments for software and other intangibles	(23,197)
Net cash used for investments	$(116,616)

Cash flows from financing activities:	
Proceeds from issuance of long-term debt	$ 107,440
Purchase of common stock for treasury	(43,552)
Issuance of common stock...	15,916
Net short-term borrowing under credit facilities	(6,079)
Net cash provided by financing activities	$ 73,725

Ties into
balance
sheet ———→

Net increase in cash and short-term investments.......................	$ 82,544
Cash and short-term investments at beginning of year	192,433
Cash and short-term investments at end of year	$ 274,977

Supple- ———→
mentary
schedule
uses the
"indirect"
method

Reconciliation of net income to net cash provided by operations:	
Net income	$ 67,961
Depreciation and amortization	33,827
(Increase) in accounts receivable	(10,028)
(Increase) in inventory	(6,095)
Increase (decrease) in accounts payable and accrued expenses	16,569
Net change in other working capital	23,201
Net cash provided by operations	$ 125,435

Always ———→
important

The accompanying notes are an integral part of the consolidated
financial statements.

END-OF-CHAPTER REVIEW

SUMMARY OF CHAPTER LEARNING OBJECTIVES

1 Explain the purpose and usefulness of a statement of cash flows.
The purpose of a statement of cash flows is to provide information about
the cash receipts and cash payments of the entity, and also about its
investing and financing activities. Readers of financial statements use
this information to assess the solvency of a business and to evaluate its

ability to generate positive cash flows in future periods, pay dividends, and finance growth.

2 **Describe how cash transactions are classified within a statement of cash flows.**
Cash flows are classified into the categories of (1) operating activities, (2) investing activities, and (3) financing activities. Receipts and payments of interest are classified as operating activities.

3 **Compute the major cash flows relating to operating activities.**
The major operating cash flows are (1) cash received from customers, (2) interest and dividends received, (3) cash paid to suppliers and employees, (4) interest paid, and (5) income taxes paid. These cash flows are computed by converting the income statement amounts for revenue, cost of goods sold, and expenses from the accrual basis to the cash basis. This is done by adjusting the income statement amounts for changes occurring over the period in related balance sheet accounts.

4 **Explain why net income differs from net cash flow from operating activities.**
Net income differs from net operating cash flow for several reasons. One reason is "noncash" expenses, such as depreciation and the amortization of intangible assets. These expenses, which require no cash outlays, reduce net income but do not affect net cash flow. Another reason is the many timing differences existing between the recognition of revenue and expense and the occurrence of the underlying cash flows. Finally, nonoperating gains and losses enter into the determination of net income, but the related cash flows are classified as investing or financing activities, not operating activities.

5 **Distinguish between the direct and indirect methods of reporting operating cash flow.**
The direct and indirect methods are alternative formats for reporting net cash flow from operating activities. The ***direct*** method shows the specific cash inflows and outflows comprising the operating activities of the business. Under the ***indirect*** method, the computation begins with accrual-based net income, and then shows adjustments necessary to arrive at net cash flow from operating activities. Both methods result in the same dollar amount of net cash flow from operating activities.

6 **Compute the cash flows relating to investing and financing activities.**
Cash flows from investing and financing activities can be determined by examining the entries in the related asset and liability accounts, along with any related gains or losses shown in the income statement. Debit entries in asset accounts represent purchases of assets (an investing activity). Credit entries in asset accounts represent the cost of assets sold. (However, the amount of these credit entries must be adjusted by any gains or losses recognized on these sales transactions.)
Debit entries to liability accounts represent repayment of debt, while credit entries represent borrowing. Both types of transactions are classified as financing activities. Other financing activities include the issuance of stock (indicated by credits to the paid-in capital accounts) and payment of dividends (indicated by debit entries in the Retained Earnings account).

7 Explain why and how noncash investing and financing activities are disclosed in a statement of cash flows.

One purpose of the statement of cash flows is to provide information about all investing and financing activities. Therefore, if these activities have "noncash" elements, such as the issuance of capital stock in exchange for land, the noncash aspects of the transactions are disclosed in a supplementary schedule that accompanies the statement of cash flows.

*8 Compute net cash flow from operating activities using the indirect method.

The indirect method uses net income (as reported in the income statement) as the starting point in the computation of net cash flow from operating activities. Adjustments to net income necessary to arrive at net cash flow from operating activities fall into the following three categories:

■ "Noncash" expenses
■ Timing differences
■ "Nonoperating" gains and losses

In effect, the adjustments reconcile net income (accrual basis) to net cash flow from operating activities. Specific adjustments from each of the above three categories are illustrated in the Summary Diagram of the Indirect Method on page 897.

Whether you are an investor, a manager, or a taxpayer, you need to understand the difference between cash flows and the accrual basis of accounting. Accrual-based information is useful in determining the profitability and the financial position of a business—especially a business of considerable financial strength. But in evaluating such factors as solvency, the prospects for short-term survival, and the ability of a business to seize investment opportunities, cash flows may be more relevant than accrual-based measurements.

KEY TERMS INTRODUCED OR EMPHASIZED IN CHAPTER 19

Accrual basis   A method of summarizing operating results in terms of revenue earned and expenses incurred, rather than cash receipts or cash payments.

Cash basis   A method of summarizing operating results in terms of cash receipts and cash payments, rather than revenue earned or expenses incurred.

Cash equivalents   Highly liquid short-term investments, such as Treasury bills, money market funds, and commercial paper. For purposes of preparing a statement of cash flows, money held in cash equivalents is still viewed as "cash." Thus, transfers between a bank account and cash equivalents are not considered receipts or disbursements of cash.

Cash flows   A term describing both cash receipts (inflows) and cash payments (outflows).

Direct method   A method of reporting net cash flow from operating activities by listing specific types of cash inflows and outflows. This is the method recommended by the FASB, but the ***indirect method*** is an allowable alternative.

---

*   *Supplemental Topic A, "The Indirect Method"*

Financing activities Transactions such as borrowing, repaying borrowed amounts, raising equity capital, or making distribution to owners. The cash effects of these transactions are reported in the financing activities section of a statement of cash flows. Noncash aspects of these transactions are disclosed in a supplementary schedule.

Indirect method A format of reporting net cash flow from operating activities that reconciles this figure with the amount of net income shown in the income statement. An alternative to the *direct method.*

Investing activities Transactions involving acquisitions or sales of investments or plant assets. The cash aspects of these transactions are shown in the investing activities section of a statement of cash flows. Noncash aspects of these transactions are disclosed in a supplementary schedule to this financial statement.

Operating activities Transactions entering into the determination of net income, with the exception of gains and losses relating to financing or investing activities. The category includes such transactions as selling goods or services, earning investment income, and incurring costs and expenses. The cash effects of these transactions are reflected in the operating activities section of a statement of cash flows.

Statement of cash flows A financial statement designed to provide information about the cash receipts, cash payments, investing activities, and financing activities of a business. Useful in evaluating the solvency of the business.

DEMONSTRATION PROBLEM FOR YOUR REVIEW

You are the chief accountant for American Modem. Your assistant has prepared an income statement for the current year and has also developed the following "Additional Information" by analyzing changes in the company's balance sheet accounts.

AMERICAN MODEM
Income Statement
For the Year Ended December 31, 19__

Revenue:		
Net sales..		$9,500,000
Interest income...		320,000
Gain on sales of marketable securities		70,000
Total revenue and gains		$9,890,000
Costs and expenses:		
Cost of goods sold...	$4,860,000	
Operating expenses (including depreciation of $700,000)........	3,740,000	
Interest expense..	270,000	
Income taxes...	300,000	
Loss on sales of plant assets.................................	90,000	
Total costs, expenses, and losses.........................		9,260,000
Net income...		$ 630,000

Information about changes in the company's balance sheet accounts over the year is summarized below:

1 Accounts receivable decreased by $85,000.

2 Accrued interest receivable increased by $15,000.

3 Inventory decreased by $280,000, and accounts payable to suppliers of merchandise decreased by $240,000.

4 Short-term prepayments of operating expenses decreased by $18,000, and accrued liabilities for operating expenses increased by $35,000.

5 The liability for accrued interest payable decreased by $16,000 during the year.

6 The liability for accrued income taxes payable increased by $25,000 during the year.

7 The following schedule summarizes the total debit and credit entries during the year in other balance sheet accounts:

	Debit Entries	Credit Entries
Marketable securities	$ 120,000	$ 210,000
Notes receivable (cash loans made to others)	250,000	190,000
Plant assets (see paragraph 8)	3,800,000	360,000
Notes payable (short-term borrowing)	620,000	740,000
Bonds payable		1,100,000
Capital stock		50,000
Additional paid-in capital (from issuance of stock)		840,000
Retained earnings (see paragraph 9 below)	320,000	630,000

8 The $360,000 in credit entries to the plant asset accounts are net of any debits to accumulated depreciation when plant assets were retired. Thus, the $360,000 in credit entries represents the **book value** of all plant assets sold or retired during the year.

9 The $320,000 debit to retained earnings represents dividends declared and paid during the year. The $630,000 credit entry represents the net income shown in the income statement.

10 All investing and financing activities were cash transactions.

11 Cash and cash equivalents amounted to $448,000 at the beginning of the year, and to $330,000 at year-end.

INSTRUCTIONS You are to prepare a statement of cash flows for the current year, following the format illustrated on page 878. Cash flow from operating activities is to be determined by the **direct method.** Place brackets around dollar amounts representing cash outlays. Show separately your computations of the following amounts:

1 Cash received from customers

2 Interest received

3 Cash paid to suppliers and employees

4 Interest paid

5 Income taxes paid

6 Proceeds from sales of marketable securities

7 Proceeds from sales of plant assets

8 Proceeds from issuing capital stock

SOLUTION TO DEMONSTRATION PROBLEM

AMERICAN MODEM
Statement of Cash Flows
For the Year Ended December 31, 19___

Cash flows from operating activities:

Cash received from customers (1)	$ 9,585,000	
Interest received (2)	305,000	
Cash provided by operating activities		$ 9,890,000
Cash paid to suppliers and employees (3)	$(7,807,000)	
Interest paid (4)	(286,000)	
Income taxes paid (5)	(275,000)	
Cash disbursed for operating activities		(8,368,000)
Net cash flow from operating activities		$ 1,522,000

Cash flows from investing activities:

Purchases of marketable securities	$ (120,000)	
Proceeds from sales of marketable securities (6)	280,000	
Loans made to borrowers	(250,000)	
Collections on loans	190,000	
Cash paid to acquire plant assets	(3,800,000)	
Proceeds from sales of plant assets (7)	270,000	
Net cash used by investing activities		(3,430,000)

Cash flow from financing activities:

Proceeds from short-term borrowing	$ 740,000	
Payments to settle short-term debts	(620,000)	
Proceeds from issuing bonds payable	1,100,000	
Proceeds from issuing capital stock (8)	890,000	
Dividends paid	(320,000)	
Net cash provided by financing activities		1,790,000
Net increase (decrease) in cash		$ (118,000)
Cash and cash equivalents, beginning of year		$ 448,000
Cash and cash equivalents, end of year		$ 330,000

Supporting computations:

(1) Cash received from customers:

Net sales	$ 9,500,000
Add: Decrease in accounts receivable	85,000
Cash received from customers	**$ 9,585,000**

(2) Interest received:

Interest income	$ 320,000
Less: Increase in accrued interest receivable	15,000
Interest received	**$ 305,000**

(3) Cash paid to suppliers and employees:

Cash paid for purchases of merchandise:

Cost of goods sold	$ 4,860,000
Less: Decrease in inventory	280,000
Net purchases	$ 4,580,000
Add: Decrease in accounts payable to suppliers	240,000
Cash paid for purchases of merchandise	**$ 4,820,000**

Cash paid for operating expenses:

Operating expenses			$ 3,740,000
Less: Depreciation (a "noncash" expense)	$	700,000	
Decrease in prepayments		18,000	
Increase in accrued liabilities for			
operating expenses		35,000	753,000
Cash paid for operating expenses			$ 2,987,000
Cash paid to suppliers and employees ($4,820,000 + $2,987,000)			$ 7,807,000

(4) Interest paid:

Interest expense	$ 270,000
Add: Decrease in accrued interest payable	16,000
Interest paid	$ 286,000

(5) Income taxes paid:

Income taxes expense	$ 300,000
Less: Increase in accrued income taxes payable	25,000
Income taxes paid	$ 275,000

(6) Proceeds from sales of marketable securities:

Cost of marketable securities sold (credit entries to the	
Marketable Securities account)	$ 210,000
Add: Gain reported on sales of marketable securities	70,000
Proceeds from sales of marketable securities	$ 280,000

(7) Proceeds from sales of plant assets:

Book value of plant assets sold (paragraph 8)	$ 360,000
Less: Loss reported on sales of plant assets	90,000
Proceeds from sales of plant assets	$ 270,000

(8) Proceeds from issuing capital stock:

Amounts credited to the Capital Stock account	$ 50,000
Add: Amounts credited to Additional Paid-in Capital account	840,000
Proceeds from issuing capital stock	$ 890,000

SELF-TEST QUESTIONS

Answers to these questions appear on page 921.

1 The statement of cash flows is designed to assist users in assessing each of the following, *except:*

a The ability of a company to remain solvent.

b The company's profitability.

c The major sources of cash receipts during the period.

d The reasons why net cash flow from operating activities differs from net income.

2 Which of the following is *not* included in the statement of cash flows, or in a supplementary schedule accompanying the statement of cash flows?

a Disclosure of the amount of cash invested in money market funds during the accounting period

b A reconciliation of net income to net cash flow from operating activities

c Disclosure of investing or financing activities that did not involve cash

d The amount of cash and cash equivalents owned by the business at the end of the accounting period

3 The cash flows shown in the statement of cash flows are grouped into the following major categories:

   a Operating activities, investing activities, and financing activities

   b Cash receipts, cash disbursements, and noncash activities

   c Direct cash flows and indirect cash flows

   d Operating activities, investing activities, and collecting activities

4 Shown below is a list of various cash payments and cash receipts:

Cash paid to suppliers and employees	*$400,000*
Dividends paid	*18,000*
Interest paid	*12,000*
Purchases of plant assets	*45,000*
Interest and dividends received	*17,000*
Payments to settle short-term debt	*29,000*
Income taxes paid	*23,000*
Cash received from customers	*601,000*

   Based only upon the above items, net cash flow from operating activities is:
   a $138,000   b $91,000   c $183,000   d $120,000

5 During the current year, two transactions were recorded in the Land account of Nolan Industries. One involved a debit of $320,000 to the Land account; the second was a $210,000 credit to the Land account. Nolan Industries' income statement for the year reported a loss on sale of land in the amount of $25,000. All transactions involving the Land account were cash transactions. These transactions would be shown in the statement of cash flows as:

   a $320,000 cash provided by investing activities, and $210,000 cash disbursed for investing activities.

   b $210,000 cash provided by investing activities, and $320,000 cash disbursed for investing activities.

   c $235,000 cash provided by investing activities, and $320,000 cash disbursed for investing activities.

   d $185,000 cash provided by investing activities, and $320,000 cash disbursed for investing activities.

ASSIGNMENT MATERIAL

DISCUSSION QUESTIONS

1 A recent headline in the business section of a newspaper referred to the statement of cash flows as a "new" financial statement. Why?

2 Why does the FASB ask companies not to use the term *funds* in a statement of cash flows?

3 Briefly state the purposes of a statement of cash flows.

4 Does a statement of cash flows or an income statement best measure the profitability of a financially sound business? Explain.

5 Two supplementary schedules usually accompany a statement of cash flows. Briefly explain the content of these schedules.

6 Give two examples of cash receipts and two examples of cash payments which fall into each of the following classifications:

a Operating activities

b Investing activities

c Financing activities

7 Why are payments and receipts of interest classified as operating activities rather than as financing or investing activities?

8 Define **cash equivalents** and list three examples.

9 During the current year, Delta Corporation transferred $300,000 from its bank account into a money market fund. Will this transaction appear in a statement of cash flows? If so, in which section? Explain.

10 In the long run, is it more important for a business to have positive cash flows from its operating activities, investing activities, or financing activities? Why?

11 Of the three types of business activities summarized in a cash flow statement, which type is **least** likely to show a positive net cash flow in a successful, growing business? Explain your reasoning.

12 The items and amounts listed in a balance sheet and an income statement correspond to specific accounts in a company's ledger. Is the same true about the items and amounts in a statement of cash flows? Explain.

13 Marathon, Inc., had net sales for the year of $840,000. Accounts receivable increased from $90,000 at the beginning of the year to $162,000 at year-end. Compute the amount of cash collected during the year from customers.

14 Describe the types of cash payments summarized by the caption "Cash paid to suppliers and employees."

15 Identify three factors that may cause net income to differ from net cash flow from operating activities.

16 Briefly explain the difference between the direct and indirect methods of computing net cash flow from operating activities. Which method results in the higher net cash flow?

17 Are cash payments of accounts payable viewed as operating activities or investing activities? Referring to the statement of cash flows illustrated on page 878, state the caption that includes amounts paid on accounts payable.

18 Discount Club acquired land by issuing $500,000 worth of capital stock. No cash changed hands in this transaction. Will the transaction be disclosed in the company's statement of cash flows? Explain.

19 The only transaction recorded in the plant asset accounts of Rogers Corporation in the current year was a $150,000 credit to the Land account. Assuming that this credit resulted from a cash transaction, does this entry indicate a cash receipt or a cash payment? Should this $150,000 amount appear in the statement of cash flows, or is some adjustment necessary.

20 During the current year, the following credit entries were posted to the paid-in capital accounts of Moser Shipyards:

Capital Stock	*$10,000,000*
Additional Paid-in Capital	*98,500,000*

Explain the type of cash transaction that probably caused these credit changes, and illustrate the presentation of this transaction in a statement of cash flows.

21 At the beginning of the current year, Burnside Corporation had dividends payable of $1,200,000. During the current year, the company declared cash dividends of $3,600,000, of which $900,000 appeared as a liability at year-end. Determine the amount of cash dividends **paid** during this year.

EXERCISES

EXERCISE 19-1
Accounting Terminology

Listed below are nine technical accounting terms introduced or emphasized in this chapter.

Cash flow	*Income statement*	*Operating activities*
Direct method	*Statement of cash flows*	*Investing activities*
Indirect method	*Cash equivalents*	*Financing activities*

Each of the following statements may (or may not) describe one of these technical terms. For each statement, indicate the term described, or answer "None" if the statement does not correctly describe any of the terms.

a Transactions involving investments by owners, issuance and repayment of debt, and the payment of dividends.

b The financial statement showing the financial position of the business at one particular date.

c A term that describes either a cash receipt or a cash disbursement.

d The process of recognizing revenue as it is earned and expenses as they are incurred, regardless of when cash is received or paid.

e The method of reporting net cash flow from operating activities that is favored by the FASB.

f An asset consisting of readily marketable investments in the stocks and bonds of large corporations.

g The section of a statement of cash flows that includes purchases of plant assets.

h The financial statement that best describes the profitability of a business receiving most of its revenue in cash.

EXERCISE 19-2
Computing Cash Flows

An analysis of the Marketable Securities controlling account of Dixie Mills, Inc., shows the following entries during the year:

Balance, January	$390,000
Debit entries .... Purchases	125,000
Credit entries .... Cost security sold	(140,000)
Balance, December 31	$375,000

In addition, the company's income statement includes a $27,000 loss on sales of marketable securities. None of the company's marketable securities is considered a cash equivalent.

INSTRUCTIONS Compute the amounts that should appear in the statement of cash flows as:

a Purchases of marketable securities.

b Proceeds from sales of marketable securities.

**EXERCISE 19-3
Comparing Net
Sales and
Cash Receipts**

During the current year, Grafton Labs made cash sales of $250,000 and credit sales of $490,000. During the year, accounts receivable decreased by $32,000.

a Compute for the current year the amounts of:

   1 Net sales reported as revenue in the income statement

   2 Cash received from collecting accounts receivable

   3 Cash received from customers

b Write a brief statement explaining why cash received from customers differs from the amount of net sales.

**EXERCISE 19-4
Computing
Cash Paid for
Purchases of
Merchandise**

The general ledger of Nitro Tech provides the following information relating to purchases of merchandise:

	End of Year	Beginning of Year
Inventory..	$820,000	$780,000
Accounts payable to merchandise suppliers	430,000	500,000

The company's cost of goods sold during the year was $2,875,000.

INSTRUCTIONS

Compute the amount of cash payments made during the year to suppliers of merchandise.

**EXERCISE 19-5
Reporting
Lending Activi-
ties and Inter-
est Revenue**

During the current year, Otay Savings and Loan Association made new loans of $12 million. In addition, the company collected $36 million from borrowers, of which $31 million was interest revenue. Explain how these cash flows will appear in the company's statement of cash flows, indicating the classification and the dollar amount of each cash flow.

**EXERCISE 19-6
Disclosing
"Non-cash"
Investing and
Financing Ac-
tivities**

During the current year, Nordic Co. purchased a factory from Fisher Industries. The journal entry made to record this transaction is shown below:

Land..	500,000	
Buildings	750,000	
Equipment	1,800,000	
Mortgage Payable		2,100,000
Cash..		950,000

This was Nordic Co.'s only purchase of plant assets during the year. Nordic Co. prepares a supplementary schedule to its statement of cash flows for the purpose of disclosing any "noncash" aspects of investing and financing activities.

INSTRUCTIONS

a Prepare the supplementary schedule to disclose the "noncash" aspects of this transaction. Follow the general format illustrated on page 889.

b Illustrate the presentation of this transaction in Nordic Co.'s statement of cash flows. Begin your illustration by indicating the section of the statement (operating, investing, or financing activities) in which this transaction will appear.

EXERCISE 19-7
Format of a Statement of Cash Flows

The accounting staff of Carolina Crafts, Inc., has assembled the following information for the year ended December 31, 1994:

Cash and cash equivalents, beginning of year	$ 45,200
Cash and cash equivalents, end of year	64,200
Cash paid to acquire plant assets	21,000
Proceeds from short-term borrowing	10,000
Loans made to borrowers	5,000
Collections on loans (excluding interest)	4,000
Interest and dividends received	17,000
Cash received from customers	795,000
Proceeds from sales of plant assets	9,000
Dividends paid	65,000
Cash paid to suppliers and employees	635,000
Interest paid	19,000
Income taxes paid	71,000

INSTRUCTIONS

Using this information, prepare a formal statement of cash flows. Include a proper heading for the financial statement, and classify the given information into the categories of operating activities, investing activities, and financing activities. Net cash flows from operating activities are determined by the direct method. Place brackets around the dollar amounts of all cash disbursements.

*EXERCISE 19-8
An Analysis of Possible Reconciling Items

An analysis of the annual financial statements of Waste Disposal Corporation reveals the following:

a   The company had a $4 million extraordinary loss from the early retirement of bonds payable.

b   Depreciation for the year amounted to $9 million.

c   During the year, $2 million in cash was transferred from the company's checking account into a money market fund.

d   Accounts receivable from customers increased by $5 million over the year.

e   Cash received from customers during the year amounted to $165 million.

f   Prepaid expenses decreased by $1 million over the year.

g   Dividends declared during the year, $7 million; dividends paid during the year, $6 million.

h   Accounts payable (to suppliers of merchandise) increased by $3 million during the year.

i   The liability for accrued income taxes payable amounted to $5 million at the beginning of the year and $3 million at year-end.

INSTRUCTIONS

In the computation of net cash flow from operating activities by the indirect method, explain whether each of the above items should be *added to net income,* *deducted from net income,* or *omitted from the computation.* Briefly explain your reasons for each answer.

---

*   *Supplemental Topic A, "The Indirect Method"*

*EXERCISE 19-9
Computation of
Net Cash Flow
from Operating
Activities—
Indirect
Method*

The data below are taken from the income statement and balance sheets of All Night Pharmacies, Inc.:

	Dec. 31 1994	Jan. 1 1994
Income statement:		
Net income	$400,000	
Depreciation expense	120,000	
Amortization of intangible assets	40,000	
Gain on sale of plant assets	80,000	
Loss on sale of investments	35,000	
Balance sheets:		
Accounts receivable	$335,000	$380,000
Inventory	503,000	575,000
Prepaid expenses	22,000	10,000
Accounts payable (to merchandise suppliers)	379,000	410,000
Accrued expenses payable	180,000	155,000

INSTRUCTIONS

Using this information, prepare a partial statement of cash flows for the year ended December 31, 1994, showing the computation of net cash flow from operating activities by the *indirect* method.

PROBLEMS

Group A

PROBLEM 19A-1
**Classifying
Cash Flows**

Among the transactions of Miyota Communications were the following:

a Made payments on accounts payable to merchandise suppliers.

b Paid the principal amount of a note payable to First Bank.

c Paid interest charges relating to a note payable to First Bank.

d Issued bonds payable for cash; management plans to use this cash in the near future to expand manufacturing and warehouse capabilities.

e Paid salaries to employees in the finance department.

f Collected an account receivable from a customer.

g Transferred cash from the general bank account into a money market fund.

h Used the cash received in **d,** above, to purchase land and building suitable for a manufacturing facility.

i Made a year-end adjusting entry to recognize depreciation expense.

j At year-end, purchased for cash an insurance policy covering the next 12 months.

k Paid the quarterly dividend on preferred stock.

l Paid the semiannual interest on bonds payable.

m Received a quarterly dividend from an investment in the preferred stock of another corporation.

n Sold for cash an investment in the preferred stock of another corporation.

o Received cash upon the maturity of an investment in cash equivalents.

---

*   *Supplemental Topic A, "The Indirect Method"*

INSTRUCTIONS Most of the preceding transactions should be included among the activities summarized in a statement of cash flows. For each transaction that should be included in this statement, indicate whether the transaction should be classified as an operating activity, an investing activity, or a financing activity. If the transaction ***should not be included*** in the current year's statement of cash flows, briefly explain why not. (Assume that the net cash flow from operating activities is determined by the ***direct method.***)

PROBLEM 19A-2
Reporting Operating Cash Flow by the Direct Method

The following income statement and selected balance sheet account data are available for Satellite Transmissions, Inc., at December 31:

SATELLITE TRANSMISSIONS, INC.
Income Statement
For the Year Ended December 31, 19__

Revenue:

Net sales..	$2,850,000
Dividend income	104,000
Interest income...	70,000
Gain on sales of marketable securities	4,000
Total revenue and gains	$3,028,000

Costs and expenses:

Cost of goods sold	$1,550,000	
Operating expenses	980,000	
Interest expense..	185,000	
Income taxes...	110,000	
Total costs and expenses		2,825,000
Net income...		$ 203,000

Selected account balances:	End of Year	Beginning of Year
Accounts receivable	$650,000	$720,000
Accrued interest receivable	9,000	6,000
Inventories	800,000	765,000
Short-term prepayments	20,000	15,000
Accounts payable (merchandise suppliers)	570,000	562,000
Accrued operating expenses payable.......................	65,000	94,000
Accrued interest payable	21,000	12,000
Accrued income taxes payable.............................	22,000	35,000

ADDITIONAL INFORMATION

1 Dividend revenue is recognized on the cash basis. All other income statement amounts are recognized on the accrual basis.

2 Operating expenses include depreciation expense of $115,000.

INSTRUCTIONS Prepare a partial statement of cash flows, including only the operating activities section of the statement. Use the ***direct method,*** including the captions illustrated on page 878. Place brackets around numbers representing cash payments. Show supporting computations for the amounts of:

1 Cash received from customers

2 Interest and dividends received

3 Cash paid to suppliers and employees

4 Interest paid

5 Income taxes paid

**PROBLEM 19A-3
Reporting In-
vesting Activi-
ties**

An analysis of the income statement and the balance sheet accounts of Franklin Optical at December 31 provides the following information:

Income statement items:

Gain on sale of marketable securities	$ 42,000
Loss on sales of plant assets	33,000

Analysis of balance sheet accounts:

Marketable Securities account:

Debit entries	$ 81,000
Credit entries	90,000

Notes Receivable account:

Debit entries	210,000
Credit entries	162,000

Plant and equipment accounts:

Debit entries to plant asset accounts......................................	186,000
Credit entries to plant asset accounts	120,000
Debit entries to accumulated depreciation accounts	75,000

**ADDITIONAL
INFORMATION**

1 Except as noted in **4,** below, payments and proceeds relating to investing transactions were made in cash.

2 The marketable securities are not cash equivalents.

3 All notes receivable relate to cash loans made to borrowers, not to receivables from customers.

4 Purchases of new equipment during the year ($186,000) were financed by paying $60,000 in cash and issuing a long-term note payable for $126,000.

5 Debits to the accumulated depreciation account are made whenever depreciable plant assets are retired. Thus, the book value of plant assets retired during the year was $45,000 ($120,000 − $75,000).

INSTRUCTIONS

a Prepare the ***Investing activities*** section of a statement of cash flows. Show supporting computations for the amounts of (1) proceeds from sales of marketable securities and (2) proceeds from sales of plant assets. Place brackets around numbers representing cash outflows.

b Prepare the supporting schedule that should accompany the statement of cash flows in order to disclose the "noncash" aspects of the company's investing and financing activities.

PROBLEM 19A-4
Format of a
Statement of
Cash Flows

The accounting staff of Educators' Outlet, Inc., has assembled the following information for the year ended December 31, 19__:

Cash sales	$ 800,000
Credit sales	2,500,000
Collections on accounts receivable...............................	2,200,000
Cash transferred from the money market fund to the	
general bank account...	250,000
Interest and dividends received	100,000
Purchases (all on account)...	1,800,000
Payments on accounts payable to merchandise suppliers	1,500,000
Cash payments for operating expenses	1,050,000
Interest paid	180,000
Income taxes paid..	95,000
Loans made to borrowers...	500,000
Collections on loans (excluding receipts of interest)	260,000
Cash paid to acquire plant assets..................................	3,100,000
Book value of plant assets sold....................................	660,000
Loss on sales of plant assets......................................	80,000
Proceeds from issuing bonds payable................................	2,500,000
Dividends paid	120,000
Cash and cash equivalents, beginning of year	446,000
Cash and cash equivalents, end of year	–?–

INSTRUCTIONS

Prepare a statement of cash flows in the format illustrated on page 878. Place brackets around amounts representing cash outflows. Use the ***direct method*** of reporting cash flows from operating activities.

    Many of the items above will be listed in your statement without change. However, you will have to combine certain given information to compute the amounts of (1) collections from customers, (2) cash paid to suppliers and employees, and (3) proceeds from sales of plant assets. (Hint: Not every item listed above is used in preparing a statement of cash flows.)

PROBLEM 19A-5
Preparing a
Statement of
Cash Flows: A
Comprehensive
Problem

The accounting department of Inland Waste Management, Inc., has prepared an income statement for the current year and also has developed the "Additional Information" listed below by analyzing changes in the company's balance sheet accounts.

INLAND WASTE MANAGEMENT, INC.
Income Statement
For the Year Ended December 31, 19__

Revenue:		
Net sales..		$2,450,000
Interest revenue		130,000
Gain on sales of plant assets		10,000
Total revenue and gains		$2,590,000
Costs and expenses:		
Cost of goods sold	$1,300,000	
Operating expenses (including depreciation of $200,000)	825,000	
Interest expense..	100,000	
Income taxes..	95,000	
Loss on sales of marketable securities	30,000	
Total costs, expenses, and losses.............................		2,350,000
Net income..		$ 240,000

ADDITIONAL INFORMATION

Information about changes in the company's balance sheet accounts over the year is summarized below:

1 Accounts receivable decreased by $50,000.

2 Accrued interest receivable increased by $15,000.

3 Inventory increased by $100,000, and accounts payable to suppliers of merchandise increased by $80,000.

4 Short-term prepayments of operating expenses decreased by $8,000, and accrued liabilities for operating expenses increased by $40,000.

5 The liability for accrued interest payable decreased by $4,000 during the year.

6 The liability for accrued income taxes payable increased by $9,000 during the year.

7 The following schedule summarizes the total debit and credit entries during the year in other balance sheet accounts:

	Debit Entries	Credit Entries
Marketable securities	$185,000	$170,000
Notes receivable (cash loans made to borrowers)	210,000	250,000
Plant assets (see paragraph 8)	625,000	50,000
Notes payable (short-term borrowing)	340,000	225,000
Capital stock		25,000
Additional paid-in capital—capital stock		375,000
Retained earnings (see paragraph 9 below)	150,000	240,000

8 The $50,000 in credit entries to the plant assets account are net of any debits to accumulated depreciation when plant assets were retired. Thus, the $50,000 in credit entries represents the **book value** of all plant assets sold or retired during the year.

9 The $150,000 debit to retained earnings represents dividends declared and paid during the year. The $240,000 credit entry represents the net income shown in the income statement.

10 All investing and financing activities were cash transactions.

11 Cash and cash equivalents amounted to $210,000 at the beginning of the year, and to $303,000 at year-end.

INSTRUCTIONS

You are to prepare a statement of cash flows for the current year, following the format illustrated on page 878. Cash flows from operating activities are to be presented using the direct method. Place brackets around dollar amounts representing cash outlays. Show separately your computations of the following amounts:

1 Cash received from customers

2 Interest received

3 Cash paid to suppliers and employees

4 Interest paid

5 Income taxes paid

6 Proceeds from sales of marketable securities

7 Proceeds from sales of plant assets

8 Proceeds from issuing capital stock

***PROBLEM 19A-6
Reporting Operating Cash Flow—Indirect Method**

Using the information presented in Problem **19A-2,** prepare a partial statement of cash flows for the current year, showing the computation of net cash flow from operating activities by the **indirect method.** Use the format and captions illustrated on page 893.

---

*   *Supplemental Topic A, "The Indirect Method"*

Group B

PROBLEM 19B-1
Classifying
Cash Flows

Fifteen business transactions of Columbia Publishing Co. are listed below:

a Declared a dividend to be paid early next year.

b At year-end, purchased for cash an insurance policy covering the next 12 months.

c Purchased short-term Treasury bills for cash.

d Made payments on accounts payable to merchandise suppliers.

e Issued bonds payable for cash; management plans to use this cash in the near future to modernize production facilities.

f Sold marketable securities at a loss.

g Collected principal amounts due on a loan (a note receivable).

h Collected interest due on the note receivable described in **g,** above.

i Used the cash received in **e,** above, for the purpose of modernizing production facilities.

j Made a semiannual interest payment on bonds payable.

k Collected an account receivable from a customer.

l Transferred cash from a money market fund into the general bank account.

m Made a year-end adjusting entry to recognize depreciation expense.

n Paid salaries to employees in the accounting and finance departments.

o Paid a dividend declared in the prior year.

INSTRUCTIONS

Most of the preceding transactions should be included among the activities summarized in a statement of cash flows. For each transaction that should be included in this statement, indicate whether the transaction should be classified as an operating activity, investing activity, or financing activity. If the transaction should *not be included* in the current year's statement of cash flows, briefly explain why not. (Assume that the net cash flow from operating activities is determined by the *direct method.*)

PROBLEM 19B-2
Reporting Operating Cash Flow by the Direct Method

The following income statement and selected balance sheet account data are available for Child's Play, Inc., at December 31, of the current year:

CHILD'S PLAY, INC.
Income Statement
For the Year Ended December 31, 19___

Revenue:		
Net sales...		$3,100,000
Interest income..		50,000
Dividend income		47,000
Total revenue		$3,197,000
Costs and expenses:		
Cost of goods sold..	$1,850,000	
Operating expenses	920,000	
Interest expense...	140,000	
Income taxes..	90,000	
Loss on sales of plant assets	7,000	
Total costs, expenses, and losses...........................		3,007,000
Net income..		$ 190,000

	End of Year	Beginning of Year
Selected account balances:		
Accounts receivable	$780,000	$700,000
Accrued interest receivable	6,000	8,000
Inventories	670,000	690,000
Short-term prepayments	18,000	22,000
Accounts payable (merchandise suppliers)	577,000	590,000
Accrued operating expenses payable	38,000	21,000
Accrued interest payable	13,000	19,000
Accrued income taxes payable	36,000	28,000

ADDITIONAL INFORMATION

1 Dividend revenue is recognized on the cash basis. All other income statement amounts are recognized on the accrual basis.

2 Operating expenses include depreciation expense of $105,000.

INSTRUCTIONS

Prepare a partial statement of cash flows, including only the operating activities section of the statement. Use the format and captions illustrated on page 878. Net cash flow from operating activities is to be presented using the ***direct method.*** Place brackets around amounts representing cash payments. Show supporting computations for the amounts of:

1 Cash received from customers

2 Interest and dividends received

3 Cash paid to suppliers and employees

4 Interest paid

5 Income taxes paid

PROBLEM 19B-3 Reporting Investing Activities

An analysis of the income statement and the balance sheet accounts of Caravan Imports at December 31 provides the following information:

Income statement items:	
Gain on sales of plant assets	$ 9,000
Loss on sales of marketable securities	15,000
Analysis of balance sheet accounts:	
Marketable Securities account:	
Debit entries	$ 74,000
Credit entries	62,000
Notes Receivable account:	
Debit entries	52,000
Credit entries	60,000
Plant and equipment accounts:	
Debit entries to plant asset accounts	130,000
Credit entries to plant asset accounts	140,000
Debit entries to accumulated depreciation accounts	100,000

ADDITIONAL INFORMATION

1 Except as noted in **4,** below, payments and proceeds relating to investing transactions were made in cash.

2 The marketable securities are not cash equivalents.

3 All notes receivable relate to cash loans made to borrowers, not to receivables from customers.

4 Purchases of new equipment during the year ($130,000) were financed by paying $50,000 in cash and issuing a long-term note payable for $80,000.

5 Debits to the accumulated depreciation account are made whenever depreciable plant assets are sold or retired. Thus, the book value of plant assets sold or retired during the year was $40,000 ($140,000 − $100,000).

INSTRUCTIONS

a Prepare the ***Investing activities*** section of a statement of cash flows. Show supporting computations for the amounts of (1) proceeds from sales of marketable securities and (2) proceeds from sales of plant assets. Place brackets around amounts representing cash outflows.

b Prepare the supplementary schedule that should accompany the statement of cash flows in order to disclose the "noncash" aspects of the company's investing and financing activities.

PROBLEM 19B-4
Preparing a
Statement of
Cash Flows

The accounting staff of TeleGift Corporation has assembled the following information for the year ended December 31, 19__:

Cash sales	$ 402,000
Credit sales	3,420,000
Collections on accounts receivable...	3,193,000
Cash transferred from the money market fund to the general bank account....	180,000
Interest and dividends received	40,000
Purchases (all on account)...	1,950,000
Payments on accounts payable to merchandise suppliers	2,036,000
Cash payments for operating expenses	822,000
Interest paid	99,000
Income taxes paid...	180,000
Loans made to borrowers..	220,000
Collections on loans (excluding receipts of interest)	145,000
Cash paid to acquire plant assets...	1,640,000
Book value of plant assets sold...	70,000
Gain on sales of plant assets	35,000
Proceeds from issuing capital stock..	1,355,000
Dividends paid	180,000
Cash and cash equivalents, beginning of year	297,000
Cash and cash equivalents, end of year	−?−

INSTRUCTIONS

Prepare a statement of cash flows in the format illustrated on page 878. Place brackets around amounts representing cash outflows. Use the ***direct method*** of reporting cash flows from operating activities.

Many of the items above will be listed in your statement without change. However, you will have to combine certain given information to compute the amounts of (1) collections from customers, (2) cash paid to suppliers and employees, and (3) proceeds from sales of plant assets.

PROBLEM 19B-5
Preparing a Statement of Cash Flows: A Comprehensive Problem

You are the controller for Barraza Industries, Inc. Your staff has prepared an income statement for the current year, and has also developed the following "Additional Information" by analyzing changes in the company's balance sheet accounts.

BARRAZA INDUSTRIES, INC.
Income Statement
For the Year Ended December 31, 19—

Revenue:

Net sales...		$3,200,000
Interest revenue		40,000
Gain on sales of marketable securities		34,000
Total revenue and gains		$3,274,000

Costs and expenses:

Cost of goods sold	$1,620,000	
Operating expenses (including depreciation of $150,000)	1,240,000	
Interest expense...	42,000	
Income taxes..	100,000	
Loss on sales of plant assets.................................	12,000	
Total costs, expenses, and losses.......................................		3,014,000
Net income..		$ 260,000

ADDITIONAL INFORMATION

Information about changes in the company's balance sheet accounts over the year is summarized below:

1 Accounts receivable increased by $60,000.

2 Accrued interest receivable decreased by $2,000.

3 Inventory decreased by $60,000, and accounts payable to suppliers of merchandise decreased by $16,000.

4 Short-term prepayments of operating expenses increased by $6,000, and accrued liabilities for operating expenses decreased by $8,000.

5 The liability for accrued interest payable increased by $4,000 during the year.

6 The liability for accrued income taxes payable decreased by $14,000 during the year.

7 The following schedule summarizes the total debit and credit entries during the year in other balance sheet accounts:

	Debit Entries	Credit Entries
Marketable securities	$ 60,000	$ 38,000
Notes receivable (cash loans made to borrowers)................	44,000	28,000
Plant assets (see paragraph 8 below)	500,000	36,000
Notes payable (short-term borrowing)	92,000	32,000
Capital stock		20,000
Additional paid-in capital—capital stock		150,000
Retained earnings (see paragraph 9 below)	120,000	250,000

8 The $36,000 in credit entries to the plant assets account are net of any debits to accumulated depreciation when plant assets were retired. Thus, the $36,000 in credit entries represents the book value of all plant assets sold or retired during the year.

9 The $120,000 debit to retained earnings represents dividends declared and paid during the year. The $260,000 credit entry represents the net income shown in the income statement.

10 All investing and financing activities were cash transactions.

11 Cash and cash equivalents amounted to $244,000 at the beginning of the year, and to $164,000 at year-end.

INSTRUCTIONS You are to prepare a statement of cash flows for the current year, following the format illustrated on page 878. Use the ***direct method*** of reporting cash flows from operating activities. Place brackets around dollar amounts representing cash outflows. Show separately your computations of the following amounts:

1 Cash received from customers

2 Interest received

3 Cash paid to suppliers and employees

4 Interest paid

5 Income taxes paid

6 Proceeds from sales of marketable securities

7 Proceeds from sales of plant assets

8 Proceeds from issuing capital stock

*PROBLEM 19B-6
Reporting Operating Cash Flow—Indirect Method

Using the information presented in Problem **19B-2,** prepare a partial statement of cash flows for the current year, showing the computation of net cash flow from operating activities by the ***indirect method.*** Use the format and captions illustrated on page 893.

CASES AND UNSTRUCTURED PROBLEMS

CASE 19-1
Another Look at Allison Corporation

This case is based upon the statement of cash flows for Allison Corporation, illustrated on page 892. You are to use this statement to evaluate the company's ability to continue paying the current level of dividends—$40,000 per year. The following information also is available:

1 The net cash flow from operating activities shown in the statement is relatively "normal" for Allison Corporation. In fact, net cash flows from operating activities have not varied by more than a few thousand dollars in any of the last three years.

2 The net outflow for investing activities was unusually high, because the company modernized its production facilities during the year. The "normal" investing cash outflow is about $45,000 per year, the amount required to replace existing plant assets as they are retired. Over the long run, marketable securities transactions and lending transactions have a very small impact upon Allison's net cash flow from investing activities.

3 The net cash flow from financing activities was unusually large in the current year, because of the issuance of bonds payable and capital stock. These securities were issued to finance the modernization of the production facilities. In a typical year, financing activities include only short-term borrowing transactions and payments of dividends.

---

* *Supplemental Topic A, "The Indirect Method"*

INSTRUCTIONS

a Based solely upon the company's past performance, do you believe that the $40,000 annual dividend payments are secure? That is, does the company appear able to pay this amount in dividends every year without putting any strain on its cash position? Do you think it more likely that Allison Corporation will increase or decrease the amount of dividends that it pays? Explain fully.

b Should any of the "unusual" events appearing in the statement of cash flows for the current year affect your analysis of the company's ability to pay future dividends? Explain.

**CASE 19-2
Lookin' Good?**

It is late summer and National Motors, an auto manufacturer, is facing a financial crisis. A large issue of bonds payable will mature next March, and the company must issue stock or new bonds to raise the money to retire this debt. Unfortunately, profits and cash flows have been declining over recent years. Management fears that if cash flows and profits do not improve in the current year, the company will not be able to raise the capital needed to pay off the maturing bonds. Therefore, members of management have made the following proposals to improve the cash flows and profitability that will be reported in the financial statements dated this coming December 31.

1 Switch from the LIFO method to the FIFO method of valuing inventories. Management estimates that the FIFO method will result in a lower cost of goods sold but in higher income taxes for the current year. However, the additional income taxes will not actually be paid until early next year.

2 Switch from the sum-of-the-years'-digits method of depreciation to the straight-line method and also lengthen the useful lives over which assets are depreciated. (These changes would be made only for financial reporting purposes, not for income tax purposes.)

3 Pressure dealers to increase their inventories—in short, to buy more cars. (The dealerships are independently owned; thus, dealers are the "customers" to whom National Motors sells automobiles.) It is estimated that this strategy could increase sales for the current year by 5%. However, any additional sales in the current year would be almost entirely offset by fewer sales to dealers in the following year.

4 Require dealers to pay for purchases more quickly. Currently, dealers must pay for purchases of autos within 60 days. Management is considering reducing this period to 30 days.

5 Pass up cash discounts offered for prompt payment (i.e., 2/10, n/30) and do not pay any bills until the final due date.

6 Borrow at current short-term interest rates (about 10%) and use the proceeds to pay off long-term debt bearing an interest rate of 13%.

7 Substitute stock dividends for the cash dividends currently paid on capital stock.

INSTRUCTIONS

a Prepare a schedule with four columns. The first column is to be headed "Proposals," and is to contain the paragraph numbers of the seven proposals listed above. The next three columns are to be headed with the following financial statement captions: (1) "Net income," (2) "Net cash flow from operating activities," and (3) "Cash."

For each of the seven proposals in the left column, indicate whether you expect the proposal to "Increase," "Decrease," or have "No Effect" in the current year upon each of the financial statement captions listed in the next three columns. (**Note:** Only a few months remain in the current year. Therefore, you are to determine the **short-term** effects of these proposals.)

b For each of the seven proposals, write a short paragraph explaining the reasoning behind your answers to part **a.**

*CASE 19-3
Analysis of
Data from an
Annual Report

Shown below is an excerpt from a recent annual report of **The Upjohn Company** (Dollar amounts are in thousands.)

Cash flows from operations:

Net income..	$353,418
Adjustments to reconcile net income to net cash provided (required) by operations:	
Depreciation and amortization	102,945
Deferred income taxes..	(8,540)
Other	(6,232)
Changes in:	
Accounts receivable..	(48,756)
Inventory...	(9,169)
Accounts payable	63,505
Income taxes payable	14,003
Other current and noncurrent assets	(47,184)
Other current and noncurrent liabilities.................................	14,682
Net cash provided by operations	**$428,672**

The company did not state whether the changes in the balance sheet accounts listed were increases or decreases, apparently assuming that the reader of the financial statements could determine this from the effect of each adjustment upon net income. (Of course, this information also may be determined by comparing the company's balance sheets at the beginning and end of the year.)

INSTRUCTIONS

By analyzing the effects of the adjustments upon net income in the above schedule, indicate whether the balance in each of the four accounts listed below *increased* or *decreased* over the year. Explain the reasoning behind your answer.

a Accounts receivable

b Inventories

c Accounts payable

d Income taxes payable

ANSWERS TO SELF-TEST QUESTIONS

1 b   2 a   3 a   4 c   5 d

---

*   *Supplemental Topic A, "The Indirect Method"*

20 Analysis and Interpretation of Financial Statements

In preceding chapters we have explained how decision makers analyze, interpret, and use various types of accounting information. Now we are ready to examine a complete set of financial statements, and to see how investors and creditors may use these statements in evaluating the profitability, solvency, and future prospects of a business. A major goal of this chapter is to demonstrate how different types of investors select the accounting information that is most relevant to their decisions.

After studying this chapter you should be able to meet these Learning Objectives:

1 *Put a company's net income into perspective by relating it to sales, assets, and stockholders' equity.*

2 *Describe several sources of financial information about a business.*

3 *Explain the uses of dollar and percentage changes, trend percentages, component percentages, and ratios.*

4 *Discuss the "quality" of a company's earnings, assets, and working capital.*

5 *Analyze financial statements from the viewpoints of common stockholders, creditors, and others.*

6 *Compute the ratios widely used in financial statement analysis and explain the significance of each.*

*F*inancial statements are the instrument panel of a business enterprise. They constitute a report on managerial performance, attesting to managerial success or failure and flashing warning signals of impending difficulties. To read a complex instrument panel, one must understand the gauges and their calibration to make sense out of the array of data they convey. Similarly, one must understand the inner workings of the accounting system and the significance of various financial relationships to interpret the data appearing in financial statements. To a reader with a knowledge of accounting, a set of financial statements tells a great deal about a business enterprise.

The financial affairs of a business may be of interest to a number of different groups: management, creditors, investors, politicians, union officials, and government agencies. Each of the groups has somewhat different needs, and accordingly each tends to concentrate on particular aspects of a company's financial picture.

What Is Your Opinion of the Level of Corporate Profits?

OBJECTIVE 1
Put a company's net income into perspective by relating it to sales, assets, and stockholders' equity.

As a college student who has completed (or almost completed) a course in accounting, you have a much better understanding of corporate profits than do people who have never studied accounting. The level of earnings of large corporations is a controversial topic, a favorite topic in many political speeches and at cocktail parties. Many of the statements one reads or hears from these sources are emotional rather than rational, fiction rather than fact. Public opinion polls show that the public believes the average manufacturing company has an after-tax profit of about 30% of sales, when in fact such profit has been *about 5% of sales* in recent years. A widespread public belief that profits are six times the actual rate may lead to some unwise legislation.

CASE IN POINT General Motors in an annual report a few years ago showed a net income of $321 million. This profit may sound like a huge amount, but it was only one-half of 1% of GM's sales. Thus, of every dollar received as revenue, only $\frac{1}{2}$ cent represented profit for GM. On a $10,000 car, this was a profit of $50. Actually, earning only $321 million in a year must be regarded as very poor performance for a corporation the size of General Motors. Shortly afterward, however, GM set new records for both sales and earnings. Net income was $4.5 billion and represented about $5\frac{1}{2}$ cents profit on each dollar of sales. That was a profit of $550 on a $10,000 automobile.

An in-depth knowledge of accounting does not enable you to say at what level corporate earnings *should be;* however, a knowledge of accounting does enable you to read audited financial statements that show what the level of corporate earnings *actually is.* Moreover, you are aware the information in published financial statements of corporations has been audited by CPA firms and has been reviewed in detail by government agencies, such as the Securities and Exchange Commission (SEC) and the Internal Revenue Service (IRS). Consequently, you know that the profits reported in these published financial statements are reasonably reliable; they have been determined in accordance with generally accepted accounting principles and verified by independent experts.

Some Specific Examples of Corporate Earnings . . . and Losses

Not all leading corporations earn a profit every year. For the ten years from 1981 through 1990, Pan American Airways reported a net loss each year. Late in 1991 Pan Am—America's "flagship" airline—ceased operations. Many American corporations had a bad year in 1991. Each of the "Big Three" American automakers reported huge losses. Even IBM sustained a net loss—the first in the company's 80-year history.

The oil companies have been particularly subject to criticism for so-called excessive profits, so let us briefly look at the profits of Exxon, the world's largest oil company. A recent annual report of Exxon (audited by Price Waterhouse) shows that profits amounted to a little over $3.5 billion. Standing alone, that figure seems enormous—but we need to look a little farther. The total revenue of Exxon was over $95 billion, so net income amounted to less than 4% of sales. On the other hand, income taxes, excise taxes, and other taxes and duties levied upon Exxon amounted to more than $27 billion, or about $7\frac{1}{2}$ times as much as the company's profit. Thus, taxation represents a far greater portion of the cost of a gallon of gasoline than does the oil company's profit.

There are many ways of appraising the adequacy of corporate earnings. Certainly, earnings should be compared with total assets and with invested capital as well as with sales. In this chapter we shall look at a number of ways of evaluating corporate profits and solvency.

Sources of Financial Information

*OBJECTIVE 2
Describe several sources of financial information about a business.*

For the most part, our discussion will be limited to the kind of analysis that can be made by "outsiders" who do not have access to internal accounting records. Investors must rely to a considerable extent on financial statements in published annual and quarterly reports. In the case of largely publicly owned corporations, additional information is filed with the SEC and is available to the public.

The SEC requires large corporations to include in their annual reports a ***discussion and analysis*** by top management of the results of the company's operations and of its current financial position. In this section of the annual report, management is required to highlight favorable and unfavorable trends, and to identify significant events and existing uncertainties affecting the company's financial condition. (This element of an annual report is illustrated in Comprehensive Problem 5, on pages 974–975.)

Many financial analysts also study the financial position and future prospects of publicly owned corporations and sell their analyses, conclusions, and investment recommendations for a fee. For example, detailed financial analyses of most large corporations are published weekly by Moody's Investors Service, Standard & Poor's, and The Value Line Investment Survey. Anyone may subscribe to these investment advisory services.

Bankers and major creditors usually are able to obtain detailed financial information from borrowers simply by requesting it as a condition for granting a loan. Suppliers and other trade creditors may obtain some financial information about almost any business from credit-rating agencies, such as Dunn & Bradstreet.

Comparative Financial Statement

Significant changes in financial data are easy to see when financial statement amounts for two or more years are placed side by side in adjacent columns. Such a statement is called a ***comparative financial statement.*** The amounts for the most recent year are usually placed in the left-hand money column. Both the balance sheet and the income statement are often prepared in the form of comparative statements. A highly condensed comparative income statement covering three years is shown below.

Condensed three-year income statement

BENSON CORPORATION **Comparative Income Statement** **For the Years Ended December 31, 1994, 1993, and 1992** **(in thousands of dollars)**			
	1994	*1993*	*1992*
Net sales	*$600*	*$500*	*$400*
Cost of goods sold	*370*	*300*	*235*
Gross profit	*$230*	*$200*	*$165*
Expenses	*194*	*160*	*115*
Net income	*$ 36*	*$ 40*	*$ 50*

Tools of Analysis

Few figures in a financial statement are highly significant in and of themselves. It is their relationship to other quantities or the amount and direction of change that is important. Analysis is largely a matter of establishing significant relationships and identifying changes and trends. Four widely used analytical techniques are (1) dollar and percentage changes, (2) trend percentages, (3) component percentages, and (4) ratios.

OBJECTIVE 3
Explain the uses of dollar and percentage changes, trend percentages, component percentages, and ratios.

Dollar and Percentage Changes

The dollar amount of change from year to year is significant, but expressing the change in percentage terms adds perspective. For example, if sales this year have increased by $100,000, the fact that this is an increase of 10% over last year's sales of $1 million puts it in a different perspective than if it represented a 1% increase over sales of $10 million for the prior year.

The dollar amount of any change is the difference between the amount for a ***comparison*** year and for a ***base*** year. The percentage change is computed by dividing the amount of the change between years by the amount for the base year. This is illustrated in the tabulation below, using data from the comparative income statement above.

| | In Thousands | | | Increase or (Decrease) | | | |
| | | | | 1994 over 1993 | | 1993 over 1992 | |
	Year 1994	Year 1993	Year 1992	Amount	%	Amount	%
Net sales.............	$600	$500	$400	$100	20%	$100	25%
Net income..........	36	40	50	(4)	(10%)	(10)	(20%)

Dollar and percentage changes

Although net sales increased $100,000 in both 1993 and 1994, the percentage of change differs because of the shift in the base from 1992 to 1993. These calculations present no problems when the figures for the base year are positive amounts. If a negative amount or a zero amount appears in the base year, however, a percentage change cannot be computed. Thus if Benson Corporation had incurred a net loss in 1993, the percentage change in net income from 1993 to 1994 could not have been calculated.

Evaluating Percentage Changes in Sales and Earnings Computing the percentage changes in sales, gross profit, and net income from one year to the next gives insight into a company's rate of growth. If a company is experiencing growth in its economic activities, sales and earnings should increase at **more than the rate of inflation.** Assume, for example, that a company's sales increase by 6% while the general price level rises by 10%. It is probable that the entire increase in the dollar amount of sales may be explained by inflation, rather than by an increase in sales volume (the number of units sold). In fact, the company may well have sold **fewer** goods than in the preceding year.

In measuring the dollar or percentage change in **quarterly** sales or earnings, it is customary to compare the results of the current quarter with those of the **same quarter in the preceding year.** Use of the same quarter of the preceding year as the base period prevents our analysis from being distorted by seasonal fluctuations in business activity.

Percentages Become Misleading When the Base Is Small Percentage changes may create a misleading impression when the dollar amount used as a base is unusually small. Occasionally we hear a television newscaster say that a company's profits have increased by a very large percentage, such as 900%. The initial impression created by such a statement is that the company's profits must now be excessively large. But assume, for example, that a company had net income of $100,000 in its first year; that in the second year net income drops to $10,000; and that in the third year net income returns to the $100,000 level. In this third year, net income has increased by $90,000, representing a 900% increase over the profits of the second year. What needs to be added is that this 900% increase in profits in the third year **exactly offsets** the 90% decline in profits in the second year.

Few people realize that a 90% decline in earnings must be followed by a 900% increase just to get back to the starting point.

CASE IN POINT In the third quarter of 1979, General Motors earned $21.4 million, as compared with $527.9 million in the third quarter of 1978. This represented a 96% decline in third quarter profits, computed as follows:

Decline in profits ($527.9 − $21.4)	*$506.5*
Base period earnings (third quarter, 1978)	*$527.9*
Percentage decrease ($506.5 ÷ $527.9)	*96%*

How much of an increase in profits would be required in the third quarter of 1980 for profits to return to the 1978 level? Many people erroneously guess 96%. However, the correct answer is an astounding 2,367%, computed as follows:

Required increase to reach 1978 profit level (from $21.4 to $527.9)	*$506.5*
Base period earnings (third quarter, 1979)	*$ 21.4*
Required percentage increase ($506.5 ÷ $21.4)	*2,367%*

Unfortunately for GM, the company's 1980 profits did not return to 1978 levels. Instead, the company lost a then record-setting $567 million in the third quarter of 1980.

Trend Percentages

The changes in financial statement items from a base year to following years are often expressed as ***trend percentages*** to show the extent and direction of change. Two steps are necessary to compute trend percentages. First, a base year is selected and each item in the financial statements for the base year is given a weight of 100%. The second step is to express each item in the financial statements for following years as a percentage of its base-year amount. This computation consists of dividing an item such as Sales in the years after the base year by the amount of Sales in the base year.

For example, assume that 1989 is selected as the base year and that Sales in the base year amounted to $300,000 as shown below. The trend percentages for Sales are computed by dividing the Sales amount of each following year by $300,000. Also shown in the illustration are the yearly amounts of net income. The trend percentages for net income are computed by dividing the Net Income amount for each following year by the base-year amount of $15,000.

	1994	*1993*	*1992*	*1991*	*1990*	*1989*
Sales	*$450,000*	*$360,000*	*$330,000*	*$320,000*	*$312,000*	*$300,000*
Net income...........	*22,950*	*14,550*	*21,450*	*19,200*	*15,600*	*15,000*

When the computations described above have been made, the trend percentages will appear as shown below.

	1994	*1993*	*1992*	*1991*	*1990*	*1989*
Sales	*150%*	*120%*	*110%*	*107%*	*104%*	*100%*
Net income..............................	*153%*	*97%*	*143%*	*128%*	*104%*	*100%*

The above trend percentages indicate a very modest growth in sales in the early years and accelerated growth in 1993 and 1994. Net income also shows an increasing growth trend with the exception of the year 1993, when net income declined despite a solid increase in sales. This variation could have resulted from an unfavorable change in the gross profit margin or from unusual expenses. However, the problem was overcome in 1994 with a sharp rise in net income. Overall the trend percentages give a picture of a profitable growing enterprise.

As another example, assume that sales are increasing each year but that the cost of goods sold is increasing at a faster rate. This means that the gross profit margin is shrinking. Perhaps the increases in sales are being achieved through excessive price cutting. The company's net income may be declining even though sales are rising.

Component Percentages

Component percentages indicate the ***relative size*** of each item included in a total. For example, each item on a balance sheet could be expressed as a percentage of total assets. This shows quickly the relative importance of current and noncurrent assets as well as the relative amount of financing obtained from current creditors, long-term creditors, and stockholders. By computing component percentages for several successive balance sheets, we can see which items are increasing in importance and which are becoming less significant.

Common Size Income Statement   Another application of component percentages is to express all items in an income statement as a percentage of net sales. Such a statement is called a common size income statement. A condensed income statement in dollars and in common size form is illustrated below.

Income Statement

	Dollars		Component Percentages	
	1994	1993	1994	1993
Net sales...................................	$1,000,000	$600,000	100.0%	100.0%
Cost of goods sold	700,000	360,000	70.0	60.0
Gross profit on sales	$ 300,000	$240,000	30.0%	40.0%
Expenses (including income taxes)..........	250,000	180,000	25.0	30.0
Net income.................................	$ 50,000	$ 60,000	5.0%	10.0%

Are the year-to-year changes favorable?

Looking only at the component percentages, we see that the decline in the gross profit rate from 40% to 30% was only partially offset by the decrease in expenses as a percentage of net sales, causing net income to decrease from 10% to 5% of net sales.

Ratios

A ratio is a simple mathematical expression of the relationship of one item to another. Every percentage may be viewed as a ratio—that is, one number expressed as a percentage of another.

Ratios may be stated in several ways. To illustrate, let us consider the current ratio, which expresses the relationship between current assets and current liabilities. If current assets are $100,000 and current liabilities are $50,000, we may say either that the current ratio is 2 to 1 (which is written as 2:1) or that current assets are 200% of current liabilities. Either statement correctly summarizes the relationship—that is, that current assets are twice as large as current liabilities.

If a ratio is to be useful, the two amounts being compared must be logically related. Our interpretation of a ratio often requires investigation of the underlying data.

Comparative Data in Annual Reports of Major Corporations

The annual reports of major corporations usually contain comparative balance sheets covering two years and comparative income statements for three years. Supplementary schedules showing sales, net income, and other key amounts are often presented for periods of five to 10 years. Shown below are selected items from an annual report of The Coca-Cola Company showing some interesting trends for a five-year period.

THE COCA-COLA COMPANY
(Dollars in millions, except per share data)

	1989	1988	1987	1986	1985
Net sales	$8,966	$8,338	$7,658	$6,977	$5,879
Net income	1,724	1,045	916	934	722
Net earnings per share	4.92	2.85	2.43	2.42	1.84
Dividends per share	1.36	1.20	1.12	1.04	.99
Market price per share (year-end)	77.25	44.63	38.13	37.75	28.17

Standards of Comparison

In using dollar and percentage changes, trend percentages, component percentages, and ratios, financial analysts constantly search for some standard of comparison against which to judge whether the relationships that they have found are favorable or unfavorable. Two such standards are (1) the past performance of the company and (2) the performance of other companies in the same industry.

Past Performance of the Company   Comparing analytical data for a current period with similar computations for prior years affords some basis for judging whether the condition of the business is improving or worsening. This comparison of data over time is sometimes called **horizontal** or **trend** analysis, to express the idea of reviewing data for a number of consecutive periods. It is distinguished from **vertical** or **static** analysis, which refers to the review of the financial information for only one accounting period.

In addition to determining whether the situation is improving or becoming worse, horizontal analysis may aid in making estimates of future prospects.

Because changes may reverse their direction at any time, however, projecting past trends into the future is always a somewhat risky statistical pastime.

A weakness of horizontal analysis is that comparison with the past does not afford any basis for evaluation in absolute terms. The fact that net income was 2% of sales last year and is 3% of sales this year indicates improvement, but if there is evidence that net income **should be** 7% of sales, the record for both years is unfavorable.

Industry Standard   The limitations of horizontal analysis may be overcome to some extent by finding an appropriate "yardstick" against which to measure a particular company's performance. The yardsticks most widely used by most analysts are the performance of comparable companies and the average performance of several companies in the same industry.[1]

Assume, for example, that the revenue of Alpha Airlines drops by 5% during the current year. If the revenue for the airlines industry had dropped an average of 15% during this year, Alpha's 5% decline might be viewed as a **favorable** performance. As another example, assume that Omega Co. earns a net income equal to 2% of net sales. This would be substandard if Omega were a manufacturer of commercial aircraft, but it would be satisfactory performance if it were a grocery chain.

When we compare a given company with its competitors or with industry averages, our conclusions will be valid only if the companies in question are reasonably comparable. Because of the large number of diversified companies formed in recent years, the term **industry** is difficult to define, and companies that fall roughly within the same industry may not be comparable in many respects. For example, one company may engage only in the marketing of oil products; another may be a fully integrated producer from the well to the gas pump, yet both are said to be in the "oil industry."

Quality of Earnings

*OBJECTIVE 4
Discuss the
"quality" of
a company's
earnings,
assets, and
working
capital.*

Profits are the lifeblood of a business entity. No entity can survive for long and accomplish its other goals unless it is profitable. On the other hand, continuous losses will drain assets from the business, consume owners' equity, and leave the company at the mercy of creditors. In assessing the prospects of a company, we are interested not only in the total **amount** of earnings but also in the **rate** of earnings on sales, on total assets, and on owner's equity. In addition, we must look at the **stability** and **source** of earnings. An erratic earnings performance over a period of years, for example, is less desirable than a steady level of earnings. A history of increasing earnings is preferable to a "flat" earnings record.

A breakdown of sales and earnings by **major product lines** is useful in evaluating the future performance of a company. Publicly owned companies include with their financial statements supplementary schedules showing sales and profits by product line and by geographical area. These schedules assist financial analysts in forecasting the effect upon the company of changes in consumer demand for particular types of products.

---

[1]   Industry data are available from a number of sources. For example, Robert Morris Associates publishes *Annual Statement Studies* which include data from many thousands of annual reports, grouped into several hundred industry classifications. Industry classifications are subdivided further by company size. Dun & Bradstreet, Inc., annually publishes *Key Business Ratios* for more than 800 lines of business.

Financial analysts often express the opinion that the earnings of one company are of higher quality than earnings of other similar companies. This concept of *quality of earnings* arises because each company management can choose from a variety of accounting principles and methods, all of which are considered generally acceptable. A company's management often is under heavy pressure to report rising earnings, and accounting policies may be tailored toward this objective. We have already pointed out the impact on current reported earnings of the choice between the LIFO and FIFO methods of inventory valuation and the choice of depreciation policies. In judging the quality of earnings, the financial analyst should consider whether the accounting principles and methods selected by management lead to a conservative measurement of earnings or tend to inflate reported earnings.

Quality of Assets and the Relative Amount of Debt

Although a satisfactory level of earnings may be a good indication of the company's long-run ability to pay its debts and dividends, we must also look at the composition of assets, their condition and liquidity, the relationship between current assets and current liabilities, and the total amount of debt outstanding. A company may be profitable and yet be unable to pay its liabilities on time; sales and earnings may appear satisfactory, but plant and equipment may be deteriorating because of poor maintenance policies; valuable patents may be expiring; substantial losses may be imminent due to slow-moving inventories and past-due receivables. Companies with large amounts of debt often are vulnerable to increases in interest rates and to even temporary reductions in cash inflows.

Impact of Inflation

During a period of significant inflation, financial statements prepared in terms of historical costs do not reflect fully the economic resources or the real income (in terms of purchasing power) of a business enterprise. The FASB recommends that companies include in their annual reports supplementary schedules showing the effects of inflation upon their financial statements. Inclusion of these supplementary disclosures is voluntary, not mandatory. Most companies do *not* include these supplementary schedules because of the high cost of developing this information.

Illustrative Analysis for Seacliff Company

Keep in mind the above discussion of analytical principles as you study the illustrative financial analysis which follows. The basic information for our analysis is contained in a set of condensed two-year comparative financial statements for Seacliff Company shown below and on the following pages. Summarized statement data, together with computations of dollar increases and decreases, and component percentages where applicable, have been compiled. For convenience in this illustration, relatively small dollar amounts have been used in the Seacliff Company financial statements.

Using the information in these statements, let us consider the kind of analysis that might be of particular interest to (1) common stockholders, (2) long-term creditors, (3) preferred stockholders, and (4) short-term creditors.

SEACLIFF COMPANY
Comparative Income Statement
For the Years Ended December 31, 1994 and December 31, 1993

	1994	1993	Increase or (Decrease) Dollars	%	Percentage of Net Sales 1994	1993
Net sales	$900,000	$750,000	$150,000	20.0	100.0	100.0
Cost of goods sold	530,000	420,000	110,000	26.2	58.9	56.0
Gross profit on sales	$370,000	$330,000	$ 40,000	12.1	41.1	44.0
Operating expenses:						
Selling expenses:	$117,000	$ 75,000	$ 42,000	56.0	13.0	10.0
General and administrative expenses	126,000	95,000	31,000	32.6	14.0	12.7
Total operating expenses	$243,000	$170,000	$ 73,000	42.9	27.0	22.7
Operating income	$127,000	$160,000	$(33,000)	(20.6)	14.1	21.3
Interest expense	24,000	30,000	(6,000)	(20.0)	2.7	4.0
Income before income taxes	$103,000	$130,000	$(27,000)	(20.8)	11.4	17.3
Income taxes	28,000	40,000	(12,000)	(30.0)	3.1	5.3
Net income	$ 75,000	$ 90,000	$(15,000)	(16.7)	8.3	12.0
Earnings per share of common stock	$13.20	$20.25	$(7.05)	(34.8)		

SEACLIFF COMPANY
Statement of Retained Earnings
For the Years Ended December 31, 1994 and December 31, 1993

	1994	1993	Increase or (Decrease) Dollars	%
Retained earnings, beginning of year	$176,000	$115,000	$61,000	53.0
Net income	75,000	90,000	(15,000)	(16.7)
	$251,000	$205,000	$46,000	22.4
Less: Dividends on common stock ($5.00 per share in 1991, $4.80 per share in 1992)	$ 24,000	$ 20,000	$ 4,000	20.0
Dividends on preferred stock ($9 per share)	9,000	9,000		
	$ 33,000	$ 29,000	$ 4,000	13.8
Retained earnings, end of year	$218,000	$176,000	$42,000	23.9

SEACLIFF COMPANY
Condensed Comparative Balance Sheet*
December 31, 1994 and December 31, 1993

Assets	1994	1993	Increase or (Decrease) Dollars	%	Percentage of Total Assets 1994	1993
Current assets	$390,000	$288,000	$102,000	35.4	41.1	33.5
Plant and equipment (net)	500,000	467,000	33,000	7.1	52.6	54.3
Other assets (loans to officers)	60,000	105,000	(45,000)	(42.9)	6.3	12.2
Total assets	$950,000	$860,000	$ 90,000	10.5	100.0	100.0
Liabilities & Stockholders' Equity						
Liabilities:						
Current liabilities	$112,000	$ 94,000	$ 18,000	19.1	11.8	10.9
12% long-term note payable	200,000	250,000	(50,000)	(20.0)	21.1	29.1
Total liabilities	$312,000	$344,000	$(32,000)	(9.3)	32.9	40.0
Stockholders' equity:						
9% preferred stock, $100 par, callable at 105	$100,000	$100,000			10.5	11.6
Common stock, $50 par	250,000	200,000	$ 50,000	25.0	26.3	23.2
Additional paid-in capital	70,000	40,000	30,000	75.0	7.4	4.7
Retained earnings	218,000	176,000	42,000	23.9	22.9	20.5
Total stockholders' equity	$638,000	$516,000	$122,000	23.6	67.1	60.0
Total liabilities & stockholders' equity	$950,000	$860,000	$ 90,000	10.5	100.0	100.0

* In order to focus attention on important subtotals, this statement is highly condensed and does not show individual asset and liability items. These details will be introduced as needed in the next discussion. For example, a list of Seacliff Company's current assets and current liabilities appears on page 941.

SEACLIFF COMPANY
Condensed Comparative Statement of Cash Flows
For the Years Ended December 31, 1994 and December 31, 1993

	1994	1993	Increase or (Decrease) Dollars	%
Cash flows from operating activities:				
Net cash flow from operating activities	$ 19,000	$ 95,000	$(76,000)	(80.0)
Cash flows from investing activities:				
Purchases of plant assets	(63,000)	(28,000)	(35,000)	125.0
Collections of loans from officers	45,000	(35,000)	80,000	N/A*
Net cash used by investing activities	$(18,000)	$(63,000)	$ 45,000	(71.4)
Cash flows from financing activities:				
Dividends paid	$(33,000)	$(29,000)	$ (4,000)	13.7
Repayment of long-term debt	(50,000)	-0-	(50,000)	N/A*
Proceeds from issuing capital stock	80,000	-0-	80,000	N/A*
Net cash used by financing activities	$ (3,000)	$(29,000)	$ 26,000	(89.6)
Net increase (decrease) in cash and cash equivalents	$ (2,000)	$ 3,000	$ (5,000)	N/A*
Cash and cash equivalents, beginning of the year	40,000	37,000	3,000	.1
Cash and cash equivalents, end of the year	$ 38,000	$ 40,000	$ (2,000)	(.1)

* N/A indicates that computation of the percentage change is not appropriate. Percentages changes cannot be determined if the base year is zero, or if a negative amount (cash outflow) changes to a positive amount (cash inflow).

Analysis by Common Stockholders

OBJECTIVE 5
Analyze
financial
statements
from the
viewpoints
of common
stockholders,
creditors,
and others.

Common stockholders and potential investors in common stock look first at a company's earnings record. Their investment is in shares of stock, so ***earnings per share and dividends per share*** are of particular interest.

Earnings per Share of Common Stock   As indicated in Chapter 15, earnings per share of common stock are computed by dividing the income applicable to the common stock by the weighted-average number of shares of common stock outstanding during the year. Any preferred dividend requirements must be subtracted from net income to determine income applicable to common stock, as shown in the following computations for Seacliff Company:

Earnings per Share of Common Stock

Earnings re-
lated to num-
ber of common
shares out-
standing

		1994	1993
Net income..		$75,000	$90,000
Less: Preferred dividend requirements		9,000	9,000
Income applicable to common stock	(a)	$66,000	$81,000
Shares of common stock outstanding, during the year	(b)	5,000	4,000
Earnings per share of common stock (a ÷ b)		$13.20	$20.25

Notice that earnings per share have decreased by ***$7.05*** in 1994, representing a decline of nearly ***35%*** from their level in 1993 ($7.05 ÷ $20.25 = 34.8%). Common stockholders consider a decline in earnings per share to be an extremely unfavorable development. A decline in earnings per share generally represents a decline in the profitability of the company, and creates doubt as to the company's prospects for future growth.

With such a significant decline in earnings per share, we should expect to see a ***substantial*** decline in the market value of Seacliff's common stock during 1994. [For purposes of our illustration, we will assume the common stock had a market value of ***$160*** at December 31, 1993 and of ***$132*** at the end of 1994. This drop of $28 per share represents a ***17½%*** decline in the market value of every common stockholder's investment ($28 decline ÷ $160 = 17.5%).]

Price-Earnings Ratio   The relationship between the market price of common stock and earnings per share is so widely recognized that it is expressed as a ratio, called the price-earnings ratio (or ***p/e*** ratio). The p/e ratio is determined by dividing the market price per share by the annual earnings per share.

The average p/e ratio of the 30 stocks included in the Dow-Jones Industrial Average has varied widely in recent years, ranging from a low of about 10 to a high of about 18. The outlook for future earnings is the major factor influencing a company's p/e ratio. Companies with track records of rapid growth may sell at p/e ratios of perhaps 20 to 1, or even higher. Companies with "flat" earnings or earnings expected to decline in future years often sell at price-earnings ratios below, say, 10 to 1.

At the end of 1993, Seacliff's p/e ratio was approximately ***8 to 1*** ($160 ÷ $20.25 = 7.9), suggesting that investors ***were expecting*** earnings to decline in 1994. At December 31, 1994, the price earnings ratio was ***10 to 1***

($132 ÷ $13.20 = 10.0). A p/e ratio in this range suggests that investors expect future earnings to stabilize around the current level.

Dividend Yield Dividends are of prime importance to some stockholders but a secondary factor to others. In other words, some stockholders invest primarily to receive regular cash income, while others invest in stocks principally with the hope of securing capital gains through rising market prices. If a corporation is profitable and retains its earnings for expansion of the business, the expanded operations should produce an increase in the net income of the company and thus tend to make each share of stock more valuable.

In comparing the merits of alternative investment opportunities, we should relate earnings and dividends per share to the ***market value*** of the stock. Dividends per share divided by market price per share determine the ***yield*** rate of a company's stock. Dividend yield is especially important to those investors whose objective is to maximize the dividend revenue from their investments.

Summary of Earnings and Dividend Data for Seacliff The relationships of Seacliff's per-share earnings and dividends to its year-end stock prices are summarized below:

Earnings and Dividends per Share of Common Stock

	Date	Assumed Market Value per Share	Earnings per Share	Price-Earnings Ratio	Dividends per Share	Dividend Yield, %
Earnings and dividends related to market price of common stock	*Dec. 31, 1993...........*	*$160*	*$20.25*	*8*	*$5.00*	*3.1*
	Dec. 31, 1994...........	*132*	*13.20*	*10*	*4.80*	*3.6*

The decline in market value during 1994 presumably reflects the decreases in both earnings and dividends per share. Investors appraising this stock at December 31, 1994, should consider whether a price-earning ratio of ***10*** and a dividend yield of ***3.6%*** represent a satisfactory situation in the light of alternative investment opportunities. These investors will also place considerable weight on estimates of the company's prospective future earnings and the probable effect of such estimated earnings on the market price of the stock and on dividend payments.

Book Value per Share of Common Stock The procedures for computing book value per share were fully described in Chapter 14 and will not be repeated here. We will, however, determine the book value per share of common stock for the Seacliff Company:

Book Value per Share of Common Stock

		1994	1993
Why did book value per share increase?	*Total stockholders' equity ....*	*$638,000*	*$516,000*
	Less: Equity of preferred stockholders (1,000 shares at		
	* call price of $105) ....*	*105,000*	*105,000*
	Equity of common stockholders................................. (a)	*$533,000*	*$411,000*
	Shares of common stock outstanding .... (b)	*5,000*	*4,000*
	Book value per share of common stock (a ÷ b)	*$106.60*	*$102.75*

Book value indicates the net assets represented by each share of stock. This statistic is often helpful in estimating a reasonable price for a company's stock, especially for small corporations whose shares are not publicly traded. However, if a company's future earnings prospects are unusually good or unusually poor, the market price of its shares may differ significantly from their book value.

Revenue and Expense Analysis The trend of earnings of Seacliff Company is unfavorable, and stockholders will want to know the reasons for the decline in net income. The comparative income statement on page 932 shows that despite a 20% increase in net sales, net income fell from $90,000 in 1993 to $75,000 in 1994, a decline of 16.7%. As a percentage of net sales, net income fell from 12% to only 8.3%. The primary causes of this decline were the increases in selling expenses (56.0%), in general and administrative expenses (32.6%), and in the cost of goods sold (26.2%), all of which exceeded the 20% increase in net sales.

Let us assume that further investigation reveals Seacliff Company decided in 1994 to reduce its sales prices in an effort to generate greater sales volume. This would explain the decrease in gross profit rate from 44% to 41.1% of net sales. Since the dollar amount of gross profit increased $40,000 in 1994, the strategy of reducing sales prices to increase volume would have been successful if there had been little or no increase in operating expenses. However, operating expenses rose by $73,000, resulting in a $33,000 decrease in operating income.

The next step is to find which expenses increased and why. An investor may be handicapped here, because detailed operating expenses are not usually shown in published financial statements. Some conclusions, however, can be reached on the basis of even the condensed information available in the comparative income statement for Seacliff Company shown on page 932.

The substantial increase in selling expenses presumably reflects greater selling effort during 1994 in an attempt to improve sales volume. However, the fact that selling expenses increased $42,000 while gross profit increased only $40,000 indicates that the cost of this increased sales effort was not justified in terms of results. Even more disturbing is the increase in general and administrative expenses. Some growth in administrative expenses might be expected to accompany increased sales volume, but because some of the expenses are fixed, the growth generally should be ***less than proportional*** to any increase in sales. The increase in general and administrative expenses from 12.7 to 14% of sales would be of serious concern to informed investors.

Management generally has greater control over operating expenses than over revenue. The ***operating expense ratio*** is often used as a measure of management's ability to control its operating expenses. The unfavorable trend in this ratio for Seacliff Company is shown below:

Operating Expense Ratio

	1994	1993
Operating expenses	(a) $243,000	$170,000
Net sales	(b) $900,000	$750,000
Operating expense ratio (a ÷ b)	27.0%	22.7%

Does a higher operating expense ratio indicate higher net income?

If management were able to increase the sales volume while at the same time increasing the gross profit rate and decreasing the operating expense ratio, the effect on net income could be quite dramatic. For example, if in 1993 Seacliff Company can increase its sales by 11% to $1,000,000, increase its gross profit rate from 41.1 to 44%, and reduce the operating expense ratio from 27 to 24%, its operating income will increase from $127,000 to $200,000 ($1,000,000 − $560,000 − $240,000), an increase of over 57%.

Return on Investment (ROI)

The rate of return on investment (often called ROI) is a measure of management's efficiency in using available resources. Regardless of the size of the organization, capital is a scarce resource and must be used efficiently. In judging the performance of branch managers or of companywide management, it is reasonable to raise the question: What rate of return have you earned on the resources under your control? The concept of return on investment can be applied to a number of situations: for example, evaluating a branch, a total business, a product line, or an individual investment. A number of different ratios have been developed for the ROI concept, each well suited to a particular situation. We shall consider the ***return on assets*** and the ***return on common stockholders' equity*** as examples of the return on investment concept.

Return on Assets An important test of management's ability to earn a return on funds supplied from all sources is the rate of return on total assets.

The income figure used in computing this ratio should be ***operating income,*** since interest expense and income taxes are determined by factors other than the efficient use of resources. Operating income is earned throughout the year and therefore should be related to the ***average*** investment in assets during the year. The computation of this ratio of Seacliff Company is shown below:

Percentage Return on Assets

		1994	1993
Operating income	(a)	$127,000	$160,000
Total assets, beginning of year	(b)	$860,000	$820,000
Total assets, end of year	(c)	$950,000	$860,000
Average investment in assets [(b + c) ÷ 2]	(d)	$905,000	$840,000
Return on assets (a ÷ d)		14%	19%

Earnings related to investment in assets

This ratio shows that the rate of return earned on the company's assets has fallen off in 1994. Before drawing conclusions as to the effectiveness of Seacliff's management, however, we should consider the trend in the return on assets earned by other companies of similar kind and size.

Return on Common Stockholders' Equity Because interest and dividends paid to creditors and preferred stockholders are fixed in amount, a company may earn a greater or smaller return on the common stockholders' equity than on its total assets. The computation of return on stockholders' equity for Seacliff Company is shown below:

Return on Common Stockholders' Equity

		1994	1993
Net income..		$ 75,000	$ 90,000
Less: Preferred dividend requirements		9,000	9,000
Net income applicable to common stock	(a)	$ 66,000	$ 81,000
Common stockholders' equity, beginning of year	(b)	$416,000	$355,000
Common stockholders' equity, end of year....................	(c)	$538,000	$416,000
Average common stockholders' equity [(b + c) ÷ 2]	(d)	$477,000	$385,500
Return on common stockholders' equity (a ÷ d)		13.8%	21.0%

Does the use of leverage benefit common stockholders?

In both years, the rate of return on common stockholders' equity was higher than the 12% rate of interest paid to long-term creditors or the 9% dividend rate paid to preferred stockholders. This result was achieved through the favorable use of leverage.

Leverage

The term *leverage* means operating a business with borrowed money. If the borrowed capital can be used in the business to earn a return *greater* than the cost of borrowing, then the net income and the return on common stockholders' equity will *increase.* In other words, if you can borrow money at 12% and use it to earn 20%, you will benefit by doing so. However, leverage can act as a "double-edged sword"; the effects may be favorable or unfavorable to the holders of common stock.

If the rate of return on total assets should fall *below* the average rate of interest on borrowed capital, leverage will *reduce* net income and the return on common stockholders' equity. In this situation, paying off the loans that carry high interest rates would appear to be a logical move. However, most companies do not have enough cash to retire long-term debt on short notice. Therefore, the common stockholders may become "locked in" to the unfavorable effects of leverage.

In deciding how much leverage is appropriate, the common stockholders should consider the *stability* of the company's return on assets as well as the relationship of this return to the average cost of borrowed capital. If a business incurs so much debt that it becomes unable to meet the required interest and principal payments, the creditors may force liquidation or reorganization of the business.

Equity Ratio One indicator of the amount of leverage used by a business is the equity ratio. This ratio measures the proportion of the total assets financed by stockholders, as distinguished from creditors. It is computed by dividing total stockholders' equity by total assets. A *low* equity ratio indicates an extensive use of leverage, that is, a large proportion of financing provided by creditors. A high equity ratio, on the other hand, indicates that the business is making little use of leverage.

The equity ratio at year-end for Seacliff is determined as follows:

$A = L + OE$

Equity Ratio

Proportion of assets financed by stockholders

		1994	1993
Total stockholders' equity	(a)	$638,000	$516,000
Total assets (or total liabilities & stockholders' equity)	(b)	$950,000	$860,000
Equity ratio (a ÷ b)		67.2%	60.0%

Seacliff Company has a higher equity ratio in 1994 than in 1993. Is this favorable or unfavorable?

From the viewpoint of the common stockholder, a low equity ratio will produce maximum benefits if management is able to earn a rate of return on assets greater than the rate of interest paid to creditors. However, a low equity ratio can be very **unfavorable** if the return on assets falls **below** the rate of interest paid to creditors. Since the return on total assets earned by Seacliff Company has declined from 19% in 1993 to a relatively low 14% in 1994, the common stockholders probably would **not** want to risk a low equity ratio. The action by management in 1994 of retiring $50,000 in long-term liabilities will help to protect the common stockholders from the unfavorable effects of leverage if the rate of return on assets continues to decline.

Analysis by Long-Term Creditors

Bondholders and other long-term creditors are primarily interested in three factors: (1) the rate of return on their investment, (2) the firm's ability to meet its interest requirements, and (3) the firm's ability to repay the principal of the debt when it falls due.

Yield Rate on Bonds   The yield rate on bonds or other long-term indebtedness cannot be computed in the same manner as the yield rate on shares of stock, because bonds, unlike stocks, have a definite maturity date and amount. The ownership of a 12%, 10-year, $1,000 bond represents the right to receive $120 each year for 10 years plus the right to receive $1,000 at the end of 10 years. If the market price of this bond is $950, the yield rate on an investment in the bond is the rate of interest that will make the present value of these two contractual rights equal to $950. When bonds sell at maturity value, the yield rate is equal to the bond interest rate. *The yield rate varies inversely with changes in the market price of the bond.* If interest rates rise, the market price of existing bonds will fall; if interest rates decline, the price of bonds will rise. If the price of a bond is above maturity value, the yield rate is less than the bond interest rate; if the price of a bond is below maturity value, the yield rate is higher than the bond interest rate.

Interest Coverage Ratio   Bondholders feel that their investments are relatively safe if the issuing company earns enough income to cover its annual interest obligations by a wide margin.

A common measure of creditors' safety is the ratio of operating income available for the payment of interest to the annual interest expanse, called the **interest coverage ratio.** This computation for Seacliff Company would be:

Interest Coverage Ratio

		1994	1993
Long-term creditors watch this ratio	Operating income (before interest and income taxes)	(a) $127,000	$160,000
	Annual interest expense	(b) $ 24,000	$ 30,000
	Interest coverage (a ÷ b)	5.3 times	5.3 times

The ratio remained unchanged at a satisfactory level during 1994. A ratio of 5.3 times interest earned would be considered strong in many industries. In the electric utilities industry, for example, the interest coverage ratio for the leading companies presently averages about 3, with the ratios of individual companies varying from 2 to 6.

Debt Ratio   Long-term creditors are interested in the percentage of total assets financed by debt, as distinguished from the percentage financed by stockholders. The percentage of total assets financed by debt is measured by the debt ratio. This ratio is computed by dividing total liabilities by total assets, shown below for Seacliff Company.

Debt Ratio

		1994	1993
What portion of total assets is financed by creditors?	Total liabilities	(a) $312,000	$344,000
	Total assets (or total liabilities & stockholders' equity)	(b) $950,000	$860,000
	Debt ratio (a ÷ b)	32.8%	40.0%

From a creditor's viewpoint, the lower the debt ratio (or the higher the equity ratio) the better, since this means that stockholders have contributed the bulk of the funds to the business, and therefore the margin of protection to creditors against a shrinkage of the assets is high.

Analysis by Preferred Stockholders

Some preferred stocks are convertible into common stock at the option of the holder. However, many preferred stocks do not have the conversion privilege. If a preferred stock is convertible, the interests of the preferred stockholders are similar to those of common stockholders. If a preferred stock is not convertible, the interests of the preferred stockholders are more like those of long-term creditors.

Preferred stockholders are interested in the yield on their investment. The yield is computed by dividing the dividend per share by the market value per share. The dividend per share of Seacliff Company preferred stock is $9. If we assume that the market value at December 31, 1994, is $75 per share, the yield rate at that time would be 12% ($9 ÷ $75).

The primary measurement of the safety of an investment in preferred stock is the ability of the firm to meet its preferred dividend requirements. The best test of this ability is the ratio of the net income to the amount of the annual preferred dividends, as follows:

Preferred Dividends Coverage Ratio

		1994	1993
Is the preferred dividend safe?	Net income	(a) $75,000	$90,000
	Annual preferred dividend requirements	(b) $ 9,000	$ 9,000
	Preferred dividend coverage (a ÷ b)	8.3 times	10 times

Although the margin of protection declined in 1994, the annual preferred dividend requirement still appears well protected.

As previously discussed in Chapter 14 (page 663) the market price of a preferred stock tends to **vary inversely** with interest rates. When interest rates are moving up, preferred stock prices tend to decline, when interest rates are dropping, preferred stock prices rise.

Analysis by Short-Term Creditors

Bankers and other short-term creditors share the interest of stockholders and bondholders in the profitability and long-run stability of a business. Their primary interest, however, is in the current position of the firm—its ability to generate sufficient funds (working capital) to meet current operating needs and to pay current debts promptly. Thus the analysis of financial statements by a banker considering a short-term loan, or by a trade creditor investigating the credit status of a customer, is likely to center on the working capital position of the prospective debtor.

Amount of Working Capital   The details of the working capital of Seacliff Company are shown below:

SEACLIFF COMPANY
Comparative Schedule of Working Capital
As of December 31, 1994 and December 31, 1993

	1994	1993	Increase or (Decrease) Dollars	%	Percentage of Total Current Items 1994	1993
Current assets:						
Cash	$ 38,000	$ 40,000	$ (2,000)	(5.0)	9.7	13.9
Receivables (net)	117,000	86,000	31,000	36.0	30.0	29.9
Inventories	180,000	120,000	60,000	50.0	46.2	41.6
Prepaid expenses	55,000	42,000	13,000	31.0	14.1	14.6
Total current assets	$390,000	$288,000	$102,000	35.4	100.0	100.0
Current liabilities:						
Notes payable to creditors	$ 14,600	$ 10,000	$ 4,600	46.0	13.1	10.7
Accounts payable........	66,000	30,000	36,000	120.0	58.9	31.9
Accrued liabilities........	31,400	54,000	(22,600)	(41.9)	28.0	57.4
Total current liabilities	$112,000	$ 94,000	$ 18,000	19.1	100.0	100.0
Working capital	$278,000	$194,000	$84,000	43.3		

The amount of working capital is measured by the **excess of current assets over current liabilities.** Thus, working capital represents the amount of cash, near-cash items, and cash substitutes (prepayments) on hand after providing for payment of all current liabilities.

This schedule shows that current assets increased $102,000, while current liabilities rose by only $18,000, with the result that working capital increased $84,000.

Quality of Working Capital   In evaluating the debt-paying ability of a business, short-term creditors should consider the quality of working capital as well as the total dollar amount. The principal factors affecting the quality of working capital are (1) the nature of the current assets and (2) the length of time required to convert these assets into cash.

The preceding schedule shows an unfavorable shift in the composition of Seacliff Company's working capital during 1994; cash decreased from 13.9% to 9.7% of current assets, while inventory rose from 41.6% to 46.2%. Inventory is a less liquid resource than cash. Therefore, the quality of working capital is not as liquid as in 1993. *Turnover rates* (or *ratios*) may be used to assist short-term creditors in estimating the time required to turn assets such as receivables and inventory into cash.

Accounts Receivable Turnover Rate   As explained in Chapter 8, the accounts receivable turnover rate indicates how quickly a company converts its accounts receivable into cash. The accounts receivable turnover *rate* is determined by dividing net sales by the average balance of accounts receivable.[2] The number of *days* required (on average) to collect accounts receivable then may be determined by dividing the number of days in a year (365) by the turnover rate. These computations are shown below using the data in our Seacliff example:

Accounts Receivable Turnover

	1994	1993
Net sales...	(a) $900,000	$750,000
Receivables, beginning of year..................................	$ 86,000	$ 80,000
Receivables, end of year...	$117,000	$ 86,000
Average receivables	(b) $101,500	$ 83,000
Receivable turnover per year (a ÷ b)	8.9 times	9.0 times
Average number of days to collect receivables (divide 365 days by receivable turnover)..............................	41 days	41 days

Are customers paying promptly?

There has been no significant change in the average time required to collect receivables. The interpretation of the average age of receivables depends upon the company's credit terms and the seasonal activity immediately before year-end. For example, if the company grants 30-day credit terms to its customers, the above analysis indicates that accounts receivable collections are lagging. If the terms are for 60 days, however, collections are being made ahead of schedule.

Inventory Turnover Rate   The inventory turnover rate indicates how many times during the year the company is able to sell a quantity of goods equal to its average inventory. Mechanically, this rate is determined by dividing the cost of goods sold for the year by the average amount of inventory on hand during the year. The number of days required to sell this amount of inventory may be determined by dividing 365 days by the turnover rate.

---

[2]   Ideally, the accounts receivable turnover is computed by dividing net *credit* sales by the *monthly* average of receivables. Such detailed information, however, generally is not provided in annual financial statements.

These computations were explained in Chapter 9, and are demonstrated below using the data of Seacliff Company:

Inventory Turnover

		1994	1993
Cost of goods sold	(a)	$530,000	$420,000
Inventory, beginning of year		$120,000	$100,000
Inventory, end of year		$180,000	$120,000
Average inventory	(b)	$150,000	$110,000
Average inventory turnover per year (a ÷ b)		3.5 times	3.8 times
Average number of days to sell inventory (divide 365 days by inventory turnover)		104 days	96 days

The trend indicated by this analysis is unfavorable, since the length of time required for Seacliff to turn over (sell) its inventory is increasing.

Companies that have low gross profit rates often need high inventory turnover rates in order to operate profitably. This is merely another way of saying that if the gross profit rate is low, a high volume of transactions is necessary to produce a satisfactory amount of profits. Companies that sell "high markup" items, such as jewelry stores and art galleries, can operate successfully with much lower inventory turnover rates.

Operating Cycle In Chapter 5 we defined the term *operating cycle* as the average time period between the purchase of merchandise and the conversion of this merchandise back into cash. In other words, the merchandise acquired for inventory is gradually converted into accounts receivable by selling goods to customers on credit, and these receivables are converted into cash through the process of collection. The word *cycle* refers to the circular flow of assets from cash to inventory to receivables and back into cash.

Seacliff's operating cycle in 1994 was approximately 145 days, computed by adding the 104 days required to turn over inventory and the average 41 days required to collect receivables. This compares to an operating cycle of only 137 days in 1993, computed as 96 days to dispose of the inventory plus 41 days to collect the resulting receivables. From the viewpoint of short-term creditors, the shorter the operating cycle, the higher the quality of the borrower's working capital. Therefore, these creditors would regard the lengthening of Seacliff Company's operating cycle as an unfavorable trend.

Current Ratio The current ratio (current assets divided by current liabilities) expresses the relationship between current assets and current liabilities. As debts come due, they must be paid out of current assets. Therefore, short-term creditors frequently compare the amount of current assets with the amount of current liabilities. The current ratio indicates a company's short-run, debt-paying ability. It is a measure of liquidity and of solvency. A strong current ratio provides considerable assurance that a company will be able to meet its obligations coming due in the near future. The current ratio for Seacliff Company is computed as follows:

Current Ratio

Does this indicate satisfactory debt-paying ability?

	1994	1993
Total current assets	(a) $390,000	$288,000
Total current liabilities	(b) $112,000	$ 94,000
Current ratio (a ÷ b)	3.5	3.1

A widely used rule of thumb is that a current ratio of 2 to 1 or better is satisfactory. By this standard, Seacliff Company's current ratio appears quite strong. Creditors tend to feel that the higher the current ratio the better. From a managerial point of view, however, there is an upper limit. Too high a current ratio may indicate that capital is not being used productively in the business.

Use of both the current ratio and the amount of working capital helps to place debt-paying ability in its proper perspective. For example, if Company X has current assets of $200,000 and current liabilities of $100,000 and Company Y has current assets of $2,000,000 and current liabilities of $1,900,000, each company has $100,000 of working capital, but the current position of Company X is clearly superior to that of Company Y. The current ratio for Company X is quite satisfactory at 2 to 1, but Company Y's current ratio is very low—only slightly above 1 to 1.

As another example, assume that Company A and Company B both have current ratios of 3 to 1. However, Company A has working capital of $50,000 and Company B has working capital of $500,000. Although both companies appear to be good credit risks, Company B would no doubt be able to qualify for a much *larger* bank loan than would Company A.

Quick Ratio   Because inventories and prepaid expenses are further removed from conversion into cash than other current assets, a statistic known as the **quick ratio** is sometimes computed as a supplement to the current ratio. The quick ratio compares the highly liquid current assets (cash, marketable securities, and receivables) with current liabilities. Seacliff Company has no marketable securities; its quick ratio is computed as follows:

Quick Ratio

A measure of liquidity

	1994	1993
Quick assets (cash and receivables)	(a) $155,000	$126,000
Current liabilities	(b) $112,000	$ 94,000
Quick ratio (a ÷ b)	1.4	1.3

Here again the analysis reveals a favorable trend and a strong position. If the credit periods extended to customers and granted by creditors are roughly equal, a quick ratio of 1.0 or better is considered satisfactory.

Unused Lines of Credit   From the viewpoint of a short-term creditor, a company's unused lines of credit represent a "resource" almost as liquid as cash. An unused line of credit means that a bank has agreed in advance to lend the company any amount, up to the specified limit. As long as this line of credit remains available, creditors know that the business can borrow cash quickly and easily for any purpose, including payments of creditors' claims.

Existing unused lines of credit are ***disclosed*** in notes accompanying the financial statements.

Cash Flow Analysis

In Chapter 19 we stressed the importance of a company being able to generate sufficient cash flow from its operations. In 1993, Seacliff generated a net cash flow of $95,000 from its operating activities—a relatively "normal" amount, considering that net income for the year was $90,000. This $95,000 net cash flow remained ***after*** payment of interest to creditors and amounted to more than three times the dividends paid to stockholders. Thus, in 1993 the net cash flow from operating activities appeared quite sufficient to ensure that Seacliff could pay its interest obligations and also pay dividends.

In 1994, however, net cash flow from operating activities declined to only $19,000, an amount far below the company's $75,000 net income and less than one-half of the amount of dividends paid. Stockholders and creditors alike would view this dramatic decline in cash flow as a negative and potentially dangerous development.

A reconciliation of Seacliff's net income in 1994 with its net cash flow from operating activities is shown below:

Why was the cash flow from operations so low?

Net income...		$ 75,000
Add:		
Depreciation expense...	$30,000	
Increase in notes payable to suppliers	4,600	
Increase in accounts payable	36,000	70,600
		$145,600
Less:		
Increase in accounts receivable...................................	$31,000	
Increase in inventories	60,000	
Increase in prepaid expenses	13,000	
Decrease in accrued liabilities	22,600	126,600
Net cash flow from operating activities		$ 19,000

(As explained in Chapter 19, the FASB requires companies to provide this type of reconciliation either in the statement of cash flows or in a supplemental schedule.)

The primary reasons for Seacliff's low net operating cash flow appear to be the growth in uncollected accounts receivable and inventories, and the substantial reduction in accrued liabilities. Given the significant increase in sales during 1994, the increase in accounts receivable is to be expected. The large reduction in accrued liabilities probably is a one-time event, not likely to recur next year. The large increase in inventory, however, may have reduced Seacliff's liquidity unnecessarily.

Seacliff's financial position would appear considerably stronger if its increased sales volume were supplied by a higher ***inventory turnover rate,*** instead of a larger inventory.

Usefulness of the Notes to Financial Statements

A set of financial statements normally is accompanied by several pages of *notes,* disclosing information useful in interpretation of the statements. Users should view these notes as an *integral part* of the financial statements.

In our preceding chapters, we have identified many items which are disclosed in notes to the financial statements. Among the most useful disclosures are (a) a summary of the accounting methods in use, (b) material loss contingencies, (c) current market value of financial instruments, (d) identification of the assets pledged to secure specific liabilities, (e) maturity dates of significant liabilities, (f) unused lines of credit, and (g) preferred stock dividends in arrears. The notes also supplement the financial statements by providing further explanation of such items as extraordinary gains and losses, changes in accounting principle, and significant financial events occurring after the balance sheet date.

In summary, the notes often contain information *essential* to a proper interpretation of the company's financial position, operating results, and future prospects.

Summary of Analytical Measurements

OBJECTIVE 6 Compute the ratios widely used in financial statement analysis and explain the significance of each.

The basic ratios and other measurements discussed in this chapter and their significance are summarized below.

The student should keep in mind the fact that the full significance of any of these ratios or other measurements depends on the *direction of its trend* and its *relationship to some predetermined standard* or industry average.

Ratio or Other Measurement	Method of Computation	Significance
1 Earnings per share of common stock	$\dfrac{\text{Net income} - \text{preferred dividends}}{\text{Shares of common outstanding}}$	Indicates the amount of earnings applicable to a share of common stock.
2 Price-earnings ratio	$\dfrac{\text{Market price per share}}{\text{Earnings per share}}$	Indicates if price of stock is in line with earnings.
3 Dividend yield	$\dfrac{\text{Dividend per share}}{\text{Market price per share}}$	Shows the rate of return earned by stockholders based on current price for a share of stock.
4 Book value per share of common stock	$\dfrac{\text{Common stockholders' equity}}{\text{Shares of common outstanding}}$	Measures the recorded value of net assets behind each share of common stock.
5 Operating expense ratio	$\dfrac{\text{Operating expenses}}{\text{Net sales}}$	Indicates management's ability to control expenses.
6 Return on assets	$\dfrac{\text{Operating income}}{\text{Average total assets}}$	Measures the productivity of assets regardless of capital structure.

7 Return on common stockholders' equity	$$\frac{\text{Net income} - \text{preferred dividends}}{\text{Average common stockholders' equity}}$$	Indicates the earning power of common stock equity.
8 Equity ratio	$$\frac{\text{Total stockholders' equity}}{\text{Total assets}}$$	Shows the protection to creditors and the extent of leverage being used.
9 Debt ratio	$$\frac{\text{Total liabilities}}{\text{Total assets}}$$	Indicates the percentage of assets financed through borrowing; it shows the extent of leverage being used.
10 Interest coverage ratio	$$\frac{\text{Operating income}}{\text{Annual interest expense}}$$	Measures the coverage of interest requirements, particularly on long-term debt.
11 Preferred dividends coverage ratio	$$\frac{\text{Net income}}{\text{Annual preferred dividends}}$$	Shows the adequacy of current earnings to cover dividends on preferred stocks.
12 Working capital	Current assets − current liabilities	Measures short-run debt-paying ability.
13 Inventory turnover rate	$$\frac{\text{Cost of goods sold}}{\text{Average inventory}}$$	Indicates marketability of inventory and reasonableness of quantity on hand.
14 Accounts receivable turnover rate	$$\frac{\text{Net sales}}{\text{Average receivables}}$$	Indicates reasonableness of accounts receivable balance and effectiveness of collections.
15 Current ratio	$$\frac{\text{Current assets}}{\text{Current liabilities}}$$	Measures short-run debt-paying ability.
16 Quick ratio	$$\frac{\text{Quick assets}}{\text{Current liabilities}}$$	Measures the short-term liquidity of a firm.

END-OF-CHAPTER REVIEW

SUMMARY OF CHAPTER LEARNING OBJECTIVES

1 **Put a company's net income into perspective by relating it to sales, assets, and stockholders' equity.**
To judge the adequacy of a corporation's net income, we need to relate the dollar amount of net income to the company's annual sales, to the amount of its assets, and to the stockholders' equity. A net income of $1 million may represent very good earnings or very poor earnings depending upon the size of operations and amounts invested.

2 **Describe several sources of financial information about a business.**
Sources of information about a business include the company's annual report, quarterly reports, and data available from financial investment services and credit rating agencies.

3 Explain the uses of dollar and percentage changes, trend percentages, component percentages, and ratios.

Analysis of financial statements should indicate whether a company's earnings and solvency are on the upgrade or are deteriorating. The dollar change in any item is the difference between the amount for a **comparison** year and for a **base** year. The percentage change is computed by dividing the change between years by the amount for the base year.

Trend percentages are useful to compare performance in each of a series of years with a selected base year. Thus, the rate of growth in sales is revealed by trend percentages.

Component percentages indicate the relative size of each item included in a total. Thus, each item on a balance sheet may be expressed as a percentage of total assets. Each item on an income statement may be expressed as a percentage of net sales.

4 Discuss the "quality" of a company's earnings, assets, and working capital.

The concept of "quality" of earnings exists because each company management can choose from a variety of accounting principles and methods all of which are considered generally accepted. For example, the choice between straight-line depreciation and accelerated depreciation leads to different reported earnings. In judging the quality of earnings, the financial analyst considers whether the accounting principles and methods selected by management lead to a conservative measurement of earnings or tend to inflate earnings. The trend of earnings, their stability, and source are also significant in judging quality of earnings.

The quality of assets and of working capital are affected by such factors as the nature and liquidity of assets and the maturity dates of liabilities.

5 Analyze financial statements from the viewpoints of common stockholders, creditors, and others.

Investors in **common stocks** are interested primarily in **future profitability, dividends,** and the **market price** of the common shares. Therefore, these investors look at the **trend** in such measures of profitability as return on assets, return on equity, and earnings per share, and also the trend in dividend payments and cash flow from operating activities. They also are interested in measures which place stock price into perspective, such as the price-earnings ratio and dividend yield.

Long-term creditors are interested primarily in the **yield** on their investment and in the **borrower's ability to make its principal and interest payments on schedule.**

Short-term creditors are primarily interested in the borrower's **liquidity** as indicated by such measurements as cash flow from operating activities, unused lines of credit, the current ratio, quick ratio, and inventory and receivables turnover ratios.

6 Compute the ratios widely used in financial statement analysis and explain the significance of each.

The ratios widely used in financial statement analysis, the methods of computation, and the significance of each ratio are summarized in the table on pages 946–947.

This chapter concludes our emphasis upon financial accounting—the preparation and interpretation of the accounting information included in financial statements. In the remaining chapters of this text, we will shift our emphasis to managerial accounting—the use of accounting information by managers in planning and controlling business operations. In these chapters you will encounter many new terms and concepts; however, you will find your background in financial accounting to be extremely useful.

KEY TERMS INTRODUCED OR EMPHASIZED IN CHAPTER 20

Comparative financial statements Financial statement data for two or more successive years placed side by side in adjacent columns to facilitate study of changes.

Component percentage The percentage relationship of any financial statement item to a total including that item. For example, each type of asset as a percentage of total assets.

Horizontal analysis Comparison of the change in a financial statement item such as inventories during two or more accounting periods.

Leverage Refers to the practice of financing assets with borrowed capital. Extensive leverage creates the possibility for the rate of return on common stockholders' equity to be substantially above or below the rate of return on total assets. When the rate of return on total assets exceeds the average cost of borrowed capital, leverage increases net income and the return on common stockholders' equity. However, when the return on total assets is less than the average cost of borrowed capital, leverage reduces net income and the return on common stockholders' equity.

Quality of assets The concept that some companies have assets of better quality than others, such as well-balanced composition of assets, well-maintained plant and equipment, and receivables that are all current. A lower quality of assets might be indicated by poor maintenance of plant and equipment, slow-moving inventories with high danger of obsolescence, past-due receivables, and patents approaching an expiration date.

Quality of earnings Earnings are said to be of high quality if they are stable, the source seems assured, and the methods used in measuring income are conservative. The existence of this concept suggests that the range of alternative but acceptable accounting principles may still be too wide to produce financial statements that are comparable.

Rate of return on investment (ROI) A measure of management's ability to earn a satisfactory return on the assets under its control. Numerous variations of the ROI concept are used, such as return on total assets, return on total stockholders' equity, and return on common stockholders' equity.

Ratios See pages 946–947 for list of ratios, methods of computation, and significance.

Trend percentages The purpose of computing trend percentages is to measure the increase or decrease in financial items (such as sales, net income, cash, etc.) from a selected base year to a series of following years. For example, the dollar amount of net income each year is divided by the base year net income to determine the trend percentage.

Vertical analysis Comparison of a particular financial statement item to a total including that item, such as inventories as a percentage of current assets, or operating expenses in relation to net sales.

DEMONSTRATION PROBLEM FOR YOUR REVIEW

The accounting records of King Corporation showed the following balances at the end of 1993 and 1994:

	1994	1993
Cash	$ 35,000	$ 25,000
Accounts receivable (net)	91,000	90,000
Inventory	160,000	140,000
Short-term prepayments	4,000	5,000
Investment in land	90,000	100,000
Equipment	880,000	640,000
Less: Accumulated depreciation	(260,000)	(200,000)
Total assets	$1,000,000	$ 800,000

	1994	1993
Accounts payable	$ 105,000	$ 46,000
Income taxes payable and other accrued liabilities	40,000	25,000
Bonds payable—8%	280,000	280,000
Premium on bonds payable	3,600	4,000
Capital stock, $5 par	165,000	110,000
Retained earnings	406,400	335,000
Total liabilities and stockholders' equity	$1,000,000	$ 800,000

	1994	1993
Sales (net of discounts and allowances)	$2,200,000	$1,600,000
Cost of goods sold	1,606,000	1,120,000
Gross profit on sales	$ 594,000	$ 480,000
Expenses (including $22,400 interest expense)	(336,600)	(352,000)
Income taxes	(91,000)	(48,000)
Net income	$ 166,400	$ 80,000

Cash dividends of $40,000 were paid and a 50% stock dividend was distributed early in 1994. All sales were made on credit at a relatively uniform rate during the year. Inventory and receivables did not fluctuate materially. The market price of the company's stock on December 31, 1994, was $86 per share; on December 31, 1993, it was $43.50 (before the 50% stock dividend distributed in 1994).

INSTRUCTIONS Compute the following for 1994 and 1993:

1 Quick ratio.

2 Current ratio.

3 Equity ratio.

4 Debt ratio.

5 Book value per share of capital stock (based on shares outstanding after 50% stock dividend in 1994).

6 Earnings per share of capital stock.

7 Price-earnings ratio.

8 Gross profit percentage.

9 Operating expense ratio.

10 Net income as a percentage of net sales.

11 Inventory turnover. (Assume an average inventory of $150,000 for both years.)

12 Accounts receivable turnover. (Assume average accounts receivable for $90,000 for 1993.)

13 Interest coverage ratio.

SOLUTION TO DEMONSTRATION PROBLEM

	1994	*1993*
(1) Quick ratio:		
$126,000 ÷ $145,000	.9 to 1	
$115,000 ÷ $71,000		1.6 to 1
(2) Current ratio:		
$290,000 ÷ $145,000	2 to 1	
$260,000 ÷ $71,000		3.7 to 1
(3) Equity ratio:		
$571,400 ÷ $1,000,000	57%	
$445,000 ÷ $800,000		56%
(4) Debt ratio:		
$428,600 ÷ $1,000,000	43%	
$355,000 ÷ $800,000		44%
(5) Book value per share of capital stock:		
$571,400 ÷ 33,000 shares	$17.32	
$445,000 ÷ 33,000* shares		$13.48
(6) Earnings per share of capital stock:		
$166,400 ÷ 33,000 shares	$5.04	
$80,000 ÷ 33,000* shares		$2.42
(7) Price-earnings ratio:		
$86 ÷ $5.04	17 times	
$43.50 ÷ 1.5* = $29, adjusted market price;		
$29 ÷ $2.42		12 times
(8) Gross profit percentage:		
$594,000 ÷ $2,200,000	27%	
$480,000 ÷ $1,600,000		30%
(9) Operating expense ratio:		
($336,600 − $22,400) ÷ $2,200,000	14%	
($352,000 − $22,400) ÷ $1,600,000		20.6%
(10) Net income as a percentage of net sales:		
$166,400 ÷ $2,200,000	7.6%	
$80,000 ÷ $1,600,000		5%
(11) Inventory turnover:		
$1,606,000 ÷ $150,000	10.7 times	
$1,120,00 ÷ $150,000		7.5 times
(12) Accounts receivable turnover:		
$2,200,000 ÷ $90,500	24.3 times	
$1,600,000 ÷ $90,000		17.8 times
(13) Interest coverage ratio:		
($166,400 + $22,400 + $91,000) ÷ $22,400	12.5 times	
($80,000 + $22,400 + $48,000) ÷ $22,400		6.7 times

*   Adjusted retroactively for 50% stock dividend.

SELF-TEST QUESTIONS

Answers to these questions appear on page 967.

1 Which of the following is **not** an accurate statement?

   a Expressing the various items in the income statement as a percentage of net sales illustrates the use of component percentages.

   b An increase in the market price of bonds causes the yield rate to decline.

   c A high debt ratio is viewed favorably by long-term creditors as long as the number of times interest earned is at least 1.

   d In measuring the dollar or percentage change in quarterly sales or earnings, it is appropriate to compare the results of the current quarter with those of the same quarter in the preceding year.

2 Which of the following actions will improve the "quality" of earnings, even though the total dollar amount of earnings may not increase?

   a Increasing the uncollectible accounts expense from 1% to 2% of net credit sales to reflect current conditions.

   b Switching from an accelerated method to the straight-line method for depreciating assets.

   c Changing from LIFO to the FIFO method of inventory valuation during a period of rising prices.

   d Lengthening the estimated useful lives of depreciable assets.

3 Hunter Corporation's net income was $400,000 in 1993 and $160,000 in 1994. What percentage increase in net income must Hunter achieve in 1995 to offset the decline in profits in 1994?

   a 60%   **b** 150%   **c** 600%   **d** 67%

4 Of the following situations, which would be considered the most favorable for the common stockholders?

   a The company stops paying dividends on its cumulative preferred stock; the price-earnings ratio of common stock is low.

   b Equity ratio is high; return on assets exceeds the cost of borrowing

   c Book value per share of common stock is substantially higher than market value per share; return on common stockholders' equity is less than the rate of interest paid to creditors.

   d Equity ratio is low; return on assets exceeds the cost of borrowing.

5 During 1994, Ganey Corporation had sales of $4,000,000, all on credit. Accounts receivable averaged $400,000 and inventory levels averaged $250,000 throughout the year. If Ganey's gross profit rate during 1994 was 25% of net sales, which of the following statements are correct? (More than one statement may be correct. Assume 360 days in a year.)

   a Ganey "turns over" its accounts receivable more times per year than it turns over its average inventory.

   b Ganey collects the amount of its average accounts receivable in about 36 to 37 days.

   c Ganey's operating cycle is 66 days.

   d The quality of Ganey's working capital would improve if the company could reduce its inventory and receivables turnover rates.

ASSIGNMENT MATERIAL

DISCUSSION QUESTIONS

1 a What groups are interested in the financial affairs of publicly owned corporations?

 b List some of the more important sources of financial information for investors.

2 In financial statement analysis, what is the basic objective of observing trends in data and ratios? Suggest some other standards of comparison.

3 In financial statement analysis, what information is produced by computing a ratio that is not available in a simple observation of the underlying data?

4 Distinguish between *trend percentages* and *component percentages.* Which would be better suited to analyzing the change in sales over a term of several years?

5 "Although net income declined this year as compared with last year, it increased from 3% to 5% of net sales." Are sales increasing or decreasing?

6 Differentiate between *horizontal* and *vertical* analysis.

7 Assume that Chemco Corporation is engaged in the manufacture and distribution of a variety of chemicals. In analyzing the financial statements of this corporation, why would you want to refer to the ratios and other measurements of companies in the chemical industry? In comparing the financial results of Chemco Corporation with another chemical company, why would you be interested in the accounting practices used by the two companies?

8 Explain how the following accounting practices will tend to raise or lower the quality of a company's earnings. (Assume the continuance of inflation.)

 a Adoption of an accelerated depreciation method rather than straight-line depreciation.

 b Adoption of FIFO rather than LIFO for the valuation of inventories.

 c Adoption of a 7-year life rather than a 10-year life for the depreciation of equipment.

9 What single ratio do you think should be of greatest interest to:

 a A banker considering a short-term loan?

 b A common stockholder?

 c An insurance company considering a long-term mortgage loan?

10 Modern Company earned a 16% return on its total assets. Current liabilities are 10% of total assets. Long-term bonds carrying a 13% coupon rate are equal to 30% of total assets. There is no preferred stock. Is this application of leverage favorable or unfavorable from the viewpoint of Modern Company's stockholders?

11 In deciding whether a company's equity ratio is favorable or unfavorable, creditors and stockholders may have different views. Why?

12 Ahi Co. has a current ratio of 3 to 1. Ono Corp. has a current ratio of 2 to 1. Does this mean that Ahi's operating cycle is longer than Ono's? Why?

13 An investor states, "I bought this stock for $50 several years ago and it now sells for $100. It paid $5 per share in dividends last year so I'm earning 10% on my investment." Criticize this statement.

14 Alpine Products experiences a considerable seasonal variation in its business. The high point in the year's activity comes in November, the low point in July. During which month would you expect the company's current ratio to be higher? If the company were choosing a fiscal year for accounting purposes, how would you advise them?

15 Auto Parts' inventory turnover and accounts receivable turnover both increased from 1993 to 1994, but net income decreased. Can you offer some possible reasons for this?

16 Is the rate of return on investment (ROI) intended primarily to measure liquidity, solvency, or some other aspect of business operations? Explain.

17 Mention three financial amounts to which corporate profits can logically be compared in judging their adequacy or reasonableness.

18 Under what circumstances would you consider a corporate net income of $1 million for the year as being unreasonably low? Under what circumstances would you consider a corporate profit of $1 million as being unreasonably high?

EXERCISES

EXERCISE 20-1
Accounting
Terminology

Listed below are nine technical accounting terms introduced or emphasized in this chapter.

Inventory turnover	Trend percentages	Leverage
Operating cycle	Vertical analysis	Yield
Price-earning ratio	Return on assets	Quick ratio

Each of the following statements may (or may not) describe one of these technical terms. For each statement, indicate the accounting term described, or answer "None" if the statement does not correctly describe any of the terms.

a The proportion of total assets financed by stockholders, as distinguished from creditors.

b Market price per common share divided by earnings per common share.

c Changes in financial statement items from a base year to following years expressed as a percentage of the base year amount and designed to show the extent and direction of change.

d Dividends per share divided by market price per share.

e Average time period between the purchase of merchandise and the conversion of this merchandise back into cash.

f Study of relationships among the data of a single accounting period.

g Net sales divided by average inventory.

h Comparison of highly liquid current assets (cash, marketable securities, and receivables) with current liabilities.

i Buying assets with money raised by borrowing.

EXERCISE 20-2
Percentage
Changes

Selected information taken from financial statements of Lopez Company for two successive years follows. You are to compute the percentage change from 1993 to 1994 whenever possible.

	1994	1993
a Accounts receivable..	$126,000	$150,000
b Marketable securities	-0-	250,000
c Retained earnings...	80,000	(80,000)
d Notes receivable	120,000	-0-
e Notes payable..	860,000	800,000
f Cash	82,400	80,000
g Sales	990,000	900,000

EXERCISE 20-3
Intuition versus Calculation

Tait Corporation had net income of $4 million in its first year. In the second year, net income decreased by 75%. In the third year, due to an improved business environment, net income increased by 250%.

INSTRUCTIONS

a Prior to making any computations, do you think Tait's net income was higher or lower in the third year than in the first year?

b Compute Tait's net income for the second year and for the third year. Do your computations support your initial response in part **a**?

EXERCISE 20-4
Trend Percentages

Compute **trend percentages** for the following items taken from the financial statements of Water-Wise Plumbing Fixtures over a five-year period. Treat 1990 as the base year. State whether the trends are favorable or unfavorable. (Dollar amounts are stated in thousands.)

	1994	1993	1992	1991	1990
Sales	$85,000	$74,000	$61,500	$59,000	$50,000
Cost of goods sold	$58,500	$48,000	$40,500	$36,000	$30,000

EXERCISE 20-5
Common Size Income Statements

Prepare **common size** income statements for Toyoda Company, a sole proprietorship, for the two years shown below by converting the dollar amounts into percentages. For each year, sales will appear as 100% and other items will be expressed as a percentage of sales. (Income taxes are not involved as the business is not incorporated.) Comment on whether the changes from 1993 to 1994 are favorable or unfavorable.

	1994	1993
Sales	$500,000	$400,000
Cost of goods sold	330,000	268,000
Gross profit	$170,000	$132,000
Operating expenses	140,000	116,000
Net income...	$ 30,000	$ 16,000

EXERCISE 20-6
Ratios for a Retail Store

Selected financial data for Vashon's, a retail store, appear below. Since monthly figures are not available, the average amounts for inventories and for accounts receivable should be based on the amounts shown for the beginning and end of 1994.

	1994	1993
Sales (terms 2/10, n/30)...	$750,000	$600,000
Cost of goods sold	495,000	408,000
Inventory at end of year	85,500	94,500
Accounts receivable at end of year.................................	87,500	100,000

INSTRUCTIONS Compute the following for 1994:

a Gross profit percentage

b Inventory turnover

c Accounts receivable turnover

EXERCISE 20-7
Computing Ratios

A condensed balance sheet for Durham Corporation prepared at the end of the year appears below.

Assets		Liabilities & Stockholders' Equity	
Cash	$ 55,000	Notes payable (due in 6 months)	$ 40,000
Accounts receivable	155,000	Accounts payable	110,000
Inventory	270,000	Long-term liabilities	330,000
Prepaid expenses	60,000	Capital stock, $5 par	300,000
Plant & equipment (net)	570,000	Retained earnings	420,000
Other assets	90,000		
Total	$1,200,000	Total	$1,200,000

During the year the company earned a gross profit of $1,116,000 on sales of $2,790,000. Accounts receivable, inventory, and plant assets remained almost constant in amount throughout the year.

INSTRUCTIONS

Compute the following:

a Current ratio
b Quick ratio
c Working capital
d Equity ratio
e Accounts receivable turnover (all sales were on credit)
f Inventory turnover
g Book value per share of capital stock

EXERCISE 20-8
Current Ratio, Debt Ratio, and Earnings per Share

Selected items from successive annual reports of Hastings, Inc., appear below.

	1994	1993
Total assets (40% of which are current)	$400,000	$325,000
Current liabilities	$ 80,000	$100,000
Bonds payable, 12%	100,000	50,000
Capital stock, $5 per value	100,000	100,000
Retained earnings	120,000	75,000
Total liabilities & stockholders' equity	$400,000	$325,000

Dividends of $26,000 were declared and paid in 1994.

INSTRUCTIONS

Compute the following:

a Current ratio for 1994 and 1993
b Debt ratio for 1994 and 1993
c Earnings per share for 1994

EXERCISE 20-9
Ratio Analysis for Two Similar Companies

Selected data from the financial statements of Italian Marble Co. and Toro Stone Products for the year just ended follow. Assume that for both companies dividends declared were equal in amount to net earnings during the year and therefore stockholders' equity did not change. The two companies are in the same line of business.

	Italian Marble Co.	Toro Stone Products
Total liabilities..	$ 200,000	$ 100,000
Total assets	800,000	400,000
Sales (all on credit)..	1,800,000	1,200,000
Average inventory	240,000	140,000
Average receivables	200,000	100,000
Gross profit as a percentage of sales	40%	30%
Operating expenses as a percentage of sales.................	36%	25%
Net income as a percentage of sales	4%	5%

INSTRUCTIONS Compute the following for each company:

a Net income

b Net income as a percentage of stockholders' equity

c Accounts receivable turnover

d Inventory turnover

PROBLEMS

Note: In this chapter, we provide an unusually wide variety of problem assignments. In order to make the full range of these assignments available to all users of the text, we present them in one consecutive series, rather than splitting them into A and B groups. This entire series is supported in both the Group A and Group B accounting work sheets.

PROBLEM 20-1
Analysis to Identify Favorable and Unfavorable Trends

The following information was developed from the financial statements of Custom Logos, Inc. At the beginning of 1994, the company's former supplier went bankrupt, and the company began buying merchandise from another supplier.

	1994	1993
Gross profit on sales	$1,008,000	$1,134,000
Income before income taxes	230,400	252,000
Net income...	172,800	189,000
Net income as a percentage of net sales	6.0%	7.5%

INSTRUCTIONS a Compute the net sales for each year.

b Compute the cost of goods sold in dollars and as a percentage of net sales for each year.

c Compute operating expenses in dollars and as a percentage of net sales for each year. (Income taxes expense is not an operating expense.)

d Prepare a condensed comparative income statement for 1993 and 1994. Include the following items: net sales, cost of goods sold, gross profit, operating expenses, income before income taxes, income taxes expense, and net income. Omit earnings per share statistics.

e Identify the significant favorable trends and unfavorable trends in the performance of Custom Logos, Inc. Comment on any unusual changes.

PROBLEM 20-2
Comparing Operating Results with Average Performance in the Industry

Sub Zero, Inc., manufactures camping equipment. Shown below for the current year are the income statement for the company and a common size summary for the industry in which the company operates. (Notice that the percentages in the right-hand column are **not** for Sub Zero, Inc., but are average percentages for the industry.)

	Sub Zero, Inc.	Industry Average
Sales (net)	$20,000,000	100%
Cost of goods sold	9,800,000	57
Gross profit on sales	$10,200,000	43%
Operating expenses:		
Selling	$ 4,200,000	16%
General and administrative	3,400,000	20
Total operating expenses	$ 7,600,000	36%
Operating income	$ 2,600,000	7%
Income taxes	1,200,000	3
Net income	$ 1,400,000	4%
Return on assets	23%	14%

INSTRUCTIONS

a Prepare a two-column common size income statement. The first column should show for Sub Zero, Inc., all items expressed as a percentage of net sales. The second column should show as an industry average the percentage data given in the problem. The purpose of this common size statement is to compare the operating results of Sub Zero, Inc., with the average for the industry.

b Comment specifically on differences between Sub Zero, Inc., and the industry average with respect to gross profit on sales, selling expenses, general and administrative expenses, operating income, net income, and return on assets. Suggest possible reasons for the more important disparities.

PROBLEM 20-3
Ratios Based on Balance Sheet and Income Statement Data

Barnum Corporation has issued common stock only. The company has been successful and has a gross profit rate of 25%. The information shown below was derived from the company's financial statements.

Beginning inventory	$ 700,000
Ending inventory	800,000
Average accounts receivable	250,000
Average common stockholders' equity	1,800,000
Sales (80% on credit)	4,000,000
Net income	225,000

INSTRUCTIONS

On the basis of the above information, compute the following (assume 365 days in a year):

a Accounts receivable turnover and the average number of days required to collect the accounts receivable

b The inventory turnover and the average number of days required to turn over the inventory

c Length of Barnum Corporation's operating cycle

d Return on common stockholders' equity

PROBLEM 20-4
Ratios;
Consider
Advisability of
Incurring Long-
Term Debt

At the end of the year, the following information was obtained from the accounting records of Carleton Office Products:

Sales (all on credit)	$2,700,000
Cost of goods sold	1,755,000
Average inventory	351,000
Average accounts receivable	300,000
Interest expense	45,000
Income taxes	84,000
Net income	159,000
Average investment in assets	1,800,000
Average stockholders' equity	795,000

INSTRUCTIONS a From the information given, compute the following:

1 Inventory turnover

2 Accounts receivable turnover

3 Total operating expenses

4 Gross profit percentage

5 Return on average stockholders' equity

6 Return on average assets

b Carleton has an opportunity to obtain a long-term loan at an annual interest rate of 12% and could use this additional capital at the same rate of profitability as indicated above. Would obtaining the loan be desirable from the viewpoint of the stockholders? Explain.

PROBLEM 20-5
Ratios;
Consider
Advisability of
Incurring Long-
Term Debt—
A Second
Problem

At the end of the year, the following information was obtained from the accounting records of Santa Fe Boot Co.

Sales (all on credit)	$800,000
Cost of goods sold	480,000
Average inventory	120,000
Average accounts receivable	80,000
Interest expense	6,000
Income taxes	8,000
Net income for the year	36,000
Average investment in assets	500,000
Average stockholders' equity	400,000

The company declared no dividends of any kind during the year and did not issue or retire any capital stock.

INSTRUCTIONS a From the information given, compute the following for the year:

1 Inventory turnover

2 Accounts receivable turnover

3 Total operating expenses

4 Gross profit percentage

5 Return on average stockholders' equity

6 Return on average assets

b Santa Fe Boot Co. has an opportunity to obtain a long-term loan at an annual interest rate of 12% and could use this additional capital at the same rate of profitability as indicated above. Would obtaining the loan be desirable from the viewpoint of the stockholders? Explain.

PROBLEM 20-6
Analysis and Interpretation from Viewpoint of Short-Term Creditor

Shown below are selected financial data for Mondo Corporation and Global, Inc., at the end of the current year.

	Mondo Corporation	Global, Inc.
Net sales (all on credit)	$1,440,000	$1,190,000
Cost of goods sold	1,260,000	825,000
Cash	36,000	70,000
Accounts receivable (net)	180,000	140,000
Inventory	504,000	165,000
Current liabilities	240,000	150,000

Assume that the year-end balances shown for accounts receivable and for inventory also represent the average balances of these accounts throughout the year.

INSTRUCTIONS

a For each company, compute the following:

1 Working capital.

2 Current ratio.

3 Quick ratio.

4 Number of times inventory turned over during the year and the average number of days required to turn over inventory.

5 Number of times accounts receivable turned over during the year and the average number of days required to collect accounts receivable. (Round to the nearest day.)

6 Operating cycle.

b From the viewpoint of a short-term creditor, comment upon the *quality* of each company's working capital. To which company would you prefer to sell $50,000 in merchandise on a 30-day open account?

PROBLEM 20-7
Ratios: Evaluation of Two Companies

Shown below are selected financial data for Another World and Imports, Inc., at the end of the current year:

	Another World	Imports, Inc.
Net credit sales	$675,000	$560,000
Cost of goods sold	504,000	430,000
Cash	51,000	20,000
Accounts receivable (net)	75,000	70,000
Inventory	84,000	150,000
Current liabilities	105,000	100,000

Assume that the year-end balances shown for accounts receivable and for inventory also represent the average balances of these items throughout the year.

INSTRUCTIONS

a For each of the two companies, compute the following:

1 Working capital.

2 Current ratio.

3 Quick ratio.

4 Number of times inventory turned over during the year and the average number of days required to turn over inventory. (Round computation to the nearest day.)

5 Number of times accounts receivable turned over during the year and the average number of days required to collect accounts receivable. (Round computation to the nearest day.)

6 Operating cycle.

b From the viewpoint of a short-term creditor, comment upon the *quality* of each company's working capital. To which company would you prefer to sell $20,000 in merchandise on a 30-day open account?

PROBLEM 20-8
Evaluating
Short-Term
Debt-Paying
Ability

Listed below is the working capital information for Imperial Products, Inc., at the beginning of the year.

Cash..	*$405,000*
Temporary investments in marketable securities	*216,000*
Notes receivable—current	*324,000*
Accounts receivable	*540,000*
Allowance for doubtful accounts	*27,000*
Inventory...	*432,000*
Prepaid expenses	*54,000*
Notes payable within one year	*162,000*
Accounts payable	*445,500*
Accrued liabilities	*40,500*

The following transactions are completed during the year:

0 Sold on account inventory costing $72,000 for $65,000.

1 Issued additional shares of capital stock for cash, $800,000.

2 Sold temporary investments costing $60,000 for $54,000 cash.

3 Acquired temporary investments, $105,000. Paid cash.

4 Wrote off uncollectible accounts, $18,000.

5 Sold on account inventory costing $75,000 for $90,000.

6 Acquired plant and equipment for cash, $480,000.

7 Declared a cash dividend, $240,000.

8 Declared a 10% stock dividend.

9 Paid accounts payable, $120,000.

10 Purchased goods on account, $90,000.

11 Collected cash on accounts receivable, $180,000.

12 Borrowed cash from a bank by issuing a short-term note, $250,000.

INSTRUCTIONS

a Compute the amount of quick assets, current assets, and current liabilities at the beginning of the year as shown by the above account balances.

b Use the data compiled in part **a** to compute: (1) current ratio; (2) quick ratio; and (3) working capital.

c Indicate the effect (Increase, Decrease, and No Effect) of each independent transaction listed above on the current ratio, quick ratio, working capital, and net cash flow from operating activities. Use the following four-column format (item **0** is given as an example):

Effect on

Item	Current Ratio	Quick Ratio	Working Capital	Net Cash Flow from Operating Activities
0	Decrease	Increase	Decrease	No Effect

**PROBLEM 20-9
Effects of Transactions on Various Ratios**

Listed in the left-hand column below is a series of 12 business transactions and events relating to the activities of Wabash Industries. Opposite each transaction is listed a particular ratio used in financial analysis.

Transaction	Ratio
(1) Purchased inventory on open account.	Quick ratio
(2) A larger physical volume of goods was sold at smaller unit prices.	Gross profit percentage
(3) Corporation declared a cash dividend.	Current ratio
(4) An uncollectible account receivable was written off against the allowance account.	Current ratio
(5) Issued additional shares of common stock and used proceeds to retire long-term debt.	Debt ratio
(6) Paid stock dividend on common stock, in common stock.	Earnings per share
(7) Conversion of a portion of bonds payable into common stock. (Ignore income taxes.)	Interest coverage ratio
(8) Appropriated retained earnings.	Rate of return on stockholders' equity
(9) During period of rising prices, company changed from FIFO to LIFO method of inventory pricing.	Inventory turnover
(10) Paid a previously declared cash dividend.	Debt ratio
(11) Purchased factory supplies on open account.	Current ratio (assume that ratio is greater than 1:1)
(12) Issued shares of capital stock in exchange for patents.	Equity ratio

INSTRUCTIONS What effect would each transaction or event have on the ratio listed opposite to it; that is, as a result of this event would the ratio increase, decrease, or remain unchanged? Your answer for each of the 12 transactions should include a brief explanation.

**PROBLEM 20-10
Building Financial Statements from Limited Information, Including Ratios**

Pete Mitchell, the accountant for Hercules Construction, prepared the year-end financial statements, including all ratios, and was invited to bring them along on a wilderness retreat with the executives of the corporation. To his embarrassment, he found that only certain fragmentary information had been placed in his briefcase and the completed statements had been left in his office. One hour before Mitchell was to present the financial statements to the executives, he was able to come up with the following information:

HERCULES CONSTRUCTION
Balance Sheet
December 31, 19—
(in thousands of dollars)

Assets			Liabilities & Stockholders' Equity		
Current assets:			Current liabilities		$?
Cash......................		?	Long-term debt, 8%		
Accounts receivable			interest		?
(net)		?	Total liabilities...................		$?
Inventory.................		?	Stockholders' equity:		
Total current			Capital stock, $5 par..........	$300	
assets		$?	Retained earnings	100	
Plant assets:			Total stockholders'		
Machinery and			equity............................		400
equipment	$580				
Less: Accumulated					
depreciation.....	80	500	Total liabilities & stockholders'		
Total assets		$?	equity............................		$?

HERCULES CONSTRUCTION
Income Statement
For the Year Ended December 31, 19—
(in thousands of dollars)

Net sales...	$?
Cost of goods sold.	?
Gross profit on sales (25% of net sales)..	$?
Operating expenses	?
Operating income (10% of net sales)	$?
Interest expense..	28
Income before income taxes	$?
Income taxes—40% of income before income taxes.............................	?
Net income..	$60

ADDITIONAL INFORMATION

1 The equity ratio was 40%; the debt ratio was 60%.

2 The only interest expense was on the long-term debt.

3 The beginning inventory was $150,000; the inventory turnover was 4.8 times.

4 The current ratio was 2 to 1; the quick ratio was 1 to 1.

5 The beginning balance in accounts receivable was $80,000; the accounts receivable turnover for the year was 12.8 times. All sales were made on account.

INSTRUCTIONS The accountant asks you to help complete the financial statements for Hercules Construction, using only the information available. Present supporting computations and explanations for all amounts appearing in the balance sheet and the income statement. Hint: In completing the income statement, start with the net income figure (60% of income before income taxes) and work up.

**PROBLEM 20-11
Analysis and
Interpretation
from Viewpoint
of Common
Stockholders
and of Bond-
holders**

The following financial information for Continental Transfer Co. and American Van Lines (except market price per share of stock) is stated in ***thousands of dollars.*** The figures are as of the end of the current year. The two companies are in the same industry and are quite similar as to operations, facilities, and accounting methods. Assume that both companies pay income taxes equal to 50% of income before income taxes.

Assets	Continental Transfer Co.	American Van Lines
Current assets	$ 97,500	$132,320
Plant and equipment	397,500	495,680
Less: Accumulated depreciation	(55,000)	(78,000)
Total assets	$440,000	$550,000

Liabilities & Stockholders' Equity		
Current liabilities	$ 34,000	$ 65,000
Bonds payable, 12%, due in 15 years........................	120,000	100,000
Capital stock, no par	150,000	200,000
Retained earnings	136,000	185,000
Total liabilities & stockholders' equity	$440,000	$550,000

Analysis of retained earnings:		
Balance, beginning of year.................................	$125,200	$167,200
Net income for the year.....................................	19,800	37,400
Dividends	(9,000)	(19,600)
Balance, end of year..	$136,000	$185,000
Market price of capital stock, per share	$30	$61
Number of shares of capital stock outstanding	6 million	8 million

INSTRUCTIONS

a Compute for each company:

   1 The interest coverage ratio (number of times bond interest was earned during the current year). (Remember to use ***operating income*** rather than net income in determining the coverage of interest expense.)

   2 The debt ratio.

b In light of the information developed in **a** above, write a paragraph indicating which company's bonds you think would trade in the market at the higher price. Which would probably provide the higher yield? Explain how the ratios developed influence your answer. (It may be assumed that the bonds were issued several years ago and are traded on an organized securities exchange.)

c For each company compute the dividend yield, earnings per share, the price-earnings ratio, and the book value per share. (Show supporting computations. Remember that dollar amounts in the problem are in thousands of dollars, that is, three zeros omitted.)

d Assume that you expect both companies to grow at the same rate. Express an opinion, based solely on the data developed in **c** above, as to which company's stock is a better investment at the present market price.

PROBLEM 20-12
A Financial
Taste Test

Selected data from recent annual reports of *The Coca-Cola Company* and *Pep-siCo, Inc.* (and subsidiaries) are shown below. (Dollar amounts are stated in millions.)

	Coca-Cola	PepsiCo*
Balance sheet statistics:		
At year-end:		
Quick assets	$2,002	$ 2,774
Current assets	3,604	3,551
Total assets	8,283	15,127
Current liabilities	3,658	3,692
Total liabilities..	4,798	11,236
Total stockholders' equity	3,485	3,891
Average throughout the year:		
Accounts receivable	802	1,110
Inventory...	784	494
Total assets	7,867	13,131
Total stockholders' equity	3,415	3,526
Income statement statistics:		
Net sales...	8,966	15,242
Cost of goods sold	3,892	7,468
Interest expense..	308	610
Operating income	1,726	1,783
Net income..	1,724	901

* More than one-half of PepsiCo's revenue and profits stem from its snack food and restaurant operations, rather than from soft drink sales.

INSTRUCTIONS

a Compute the following for each company:

1 Net income as a percentage of sales

2 Return on assets

3 Return on equity

4 Working capital

5 Accounts receivable turnover rate

6 Inventory turnover rate

7 Quick ratio

8 Debt ratio

9 Interest coverage ratio

b Both Coca-Cola and PepsiCo are highly successful companies with excellent credit ratings. Based on your analysis in part **a**, however, indicate which of these companies you believe:

1 Provides the greatest degree of safety for its ***short-term*** creditors.

2 Provides the greatest degree of safety for its ***long-term*** creditors.

3 Would have the higher p/e ratio (that is, the stock would sell at the greater market value relative to the current earnings per share).

In each case, ***explain your reasoning.***

CASES AND UNSTRUCTURED PROBLEMS

CASE 20-1
Season's
Greetings

Holiday Greeting Cards is a local company organized late in July of 1993. The company's net income for each of its first six calendar quarters of operations is summarized below. The amounts are stated in thousands of dollars.

	1994	1993
First quarter (January through March)	$ 253	—
Second quarter (April through June)	308	—
Third quarter (July through September)	100	$ 50
Fourth quarter (October through December)	450	500
Total for the calendar year	$1,111	$550

Glen Wallace reports the business and economic news for a local radio station. On the day that Holiday Greeting Cards released the above financial information, you heard Wallace make the following statement during his broadcast: "Holiday Greeting Cards enjoyed a 350% increase in its profits for the fourth quarter, and profits for the entire year were up by over 100%."

INSTRUCTIONS
a Show the computations that Wallace probably made in arriving at his statistics. (Hint: Wallace did not make his computations in the manner recommended in this chapter. His figures, however, can be developed from the financial data above.)

b Do you believe that Wallace's percentage changes present a realistic impression of Holiday Greeting Cards' rate of growth in 1994? Explain.

c What figure would you use to express the percentage change in Holiday's fourth quarter profits in 1994? Explain why you would compute the change in this manner.

CASE 20-2
Limit on
Dividends

During each of the last 10 years, Reese Corporation has increased the common stock dividend per share by about 10%. Total dividends now amount to $9 million per year, consisting of $2 million paid to preferred stockholders and $7 million paid to common stockholders. The preferred stock is cumulative but not convertible. Annual net income had been rising steadily until two years ago, when it peaked at $44 million. Last year, increased competition caused net income to decline to $37 million. Management expects income to stabilize around this level for several years. This year, Reese Corporation issued bonds payable. The contract with bondholders requires Reese Corporation to limit total dividends to not more than 25% of net income.

INSTRUCTIONS
Evaluate this situation from the perspective of:

a Common stockholders

b Preferred stockholders

CASE 20-3
Improving
Cash Flow

Reynolds Labs develops and manufactures pharmaceutical products. The company has been growing rapidly during the past 10 years, due primarily to having discovered, patented, and successfully marketed dozens of new products. Profits have increased annually by 30% or more. The company pays no dividend but has a very high price-earnings ratio. Due to its rapid growth and large expenditures for research and development, the company has experienced occasional cash shortages. To solve this problem, Reynolds has decided to improve its cash position by (1) requiring customers to pay for products purchased on account from the company in 30 days instead of 60 days and (2) reducing expenditures for research and development by 20%.

INSTRUCTIONS   Evaluate this situation from the perspective of:

    a Short-term creditors.

    b Common stockholders.

CASE 20-4
Declining
Interest Rate

Metro Utilities has outstanding 16 issues of bonds payable, with interest rates ranging from $5\frac{1}{2}\%$ to 14%. The company's rate of return on assets consistently averages 12%. Almost every year, the company issues additional bonds to finance growth, to pay maturing bonds, or to call outstanding bonds when advantageous. During the current year, long-term interest rates have fallen dramatically. At the beginning of the year, these rates were between 12% and 13%; now, however, they are down to between 8% and 9%. Management currently is planning a large 8% bond issue.

INSTRUCTIONS   Evaluate this situation from the perspective of:

    a Holders of $5\frac{1}{2}\%$ bonds, maturing in 11 years but callable now at 103.

    b Holders of 14% bonds, maturing in 23 years but callable now at 103.

    c Common stockholders.

ANSWERS TO SELF-TEST QUESTIONS

1 c   **2** a   **3** b   **4** d   **5** b, c

COMPREHENSIVE PROBLEM 5

RUBBERMAID INCORPORATED

ANALYSIS OF THE FINANCIAL STATEMENTS OF A PUBLICLY OWNED CORPORATION

The purpose of this Comprehensive Problem is to acquaint you with the financial statements of a publicly owned company. The financial statements included in the 1990 annual report of **Rubbermaid Incorporated** (the company) were selected because they illustrate many of the financial reporting issues discussed in this textbook. Notice that several pages of explanatory notes are included with the basic statements. These explanatory notes supplement the condensed information in the financial statements and are intended to carry out the generally accepted accounting principle of adequate disclosure.

This Comprehensive Problem is subdivided into three parts. **Part 1** is designed to familiarize you with the content of these financial statements. **Part 2** requires analysis from the viewpoint of a short-term creditor, and **Part 3,** from the perspective of a stockholder.

NOTES TO CONSOLIDATED FINANCIAL STATEMENTS

(Dollars in thousands except per share amounts)

1. SUMMARY OF SIGNIFICANT ACCOUNTING POLICIES

Principles of Consolidation:
The consolidated financial statements include the accounts of Rubbermaid Incorporated and its subsidiary companies, all of which are wholly-owned except for Rubbermaid-Allibert (see note 2). All significant intercompany profits, transactions and balances have been eliminated in consolidation.

Cash Equivalents:
The Company considers all short-term investments with a maturity at date of purchase of three months or less to be cash equivalents.

Inventories:
Inventories are stated at the lower of cost or market, with cost determined using the last-in, first-out (LIFO) method for 79% and 71% of inventories in 1990 and 1989, respectively. The cost of the remaining inventories for each respective year is determined using the first-in, first-out (FIFO) method.

Property, Plant and Equipment:
Property, plant and equipment is stated at cost less depreciation and amortization accumulated to date. Depreciation and amortization are computed on the straight-line method over the estimated useful lives of the assets.

Net Earnings Per Common Share:
Net earnings per Common Share is based on the average number of Common Shares outstanding during each year. Average shares used in the calculations were 79,843,759, 79,624,590 and 79,464,178 in 1990, 1989 and 1988, respectively.

Reclassifications:
Certain prior years' amounts have been reclassified to conform to the current year presentation.

2. ACQUISITIONS AND JOINT VENTURES

Acquisitions:
In October 1990, 6,236,758 Common Shares were issued in exchange for all the outstanding Common Shares of Eldon Industries, Inc. (Eldon), primarily a manufacturer and marketer of office products.

The acquisition has been accounted for as a pooling of interests, and accordingly, the accompanying financial information has been restated to include the accounts of Eldon for all periods presented.

Net sales and net earnings of the separate companies for the period preceding the acquisition were:

	January 1, 1990 Through October 29, 1990	Years Ended December 31, 1989	1988
Net Sales:			
Rubbermaid	$1,184,249	$1,343,873	$1,193,539
Eldon	88,732	108,492	98,045
Combined	$1,272,981	$1,452,365	$1,291,584
Net Earnings:			
Rubbermaid	$ 117,366	$ 116,410	$ 99,290
Eldon	6,440	8,574	7,568
Combined	$ 123,806	$ 124,984	$ 106,858

In June 1990, the Company also acquired EWU AG, a manufacturer and marketer of commercial floor care supplies and equipment, through a cash transaction accounted for as a purchase. The results of operations of EWU AG have been included in the accompanying consolidated financial statements from June 13, 1990, the acquisition date. Pro forma consolidated financial information is not considered significant and has been omitted.

Joint Ventures:
In January 1990, the Company completed the formation of a joint venture, Curver Rubbermaid Group, with the Dutch conglomerate, DSM, giving the Company a 40% ownership interest which is being accounted for by the equity method. Curver Rubbermaid Group manufactures and markets plastic and rubber housewares for Europe, the Middle East and North Africa.

In 1989, the Company formed a joint venture with Allibert, S.A., a French corporation, giving the Company a 50% ownership interest and management control. The joint venture, Rubbermaid-Allibert, manufactures and markets casual resin furniture for North America.

3. INVENTORIES

A summary of inventories follows:

	1990	1989
FIFO cost:		
Raw materials	$ 68,791	$ 63,961
Work-in-process	11,752	12,785
Finished goods	159,941	146,795
	240,484	223,541
Excess of FIFO over LIFO cost	(23,676)	(24,016)
	$ 216,808	$ 199,525

4. PROPERTY, PLANT AND EQUIPMENT, NET

The components of property, plant and equipment are summarized below:

	1990	1989
Land and land improvements	$ 18,169	$ 16,839
Buildings	182,122	173,995
Machinery and equipment	487,028	457,892
	687,319	648,726
Accumulated depreciation	(341,340)	(319,080)
	345,979	329,646
Additions in progress	59,541	49,461
	$ 405,520	$ 379,107

5. NOTES PAYABLE AND LONG-TERM DEBT

Notes payable includes $8,500 of variable rate industrial revenue bonds at December 31, 1990 and 1989. Although the bonds mature in 2009, they are classified as short-term debt since annually the bondholders may elect to continue their investment or return the bonds at which time they can be redeemed or resold.

Long-term debt at December 31, 1990 and 1989 is summarized as follows:

	1990	1989
Industrial revenue bonds – rates ranging from 5 3/4% to 11 1/8% with maturities through 2012	$ 34,608	$ 35,930
Other	6,491	17,740
	41,099	53,670
Less current portion	1,908	3,376
	$ 39,191	$ 50,294

The aggregate principal payments due on the long-term debt for the five years subsequent to December 31, 1990 are as follows:

1991	1992	1993	1994	1995
$1,908	$11,060	$2,687	$2,626	$2,698

6. ACCRUED LIABILITIES

Accrued liabilities at December 31, 1990 and 1989 consist of the following:

	1990	1989
Compensation and commissions	$ 27,235	$ 27,142
Retirement plans	16,930	17,171
Other	71,272	58,434
	$115,437	$102,747

7. EMPLOYEE BENEFIT AND RETIREMENT PLANS

The Company provides retirement benefits primarily through noncontributory defined contribution plans. The cost of these plans aggregated $16,889, $15,312 and $14,820 for the years ended December 31, 1990, 1989 and 1988, respectively.

The Company's Restricted Stock Incentive Plans provide for Common Share awards to be made to key management associates with restrictions as to disposition and subject to forfeiture upon termination of employment or if certain performance goals are not achieved. The plans also provide for supplemental cash awards in the event performance goals are exceeded. During 1990, 1989 and 1988, 91,791, 114,192 and 91,688 Common Shares were awarded and 9,574, 27,056 and 22,972 shares were forfeited, respectively.

The Company also maintains an incentive plan for participating officers and key management associates and a Voluntary Employee Beneficiary Association (VEBA).

8. RESEARCH AND DEVELOPMENT COSTS

Research and development costs relating to both future and present products are charged to selling, general and administrative expenses as incurred. These costs aggregated $16,121, $16,072 and $13,493 for the years ended December 31, 1990, 1989 and 1988, respectively.

9. INCOME TAXES

Income taxes are summarized as follows:

	1990	1989	1988
Current:			
Federal	$ 71,610	$ 66,117	$ 64,858
State and local	9,716	8,965	7,494
Foreign	6,455	7,968	5,865
	87,781	83,050	78,217
Deferred:			
Federal	(940)	(3,516)	(12,573)
State and local	73	(410)	(1,521)
Foreign	835	572	849
	(32)	(3,354)	(13,245)
	$ 87,749	$ 79,696	$ 64,972

Deferred income taxes arising from timing differences between financial and tax reporting relate to the following:

	1990	1989	1988
Excess tax over book depreciation	$ 4,351	$ 5,001	$ 8,215
Installment sales	–	(1,710)	(13,224)
Other	(4,383)	(6,645)	(8,236)
	$ (32)	$ (3,354)	$(13,245)

Earnings before income taxes aggregated $215,291, $188,189 and $156,141 for domestic operations and $15,978, $16,491 and $15,689 for foreign operations in 1990, 1989 and 1988, respectively. Total tax expense as a percent of pretax income differs from the amounts computed by applying the U.S. federal income tax rate of 34% to earnings before income taxes primarily due to the effect of state and local income tax expense.

10. COMMON SHARES

Under the Company's Rights Agreement, each shareholder has the right to purchase from the Company one Common Share at a price that is currently $125 per share. The rights are only exercisable in the event a person acquires or commences a tender offer or exchange offer for 20% or more of the Company's outstanding Common Shares.

In the event that a person who owns 20% or more of the Company's outstanding Common Shares merges into the Company, engages in one of a number of self-dealing transactions or increases ownership to 25% or more, each right would entitle its holder to purchase the Company's Common Shares having a market value equal to twice the right's exercise price.

In the event that the Company engages in a merger or other business transaction in which the Company is not the surviving corporation, engages in a merger or other business combination transaction in which its Common Shares are changed or exchanged or 50% or more of the Company's assets or earning power are sold, each right would entitle its holder to purchase common shares of the acquiring, surviving or resulting person having a market value equal to twice the right's exercise price.

The rights expire June 24, 1996, and may be redeemed by the Company at a cost that is currently $.025 per right, prior to the occurrence of the events described in the preceding two paragraphs.

CONSOLIDATED FINANCIAL SUMMARY

(Dollars in thousands except per share amounts)

		1990	1989	1988	1987
OPERATING RESULTS	Net sales	$1,534,013	$1,452,365	$1,291,584	$1,096,055
	Cost of sales	1,014,526	967,563	886,850	727,927
	Selling, general and administrative expenses	286,647	268,148	221,497	199,145
	Other charges (credits), net	1,571	11,974	11,407	10,761
	Earnings before income taxes	231,269	204,680	171,830	158,222
	Income taxes	87,749	79,696	64,972	67,499
	Net earnings	$ 143,520	$ 124,984	$ 106,858	$ 90,723
	Per Common Share	$ 1.80	$ 1.57	$ 1.34	$ 1.15
	% to sales	9.4%	8.6%	8.3%	8.3%
FINANCIAL POSITION	Current assets	$ 602,697	$ 567,307	$ 452,639	$ 418,563
	Property, plant and equipment, net	405,520	379,107	347,677	310,017
	Intangible and other assets, net	106,033	38,591	42,389	45,748
	Total assets	$1,114,250	$ 985,005	$ 842,705	$ 774,328
	Current liabilities	$ 235,300	$ 215,121	$ 197,431	$ 209,771
	Deferred taxes, credits and other liabilities	71,555	67,114	47,471	47,585
	Long-term debt	39,191	50,294	39,023	40,042
	Shareholders' equity	768,204	652,476	558,780	476,930
	Total liabilities and shareholders' equity	$1,114,250	$ 985,005	$ 842,705	$ 774,328
	Long-term debt as a % of total capitalization	5%	8%	7%	8%
	Working capital	$ 367,397	$ 352,186	$ 255,208	$ 208,792
	Current ratio	2.56	2.64	2.29	2.00
OTHER DATA	Average Common Shares outstanding (000)	79,844	79,625	79,464	79,234
	Return on average shareholders' equity	20.2%	20.6%	20.6%	20.8%
	Cash dividends paid	$ 42,621	$ 35,975	$ 29,520	$ 24,581
	Cash dividends paid per Common Share	$ .54	$ .46	$ .38	$ .32
	Shareholders' equity per Common Share	$ 9.60	$ 8.20	$ 7.04	$ 6.02
	Stock price range - NYSE	$ 45-31	$ 38-25	$ 27-21	$ 35-19
	Additions to property, plant and equipment	$ 103,720	$ 89,787	$ 87,333	$ 104,429
	Depreciation expense	$ 55,346	$ 57,341	$ 46,134	$ 44,155
	Number of shareholders - year end	13,305	11,225	10,482	10,104
	Average number of associates	9,304	9,098	8,643	7,512

All appropriate data have been adjusted for
the acquisitions accounted for as pooling of
interests and for stock splits.

1986	1985	1984	1983	1982	1981	1980
$864,721	$747,858	$676,660	$555,789	$462,792	$434,021	$375,758
554,421	488,169	458,803	366,425	306,190	289,748	261,448
166,954	140,203	118,915	103,608	90,336	82,731	67,634
684	3,233	803	2,189	3,619	2,457	3,047
142,662	116,253	98,139	83,567	62,647	59,085	43,629
67,658	53,965	44,010	38,742	29,828	28,796	20,795
$ 75,004	$ 62,288	$ 54,129	$ 44,825	$ 32,819	$ 30,289	$ 22,834
$ .95	$ .79	$ .69	$ .58	$ .44	$ .40	$ .30
8.7%	8.3%	8.0%	8.1%	7.1%	7.0%	6.1%
$332,655	$309,336	$270,989	$232,226	$169,879	$137,074	$111,055
248,224	210,929	171,836	138,078	138,003	138,858	142,917
45,780	13,041	9,826	8,151	8,112	7,909	1,076
$626,659	$533,306	$452,651	$378,455	$315,994	$283,841	$255,048
$156,456	$133,116	$114,970	$ 87,061	$ 65,342	$ 65,821	$ 56,117
40,013	28,713	23,172	19,317	17,166	17,528	16,486
35,668	34,071	27,559	28,589	29,873	24,400	25,266
394,522	337,406	286,950	243,488	203,613	176,092	157,179
$626,659	$533,306	$452,651	$378,455	$315,994	$283,841	$255,048
9%	10%	9%	11%	13%	13%	15%
$176,199	$176,220	$156,019	$145,165	$104,537	$ 71,253	$ 54,938
2.13	2.32	2.36	2.67	2.60	2.08	1.98
79,032	78,794	78,620	76,967	74,722	75,531	75,621
20.5%	20.0%	20.4%	20.1%	17.3%	18.2%	15.0%
$ 19,771	$ 15,907	$ 13,224	$ 11,277	$ 9,995	$ 8,558	$ 7,408
$ .26	$ .225	$ .195	$ .175	$ .157	$ .135	$ .12
$ 5.00	$ 4.29	$ 3.66	$ 3.14	$ 2.76	$ 2.40	$ 2.10
$ 29-17	$ 17-11	$ 11-8	$ 13-7	$ 8-4	$ 5-3	$ 4-3
$ 71,587	$ 71,665	$ 55,615	$ 29,275	$ 21,433	$ 23,873	$ 37,370
$ 34,135	$ 31,607	$ 23,473	$ 20,054	$ 18,450	$ 17,280	$ 16,466
8,379	6,332	5,722	5,168	4,775	4,305	4,711
6,509	5,934	5,374	4,815	4,645	4,612	4,585

PART 1
An Overview of the Statements and the Related Notes, Schedules, and Reports

Published financial statements include not only the statements themselves, but also the following reports and supplementary information:

- The report of the company's independent auditors (page 968).
- A report by management describing its responsibility for the statements (page 971).
- The notes accompanying the statements (pages 972–974).
- Segment information, indicating the various industries and the geographic regions in which the company operates (page 974).
- Quarterly information about operating results, stock prices, earnings per share, and dividends (page 974).
- Management's discussion and analysis of the company's financial condition and the results of operations (pages 974–975).
- A 10-year summary of key financial statistics (pages 976–977).

Our objective in **Part 1** of this comprehensive problem is to acquaint you with the form and content of these elements of the financial presentation.

INSTRUCTIONS

Answer each of the following questions and briefly explain *where* in the statements, notes, reports by management or by the auditors, or special schedules you located the information used in your answer.

a The comparative financial statements include balance sheets for two years, and statements of income, cash flows, and stockholders' equity for three years. Were all of these statements audited by a firm of independent accountants? Name the firm that audited some or all of these statements. What were the auditors' conclusions?

b Who is responsible for the content of these statements—management, the company's board of directors, or the auditors? In general terms, what measures have been undertaken by *management* to ensure the reliability of these statements?

c Write out the amount of the company's net sales in 1990 using words, rather than numbers.

d How much cash did Rubbermaid spend during 1990 on additions to plant, property, and equipment? In income taxes?

e The comparative balance sheets for 1989 and 1990 indicate that Rubbermaid issued additional shares of capital stock in 1990, but the statement of cash flows shows no proceeds. What happened?

f Are inventories valued using LIFO, FIFO, or some other method?

g Does Rubbermaid have an unusually large amount of debt maturing in any of the next five years? If so, does this amount of maturing debt appear to threaten the company's solvency?

h Does it appear that any lawsuits of material amount are pending against the company?

i Within how many industries does the company operate? Identify these industries. What percentage of the company's net sales were made outside of the United States in 1990? In 1989?

j What was the amount of net income earned during the *second quarter* of 1990? What was the percentage increase or decrease relative to the second quarter of 1989?

k Oil is the principal raw material in the manufacture of many plastic products. Late in 1990, the cost of oil more than doubled as the world braced itself for war in the Persian Gulf. How did this situation affect Rubbermaid?

    l Indicate for the years *1990* and *1985* the following per share amounts: (1) earnings, (2) cash dividends, (3) book value, and (4) stock price range (high and low).

    m Does management indicate a policy or objective with respect to the amount of dividends to be paid each year?

PART 2
Evaluation of
Credit Worthi-
ness

Assume that in early 1991 you are the credit manager of a company which sells materials used in the manufacture of plastic and rubber products. Rubbermaid wants to make credit purchases from your company of between $5 million and $10 million per month, with payment due in 60 days.

INSTRUCTIONS

    a As general background, read *Management's Discussion and Analysis* of the company's financial condition and the results of its operations on pages 974–975. Next, compute the following for the years ended December 31, 1990 and 1989. (Follow the company's policy of stating dollar amounts in thousands. Round percentages to $\frac{1}{10}$ of 1%, and other computations to one decimal place.)

        1 Current ratio.

        2 Quick ratio.

        3 Working capital.

        4 Percentage of working capital comprised of cash and cash equivalents.

        5 Percentage changes in cash and cash equivalents from the preceding year (At the end of 1988, cash and cash equivalents amounted to $33,683.)

        6 Accounts receivable turnover rate and the average number of days required to collect accounts receivable (Assume that average accounts receivable during 1989 amounted to $225 million.)

        7 Inventory turnover rate and number of days required to sell the average amount of inventory (Average inventory during 1989 amounted to $168 million.)

        8 The excess (or shortfall) in the company's net cash flow from operating activities over (or below) the sum of (a) cash paid to acquire property, plant, and equipment, and (b) dividends paid to stockholders.

    b Does the company have lines of credit which could assist it in meeting its short-term obligations for cash payments?

    c Based upon your above analyses, does this company's liquidity appear to have ***increased*** or ***decreased*** during 1990? Explain. If you indicated that liquidity has decreased, explain whether you consider this a serious problem.

    d Your company assigns each customer one of the four credit ratings listed below. Assign a credit rating to Rubbermaid and write a memorandum explaining your decision. (In your memorandum, you may use any of your computations in parts **a** or **b**, and may refer to other information in the financial statements.)

POSSIBLE
CREDIT
RATINGS

    A **Outstanding.** Little or no risk of inability to pay. For customers in this category, we fill any reasonable order, without imposing a credit limit. The customer's credit is reevaluated annually.

    B **Good.** Customer has good debt-paying ability, but is assigned a credit limit which is reviewed every six months. Orders above the established credit limit are accepted only on a cash basis.

    C **Marginal.** Customer appears sound, but credit should be extended only on a 30-day basis with a relatively low credit limit. Credit status and credit limit are reevaluated every 90 days.

    D **Unacceptable.** Customer does not qualify for credit.

PART 3
Analysis of
Common Stock

Assume that you are an investment advisor who publishes a monthly newsletter with recommendations to your clients as to whether to buy, hold, or sell specific stocks. One of the common stocks that you will evaluate this month is Rubbermaid. It is now early 1991, and the price of the company's common stock is **$45** per share.

INSTRUCTIONS

a As general background, read *Management's Discussion and Analysis* of the company's financial condition and the results of its operations on pages 974–975. Next, compute the following for the years ended December 31, 1990 and 1989. (Follow the company's policy of stating dollar amounts in thousands, except for per share amounts. Round percentage computations to $\frac{1}{10}$ of 1%.)

   1 Price-earnings ratio. (For 1990, use the current stock price of $45 per share; for 1989, use the high stock price for the year.)

   2 Dividend yield. (Use the stock prices indicated in item **1**.)

   3 Return on average total assets. Assume that average total assets in 1989 amounted to $913,855 (thousand).

   4 Return on average stockholders' equity. Assume that average stockholders' equity during 1989 amounted to $605,628 (thousand).

   5 Equity ratio.

b Prepare trend analyses of (1) net sales, (2) net income, (3) dividends per share, and (4) highest market price per share for the three years from 1988 through 1990. (Use 1988 as the base year, which will be stated at 100% in each trend analysis. Round to the nearest percent.)

c Rubbermaid has consistently followed a policy of increasing each year the cash dividend per share paid to holders of the common stock. Write a memorandum evaluating the company's ability to continue this policy. As a basis for this memorandum, review the trends in the company's net income and earnings per share, and also review the statement of cash flows.

d Write a brief memorandum on the topic of leverage as it relates to Rubbermaid. Does the company make extensive use of long-term debt financing? Assuming that long-term interest rates are about 9%, would the use of long-term debt as a means of financing future growth be desirable from the viewpoint of common stockholders?

e Write a brief memorandum on the "quality" of the company's earnings. As a basis for this memorandum, review trends in the comparative income statements and in the 10-year summary. Also consider management's decision and analysis of the company's operations results.

f Write a statement for your newsletter in which you recommend that your clients take one of the following actions with respect to Rubbermaid's common stock:

   Buy (Your most positive recommendation; you think the market price of the stock will go up.)

   Sell (Your most negative recommendation; you feel that the stock is overpriced and will fall in value.)

   Hold (A relatively neutral position: you feel that the stock is priced at a fair value with good but not exceptional prospects.)

Explain the reasoning behind your recommendation.

   In addition to the information developed in other parts of this problem, your recommendation should consider the following facts about the economic environment in early 1991.

The country had recently entered a recession. Corporate profits were declining in many industries. However, the crisis in the Persian Gulf had just been resolved, the price of oil had dropped by nearly 50% in the past several months, and interest rates were coming down rapidly. Many economists were forecasting an end to the recession within six months, to be followed by a period of modest economic growth. Stock prices were highly volatile. Overall, however, the stock market was near its record high.

Dividend yields for growth-oriented companies ranged from zero to about 3%; for slow-growth companies, yields were from 5% to 7%. Companies with slow but reliable rates of growth, such as telephone companies, were selling at p/e ratios of between 14 to 1 and 17 to 1. Some fast-growth companies, such as *Microsoft,* were trading at p/e ratios in excess of 30 to 1.

g Look up the current market price of Rubbermaid's common stock in the financial pages of a newspaper. (The stock trades on the New York Stock Exchange.) How did your recommendation work out in the long run?

Managerial Accounting: Cost Accounting Systems

*T*he next two chapters provide the basic foundation for our study of managerial accounting. In these chapters, we will show how accounting systems can measure the cost of manufacturing specific products and of performing specific services.

Part 7 concludes with a Comprehensive Problem providing a review of both process and job order cost accounting systems.

21 Introduction to Managerial Accounting; Accounting for Manufacturing Operations

Chapter 21 is the first of six chapters emphasizing the specialized use of accounting information by managers. In the opening pages, we contrast managerial accounting with financial accounting. The major purpose of this chapter, however, is to introduce accounting concepts relating to manufacturing activities. We explain the nature of manufacturing costs, with emphasis upon the idea that these are "product costs" not "period costs." Next, we illustrate the "flow" of manufacturing costs through perpetual inventory records. A distinction is drawn between direct and indirect manufacturing costs, and the use of overhead application rates is explained and illustrated. Finally, we illustrate the schedule of cost of finished goods manufactured, which summarizes the relationships between manufacturing costs and completed units of product.

After studying this chapter you should be able to meet these Learning Objectives:

1 *Distinguish between the fields of managerial accounting and financial accounting.*
2 *Describe the three basic types of manufacturing cost.*
3 *Distinguish between product costs and period costs and explain how product costs are offset against revenue.*
4 *Describe how manufacturing costs "flow" through perpetual inventory accounts.*
5 *Distinguish between direct and indirect manufacturing costs.*
6 *Explain the purpose of overhead application rates and the importance of basing these rates upon significant "cost drivers."*
7 *Prepare a schedule of the cost of finished goods manufactured.*

INTRODUCTION TO MANAGERIAL ACCOUNTING

OBJECTIVE 1 Distinguish between the fields of managerial accounting and financial accounting.

In preceding chapters we have emphasized the topic of financial accounting. The term *financial accounting* refers to the preparation and use of accounting information describing the financial position and operating results of a business entity. Financial accounting serves as the basis for the preparation of both financial statements and income tax returns. Because financial statements are used by outsiders, such as creditors, stockholders, and potential investors, the information in these statements is presented in conformity with *generally accepted accounting principles.* Although income tax rules differ somewhat from generally accepted accounting principles, there are many similarities between these two sets of reporting standards.

Beginning with this chapter, we shall shift our emphasis toward the field of managerial accounting. *Managerial accounting* (or management accounting) involves the preparation and use of accounting information designed to assist managers in planning and controlling the operations of the business, and in decision making. In short, managerial accounting information is designed to meet the needs of *insiders,* rather than decision makers *outside* the business entity.

Since managerial accounting reports are used exclusively by management, their content is *not* governed by generally accepted accounting principles or income tax rules. Rather, managerial accounting reports should contain whatever information *best suits the needs of the decision maker.* The greatest challenge to managerial accountants is providing managers with the information that is most relevant to a particular business decision.

The diagram on the following page compares the basic characteristics of financial and managerial accounting. Notice that both types of accounting information are developed within the same accounting system. Thus, the accounting system of a business should be able to provide the special types of information needed by management, as well as to meet the company's financial reporting requirements.

Interdisciplinary Nature of Managerial Accounting

In meeting the information needs of management, managerial accountants often must obtain estimates and data from experts in fields other than accounting. For example, many managerial accounting reports are forecasts of future operating results. Forecasting the sales of a multinational corporation, however, may involve marketing research, assumptions about future economic conditions, an understanding of international trade agreements, and familiarity with numerous foreign cultures. Managerial accountants do not need personal expertise in each of these areas, but they must have a broad understanding of the company's business environment.

To encourage a professional level of training and competence for managerial accountants, the Institute of Certified Management Accountants sponsors a Certified Management Accounting (CMA) program. To become a *CMA,* an individual must meet educational and experience requirements, and also pass a rigorous five-part examination.

THE ACCOUNTING SYSTEM

FINANCIAL ACCOUNTING

Purpose

To provide a wide variety of decision makers with useful information about the financial position and operating results of a business entity.

Types of Reports

Financial statements, income tax returns, and special reports, such as loan applications and reports to regulatory agencies.

Standards for Presentation

In financial statements, generally accepted accounting principles. In income tax returns, tax regulations.

Reporting Entity

Usually the company viewed as a whole.

Time Periods Covered

Usually a year, quarter, or month. Most reports focus upon completed periods. Emphasis is placed on the current (latest) period, with prior periods often shown for comparison.

MANAGERIAL ACCOUNTING

Purpose

To provide managers with information useful in planning and controlling business operations, and in making managerial decisions.

Types of Reports

Many different types of reports, depending upon the nature of the business and the specific information needs of management.

Standards for Presentation

No specific rules; whatever information is most relevant to the needs of management.

Reporting Entity

Usually a subdivision of the business, such as a department, a product line, or a type of activity.

Time Periods Covered

Any period: year, quarter, month, week, day, even a work shift. Some reports are historical in nature; others focus on estimates of results expected in future periods.

Users of the Information

Outsiders as well as managers. For financial statements, these outsiders include stockholders, creditors, prospective investors, tax and regulatory authorities, and the general public. Income tax returns normally go only to tax authorities.

Users of the Information

Management (different reports to different managers). Managerial accounting reports usually are not distributed to outsiders.

Our Approach to Managerial Accounting

In this introductory textbook, we divide our discussion of managerial accounting into three broad categories: (1) *cost accounting* (with an emphasis on determining the cost of manufactured products), (2) the use of accounting information in *planning and controlling* business operations, and (3) *tailoring accounting information* for use in specific managerial decisions. These closely related topics provide an overview of the nature and use of managerial accounting information. Many topics, however, remain to be explored; the study of managerial accounting may be continued throughout a professional career.

Cost Accounting   In order to plan and control the activities of a business, management must first have information about the costs involved in performing different business operations. This information about costs will help management in determining whether specific activities are profitable and whether the various departments within the business are operating efficiently. The accounting concepts and practices for measuring the cost of performing different business activities and of manufacturing various products are called ***cost accounting.***

Let us consider, for example, a company that manufactures several different products. The company's accounting system should provide information about the cost of manufacturing ***each product*** and the cost of conducting other business activities, such as operating the accounting, personnel, and marketing departments. We will discuss accounting for the costs of manufactured products in the remainder of this chapter and in Chapter 22. Measuring the cost of performing other business activities will be discussed in Chapter 24.

Planning and Control   The term ***planning*** refers to setting objectives or goals for future performance. Often, these objectives are stated in terms of dollar amounts, such as achieving "net sales of $10 million in the coming year."

Control refers to monitoring the extent to which these planned objectives are being accomplished and to taking corrective action when actual results differ from the plan. In Chapters 23, 24, and 25, we focus upon the use of accounting information in planning and controlling business operations.

Tailoring Information to Specific Decisions   Managerial accounting information often is collected and arranged to assist a particular manager in making a specific business decision. This process is explained and illustrated in Chapter 26.

Overlap of Managerial and Financial Accounting

It is useful to recognize that financial and managerial accounting are ***not*** two entirely separate disciplines. Financial accounting information is widely used in many managerial decisions. For example, managers daily use information about sales, expenses, and income taxes in many business decisions. However, managers also require additional information, such as revenue and expenses broken down by department or by product line. Thus, much managerial accounting information is actually financial accounting information, rearranged to suit a particular managerial purpose.

As you progress through the remaining chapters, you should encounter many familiar accounting terms and concepts. However, you will also encounter new terms and concepts, as well as new ways of interpreting familiar accounting information.

ACCOUNTING FOR MANUFACTURING OPERATIONS

One area in which managerial and financial accounting overlap is in accounting for manufacturing activities. A merchandising company buys its inventory in a ready-to-sell condition. Therefore, the cost of this merchandise is simply the purchase price. A ***manufacturing*** company, on the other hand, ***produces*** the goods that it sells. In this case, the cost of the merchandise consists of various ***manufacturing costs,*** including the cost of the raw materials used in the production process, wages earned by factory workers, and all of the other costs of operating a factory.[1]

In a manufacturing company, manufacturing costs are of vital importance both to managerial and financial accountants. Managerial accountants must supply managers with prompt and reliable information about manufacturing costs for use in such decisions as:

- What sales price must we charge for our products to earn a reasonable profit?
- Can we produce a particular type of product at a cost which will enable us to sell it at a competitive price?
- Would it be less expensive for us to buy certain parts used in our products, or to manufacture these parts in our plant?
- Should we install a more highly automated assembly line?

Financial accountants need information about manufacturing costs in order to determine the cost of a manufacturing company's inventories and its cost of goods sold.

Types of Manufacturing Costs

OBJECTIVE 2
Describe the three basic types of manufacturing cost.

A typical manufacturing company buys raw materials and, through the efforts of factory workers and the use of machines, converts these materials into finished products. Manufacturing costs may be divided into three broad categories:

1 **Direct materials**—the cost of the materials and component parts used in the manufacture of the finished products.

2 **Direct labor costs**—wages and other payroll costs relating to employees who work directly on the goods being manufactured, either by hand or with tools.

3 **Manufacturing overhead**—a "catch-all" classification, including all manufacturing costs ***other than*** the costs of direct materials and direct labor. Examples include depreciation on machinery, supervisors' salaries, factory utilities, and equipment repairs.

Manufacturing costs are ***not*** regarded as expenses of the current period; rather they are costs of ***creating inventory.*** For this reason, manufacturing costs are often called ***inventoriable costs,*** or ***product costs.***

Product Costs and Period Costs

The terms ***product costs*** and ***period costs*** are helpful in explaining the difference between manufacturing costs and expenses. ***Product costs*** are

---

[1] Manufacturing costs are the cost of producing inventory, which is an asset. Therefore, these expenditures are termed ***costs,*** rather than ***expenses.*** Unexpired costs are assets; expired costs are expenses.

OBJECTIVE 3 Distinguish between product costs and period costs and explain how product costs are offset against revenue.

the costs of purchasing or manufacturing inventory. Thus, until the related goods are sold, product costs **represent inventory,** which is an asset. When the goods are sold, the product costs are deducted from revenue as the cost of goods sold.

Costs that are associated with time periods, rather than with the purchase or manufacture of inventory, are termed **period costs.** Period costs are charged directly to expense accounts on the assumption that the benefits are received in the same period as the cost is incurred. Period costs include all selling expenses, general and administrative expenses, interest expense, and income taxes expense—in short, all the items classified in an income statement as "expense."

The "flow" of product costs and of period costs through financial statements is shown in the following diagram:

Product costs become inventory

Period costs become expense

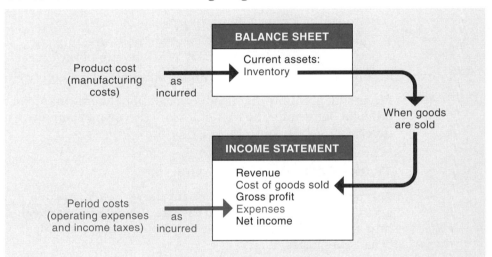

To illustrate this distinction, let us consider two costs which, on the surface, appear quite similar: depreciation on a direct materials warehouse and depreciation on a finished goods warehouse. Depreciation on the direct materials warehouse is a **product cost,** because this cost relates to the manufacturing process. Once the manufacturing process is complete and the goods are available for sale, however, storage costs are viewed as a selling expense. Thus, the depreciation on the finished goods warehouse is a **period cost.**

Product Costs and the Matching Principle The distinction between product costs and period costs may be explained by the **matching principle**— the idea that revenue should be offset by the costs incurred in generating that revenue. To illustrate, consider a real estate developer who starts construction on a tract of 10 homes in 1994. During the year, the developer spends $100,000 on each house ($1 million in total) in materials, construction wages, and overhead. At the end of 1994, all 10 houses are complete, but none has yet been sold. How much of the $1 million for construction costs should the developer recognize as expense in 1994?

The answer is **none.** These costs are not related to any revenue earned by the developer in 1994, but they are related to revenue that the developer will earn when the houses are sold. Therefore, at the end of 1994, the

$1 million of product costs should appear in the developer's balance sheet as *inventory.* As each house is sold, $100,000 will be deducted from the sales revenue as the cost of goods sold. In this way, the developer's income statements in future periods will reflect properly both the revenue and the cost of each sale.

Inventories of a Manufacturing Business

In the preceding example, the houses all were completed by the end of 1994, so our developer's inventory consisted only of finished goods. Manufacturing companies, however, normally have *three types* of inventories:

1 **Materials inventory**—direct materials on hand and available for use in the manufacturing process.

2 **Work in process inventory**—partially completed goods upon which production activities have been started but not yet completed.

3 **Finished goods inventory**—finished products available for sale to customers.

All three of these inventories are shown in the balance sheet at cost and are classified as current assets. The cost of the materials inventory is based upon purchase prices; the costs of the work in process inventory and of the finished goods inventory are based upon the manufacturing costs incurred in producing these units.

Manufacturing companies may use either a perpetual or a periodic inventory system. Perpetual systems have many advantages, however, such as providing managers with up-to-date information about the amounts of inventory on hand and the per-unit costs of manufacturing products. For these reasons, virtually all large manufacturing companies use perpetual inventory systems. Also, the flow of manufacturing costs through the inventory accounts and into the cost of goods sold is most easily illustrated in a perpetual inventory system. Therefore, we will assume the use of a perpetual inventory system in our discussion of manufacturing activities.

Flow of Costs Parallels the Physical Flow of Goods

*OBJECTIVE 4
Describe
how manu-
facturing
costs "flow"
through
perpetual
inventory
accounts.*

When a perpetual inventory system is in use, the flow of manufacturing costs through the company's ledger accounts closely parallels the physical flow of goods through the production process. This relationship is illustrated in the diagram on page 992. The green shaded boxes in the bottom portion of this diagram represent the *ledger accounts* used by a manufacturing company in accounting for manufacturing costs.

Accounting for Manufacturing Costs: An Illustration

The diagram introduces six ledger accounts used in accounting for manufacturing activities: (1) Materials Inventory, (2) Direct Labor, (3) Manufacturing Overhead, (4) Work in Process Inventory, (5) Finished Goods Inventory, and (6) Cost of Goods Sold.

The manner in which manufacturing costs "flow through" these accounts is illustrated on page 993. The data in this illustration represent

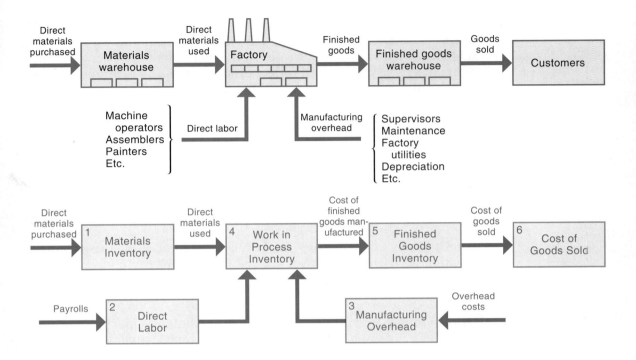

the manufacturing costs of Allied Manufacturing Company during 1994. (The debit and credit entries appearing in this illustration summarize numerous transactions recorded by Allied throughout the year.)

Our use of several colors in this illustration is intended to help you follow the flow of manufacturing costs through the accounts. The beginning balances in the three inventory accounts are shown in black. Manufacturing costs are shown in red, as are the arrows showing the transfers of these costs from one account to another. Account balances at year-end, which will appear in the company's financial statements, are shown in blue.

Let us now look more closely at the flow of manufacturing costs through these ledger accounts.

Materials Inventory

The Materials Inventory account is used to record purchases of direct materials and the use of these materials in the manufacturing process. **Direct materials** are those raw materials and component parts that become an integral part of the finished product, and that can be traced conveniently and directly into the quantity of finished goods manufactured. For example, the direct materials used by an automaker include sheet steel, glass, plastic, tires, transmissions, and batteries. The completed automobiles assembled from these components are the automaker's finished goods.

The terms **direct materials** and **finished goods** are defined from the viewpoint of each manufacturing company. For example, Ford Motor Company views tires as a direct material; the Goodyear Tire & Rubber Company, however, views tires as finished goods.

In a perpetual inventory system, purchases of direct materials are debited directly to the Materials Inventory account. As these materials are

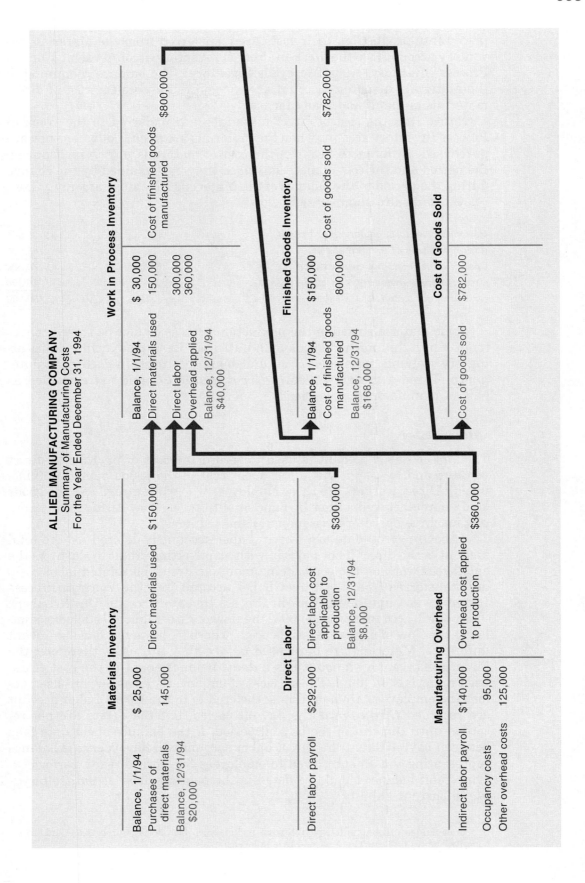

ALLIED MANUFACTURING COMPANY
Summary of Manufacturing Costs
For the Year Ended December 31, 1994

Materials Inventory

Balance, 1/1/94	$ 25,000	Direct materials used
Purchases of direct materials	145,000	
Balance, 12/31/94 $20,000		

$150,000

Work in Process Inventory

Balance, 1/1/94	$ 30,000	Cost of finished goods manufactured
Direct materials used	150,000	
Direct labor	300,000	
Overhead applied	360,000	
Balance, 12/31/94 $40,000		

$800,000

Direct Labor

Direct labor payroll	$292,000	Direct labor cost applicable to production
		Balance, 12/31/94 $8,000

$300,000

Finished Goods Inventory

Balance, 1/1/94	$150,000	Cost of goods sold
Cost of finished goods manufactured	800,000	
Balance, 12/31/94 $168,000		

$782,000

Manufacturing Overhead

Indirect labor payroll	$140,000	Overhead cost applied to production
Occupancy costs	95,000	
Other overhead costs	125,000	

$360,000

Cost of Goods Sold

Cost of goods sold	$782,000

placed into production, their costs are transferred from the Materials Inventory account into the Work in Process Inventory account (debit Work in Process Inventory, credit Materials Inventory). The balance remaining in the Materials Inventory account at year-end represents the cost of direct materials on hand and ready for use.

Notice that the cost of direct materials is transferred to the Work in Process Inventory account when the materials are *used,* not when they are purchased. Differences between the cost of materials *purchased* during the period and the cost of materials *used* may be explained by the change during the period in the balance of the Materials Inventory account. These relationships are summarized below:

Materials inventory, beginning of the year	$ 25,000
Add: Purchases of direct materials	145,000
Cost of direct materials available for use	$170,000
Less: Materials inventory, end of the year	20,000
Cost of direct materials used	$150,000

Some materials used in the production process cannot be traced conveniently into the finished goods manufactured. Examples include lubricating oil, welding materials, glue, and materials used in factory maintenance. These items are called *indirect materials* and are classified as part of manufacturing overhead.

Direct Labor

The Direct Labor account is used to record the cost of payrolls to direct workers and to assign this direct labor cost to the goods being manufactured.[2] Direct workers are those employees who work directly on the goods being manufactured, either by hand or with tools. They include, for example, machine operators, assemblers, and painters.

At each payroll date, the Direct Labor account is debited for the total amount of the direct labor payroll, with an offsetting credit to Cash. As the employees work on the goods being manufactured, the related labor costs are transferred from the Direct Labor account into the Work in Process Inventory account (debit Work in Process Inventory, credit Direct Labor).

In our T accounts on page 993, the flow of direct labor costs looks similar to the flow of direct materials costs. There is, however, one significant difference. Materials are purchased *before* they are used; therefore, the Materials Inventory account has a *debit* balance equal to the cost of unused materials on hand. The services of employees, however, are used before the employees are paid. Thus, the credits to the Direct Labor account are recorded *throughout* the payroll period, but the debits are not recorded until the *end* of the payroll period. If the balance sheet date falls between payroll dates, the Direct Labor account will have a *credit* balance representing the amount owed to employees for work already performed. This credit balance should be listed in the balance sheet as *wages payable,* a current liability.

---

[2] As explained in Chapter 11, payroll costs include such factors as payroll taxes and "fringe benefits," as well as the wages earned by employees.

Many employees in a manufacturing plant do not work directly on the goods being manufactured. Examples of these indirect workers include supervisors, timekeepers, maintenance personnel, and plant security guards. ***Indirect labor*** costs are considered part of manufacturing overhead rather than being included in direct labor costs.

Manufacturing Overhead

The Manufacturing Overhead account is used to record all costs classified as "overhead," and also to assign these costs to the products being manufactured. Manufacturing overhead is a broad category of manufacturing costs, representing all manufacturing costs ***other than*** direct materials and direct labor. Examples of manufacturing costs classified as overhead include:

1 **Indirect materials used**

   a Factory supplies that do not become an integral part of the finished goods, such as lubricating oil and parts used to maintain or repair equipment.

   b Materials that become an integral part of the finished goods, but would be traceable into the products only with great effort and expense. Examples include glue, welding materials, and staples.

2 **Indirect labor costs**

   a Supervisors' salaries

   b Salaries of factory maintenance, medical, and security personnel

3 **Plant occupancy costs**

   a Rent or depreciation on buildings

   b Insurance on buildings; property taxes on land and buildings

   c Maintenance and repairs on buildings

   d Utilities—gas, electricity, water, and telephone

4 **Machinery and equipment costs**

   a Rent or depreciation on machinery

   b Insurance and property taxes on machinery

   c Maintenance and repairs on machinery

5 **Cost of compliance with federal, state, and local regulations**

   a Meeting factory safety requirements

   b Disposal of hazardous waste materials

   c Control over factory emissions (meeting clean air standards)

These are only examples; because of the diverse nature of manufacturing companies, it is not possible to prepare a complete list of all types of overhead costs. As there are many different types of overhead costs, Manufacturing Overhead is a controlling account. Subsidiary records are maintained to keep track of the different types of overhead costs.

Selling expenses and general and administrative expenses do ***not*** relate to the manufacturing process and are ***not*** included in manufacturing overhead. Certain costs, such as insurance, property taxes, and utilities, may be applicable in part to manufacturing operations and in part to administrative and selling functions. In such cases, these costs should be ***apportioned*** among manufacturing overhead, general and administrative expense, and selling expense accounts.

Recording Overhead Costs   The Manufacturing Overhead account is debited to record any cost classified as "overhead." Examples of costs debited to this account include purchases of indirect materials, payments of indirect labor payrolls, payments of factory utilities, and recording depreciation on machinery. The account credited may vary, depending upon the nature of the overhead cost. For example, in recording purchases of indirect materials or factory utilities, the account credited usually will be Cash or Accounts Payable. In recording depreciation on machinery, however, the account credited is Accumulated Depreciation.

As the items included in total overhead costs are "consumed" by production activities, the related costs are transferred from the Manufacturing Overhead account into the Work in Process Inventory account (debit Work in Process Inventory, credit Manufacturing Overhead). In the course of the year, all the overhead costs incurred should be assigned to units of product manufactured. Thus, at year-end, the Manufacturing Overhead account should have a zero balance.[3]

Direct and Indirect Manufacturing Costs

OBJECTIVE 5
Distinguish between direct and indirect manufacturing costs.

The costs of direct materials and direct labor may be traced conveniently and directly into specific units of product. Consider, for example, a company that manufactures many types of fine furniture. It is relatively easy to determine the cost of the wood and the cost of the direct labor that go into making a particular dining table. For this reason, accountants call these items ***direct*** manufacturing costs.

Overhead, however, is an ***indirect cost.*** Consider, for example, the types of costs that a furniture manufacturer classifies as overhead. These costs include property taxes on the factory, depreciation on tools and equipment, supervisors' salaries, and repairs to equipment. How much of these indirect costs should be assigned to the dining table?

There is no easy answer to this question. By definition, indirect costs ***cannot*** be traced easily and directly into specific units of product. These costs often relate to manufacturing operations viewed ***as a whole,*** rather than to specific units of product. However, we cannot ignore indirect manufacturing costs. In many companies, overhead is by far the largest of the three basic categories of manufacturing costs. Therefore, manufacturing companies must develop a method of allocating an appropriate portion of total manufacturing overhead to each product manufactured. The allocation of overhead costs to production is accomplished through the use of ***overhead application rates.***

Overhead Application Rates

An overhead application rate is a device used to assign appropriate amounts of manufacturing overhead to specific units of manufactured

---

[3]   The disposition of over- or underapplied overhead will be discussed in Chapter 22.

OBJECTIVE 6
Explain the purpose of overhead application rates and the importance of basing these rates upon significant "cost drivers."

products. The rate expresses the expected relationship between manufacturing overhead and some ***activity base*** that can be traced directly to the manufactured products. Manufacturing overhead is then assigned to products ***in proportion*** to this activity base.

The overhead application rate is determined at the beginning of the accounting period, based upon estimated amounts. The formula is:

$$\text{Overhead Application Rate} = \frac{\text{Estimated Overhead Costs}}{\text{Estimated Units in the Activity Base}}$$

The mechanics of computing and using an overhead application rate are quite simple. The challenging problems for accountants are (1) selecting an appropriate activity base, and (2) making reliable estimates of total overhead costs for the period and of the units in the activity base.[4] Let us first address the easy topic—mechanics.

Computation and Use of an Overhead Application Rate   Assume that at the beginning of 1994, Allied Manufacturing Company makes the following estimates relating to its manufacturing activities for the coming year:

Estimated total manufacturing overhead costs for the year...............	*$360,000*
Estimated total direct labor cost for the year	*$300,000*
Estimated machine hours for the year....................................	*10,000 hours*

Using this estimated data, we will illustrate the computation and use of an overhead application rate under two independent assumptions:

*Assumption 1: **Allied uses direct labor cost as the "activity base" in the application of overhead costs.***
In this case, the overhead application rate will be ***120% of direct labor cost*** ($360,000 estimated overhead ÷ $300,000 estimated direct labor cost = 120%). Manufacturing overhead will be assigned to manufactured units in proportion to the direct labor cost assigned to those units. Thus, if $2,000 in direct labor is charged to specific units of product, $2,400 of overhead will be charged to these units ($2,000 direct labor cost × 120% overhead application rate = $2,400).

*Assumption 2: **Allied uses machine hours as the activity base.***
In this case, the overhead application rate will be ***$36 per machine hour*** ($360,000 ÷ 10,000 hours). Using this approach, manufacturing overhead costs will be assigned to units based upon the number of machine hours used in producing the units. If 10 machine hours are needed to manufacture a particular group of units, those units will be charged with $360 in overhead costs (10 hours × $36 per hour).

What "Drives" Overhead Costs?

For the use of an overhead application rate to provide reliable results, the activity base must be a significant "driver" of overhead costs. A ***cost driver***

---

[4]   Errors in estimating the amount of total overhead costs for the coming period or the number of units in the activity base will cause differences between the actual overhead incurred and the amounts assigned to units manufactured. These differences usually are small and are eliminated by an adjusting entry at the end of the accounting period. We will address this issue in Chapter 22.

is an activity base that is a ***causal factor*** in the incurrence of overhead costs.

In the past, direct labor costs (or direct labor hours) often were viewed as the primary driver of overhead costs. Products that required more direct labor often required more indirect labor (supervision), more wear and tear on machinery (maintenance and depreciation), and greater use of factory supplies and of electricity. Therefore, many manufacturing companies followed the practice of allocating all overhead costs to production in proportion to direct labor costs (or hours).

As factories have become more highly automated, direct labor has become much less of a causal factor in many overhead costs. Today, many manufacturing companies find that activity bases such as machine-hours, computer time, or the number of component parts to be assembled result in a more realistic allocation of overhead costs.

The Use of Multiple Overhead Application Rates   In an effort to determine the "true" cost of manufacturing different types of products, many companies are refining the techniques used in associating overhead costs with specific units of production. These companies may use different overhead application rates in allocating different types of overhead costs. For example, supervision costs may be allocated to production based upon direct labor cost, whereas maintenance and depreciation on factory machines may be allocated on the basis of machine-hours. Different application rates also may be used in each production department and in applying overhead costs to different types of products.

The key point is that each manufactured product should be charged with the overhead costs ***generated by*** the manufacture of that product. If the activity base used in applying overhead costs is ***not*** the primary cost driver, the relative production cost of different products may be ***significantly distorted.*** This, in turn, may lead to faulty decisions by management.

CASE IN POINT   A large dairy products company allocated its overhead costs to production in proportion to the amount of butterfat used in each product. The quantity of butterfat used in producing a product had been a major driver of overhead costs until the dairy began producing dehydrated milk.

The manufacture of dehydrated milk required the use of expensive machinery and greatly increased overhead costs. However, the dehydrated milk contained almost no butterfat. Based on the "butterfat method" of allocating overhead costs, the increased overhead stemming from the manufacture of dehydrated milk was allocated primarily to ice cream and other products high in butterfat. The cost of manufacturing dehydrated milk appeared to be quite low, because almost no overhead costs were allocated to this product.

As a result of the distorted cost figures, management cut back on the production of ice cream and increased production of dehydrated milk. This strategy, however, resulted in a substantial decline in the company's profitability. Only after a business consultant pointed out the improper allocation of overhead costs did management learn that ice cream was the company's most profitable product and that dehydrated milk was being sold to customers at a price below its actual production cost.

The Increasing Importance of Proper Overhead Allocation   In today's global economy, competition among manufacturing companies is greater than ever before. If a company is to determine whether it can compete effectively in this marketplace, it must first know with some precision its per-unit cost of manufacturing its products. In highly automated factories, overhead often is the largest of the three basic categories of manufacturing costs. Therefore, the proper allocation of overhead costs is one of the major challenges facing managerial accountants.

Work in Process Inventory, Finished Goods Inventory, and the Cost of Goods Sold

The Work in Process Inventory account is used (1) to accumulate the manufacturing costs relating to all units of product worked on during the period and (2) to allocate these costs between those units completed during the period and those that are only partially completed at year-end.

As materials are placed into production and manufacturing activities take place, the related manufacturing costs are debited to the Work in Process Inventory account. The flow of manufacturing costs into this inventory account is consistent with the idea that manufacturing costs are ***product costs,*** rather than period costs.

As specific units are completed, the cost of manufacturing them is transferred from the Work in Process Inventory account to the Finished Goods Inventory account. Thus, the balance in the Work in Process account represents only the manufacturing costs associated with units still "in process."

Notice that manufactured products are classified as finished goods only ***after*** all manufacturing processes have been completed. Therefore, any costs of storing, marketing, or delivering finished goods are regarded as ***selling expenses,*** not manufacturing costs. When units of finished goods are sold, their cost is transferred from the Finished Goods Inventory account to the Cost of Goods Sold account.

The Need for Per-Unit Cost Data   Transferring the cost of specific units from one account to another requires knowledge of the ***per-unit cost***— that is, the total manufacturing costs assigned to specific units. (The determination of unit cost is one of the primary goals of every ***cost accounting system*** and will be explained and illustrated in the following chapter.)

Unit costs are of importance to both financial and managerial accountants. Financial accountants use unit costs in recording the transfer of completed units from the Work in Process account to the Finished Goods account and also in recording the cost of goods sold. Thus, both a manufacturing company's inventory of finished goods and its costs of goods sold are based upon the ***cost of manufacturing*** the related units of product. Managerial accountants use unit costs in developing information to assist management in making pricing decisions, evaluating the efficiency of current operations, and planning future operations.

Schedule of the Cost of Finished Goods Manufactured

OBJECTIVE 7
Prepare a
schedule of
the cost of
finished
goods manu-
factured.

Most manufacturing companies prepare a **schedule of the cost of finished goods manufactured** to provide managers with an overview of the costs relating to manufacturing activities during the period. Using the data in our illustration on page 993, a schedule of the cost of finished goods manufactured for Allied Manufacturing Company is shown below.

ALLIED MANUFACTURING COMPANY
Schedule of the Cost of Finished Goods Manufactured
For the Year Ended December 31, 1994

Work in process inventory, beginning of the year		$ 30,000
Manufacturing cost assigned to production:		
Direct materials used	$150,000	
Direct labor	300,000	
Manufacturing overhead	360,000	
Total manufacturing costs		810,000
Total cost of all work in process during the year		$840,000
Less: Work in process inventory, end of the year		(40,000)
Cost of finished goods manufactured		$800,000

Notice that all the amounts used in this schedule may be obtained from the Work in Process Inventory account illustrated on page 993. In short, the schedule of cost of finished goods manufactured summarizes the flow of manufacturing costs into and out of the Work in Process Inventory account.

Purpose of the Schedule   A schedule of the cost of finished goods manufactured is **not** a formal financial statement. Rather, it is intended primarily to assist managers in understanding and evaluating the overall cost of manufacturing the company's products. By comparing these schedules for successive periods, for example, managers can determine whether direct labor or manufacturing overhead is rising or falling as a percentage of total manufacturing costs. The schedule is also helpful in developing information about unit costs.

If the company manufactures only a single product, the **cost per unit** of manufactured product is equal to the **cost of finished goods manufactured** divided by the **number of units produced.**[5] For example, if Allied produced **10,000** finished units during 1994, the average cost per unit was **$80** ($800,000 ÷ 10,000 units). Knowing the manufacturing cost per unit is useful to managers in setting sales prices, in evaluating the efficiency of manufacturing operations, and in deciding whether the company should devote more or less of its resources to manufacturing this product.

---

[5]   Many companies, of course, produce more than a single product. In this case, the company's accounting records should include separate work in process inventory accounts for each type of product. A separate schedule of the cost of finished goods manufactured then may be prepared for **each product line.**

Financial Statements of a Manufacturing Company

Let us now illustrate how the data used in our example will be reported in the 1994 income statement and balance sheet of Allied Manufacturing Company.

The company's 1994 income statement is illustrated below.

ALLIED MANUFACTURING COMPANY
Income Statement
For the Year Ended December 31, 1994

Sales...		$1,300,000
Cost of goods sold		782,000
Gross profit on sales		$ 518,000
Operating expenses:		
Selling expenses...	$135,000	
General and administrative expenses	265,000	
Total operating expenses...........................		400,000
Income from operations		$ 118,000
Less: Interest expense		18,000
Income before income taxes...........................		$ 100,000
Income taxes expenses		30,000
Net income		$ 70,000

Notice that no manufacturing costs appear among the company's expenses. Manufacturing costs appear in two places in a manufacturer's financial statements. The cost of manufacturing units *sold* during the period appears in the income statement as the ***cost of goods sold.*** Manufacturing costs associated with goods *still on hand* are classified as *inventory* and appear in the company's balance sheet. The balance sheet presentation of Allied's three types of inventory is illustrated below:

ALLIED MANUFACTURING COMPANY
Partial Balance Sheet
December 31, 1994

Notice the three types of inventory

Current assets:		
Cash and cash equivalents		$ 60,000
Accounts receivable (net of allowance for doubtful accounts)		190,000
Inventories:		
Materials...	$ 20,000	
Work in process...	40,000	
Finished goods..	168,000	228,000
Total current assets		$478,000

Allied's balance sheet also should include a current liability for wages payable, representing the $8,000 credit balance in the Direct Labor account. The credit balance in the Direct Labor account indicates that direct workers have rendered services costing $8,000 since the last payroll date.

END-OF-CHAPTER REVIEW

SUMMARY OF CHAPTER LEARNING OBJECTIVES

1 **Distinguish between the fields of managerial accounting and financial accounting.**

Managerial accounting involves the preparation and use of accounting information designed to assist management in planning and controlling business operations and in making various managerial decisions. Managerial accounting information may be specifically tailored to the decision at hand.

Financial accounting, in contrast, provides "general-purpose" information describing the financial position and operating results of an organization. Financial accounting information is prepared in accordance with recognized standards and is designed primarily to assist investors and creditors in making resource allocation decisions.

2 **Describe the three basic types of manufacturing cost.**

Direct materials used consist of the parts and materials which become part of the finished products. Direct labor cost consists of the wages paid to factory employees who work directly on the products being manufactured. Manufacturing overhead includes all manufacturing costs *other than* the cost of materials used and direct labor. Examples of manufacturing overhead include depreciation of machinery and the plant security service.

3 **Distinguish between product costs and period costs and explain how product costs are offset against revenue.**

Product costs are the costs of *creating* inventory. They are treated as assets until the related goods are sold, at which time the product costs are deducted from revenue as the cost of goods sold. Thus, goods manufactured this year but not sold until next year are deducted from next year's revenue.

Period costs are charged to expense in the accounting period in which they are incurred. Period costs are not related to production of goods; consequently, they are deducted from revenue on the assumption that the benefits obtained from the expenditures are received in the same period as the costs are incurred. Period costs include general and administrative expense, selling expense, and income taxes expense.

4 **Describe how manufacturing costs "flow" through perpetual inventory accounts.**

Manufacturing costs originally are recorded in controlling accounts such as Materials Inventory, Direct Labor, and Manufacturing Overhead. As these costs become applicable to goods placed into production, they are transferred from these manufacturing cost accounts to the Work in Process Inventory account. As units are completed, their cost is transferred from the Work in Process account to Finished Goods Inventory. Then, when units are sold, their costs are transferred from Finished Goods Inventory to the Cost of Goods Sold account.

5 **Distinguish between direct and indirect manufacturing costs.**

Direct manufacturing costs (direct materials and direct labor) can be identified with specific products. Indirect manufacturing costs are the many elements of manufacturing overhead which apply to factory operations as a whole and cannot be traced to specific products.

6 **Explain the purpose of overhead application rates and the importance of basing these rates upon significant "cost drivers."** An overhead application rate is a device used to assign appropriate amounts of overhead costs to specific units of output (manufactured products). Overhead is an indirect cost, which cannot be directly associated with specific output. However, the overhead application rate expresses the relationship between overhead costs and some *activity base* that can be traced directly to specific units. The activity base should be the major *driver* (causal factor) of overhead costs; if the activity base is not the cost driver, the relative production cost of different products may be significantly distorted.

7 **Prepare a schedule of the cost of finished goods manufactured.** This schedule summarizes the flow of manufacturing costs into and out of the Work in Process Inventory account. Its purpose is to assist management in understanding and evaluating manufacturing costs incurred in the period.

   To prepare this schedule, we start by listing the work in process inventory at the beginning of the year. To this amount we add the materials used, direct labor costs, and overhead for the period. Combining these four items indicates the total cost of all work in process during the period. A final step is deducting the cost of work still in process at the end of the period. This gives us the *cost of finished goods manufactured* during the period.

The terminology and concepts introduced in this chapter will be used extensively throughout the remaining chapters in this text. In Chapter 22, for example, we discuss cost accounting systems that determine the per-unit cost of each manufactured product. In Chapters 23 through 26, we explore uses of accounting information in planning and controlling business operations. Most of the examples and illustrations used in these chapters will involve manufacturing activities.

KEY TERMS INTRODUCED OR EMPHASIZED IN CHAPTER 21

Cost accounting The accounting concepts and practices used in determining the costs of manufacturing various products or of performing different business activities.

Cost driver An activity base that can be traced directly into units produced and that serves as a causal factor in the incurrence of overhead costs. Serves as an activity base in an *overhead application rate.*

Cost of finished goods manufactured The manufacturing costs relating to units of manufactured product completed during the period.

Direct labor Payroll costs for employees who work directly on the products being manufactured, either by hand or with tools.

Direct manufacturing cost A manufacturing cost that can be traced conveniently and directly into the quantity of finished goods manufactured. Examples include *direct materials* and *direct labor.*

Direct materials Materials and component parts that become an integral part of the manufactured goods and can be traced directly into the finished products.

Financial accounting Developing and interpreting information describing the financial position and operating results of a business entity, often for use by decision makers outside the entity.

Finished goods inventory The completed units that have emerged from the manufacturing process and are on hand available for sale.

Indirect labor Payroll costs relating to factory employees who do not work directly upon the goods being manufactured. Examples are wages of security guards and maintenance personnel. Indirect labor costs are classified as *manufacturing overhead.*

Indirect manufacturing cost A manufacturing cost that cannot be conveniently traced into the specific products being manufactured. Examples include property taxes, depreciation on machinery, and other types of *manufacturing overhead.*

Indirect materials Materials used in the manufacturing process that cannot be traced conveniently to specific units of production. Examples include lubricating oil, maintenance supplies, and glue. Indirect materials are accounted for as part of *manufacturing overhead.*

Inventoriable costs See *product costs.*

Managerial accounting Developing and interpreting accounting information specifically suited to the needs of a company's management.

Manufacturing costs The cost of manufacturing goods that will be sold to customers. The basic types of manufacturing costs are *direct materials used, direct labor,* and *manufacturing overhead.*

Manufacturing overhead A "catch-all" category including all manufacturing costs other than the costs of *direct materials used* and *direct labor.*

Materials inventory The cost of direct materials on hand and available for use in the manufacturing process.

Overhead application rate A device used to assign overhead costs to the units being manufactured. Expresses the relationship between estimated overhead costs and some activity base that can be traced directly to manufactured units. Results in overhead costs being applied to units produced in proportion to the selected activity base.

Period costs Costs that are charged to expense accounts in the period that the costs are incurred. Includes all items classified as "expense."

Perpetual inventory system A system in which transactions increasing or decreasing inventory are recorded directly in the inventory accounts, thus creating an up-to-date record of the level of inventories and the flow of costs into and out of the inventory accounts.

Product costs The costs of purchasing or manufacturing inventory. Until the related goods are sold, these product costs represent an asset—inventory. Once the goods are sold, these costs are deducted from revenue as the cost of goods sold.

Schedule of the cost of finished goods manufactured A schedule summarizing the flow of manufacturing costs into and out of the Work in Process Inventory account. Intended to assist managers in evaluating manufacturing costs.

Work in process inventory Goods at any stage of the manufacturing process short of completion. As these units are completed, they become finished goods.

DEMONSTRATION PROBLEM FOR YOUR REVIEW

The following T accounts summarize the flow of manufacturing costs during the current year through the ledger accounts of Marston Manufacturing Company:

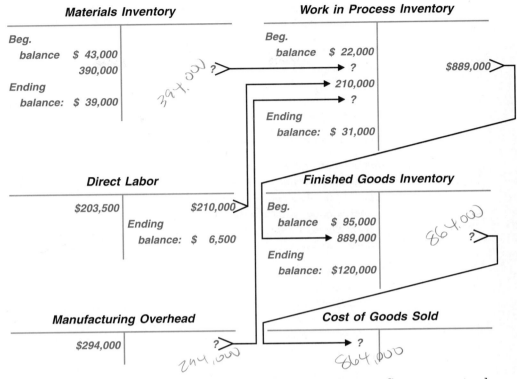

INSTRUCTIONS From the data supplied above, indicate the following amounts. Some amounts already appear in the T accounts; others require short computations.

a Purchases of direct materials

b Direct materials used during the year

c Direct labor costs assigned to production

d The year-end liability to direct workers for wages payable

e The overhead costs applied to production during the year, assuming that overhead was applied at a rate equal to 140% of direct labor costs

f Total manufacturing costs charged to production during the year

g The cost of finished goods manufactured

h The cost of goods sold

i The total costs classified as "inventory" in the year-end balance sheet

SOLUTION TO DEMONSTRATION PROBLEM

a Purchases of direct materials $390,000

b Computation of direct materials used:

Materials inventory, beginning of year	$ 43,000
Purchases of direct materials	390,000
Direct materials available for use	$433,000
Less: Materials inventory, end of year	39,000
Direct materials used	$394,000

c Direct labor costs assigned to production $210,000

d Year-end liability for direct wages payable .... $ 6,500

e *Overhead costs applied during the year*
  ($210,000 direct labor costs × 140%) $294,000

f *Total manufacturing costs charged to production:*
  Direct materials used (part b) $394,000
  Direct labor costs assigned to production 210,000
  Manufacturing overhead applied (part e) 294,000
    Total manufacturing costs charged to production $898,000

g *Cost of finished goods manufactured* $889,000

h *Computation of cost of goods sold:*
  Beginning inventory of finished goods .... $ 95,000
  Cost of finished goods manufactured 889,000
  Cost of goods available for sale $984,000
  Less: Ending inventory of finished goods 120,000
  Cost of goods sold $864,000

i *Total year-end inventory:*
  Materials .... $ 39,000
  Work in process 31,000
  Finished goods 120,000
    Total inventory $190,000

SELF-TEST QUESTIONS

Answers to these questions appear on page 1019.

1 Indicate which of the following statements are more descriptive of managerial accounting than of financial accounting. (More than one answer may be appropriate.)

  a Recognized standards are used for presentation.

  b Information is tailored to the needs of individual decision makers.

  c Information is more widely distributed.

  d Emphasis is on expected future results.

2 In a manufacturing company, the costs debited to the Work in Process Inventory account represent:

  a Direct materials used, direct labor, and manufacturing overhead.

  b Cost of finished goods manufactured.

  c Period costs and product costs.

  d None of the above; the types of costs debited to this account will depend upon the type of products being manufactured.

3 The Work in Process Inventory account had a beginning balance of $4,200 on February 1. During February, the cost of direct materials used was $29,000 and direct labor cost applied to production was $3,000. Overhead is applied at the rate of $20 per direct labor hour. During February, 180 direct labor hours were used in the production process. If the cost of finished goods manufactured was $34,100, compute the balance in the Work in Process Inventory account at the **end** of February.

  a $9,900   b $1,500   c $2,100   d $5,700

4 The purpose of an overhead application rate is to:

  a Assign an appropriate portion of indirect manufacturing costs to each product manufactured.

  b Determine the type and amount of costs to be debited to the Manufacturing Overhead account.

  c Charge the Work in Process Inventory account with the appropriate amount of direct manufacturing costs.

  d Allocate manufacturing overhead to expense in proportion to the number of units manufactured during the period.

5 The accounting records of Newport Mfg. Co. include the following information for 1994:

	Dec. 31	Jan. 1
Inventory of work in process	$ 20,000	$10,000
Inventory of finished goods	80,000	60,000
Direct materials used	200,000	
Direct labor	120,000	
Manufacturing overhead (150% of direct labor)	180,000	
Selling expenses	150,000	

Indicate which of the following are correct. (More than one answer may be correct.)

  a Amount debited to the Work in Process Inventory account during 1994, $500,000

  b Cost of finished goods manufactured, $490,000

  c Cost of goods sold, $470,000

  d Total manufacturing costs for the year, $650,000

ASSIGNMENT MATERIAL

DISCUSSION QUESTIONS

1 Briefly distinguish between managerial and financial accounting information in terms of (a) the intended users of the information and (b) the purpose of the information.

2 Briefly explain what is meant by the terms *managerial accounting* and *cost accounting.* Are the two terms related to one another? Explain.

3 Are financial accounting and managerial accounting two entirely separate disciplines? Explain.

4 Is managerial accounting information developed in conformity with generally accepted accounting principles or some other set of prescribed standards? Explain.

5 What are the three basic types of manufacturing costs?

6 A manufacturing firm has three inventory controlling accounts. Name each of the accounts, and describe briefly what the balance in each at the end of any accounting period represents.

7 Explain the distinction between *product costs* and *period costs.* Why is this distinction important?

8 Is the cost of disposing of hazardous waste materials resulting from factory operations a product cost or a period cost? Explain.

9 During the current year, Coronado Boat Yard has incurred manufacturing costs of $420,000 in building three large sailboats. At year-end, each boat is about 70% complete. How much of these manufacturing costs should be recognized as expense in Coronado Boat Yard's income statement for the current year? Explain.

10 What amounts are **debited** to the Materials Inventory account? What amounts are **credited** to this account? What type of balance (debit or credit) is this account likely to have at year-end? Explain.

11 During the current year the net cost of direct materials purchased by a manufacturing firm was $340,000, and the direct material inventory increased by $20,000. What was the cost of direct materials **used** during the year?

12 What amounts are debited to the Direct Labor account during the year? What amounts are credited to this account? What type of balance (debit or credit) is this account likely to have at year-end? Explain.

13 The illustration on page 1005 includes six ledger accounts. Which of these six accounts often have balances at year-end that appear in the company's formal financial statements? Briefly explain how these balances will be classified in the financial statements.

14 Explain the distinction between a **direct** manufacturing cost and an **indirect** manufacturing cost. Provide two examples of each type of cost.

15 Argo Mfg. Co. uses approximately $1,200 in janitorial supplies to clean the work area and factory equipment each month. Should this $1,200 be included in the cost of direct materials used? Explain.

16 What is meant by the term **overhead application rate?**

17 What is meant by the term **overhead cost driver?** How does the cost driver enter into computation of an overhead application rate?

18 Identify two possible overhead cost drivers for a company that:
   a Manufactures handmade furniture using skilled craftspersons and small hand tools.
   b Manufactures microchips for computers using an assembly line of computer-driven robots.

19 What amounts are **debited** to the Work in Process Inventory account during the year? What amounts are **credited** to this account? What does the year-end balance in this account represent?

20 What amounts are **debited** to the Finished Goods Inventory account during the year? What amounts are **credited** to this account? What type of balance (debit or credit) is this account likely to have at year-end?

21 Briefly describe the computation of the cost of finished goods manufactured as it appears in a schedule of the cost of finished goods manufactured.

22 A schedule of the cost of finished goods manufactured is a helpful tool in determining the per-unit cost of manufactured products. Explain several ways in which information about per-unit manufacturing costs is used by (a) managerial accountants and (b) financial accountants.

CHAPTER 21 / MANAGERIAL ACCOUNTING; ACCOUNTING FOR MANUFACTURING OPERATIONS ■ *1009*

EXERCISES

**EXERCISE 21-1
Accounting
Terminology**

Listed below are nine technical accounting terms introduced or emphasized in this chapter:

Work in Process Inventory	Period costs	Cost of finished goods manufactured
Overhead application rate	Product costs	Cost of Goods Sold
Manufacturing overhead	Cost accounting	Managerial accounting

Each of the following statements may (or may not) describe one of these technical terms. For each statement, indicate the accounting term described, or answer "None" if the statement does not correctly describe any of the terms.

a The preparation and use of accounting information designed to assist managers in planning and controlling the operations of a business.

b All manufacturing costs other than direct materials used and direct labor.

c A means of assigning indirect manufacturing costs to work in process during the period.

d A manufacturing cost that can be traced conveniently and directly into manufactured units of product.

e The techniques and procedures used in determining the cost of manufacturing a specific product or performing a particular type of business activity.

f The account debited at the time that the Manufacturing Overhead account is credited.

g The amount transferred from the Work in Process Inventory account to the Finished Goods Inventory account.

h Costs that are debited directly to expense accounts when the costs are incurred.

**EXERCISE 21-2
Basic Types of
Manufacturing
Costs**

Into which of the three elements of manufacturing cost would each of the following be classified?

a Tubing used in manufacturing bicycles

b Wages paid by an automobile manufacturer to employees who test-drive completed automobiles

c Property taxes on machinery

d Gold bullion used by a jewelry manufacturer

e Wages of assembly-line workers who package frozen food

f Salary of plant superintendent

g Electricity used in factory operations

h Salary of a nurse in a factory first-aid station

**EXERCISE 21-3
Product Costs
and Period
Costs**

Indicate whether each of the following should be considered a ***product cost*** or a ***period cost***. If you identify the item as a product cost, also indicate whether it is a ***direct*** or an ***indirect*** cost. For example, the answer to item **0** is "indirect product cost." Begin with item **a**.

0 Property taxes on factory building

a Cost of disposal of hazardous waste materials to a chemical plant

b Amounts paid by a mobile home manufacturer to a subcontractor who installs plumbing in each mobile home

c Depreciation on sales showroom fixtures

d Salaries of security guards in administrative office building e Salaries of factory security guards

f Salaries of office workers in the credit department

g Depreciation on raw materials warehouse

h Income taxes on a profitable manufacturing company

EXERCISE 21-4
Flow of Costs through Manufacturing Accounts

The information below was taken from the accounting records of Craftsman Products for the current year:

Work in process inventory, beginning of the year	$ 31,000
Cost of direct materials used	260,000
Direct labor cost applied to production	100,000
Cost of finished goods manufactured	665,000

Overhead is applied to production at a rate of $30 per machine hour. During the current year, 10,000 machine hours were used in the production process.

Compute the amount of the work in process inventory on hand at year-end.

EXERCISE 21-5
Computation and Use of an Overhead Application Rate

The production manager of Del Mar Manufacturing Co. has made the following estimates for the coming year:

Estimated manufacturing overhead	$1,200,000
Estimated direct labor costs	$ 500,000
Estimated machine hours	80,000 hours

INSTRUCTIONS

a Compute the overhead application rate based on:

1 Direct labor cost.

2 Machine hours.

b Assume that the manufacture of a particular product requires $2,000 in direct materials, $400 in direct labor, and 62 machine hours. Determine the total cost of manufacturing this product assuming that the overhead application rate is based upon:

1 Direct labor cost.

2 Machine hours.

EXERCISE 21-6
Preparing a Schedule of the Cost of Finished Goods Manufactured

The accounting records of NuTronics, Inc., include the following information for the year ended December 31, 1994:

	Dec. 31	Jan. 1
Inventory of materials	$ 24,000	$20,000
Inventory of work in process	8,000	12,000
Inventory of finished goods	90,000	80,000
Direct materials used	210,000	
Direct labor	120,000	
Selling expenses	170,000	
General and administrative expenses	140,000	

Overhead is applied to production at a rate of 160% of direct labor costs.

INSTRUCTIONS

a Prepare a schedule of the cost of finished goods manufactured. (Not all of the data given above is used in this schedule.)

b Assume that the company manufactures a single product and that 20,000 units were completed during the year. What is the average per-unit cost of manufacturing this product?

17.88

EXERCISE 21-7
Overhead Cost Drivers; Determination and Use of Unit Cost

During June, Assembly Department no. 4 of Riverside Electronics produced 10,000 Model 201 computer keyboards. Assembly of these units required 1,230 hours of direct labor at a cost of $22,000, direct materials costing $265,800, and 2,400 hours of machine time. Based upon an analysis of overhead costs at the beginning of the year, overhead is applied to keyboards using the following formula:

Overhead = 80% of Direct Labor Cost + $30 per Machine-Hour

INSTRUCTIONS

a Compute the total amount of overhead cost applied to the 10,000 keyboards.

b Compute the *per-unit cost* of manufacturing these keyboards.

c Briefly explain *why* the department might use *two separate activity bases* in applying overhead costs to one type of product.

d Identify at least two types of overhead costs that might be "driven" by each of the two cost drivers indicated in this situation.

e What appears to be the *primary* driver of overhead costs in the manufacture of keyboards?

f Compute the gross profit that will result from the sale of 2,000 of these keyboards at a sales price of $60 each.

PROBLEMS

Group A

PROBLEM 21A-1
An Introduction to Product Costs

Aqua-Craft manufactures fiberglass ski boats. The manufacturing costs incurred during the first year of operations are shown below:

Direct materials purchased	$224,500
Direct materials used	215,600
Direct labor assigned to production	180,000
Manufacturing overhead	342,000
Cost of finished goods manufactured (112 boats).............................	706,000

During the year, 112 completed boats were manufactured, of which 100 were sold. (Assume that the amounts of the ending inventory of finished goods and the cost of goods sold are determined using the average per-unit cost of manufacturing a completed boat.)

INSTRUCTIONS

a Compute each of the following and show all computations:

  1 The average per-unit cost of manufacturing a completed boat during the current year

  2 The year-end balances of the inventories of materials, work in process, and finished goods

  3 The cost of goods sold during the year

b For the current year, the costs of direct materials purchased, direct labor assigned to production, and manufacturing overhead total $746,500. Is this the amount of the manufacturing costs deducted from revenue in the current year? Explain fully.

PROBLEM 21A-2
Flow of Manufacturing Costs through Ledger Accounts

The "flow" of manufacturing costs through the ledger accounts of Superior Locks, Inc., in the current year is illustrated below in summarized form:

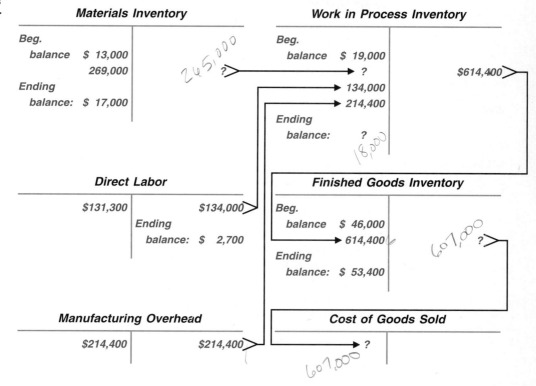

Materials Inventory

Beg.	
balance $ 13,000	
269,000	245,000 ?
Ending	
balance: $ 17,000	

Work in Process Inventory

Beg.	
balance $ 19,000	
?	$614,400
134,000	
214,400	
Ending	
balance: ? 18,000	

Direct Labor

$131,300	$134,000
Ending	
balance: $ 2,700	

Finished Goods Inventory

Beg.	
balance $ 46,000	607,000 ?
614,400	
Ending	
balance: $ 53,400	

Manufacturing Overhead

$214,400	$214,400

Cost of Goods Sold

?	
607,000	

INSTRUCTIONS

Indicate the amounts requested below. Some amounts are shown in the T accounts above; others require short computations. (Show all computations.)

a Purchases of direct materials

b The cost of direct materials used

c Direct labor costs assigned to production

d The year-end liability for direct wages payable

e The overhead application rate in use throughout the year, assuming that overhead is applied as a percentage of direct labor costs

f Total manufacturing costs charged to the Work in Process Inventory account during the current year

g The cost of finished goods manufactured

h The year-end balance in the Work in Process Inventory account

i The cost of goods sold

j The total amount of "inventory" listed in the year-end balance sheet

PROBLEM 21A-3
Flow of Manufacturing Costs: A Comprehensive Problem

The balances in the perpetual inventory accounts of Sunnyvale Manufacturing Co. at the beginning and end of the current year are as follows:

	End of Year	Beginning of Year
Inventory accounts:		
Materials	$25,800	$22,000
Work in process	8,000	5,000
Finished goods inventory	24,000	38,000

The total dollar amounts debited and credited during the year to the accounts used in recording manufacturing activities are summarized below:

Account:	Debit Entries	Credit Entries
Materials Inventory	$410,000	$?
Direct Labor	189,000	192,000
Manufacturing Overhead	393,600	393,600
Work in Process Inventory	?	?
Finished Goods Inventory	?	?

INSTRUCTIONS

a Using this data, state or compute for the year the amounts of:

1 Direct materials purchased

2 Direct materials used

3 Payments of direct labor payrolls

4 Direct labor cost assigned to production

5 The overhead application rate used during the year, assuming that overhead was applied as a percentage of direct labor costs

6 Total manufacturing costs charged to the Work in Process Inventory account during the year

7 The cost of finished goods manufactured

8 Cost of goods sold

9 The total amount to be classified as "inventory" in the year-end balance sheet

b Prepare a schedule of the cost of finished goods manufactured.

PROBLEM 21A-4
Flow of Manufacturing Costs

Shown below are 1994 data regarding Talking Teddy, one of the major products manufactured by St. Nicholas Toy Co.:

Purchases of direct materials	$332,000
Direct materials used	333,600
Direct labor payrolls (paid during the year)	176,700
Direct labor costs assigned to production	180,000
Manufacturing overhead (incurred and applied)	288,000

During the year 60,000 units of this product were manufactured and 62,100 units were sold. Selected information concerning inventories during the year is shown below:

12,800
+ 332,000
233,600

	Dec. 31	Jan. 1
	11,200	
Materials	$?	$ 12,800
Work in process	4,700	4,100
Finished goods, Jan. 1 (3,000 units @ $13)	?	39,000

INSTRUCTIONS

a Prepare a schedule of the cost of finished goods manufactured for this product in 1994.

b Compute the average unit cost of Talking Teddies completed in 1994.

c Compute the cost of Talking Teddies goods sold during the year. Assume that there is a first-in, first-out (FIFO) flow through the Finished Goods Inventory account and that all units completed in 1994 are assigned the per-unit cost determined in part **b**.

d Compute the amount of "inventory" relating to this product that will be listed in the company's balance sheet at December 31, 1994. (Show supporting computations for the year-end amounts of materials inventory and finished goods inventory.)

e Explain where the $180,000 in direct labor costs assigned to production in 1994 affect the company's 1994 income statement and balance sheet.

PROBLEM 21A-5
"I Don't Need an Accountant . . . ."

Early in the year, John Raymond founded Raymond Engineering Co. for the purpose of manufacturing a special flow control valve which he had designed. Shortly after year-end, the company's accountant was injured in a skiing accident, and no year-end financial statements have been prepared. However, the accountant had correctly determined the year-end inventories at the following amounts:

Materials	$46,000
Work in process	31,500
Finished goods (3,000 units)	88,500

As this was the first year of operations, there were no beginning inventories.

While the accountant was in the hospital, Raymond improperly prepared the following income statement from the company's accounting records:

Net sales		$610,600
Cost of goods sold:		
Purchases of direct materials	$181,000	
Direct labor costs assigned to production	110,000	
Manufacturing overhead applied to production	170,000	
Selling expenses	70,600	
Administrative expenses	132,000	
Total costs		663,600
Net loss for year		$ (53,000)

Raymond was very disappointed in these operating results. He states, "Not only did we lose more than $50,000 this year, but look at our unit production costs. We sold 10,000 units this year at a cost of $663,600; that amounts to a cost of $66.36 per unit. I know some of our competitors are able to manufacture similar valves for about $35 per unit. I don't need an accountant to know that this business is a failure."

INSTRUCTIONS

a Prepare a schedule of the cost of finished goods manufactured for the year. (As there were no beginning inventories, your schedule will start with "Manufacturing costs assigned to production:.") Show a supporting computation for the cost of direct materials used during the year.

b Compute the average cost per unit manufactured.

c Prepare a corrected income statement for the year, using the multiple-step format. If the company has earned any operating income, assume an income tax rate of 30%. (Omit earnings per share figures.)

d Explain whether you agree or disagree with Raymond's remarks that the business is unprofitable and that its unit cost of production ($66.36, according to Raymond) is much higher than that of competitors (around $35). If you disagree with Raymond, explain any errors or shortcomings in his analysis.

Group B

PROBLEM 21B-1
**An Introduc-
tion to Product
Costs**

Explorer, Inc., began operations early in the current year building luxury motor
homes. During the year the company started and completed 50 motor homes at a
cost of $52,000 per unit. Forty-eight of these completed motor homes were sold for
$80,000 each. In addition, the company had 5 partially completed motor homes in
its factory at year-end. Total costs incurred during the year (summarized alphabetically) were as follows:

Direct materials used	$ 700,000
Direct labor applied to production.	800,000
Income taxes expense	105,000
General and administrative expenses.	480,000
Manufacturing overhead	1,280,000
Selling expenses	550,000

INSTRUCTIONS

Compute for the current year:

a   Total manufacturing costs charged to work in process during the period

b   Cost of finished goods manufactured

c   Cost of goods sold

d   Gross profit on sales

e   Ending inventories of (1) work in process and (2) finished goods

PROBLEM 21B-2
**Flow of Manu-
facturing Costs
through Per-
petual Inven-
tory Records**

The following T accounts summarize the flow of manufacturing costs during the
current year through the ledger accounts of Intruder Alert, Inc.

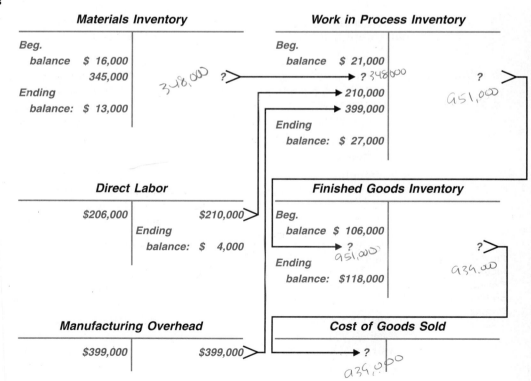

INSTRUCTIONS From the data supplied above, indicate the following amounts. Some amounts are shown in the T accounts; others require short computations. (Show all computations.)

a Purchases during the year of direct materials

b The cost of direct materials used

c Direct labor payrolls paid during the year

d Direct labor costs assigned to production

e The overhead application rate in use during the year, assuming that overhead is applied as a percentage of direct labor costs

f Total manufacturing costs charged to the Work in Process Inventory account during the year

g The cost of finished goods manufactured

h The cost of goods sold

i The total costs to be classified as "inventory" in the year-end balance sheet

PROBLEM 21B-3
Schedule of the Cost of Finished Goods Manufactured; Use of Unit Costs in Financial Statements

The accounting records of Scott Mfg. Co. include the following information relating to the current year:

	Dec. 31	Jan. 1
Materials inventory	$ 20,000	$ 25,000
Work in process inventory	37,500	40,000
Finished goods inventory, Jan. 1 (10,000 units @ $21 per unit)	?	210,000
Purchases of direct materials during year	285,000	
Direct labor costs assigned to production	240,000	
Manufacturing overhead applied to production.....................	457,500	

The company manufactures a single product; during the current year, **45,000** units were manufactured and **40,000** units were sold.

INSTRUCTIONS a Prepare a schedule of the cost of finished goods manufactured for the current year. (Show a supporting computation of the cost of direct materials *used* during the year.)

b Compute the average per-unit cost of production during the current year.

c Compute the cost of goods sold during the year, assuming that the FIFO (first-in, first-out) method of inventory costing is used.

d Compute the cost of the inventory of finished goods at December 31 of the current year, assuming that the FIFO (first-in, first-out) method of inventory costing is used.

PROBLEM 21B-4
Flow of Manufacturing Costs: A Comprehensive Problem

Shown below are the beginning and ending balances in the inventory accounts of ProTools, Inc., for 1994:

	End of Year	Beginning of Year
Inventory accounts:		
Materials	$52,000	$47,000
Work in process...	24,000	26,000
Finished goods inventory	?	98,000

The amounts debited and credited during the year to the accounts used in recording manufacturing costs are summarized below:

	Debit Entries	Credit Entries
Account:		
Materials Inventory	$ 690,000	$?
Direct Labor	395,000	400,000
Manufacturing Overhead	880,000	880,000
Cost of Goods Sold	1,975,000	-0-
Work in Process Inventory	?	?
Finished Goods Inventory	?	?

INSTRUCTIONS

a Using the above information, state (or compute) for 1994 the amounts of:

1 Direct materials purchased

2 Direct materials used

3 Direct labor payrolls paid during the year

4 Direct labor costs assigned to units being manufactured

5 The year-end liability for direct wages payable

6 The overhead application rate, assuming that overhead costs are applied to units being manufactured in proportion to direct labor costs

7 Total manufacturing costs debited to the Work in Process Inventory account

8 Cost of finished goods manufactured

9 Ending inventory of finished goods

b Prepare a schedule of the cost of finished goods manufactured for the year.

PROBLEM 21B-5
Effect on Income Statement of Errors in Handling Manufacturing Costs

William Nelson, the chief accountant of West Texas Guitar Company, was injured in an automobile accident shortly before the end of the company's first year of operations. At year-end, a clerk with a very limited understanding of accounting prepared the following income statement, which is unsatisfactory in several respects:

WEST TEXAS GUITAR COMPANY
Income Statement
For the Year Ended December 31, 19__

Net sales		$1,300,000
Cost of goods sold:		
Purchases of direct materials	$ 460,000	
Direct labor	225,000	
Indirect labor	90,000	
Depreciation on machinery—factory	50,000	
Rent	144,000	
Insurance	16,000	
Utilities	28,000	
Miscellaneous manufacturing overhead	34,600	
Other operating expenses	273,800	
Dividends declared on capital stock	46,000	
Cost of goods sold		(1,367,400)
Loss for year		$ (67,400)

You are asked to help management prepare a corrected income statement for the first year of operations. Management informs you that 60% of the rent, insurance, and utilities apply to factory operations, and that the remaining 40% should be classified as operating expense. Also, the correct ending inventories are as follows:

Material	$ 38,000
Work in process	10,000
Finished goods	110,400

As this is the first year of operations, there were no beginning inventories.

INSTRUCTIONS

a Identify the shortcomings and errors in the above income statement. Based upon the shortcomings you have identified, explain whether you would expect the company's actual net income for the first year of operations to be higher or lower than the amount shown.

b Prepare schedules to determine:

1 The cost of direct materials used.

2 Total manufacturing overhead.

c Prepare a schedule of cost of finished goods manufactured during the year. (Use the amounts computed in part **b** as the costs of direct materials used and manufacturing overhead.)

d Prepare a corrected income statement for the year, using a multiple-step format. Assume that income taxes expense amounts to 30% of income before income taxes.

CASES AND UNSTRUCTURED PROBLEMS

CASE 21-1
Poor Drivers Are Cost Drivers

Ye Olde Bump & Grind, Inc., is an automobile body and fender repair shop. Repair work is done by hand and with the use of small tools. Customers are billed based on time (direct labor hours) and materials used in each repair job.

The shop's overhead costs consist primarily of indirect materials (welding materials, metal putty, and sandpaper), rent, indirect labor, and utilities. Rent is equal to a percentage of the shop's gross revenue for each month. The indirect labor relates primarily to ordering parts and processing insurance claims. The amount of indirect labor, therefore, tends to vary with the size of each job.

Henry Lee, manager of the business, is considering using either direct labor hours or number of repair jobs as the basis for allocating overhead costs. He has estimated the following amounts for the coming year:

Estimated total overhead	123,000
Estimated direct labor hours	10,000
Estimated number of repair jobs	300

INSTRUCTIONS

a Compute the overhead application rate based on:

1 Direct labor hours.

2 Number of repair jobs.

b Shown below is information for two repair jobs:

Job 1 Repair a dented fender. Direct material used, $25; direct labor hours, 5; direct labor cost, $75.

Job 2 Repair an automobile involved in a serious collision. Direct materials used, $3,800; direct labor hours, 200; direct labor cost, $3,000.

Determine the **total cost** of each repair job, assuming that overhead costs are applied to each job based upon:

1 Direct labor hours.

2 Number of repair jobs.

c Discuss the results obtained in part **b**. Which overhead application method appears to provide the more realistic results. Explain the reasoning behind your answer, addressing the issue of what "drives" overhead costs in this business.

CASE 21-2
The Meadowbrooke Miracle

Prescott Manufacturing operates several plants, each of which produces a different product. Early in the current year, John Walker was hired as the new manager of the Meadowbrooke Plant. At year-end, all the plant managers are asked to summarize the operations of their plants at a meeting of the company's board of directors. John Walker displayed the following information on a chart as he made his presentation:

	Current Year	Last Year
Inventories of finished goods:		
Beginning of the year (30,000 units in the current year and 10,000 units last year)	$ 255,000	$ 85,000
End of the year (20,000 units in the current year and 30,000 last year)	202,000	255,000
Cost of finished goods manufactured	909,000	1,020,000

Walker made the following statements to the board: "As you know, sales volume has remained constant for the Meadowbrooke Plant. Both this year and last, our sales amounted to 100,000 units. We have made real gains, however, in controlling our manufacturing costs. Through efficient plant operations, we have reduced our cost of finished goods manufactured by over $100,000 from last year's levels. These economies are reflected in a reduction of the manufacturing cost per unit sold from $10.20 last year ($1,020,000 ÷ 100,000 units) to $9.09 in the current year ($909,000 ÷ 100,000 units)."

Father Alan Carter is president of St. Mary's University and is a member of Prescott Manufacturing's board of directors. However, Father Carter has little background in the accounting practices of manufacturing companies, and he asks you for assistance in evaluating Walker's statements.

INSTRUCTIONS

a As a preliminary step to your analysis, compute the following for the Meadowbrooke Plant in each of the two years:

1 Cost of goods sold

2 Number of finished units manufactured

3 Average cost per unit manufactured

4 Average cost per unit sold

b Evaluate the statements made by Walker. Comment specifically upon Walker's computation of the manufacturing cost of units sold and upon whether it appears that the reduction in the cost of finished goods sold was achieved through more efficient operations.

ANSWERS TO SELF-TEST QUESTIONS

1 b, d   2 a   3 d   4 a   5 a, b, c

22 Cost Accounting Systems

$\mathbf{H}$ow much does it cost Apple Computer to manufacture each Macintosh? If you are a manager at Apple, you need this information. You need it to set selling prices, to determine the cost of goods sold, to evaluate the efficiency of the company's manufacturing operations, and to plan for the future. In this chapter, we show how manufacturing companies use cost accounting systems to determine on a timely basis the per-unit cost of each product manufactured. Both job order and process cost systems are illustrated and explained.

Several recent developments in the field of cost accounting, including activity-based costing and just-in-time (JIT) systems, are discussed in the Supplemental Topic section at the end of the chapter.

After studying this chapter, you should be able to meet these Learning Objectives:

1 *Explain the purpose of a cost accounting system.*

2 *Explain the characteristics of a job order cost accounting system.*

3 *Describe the purpose and the content of a job cost sheet.*

4 *Explain the characteristics of a process cost accounting system.*

5 *Define and compute "equivalent full units" of production.*

6 *Prepare a process cost summary for a production department using a process cost system.*

*7 *Distinguish between "value-adding" activities and "non-value-adding" activities in a manufacturing business.*

*8 *Describe activity-based costing and explain the potential benefits of this technique.*

*9 *Explain the nature and goals of a JIT manufacturing system.*

---

* *Supplemental Topic, "The New Manufacturing Environment"*

*A*ssume that during the current month, Tri-State Manufacturing Co. incurs manufacturing costs of $10 million. At month-end, how much of this $10 million represents the cost of finished goods manufactured, and how much is applicable to goods still in process at month-end? If the company produces 20 different types of products, should the manufacturing costs be allocated among these products? Answers to these questions can only be provided by the company's ***cost accounting system.***

What Is a Cost Accounting System?

OBJECTIVE 1
Explain the purpose of a cost accounting system.

A cost accounting system consists of the techniques, forms, and accounting records used to develop timely information about the cost of manufacturing specific products and of performing specific functions. Because cost accounting systems are most widely used in manufacturing companies, we will focus upon the use of these systems to determine the cost of manufactured products. However, the concepts of cost accounting are applicable to a wide range of business situations. For example, banks, accounting firms, and governmental agencies all use cost accounting systems to determine the cost of performing various service functions.

CASE IN POINT   Congress recently passed legislation requiring hospitals to measure and report the average unit costs of their "products." The products are defined as specific types of medical services, such as heart transplants, tonsillectomies, and deliveries (births). Thus, hospitals must develop cost accounting systems capable of determining the average cost of providing each of these types of service.

In a manufacturing company, cost accounting serves two important managerial objectives: (1) to determine the per-unit cost of each manufactured product and (2) to provide management with information that will be useful in planning future business operations and in controlling costs. ***Unit costs*** are determined by relating manufacturing costs—the costs of direct materials used, direct labor, and manufacturing overhead—to the number of units manufactured.

A "unit" of product is defined differently in different industries. We tend to think of "units" as individual physical products, such as automobiles or television sets. In other industries, however, the number of units manufactured may be stated as a number of tons, gallons, barrels, pounds, board-feet, or other appropriate unit of measure.[1]

Unit costs provide the basis for inventory valuation and measurement of the cost of goods sold. They also provide managers with information useful in setting selling prices, deciding what products to manufacture, and evaluating the efficiency of operations.

Controlling costs refers to keeping costs down to reasonable levels. When a cost accounting system provides timely information about unit costs, managers are able to react quickly should costs begin to rise to unac-

---

[1]   Some service industries also express their operating costs on a per-unit basis. The "units of product" used in the airline industry, for example, are ***passenger-miles*** flown.

ceptable levels. By comparing current unit costs with budgets, past performance, and other yardsticks, managers are able to identify those areas in which corrective actions are most needed.

Two Basic Types of Cost Accounting Systems

There are two distinct types of cost accounting systems: job order cost systems and process cost systems. Both systems produce the same end results: timely information about manufacturing costs, inventories on hand, and unit costs.

Job order cost systems are used by companies that manufacture "one-of-a-kind" products or that tailor products to the specifications of individual customers. In a job order cost system, the costs of materials used, direct labor, and manufacturing overhead are accumulated separately for each job. A "job" represents the goods manufactured at one time to fill a particular order. If the job contains more than one unit of product, unit costs are determined by dividing the total costs charged to the job by the number of units manufactured.

Construction companies use job order cost systems because each construction project has unique characteristics that affect its cost. Job order cost systems also are used by shipbuilders, motion picture studios, defense contractors, print shops, and furniture makers. In addition, these systems are widely used in service-type businesses, including repair shops, hospitals, accounting firms, and law firms.

Process cost systems are used by companies that produce a "steady stream" of nearly identical products over a long period of time. In a process cost system, the focal points in accumulating manufacturing costs are the individual *production departments* (or *processes*) involved in the production cycle. As a first step, the costs of materials used, direct labor, and overhead applicable to each production department are compiled for a given period of time (usually one month). The average cost of running a unit of product through each production department then is determined by dividing the departmental costs by the number of units processed during the period. If a product passes through two or more processing departments, the unit costs of performing each process are combined to determine the unit cost of the finished good.

Companies that use process cost systems include oil refineries, power plants, soft-drink bottlers, breweries, flour mills, and most "assembly-line" or "mass-production" manufacturing operations.

The type of cost accounting system best suited to a particular company *depends upon the nature of the company's manufacturing operations.* Both job order and process cost systems are widely used. In fact, a given company may use a job order cost system to account for some of its production activities, and a process cost system to account for others. In the following sections of this chapter, we will illustrate and explain each of these cost accounting systems.

JOB ORDER COST SYSTEMS

The distinguishing characteristic of a job order cost system is that manufacturing costs are accumulated *separately for each job.* As explained in

OBJECTIVE 2
Explain the
characteris-
tics of a job
order cost
accounting
system.

Chapter 21, manufacturing costs are charged (debited) to the Work in Process Inventory account. In a job cost system, Work in Process Inventory is a controlling account, supported by a subsidiary ledger showing the manufacturing costs charged to each job. The accounts in this subsidiary ledger are called ***job cost sheets.***

The Job Cost Sheet

Job cost sheets are the heart of a job order cost system. A separate job cost sheet is prepared for each job and is used to accumulate a record of all manufacturing costs charged to the job. Once the job is finished, the job cost sheet indicates the cost of the finished goods manufactured and provides the information necessary to compute the unit costs of production.

OBJECTIVE 3
Describe the
purpose and
the content
of a job cost
sheet.

Direct manufacturing costs (direct materials used and direct labor) are recorded on the job cost sheet as quickly as these costs can be traced to the job. Once the job is complete, overhead costs are applied using an overhead application rate. Shown on the following page is a completed job cost sheet of the Oak & Glass Furniture Co. This "job" involved the manufacture of 100 dining tables of a particular style.

Throughout the production process, manufacturing costs traceable to the job are accumulated in the "Costs charged to this job" section of the job cost sheet. The "Cost summary" section is filled in when the job is completed.

The total cost of completing job no. 831 is ***$75,000.*** Upon completion of the job, this amount should be transferred from the Work in Process Inventory account to the Finished Goods Inventory account. The unit cost figures shown in the job cost sheet are determined by dividing the total manufacturing costs by the 100 units manufactured.

Flow of Costs in a Job Cost System: An Illustration

On pages 1026 and 1027, we expand our example of Oak & Glass Furniture Co. to illustrate the flow of costs through a complete but simple job cost accounting system.

This flowchart summarizes the company's manufacturing operations during the month of January. Notice that each of the inventory controlling accounts (Materials, Work in Process, and Finished Goods) is supported by a subsidiary ledger.

In our flowchart, all subsidiary ledger accounts are shown in T account form to conserve space. In practice, the individual job cost sheets serve as the subsidiary ledger for the Work in Process Inventory controlling account. Also, the subsidiary ledger accounts for direct materials and finished goods would have additional columns providing detailed information as to quantities on hand and unit costs.

We will now use our example of Oak & Glass Furniture Co. to explain the flow of manufacturing costs through a job order cost accounting system.

Accounting for Direct Materials

In a perpetual inventory system, purchases of direct materials are posted from the purchases journal to the accounts in the materials subsidiary

OAK & GLASS FURNITURE CO.
JOB COST SHEET
831

Product _French Court dining tables_

Date started _4/03/94_

Number of units manufactured _100_

Date completed _4/21/94_

Costs Charged to This Job

Manufacturing Department	Direct Materials	Direct Labor		Manufacturing Overhead	
		Hours	Cost	Rate	Cost Applied
Milling & Carving	$10,000	700	$14,000	150%	$21,000
Finishing	15,000	300	6,000	150%	9,000

Cost Summary and Unit Costs

	Total Costs	Unit Costs
Direct materials used	$25,000	$250
Direct labor	20,000	200
Manufacturing overhead applied	30,000	300
Cost of finished goods manufactured (100 tables)	$75,000	$750

ledger. The entries in the subsidiary ledger indicate the type, quantity, and cost of the material purchased. At the end of each month, a summary entry is made debiting the Materials Inventory controlling account for the total cost of direct materials purchased during the period. (The offsetting credit normally is to Accounts Payable.)

To obtain materials for use in the production process, the production department must issue a **_materials requisition_** form to the materials warehouse. This requisition shows the quantity of materials needed and the job on which these materials will be used.

Copies of these requisitions are sent to the accounting department, where the cost of the materials placed into production is determined from the materials subsidiary ledger. The cost of the requisitioned materials is entered on the requisition form and in the subsidiary ledger accounts. In the subsidiary ledgers, usage of direct materials is recorded by (1) entering the cost of the materials used on the appropriate job cost sheet and (2) crediting the materials subsidiary ledger.

At month-end, all the materials requisitions issued during the month are totaled, and the following summary entry is made in the controlling accounts:

Recording materials used during the month

Work in Process Inventory	*50,000*	
Materials Inventory		*50,000*

To record the cost of all direct materials placed into production during January.

Accounting for Direct Labor Costs

Debits to the Direct Labor account arise from making payments to direct factory workers; the offsetting credit is to the Cash account.[2] Payments to ***indirect*** factory workers (such as supervisors and security guards) are debited to Manufacturing Overhead, not to the Direct Labor account.

The Direct Labor account is credited as direct labor is ***used***—that is, as employees work on specific jobs. A number of mechanical and computerized means have been developed for determining the direct labor cost applicable to each job. One common method is to prepare ***time cards*** for each employee, showing the number of hours worked on each job, the employee's rate of pay, and the direct labor cost chargeable to each job. These time cards become the basis for preparing factory payrolls and also for posting direct labor costs to the work in process subsidiary ledger accounts (job cost sheets).

At the end of each month, a summary entry is made debiting Work in Process Inventory and crediting the Direct Labor account for all direct labor costs assigned to jobs during the month. For Oak & Glass, this entry is:

Recording direct labor costs

Work in Process Inventory	*60,000*	
Direct Labor		*60,000*

To record in the general ledger all direct labor costs charged to jobs during January.

Notice that the Direct Labor account is debited when employees are ***paid,*** but is credited for the cost of work ***performed*** on jobs. Work is performed on a daily basis, but employees are paid only at periodic intervals, such as every two weeks. Thus, the direct labor cost charged to jobs does not necessarily equal the amount paid to employees during the month. In our example, $60,000 of direct labor was assigned to the three jobs in process, but payments to employees totaled only $52,000. Thus, the $8,000 credit balance of the Direct Labor account at month-end represents a ***liability for accrued wages payable.***

---

[2] To the extent that amounts are withheld from employees' pay for such purposes as income taxes and social security taxes, the offsetting credits are to various current liability accounts. Accounting for payrolls was discussed in Chapter 11.

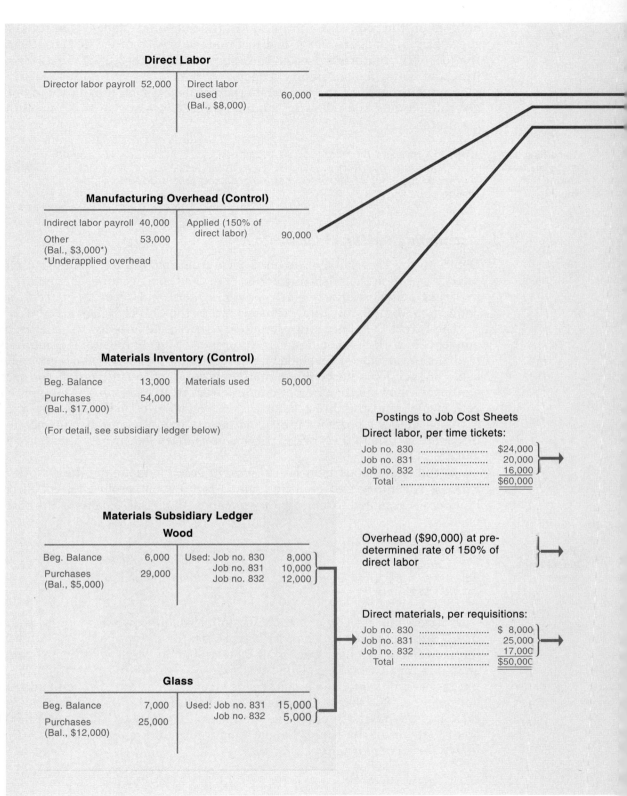

Direct Labor

Director labor payroll	52,000	Direct labor used (Bal., $8,000)	60,000

Manufacturing Overhead (Control)

Indirect labor payroll	40,000	Applied (150% of direct labor)	90,000
Other	53,000		
(Bal., $3,000*)			
*Underapplied overhead			

Materials Inventory (Control)

Beg. Balance	13,000	Materials used	50,000
Purchases	54,000		
(Bal., $17,000)			

(For detail, see subsidiary ledger below)

Materials Subsidiary Ledger
Wood

Beg. Balance	6,000	Used: Job no. 830	8,000
Purchases	29,000	Job no. 831	10,000
(Bal., $5,000)		Job no. 832	12,000

Glass

Beg. Balance	7,000	Used: Job no. 831	15,000
Purchases	25,000	Job no. 832	5,000
(Bal., $12,000)			

Postings to Job Cost Sheets

Direct labor, per time tickets:

Job no. 830	$24,000
Job no. 831	20,000
Job no. 832	16,000
Total	$60,000

Overhead ($90,000) at pre-determined rate of 150% of direct labor

Direct materials, per requisitions:

Job no. 830	$ 8,000
Job no. 831	25,000
Job no. 832	17,000
Total	$50,000

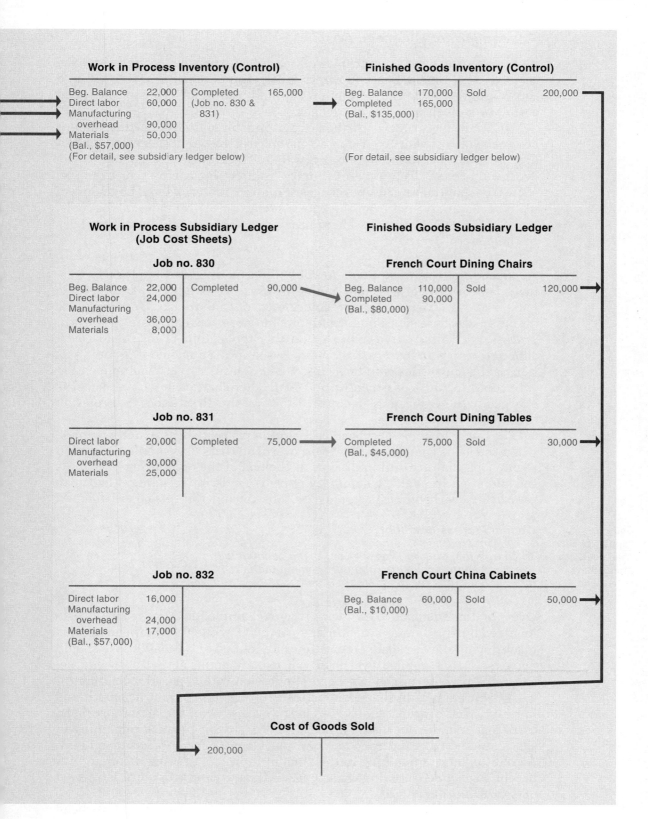

Work in Process Inventory (Control)

Beg. Balance	22,000	Completed	165,000
Direct labor	60,000	(Job no. 830 &	
Manufacturing		831)	
overhead	90,000		
Materials	50,000		
(Bal., $57,000)			

(For detail, see subsidiary ledger below)

Finished Goods Inventory (Control)

Beg. Balance	170,000	Sold	200,000
Completed	165,000		
(Bal., $135,000)			

(For detail, see subsidiary ledger below)

**Work in Process Subsidiary Ledger
(Job Cost Sheets)**

Finished Goods Subsidiary Ledger

Job no. 830

Beg. Balance	22,000	Completed	90,000
Direct labor	24,000		
Manufacturing			
overhead	36,000		
Materials	8,000		

French Court Dining Chairs

Beg. Balance	110,000	Sold	120,000
Completed	90,000		
(Bal., $80,000)			

Job no. 831

Direct labor	20,000	Completed	75,000
Manufacturing			
overhead	30,000		
Materials	25,000		

French Court Dining Tables

Completed	75,000	Sold	30,000
(Bal., $45,000)			

Job no. 832

Direct labor	16,000
Manufacturing	
overhead	24,000
Materials	17,000
(Bal., $57,000)	

French Court China Cabinets

Beg. Balance	60,000	Sold	50,000
(Bal., $10,000)			

Cost of Goods Sold

200,000	

Accounting for Overhead Costs

Manufacturing overhead includes all manufacturing costs *other than* the costs of direct materials and direct labor. Manufacturing Overhead is a controlling account; the details of the many different types of overhead costs are kept in a subsidiary ledger.

The Manufacturing Overhead account is debited for the *actual* amount of overhead costs incurred during the period. In our illustration, actual overhead costs in January total $93,000. These costs are posted to the overhead account from several sources. Indirect labor costs, for example, come from payroll records; purchases of indirect materials and payments of utility bills are posted from the voucher register or from special journals, and depreciation of plant assets comes from end-of-period adjusting entries in the general journal.

Application of Overhead Costs to Jobs   As explained in Chapter 21, overhead is an *indirect* cost and cannot be traced conveniently into specific jobs or units. Therefore, a predetermined *overhead application rate* often is used to assign appropriate amounts of overhead costs to work in process. (An alternative approach to the application of overhead costs, called *activity-based costing,* is discussed in a Supplemental Topic section at the end of this chapter.) Oak & Glass uses an overhead application rate equal to *150% of direct labor cost.* Therefore, each job cost sheet is charged with overhead costs equal to 150% of the direct labor cost relating to the job.

The entry to apply overhead costs to the job cost sheet usually is made when the job is completed. However, overhead costs also should be applied to any jobs that are still in process at the end of the accounting period. At the end of each month, a summary entry is made in the general ledger to record all overhead costs applied to jobs during the period, as follows:

Entry to "apply" overhead costs to production

Work in Process Inventory	*90,000*	
Manufacturing Overhead		*90,000*
To charge the Work in Process controlling account with overhead costs applied to jobs during the month (150% of direct labor costs for the month; $60,000 × 150% = $90,000).		

Over- or Underapplied Overhead   In our example, actual overhead costs incurred during January amounted to $93,000, while the overhead applied to jobs using the overhead application rate totaled only $90,000. We should not expect that applied overhead will exactly equal actual overhead because the predetermined overhead application rate is based on estimates.

A debit balance in the Manufacturing Overhead account at month-end indicates that overhead applied to jobs was *less* than the actual overhead costs incurred during the month. Therefore, a debit balance remaining in the Manufacturing Overhead account is called *underapplied overhead.* A credit balance remaining in the amount indicates that overhead applied to jobs *exceeded* actual overhead costs; thus, a credit balance is termed *overapplied overhead.*

The month-end balances remaining in the Manufacturing Overhead account normally are allowed to accumulate throughout the year. These amounts tend to "balance out" from month to month, and the amount of overapplied or underapplied overhead at year-end usually *is not material* in dollar amount. In this case, the year-end balance in the Manufacturing Overhead account may be closed *directly into the Cost of Goods Sold,* on the grounds that most of the error is applicable to goods sold during the year. If the year-end balance in the overhead account *is material* in dollar amount, it should be apportioned among the Work in Process Inventory, Finished Goods Inventory, and Cost of Goods Sold accounts.

Accounting for Completed Jobs

We have now explained how manufacturing costs are charged (debited) to the Work in Process Inventory account, and also how the costs of specific jobs are separately accumulated on job cost sheets.

As each job is completed, the job cost sheet is removed from the work in process subsidiary ledger and the manufacturing costs on the sheet are totaled to determine the cost of finished goods manufactured. This cost then is transferred from the Work in Process Inventory account to the Finished Goods Inventory account.

During January, Oak & Glass completed work on job nos. 830 and 831. The entries to record completion of these jobs are illustrated below:

Entries to record completed jobs

Finished Goods Inventory......................................	90,000	
Work in Process Inventory..............................		90,000

To record completion of job no. 830, consisting of 600 French Court dining chairs (unit cost, $150).

Finished Goods Inventory......................................	75,000	
Work in Process Inventory..............................		75,000

To record completion of job no. 831, consisting of 100 French Court dining tables (unit cost, $750).

As sales of these units occur, the unit cost figure will be used in determining the cost of goods sold. For example, the sale of 40 of the French Court dining tables at a total sales price of $48,000 is recorded below:

Accounts Receivable (Anthony's Fine Furniture)	48,000	
Sales		48,000

Sold 40 French Court dining tables on account, terms 2/10, n/30.

Cost of Goods Sold	30,000	
Finished Goods Inventory		30,000

To record the cost of the 40 French Court dining tables sold to Anthony's Fine Furniture (40 × $750 cost per unit = $30,000).

Job Order Cost Systems in Service Industries

In the preceding discussion, we have emphasized the use of job order cost systems in manufacturing companies. However, many service industries also use these systems to accumulate the costs of servicing a particular customer.

In a hospital, for example, each patient represents a separate "job," and the costs of caring for the patient are accumulated on a job cost sheet. Costs of such items as medicine, blood transfusions, and x-rays represent the usage of direct materials; services rendered by doctors are direct labor. The costs of nursing, meals, linen service, and depreciation of the hospital building and equipment all are part of the hospital's overhead. In a hospital, overhead usually is applied to each patient's account at a daily rate.

PROCESS COST SYSTEMS

As emphasized in the preceding section, job order cost systems are appropriate when each unit of product, or each "batch" of production, is manufactured to different specifications. In order to operate a job order system, it is necessary to be able to *identify the units* included in each job at every stage of the production process. What happens, then, when a company produces a continuous stream of identical products, such as bottles of beer or kilowatts of electricity? The answer is that these companies use *process cost systems,* rather than job order systems.

Characteristics of a Process Cost System

OBJECTIVE 4
Explain the characteristics of a process cost accounting system.

The manufacture of any product usually involves several specific steps, or manufacturing *processes.* For accounting purposes, each manufacturing process is viewed as a separate processing department. A separate Work in Process Inventory account is maintained for each processing department; this account is charged (debited) with all manufacturing costs incurred in performing the process during the current accounting period.[3] At the end of the period, the per-unit cost of performing the process is determined by dividing the costs charged to the departmental work in process account by the number of units processed during the period. The cost of a finished unit is determined by combining the per-unit cost of performing each process involved in the unit's manufacture.

Flow of Costs in a Process Cost System

To illustrate the basic features of a process cost system, assume that Baker Labs manufactures a nonprescription cold remedy called Conquest. Two processing departments are involved in the manufacture of Conquest: the Mixing Department and the Packaging Department. In the Mixing Department, the various chemicals used to make the cold remedy are blended together. The product is then transferred to the Packaging Department, where it is sealed in small "tamper-proof" packages. Packages of Conquest are the company's finished product; these packages are stored in a warehouse and shipped to customers (drug stores and grocery stores) as orders are received.

The flow of manufacturing costs through the process cost system of Baker Labs during the month of July is summarized on the next page. Notice that a separate Work in Process Inventory account is used for *each production process,* enabling accountants to accumulate separately the manufacturing costs relating to each process. As the Mixing Department

---

[3] One objective of a cost accounting system is to provide managers with *timely* information as to manufacturing costs. Therefore, the time period used in a process cost system usually is one month or less.

Cost flow diagram for process costing—notice the departmental Work in Process accounts

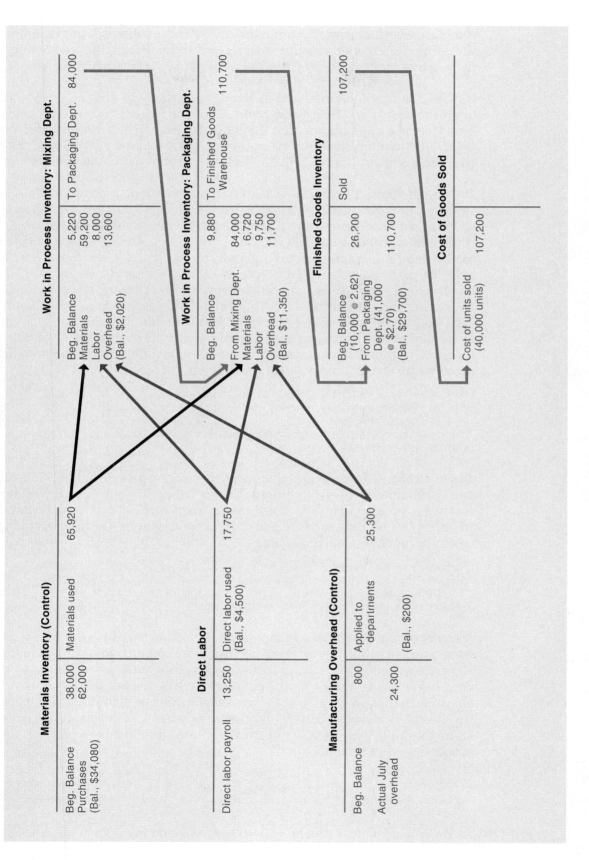

completes work on specific units, the cost of these units is transferred into the Work in Process Inventory account for the Packaging Department. Only when units emerge from the Packaging Department are they regarded as finished goods.

The cost flows summarized in this illustration will now be used to explain the operation of a process cost accounting system. Our illustration is based on the assumption that Baker Labs uses the ***first-in, first out*** (FIFO) method of inventory valuation. (Other inventory valuation methods, such as average cost, will be discussed in the cost accounting course.)

Direct Materials Purchases of materials are debited to the Materials Inventory controlling account, and a subsidiary ledger is maintained showing the unit cost and quantity on hand for each type of direct materials.

To obtain direct materials for use in production, the Processing Departments must issue materials requisition forms, and copies of these forms are sent to the Accounting Department. (Direct materials used in the Mixing Department include various chemicals; direct materials used in the Packaging Department are the "tamper-proof" containers.) The Accounting Department immediately updates the materials subsidiary ledger and, at the end of the month, makes a summary entry to charge the departmental work in process accounts for all direct materials requisitioned during the month. The summary entry for July appears below.

Work in Process Inventory: Mixing Department	*59,200*	
Work in Process Inventory: Packaging Department	*6,720*	
Materials Inventory		*65,920*
To record the cost of direct materials requisitioned for use in		
production during July.		

Direct Labor During July, payments to direct workers totaled $13,250, and this amount was debited to the Direct Labor account. The direct labor cost used within each processing department during July is determined from employees' time cards. The month-end entry to record the direct labor costs chargeable to each department is:

Work in Process: Mixing Department	*8,000*	
Work in Process: Packaging Department	*9,750*	
Direct Labor		*17,750*
To record the cost of direct labor used in July.		

Manufacturing Overhead During July, actual overhead costs of $24,300 were charged to the Manufacturing Overhead account. Baker Labs follows a policy of applying overhead costs to production ***as a percentage of direct labor costs.*** (Later in this chapter, we will discuss the alternative of charging actual overhead costs to production.) At the beginning of the year, the company developed the following overhead application rates, based upon the budgeted amounts of overhead and direct labor costs for each processing department:

Mixing Department	*170% of direct labor cost*
Packaging Department	*120% of direct labor cost*

At the end of July, the following entry is made to apply overhead to the departmental Work in Process Inventory accounts:

Work in Process Inventory: Mixing Department	*13,600*	
Work in Process Inventory: Packaging Department	*11,700*	
Manufacturing Overhead.............................		*25,300*

To apply overhead costs to departments, based on direct
labor costs (Mixing Dept., $8,000 × 170% = $13,600; Packaging
Dept., $9,750 × 120% = $11,700).

Notice that the Manufacturing Overhead controlling account had a debit balance of $800 at the beginning of July. This debit balance represented a small amount of ***underapplied overhead*** that had accumulated over the first half of the year. In July, however, applied overhead exceeds actual overhead costs by $1,000. Thus, at the end of July, the overhead account has a credit balance of $200, representing a small amount of ***overapplied overhead.*** Throughout the year, the balances in the overhead account are allowed to carry forward from month to month. At year-end, any remaining balance normally is closed out to the Cost of Goods Sold account.[4]

Equivalent Full Units—The Key to Determining Unit Cost

A basic objective of a process cost system is to determine the unit cost of direct materials, direct labor, and overhead for each manufacturing process or department. These unit costs become the basis for valuing inventories and for tracing the flow of costs through the departmental work in process accounts and finally to Finished Goods Inventory and to Cost of Goods Sold.

If all units of product in a given department are ***completely processed*** (started and completed) during the period, computing unit costs is a simple matter of dividing the departmental costs by the number of units processed. In most cases, however, there are unfinished units of product on hand at the beginning as well as at the end of the accounting period. When some of the units on hand are unfinished, we cannot compute unit costs merely by dividing total costs by the number of units worked on, for this would assign the same unit cost to finished and unfinished goods. If completed and partially completed units of product are expressed in ***equivalent full units*** of completed product, however, this difficulty is overcome. Meaningful unit costs can then be determined by dividing the total cost by the equivalent full units produced. This computation is illustrated below for direct materials:

Units Costs Based on Equivalent Full Units

$$\text{Materials Cost per Unit} = \frac{\text{Total Cost of Direct Materials Used During Month}}{\text{Equivalent Full Units Produced During Month}}$$

OBJECTIVE 5
Define and compute "equivalent full units" of production.

What Are "Equivalent Full Units"? Equivalent full units are a measure of the ***work done*** in a given accounting period. The concept of an equivalent full unit is based on the assumption that creating two units, each of which is 50% complete, represents the ***same amount of work*** as does producing one finished unit. Similarly, producing 1,000 units that are 25% complete is viewed as equivalent to 250 full units of production.

---

[4]   As explained earlier in this chapter, if the year-end balance in the overhead account is material in dollar amount, it should be apportioned among the Cost of Goods Sold, Finished Goods Inventory, and Work in Process Inventory accounts, based on the relative balances in each account. This allocation procedure is seldom necessary.

The work accomplished by a manufacturing department during a given accounting period may include (1) completing units which were already in process at the beginning of the period, (2) working on units started and completed during the current period, and (3) working on units which are still in process at the end of the current period. If we are to measure the work accomplished by the department, we must determine the equivalent full units of production represented *by each of these three types of work effort.*

To illustrate this concept, we will use the production activities of Baker Labs during the month of July. Assume that the production managers of the company's two processing departments provide the following summary of the *numbers of units* processed within their departments during July. (Notice that the following schedule describes the *extent of completion* of units in process at the beginning and end of the month.)

Production Summary—in Units
for the Month Ended July 31, 1994

	Mixing Department	Packaging Department
Units in process, July 1	5,000[a]	4,000[c]
Units started and completed in July	37,000	37,000
Units completed and transferred to next department or to finished goods in July	42,000	41,000
Units in process, July 31	4,000[b]	5,000[d]

[a] 60% complete as to materials and conversion costs on July 1.
[b] 25% complete as to materials and conversion costs on July 31.
[c] 100% complete as to materials and 75% complete as to conversion costs on July 1.
[d] 100% complete as to materials and 20% complete as to conversion costs on July 31.

In describing the extent of completion of the units in process, notice the use of the term *conversion costs.* This term is used to describe the costs of both direct labor *and* manufacturing overhead, as these are the costs of converting direct materials into finished goods.

The number of equivalent full units of production processed by the Mixing Department during July is determined as follows:

Computation of Equivalent Full Units—Mixing Department
(Direct Materials and Conversion Costs)

	Units ×	Portion Completed in July =	Equivalent Full Units Produced
Units in process at the beginning of July (60% completed in June as to materials and conversion costs)	5,000	40%	2,000
Units started and completed in July	37,000	100%	37,000
Units completed and transferred to Packaging Dept. in July	42,000		
Units in process at the end of July (25% complete as to materials and conversion costs)	4,000	25%	1,000
Equivalent full units of production during July			40,000

Although 42,000 units of product were completed and transferred to the Packaging Department, the actual amount of work accomplished in the

Mixing Department during July was equivalent to producing only **40,000 "full" units.** The work performed in July consists of 2,000 equivalent full units of work (40% of 5,000) to complete the beginning inventory of work in process, 37,000 equivalent full units of work to start and complete additional units during July, and 1,000 equivalent full units (25% of 4,000) on the units still in process at month-end.

Conversion costs normally are added to units of product at a uniform rate throughout the production process. Thus, units that are 25% complete are assigned 25% of the per-unit conversion costs. In the Mixing Department, direct materials also are added to units at a uniform rate. Therefore, the equivalent number of full units produced in the department is **the same** with respect to materials used and conversion costs.

Materials and Conversion Costs Added at Different Rates   It is not unusual for materials and conversion costs to be added to units of product at **different** rates. For example, 100% of the materials needed to produce finished goods may be placed into production at the beginning of the production process. In these situations, the number of equivalent full units produced during the period must be **computed separately** for materials and for conversion costs.

To illustrate, assume that in the Packaging Department of Baker Labs, all direct materials are placed into production at the **beginning** of the production process, but that conversion costs are applied at a **uniform rate** throughout the process. The equivalent number of full units produced is computed separately for materials used and for conversion costs, as illustrated below.

Computation of Equivalent Full Units—Packaging Department

	Units ×	Portion Completed = in July	Equivalent Full Units Produced
Direct Materials:			
Units in process at the beginning of July (100% completed in June as to materials)	4,000	-0-	-0-
Units started and completed in July	37,000	100%	37,000
Units completed and transferred to Finished Goods Warehouse in July	41,000		
Units in process at the end of July (100% complete as to materials)	5,000	100%	5,000
Equivalent full units of production during July— direct materials			42,000
Conversion Costs:			
Units in process at the beginning of July (75% completed in June as to conversion costs)	4,000	25%	1,000
Units started and completed in July	37,000	100%	37,000
Units completed and transferred to Finished Goods Warehouse in July	41,000		
Units in process at the end of July (20% complete as to conversion costs)	5,000	20%	1,000
Equivalent full units of production during July— conversion costs			39,000

In the Packaging Department, enough direct materials were placed into production to produce 42,000 units of product. However, the amount of labor and overhead used was sufficient to produce only 39,000 equivalent full units. Thus, the equivalent full units of production by the department during July **differ** with respect to materials and to conversion costs.

Determining Unit Costs

At the end of each month, the Accounting Department prepares a ***process cost summary*** for each production department. These cost summaries are specially designed working papers, upon which accountants (1) summarize the manufacturing costs charged to each department, (2) determine the departmental unit costs of production, and (3) allocate the departmental manufacturing costs between completed units and work still in process at month-end.

Process Cost Summary for the Mixing Department

The process cost summary for the Mixing Department is illustrated below:

BAKER LABS
Process Cost Summary—Mixing Department
For the Month Ended July 31, 1994

	Total Costs ÷	Equivalent Full Units =	Unit Cost
Costs charged to the department and unit costs:			
Work in process inventory, beginning of July	$ 5,220		
Manufacturing costs charged to the department during July:			
Direct materials used	59,200	40,000	$1.48
Direct labor	8,000	40,000	0.20
Manufacturing overhead	13,600	40,000	0.34
Unit cost per equivalent full unit processed during July ...			$2.02
Total costs to be accounted for	$86,020		
Allocation of costs charged to the department:			
Work in process inventory, end of July (4,000 units, 25% complete as to all costs; 4,000 units × $2.02 per full unit × 25%)	$ 2,020		
Cost of units completed and transferred to Packaging Department (42,000 units):			
Total cost (86,020 − $2,020)	84,000		
Unit cost ($84,000 ÷ 42,000 completed units)			$2.00
Total costs accounted for	$86,020		

Notice all costs are allocated

Notice two unit costs

We will now explain the steps in the preparation of this working paper.

Step 1: Summarize the Manufacturing Costs Charged to the Department
The top portion of the process cost summary begins with a list of all manufacturing costs applicable to units worked during July. These costs include the beginning inventory of work in process and all manufacturing costs

OBJECTIVE 6
*Prepare a
process cost
summary for
a production
department
using a pro-
cess cost sys-
tem.*

charged to the department during July. Notice that the sum of these costs, $86,020, is labeled "Total costs to be accounted for." As we shall see, "accounting for" these costs means assigning them either to units completed during July, or to units still in process at July 31. The information needed to complete the "Total costs" column is found in the debit side of the departmental work in process account (page 1031).

Step 2: Determine Unit Costs   The second step in preparing a process cost summary is to determine the per-unit cost of the manufacturing activities performed by the department during the month. This is accomplished by dividing each of the three categories of manufacturing costs incurred during July by the *equivalent full units* of production for the month.

For example, during July the Mixing Department used direct materials costing $59,200. Our computations above show that the department produced the equivalent of 40,000 full units. Therefore, each equivalent full unit produced by the Mixing Department during July required an average of *$1.48* in direct materials costs ($59,200 ÷ 40,000 units = $1.48 per unit). Similar computations are made to compute the per-unit costs of direct labor and manufacturing overhead.[5] These three unit costs then are combined, indicating an average cost of *$2.02* for each *equivalent full unit* produced by the Mixing Department during July.

Step 3: Allocate the Costs Charged to the Department between Completed Units and Units Still in Process   Once the per-unit manufacturing costs have been determined, we may allocate our $86,020 in "Total costs to be accounted for" between the two types of departmental output—units completed and transferred to the Packaging Department, and units still in process in the Mixing Department at month-end. This allocation of costs is illustrated in the bottom section of the process cost summary.

We could use the unit cost figures from the top section of our cost summary to compute separately the cost of the ending inventory of work in process and the cost of units completed during the period. However, it is *not necessary* to compute both of these amounts in this manner. It is quicker and easier to use unit costs to compute only the value of the ending inventory of work in process. We may then simply *assign the remainder* of the $86,020 total costs to the units completed during July.

Baker Labs uses the first-in, first-out (FIFO) method of inventory valuation; therefore, the ending inventory of work in process is valued using the *most recent* unit costs—namely, those incurred during July. Work in process in the Mixing Department at July 31 amounts to 4,000 units, each of which is 25% complete with respect to all manufacturing costs. Therefore, the cost of this ending inventory is *$2,020* (4,000 units × $2.02 × 25%).

Deducting this $2,020 from the $86,020 total costs to be accounted for leaves a remainder of *$84,000,* representing the cost of units completed by

---

[5]   In determining the unit cost of work done in July, we do not express the $5,220 beginning inventory of work in process on a per-unit basis, as these manufacturing costs were incurred in June.

the Mixing Department during July.[6] The $2.00 unit cost of these completed goods is determined by dividing their total cost ($84,000) by the number of completed units (42,000).

Upon completion of the process cost summary, the following journal entry is made to summarize the cost of units completed by the Mixing Department during the month:[7]

Cost of units transferred from one processing department to the next.

Work in Process Inventory: Packaging Department	*84,000*	
Work in Process Inventory: Mixing Department		*84,000*
To record the cost of 42,000 units transferred from the Mixing Department to the Packaging Department during July. (Unit cost, $84,000 ÷ 42,000 units = $2.00.)		

Unit Cost of Completed Products Notice that the average cost of units ***completed*** during July ($2.00) differs slightly from the average cost of manufacturing an ***equivalent full unit*** of product during the month ($2.02). The reason for this small difference is that the cost of producing an equivalent full unit is based ***entirely upon manufacturing costs incurred during July.*** Some of the units completed during July, however, received part of their processing during June.[8]

Each of these two unit costs is important and serves a separate purpose. The $2.02 per unit is the ***most current*** unit cost figure; therefore, this amount is helpful in evaluating the efficiency of the Mixing Department during July. Also, this current unit cost is used in valuing the ending inventory of work in process under the FIFO method.

The $2.00 unit cost, on the other hand, is the average cost incurred in manufacturing the 42,000 units ***completed*** during July. This is the unit cost that will be carried forward into the process cost summary of the Packaging Department and, eventually, into the Finished Goods Inventory and Cost of Goods Sold accounts.

---

[6] The $84,000 cost of the 42,000 units completed by the Mixing Department during July may be verified as follows:

Work in process inventory, July 1 (5,000 units, 60% complete)		*$ 5,220*
Costs added in July to complete these 5,000 units:		
Direct materials used (5,000 units × $1.48 × 40%)	*$ 2,960*	
Direct labor (5,000 units × $0.20 × 40%)	*400*	
Manufacturing overhead (5,000 units × $0.34 × 40%)	*680*	*4,040*
Total cost of first 5,000 units completed in July		*$ 9,260*
Cost of 37,000 units started and completed during July:		
Direct materials used (37,000 units × $1.48)	*$54,760*	
Direct labor (37,000 units × $0.20)	*7,400*	
Manufacturing overhead (37,000 units × $0.34)	*12,580*	
Total cost of next 37,000 units completed during July		*74,740*
Cost of 42,000 units completed and transferred to Packaging Department during July		*$84,000*

[7] In practice, it is not necessary to wait until a monthly process cost summary is completed to record transfers of completed units from production departments. These transfers may be recorded at any time using ***standard costs*** (estimated amounts). Standard cost systems are discussed in Chapter 25.

[8] In our illustration, 5,000 of the units completed in July received 60% of their processing in June.

Process Cost Summary for the Packaging Department

The process cost summary for the Packaging Department is illustrated below. In most respects, this schedule parallels that prepared for the Mixing Department. There are, however, several new features that deserve attention.

BAKER LABS
Process Cost Summary—Packaging Department
For the Month Ended July 31, 1994

	Total Costs	÷ Equivalent Full Units	= Unit Cost
Costs charged to the department and unit costs:			
Work in process inventory, beginning of July..........	$ 9,880		
Cost of 42,000 units transferred in from Mixing			
Department during July.............................	84,000		$2.00
Manufacturing costs added by Packaging Department during July:			
Direct materials used	6,720	42,000	.16
Direct labor	9,750	39,000	.25
Manufacturing overhead	11,700	39,000	.30
Unit cost per equivalent unit processed during July ...			$2.71
Total costs to be accounted for	$122,050		
Allocation of costs charged to the department:			
Work in process inventory, end of July (5,000 units, 100% complete as to materials, 20% as to conversion costs):			
Cost of units transferred in from the Mixing			
Department (5,000 units × $2.00)	$ 10,000		
Direct materials added (5,000 units × $.16 × 100%)...	800		
Direct labor (5,000 units × $.25 × 20%)	250		
Manufacturing overhead (5,000 units × $.30 × 20%) ..	300		
Total cost of work in process inventory at July 31 .	$ 11,350		
Cost of units completed and transferred to Finished Goods Warehouse (41,000 units):			
Total cost ($122,050 − $11,350)....................	110,700		
Unit cost ($110,700 ÷ 41,000 finished units)............			$2.70
Total costs accounted for............................	$122,050		

First, notice that the manufacturing costs charged to the Packaging Department include the ***cost of units transferred in from the Mixing Department*** during the month. The $84,000 cost of these units, and also the $2.00 unit cost, were computed in the process cost summary of the Mixing Department (page 1036). From the viewpoint of the Packaging Department, the units transferred in from the Mixing Department are a form of direct material to be used in the packaging process.

Second, notice that ***different amounts*** of equivalent full units of production are used in computing the unit costs of materials and conversion costs (direct labor and manufacturing overhead). We explained earlier in this chapter that in the Packaging Department, 100% of the direct materials are placed into production at the start of the production process, while conversion costs are applied uniformly throughout the process. As a result, the equivalent full units of production turned out by the department may **differ** with respect to materials and to conversion costs. (The equivalent full units of production for the Packaging Department in July were computed in the schedules illustrated above.)

A third new feature in the process cost summary of the Packaging Department is the itemizing of the various cost elements included in the ending inventory of work in process. Since these units are 100% complete as to materials, but only 20% complete as to conversion costs, the amount of each manufacturing cost to be included in these units must be computed separately. Also note that the costs transferred in from the Mixing Department, amounting to $2.00 per unit, are included in the cost of the 5,000 units in process at July 31.

All of the $122,050 in costs charged to the Packaging Department during July are applicable either to units still in process at July 31 or to units completed during the month. Since we have assigned $11,350 of these costs to the ending inventory of work in process, the remaining $110,700 ($122,050 − $11,350) represents the cost of the 41,000 units completed during July. The entry to transfer the cost of goods completed by the Packaging Department during July to the Finished Goods Inventory account is:

Finished Goods Inventory....................................	*110,700*	
Work in Process Inventory: Packaging Department		*110,700*

To record the cost of 41,000 units of finished goods completing the production process during July. (Unit cost, $110,700 ÷ 41,000 units = $2.70.)

As these finished units are sold, their cost will be transferred from the Finished Goods Inventory account to the Cost of Goods Sold at a rate of $2.70 per unit.

Process Cost Systems: Actual Overhead or Applied Overhead?

In our example of a process cost system, we used an **overhead application rate** to charge an appropriate amount of manufacturing overhead to the departmental work in process accounts each month. We mentioned, however, that the possibility of using **actual overhead costs** would be discussed later in the chapter.

In a process cost system, overhead is not charged to the departmental work in process accounts until the end of the accounting period. Therefore, it is possible to charge these accounts with the actual overhead costs incurred during the month, rather than with the amount of overhead indicated by using an overhead application rate.[9] In fact, many manufacturing companies **do** charge production departments with actual overhead costs on a monthly basis.

At first glance, charging the actual overhead costs to production departments has great appeal. For one thing, this approach eliminates the prob-

---

[9] Actual overhead **cannot** be applied to specific jobs in a job order cost system, because actual overhead costs for the month are **not known** at the time that specific jobs are completed. Therefore, all companies with job order cost systems use overhead application rates.

lem of accounting for overapplied or underapplied overhead. However, the use of an overhead application rate often provides **more useful** unit cost information, especially if (1) some major overhead costs occur at infrequent intervals or (2) the volume of production varies from month to month.

Costs Occurring at Infrequent Intervals

Some overhead costs occur at infrequent intervals, rather than uniformly from month to month. Examples include repairs and refurbishing projects. If actual overhead costs are assigned to production on a monthly basis, the entire amount of these infrequent costs is assigned to the units produced during the month in which the cost happens to occur; none of the cost is borne by units produced in other months.

To illustrate, assume that Baker Labs shuts down its factory for two weeks every August to repair equipment and repaint the building. It is not reasonable to say that these actions relate only to the limited number of units produced during the remainder of August. Obviously, these annual costs relate to production throughout the year.

An overhead application rate avoids the "infrequent cost" problem, because the rate is based upon the estimated cost for the **entire year.** Thus, the costs of infrequent events, such as repairs, are spread uniformly over units produced throughout the year.

Fluctuations in the Level of Production

A second problem in the use of actual overhead costs may arise if the number of units produced fluctuates from month to month. This problem stems from the fact that many elements of manufacturing overhead are fixed costs, rather than variable costs.

Fixed costs are those that tend to remain relatively fixed (constant) from month to month. Examples of fixed overhead costs include the monthly salary paid to the plant manager, and the depreciation, property taxes, and insurance on plant assets. **Variable costs,** in contrast, are those that **change in approximate proportion to the level of production.** Examples of variable overhead costs include factory utilities and the costs of some indirect materials used in the manufacturing process.[10]

Because many overhead costs are fixed, total monthly overhead **does not** vary in direct proportion to the number of units produced. Thus, if we allocate actual overhead costs incurred each month to output for that month, the unit cost of production may vary widely from month to month. In months of high output, per-unit overhead costs would be relatively low; in months of low output, per-unit overhead costs would be relatively high.

To illustrate, assume that Drew Corporation has the capacity to produce 10,000 units per month. Fixed overhead costs are **$120,000 per month,** and variable overhead amounts to **$2 per unit** manufactured. The overhead costs per unit at different levels of output are as follows:

---

[10] The concepts of fixed and variable costs extend to many costs and expenses other than manufacturing overhead. The costs of direct materials and direct labor, for example, are variable costs. These concepts are explored further in Chapter 23.

Overhead Costs per Unit at Different Level of Output

	Level of Output		
	10,000 Units	8,000 Units	6,000 Units
Fixed overhead costs.....................................	$120,000	$120,000	$120,000
Variable overhead costs ($2 per unit)....................	20,000	16,000	12,000
Total overhead costs (a)	$140,000	$136,000	$132,000
Units produced (b)	10,000	8,000	6,000
Overhead cost per unit (a) ÷ (b)........................	$14	$17	$22

For most business purposes, management needs to know the "normal" unit cost of producing a product, not monthly costs that vary significantly depending upon the volume of production. Again, this problem is solved by using an overhead application rate. As the application rate is based upon budgeted overhead for the entire year, the fixed overhead costs are "averaged out" over all units, regardless of whether the units are produced in a high-volume month or a low-volume month.

Using Actual Overhead May Work Well in Large Companies   The problems that we have described above are far more likely to arise in small companies than in large ones. In large companies, such costs as maintenance and repairs do not vary much from month to month. Also, most large companies are able to schedule their production so as to produce approximately the same number of units each month. Thus, for a large company using a process cost system, charging the work in process accounts with the actual amount of monthly overhead costs may work just as well as using an overhead application rate.

■ ■ ■ * *Supplemental Topic*
The New Manufacturing Environment

In recent years, the competition among manufacturing companies has become international in scope. If American companies cannot produce quality products at competitive prices, the market soon is lost to efficient foreign producers.

CASE IN POINT   The widespread ownership of television sets began in the United States. For years, American corporations such as General Electric, RCA, and Zenith were the leading television manufacturers. The United States still represents the world's largest market for television sets. As of 1989, however, this market was being supplied entirely by foreign producers; ***no*** television picture tubes were being manufactured in the United States.

To compete effectively in today's global economy, American manufacturing companies must strive constantly to improve the efficiency of their manufacturing processes and the quality of their products. Cost accounting systems can aid managers in achieving these goals by providing more detailed and more accurate information about unit costs, and by developing useful measurements of product quality.

THE USEFULNESS OF DETAILED INFORMATION

In this chapter, we have illustrated how a cost accounting system determines separately the cost of performing various manufacturing processes. Our Baker Labs example included two major processes—mixing and packaging. Such broad definitions of "processes" are satisfactory for developing information for financial statements, but not for use by management in evaluating the ***efficiency*** of business operations.

To enable managers to evaluate the efficiency of business operations, a cost accounting system ideally should measure separately the cost of each step, activity, and use of materials in the manufacturing process. Accounting systems also should be ***cost-effective,*** however; meaning that the cost of developing information should not exceed its value to the intended users.

With the aid of computers, managerial accountants are finding that they economically can develop more detailed unit cost information than they previously thought possible. This detailed information often highlights opportunities for significant cost savings.

CASE IN POINT   If you fly first class on American Airlines, your dinner salad probably will contain only one black olive. The company's cost accounting system revealed that reducing the number of olives in these salads from 2 to 1 would reduce operating costs by more than $40,000 per year.

H. J. Heinz Company made a similar discovery. By placing one label on its large catsup bottles instead of two, the company reduced its annual manufacturing costs by several hundred thousand dollars.

"Value-Adding" and "Non-Value-Adding" Activities   As stated previously, cost considerations may limit the extent of detailed information which is developed. Of particular importance however, is measuring separately the costs of performing ***non-value-adding activities.***

OBJECTIVE 7
Distinguish between "value-adding" activities and "non-value-adding" activities in a manufacturing business.

An ***activity*** is any repetitive action performed in the conduct of business operations. Activities that increase the worth of a product (or service) ***to the customer*** are said to be "value-adding" activities. Non-value-adding activities are those functions that ***do not*** directly increase the worth of the product to the consumer. Therefore, cost savings achieved through the reduction or elimination of non-value-adding activities usually ***do not lessen customer satisfaction.***

A few examples of activities often classified as value-adding or as non-value-adding activities are as follows:

Value-Adding Activities	*Non-Value-Adding Activities*
Product design	Inventory storage and handling
Manufacture and assembly	Machinery setup and idle time
Packaging	Storing work in process awaiting further
Delivery	processing
Technical support services	Production of excess quantities of
after sale	finished goods
Extension of credit	Quality control inspections and
	rework of defective units
	Spoilage, breakage, and scrapping of
	defective output

Our classification of quality control inspections and the rework of defective units as non-value-adding activities requires additional explanation. Quality, of course, adds value to the product. However, inspections and rework would ***not be necessary*** if the manufacturing process ***had been performed properly in the first place.*** Therefore, these activities may be viewed as the "cost" of errors or inefficiencies in the production process. Mistakes and inefficiencies do not add value.

Whether or not a specific activity "adds value" to the product may vary from one situation to the next. For example, most customers probably regard quality control inspections of newly manufactured aircraft engines as a value-adding activity.

In summary, non-value-adding activities are ***unnecessary,*** and the costs relating to these activities ***should be minimized.*** The concepts of value-adding and non-value-adding activities are applicable to ***all aspects*** of business operations, not merely to manufacturing activities.

ACTIVITY-BASED COSTING (ABC)

OBJECTIVE 8
Describe activity-based costing and explain the potential benefits of this technique.

Activity-based costing is a technique of allocating overhead costs among different types of manufactured products using a wide variety of cost drivers.[11] Activity-based costing serves two basic purposes. First, it forces careful consideration of the factors that drive specific overhead costs. This analysis may bring to light means of reducing these costs. Second, activity-based costing results in a more accurate measurement of unit cost than is achieved through the use of a single overhead application rate. A realistic knowledge of unit cost is a prerequisite to setting sales prices at levels that are both profitable and competitive.

The allocation of overhead costs through activity-based costing involves the following steps:

1 Subdivide total overhead costs into specific activities, and determine the cost driver(s) for each activity.

---

[11] Activity-based-costing procedures also may be applied to activities ***other than*** overhead. Examples include marketing and distribution activities, billing, and providing services either within the organization or to customers. Our discussion of ABC, however, is limited to activities classified as manufacturing overhead.

2 Forecast for the coming year (a) the cost of each overhead activity, (b) the level of cost driver activity, (c) the number of units of each type of product to be manufactured, and (d) the percentage of cost driver activity relating to each type of product manufactured.

3 Using the relative percentages of cost driver activity, allocate each type of overhead cost among the product lines.

4 Express the estimated overhead costs applicable to each type of product as a per-unit dollar amount.

5 Apply overhead costs to units of production using the estimated per-unit amounts.

An Illustration of Activity-Based Costing

To illustrate the basic concept of activity-based costing, we will use this approach to determine how selected overhead costs might be allocated among three products.

Assume that Arc Electronics manufactures three products, which we will call A, B, and C. The schedule on page 1046 summarizes the determination of the overhead costs relating to the ordering, storage, and handling of direct materials that will be charged to each unit of production during the year.

Arc's managerial accountants began this process by identifying the major overhead activities involved in the ordering, storage, and handling of direct materials—and also identifying the related cost drivers. Next, they forecast the cost of each overhead activity, the activity base (cost driver), and the percentage of this activity base applicable to each product line.

Often, the percentage of cost driver activity applicable to each product line is based upon the estimated *number of transactions* involving that product. (With respect to ordering materials, for example, each issuance of a purchase order may be viewed as one "transaction.") For this reason, activity-based costing sometimes is called *transaction-based costing.*

The dollar amount of each overhead activity charged to a specific product line is determined by applying the percentage of cost driver activity for that product line to the estimated annual cost of the overhead activity. Finally, a *per-unit application rate* is determined by dividing the total cost applicable to that product line by the estimated number of units to be produced. As units are produced, they will be charged with materials-handling costs based upon this per-unit application rate. (Of course, per-unit application rates also are developed for the other elements of manufacturing overhead.)

Benefits of Activity-Based Costing

Let us briefly discuss two benefits of activity-based costing.

First, management is made aware of the various factors comprising overhead costs. This may direct managers' attention to areas in which costs may be reduced. For example, the cost of inspecting materials ordered for product C is expected to total $40,000 in the coming year. Perhaps this cost could be reduced or eliminated if these materials were ordered from a more quality-oriented supplier. Also the costs of storing materials used in the manufacture of product A are expected to total $54,000 this year. Perhaps

ARC ELECTRONICS
Determination of Certain Overhead Costs per Unit
Using Activity-Based Costing Procedures
for the Year Ended December 31, 19___

Overhead Activities (Relating to Materials)	Estimated Annual Cost	Cost Driver	Percentage A	B	C	Dollars A	B	C
Ordering materials and stocking incoming shipments	$170,000	Number of purchase orders	20%	30%	50%	$34,000	$51,000	$ 85,000
Inspecting incoming shipments	40,000	Inspection hours	0%	0%	100%	-0-	-0-	40,000
Storage of materials	90,000	Square footage of storage space	60%	10%	30%	54,000	9,000	27,000
Moving materials into production	10,000	Number of production runs	20%	50%	30%	2,000	5,000	3,000
Total	$310,000					$90,000	$65,000	$155,000
Scheduled number of units to be manufactured during the year						45,000	100,000	50,000
Materials handling overhead costs to be applied per unit						$2.00	$0.65	$3.10

these storage costs could be reduced by ordering smaller quantities of these materials and having shipments delivered more frequently.

Second, notice the use of *four different cost drivers* in allocating only these few types of overhead costs. The purpose of this detailed allocation is to associate overhead costs *as closely as possible* with the units generating these costs.

JUST-IN-TIME MANUFACTURING SYSTEMS

OBJECTIVE 9
*Explain the
nature and
goals of a
JIT manu-
facturing
system.*

Much attention recently has been given to just-in-time *(JIT)* manufacturing systems. The phrase "just in time" refers to acquiring materials and manufacturing goods only as needed to fill customers' orders. JIT systems sometimes are described as "demand pull" manufacturing, because production occurs only in response to customer demand. This contrasts with the more traditional "supply push" systems, in which the manufacturer simply produces as many goods as possible.

A JIT system is characterized by extremely small or nonexistent inventories of materials, work in process, and finished goods. Materials arrive only as needed by the production departments—sometimes within a few hours of their scheduled use. Work in process flows quickly from one production process to the next, without moving temporarily into storage facilities. Finished goods are not produced in excess of existing customer orders.

Storing large amounts of inventory can be costly. Among the costs generated by the storage function are the acquisition and operation of storage facilities, insurance, the cost of money "tied-up" in the inventory, and potential losses which may be incurred from spoilage or obsolescence. One goal of a JIT system is the reduction or elimination of storage costs, because these costs *do not add value* to the product.[12]

JIT is much more, however, than an approach to inventory management. It is the philosophy of *eliminating non-value-adding activities* and *increasing product quality* throughout the manufacturing process.[13]

JIT Systems and Product Quality

Perhaps the most significant benefit of a successful JIT system is the overall contribution which the system can make to product quality.

If materials are purchased and goods are produced "just in time," the production process must be performed "just right." No inventories of spare materials or of finished goods are available to "take up the slack" if defective materials must be returned to the supplier or if finished goods must be reworked. Therefore, *everyone involved in the manufacturing process must strive toward a "zero defects" level of performance.*

At first glance, it may appear that the JIT concept involves great risk that quality goods will not be completed on schedule. If materials do not arrive on time, or if they are defective, the entire manufacturing process

---

[12] Factors to be considered in determining the optimal size of inventories are discussed in Chapter 9.

[13] JIT refers to the movement of goods and, therefore, to manufacturing processes. However, the goals of eliminating inefficiency and improving quality can be extended to many other types of organizational activities. The extension of the JIT philosophy *throughout the organization* is called *total quality management (TQM).*

may be forced to shut down until more materials can be obtained. Similarly, if some of the finished goods are defective, sales opportunities—and customers—may be lost.

Interestingly, however, many manufacturing companies have found that a nearly zero-defects level of production ***can be achieved*** when this goal becomes a priority recognized throughout the organization.

Zero Defects Starts with Reliable Suppliers As previously stated, defective materials can force the entire production process in a JIT system to shut down. Therefore, the purchasing department of a JIT manufacturer seeks suppliers that can provide ***quality materials on a reliable schedule.*** Once specific suppliers have proven their reliability, the JIT manufacturer can dispense with quality inspections of incoming materials, thus eliminating another non-value-adding activity.

Product Design Plays a Critical Role In a JIT system, product quality is "designed-in" and "manufactured-in," rather than being achieved through "inspecting-out" of defective units at the end of the manufacturing process. When zero defects becomes the goal, products are ***designed in a manner that simplifies the manufacturing process and reduces the risk of defects.***

The Need for a Multiskilled Work Force In a JIT system, goods are produced only as needed. Therefore, workers and machinery must be versatile—that is, able to shift quickly from the manufacture of one product to another. Workers must learn to perform various tasks and to operate different machines. Many companies have found that this concept of ***flexible manufacturing*** increases employees' morale, skill, and productivity.

Workers are trained to ***recognize and correct defects as they occur,*** rather than allowing defective products to continue down the assembly line. This approach eliminates (or greatly reduces) the need for inspecting finished units and for scrapping or reworking defective finished goods.

Machinery, Too, Plays a Vital Role In a JIT system, machines used in sequential manufacturing processes are located next to one another in order to achieve a smooth and rapid flow of work in process. This factory arrangement minimizes the movement of work in process and "wait-time."

Machinery downtime can interrupt the entire production process. Therefore ***equipment reliability*** is a vital consideration in machinery-acquisition decisions. Also, maintenance is performed on a ***preventive basis,*** rather than only when a breakdown occurs. Production workers are trained to maintain the machinery and to make routine repairs themselves.

Accounting Implications of a JIT System

A JIT cost accounting system possesses characteristics of ***both*** job order and process cost accounting systems. The concept of flexible manufacturing—producing different products as they are needed—means that units are produced in batches, or "jobs." However, a basic goal of a JIT system is to eliminate or minimize non-value-adding activities. Therefore, the accounting system must measure separately the costs of many specific processes performed in the course of each job—especially the costs associated with non-value-adding activities.

In order to bring to management's attention the costs and cost drivers associated with non-value-adding activities, JIT systems normally utilize activity-based costing.

The Need for Time Measurements Timing is all-important in a JIT system. Therefore, a JIT cost accounting system measures the ***time*** required for each manufacturing process. These time measurements are essential for scheduling production activities in a manner that avoids "bottlenecks" and ensures that jobs are completed "just in time."

Measures of Efficiency in a JIT System The length of time required for a product to pass completely through a manufacturing process is called ***cycle time.*** Cycle time often is viewed as containing four separate elements: (1) processing time, (2) storage and waiting time, (3) movement-time, and (4) inspection-time. ***Only during processing time, however, is value added to the product.*** Ideally, the other elements of cycle time should be reduced as much as possible.

A widely used measure of the efficiency of a JIT system is the ***manufacturing efficiency ratio*** (or throughput ratio). This measure expresses the time spent in value-adding activities (such as processing) as a percentage of total cycle time, as follows:

$$\text{Manufacturing Efficiency Ratio} = \frac{\text{Value-Adding Time}}{\text{Cycle Time}}$$

The manufacturing efficiency ratio may be applied to specific production processes or to the manufacturing process viewed as a whole. (When the manufacturing process is viewed as a whole, cycle time begins with the arrival of direct materials and ends with the shipment of the finished goods.)

The basic purpose of the manufacturing efficiency ratio is to highlight the percentage of time spent in non-value-adding activities. The optimal efficiency ratio is ***100%,*** which indicates that ***no*** time is being spent on non-value-adding activities. In practice, however, this ratio is always less than 100%. If a manufacturing company has not made a concerted effort to reduce its non-value-adding activities, its manufacturing efficiency ratio often is less than 10%.

Accounting for Scrap and Spoilage Prior to the recent emphasis on efficiency and control of costs, most manufacturing companies considered some amount of scrap, waste, and defective units as "normal spoilage." As long as spoilage costs remained within an "acceptable" range, they were not accounted for separately. Thus, spoilage simply became part of the total manufacturing cost assigned to completed units.

When a company is striving to achieve a zero-defects level of performance, ***no*** amount of spoilage is viewed as "acceptable." Therefore, the accounting system should ***record separately*** even amounts of spoilage which are immaterial in dollar amount, and should associate these costs with specific production processes.

Accounting for such small amounts of spoilage in this manner is ***not necessary for financial statement purposes.*** Rather, the purpose is to focus attention throughout the organization on the zero-defects target, and to emphasize the importance of quality in a JIT system.

Measuring Quality Accounting systems in JIT companies measure ***quality,*** as well as costs and cycle times. One widely used measure of production quality is ***defects per million*** units produced. In some companies, defect rates have been reduced to less than one defective part per million units of production. Other measures of quality include merchandise returns, numbers of warranty claims, customer complaints, and the results of customer satisfaction polls.

A JIT system does not, in itself, ensure quality. Rather, it establishes ***striving for quality*** as a basic goal of the organization.

A Concluding Comment . . .

The principles of JIT manufacturing offer many benefits to manufacturing companies. Among the most significant are:

1 A reduction in unit cost through increased efficiency and the reduction or elimination of non-value-adding activities.

2 Constant improvement in product quality.

3 Greater challenge, variety, and responsibility for production workers.

4 Reduction in the risk that not all output can be sold.

The most commonly cited characteristic of JIT systems—maintenance of inventories at near-zero levels—is ***not appropriate for all companies.*** If a company does not have access to highly reliable sources of supply, it should maintain reasonable inventories of materials. If the company has a lengthy cycle time, or if it cannot achieve a nearly zero-defects level of production, it should consider maintaining an adequate inventory of finished goods to ensure prompt deliveries to customers. ***All*** companies, however, can benefit from the basic ***philosophy*** of the JIT approach, which is ***striving to eliminate inefficiency and to improve product quality.***

CASE IN POINT JIT and other applications of total quality management (TQM) are widely cited as contributing to the industrial rebirth of Japan. After World War II, Japan was a nation with a shattered economy and little manufacturing capacity. Throughout the 1950s, Japanese products were regarded as "cheap imitations" of American goods. Today, however, Japan is recognized worldwide as an efficient producer of high-quality products.

Interestingly, the concepts of JIT and TQM so successfully adopted by many Japanese companies are based in large part upon the management theories of W. Edwards Deming, an American statistician.

END-OF-CHAPTER REVIEW

SUMMARY OF CHAPTER LEARNING OBJECTIVES

1 **Explain the purpose of a cost accounting system.**
The purpose of a cost accounting system is to provide current information about the total cost and the per-unit cost of manufacturing a prod-

uct or performing a service. This information is used by financial accountants to value inventories and the cost of goods sold, and by managerial accountants for controlling costs and planning future operations.

2 Explain the characteristics of a job order cost accounting system.
A job order cost system measures the total cost and the per-unit cost of each "job"—that is, each specific batch of production. All the manufacturing costs relating to the job are accumulated on a job cost sheet. Once the job is complete, unit cost is determined by dividing the total cost of the job by the number of units produced.

3 Describe the purpose and the content of a job cost sheet.
The purpose of a job cost sheet is to keep track of all manufacturing costs relating to a particular job. Each job cost sheet shows the cost of all the materials, direct labor, and factory overhead charged to the job. The job cost sheets of all jobs in process serve as a subsidiary ledger supporting the balance of the Work in Process Inventory controlling account.

4 Explain the characteristics of a process cost accounting system.
A process cost system measures the manufacturing costs incurred by each manufacturing process or department during the accounting period. The unit cost of each process then is determined by dividing the manufacturing costs assigned to the department by the equivalent full units of production. The cost of a finished unit is the sum of the unit costs of performing each process in the unit's manufacture.

5 Define and compute "equivalent full units" of production.
Equivalent full units of production is a measure of the work done by a production department during the accounting period. The concept of an "equivalent full unit" is based upon the idea that creating two units, each of which is 50% complete, represents the same amount of "work" as does completing one finished unit. The equivalent full units of production for a department are computed by considering the amount of work performed on (1) units already in process at the beginning of the period, (2) units started and completed during the period, and (3) units still in process at the end of the period.

6 Prepare a process cost summary for a production department using a process cost system.
A process cost summary is prepared for each manufacturing process or each production department. These reports (1) summarize the manufacturing costs charged to a department during the accounting period, (2) compute the unit cost of performing the production process during the period, and (3) allocate the manufacturing costs charged to the department between completed units and the ending inventory of work in process.

*7 Distinguish between "value-adding" activities and "non-value-adding" activities in a manufacturing business.
Value-adding activities are functions that add value to a product from the customer's point of view. Non-value-adding activities may be conve-

---

* *Supplemental Topic, "The New Manufacturing Environment"*

nient for the producer, but they do not add value to the product. Therefore, non-value-adding activities represent inefficiencies in production and delivery of the product.

*8 Describe activity-based costing and explain the potential benefits of this technique.
Activity-based costing (ABC) is a method of allocating the costs of different overhead activities among products using a wide variety of cost drivers. The primary benefits of ABC are (1) the factors driving each type of overhead cost are brought to management's attention, and (2) management has a more precise measurement of actual unit cost than results from use of a more broadly based overhead application rate.

*9 Explain the nature and goals of a JIT manufacturing system.
In a JIT system, materials are acquired and goods are produced "just in time" to meet sales requirements. Thus, production is "pulled" by customer demand, rather than "pushed" by an effort to produce inventory. The goals of a JIT system are to eliminate (minimize) non-value-adding activities and to increase the focus upon product quality throughout the production process.

In this chapter we emphasize the determination of unit cost. Unit cost data play a key role in each of the four remaining chapters. We will see that unit cost data are useful in a wide variety of managerial decisions. A second concept introduced in this chapter—the distinction between fixed and variable costs—also plays an important role in many managerial decisions. The distinctions between fixed and variable costs are discussed further in the next chapter.

KEY TERMS INTRODUCED OR EMPHASIZED IN CHAPTER 22

Activity-based costing (ABC) The technique of assigning the cost of each overhead activity to products in proportion to the extent that manufacture of the product drives that specific overhead activity. Also called *transaction-based costing.*

Conversion costs Manufacturing costs incurred in the process of converting direct materials into finished goods. Conversion costs include both direct labor and manufacturing overhead.

Cycle time The length of time for a product to pass completely through a specific manufacturing process, or the manufacturing process viewed as a whole. Used as a measure of efficiency in JIT systems.

Defects per million The number of defective units per million units produced. Used as a measure of product quality.

Equivalent full units of production A measure of the work done during an accounting period. Includes work done on beginning and ending inventories of work in process as well as work on units completely processed during the period.

Fixed cost A cost that does not vary in direct response to changes in the level of activity.

Job cost sheet A record used in a job order cost system to summarize the manufacturing costs (materials, labor, and overhead) applicable to each job, or batch of

---

*   *Supplemental Topic, "The New Manufacturing Environment"*

production. Job cost sheets may be viewed as a subsidiary ledger supporting the balance of the Work in Process Inventory control account.

Job order cost system   A cost accounting system under which the focal point of costing is a quantity of product known as a *job* or *lot.* Costs of direct materials, direct labor, and manufacturing overhead applicable to each job are compiled to arrive at average unit cost.

Just-in-time (JIT) manufacturing systems   A modern approach to manufacturing aimed at reducing or eliminating non-value-adding activities, such as maintenance of inventories. Focuses upon both efficiency and product quality.

Manufacturing efficiency ratio   Processing time stated as a percentage of cycle time. Used as a measure of efficiency in JIT systems.

Non-value-adding activity   An activity within the manufacturing process that does not add value to the product. Storage of inventory is an example.

Overhead application rate   A device used to apply a "normal" amount of overhead costs to work in process. The rate is predetermined at the beginning of the year and expresses the percentage relationship between estimated total overhead for the year and the estimated total of some "cost driver," such as direct labor hours, direct labor costs, or machine hours. Use of the overhead application rate causes overhead to be charged to work in process in proportion to the amount of "cost driver" traceable to those units.

Over- or underapplied overhead   The difference between the actual manufacturing overhead incurred during the period and the amount applied to work in process by use of a predetermined overhead application rate.

Process cost summary   A schedule prepared for each production process or department in a process cost system. Shows the costs charged to the department during the period, the computation of unit manufacturing costs, and the allocation of departmental costs between units completed during the period and the ending inventory of work in process.

Process cost system   A cost accounting system used mostly in industries such as petroleum or chemicals characterized by continuous mass production. Costs are not assigned to specific units but to a manufacturing process or department.

Total quality management (TQM)   An approach to eliminating wasteful activities and improving quality throughout the organization. The philosophy behind JIT manufacturing systems.

Transaction-based costing   See *activity-based costing.*

Value-adding activity   An activity which, from the customers' viewpoint, adds value to the product. Actual manufacture and assembly functions are examples.

Variable cost   A cost that changes in approximate proportion to some level of activity, such as the level of production. The cost of direct materials used is a variable cost.

Zero defects   The goal of defect-free production. Although some defects actually do occur, they are so infrequent and are so quickly corrected as not to interfere with a JIT manufacturing system.

DEMONSTRATION PROBLEM FOR YOUR REVIEW

Sumasani Corp. manufactures EndAll, an electronic unit that plays a wide variety of video games on a television set. The units are entirely assembled in one production department. All manufacturing costs are incurred at a uniform rate throughout the production process. The following information is available for the month of March:

EXERCISE 22-6
Preparing
Journal Entries
in a Process
Cost System

Shamrock Industries uses a process cost system. Products are processed succes-sively by the Cutting Department and the Assembly Department and are then transferred to the finished goods warehouse. Shown below is cost information for the Assembly Department during the month of June:

Cost of work in process at June 1		$ 19,000
Cost of units transferred in from Cutting Department during June		72,500
Manufacturing costs added in Assembly Department:		
Direct materials used	$44,000	
Direct labor	6,100	
Manufacturing overhead	17,400	67,500
Total costs to be accounted for		$159,000

The total cost of finished goods manufactured during June amounted to $136,800.

INSTRUCTIONS   Prepare journal entries to summarize for the month of June (1) the transfer of production from the Cutting Department to the Assembly Department, (2) the manufacturing costs incurred by the Assembly Department, and (3) the transfer of completed units from the Assembly Department to the finished goods warehouse.

EXERCISE 22-7
Computing
Unit Costs

Given below are the production data for Department No. 1 for the first month of operation:

Costs charged to Department No. 1:	
Direct materials used	$30,900
Direct labor	11,440
Manufacturing overhead	57,200
Total	$99,540

During this first month, 3,000 units were placed into production; 2,800 units were completed and the remaining 200 units are **100% completed** as to material and **30% completed** as to direct labor and overhead.

INSTRUCTIONS   You are to compute the following:

a Unit cost of direct material used.

b Equivalent full units of production for direct labor and factory overhead.

c Unit cost of direct labor.

d Unit cost of manufacturing overhead.

e Total cost of the 200 units in process at month-end.

f Total cost of the 2,800 units completed during the month. (Use a FIFO flow assumption, although it does not matter as there is no beginning inventory of work in process.)

EXERCISE 22-8
Evaluating
Departmental
Performance

Shown below in the left-hand column are the unit costs relating to the manufactur-ing activities of the Packaging Department of Baker Labs in the month of July. (These unit costs are taken directly from the process cost summary on page 1039.) Assume that the right-hand column indicates the unit costs **budgeted** for the Packaging Department—that is, the unit costs that managers had **expected** the department to incur during the month.

	Unit Costs	
	Actual	*Budgeted*
Manufacturing cost charged to the Packaging Department:		
Units transferred in from the Mixing Department	$2.00	$2.15
Manufacturing costs added by the Packaging Department:		
Direct materials requisitioned	.16	.16
Direct labor	.25	.20
Manufacturing overhead (120% of direct labor cost)	.30	.24
Unit cost per equivalent unit processed during July	$2.71	$2.75

Based upon this information, did the Packaging Department perform as well during July as managers had expected? Explain.

*EXERCISE 22-9
Characteristics of JIT Systems

Indicate whether the following characteristics are more closely associated with a JIT manufacturing system or with a traditional "supply push" system. Explain your reasons for each answer.

a High inventory turnover rate

b Low manufacturing efficiency ratio

c Thorough quality control inspection of each finished unit

d Short cycle time

e Continuous focus upon the production of a single type of product

f Low rate of defects in finished goods

g Increased emphasis upon product design

*EXERCISE 22-10
Evaluation of JIT Systems

Just-in-time (JIT) manufacturing systems are receiving much attention in today's business world.

a Explain the nature of a JIT manufacturing system.

b Why is the quality of materials and finished products of greater importance in a JIT system than in a system that maintains sizable inventories?

c Why do JIT systems often utilize activity-based costing procedures?

d Identify four areas of potential cost savings often associated with JIT systems.

e Identify three separate conditions which might make it ***unwise*** for a company to attempt operating at the near-zero levels of materials and finished goods inventories often associated with JIT systems.

f Does the JIT philosophy offer any potential benefits to a company that decides ***not*** to minimize its inventory levels?

---

* *Supplemental Topic, "The New Manufacturing Environment"*

*EXERCISE 22-11
Measurement and Evaluation of Manufacturing Efficiency

The activities involved in the manufacture of a particular model piano at von Rohen Piano Co. are listed below, along with the average number of days required for each activity:

Activity	Days
Inspection of incoming shipments of materials	2
Direct materials kept in storage	45
Processing by Milling Department	12.5
Partially completed pianos and components kept in storage between processing activities	20
Processing by Staining and Finishing Department	8
Processing by Assembly Department	3
Inspection	1
Correcting defects	4
Tuning	5
Storage of finished units awaiting sale	33
Packaging for shipment	1
Total cycle time	130.0

INSTRUCTIONS

a List the value-adding activities in the company's production cycle and the times required to complete these activities.

b Compute the manufacturing efficiency ratio for the entire production cycle, from the receipt of materials through the shipment of finished goods. (Round to the nearest percent.)

c Suggest several specific steps likely to increase the manufacturing efficiency ratio, and explain how each of these steps may reduce the company's overall costs.

PROBLEMS

Group A

PROBLEM 22A-1
Job Order Cost System: A Short Problem

Chesapeake Sailmakers uses a job order cost accounting system. Manufacturing overhead is charged to individual jobs through the use of a predetermined overhead rate based on direct labor costs. The following information appears in the company's Work in Process Inventory controlling account for the month of June:

Debits to account:	
Balance, June 1	$ 7,200
Direct materials	12,000
Direct labor	9,000
Manufacturing overhead (applied to jobs as 150% of direct labor cost)	13,500
Total debits to account	$41,700
Credits to account:	
Transferred to Finished Goods Inventory account	33,200
Balance, June 30	$ 8,500

INSTRUCTIONS

a Assuming that the direct labor charged to the jobs still in process at June 30 amounts to $2,100, compute the amount of manufacturing overhead and the amount of direct materials which have been charged to these jobs as of June 30.

---

* *Supplemental Topic, "The New Manufacturing Environment"*

b Prepare general journal entries to summarize:

1 The manufacturing costs (direct materials, direct labor, and overhead) charged to production during June.

2 The transfer of production completed during June to the Finished Goods Inventory account.

3 The cash sale of 90% of the merchandise completed during June at a total sales price of $46,500. Show the related cost of goods sold in a separate journal entry.

**PROBLEM 22A-2
Job Order Cost
System: A
Comprehensive
Problem**

Georgia Woods, Inc., manufactures furniture to customers' specifications and uses a job order cost system. A predetermined overhead rate is used in applying manufacturing overhead to individual jobs. In Department One, overhead is applied on the basis of machine-hours, and in Department Two, on the basis of direct labor hours. At the beginning of the current year, management made the following budget estimates to assist in determining the overhead application rate:

	Department One	Department Two
Direct labor cost	$300,000	$225,000
Direct labor hours	20,000	15,000
Manufacturing overhead	$420,000	$337,500
Machine-hours	12,000	7,500

Production of a batch of custom furniture ordered by City Furniture (job no. 58) was started early in the year and completed three weeks later on January 29. The records for this job show the following cost information:

	Department One	Department Two
Job order for City Furniture (job no. 58):		
Direct materials cost	$10,100	$ 7,600
Direct labor cost	$16,500	$11,100
Direct labor hours	1,100	740
Machine-hours	750	500

Selected additional information for January is given below:

	Department One	Department Two
Direct labor hours—month of January	1,600	1,200
Machine-hours—month of January	1,100	600
Manufacturing overhead incurred in January	$39,010	$26,540

INSTRUCTIONS

a Compute the predetermined overhead rate for each department.

b What is the total cost of the furniture produced for City Furniture?

c Prepare the entries required to record the sale (on account) of the furniture to City Furniture. The sales price of the order was $147,000.

d Determine the over- or underapplied overhead for each department at the end of January.

**PROBLEM 22A-3
Process Cost
System: A
Short but Com-
prehensive
Problem**

One of the primary products of Magic Touch is the Shutterbug, an instant camera, which is processed successively in the Assembly Department and the Lens Department, and then transferred to the company's sales warehouse. After having been shut down for three weeks as a result of a materials shortage, the company resumed production of Shutterbugs on May 1. The flow of **units of product** through the departments during May is shown below.

Assembly Department Work in Process		Lens Department Work in Process	
Started in process— 30,000 units	To Lens Dept.— 25,000 units	From Assembly Dept.—25,000 units	To warehouse— 21,000 units

Neither department had any units in process at May 1. Departmental manufacturing costs applicable to Shutterbug production for the month of May were as follows:

	Assembly Department	Lens Department
Units transferred from Assembly Department		$?
Direct materials	$164,700	67,900
Direct labor	67,500	45,200
Manufacturing overhead	118,800	135,600
Total manufacturing costs	$351,000	$?

Unfinished goods in each department at the end of May were on the average 40% complete, with respect to both direct materials and conversion costs.

INSTRUCTIONS

a Determine the equivalent full units of production in each department during May.

b Compute unit production costs in each department during May.

c Prepare the necessary journal entries to record the transfer of product out of the Assembly Department and the Lens Department during May.

**PROBLEM 22A-4
Process Costs:
Cost Report
and Journal
Entries**

Aladdin Electric manufactures several products, including an electric garage door opener called the Door Tender. Door Tenders are completely processed in one department and are then transferred to the finished goods warehouse. All manufacturing costs are applied to Door Tender units at a uniform rate throughout the production process. The following information is available for July:

Beginning inventory of work in process	$ 21,220
Manufacturing costs incurred in July:	
Direct materials used	56,100
Direct labor	29,920
Manufacturing overhead applied	82,280
Total costs to be accounted for	$189,520

The beginning inventory consisted of 400 units which had been 60% completed during June. In addition to completing these units, the department started and completed another 1,500 units during July and started work on 300 more units which were 70% completed at July 31.

INSTRUCTIONS   a Compute the equivalent full units of production in July.

b Prepare a process cost summary for the department for the month of July, as illustrated on page 1039. Use the July unit cost figures to determine the cost of the ending inventory of work in process. (This represents a **FIFO** flow assumption.)

c Prepare journal entries to record (1) the manufacturing costs charged to the department during July and (2) the transfer of 1,900 completed units to the finished goods warehouse.

PROBLEM 22A-5
Process Costs:
A Second
Comprehensive
Problem

Saf-T-File, Inc., manufactures metal filing cabinets and uses a process cost system. The cabinets pass through a series of production processes, one of which is the Lock Assembly Department. The costs charged to the Lock Assembly Department during April, along with a summary of the units worked on by the department, are shown below:

Costs charged to the Lock Assembly Department:

Work in process, April 1	$ 29,840
Cost of 2,000 units transferred in from the Drawer Assembly Department	
during April ($52 per unit)	104,000
Manufacturing costs added by the Lock Assembly Department during April:	
Direct materials	8,200
Direct labor	3,800
Manufacturing overhead (applied as 150% of direct labor costs)	5,700
Total costs to be accounted for	$151,540

Units worked on during April:

Work in process, April 1 (100% complete as to materials, 80% complete as	
to conversion costs)...	500
Units started and completed during April....................................	1,600
Units completed and transferred to the Painting Department during April	2,100
Work in process, May 31 (100% complete as to materials, 50% complete	
as to conversion costs)...	400

INSTRUCTIONS   a Compute separately the equivalent full units of production during April for (1) materials and (2) conversion costs (direct labor and overhead).

b Prepare a process cost summary for April, following the format illustrated on page 1039. Use the April unit cost figures to value the ending inventory of work in process; the remainder of the $151,540 total cost to be accounted for may be assigned to units transferred from the Lock Assembly Department to the Painting Department (a **FIFO** flow assumption).

c Prepare journal entries to record:

1 Transfer of the 2,000 units from the Drawer Assembly Department into the Lock Assembly Department.

2 Manufacturing costs added by the Lock Assembly Department during April. (You may show all three elements of manufacturing costs in one compound journal entry.)

3 Transfer of the 2,100 completed units from the Lock Assembly Department to the Painting Department. (Hint: These units are not finished goods.)

PROBLEM 22A-6
Manufacturing
Overhead and
Fluctuations in
Production Vol-
ume

John Park is the founder and president of Park West Engineering. One of the company's principal products is sold exclusively to BigMart, a national chain of retail stores. BigMart buys a large quantity of the product in the first quarter of each year but buys successively smaller quantities in the second, third, and fourth quarters. Park West cannot produce in advance to meet the big first-quarter sales requirement, because BigMart frequently makes minor changes in the specifications for the product. Therefore, Park West must adjust its production schedules to fit BigMart's buying pattern.

In Park West's cost accounting system, unit costs are computed quarterly on the basis of actual materials, labor, and manufacturing overhead costs charged to work in process at the end of each quarter. At the close of the current year, Park received the following cost report, by quarters, for the year. (Fixed overhead represents items of manufacturing costs that remain relatively constant month by month; variable overhead includes those costs that tend to move up and down in proportion to changes in the volume of production.)

	First Quarter	Second Quarter	Third Quarter	Fourth Quarter
Direct materials used	$ 78,000	$ 60,000	$ 42,000	$22,000
Direct labor	80,000	60,000	40,000	20,000
Fixed overhead (actual)	30,000	30,000	30,000	30,000
Variable overhead (actual)	48,000	39,000	29,000	14,000
Total manufacturing cost	$236,000	$189,000	$141,000	$86,000
Equivalent full units produced	40,000	30,000	20,000	10,000
Unit production cost.........................	$ 5.90	$ 6.30	$ 7.05	$ 8.60

Park is concerned about the steadily rising unit costs. He states, "We have a contract to produce 50,000 units for BigMart next quarter at a unit sales price of $8.50. If this sales price won't even cover our unit production costs, I'll have to cancel the contract. But before I take such drastic action, I'd like to study our method of computing unit costs to see if we might be doing something wrong."

INSTRUCTIONS

a As the first step in your study, determine the ***unit cost*** of each cost element (materials, labor, fixed overhead, and variable overhead) in the first quarter and in the fourth quarter of the current year.

b Based on your computation in part **a**, which cost element is primarily responsible for the increase in unit production costs? Explain why you think the unit cost for this cost element has been rising throughout the year.

c Compute an overhead application rate for Park West Engineering which expresses total overhead ***for the year*** (including both fixed and variable overhead) as a percentage of direct labor costs.

d Redetermine the unit production cost for each quarter using the overhead application rate to apply overhead costs.

e Determine the expected unit cost of producing 50,000 units next quarter. (Assume that unit costs for materials and direct labor remain the same as in the fourth quarter and use the overhead application rate to determine the unit cost of applied overhead.)

f Explain to Park how Park West might improve its procedures for determining unit production costs. Also explain whether Park West reasonably can expect to recover its production costs next quarter if it sells 50,000 units to BigMart at a unit sales price of $8.50.

Group B

PROBLEM 22B-1
Journal Entries to Record Basic Cost Flows

The following information relates to the manufacturing operations of O'Shaughnessy Mfg. Co. during the month of March. The company uses a job order cost accounting system.

a Purchases of direct materials during the month amount to $59,700. (All purchases were made on account.)

b Materials requisitions issued by the production department during the month total $56,200.

c Time cards of direct workers show 2,000 hours worked on various jobs during the month, for total direct labor cost of $30,000.

d Direct workers were paid $26,300 in March.

e Actual overhead costs for the month amount to $34,900 (for simplicity, you may credit Accounts Payable).

f Overhead is applied to jobs at a rate of $18 per direct labor hour.

g Jobs with total accumulated costs of $116,000 were completed during the month.

h During March, units costing $128,000 were sold for $210,000. (All sales were made on account.)

INSTRUCTIONS Prepare general journal entries to summarize each of these transactions in the company's general ledger accounts.

PROBLEM 22B-2
Job Order Cost System: A Comprehensive Problem

Precision Instruments, Inc., uses a job order cost system and applies manufacturing overhead to individual jobs by using predetermined overhead rates. In Department A overhead is applied on the basis of machine-hours, and in Department B on the basis of direct labor hours. At the beginning of the current year, management made the following budget estimates as a step toward determining the overhead application rates:

	Department A	Department B
Direct labor	$420,000	$300,000
Manufacturing overhead	$540,000	$412,500
Machine-hours	18,000	1,900
Direct labor hours	28,000	25,000

Production of 4,000 tachometers (job no. 399) was started in the middle of January and completed two weeks later. The cost records for this job show the following information:

	Department A	Department B
Job no. 399 (4,000 units of product):		
Cost of materials used on job.........................	$6,800	$4,500
Direct labor cost	$8,100	7,200
Direct labor hours.....................................	540	600
Machine-hours	250	100

INSTRUCTIONS

a Determine the overhead rate that should be used for each department in applying overhead costs to job no. 399.

b What is the total cost of job no. 399, and the unit cost of the product manufactured on this production order?

c Prepare the journal entries required to record the sale (on account) of 1,000 of the tachometers to SkiCraft Boats. The total sales price was $19,500.

d Assume that actual overhead costs for the year were $517,000 in Department A and $424,400 in Department B. Actual machine-hours in Department A were 17,000, and actual direct labor hours in Department B were 26,000 during the year. On the basis of this information, determine the over- or underapplied overhead in each department for the year.

PROBLEM 22B-3
Process Costs:
Journal Entries

After having been shut down for two months during a strike, Oshima Appliance Co. resumed operations on August 1. One of the company's products is a dishwasher which is successively processed by the Tub Department and the Motor Department before being transferred to the finished goods warehouse. Shown below are data concerning the units produced and costs incurred by the two manufacturing departments during August:

Production Summary—in Units

	Tub Department	Motor Department
Units placed in production....................................	1,700	900
Less: Units in process, Aug. 31	800	400
Units completed during August	900	500

Costs Charged to the Departments

	Tub Department	Motor Department
Transferred in from Tub Department..........................		$?
Direct materials used	$54,000	57,600
Direct labor	30,000	10,400
Manufacturing overhead	46,500	14,400

Due to the strike, there were no units in process at August 1 in either department. The units in process in both departments at August 31 are 75% complete with respect to both materials and conversion costs.

INSTRUCTIONS

a Compute the equivalent full units of production in August for each department.

b Compute the unit production costs for August in each department. (Include in the product costs of the Motor Department the cost of the 900 units transferred in from the Tub Department.)

c Use the August unit cost figures to determine the cost of the ending inventory of work in process in each department at August 31.

d Prepare the journal entries required to record the transfer of completed units out of each of the two departments during August.

PROBLEM 22B-4
Process Costs:
A Comprehensive Problem

Universal Corp. has one production department and uses a process cost system. The following data is available as to the costs of production and the number of units worked on during the month of May:

Costs charged to the production department:	
Work in process, May 1...	$ 25,400
Manufacturing costs added during May:	
Direct materials	137,400
Direct labor	56,000
Manufacturing overhead (applied as 180% of direct labor costs)............	100,800
Total costs to be accounted for	$319,600

Units worked on during May:	
Work in process, May 1 (40% complete as to materials, 60% complete as to conversion costs)	2,000
Units started and completed during May	8,000
Finished goods produced during May	10,000
Work in process, May 31 (75% complete as to materials, 80% complete as to conversion costs)...	3,000

INSTRUCTIONS a Compute separately the equivalent full units of production during May for (1) materials and (2) conversion costs (direct labor and overhead).

b Prepare a process cost summary for May, following the format illustrated on page 1039. Use the May unit cost figures to value the ending inventory of work in process; the remainder of the $319,600 total costs to be accounted for are to be assigned to the units completed during the month (a *FIFO* flow assumption).

c Prepare journal entries to record for the month:

1 The manufacturing costs charged to production. (Use one compound journal entry to record all three types of manufacturing costs.)

2 The transfer of the 10,000 completed units to the finished goods warehouse.

PROBLEM 22B-5
Process Costs:
A Second
Comprehensive
Problem

Dayton Chemical, Inc., manufactures a fertilizer concentrate, called PH Max. This product passes through four successive production processes, identified as Departments No. 1, 2, 3, and 4. After processing by Department No. 4, the product is transferred to a warehouse as finished goods inventory.

In Department No. 4, all direct materials needed to complete PH Max are added at the beginning of processing. The accounting department has accumulated the following information relating to processing in Department No. 4 during the month of April:

Costs charged to Department No. 4:	
Work in process inventory, April 1 (40,000 units, 100% complete as to	
materials, 75% complete as to conversion costs)	*$ 387,000*
Cost of 140,000 units transferred in from Department No. 3 during	
April (unit cost = $5)	*700,000*
Manufacturing costs added in Department No. 4 during April:	
Direct materials added	*280,000*
Direct labor	*125,000*
Manufacturing overhead	*375,000*
Total costs to be accounted for	*$1,867,000*

During April, the 40,000 units in process at April 1 and 90,000 of the units transferred in from Department No. 3 were completed and transferred to the warehouse. The remaining 50,000 units transferred in from Department No. 3 are still in process at April 30, and are 100% complete as to materials and 50% complete as to conversion costs (direct labor and overhead).

INSTRUCTIONS a Compute the equivalent full units of production during April. (Separate computations are required for materials and for conversion costs.)

b Prepare a process cost summary for Department No. 4 for the month of April. Use the April unit cost figures to determine the cost of work in process at April 30; the remainder of the $1,867,000 in total costs applies to units completed during the month (the FIFO method of valuing inventory).

c Prepare journal entries to record:

1 The transfer of the 140,000 units from Department No. 3 into Department No. 4.

2 The manufacturing costs added by Department No. 4 during April.

3 The transfer of the 130,000 completed units from Department No. 4 to the finished goods warehouse.

CASES AND UNSTRUCTURED PROBLEMS

*CASE 22-1
ABC

Rotron Mfg. Corp. manufactures two automotive products: airbags and passive-restraint seat belts. Shown below are the forecast amounts of three manufacturing overhead costs for the coming year:

Direct materials storage	$ 300,C00
Supervision (indirect labor)	900,C00
Quality control inspection of finished goods	1,200,C00
Total	$2,400,C00

The company also has developed the following forecasts of factors which might be useful in assigning overhead costs to units produced:

	Airbags	Seat Belts
Number of incoming materials shipments	12	24
Square footage of warehouse space used in direct materials storage	8,000	2,C00
Units scheduled for manufacture	1,000,000	2,000,C00
Direct labor hours	400,000	200,C00
Machine-hours	300,000	50,C00
Inspection (minutes per unit)	2.5	.25

INSTRUCTIONS

a Assume that all overhead costs are assigned to production on the basis of direct labor hours. Determine the amount of the $2,400,000 in overhead costs listed above that will be assigned to *each unit* of (1) airbags and (2) seat belts scheduled for production in the coming year.

b Assume that Rotron uses activity-based costing. The following cost drivers are used in assigning the selected overhead costs to production:

Overhead Cost	Cost Driver
Direct materials storage costs	Square footage of storage space
Supervision	Direct labor hours
Quality control inspection	Total inspection time

Using these criteria, determine the per-unit amount of each of the three overhead costs which would be assigned to airbags and to seat belts. Also indicate for each product the total of these three per-unit costs.

c Which method of assigning overhead costs do you believe results in the more accurate measure of unit cost? Explain your reasoning.

d Identify two areas of potential cost savings relating to the manufacture of airbags. Indicate how cost savings might be achieved in each of these areas.

*CASE 22-2
Just-in-Time
Frozen Dinners

Healthy Times produces four types of frozen TV dinners that it sells to supermarkets and independent grocery stores. The company operates from two locations: a manufacturing plant and a refrigerated warehouse located a few blocks away. (Administrative offices are located in the manufacturing plant.)

The types of dinners to be produced each week is scheduled a week in advance, based upon customer orders. The *number* of dinners produced, however, is always

---

the same. The company runs its production facilities at full capacity—20,000 units per day—to minimize fixed manufacturing costs per unit.

Every Friday, local suppliers deliver to Healthy Times' factory the fresh vegetables, chicken, fish, and other ingredients required for the following week's production. (Materials are abundant in the region.) These ingredients then are cut into meal-sized portions, "fresh frozen" using special equipment, and transported by truck to the refrigerated warehouse. The company maintains an inventory of frozen ingredients equal to approximately two weeks' production.

Every day, ingredients for 20,000 dinners are brought by truck from the warehouse to the factory. All dinners produced in a given production run must be of the same type. However, production workers can make the machinery "setup" changes necessary to produce a different type of frozen dinner in about 10 minutes.

Monday through Thursday, Healthy Times produces one type of dinner each day. On Friday, it manufactures whatever types of dinner are needed to "balance" its inventories. Completed frozen dinners are transported back to the refrigerated warehouse on a daily basis.

Frozen dinners are shipped daily from the warehouse to customers. All shipments are sent by independent carriers. Healthy Times usually maintains about a 10-day inventory of frozen dinners in the warehouse. Recently, however, daily sales have been averaging about 2,000 units less than the level of production, and the finished goods inventory has swelled to a 25-day supply.

Marsha Osaka, the controller of Healthy Times, recently read about the JIT inventory system used by Toyota in its Japanese production facilities. She is wondering whether a JIT system might benefit Healthy Times.

INSTRUCTIONS a In **general terms,** describe a JIT manufacturing system. Identify the basic goals of a JIT manufacturing system and any basic conditions which must exist for the system to operate efficiently.

b Identify any non-value-adding activities in Healthy Times' operations which might be reduced or eliminated in a JIT system. Also identify specific types of costs that might be reduced or eliminated.

c Assume that Healthy Times **does** adopt at JIT manufacturing system. Prepare a description of the company's operations under such a system. (Your description should be similar in depth to the description provided above.)

d Explain whether or not you think that a JIT system would work for Healthy Times. Provide specific reasons supporting your conclusion.

ANSWERS TO SELF-TEST QUESTIONS

1 b   2 c   3 a, c, d   4 a   5 d   6 a, c

COMPREHENSIVE PROBLEM 6

APEX COMPUTER, INC.

JOB ORDER AND PROCESS COST ACCOUNTING SYSTEMS

Apex Computer, Inc., manufactures and sells 10 different models of small computers, each using different combinations of micro-processors, disc drives, number of expansion slots, and other features. Some models are lap-tops, some are desk-tops, and others are workstations designed for networking. Production departments that manufacture standardized computer components, such as keyboards or monitors, use process cost accounting systems. However, the Computer Assembly Department sequentially assembles batches of from 5,000 to 10,000 of whichever model computer is most in demand. Therefore, the Computer Assembly Department uses a job order cost accounting system.

In **Part 1** of this Comprehensive Problem, we look at the accounting practices of the Computer Assembly Department—a job order cost accounting system. In **Part 2,** we focus upon the Keyboard Assembly Department, which uses a process cost accounting system.

Computer Assembly Department

PART 1
Job Order Cost Accounting Systems

The Computer Assembly Department uses a *job order* cost accounting system, with each job representing assembly of between 5,000 and 10,000 units of a particular model of computer. Once assembly is completed, the computers are transferred to the Finished Goods Warehouse and are available for sale.

Late in May 1994, the Computer Assembly Department began job no. 2140, the assembly of 10,000 model AC10 lap-top computers. This job was partially complete on May 31, and was completed on June 9. The job cost sheet included the following costs for materials and for direct labor as of May 31 and June 9 (the June 9 costs include those charged through May 31):

	Costs Charged to Job as of:	
	May 31	June 9
Direct materials requisitioned	$ 657,200	$2,290,300
Manufactured products requisitioned	$1,058,000	$4,723,700
Number of component parts requisitioned	12,000	65,000
Direct labor	$ 12,000	$ 56,000

Accounting Policies and Other Data

1 Manufacturing overhead is applied to jobs at the predetermined rate of $2 per component part requisitioned. (Note that the number of parts requisitioned is listed in the job cost sheet.)

2 Direct materials represent parts purchased from others in a ready-to-use condition. Therefore, requisition of these parts is recorded by crediting the Materials Inventory controlling account.

3 Manufactured parts are components manufactured by Apex's other production departments and stored in the Components Warehouse. The requisition of these parts is recorded by crediting the Work in Process Inventory, Components controlling account.

4 Units completed by the Computer Assembly Department are classified as finished goods.

5 The specific identification method is used in transferring costs from the Finished Goods Inventory account to the Cost of Goods Sold account.

INSTRUCTIONS

a Compute the total cost of completing job no. 2140, and the per-unit cost of the 10,000 lap-top computers manufactured.

b Prepare general journal entries to summarize:

1 The manufacturing costs charged to job no. 2140 through the end of May. (Include manufacturing overhead.)

2 The manufacturing costs charged to job no. 2140 during June. (Include manufacturing overhead.)

3 The completion of the job and the transfer of the computers to the Finished Goods Warehouse.

c On June 28, Apex sells 4,000 of the lap-top computers in job no. 2140 to MicroCity, a national computer retailer. The sales price was $1,200 per unit; terms, 2/10, n/30.

1 Prepare the journal entries to record this sale (use separate entries to record revenue and to record the cost of goods sold).

2 Briefly explain how the total costs charged to job no. 2140 (per part **a**) will be shown in Apex's financial statements for the month ended June 30, 1994.

d Assume that during 1994, actual manufacturing overhead for the Computer Assembly Department amounted to $2,372,740, and that during the year the department requisitioned for assembly a total of 1,180,340 component parts.

1 Compute the amount of over- or underapplied overhead for the year.

2 Prepare a journal entry to close the Manufacturing Overhead controlling account at year-end, assuming that the amount of over- or underapplied overhead was not material in dollar amount.

The Keyboard Assembly Department

PART 2
Process Cost
Accounting
Systems

One of the production departments of Apex Computer, Inc., that uses a process cost accounting system is the Keyboard Assembly Department. The plastic frames for keyboards are produced in Apex's Plastic Molding Department. Those frames are then transferred to the Keyboard Assembly Department, where the production process is completed. Completed keyboards are transferred to the Components Warehouse where they are stored until they are needed by the Computer Assembly Department.

The accounting department has accumulated the following information relating to processing in the Keyboard Assembly Department during the month of June, 1994:

Costs charged to Keyboard Assembly Department:	
Work in process inventory, June 1	*$ 47,696*
Cost of 16,600 plastic keyboard frames transferred in from Plastic	
Molding Department during June (unit cost, $1.06)	*17,596*
Manufacturing costs added in Keyboard Assembly Department during June:	
Direct materials added	*157,700*
Direct labor	*40,040*
Manufacturing overhead	*48,048*
Total costs to be accounted for	*$311,080*

Keyboards worked on during June:

Units in process, June 1 (100% complete as to materials, 30% complete as to conversion costs)	*4,000*
Units started and completed during June	*13,600*
Units completed and transferred to Components Warehouse during June	*17,600*
Units in process, June 30 (100% complete as to materials, 60% complete as to conversion costs)	*3,000*

Accounting Policies and Other Data

1 All direct materials needed to complete Keyboards are placed into production at the start of the manufacturing process.

2 The FIFO inventory method is used in valuing the ending inventories of work in process and in determining the cost of completed keyboards transferred to the Components Warehouse.

3 Transfers of completed keyboards to the Components Warehouse are recorded by debiting a controlling account entitled Work in Process Inventory, Components.

INSTRUCTIONS

a Compute separately the equivalent full units of production in June by the Keyboard Assembly Department with respect to (1) materials and (2) conversion costs.

b Prepare a process cost report for the Keyboard Assembly Department for the month of June.

c Prepare journal entries to record for June the:

1 Transfer of 16,600 plastic keyboard frames from the Plastic Department into the Keyboard Assembly Department.

2 Manufacturing costs incurred in the Keyboard Assembly Department.

3 Transfer of 17,600 completed keyboards from the Keyboard Assembly Department to the Components Warehouse. (Note: these keyboards are *not* viewed as finished goods.)

8 Managerial Accounting: Planning and Control

Managers are responsible for planning and controlling the activities of the business. The functions of planning and control are closely related. Planning is the process of setting financial and operational goals for the business and deciding upon the strategies and actions for achieving these goals. Exercising control means monitoring actual operating results, comparing those results to the plan, and taking corrective action when actual results fall below expectation.

23 Cost-Volume-Profit Analysis

This chapter has two major objectives. Our first is to explain how various costs respond to changes in the level of business activity. An understanding of these relationships is essential to developing successful business strategies and to planning future operations. Our second objective is to show how managers may use cost-volume-profit analysis in a wide variety of business decisions. We illustrate and explain the use of a "break-even" graph—a basic tool of cost-volume-profit analysis. Also, we discuss the concept of "contribution margin." In tailoring this concept to specific managerial decisions, we show how contribution margin may be expressed on a per-unit basis, as a percentage of sales, and in relation to available units of a scarce resource.

After studying this chapter, you should be able to meet these Learning Objectives:

1 *Explain how fixed, variable, and semivariable costs respond to changes in the level of business activity.*

2 *Use the high-low method to separate the fixed and variable elements of a semivariable cost.*

3 *Prepare a cost-volume-profit (break-even) graph.*

4 *Explain contribution margin; compute contribution margin per unit and contribution margin ratio.*

5 *Determine the sales volume required to earn a desired level of operating income.*

6 *Use the contribution margin ratio to estimate the effect upon operating income of changes in sales volume.*

7 *Use cost-volume-profit relationships in evaluating various marketing strategies.*

8 *Determine the sales mix that will maximize the contribution margin per unit of a scarce resource.*

*O*ne of the most important analytical tools used by many managers is cost-volume-profit analysis (or ***CVP analysis***). CVP analysis is a means of learning how costs and profits behave in response to changes in the level of business activity. An understanding of these relationships is essential in developing plans and budgets for future business operations. In addition, analysis assists managers in predicting the effects of various decisions and strategies upon the operating income of the business. In our discussion of cost-volume-profit relationships, the term "cost" is used to describe both manufacturing costs and operating expenses.

Cost-volume-profit analysis may be used by managers to answer questions such as the following:

■ What level of sales must be reached to cover all expenses, that is, to break even?

■ How many units of a product must be sold to earn a given operating income?

■ What will happen to our profitability if we expand capacity?

■ What will be the effect of changing compensation of sales personnel from fixed monthly salaries to a straight commission of 10% on sales?

■ If we increase our spending on advertising to $100,000 per month, what increase in sales volume will be required to maintain our current level of income from operations?

Cost-volume-profit relationships are useful not only to management but also to creditors and investors. The ability of a business to pay its debts and to increase its dividend payments, for example, depends largely upon its ability to generate earnings. Assume that a company's sales volume is expected to increase by 10% during the next year. What will be the effect of this increase in sales volume upon the company's net income? The answer depends upon how the company's costs behave in response to this increase in the level of business activity.

The concepts of cost-volume-profit analysis may be applied to the business as a whole; to individual segments of the business such as a division, a branch, or a department; or to a particular product line.

Cost-Volume Relationships

OBJECTIVE 1 Explain how fixed, variable, and semivariable costs respond to changes in the level of business activity.

To illustrate the relationships between costs and the level of activity, we shall first consider cost behavior in a simple and familiar setting, the cost of operating a personal automobile. Suppose that someone tells you that the average annual cost of owning and operating an automobile is $2,700. Obviously, each individual driver does not incur an annual cost of exactly $2,700. In large part, the annual cost of owning an automobile depends upon how much you drive.

The Activity Base   In studying cost behavior, we first look for some measurable concept of volume or activity that serves as a ***cost driver***—that is, has a strong influence on the amount of cost incurred. We then try to find out how costs change in response to changes in the level of this activity. The unit of measure used to define the selected cost driver is called the ***activity base.***

An activity base may be units of key production input, such as tons of peaches processed or direct labor hours worked. (We have seen in prior chapters that manufacturing overhead costs often are expressed in terms of an activity base such as direct labor costs, direct labor hours, or machine-hours.) Alternatively, the activity base may be based upon output, such as equivalent full units of production, units sold, or dollars of sales revenue.

Most airlines consider passenger-miles flown to be their major cost driver and use this measurement as the activity base for studying the behavior of their operating costs. Retail stores, on the other hand, usually find total dollar sales to be the most significant activity base in cost analysis. In our example involving the operation of an automobile, we will use *miles driven* during the year as our activity base.

Once an appropriate activity base has been selected, we can classify all operating costs into one of the following three broad categories.

Fixed Costs (or Fixed Expenses)   *Fixed* costs are those costs and expenses that *do not change* significantly in response to changes in the activity base. For example, the annual licensing fee is an example of a fixed cost in the operation of an automobile, as this cost remains constant regardless of the number of miles driven. In a business entity, fixed costs include monthly salaries to office workers and executives, depreciation, property taxes, and many types of insurance protection.

Variable Costs (Variable Expenses)   A *variable* cost is one that rises or falls in direct proportion to changes in the activity base. For example, if the activity base increases by 10%, a variable cost increases by approximately 10%. In our example involving the operation of an automobile, gasoline is a variable cost that changes in response to the number of miles driven.

In manufacturing operations, the costs of direct materials and direct labor are variable costs with respect to the number of units manufactured. For an airline, fuel expense is a variable cost that responds to changes in the number of passenger-miles flown. In retailing, the cost of goods sold and sales commissions expense are examples of variable costs that respond closely to changes in total dollar sales.

Semivariable Costs (Semivariable Expenses)   *Semivariable* costs also are called *mixed* costs, because *part of the cost is fixed* and *part is variable.* A great many business costs are semivariable. Telephone expense, for example, includes both a fixed element (the "base rate" charged by the telephone company each month) and a variable element (the additional charges for long-distance calls).

The concept of a semivariable cost usually applies when we combine a variety of different costs into one broad category. For example, manufacturing overhead includes both fixed costs, such as property taxes, and variable costs, such as supplies used and utilities expense. Therefore, total manufacturing overhead behaves as a semivariable cost.

In our example involving the operation of an automobile, we will use depreciation to illustrate the concept of a semivariable cost. With respect to automobiles, some depreciation occurs simply with the passage of time, without regard to miles driven. This represents the "fixed portion" of depreciation expense. However, the more miles an automobile is driven each year, the faster it depreciates. Thus, part of the total depreciation expense is a variable cost. (A technique for determining the fixed and variable portions of a semivariable expense will be illustrated and explained later in this chapter.)

Automobile Costs—Graphic Analysis   To illustrate cost-volume behavior, we shall assume the following somewhat simplified data to describe the cost of owning and operating a typical automobile:

Type of Cost	Amount
Fixed costs:	
Insurance	*$430 per year*
License fee	*70 per year*
Variable costs:	
Gasoline, oil, servicing	*8 cents per mile*
Semivariable costs:	
Depreciation	*$1,000 per year plus 4 cents per mile*

We can express these cost-volume relationships graphically. The relation between volume (miles driven per year) and the three types of cost, both separately and combined, is shown in the following diagrams.

GRAPHIC ANALYSIS OF AUTOMOBILE COSTS

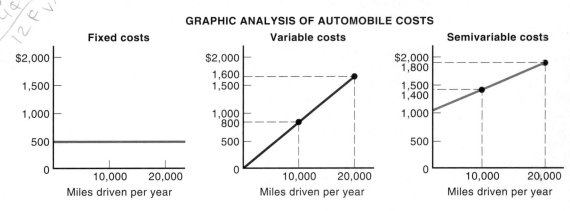

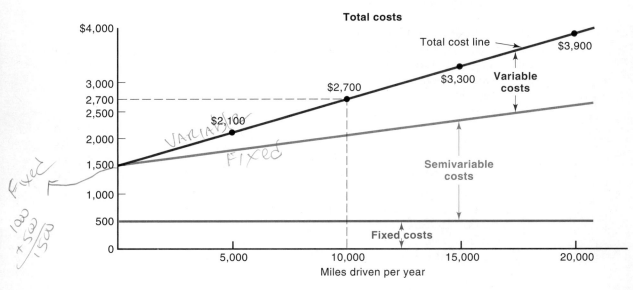

Total costs

We can read from the total costs graph the estimated annual automobile cost for any assumed mileage. For example, an owner who expects to drive 10,000 miles in a given year may estimate the total cost at $2,700 or 27.0 cents per mile. By combining all the fixed and variable elements of cost, we can generalize the cost-volume relationship and state simply that the cost of owning an automobile is ***$1,500 per year plus 12 cents per mile*** driven during the year.

The effect of volume on unit (per-mile) costs can be observed by converting total cost figures to average unit costs as follows:

Cost per Mile of Owning and Using an Automobile

<table>
<tr><td>Miles driven</td><td>5,000</td><td>10,000</td><td>15,000</td><td>20,000</td></tr>
<tr><td>Costs:</td><td></td><td></td><td></td><td></td></tr>
<tr><td>Fully variable (8 cents per mile)</td><td>$ 400</td><td>$ 800</td><td>$1,200</td><td>$1,600</td></tr>
<tr><td>Semivariable:</td><td></td><td></td><td></td><td></td></tr>
<tr><td>Variable portion (4 cents per mile)</td><td>200</td><td>400</td><td>600</td><td>800</td></tr>
<tr><td>Fixed portion</td><td>1,000</td><td>1,000</td><td>1,000</td><td>1,000</td></tr>
<tr><td>Completely fixed ($430 + $70)</td><td>500</td><td>500</td><td>500</td><td>500</td></tr>
<tr><td>Total costs</td><td>$2,100</td><td>$2,700</td><td>$3,300</td><td>$3,900</td></tr>
<tr><td>Cost per mile</td><td>$ 0.42</td><td>$ 0.27</td><td>$ 0.22</td><td>$0.195</td></tr>
</table>

Note decrease in cost per mile as use increases

The average unit-cost behavior of operating an automobile may be presented graphically as shown below:

Average cost per mile of driving a car

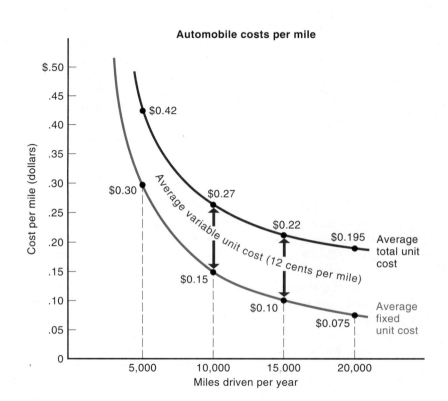

Automobile costs per mile

Behavior of Unit Costs

Total variable costs rise and fall in approximate proportion to changes in the activity base. Therefore, variable costs per unit **remain relatively constant.** Notice in our preceding example that variable costs amount to 12 cents per mile, regardless of the number of miles driven.

Fixed costs, on the other hand, **do not** vary with changes in the activity base. Therefore, fixed costs per unit **decline as the level of activity increases.** Notice in our example that fixed costs amount to 30 cents per mile for an automobile driven 5,000 miles each year, but amount to only 15 cents per mile for an automobile driven 10,000 miles.

Cost Advantage for Intensive Use of Facilities   What does the behavior of these unit costs mean to a business entity? In short, **a business can reduce its overall per-unit costs by using its facilities more intensively.** To illustrate, assume that an automobile plant incurs fixed costs of $8.4 million per month and has the capacity to produce 7,000 automobiles per month. The fixed cost per automobile manufactured is shown below at three different levels of production:

Fixed Costs per Month	Level of Production	Fixed Cost per Unit
$8,400,000	4,000 cars	$2,100
8,400,000	6,000 cars	1,400
8,400,000	7,000 cars	1,200

Notice that by producing 7,000 cars per month, the automaker's manufacturing costs are **$900 less** per automobile than if the automaker produces only 4,000 cars each month ($2,100 − $1,200 = $900). This "cost advantage" results from fully utilizing the company's production facilities and, therefore, spreading the company's fixed costs over as many units as possible. Unless overtime costs are incurred, **every business benefits from using its facilities more intensively.** This benefit is most apparent in business operations with relatively high fixed costs, such as automakers, utility companies, airlines, chemical manufacturers, and other companies with large investments in plant assets or large commitments to research and development.

CASE IN POINT   General Motors is the world's largest automaker; it sells more than twice as many automobiles each year as does its archrival, Ford Motor Company. Yet for much of the late 1980s, Ford earned larger profits than GM. The variable costs of manufacturing an automobile were similar at Ford and GM. The key to Ford's impressive profitability was its ability to operate its plants at nearly full capacity. Weekend shifts were part of Ford's normal workweek. As a result, Ford incurred much lower fixed costs per car than did its American competitors. This "cost advantage" enabled Ford to price its cars competitively and still earn a higher profit margin than either GM or Chrysler.

Cost Behavior in Business

Cost relationships in a business are seldom as simple as those in our example involving the operation of an automobile. However, the operating costs of all businesses exhibit variable, semivariable, and fixed characteristics.

Some business costs increase in lump-sum steps as shown in graph **(a)** below rather than in continuous increments. For example, when production reaches a point where another supervisor and crew must be added, a lump-sum addition to labor costs occurs at this point. Other costs may vary along a curve rather than a straight line, as in graph **(b).** For example, when overtime must be worked to increase production, the labor cost per unit may rise more rapidly than volume because of the necessity of paying an overtime premium to employees.

"Stair-step" and curvilinear costs

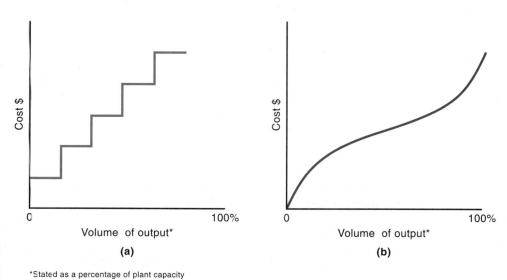

(a)

(b)

*Stated as a percentage of plant capacity

Taking all the possible variations of cost behavior into account would add greatly to the complexity of cost-volume analysis. How far from reality are the assumed straight-line relationships? Fortunately, there are two factors that make straight-line approximations of cost behavior useful for analytical purposes.

First, unusual patterns of cost behavior tend to offset one another. If we were to plot actual total costs incurred by a business over a time period in which volume changes occurred, the result might appear as in the cost-volume graph **(a)** on the next page. Total cost often moves in close approximation to a straight-line pattern when the various "stair-step" and curvilinear cost patterns of individual costs are combined.

Second, unusual patterns of cost behavior are most likely to occur at extremely high or extremely low levels of volume. For example, if output were increased to near 100% of plant capacity, variable costs would curve sharply upward because of payments for overtime. An extreme decline in volume, on the other hand, might require shutting down plants and extensive layoffs, thereby reducing some expenditures which are usually considered fixed costs. Most businesses, however, operate somewhere between perhaps 45% and 80% of capacity and try to avoid large fluctuations in volume. For a given business, the probability that volume will vary outside of a fairly narrow range is usually remote. The range over which output may be expected to vary is called the ***relevant range,*** as shown in graph **(b)** below. Within this relevant range, the assumption that total costs vary in straight-line relation to changes in volume is reasonably realistic for most companies.

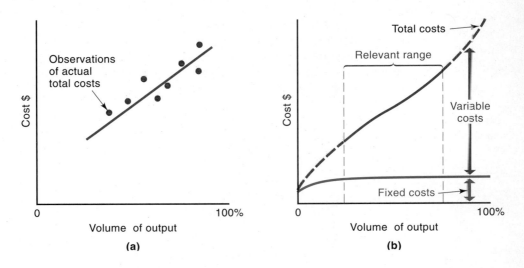

(a)

(b)

Analysis of Semivariable Costs: Determining the Fixed and Variable Elements

The study of relationships between costs and the level of activity is simplified when all costs may be classified either as fixed or variable. Therefore, we divide semivariable costs into two elements: (1) the fixed portion and (2) the variable portion.

OBJECTIVE 2
Use the
high-low
method to
separate the
fixed and
variable ele-
ments of a
semivariable
cost.

Several mathematical techniques may be used to determine the fixed and variable elements of a semivariable cost or mixed cost. One approach, called the ***high-low method,*** is illustrated below.[1]

High-Low Method To illustrate the high-low method, assume that some portion of the monthly maintenance cost of Ross Mfg. Co. is fixed and that some portion of this cost varies with the level of production. The levels of production and of maintenance cost for the first six months of the year are shown below:

Month	Equivalent Full Units of Production	Maintenance Cost
January	7,200	$4,790
February	7,000	4,700
March	7,700	5,100
April	8,400	5,430
May	9,000	5,700
June	8,600	5,600

---

[1] Other approaches to determining the fixed and variable elements of a semivariable cost include the least squares method and regression analysis. These techniques are discussed in the cost accounting course.

To find the variable portion of this cost, we relate the change in the cost to the change in the activity base between the months of highest and lowest production activity:

	Equivalent Full Units of Production	Maintenance Cost
Highest level of activity base	9,000	$5,700
Lowest level of activity base	7,000	4,700
Changes	2,000	$1,000

Notice that a 2,000-unit increase in production caused a $1,000 increase in maintenance cost. Therefore, the variable element of this cost may be estimated at $1,000/2,000 units, or **$0.50 per equivalent full unit of production.**

To determine the fixed portion of the monthly maintenance cost, we take the total monthly cost at either the high point or low point and deduct the variable maintenance cost at that level of activity. This computation follows, starting with the total monthly maintenance cost at the high point of activity:

$$\text{Fixed Cost} = \text{Total Cost} - \text{Variable Cost}$$
$$= \$5,700 - (\$0.50 \text{ per unit} \times 9,000 \text{ units})$$
$$= \$5,700 - \$4,500$$
$$= \$1,200 \text{ per month}$$

We have now developed a **cost formula** for monthly maintenance cost: **$1,200 fixed cost + $0.50 per equivalent full unit of production.** This formula may be used in evaluating the reasonableness of maintenance costs incurred in past periods, and also in forecasting costs likely to be incurred in the future. For example, what amount of maintenance cost should Ross Mfg. Co. expect in a month in which the company has scheduled 8,000 equivalent full units of production? The answer is approximately **$5,200,** determined as follows:

Monthly fixed cost..	$1,200
Variable cost ($0.50 × 8,000 equivalent full units)	4,000
Total estimated maintenance cost	$5,200

Cost Classifications

Once semivariable costs and expenses have been subdivided into fixed and variable elements, we may summarize the relationships among revenue, costs (and expenses), and profit as follows:

Classifications used in CVP analysis

Revenue − Variable Costs − Fixed Costs = Operating Income

Remember, we are using the term **cost** to include both manufacturing costs **and** operating expenses.

Notice that this formula leads to the determination of **operating income,** rather than net income. This is because income taxes expense and nonoperating gains and losses do not meet the criteria of either variable costs or fixed costs. Therefore, the term **profit** in cost-volume-profit analysis always refers to **operating income, not net income.**

Cost-volume-profit analysis often is called **break-even analysis,** a reference to the point at which a business moves from a loss to a profit position. This **break-even point** may be defined as the level of activity at which operating income is equal to **zero;** thus, revenue is exactly equal to the sum of the variable costs and fixed costs.

Cost-Volume-Profit Analysis: An Illustration

A simple business situation will be used to illustrate the kinds of information that can be derived from cost-volume-profit analysis. Hannigan's Ice Cream Company has a chain of stores located throughout a large city, selling a variety of ice cream products. Although the company sells many ice cream products of different size, we shall assume that volume of business is measured in gallons of ice cream sold. The company buys its ice cream from a dairy at a price of $4.20 per gallon. Retail sales prices vary depending upon the item and quantity purchased by a customer, but revenue consistently **averages** $12 per gallon of ice cream sold. Monthly operating statistics for a typical store are shown below:

HANNIGAN'S ICE CREAM COMPANY
Monthly Operating Data—
Typical Retail Store

		Variable Expenses per Gallon	Variable Expenses as Percentage of Sales Price
Average selling price		*$12.00*	*100%*
Cost of ice cream		*$ 4.20*	*35.0%*
	Fixed Expenses		
Monthly operating expenses:			
Manager's salary	*$2,400*		
Wages	*3,720+*	*.24*	*2.0*
Store rent	*1,600*		
Utilities	*180+*	*.06*	*.5*
Insurance and depreciation	*280*		
Miscellaneous	*820+*	*.30*	*2.5*
Total expenses (except for income taxes)....	*$9,000+*	*$4.80*	*40.0%*
Unit contribution margin and contribution			
margin ratio (discussed on pages			
1088–1089)		*$7.20*	*60.0%*

Note variable and fixed cost elements (margin note)

$12 / $4.20 (handwritten note)

DIR LABOR (handwritten note)

overhead (handwritten note)

Notice that income taxes expense is not included among the monthly operating expenses. Income taxes are neither a fixed nor a variable cost because they depend upon the amount of taxable income, rather than sales volume.[2]

CVP analysis may be performed either by stating the cost-volume-profit relationships in the form of mathematical formulas or by illustrating them visually in a graph. Let us begin with graphic analysis.

---

[2] Determination of the income taxes expense applicable to a corporation's pretax income is discussed in Chapter 18.

Preparing and Using a Break-Even Graph

OBJECTIVE 3
*Prepare a
cost-volume-
profit
(break-even)
graph.*

A *cost-volume-profit* (or *break-even*) graph for a typical Hannigan's Ice Cream store, based on the preceding data, is shown below.

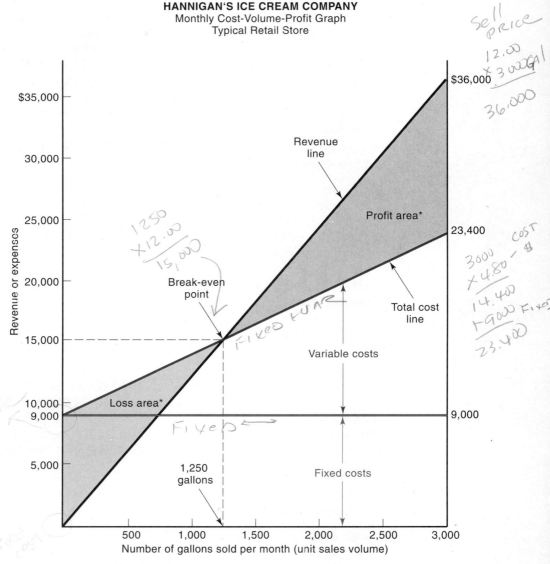

HANNIGAN'S ICE CREAM COMPANY
Monthly Cost-Volume-Profit Graph
Typical Retail Store

* Profit and loss areas represent income or loss before income taxes

The horizontal axis represents the activity base, which for a Hannigan's store is the number of gallons of ice cream sold per month. Since none of the company's stores sells more than 3,000 gallons per month, this is assumed to be the upper limit of the relevant range. The vertical axis of the graph is in dollars of revenue or costs (expenses).

The steps in drawing this graph are as follows:

1 Draw the total revenue line. This line runs from $0 revenue at zero sales volume to $36,000 in revenue at the maximum sales volume of

3,000 gallons per month. (Notice that the revenue line increases at a rate of $12 per gallon sold.)

2 Draw the fixed cost line. This is a horizontal line representing a constant $9,000 monthly amount at all volume levels.

3 Starting at the $9,000 fixed cost line, draw a line representing variable costs. This line will rise at the rate of $4.80 per gallon of ice cream sold. Any two points may be used in drawing the variable cost line, such as $0 in variable costs at zero gallons, and $14,400 in variable costs at 3,000 gallons ($4.80 per gallon × 3,000 gallons = $14,400). **Remember,** however, to add the $9,000 in fixed costs to the variable costs in finding the points for drawing the variable cost line. When the variable cost line is drawn starting "on top" of the fixed costs, it **also serves as the total cost line.**

4 Label the point at which the revenue line crosses the total cost line as the **break-even point.**

The operating profit or loss expected at any sales volume may be read from the cost-volume-profit graph. For example, the break-even point (zero profit) for a Hannigan's store is at **1,250** gallons per month, or $15,000 in sales revenue. At this point, total revenue is exactly equal to total costs and expenses, as verified below:

Computation verifying the break-even point in our graph

Revenue (1,250 gallons × $12 per gallon)		*$15,000*
Costs and expenses:		
Fixed	*$9,000*	
Variable (1,250 gallons × $4.80 per gallon)	*6,000*	*15,000*
Operating income		*$ -0-*

On the other hand, if a sales volume of 3,000 gallons per month is achieved, the monthly operating income will amount to $12,600 ($36,000 revenue, less $23,400 in total costs).

We will now explore the use of several mathematical formulas which will enable us to focus more quickly and easily upon specific cost-volume-profit relationships.

OBJECTIVE 4
Explain contribution margin; compute contribution margin per unit and contribution margin ratio.

Contribution Margin: A Key Relationship

Variable costs vary in direct proportion to revenue. Thus, the generation of an additional dollar of revenue also generates some amount of variable costs. The operating data for our Hannigan's ice cream stores (page 1086) indicate that variable costs (such as the cost of ice cream) account for 40% of the company's sales revenue. Thus, for every $100 in revenue, the company may expect to pay out $40 to cover the related variable costs. The remaining $60 is called the **contribution margin.**

The contribution margin is the **amount of revenue in excess of variable costs.** This portion of the revenue is available to cover the company's fixed costs and, after all fixed costs have been covered, provide an operating profit. The allocation of the average revenue dollar between the variable costs relating to the sale and the contribution margin is illustrated below for a typical Hannigan's store:

40¢ of each revenue dollar is consumed by variable expenses relating to the sale.

60¢ of each revenue dollar is available to cover fixed expenses and operating income. This is called the *contribution margin*.

Contribution margin may be expressed either as a total dollar amount for the period (total revenue minus total variable costs) or as an amount per unit (unit sales price minus variable costs per unit). For example, the contribution margin *per gallon* of ice cream sold at a typical Hannigan's store is *$7.20,* computed as follows (per-gallon data from page 1086):

Unit Contribution Margin = Unit Sales Price − Variable Costs per Unit
= $12.00 − $4.80
= $7.20

Contribution Margin Ratio In CVP analysis, it is often useful to express contribution margin as a *percentage of revenue.* This percentage, called the ***contribution margin ratio,*** may be computed using either the total contribution margin or the contribution margin per unit. The relationships are as follows:

$$\text{Contribution Margin Ratio} = \frac{\text{Total Contribution Margin}}{\text{Total Revenue}}$$

and/or

$$\text{Contribution Margin Ratio} = \frac{\text{Unit Contribution Margin}}{\text{Unit Sales Price}}$$

Using the per-unit data on page 1086, the contribution margin ratio of a typical Hannigan's store is *60%,* computed as follows:

$$\text{Contribution Margin Ratio} = \frac{\$7.20}{\$12.00} = \textbf{60\%}$$

A contribution margin of 60% means that 60% of the revenue earned in a Hannigan's store contributes toward covering fixed costs and providing operating income. The other 40% of revenue earned is consumed by variable expenses.

Let us now see how management makes use of such measurements as contribution margin and contribution margin ratio.

OBJECTIVE 5
Determine the sales volume required to earn a desired level of operating income.

How Many Units Must We Sell?

The concept of contribution margin provides a quick means of determining the ***unit sales volume*** required for a business to break even or to earn any desired level of operating income. Break-even sales volume can be of vital importance, especially to companies deciding whether to introduce a new product line, build a new plant, or, in some cases, remain in business.

CASE IN POINT   Chrysler Corp., widely believed to be heading for bankruptcy during the early 1980s, undertook a severe cost-cutting program and altered marketing strategies in an effort to lower the company's breakeven point. In 1981, Chrysler had a break-even point of 1,413,000 vehicles; sales amounted to 1,282,000 vehicles and the company incurred substantial losses. For 1982, the company was able to reduce its break-even point to 1,244,000 vehicles. Chrysler surprised many people in the financial community by returning to profitable operations in 1982 with sales of approximately 1,400,000 vehicles. This "turnaround year" may well have saved Chrysler Corp. Notice, however, that the 1982 sales volume would have resulted in a net loss had Chrysler not been able to lower its break-even point.

To illustrate the relationship between sales volume and contribution margin, assume that we want to know how many gallons of ice cream a Hannigan's store must sell to break even. At the break-even point, the store must earn a contribution large enough to cover all fixed costs. The data on page 1086 show that the monthly fixed costs amount to **$9,000,** and that the contribution margin per gallon of ice cream is **$7.20** ($12.00 sales price minus $4.80 variable costs). If the sale of each gallon covers $7.20 of fixed costs, how many gallons must be sold to cover monthly fixed costs of $9,000? The answer is 1,250 gallons per month, as shown below:

$$\text{Sales Volume (in units)} = \frac{\$9,000}{\$7.20 \text{ per gallon}} = 1{,}250 \text{ gallons per month}$$

Notice that this answer corresponds to the sales volume shown in the cost-volume-profit graph on page 1087.

The reasoning in our above analysis may be summarized by the following formula:

$$\text{Sales Volume (in units)} = \frac{\text{Fixed Costs} + \text{Target Profit}}{\text{Unit Contribution Margin}}$$

With this formula, we may find not only the break-even sales volume (at which operating income is zero), but also the unit sales volume needed to achieve **any desired level of operating income.** For example, how many gallons of ice cream must be sold for a Hannigan's store to earn a monthly operating income of **$4,500?**

$$\text{Sales Volume (in units)} = \frac{\$9,000 + \$4,500}{\$7.20} = 1{,}875 \text{ gallons per month}$$

Finding Required Dollar Sales Volume   To find the **dollar sales volume** needed to earn a given level of operating income, we could first compute the required unit sales and then multiply our answer by the unit sales price. Using the data from our preceding example, a Hannigan's store expecting to earn a monthly operating income of $4,500 would need sales revenue of $22,500 (1,875 gallons × $12 per gallon).

As a more direct approach, we may compute the required dollar sales volume by substituting the **contribution margin ratio** for the contribution margin per unit in our sales volume formula. The formula then becomes:

$$\text{Sales Volume (in dollars)} = \frac{\text{Fixed Costs} + \text{Target Profit}}{\text{Contribution Margin Ratio}}$$

To illustrate, let us again compute the sales volume required for a Hannigan's store to earn a monthly operating income of $4,500:

$$\text{Sales Volume (in dollars)} = \frac{\$9,000 + \$4,500}{.60} = \textbf{\$22,500 per month}$$

Margin of Safety The amount by which actual sales volume **exceeds** the break-even sales volume is called the margin of safety. This is the dollar amount by which sales could **decline** before the company will incur an operating loss. A typical Hannigan's store has a break-even sales volume of $15,000 per month.

$$\text{Sales Volume (in dollars)} = \frac{\$9,000}{.60} = \textbf{\$15,000 per month}$$

Therefore, a store with actual sales of $22,500 has a **margin of safety** of $7,500; a store with sales of $25,000 has a margin of safety of **$10,000** ($25,000 − $15,000).

The margin of safety provides us with a quick means of estimating operating income at any sales volume above the break-even point, as shown below:

Operating Income = Margin of Safety × Contribution Margin Ratio

The rationale for this formula stems from the fact that the margin of safety represents sales dollars **in excess of** the break-even point. Therefore, fixed costs have already been covered and the **entire contribution margin from these sales increases operating income.**

To illustrate this concept, let us estimate the operating income of a Hannigan's store with a sales volume of $22,500, which is $7,500 above the break-even point. The estimated operating income is **$4,500** ($7,500 × 60%). (Notice that this answer is consistent with our earlier computations.)

Changes in Operating Income The contribution margin ratio in our example is 60%, which means that 60 cents out of every revenue dollar goes toward covering fixed costs (which reduces an operating loss) or toward increasing operating income. Thus, every additional dollar of sales improves Hannigan's profit picture by 60 cents. Conversely, a $1 sales decline lowers profitability by 60 cents. This relationship may be summarized as follows:

$$\frac{\text{Change in}}{\text{Operating Income}} = \frac{\text{Change in}}{\text{Sales Volume}} \times \frac{\text{Contribution}}{\text{Margin Ratio}}$$

OBJECTIVE 6 Use the contribution margin ratio to estimate the effect upon operating income of changes in sales volume.

To illustrate, let us assume that the sales volume at a given ice cream store increases from $15,000 (the break-even point) to $22,500, an increase of $7,500. According to the above equation, the operating income of the store should increase by **$4,500** ($7,500 × 60%). This increase may be verified by reference to our earlier calculations. On page 1088, we showed that a sales volume of $15,000 is the break-even point for a Hannigan's store; operating income at this sales volume, therefore, is zero. Also, in an earlier section, we determined that the sales volume required to earn a target profit of $4,500 is $22,500.

Using Cost-Volume-Profit Relationships

OBJECTIVE 7 Use cost-volume-profit relationships in evaluating various marketing strategies.

Cost-volume-profit relationships are widely used during the budgeting process to set sales targets, and to estimate costs and expenses. In addition, these relationships can provide information which is useful in a wide variety of planning decisions. To illustrate, let us consider several ways in which cost-volume-profit relationships might be used by the management of Hannigan's Ice Cream Company in planning marketing strategies:

1 **Question:** To increase volume, management is considering a policy of giving greater discounts on gallon and half-gallon packages of ice cream. It is estimated that the effect of this pricing policy would be to reduce the average selling price per gallon by $1.20 (that is, from $12 per gallon to $10.80). Management is interested in knowing the effect of such a price reduction on the **number of gallons** of ice cream a store must sell to break even.

Analysis: The proposed change in average sales price changes the contribution margin per gallon of ice cream from $7.20 to $6.00, as shown below:

$$\text{Unit Contribution Margin} = \text{Unit Sales Price} - \text{Variable Costs per Unit}$$
$$= \$10.80 - \$4.80$$
$$= \$6.00$$

The fixed operating expenses remain unchanged by this pricing decision. Therefore, the unit sales volume **to break even** under the new pricing situation would be:

$$\text{Sales Volume (in units)} = \frac{\text{Fixed Costs} + \text{Target Profit}}{\text{Unit Contribution Margin}}$$
$$= \frac{\$9,000 + \$0}{\$6.00}$$
$$= \textbf{1,500 gallons per month}$$

This new break-even point, 1,500 gallons, is 20% higher than the present 1,250 gallon break-even volume. Thus, management should be advised that the proposed pricing policy is desirable only if the unit sales volume per store can be expected to increase 20% per month as a result of the lower sales prices on gallon and half-gallon packages.

2 **Question:** Management is considering a change in the method of compensating store managers. Instead of a fixed salary of $2,400 per month, it is proposed that managers be put on a salary of $1,740 per month plus a commission of 72 cents per gallon of sales. The present average monthly operating income per store is $3,000 on sales of $20,000 (Proof: $20,000 × 60% − $9,000 = $3,000). What sales revenue per store will be necessary to produce the same monthly income to Hannigan's under the proposed incentive compensation arrangement?

Analysis: This proposal involves a change in both the contribution margin ratio and the fixed monthly operating expenses. Adding 72 cents per gallon to variable costs raises the total variable cost to $5.52 per gallon and reduces the contribution margin ratio to 54%, as computed below: *was 60%*

$$\text{Contribution Margin Ratio} = \frac{\text{Unit Sales Price} - \text{Variable Costs per Unit}}{\text{Unit Sales Price}}$$

$$= \frac{\$12.00 - \$5.52}{\$12.00}$$

$$= 54\%$$

Cutting the manager's salary from $2,400 to $1,740 per month will reduce monthly fixed costs from $9,000 to $8,340. The sales volume required to produce a monthly operating income of $3,000 may be computed as follows:

$$\text{Sales Volume (in dollars)} = \frac{\text{Fixed Costs} + \text{Target Profit}}{\text{Contribution Margin Ratio}}$$

$$= \frac{\$8,340 + \$3,000}{.54}$$

$$= \$21,000 \text{ per month}$$

To produce the same $3,000 per month operating income under the new compensation plan, sales volume per store would have to be increased by $1,000 (or $83\frac{1}{3}$ gallons) over the current monthly sales volume of $20,000. The issue thus boils down to whether the incentive compensation arrangement will induce store managers to increase volume by more than $83\frac{1}{3}$ gallons per month. Cost-volume-profit analysis does not answer this question, but it provides the information which enables management to exercise its judgment intelligently.

3 *Question:* Hannigan's Ice Cream Company stores are now open 12 hours each day (from 9 A.M. to 9 P.M.). Management is considering a proposal to decrease store hours by opening two hours later each morning. It is estimated that this policy would reduce sales volume by an average of 125 gallons per month and would cut fixed costs (utilities and wages) by $1,100 per month. Would it pay the company to change its store hours?

Analysis: The loss of 125 gallons of sales per month would decrease revenue by $1,500 (125 × $12). This would result in the loss of contribution margin of $900 ($1,500 × 60%). Therefore, whether the reduction in store hours would increase operating income per store may be determined as follows:

Reduction in fixed costs	$1,100
Less: Loss of contribution margin ($1,500 × 60%)	900
Prospective increase in monthly operating income per store	$ 200

Importance of Sales Mix in Cost-Volume-Profit Analysis

In our example of Hannigan's Ice Cream Company, we assumed that the contribution margin ratio **averaged** 60% of sales expressed in dollars and that the **average** selling price was $12 per gallon of ice cream sold. Let us now change our example and assume that a detailed analysis indicated that ice cream is actually sold in the following varieties:

	Hand-packed Quart	Prepackaged Half-gallon	Cones and Novelties
Unit sales price	$4.00	$5.00	$1.60
Less: Variable costs per unit...................	1.50	2.50	.40
Unit contribution margin	$2.50	$2.50	$1.20
Contribution margin ratio (unit contribution margin ÷ sales price)	62.5%	50%	75%
Break-even sales volume, assuming that only the one type of product is sold (fixed costs, $9,000, divided by contribution margin ratio) .	$14,400	$18,000	$12,000

Earlier in this chapter we stated that Hannigan's Ice Cream Company is now selling a certain *mix* of the three sizes and that a sales volume of $15,000 is required to break even ($9,000 ÷ *average* contribution margin ratio of 60%). If ice cream were sold exclusively in quarts, sales of $14,400 would be required to break even; if only half-gallon packages were sold, the break-even sales volume would be $18,000; if only cones and novelties were sold, the break-even sales volume would be $12,000. The reason the break-even sales volume differs for each size is because each size yields a different contribution margin per dollar of sales (contribution margin ratio). *The higher the contribution margin ratio, the lower the sales volume that is required to cover a given amount of fixed expenses.*

The amount of operating income earned by a business unit depends not only on the volume of sales and the ability to control expenses, but also on the *quality* of sales. At any given sales volume, selling products with high contribution margin ratios is more profitable than selling products with low contribution margin ratios. Thus, sales with high contribution margin ratios are said to be *high-quality sales.* A shift from low-margin sales to high-margin sales can increase net income even though total sales volume may decline. On the other hand, a shift from high-margin to low-margin sales can cause profits to fall even though total sales may increase.

Contribution Margin per Unit of Scarce Resource

The contribution margin approach is useful to management in deciding what products to manufacture (or purchase for resale) and what products

to eliminate when certain factors of production are available only in limited quantity. One of the important functions of management is to develop the most profitable uses of such scarce resources as raw materials, skilled labor, high-cost equipment, and factory floor space.

Assume that you are offered two equally satisfactory jobs, one paying $6 per hour and one paying $9 per hour. Since your time is scarce and you wish to maximize the pay that you receive for an hour of your time, you would naturally choose the job paying $9 per hour. For the same reason, if a company has the capacity to utilize only 100,000 direct labor hours per year, management would want to use this capacity in such a way as *to produce the maximum contribution margin per hour of direct labor.*

To illustrate this concept, assume that Optic Corporation is considering the production of three products. The contribution margin per direct labor hour required to produce each of the three products is estimated as follows:

OPTIC CORPORATION
Contribution Margin per Hour of Direct Labor

	Unit Sales Price	−	Variable Expenses	=	Unit Contribution Margin	÷	Direct Labor Hours Required per Unit Produced	=	Contribution Margin per Direct Labor Hour
A ...	$100		$60		$40		10		$ 4
B ...	80		50		30		5		6
C ...	60		40		20		2		10

Should output of product C be expanded?

Notice that the manufacture of a unit of product A requires 10 hours of direct labor and generates $40 in contribution margin; a unit of product B requires only 5 hours of direct labor and yields $30 of contribution margin; finally, product C requires only 2 hours of direct labor and yields $20 in contribution margin. Thus, product C produces the ***largest amount of contribution margin per hour of direct labor.*** Even though product A has the highest contribution margin per unit ($40) and the highest contribution margin ratio (40%), it is the least profitable of the three products in terms of contribution margin ***per hour of direct labor.***

When a company's total output is limited by the scarcity of one particular resource, the company should attempt to maximize the contribution margin per unit of this scarce resource. To illustrate this idea, the following table shows the amounts of contribution margin that Optic would earn if it devoted all 100,000 available direct labor hours exclusively to the manufacture of each of the three products under consideration:

Product	Total Capacity (Hours)	×	Contribution Margin per Hour of Direct Labor	=	Total Contribution Margin If Only One Product Is Manufactured
A	100,000		$ 4		$ 400,000
B	100,000		6		600,000
C	100,000		10		1,000,000

Which is the most profitable product?

This schedule clearly shows that the company can maximize its contribution margin and, therefore, its operating income by concentrating its manufacturing efforts on ***product C.***

In most cases, however, a company cannot simply devote all of its efforts to manufacturing the single product that is the most profitable. For example, the demand for product C may not be sufficient to allow the company to sell all the units of this product that it can produce. In this case, the company should produce units of product B after it has met the demand for product C. It should produce product A only after it has met the total demand for both products B and C.

Another consideration is that the production and sale of products A or B may be ***necessary to support the sales of product C.*** Often, the profit margins are much lower on these "supporting" products. Gillette, for example, manufactures blade-razors which it sells at or below cost. Why? The answer is that the sale of razors promotes the sale of razor blades, which are products with a high contribution margin.

In conclusion, most companies are not able to devote all their manufacturing efforts to the single product that provides the highest contribution margin per unit of the resource that limits the company's production. However, if the sales of different products are independent of one another, the company will maximize its total contribution margin by first meeting the demand for those products with the highest contribution margins *per unit of this scarce resource.*

Assumptions Underlying Cost-Volume-Profit Analysis

In cost-volume-profit analysis, accountants assume the following:

1 Sales price per unit remains constant.
2 If more than one product is sold, the proportion of the various products sold (sales mix) is assumed to be constant.
3 Fixed costs (expenses) remain constant at all levels of sales within the assumed relevant range of activity.
4 Variable costs (expenses) remain constant as a percentage of sales revenue.
5 For a business engaged in manufacturing, the number of units produced is assumed to be equal to the number of units sold.

These assumptions simplify cost-volume-profit analysis. In actual practice, however, some of these assumptions may not hold true. However, cost-volume-profit analysis is still a useful planning tool for management. As changes take place in selling prices, sales mix, expenses, and production levels, management should update and revise its analysis.

Summary of Basic Cost-Volume-Profit Relationships

In this chapter, we have demonstrated a number of ratios and mathematical relationships which are useful in cost-volume-profit analysis. For your convenience, these relationships are summarized below:

Measurement	Method of Computation
Contribution margin	Sales Revenue − Total Variable Costs
Unit contribution margin	Unit Sales Price − Variable Costs per Unit
Contribution margin ratio	$\dfrac{\text{Unit Sales Price} - \text{Variable Costs per Unit}}{\text{Unit Sales Price}}$
	or
	$\dfrac{\text{Sales} - \text{Total Variable Costs}}{\text{Sales}}$
Sales volume (in units)	$\dfrac{\text{Fixed costs} + \text{Target Profit*}}{\text{Unit Contribution Margin}}$
Sales volume (in dollars)	$\dfrac{\text{Fixed costs} + \text{Target Profit*}}{\text{Contribution Margin Ratio}}$
Margin of safety	Actual Sales Volume − Break-Even Sales Volume
Operating income	Margin of Safety × Contribution Margin Ratio
Change in operating income	Change in Sales Volume × Contribution Margin Ratio

* Target "profit" represents target **operating income.**

END-OF-CHAPTER REVIEW

SUMMARY OF CHAPTER LEARNING OBJECTIVES

1   **Explain how fixed, variable, and semivariable costs respond to changes in the level of business activity.**
Fixed costs (fixed expenses) remain unchanged despite changes in sales volume, while variable costs (or expenses) change in direct proportion to changes in sales volume. With a semivariable cost, part of the cost is fixed and part is variable. Semivariable costs change in response to a change in the level of activity, but they change by less than a proportionate amount.

2   **Use the high-low method to separate the fixed and variable elements of a semivariable cost.**
This technique is based upon analysis of a semivariable cost occurring at two levels of activity: the highest and the lowest activity levels during a reasonable time frame. To determine the variable portion of a semivariable cost, the change in cost is divided by the change in activity level, yielding the variable cost per unit. The fixed cost is then determined by deducting total variable cost from total semivariable cost at any activity level. The fixed cost and the variable cost per unit are then used to develop a cost formula for the semivariable cost.

3   **Prepare a cost-volume-profit (break-even) graph.**
The vertical axis on a break-even graph is dollars of revenue or costs, and the horizontal axis is unit sales. Lines are plotted on the graph showing revenue and total costs. The vertical distance between these lines represents the amount of operating income (or loss). The lines intersect at the break-even point.

4   **Explain contribution margin; compute contribution margin per unit and contribution margin ratio.**
Contribution margin is the excess of revenue over variable costs. Thus, it represents the amount of revenue available to cover fixed costs and to provide an operating profit. Contribution margin may be expressed in total dollars, on a per-unit basis (sales price per unit minus variable costs per unit), or as a percentage of sales. Contribution margin stated as a percentage of sales price is called the *contribution margin ratio.*

5   **Determine the sales volume required to earn a desired level of operating income.**
The sales volume *(in units)* required to earn a target profit is equal to the sum of the fixed costs plus the target profit, divided by the *unit* contribution margin. To determine the sales volume in *dollars,* the sum of the fixed costs plus the target profit is divided by the *contribution margin ratio.* These formulas are summarized on page 1096.

6   **Use the contribution margin ratio to estimate the effect upon operating income of changes in sales volume.**
Multiplying the expected dollar change in sales volume by the contribution margin ratio indicates the expected change in operating income.

7   **Use cost-volume-profit relationships in evaluating various marketing strategies.**
Through cost-volume-profit analysis, we may estimate the effects upon operating income of changes in sales price, unit sales volume, and the

level of expenses. The use of CVP analysis to evaluate various marketing strategies is demonstrated on pages 1092 and 1093.

8 **Determine the sales mix that will maximize the contribution margin per unit of a scarce resource.**
The quantity of goods or services which a business can produce often is limited by the scarcity of a particular resource, such as direct labor hours or machine hours. In these cases, the company can maximize its profits by producing those products with the highest contribution margin per unit of the scarce resource.

An understanding of cost behavior—the manner in which costs normally respond to changes in the level of activity—is required in each remaining chapter of this textbook. In these chapters, we will explore the use of accounting information in evaluating the performance of managers and departments, in planning future business operations, and in making numerous types of managerial decisions. The concepts and terminology introduced in Chapter 23 will be used extensively in these discussions.

KEY TERMS INTRODUCED OR EMPHASIZED IN CHAPTER 23

Activity base   The scale used in measuring an activity which serves as a **cost driver** of variable and semivariable cost.

Break-even point   The level of sales at which a company neither earns an operating profit nor incurs a loss. Revenue exactly covers costs and expenses.

Cost driver   A type of activity that has a causal effect in the occurrence of a particular cost.

Cost formula   A mathematical statement expressing the expected amount of a cost in terms of the fixed element of the cost and/or the portion of the cost that varies in response to changes in some activity base. For example, the cost formula for a semivariable cost might be: $2,500 per month, plus 5% of net sales.

Contribution margin   Sales minus variable costs. The portion of sales revenue which is not consumed by variable costs and, therefore, is available to cover fixed costs and contribute to operating income.

Contribution margin per unit   The excess of unit sales price over variable cost per unit; the dollar amount contributed by the sale **of each unit** toward covering fixed costs and generating operating income.

Contribution margin ratio   The contribution margin expressed as a percentage of sales price. Represents the percentage of each revenue dollar which is available to cover fixed costs or to provide an operating profit.

Fixed costs   Costs and expenses that remain unchanged despite changes in the level of the activity base.

High-low method   A method of dividing a semivariable (or mixed) cost into its fixed and variable elements by relating the change in the cost to the change in the activity base between the highest and lowest levels of observed activity.

Margin of safety   Amount by which actual sales exceed the break-even point.

Relevant volume range   The span or range of output over which output is likely to vary and assumptions about cost behavior are generally valid. Excludes extreme volume variations.

Semivariable costs   Costs and expenses that respond to change in the level of the activity base by less than a proportionate amount.

Variable costs   Costs and expenses that vary directly and proportionately with changes in the level of the activity base.

DEMONSTRATION PROBLEM FOR YOUR REVIEW

The management of the Fresno Processing Company has engaged you to assist in the development of information to be used for managerial decisions.

The company has the capacity to process 20,000 tons of cottonseed per year. The yield from a ton of cottonseed is as shown below.

Product	Average Yield per Ton* of Cottonseed	Average Selling Price	Total Revenue
Oil......................................	400 pounds	$ 0.25 per pound	$100
Meal	600 pounds	160.00 per ton	48
Hulls.....................................	800 pounds	100.00 per ton	40
Lint......................................	200 pounds	0.06 per pound	12
Total	2,000 pounds		$200

*   There are 2,000 pounds in a ton.

A special marketing study revealed that the company can expect to sell its entire output for the coming year at the average selling prices listed above.

You have determined the company's cost structure to be as follows:

Cost of cottonseed:	$80 per ton
Processing costs:	
Variable:	$26 per ton of cottonseed processed
Fixed:	$340,000 per year at all levels of production
Marketing costs:	All variable, $44 per ton of all products sold
Administrative costs:	All fixed, $300,000 per year at all levels of production and sales activity

INSTRUCTIONS

a   Compute (1) the contribution margin and (2) the contribution margin ratio per ton of cottonseed processed.

b   Compute the break-even sales volume in (1) dollars and (2) tons of cottonseed.

c   Assume that the company's budget calls for an operating income of $240,000. Compute the sales volume required to reach this profit objective, stated (1) in dollars and (2) in tons of cottonseed.

d   Compute the maximum amount that the company can afford to pay per ton of raw cottonseed and still break even by processing and selling 16,000 tons during the current year.

SOLUTION TO DEMONSTRATION PROBLEM

a (1) *Total revenue per ton of cotton seed*		$200
Less: Variable Costs:		
Cottonseed	$80	
Processing	26	
Marketing...	44	150
Unit contribution margin ($200 − $150).................................		$ 50
(2) *Contribution margin ratio ($50 ÷ $200)*		25%

b **(1)** *Break-even dollar sales volume:*

Fixed costs ($340,000 + $300,000)	$ 640,000
Contribution margin ratio **(part a)**.....................................	25%
Break-even dollar sales volume ($640,000 ÷ .25).....................	$2,560,000

(2) *Break-even unit sales volume (in tons):*

Fixed costs (per above)	$ 640,000
Unit contribution margin **(part a)**......................................	$ 50
Break-even unit sales volume, stated in tons of	
cottonseed products ($640,000 ÷ $50).............................	12,800

(Alternative computation: break-even dollar sales volume, $2,560,000, divided by unit sales price, $200, equals 12,800 tons.)

c **(1)** *Required dollar sales volume:*

Fixed expenses	$ 640,000
Add: Target profit	240,000
Required contribution margin..	$ 880,000
Contribution margin ratio **(part a)**....................................	25%
Required dollar sales volume.......................................	$3,520,000

(2) *Required unit sales volume:*

Required dollar sales volume [from (1)]	$3,520,000
Unit sales price	$ 200
Required unit sales volume, in tons	
($3,520,000 ÷ $200)...	17,600

(Alternative computation: required contribution margin to cover fixed expenses and target profit, $880,000, [part c(1)], divided by unit contribution margin, $50 per ton, equals 17,600 tons.)

d

Total revenue (16,000 tons × $200).....................................		$3,200,000
Less: Costs other than cottonseed:		
Processing (16,000 tons × $26)	$416,000	
Marketing (16,000 tons × $44)	704,000	
Fixed costs	640,000	1,760,000
Maximum amount that can be paid for 16,000 tons of		
cottonseed, while allowing company to break even.....................		$1,440,000
Maximum amount that can be paid per ton of cottonseed, while		
allowing company to break even ($1,440,000 ÷ 16,000 tons).............		$90

SELF-TEST QUESTIONS

Answers to these questions appear on page 1112.

1 During the current year, the net sales of Ridgeway, Inc., were 10% below last year's level. You should expect Ridgeway's semivariable costs to:

  a   Decrease in total, but increase as a percentage of net sales.

  b   Increase in total and increase as a percentage of net sales.

  c   Decrease in total and decrease as a percentage of net sales.

  d   Increase in total, but decrease as a percentage of net sales.

2   Shown below are the monthly high and low levels of direct labor hours and of total manufacturing overhead for Apex Mfg. Co.:

	Direct Labor Hours	Total Manufacturing Overhead
Highest observed level.......................................	6,000	$17,000
Lowest observed level	4,000	14,000

In a month in which 5,000 direct labor hours are used, the ***fixed element*** of total manufacturing overhead costs should be approximately:

a $15,500.   b $8,000.   c $7,500.   d $8,000 plus $1.50 per unit.

3   Marston Company sells a single product at a sales price of $50 per unit. Fixed costs total $15,000 per month, and variable costs amount to $20 per unit. If management reduces the sales price of this product by $5 per unit, the sales volume needed for the company to break-even will:

a Increase by $5,000.   c Increase by $2,000.

b Increase by $4,500.   d Remain unchanged.

4   Becker Auto Supply earns an average contribution margin ratio of 40% on its sales. The store manager estimates that by spending an additional $5,000 per month for radio advertising, the store will be able to increase its operating income by $3,000 per month. The manager is expecting the radio advertising to increase monthly dollar sales volume by:

a $12,500.   b $8,000.   c $7,500.   d Some other amount.

5   Elco Corporation manufactures two products. Data concerning these products is shown below:

	Product A	Product B
Total monthly demand for product..........................	1,000 units	500 units
Sales price per unit...	$400	$500
Contribution margin ratio	30%	40%
Direct labor hours to manufacture each unit	5	10

Elco's productive capacity is limited by the availability of only 6,500 direct labor hours each month. If the company is to maximize its operating income, how many units of product B should Elco produce each month?

a None   b 150   c 500   d Some other amount

ASSIGNMENT MATERIAL

DISCUSSION QUESTIONS

1 Why is it important for management to understand cost-volume-profit relationships?

2 What is an ***activity base*** and why is it important in analyzing cost behavior?

3 What is the effect of an increase in activity upon:

a   Total variable costs.

b   Variable costs per unit of activity.

4 What is the effect of an increase in activity upon:

a Total fixed costs.

b Fixed costs per unit of activity.

5 The simplifying assumption that costs and volume vary in straight-line relationships makes the analysis of cost behavior much easier. What factors make this a reasonable and useful assumption in many cases?

6 Define the **relevant range** of activity.

7 Explain how the high-low method determines:

a The variable portion of a semivariable cost.

b The fixed portion of a semivariable cost.

8 Define (a) **contribution margin** and (b) **contribution margin ratio.**

9 What important relationships are shown on a cost-volume-profit (break-even) graph?

10 Klein Company has an average contribution margin ratio of 35%. What dollar sales volume per month is necessary to produce a monthly operating income of $30,000, if fixed costs are $145,000 per month?

11 Explain how the unit contribution margin can be used to determine the unit sales required to break even.

12 Hurst Company has variable costs of $26 per unit and a contribution margin ratio of 35%. Compute the selling price per unit.

13 Define **margin of safety.**

14 Explain the probable effect upon operating income of a $19,000 increase in sales volume by a company with variable costs of $75 per unit and a contribution margin ratio of 40%.

15 An executive of a large American steel company put the blame for lower net income for a recent fiscal period on the "shift in product mix to a higher proportion of export sales." Sales for the period increased slightly while net income declined by 28%. Explain how a change in product (sales) mix to a higher proportion in export sales would result in a lower level of net income.

16 Why is it helpful to know the approximate amount of contribution margin generated from the use of a scarce resource such as a machine-hour or an hour of direct labor?

17 The president of an airline blamed a profit squeeze on "unwise and unjustifiable promotional fares." He pointed out that 50% of the company's revenue came from "discount fares." Explain why discount fares tend to reduce net income and point out circumstances in which a discount from the regular price of a plane fare could **increase** net income.

EXERCISES

EXERCISE 23-1
Accounting Terminology

Listed below are nine technical accounting terms introduced in this chapter:

Variable costs	Relevant range	Contribution margin ratio
Break-even point	Fixed costs	Semivariable costs
Margin of safety	Sales mix	Unit contribution margin

Each of the following statements may (or may not) describe one of these technical terms. For each statement, indicate the accounting term described, or answer "None" if the statement does not correctly describe any of the terms.

a The level of sales at which revenue exactly equals costs and expenses.

b Costs that remain unchanged despite changes in sales volume.

c The span over which output is likely to vary and assumptions about cost behavior generally remain valid.

d Contribution margin per unit expressed as a percentage of unit sales price.

e Unit sales price minus variable costs per unit.

f The amount by which sales volume exceeds the break-even point.

g Costs that respond to changes in sales volume by less than a proportionate amount.

h Operating income less variable costs.

EXERCISE 23-2
Patterns of Cost Behavior

Explain the effects of an increase in the volume of activity upon the following costs. (Assume volume remains within the relevant range.)

a Total variable costs

b Variable costs per unit

c Total fixed costs

d Fixed costs per unit

e Total semivariable costs

f Semivariable costs per unit

EXERCISE 23-3
Classification of Various Costs

Explain whether you regard each of the following costs or categories of costs as fixed, variable, or semivariable with respect to net sales. Briefly explain your reasoning. If you do not believe that a cost fits into any of these classifications, explain.

a The cost of goods sold.

b Salaries to salespeople. (These salaries include a monthly minimum amount, plus a commission on all sales.)

c Income taxes expense.

d Property taxes expense.

e Depreciation expense on a sales showroom, based upon the straight-line method of depreciation.

f Depreciation expense on a sales showroom, based upon the double-declining-balance method of depreciation.

EXERCISE 23-4
High-Low Method of Cost Analysis

The following information is available regarding the total manufacturing overhead of Drew Mfg. Co. for a recent four-month period:

	Machine-Hours	Manufacturing Overhead
March	3,000	$122,250
April	2,500	114,000
May	3,500	132,750
June	4,000	141,000

a Use the high-low method to determine:

1 The variable element of manufacturing overhead costs per machine-hour.

2 The fixed element of monthly overhead cost.

b Use the cost relationships determined in part **a** to estimate the total manufacturing overhead expected to be incurred at an activity level of 3,800 machine-hours.

EXERCISE 23-5
Using a Cost Formula

City Ambulance Service estimates the monthly cost of responding to emergency calls to be $19,500 plus $110 per call.

a In a month in which the company responds to 125 emergency calls, determine the estimated:

1 Total cost of responding to emergency calls.

2 Average cost of responding to emergency calls.

b Assume that in a given month, the number of emergency calls was unusually low. Would you expect the average cost of responding to emergency calls during this month to be higher or lower than in other months? Explain.

EXERCISE 23-6
Using a Cost Formula

Through using the high-low method, Regency Hotels estimates the total costs of providing room service meals to amount to $5,950 per month, plus 30% of room service revenue.

a What is the contribution margin ratio of providing room service meals?

b What is the break-even point for room service operations in terms of total room service revenue?

c What would you expect to be the total cost of providing room service in a month in which room service revenue amounts to $15,000?

EXERCISE 23-7
Computing Required Sales Volume

Information concerning a product manufactured by Ames Brothers appears below:

Sales price per unit.	$ 70
Variable cost per unit.	43
Total fixed manufacturing and operating costs (per month).	405,000

Determine the following:

a The unit contribution margin

b The number of units that must be sold each month to break even

c The unit sales level that must be reached in order to earn an operating income of $270,000 per month

EXERCISE 23-8
Computing Sales Volume

Porter Corporation has fixed costs of $660,000, variable costs of $24 per unit, and a contribution margin ratio of 40%.

Compute the following:

a Unit sales price, and unit contribution margin for the above product

b The sales volume in units required for Porter Corporation to earn an operating income of $300,000

c The dollar sales volume required for Porter Corporation to earn an operating income of $300,000

EXERCISE 23-9
Computing Contribution Margin Ratio and Margin of Safety

The information shown below relates to the only product sold by Harper Company:

Sales price per unit..	$ 24
Variable cost per unit...	18
Fixed costs per year..	240,000

a Compute the contribution margin ratio and the dollar sales volume required to break even.

b Assuming that the company sells 75,000 units during the current year, compute the margin of safety sales volume (dollars).

EXERCISE 23-10
Relating Contribution Margin Ratio to Sales Price

Firebird Mfg. Co. has a contribution margin ratio of 45% and must sell 25,000 units at a price of $80 each in order to break even. Compute:

a Total fixed costs.

b Variable costs per unit.

EXERCISE 23-11
Computing the Break-Even Point

Malibu Corporation has fixed costs of $36,000 per month. It sells two products as follows:

	Sales Price	Variable Costs	Contribution Margin
Product no. 1	$10	$4	$6
Product no. 2	10	7	3

a What monthly dollar sales volume is required to break even if two units of product no. 1 are sold with one unit of product no. 2?

b What monthly dollar sales volume is required to break even if one unit of product no. 1 is sold with two units of product no. 2?

EXERCISE 23-12
Cost-Volume-Profit Relationships

For each of the six independent situations below, compute the missing amounts.

a Only one product is manufactured:

	Sales	Variable Costs	Contribution Margin per Unit	Fixed Costs	Operating Income	Units Sold
(1)	$_____	$120,000	$20	$_____	$25,000	4,000
(2)	180,000	_____	____	45,000	30,000	5,000
(3)	600,000	_____	30	150,000	90,000	____

b Many products are manufactured:

	Sales	Variable Costs	Contribution Margin Ratio	Fixed Costs	Operating Income
(1)	$900,000	$720,000	___%	$_____	$95,000
(2)	600,000	_____	40%	_____	75,000
(3)	_____	_____	30%	90,000	60,000

EXERCISE 23-13
Evaluating a Marketing Strategy

Chaps & Saddles, a retailer of tack and western apparel, earns an average contribution margin of 45% on its sales volume. Recently, the advertising manager of a local "country" radio station offered to run numerous radio advertisements for Chaps & Saddles at a monthly cost of $1,800.

Compute the amount by which the proposed radio advertising campaign must increase Chaps & Saddles' monthly sales volume to:

a Pay for itself.

b Increase operating income by $1,000 per month. (Round computations to the nearest dollar.)

PROBLEMS

Group A

PROBLEM 23A-1
Using Cost-Volume-Profit Formulas

MURDER TO GO! writes and manufactures murder mystery parlour games which it sells to retail stores. Shown below is per-unit information relating to the manufacture and sale of this product.

Unit sales price	$ 28
Variable cost per unit	7
Fixed costs per year	240,000

INSTRUCTIONS

Determine the following, showing as part of your answer the formula which you used in your computation. For example, the formula used to determine the contribution margin ratio (part **a**) is:

$$\text{Contribution Margin Ratio} = \frac{\text{Unit Sales Price} - \text{Variable Costs per Unit}}{\text{Unit Sales Price}}$$

a Contribution margin ratio

b Sales volume (in dollars) required to break even

c Sales volume (in dollars) required to earn an annual operating income of $450,000

d The margin of safety sales volume if annual sales total 40,000 units

e Operating income if annual sales total 40,000 units

PROBLEM 23A-2
Setting Sales Price and Computing the Break-Even Point

Thermal Tent, Inc., is a newly organized manufacturing business which plans to manufacture and sell 50,000 units per year of a new product. The following estimates have been made of the company's costs and expenses (other than income taxes):

	Fixed	Variable per Unit
Manufacturing costs:		
Direct materials		$47
Direct labor		32
Manufacturing overhead	$340,000	4
Period expenses:		
Selling expenses		1
Administrative expenses	200,000	
Totals	$540,000	$84

INSTRUCTIONS

a What should the company establish as the sales price per unit if it sets a target of earning an operating income of $260,000 by producing and selling 50,000 units during the first year of operations? (Hint: First compute the required contribution margin per unit.)

b At the unit sales price computed in part **a**, how many units must the company produce and sell to break even? (Assume all units produced are sold.)

c What will be the margin of safety (in dollars) if the company produces and sells 50,000 units at the sales price computed in part **a**? Using the margin of safety, compute operating income at 50,000 units.

d Assume that the marketing manager feels that the price of this product must be no higher than $94 in order to ensure market penetration. Will setting the sales price at $94 enable Thermal Tent to break even, given the plans to manufacture and sell 50,000 units? Explain your answer.

PROBLEM 23A-3
Preparing a "Break-Even" Graph

Stop-n-Shop operates a downtown parking lot containing 800 parking spaces. The lot is open 2,500 hours per year. The parking charge per car is 50 cents per hour; the average customer parks two hours. Stop-n-Shop rents the lot for $7,250 per month. The lot supervisor is paid $24,000 per year. Five employees who handle the parking of cars are paid $300 per week for 50 weeks, plus $600 each for the two-week vacation period. Employees rotate vacations during the slow months when four employees can handle the reduced load of traffic. Lot maintenance, payroll taxes, and other costs of operating the parking lot include fixed costs of $3,000 per month and variable costs of 5 cents per parking-space hour.

INSTRUCTIONS

a Draw a cost-volume-profit graph for Stop-n-Shop on an annual basis. Use thousands of parking-space hours as the measure of volume of activity. [Stop-n-Shop has an annual capacity of 2 million parking-space hours (800 spaces × 2,500 hours per year).]

b What is the contribution margin ratio? What is the annual break-even point in dollars of parking revenue?

c Suppose that the five employees were taken off the hourly wage basis and paid 30 cents per car parked, with the same vacation pay as before. (1) How would this change the contribution margin ratio and total fixed costs? Hint: The variable costs per parking-space hour will now include 15 cents, or one-half of the 30 cents paid to employees per car parked, because the average customer parks for two hours. (2) What annual sales revenue would be necessary to produce operating income of $300,000 under these circumstances?

PROBLEM 23A-4
Determining Optimal Sales Mix

Priestley Equipment Company manufactures three different products. The estimated demand for the products for the current year is such that production will not be able to keep pace with incoming orders. Some pertinent data for each product are listed below:

Product	Estimated Unit Sales	Sales Price	Direct Material Cost	Direct Labor Cost	Variable Manufacturing Overhead
A	15,000	$65	$9	$30	$2 4|
B	8,000	37	3	15	1 /9
C	2,500	55	6	20	1 27

Direct labor costs an average of $10 per hour.

INSTRUCTIONS

a Prepare a schedule showing the contribution margin per one unit of each product and also the contribution margin per one hour of direct labor applied to the production of each class of product.

b If you were able to reduce the production of one of the products in order to meet the demand for the others, what would that product be? Why? Assume that available direct labor hours represent the scarce resource which limits total output.

c Assume that the 45,000 hours of direct labor now used to produce product A are used to produce additional units of product C. What would be the effect on total contribution margin?

PROBLEM 23A-5
Cost-Volume-Profit Analysis; Preparing a Graph

Simon Teguh is considering investing in a vending machine operation involving 20 vending machines located in various plants around the city. The machine manufacturer reports that similar vending machine routes have produced a sales volume ranging from 800 to 1,000 units per machine per month. The following information is made available to Teguh in evaluating the possible profitability of the operation.

1 An investment of $45,000 will be required, $9,000 for merchandise and $36,000 for the 20 machines.

2 The machines have a service life of five years and no salvage value at the end of that period. Depreciation will be computed on the straight-line basis.

3 The merchandise (candy and soft drinks) retails for an average of 75 cents per unit and will cost Teguh an average of 25 cents per unit.

4 Owners of the buildings in which the machines are located are paid a commission of 5 cents per unit of candy and soft drinks sold.

5 One person will be hired to service the machines. The salary will be $1,500 per month.

6 Other expenses are estimated at $600 per month. These expenses do not vary with the number of units sold.

INSTRUCTIONS

a Determine the unit contribution margin and the break-even volume in units and in dollars per month.

b Draw a monthly cost-volume-profit graph for sales volume up to 1,000 units per machine per month.

c What sales volume in units and in dollars per month will be necessary to produce an operating income equal to a 30% annual return on Teguh's $45,000 investment? (Round to the nearest unit.)

d Teguh is considering offering the building owners a flat rental of $30 per machine per month in lieu of the commission of 5 cents per unit sold. What effect would this change in commission arrangement have on his ***monthly*** break-even volume in terms of units?

Group B

PROBLEM 23B-1
Introduction to Cost-Volume-Profit Formulas

Shown below is information relating to the only product sold by EnviroPure, Inc.:

Unit sales price	$ 85
Variable cost per unit	34
Fixed costs per year	390,000

INSTRUCTIONS

Determine the following, showing as part of your answer the formula or relationships you used in your computations. For example, the formula used to determine the contribution margin ratio (part **a**) is:

$$\text{Contribution Margin Ratio} = \frac{\text{Unit Sales Price} - \text{Variable Costs per Unit}}{\text{Unit Sales Price}}$$

a Contribution margin ratio

b Dollar sales volume required to break even

c Dollar sales volume required to earn an annual operating income of $900,000

d The margin of safety if annual sales total 30,000 units

e Operating income if annual sales total 30,000 units

PROBLEM 23B-2
Estimating
Costs and
Profits

High Rollers, Inc., manufactures rollerblades. For the coming year, the company has budgeted the following costs for the production and sale of 30,000 pairs of skates.

	Budgeted Costs	Budgeted Costs per Pair	Percentage of Costs Considered Variable
Direct materials	$ 630,000	21	100%
Direct labor	300,000	10	100
Manufacturing overhead (fixed and variable).......	720,000	24	25
Selling and administrative expenses..............	600,000	20	20
Totals..	$2,250,000	$75	

INSTRUCTIONS

a Compute the sales price per unit that would result in a budgeted operating income of $900,000, assuming that the company produces and sells 30,000 pairs. (Hint: First compute the budgeted sales revenue needed to produce this operating income.)

b Assuming that the company decides to sell the skates at a unit price of $121 per pair, compute the following:

1 Total fixed costs budgeted for the year

2 Variable costs per unit

3 The unit contribution margin

4 The number of pairs that must be produced and sold annually to break even at a sales price of $121 per pair

PROBLEM 23B-3
Drawing a
Cost-Volume-
Profit Graph

Rainbow Paints operates a chain of retail paint stores. Although the paint is sold under the Rainbow label, it is purchased from an independent paint manufacturer. Guy Walker, president of Rainbow Paints, is studying the advisability of opening another store. His estimates of monthly costs for the proposed location are:

Fixed costs:

Occupancy costs..	$3,160
Salaries...	3,640
Other..	1,200
Variable costs (including cost of paint)....................................	$6 per gallon

Although Rainbow stores sell several different types of paint, monthly sales revenue consistently averages $10 per gallon sold.

INSTRUCTIONS

a Compute the contribution margin ratio and the break-even point in dollar sales and in gallons sold for the proposed store.

b Draw a monthly cost-volume-profit graph for the proposed store, assuming 3,000 gallons per month as the maximum sales potential.

c Walker thinks that the proposed store will sell between 2,200 and 2,600 gallons of paint per month. Compute the amount of operating income that would be earned per month at each of these sales volumes.

PROBLEM 23B-4
Determining the Most Profitable Product Given Scarce Resources

Optical Instruments produces two models of binoculars. Information for each model is shown below:

	Model 100	Model 101
Sales price per unit...	$200	$135
Costs and expenses per unit:		
Direct materials	$51	$38
Direct labor	33	30
Manufacturing overhead (applied at the rate of $18		
per machine-hour, $\frac{1}{3}$ of which is fixed and		
$\frac{2}{3}$ variable)	36	18
Variable selling expenses	30	15
Total costs and expenses per unit	150	101
Profit per unit	$ 50	$ 34
Machine-hours required to produce one unit..................	2	1

Total manufacturing overhead amounts to $180,000 per month, one-third of which is fixed. The demand for either product is sufficient to keep the plant operating at full capacity of 10,000 machine-hours per month. Assume that ***only one product is to be produced in the future.***

INSTRUCTIONS

a Prepare a schedule showing the contribution margin per machine-hour for each product.

b Explain your recommendation as to which of the two products should be discontinued.

PROBLEM 23B-5
Analyzing the Effects of Changes in Costs

Precision Systems manufactures tape decks and currently sells 18,500 units annually to producers of sound reproduction systems. Jay Wilson, president of the company, anticipates a 15% increase in the cost per unit of direct labor on January 1 of next year. He expects all other costs and expenses to remain unchanged. Wilson has asked you to assist him in developing the information he needs to formulate a reasonable product strategy for next year.

You are satisfied that volume is the primary factor affecting costs and expenses and have separated the semivariable costs into their fixed and variable segments. Beginning and ending inventories remain at a level of 1,000 units.

Below are the current-year data assembled for your analysis:

Sales price per unit..		$100
Variable costs per unit:		
Direct materials	$10	
Direct labor	20	
Manufacturing overhead and selling and administrative		
expenses	30	60
Contribution margin per unit (40%).........................		$ 40
Fixed costs		$390,000

INSTRUCTIONS

a What increase in the selling price is necessary to cover the 15% increase in direct labor cost and still maintain the current contribution margin ratio of 40%?

b How many tape decks must be sold to maintain the current operating income of ***$350,000*** if the sales price remains at $100 and the 15% wage increase goes into effect? (Hint: First compute the unit contribution margin.)

c Wilson believes that an additional $700,000 of machinery (to be depreciated at 20% annually) will increase present capacity (20,000 units) by 25%. If all tape decks produced can be sold at the present price of $100 per unit and the wage increase goes into effect, how would the estimated operating income before capacity is increased compare with the estimated operating income after capacity is increased? Prepare schedules of estimated operating income at full capacity *before* and *after* the expansion.

CASES AND UNSTRUCTURED PROBLEMS

CASE 23-1
Iacocca's
Dilemma

Assume that you are part of the new management team which has taken over the management of a large diversified automobile manufacturer that is in serious financial condition. Despite several years of large losses, the company's previous management has made practically no changes in the company's operations. The automobiles manufactured by the company are satisfactory in terms of size, style, and fuel economy.

INSTRUCTIONS

a Suggest some actions you might consider in an effort to reduce:

1 Fixed costs.

2 Variable costs per automobile.

b Suggest some ways other than cost reductions by which the company may be able to lower its break-even point.

CASE 23-2
Evaluating
Marketing
Strategies

Purple Cow operates a chain of drive-ins selling primarily ice cream products. The following information is taken from the records of a typical drive-in now operated by the company:

Average selling price of ice cream per gallon	$	*14.80*
Number of gallons sold per month		*3,000*
Variable costs per gallon:		
Ice cream	*$4.60*	
Supplies (cups, cones, toppings, etc.)	*2.20*	
Total variable expenses per gallon	$	*6.80*
Fixed costs per month:		
Rent on building		*$ 2,200.00*
Utilities and upkeep		*760.00*
Wages, including payroll taxes		*4,840.00*
Manager's salary, including payroll taxes but excluding any bonus		*2,500.00*
Other fixed expenses		*1,700.00*
Total fixed costs per month		*$12,000.00*

Based on these data, the monthly break-even sales volume is determined as follows:

$$\frac{\$12,000 \text{ (fixed costs)}}{\$8.00 \text{ (contribution margin per unit)}} = 1{,}500 \text{ gallons (or } \$22{,}200)$$

INSTRUCTIONS

a Currently, all store managers have contracts calling for a bonus of 20 cents per gallon for each gallon sold *beyond* the break-even point. Compute the number of gallons of ice cream that must be sold per month in order to earn a monthly operating income of $10,000 (round to the nearest gallon).

b In order to increase operating income, the company is considering the following two alternatives:

1 Reduce the selling price by an average of $2.00 per gallon. This action is expected to increase the number of gallons sold by 20%. (Under this plan, the manager would be paid a salary of $2,500 per month without a bonus.)

2 Spend $3,000 per month on advertising without any change in selling price. This action is expected to increase the number of gallons sold by 10%. (Under this plan, the manager would be paid a salary of $2,500 per month without a bonus.)

Which of these two alternatives would result in the higher monthly operating income? How many gallons must be sold per month under each alternative in order for a typical outlet to break even? Provide schedules in support of your answers.

c Draft a memo to management indicating your recommendations with respect to these alternative marketing strategies.

ANSWERS TO SELF-TEST QUESTIONS

1 a   **2** b   **2** c (from $25,000 to $27,000)   **4** d ($20,000)   **5** b

Measuring and Evaluating Segment Performance

In this chapter, we focus upon measuring the performance of divisions, departments, and other segments of a business organization. Emphasis is placed upon such topics as responsibility accounting, developing segmented income statements that show subtotals for contribution margin and segment margin, and the use of segment information in evaluating the performance of segments and segment managers.

As a Supplemental Topic we also explore variable costing—a technique for rearranging the information generated by a conventional cost accounting system into a format that is better suited to many types of managerial decisions.

After studying this chapter, you should be able to meet these Learning Objectives:

1 *Explain the need for segment information and describe a responsibility accounting system.*

2 *Prepare segment income statements showing contribution margin and segment margin.*

3 *Distinguish between traceable and common fixed costs.*

4 *Explain the usefulness of contribution margin and segment margin in making short-term and long-term decisions.*

*5 *Explain the differences between full costing and variable costing.*

*6 *Use a variable costing income statement in cost-volume-profit analysis.*

*7 *Explain why short-term fluctuation in the level of production may distort key measurements of segment performance under full costing.*

---

* *Supplemental Topic, "Variable Costing"*

SEGMENTS OF A BUSINESS

Most businesses are organized into a number of different subunits that perform different functions. For example, a manufacturing company typically has departments specializing in purchasing, production, sales, shipping, accounting, finance, and personnel. Production departments and sales departments often are further subdivided along different product lines or geographical areas. Organizing a business in this manner enables managers and employees to specialize in specific types of business activity. Also, this type of organization helps to establish clear lines of managerial responsibility.

Companies use many different names to describe their internal operating units, including divisions, departments, branches, product lines, and sales territories. In our discussion, we generally will use the term **segment** to describe a subunit within a business organization. A designated manager is responsible for directing the activities of each segment within a business organization. Therefore, we also describe segments of a business as **responsibility centers.**

In most business organizations, large responsibility centers are further subdivided into smaller ones. Consider, for example, a retail store within a chain such as Sears or Walmart. Each store is a responsibility center under the control of a store manager. However, each store is further divided into many separate sales departments, such as appliances, automotive products, and sporting goods. Each sales department also is a responsibility center, under the control of a department manager. These department managers report to, and are supervised by, the store manager.

The Need for Information about Segment Performance

An income statement measures the overall performance of a business entity. However, managers also need accounting information measuring the performance of **each segment** within the business organization. This segment information assists managers in:

1 **Planning and allocating resources.** Management needs to know how well various segments of the business are performing in order to set future performance goals and to allocate resources to those segments offering the greatest profit potential. If one product line is more profitable than another, for example, the company's overall profitability may increase by allocating more production capacity to the more profitable product.

2 **Controlling operations.** One use of segment data is to identify those portions of the business that are performing inefficiently or below expectations. When revenue lags, or costs become excessive, segment information helps to focus management's attention upon the segments responsible for the poor performance. If a segment of the business is unprofitable, perhaps it should be discontinued.

3 **Evaluating the performance of segment managers.** As each segment is an area of managerial responsibility, the performance of the segment provides one basis for evaluating the skills of the segment manager.

Thus, measuring the performance of each segment in the business organization is an important function of any accounting system designed to meet the needs of management.

Profit Centers, Investment Centers, and Cost Centers

The segments of a business may be viewed as profit centers, as investment centers, or as cost centers.

Profit Centers   A profit center is a segment of the business that generates **both revenue and costs.**[1] Examples of profit centers include product lines, sales territories, retail outlets, and the specific sales departments within each retail outlet. Even an individual salesperson may be viewed as a profit center within a business organization.

Profit centers are evaluated primarily upon their profitability. Thus, **segmented income statements** are prepared showing the revenue and costs applicable to each profit center. The revenue and costs of each segment may then be compared with budgeted amounts, with the segment's performance in past periods, and, most importantly, with the profitability of other profit centers within the organization. For example, supermarkets view every product line as a separate profit center. Because supermarkets have limited shelf space, they may discontinue even profitable product lines if the related shelf space can be used for still more profitable products.

Investment Centers   Some profit centers also qualify as investment centers. An **investment center** is a profit center for which management is able to measure objectively the cost of the assets used in the center's operations.

The performance of an investment center may be evaluated using return on investment (ROI) measurements. The most common of these measures is **return on assets,** in which the operating income (or **segment margin**) of the segment is expressed as a percentage of the average total assets utilized by the segment during the period.

Not all profit centers can be evaluated as investment centers. For example, if a profit center shares the use of common facilities with other segments of the business, it may be difficult to determine the "amount invested" in the profit center. Thus, profit centers that share common facilities usually are evaluated upon their profitability, but this profitability is not expressed as a "return on investment."

To illustrate the distinction between investment centers and other profit centers, consider a hotel within a national hotel chain, and also the coffee shop within this hotel. Both the hotel and the coffee shop are profit centers. The hotel, however, is also an investment center, because management can readily identify those assets used in the operations of the hotel. The assets utilized by the coffee shop, on the other hand, cannot be determined with anywhere near the same degree of objectivity. For example, the coffee shop uses a small portion of the land, building, and parking lot of the

---

[1]   In this chapter, we will continue the convenient practice of using the term **costs** to describe both costs (such as the cost of goods sold) and expenses.

hotel. Any allocation of such assets among the subunits within the hotel (the coffee shop, dining room, lounge, and guest rooms) would be highly arbitrary. Thus, the coffee shop would be evaluated as a profit center, but not as an investment center.

Cost Centers A *cost center* is a segment of the business that incurs costs (or expenses) but does not directly generate revenue.[2] Production departments in a manufacturing company are examples of cost centers. Service departments, such as accounting, finance, maintenance, and the legal department also are cost centers. Service departments provide services to other segments within the business but do not sell goods or services directly to customers.

Cost centers are evaluated primarily upon (1) their ability to control costs and (2) the *quantity* and the *quality* of the services that they provide to the business organization. As cost centers do not directly generate revenue, segmented income statements are not prepared for these segments of the business. However, the accounting system must accumulate separately the costs incurred by each cost center.

In some cases, costs provide an objective basis for evaluating the performance of a cost center. For example, production departments are evaluated primarily upon the unit costs incurred in manufacturing inventory. For many cost centers, however, nonfinancial criteria are extremely important in assessing the segment's performance. In evaluating the performance of a maintenance department, for example, the question of whether plant assets are maintained in good operating order is an important consideration. Evaluating the performance of an accounting department is even more subjective. Management must compare the costs incurred by the department with the "value" of the department's services to the business. These services include not only meeting the company's financial and income tax reporting requirements, but also providing managers with the information necessary to run the business.

RESPONSIBILITY ACCOUNTING SYSTEMS

*OBJECTIVE 1
Explain the
need for seg-
ment infor-
mation and
describe a
responsibil-
ity account-
ing system.*

An accounting system designed to measure the performance of each responsibility center within a business is termed a *responsibility accounting system.* Measuring performance along the lines of managerial responsibility is an important managerial tool. A responsibility accounting system holds individual managers accountable for the performance of the business segments under their control. In addition, such systems provide top management with information useful in identifying the strong and the weak segments throughout the business organization.

The operation of a responsibility accounting system involves three basic steps. First, *budgets* are prepared for each responsibility center. These budgets serve as targets, with which the segment's actual performance will be compared. Second, the accounting system *measures the performance* of each responsibility center. Third, timely *performance reports* are pre-

---

2   Cost centers sometimes generate insignificant amounts of revenue, but the direct generation of revenue is incidental to the basic purpose of the segment.

pared, comparing the actual performance of each segment with the budgeted amounts. Frequent performance reports help segment managers keep their segments' performance "on target," and they also assist top management in evaluating the performance of each segment and segment manager.

In this chapter, we emphasize the second step in the operation of a responsibility accounting system—measuring the performance of each responsibility center. The use of budgets and of performance reports is discussed in the following chapter.

Responsibility Accounting: An Illustration

OBJECTIVE 2
Prepare segment income statements showing contribution margin and segment margin.

The diagram on the following page shows in condensed form how the monthly performance of profit centers is measured and reported in the responsibility accounting system. The company in our example, NuTech Electronics, is first segmented into two divisions: retail sales and special orders. The Retail Sales Division is further segmented into two stores; each store has two profit centers—a department that sells merchandise and a department that repairs electronic appliances for customers.[3]

As you read down the NuTech illustration, you are looking at smaller and smaller parts of the company. The recording of revenue and costs must begin at the **bottom** of the illustration—that is, for the **smallest** areas of managerial responsibility. If income statements are to be prepared for each profit center in the 42d St. Store, for example, NuTech's chart of accounts must be sufficiently detailed to measure separately the revenue and costs of these departments. The income statements for larger responsibility centers then may be prepared primarily by combining the amounts appearing in the income statements of the smaller subunits. Notice, for example, that the total sales of the 42d St. Store ($200,000) are equal to the sum of the sales reported by the two profit centers within the store ($180,000 and $20,000).

Assigning Revenue and Costs to Segments of a Business

In segment income statements, revenue is assigned first to the profit center responsible for earning that revenue. Assigning revenue to the proper department is relatively easy. Electronic cash registers, for example, automatically classify sales revenue by the department of origin.

In assigning costs to segments of a business, two concepts generally are applied:

1 **Costs are classified into the categories of variable costs and fixed costs.**[4] When costs are classified in this manner, a subtotal may be developed in the income statement showing the **contribution margin** of the business segment. Arranging an income statement in this

---

[3] NuTech also prepares segment income statements showing the profit centers in the Special Orders Division and in the Baker St. Store. To conserve space, these statements are not included in our illustration.

[4] In Chapter 23, we discussed techniques such as the "high-low method" for separating semi-variable costs such as sales salaries and telephone expense into their variable and fixed elements.

ILLUSTRATION OF A RESPONSIBILITY ACCOUNTING SYSTEM

Segments defined as divisions

	Entire Company	Segments	
		Retail Division	Special Orders Division
Sales	$900,000	$500,000	$400,000
Variable costs	400,000	240,000	160,000
Contribution margins	$500,000	$260,000	$240,000
Fixed costs traceable to divisions	360,000	170,000	190,000
Division segment margins	$140,000	$ 90,000	$ 50,000
Common fixed costs	40,000		
Operating income	$100,000		
Income taxes expense	35,000		
Net income	$ 65,000		

Segments defined as stores in the Retail Division

	Retail Division	Segments	
		42d St. Store	Baker St. Store
Sales	$500,000	$200,000	$300,000
Variable costs	240,000	98,000	142,000
Contribution margins	$260,000	$102,000	$158,000
Fixed costs traceable to stores	140,000	60,000	80,000
Store segment margins	$120,000	$ 42,000	$ 78,000
Common fixed costs	30,000		
Segment margin for division	$ 90,000		

Segments defined as profit centers (departments) in the 42d St. Store

	42d St. Store	Segments	
		Sales Department	Repairs Department
Sales	$200,000	$180,000	$ 20,000
Variable costs	98,000	90,000	8,000
Contribution margins	$102,000	$ 90,000	$ 12,000
Fixed costs traceable to departments	32,000	18,000	14,000
Departmental segment margins	$ 70,000	$ 72,000	$ (2,000)
Common fixed costs	28,000		
Segment margin for store	$ 42,000		

manner is termed the ***contribution margin approach*** and is widely used in preparing reports for use by managers.

2 **Each segment is charged with only those costs that are directly traceable to that segment.** A cost is "directly traceable" to a particular segment if that segment is ***solely responsible*** for the cost being

incurred. Thus, traceable costs should ***disappear if the segment is discontinued.***

The question of whether a cost is traceable to a particular department is not always clear-cut. In assigning costs to segments of a business, accountants often must exercise professional judgment.

CASE IN POINT The sales department of a large manufacturing company used to request many "Rush" orders from the production department. To fill these rush orders, the production department had to work overtime, which caused the production department to incur labor costs well in excess of budgeted amounts. The company's controller modified the responsibility accounting system to charge the ***sales department*** with the extra labor cost of processing rush orders. After this change was made, the sales department made a greater effort to give the production department adequate notice of all sales orders. As a result, the number of costly rush orders was substantially reduced.

Variable Costs

In segmented income statements, variable costs are those costs that change in approximate proportion to changes in sales volume. Examples of variable costs include the cost of goods sold and commissions paid to salespeople. Because variable costs are directly related to revenue, they usually are traceable to the profit center generating the revenue. If a profit center were eliminated, all of that center's variable costs should disappear.

Contribution Margin

Contribution margin (revenue minus variable costs) is an important tool for cost-volume-profit analysis. For example, the effect of a change in sales volume upon operating income may be estimated by either (1) multiplying the change in unit sales by the contribution margin per unit or (2) multiplying the dollar change in sales volume by the contribution margin ratio. (To assist in this type of analysis, segmented income statements often include percentages, as well as dollar amounts. A segmented income statement with percentage columns is illustrated on page 1122.)

Contribution margin expresses the relationship between revenue and variable costs but ignores fixed costs. Thus, contribution margin is primarily a ***short-run*** planning tool. It is useful primarily in decisions relating to price changes, short-run promotional campaigns, or changes in the level of output that will not significantly affect fixed costs. For longer-term decisions, such as whether to build a new plant or close a particular profit center, managers must consider fixed costs as well as contribution margin.

Fixed Costs

For a business to be profitable, total contribution margin must exceed total fixed costs. However, many fixed costs cannot be easily traced to specific

OBJECTIVE 3
Distinguish
between
traceable
and common
fixed costs.

segments of the business. Thus, a distinction is often drawn in segment income statements between ***traceable fixed costs*** and ***common fixed costs.***

Traceable Fixed Costs

Traceable fixed costs are those that can be easily traced to a specific segment of the business, and that arise because of that segment's existence. In short, traceable fixed costs ***could be eliminated*** if the segment were closed. Examples of traceable fixed costs include the salaries of the segment's employees, and depreciation and other costs relating to fixtures or equipment used exclusively by that segment.

In determining whether a specific profit center adds to the profitability of the business, it is reasonable to deduct from the center's contribution margin any traceable fixed costs. In a segmented income statement, contribution margin less traceable fixed costs is termed ***segment margin,*** as illustrated in the NuTech Electronics example earlier.

Common Fixed Costs

Common fixed costs (or indirect fixed costs) ***jointly benefit several segments*** of the business. The level of these fixed costs usually would not change significantly even if one of the segments deriving benefits from these costs were discontinued.

Consider, for example, a large department store, such as a Broadway or a Nordstrom. Every department in the store derives some benefit from the store building. However, such costs as depreciation and property taxes on the store will continue at current levels even if one or more of the departments within the store is discontinued. Thus, from the viewpoint of the segments within the store, depreciation on the building is a common fixed cost.

Common fixed costs cannot be assigned to specific subunits except by arbitrary means, such as in proportion to relative sales volume or square feet of space occupied. In an attempt to measure the "overall profitability" of each profit center, some businesses allocate common fixed costs to segments along with traceable costs. A more common approach, however, is to charge each profit center only with those costs ***directly traceable*** to that segment of the business. In this text, we follow this latter approach.

Activity-based costing, discussed in the Supplemental Topic section following Chapter 22, greatly increases the portion of a company's total costs that are traceable to specific business segments.

Common Fixed Costs Include Costs Traceable to Service Departments In a segmented income statement, the category of traceable fixed costs usually includes only those fixed costs ***traceable to profit centers.*** Costs traceable to ***service departments,*** such as the accounting department, benefit many segments of the business. Thus, the costs of operating service departments are classified in a segmented income statement as common fixed costs. For example, the $28,000 in common fixed costs shown in the segmented income statement of NuTech's 42d St. Store includes the costs of operating the store's accounting, security, and maintenance departments, as well as other "storewide" costs such as depreciation, utilities expense, and the store manager's salary.

Service departments are evaluated as cost centers. Therefore, the responsibility accounting system should accumulate separately the costs traceable to each service department.

Common Fixed Costs Are Traceable to Larger Responsibility Centers All costs are traceable to *some level* of the organization. To illustrate this concept, a portion of the responsibility accounting system of NuTech Electronics is repeated below, with emphasis upon the fixed costs in the 42d St. Store:

Segments defined as stores in the Retail Division

		Segments	
	Retail Division	*42d St. Store*	*Baker St. Store*
Sales	*$500,000*	*$200,000*	*$300,000*
Variable costs	240,000	98,000	142,000
Contribution margins	*$260,000*	*$102,000*	*$158,000*
Fixed costs traceable to stores	140,000	▶ 60,000	80,000
Store segment margins	*$120,000*	*$ 42,000*	*$ 78,000*
Common fixed costs	30,000		
Segment margin for division	*$ 90,000*		

*Segments defined as profit centers (departments) in the
42d St. Store*

		Segments	
	42d St. Store	*Sales Department*	*Repairs Department*
Sales	*$200,000*	*$180,000*	*$ 20,000*
Variable costs	98,000	90,000	8,000
Contribution margins	*$102,000*	*$ 90,000*	*$ 12,000*
Fixed costs traceable to departments	32,000—	18,000	14,000
Departmental segment margins	*$ 70,000*	*$ 72,000*	*$ (2,000)*
Common fixed costs	28,000—		
Segment margin for store	*$ 42,000*		

We have made the point that certain "storewide" costs, such as the operation of the maintenance department and the store manager's salary, are not traceable to the specific profit centers within the store. These costs are, however, easily traceable to the 42d St. Store. Therefore, whether these costs are classified as "traceable" or "common" depends upon whether we define the business segments as stores or as departments within the stores.

As we move up a responsibility reporting system to broader and broader areas of responsibility, common costs at the lower levels of managerial responsibility *become traceable costs* as they fall under the control of the managers of larger responsibility centers.

Segment Margin

OBJECTIVE 4
Explain the usefulness of contribution margin and segment margin in making short-term and long-term decisions.

We have mentioned that contribution margin is an excellent tool for evaluating the effects of short-run decisions upon profitability. **Segment margin** is a **longer-run** measure of profitability because it takes into consideration any fixed costs traceable to the segment. Thus, segment margin more useful than contribution margin for making long-term decisions that involve changes in fixed costs. Examples of such "long-run" decisions include whether to expand plant capacity or eliminate a profit center that is performing poorly.

To illustrate, assume that Pioneer Mfg. Co. manufactures and sells two products—car radios and cellular telephones. The company's monthly income statement, segmented by product line, is shown below. In this segmented income statement, we illustrate the common practice of including **component percentages** as well as dollar amounts.

	Entire Company		Product Car Radios		Cellular Telephones	
	Dollars	%	Dollars	%	Dollars	%
Sales	$200,000	100	$100,000	100	$100,000	100
Variable costs	100,000	50	60,000	60	40,000	40
Contribution margins	$100,000	50	$ 40,000	40	$ 60,000	60
Fixed costs traceable to product lines	56,000	28	12,000	12	44,000	44
Product segment margins	$ 44,000	22	$ 28,000	28	$ 16,000	16
Common fixed costs	26,000	13				
Operating income	$ 18,000	9				
Income taxes expense	6,000	3				
Net income	$ 12,000	6				

Which is the company's most profitable product? The answer depends upon whether you are making short-run decisions, which usually do not change fixed costs, or long-run decisions, in which changes in fixed costs become important factors.

First, let us consider short-run decisions. Assume that management believes a $2,000 per month radio advertising campaign would increase the monthly sales of whichever product is advertised by 10% ($10,000). Which product will it be most profitable to advertise? The answer is **cellular telephones,** because of the higher **contribution margin ratio** of this product (60% as compared to 40% for car radios). Selling an additional $10,000 of cellular telephones will generate $6,000 in contribution margin, whereas selling an additional $10,000 of radios will generate only $4,000.

Now let us take a longer-run view. Assume that the company must discontinue one of these products. Which product should the company **continue to produce?** The answer is **car radios.** After considering fixed costs traceable to each product, car radios contribute $28,000 to the company's operating income, whereas cellular telephones contribute only $16,000. Stated another way, if the cellular telephone product line is discontinued, all the revenue, variable costs, and traceable fixed costs relating to this product should disappear. In short, the company would lose the $16,000 monthly **segment margin** now produced by this product line. This, of course, is preferable to losing the $28,000 monthly segment margin produced by the car radio product line.

In summary, in making short-run decisions that do not affect fixed costs, managers should attempt to generate the most **contribution margin** for the additional costs incurred. This usually means emphasizing those segments with the highest contribution margin ratios. In evaluating a segment as a long-term investment, however, managers must consider the ability of the segment to cover its fixed costs. Thus, in the long run managers should emphasize growth in those segments with the highest **segment margins** and **segment margin ratios.**

When a segment is evaluated as an investment center, segment margin generally is used as the "income" figure in making any ROI computations. Thus, the return on assets for an investment center would be computed as segment margin divided by the average assets utilized by the segment.

When Is a Segment "Unprofitable"?

In deciding whether a specific profit center is "unprofitable," management should consider several factors. Segment margin, however, is a good starting point. Segment margin indicates whether the profit center earns enough contribution margin to cover the fixed costs traceable to that segment of the business.

To illustrate, consider the segmented income statement for the 42d St. Store of NuTech Electronics:

	42d St. Store	Segments	
		Sales Department	Repairs Department
Sales	$200,000	$180,000	$ 20,000
Variable costs	98,000	90,000	8,000
Contribution margins	$102,000	$ 90,000	$ 12,000
Fixed costs traceable to departments	32,000	18,000	14,000
Departmental segment margins	$ 70,000	$ 72,000	$ (2,000)
Common fixed costs	28,000		
Segment margin for store.....................	$ 42,000		

According to this data, discontinuing the Repairs Department should eliminate the $20,000 in revenue, and also $22,000 in costs ($8,000 variable costs, plus $14,000 in traceable fixed costs). Thus, closing the Repairs Department might well increase the profitability of the store by **$2,000**—the negative segment margin reported by the Repairs Department.

In deciding whether or not to close the Repairs Department, managers should also consider other factors. For example, does the existence of the Repairs Department contribute to merchandise sales? What alternative use could be made of the space now used by the Repairs Department? These factors will be considered in greater depth in Chapter 26.

Evaluating Segment Managers

Some costs traceable to a segment are simply beyond the segment manager's immediate control. Examples include depreciation expense and property taxes on plant assets. If a segment is saddled with high costs that are beyond the segment manager's control, the segment may perform poorly even if the segment manager is doing an excellent job.

As a response to this problem, some companies subdivide the fixed costs traceable to each segment into the subcategories of **controllable fixed costs** and **committed fixed costs.** Controllable fixed costs are those under the segment manager's immediate control, such as salaries and advertising. Committed fixed costs are those which the segment manager cannot readily change, such as depreciation. In the segmented income statement, controllable fixed costs are deducted from contribution margin to arrive at a subtotal called **performance margin.** Committed fixed costs then are deducted to determine segment margin.

Subdividing traceable costs in this manner draws a distinction between the performance of the segment manager and the profitability of the segment as a long-term investment. The performance margin includes only the revenue and costs **under the segment manager's direct control** and is a useful tool in evaluating the manager's skill. Segment margin, however, remains the best measure of the segment's long-term profitability.

Arguments against Allocating Common Fixed Costs to Segments

We have mentioned that some companies follow a policy of allocating common fixed costs among the segments benefiting from these costs. The bases used for allocating common costs are necessarily arbitrary, such as relative sales volume, or square feet of floor space occupied by the segment. In a segmented income statement, segment margin less common fixed costs allocated to the segment usually is called "operating income."

We do **not** recommend this practice, for several reasons:

1 **Common fixed costs often would not change even if a segment were eliminated.**   Therefore, an allocation of these costs only distorts the amount contributed by each segment to the income of the company.

    To illustrate this point, assume that $10,000 in common costs are allocated to a segment that has a segment margin of only $4,000. Also assume that total common costs would not change even if the segment were eliminated. The allocation of common costs makes the segment **appear** to be unprofitable, showing an operating loss of $6,000 ($4,000 segment margin, less $10,000 in allocated common fixed costs). However, closing the segment would actually **reduce** the company's income by **$4,000,** as the segment's $4,000 segment margin would be lost, but common fixed costs would not change.

2 **Common fixed costs are not under the direct control of the segment managers.**   Therefore, allocating these costs to the segments does not assist in evaluating the performance of segment managers.

3 **Allocation of common fixed costs may imply changes in segment profitability that are unrelated to segment performance.**

To illustrate this point, assume that $50,000 in monthly common fixed costs are allocated equally to each of five profit centers. Thus, each profit center is charged with **$10,000** of these costs. Now assume that one of the profit centers is discontinued but that the monthly level of common fixed costs does not change. Each of the four remaining profit centers will now be charged with **$12,500** in common fixed costs ($50,000 ÷ 4). Thus, the continuing profit centers are made to appear less profitable because of an event (closure of the fifth profit center) that is **unrelated** to their activities.

Nonfinancial Objectives and Information

Thus far, we have emphasized measuring the financial performance of segments within a business organization. In addition, many firms specify **nonfinancial** objectives which they consider important to their basic goals. A responsibility accounting system may be designed to gather much nonfinancial information about each responsibility center.

CASE IN POINT Among the factors used by McDonald's Corporation to evaluate a restaurant manager is the manager's performance on the company's QSC standards. "QSC" stands for "quality, service, and cleanliness." Each restaurant manager periodically is rated on these standards by a member of McDonald's supervisory staff. Among the many items listed on McDonald's QSC rating forms are:
Quality: Temperature, appearance, quantity, and taste of food servings.
Service: Appearance and general conduct of employees; use of proper procedures in greeting customers.
Cleanliness: Cleanliness in all areas in the kitchen, front counter, tables, and restrooms. Appearance of building exterior and parking lot.

■ ■ ■ ■ * Supplemental Topic
Variable Costing

OBJECTIVE 5 Explain the differences between full costing and variable costing.

Our preceding examples of income statements showing contribution margin and segment margin are based upon the activities of merchandising companies. In a merchandising company, the entire cost of goods sold represents a variable cost. In the financial statements of a manufacturing company, however, the cost of goods sold is based upon manufacturing costs—some of which are variable, and some of which are fixed. The conventional practice of including both variable and fixed manufacturing costs in the valuation of inventories and in the cost of goods sold is called **full costing.** Full costing is the method **required** by generally accepted accounting principles and by income tax regulations.

For the purposes of making managerial decisions, it is often more useful to have an income statement in which variable and fixed costs are shown separately and a subtotal is shown indicating contribution margin. Arranging the income statement of a manufacturing company in this format involves a technique called **variable costing.**

Under variable costing, the cost of goods sold includes only **variable** manufacturing costs. Fixed manufacturing costs are viewed as **period costs** and are deducted separately in the income statement after the determination of contribution margin. Before discussing variable costing further, let us briefly review some of the basic concepts of accounting for manufacturing costs.

Full Costing: The Traditional View of Product Costs

In Chapter 21, we made the distinction between **product costs** and **period costs.** Product costs are the costs of manufacturing inventory and are debited to the Work-in-Process Inventory account. From this account, product costs flow into the Finished Goods Inventory account and then into the Cost of Goods Sold. Thus, product costs are offset against revenue in the period in which the related goods are **sold.** Period costs, on the other hand, are charged directly to expense accounts and are deducted from revenue in the period in which the **cost is incurred.**

Under full costing, **all manufacturing costs are treated as product costs,** regardless of whether these costs are "variable" or "fixed." As all manufacturing costs are "absorbed" into the cost of manufactured products, full costing often is termed **absorption** costing.

Variable Costing: A Different View of Product Costs

Some manufacturing costs are variable costs and some manufacturing costs are fixed costs. The costs of direct materials used and of direct labor, for example, are variable costs. Manufacturing overhead, on the other hand, consists primarily of fixed costs. Examples of "fixed" overhead costs include depreciation on plant assets and salaries to supervisors, security guards, and maintenance personnel.

Under variable costing, only the **variable** manufacturing costs are viewed as product costs; **fixed manufacturing costs are viewed as period costs.** Thus, fixed overhead costs are classified as expenses of the current period, rather than flowing into the inventory accounts and the Cost of Goods Sold account. The diagrams on the facing page illustrate the flow of costs under full costing and variable costing.

In reports intended for use by managers, variable costing has two distinct advantages over full costing:

1 The format of the variable costing income statement easily lends itself to cost-volume-profit analysis.

2 Segment margin (or income from operations) is **not affected** by short-run fluctuations in the level of production.

Illustration of Variable Costing

The differences between variable costing and full costing may be further illustrated by preparing a partial income statement under each of these methods. Assume, for example, that on June 1, 1994, Hamilton Mfg. Co.

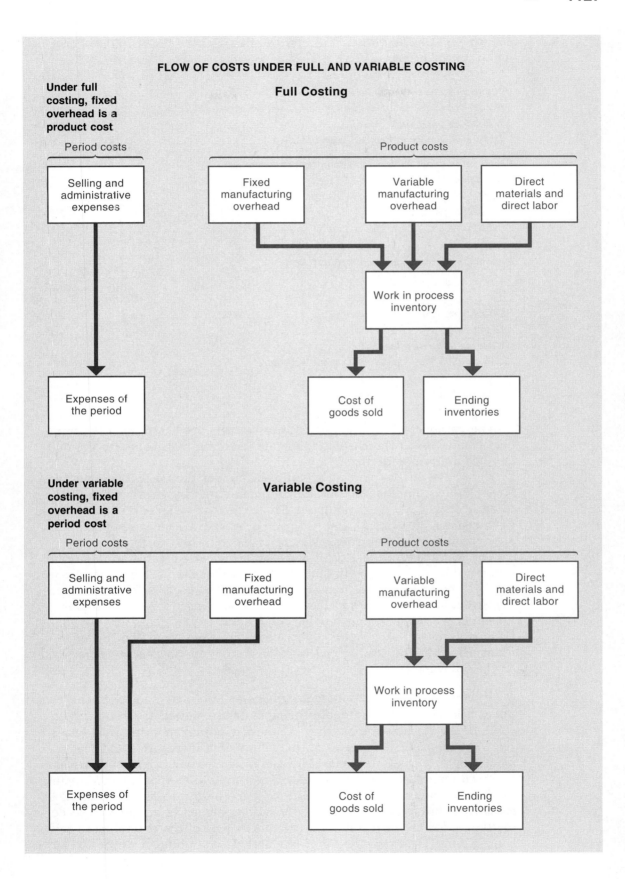

FLOW OF COSTS UNDER FULL AND VARIABLE COSTING

opened its Nashville Plant. Data for the first month of operations of this plant appear below:

Units manufactured and units sold:

Number of units manufactured (all completed by June 30)	11,000
Number of units sold	10,000
Units in inventory of finished goods at June 30............................	1,000

Sales revenue and selling and administrative expenses:

Net sales (10,000 units sold @ $20)	$200,000
Selling and administrative expenses:	
Variable ($2 per unit sold)	20,000
Fixed	30,000

Manufacturing costs (per unit manufactured):

	Full Costing	Variable Costing
Direct materials	$ 4	$ 4
Direct labor	3	3
Manufacturing overhead:		
Fixed ($55,000 ÷ 11,000 units manufactured)....................	5	-0-
Variable..	1	1
Total cost per unit manufactured...............................	$13	$ 8

The variable selling and administrative costs are based upon the number of units **sold,** whereas variable manufacturing costs relate to the number of units **manufactured.**

Notice the difference in "total unit cost" under the two costing methods. Under full costing, the $55,000 in fixed manufacturing overhead is allocated to the 11,000 units produced. Thus, the cost assigned to each finished unit includes $5 of fixed manufacturing overhead. Under variable costing, only variable manufacturing costs are included in unit cost.

The treatment of these fixed manufacturing costs creates an important difference between full costing and variable costing. Under full costing, we will use the **$13** unit cost to determine the cost of goods sold and the ending inventory. Under variable costing, the cost of goods sold and ending inventory will be determined using the **$8** unit cost.

Partial income statements and the ending inventory at the Nashville Plant using the full costing and variable costing approaches are illustrated on the following page.

Treatment of Fixed Manufacturing Costs We have made the point that under full costing, fixed manufacturing costs are viewed as **product** costs, while under variable costing they are viewed as **period** costs. Now let us see what that means in terms of the valuation of inventories and the amount of profit (segment margin) reported under our two costing methods.

Fixed manufacturing costs in our illustration total $55,000 and amount to $5 for each unit manufactured. If we view these costs as **product costs**—the full costing approach—the costs assigned to any units sold during the period are deducted from revenue as part of the cost of goods sold. During June, the Nashville Plant produced 11,000 units, of which 10,000

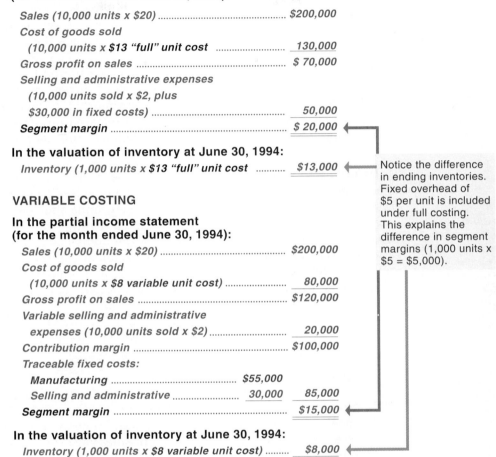

FULL COSTING

In the partial income statement
(for the month ended June 30, 1994):

Fixed overhead viewed as a product cost

Sales (10,000 units x $20)	*$200,000*
Cost of goods sold	
(10,000 units x $13 "full" unit cost	*130,000*
Gross profit on sales	*$ 70,000*
Selling and administrative expenses	
(10,000 units sold x $2, plus	
$30,000 in fixed costs)	*50,000*
Segment margin	*$ 20,000*

In the valuation of inventory at June 30, 1994:

Inventory (1,000 units x $13 "full" unit cost	*$13,000*

Notice the difference in ending inventories. Fixed overhead of $5 per unit is included under full costing. This explains the difference in segment margins (1,000 units x $5 = $5,000).

VARIABLE COSTING

In the partial income statement
(for the month ended June 30, 1994):

Sales (10,000 units x $20)		*$200,000*
Cost of goods sold		
(10,000 units x $8 variable unit cost)		*80,000*
Gross profit on sales		*$120,000*
Variable selling and administrative		
expenses (10,000 units sold x $2)		*20,000*
Contribution margin		*$100,000*

Fixed overhead viewed as a period cost

Traceable fixed costs:		
Manufacturing	*$55,000*	
Selling and administrative	*30,000*	*85,000*
Segment margin		*$15,000*

In the valuation of inventory at June 30, 1994:

Inventory (1,000 units x $8 variable unit cost)	*$8,000*

were sold. Under full costing, the per-unit cost is ***$13,*** including $5 per unit in fixed costs. Notice that the cost of goods sold in the full costing income statement is ***$130,000*** (10,000 units sold × $13), and ending inventory under full costing is ***$13,000*** (1,000 units × $13). Thus, ***$50,000*** of fixed manufacturing cost is ***included in the cost of goods sold*** (10,000 units sold × $5 per unit), and ***$5,000*** is ***included in the ending inventory*** of finished goods (1,000 units in inventory × $5 per unit).

Under variable costing, fixed manufacturing costs are treated as a ***period cost.*** The ***entire $55,000 is deducted from revenue;*** none is included in the cost assigned to inventory. (Notice that under variable costing, ending inventory is valued at only ***$8*** per unit, the ***variable*** costs of production.)

How do the different treatments accorded to fixed costs affect the amount of segment margin shown in the income statement? The answer is that fixed manufacturing costs may be ***deferred to future periods*** under the full costing method. Instead of being deducted from revenue immediately, fixed manufacturing costs relating to units in inventory are "carried forward" as part of the cost of this inventory. These costs will be "released" from inventory and included in the cost of goods sold in the period in which these goods are *sold.* In our illustration, $5,000 in fixed manufacturing cost was deferred into inventory under the full costing approach. This explains why both the value assigned to ending inventory and the reported amount of segment margin are $5,000 higher under full costing.

In summary, full costing results in a higher segment margin than does variable costing *when inventories are increasing* and fixed manufacturing costs are being deferred. In periods in which inventory *declines,* however, full costing results in a *lower* segment margin, because the fixed costs previously deferred into inventory are released into the Cost of Goods Sold account. This situation is illustrated later in this chapter.

OBJECTIVE 6
Use a variable costing income statement in CVP analysis.

Using a Variable Costing Income Statement The *variable costing* income statement readily lends itself to cost-volume-profit analysis. To illustrate, let us use this income statement to determine the dollar sales volume needed for the Nashville Plant to earn a monthly segment margin of $50,000. As a first step, we may compute the plant's contribution margin ratio directly from the income statement, as follows: $100,000 contribution margin ÷ $200,000 net sales = **50%.** We may then compute the required sales volume using the following cost-volume-profit relationships:

$$\text{Sales Volume} = \frac{\text{Fixed Costs} + \text{Target Segment Margin}}{\text{Contribution Margin Ratio}}$$

$$= \frac{\$85,000 + \$50,000}{.50} = \underline{\underline{\$270,000}}$$

Fluctuations in the Level of Production

Two accounting measurements widely used in evaluating the performance of a manufacturing segment of a business are the unit cost of manufactured products and segment margin. A significant shortcoming in the full costing approach is that both of these performance measurements are affected by short-term fluctuation in the level of production. This complicates the process of evaluating the performance of a segment. The manager performing the evaluation must determine whether changes in unit cost and in segment margin represent important changes in performance or merely the effects of a temporary change in the number of units produced.

OBJECTIVE 7
Explain why short-term fluctuation in the level of production may distort key measurements of segment performance under full costing.

This problem arises because under full costing, fixed manufacturing costs are included in the cost of finished goods manufactured. If the level of production temporarily rises, fixed costs per unit will decline. If production temporarily declines, fixed costs per unit will increase. In either case, the changes in fixed costs per unit will also affect total unit manufacturing cost.

In addition to causing changes in unit cost, fluctuations in the level of production may cause some fixed costs to be deferred into inventory, or released from inventory. For example, if production rises *above* the level of current sales, some of the fixed costs of the period are *deferred* into inventory, rather than being offset against the revenue of the current period. If production temporarily falls *below* the level of sales, the fixed costs of prior periods are *released* from inventory and charged against the revenue of the current period.

Most accountants agree that short-term fluctuations in the level of production, by themselves, do **not** represent changes in the profitability of a segment. Profits result from sales, not merely from production. An advantage of variable costing is that unit cost, contribution margin, and segment margin—all important measurements of segment performance—are **not affected** by short-run fluctuations in the level of production.

To illustrate this point, we will use the operating data for the Jogman Division of Yato Mfg. Co. during 1994 and 1995, illustrated below and on the following page. In this illustration, sales, variable costs per unit, and total fixed costs remain **unchanged** in each of the two years. The only change is a temporary fluctuation in the level of production; during 1994, the division produces **60,000** units and in 1995 it produces only **40,000** units. (To simplify this illustration, we assume that the segment has no beginning inventory and that all selling and administrative expenses are fixed costs.)

Operating Data for the Jogman Division

	1994 & 1995
Annual unit sales..	50,000
Unit sales price	$ 18
Annual net sales (50,000 × $18)	900,000
Annual fixed costs:	
Manufacturing..	240,000
Selling and administrative	130,000

	1994	1995
Number of units manufactured	60,000	40,000
Cost per unit manufactured (full costing):		
Variable manufacturing costs	$ 7	$ 7
Fixed manufacturing costs ($240,000 divided by number		
of units manufactured during the year)	4	6
Total unit cost of finished goods manufactured (full costing)	$11	$13

Income Statements for the Jogman Division

Full Costing

	1994		1995	
Sales (50,000 units).....................................		$900,000		$900,000
Cost of goods sold:				
Beginning inventory	$ -0-		$110,000	
Cost of finished goods manufactured ...	660,000[a]		520,000[c]	
Cost of goods available for sale	$660,000		$630,000	
Less: Ending inventory	110,000[b]		-0-	
Cost of goods sold...............................		550,000		630,000
Gross profit..		$350,000		$270,000
Selling and administrative expenses....................		130,000		130,000
Segment margin......................................		$220,000		$140,000

[a]   60,000 units @ $11 per unit.
[b]   10,000 units @ $11 per unit.
[c]   40,000 units @ $13 per unit.

Variable Costing

	1994		1995	
Sales (50,000 units).....................................		$900,000		$900,000
Variable cost of goods				
sold (50,000 units @ $7)..............................		350,000		350,000
Contribution margin		$550,000		$550,000
Traceable fixed costs:				
Manufacturing...........................	$240,000		$240,000	
Selling and administrative	130,000	370,000	130,000	370,000
Segment margin..		$180,000		$180,000

Analysis of the Illustration Remember the basic facts of our illustration: nothing has changed at the Jogman Division from 1994 to 1995 *except for the level of production.* Notice that in the variable costing income statements, the Jogman Division reports the *same amounts* of contribution margin and segment margin in 1994 and 1995. The unit cost of finished goods manufactured, $7, also remained unchanged. Thus, the key measurements of segment performance are *not affected* by the change in the level of production. Under variable costing, contribution margin and segment margin change only when there is a change in (1) sales revenue, (2) variable costs per unit, or (3) fixed costs incurred during the period.

Under full costing, however, changes in the level of production *can* cause significant changes in key measurements of performance. These changes result from both the change in fixed costs per unit and fixed costs being deferred into inventory or released from inventory. Let us now look at the reasons behind the fluctuation in the amounts of segment margin reported in our example under the full costing approach.

1994: More units are produced than sold Notice that under full costing in 1994, fixed manufacturing costs amounted to $4 per unit ($240,000 ÷ 60,000 units manufactured). During 1994, the Jogman Division manufactured 10,000 more units than it sold. Thus, under full costing, $40,000 in fixed manufacturing costs were deferred into ending inventory. This deferral of fixed costs explains why the segment margin reported in 1994 is $40,000 higher than the segment margin shown in the variable costing income statement.

1995: Fewer units are produced than sold Now consider the results reported under full costing in 1995. In this year, unit sales exceeded production by 10,000 units. As the inventory is drawn down, the $40,000 in fixed costs deferred in 1994 become part of the cost of goods sold in 1995. Thus, the segment margin is $40,000 lower than that shown under variable costing.

Summary Because the full costing method associates fixed manufacturing costs with units of production, the amount of fixed manufacturing cost offset against revenue varies with the relationship between the number of units produced and the number sold. If production temporarily exceeds unit sales, some fixed manufacturing costs are deferred to future periods, and segment margin will be higher than would be reported under variable costing. If fewer units are produced during the period than are sold, fixed costs deferred in prior periods are offset against current revenue as inventory is drawn down. Thus, segment margin reported for the current period will be lower than would result from variable costing.

Under variable costing, the level of production has **no effect** upon segment margin, because all fixed manufacturing costs are offset against revenue as they are incurred, **regardless** of the level of production.

In the long run, the total amounts of segment margin reported under full costing and variable costing should be very similar. Over the long run, the number of units produced tends to equal the number of units sold. In the short run, however, variable costing provides managers with the more reliable measurement of the performance of segments engaged in manufacturing activities.

Why Is Variable Costing Unacceptable for Use in Financial Statements?

We have shown that in several respects, variable costing may be more useful than full costing as a basis for many managerial decisions. Why then is variable costing not also used in financial statements and income tax returns? The answer to this question is that variable costing omits fixed manufacturing costs from the valuation of the ending inventory. Financial accountants and income tax authorities argue that variable costing significantly understates the "full" cost of manufacturing this asset. As a result of understating ending inventories, variable costing may understate net income, especially for a growing business with steadily increasing inventories.

END-OF-CHAPTER REVIEW

SUMMARY OF CHAPTER LEARNING OBJECTIVES

1 **Explain the need for segment information and describe a responsibility accounting system.**
Segment information presents separately the operating results of each segment within the organization. In a responsibility accounting system, segments are defined as responsibility centers. The segment information then holds managers accountable for the performance of the segments under their control.

2 **Prepare segment income statements showing contribution margin and segment margin.**
In segment income statements, revenue is assigned to the profit center responsible for generating that revenue. Two concepts are used in assigning and classifying expenses. First, each segment is charged only with those costs **directly traceable** to the segment. Second, costs charged to the segment are subdivided between the categories of variable costs and fixed costs. Subtracting variable costs from segment revenue indicates the segment's **contribution margin;** then, subtracting traceable fixed costs indicates the segment's **segment margin.**

3 Distinguish between traceable and common fixed costs.

Traceable fixed costs are fixed costs that arise because of the existence of a particular segment and could be eliminated if the segment were closed. Common fixed costs jointly benefit two or more segments of the business and cannot be allocated between these segments except by arbitrary means.

4 Explain the usefulness of contribution margin and segment margin in making short-term and long-term decisions.

Fixed costs generally cannot be changed in the short run. Therefore, the affects of short-run strategies upon operating income are equal to the change in *contribution margin* (revenue less variable costs). In the long run, however, strategies may affect changes in the fixed costs traceable to a segment. Therefore, the profitability of long-run strategies may be evaluated in terms of changes in *segment margin* (revenue less variable costs and less traceable fixed costs).

*5 Explain the differences between full costing and variable costing.

Under full costing, fixed manufacturing costs are viewed as product costs and are included in the cost of finished goods manufactured. Under variable costing, fixed manufacturing costs are treated as period expenses. An income statement prepared on a variable costing basis is useful for cost-volume-profit analysis; however, variable costing is *not acceptable* for use in published financial statements or income tax returns.

*6 Use a variable costing income statement in CVP analysis.

In a variable costing income statement, costs are subdivided into the classifications of variable costs and fixed costs. This classification permits arranging an income statement in a manner showing subtotals for contribution margin and total fixed costs—two key amounts in cost-volume-profit analysis.

*7 Explain why short-term fluctuation in the level of production may distort key measurements of segment performance under full costing.

Under full costing, fixed manufacturing costs are assigned to the units produced during the period. Thus, unit cost falls with increases in production level, but rises with decreases. Unit costs comprise the cost of goods sold. Therefore, temporary fluctuations in the level of production may affect the cost of goods sold and, in turn, such performance measures as contribution margin and segment margin.

One purpose of this chapter is to "tie together" many of the concepts introduced in our three preceding managerial accounting chapters. Notice, for example, how such concepts as the distinction between variable costs and fixed costs, cost-volume-profit relationships, the nature of period costs and product costs, and the flow of manufacturing costs through an accounting system have played major roles in our evaluation of segment performance. In the next chapter, we introduce the topic of budgeting. The budget provides one of the major standards with which current performance is compared.

---

* *Supplemental Topic, "Variable Costing"*

KEY TERMS INTRODUCED OR EMPHASIZED IN CHAPTER 24

Absorption costing   See **full costing.**

Committed fixed costs   Fixed costs that are traceable to a segment of a business but which, in the short run, cannot readily be changed by the segment manager.

Common fixed costs   Fixed costs that are of joint benefit to several segments of a business. Thus, these common costs cannot be traced to the segments deriving benefit, except by arbitrary means.

Contribution margin   Revenue less variable costs; also, the amount of revenue available to contribute toward fixed costs and operating income (or **segment margin**). The key statistic for most types of cost-volume-profit analysis.

Contribution margin approach   Arranging a segmented income statement in a manner that develops **contribution margin** as a subtotal. Requires dividing costs and expenses into the categories of variable costs and fixed costs.

Controllable fixed costs   Fixed costs that are under the direct control of the segment manager.

Cost center   A segment of the business that incurs costs but that does not directly generate revenue.

Direct costing   See **variable costing.**

Full costing   The traditional method of product costing in which both fixed and variable manufacturing costs are treated as product costs and charged to inventories. Also called **absorption costing.**

Investment center   A profit center for which the amount of assets invested in the segment may be readily identified. When a profit center meets this criterion, its performance may be evaluated using return on investment (ROI) techniques, such as return on assets.

Performance margin   A subtotal in a segmented income statement designed to assist in evaluating the performance of a segment manager based solely upon revenue and expenses under the manager's control. Consists of contribution margin less the controllable fixed costs traceable to the department.

Period costs   Costs that are deducted as expense in the period in which they are incurred, rather than being debited to asset accounts.

Product costs   Costs that become part of the inventory value of work-in-process and finished goods. These costs are deducted from revenue in the period that the related goods are sold.

Profit center   A segment of a business that directly generates revenue, as well as incurring costs.

Responsibility accounting system   An accounting system that separately measures the performance of each responsibility center in the organization.

Responsibility center   A segment of a business for which a particular manager is in charge and held responsible for the segment's performance.

Segment   A subunit within a business organization. A segment of a business conducts specific types of business activity and is under the control of a designated manager.

Segment margin   Revenue less variable costs and traceable fixed costs. A long-run measure of the profitability of a profit center. Consists of the revenue and costs likely to disappear if the segment were eliminated.

Segmented income statement   An income statement that subdivides the operating results of a business segment among the profit centers comprising that segment.

Traceable fixed costs Fixed costs that are directly traceable to a specific segment of a business. These costs usually would be eliminated if the segment were discontinued.

Variable costing The technique of product costing in which only the variable manufacturing costs are regarded as product costs. Fixed manufacturing costs are treated as period costs. Useful for managerial purposes, but not acceptable for use in financial statements or income tax returns. Also called ***direct costing.***

DEMONSTRATION PROBLEM FOR YOUR REVIEW

Burnham Mfg. Co. operates two plants that produce and sell a single product. Shown below are the operating results of both plants during 1994, the company's first year of operations:

	Riverville Plant	Truesdale Plant
Sales (40,000 units at $50)	$2,000,000	$2,000,000
Per unit costs:		
Variable manufacturing costs	$ 15	$ 18
Variable selling and administrative	3	4
Traceable fixed costs:		
Manufacturing overhead	$ 600,000	$ 400,000
Selling and administrative	150,000	150,000

During 1994, both plants produced 50,000 units, of which 40,000 were sold. Common fixed costs relating to both plants amount to $500,000.

INSTRUCTIONS

a Determine the variable cost of goods sold at each plant, using variable costing.

b Prepare a partial income statement for Burnham Mfg. Co., segmented by plant and using the contribution margin approach. Conclude this income statement with the company's income from operations.

c Compute the cost of goods sold at each plant using full costing.

d Prepare a partial income statement for the entire company determining income from operations using the full costing approach. (Show the cost of goods sold as a single figure.)

e Explain the difference in the amounts of income from operations reported in parts **b** and **d**.

SOLUTION TO DEMONSTRATION PROBLEM

a

	Riverville Plant	Truesdale Plant
Variable cost of goods sold (variable costing):		
Riverville Plant: $15 variable manufacturing costs × 40,000 units manufactured	$600,000	
Truesdale Plant: $18 variable manufacturing costs × 40,000 units manufactured		$720,000

b Segmented income statement:

	Burnham Mfg. Co.	Riverville Plant	Truesdale Plant
Sales	$4,000,000	$2,000,000	$2,000,000
Variable costs:			
Cost of goods sold *(part a)*	$1,320,000	$ 600,000	$ 720,000
Selling and administrative	280,000	120,000	160,000
Total variable costs	$1,600,000	$ 720,000	$ 880,000
Contribution margin	$2,400,000	$1,280,000	$1,120,000
Traceable fixed costs:			
Manufacturing	$1,000,000	$ 600,000	$ 400,000
Selling and administrative	300,000	150,000	150,000
Total traceable fixed costs	$1,300,000	$ 750,000	$ 550,000
Plant segment margins	$1,100,000	$ 530,000	$ 570,000
Common fixed costs	500,000		
Income from operations	$ 600,000		

c

	Riverville Plant	Truesdale Plant
Cost of goods sold (full costing):		
Variable manufacturing costs:		
Riverville Plant ($15 × 40,000 units)	$ 600,000	
Truesdale Plant ($18 × 40,000 units)		$ 720,000
Fixed manufacturing costs:		
Riverville Plant ($600,000 ÷ 50,000 units = $12 per unit; $12 × 40,000 units sold)	480,000	
Truesdale Plant ($400,000 ÷ 50,000 units = $8 per unit; $8 × 40,000 units sold)		320,000
Cost of goods sold (full costing)	$1,080,000	$1,040,000

d
BURNHAM MFG. CO.
Partial Income Statement—Full Costing
For the Year Ended December 31, 1994

Sales		$4,000,000
Cost of goods sold [$1,080,000 + $1,040,000 *(part c)*]		2,120,000
Gross profit on sales		$1,880,000
Selling and administrative expenses:		
Variable ($120,000 + $160,000)	$280,000	
Fixed ($150,000 + $150,000 + $500,000)	800,000	1,080,000
Income from operations		$ 800,000

e The difference in the amount of income from operations is explained by the fixed manufacturing costs deferred into inventory under the full costing method, as shown below. (The fixed manufacturing costs per unit were determined in part **c**).

Income from operations: variable costing (part b)		*$600,000*
Add: Fixed manufacturing costs deferred into inventory		
under full costing:		
Riverville Plant (10,000 units × $12 per unit)	*$120,000*	
Truesdale Plant (10,000 units × $8 per unit)	*80,000*	*200,000*
Income from operations: full costing (part d)		*$800,000*

SELF-TEST QUESTIONS

Answers to these questions appear on page 1150.

1   Which of the following is a common fixed cost to the sales departments in a department store?

  a   Salaries of store security personnel.

  b   Salaries of sales department managers.

  c   Cost of goods sold.

  d   Depreciation on fixtures used exclusively in a specific sales department.

2   In preparing an income statement that measures contribution margin and segment margin, two concepts are applied in classifying costs. One is whether the costs are variable or fixed. The other is whether the costs are:

  a   Product costs or period costs.

  b   Traceable to the segment.

  c   Under the control of the segment manager.

  d   Higher or lower than the budgeted amount.

3   A subtotal used in evaluating the performance of a segment manager, as distinct from the performance of the segment, is:

  a   Contribution margin, less traceable fixed costs.

  b   Sales, less committed costs.

  c   Contribution margin, plus fixed costs deferred into inventory.

  d   Contribution margin, less controllable fixed costs.

4   An investment center has annual sales of $500,000, a contribution margin ratio of 40%, and traceable fixed costs of $80,000. Average assets invested in the center are $600,000. Which of the following statements are correct? (More than one answer may be correct.)

  a   Variable costs amount to $300,000.

  b   Segment margin amounts to $200,000.

  c   Segment margin represents a 20% return on assets.

  d   If $10,000 in additional advertising would result in $60,000 in additional sales, segment margin would increase by $14,000.

*5   During its first year of operations, Marco Mfg. Co. manufactured 5 million units, of which 4 million were sold. Manufacturing costs for the year were as follows:

Fixed manufacturing costs	*$10,000,000*
Variable manufacturing costs	*$3 per unit*

  Which of the following answers is correct? (In all cases, assume that unit sales for the year remain at 4 million; more than one answer may be correct.)

---
*   *Supplemental Topic, "Variable Costing"*

a Under variable costing, income from operations will be $2,000,000 less than full costing.

b Under full costing, the cost of goods sold would have been $2 million greater if Marco had manufactured only 4 million units during the year.

c Under variable costing, the amount of manufacturing costs deducted from revenue during the year will be $12 million, regardless of the number of units manufactured.

d Under full costing, Marco's net income would have been higher for the first year of operations if more units had been manufactured.

ASSIGNMENT MATERIAL

DISCUSSION QUESTIONS

1 What are some of the uses that management may make of accounting information about individual segments of the business?

2 Explain how a responsibility accounting system can assist managers in controlling the costs of a large business organization.

3 Distinguish among a *cost center,* a *profit center,* and an *investment center,* and give an example of each.

4 Marshall's Grocery Store has a small bakery that sells coffee and baked goods at very low prices. (For example, coffee and one doughnut cost 25 cents.) The basic purpose of the bakery is to attract customers to the store and to make the store "smell like a bakery." In each period, costs traceable to the bakery exceed revenue. Would you evaluate the bakery as a cost center or as a profit center? Explain.

5 In general terms, describe the criteria that should be considered in evaluating the performances of a *cost center.*

6 What is a *responsibility accounting system?*

7 The operation of a responsibility accounting system involves three basic steps. In this chapter, we emphasize the second step: measuring the performance of each responsibility center. List all three steps in the logical sequence of occurrence.

8 In a responsibility accounting system, should the recording of revenue and costs begin at the largest areas of responsibility or the smallest? Explain.

9 In the segmented income statements illustrated in this chapter, two concepts are used in classifying costs. What are these concepts?

10 Distinguish between *traceable* and *common* fixed costs. Give an example of each type of fixed cost for an auto dealership that is segmented into a sales department and a service department.

11 How do the costs of operating *service departments* (organized as cost centers) appear in a segmented income statement?

12 DeskTop, Inc., operates a national sales organization. The income statements prepared for each sales territory are segmented by product line. In these income statements, the sales territory manager's salary is treated as a common fixed cost. Will this salary be viewed as a common fixed cost at all levels of the organization? Explain.

13 Assume that Department A has a higher contribution margin ratio, but a lower segment margin ratio, than Department B. If $10,000 in advertising is expected to increase the sales of either department by $50,000, in which department can the advertising dollars be spent to the best advantage?

14 Criticize the following statement: "In our business, we maximize profits by closing any department that does not show a segment margin ratio of at least 15%."

15 What is the relationship between contribution margin and segment margin? Explain how each of these measurements is useful in making managerial decisions.

16 What does a consistently negative segment margin imply will happen to the operating income of the business if the segment is closed? Why? Identify several other factors that should be considered in deciding whether or not to close the segment.

17 Briefly explain the distinction between ***controllable*** fixed costs and ***committed*** fixed costs. Also explain the nature and purpose of performance margin in a segmented income statement.

18 The controller of Fifties, a chain of drive-in restaurants, is considering modifying the monthly segmented income statements by charging all costs relating to operations of the corporate headquarters to the individual restaurants in proportion to each restaurant's gross revenue. Do you think that this would increase the usefulness of the segmented income statement in evaluating the performance of the restaurants or the restaurant managers? Explain.

*19 Distinguish between ***variable costing*** and ***full costing.*** Which method is used in financial statements? Which method is used in income tax returns?

*20 Explain why a variable costing income statement provides a better basis for cost-volume-profit analysis than does a full costing income statement.

*21 Rose Speakers, a division of Innovative Sound, temporarily increases production to exceed unit sales, thereby causing its inventory of finished goods to increase. Explain the effect of this action upon the segment margin reported by Rose under (a) full costing and (b) variable costing.

EXERCISES

EXERCISE 24-1
Accounting Terminology

Listed below are nine technical accounting terms introduced or emphasized in this chapter:

Segment margin	*Variable costing*	*Common fixed costs*
Contribution margin	*Full costing*	*Traceable fixed costs*
Performance margin	*Product costs*	*Committed fixed costs*

Each of the following statements may (or may not) describe one of these technical terms. For each statement, indicate the accounting term described, or answer "None" if the statement does not correctly describe any of the terms.

a The costs deducted from contribution margin to determine segment margin.

b The method of assigning manufacturing costs to inventories and to the cost of goods sold that is required under generally accepted accounting principles.

c Fixed costs that are readily controllable by the segment manager.

---

* *Supplemental Topic, "Variable Costing"*

d A subtotal in a segmented income statement, equal to segment margin plus committed fixed costs.

e The subtotal in a segmented income statement that is most useful in evaluating the short-run effect of various marketing strategies upon the income of the business.

f The subtotal in a segmented income statement that comes closest to indicating the change in income from operations that would result from closing a particular segment of the business.

g A technique that makes the income statement of a manufacturing segment readily suitable to cost-volume-profit analysis.

EXERCISE 24-2
Types of Responsibility Centers

Indicate whether each of the following should be evaluated as an investment center, a profit center (other than an investment center), or a cost center. Briefly explain the reasoning behind your answer.

a An individual restaurant within a chain of restaurants.

b A restaurant within a department store, owned by the department store.

c A kitchen within a hospital that prepares meals for patients. (Patients are billed for time spent in the hospital but are not charged separately for meals.)

EXERCISE 24-3
Classification of Costs in a Segmented Income Statement

The controller of Maxwell Department Store is preparing an income statement, segmented by sales departments and including subtotals for contribution margin, performance margin, and segment margin. Indicate the appropriate classification of the seven items (**a** through **g**) listed below. Select from the following cost classifications:
Variable costs
Traceable fixed costs—controllable
Traceable fixed costs—committed
Common fixed costs
None of the above

a Cost of operating the store's accounting department.

b Cost of advertising specific product lines (classify as a fixed cost).

c Sales taxes on merchandise sold.

d Depreciation on the hydraulic lifts used in the Automotive Service Department.

e Salaries of departmental sales personnel.

f Salary of the store manager.

g Cost of merchandise sold in the Sportswear Department.

EXERCISE 24-4
Preparing a Segmented Income Statement

MicroPress is segmented into two product lines—software and hardware. During the current year, the two product lines reported the following results (dollar amounts are stated in thousands):

	Software	*Hardware*
Sales	*$450,000*	*$600,000*
Variable costs (as a percentage of sales)	*30%*	*58%*
Traceable fixed costs	*189,000*	*168,000*

In addition, fixed costs common to both product lines (stated in thousands of dollars) amounted to $31,500.

Prepare a segmented income statement showing percentages as well as dollar amounts (stated in thousands). Conclude your statement with income from operations for the business, and with segment margin for each product line.

b Assume that the sales of both products by Division 1 are equal to total manufacturing capacity. To increase sales of either product, the company must increase manufacturing facilities, which means an increase in traceable fixed costs in approximate proportion to the expected increase in sales. In this case, which product line would you recommend expanding? Explain.

c The segmented income statement for Division 1 includes $21,000 in common fixed costs. What happens to these fixed costs in the income statements segmented by division?

d Assume that in April, the monthly sales in Division 2 increase to $200,000. Compute the expected effect of this change upon the operating income of the company (assume no other changes in revenue or cost behavior).

e Prepare an income statement for Butterfield, Inc., segmented by divisions, under the assumption stated in part **d**. Organize this income statement in the format illustrated above, including columns for percentages.

PROBLEM 24B-4
Allocating Fixed Costs to Segments

You have just been hired as the controller of Land's End Hotel. The hotel prepares monthly segmented income statements in which all fixed costs are allocated among the various profit centers in the hotel, based upon the relative amounts of revenue generated by each profit center.

Robert Chamberlain, manager of the hotel dining room, argues that this approach understates the profitability of his department. "Through developing a reputation as a fine restaurant, the dining room has significantly increased its revenue. Yet the more revenue we earn, the larger the percentage of the hotel's operating costs that are charged against our department. Also, whenever vacancies go up, rental revenue goes down, and the dining room is charged with a still greater percentage of overall operating costs. Our strong performance is concealed by poor performance in departments responsible for keeping occupancy rates up." Chamberlain suggests that fixed costs relating to the hotel should be allocated among the profit centers based upon the number of square feet occupied by each department.

Debra Mettenburg, manager of the Sunset Lounge, objects to Chamberlain's proposal. She points out that the lounge is very big, because it is designed for hotel guests to read, relax, and watch the sunset. Although the lounge does serve drinks, the revenue earned in the lounge is small in relation to its square footage. Many guests just come to the lounge for the free hors d'oeuvres and don't even order a drink. Chamberlain's proposal would cause the lounge to appear unprofitable; yet a hotel must have some "open space" for its guests to sit and relax.

INSTRUCTIONS

a Separately evaluate the points raised by each of the two managers.

b Suggest your own approach to allocating the hotel's fixed costs among the various profit centers.

*PROBLEM 24B-5
Variable Costing

At the beginning of the current year, Tender Age, Inc., opened its Lewiston Plant to manufacture baby strollers. During the year, 200,000 strollers were manufactured, of which 175,000 were sold at a unit sales price of $150. Variable manufacturing costs for the year amounted to $9,000,000, and fixed manufacturing costs totaled $3,600,000. Variable selling and administrative expenses were $1,575,000, and traceable fixed selling and administrative expenses were $2,700,000.

INSTRUCTIONS

a Prepare a schedule showing variable, fixed, and total manufacturing costs per unit.

---

* *Supplemental Topic, "Variable Costing"*

b Prepare partial income statements (ending with segment margin) for the Lewiston Plant for the current year using:

1 Full costing

2 Variable costing

c Briefly explain the difference in the amount of segment margin reported in the two income statements for the segment.

d Using the data contained in the variable costing income statement, compute (1) the contribution margin per unit sold and (2) the number of strollers which must be manufactured and sold annually for the Lewiston Plant to cover its fixed costs—that is, to break even.

CASES AND UNSTRUCTURED PROBLEMS

Advance Electronics opened its new Jefferson Plant at the beginning of the current year to manufacture a burglar alarm. During the year, the Jefferson Plant manufactured 120,000 burglar alarms, of which 100,000 were sold and 20,000 remain on hand as finished goods inventory. There was no work-in-process inventory at year-end. An income statement for the Jefferson Plant, prepared in conventional (full costing) form, is shown below:

ADVANCE ELECTRONICS—JEFFERSON PLANT
Income Statement
For First Year of Operations

Sales (100,000 units @ $90)		$9,000,000
Cost of goods sold:		
Manufacturing costs (120,000 units @ $63)	$7,560,000	
Less: Ending inventory (20,000 units @ $63)	1,260,000	6,300,000
Gross profit on sales		$2,700,000
Selling and administrative expenses:		
Variable ($12 per unit sold)	$1,200,000	
Fixed	1,275,000	2,475,000
Segment margin		$ 225,000

The $7,560,000 in total manufacturing costs consisted of the following cost elements:

Direct materials used		$2,700,000
Direct labor		2,160,000
Manufacturing overhead:		
Variable	$ 900,000	
Fixed	1,800,000	2,700,000
Total manufacturing costs		$7,560,000

The manager of the Jefferson Plant is proud of the $225,000 operating income reported for the first year of operations. However, the controller of Advance Electronics, an advocate of variable costing, makes the following statement: "The only reason that the Jefferson Plant shows a profit is that $300,000 of fixed costs are deferred in the ending inventory figure. Actually a sales volume of 100,000 units is below the break-even point."

* *Supplemental Topic, "Variable Costing"*

BUDGETING: THE BASIS FOR PLANNING AND CONTROL

A budget is a comprehensive *financial plan* setting forth the expected route for achieving the financial and operational goals of an organization. Budgeting is an essential step in effective financial planning. Even the smallest business will benefit from preparing a formal written plan for its future operations, including the expected levels of sales, expenses, net income, cash receipts, and cash outlays.

The use of a budget is a key element of financial planning and also of the managerial function of controlling costs. To control costs, the managers of all units of the company compare actual costs incurred with the budgeted amounts and take action to correct excessive costs. Thus, controlling costs means keeping actual costs in line with a financial plan.

Virtually all economic entities—businesses, governmental agencies, universities, churches, and individuals—engage in some form of budgeting. For example, a college student with limited financial resources may prepare a list of expected monthly cash payments to see that they do not exceed expected monthly cash receipts. This list is a simple form of cash budget. Business managers must plan (budget) to achieve profit objectives as well as to meet the financial obligations of the business as they become due. Administrators of nonprofit organizations and governmental agencies must plan to accomplish the objectives of the organization with the available resources.

While all businesses engage in some degree of planning, the extent to which plans are formalized in written budgets varies from one business to another. Large well-managed companies generally have carefully developed budgets for every aspect of their operations. Inadequate or sloppy budgeting is a characteristic of companies with weak or inexperienced management.

Benefits Derived from Budgeting

OBJECTIVE 1 Discuss the benefits that a company may derive from a formal budgeting process.

A budget is a forecast of future events. In fact, the process of budgeting is often called *financial forecasting.* Careful planning and preparation of a formal budget benefit a company in many ways, including:

1 **Enhanced managerial perspective.** On a day-to-day basis, most managers focus their attention upon the routine problems of running the business. In preparing a budget, however, managers are forced to consider all aspects of a company's internal activities and also to make estimates of future economic conditions, including costs, interest rates, demand for the company's products, and the level of competition. Thus, budgeting increases management's awareness of the company's external economic environment.

2 **Advance warning of problems.** Since the budget shows the expected results of future operations, management is forewarned of financial problems. If, for example, the budget shows that the company will run short of cash during the summer months, management has advance warning of the need to hold down expenditures or to obtain additional financing.

3 Coordination of activities. Preparation of a budget provides management with an opportunity to coordinate the activities of the various departments within the business. For example, the production department should be budgeted to produce approximately the same quantity of goods as the sales department is budgeted to sell. A written budget shows departmental managers in quantitative terms exactly what is expected of their departments during the upcoming period.

4 Performance evaluation. Budgets show the expected costs and expenses for each department as well as the expected output, such as revenue to be earned or units to be produced. Thus, the budgets provide a yardstick with which each department's actual performance may be measured.

Establishing Budgeted Amounts

OBJECTIVE 2 Explain two "philosophies" that may be used in setting budgeted amounts.

Comparisons of actual performance with budgeted amounts are widely used in evaluating the performance of departments and of departmental managers. There are today two basic philosophies as to the levels at which budgeted amounts should be set. We will identify these philosophies as (1) the **behavioral** approach and (2) the **total quality management** approach. We will first discuss the behavioral approach, which currently is the more widely used budgeting philosophy.

The "Behavioral" Approach The assumption underlying the behavioral approach is that departmental managers will be most highly motivated if they view the budget as a **"fair"** basis for evaluating departmental performance. Therefore, budgeted amounts are set at **reasonable and achievable levels;** that is, at levels which **can be achieved** through reasonably efficient operations. A department which operates in a highly efficient manner should be able to **exceed** the budgeted level of performance. Failure to stay "within the budget," in contrast, is viewed as an unacceptable level of performance.

The "Total Quality Management" Approach A basic premise of total quality management is that every individual and segment of the organization constantly should strive for improvement. The entire organization is committed to the goal of **completely eliminating** inefficiency and non-value-adding activities. In short, the organization strives to achieve **perfection** in all aspects of its operations.

As a step toward achieving this goal, budgeted amounts may be set at levels representing **absolute efficiency.** Departments generally will fall somewhat short of achieving this level of performance. However, even small failures to achieve the budgeted performance serve to direct management's attention toward those areas in which there is "room for improvement."

Selecting and Using a Budgeting Approach The approach used in setting budget amounts reflects the philosophy and goals of top management. Under either approach, however, departmental managers should **participate actively** in the budgeting process. Departmental managers generally are the best source of information as to the levels of performance which can be achieved within their departments. Also, these managers should understand both the intended purpose of the budget and the philosophy underlying the development of budgeted amounts.

In comparing actual performance with budgeted amounts, top management should consider the philosophy used in developing the budgeted amounts. If a behavioral approach was employed, a highly efficient department often may *exceed* the budgeted level of performance. If a total quality management approach was used, a highly efficient department should fall *slightly short* of the budget standards.

In the remainder of this chapter and in our assignment material, we will assume that budgeted amounts are set at *reasonable and achievable levels* (that is, the behavioral approach). Using this approach will enable us to illustrate and discuss actual levels of performance both above and below budgeted levels.

The Budget Period

As a general rule, the period covered by a budget should be long enough to show the effect of managerial policies but short enough so that estimates can be made with reasonable accuracy. This suggests that different types of budgets should be made for different time spans.

Capital expenditures budgets, which summarize plans for major investments in plant and equipment, might be prepared to cover plans for as long as 5 to 10 years. Projects such as building a new factory or an oil refinery require many years of planning and expenditures before the new facilities are ready for use.

Most operating budgets and financial budgets cover a period of one fiscal year. Companies often divide these annual budgets into four quarters, with budgeted figures for each quarter. The first quarter is then subdivided into budgeted figures for each month, while only quarterly figures are shown for the last three quarters. As the end of the quarter nears, the budget for the next quarter is reviewed, revised for any changes in economic conditions, and divided into monthly budget figures. This process assures that the budget is reviewed at least several times each year and that the budgeted figures for the months just ahead are based upon current conditions and estimates. In addition, budgeted figures for relatively short periods of time enable managers to compare actual performance to the budget without waiting until year-end.

Continuous Budgeting   An increasing number of companies follow a policy of continuous budgeting, whereby a new month is added to the end of the budget as the current month draws to a close. Thus, the budget always covers the upcoming 12 months. The principal advantage of continuous budgeting is that it "stabilizes" the planning horizon at one year ahead. Under the fiscal year approach, the planning period becomes shorter as the year progresses. Also, continuous budgeting forces managers into a continuous review and reassessment of the budget estimates and the company's current progress.

The Master Budget: A "Package" of Related Budgets

OBJECTIVE 3
Describe the
elements of
a master
budget.

The "budget" is not a single document. Rather, the **master budget** consists of a number of interrelated budgets which together summarize all the planned activities of the business. The elements of a master budget vary, depending upon the size and nature of the business. However, a typical master budget for a manufacturing business includes:

1 Operating budgets
  a Sales forecast
  b Production schedule (stated in number of units to be produced)
  c Manufacturing expense budget
  d Operating expense budget
  e Budgeted income statement
2 Capital expenditures budget
3 Financial budgets
  a Cash budget
  b Budgeted balance sheet

Some elements of the master budget are **segmented by responsibility centers.** The budgeted income statement, for example, is segmented to indicate the budgeted revenue and expenses of each profit center. The cash budget is segmented to show the budgeted cash flows for each cost center as well as each revenue center. The production schedule and manufacturing cost budget may be segmented to indicate the unit production and manufacturing costs budgeted for each production process. The portion of the budget relating to an individual responsibility center is called a **responsibility budget.** As explained in Chapter 24, responsibility budgets are an important element of a responsibility accounting system.

The many budgets and schedules comprising the master budget are closely interrelated. Some of these relationships are illustrated in the diagram on the following page.

Steps in Preparing a Master Budget

OBJECTIVE 4
Prepare any
of the bud-
gets or sup-
porting
schedules
included in
a master
budget.

Some parts of the master budget should not be prepared until other parts have been completed. For example, the budgeted financial statements are not prepared until the sales, manufacturing, and operating expense budgets are available. A logical sequence of steps for preparing the annual elements of the master budget is described below. (Through the use of color, these steps also are illustrated in our diagram of the elements of the budget.)

1 **Prepare a sales forecast.**   The sales forecast is the starting point in the preparation of a master budget. This forecast is based upon past experience, estimates of general business and economic conditions, and expected levels of competition. A forecast of the expected level of sales is a prerequisite to scheduling production and to budgeting revenue and variable costs.

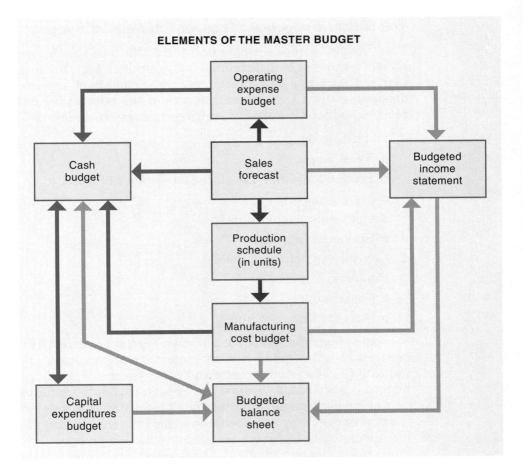

To emphasize the central role of the sales forecast in the budgeting process, the sales forecast in our budget diagram is shown in red. The arrows indicate that information "flows" from this forecast into several other budgets.

2 **Prepare budgets for production, manufacturing costs, and operating expenses.** Once the level of sales has been forecast, production may be scheduled and estimates made of the expected manufacturing costs and operating expenses for the year (red arrows). These elements of the master budget depend upon both the level of sales and cost-volume relationships.

3 **Prepare a budgeted income statement.** The budgeted income statement is based upon the sales forecast, the manufacturing costs comprising the cost of goods sold, and the budgeted operating expenses (green arrows).

4 **Prepare a cash budget.** The cash budget is a forecast of the cash receipts and cash payments for the budget period. As shown by the blue arrows in the budget diagram, the cash budget is affected by many of the other budget estimates.

The budgeted level of cash receipts depends upon the sales forecast, credit terms offered by the company, and the company's experience in collecting amounts receivable from customers. Budgeted cash payments depend upon the forecasts of manufacturing costs, operating expenses, and capital expenditures, as well as the credit terms offered by suppliers. Anticipated borrowing, debt repayment, cash dividends, and issuances of capital stock also are reflected in the cash budget.

5 **Prepare a budgeted balance sheet.** A projected balance sheet cannot be prepared until the effects of cash transactions upon various asset, liability, and owners' equity accounts have been determined. In addition, the balance sheet is affected by budgeted capital expenditures and budgeted net income (pink arrows).

The capital expenditures budget covers a span of many years. This budget is continuously reviewed and updated, but it is not prepared anew on an annual basis.

Preparing the Master Budget: An Illustration

To illustrate the preparation of a master budget, assume that Berg Company makes and sells a single product. Management has asked for a master budget for the first and second quarter of the coming year. The balance sheet for Berg Company at January 1 is shown below:

BERG COMPANY
Balance Sheet
January 1, Current Year

Assets

Current assets:		
Cash		$ 75,000
Receivables		82,000
Inventories:		
Direct materials	$ 25,000	
Finished goods (FIFO method)	52,000	77,000
Prepayments		21,000
Total current assets		$255,000
Plant and equipment:		
Buildings and equipment	$970,000	
Less: Accumulated depreciation	420,000	
Total plant and equipment		550,000
Total assets		$805,000

Liabilities & Stockholders' Equity

Current liabilities:		
Notes payable, 12% ($40,000 payable quarterly)		$160,000
Other current payables		78,000
Income taxes payable		25,000
Total current liabilities....................................		$263,000
Stockholders' equity:		
Capital stock, no par, 100,000 shares outstanding	$350,000	
Retained earnings	192,000	542,000
Total liabilities & stockholders' equity		$805,000

Sales of the company's product are seasonal; sales during the second quarter are expected to exceed first-quarter sales by 50%. However, the economies of a stable level of production have led management to schedule production of **120,000** units in both the first and second quarters.

Operating Budget Estimates The various operating budgets (except for the budgeted income statement) for each of the first two quarters are shown below:

BERG COMPANY
Operating Budget Estimates
First and Second Quarters of the Current Year

Schedule		1st Quarter	2nd Quarter
A1	*Sales forecast:*		
	Selling price per unit:..............................	$ 3.00	$ 3.00
	Budgeted sales (in units)	100,000	150,000
	Budgeted sales (in dollars)	$300,000	$450,000
A2	*Production schedule (in units):*		
	Budgeted sales (**A1**)..................................	100,000	150,000
	Add: Ending inventory of finished goods	50,000	20,000
	Units budgeted to be available for sale	150,000	170,000
	Less: Beginning inventory of finished goods	30,000	50,000
	Planned production of finished goods	120,000	120,000

		Per Quarter
A3	*Manufacturing cost estimates:*	
	Variable costs:	
	Per unit manufactured:	
	Direct materials	$ 0.50
	Direct labor	0.60
	Variable manufacturing overhead	0.30
	Fixed costs (per quarter):	
	Manufacturing overhead	$ 42,000
A4	*Manufacturing cost budget (for 120,000 units):*	
	Direct materials used ($0.50 per unit)	$ 60,000
	Direct labor ($0.60 per unit)	72,000
	Variable manufacturing overhead ($0.30 per unit)	36,000
	Fixed manufacturing overhead	42,000
	Total cost of finished goods manufactured	$210,000
	Cost per unit ($210,000 ÷ 120,000 units)	$1.75

Schedule		1st Quarter	2nd Quarter
A5	*Ending finished goods inventory:*		
	50,000 units at $1.75 (**A4**)	$ 87,500	
	20,000 units at $1.75 (**A4**)		$ 35,000
A6	*Operating expense budget:*		
	Variable expenses ($0.30 × units sold)...............	$ 30,000	$ 45,000
	Fixed expenses	70,000	70,000
	Total selling and administrative expense	$100,000	$115,000

Estimates of unit sales and sales prices per unit (Schedule *A1*) are based upon future marketing plans and forecasts of future economic conditions. The production schedule (Schedule *A2*) reflects both the decision to stabilize production and a decision to reduce the inventory of finished goods from its January 1 level of 30,000 to 20,000 units at the end of the second quarter. (Notice that the inventory of finished goods must rise to 50,000 units at the end of the first quarter in order to meet the budgeted sales and ending inventory of the second quarter.)

The cost estimates in Schedule *A3* provide the basis for budgeting manufacturing costs. Schedule *A4,* the manufacturing budget, indicates the budgeted cost of producing 120,000 finished units in each quarter.

Schedule *A5* shows the dollar value of the ending inventories of finished goods that will be on hand if the targets in the sales budget and the manufacturing budget are met. Schedule *A6,* the operating expense budget, summarizes numerous estimates made by departmental managers in light of the budgeted sales volume.

Budgeted Income Statement   The budgeted income statements for each quarter shown below are based upon the estimates in Schedules *A1* through *A6*. In addition, these income statements include budgeted amounts for interest expense and income taxes expense. The $160,000 note payable in the January 1 balance sheet is a bank loan payable in quarterly installments of $40,000, plus accrued interest, due at the end of each quarter. Interest at 12% per year, or 3% per quarter, is computed on the outstanding balance of $160,000 during the first quarter, and on $120,000 during the second quarter. Income tax expense is budgeted at 40% of income before income taxes.

BERG COMPANY
Budgeted Income Statements
First Two Quarters of Current Year

	1st Quarter	2nd Quarter
Sales (A1)...	$300,000	$450,000
Cost of goods sold:		
Finished goods, beginning inventory	$ 52,000	$ 87,500
Cost of finished goods manufactured (A4)..............	210,000	210,000
Cost of goods available for sale	$262,000	$297,500
Less: Finished goods, ending inventory (A5)	87,500	35,000
Cost of goods sold	$174,500	$262,500
Gross profit on sales	$125,500	$187,500
Operating expenses:		
Selling and administrative expenses (A6)................	$100,000	$115,000
Interest expense......................................	4,800	3,600
Total operating expenses	$104,800	$118,600
Income before income taxes	$ 20,700	$ 68,900
Income taxes (40% of income before income taxes)........	8,280	27,560
Net income...	$ 12,420	$ 41,340

Here is what quarterly income should be (margin note)

The budgeted income statement shows the effects that our budgeted activities are expected to have upon revenue, expense, and net income. We are now ready to estimate the cash flows required by implementing our operating budgets and also to determine the effects of the budgeted activities upon balance sheet accounts.

Financial Budget Estimates The estimates and data necessary to prepare a cash budget and budgeted balance sheet for each quarter follow. (The amounts used in the preparation of the cash budget are highlighted in red.)

BERG COMPANY
Financial Budget Estimates
First and Second Quarters of Current Year

Schedule		1st Quarter	2nd Quarter
B1	*Budgeted direct materials purchases and inventory:*		
	Direct materials used *(A4)*	$ 60,000	$ 60,000
	Desired ending inventory	40,000	40,000
	Direct materials available for use	$100,000	$100,000
	Less: Inventory at beginning of quarter	25,000	40,000
	Budgeted direct materials purchases................	$ 75,000	$ 60,000

B2 *Means of financing costs and expenses:*

	Total	Current Payables	Expiration of Prepayments	Depreciation
First quarter:				
Direct materials purchases *(B1)*	$ 75,000	$ 75,000		
Direct labor *(A4)*	72,000	72,000		
Manufacturing overhead— variable and fixed *(A4)*	78,000	64,000	$4,400	$ 9,600
Selling and administrative expense *(A6)*	100,000	94,600	3,000	2,400
Total	$325,000	$305,600	$7,100	$12,000
Second quarter:				
Direct materials purchases *(B1)*	$ 60,000	$ 60,000		
Direct labor *(A4)*	72,000	72,000		
Manufacturing overhead— variable and fixed *(A4)*	78,000	64,400	$4,000	$ 9,600
Selling and administrative expense *(A6)*	115,000	109,500	3,100	2,400
Total	$325,000	$305,900	$7,100	$12,000

Schedule		1st Quarter	2nd Quarter
B3	*Payments on current payables:*		
	Balance at beginning of quarter.......................	$ 78,000	$101,500
	Increase in payables during quarter *(B2)*	305,600	305,900
	Total payables during quarter.......................	$383,600	$407,400
	Estimated balance at end of quarter (given)...	101,500	85,000
	Payments on current payables during quarter	$282,100	$322,400

Schedule		1st Quarter	2nd Quarter
B4	**Prepayments budget:**		
	Balance at beginning of quarter......................	$ 21,000	$ 15,600
	Estimated cash expenditure during quarter...........	2,000	12,000
	Total prepayments	$ 23,000	$ 27,600
	Expiration of prepayments (B2)......................	7,400	7,100
	Prepayments at end of quarter......................	$ 15,600	$ 20,500
B5	**Debt service budget:**		
	Liability to bank at beginning of quarter..............	$160,000	$120,000
	Interest expense for the quarter......................	4,800	3,600
	Total principal plus accrued interest	$164,800	$123,600
	Cash payments (principal and interest)..............	44,800	43,600
	Liability to bank at end of quarter...................	$120,000	$ 80,000
B6	**Budgeted income taxes:**		
	Income tax liability at beginning of quarter	$ 25,000	$ 8,280
	Estimated income taxes for the		
	quarter (per budgeted income statement)...........	8,280	27,560
	Total accrued income tax liability	$ 33,280	$ 35,840
	Cash payments (tax liability at beginning		
	of quarter)	25,000	8,280
	Income tax liability at end of quarter	$ 8,280	$ 27,560
B7	**Estimated cash receipts from customers:**		
	Balance of receivables at beginning of year	$ 82,000	
	Collections on first-quarter sales of		
	$300,000 ($\frac{2}{3}$ in first quarter and $\frac{1}{3}$ in second)........	200,000	$100,000
	Collections on second-quarter sales of		
	$450,000 ($\frac{2}{3}$ in second quarter)		300,000
	Cash receipts from customers	$282,000	$400,000
B8	**Budgeted accounts receivable:**		
	Balance at the beginning of the quarter	$ 82,000	$100,000
	Sales on open account during quarter (A1)...........	300,000	450,000
	Total accounts receivable.........................	$382,000	$550,000
	Less: Estimated collections on accounts		
	receivable (B7).....................................	282,000	400,000
	Estimated accounts receivable balance		
	at end of quarter	$100,000	$150,000

Let us now briefly discuss each of these schedules:

Schedule B1 In our manufacturing budget (page 1158), we estimated the cost of direct materials expected to be *used* in our manufacturing process at $60,000. In preparing a cash budget, however, we need to know the cost of direct materials to be *purchased* each quarter, rather than used. In budgeting purchases of direct materials, we must consider both the expected use of materials and the desired direct materials inventory at the end of each quarter.

Let us assume that the production supervisor feels that the January 1 inventory of materials of $25,000 is too low. The supervisor recommends that the materials inventory be increased to $40,000 and maintained at that level. Schedule *B1* calculates the purchases of direct materials required to achieve this desired inventory level while allowing for the use of $60,000 of materials each quarter.

Schedule B2   The next step in preparing a cash budget is to estimate the portion of our budgeted costs and expenses which must be **paid in cash** in the near future. Costs and expenses may be financed in any of three ways: through (1) current payables (including accounts payable, accrued expenses payable, and immediate cash payments), (2) expiration of prepaid expenses, and (3) depreciation of plant assets.

Schedule *B2* shows how the budgeted costs and expenses of Berg Company are expected to be financed. The column headed "Current Payables" indicates the portion of the costs and expenses to be paid in cash or financed by current liabilities. Examples of these items include purchases of direct materials (whether for cash or on account), factory payrolls, and utilities bills. The column headed "Expiration of Prepayments" includes costs and expenses stemming from the expiration of short-term prepayments, such as unexpired insurance and prepaid rent.

The budgeted manner of financing the costs and expenses listed in Schedule *B2* is based upon an analysis of the prepaid expenses at the beginning of the first quarter and upon computations of depreciation on plant assets. All costs and expenses other than those resulting from depreciation or the expiration of prepayments require future cash payments and, therefore, are listed as current payables.

Schedule B3   The purpose of this schedule is to estimate the cash payments required each quarter for the costs and expenses classified as current payables in Schedule *B2*. The starting point in Schedule *B3* is the balance of the current payables at the beginning of the first quarter ($78,000), which is taken from the January 1 balance sheet on page 1157. To this amount, we add the $305,600 shown in Schedule *B2* as the total current payables budgeted to arise during the first quarter. From this subtotal ($383,600), we subtract the estimated balance of current payables at the end of the quarter to determine the cash payments to be made during the first quarter. The $101,500 balance of current payables at the end of the first quarter was estimated by Berg Company's treasurer after an analysis of suppliers' credit terms.

Similar computations are made for the second quarter. The beginning balance of current payables for the second quarter is the ending balance from the first quarter. Again, the amount payable at the end of the second quarter ($85,000) was estimated by the treasurer.

Schedule B4   This schedule budgets the expected cash payments for prepaid expenses during the period. These payments were estimated by the treasurer after considering the amount of prepaid expenses at January 1 and the expiration of these items indicated in Schedule *B2*.

Schedule B5   This schedule summarizes the cash payments required on Berg Company's bank loan during the budget period. The loan agreement calls for quarterly payments of $40,000 plus the interest accrued during the quarter. Interest is computed at an annual rate of 12%, or 3% per quarter. Thus, the interest amounts to $4,800 for the first quarter ($160,000 loan $\times$ 3%) and $3,600 in the second ($120,000 outstanding balance $\times$ 3%).

Schedule B6 The budgeted cash payments for income tax expense are summarized in Schedule *B6*. Each quarter, Berg Company makes income tax payments equal to its income tax liability at the beginning of that quarter.

Schedule B7 All of Berg Company's sales are made on account. Therefore, the sole source of the company's cash receipts is the collection of accounts receivable. The credit manager estimates that two-thirds of the sales in any quarter will be collected in that quarter and that the remaining one-third will be collected in the following quarter. Schedule *B7* indicates the budgeted cash collections under these assumptions. (Losses from uncollectible accounts are ignored in our example.)

Schedule B8 This schedule indicates the effect that credit sales (from the sales budget) and collections from customers (Schedule *B7*) are expected to have upon the balance of accounts receivable. The balances shown for accounts receivable at the end of each quarter are carried forward to the budgeted balance sheets on page 1164.

Cash Budget The information derived from the financial budget schedules is the basis for the following quarterly cash budget.

BERG COMPANY
Cash Budget
First Two Quarters of Current Year

	1st Quarter	2nd Quarter
Cash balance at beginning of quarter	$ 75,000	$ 3,100
Cash receipts:		
Cash received from customers (B7)	282,000	400,000
Total cash available	$357,000	$403,100
Cash payments:		
Payment of current payables (B3)	$282,100	$322,400
Prepayments (B4)	2,000	12,000
Payments on notes, including interest (B5)	44,800	43,600
Income tax payments (B6)	25,000	8,280
Total disbursements	$353,900	$386,280
Cash balance at end of the quarter	$ 3,100	$ 16,820

Projected cash flow and ending cash balance

The cash budget is an important tool for forecasting whether the company will be able to meet its obligations as they mature. Often the cash budget may indicate a need for short-term borrowing or other measures to generate or conserve cash in order to keep the company solvent. Remember that one of the principal reasons for preparing budgets is to give advance warning of potential problems such as cash shortages.

Budgeted Balance Sheet We now have the necessary information to forecast the financial position of the Berg Company at the end of each of the next two quarters. The budgeted balance sheets are illustrated on the following page. Budget schedules from which various figures on the balance sheets have been derived are indicated parenthetically.

BERG COMPANY
Budgeted Balance Sheets
As of the End of First Two Quarters of Current Year

Assets	*1st Quarter*	*2nd Quarter*
Current assets:		
Cash *(per cash budget)*	$ 3,100	$ 16,820
Receivables *(B8)*	100,000	150,000
Inventories:		
Direct materials *(B1)*.............................	40,000	40,000
Finished goods *(A5)*	87,500	35,000
Prepayments *(B4)*	15,600	20,500
Total current assets	$246,200	$262,320
Plant and equipment:		
Buildings and equipment	$970,000	$970,000
Less: Accumulated depreciation *(B2)*.................	(432,000)	(444,000)
Total plant and equipment	$538,000	$526,000
Total assets	$784,200	$788,320

Liabilities & Stockholders' Equity		
Current liabilities:		
Notes payable, 12% *(B5)*	$120,000	$ 80,000
Other current payables *(B3)*.........................	101,500	85,000
Income taxes payable *(B6)*	8,280	27,560
Total current liabilities	$229,780	$192,560
Stockholders' equity:		
Capital stock, no par, 100,000 shares issued		
and outstanding.......................................	$350,000	$350,000
Retained earnings, beginning of quarter	192,000	204,420
Net income for the quarter *(per budgeted*		
income statements)....................................	12,420	41,340
Total stockholders' equity	$554,420	$595,760
Total liabilities & stockholders' equity	$784,200	$788,320

Projected quarterly balance sheet

Using Budgets Effectively

Earlier in this chapter, we noted several ways in which budgeting benefits an organization. One benefit, an increased awareness by managers of the company's operations and its business environment, may be received even if the completed budget is promptly filed and forgotten. In preparing a budget, managers are forced to consider carefully all aspects of the company's activities. This study and analysis should, in itself, enable managers to do a better job of managing.

The primary benefits of budgeting, however, stem from the uses made of the budgeted information. Among these benefits are (1) advance warning of conditions that require advance corrective action, (2) coordination of the activities of all the departments within the organization, and (3) the creation of standards for evaluating the performance of company personnel. Let us consider how the master budget for Berg Company might serve these functions.

An Advance Warning of Potential Trouble One of the major concerns of the management of Berg Company was the ability of the company to meet the quarterly payments on its loan obligations. The cash budget for the first two quarters of the year indicates that the cash position of the company at the end of each quarter will be precariously low. A cash balance of $3,100 is forecast at the end of the first quarter, and a balance of $16,820 at the end of the second quarter. If all goes well the payments *can* be met, but there is little margin for error in the estimates.

When confronted with such a forecast, management should take steps in advance to prevent the cash balance from dropping as low as the budgeted amounts. It may be possible to obtain longer credit terms from suppliers and thus reduce payments on accounts payable during the first two quarters. The company may decide to let inventories fall below scheduled levels in order to reduce cash payments relating to manufacturing costs. An extension of the terms of the note payable might be sought, or the possibility of long-term financing might be considered. If any or all of these steps were taken, it would be necessary to revise the budget estimates accordingly. The fact that management is *forewarned* of this condition several months before it happens illustrates one of the prime values of budgeting.

Coordination of the Activities of Departments   The budget provides a comprehensive plan for all the departments to work together in a coordinated manner. For example, the production department knows the quantity of goods which must be produced to meet the expected needs of the sales department. The purchasing department knows the quantities of direct materials which must be ordered to meet the requirements of the production department. Responsibility budgets inform every segment manager of the level of performance expected of his or her responsibility center during the budget period.

A Yardstick for Evaluating Managerial Performance   Comparison of actual results with budgeted amounts is a common means of evaluating the performance of segment managers. As discussed in Chapter 24, the evaluation of performance should be based only upon those revenues and costs which are *under the control* of the person being evaluated. Therefore, in a responsibility budget, budgeted fixed costs should be subdivided into the categories of *controllable costs* and *committed costs.*

Performance may become difficult to evaluate if the actual level of activity (either sales or production) differs substantially from the level originally budgeted. Assume, for example, that sales for the first quarter are considerably higher than forecast. Not only will revenue differ substantially from the originally budgeted amount, but so will variable costs, production levels, cash flows, and the March 31 balance sheet amounts. Thus, the usefulness of the original budget as a yardstick for evaluating performance is greatly reduced. The solution to this problem lies in *flexible budgeting.*

Flexible Budgeting

A *flexible budget* is one that can be easily adjusted to show budgeted revenue, costs, and cash flows at different levels of activity. Thus, if a change in volume lessens the usefulness of the original budget, a new bud-

OBJECTIVE 5
Prepare a
flexible bud-
get and ex-
plain its
usefulness.

get may be prepared quickly that reflects the actual level of activity for the period.

To illustrate the usefulness of a flexible budget, assume that Harold Stone, production manager of Berg Company, is presented with the following performance report at the end of the first quarter of the current year. This performance report compares the manufacturing costs originally budgeted for the quarter (Schedule *A4* on page 1158) with the actual results.

BERG COMPANY
Performance Report for Production Department
For the Quarter Ended March 31, 19—

120,000 units

Is this good or poor performance?

	Budgeted	Actual	Over or (Under) Budget
Manufacturing costs:			
Direct materials used	$ 60,000	$ 63,800	$ 3,800
Direct labor	72,000	76,500	4,500
Variable overhead	36,000	38,000	2,000
Fixed overhead.............................	42,000	42,400	400
Total manufacturing costs	$210,000	$220,700	$10,700

At first glance, it appears that the production manager's cost control performance is quite poor, since all production costs exceeded the budgeted amounts. However, we have deliberately omitted one piece of information from this performance report. To meet unexpectedly high customer demand for the company's product, the production department produced **130,000** units, instead of the **120,000** units originally budgeted for the first quarter.

Under these circumstances, we should reevaluate our conclusions concerning the manager's ability to control manufacturing costs. At this higher level of production, variable manufacturing costs should naturally exceed the originally budgeted amounts. In order to evaluate the performance of the production manager, the budget must be adjusted to indicate the levels of cost that should be incurred in manufacturing 130,000 units.

Flexible budgeting may be viewed as combining the concepts of budgeting and cost-volume-profit analysis. Using the cost-volume-profit estimates in Schedule *A3* (page 1158), the manufacturing cost budget for Berg Company may be revised to reflect any level of production. For example, in the following schedule these relationships are used to forecast quarterly manufacturing costs at three different levels of production:

Test

	Level of Production (In Units)		
	110,000	120,000	130,000
Manufacturing cost estimates from Schedule A3:			
Variable costs:			
Direct materials ($0.50 per unit).....................	$ 55,000	$ 60,000	$ 65,000
Direct labor ($0.60 per unit)........................	66,000	72,000	78,000
Manufacturing overhead ($0.30 per unit).............	33,000	36,000	39,000
Fixed costs:			
Manufacturing overhead	42,000	42,000	42,000
Total manufacturing costs	$196,000	$210,000	$224,000

Notice that budgeted *variable* manufacturing costs change with the level of production, but that budgeted *fixed* costs remain the same.

Let us modify the performance report for the production department to reflect the actual *130,000* unit level of production achieved during the first quarter:

BERG COMPANY
Performance Report for Production Department
For the Quarter Ended March 31, 19___

		Level of Production (In Units)			Actual Costs Over or (Under) Flexible Budget
		Originally Budgeted 120,000	Flexible Budget 130,000	Actual 130,000	
Flexible budget shows a different picture	*Manufacturing costs:*				
	Direct materials used	$ 60,000	$ 65,000	$ 63,800	$(1,200)
	Direct labor	72,000	78,000	76,500	(1,500)
	Variable overhead	36,000	39,000	38,000	(1,000)
	Fixed overhead................	42,000	42,000	42,400	400
	Total manufacturing costs	$210,000	$224,000	$220,700	$(3,300)

This comparison paints quite a different picture from the performance report on the preceding page. Considering the actual level of production, the production manager has kept all manufacturing costs below budgeted amounts, with the exception of fixed overhead (most of which may be committed costs).

The techniques of flexible budgeting also may be applied to profit centers by applying cost-volume-profit relationships to the actual level of *sales* achieved.

Computers and Flexible Budgeting   Adjusting the entire budget to reflect a different level of sales or production would be a sizable task in a manual system. In a computer-based system, however, it can be done quickly and easily. Once the cost-volume-profit relationships have been entered into the budgeting program, the computer almost instantly can perform the computations to generate a complete master budget for any level of business activity.

Many businesses use their budgeting software to generate complete budgets under many different assumptions. These companies use this software as a planning tool to assess the expected impact of changes in sales, production, or other key variables upon all aspects of their business operations.

STANDARD COSTS: FOCUSING ATTENTION ON COST VARIANCES

In Chapter 22 we saw how cost accounting systems are used to determine the actual cost to manufacture products or to perform specific manufacturing processes. A cost accounting system becomes even more useful when it

OBJECTIVE 6
Explain how
standard
costs assist
managers in
controlling
the costs of
a business.

includes the budgeted amounts for direct materials, labor, and manufacturing overhead to serve as standards for comparison with the actual costs. The budgeted amounts used in a cost accounting system are called *standard costs.* Standard costs may be used in both job order and process cost accounting systems.

The standard cost is the cost that *should be* incurred to produce a product *under normal conditions.* Thus, comparison of actual costs with the predetermined standard alerts managers to those areas in which the actual costs appear excessive. Assume, for example, that the standard (budgeted) cost of making a product is $10 per unit. If job no. 430, which requires 1,000 units of the product, has an average unit cost of $12.50, management should investigate immediately to determine why actual costs exceeded the standard by such a large margin (25%).

Cost accountants often speak of the "standard" materials cost and the "standard" labor cost: Remember that these "standard" costs are actually *budgeted* costs.

Establishing and Revising Standards

Standard costs are established during the budgeting process. Along with the budget, standard costs should be reviewed periodically and revised if significant changes occur in production methods or the prices paid for materials, labor, or overhead. When actual costs exceed standard costs because of waste or inefficiency, however, the standard costs should *not* be revised upward. The standard cost for direct materials, for example, would not be changed if some of the materials placed in production were spoiled because of carelessness by employees. The standard cost for direct material would be changed, however, if the price of the materials were increased by the supplier. Similarly, the standard cost for labor would not be changed merely because excessive hours of labor were wasted; but it would be changed if laborsaving equipment were installed or if new contracts with labor unions called for increased wage rates.

Cost Variances

Even though standard costs are carefully set and are revised as conditions change, actual costs will still vary somewhat from standard costs. The differences between standard costs and actual costs are called *cost variances.* Cost variances for materials, labor, and overhead result from a variety of different causes. Thus, in evaluating the efficiency of manufacturing operations, these cost variances should be measured and analyzed. As might be expected, different managers within the organization are responsible for different types of cost variances.

When standard costs are used in a cost accounting system, the costs charged to the Work in Process Inventory, Finished Goods Inventory, and Cost of Goods Sold accounts are *standard costs, not actual costs.* Any differences between the actual and standard costs are recorded in *cost variance accounts.* A separate cost variance account is used for each type of cost variance. Thus, the cost accounting system provides managers with information as to the *nature and amount* of all differences between the actual and budgeted manufacturing costs.

A cost variance is said to be **favorable** when actual costs are less than standard costs. When actual costs exceed standard costs, the cost variance is said to be **unfavorable.**

Illustration of Standard Costs

To illustrate the use of standard costs and the computation of cost variances, assume that product C is one of the products produced by Briar Mfg. Co. The company produces an average of **6,000 units** of product C per month. The standard manufacturing cost per unit, assuming production at the average level of 6,000 units per month, is shown below:

Direct materials (3 pounds @ $5.00)		$15
Direct labor (2.0 hours @ $12.00 per hour)		24
Manufacturing overhead (based upon 12,000 standard direct labor hours):		
Fixed ($120,000 ÷ 6,000 units)	$20	
Variable	1	21
Standard cost per unit of finished goods		$60

During March, Briar Mfg. Co. deliberately reduced the level of its finished goods inventory by scheduling and producing only 5,000 units of product C. Actual manufacturing costs incurred during March were as follows:

Direct materials (14,500 pounds @ $5.20)		$ 75,400
Direct labor (9,800 hours × $13)		127,400
Manufacturing overhead:		
Fixed	$122,020	
Variable	6,180	128,200
Total manufacturing costs incurred in March		$331,000

There was no work in process at either the beginning or the end of March.

By comparing the actual costs incurred in March to the standard costs, we can determine the net cost variance for the month:

Actual costs (above)	$331,000
Standard cost for producing 5,000 units (5,000 units × $60)	300,000
Net unfavorable cost variance (excess of actual costs over standard costs)	$ 31,000

Actual costs incurred during the month **exceeded** the standard cost of producing 5,000 units by **$31,000.** In planning corrective action, management needs to know the specific causes of this $31,000 unfavorable cost variance. By comparing each element of manufacturing cost (direct materials, direct labor, and overhead) to the related standard costs, we can explain the net cost variance for March in greater detail. Let us begin by determining the portion of this variance which is attributable to the price and the quantity of direct materials used in March.

Materials Price and Materials Quantity Variances

*OBJECTIVE 7
Compute the
materials,
labor, and
overhead
variances
and explain
the meaning
of each cost
variance.*

In establishing the standard material cost for each unit of product, two factors were considered: (1) the **quantity** of materials that should have been used in making a unit of finished product and (2) the **prices** that should have been paid in acquiring this quantity of materials. Therefore, the total materials cost variance may result from differences between standard and actual **quantities** of materials used or between standard and actual **prices paid** for materials, or from a combination of these two factors. This can be illustrated by the following diagram:

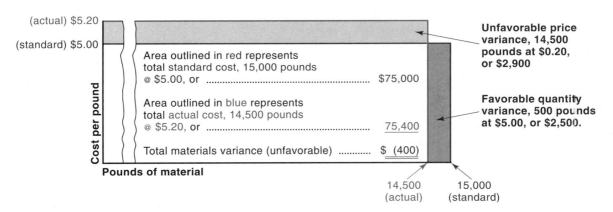

The $400 excess of actual materials cost over the standard materials cost was caused by two factors: (1) a $2,900 unfavorable **materials price variance** and (2) a $2,500 favorable **materials quantity variance.**

The unfavorable **materials price variance** results from the fact that each of the 14,500 pounds of direct material used during the period cost **20 cents more** than the standard $5 price. The materials price variance is the responsibility of the manager responsible for purchasing materials—namely, the purchasing agent.

A formula for computing the materials price variance is illustrated below:

Materials Price Variance = Actual Quantity Used × (Standard Price − Actual Price)
= 14,500 pounds × ($5.00 − $5.20)
= −$2,900 (or $2,900 Unfavorable)

(All of our variance formulas result in a negative number when the variance is unfavorable, and a positive number when the variance is favorable.)

The favorable **materials quantity variance** of $2,500 resulted from the production department using **500 fewer pounds of material** than allowed by the 3 pound per-unit standard in producing 5,000 units of finished product. This variance indicates that the production supervisors are doing a good job in seeing that materials are used efficiently in the production process. The materials quantity variance may be computed as shown below:

Materials Quantity Variance = Standard Price × (Standard Quantity − Actual Quantity)
= $5 × (15,000 pounds − 14,500 pounds)
= $2,500 Favorable

The two materials cost variances may be summarized as follows:

Actual Quantity at Actual Price 14,500 lb × $5.20 $75,400	Actual Quantity at Standard Price 14,500 lb × $5.00 $72,500	Standard Quantity at Standard Price 15,000 lb × $5.00 $75,000
	Materials Price Variance **$2,900 Unfavorable**	**Materials Quantity Variance** **$2,500 Favorable**

Total Materials Variance, $400 Unfavorable

The journal entry to record the cost of materials used during March, and the related cost variances, is shown below:

Work in Process Inventory (standard cost).....................	*75,000*	
Materials Price Variance (unfavorable)	*2,900*	
Materials Quantity Variance (favorable)		*2,500*
Direct Materials Inventory (actual cost)		*75,400*
To record cost of direct materials used in March.		

Notice that the Work in Process account is debited for the **standard cost** of materials used, but that the Materials Inventory account is credited for the actual cost of materials used. The differences between the standard and actual costs of materials used are recorded in the two **cost variance accounts.**[1] Unfavorable variances are recorded by debit entries, because they represent costs in excess of the standard cost; favorable variances are recorded by credit entries, because they represent cost savings relative to the standard amounts.

Labor Rate and Labor Efficiency Variances

Briar incurred actual direct labor costs of $127,400 in March, although the standard labor cost of producing 5,000 finished units is only $120,000 (5,000 units × 2 labor hours per unit × $12 per hour). Thus, the company incurred an unfavorable total labor cost variance of **$7,400.** We can gain additional insight into the reasons for this excessive labor cost by dividing the total labor variance into a labor rate variance and a separate labor efficiency variance.

Actual labor costs are a function of (1) the wage rate paid to direct labor workers and (2) the number of direct labor hours worked. A **labor rate variance** shows the extent to which differences between actual and standard hourly wage **rates** contribute to the total labor variance. The **labor efficiency variance** indicates the extent to which the total labor variance results from differences between the budgeted and actual number of **labor hours** required in the production process.

The labor rate variance is equal to the actual number of hours worked, multiplied by the difference between the standard and actual hourly wage rates. The computation of the labor rate variance for Briar in March is as follows:

Labor Rate Variance = Actual Labor Hours × (Standard Hourly Rate − Actual Hourly Rate)
= 9,800 hours × ($12.00 − $13.00)
= −$9,800 (or $9,800 Unfavorable)

---

[1] An alternative is to record the materials price variance at the time that the materials are purchased. Such alternatives are discussed in the cost accounting course.

An ***unfavorable*** labor rate variance may result from using highly paid employees to perform lower payscale jobs or from poor scheduling of production that results in unnecessary overtime.[2] The production manager is responsible for assigning employees to production tasks and also for scheduling production. Therefore, the production manager is responsible for labor rate variances.

The labor efficiency variance (also called labor usage variance) is a measure of workers' productivity. This variance is favorable if workers are able to complete the scheduled production in fewer hours than are allowed by the standard. An unfavorable labor efficiency variance represents excessive labor costs resulting from wasted time or low levels of hourly productivity. The labor efficiency variance is computed by multiplying the standard hourly wage rate by the difference between the standard and actual number of direct labor hours used, as shown below:

Labor Efficiency Variance = Standard Hourly Rate × (Standard Hours − Actual Hours)
= $12.00 per hour × (10,000 hours − 9,800 hours)
= $2,400 Favorable

The ***favorable*** labor efficiency variance indicates that direct workers were able to complete the scheduled level of production in ***less time*** than was allowed in the standard cost estimates. Production managers are responsible for the productivity of direct workers and, therefore, for the labor efficiency variance.

The two labor cost variances may be summarized as follows:

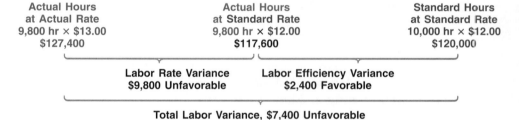

Actual Hours at Actual Rate	Actual Hours at Standard Rate	Standard Hours at Standard Rate
9,800 hr × $13.00	9,800 hr × $12.00	10,000 hr × $12.00
$127,400	$117,600	$120,000

Labor Rate Variance $9,800 Unfavorable   Labor Efficiency Variance $2,400 Favorable

Total Labor Variance, $7,400 Unfavorable

The journal entry to record direct labor costs relating to work performed in March is:

Work in Process Inventory (standard cost)...................	*120,000*	
Labor Rate Variance	*9,800*	
Labor Efficiency Variance.............................		*2,400*
Direct Labor (actual cost).............................		*127,400*

To record cost of direct labor used in March.

Both the labor rate and the labor efficiency variances are controllable by the production manager. Often, these variances are closely related. For example, assume that during March the production manager decided to use more highly skilled workers to manufacture product C. This strategy could explain both the unfavorable labor rate variance and the favorable labor efficiency variance, as the more highly skilled workers receive a higher hourly wage and also should work faster than less skilled workers.

In this case, however, the production manager's strategy did not pay off. The cost savings resulting from increased productivity ($2,400) were not

---

[2] If the scheduled level of production requires overtime even with efficient scheduling, the overtime wage rate should be reflected in the standard cost.

sufficient to offset the additional costs from the higher hourly wage rates ($9,800). After reviewing these cost variances, the production manager probably will return to the approach of using lower paid workers in the production of product C.

Manufacturing Overhead Variances

The difference between actual manufacturing overhead costs and the standard overhead cost charged to production is called the ***overhead variance.*** Whereas direct materials and direct labor are ***variable*** costs, manufacturing overhead consists primarily of ***fixed*** costs. Therefore, the analysis of the overhead variance differs somewhat from the analysis of the materials and labor variances. The total overhead variance may be subdivided into three or four subvariances. In our discussion, however, we will follow the more common accounting practice of dividing the total overhead variance into two elements: the spending variance and the volume variance.[3]

The Overhead Spending Variance   The most important element of the overhead variance is the ***spending variance***—that is, the difference between overhead shown in a ***flexible budget*** and actual overhead expenditures during the period. The overhead spending variance of Briar Mfg. Co. in March may be computed as follows:

Overhead per flexible budget at 5,000 units of production:		
Fixed	$120,000	
Variable ($1 per unit × 5,000 units)	5,000	$125,000
Actual overhead in March:		
Fixed	$122,020	
Variable	6,180	128,200
Overhead spending variance (unfavorable)		$ (3,200)

The overhead spending variance is the responsibility of the production manager. Presumably, most of the overhead spending variance represents differences between budgeted and actual amounts of ***controllable*** overhead costs. For this reason, the spending variance is sometimes called the ***controllable*** overhead variance. If a significant portion of the spending variance results from differences between the budgeted and actual amounts of ***committed*** costs, the overhead cost standards should be revised.

The Volume Variance   The overhead spending variance has shown us the difference between the amount of overhead included in a flexible budget and the actual overhead costs incurred. The ***volume variance*** represents the difference between overhead ***applied to work in process*** (at standard cost) and the overhead per the flexible budget.

In a standard cost system, overhead is applied (debited) to the Work in Process Inventory account using a standard per-unit cost. On page 1169,

---

[3] "Three-way" and "four-way" analysis of the overhead variance will be illustrated and explained in the cost accounting course.

we computed the standard per-unit cost of manufacturing overhead at $21. Thus, the Work in Process Inventory account will be debited with $21 in overhead costs for each unit produced.

A temporary problem may arise when overhead is applied at a standard per-unit amount. Using a standard unit cost to apply overhead means that the total amount of applied overhead will **vary directly with the number of units produced.** In essence, a standard cost system treats overhead as a **variable cost.** In reality, however, overhead consists primarily of **fixed costs.**

To illustrate the temporary distortions that may result from using a standard unit cost to apply overhead to Work in Process Inventory, let us compare applied overhead to flexible budget overhead for Briar at three different levels of monthly production.

	Actual Production (In Units)		
	5,000	6,000	7,000
Overhead applied to Work in Process			
Inventory using $21 per unit standard cost	$105,000	$126,000	$147,000
Overhead per flexible budget:			
Fixed	$120,000	$120,000	$120,000
Variable ($1 per unit)	5,000	6,000	7,000
Total overhead per flexible budget	$125,000	$126,000	$127,000
Volume variances—favorable (unfavorable)	$ (20,000)	$ –0–	$ 20,000

Notice that when actual production is 6,000 units per month, the "normal" level of production, there is no volume variance. This is because our $21 standard cost figure **assumes** the 6,000 unit per month level of production. As shown on page 1169, the $21 per-unit standard cost **includes $20 per-unit in fixed costs** ($120,000 budgeted fixed overhead ÷ 6,000 units). Whenever actual production is less than 6,000 units, less than $120,000 in fixed overhead costs will be applied to production. In March, for example, only **5,000** units were produced. Thus, use of a standard cost that includes **$20** per unit in fixed overhead applies only **$100,000** in fixed overhead costs to work in process. The remaining $20,000 in fixed overhead budgeted for the month is recorded as an **unfavorable** volume variance. This unfavorable volume variance actually represents **underapplied overhead.**

The situation reverses whenever actual production exceeds the normal level. When actual monthly production is **greater** than 6,000 units, use of a standard unit cost applies **more than** $120,000 in fixed overhead costs to work in process. Comparison of the applied overhead to the budget then indicates a **favorable** volume variance. This favorable variance should be viewed as **overapplied** overhead.

The key point is that **volume variances represent over- or underapplied overhead;** they occur automatically whenever actual production differs from the average level of production assumed in computing the standard overhead cost per unit. Over time, actual production should average approximately the level used in developing the standard cost. Thus, the favorable and unfavorable volume variances should "balance out" over the year.

As long as the production department is producing the desired number of units, volume variances do ***not*** indicate either strong or poor performance. Volume variances are the natural result of variations in the scheduled level of production from month to month. Scheduled production may vary from month to month because of such factors as seasonal sales demand, an effort to increase or decrease inventories, or holidays and vacations. Thus, unless the production department fails to produce the scheduled number of units, no manager should be considered "responsible" for a volume variance.

Summary of the Overhead Cost Variances The two overhead variances incurred in March by Briar Mfg. Co. may be summarized as follows:

Actual Overhead		Overhead per Flexible Budget		Overhead Applied at Standard Cost
Fixed .	$122,020	Fixed	$120,000	5,000 units × $21
Variable	6,180	Variable (5,000 × $1)	5,000	
Total ..	$128,200	Total..............	$125,000	$105,000

Spending Variance
$3,200 Unfavorable

Volume Variance
$20,000 Unfavorable

Total Overhead Variance, $23,200 Unfavorable

The journal entry to apply overhead costs to production in March, and to record the overhead cost variances, is:

Work in Process Inventory (standard cost).................	*105,000*	
Overhead Spending Variance.............................	*3,200*	
Overhead Volume Variance..................................	*20,000*	
Manufacturing Overhead (actual)......................		*128,200*

To assign overhead costs to 5,000 units of production at standard rate of $21 per unit, and to record overhead cost variances.

Valuation of Finished Goods

In a standard cost system, only standard costs are debited to the Work in Process Inventory account. Thus, finished goods manufactured are valued at standard cost as they are transferred into the Finished Goods Inventory account and the Cost of Goods Sold account. The entry made at the end of March to record the completion of 5,000 units of product C is shown below:

Finished Goods Inventory: Product C	*300,000*	
Work in Process Inventory: Product C.................		*300,000*

To record completion during March of 5,000 units of product C at standard cost (5,000 units × $60 per unit = $300,000).

Notice that the inventory of finished goods is valued at ***standard cost.*** As units of product C are sold, this standard cost will be transferred into the Cost of Goods Sold account.

Disposition of Cost Variance Accounts The balances in the variance accounts represent differences between actual manufacturing costs and the standard costs used in the valuation of finished goods inventory and the cost of goods sold. These balances are allowed to accumulate in the variance accounts from month to month. Hopefully, the favorable and unfavorable variances will "balance out" over the year, and only a small balance will remain in each variance account at year-end. In this case, the variance accounts are simply closed into the cost of goods sold, since most of the difference between actual and standard cost is applicable to goods sold during the year.

However, if the net cost variance for the year is ***material in dollar amount,*** it should be apportioned among the Work in Process Inventory, Finished Goods Inventory, and Cost of Goods Sold accounts in order to restate these accounts at actual cost.

Evaluation of Cost Variances

We have now computed six separate cost variances to explain in greater detail the $31,000 net unfavorable cost variance incurred by Briar Mfg. Co. in March. These variances are summarized below:

Cost variances:		
Materials price variance—unfavorable	$ (2,900)	
Materials quantity variance—favorable	2,500	
Total materials variance—unfavorable		$ (400)
Labor rate variance—unfavorable	$ (9,800)	
Labor efficiency variance—favorable	2,400	
Total labor variance—unfavorable		(7,400)
Overhead spending variance—unfavorable	$ (3,200)	
Overhead volume variance—unfavorable	(20,000)	
Total labor variance—unfavorable		(23,200)
Net unfavorable cost variance in March		$(31,000)

This summary should assist managers in identifying problem areas and in controlling costs in future months. For example, the unfavorable materials price variance highlights the fact that the purchasing department should be able to purchase the direct materials used in product C at a lower cost. The favorable materials quantity variance, in contrast, indicates that the production department is using materials in a very efficient manner.

However, the production manager has a serious problem with respect to labor rates. The large unfavorable labor variance indicates that the strategy of using more highly paid workers in manufacturing product C is not cost effective. Therefore, the manager should change this strategy and return to using lower payscale workers in the manufacture of this product.

The overhead spending variance also indicates excessive levels of expenditures. Now that managers are alerted to this problem, they should look more carefully for opportunities to reduce overhead costs. The large negative volume variance should not be a matter of concern—this variance resulted automatically from the deliberate action of scheduling only 5,000 units of production in March. As soon as production returns to the normal level of 6,000 units per month, this variance will disappear.

Summary of Cost Variances

For your convenience, the six cost variances discussed in this chapter are summarized below.

Variance	Computation	Responsible Manager
Materials:		
Price variance	Actual Quantity × (Standard Price − Actual Price)	Purchasing agent
Quantity variance	Standard Price × (Standard Quantity − Actual Quantity)	Production manager
Labor:		
Rate variance	Actual Hours × (Standard Hourly Rate − Actual Hourly Rate)	Production manager
Efficiency (usage) variance	Standard Hourly Rate × (Standard Hours − Actual Hours)	Production manager
Overhead:		
Spending variance	Overhead per Flexible Budget − Actual Overhead	Production manager (to extent variance relates to controllable costs)
Volume variance	Applied Overhead (at Standard Rate) − Overhead per Flexible Budget	None—this variance results from scheduling production at any level other than "normal"

END-OF-CHAPTER REVIEW

SUMMARY OF CHAPTER LEARNING OBJECTIVES

1 **Discuss the benefits that a company may derive from a formal budgeting process.**
The benefits of budgeting are simply the benefits which come from "thinking ahead." Budgeting helps to coordinate the activities of the different departments, provides a basis for evaluating departmental performance, and often provides managers with advance warning of possible problems. In addition, budgeting forces management to estimate future economic conditions, including costs of materials, demand for the company's products, and interest rates.

2 **Explain two "philosophies" that may be used in setting budgeted amounts.**
The most widely used approach is to set budgeted amounts at levels which are *reasonably achievable* under "normal" operating conditions. The goal in this case is to make the budget a fair and reasonable basis for evaluating performance.
    An alternative is to budget an "ideal" level of performance. Under this approach, departments normally fall somewhat short of budgeted performance, but the variations may identify areas in which improvement is possible.

3 Describe the elements of a master budget.

A "master budget" actually is a group of related budgets and forecasts which together summarize all the planned activities of the business. For example, a master budget usually includes a sales forecast, a production schedule, a manufacturing costs budget, an operating expense budget, a cash budget, a capital expenditures budget, and projected financial statements. The number and type of individual budgets and schedules which make up the master budget depend upon the size and nature of the business.

4 Prepare any of the budgets or supporting schedules included in a master budget.

Preparation of any budget (or supporting schedule) involves two basic considerations. First, the budgeted levels of performance should be reasonable and achievable. Second, the activity summarized in the budget should be coordinated with the related activities budgeted for other departments. For example, a production schedule should be realistic in terms of plant capacity and available labor and materials. However, it also should be coordinated with the company's sales forecast and the budgeted level of production costs.

5 Prepare a flexible budget and explain its usefulness.

A flexible budget shows budgeted revenue, costs, and profits for different levels of business activity. Thus, a flexible budget can be used to evaluate the efficiency of departments throughout the business even if the actual level of business activity differs from management's original estimates. The amounts included in a flexible budget at any given level of activity are based upon cost-volume-profit relationships.

6 Explain how standard costs assist managers in controlling the costs of a business.

Standard costs are the "expected" (or budgeted) costs per unit. When standard costs are used in a cost accounting system, differences between actual costs and budgeted costs are immediately recorded in the accounting records as cost variances. Thus, any "cost overruns" or other variations from the budget are promptly brought to management's attention.

7 Compute the materials, labor, and overhead variances and explain the meaning of each cost variance.

Cost variances are computed by comparing actual costs to standard costs and explaining the reasons for any differences. Differences in the cost of materials used may be caused either by variations in the price paid to purchase materials or in the quantity of materials used. Differences in the cost of direct labor may be caused by variations in wage rates or in the number of hours worked. Variances from budgeted levels of factory overhead may be caused by differences in outlays for controllable overhead expenditures or in the actual and budgeted levels of production.

Chapter 25 serves as something of a "capstone" for the preceding several chapters. The preparation of a budget and the use of standard costs draw heavily upon the concepts of product costing, cost-volume-profit analysis, and responsibility accounting. When these concepts and tools are brought together in a well-designed accounting system, managers are provided with a wealth of information useful in planning and controlling the operations of every segment of the business. In our next and final chapter, we will see how managers select and utilize the information most relevant to specific types of business decisions.

KEY TERMS INTRODUCED OR EMPHASIZED IN CHAPTER 25

Budget A plan or forecast for a future period expressed in quantitative terms. Establishes objectives and aids in evaluating subsequent performance.

Continuous budgeting A technique of extending the budget period by one month as each month passes. Therefore, the budget always covers the upcoming 12 months.

Cost variance A difference between the actual level of cost incurred and the standard (budgeted) level for the cost. The total cost variance may be subdivided into separate cost variances indicating the amount of variance attributable to specific causal factors.

Flexible budget A budget that can readily be revised to reflect budgeted amounts given the actual levels of activity (sales and production) achieved during the period. Makes use of cost-volume-profit relationships to restate the master budget for the achieved level of activity.

Labor efficiency variance The portion of the total labor variance caused by a difference between the standard and actual number of labor hours to complete the task. Computed as *Standard hourly rate × (Standard hours − Actual hours).* Also called labor usage variance.

Labor rate variance The portion of the total labor variance caused by a difference between the standard hourly wage rate and the rate actually paid to workers. Usually stems from overtime or using workers at a different payscale than assumed in developing the standard cost. Computed as *Actual hours × (Standard hourly rate − Actual hourly rate).*

Master budget An overall financial and operating plan, including budgets for all aspects of business operations and for all responsibility centers.

Materials price variance The portion of the total materials variance caused by paying a different price to purchase materials than was assumed in the standard cost. Computed as *Actual quantity × (Standard unit price − Actual unit price).*

Materials quantity variance The portion of the total materials variance caused by using more or less material in the production process than is called for in the standards. Computed as *Standard unit price × (Standard quantity − Actual quantity).*

Overhead spending variance The portion of the total overhead variance caused by incurring more overhead costs than are indicated in a flexible budget prepared for the actual level of activity achieved.

Performance report A schedule comparing the actual and budgeted performance of a particular responsibility center.

Responsibility budget A portion of the master budget showing the budgeted performance of a particular responsibility center within the organization.

Standard cost The budgeted cost that should be incurred under normal, efficient conditions.

Standard cost system An accounting system in which inventories and the cost of goods sold are valued at standard costs, and cost variances are separately accumulated in cost variance accounts. A tool for promptly alerting management to significant cost variances.

Volume variance   The portion of the total overhead variance that results from a difference between the actual level of production and the "normal" level assumed in computing the standard unit cost. In effect, the volume variance is a misallocation of fixed overhead costs and often is not relevant in evaluating segment performance.

SELF-TEST QUESTIONS

Answers to these questions appear on page 1193.

1   Which of the following statements correctly describe relationships within the master budget? (More than one answer may be correct.)

a   The manufacturing budget is based in large part upon the sales forecast.

b   In many elements of the master budget, the amounts budgeted for the upcoming quarter are reviewed and subdivided into monthly budget figures.

c   The manufacturing cost budget affects the budgeted income statement, the cash budget, and the budgeted balance sheet.

d   The capital expenditures budget has a greater effect upon the budgeted income statement than it does upon the budgeted balance sheet.

2   During the first quarter of its operations, Morris Mfg. Co. expects to sell 50,000 units and create an ending inventory of 20,000 units. Variable manufacturing costs are budgeted at $10 per unit, and fixed manufacturing costs at $100,000 per quarter. The company's treasurer expects that 80% of the variable manufacturing costs will require cash payment during the quarter and that 20% will be financed through accounts payable and accrued liabilities. Only 50% of the fixed manufacturing costs are expected to require cash payments during the quarter.

In the cash budget, payments for manufacturing costs during the quarter will total:

a $800,000   b $610,000   c $600,000   d $450,000

3   Rodgers Mfg. Co. prepares a flexible budget. The original budget forecast sales of 100,000 units @ $20, and operating expenses of $300,000 fixed, plus $2 per unit. Production was budgeted at 100,000 units. Actual sales and production for the period totaled 110,000 units. When the budget is adjusted to reflect these new activity levels, which of the following budgeted amounts will increase, but by *less than* 10%?

a   Sales revenue.

b   Variable manufacturing costs.

c   Fixed manufacturing costs.

d   Total operating expenses.

4   For the number of equivalent full units actually produced, the flexible budget called for the use of 9,500 pounds of materials at a standard cost of $10 per pound. The production department actually used 10,000 pounds of materials costing $9.90 per pound. The production manager should be considered responsible for:

a   An unfavorable cost variance of $4,000.

b   A favorable price variance of $1,000.

    c An unfavorable quantity variance of $5,000.

    d None of the above; the flexible budget should be adjusted to reflect the use of 10,000 pounds of material.

5 An unfavorable volume variance indicates that:

    a Total fixed overhead exceeded budgeted amounts.

    b Variable overhead per unit exceeded budgeted amounts.

    c The production department failed to produce the quantity of units called for in the production schedule.

    d The actual production for the period was less than the normal volume used in establishing the standard unit cost.

ASSIGNMENT MATERIAL

DISCUSSION QUESTIONS

1 Explain the relationship between the managerial functions of *planning* and *controlling costs.*

2 Briefly explain at least three ways in which a business may expect to benefit from preparing a formal budget.

3 Criticize the following quotation:
    "At our company, budgeted revenue is set so high and budgeted expenses so low that no department can ever meet the budget. This way, department managers can never relax; they are motivated to keep working harder no matter how well they are already doing."

4 Identify at least five budgets or schedules which are often included in the master budget of a manufacturing business.

5 List in a logical sequence the major steps in the preparation of a master budget.

6 Why is the preparation of a sales forecast one of the earliest steps in preparing a master budget?

7 What are *responsibility budgets?* What responsibility segments would serve as the basis for preparing responsibility sales budgets in a large retail store, such as **Sears** or **Nordstrom?**

8 What is a *flexible budget?* Explain how a flexible budget increases the usefulness of budgeting as a means of evaluating performance.

9 An article in *Business Week* stated that approximately one-third of the total federal budget is considered "controllable." What is meant by a budgeted expenditure being controllable? Give two examples of government expenditures that may be considered "noncontrollable."

10 Define *standard costs* and briefly indicate how they may be used by management in planning and control.

11 What is wrong with the following statement: "There are three basic kinds of cost accounting systems: job order, process, and standard"?

12 Once standard costs are established, what conditions would require that standards be revised?

13 List the variances from standard cost that are generally computed for direct materials, direct labor, and manufacturing overhead.

14 Would a production manager be equally responsible for an unfavorable materials price variance and an unfavorable materials quantity variance? Explain.

15 What is meant by a favorable labor efficiency variance? How is the labor efficiency variance computed?

16 Explain the cause of an unfavorable and of a favorable overhead *volume variance.*

17 Why is an unfavorable overhead volume variance not usually considered in evaluating the performance of the production department manager?

EXERCISES

EXERCISE 25-1
Accounting
Terminology

Listed below are nine technical accounting terms introduced in this chapter:

Overhead spending variance	Materials price variance	Materials quantity variance
Labor rate variance	Master budget	Standard costs
Labor efficiency variance	Flexible budget	Volume variance

Each of the following statements may (or may not) describe one of these technical terms. For each statement, indicate the accounting term described, or answer "None" if the statement does not correctly describe any of the terms.

a The additional cost or cost savings resulting from the actual number of required hours of direct labor differing from standard.

b A budget showing cost levels which departmental managers may not exceed without written permission from top management.

c The budgeted costs of producing a product under normal conditions.

d An overall financial plan for the operation of a business, which includes separate budgets or supporting schedules for each aspect of business operations.

e A variance that is always favorable when more units are sold than are produced during the period.   *I could be inventory*

f The difference between actual manufacturing overhead and the level of overhead budgeted for the level of output actually achieved.

g A budget which may be readily adjusted to show budgeted amounts at different possible levels of output.

h The difference between the standard and actual unit cost of materials used, multiplied by the actual quantity of materials used.

EXERCISE 25-2
Budgeting Purchases and Cash Payments

The following information is taken from the manufacturing budget and budgeted financial statements of Wexler Fabrication:

Direct materials inventory, Jan. 1	$ 62,000
Direct materials inventory, Dec. 31	75,000
Direct materials budgeted for use during the year	220,000
Accounts payable to suppliers of direct materials, Jan. 1	48,000
Accounts payable to suppliers of direct materials, Dec. 31	60,000

INSTRUCTIONS

Compute the budgeted amounts for:

a Purchases of direct materials during the year.

b Cash payments during the year to suppliers of direct materials.

EXERCISE 25-3
Budgeting
Cash Receipts

Sales on account for the first two months of the current year are budgeted as follows:

January	$600,000
February	800,000

All sales are made on terms of 2/10, n/30; collections on accounts receivable are typically made as follows:

Collections within the month of sale:	
Within discount period	60%
After discount period	15%
Collections within the month following sale:	
Within discount period	15%
After discount period	7%
Returns, allowances, and uncollectibles	3%
Total	100%

INSTRUCTIONS Compute the estimated cash collections on accounts receivable for the month of *February*.

EXERCISE 25-4
Preparing a
Flexible Budget

The flexible budget at the 70,000-unit and the 80,000-unit level of activity is shown below:

	70,000 Units	80,000 Units	90,000 Units
Sales	$1,400,000	$1,600,000	$
Cost of goods sold	840,000	960,000	
Gross profit on sales	$ 560,000	$ 640,000	$
Operating expenses ($90,000 fixed)	370,000	410,000	
Operating income	$ 190,000	$ 230,000	$
Income taxes (30% of operating income)	57,000	69,000	
Net income	$ 133,000	$ 161,000	$

INSTRUCTIONS Complete the flexible budget at the 90,000-unit level of activity. Assume that the cost of goods sold and variable operating expenses vary directly with sales and that income taxes remain at 30% of operating income.

EXERCISE 25-5
More on
Flexible Budgeting

The cost accountant for Amalfi Leather Goods prepared the following monthly performance report relating to the Finishing Department:

	Budgeted Production (10,000 Units)	Actual Production (11,000 Units)	Variances Favorable	Variances Unfavorable
Direct materials used	$300,000	$320,000		$20,000
Direct labor	100,000	115,000		15,000
Variable manufacturing overhead	20,000	21,500		1,500
Fixed manufacturing overhead	150,000	149,200	$800	

INSTRUCTIONS Prepare a revised performance report in which the variances are computed by comparing the actual costs incurred with estimated costs *using a flexible budget* for 11,000 units of production.

EXERCISE 25-6
Relationships among Standard Costs, Actual Costs, and Cost Variances

The standard costs and variances for direct materials, direct labor, and factory overhead for the month of May are given below:

	Standard Cost	Variances Unfavorable	Variances Favorable
		Variances	
	Standard Cost	*Unfavorable*	*Favorable*
Direct materials	$ 90,000		
Price variance		$4,500	
Quantity variance			$2,700
Direct labor	180,000		
Rate variance			1,800
Efficiency variance		5,400	
Manufacturing overhead	270,000		
Spending variance			3,600
Volume variance			2,400

INSTRUCTIONS Determine the **actual costs** incurred during the month of May for direct materials, direct labor, and manufacturing overhead.

EXERCISE 25-7
Computing Materials Cost Variances

One of the products of Hearts & Flowers is a one-pound box of chocolate candy, packaged in a box bearing the customer's logo. (Minimum order, 100 boxes.) The standard cost of the chocolate candy used is $2 per pound. During November, 20,000 of these one-pound boxes were produced, requiring 20,800 pounds of chocolate candy at a total direct materials cost of $42,640.

Determine the materials price variance and quantity variance with respect to the candy used producing this product.

EXERCISE 25-8
Computing Labor Cost Variances

One of the most popular products of Loring Glassworks is a hand-decorated vase. The company's standard cost system calls for .75 hours of direct labor per vase, at a standard wage rate of $8.25. During September, Loring produced 4,000 vases at an actual direct labor cost of $24,464 for 2,780 direct labor hours.

INSTRUCTIONS a What was the average hourly pay rate of the direct workers producing the vases in September?

b Compute the labor rate and efficiency variances for the month.

c Was using workers on the payscale indicated in part **a** an effective strategy? Explain.

EXERCISE 25-9
Computing Overhead Cost Variances

From the following information for Alfred Industries, compute the overhead spending variance and the volume variance.

Standard manufacturing overhead based on normal monthly volume:		
Fixed ($300,000 ÷ 20,000 units)	$15.00	
Variable ($100,000 ÷ 20,000 units)	5.00	$20.00
Units actually produced in current month		18,000 units
Actual overhead costs incurred (including $300,000 fixed)		$383,800

EXERCISE 25-10
Elements of the Materials Cost Variances

The following computation of the materials variances of Weitzen Foods is incomplete. The missing data is labeled **(a)** through **(d)**.

Materials price variance = 3,640 pounds × [**(a)** standard price − $9.00 actual price] .... $910 Unfavorable

Materials quantity variance = **(b)** × [3,800 pounds − **(c)** actual quantity] . $ **(d)**

INSTRUCTIONS	Supply the missing data for items *(a)* through *(d)*. Prepare a caption describing the item, as well as indicating the dollar amount of physical quantity. Briefly explain each answer, including how you determined the amount.
EXERCISE 25-11 **Computing Materials and Labor Variances**	Nolan Mills uses a standard cost system. During May, Nolan manufactured 15,000 pillowcases, using 27,000 yards of fabric costing $3.05 per yard and incurring direct labor costs of $19,140 for 3,300 hours of direct labor. The standard cost per pillowcase assumes 1.75 yards of fabric at $3.10 per yard, and 0.2 hours of direct labor at $5.95 per hour.
INSTRUCTIONS	**a** Compute both the price variance and quantity variance relating to direct materials used in the manufacture of pillowcases in May.
	b Compute both the rate variance and efficiency variance for direct labor costs incurred in manufacturing pillowcases in May.
EXERCISE 25-12 **Causes of Cost Variances**	For each of the following variances, briefly explain at least one probable cause and indicate the departmental manager (if any) responsible for the variance.
	a A favorable materials price variance.
	b An unfavorable labor rate variance.
	c A favorable volume variance.
	d An unfavorable materials quantity variance.

PROBLEMS

Group A

PROBLEM 25A-1 **Budgeting Manufacturing Overhead**	Yung Hsin, Inc., manufactures a component which is processed successively by Department A and Department B. Manufacturing overhead is applied to units of production at the following standard costs:

	Manufacturing Overhead Per Unit		
	Fixed	*Variable*	*Total*
Department A	$14.40	$6.80	$21.20
Department B	10.40	4.90	15.30

These standard manufacturing overhead costs per unit are based on a normal volume of production of 5,000 units per month. In January, variable manufacturing overhead is expected to be *15%* above standard in Department B because of scheduled repairs to equipment. The company plans to produce 4,500 units during January.

INSTRUCTIONS	Prepare a budget for manufacturing overhead costs in January. Use column headings as follows: Total, Department A, and Department B.
PROBLEM 25A-2 **Short Budgeting Problem**	Harmony Corporation at present manufactures and sells a single product. In preparing the budget for the first quarter, the company's cost accountant has assembled the following information:

	Units	*Dollars*
Sales (budgeted)	150,000	$12,150,000
Finished goods inventory, Jan. 1 (actual)	30,000	1,080,000
Finished goods inventory, Mar. 31 (budgeted)	20,000	?
Cost of finished goods manufactured (budgeted manufacturing cost is $39 per unit)	?	?

The company uses the first-in, first-out method of pricing its inventory of finished goods.

INSTRUCTIONS   Compute the following budgeted quantities or dollar amounts:

a   Planned production of finished goods (in units).

b   Cost of finished goods manufactured.

c   Finished goods inventory, Mar. 31. (Remember to use the first-in, first-out method in pricing the inventory.)

d   Cost of goods sold.

**PROBLEM 25A-3
Preparing a
Cash Budget**

Barnum Distributors wants a projection of cash receipts and cash payments for the month of November. On November 28, a note will be payable in the amount of $98,500, including interest. The cash balance on November 1 is $29,600. Accounts payable to merchandise creditors at the end of October were $217,000.

The company's experience indicates that 70% of sales will be collected during the month of sale, 20% in the month following the sale, and 7% in the second month following the sale; 3% will be uncollectible. The company sells various products at an average price of $11 per unit. Selected sales figures are shown below:

	Units
September—actual	40,000
October—actual	60,000
November—estimated	80,000
December—estimated	50,000
Total estimated for the current year	800,000

Because purchases are payable within 15 days, approximately 50% of the purchases in a given month are paid in the following month. The average cost of units purchased is $7 per unit. Inventories at the end of each month are maintained at a level of 2,000 units plus 10% of the number of units that will be sold in the following month. The inventory on October 1 amounted to 8,000 units.

Budgeted operating expenses for November are $220,000. Of this amount, $90,000 is considered fixed (including depreciation of $35,000). All operating expenses, other than depreciation, are paid in the month in which they are incurred.

The company expects to sell fully depreciated equipment in November for $8,400 cash.

INSTRUCTIONS   Prepare a cash budget for the month of November, supported by schedules of cash collections on accounts receivable and cash payments for purchases of merchandise.

**PROBLEM 25A-4
Preparing and
Using a Flexi-
ble Budget**

Four Flags is a retail department store. The following cost-volume relationships were used in developing a flexible budget for the company for the current year:

	Yearly Fixed Expenses	Variable Expenses per Sales Dollar
Cost of merchandise sold		$0.600
Selling and promotion expense	$ 210,000	0.082
Building occupancy expense	186,000	0.022
Buying expense	150,000	0.040
Delivery expense	111,000	0.010
Credit and collection expense	72,000	0.002
Administrative expense	531,000	0.003
Totals	$1,260,000	$0.759

Management expected to attain a sales level of $12 million during the current year. At the end of the year the actual results achieved by the company were as follows:

Net sales	10,500,000
Cost of goods sold	6,180,000
Selling and promotion expense	1,020,000
Building occupancy expense	420,000
Buying expense	594,000
Delivery expense	183,000
Credit and collection expense	90,000
Administrative expense	564,000

INSTRUCTIONS

a Prepare a schedule comparing the actual results with flexible budget amounts developed for the actual sales volume of $10,500,000. Organize your schedule as a partial multiple-step income statement, ending with operating income. Include separate columns for (1) flexible budget amounts, (2) actual amounts, and (3) any amount over or (under) budget. Use the cost-volume relationships given in the problem to compute the flexible budget amounts.

b Write a statement evaluating the company's performance in relation to the plan reflected in the flexible budget.

PROBLEM 25A-5
Basic Standard Cost Problem

AgriChem Industries manufactures fertilizer concentrate and uses a cost system. The fertilizer is produced in 500-pound batches; the normal level of production is 250 batches of fertilizer per month. The standard costs per batch are shown below:

	Standard Costs per Batch
Direct materials:	
Various chemicals (500 lbs. per batch @ $0.60/lb.)	$300
Direct labor:	
Preparation and blending (25 hrs. per batch @ $7.00/hr.)	175
Manufacturing overhead:	
Fixed ($50,000 per month ÷ 250 batches)	$200
Variable (per batch)	25	225
Total standard cost per batch of fertilizer	$700

During January, the company temporarily reduced the level of production to 200 batches of fertilizer. Actual costs incurred in January were as follows:

Direct materials (102,500 lbs. @ $0.57/lb.)	$ 58,425
Direct labor (4,750 hrs. @ $6.80/hr.)	32,300
Manufacturing overhead	54,525
Total actual costs (200 batches)	$145,250
Standard cost of 200 batches (200 batches × $700 per batch)	140,000
Net unfavorable cost variance	$ 5,250

INSTRUCTIONS You have been engaged to explain in detail the elements of the $5,250 net unfavorable cost variance, and to record the manufacturing costs for January in the company's standard cost accounting system.

a As a first step, compute the materials price and quantity variances, the labor rate and efficiency variances, and the overhead spending and volume variances for the month.

   b Prepare journal entries to record the flow of manufacturing costs through the standard cost system and the related cost variances. Make separate entries to record the costs of direct materials used, direct labor, and manufacturing overhead. Work in Process Inventory is to be debited only with standard costs.

PROBLEM 25A-6
Computation, Recording, and Analysis of Cost Variances

Heritage Furniture Co. uses a standard cost system. One of the company's most popular products is an oak entertainment center that looks like an old ice box but houses a television, stereo, or other electronic components. The per-unit standard costs of the entertainment center, assuming a "normal" volume of 1,000 units per month, are as follows:

Direct materials, 100 board feet of wood at $1.30 per foot............................		$130.00
Direct labor, 5 hours at $8.00 per hour..		40.00
Manufacturing overhead (applied at $22 per unit)		
Fixed ($15,000 ÷ 1,000 units of normal production)...................	$15.00	
Variable..	7.00	22.00
Total standard unit cost..		$192.00

During July, 800 entertainment centers were scheduled and produced at the following actual unit costs:

Direct materials, 110 feet at $1.20 per foot..	$132.00
Direct labor, $5\frac{1}{2}$ hours at $7.80 per hour....................................	42.90
Manufacturing overhead, $18,480 ÷ 800 units......................................	23.10
Total actual unit cost..	$198.00

INSTRUCTIONS

   a Compute the following cost variances for the month of July:

      1 Materials price variance.

      2 Materials quantity variance.

      3 Labor rate variance.

      4 Labor efficiency variance.

      5 Overhead spending variance.

      6 Volume variance.

   b Prepare journal entries to assign manufacturing costs to the Work in Process Inventory account and to record cost variances for July. Use separate entries for (1) direct materials, (2) direct labor, and (3) overhead costs.

   c Comment upon any significant problems or areas of cost savings revealed by your computation of cost variances. Also comment on any possible causal relationships between significant favorable and unfavorable cost variances.

Group B

PROBLEM 25B-1
Budgeting Labor Costs

Sun Valley Naturals manufactures a product which is first dry roasted and then packed for shipment to customers. The standard direct labor cost per pound of product in each process follows:

Process	Direct Labor Hours per Pound	Standard Direct Labor Cost per Hour
Dry roasting...	.024	$7.50
Packing..	.015	6.00

The budget for November calls for the production of 150,000 pounds of product. The expected labor cost in the dry roasting department is expected to be 7% above standard for the month of November as a result of higher wage rates and inefficiencies in the scheduling of work. The expected cost of labor in the packing room is expected to be 5% below standard because of a new arrangement of equipment.

INSTRUCTIONS   Prepare a budget for direct labor costs for November. Use column headings as follows: Total, Dry Roasting, and Packing.

PROBLEM 25B-2
Budgeting Production Inventories, and the Cost of Sales

Welsh Scientific manufactures and sells a single product. In preparing the budget for the current quarter, the company's controller has assembled the following information:

	Units	Dollars
Sales (budgeted)	126,000	$4,410,000
Finished goods inventory, beginning of the quarter	31,200	594,000
Finished goods inventory, end of the quarter	24,000	?
Cost of finished goods manufactured (budgeted manufacturing cost is $20 per unit)	?	?

The company uses the weighted-average method of pricing its inventory of finished goods.

INSTRUCTIONS   Compute the following budgeted quantities or dollar amounts:

a   Planned production of finished goods (in units).

b   Cost of finished goods manufactured.

c   Finished goods inventory, end of the quarter. (Remember that in using the weighted-average method you must first compute the average cost of units available for sale.)

d   Cost of goods sold.

PROBLEM 25B-3
Flexible Budgeting

Braemar Saddlery uses departmental budgets and performance reports in planning and controlling its manufacturing operations. The following annual performance report for the custom saddle production department was presented to the president of the company.

	Budgeted Costs for 5,000 Units		Actual Costs Incurred	Over or (Under) Budget
	Per Unit	Total		
Variable manufacturing costs:				
Direct materials	$ 30.00	$150,000	$171,000	$21,000
Direct labor	48.00	240,000	261,500	21,500
Indirect labor...........................	15.00	75,000	95,500	20,500
Indirect materials, supplies, etc...........	9.00	45,000	48,400	3,400
Total variable manufacturing costs	$102.00	$510,000	$576,400	$66,400
Fixed manufacturing costs:				
Lease rental.............................	$ 9.00	$ 45,000	$ 45,000	None
Salaries of foremen......................	24.00	120,000	125,000	$ 5,000
Depreciation and other	15.00	75,000	78,600	3,600
Total fixed manufacturing costs	$ 48.00	$240,000	$248,600	$ 8,600
Total manufacturing costs	$150.00	$750,000	$825,000	$75,000

Although a production volume of 5,000 saddles was originally budgeted for the year, the actual volume of production achieved for the year was **6,000** saddles. The company does not use standard costs; direct materials and direct labor are charged to production at actual cost. Factory overhead is applied to production at the predetermined rate of 150% of the actual direct labor cost.

After a quick glance at the performance report showing an unfavorable manufacturing cost variance of $75,000, the president said to the accountant: "Fix this thing so it makes sense. It looks as though our production people really blew the budget. Remember that we exceeded our budgeted production schedule by a significant margin. I want this performance report to show a better picture of our ability to control costs."

INSTRUCTIONS

a Prepare a revised performance report for the year on a flexible budget basis. Use the same format as the production report above, but revise the budgeted cost figures to reflect the actual production level of **6,000** saddles.

b In a few sentences compare the original performance report with the revised report.

c What is the amount of over- or underapplied manufacturing overhead for the year? (Note that a standard cost system is not used.)

PROBLEM 25B-4
Preparing a
Cash Budget

Jake Marley, owner of Marley Wholesale, is negotiating with the bank for a $200,000, 90-day, 12% loan effective July 1 of the current year. If the bank grants the loan, the proceeds will be $194,000, which Marley intends to use on July 1 as follows: pay accounts payable, $150,000; purchase equipment, $16,000; add to bank balance, $28,000.

The current working capital position of Marley Wholesale, according to financial statements as of June 30, is as follows:

Cash in bank...	$ 20,000
Receivables (net of allowance for doubtful accounts)	160,000
Merchandise inventory...	90,000
Total current assets	$270,000
Accounts payable (including accrued operating expenses)	150,000
Working capital..	$120,000

The bank loan officer asks Marley to prepare a forecast of his cash receipts and cash payments for the next three months to demonstrate that the loan can be repaid at the end of September.

Marley has made the following estimates, which are to be used in preparing a three-month cash budget: Sales (all on open account) for July, $300,000; August, $360,000; September, $270,000; and October, $200,000. Past experience indicates that 80% of the receivables generated in any month will be collected in the month following the sale, 19% in the second month following the sale, and 1% will prove uncollectible. Marley expects to collect $120,000 of the June 30 receivables in July, and the remaining $40,000 in August.

Cost of goods sold has averaged consistently about 65% of sales. Operating expenses are budgeted at $36,000 per month plus 8% of sales. With the exception of $4,400 per month depreciation expense, all operating expenses and purchases are on open account and are paid in the month following their incurrence.

Merchandise inventory at the end of each month should be sufficient to cover the following month's sales.

INSTRUCTIONS

a Prepare a monthly cash budget showing estimated cash receipts and cash payments for July, August, and September, and the cash balance at the end of each month. Supporting schedules should be prepared for estimated collections on receivables, estimated merchandise purchases, and estimated payments for operating expenses and of accounts payable for merchandise purchases.

b On the basis of this cash forecast, write a brief report to Marley explaining whether he will be able to repay the $200,000 bank loan at the end of September.

**PROBLEM 25B-5
Using Standard
Costs**

American Hardwood Products uses standard costs in a process cost system. At the end of the current month, the following information is prepared by the company's cost accountant:

	Direct Materials	Direct Labor	Manufacturing Overhead
Actual costs incurred.............................	$96,000	$82,500	$123,240
Standard costs	90,000	84,000	115,500
Materials price variance (favorable)................	2,400		
Materials quantity variance (unfavorable)	8,400		
Labor rate variance (favorable).....................		3,000	
Labor efficiency variance (unfavorable).............		1,500	
Overhead spending variance (unfavorable)			3,240
Overhead volume variance (unfavorable)			4,500

The total standard cost per unit of finished product is $30. During the current month, 9,000 units were completed and transferred to the finished goods inventory and 8,800 units were sold. The inventory of work in process at the end of the month consists of 1,000 units which are 65% completed. There was no inventory in process at the beginning of the month.

INSTRUCTIONS

a Prepare journal entries to record all variances and the costs incurred (at standard) in the Work in Process account. Prepare separate compound entries for (1) direct materials, (2) direct labor, and (3) manufacturing overhead.

b Prepare journal entries to record (1) the transfer of units finished to the Finished Goods Inventory account and (2) the cost of goods sold (at standard) for the month.

c Assuming that the company operated at 90% of its normal capacity during the current month, what is the amount of the fixed manufacturing overhead per month?

**PROBLEM 25B-6
Computing and
Recording
Cost Variances**

The accountants for Polyglaze, Inc., have developed the following information regarding the standard cost and the actual cost of a product manufactured in June:

	Standard Cost	Actual Cost
Direct materials:		
Standard: 10 ounces at $0.15 per ounce............................	$1.50	
Actual: 11 ounces at $0.16 per ounce		$1.76
Direct labor:		
Standard: .50 hours at $10.00 per hour	5.00	
Actual: .45 hours at $10.40 per hour................................		4.68
Manufacturing overhead:		
Standard: $5,000 fixed cost and $5,000 variable cost for		
10,000 units normal monthly volume	1.00	
Actual: $5,000 fixed cost and $4,600 variable cost for 8,000		
units actually produced in June.....................................		1.20
Total unit cost...	$7.50	$7.64

INSTRUCTIONS

a Compute the materials price variance and the materials quantity variance, indicating whether each is favorable or unfavorable. Prepare the journal entry to record the cost of direct materials used during June in the Work in Process account (at standard).

b Compute the labor rate variance and the labor efficiency variance, indicating whether each is favorable or unfavorable. Prepare the journal entry to record the cost of direct labor used during June in the Work in Process account (at standard).

c Compute the overhead spending variance and the overhead volume variance, indicating whether each is favorable or unfavorable. Prepare the journal entry to assign overhead cost to production in June.

CASES AND UNSTRUCTURED PROBLEMS

CASE 25-1
It's Not My Fault

Cabinets, Cabinets, Inc., is a large manufacturer of modular kitchen cabinets, sold primarily to builders and developers. The company uses standard costs in a responsibility accounting system. Standard production costs have been developed for each type of cabinet; these costs, and any cost variances, are charged to the production department. A budget also has been developed for the sales department. The sales department is credited with the gross profit on sales (measured at standard costs) and is charged with selling expenses and any variations between budgeted and actual selling expenses.

In early April, the manager of the sales department asked the production department to fill a "rush" order of kitchen cabinets for a tract of 120 homes. The sales manager stated that the entire order must be completed by May 31. The manager of the production department argued that an order of this size would take 12 weeks to produce. The sales manager answered, "The customer needs it on May 31, or we don't get the business. Do you want to be responsible for our losing a customer who makes orders of this size?"

Of course, the production manager did not want to take that responsibility. Therefore, he gave in and processed the rush order by having production personnel work overtime through April and May. As a result of the overtime, the performance reports for the production department in those months showed large, unfavorable labor rate variances. The production manager, who in the past had prided himself on "coming in under budget," now has very ill feelings toward the sales manager. He also has stated that the production department will never again accept a "rush" order.

INSTRUCTIONS

a Identify any problem which you see in the company's standard cost system or in the manner in which cost variances are assigned to the responsible managers.

b Make recommendations for changing the cost accounting system to reduce or eliminate any problems which you have identified.

CASE 25-2
Determination and Use of Standard Costs

Armstrong Chemical began operations in January. The company manufactures an acrylic floor wax called Tough-Coat. The following standard cost estimates were developed several months before the company began operations, based upon an estimated production of 1,000,000 units:

Material X-1 (one ounce)	$1.00
Material X-2 (one pound)	.50
Direct labor	.80
Manufacturing overhead ($1,400,000 ÷ 1,000,000 units)	1.40
Total estimated standard cost per unit	$3.70

During the year, 1,000,000 units of Tough-Coat were actually produced and 900,000 units were sold. Actual costs incurred during the year were:

Material X-1 purchased, 1,200,000 ounces @ $0.70	$ 840,000
Material X-2 purchased, 1,150,000 pounds @ $0.50	575,000
Direct labor	880,000
Manufacturing overhead	1,400,000
Total production cost incurred during the year.............................	$3,695,000

The company's inventories at the end of the year consisted of the following, with the Finished Goods inventory stated at standard cost:

Direct materials:		
Material X-1, 200,000 ounces @ $0.70	$140,000	
Material X-2, 100,000 pounds @ $0.50	50,000	$190,000
Finished Goods:		
Tough-Coat, 100,000 units @ $3.70 standard cost		370,000
Total inventory at December 31		$560,000

The independent certified public accountant who has been engaged to audit the company's financial statements wants to adjust the valuation of Finished Goods inventory to "a revised standard cost" which would take into account the favorable price variance on material X-1 ($0.30 per ounce) and the 10% wage increase early in the year. (An unfavorable quantity variance on material X-2 was caused by spoilage in production; the CPA feels no adjustment to the standard should be made for this type of item.)

The president of the company objects on the following grounds: "Such a revision is not necessary because the cost of material X-1 already shows signs of going up and the wage increase was not warranted because the productivity of workers did not increase one bit. Furthermore, if we revise our inventory figure of $560,000, our operating income will be reduced from the current level of $50,000." You are called in by the president to help resolve the controversy.

INSTRUCTIONS

a   Do you agree with the president that revision of the $3.70 standard cost figure is not necessary?

b   Assume that you conclude that the standards for this first year of operations should be revised. Compute a "revised standard cost per unit" and determine the value to be assigned to the ending inventory of finished units using this revised standard cost.

c   What effect would this revaluation of Finished Goods inventory have upon the company's operating income?

d   Using the *original* standards, compute the following:

1   Materials price variance and quantity variance for material X-1

2   Materials price variance and quantity variance for material X-2

3   Total direct labor variance (do not separate into rate variance and usage variance.)

4   Total manufacturing overhead variance

ANSWERS TO SELF-TEST QUESTIONS

1 a, b, c   2 b (70,000 units × $10 per unit × 80%) + ($100,000 × 50%) = $610,000   3 d   4 c   5 d

26 Relevant Information, Incremental Analysis, and Capital Budgeting

In this chapter, we discuss several analytical techniques which aid managers in making a variety of business decisions. First, we explain the nature of "relevant" information and show how incremental analysis is used to identify and evaluate this information. Emphasis is given to the relevance of opportunity costs and to the irrelevance of sunk costs.

Our second major topic is capital budgeting—the process of planning and evaluating proposals for investments in plant assets. We illustrate and explain the widely used capital budgeting techniques of payback period, return on average investment, and discounting future cash flows.

We also emphasize the need for managers to be aware of (1) nonfinancial considerations, (2) the long-run implications of their actions, and (3) the possible existence of additional, more advantageous courses of action.

After studying this chapter you should be able to meet these Learning Objectives:

1 *Identify the financial information relevant to a particular business decision.*

2 *Use incremental analysis to evaluate alternative courses of action.*

3 *Discuss the relevance of opportunity costs, sunk costs, and out-of-pocket costs in making business decisions.*

4 *Determine the effect upon operating income of discontinuing a product line.*

5 *Explore a decision: be aware of the nonfinancial considerations, and creatively search for a better course of action.*

6 *Evaluate capital budgeting proposals using (a) the payback period, (b) return on average investment, and (c) discounted future cash flows.*

THE CONCEPT OF RELEVANT INFORMATION

OBJECTIVE 1
Identify the
financial
information
relevant to a
particular
business
decision.

Many types of information may be relevant to a given business decision. For example, information as to the number of jobs to be created or the expected effect of a decision upon the environment or upon public opinion may be quite relevant. Our discussion, however, will be limited to relevant *financial* information—namely, costs and revenue.

All business decisions involve a choice among alternative courses of action. The only information relevant to a decision is that information *which varies among the alternative courses of action being considered.* Costs, revenue, or other factors which *do not vary* among alternative courses of action *are not relevant* to the decision.

To illustrate the concept of relevant information, assume that the sawmill of Sierra Lumber is closed because of a labor strike expected to last for several months. During the strike, Sierra Lumber is incurring costs at the mill of $15,000 per week. (These costs include depreciation, interest expense, and salaries to nonstriking employees.) Assume also that a film company has offered to rent the mill for one week at a price of $10,000 in order to shoot scenes for a new James Bond movie. If the mill is rented to the film company, Sierra's management estimates that clean-up costs will amount to approximately $2,000 after shooting is completed. Based solely upon this information, would it be profitable to rent the closed sawmill to the film company?

If the mill is rented to the film company, the profitability of the mill during that week may be measured as follows:

Revenue		$10,000
Costs and expenses:		
Weekly sawmill expenses	$15,000	
Clean-up cost	2,000	17,000
Operating income (loss)		$ (7,000)

However, not all the information in this income statement is *relevant* to the decision at hand. The $15,000 in weekly sawmill expenses will continue *whether or not* the mill is rented to the film company.

OBJECTIVE 2
Use incre-
mental
analysis to
evaluate al-
ternative
courses of
action.

The relevant factors in this decision are the *differences* between the costs incurred and revenue earned under the alternative courses of action (renting or not renting.) These differences are often called the *incremental* costs and revenue. An incremental analysis of the Sierra Lumber decision is shown as follows:

	Reject Offer	Accept Offer	Incremental Analysis
Revenue	$ 0	$10,000	$10,000
Costs and expenses:			
Weekly sawmill expenses	(15,000)	(15,000)	
Estimated clean-up costs	0	(2,000)	(2,000)
Operating income (loss)	$(15,000)	$ (7,000)	$ 8,000

The incremental analysis shows that accepting the film company's offer results in $10,000 of incremental revenue, but only $2,000 in incremental costs. Thus, renting the sawmill to the company will benefit Sierra by reducing its operating loss for the week by $8,000.

Accepting Special Orders

A more commonplace example of the need to identify relevant information is the decision of whether to accept an order for an additional volume of business at special terms.

To illustrate, assume that one product of Zing Golf Products is golf balls. The company has the capacity to produce 2 million golf balls per month, but actually manufactures only 800,000 balls per month, as this is all that it is able to sell. The balls normally sell for **$1.25** apiece; the cost of manufacturing 800,000 balls in a month amounts to $480,000, or **$0.60** per ball, as shown below:

Manufacturing costs:	
Variable ($0.20 per ball × 800,000 balls).....................................	$160,000
Fixed	320,000
Total cost of manufacturing 800,000 balls per month......................	$480,000
Average manufacturing cost per ball ($480,000 ÷ 800,000 balls).................	$0.60

Now assume that Zing Golf Products receives an offer from a foreign company to purchase 500,000 "private label" golf balls per month. These balls will be imprinted with the name of the foreign company, not with Zing's name. In fact, golfers who purchase the balls will never know that they were manufactured by Zing. These balls will be sold only in the foreign country, and will not affect Zing's regular sales to its own customers. However, the foreign country offers to pay Zing only **$250,000** (or 50 cents per ball) for this special order. Would it be profitable for Zing to accept this order?

At first glance, it appears unprofitable for Zing to accept this special order. Not only is the sales price of $0.50 per ball much less than the regular sales price, it is even less than Zing's $0.60 average per-unit cost of manufacturing golf balls. Let us look, however, at the incremental monthly revenue and manufacturing costs that should result from accepting this special order:

	Production Level		
	Normal (800,000 Balls)	**With Special Order (1,300,000 Balls)**	**Incremental Analysis**
Sales:			
Regular sales @ $1.25..............	$1,000,000	$1,000,000	$ –0–
Special order......................		250,000	250,000
Manufacturing costs:			
Variable ($0.20 per ball)............	(160,000)	(260,000)	(100,000)
Fixed manufacturing costs per month	(320,000)	(320,000)	–0–
Gross profit on golf ball sales	$ 520,000	$ 670,000	$150,000

A special order is profitable if incremental revenue exceeds incremental costs

This analysis shows that accepting the special order will generate incremental revenue of $250,000, and incremental costs of only $100,000.

Therefore, accepting the special order will *increase* Zing's monthly gross profit on golf ball sales *by $150,000.*

The relevant factors in this type of decision are the incremental revenue that will be earned and the additional (incremental) costs that will be incurred by accepting the special order. The only incremental costs of filling the special order are the related *variable* manufacturing costs; accepting the order will *not* increase fixed manufacturing costs. Thus, the $0.60 "average manufacturing cost," which includes fixed costs per unit, is *not relevant* to the decision.[1]

In evaluating the merits of a special order such as the one received by Zing, managers should consider the effect that filling the order might have upon the company's regular sales volume and sales prices. Obviously, it would not be wise for Zing to sell golf balls at 50 cents apiece to a domestic company which might then try to sell the balls to Zing's regular customers for less than Zing's regular sales price ($1.25 per ball). Management should also consider how Zing's large regular customers might react if "word gets out" about Zing accepting this special order. Might these customers also demand the $0.50 per-ball price?

In summary, incremental analysis is a useful tool for evaluating the effects of expected short-term changes in revenue and in costs. Managers should always be alert, however, to the long-run implications of their actions.

Make or Buy Decisions

In many manufacturing operations, a company must decide whether (1) to produce a certain component part required in the assembly of its finished products or (2) to buy the component part from outside suppliers. If the company is currently producing a component part which could be purchased at a lower cost from outsiders, profits *may* be increased by a decision to buy the part and utilize the company's own manufacturing resources for other purposes.

For example, if a company can buy for $5 per unit a part which costs the company $6 per unit to produce, the choice seems to be clearly in favor of buying. But the astute reader will quickly raise the question, "What is included in the cost of $6 per unit?" Assume that the $6 unit cost of producing a normal required volume of 10,000 units per month was determined as follows:

Manufacturing costs:	
Direct materials	$ 8,000
Direct labor	12,500
Variable overhead	10,000
Fixed overhead per month	29,500
Total cost of manufacturing 10,000 units per month........................	$60,000
Average manufacturing cost per unit ($60,000 ÷ 10,000 units)	$6

---

[1] In our discussion, we evaluate only the *profitability* of accepting this order. Some countries have "antidumping" laws that legally prohibit a foreign company from selling its products in that country at a price below the average "full" manufacturing cost per unit. Zing should, of course, consider the legal as well as economic implications of accepting this order.

A review of operations indicates that if the production of this part were discontinued, all the cost of direct materials and direct labor plus $9,000 of variable overhead would be eliminated. In addition, $2,500 of the fixed overhead would be eliminated. These, then, are the **relevant costs** in producing the 10,000 units of the component part, and we can summarize them as follows:

Is it cheaper to make or to buy?

	Make the Part	*Buy the Part*	*Incremental Analysis*
Manufacturing costs for 10,000 units:			
Direct materials	$ 8,000		$ 8,000
Direct labor	12,500		12,500
Variable overhead	10,000	$ 1,000	9,000
Fixed overhead.................................	29,500	27,000	2,500
Purchase price of part, $5 per unit		50,000	(50,000)
Total cost to acquire part	$60,000	$78,000	$(18,000)

Our analysis shows that making the part will cost $60,000 per month, while buying the part will cost $78,000. Thus, the company will save $18,000 per month by continuing to make the part.

In our example, we assumed that only part ($9,000) of the variable overhead incurred in producing the part would be eliminated if the part were purchased. We also assumed that $2,500 of the fixed overhead could be eliminated if the part were purchased. The purpose of these assumptions was to show that not all variable costs are incremental, and that some fixed costs may be incremental in a given situation.

Opportunity Costs

OBJECTIVE 3 Discuss the relevance of opportunity costs, sunk costs, and out-of-pocket costs in making business decisions.

At this stage of our discussion, it is appropriate to introduce the topic of opportunity costs. An **opportunity cost** is the benefit which could have been obtained **by following another course of action.** For example, assume that you pass up a summer job which pays $2,400 in order to attend summer school. The $2,400 may be viewed as an opportunity cost of attending summer school.

Opportunity costs are **not recorded** in the accounting records, but they are an important factor in many business decisions. Ignoring opportunity costs is a common source of error in cost analyses. In our preceding example, we determined that the company could save $18,000 per month by continuing to manufacture a particular part, rather than buying it from an outside supplier. Assume, however, that the production facilities used to make the part could instead be used to manufacture a product which would increase the company's profitability by $25,000 per month. Obviously, the company should not forgo a $25,000 profit in order to save $18,000. When this $25,000 **opportunity cost** is considered, it becomes evident that the company should buy the part and use its productive facilities to produce the more profitable product.

Sunk Costs versus Out-of-Pocket Costs

The only costs relevant to a decision are those costs which vary among the alternative courses of action being considered. A **sunk cost** is one which has **already been incurred** by past actions. Sunk costs are **not relevant** to decisions because they ***cannot be changed*** regardless of what decision is made. The term ***out-of-pocket cost*** is often used to describe costs which have ***not yet*** been incurred and which ***may vary*** among the alternative courses of action. Out-of-pocket costs, therefore, are relevant in making decisions.

Scrap or Rebuild Defective Units

To illustrate the irrelevance of sunk costs, assume that 500 television sets which cost $80,000 to manufacture are found to be defective and management must decide what to do with them. These sets may be sold "as is" for $30,000, or they can be rebuilt and placed in good condition at an additional out-of-pocket cost of $60,000. If the sets are rebuilt, they can be sold for the regular price of $100,000. Should the sets be sold "as is" or rebuilt?

Regardless of whether the sets are sold or rebuilt, the $80,000 sunk cost has already been incurred. The relevant considerations in the decision to sell the sets in their present condition or to rebuild are the ***incremental revenue*** and the ***incremental cost.*** By rebuilding the sets, the company will realize $70,000 more revenue than if the sets are sold "as is." The incremental cost necessary to obtain this incremental revenue is the $60,000 cost of rebuilding the sets. Thus, the company will be $10,000 better off ($70,000 − $60,000) if it rebuilds the sets.

Whether to Discontinue an Unprofitable Product Line

Management often must decide whether a company's overall profitability can be improved by discontinuing one or more product lines. The concepts of incremental analysis and of opportunity costs play important roles in such decisions.

OBJECTIVE 4 Determine the effect upon operating income of discontinuing a product line.

To illustrate, assume that Auto Sound Co. manufactures three products: an economy model car radio, a deluxe car radio that includes a tape deck, and speakers for automobile sound systems. In recent years, increased competition has forced the company to reduce the sales price of its deluxe radios to the point that this product line now has a negative segment margin. A partial income statement for the current month, segmented by product lines, appears below:

AUTO SOUND CO.
Partial Income Statement, Segmented by Product Line
For the Current Month

Should the deluxe radio be discontinued?

	Auto Sound Co.	Economy Radios	Deluxe Radios	Speakers
		Products		
Sales	$600,000	$300,000	$100,000	$200,000
Variable costs	320,000	170,000	70,000	80,000
Contribution margins	$280,000	$130,000	$ 30,000	$120,000
Fixed costs traceable to product lines	100,000	30,000	40,000	30,000
Product segment margins	$180,000	$100,000	$ (10,000)	$ 90,000
Common fixed costs	80,000			
Income from operations	$100,000			

Management is considering whether or not to discontinue deluxe radios. As discussed in Chapter 24, the revenue, variable costs, and fixed costs traceable to a business segment are likely to disappear if that segment is discontinued. Thus, discontinuing the deluxe radio should *eliminate* the $10,000 negative monthly segment margin of that product line. At first glance, we might assume that Auto Sound's monthly operating income should then increase by this amount. However, several other factors must be considered. Two such factors are:

1 How will discontinuing the sale of deluxe radios affect sales of the company's *other products?*
2 What *alternative use* might be made of the production facilities now used in manufacturing deluxe radios?

Competing Products and Complementary Products Many companies offer customers several products that compete directly with one another. For example, Auto Sound's economy model and deluxe model radios are competing products—most customers will buy one or the other, but not both. If the deluxe radio is discontinued, it is logical to expect some increase in the sales of economy radios. Some customers, no longer able to buy the deluxe model, will instead purchase the economy model. Assume that management estimates that sales of the economy radio will *increase by 5%* if the deluxe radio is discontinued.

Companies often also sell complementary products. Complementary products are those for which sales of one may contribute to sales of the other. Assume, for example, that many buyers of Auto Sound Co.'s deluxe radios also buy a set of the company's speakers. Therefore, discontinuing the sale of deluxe radios can be expected to reduce sales of speakers. Management estimates that speaker sales will *decline by 20%* if the deluxe radio is discontinued.

Incremental Analysis To illustrate the effects of expected changes in the sales of other products, we will temporarily assume that no alternative use will be made of the facilities now used in manufacturing deluxe radios. In this case, an incremental analysis of the expected effects of discontinuing the deluxe radio product line is shown below:

Increases in monthly operating income expected from discontinuing the deluxe radio product line:

Elimination of negative monthly segment margin of deluxe radio product line	$10,000
Additional contribution margin from expected 5% increase in sales of economy radios ($130,000 × 5%)	6,500
Total expected increases in operating income	$16,500

Decreases in monthly operating income expected from discontinuing deluxe radio product line:

Decrease in contribution margin from expected 20% decrease in speaker sales ($120,000 × 20%)	(24,000)
Estimated increase (decrease) in monthly operating income if deluxe radio product line is discontinued	$(7,500)

This analysis indicates that although the deluxe radio line has a negative segment margin, discontinuing this product would cause the company's monthly operating income to *decrease* by $7,500. The reason that operating income would decline is not the disappearance of the revenue and costs relating to the deluxe radio segment of the business, but rather the expected loss in contribution margin from sales of speakers—a highly profitable complementary product.

The loss in contribution margin from speaker sales is an *opportunity cost* of discontinuing the deluxe radio line. However, continuing to produce the deluxe radios also may involve an opportunity cost—namely the segment margin of a more profitable product line that might be produced in place of deluxe radios.

Alternative Use of the Facilities   Let us now assume that if the deluxe radio line is discontinued Auto Sound Co. will use the related production facilities to manufacture car phones. Management estimates that the manufacture and sale of car phones will produce a positive segment margin of $50,000 per month. Sales of car phones are not expected to have any effect upon sales of economy radios or speakers. Therefore, the effects of discontinuing the deluxe radios upon these two product lines remains the same as in our preceding analysis. An incremental analysis of manufacturing car phones instead of deluxe car radios follows:

Increases in monthly operating income expected from manufacturing car phones instead of deluxe radios:

Elimination of negative monthly segment margin of deluxe radio product line	$10,000
Expected monthly segment margin from new car phone product line	50,000
Additional contribution margin from expected 5% increase in sales of economy radios ($130,000 × 5%)	6,500
Total expected increases in operating income	$66,500

Decreases in monthly operating income expected from manufacturing car phones instead of deluxe radios:

Decrease in contribution margin from expected 20% decline in speaker sales ($120,000 × 20%)	(24,000)
Estimated increase in operating income if deluxe radio product line is discontinued	$42,500

This analysis indicates that operating income will *increase* by $42,500 per month if the company uses its production facilities to manufacture car phones instead of deluxe radios.

Other Factors to Be Considered   There are, of course, other factors to consider in a decision of whether to discontinue a product line. Perhaps a company wants to avoid laying-off employees, especially if these workers may be needed in the near future to produce new products. Perhaps a company wants to maintain a reputation for offering its customers a "full line" of products, or "state-of-the-art" products, even if it cannot earn a profit from every product line. Perhaps an "unprofitable" product line is an effective "loss leader," which attracts customers who also buy the compa-

OBJECTIVE 5
Explore a
decision: be
aware of the
nonfinancial
considera-
tions, and
creatively
search for a
better course
of action.

ny's profitable products. (Auto Sound's deluxe radio is an effective "loss leader," because sales of this product generate enough contribution margin from additional sales of speakers to more than cover the losses of the deluxe radio segment.)

Looking for Better Alternatives   Incremental analysis is an excellent tool for evaluating alternative courses of action. However, managers should not automatically follow the first course of action that holds a promise of increased profitability. Rather, managers and accountants should always be alert to the possibility of even more satisfactory alternatives. Often, a careful review of the incremental analysis of one possible decision will offer clues to additional, more profitable alternatives.

Consider, for example, our incremental analysis on the preceding page. The principal benefit to be derived from discontinuing the deluxe radio product line is that the company's production facilities can be used more profitably in manufacturing car phones. The one drawback in discontinuing the deluxe radios is the expected loss in contribution margin from a decline in speaker sales. These facts suggest an alternative course of action: perhaps Auto Sound should continue to sell deluxe radios, but should **buy** these radios from an outside supplier ***instead of manufacturing them.*** The company could then use its production facilities to manufacture car phones, while continuing to sell deluxe radios and speakers at the current sales level. The effects of this alternative also may be evaluated through the technique of incremental analysis.

CAPITAL BUDGETING

OBJECTIVE 6
Evaluate
capital bud-
geting pro-
posals using
(a) the pay-
back period,
(b) return
on average
investment,
and (c) dis-
counted fu-
ture cash
flows.

In terms of dollar amounts, some of the most significant decisions made by management involve expenditures to acquire plant assets. The process of planning and evaluating proposals for investment in plant assets is called **capital budgeting.** Capital budgeting decisions are complicated by the fact that the decision must be made from estimates of future operating results, which by their nature involve a considerable degree of uncertainty. Yet these decisions are crucial to the long-run financial health of a business enterprise. Not only are large amounts of money committed for long periods of time, but many capital budgeting decisions are difficult or impossible to reverse once the funds have been committed and the project has begun. Thus, companies may benefit from good capital budgeting decisions and suffer from poor ones for many years.

Many nonfinancial factors are considered in making capital budgeting decisions. For example, many companies give high priority to creating new jobs and avoiding layoffs. However, it is also essential that investments in plant assets earn a satisfactory return on the funds invested. Without this return, investors will not be willing to make funds available to finance the project and the company will not be able to generate sufficient funds for future investment projects.

Capital budgeting is a broad field, involving many sophisticated techniques for evaluating the financial and nonfinancial considerations. We shall limit our discussion in this area to three of the most common techniques of evaluating investment opportunities: payback period, return on average investment, and discounted cash flow analysis.

To illustrate these techniques, let us assume that Tanner Corporation is considering several alternative investments, including the purchase of equipment to produce a new product. The equipment costs $450,000 has a 10-year service life, and an estimated salvage value of $50,000. Tanner Corporation estimates that production and sale of the new product will increase the company's net income by $50,000 per year, computed as follows:

Estimated sales of new product..		$400,000
Deduct estimated expenses:		
Depreciation on new equipment [($450,000 − $50,000) ÷ 10 years].	$ 40,000	
Manufacturing costs other than depreciation	220,000	
Additional selling and general expenses	60,000	320,000
Estimated increase in before-tax income		$ 80,000
Less: Additional income taxes (37½%)...		30,000
Estimated increase in net income...		$ 50,000

Most capital budgeting techniques involve analysis of the estimated annual net cash flows pertaining to the investment. Annual net cash flow is the excess of cash receipts over cash payments in a given year. In our example, assume that all revenue is received in cash and all expenses other than depreciation are paid in cash. Tanner Corporation should expect an annual **net cash flow of $90,000** from sales of the new product ($400,000 − $220,000 − $60,000 − $30,000). Note that annual net cash flow exceeds estimated net income ($50,000) by the amount of the depreciation expense ($40,000). This is because none of the cash received from revenue is paid out for depreciation expense. (Other differences which may exist between net income and net cash flow were discussed in Chapter 19.)

Payback Period

The **payback period** is the length of time necessary to recover the entire cost of an investment from the resulting annual net cash flow. In our example, the payback period is computed as follows:

$$\frac{\text{Amount to Be Invested}}{\text{Estimated Annual Net Cash Flow}} = \frac{\$450,000}{\$90,000} = 5 \text{ years}$$

In selecting among alternative investment opportunities, a short payback period is considered desirable because the sooner the amount of the investment is recovered, the sooner the funds may be put to other use. A short payback period also reduces the risk that changes in economic conditions will prevent full recovery of the investment. Before an investment can be considered profitable, the life of the investment must exceed the payback period. However, the payback period ignores the total life and, therefore, the total profitability of the investment. For this reason, the payback period should never be the only factor considered in a major capital budgeting decision.

Return on Average Investment

The **return on investment (ROI)** is the average annual net income from an investment expressed as a percentage of the **average** amount invested. Tanner Corporation will have to invest $450,000 in the new equipment, but each year depreciation will reduce the carrying value of this asset by $40,000. Since the annual cash flow will exceed net income by this amount, we may view depreciation expense as providing for the recovery of the amount originally invested. Thus, the amount invested in the equipment at any given time is represented by the carrying value (cost less accumulated depreciation) of the asset.

When straight-line depreciation is used, the carrying value of an asset decreases uniformly over the asset's life. Thus, the average carrying value is equal to an amount halfway between the asset's original cost and its salvage value. (When the expected salvage value is zero, the average investment is simply one-half of the original investment.) Mathematically, the average amount invested over the life of an asset may be determined as follows:

$$\text{Average Investment} = \frac{\text{Original Cost} + \text{Salvage Value}}{2}$$

Thus, Tanner Corporation will have an average investment in the new equipment of ($450,000 + $50,000) ÷ 2, or $250,000. We may compute the expected rate of return on this average investment as follows:

$$\frac{\text{Average Estimated Net Income}}{\text{Average Investment}} = \frac{\$50,000}{\$250,000} = 20\%$$

In deciding whether 20% is a satisfactory rate of return, Tanner Corporation should consider such factors as the rate of return available from alternative investment opportunities, the risk involved in actually realizing the expected rate of return, the corporation's cost of capital, and the nonfinancial factors relating to the investment. In comparing alternative investment opportunities, management usually prefers the investment with the **lowest risk, highest rate of return,** and **shortest payback period.** Of course, the same investment is seldom superior to all others in every respect. Thus, managers must consider many subjective factors in making their decisions.

A weakness in the concept of return on average investment is the failure to consider the **timing** of the future cash flows. Computing the average annual net income, for example, ignores the question of whether the cash receipts will occur early or late in the life of the investment. Also, computing the average investment in the equipment fails to consider whether the purchase price of the equipment must be paid in advance or in installments stretching over a period of years. A technique which does take into account the timing of cash flows is called **discounting** future cash flows.

Discounting Future Cash Flows

As explained in Chapter 16, the present value of a future cash flow is the amount that a knowledgeable investor would pay today for the right to receive that future amount. The exact amount of the present value depends upon (1) the amount of the future payment, (2) the length of time until the future amount will be received, and (3) the rate of return required by the investor. **Discounting** is the process of determining the present value of cash flows.

The use of present value tables to discount future cash flows is demonstrated in Appendix C, entitled Applications of Present Value, located at the end of this text. (Readers who are not familiar with the concept of present value and with the use of present value tables should read this appendix before continuing with this chapter.) For your convenience, the two present value tables presented in the appendix are repeated below and on the following page.

Table 1 shows the present value of a single lump-sum payment of $1 to be received *n* periods (years) in the future. **Table 2** shows the present value of a $1 annuity—that is, $1 to be received each year for *n* consecutive years. For illustrative purposes, both tables have been kept short. They include only selected discount rates and extend for a limited number of periods. However, the tables contain the appropriate rates and periods for all problem material in this chapter.

The discount rate may be viewed as the investor's required rate of return. The present value of the future cash flows is the maximum amount that the investor may pay for the investment and still expect to earn the required rate of return. Therefore, an investment is considered desirable when its cost is less than the present value of the expected future cash flows. Conversely, an investment is undesirable when its cost is greater than the present value of expected future cash flows.

TABLE 1
Present Values of $1 Due in *n* Periods*

Number of Periods (n)	1%	1½%	5%	6%	8%	10%	12%	15%	20%
1	.990	.985	.952	.943	.926	.909	.893	.870	.833
2	.980	.971	.907	.890	.857	.826	.797	.756	.694
3	.971	.956	.864	.840	.794	.751	.712	.658	.579
4	.961	.942	.823	.792	.735	.683	.636	.572	.482
5	.951	.928	.784	.747	.681	.621	.567	.497	.402
6	.942	.915	.746	.705	.630	.564	.507	.432	.335
7	.933	.901	.711	.665	.583	.513	.452	.376	.279
8	.923	.888	.677	.627	.540	.467	.404	.327	.233
9	.914	.875	.645	.592	.510	.424	.361	.284	.194
10	.905	.862	.614	.558	.463	.386	.322	.247	.162
20	.820	.742	.377	.312	.215	.149	.104	.061	.026
24	.788	.700	.310	.247	.158	.102	.066	.035	.013
36	.699	.585	.173	.123	.063	.032	.017	.007	.001

* The present value of $1 is computed by the formula $p = 1/(1 + i)^n$, where p is the present value of $1, i is the discount rate, and n is the number of periods until the future cash flow will occur. Amounts in this table have been rounded to three decimal places and are shown for a limited number of periods and discount rates. Many calculators are programmed to use this formula and can compute present values when the future amount is entered along with values for i and n.

TABLE 2
Present Values of $1 to Be Received Periodically for *n* Periods

Number of Periods (n)	Discount Rate								
	1%	1½%	5%	6%	8%	10%	12%	15%	20%
1	0.990	0.985	0.952	0.943	0.926	0.909	0.893	0.870	0.833
2	1.970	1.956	1.859	1.833	1.783	1.736	1.690	1.626	1.528
3	2.941	2.912	2.723	2.673	2.577	2.487	2.402	2.283	2.106
4	3.902	3.854	3.546	3.465	3.312	3.170	3.037	2.855	2.589
5	4.853	4.783	4.329	4.212	3.993	3.791	3.605	3.352	2.991
6	5.795	5.697	5.076	4.917	4.623	4.355	4.111	3.784	3.326
7	6.728	6.598	5.786	5.582	5.206	4.868	4.564	4.160	3.605
8	7.652	7.486	6.463	6.210	5.747	5.335	4.968	4.487	3.837
9	8.566	8.361	7.108	6.802	6.247	5.759	5.328	4.772	4.031
10	9.471	9.222	7.722	7.360	6.710	6.145	5.650	5.019	4.192
20	18.046	17.169	12.462	11.470	9.818	8.514	7.469	6.259	4.870
24	21.243	20.030	13.799	12.550	10.529	8.985	7.784	6.434	4.937
36	30.108	27.661	16.547	14.621	11.717	9.677	8.192	6.623	4.993

The higher the discount rate being used, the lower will be the resulting present value. Therefore the investor will be interested in the investment only at a lower price. The "appropriate" discount rate for determining the present value of a specific investment depends upon the nature of that investment, the alternative investment opportunities available, and the investor's cost of capital.

Let us now apply the concept of discounting cash flows to our continuing example of the Tanner Corporation. We shall assume that Tanner Corporation requires a 15% annual rate of return on investments in new plant assets. The $450,000 investment in equipment is expected to produce annual net cash flows of $90,000 for 10 years. *Table 2* indicates that the present value of $1 to be received annually for 10 years, discounted at an annual rate of 15%, is *5.019.* Therefore, the present value of $90,000 received annually for 10 years is $90,000 × 5.019 or *$451,710.*

In addition to the annual cash flows, Tanner Corporation expects to receive $50,000 in salvage value for the equipment at the end of the tenth year. Referring to *Table 1* (page *1205*), we see that the present value of $1 due in 10 years, discounted at 15% per year, is *.247.* Thus, the present value of $50,000 to be received 10 years hence is $50,000 × .247, or *$12,350.* We may now analyze the proposal to invest in the equipment as follows:

Present value of expected annual cash flows ($90,000 × 5.019)	$451,710
Present value of proceeds from disposal of equipment ($50,000 × .247)	12,350
Total present value of future cash flows	$464,060
Amount to be invested (payable in advance)	450,000
Net present value of proposed investment	$ 14,060

This analysis indicates that the present value of the expected net cash flows from the investment, discounted at an annual rate of 15%, amounts to $464,060. This is the maximum amount which Tanner Corporation could afford to invest in the project and still expect to earn the required 15% annual rate of return. Since the actual cost of the investment is only $450,000, Tanner Corporation can expect to earn more than 15%.

The *net present value* of the proposal is the difference between the total present value of the net cash flows and the cost of the investment. When the net present value is equal to zero, the investment provides a rate of return *exactly equal* to the rate used in discounting the cash flows. A *positive* net present value means that the investment provides a rate of return *greater than the discount rate;* a *negative* net present value means that the investment yields a return of *less* than the discount rate. Since the discount rate is usually the minimum rate of return required by the investor, proposals with a positive net present value are considered acceptable and those with a negative net present value are viewed as unacceptable.

Replacement of Old Equipment

A problem often facing management is whether it should buy new and more efficient equipment or whether it should continue to use existing equipment. Assume, for example, that the Ardmore Company is meeting increasing competition in the sale of product Q. The sales manager believes the source of the trouble is that competitors have installed more efficient equipment, which has enabled them to reduce prices. The issue raised therefore is whether Ardmore Company should: (1) buy new equipment at a cost of $120,000, or (2) continue using its present equipment. We will make the simplifying assumption that both the new equipment and present equipment have a remaining useful life of five years and neither will have any residual value. The new equipment will produce substantial savings in direct labor, direct materials, and manufacturing overhead costs. The company does not believe the use of new equipment will have any effect on sales volume, so the decision rests entirely on whether cost savings are possible.

The old equipment has a book value of $100,000 but can be sold for only $20,000 if it is replaced. At first glance, the resulting $80,000 loss on disposal appears to be a good reason for not replacing the old equipment. However, the cost of the old equipment is a *sunk cost* and is not relevant to the decision. If the old machinery is sold, its book value contributes to the amount of the loss; if the old machinery is retained, its book value will be recognized as expense through future charges to depreciation. Thus, this cost cannot be avoided by Ardmore Company regardless of which decision is made. From a present value standpoint, there is some benefit to recognizing this sunk cost as a loss in the current period inasmuch as the related tax reduction will occur this year rather than over the remaining life of the equipment.

In deciding whether to replace the old equipment, Ardmore Company should determine the *present value of the incremental net cash flows* resulting from replacement of the old machinery. This present value may then be compared with the cost of the new equipment to determine whether the investment will provide the required rate of return. To compute the incremental annual net cash flow from replacing the old equipment, management must consider both the annual cash savings in manufacturing costs and the difference in annual income taxes. Income taxes will differ under the alternative courses of action because of differences in (1) variable manufacturing costs and (2) annual depreciation expense.

Let us assume that the new machinery will result in a $34,000 annual cash savings in variable manufacturing costs. However, annual depreciation on the new equipment will be $24,000 ($120,000 ÷ 5 years), whereas annual depreciation on the old equipment is $20,000 ($100,000 ÷ 5 years). This $4,000 increase in depreciation expense means that purchase of the new equipment will ***increase*** taxable income by $30,000 per year ($34,000 cost savings less $4,000 additional depreciation). Assuming a tax rate of 40%, purchase of the new equipment will increase annual income tax expense by $12,000 ($30,000 × 40%). The incremental annual ***net cash flow*** from owning the new machinery, therefore, amounts to ***$22,000*** ($34,000 cost savings less $12,000 additional income tax expense).

We shall assume that Ardmore Company requires a 12% return on investments in plant assets. Referring to the annuity table on page 1206, we see that the present value of $1 received annually for five years is ***3.605***. Therefore, $22,000 received annually for five years, discounted at an annual rate of 12%, has a present value of ***$79,310*** ($22,000 × 3.605). In addition to the present value of the annual net cash flows, however, we must consider two other factors: (1) the proceeds from sale of the old equipment and (2) the tax savings resulting from the loss on disposal.

The $20,000 proceeds from sale of the old equipment will be received immediately and, therefore, have a present value of ***$20,000.*** The $80,000 loss on disposal results in a $32,000 reduction in income taxes payable at the end of the first year ($80,000 × 40%). The present value of $32,000 one year hence discounted at 12% is ***$28,576*** ($32,000 × .893), as determined from a present value table.

We may now determine the net present value of the proposal to replace the old equipment with new equipment as follows:

Present value of incremental annual cash flows ($22,000 × 3.605)	*$ 79,310*
Present value of proceeds from sale of old equipment	*20,000*
Present value of tax savings from loss on disposal ($32,000 × .893)	*28,576*
Total present value	*$127,886*
Amount to be invested	*120,000*
Net present value	***$ 7,886***

Since the total present value of all future cash flows from acquiring the new equipment exceeds the cost of the investment, Ardmore Company should replace the old equipment with new.

Concluding Comments

We have merely scratched the surface in discussing the possible kinds of analyses that might be prepared in making decisions. The brief treatment in this chapter, however, has been sufficient to establish the basic principles that lie behind such analyses. The most profitable course of action is determined by studying the costs and revenue that are *incremental* to the particular alternatives under consideration. The relevant information generally involves making *estimates* about the future. As a result, such information is subject to some degree of error. Of course it is important to remember that many nonfinancial factors may be brought into the decision picture after the quantitative analysis has been made.

END-OF-CHAPTER REVIEW

SUMMARY OF CHAPTER LEARNING OBJECTIVES

1 **Identify the financial information relevant to a particular business decision.**
Only that information which *varies* among the alternative courses of action being considered is relevant to the decision. Costs or revenue which do not vary among the alternative courses of action are not relevant to the decision.

2 **Use incremental analysis to evaluate alternative courses of action.**
Incremental analysis is the technique of comparing one course of action to another by determining the *differences* expected to arise in revenue and in costs.

3 **Discuss the relevance of opportunity costs, sunk costs, and out-of-pocket costs in making business decisions.**
An *opportunity cost* is the benefit which could have been obtained by pursuing another course of action. Opportunity costs often are subjective, but they are important considerations in any business decision. *Sunk costs,* on the other hand, have already been incurred as a result of past actions. These costs cannot be changed regardless of the action taken and are not relevant to the decision at hand. *Out-of-pocket costs* will be incurred in the future and are relevant if they will vary among the possible courses of action.

4 **Determine the effect upon operating income of discontinuing a product line.**
To determine the effects of discontinuing a product line, we must look at both the increases and decreases which may result in the level of operating income. In addition to the lost contribution margin from the discontinued line, factors to be considered include the effects upon sales of other products, opportunity costs, and possible reductions in "fixed" costs.

5 **Explore a decision: be aware of the nonfinancial considerations, and creatively search for a better course of action.**
Our goal in this chapter is to emphasize the types of information *relevant* to a particular business decision. Both financial and nonfinancial information are relevant to business decisions. Examples of relevant *nonfinancial* information include, legal and ethical considerations, and the long-run effects of decisions upon company image, employee morale, and the environment. Also, managers should search creatively for alternative courses of action. Unless a company selects the best pos-

sible course of action, it incurs an opportunity cost. Opportunity costs are not recorded in the accounting records, but they may determine the success or failure of a business enterprise.

6 **Evaluate capital budgeting proposals using (a) the payback period, (b) return on average investment, and (c) discounted future cash flows.**

The payback period is the length of time needed to recover the cost of an investment from the resulting net cash flows. However, this type of investment analysis fails to consider the total life and overall profitability of the investment.

Return on average investment expresses the average estimated net income from the investment as a percentage of the average investment. This percentage represents the "rate of return" earned on the investment. A shortcoming is that "average" estimated net income ignores the timing of future cash flows. Therefore, no consideration is given to the "time value" of money.

Discounting future cash flows determines the ***net present value*** of an investment proposal. Proposals with a positive net present value usually are considered acceptable, while proposals with a negative net present value are considered unacceptable. This technique considers both the life of the investment and the timing of future cash flows.

This book has introduced you to the basic concepts of financial accounting, managerial accounting, and, to a lesser extent, income taxes. We are confident that you will find this background useful throughout your career. However, we also recommend that you continue your study of accounting with additional courses. We particularly recommend a course in cost accounting, and the first course in income taxes.

KEY TERMS INTRODUCED OR EMPHASIZED IN CHAPTER 26

Capital budgeting   The process of planning and evaluating proposals for investments in plant assets.

Discount rate   The required rate of return used by an investor to discount future cash flows to their present value.

Discounted cash flows   The present value of expected future cash flows.

Incremental (or differential) cost   The difference between the total costs of alternative courses of action.

Incremental (or differential) revenue   The difference between the revenue amounts provided by alternative courses of action.

Net present value   The excess of the present value of the net cash flows expected from an investment over the amount to be invested. Net present value is one method of ranking alternative investment opportunities.

Opportunity cost   The benefit foregone by not pursuing an alternative course of action. Opportunity costs are not recorded in the accounting records, but are important in making many types of business decisions.

Payback period   The length of time necessary to recover the cost of an investment through the cash flows generated by that investment. Payback period is one criterion used in making capital budgeting decisions.

Present value   The amount of money today which is considered equivalent to a cash inflow or outflow expected to take place in the future. The present value of money is always less than the future amount, since money on hand today can be invested to become the equivalent of a larger amount in the future.

Relevant information Information which should be given consideration in making a specific decision and which varies among the alternative courses of action being considered.

Return on average investment The average annual net income from an investment expressed as a percentage of the average amount invested. Return on average investment is one method of ranking alternative investment opportunities according to their relative profitability.

Sunk cost A cost which has irrevocably been incurred by past actions. Sunk costs are irrelevant to decisions regarding future actions.

SELF-TEST QUESTIONS

Answers to these questions appear on page 1223.

The following data relate to questions 1 and 2

One of Phoenix Computer's products is WizardCard. The company currently produces and sells 30,000 WizardCards per month, although it has the plant capacity to produce 50,000 units per month. At the 30,000 unit-per-month level of production, the per-unit cost of manufacturing WizardCards is $45, consisting of $15 in variable costs and $30 in fixed costs. Phoenix sells WizardCards to retail stores for $90 each. Computer Marketing Corp. has offered to purchase 10,000 WizardCards per month at a reduced price. Phoenix can manufacture these additional units with no change in fixed manufacturing costs.

1 In deciding whether to accept this special order from Computer Marketing Corp., Phoenix should be **least** concerned with:

   a What Computer Marketing Corp. intends to do with the WizardCards.

   b The $45 average cost of manufacturing WizardCards.

   c The opportunity cost of not accepting the order.

   d The incremental cost of manufacturing an additional 10,000 WizardCards per month.

2 Assume that Phoenix decides to accept the special order at a unit sales price that will add $400,000 per month to its operating income. The unit price of the special order will be:

   a $85   b $70   c $55   d Some other amount

3 The contribution margin ratios and monthly segment margins of three products sold by Video Game Corp. are as follows:

	Product 1	Product 2	Product 3
Contribution margin ratio	20%	40%	60%
Monthly segment margin..........................	$(4,000)	$15,000	$10,000

Management is considering discontinuing product 1. This action is expected to eliminate all costs traceable to product 1, increase monthly sales of product 2 by $10,000, decrease monthly sales of product 3 by $5,000, and have no effect on common fixed costs. Based upon these facts, discontinuing product 1 should cause the company's monthly operating income to:

   a Increase by $4,000   c Decrease by $3,000

   b Increase by $9,000   d None of the above

4 Western Mfg. Co. is considering two capital budgeting proposals, each with a 10-year life, and each requiring an initial cash outlay of $50,000. Proposal A shows a higher return on average investment than Proposal B, but Proposal B shows the higher net present value. The most probable explanation is that:

  a Expected cash inflows tend to occur earlier in Proposal B.

  b Total expected cash inflows are greater in Proposal B.

  c The payback period is shorter in Proposal A.

  d The discounted future cash flows approach makes no provision for recovery of the original $50,000 investment.

5 Copy Center is considering replacing its old copying machine, which has a $3,200 book value, with a new one. Discounted cash flow analysis of the proposal to acquire the new machine shows an estimated net present value of $2,800. If the new machine is acquired, the old machine will have no resale value and will be given away. The loss on disposal of the old machine:

  a Is an opportunity cost of purchasing the new machine.

  b Exceeds the net present value of the new machine, indicating that the new machine should not be acquired.

  c Has already been deducted from future revenue in arriving at the $2,800 net present value of the new machine.

  d Is a sunk cost and is not relevant to the decision at hand, except as it affects the timing of income tax payments.

ASSIGNMENT MATERIAL

DISCUSSION QUESTIONS

1 What is the basic characteristic of "relevant" information?

2 A company regularly sells 100,000 washing machines at an average price of $250. The average cost of producing these machines is $180. Under what circumstances might the company accept an order for 20,000 washing machines at $175 per machine?

3 The Calcutta Corporation produces a large number of products. The costs per unit for one product, a fishing reel, are shown below:

Direct materials and direct labor	$7.00
Variable factory overhead	4.00
Fixed factory overhead	2.00

The company recently decided to buy 10,000 fishing reels from another manufacturer for $12.50 per unit because "it was cheaper than our cost of $13.00 per unit." Evaluate the decision only on the basis of the cost data given.

4 Define **opportunity costs** and explain why they represent a common source of error in making cost analyses.

5 What is the difference between a **sunk cost** and an **out-of-pocket cost?**

6 Briefly discuss the type of information you would want before deciding to discontinue the production of a major line of products.

7 Indicate several reasons why management might decide **not** to discontinue a product line that consistently incurs a negative segment margin.

8 What is *capital budgeting?* Why are capital budgeting decisions crucial to the long-run financial health of a business enterprise?

9 A company invests $100,000 in plant assets with an estimated 20-year service life and no salvage value. These assets contribute $10,000 to annual net income when depreciation is computed on a straight-line basis. Compute the payback period and explain your computation.

10 What is the major shortcoming of using the payback period as the only criterion in making capital budgeting decisions?

11 What factors should an investor consider in appraising the adequacy of the rate of return from a specific investment proposal?

12 Discounting a future cash flow at 15% results in a lower present value than does discounting the same cash flow at 10%. Explain why.

13 What factors determine the present value of a future cash flow?

14 Discounting cash flows takes into consideration one characteristic of the earnings stream which is ignored in the computation of return on average investment. What is this characteristic and why is it important?

15 Explain why the book value of existing equipment is not relevant in deciding whether the equipment should be scrapped (without realizing any proceeds) or continued in use.

EXERCISES

EXERCISE 26-1
Accounting
Terminology

Listed below are nine technical accounting terms introduced or emphasized in this chapter:

Opportunity cost	Sunk cost	Out-of-pocket cost
Net present value	Payback period	Incremental analysis
Capital budgeting	Estimated useful life	Relevant information

Each of the following statements may (or may not) describe one of these technical terms. For each statement, indicate the accounting term described, or answer "None" if the statement does not correctly describe any of the terms.

a Examination of differences between costs to be incurred and revenues to be earned under alternative courses of action.

b A cost incurred in the past which cannot be changed as a result of future actions.

c Costs and revenues which are expected to vary, depending upon the course of action decided upon.

d The benefit foregone by not pursuing an alternative course of action.

e The process of planning and evaluating proposals for investments in plant assets.

f The average annual net income from an investment expressed as a percentage of the average amount invested.

g Length of time necessary to recover the entire cost of an investment from resulting annual net cash flow.

h A cost which has not yet been incurred which will require payment and which may vary among alternative courses of action.

PROBLEMS

Group A

**PROBLEM 26A-1
Evaluating a
Special Order**

D. Lawrance designs and manufactures fashionable men's clothing. For the coming year, the company has scheduled production of 30,000 suede jackets. The budgeted costs for this product are shown below:

	Unit Costs (30,000 Units)	Total
Variable manufacturing costs	$51	$1,530,000
Variable selling expenses	15	450,000
Fixed manufacturing costs	8	240,000
Fixed operating expenses	6	180,000
Total costs and expenses	$80	$2,400,000

The management of D. Lawrance is considering a special order from Discount House for an additional 10,000 jackets. These jackets would carry the Discount House label, rather than that of D. Lawrance. In all other respects, they would be identical to the regular D. Lawrance jackets.

Although D. Lawrance sells its regular jackets to retail stores at a price of $120 each, Discount House has offered to pay only $69 per jacket. However, no sales commissions are involved on this special order, so D. Lawrance would incur variable selling expenses of only $3 per unit on these jackets, rather than the regular $15. Accepting the order would cause no change in D. Lawrance's fixed costs or fixed operating expenses. D. Lawrance has enough plant capacity to produce 45,000 jackets per year.

INSTRUCTIONS

a Using incremental revenue and incremental costs, compute the expected effect of accepting this special order upon D. Lawrance's operating income.

b Briefly discuss any other factors which you believe D. Lawrance's management should consider in deciding whether to accept this special order. You may include nonfinancial as well as financial considerations.

**PROBLEM 26A-2
Make or Buy
Decision**

Guaranteed Tools manufactures an electric motor which it uses in several of its products. Management is considering whether to continue manufacturing the motors, or whether to buy them from an outside source. The following information is available:

1 The company needs 10,000 motors per year. The motors can be purchased from an outside supplier at a cost of $20 per unit.

2 The cost of manufacturing the motors is $25 per unit, computed as follows:

Direct materials	$ 65,000
Direct labor	55,000
Factory overhead:	
Variable	70,000
Fixed	60,000
Total manufacturing costs	$250,000
Cost per unit ($250,000 ÷ 10,000 units)	$25

3 Discontinuing the manufacture of motors will eliminate all of the raw materials and direct labor costs, but will eliminate only 60% of the variable factory overhead costs.

4   If the motors are purchased from an outside source, certain machinery used in the production of motors will be sold at its book value. The sale of this machinery will reduce fixed factory overhead costs by $3,600 for depreciation and $400 for property taxes. No other reductions in fixed factory overhead will result from discontinuing production of the motors.

INSTRUCTIONS   a   Prepare a schedule in the format illustrated on page 1198 to determine the incremental cost or benefit of buying the motors from the outside supplier. Based on this schedule, would you recommend that the company manufacture the motors or buy them from the outside source?

b   Assume that if the motors are purchased from the outside source, the factory space previously used to produce motors can be used to manufacture an additional 7,000 power trimmers per year. Power trimmers have an estimated contribution margin of $8 per unit. The manufacture of the additional power trimmers would have no effect upon fixed factory overhead. Would this new assumption change your recommendation as to whether to make or buy the motors? In support of your conclusion, prepare a schedule showing the incremental cost or benefit of buying the motors from the outside source and using the factory space to produce additional power trimmers.

PROBLEM 26A-3
Discontinuing a Product Line

Ski America is a small airline flying out of Denver. The company has only enough planes to service three routes, connecting Denver with San Francisco, and with the Colorado ski resorts of Aspen and Vail. Typical monthly operating data for these three routes are summarized below:

	San Francisco	%	Aspen	%	Vail	%
Passengers per month.............	1,000		1,200		900	
	Dollars	%	Dollars	%	Dollars	%
Sales	$400,000	100	$240,000	100	$270,000	100
Variable costs	40,000	10	12,000	5	13,500	5
Contribution margins	$360,000	90	$228,000	95	$256,500	95
Traceable fixed costs	408,000	102	96,000	40	113,400	42
Segment margins..................	$ (48,000)	(12)	$132,000	55	$143,100	53

Management is concerned about the losses incurred each month on the San Francisco route, and also has an opportunity to use the plane now serving San Francisco to establish a new Denver to Durango route. Management estimates that the Denver-Durango route would generate a positive monthly segment margin of $50,000. However, many of the passengers flying the San Francisco route with Ski America also "book through" on either the Aspen or Vail flights. Ski America's management knows that cancelling service to San Francisco will cause a loss of passengers on the Aspen and Vail routes.

By studying ticket sales, Ski America's managerial accountants have learned that 45% of the passengers flying Ski America from San Francisco continue on Ski America to Aspen, and that 36% fly Ski America into Vail. A marketing survey indicates that if the San Francisco route is cancelled, Ski America will still receive 60% of the business of those San Francisco passengers who travel from Denver to Aspen or Vail.

INSTRUCTIONS   a   Using the data about numbers of passengers, prepare a schedule showing the percentage by which monthly passenger volume is expected to decline on (1) the Aspen route, and (2) the Vail route, assuming that the San Francisco route is cancelled.

b Prepare a schedule showing the estimated effect of replacing the San Francisco route with service to Durango upon the monthly operating income of Ski America. Changes in the contribution margin generated from the Aspen and Vail routes are expected to coincide with the changes in passenger volume.

c Make a recommendation as to whether the San Francisco route should be discontinued. Also raise any points that you believe should be considered by management.

PROBLEM 26A-4
Capital Budgeting

Micro Technology is considering two alternative proposals for modernizing its production facilities. To provide a basis for selection, the cost accounting department has developed the following data regarding the expected annual operating results for the two proposals.

	Proposal 1	Proposal 2
Required investment in equipment	$360,000	$350,000
Estimated service life of equipment	8 years	7 years
Estimated salvage value	–0–	$ 14,000
Estimated annual cost savings (net cash flow)	$ 75,000	$ 76,000
Depreciation on equipment (straight-line basis)	$ 45,000	$ 48,000
Estimated increase in annual net income	$ 30,000	$ 28,000

INSTRUCTIONS

a For each proposal, compute the (1) payback period, (2) return on average investment, and (3) net present value, discounted at an annual rate of 12%. (Round the payback period to the nearest tenth of a year and the return on investment to the nearest tenth of a percent.)

b Based on your analysis in part **a,** state which proposal you would recommend and explain the reasons for your choice.

PROBLEM 26A-5
Capital Budgeting Using Three Models

Marengo is a popular restaurant located in the Chilton Resort. Management feels that enlarging the facility to incorporate a large outdoor seating area will enable Marengo to continue to attract existing customers as well as handle large banquet parties that now must be turned away. Two proposals are currently under consideration. Proposal A involves a temporary walled structure and umbrellas used for sun protection; Proposal B entails a more permanent structure with a full awning cover for use even in inclement weather. Although the useful life of each alternative is estimated to be 10 years, Proposal B results in higher salvage value due to the awning protection. The accounting department of Chilton Resort and the manager of Marengo have assembled the following data regarding the two proposals:

	Proposal A	Proposal B
Required investment	$400,000	$500,000
Estimated life of fixtures	10 years	10 years
Estimated salvage value	$ 20,000	$ 50,000
Estimated annual net cash flow	$ 80,000	$ 95,000
Depreciation (straight-line basis)	$ 38,000	$ 45,000
Estimated annual net income	?	?

INSTRUCTIONS

a For each proposal, compute the (1) payback period, (2) return on average investment, and (3) net present value discounted at management's required rate of return of 15%. Round the payback period to the nearest tenth of a year and the return on investment to the nearest tenth of a percent.

b Based upon your analysis in part **a,** state which proposal you would recommend and explain the reasons for your choice.

PROBLEM 26A-6
Capital Budgeting—Computing Annual Net Cash Flow

Toying With Nature wants to take advantage of children's current fascination with dinosaurs by adding several scale-model dinosaurs to its existing product line. Annual sales of the dinosaurs are estimated at 80,000 units at a price of $6 per unit. Variable manufacturing costs are estimated at $2.50 per unit, incremental fixed manufacturing costs (excluding depreciation) at $45,000 annually, and additional selling and general expenses related to the dinosaurs at $55,000 annually.

To manufacture the dinosaurs, the company must invest $350,000 in design molds and special equipment. Since toy fads wane in popularity rather quickly, Toying With Nature anticipates the special equipment will have a three-year service life with only a $20,000 salvage value. Depreciation will be computed on a straight-line basis. All revenue and expenses other than depreciation will be received or paid in cash. The company's combined federal and state income tax rate is 40%.

INSTRUCTIONS

a Prepare a schedule showing the estimated increase in annual net income from the planned manufacture and sale of dinosaur toys.

b Compute the annual net cash flow expected from this project.

c Compute for this project (1) payback period, (2) return on average investment, and (3) net present value, discounted at an annual rate of 15%. Round the payback period to the nearest tenth of a year and the return on average investment to the nearest tenth of a percent.

Group B

PROBLEM 26B-1
Evaluating a Special Order

Never Bored Game Company sells 600,000 units per year of a particular board game at $12.00 each. The current unit cost of the game sets is broken down as follows:

Direct materials	*$2.50*
Direct labor	*2.70*
Variable factory overhead	*1.60*
Fixed factory overhead	*2.20*
Total	*$9.00*

At the beginning of the current year, Never Bored receives a special order for 10,000 of these games per month, *for one year only* at a sales price of $8.00 per unit. A new machine with an estimated life of five years would have to be purchased for $30,000 to produce the additional units. Management thinks that it will not be able to use the new machine beyond one year and that it will have to be sold for a salvage value of approximately $20,000.

INSTRUCTIONS

Compute the estimated increase or decrease in annual operating income that will result from accepting this special order.

PROBLEM 26B-2
Make or Buy Decision

Precision Heating & Cooling manufactures thermostats which it uses in several of its products. Management is considering whether to continue manufacturing thermostats, or to buy them from an outside source. The following information is available:

1 The company needs 80,000 thermostats per year. Thermostats can be purchased from an outside supplier at a cost of $6 per unit.

2 The cost of manufacturing thermostats is $7.50 per unit, computed as follows:

Direct materials...	*$156,000*
Direct labor	*132,000*
Manufacturing overhead:	
Variable	*168,000*
Fixed...	*144,000*
Total manufacturing costs	*$600,000*
Cost per unit ($600,000 ÷ 80,000 units)	*$7.50*

3 Discontinuing the manufacture of the thermostats will eliminate all of the direct materials and direct labor costs, but will eliminate only 60% of the variable overhead costs.

4 If the thermostats are purchased from an outside source, certain machinery used in the production of thermostats will be sold at its book value. The sale of this machinery will reduce fixed overhead costs by $8,400 for depreciation and $800 for property taxes. No other reductions in fixed overhead will result from discontinuing production of the thermostats.

INSTRUCTIONS a Prepare a schedule to determine the incremental cost or benefit of buying thermostats from the outside supplier. Based on this schedule, would you recommend that the company manufacture thermostats or buy them from the outside source?

b Assume that if thermostats are purchased from the outside source, the factory space previously used to produce thermostats can be used to manufacture an additional 6,000 heat-flow regulators per year. These regulators have an estimated contribution margin of $18 per unit. The manufacture of the additional heat-flow regulators would have no effect upon fixed overhead.

Would this new assumption change your recommendation as to whether to make or buy thermostats? In support of your conclusion, prepare a schedule showing the incremental cost or benefit of buying thermostats from the outside source and using the factory space to produce additional heat-flow regulators.

PROBLEM 26B-3
Discontinuing a Product Line—Any Ideas?

Quest Corporation began business about 10 years ago manufacturing and selling ski equipment. Later it introduced a line of golf clubs, which has since become its biggest selling and most profitable product. Over the years, competition from Europe has forced the company to reduce its sales price on skis, and this product line now consistently has a negative segment margin. The company also makes a unique ski binding, which has remained profitable. Typical monthly operating data for these three product lines are shown below:

	Golf Clubs		Skis		Ski Bindings	
	Dollars	**%**	**Dollars**	**%**	**Dollars**	**%**
Sales	$500,000	100	$300,000	100	$160,000	100
Variable costs	215,000	43	225,000	75	80,000	50
Contribution margins	$285,000	57	$ 75,000	25	$ 80,000	50
Traceable fixed costs	110,000	22	90,000	30	63,800	43
Segment margins...................	$175,000	35	$ (15,000)	(5)	$ 11,200	7

Management is considering discontinuing the manufacture and sale of skis. All costs traceable to the product line would be eliminated if the product line is discontinued. Skis and bindings are sold to the same stores; therefore, management estimates that discontinuing the sale of skis would cause a 20% decline in sales of ski bindings. Golf clubs are sold to different customers, so management does not believe that golf club sales would be affected by discontinuing skis. All three product lines are manufactured in the same plant, which is operating at between 90% and 95% of capacity, due to the increasing demand for golf clubs.

INSTRUCTIONS **a** Prepare a schedule showing the estimated effect of discontinuing the manufacture and sale of skis upon Quest's monthly operating income.

b Prepare a schedule determining the expected monthly segment margin of the ski bindings product line, assuming that the ski product line is discontinued and that sales of ski bindings decline by 20%.

c Draft a memo summarizing your recommendations as to Quest's best course of action. Bring out any points that you think management should consider. Perhaps you have noticed factors that management may be overlooking.

PROBLEM 26B-4
Capital
Budgeting

Banner Equipment Co. is evaluating two alternative investment opportunities. The controller of the company has prepared the following analysis of the two investment proposals:

	Proposal A	Proposal B
Required investment in equipment	$220,000	$240,000
Estimated service life of equipment	5 years	6 years
Estimated salvage value	$ 10,000	–0–
Estimated annual net cash flow	$ 60,000	$ 60,000
Depreciation on equipment (straight-line basis)	$ 42,000	$ 40,000
Estimated annual net income	$ 18,000	$ 20,000

INSTRUCTIONS **a** For each proposed investment, compute the (1) payback period, (2) return on average investment, and (3) net present value, discounted at an annual rate of 12%. (Round the payback period to the nearest tenth of a year and the return on investment to the nearest tenth of a percent.)

b Based upon your computations in part **a,** which proposal do you consider to be the better investment? Explain.

PROBLEM 26B-5
Capital Budgeting Using Three Models

V. S. Yogurt is considering two possible expansion plans. Proposal A involves opening 10 stores in northern California at a total cost of $3,150,000. Under another strategy, Proposal B, V. S. Yogurt would focus on southern California and open six stores for a total cost of $2,500,000. Selected data regarding the two proposals has been assembled by the controller of V. S. Yogurt as follows:

	Proposal A	Proposal B
Required investment...	$3,150,000	$2,500,000
Estimated life of store locations.............................	7 years	7 years
Estimated salvage value	–0–	$ 400,000
Estimated annual net cash flow	$ 750,000	$ 570,000
Depreciation on equipment (straight-line basis)	$ 450,000	$ 300,000
Estimated annual net income	?	?

INSTRUCTIONS **a** For each proposal, compute the (1) payback period, (2) return on average investment, and (3) net present value, discounted at management's required rate of return of 15%. Round the payback period to the nearest tenth of a year and the return on investment to the nearest tenth of a percent.

b Based upon your analysis in part **a,** state which proposal you would recommend and explain the reasoning behind your choice.

PROBLEM 26B-6
Another Capital Budgeting Problem

Rothmore Appliance Company is planning to introduce a built-in blender to its line of small home appliances. Annual sales of the blender are estimated at 10,000 units at a price of $35 per unit. Variable manufacturing costs are estimated at $15 per unit, incremental fixed manufacturing costs (other than depreciation) at $40,000 annually, and incremental selling and general expenses relating to the blenders at $50,000 annually.

To build the blenders, the company must invest $240,000 in molds, patterns, and special equipment. Since the company expects to change the design of the blender every four years, this equipment will have a four-year service life with no salvage value. Depreciation will be computed on a straight-line basis. All revenue and expenses other than depreciation will be received or paid in cash. The company's combined state and federal tax rate is 40%.

INSTRUCTIONS

a   Prepare a schedule showing the estimated annual net income from the proposal to manufacture and sell the blenders.

b   Compute the annual net cash flow expected from the proposal.

c   Compute for this proposal the (1) payback period (round to the nearest tenth of a year), (2) return on average investment (round to the nearest tenth of a percent), and (3) net present value, discounted at an annual rate of 15%.

CASES AND UNSTRUCTURED PROBLEMS

CASE 26-1
Relevant Information and Opportunity Costs

McFriendly Software recently developed new spreadsheet software, Easy-Calc, which it intends to market by mail through ads in computer magazines. Just prior to introducing Easy-Calc, McFriendly receives an unexpected offer from Jupiter Computer to buy all rights to the software for $10 million cash.

a   Is the $10 million offer "relevant" financial information?

b   Describe McFriendly's opportunity cost if it (1) accepts Jupiter's offer, and (2) turns down the offer and markets Easy-Calc itself. Would these opportunity costs be recorded in McFriendly's accounting records? If so, explain the journal entry to record these costs.

c   Briefly describe the extent to which the dollar amounts of the two opportunity costs described in part **b** are known to management at the time of the decision of whether to accept Jupiter's offer.

d   Might there be any other opportunity costs to consider at the time of making this decision? If so, explain briefly.

CASE 26-2
How Much Is That Laser in the Window?

The management of Metro Printers is considering a proposal to replace some existing equipment with a new highly efficient laser printer. The existing equipment has a current book value of $2,200,000 and a remaining life (if not replaced) of 10 years. The laser printer has a cost of $1,300,000 and an expected useful life of 10 years. The laser printer would increase the company's annual cash flow by reducing operating costs and by increasing the company's ability to generate revenue. Susan Mills, controller of Metro Printers, has prepared the following estimates of the laser printer's effect upon annual earnings and cash flow:

Estimated increase in annual cash flow (before income taxes):

Incremental revenue	*$140,000*	
Cost savings (other than depreciation)	*110,000*	*$250,000*
Reduction in annual depreciation expense:		
Depreciation on existing equipment	*$220,000*	
Depreciation on laser printer	*130,000*	*90,000*
Estimated increase in income before income taxes		*$340,000*
Increase in annual income taxes (40%)		*136,000*
Estimated increase in annual net income		*$204,000*
Estimated increase in annual net cash flow ($250,000 − $136,000)		*$114,000*

Don Adams, a director of Metro Printers, makes the following observation: "These estimates look fine, but won't we take a huge loss in the current year on the sale of our existing equipment? After the invention of the laser printer, I doubt that our old equipment can be sold for much at all." In response, Mills provides the following information about the expected loss on the sale of the existing equipment:

Book value of existing printing equipment	*$2,200,000*
Estimated current sales price, net of removal costs	*200,000*
Estimated loss on sale, before income taxes	*$2,000,000*
Reduction in current year's income taxes as a result of loss (40%)	*800,000*
Loss on sale of existing equipment, net of tax savings	*$1,200,000*

Adams replies, "Good grief, our loss would be almost as great as the cost of the laser itself. Add this $1,200,000 loss to the $1,300,000 cost of the laser, we're into this new equipment for $2,500,000. I'd go along with a cost of $1,300,000, but $2,500,000 is out of the question.

INSTRUCTIONS

a Compute the net present value of the proposal to sell the existing equipment and buy the laser printer, discounted at an annual rate of 15%. In your computation, make the following assumptions regarding the timing of cash flows:

1 The purchase price of the laser printer will be paid in cash immediately.

2 The $200,000 sales price of the existing equipment will be received in cash immediately.

3 The income tax benefit from selling the equipment will be realized one year from today.

4 The annual net cash flows may be regarded as received at year-end for each of the next ten years.

b Is the cost to Metro Printers of acquiring the laser printer $2,500,000, as Adams suggests? Explain fully.

ANSWERS TO SELF-TEST QUESTIONS

1 b   2 c [$15 + ($400,000 ÷ 10,000 cards)].   3 d (Increase by $5,000. Segment margin will change as follows: product 1, +$4,000; product 2, +$4,000; product 3, −$3,000).   4 a   5 d

More about Periodic Inventory Systems

Intended for Use after Chapter 5

The purpose of this appendix is to explain in greater detail the operation of a *periodic* inventory system. As indicated in the text, virtually all large organizations are *perpetual* inventory systems. However, periodic systems are used in a number of smaller companies—particularly those which use manual accounting systems.

After studying this appendix you should be able to meet these Learning Objectives:

1 *Explain the characteristics, advantages, and disadvantages of a periodic inventory system.*

2 *Account for merchandising transactions using a periodic inventory system.*

3 *Prepare closing entries for a business using a periodic inventory system, including the entry to "reopen" the inventory account.*

Characteristics of a Periodic Inventory System

A periodic inventory system is an ***alternative*** to a perpetual inventory system. The basic characteristics of a periodic system are:

OBJECTIVE 1 Explain the characteristics, advantages, and disadvantages of a periodic inventory system.

1 During an accounting period no entries are made in the Inventory account to record the cost of merchandise purchased or sold. Purchases are recorded by debiting an account called ***Purchases.*** When merchandise is sold, the revenue is recorded, but no effort is made to record the cost of goods sold. Thus, the balance in the Inventory account remains ***unchanged*** throughout the year, and the accounting records do not indicate the cost of goods sold.

2 At the end of each year, a complete ***physical inventory*** is taken. The merchandise on hand is counted, and its cost is determined. (The procedures for assigning per-unit costs to the items in inventory are discussed in Chapter 9.)

3 As stated above, the cost of goods sold is ***not recorded*** as individual sales transactions occur. Rather, the cost of goods sold for the entire year is determined at year-end by a computation such as the one that follows:

Inventory, beginning of the year (per last year's physical count)	$ 10,000
Add: Purchases	140,000
Cost of goods available for sale during the year	$150,000
Less: Ending inventory (per this year's physical count)	12,000
Cost of goods sold	$138,000

Advantages and Disadvantages of a Periodic System   As compared with a perpetual inventory system, a periodic inventory system has one advantage: no entries are required to record the cost of goods sold relating to individual sales transactions. As a direct result, however, the accounting records do not indicate the amount of inventory on hand, or the cost of goods sold, until a complete physical inventory is taken.

Taking a complete physical inventory is both inconvenient and costly. Therefore, a physical inventory usually is taken only at year-end. Thus, a periodic inventory system is well suited to the preparation of annual financial statements, but not to preparing financial statements for shorter periods, such as quarters or months.

Another shortcoming of the periodic system is the lack of an inventory subsidiary ledger. As stated in Chapter 5, an inventory subsidiary ledger indicates by type of product the costs and quantities of merchandise sold during the period and currently in inventory. This information—absent in a periodic inventory system—is useful to management in developing marketing strategies and in deciding what products to purchase, when to reorder merchandise, and the quantities of merchandise to be purchased.

In order to manage inventories in an efficient manner, and also to meet their quarterly reporting obligations, ***all publicly owned companies use perpetual inventory systems.*** Also, all businesses with point-of-sale terminals or computerized inventory accounting systems use the perpetual approach. For a small business with a manual accounting system, however, the fact that a periodic system requires less record keeping than does a perpetual system may outweigh all other considerations.

In businesses in which accounting records are maintained manually by the owner, or by a professional accountant who visits the business on a weekly or monthly basis, a periodic inventory system may be the *only* practical means of accounting for inventory.

CASE IN POINT Dale's Market is a small grocery store, in which sales are recorded on mechanical cash registers. The daily register tapes list the retail prices of the items sold but do not identify the products in any other way. Even if Dale were willing to spend all night recording the costs of merchandise sold, he would have no place to start. His accounting system does not identify the types of products that have been sold.

A business with a manual accounting system may be able to use a perpetual inventory system if it sells a relatively small quantity of high-cost items. Examples of such businesses are antique stores, art galleries, and jewelry stores. On the other hand, a business which sells a high volume of low-cost items, such as Dale's Market, can maintain a perpetual inventory system only by installing electronic point-of-sale terminals. (The capabilities of these terminals are discussed in Chapters 5 and 6.)

Operation of a Periodic Inventory System

OBJECTIVE 2
Account for merchandising transactions using a periodic inventory system.

In a periodic inventory system, the amount of inventory on hand at the end of each accounting period is determined by physical count. The inventory at the end of one accounting period also represents the *beginning inventory* of the following period.

In summary, a periodic inventory system requires that a complete physical inventory be taken at the end of each accounting period. Annual financial statements may be prepared by taking inventory at the end of the fiscal year. The preparation of monthly financial statements, however, would require monthly inventories.[1]

Purchases of Merchandise Under a periodic inventory system, the cost of merchandise purchased for resale is recorded by debiting an account entitled *Purchases,* as shown below:

Purchases	*1,960*	
Accounts Payable (Beta Wholesale Co.)		*1,960*

Purchased merchandise on account; gross price, $2,000; terms 2/10, n/30. ($2,000, less 2% = $1,960.)

Purchases may be recorded either at the gross invoice price, or at net price—that is, net of available cash discounts. As in Chapter 5, we will record purchases at the *net* cost.

---

[1] In Chapter 9, we discuss several estimating techniques which may be used in preparing monthly or quarterly financial statements. If inventory (and the cost of goods sold) are based upon such estimating techniques, this fact should be disclosed in the financial statements.

Other Accounts Included in the Cost of Goods Sold   In our illustration on page 234, we used only three items in computing the cost of goods sold: beginning inventory, purchases, and ending inventory. In most cases, however, two additional accounts are involved in this computation: Purchase Returns and Allowances, and Transportation-in.

Purchase Returns and Allowances   When merchandise purchased from suppliers is found to be unsatisfactory, the goods may be returned or a request may be made for an allowance on the price. A return of goods to the supplier is recorded as follows:

Journal entry for return of goods to supplier

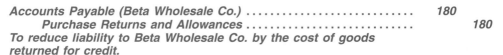

Accounts Payable (Beta Wholesale Co.) *180*
    Purchase Returns and Allowances *180*
To reduce liability to Beta Wholesale Co. by the cost of goods returned for credit.

Assuming that the purchase had been recorded at net cost, the purchase return also should be recorded at the net cost of the merchandise.

    The Purchase Returns and Allowances account may be viewed as a reduction in the cost of purchases made during the period. It is preferable to credit this "contra-purchases" account when merchandise is returned to a supplier rather than crediting the Purchases account directly. Together, these two accounts show both the total amount of purchases and the amount of cost adjustments and returns. Management is interested in the percentage relationship between goods purchased and the portion of these goods which must be returned. Returning merchandise is time-consuming and expensive and also may result in a loss of sales opportunities. Excessive returns may suggest a need to find more reliable suppliers.

Transportation-in   Transportation charges relating to merchandise are accounted for in the same manner in periodic and perpetual inventory systems. The freight charges paid on ***inbound*** shipments are debited to an account entitled ***Transportation-in,*** which is added to the cost of goods sold. Delivery costs on ***outbound*** shipments are debited to Delivery Expense, which is classified as a selling expense.

Purchase Discounts   We follow the policy of recording purchases at their net cost. Under this net method, the amount paid to the supplier will be equal to the recorded liability, assuming that payment will be made within the discount period. If payment is not made until after the discount period has expired, the purchaser must pay the gross invoice price. The additional amount paid is debited to an account entitled ***Purchase Discounts Lost,*** an expense account representing a form of interest expense. We strongly recommend this net method, as it focuses management's attention upon any failures to take advantage of available cash discounts.[2]

---

[2]   An alternative approach is to record purchases at the gross invoice price. If payment is made within the discount period, the buyer will then pay the supplier less than the recorded amount of the liability. This "cost savings" is credited to an account called Purchase Discounts Taken. Purchase Discounts Taken is a contra-purchases account, similar to Purchase Returns and Allowances. In terms of net income, the "gross method" and "net method" produce essentially the same results.

Accounting for Sales Transactions

Accounting for sales transactions is the same under periodic and perpetual inventory systems, with one notable exception. In a periodic system, no entries are made transferring costs from the Inventory account to the Cost of Goods Sold account.

To illustrate, assume that Farrow's Bait & Tackle Shop sells merchandise on account to South Shore Marina for $1,200; terms, 2/10, net/30. South Shore finds $200 worth of this merchandise defective and returns it to Farrow's immediately. South Shore then pays for the remainder of these goods within the discount period. Farrow's should record the original sales transaction as shown below:

Accounts Receivable (South Shore Marina)	1,200	
Sales		1,200
To record credit sale, terms 2/10, n/30.		

Notice that **only one entry** is needed to record a sale. The primary advantage of a periodic inventory system is that it is not necessary to record the cost of goods sold relating to individual sales transactions. (As in a perpetual inventory system, sales usually are recorded at the **gross** invoice price, not at the net amount.)

Farrow's would record the sales return by South Shore as follows:

Sales Returns and Allowances	200	
Accounts Receivable (South Shore Marina).................		200
Credit customer returned defective merchandise.		

Again, only one entry is necessary. Under a periodic inventory system, no entry is made to update the Inventory account or to adjust the cost of goods sold.

Following this sales return, South Shore owes Farrow's $1,000. If South Shore pays within the discount period, however, it may take a 2% cash discount. The entry to record the collection of this account receivable within the discount period is:

Cash...	980	
Sales Discounts	20	
Accounts Receivable (South Shore Marina).................		1,000
To record collection of account receivable within the discount period.		

Both Sales Returns & Allowances and Sales Discounts are **contra-revenue** accounts, which are deducted from gross sales revenue as a step in determining net sales. These debit balance accounts reduce the revenue of a specific time period. At the end of the period, they are closed into the Income Summary along with the company's expense accounts.

Income Statement for a Company Using a Periodic Inventory System

To pull together the concepts discussed in this appendix, let us look at a detailed income statement of a business using a periodic inventory system.

Olympic Sporting Goods is a small retail store organized as a sole proprietorship and operated by Robert Riley. The business has no external reporting responsibilities, other than determining its annual income for inclusion in Riley's personal income tax return. Also, Riley works in the store on a daily basis and is intimately familiar with the inventory on hand. Thus, Olympic Sporting Goods is able to meet Riley's needs for accounting information with a periodic inventory system. The company's 1994 income statement is illustrated below:

OLYMPIC SPORTING GOODS
Income Statement
For the Year Ending December 31, 1994

Revenue:			
Sales			$627,000
Less: Sales returns and allowances		$ 12,000	
Sales discounts		5,000	17,000
Net sales			$610,000
Cost of goods sold:			
Inventory, Jan. 1		$ 60,000	
Purchases	$375,000		
Less: Purchase returns and allowances	10,000		
Net purchases	$365,000		
Add: Transportation-in	11,000		
Delivered cost of purchases		376,000	
Cost of goods available for sale		$436,000	
Less: Inventory, Dec. 31		70,000	
Cost of goods sold			366,000
Gross profit on sales			$244,000
Operating expenses:			
Selling expenses:			
Sales salaries	$ 74,000		
Advertising	29,000		
Delivery service	7,000		
Depreciation	6,000		
Total selling expenses		$116,000	
General and administrative expenses:			
Office salaries	$ 55,000		
Utilities	2,100		
Depreciation	2,000		
Total general and administrative expenses		59,100	
Total operating expenses			175,100
Income from operations			$ 68,900
Nonoperating expenses:			
Purchase discounts lost	$ 1,000		
Interest expense	8,200		9,200
Net income			$ 59,700

Notice the computation of the cost of goods sold

Work Sheet for a Merchandising Business

In Chapter 4, we illustrated the preparation of a work sheet as a means of organizing the data used in making adjusting and closing entries and in preparing financial statements. A merchandising business using a periodic inventory system also may elect to prepare a work sheet. In fact, it is small businesses with periodic inventory systems and manual accounting records that are most likely to actually prepare such a schedule.[3]

In most respects, a work sheet prepared by a merchandising company with a periodic inventory system parallels the work sheet explained and illustrated in Chapter 4. There are, however, a few new features—namely, the Inventory account and other accounts used in recording merchandising transactions. As an illustration, a year-end work sheet for Olympic Sporting Goods is illustrated on the following page. For emphasis, the new types of accounts included in this work sheet are shown in black.

Trial Balance Columns   The trial balance columns are prepared by listing the account balances in the ledger at December 31, *prior* to making adjusting and closing entries. The Inventory account, however, is *not* up-to-date; its $60,000 balance represents the inventory at the *beginning of the year.* (A distinctive feature of the periodic inventory system is that the Inventory account is *not* updated throughout the year for purchases and sales of merchandise.)

Adjustment Columns and Adjusted Trial Balance   The adjustments required in a merchandising company at the end of the period are similar to those of a service business. In our illustration, we assume that the only adjustment needed at December 31 is an entry to record depreciation expense for the year.

The merchandising accounts (shown in black) usually do not require adjustment. Therefore, their balances are extended directly from the Trial Balance columns to the Adjusted Trial Balance columns.

Income Statement Columns   The accounts used in the determination of net income are extended from the Adjusted Trial Balance columns into the Income Statement columns. These are the revenue accounts, expense accounts, and *all accounts used in the computation of the cost of goods sold.*

Notice that the $60,000 balance in the Inventory account is extended into the *Income Statement* debit column, instead of the Balance Sheet debit column. This is because the $60,000 balance in this account represents the inventory at the *beginning* of the year. At year-end, the beginning inventory is *no longer an asset;* rather, it has become *part of the cost of goods sold.* The cost of goods sold, of course, is offset against revenue in the income statement.

Treatment of the Inventory Account   The most unique element of this work sheet is the treatment accorded to the Inventory account. As we have explained, the $60,000 beginning balance is extended into the Income State-

---

[3]   Remember that a work sheet is *not* an essential step in the accounting cycle. In essence, it is "scratch paper," upon which an accountant may work out certain entries before making entries in the accounting records. The student should regard the work sheets in this text as illustrations of accounting *processes,* not of account documents. In practice, accountants often perform the illustrated processes *without* first preparing a work sheet.

Note the treatment of the beginning and the ending inventories

OLYMPIC SPORTING GOODS
Work Sheet
For the Year Ended December 31, 1994

	Trial Balance		Adjustments		Adjusted Trial Balance		Income Statement		Balance Sheet	
	Dr	Cr	Dr	Cr	Dr	Cr	Dr	Cr	Dr	Cr
Balance sheet accounts:										
Cash	19,400				19,400				19,400	
Accounts receivable	48,300				48,300				48,300	
Inventory	60,000				60,000		60,000	70,000	70,000	
Land	52,000				52,000				52,000	
Building	160,000				160,000				160,000	
Accumulated depreciation: building		56,000		(a) 8,000		64,000				64,000
Notes payable		82,000				82,000				82,000
Accounts payable		55,000				55,000				55,000
Robert Riley, capital		115,000				115,000				115,000
Robert Riley, drawing	26,000				26,000				26,000	
Income statement accounts:										
Sales		627,000				627,000		627,000		
Sales returns and allowances	12,000				12,000		12,000			
Sales discounts	5,000				5,000		5,000			
Purchases	375,000				375,000		375,000			
Purchase returns and allowances		10,000				10,000		10,000		
Transportation-in	11,000				11,000		11,000			
Sales salaries	74,000				74,000		74,000			
Advertising expense	29,000				29,000		29,000			
Delivery service	7,000				7,000		7,000			
Office salaries	55,000				55,000		55,000			
Utilities expense	2,100				2,100		2,100			
Purchase discounts lost	1,000				1,000		1,000			
Interest expense	8,200				8,200		8,200			
	945,000	945,000								
Depreciation expense: building			(a) 8,000		8,000		8,000			
			8,000	8,000	953,000	953,000	647,300	707,000	375,700	316,000
Net income							59,700			59,700
Totals							707,000	707,000	375,700	375,700

ment debit column, not into the Balance Sheet columns. Now, however, it is time to **update** the Inventory account to show the $70,000 **ending inventory,** as determined by a physical inventory taken at year-end.

Updating the Inventory account requires **two entries** in the work sheet. Notice that the cost of the ending inventory appears both in the **Income Statement credit column** and in the **Balance Sheet debit column.** (For emphasis, these two entries are shown in red.)

Let us briefly explain the reasoning behind these entries. The cost of the ending inventory is entered into the Balance Sheet debit column because this amount will appear in the December 31 balance sheet. The amount also is entered into the Income Statement credit column because, in a periodic inventory system, the amount of ending inventory **enters into the determination of net income.**

In a periodic inventory system, the cost of goods sold is determined by **subtracting ending inventory** from the total of beginning inventory, purchases, and transportation-in. By entering the ending inventory in the Income Statement **credit** column, we in effect are **deducting** it from the sum of the beginning inventory, purchases, and transportation-in, all of which were extended into the Income Statement **debit** column.

One of the functions of the Income Statement columns is to bring together all of the accounts involved in determining the cost of goods sold. The accounts with debit balances are the beginning Inventory, Purchases, and Transportation-in; these accounts total $446,000. Against this total the two credit items of Purchase Returns & Allowances, $10,000, and ending Inventory, $70,000, are offset. The three accounts with debit balances exceed the total of the two credit balances by **$366,000;** this amount is the **cost of goods sold,** as shown in the income statement on page A-6.

Completing the Work Sheet   When all the accounts on the work sheet have been extended into the Income Statement or Balance Sheet columns, the final four columns are totaled. The net income is computed, and the work sheet completed in the same manner as illustrated in Chapter 4 for a service business.

Financial Statements

The work to be done at the end of the period is much the same for a merchandising business as for a service-type firm. First, the work sheet is completed; then, financial statements are prepared from the data in the work sheet; next, the adjusting and closing entries are entered in the journal and posted to the ledger accounts; and finally, an after-closing trial balance is prepared. This completes the annual accounting cycle.

The income statement on page A-6 was prepared from the Olympic Sporting Goods work sheet. Note particularly the arrangement of items in the cost of goods sold section of the income statement; this portion of the income statement illustrates many of the essential accounting concepts covered in this appendix.

Closing Entries

In a **perpetual** inventory system, the Cost of Goods Sold account simply is closed along with the company's expense accounts. In a **periodic** inventory

*OBJECTIVE 3
Prepare
closing en-
tries for a
business
using a peri-
odic inven-
tory system,
including
the entry to
"reopen" the
inventory
account.*

system, a single Cost of Goods Sold account is not used throughout the accounting period. Instead, separate ledger accounts are maintained for the various components of the cost of goods sold, each of which is closed at year-end. The major new elements in the closing process for a merchandising business using a periodic inventory system are the entries showing the **elimination** of the beginning inventory and the **recording** of the ending inventory.

The beginning inventory is cleared out of the Inventory account by a debit to Income Summary and a credit to Inventory. A separate entry could be made for this purpose, but we can save time by making one compound entry which will debit the Income Summary account with the balance of the beginning inventory and with the balances of all temporary accounts having debit balances.

The **temporary** accounts are those which appear in the income statement, including those which enter into the computation of the cost of goods sold. As the name suggests, the temporary accounts are used to accumulate temporarily the increases and decreases in owner's equity resulting from operation of the business. The entry to close the beginning inventory and income statement accounts with debit balances is illustrated below. (For emphasis, the Inventory account is shown in red, and other accounts relating specifically to merchandising transactions are shown in black.)

**Closing begin-
ning inventory
and income
statement ac-
counts with
debit balances**

Dec. 31	*Income Summary*	*647,300*	
	Inventory (Jan. 1)		*60,000*
	Sales Returns and Allowances		*12,000*
	Sales Discounts		*5,000*
	Purchases		*375,000*
	Transportation-in		*11,000*
	Sales Salaries		*74,000*
	Advertising Expense		*29,000*
	Delivery Service		*7,000*
	Office Salaries		*55,000*
	Utilities Expense		*2,100*
	Purchase Discounts Lost		*1,000*
	Interest Expense		*8,200*
	Depreciation Expense: Building		*8,000*
	*To close out the beginning inventory and the
income statement accounts with debit balances.*		

The preceding closing entry closes all the operating expense accounts, as well as the accounts used to accumulate the cost of goods sold. It also closes the accounts for Sales Returns and Allowances and for Sales Discounts, as well as Purchase Discounts Lost. After this first closing entry, the Inventory account has a zero balance. Therefore, it is time to record in this account the new inventory of $70,000 determined by a physical count at December 31.

To bring the ending inventory into the accounting records after the physical inventory on December 31, we could make a separate entry debiting Inventory and crediting the Income Summary account. It is more convenient, however, to combine this step with the closing of the Sales account and any other income statement accounts having credit balances, as illustrated in the following closing entry:

Closing income statement accounts with credit balances and recording ending inventory	Dec. 31	*Inventory (Dec. 31)*.............................	*70,000*	
		Sales..	*627,000*	
		Purchase Returns and Allowances...............	*10,000*	
		Income Summary...........................		*707,000*
		To record the ending inventory and to close all income statement accounts with credit balances.		

In this entry, we "close" the Sales account and the Purchase Returns and Allowances account, as each of these accounts will have a ***zero balance*** after the closing entry is posted. On the other hand, the Inventory account had been "closed" in the ***preceding*** entry, which transferred its entire balance into the Income Summary account. Therefore, debiting the Inventory account for the amount of the ending inventory should be viewed as ***"reopening"*** the Inventory account.

The remaining closing entries serve to transfer the balance of the Income Summary account to the owner's capital account and to close the drawing account, as follows:

Closing the Income Summary account and Owner's Drawing account	Dec. 31	*Income Summary*	*59,700*	
		Robert Riley, Capital...........................		*59,700*
		To close the Income Summary account.		
	Dec. 31	*Robert Riley, Capital*	*26,000*	
		Robert Riley, Drawing		*26,000*
		To close the drawing account.		

After the preceding four closing entries have been posted to the ledger, the only ledger accounts left with dollar balances will be balance sheet accounts. An after-closing trial balance should be prepared to prove that the ledger is in balance after the year-end entries to adjust and close the accounts have been recorded.

Record-Keeping Requirements in a Periodic System

At first glance, the more complex closing procedures may seem to negate the basic advantage of a periodic inventory system—that is, a reduction in the amount of required record keeping. However, recording the cost of goods sold relating to each sales transaction may require dozens, scores, or hundreds of entries ***each day.*** In contrast, the end-of-the-year closing procedures for a periodic inventory system involve only two additional elements: "closing out" the beginning inventory and "reopening" the Inventory account at the proper ending inventory amount. As closing procedures are usually handled by experienced accountants, use of a periodic system adds only a couple of minutes to the closing process.

ASSIGNMENT MATERIAL
PROBLEMS

PROBLEM A-1
Income Statement Relationships with a Periodic Inventory System

This exercise stresses the sequence and relationship of items in a multiple-step income statement for a merchandising business using a periodic inventory system. Each of the five horizontal lines in the table represents a separate set of income statement items. You are to copy the table and fill in the missing amounts. A net loss in the right-hand column is to be indicated by placing brackets before and after the amount, as for example, in line **e** (25,000).

	Net Sales	Beginning Inventory	Net Purchases	Ending Inventory	Cost of Goods Sold	Gross Profit	Expenses	Net Income or (Loss)
a	300,000	95,000	130,000	44,000	?	119,000	90,000	?
b	600,000	90,000	340,000	?	330,000	?	?	25,000
c	700,000	230,000	?	185,000	490,000	210,000	165,000	?
d	900,000	?	500,000	150,000	?	260,000	300,000	?
e	?	260,000	?	255,000	660,000	225,000	?	(25,000)

PROBLEM A-2
Journal Entries for Merchandising Transactions

Runners' World deals in a wide variety of low-priced merchandise and uses a periodic inventory system. The company's accounting policies call for recording credit sales at the gross invoice price, but recording purchases at net cost. Shown below is a partial list of the transactions occurring during May:

May 2   Purchased merchandise (running shoes) on credit from MinuteMan Shoes, $9,500. Terms, 2/10, n/30.

May 3   Paid freight charges of $45 on the shipment of merchandise purchased from MinuteMan Shoes.

May 4   Upon unpacking the shipment from MinuteMan, discovered that some of the shoes were the wrong style. Returned these shoes, which had a gross invoice price of $400 ($392 net cost) to MinuteMan and received full credit.

May 9   Sold merchandise on account to Desert Spa Hotel, $4,100. Terms, 2/10, n/30.

May 11   Paid $22 freight charges on the outbound shipment to Desert Spa Hotel.

May 12   Paid MinuteMan Shoes within the discount period the remaining amount owed for the May 2 purchase, after allowing for the purchase return on May 4.

May 16   Sold merchandise on account to Holiday Sportswear, $2,755. Terms, 2/10, n/30.

May 19   Received check from Desert Spa Hotel within the discount period in full settlement of the May 9 sale.

May 21   Holiday Sportswear returned $650 of the merchandise it had purchased on May 16. Runners' World has a policy of accepting all merchandise returns within 30 days of the date of sale without question. Full credit was given to Holiday for the returned merchandise.

INSTRUCTIONS   Prepare journal entries to record each of these transactions in the accounting records of Runners' World. Include a written explanation for each journal entry.

PROBLEM A-3
Preparing an Income Statement and Closing Entries

Listed below are the accounts relating to income of Leather Bandit for the three-month period ended March 31, 1994:

Sales	$500,000	Inventory, Jan. 1, 1994........	$170,100
Sales returns & allowances ...	15,000	Inventory, Mar. 31, 1994	
Sales discounts	7,800	(estimated).................	165,000
Purchases	302,000	Operating expenses	121,400
Purchase returns & allowances	4,500	Purchase discounts lost	400
Transportation-in	1,900	Interest expense..............	7,500

INSTRUCTIONS

a Compute the amount of net sales for the three-month period.

b Compute the cost of goods sold.

c Prepare a **condensed** multiple-step income statement. Show both net sales and the cost of goods sold as "one-line items," without showing the accounts used to compute these amounts. Interest expense and purchase discounts lost should be shown after determining income from operations.

d Prepare closing entries for the period ended March 31, 1994. Only three closing entries are required as the owner, John Brown, made no withdrawals during the year.

PROBLEM A-4
Completing a Work Sheet and Adjusting and Closing Entries

Westport Landing is a small company maintaining its accounts on a calendar-year basis and using a periodic inventory system. A four-column schedule consisting of the first four columns of a 10-column work sheet appears below.

WESTPORT LANDING
Work Sheet
For the Year Ended December 31, 19___

	Trial Balance		Adjustments	
	Debit	Credit	Debit	Credit
Balance sheet accounts:				
Cash	6,400			
Accounts receivable	16,000			
Inventory (Jan. 1)	60,000			
Unexpired insurance	4,400		(b)	2,800
Equipment............................	22,000			
Accumulated depreciation: equipment ..		6,600		(a) 2,200
Accounts payable.....................		20,400		
Jane Hill, capital		83,800		
Jane Hill, drawing......................	21,000			
Income statement accounts:				
Sales.................................		529,000		
Sales returns & allowances.............	21,000			
Sales discounts........................	8,000			
Purchases	361,000			
Purchase returns & allowances.........		18,000		
Transportation-in......................	12,000			
Advertising expense	32,000			
Rent expense..........................	25,000			
Salaries expense.......................	68,000			
Purchase discounts lost................	1,000			
	657,800	657,800		
Depreciation expense			(a) 2,200	
Insurance expense.....................			(b) 2,800	
			5,000	5,000

The completed Adjustments columns have been included in the work sheet to minimize the detail work involved. These adjustments were derived from the following information available at December 31.

a Depreciation expense for the year on equipment, $2,200.

b Insurance premiums expired during the year, $2,800.

A physical inventory taken at December 31 showed the ending inventory to be $66,000.

INSTRUCTIONS

a Prepare a 10-column work sheet following the format illustrated on page A-8. Include at the bottom of the work sheet a legend consisting of a brief explanation keyed to each adjusting entry.

b Prepare the two journal entries needed to adjust the accounts at December 31.

c Prepare the necessary journal entries to close the accounts on December 31.

PROBLEM A-5
Preparing a Work Sheet, Financial Statements, Adjusting Entries, and Closing Entries

Shown below is a trial balance prepared from the ledger of Western Supply at December 31, 19__. The accounts are maintained on a calendar-year basis and are adjusted and closed annually.

WESTERN SUPPLY
Trial Balance
December 31, 19__

Cash	$ 16,300	
Accounts receivable	49,200	
Inventory (Jan. 1, 19__)	62,000	
Unexpired insurance	1,800	
Office supplies	800	
Land	17,000	
Buildings	60,000	
Accumulated depreciation: buildings		$ 2,400
Equipment	16,000	
Accumulated depreciation: equipment		4,800
Accounts payable		47,900
Mary Lane, capital		99,500
Mary Lane, drawing	18,000	
Sales		326,000
Sales returns & allowances	4,100	
Sales discounts	1,100	
Purchases	190,000	
Purchase returns & allowances		2,000
Purchase discounts lost	400	
Transportation-in	4,800	
Salaries and wages expense	40,000	
Property taxes expense	1,100	
	$482,600	$482,600

OTHER DATA

a Examination of policies showed $600 *unexpired* insurance on December 31.

b Supplies on hand at December 31 were estimated to amount to $300.

c The buildings are being depreciated over a 25-year useful life. The equipment is being depreciated over a 10-year useful life.

d Accrued salaries payable as of December 31 were $5,000.

e Inventory of merchandise on December 31 was $44,600.

INSTRUCTIONS a Prepare a 10-column work sheet at December 31, 19__, using the format shown on page A-8.

b Prepare an income statement, a statement of owner's equity, and a classified balance sheet.

c Prepare adjusting entries.

d Prepare closing entries.

CASES AND UNSTRUCTURED PROBLEMS

CASE A-1
What Would You Expect?

In each of the following situations, indicate whether you would expect the business to use a periodic inventory system or a perpetual inventory system. Explain the reasons for your answer.

a The Frontier Shop is a small retail store that sells boots and western clothing. The store is operated by the owner, who works full time in the business, and by one part-time salesclerk. Sales transactions are recorded on an antique cash register. The business uses a manual accounting system, which is maintained by ACE Bookkeeping Service. At the end of each month, an employee of ACE visits The Frontier Shop to update its account records, prepare sales tax returns, and perform other necessary accounting services.

b Allister's Corner is an art gallery in the Soho district of New York. All accounting records are maintained manually by the owner, who works in the store on a full-time basis. The store sells three or four paintings each week, at sales prices ranging from about $5,000 to $50,000 per painting.

c A publicly owned corporation publishes about 200 titles of college-level textbooks. The books are sold to college bookstores throughout the country. Books are distributed to these bookstores from four central warehouses, located in California, Texas, Ohio, and Virginia.

d Toys-4-You operates a national chain of 86 retail toy stores. The company has a "state-of-the-art" computerized accounting system. All sales transactions are recorded on electronic point-of-sale terminals. These terminals are tied into a central computer system which provides the national headquarters with information about the profitability of each store on a weekly basis.

e Mr. Jingles, an independently owned and operated ice cream truck.

f TransComm is a small company that sells very large quantities of a single product. The product is a low-cost, 3.5 inch, double-sided, double-density computer floppy disk, manufactured by a large Japanese company. Sales are made only in large quantities, primarily to chains of computer stores and large discount stores. This year, the average sales transaction has amounted to $14,206 worth of merchandise. All accounting records are maintained by a full-time employee using commercial accounting software and a personal computer.

Manual Special Journals

Intended for Use after Chapter 6

Special journals were introduced in Chapter 6. This Appendix expands upon that introduction with specific examples and illustrations.

The basic purpose of a special journal is to record a particular type of recurring business transaction quickly and efficiently. Some special journals are machines, such as cash registers and point-of-sale terminals. Many others are handwritten accounting records. In this appendix, we illustrate and explain the use of special journals in manual accounting systems.

After studying this appendix you should be able to meet these Learning Objectives:

1   *Explain why the types and formats of special journals vary from one business to the next.*

2   *Record transactions in an appropriate special journal.*

3   *Design a special journal for efficiently recording a particular type of business transaction.*

Why Study Manual Special Journals?

Prior to the use of computers, all accounting records were maintained manually, with the assistance of some mechanical devices such as cash registers. Today more and more businesses use computers in developing accounting information. Why, then, study the "old style" manual accounting records?

We offer several answers to this question. First, manual special journals *remain in widespread use—and probably always will.* Many individuals and small businesses rely almost entirely upon manual records for developing their accounting information. Many large businesses use manual special journals on a temporary basis—whenever their computerized systems "go down." And in some situations, it simply is more convenient to record transactions in handwriting than to use a machine. Also, you will find that the study of manual special journals will *enhance your understanding* of the operation of every accounting system—large and small.

CHECK REGISTER: THE MOST COMMON SPECIAL JOURNAL OF THEM ALL

Check registers probably outnumber all other special journals combined. A check register, found inside every checkbook, is a special journal for recording all of the transactions in a particular bank checking account. Almost everyone with a checking account maintains this type of special journal.

If a business has more than one checking account, *a separate check register is maintained for each account.* When checks are printed by computer, the computer automatically maintains a check register. When checks are written "in the field," however, it often is convenient for the person issuing the check to record the transaction in the manual check register contained in checkbook. A manual check register is illustrated below:

A special journal found in every checkbook

		Check Register			
Date	Check No.	Name of Payee and Transaction Description	Amounts Deposits	Checks	Cash Balance
Mar. 31		Balance			$9,875
Apr. 1	364	Mall Mgmt. Corp. (Store rent for April)		$2,250	(2,250) $7,625
Apr. 1	365	ADP Wholesale Co. (Invoice dated Mar. 22)		3,205	(3,205) $4,420
Apr. 1		Day's cash receipts (All cash sales)	$1,950		1,950 $6,370
Apr. 2	366	. . .			

The transactions recorded in a check register may be posted periodically to the company's general ledger accounts, just as are transactions recorded in a general journal. For example, the first transactions in the illustrated check register would be posted as a debit to Rent Expense and as a credit to Cash. Some entries—such as payment of an account payable—also are posted to subsidiary ledger accounts.

Large businesses generally post these entries promptly. Small businesses sometimes leave this task for a professional accountant who visits the business only on a monthly or quarterly basis. A special feature of a manual check register, however, is a column indicating the ***current balance*** in the checking account. Thus, even if entries in the check register have not yet been posted to the general ledger, the business has an up-to-date record of the amount of cash in its checking account.

OTHER TYPES OF SPECIAL JOURNALS

OBJECTIVE 1
Explain why the types and formats of special journals vary from one business to the next.

Special journals are not all alike; each is designed for recording a ***specific type*** of business transaction. The number and format of the special journals in use at a particular business will vary with the nature and the volume of the company's transactions.

To illustrate the design and use of special journals, let us use the common example of a small merchandising operation. Ski Chalet is a ski shop with a manual accounting system. Like many small businesses with manual accounting systems, Ski Chalet uses a ***periodic inventory system.***[1]

The savings of time and effort are greatest when a separate special journal is designed to record each type of transaction that ***occurs frequently.*** In most merchandising businesses, the vast majority of transactions (perhaps 90% to 95%) fall into four major categories: (1) sales on account, (2) purchases of merchandise on account, (3) cash receipts, and (4) cash payments. Ski Chalet uses four separate special journals for recording these types of transactions, as shown below:

Types of Transactions That Occur Frequently	Corresponding Special Journal
Sales of merchandise on account	Sales journal
Purchases of merchandise on account	Purchases journal
Cash receipts	Cash receipts journal
Cash payments	Cash payments journal

In addition to these four special journals, Ski Chalet uses a ***general journal*** to record any transactions that ***do not fit*** into one of the special journals. Examples of transactions recorded in the general journal include sales returns, end-of-period adjusting entries, and closing entries.

We will now explain and illustrate the use of each of Ski Chalet's four special journals.

---

[1] Characteristics of periodic inventory systems are discussed in Chapter 5 and in Appendix A. Characteristics central to this illustration are (1) purchases of merchandise are debited to a ***Purchases*** account, rather than to the Inventory account; and (2) no entries are made recording the cost of goods sold as sales transactions occur.

Sales Journal

OBJECTIVE 2
Record
transactions
in an appro-
priate spe-
cial journal.

Ski Chalet uses its sales journal for recording only one type of transaction—**sales of merchandise on account.** If a sales transaction involves even a partial cash down payment, it is recorded in the cash receipts journal (discussed later in this appendix) rather than in the sales journal.

Ski Chalet's sales journal for the month of November is illustrated below:

Sales Journal						Page 8
Date	Account Receivable Debited	Invoice No.	Terms	✓		Amount
19___						
Nov 1	Jill Adams	301	2/10, n/30	✓		3,000
3	Harold Black	302	2/10, n/30	✓		1,400
10	C. D. Early	303	net 30	✓		900
18	Terry Frost	304	10 e.o.m.	✓		1,280
26	Nordic Ski Rentals	305	2/10, n/30	✓		8,600
28	Nordic Ski Rentals	306	2/10, n/30	✓		430
30	Total for the month					15,610

Notice that **special columns** are provided for recording each aspect of the sale. The data entered in each column can be quickly copied from the **sales invoice** prepared for each credit sale.

Advantages of the Sales Journal   Note that each of the six sales transactions is recorded on a single line. Each entry consists of a debit to a customer's account; the offsetting credit to the Sales account is understood without being written, because every transaction recorded in this special journal is a sale.

An entry in a sales journal **need not include an explanation;** if more information about the transaction is desired it can be obtained by referring to the file copy of the sales invoice. The invoice number is listed in the sales journal as part of each entry. The one-line entry in the sales journal requires much less writing than would be necessary to record a sales transaction in the general journal. Since there may be several hundred or several thousand sales transactions each month, the time saved in recording transactions in this streamlined manner becomes quite important.

Another advantage of recording transactions in special journals is that much time may be saved in posting the effects of transactions to the company's general ledger accounts.

Posting Entries from the Sales Journal   The posting of transaction data from Ski Chalet's sales journal is illustrated on the following page.

Each credit sales transaction is posted promptly as a **debit** to the customer's account in the accounts receivable **subsidiary ledger.** (These postings are illustrated in black.) Whenever a posting is made to a subsidi-

Posting a Sales Journal

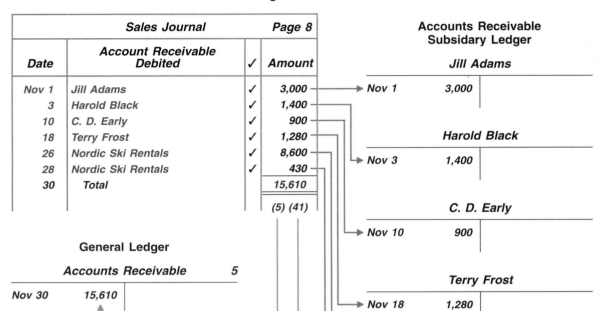

ary ledger account, a check mark (✔) is placed in the sales journal posting reference column.

Use of a special journal does not save time in posting transaction data to subsidiary ledger accounts. It does, however, save great amounts of time in posting to ***general ledger*** accounts. As we have seen in Chapter 2, all entries in a general journal are posted separately to the general ledger accounts.

In the illustrated sales journal, however, every transaction is a credit sale, to be recorded as a debit to Accounts Receivable and a credit to Sales. Instead of posting each of these transactions to the general ledger separately, we wait until month-end and then post ***one amount representing all of these credit sales.***

At month-end, the Amount column in the sales journal is ***totaled.*** This total, ***$15,610,*** is posted as a debit to the Accounts Receivable controlling account in the general ledger, and also as a credit to the Sales account. (These postings are shown in red.) The account numbers for these two general ledger accounts (5 and 41) then are placed in parentheses below the column total to show that this amount has been posted.

Notice that the amount debited to the Accounts Receivable controlling account, $15,610, is equal to the ***sum*** of the six separate amounts debited during the month to the accounts receivable subsidiary ledger.

In effect, the six credit sales transactions occurring during November were posted to the general ledger ***as one dollar amount.*** In actual practice, this one posting might represent 600, or even 6,000, separate credit sales transactions.

Purchases Journal

Ski Chalet records all of its **purchases of merchandise on account** in a special **purchases journal.** This journal is illustrated below, along with arrows indicating how the transaction data are posted to accounts in the accounts payable ledger and the general ledger.

Purchases journal and . . .

. . . posting procedures

Purchases Journal						Page 6
Date		Account Payable Credited	Invoice Date	Terms	✓	Net Cost
19__						
Nov	2	Alpine Ski Equip.	Nov 2	net 30	✓	5,210
	4	Backcountry Sports	4	2/10, n/30	✓	3,920
	10	Downhill Specialists	9	net 30	✓	1,860
	17	Heads & Tails	16	2/10, n/30	✓	2,450
	27	Quick Release Bindings Co.	25	net 30	✓	790
	30	Total for the month				14,230
						(50)(21)

General Ledger

Purchases 50

Nov 30   14,230

Accounts Payable 21

Nov 30   14,230

Accounts Payable Subsidiary Ledger

Alpine Ski Equip.

Nov 2   5,210

Backcountry Sports

Nov 4   4,000

Downhill Specialists

Nov 10   1,860

Heads & Tails

Nov 17   2,500

Quick Release Bindings Co.

Nov 27   790

Because Ski Chalet uses a **periodic** inventory system, the costs of merchandise purchased are debited to a general ledger account entitled **Purchases** rather than to the Inventory account.

Ski Chalet has a policy of taking advantage of all cash discounts offered by its suppliers. Therefore, purchases are recorded at **net cost**—that is, at invoice price **less any available cash discount.** The two columns in the purchases journal showing the credit terms and invoice date of each purchase assist the company's accounting personnel in determining when each invoice must be paid.

This purchases journal is used in recording only one type of transaction—**purchases of merchandise on account.** Cash purchases are recorded in the cash payments journal, not the purchases journal. When assets **other than** merchandise are purchased, the journal used in recording the transaction depends upon whether a cash payment is made. If assets of this type are purchased for cash, the transaction is recorded in the cash payments journal; if the acquisition is made on account, the general journal is used.

Posting the Purchases Journal Each credit purchase is posted immediately as a credit to the appropriate account in the accounts payable subsidiary ledger. As these postings are made, a check mark (✔) is placed in the purchases journal.

At the end of the month, the Amount column is totaled. This total—representing all credit purchases for the month—is posted to the general ledger as a debit to the Purchases account and as a credit to the Accounts Payable controlling account. The account numbers of these two general ledger accounts then are entered in parentheses just below the column total to show that these postings have been made.

Special Journals for Cash Transactions

A great many transactions involve either the receipt or the payment of cash. As shown earlier in this appendix, the cash receipts and cash payments of a very small business may be summarized in a check register. Most businesses, however, also maintain a separate **cash receipts journal** and **cash payments journal.**

When these special cash journals are in use, a check register is still maintained for each checking account. However, the purpose of each check register is primarily to indicate the current balance in a particular checking account. The cash receipts and cash payments journals provide more detailed information about cash transactions and are used as the basis for posting transactions to the ledger accounts.

Cash Receipts Journal

Ski Chalet's cash receipts journal is used for recording **every transaction that involves the receipt of cash.** Cash receipts arise from a variety of sources. Therefore, the cash receipts journal is more complicated than the "single-column" special journals that the company uses for recording credit sales and purchases on account.

Ski Chalet's most common source of cash receipts is the sale of merchandise for cash. As each cash sale is made, it is rung up on a cash register. At the end of the day, the total of the cash sales is computed by striking a total key on the register. This total is entered as cash sales in the cash receipts journal, which therefore contains one entry for each day's total cash sales.[2] For other types of cash receipts, such as the collection of an account receivable, a separate entry is made for each transaction.

The cash receipts journal illustrated on the following page contains entries for all of the November transactions of Ski Chalet *involving the receipt of cash.* These transactions are described below:

Nov. 1   The owner, G. G. Nuccio, made an additional investment in the business of $30,000 cash.

Nov. 1   Cash sales for the day totaled $1,200.

Nov. 2   Cash sales for the day totaled $910.

Nov. 8   Collected $2,940 from Jill Adams in full settlement of sales invoice no. 301. Payment received within the discount period.

Nov. 10   Sold a small portion of land not needed in the business for a total price of $27,000, receiving $7,000 cash and a note receivable for $20,000. The cost of the land was $25,000; thus, a $2,000 gain was realized on the sale.

Nov. 12   Collected $1,372 from Harold Black in full settlement of sales invoice no. 302. Payment received within the discount period.

Nov. 28   Collected $500 from C. D. Early as a partial payment on sales invoice no. 303.

Nov. 30   Cash sales (since Nov. 2) totaled $18,300.

Nov. 30   Obtained a $15,000 bank loan by issuing a note payable.

Columns in a Cash Receipts Journal   Notice that the illustrated cash receipts journal has several columns for recording debits and several for recording credits. Providing a separate column for debit or credit entries to a specific account *speeds up* both the recording and posting of these entries.

An entry is recorded in a special column merely by entering the dollar amount; it is not necessary to write the account title, as all entries in the column affect the same account. Also, all of the entries in a specific column have a similar effect upon the account—that is, they are either all debits or all credits. Therefore, it is not necessary to separately post each transaction to the general ledger account. Instead, all of the entries may be posted simply by posting the column total at the end of each month.

In designing a cash receipts journal, a separate column should be provided for any type of debit or credit entry that *occurs frequently.* For example, every cash receipt transaction includes a debit to the Cash account. Therefore, a column is provided for recording these debits. As Ski Chalet often collects its accounts receivable within the discount period, it includes a debit column for recording sales discounts taken by customers. When cash is received, the offsetting credit most often is to either Accounts Receivable or to Sales. Therefore, separate columns are provided for recording these credit entries.

In a manual journal, it usually is not practical to have more than eight or ten columns. Thus, "Other Accounts" columns must be included to accommodate entries to accounts for which there is no special column. A computerized system may (in effect) include separate columns for ***every***

---

[2]   To conserve space, our illustration includes daily entries for cash sales only on the first two days of the month. The remaining cash sales for the month are summarized in a single entry dated November 30.

Includes all transactions involving re-ceipt of cash

Cash Receipts Journal

Page 7

| | | | | Debits | | | | Credits | | | | |
| | | | | | Other Accounts | | | Accounts Receivable | | | Other Accounts | |
Date	Explanation	Cash	Sales Discounts	Name	LP	Amount	Account Credited	✓	Amount	Sales	LP	Amount
19__												
Nov 1	Investment by owner	30,000					G. G. Nuccio, Capital				30	30,000
1	Cash sales	1,200								1,200		
2	Cash sales	910								910		
8	Invoice 301, less 2%	2,940	60				Jill Adams	✓	3,000			
10	Sale of land	7,000		Notes Receivable	3	20,000	Land				11	25,000
							Gain on Sale of Land				40	2,000
12	Invoice 302, less 2%	1,372	28				Harold Black	✓	1,400			
28	Invoice 303, partial payment received	500					C. D. Early	✓	500			
30	Cash sales	18,300								18,300		
30	Obtained bank loan	15,000					Notes Payable				20	15,000
30	Totals for the month	77,222	88			20,000			4,900	20,410		72,000
		(1)	(43)			(X)			(5)	(41)		(X)

ledger account. In this appendix, however, we are focusing upon manual systems.

Using the Other Accounts Columns   Notice that "Other Accounts" columns are provided on both the debit and credit sides of the journal. These columns can accommodate debit or credit entries to **any** ledger account.

Space is provided in the Other Accounts columns for writing both the name of the account and the dollar amount of the debit or credit entry. For example, the entry of November 10 in the illustrated journal shows that cash and a note receivable were received when land was sold. The amount of cash received, $7,000, simply is entered in the Cash debit column; the title Notes Receivable is written in the Other Accounts debit column along with the amount of the debit to this account ($20,000). These two debits are offset by credit entries to Land, $25,000, and Gain on Sale of Land, $2,000, in the Other Accounts credit column. (Notice that a transaction which involves several "other accounts" occupies more than one line in the cash receipts journal.)

Posting the Cash Receipts Journal   Three distinct posting processes are involved for the cash receipts journal:

1 As with other special journals, amounts affecting **subsidiary ledger** accounts are posted immediately. In the cash receipts journal, these entries are the credits to the accounts receivable from specific customers. A check mark (✔) is entered in the cash receipts journal as evidence that each of these entries has been posted. (For purposes of illustration, the amounts to be posted daily to subsidiary ledgers are shown in black type.)

2 The entries to **general ledger accounts recorded in the Other Accounts column** also should be posted daily. As these postings are made, the number of the ledger account is entered in the LP (ledger page) column of the cash receipts journal opposite the item posted. (In our illustration, amounts that should be posted immediately to general ledger accounts appear in green.)

3 At month-end, each of the debit and credit amount columns is totaled. Before any column totals are posted, it is first important to determine that the sum of the debit column totals is **equal** to the sum of the credit column totals. This **crossfooting** of the journal is an error-catching procedure, similar to the preparation of a trial balance.

    After the column totals have been crossfooted, any debit or credit total **relating to a specific general ledger account** is posted to that account. This posting updates the accounts for all of the individual entries recorded in the column during the month. As evidence of this month-end posting, the number of the general ledger account is entered in parentheses just below the column total. (Column totals to be posted at month-end are illustrated in red.)

The totals of the Other Accounts columns are **not posted** at month-end for two reasons. First, these column totals often include entries affecting several different ledger accounts. Next, the individual amounts comprising these column totals have **already been posted,** as described in step **2,** above. The symbol *(X)* is placed below the totals of the Other Accounts columns to indicate that these amounts should not be posted.

Cash Payments Journal

Another widely used special journal is the cash payments journal, sometimes called the cash disbursements journal, in which **all payments of cash** are recorded. Among the more common of these transactions are payments of accounts payable to creditors, payment of operating expenses, and cash purchases of merchandise.

The cash payments journal illustrated on the following page contains entries for all November transactions of Ski Chalet which required the **payment of cash.** These transactions are:

Nov. 1 Paid Powder Bowl Mall rent on store building for November, $2,400.

Nov. 2 Purchased merchandise from Uller Products for cash, $250.

Nov. 5 Bought land, $60,000, and building, $100,000, for use as a future business site. Paid cash of $35,000 to Western Escrow Co., and signed a note payable for the $125,000 balance of the purchase price.

Nov. 17 Paid salaries of $3,600 by issuing one check for the entire payroll amount to Payroll Services, Inc.

Nov. 27 Paid $2,450 to Heads & Tails in full settlement of $2,500 purchase on Nov. 17, less 2% discount.

Nov. 27 Purchased merchandise from Mountain High for $800 cash.

Nov. 28 Purchased office supplies from Office World for $325, cash.

Nov. 29 Paid for newspaper advertising in Snow Report, $450.

Nov. 30 Paid Backcountry Sports the full $4,000 invoice amount for the purchase on Nov. 4. This invoice was inadvertently overlooked and was not paid within the discount period. (Remember, the purchase originally had been recorded at a **net price** of $3,920.

Notice in the illustrated cash payments journal that the two credit columns (Cash and Other Accounts) are located **to the left** of the three debit columns. Any sequence of columns is satisfactory as long as the column headings clearly indicate whether the account is being debited or credited. The Cash column often is placed first in both the cash receipts journal and the cash payments journal simply because this column is used in recording every transaction.

Good internal control over cash disbursements requires that all payments be made by check. The checks are serially numbered and as each transaction is entered in the cash payments journal, the check number is listed in a special column provided just to the right of the date column. An unbroken sequence of check numbers in this column gives assurance that every check issued has been recorded in the accounting records.

Posting the Cash Payments Journal The posting of the cash payments journal falls into the same phases already described for the cash receipts journal. The first phase consists of the daily posting of entries in the Accounts Payable debit column to the individual accounts of creditors in the accounts payable subsidiary ledger. Check marks (✔) are entered opposite

Includes all transactions involving payment of cash

Cash Payments Journal

Page 12

Date	Check No.	Payee	Credits: Cash	Credits: Other Accounts — Name	LP	Amount	Account Debited	Debits: Accounts Payable ✓	Amount	Debits: Purchases	Debits: Other Accounts — LP	Amount
19—												
Nov 1	420	Powder Bowl Mall	2,400				Store Rent Expense				54	2,400
2	421	Uller Products	250							250		
5	423	Western Escrow Co.	35,000	Notes Payable	20	125,000	Land				11	60,000
							Building				12	100,000
17	424	Payroll Services, Inc.	3,600				Salaries Expense				53	3,600
27	425	Heads & Tails	2,450				Heads & Tails	✓	2,450			
27	426	Mountain High	800							800		
28	427	Office World	325				Office Supplies				5	325
29	428	Snow Report	450				Advertising Expense				55	450
30	429	Backcountry Sports	4,000				Backcountry Sports	✓	3,920			
							Purchase Discounts Lost				70	80
30		Totals for the month	49,275			125,000			6,370	1,050		166,855
			(1)			(X)			(21)	(50)		(X)

those items to show that the posting has been made. (Amounts to be posted to the subsidiary ledger accounts are shown in black.)

The individual debit and credit entries in the Other Accounts columns of the cash payment journal may be posted daily or at convenient intervals during the month. As the posting of these individual items are made, the number of the ledger account debited or credited is entered in the LP (ledger page) column of the cash payments journal opposite the item posted. (Amounts to be posted to general ledger accounts on a daily basis are shown in green.)

The third phase of posting the cash payments journal is performed at the end of the month. When all the transactions of the month have been journalized, the cash payments journal is ruled as shown in our illustration, and the five money columns are totaled. The equality of debits and credits is then proved before posting.

After the totals of the cash payments journal have been proved to be in balance, the totals of the columns for Cash, Accounts Payable, and Purchases are posted to the corresponding accounts in the general ledger. (The column totals to be posted are shown in red.) The numbers of the accounts to which these postings are made are listed in parentheses just below the respective column totals in the cash payments journal. The totals of the Other Accounts columns in both the debit and credit section of this special journal are not to be posted, and the symbol *(X)* is placed below the totals of these two columns to indicate that no posting is required.

The General Journal

When all transactions involving cash or the purchase and sale of merchandise are recorded in special journals, only a few types of transactions remain to be entered in the general journal. Examples include the purchase or sale of plant and equipment on credit, the return of merchandise for credit to a supplier, and the return of merchandise by customers for credit to their accounts. The general journal is also used for adjusting and closing entries at the end of the accounting period.

The following transactions of Ski Chalet during November could not conveniently be handled in any of the four special journals and were therefore entered in the general journal.

Nov. 22 A customer, Terry Frost, returned for credit $210 worth of merchandise that had been sold to her on Nov. 18.

Nov. 28 Ski Chalet returned to a supplier, Quick Release, for credit $158 worth of the merchandise purchased on Nov. 27.

Nov. 29 Purchased for use in the business office equipment costing $3,600. Agreed to make payment within 30 days to Wolfe Computer

Each of the following three entries includes a debit or credit to a controlling account (Accounts Receivable or Accounts Payable) and also identifies by name a particular creditor or customer. When a *controlling account* is debited or credited by a general journal entry, the debit or credit must be posted *twice:* one posting to the controlling account in the *general ledger* and another posting to a customer's account or a creditor's account in a *subsidiary ledger.* This double posting is necessary to keep the controlling account in agreement with the subsidiary ledger.

General Journal   Page 4

Date		Account Titles and Explanation	LP	Dr	Cr
19__ Nov	22	Sales Returns and Allowances .... Accounts Receivable (Terry Frost).... Allowed credit to customer for return of merchandise from sale of Nov. 18.	42 5/√	210	210
	28	Accounts Payable (Quick Release)........ Purchase Returns and Allowances ... Returned to supplier for credit a portion of merchandise purchased on Nov. 27.	21/√ 51	158	158
	29	Office Equipment .... Accounts Payable (Wolfe Computer) Purchased office equipment on 30-day credit.	14 21/√	3,600	3,600

Transactions which do not "fit" in any of the special journals

For example, in the illustrated entry of November 22 for the return of merchandise by a customer, the credit part of the entry is posted twice:

1 To the Accounts Receivable controlling account in the general ledger; this posting is evidenced by listing the account number (5) in the LP column of the general ledger.

2 To the account of Terry Frost in the subsidiary ledger for accounts receivable; this posting is indicated by the check mark (✔) placed in the LP column of the general journal.

Showing the Source of Postings in Ledger Accounts

When a general journal and several special journals are in use, the ledger accounts should indicate the book of original entry from which each debit and credit was posted. An identifying symbol is placed opposite each entry in the reference column of the account. The symbols used in this text are as follows:

- **S8** meaning page 8 of the sales journal
- **P6** meaning page 6 of the purchases journal
- **CR7** meaning page 7 of the cash receipts journal
- **CP12** meaning page 12 of the cash payments journal
- **J4** meaning page 4 of the general journal

The following illustration shows a typical customer's account in a subsidiary ledger for accounts receivable:

Customer:	*C. D. Early*				Credit terms *net 30*	
					Credit limit *$2,000*	
Date			**Ref**	**Debit**	**Credit**	**Balance**
19—						
Nov	*10*		*S8*	*900*		*900*
	28		*CR7*		*500*	*400*

Notice that the Reference column shows the source of each debit and credit entry. Similar references are entered in general ledger accounts.

Reconciling Subsidiary Ledgers with Controlling Accounts

We have made the point that the balance in a controlling account should be equal to the sum of the balances of the subsidiary ledger accounts. Proving the equality is termed **reconciling** the subsidiary ledger with its controlling account. This process may bring to light errors in either the subsidiary ledger or in the controlling account.

The first step in reconciling a subsidiary ledger is to prepare a schedule of the balances of the subsidiary ledger accounts. For example, the balances in Ski Chalet's accounts receivable subsidiary ledger at November 30 are shown below. The total of this schedule should agree with the balance in the controlling account in the general ledger.

Schedule of Accounts Receivable
November 30, 19—

C. D. Early	$ 400
Terry Frost	1,070
Nordic Ski Rentals	9,030
Total (per Accounts Receivable controlling account)	$10,500

Reconciling subsidiary ledgers with their controlling accounts is an important internal control procedure and should be performed at least once a month. This procedure may disclose such errors in the subsidiary ledger as failure to post transactions, transposition or slide errors, or mathematical errors in determining the balances of specific accounts receivable or accounts payable. However, this procedure will **not** disclose an entry which was posted to the wrong account within the subsidiary ledger.

If the subsidiary ledger and controlling account are **not** in agreement, the error may be difficult to find. The disagreement may be caused by an incorrect posting or by an error in the computation of an account balance. Thus, we may need to verify postings and recompute account balances until the error is found. Fortunately, most businesses use computer programs to maintain accounts receivable records. These programs have built-in internal control procedures that effectively prevent differences between amounts posted to the subsidiary ledger and to the related controlling account.

Variations in Special Journals

OBJECTIVE 3
Design a
special jour-
nal for effi-
ciently re-
cording a
particular
type of busi-
ness trans-
action.

The number of special journals used in a business, and the number of columns in those journals, depends upon the nature of the business and the volume of the various kinds of transactions. For example, a business with a large volume of merchandise returns might establish a special **sales returns and allowances journal.**

Special Journals in Perpetual Inventory Systems   The company in our illustration in this appendix used a periodic inventory system. Periodic inventory systems are used primarily in small businesses that sell a wide variety of low cost merchandise and that have manual accounting systems. Most large businesses today use **perpetual** inventory systems, in which the Inventory and Cost of Goods Sold accounts are kept up-to-date. Of course, these large companies also have computer-based accounting systems which enable them to efficiently record the cost of goods sold relating to each sales transaction.

A small business with manual accounting records can maintain a perpetual inventory system only if the company sells a **low volume** of high-cost merchandise. Examples of such businesses include art galleries, furniture stores, and used car dealerships.

To modify the illustrated special journals for a perpetual inventory system, two basic changes are necessary:

1   The name of the Purchases columns in the purchases journal and the cash payments journal is changed to **Inventory.** Entries in these Inventory columns should be posted daily as debits to the appropriate accounts in the inventory subsidiary ledger. At month-end, the column totals are posted to the general ledger as debits to the Inventory controlling account and as credits to the Accounts Payable controlling account.

2   A **Cost of Goods Sold column** is added to the sales journal. As sales transactions are recorded in this journal, the cost of the items sold is entered in this Cost of Goods Sold column. The individual entries in this column are posted daily as credits to the inventory subsidiary ledger. At month-end, the column total is posted to the general ledgers as a debit to the Cost of Goods Sold account and a credit to the Inventory controlling account.

In Conclusion . . .   Special journals should be regarded as laborsaving devices designed to meet the needs of a particular business. Every business can benefit by using some form of special journal for recording any type of transaction that **occurs frequently.**

ASSIGNMENT MATERIAL

PROBLEMS

PROBLEM B-1
**Using a Sales
Journal and
Cash Receipts
Journal**

The accounting records of Video Games, a wholesale distributor of packaged software, include a general journal and four special journals similar to those illustrated in this appendix. The company maintains a general ledger and subsidiary ledgers for accounts receivable and accounts payable, and uses a periodic inventory system.

Among the general ledger accounts used by Video Games are:

Cash................................	10	Sales	50
Notes receivable	15	Sales returns & allowances	52
Accounts receivable	17	Sales discounts	54
Notes payable......................	30	Purchases returns & allowances	62
Accounts payable	32		

Transactions in June involving the sale of merchandise and the receipt of cash are shown below.

June 1 Sold merchandise to The Game Store for cash, $472.

June 4 Sold merchandise to Bravo Company, $8,500. Invoice no. 618; terms 2/10, n/30.

June 5 Received cash refund of $1,088 for merchandise returned to a supplier.

June 8 Sold merchandise to Micro Stores for $4,320. Invoice no. 619; terms e.o.m.

June 11 Received $2,310 cash as partial collection of a $6,310 account receivable from Olympus Corporation. Also received a note receivable for the $4,000 remaining balance due.

June 13 Received check from Bravo Company in settlement of invoice dated June 4, less discount.

June 16 Sold merchandise to Books, Etc. for $4,040. Invoice no. 620; terms 2/10, n/30.

June 16 Returned merchandise costing $960 to supplier, Software Co., for reduction of account payable.

June 20 Sold merchandise to Graphics, Inc., for $7,000. Invoice no. 621; terms 2/10, n/30.

June 21 Books, Etc. returned for credit $640 of merchandise purchased on June 16.

June 23 Borrowed $24,000 cash from a local bank, signing a six-month note payable.

June 25 Received $3,332 from Books, Etc., in full settlement of invoice dated June 16, less return on June 21 and 2% discount.

June 30 Collected from Graphics, Inc., amount of invoice dated June 20, less 2% discount.

June 30 Received a 60-day note receivable for $4,320 from Micro Stores in settlement of invoice dated June 8.

INSTRUCTIONS Record the above transactions in the appropriate journals. Use a single-column sales journal, a six-column cash receipts journal, and a two-column general journal. Foot and rule the special journals. Indicate how postings would be made by placing ledger account numbers and check marks in the appropriate columns of the journals. (You are not required to post to ledger accounts.)

PROBLEM B-2 Special Journals; Purchases and Cash Payments Poison Creek Drug Store uses a periodic inventory system and the types of manual special journals illustrated in this appendix. Among the ledger accounts used by the company are the following:

Cash................................	10	Accounts payable	30
Office supplies	18	Purchases	50
Land...............................	20	Purchase returns & allowances	52
Building............................	22	Salaries expense	60
Notes payable......................	28	Purchase discounts lost	80

The August transactions relating to the purchase of merchandise for resale and to accounts payable are listed below along with selected other transactions. It is Poison Creek Drug's policy to record purchases of merchandise at ***net cost.***

Aug. 1   Purchased merchandise from Medco Labs at a gross invoice price of $8,450. Invoice dated today; terms 2/10, n/30.

Aug. 4   Purchased merchandise from American Products at a gross invoice price of $19,300. Invoice dated August 3; terms 2/10, n/30.

Aug. 5   Returned for credit to Medco Labs defective merchandise having an invoice price of $1,200 (net cost, $1,176).

Aug. 6   Received shipment of merchandise from Tricor Corporation and their invoice dated August 5 in amount of $14,560. Terms net 30 days.

Aug. 8   Purchased merchandise from Vita-Life, Inc., $24,480. Invoice dated today; terms net 30.

Aug. 10   Purchased merchandise from King Corporation at an invoice price of $30,000. Invoice dated August 9; terms 2/10, n/30.

Aug. 10   Issued check no. 631 for $7,105 to Medco Labs in settlement of balance resulting from purchase of August 1 and purchase return of August 5.

Aug. 18   Issued check no. 632 to American Products for $19,300, in payment of the August 3 invoice. This invoice temporarily had been misplaced, and Poison Creek failed to make payment in time to take advantage of the 2% cash discount.

Aug. 18   Issued check no. 633 for $29,400 to King Corporation in settlement of invoice dated August 9, less 2% discount.

Aug. 20   Purchased merchandise for cash, $1,080. Issued check no. 634 to Candy Corp.

Aug. 21   Bought land and building for $208,800. Land was worth $64,800, and building, $144,000. Paid cash of $36,000 and signed a promissory note for the balance of $172,800. Check no. 635, in the amount of $36,000, was issued to Security Escrow Co.

Aug. 23   Purchased merchandise from Novelty Products for cash, $900. Issued check no. 636.

Aug. 26   Purchased merchandise from Ralston Company for a gross invoice price of $32,400. Invoice dated August 26, terms 2/10, n/30.

Aug. 28   Paid cash for office supplies, $270. Issued check no. 637 to Super Office, Inc.

Aug. 29   Purchased merchandise from Candy Corp. for cash, $1,890. Check no. 638.

Aug. 31   Paid salaries for August, $17,920. Issued check no. 639 to National Bank, which handles the distribution of the payroll to employees. (Ignore payroll taxes.)

INSTRUCTIONS

a   Record the transactions in the appropriate journals. Use a single-column purchases journal, a five-column cash payments journal, and a two-column general journal. Foot and rule the special journals. Make all postings to the proper general ledger accounts and to the accounts payable subsidiary ledger. (For posting references in the ledgers, assume all journals are on page no. ***5***.)

b   Prepare a schedule of accounts payable at August 31 to prove that the subsidiary ledger is in balance with the controlling account for accounts payable.

PROBLEM B-3
Using Special Journals to Record Cash Transactions

J. D. Thomas Co. wholesales furniture to interior designers and retail furniture stores. The company uses a periodic inventory system and special journals similar to those illustrated in this appendix. Purchases of merchandise are recorded at *net cost* in a purchases journal.

In this problem, you are to record only the *cash transactions* of J. D. Thomas Co. during October. These transactions are listed below:

Oct. 1   Issued check no. 734 to Furniture Trade Center in payment of store rent for October, $2,200.

Oct. 3   Purchased office equipment for $8,400 from MicroDesk, issuing check no. 735 as a $1,400 cash down payment and issuing a 90-day, 10% note payable for the $7,000 balance.

Oct. 4   The owner, J. D. Thomas, invested an additional $20,000 cash in the business.

Oct. 8   Paid an account payable to Colonial House, taking the allowable 2% cash discount. Issued check no. 736 in the amount of $14,700.

Oct. 9   Sold merchandise for cash to Southwest Design Studios, $16,300.

Oct. 10   Received $3,600 as a partial collection of an $18,000 account receivable from Myra's Interiors. Also received a $14,400 note receivable for the uncollected balance.

Oct. 12   Received $7,742 from Furniture Gallery in settlement of our $7,900 sales invoice dated Oct. 2, less 2%.

Oct. 15   Cash sales of merchandise, $18,750.

Oct. 22   Purchased merchandise from Carolina Furniture Co. for cash, $11,200. Issued check no. 737.

Oct. 25   Issued check no. 738 in payment of account payable to Fabrics Unlimited, $6,664.

Oct. 27   Purchased merchandise from Oak World, $16,700. Issued check no. 739.

Oct. 29   Received check for $17,836 from Lambert's in settlement of our $18,200 sales invoice dated Oct. 19, less 2%.

Oct. 31   Paid monthly salaries, $8,470. Issued one check, no. 740, to Merchants' Bank in the full amount of these salaries. (The bank handles the distribution of the payroll to individual employees.)

Oct. 31   Paid Merchants' Bank installment due today on a note payable. Issued check no. 741 in the amount of $1,630, representing $480 interest expense and a reduction in the balance of the note payable of the remaining $1,150.

INSTRUCTIONS   Enter the above transactions in either a six-column cash receipts journal or a five-column cash payments journal. Total the money columns in each journal and determine the equality of the debit and credit column totals.

CASES AND UNSTRUCTURED PROBLEMS

CASE B-1
Designing a Special Journal and Explaining Its Use

Leisure Clothing is a mail-order company which sells clothes to the public at discount prices. Recently Leisure Clothing initiated a new policy allowing a 10-day free trial on all clothes bought from the company. At the end of the 10-day period, the customer may either pay cash for the purchase or return the goods to Leisure Clothing. The new policy caused such a large boost in sales that, even after considering the many sales returns, the policy appeared quite profitable.

The accounting system of Leisure Clothing includes a sales journal, purchases journal, cash receipts journal, cash payments journal, and general journal. As an internal control procedure, an officer of the company reviews and initials every entry in the general journal before the amounts are posted to the ledger accounts. Since the 10-day free trial policy has been in effect, hundreds of entries recording sales returns have been entered in the general journal each week. Each of these entries has been reviewed and initialed by an officer of the firm, and the amounts have been posted to Sales Returns & Allowances and to the Accounts Receivable controlling account in the general ledger, and also to the customer's account in the accounts receivable subsidiary ledger.

Since these sales return entries are so numerous, it has been suggested that a special journal be designed to handle them. This could not only save time in journalizing and posting the entries, but also eliminate the time-consuming individual review of each of these repetitive entries by an officer of the company.

INSTRUCTIONS

a How many amounts are entered in the general journal to describe a single sales return transaction? Are these amounts the same?

b Explain why these sales return transactions are suited to the use of a special journal. Explain in detail how many money columns the special journal should have, and what postings would have to be done either at the time of the transaction or at the end of the period.

c Assume that there were 3,000 sales returns during the month. How many postings would have to be made during the month if these transactions were entered in the general journal? How many postings would have to be made if the special journal you designed in **b** were used? (Assume a one-month accounting period.)

Applications of Present Value

Intended for Use after Chapter 16

Several preceding chapters have included brief references to the concept of present value in discussions of the valuation of certain assets and liabilities. The purpose of this appendix is to discuss this concept more fully and also to demonstrate the use of present value tables as an aid to making present value computations. In addition, the appendix summarizes in one location the various applications of the present value concept which have been discussed throughout the book.

After studying this appendix you should be able to meet these Learning Objectives:

1 *Explain the concept of present value.*
2 *Identify the three factors that affect the present value of a future amount.*
3 *Compute the present value of a future amount and of an annuity using present value tables.*
4 *Discuss accounting applications of the present value concept.*

The Concept of Present Value

OBJECTIVE 1
*Explain the
concept of
present
value.*

The concept of present value has many applications in accounting, but it is most easily explained in the context of evaluating investment opportunities. In this context, the present value of an expected future cash receipt is the amount that a knowledgeable investor would pay **today** for the right to receive that future amount. The present value is always **less** than the future amount, because the investor will expect to earn a return on the investment. The amount by which the future cash receipt exceeds its present value represents the investor's profit; in short, this difference may be regarded as **interest revenue** included in the future amount.

OBJECTIVE 2
*Identify the
three factors
that affect
the present
value of a
future
amount.*

The present value of a particular investment opportunity depends upon three factors: (1) the expected dollar amount to be received in the future, (2) the length of time until the future amount will be received, and (3) the rate of return (called the **discount rate**) required by the investor. The process of determining the present value of a future cash receipt or payment is called **discounting** the future amount.

To illustrate the present value concept, assume that a specific investment is expected to result in a $1,000 cash receipt at the end of one year. An investor requiring a 10% annual rate of return would be willing to pay $909 today (computed as $1,000 ÷ 1.10) for the right to receive this future amount. This computation may be verified as follows (amounts rounded to the nearest dollar):

Amount to be invested (present value)	*$ 909*
Required return on investment ($909 × 10%)	*91*
Amount to be received in one year (future value)	*$1,000*

If the $1,000 is to be received **two years** in the future, the investor would pay only $826 for the investment today [($1,000 ÷ 1.10) ÷ 1.10]. This computation may be verified as follows (amounts rounded to the nearest dollar):

Amount to be invested (present value)	*$ 826*
Required return on investment in first year ($826 × 10%)	*83*
Amount invested after one year	*$ 909*
Required return on investment in second year ($909 × 10%)	*91*
Amount to be received in two years (future value)	*$1,000*

The amount that our investor would pay today, $826, is the **present value** of $1,000 to be received two years later, discounted at an annual rate of 10%. The $174 difference between the $826 present value and the $1,000 future amount may be regarded as the return (interest revenue) to be earned by the investor over the two-year period.

Present Value Tables

Although we can compute the present value of future amounts by a series of divisions as illustrated above, a more convenient method is available. We can use a **table of present values** to find the present value of $1 at a specified discount rate and then multiply that value by the future amount. For example, in *Table 1* below, the present value of $1 to be received in two years, discounted at an annual rate of 10%, is *$0.826.* If we multiply .826 by the expected future cash receipt of $1,000, we get an answer of $826, the same amount produced by the series of divisions in our previous illustration.

TABLE 1
Present Values of $1 Due in *n* Periods*

Number of Periods (*n*)	Discount Rate								
	1%	$1\frac{1}{2}$%	5%	6%	8%	10%	12%	15%	20%
1	.990	.985	.952	.943	.926	.909	.893	.870	.833
2	.980	.971	.907	.890	.857	.826	.797	.756	.694
3	.971	.956	.864	.840	.794	.751	.712	.658	.579
4	.961	.942	.823	.792	.735	.683	.636	.572	.482
5	.951	.928	.784	.747	.681	.621	.567	.497	.402
6	.942	.915	.746	.705	.630	.564	.507	.432	.335
7	.933	.901	.711	.665	.583	.513	.452	.376	.279
8	.923	.888	.677	.627	.540	.467	.404	.327	.233
9	.914	.875	.645	.592	.510	.424	.361	.284	.194
10	.905	.862	.614	.558	.463	.386	.322	.247	.162
20	.820	.742	.377	.312	.215	.149	.104	.061	.026
24	.788	.700	.310	.247	.158	.102	.066	.035	.013
36	.699	.585	.173	.123	.063	.032	.017	.007	.001

* The present value of $1 is computed by the formula $p = 1/(1 + i)^n$, where *p* is the present value of $1, *i* is the discount rate, and *n* is the number of periods until the future cash flow will occur. Amounts in this table have been rounded to three decimal places and are shown for a limited number of periods and discount rates. Many calculators are programmed to use this formula and can compute present values when the future amount is entered along with values for *i* and *n*.

Selecting an Appropriate Discount Rate

The *discount rate* may be viewed as the investor's required rate of return. All investments involve some degree of risk that actual future cash flows may turn out to be less than expected. Investors usually will expect a rate of return which justifies taking this risk. Under today's market conditions, investors require annual returns of between 6% and 9% on low-risk investments, such as government bonds and certificates of deposit. For relatively high-risk investments, such as the introduction of a new product line, investors may expect to earn an annual return of perhaps 15% or more.

In addition to the amount of risk involved, the "appropriate" discount rate for determining the present value of a specific investment depends upon the investor's cost of capital and the returns available from other investment opportunities. When a higher discount rate is used, the resulting present value will be lower and the investor, therefore, will be interested in the investment only at a lower price.

Discounting Annual Cash Flows

OBJECTIVE 3
Compute the
present
value of a
future
amount and
of an annu-
ity using
present
value tables.

Let us now assume that an investment is expected to produce an **annual net cash flow** of $10,000 in **each of the next three years.**[1] If Camino Company expects a 12% return on this type of investment, it may compute the present value of these cash flows as follows:

Year	Expected Net Cash Flow	×	Present Value of $1 Discounted at 12%	=	Present Value of Net Cash Flows
1	$10,000		.893		$ 8,930
2	10,000		.797		7,970
3	10,000		.712		7,120
Total present value of the investment					$24,020

This analysis indicates that the present value of the expected net cash flows from the investment, discounted at an annual rate of 12%, amounts to $24,020. This is the maximum amount that Camino Company could afford to pay for this investment and still expect to earn the 12% required rate of return.

In the preceding schedule, we multiplied each of the expected annual cash flows by the present value of $1 in the appropriate future period, discounted at 12% per year. The present values of the annual cash flows were then added to determine the total present value of the investment. Separately discounting each annual cash flow to its present value is necessary only when the cash flows vary in amount from one year to the next. Since the annual cash flows in our example are **uniform in amount,** there are two easier ways to compute the total present value.

One way is to add the three decimal figures representing the present value of $1 in the successive years (.893 + .797 + .712) and then to multiply this total (2.402) by the $10,000 annual cash flow. This approach produces the same result ($10,000 × 2.402 = $24,020) we obtained by determining the present value of each year's cash flow separately and adding the results.

An even easier approach to determining the present value of uniform annual cash flows is to refer to an **annuity table,** which shows the present value of **$1 to be received periodically** for a given number of periods. An annuity table appears on the following page and is labeled as **Table 2.**[2]

Note that the present value of $1 to be received periodically (annually) for three years, discounted at 12% per year, is **$2.402.** Thus, $10,000 received annually for three years, discounted at 12%, is **$24,020** ($10,000 × 2.402).

---

[1] An "annual net cash flow" normally is the net result of a series of cash receipts and cash payments occurring throughout the year. For convenience, we follow the common practice of assuming that the entire net cash flow for each year occurs at **year-end.** This assumption causes relatively little distortion and greatly simplifies computations.

[2] This table assumes that the periodic cash flows occur at the **end** of each period.

TABLE 2
Present Values of $1 to Be Received Periodically for *n* Periods

Number of Periods (*n*)	Discount Rate								
	1%	1½%	5%	6%	8%	10%	12%	15%	20%
1	0.990	0.985	0.952	0.943	0.926	0.909	0.893	0.870	0.833
2	1.970	1.956	1.859	1.833	1.783	1.736	1.690	1.626	1.528
3	2.941	2.912	2.723	2.673	2.577	2.487	2.402	2.283	2.106
4	3.902	3.854	3.546	3.465	3.312	3.170	3.037	2.855	2.589
5	4.853	4.783	4.329	4.212	3.993	3.791	3.605	3.352	2.991
6	5.795	5.697	5.076	4.917	4.623	4.355	4.111	3.784	3.326
7	6.728	6.598	5.786	5.582	5.206	4.868	4.564	4.160	3.605
8	7.652	7.486	6.463	6.210	5.747	5.335	4.968	4.487	3.837
9	8.566	8.361	7.108	6.802	6.247	5.759	5.328	4.772	4.031
10	9.471	9.222	7.722	7.360	6.710	6.145	5.650	5.019	4.192
20	18.046	17.169	12.462	11.470	9.818	8.514	7.469	6.259	4.870
24	21.243	20.030	13.799	12.550	10.529	8.985	7.784	6.434	4.937
36	30.108	27.661	16.547	14.621	11.717	9.677	8.192	6.623	4.993

Discount Periods of Less Than One Year

The interval between regular periodic cash flows is termed the ***discount period.*** In our preceding examples we have assumed cash flows and, therefore, discount periods of one year. Often a note or a contract may call for cash payments on a more frequent basis, such as monthly, quarterly, or semiannually. The illustrated present value tables can be used with discount periods of any length, ***but the discount rate must relate to the time interval of the discount period.*** Thus, if we use the annuity table to find the present value of a series of equal monthly cash payments, the discount rate must be expressed as a monthly interest rate.

To illustrate, assume that StyleMart purchases merchandise from Western Fashions, issuing in exchange a $96,000 note payable to be paid in 24 monthly installments of $4,000 each. As discussed in earlier chapters, both companies should record this transaction at the present value of the note. If a reasonable ***annual*** interest rate for this type of note is 12%, we should discount the monthly cash payments at the ***monthly*** rate of *1%.* The annuity table shows the present value of $1 to be received (or paid) for 24 monthly periods, discounted at 1% per month, is 21.243. Thus, the present value of the installment note issued by StyleMart is ***$84,972*** ($4,000 × 21.243).

ACCOUNTING APPLICATIONS OF THE PRESENT VALUE CONCEPT

Accounting applications of the concept of present value have been discussed at appropriate points throughout this textbook. We will now demon-

OBJECTIVE 4
Discuss accounting applications of the present value concept.

strate these applications with examples which make use of our present value tables.

Valuation of Long-Term Notes Receivable and Payable (Chapters 8 and 11)

When a long-term note receivable or payable does not bear a realistic stated rate of interest, a portion of the face amount of the note should be regarded as representing an interest charge. The amount of this interest charge can be determined by discounting the note to its present value using as a discount rate a realistic rate of interest.

To illustrate, consider our preceding example in which StyleMart purchases merchandise from Western Fashions by issuing an installment note payable with a face amount of $96,000 and no stated rate of interest. The present value of this note, discounted at the realistic market interest rate of 1% per month, was $84,972. The difference between the $96,000 face amount of the note and its present value of $84,972 is $11,028, which represents the interest charge included in the face amount.

StyleMart should use the **present value** of the note in determining the cost of the merchandise and the amount of the related net liability, as shown by the following entry:

The net liability is recorded at its present value

Inventory	*84,972*	
Discount on Notes Payable	*11,028*	
Notes Payable		*96,000*

Purchased merchandise by issuing a 24-month installment note payable with a 1% monthly interest charge included in the face amount.

The $11,028 discount represents the interest charges included in the face amount of the note. To determine how much of this discount will be recognized as interest expense each month, StyleMart should prepare an **amortization table** similar to the one illustrated on page 523. This table will be based upon 24 monthly payments of $4,000, a monthly interest rate of 1%, and an original unpaid balance (principal amount) of $84,972. Therefore, the interest expense for the first month (rounded to the nearest dollar) will be $850 ($84,972 × 1%), and the remaining $3,150 ($4,000 payment, less $850 interest expense) will reduce the unpaid principal amount. Interest expense will decline in each successive month, as a result of the decline in the unpaid principal amount.

The entries to record the first $4,000 payment on the face amount of this note and the related monthly interest expense are illustrated below:

Notes Payable	*4,000*	
Cash		*4,000*

To record $4,000 payment on a note payable.

Interest Expense	*850*	
Discount on Notes Payable		*850*

To record interest expense and amortize discount on an installment note payable with interest included in the face amount (interest expense equal to unpaid principal amount, $84,972, times 1% monthly interest rate).

Capital Budgeting (Chapter 10)[3]

Capital budgeting is the process of planning and evaluating proposals for capital expenditures, such as the acquisition of plant assets or the introduction of a new product line. Perhaps the most widely used approach in the evaluation of proposed capital expenditures is *discounting* the expected future cash flows to their *present value.*

Assume that Globe Mfg. Co. is considering a proposal to purchase new equipment in order to produce a new product. The equipment costs $400,000, has an estimated 10-year service life, and has an estimated salvage value of $50,000. Globe estimates that production and sale of the new product will increase the company's annual net cash flow by $100,000 per year for the next 10 years. If Globe requires a 15% annual rate of return on investments of this nature, the present value of these cash flows may be computed as shown below:

Present value of expected annual net cash inflows of $100,000 for 10 years, discounted at 15% per year: $100,000 × 5.019 (from Table 2, page C-5)	*$501,900*
Present value of estimated salvage value to be received at the end of the tenth year: $50,000 × .247 (from Table 1, page C-3)	*12,350*
Present value of estimated future cash inflows	*$514,250*
Less: Amount to be invested (already a present value)	*400,000*
Net present value of proposal	*$114,250*

This analysis indicates that the present value of the expected net cash flows from this investment, discounted at an annual rate of 15%, amounts to $514,250. This is the maximum amount which Globe could afford to invest in this project and still expect to earn the required 15% annual rate of return. As the cost of this investment is only $400,000, Globe can expect to earn more than its required 15% return.

The *net present value* of a proposal is the *difference* between the total present value of the future net cash flows and the cost of the investment. When the net present value is equal to zero, the investment provides a rate of return exactly equal to the rate used in discounting the cash flows. A *positive* net present value means that the investment provides a rate of return *greater* than the discount rate; a *negative* net present value means that the investment yields a return of *less* than the discount rate.

Since the discount rate usually is the minimum rate of return required by the investor, proposals with a positive net present value are considered acceptable, and those with a negative net present value are viewed as unacceptable.

Capital budgeting techniques are discussed further in courses in management accounting, cost accounting, and finance.

Estimating the Value of Goodwill (Chapter 10)

The asset goodwill may be defined as the present value of expected future earnings in excess of the normal return on net identifiable assets. One

---

[3]   Capital budgeting also is discussed in Chapter 26.

method of estimating goodwill is to estimate the annual amounts by which earnings are expected to exceed a normal return and then to discount these amounts to their present value.

To illustrate, assume that LiteHouse, a chain of restaurants, is negotiating to purchase Little Nell's, a highly profitable restaurant in Aspen, Colorado. In addition to paying for the fair market value of Little Nell's net identifiable assets, LiteHouse is willing to pay an appropriate amount for goodwill. The management of LiteHouse estimates that Little Nell's will earn at least $80,000 in excess of "normal earnings" for this size restaurant in each of the next five years. If LiteHouse requires a 20% annual return on purchased goodwill, it can pay as much as $239,280 for this expected 5-year $80,000 annuity. [$80,000 × 2.991 (from Table 2) = $239,280.]

Market Prices of Bonds (Chapter 16)

The market price of bonds may be regarded as the *present value* to bondholders of the future principal and interest payments. To illustrate, assume that a corporation issues $1,000,000 face value of 10-year, 9% bonds when the going market rate of interest is 10%. Since bond interest is paid semiannually, we must use 20 *semiannual* periods as the life of the bond issue and a 5% *semiannual* market rate of interest in our present value calculations. The expected issuance price of this bond issue may be computed as follows:

Present value of future principal payments:
  $1,000,000 due after 20 semiannual periods, discounted at 5% per period:
    $1,000,000 × .377 (from Table 1, page C-3) $377,000
Present value of future interest payments:
  $45,000 per period ($1,000,000 × 9% × ½) for 20 semiannual periods,
    discounted at 5%: $45,000 × 12.462 (from Table 2, page C-5) 560,790
Expected issuance price of bond issue $937,790

Capital Lease (Chapter 16)

A capital lease is regarded as a sale of the leased asset by the lessor to the lessee. At the date of this sale, the lessor recognizes sales revenue equal to the *present value* of the future lease payments receivable, discounted at a realistic rate of interest. The lessee also uses the present value of the future payments to determine the cost of the leased asset and the valuation of the related liability.

To illustrate, assume that on December 1, Pace Tractor uses a *capital lease* to finance the sale of a tractor to Kelly Grading Co. The tractor was carried in Pace Tractor's perpetual inventory records at a cost of $15,000. Terms of the lease call for Kelly Grading Co. to make *24* monthly payments of *$1,000* each, beginning on December 31. These lease payments include an interest charge of *1%* per month. At the end of the 24-month lease, title to the tractor will pass to Kelly Grading Co. at no additional cost.

Accounting by the Lessor (Pace Tractor) *Table 2* on page C-5 shows that the present value of $1 to be received monthly for 24 months, discounted at

1% per month, is **21.243.** Therefore, the present value of the 24 future lease payments is $1,000 × 21.243, or **$21,243.** Pace Tractor should record this capital lease as a sale of the tractor at a price equal to the present value of the lease payments, as follows:

Lease Payment Receivable (net)	*21,243*	
* Sales*		*21,243*

Financed sale of a tractor to Kelly Grading Co. using a capital lease requiring 24 monthly payments of $1,000. Payments include a 1% monthly interest charge.

Cost of Goods Sold	*15,000*	
* Inventory*		*15,000*

To record cost of tractor sold under capital lease.

Notice that the sales price of the tractor is only $21,243, even though the gross amount to be collected from Kelly Grading Co. amounts to $24,000 ($1,000 × 24 payments). The difference between these two amounts, $2,757, will be recognized by Pace Tractor as interest revenue over the life of the lease.[4]

To illustrate the recognition of interest revenue, the entry on December 31 to record collection of the first monthly lease payment (rounded to the nearest dollar) is:

Cash	*1,000*	
* Interest Revenue*		*212*
* Lease Payments Receivable (net)*		*788*

Received first lease payment from Kelly Grading Co.:

Lease payment received	*$1,000*
Interest revenue ($21,243 × 1%)	*(212)*
Reduction in lease payments receivable	*$ 788*

After this first monthly payment is collected, the present value of the lease payments receivable is reduced to $20,455 ($21,243 original balance, less $788). Therefore, the interest revenue earned during the **second** month of the lease (rounded to the nearest dollar) will be **$205** ($20,455 × 1%).[5]

Accounting by the Lessee (Kelly Grading Co.) Kelly Grading Co. also should use the present value of the lease payments to determine the cost of the tractor and the amount of the related liability, as shown below:

Leased Equipment	*21,243*	
* Lease Payment Obligation*		*21,243*

To record acquisition of a tractor through a capital lease from Pace Tractor. Terms call for 24 monthly payments of $1,000, which include a 1% monthly interest charge.

---

[4] We have elected to record the present value of the future lease payments by a single debit entry to Lease Payments Receivable. An alternative is to debit Lease Payments Receivable for the total amount of the future payments and to credit Discount on Lease Payments Receivable, a contra-asset account, for the unearned finance charges included in the contractual amount. Either approach results in the lessor recording a net receivable equal to the present value of the future lease payments.

[5] Both Pace Tractor and Kelly Grading Co. would prepare **amortization tables** showing the allocation of each lease payment between interest and the amount due.

The entry on December 31 to record the first monthly lease payment (rounded to the nearest dollar) is:

Interest Expense	*212*	
Lease Payment Obligation	*788*	
Cash		*1,000*
To record first monthly lease payment to Pace Tractor:		
Amount of payment	*$1,000*	
Interest expense ($21,243 × 1%)	*(212)*	
Reduction in lease payment obligation	*$ 788*	

Disclosure of Present Value Information (Chapters 8, 11, and 16)

The FASB currently requires companies to *disclose* in notes to their financial statements the *present value* of certain financial instruments (receivables or payables) whenever this present value differs from the recorded value by a *material amount.* These disclosure requirements may apply to long-term accounts and notes receivable and also to long-term obligations such as bonds payable. In the future, present value may serve as the basis for the balance sheet valuation of long-term financial instruments.

ASSIGNMENT MATERIAL

PROBLEMS

PROBLEM C-1
Using Present Value Tables

Use the tables on pages C-3 and C-5 to determine the present value of the following cash flows.

a $10,000 to be paid annually for seven years, discounted at an annual rate of 10%. Payments are to occur at the end of each year.

b $7,500 to be received today, assuming that money can be invested to earn 15% annually.

c $350 to be paid monthly for 24 months, with an additional "balloon payment" of $15,000 due at the end of the twenty-fourth month, discounted at a monthly interest rate of $1\frac{1}{2}\%$. The first payment is to be one month from today.

d $30,000 to be received annually for the first three years, followed by $20,000 to be received annually for the next two years (total of five years in which collections are received), discounted at an annual rate of 12%. Assume collections occur at year-end.

PROBLEM C-2
Present Value and Bond Prices

On June 30 of the current year, Rural Gas & Electric Co. issued $10,000,000 face value, 11%, 10-year bonds payable, with interest dates of December 31 and June 30. The bonds were issued at a discount, resulting in an effective *semiannual* interest rate of 6%. The company maintains its accounts on a calendar-year basis and amortizes the bond discount by the effective interest method.

INSTRUCTIONS

a Compute the issuance price for the bond issue which results in an effective semiannual interest rate of 6%. (Hint: Discount both the interest payments and the maturity value over 20 semiannual periods.)

b Prepare a journal entry to record the issuance of the bonds at the sales price you computed in part **a.**

PROBLEM C-3
Valuation of a Note Payable

On December 1, Showcase Interiors purchased a shipment of furniture from Colonial House by paying $10,500 cash and issuing an installment note payable in the face amount of $28,800. The note is to be paid in 24 monthly installments of $1,200 each. Although the note makes no mention of an interest charge, the rate of interest usually charged to Showcase Interiors in such transactions is $1\frac{1}{2}\%$ per month.

INSTRUCTIONS

a Compute the present value of the note payable, using a discount rate of $1\frac{1}{2}\%$ per month.

b Prepare the journal entries in the accounts of Showcase Interiors on:

1 December 1, to record the purchase of the furniture (debit Inventory).

2 December 31, to record the first $1,200 monthly payment on the note and to recognize interest expense for one month by the effective interest method. (Round interest expense to the nearest dollar.)

c Show how the liability for this note would appear in the balance sheet at December 31. (Assume that the note is classified as a current liability.)

PROBLEM C-4
Discounting Lease Agreements to Present Value

Metropolitan Transit District (MTD) plans to acquire a large computer system by entering into a long-term lease agreement with the computer manufacturer. The manufacturer will provide the computer system under either of the following lease agreements:

Five-year lease. MTD is to pay $2,500,000 at the beginning of the lease (delivery date) and $1,000,000 annually at the end of each of the next 5 years. At the end of the fifth year, MTD may take title to the system for an additional payment of $3,000,000.

Ten-year lease. MTD is to pay $2,000,000 at the beginning of the lease and $900,000 annually at the end of each of the next 10 years. At the end of the tenth year, MTD may take title for an additional payment of $1,300,000.

Under either proposal, MTD will buy the computer at the end of the lease. MTD is a governmental agency which does not seek to earn a profit and is not evaluating alternative investment opportunities. However, MTD does attempt to minimize its costs and it must borrow the money to finance either lease agreement at an annual interest rate of 10%.

INSTRUCTIONS

a Determine which lease proposal results in the lower cost for the computer system when the future cash outlays are discounted at an annual interest rate of 10%.

b Prepare a journal entry to record the acquisition of the computer system under the lowest cost lease agreement as determined in part **a.** (This journal entry will include the initial cash payment to the computer manufacturer required at the beginning of the lease.)

PROBLEM C-5
Capital Leases: A Comprehensive Problem

Custom Truck Builders frequently uses long-term lease contracts to finance the sale of its trucks. On November 1, 1993, Custom Truck Builders leased to Interstate Van Lines a truck carried in the perpetual inventory records at $33,520. The terms of the lease call for Interstate Van Lines to make 36 monthly payments of $1,400 each, beginning on November 30, 1993. The present value of these payments, after considering a built-in interest charge of 1% per month, is equal to the regular $42,150 sales price of the truck. At the end of the 36-month lease, title to the truck will transfer to Interstate Van Lines.

INSTRUCTIONS

a Prepare journal entries for 1993 in the accounts of Custom Truck Builders on:

1 November 1 to record the sale financed by the lease and the related cost of goods sold. (Debit Lease Payments Receivable for the $42,150 present value of the future lease payments.)

2 November 30, to record receipt of the first $1,400 monthly payment. (Prepare a compound journal entry which allocates the cash receipt between interest revenue and reduction of Lease Payments Receivable. The portion of each monthly payment recognized as interest revenue is equal to 1% of the balance of the account Lease Payments Receivable, at the beginning of that month. Round all interest computations to the nearest dollar.)

3 December 31, to record receipt of the second monthly payment.

b Prepare journal entries for 1993 in the accounts of Interstate Van Lines on:

1 November 1, to record acquisition of the leased truck.

2 November 30, to record the first monthly lease payment. (Determine the portion of the payment representing interest expense in a manner parallel to that described in part **a.**)

3 December 31, to record the second monthly lease payment.

4 December 31, to recognize depreciation on the leased truck through year-end. Compute depreciation expense by the straight-line method, using a 10-year service life and an estimated salvage value of $6,150.

c Compute the net carrying value of the leased truck in the balance sheet of Interstate Van Lines at December 31, 1993.

d Compute the amount of Interstate Van Lines' lease payment obligation at December 31, 1993.

PROBLEM C-6
Valuation of a Note Receivable with an Unrealistic Interest Rate

On December 31, Richland Farms sold a tract of land, which had cost $930,000, to Skyline Developers in exchange for $150,000 cash and a five-year, 4%, note receivable for $900,000. Interest on the note is payable annually, and the principal amount is due in five years. The accountant for Richland Farms did not notice the unrealistically low interest rate on the note and made the following entry on December 31 to record this sale:

Cash..	150,000	
Notes Receivable......................................	900,000	
Land...		930,000
Gain on Sale of Land..............................		120,000
Sold land to Skyline Developers in exchange for cash and a five-year note with interest due annually.		

INSTRUCTIONS

a Compute the present value of the note receivable from Skyline Developers at the date of sale, assuming that a realistic rate of interest for this transaction is 12%. (Hint: Consider both the annual interest payments and the principal amount of the note.)

b Prepare the journal entry on December 31 to record the sale of the land correctly. Show supporting computations for (1) the gain or loss on the sale and (2) the discount on the note receivable.

c Explain what effects the error made by Richland Farms' accountant will have upon (1) the net income in the year of the sale and (2) the combined net income of the next five years. Ignore income taxes.

International Accounting and Foreign Currency Transactions

Intended for Use after Chapter 17

This appendix addresses some special accounting issues encountered by companies which conduct part of their business in foreign countries or in foreign currencies. First, we discuss the meaning of currency exchange rates and the reasons that these rates fluctuate. The accounting for purchases and sales of merchandise in transactions that span national boundaries is illustrated and explained. Special attention is given to gains and losses caused by fluctuations in exchange rates.

After studying this appendix you should be able to meet these Learning Objectives:

1 *Translate an amount of foreign currency into the equivalent number of U.S. dollars.*
2 *Explain why exchange rates fluctuate and what is meant by a "strong" or a "weak" currency.*
3 *Compute the gain or loss on a receivable or payable stated in terms of a foreign currency when exchange rates fluctuate.*
4 *Explain how fluctuations in foreign exchange rates affect companies with receivables or payables stated in terms of foreign currencies.*

*F*rom what geographical area does Bank of America—the largest bank in California—earn most of its revenue? The answer is abroad—that is, from its operations in foreign countries. Bank of America is not alone in its pursuit of business on a worldwide basis. Most large corporations, such as Exxon, IBM, Volkswagen, and Sony, do business in many countries. Coca-Cola, for example, has operations in more than 150 countries throughout the world. Companies that do business in more than one country often are described as ***multinational*** corporations. The extent to which foreign sales contributed to the revenue of several well-known multinational corporations in a recent year is shown below.

Company	Headquarters	Total Revenues (in Millions)	% Earned from Foreign Operations
Nestles	Switzerland	$13,626	97.2
Sony	Japan	4,528	74.5
Exxon	USA	97,173	71.4
Volkswagen	Germany	15,427	67.9
Bank of America	USA	14,955	53.8
British Petroleum	Great Britain	51,353	52.3
IBM	USA	34,364	44.6
Coca-Cola	USA	6,250	42.7

Most large and well-known multinational corporations are headquartered in the highly industrialized countries, such as the United States, Japan, Great Britain, and the countries of Western Europe. Virtually every country, however, has many companies that engage in international business activity.

What Is International Accounting?

Accounting for business activities that span national borders comprises the field of international accounting. In this appendix, we emphasize accounting for transactions with foreign companies. We also briefly discuss some of the problems of preparing consolidated financial statements for American-based companies with subsidiaries located in foreign countries. Our discussion is limited to basic concepts; the details and complexities of international accounting will be covered in advanced accounting courses.

Foreign Currencies and Exchange Rates

One of the principal problems in international accounting arises because every country uses a different currency. Assume, for example, that a Japanese company sells merchandise to an American corporation. The Japanese company will want to be paid in Japanese currency—yen—but the American company's bank account contains U.S. dollars. Thus, one currency must be converted into another.

Most banks participate in an international currency exchange, which enables them to buy foreign currencies at the prevailing ***exchange rate.*** Thus, our American corporation can pay its liability to the Japanese company through the international banking system. The American company will pay its bank in dollars. The bank will then use these dollars to purchase the required amount of yen on the international currency exchange and will arrange for delivery of the yen to the Japanese company's bank.[1]

Exchange Rates A currency exchange rate is the ratio at which one currency may be converted into another. Thus, the exchange rate may be viewed as the "price" of buying units of foreign currency, stated in terms of the domestic currency (which for our purpose is U.S. dollars). Exchange rates fluctuate daily, based upon the worldwide supply and demand for particular currencies. The current exchange rate between the dollar and most major currencies is published daily in the financial press. For example, a few of the exchange rates recently listed in *The Wall Street Journal* are shown below:

Country	Currency	Exchange Rate (In Dollars)
Britain	Pound (£)	$1.7185
France	French franc (FF)	.1765
Japan	Yen (¥)	.0076
Mexico	Peso ($)	.0003
Germany	Deutsche mark (DM)	.5996

*OBJECTIVE 1
Translate
an amount
of foreign
currency
into the
equivalent
number of
U.S. dollars.*

Exchange rates may be used to determine how much of one currency is equivalent to a given amount of another currency. Assume that the American company in our preceding example owes the Japanese company 1 million yen (expressed ¥1,000,000). How many dollars are needed to settle this obligation, assuming that the current exchange rate is $.0076 per yen? To restate an amount of foreign currency in terms of the equivalent amount of U.S. dollars, we multiply the foreign currency amount by the exchange rate, as illustrated below.[2]

Amount Stated in Foreign Currency	× Exchange Rate (in Dollars) =	Equivalent Number of U.S. Dollars
¥1,000,000	× $.0076 per yen =	$7,600

This process of restating an amount of foreign currency in terms of the equivalent number of dollars is called ***translating*** the foreign currency.

Why Exchange Rates Fluctuate An exchange rate represents the "price" of one currency, stated in terms of another. These prices fluctuate, based upon supply and demand, just as do the prices of gold, silver, soybeans, and other commodities. When the demand for a particular currency exceeds supply, the price (exchange rate) rises. If supply exceeds demand, the exchange rate falls.

---

[1] Alternatively, the American company may send the Japanese company a check (or a bank draft) stated in dollars. The Japanese company can then arrange to have the dollars converted into yen through its bank in Japan.

[2] To convert an amount of dollars into the equivalent amount of a foreign currency, we would ***divide*** the dollar amount by the exchange rate. For example, $7,600 ÷ $.0076 per yen = ¥1,000,000.

OBJECTIVE 2
*Explain why
exchange
rates fluctu-
ate and
what is
meant by a
"strong" or
a "weak"
currency.*

What determines the demand and supply for particular currencies? In short, it is the quantities of the currency that traders and investors seek to buy or to sell. Buyers of a particular currency include purchasers of that country's exports and foreign investors seeking to invest in the country's capital markets. Sellers of a currency include companies within the country that are importing goods from abroad and investors within the country who would prefer to invest their funds abroad. Thus, two major factors in the demand and supply for a currency are (1) the ratio of the country's imports to its exports and (2) the real rate of return available in the country's capital markets.

To illustrate the first of these points, let us consider Japan and Great Britain. Japan exports far more than it imports. As a result, Japan's customers must buy yen in the international currency market in order to pay for their purchases. This creates a strong demand for the yen and has caused its price (exchange rate) to rise relative to most other currencies. Great Britain, on the other hand, imports more than it exports. Thus, British companies must sell British pounds in order to acquire the foreign currencies needed to pay for their overseas purchases. This has increased the supply of pounds in the currency markets, and the price of the pound has declined substantially over the last several decades.

The second factor—the international attractiveness of a country's capital markets—depends upon both political stability and the country's interest rates relative to its internal rate of inflation. When a politically stable country offers high interest rates relative to inflation, foreign investors will seek to invest their funds in that country. First, however, they must convert their funds into that country's currency. This demand tends to raise the exchange rate for that currency. High interest rates relative to the internal rate of inflation were the major reason for the strength of the U.S. dollar during the early 1980s. Later in the decade, however, lower interest rates, along with large trade deficits (imports in excess of exports), significantly reduced the value of the dollar.

Exchange Rate "Jargon" In the financial press, currencies are often described as "strong" or "weak," or as rising or falling against one another. For example, an evening newscaster might say that "A strong dollar rose sharply against the weakening British pound, but fell slightly against the Japanese yen and the Swiss franc." What does this mean about exchange rates?

To understand such terminology, we must remember that an exchange rate is simply the price of one currency *stated in terms of another currency.* Throughout this appendix, we refer to the prices of various foreign currencies stated in terms of *U.S. dollars.* In other countries, however, the U.S. dollar is a foreign currency, and its price is stated in terms of the local (domestic) currency.

To illustrate, consider our table from *The Wall Street Journal,* which shows the exchange rate for the Japanese yen to be $.0076. At this exchange rate, ¥132 is equivalent to $1 (¥132 × $.0076 per yen = $1). Thus, while we would say that the exchange rate for the Japanese yen is *$.0076,* the Japanese would say that the exchange rate for the U.S. dollar is *¥132.*

Now let us assume that the exchange rate for the yen (stated in dollars) rises to $.0080. At this exchange rate, ¥125 is equivalent to $1 (¥125 ×

$.0080 = \$1$). In the United States, we would say that the exchange rate for the yen has ***risen*** from $.0076 to $.0080. In Japan, however, they would say that the exchange rate for the dollar has ***fallen*** from ¥132 to ¥125. In the financial press, it might be said that "the yen has risen against the dollar," or that "the dollar has fallen against the yen." The two statements mean the same thing—that the yen has become more valuable relative to the dollar.

Now let us return to our original phrase, "A strong dollar rose sharply against the weakening British pound, but fell slightly against the Japanese yen and the Swiss franc." When exchange rates are stated in terms of U.S. dollars, this statement means that the price (exchange rate) of the British pound fell sharply, but the prices of the Japanese yen and the Swiss franc rose slightly. A currency is described as "strong" when its exchange rate is rising relative to most other currencies and as "weak" when its exchange rate is falling.

Accounting for Transactions with Foreign Companies

*OBJECTIVE 3
Compute the
gain or loss
on a receiv-
able or pay-
able stated
in terms of
a foreign
currency
when ex-
change rates
fluctuate.*

When an American company buys or sells merchandise in a transaction with a foreign company, the transaction price may be stipulated either in U.S. dollars or in units of the foreign currency. If the price is stated in ***dollars,*** the American company encounters no special accounting problems. The transaction may be recorded in the same manner as are similar transactions with domestic suppliers or customers.

If the transaction price is stated in terms of the ***foreign currency,*** the American company encounters two accounting problems. First, since the American company's accounting records are maintained in dollars, the transaction price must be ***translated*** into dollars before the transaction can be recorded. The second problem arises when (1) the purchase or sale is made ***on account*** and (2) the exchange rate ***changes*** between the date of the transaction and the date that the account is paid. This fluctuation in the exchange rate will cause the American company to experience either a gain or a loss in the settlement of the transaction.

Credit Purchases with Prices Stated in a Foreign Currency   Assume that on August 1 an American company buys merchandise from a British company at a price of 10 thousand British pounds (£10,000), with payment due in 60 days. The exchange rate on August 1 is $1.70 per British pound. The entry on August 1 to record this purchase (assuming use of a perpetual inventory system) is shown below:

Inventory	*17,000*	
Accounts Payable		*17,000*

*To record the purchase of merchandise from a British
company for £10,000 when the exchange rate is $1.70 per
pound (£10,000 × $1.70 = $17,000).*

Let us now assume that by September 30, when the £10,000 account payable must be paid, the exchange rate has fallen to $1.68 per British pound. If the American company had paid for the merchandise on August 1, the cost would have been $17,000. On September 30, however, only $16,800 is needed to pay the £10,000 liability (£10,000 × $1.68 = $16,800).

Thus, ***the decline in the exchange rate has saved the company $200.*** This savings is recorded in the accounting records as a ***Gain on Fluctuations in Foreign Exchange Rates.*** The entry on September 30 to record payment of the liability and recognition of this gain would be:

Accounts Payable	*17,000*	
Cash..		*16,800*
Gain on Fluctuations in Foreign Exchange Rates		*200*
To record payment of £10,000 liability to British company and		
to recognize gain from decline in exchange rate:		
Original liability (£10,000 × $1.70)	*$17,000*	
Amount paid (£10,000 × $1.68)	*16,800*	
Gain from decline in exchange rate................	*$ 200*	

Now let us assume that instead of declining, the exchange rate had ***increased*** from $1.70 on August 1 to $1.73 on September 30. Under this assumption, the American company would have to pay $17,300 in order to pay off the £10,000 liability on September 30. Thus, the company would be paying ***$300 more*** than if the liability had been paid on August 1. This additional $300 cost was caused by the increase in the exchange rate and should be recorded as a loss. The entry on September 30 would be:

Accounts Payable	*17,000*	
Loss on Fluctuations in Foreign Exchange Rates...............	*300*	
Cash..		*17,300*
To record payment of £10,000 liability to British company and		
to recognize loss from increase in exchange rate:		
Original liability (£10,000 × $1.70)..................	*$17,000*	
Amount paid (£10,000 × $1.73)	*17,300*	
Loss from decline in exchange rate................	*$ 300*	

In summary, having a liability that is fixed in terms of a foreign currency results in a gain for the debtor if the exchange rate falls between the date of the transaction and the date of payment. The gain results because fewer dollars will be needed to repay the debt than had originally been owed. An increase in the exchange rate, on the other hand, causes the debtor to incur a loss. In this case, the debtor will have to spend more dollars than had originally been owed in order to purchase the foreign currency needed to pay the debt.

Credit Sales with Prices Stated in a Foreign Currency   A company that makes credit ***sales*** at prices stated in a foreign currency also will experience gains or losses from fluctuations in the exchange rate. To illustrate, let us change our preceding example to assume that the American company ***sells*** merchandise on August 1 to the British company at a price of £10,000. We shall again assume that the exchange rate on August 1 is $1.70 per British pound and that payment is due in 60 days. The entry on August 1 to record this sale is:

Accounts Receivable	*17,000*	
Sales		*17,000*
To record sale to British company with sales price set at		
£10,000 (£10,000 × $1.70) = $17,000. To be collected in 60 days.		

In 60 days (September 30), the American company will collect from the British company the U.S. dollar equivalent of £10,000. If the exchange rate on September 30 has fallen to $1.68 per pound, the American company will collect only $16,800 (£10,000 × $1.68 = $16,800) in full settlement of its account receivable. Since the receivable had originally been equivalent to $17,000, the decline in the exchange rate has caused a loss of $200 to the American company. The entry to be made on September 30 is:

Cash	*16,800*	
Loss on Fluctuations in Foreign Exchange Rates	*200*	
* Accounts Receivable*		*17,000*
To record collection of £10,000 receivable from British		
company and to recognize loss from fall in exchange rate		
since date of sale:		
* Original sales price (£10,000 × $1.70)*	*$17,000*	
* Amount received (£10,000 × $1.68)*	*16,800*	
* Loss from decline in exchange rate*	*$ 200*	

Now consider the alternative case, in which the exchange rate rises from $1.70 at August 1 to $1.73 at September 30. In this case, the British company's payment of £10,000 will convert into $17,300, creating a gain for the American company. The entry on September 30 would then be:

Cash	*17,300*	
* Accounts Receivable*		*17,000*
* Gain on Fluctuations in Foreign Exchange Rates*..........		*300*
To record collection of £10,000 receivable from British		
company and to recognize gain from increase in exchange		
rate:		
* Original sales price (£10,000 × $1.70)*	*$17,000*	
* Amount received (£10,000 × $1.73)*	*17,300*	
* Gain from decline in exchange rate*	*$ 300*	

Adjustment of Foreign Receivables and Payables at the Balance Sheet Date

We have seen that fluctuations in exchange rates may cause gains or losses for companies with accounts payable or receivable in foreign currencies. The fluctuations in the exchange rates occur on a daily basis. For convenience, however, the company usually waits until the account is paid or collected before recording the related gain or loss. An exception to this convenient practice occurs at the end of the accounting period. An ***adjusting entry*** must be made to recognize any gains or losses that have accumulated on any foreign payables or receivables through the balance sheet date.

To illustrate, assume that on November 10 an American company buys equipment from a Japanese company at a price of 10 million yen (¥10,000,000), payable on January 10 of the following year. If the exchange rate is $.0080 per yen on November 10, the entry to record the purchase would be:

Equipment	*80,000*	
* Accounts Payable*		*80,000*
To record purchase of equipment from Japanese company at a		
price of ¥10,000,000, payable January 10 (¥10,000,000 ×		
$.0080 = $80,000).		

Now assume that on December 31, the exchange rate has fallen to $.0077 per yen. At this exchange rate, the American company's account payable is equivalent to only $77,000 (¥10,000,000 × $.0077). Gains and losses from changes in exchange rates are recognized in the period *in which the change occurs.* Therefore, the American company should make an adjusting entry to restate its liability at the current dollar-equivalent and to recognize any related gain or loss. This entry, which would be dated December 31, is as follows:

Accounts Payable	3,000	
Gain on Fluctuations in Foreign Exchange Rates		3,000
To adjust balance of ¥10,000,000 account payable to amount indicated by year-end exchange rate:		
Original account balance	$80,000	
Adjusted balance (¥10,000,000 × $.0077)	77,000	
Required adjustment	$ 3,000	

Similar adjustments should be made for any other accounts payable or receivable at year-end that are fixed in terms of a foreign currency.

If the exchange rate changes again between the date of this adjusting entry and the date that the American company pays the liability, an additional gain or loss must be recognized. Assume, for example, that on January 10 the exchange rate has risen to $.0078 per yen. The American company must now spend $78,000 to buy the ¥10,000,000 needed to pay its liability to the Japanese company. Thus, the rise in the exchange rate has caused the American company a $1,000 loss since year-end. The entry to record payment of the account on January 10 would be:

Accounts Payable	77,000	
Loss on Fluctuations in Foreign Exchange Rates	1,000	
Cash		78,000
To record payment of ¥10,000,000 payable to Japanese company and to recognize loss from rise in exchange rate since year-end:		
Account payable, December 31	$77,000	
Amount paid, January 10	78,000	
Loss from increase in exchange rate	$ 1,000	

Gains and losses from fluctuations in foreign exchange rates should be shown in the income statement following the determination of income from operations. This treatment is similar to that accorded to gains and losses from the sale of plant assets or investments.

Currency Fluctuations—Who Wins and Who Loses?

Gains and losses from fluctuations in exchange rates are sustained by companies (or individuals) that have either payables or receivables that are *fixed in terms of a foreign currency.* American companies that import foreign products usually have large foreign liabilities. Companies that export American products to other countries are likely to have large receivables stated in foreign currencies.

As foreign exchange rates (stated in dollars) *fall,* American-based importers will gain and exporters will lose. When a foreign exchange rate falls, the foreign currency becomes *less expensive.* Therefore, importers

*OBJECTIVE 4
Explain how
fluctuations
in foreign
exchange
rates affect
companies
with receiv-
ables or pay-
ables stated
in terms of
foreign cur-
rencies.*

will have to spend fewer dollars to pay their foreign liabilities. Exporters, on the other hand, will have to watch their foreign receivables become worth fewer and fewer dollars.

When foreign exchange rates *rise,* this situation reverses. Importers will lose, because more dollars are required to pay the foreign debts. Exporters will gain, because their foreign receivables become equivalent to an increasing number of dollars.

Exchange Rates and Competitive Prices   Up to this point, we have discussed only the gains and losses incurred by companies that have receivables or payables stated in terms of a foreign currency. However, fluctuations in exchange rates change the *relative prices* of goods produced in different countries. Exchange rate fluctuations may make the prices of a country's products more or less competitive both at home and to customers throughout the world. Even a small store with no foreign accounts receivable or payable may find its business operations greatly affected by fluctuations in foreign exchange rates.

Consider, for example, a small store in Kansas that sells an American-made brand of television sets. If foreign exchange rates fall, which happens when the dollar is strong, the price of foreign-made television sets will decline. Thus, the store selling American-made television sets may have to compete with stores selling imported television sets at lower prices. Also, a strong dollar makes American goods *more expensive to customers in foreign countries.* Thus, an American television manufacturer will find it more difficult to sell its products abroad.

The situation reverses when the dollar is weak—that is, when foreign exchange rates are relatively high. A weak dollar makes foreign imports more expensive to American consumers. Also, a weak dollar makes American products less expensive to customers in foreign countries.

In summary, we may say that a strong U.S. dollar *helps companies that sell foreign-made goods in the American market.* A weak dollar, on the other hand, *gives a competitive advantage to companies that sell American products both at home and abroad.*

Consolidated Financial Statements That Include Foreign Subsidiaries

In Chapter 17, we discussed the principles of preparing consolidated financial statements. These statements view the operations of the parent company and its subsidiaries as if the affiliated companies were a single business entity. Several special accounting problems arise in preparing consolidated financial statements when subsidiaries operate in foreign countries. First, the accounting records of the foreign subsidiaries must be translated into U.S. dollars. Second, the accounting principles in use in the foreign countries may differ significantly from American generally accepted accounting principles.

These problems pose interesting challenges to professional accountants and will be addressed in later accounting courses. Readers of the financial statements of American-based corporations, however, need not be concerned with these technical issues. The consolidated financial statements of these companies are expressed in U.S. dollars and conform to American generally accepted accounting principles.

ASSIGNMENT MATERIAL

DISCUSSION QUESTIONS

1 Translate the following amounts of foreign currency into an equivalent number of U.S. dollars using the exchange rates in the table on page D-3.

   a £800,000.

   b ¥350,000.

   c DM50,000.

2 Assume that an American company makes a purchase from a German company and agrees to pay a price of 2 million deutsche marks.

   a How will the American company determine the cost of this purchase for the purpose of recording it in the accounting records?

   b Briefly explain how an American company can arrange the payment of deutsche marks to a German company.

3 A recent newspaper shows the exchange rate for the British pound at $1.72 and for the yen at $.0076. Does this indicate that the pound is a stronger currency than the yen? Explain.

4 Identify two factors that tend to make the exchange rate for a country's currency rise.

5 Explain how an increase in a foreign exchange rate will affect a U.S. company that makes:

   a Credit sales to a foreign company at prices stated in the foreign currency.

   b Credit purchases from a foreign company at prices stated in the foreign currency.

   c Credit sales to a foreign company at prices stated in U.S. dollars.

6 You are the purchasing agent for an American business that purchases merchandise on account from companies in Mexico. The exchange rate for the Mexican peso has been falling against the dollar and the trend is expected to continue for at least several months. Would you prefer that the prices for purchases from the Mexican companies be specified in U.S. dollars or in Mexican pesos? Explain.

7 CompuTech is an American-based multinational corporation. Foreign sales are made at prices set in U.S. dollars, but foreign purchases are often made at prices stated in foreign currencies. If the exchange rate for the U.S. dollar has risen against most foreign currencies throughout the year, would CompuTech have recognized primarily gains or losses as a result of exchange rate fluctuations? Explain.

PROBLEMS

**PROBLEM D-1
Currency Fluctuations: Who Wins and Who Loses?**

Indicate whether each of the companies or individuals in the following independent cases would benefit more from a strong U.S. dollar (relatively low foreign exchange rates) or a weak U.S. dollar (relatively high foreign exchange rates). Provide a brief explanation of your reasoning.

   a **Boeing** (an American aircraft manufacturer that sells many planes to foreign customers).

   b A Nikon camera store in Beverly Hills, California. (Nikon cameras are made in Japan.)

    c **Toyota** (the Japanese auto manufacturer).

    d The Mexico City dealer for Caterpillar tractors (made in the U.S.).

    e An American tourist visiting England.

    f A small store that sells American-made video recorders in Toledo, Ohio. The store has no foreign accounts receivable or payable.

PROBLEM D-2
Gains and Losses from Exchange Rate Fluctuations

Europa-West is an American corporation that purchases automobiles from European manufacturers for distribution in the United States. A recent purchase involved the following events:

Nov. 12   Purchased automobiles from West Berlin Motors for DM2,000,000, payable in 60 days. Current exchange rate, $.5883 per deutsche mark. (Europa-West uses the perpetual inventory system.)

Dec. 31   Made year-end adjusting entry relating to the DM2,000,000 account payable to West Berlin Motors. Current exchange rate, $.6045 per deutsche mark.

Jan. 11   Issued a check to World Bank for $1,199,000 in full payment of the account payable to West Berlin Motors.

INSTRUCTIONS

  a Prepare in general journal form the entries necessary to record the preceding events.

  b Compute the exchange rate (price) of the deutsche mark in U.S. dollars on January 11.

PROBLEM D-3
Gains and Losses from Rate Fluctuations: an Alternative Problem

IronMan, Inc., is an American company that manufactures exercise machines and also distributes several lines of imported bicycles. Selected transactions of the company are listed below:

Oct. 4   Purchased manufacturing equipment from Rhine Mfg. Co., a German company. The purchase price was DM400,000, due in 60 days. Current exchange rate, $.5995 per deutsche mark. (Debit the Equipment account.)

Oct. 18   Purchased 2,500 racing bicycles from Ninja Cycles, a Japanese company, at a price of ¥60,000,000. Payment is due in 90 days; the current exchange rate is $.0073 per yen. (IronMan uses the perpetual inventory system.)

Nov. 15   Purchased 1,000 touring bicycles from Royal Lion Ltd., a British corporation. The purchase price was £192,500, payable in 30 days. Current exchange rate, $1.77 per British pound.

Dec. 3   Issued check to First Bank for the U.S. dollar-equivalent of DM400,000 in payment of the account payable to Rhine Mfg. Co. Current exchange rate, $.6085 per deutsche mark.

Dec. 15   Issued check to First Bank for dollar-equivalent of £192,500 in payment of the account payable to Royal Lion Ltd. Current exchange rate, $1.72 per British pound.

INSTRUCTIONS

  a Prepare entries in general journal form to record the preceding transactions.

  b Prepare the December 31 adjusting entry relating to the account payable to Ninja Cycles. The year-end exchange rate is $.0076 per Japanese yen.

PROBLEM D-4
A Comprehensive Problem on Exchange Rate Fluctuations

Wolfe Computer is an American company that manufactures portable personal computers. Many of the components for the computer are purchased abroad, and the finished product is sold in foreign countries as well as in the United States. Among the recent transactions of Wolfe are the following:

Oct. 28 Purchased from Mitsutonka, a Japanese company, 20,000 disc drives. The purchase price was ¥180,000,000, payable in 30 days. Current exchange rate, $.0075 per yen. (Wolfe uses the perpetual inventory method; debit the Inventory of Raw Materials account.)

Nov. 9 Sold 700 personal computers to the Bank of England for £534,100 due in 30 days. The cost of the computers, to be debited to the Cost of Goods Sold account, was $518,000. Current exchange rate, $1.73 per British pound. (Use one compound journal entry to record the sale and the cost of goods sold. In recording the cost of goods sold, credit Inventory of Finished Goods.)

Nov. 27 Issued a check to Inland Bank for $1,296,000 in *full payment* of account payable to Mitsutonka.

Dec. 2 Purchased 10,000 gray-scale monitors from German Optical for DM1,200,000, payable in 60 days. Current exchange rate, $.6010 per deutsche mark. (Debit Inventory of Raw Materials.)

Dec. 9 Collected dollar-equivalent of £534,100 from the Bank of England. Current exchange rate, $1.71 per British pound.

Dec. 11 Sold 10,000 personal computers to Computique, a French retail chain, for FF75,000,000, due in 30 days. Current exchange rate, $.1760 per French franc. The cost of the computers, to be debited to Cost of Goods Sold and credited to Inventory of Finished Goods, is $7,400,000.

INSTRUCTIONS

a Prepare in general journal form the entries necessary to record the preceding transactions.

b Prepare the adjusting entries needed at December 31 for the DM1,200,000 account payable to German Optical and the FF75,000,000 account receivable from Computique. Year-end exchange rates, $.5980 per deutsche mark and $.1770 per French franc. (Use a separate journal entry to adjust each account balance.)

c Compute the unit sales price of computers in U.S. dollars in either the November 9 or December 11 sales transactions. (The sales price is the same in each transaction.)

d Compute the exchange rate for the yen, stated in U.S. dollars, on November 27.

Index

Comparative data in annual reports
(*continued*):
Rubbermaid Incorporated, 976–
977
Comparative financial statements:
comprehensive illustration,
932–933
defined, 10, 925
Rubbermaid Incorporated, 968–
975
COMPAQ Computer Corporation,
777
Component percentages, 928
Comprehensive Problems (in text
sequence):
Little Bear Railroad, Inc., 102–
103
Friend With a Truck, 216–217
*Alpine Village and Nordic
Sports,* 507–508
Shadow Mountain Hotel, 783–
788
Rubbermaid Incorporated, 967–
981
Apex Computer, Inc., 1072–
1074
Computer-based accounting systems:
adjusting entries in, 132
aging accounts receivable in,
365
amortization tables in, 523
basic functions of, 8, 9, 11, 275
budgeting and, 1167
classifying data in, 279–283
closing entries in, 132
compared to manual systems,
77–79, 283–284
data base, 77–78, 279–282
design of, 275–284
illustration of, 79
internal control in, 292
inventory in, 277, 422
on-line, real-time, 277
payroll processing in, 532, 540
point-of-sale terminals in, 277
recording transactions in,
77, 132, 227
subsidiary ledgers in, 228–229
work sheets in, 185
Concentrations of credit risk, 374–
375
Conceptual framework project, 13,
615
Conservatism, concept of:
defined 110, 360
in valuation of accounts receivable, 360
in valuation of inventory, 415
in valuation of plant assets,
468
Consistency, principle of, 408, 415,
467
Consolidated Edison, 661
Consolidated entity, 800–802
Consolidated financial statements:
concept of, 800–802
with foreign subsidiaries, D-9

interpretation of, 802
preparation of, 802–811
Contingent liabilities (*see* Loss con-
tingencies)
Continuing operations, 692
Contra-asset accounts, 121, 360
Contra-revenue accounts, 250–251
Contribution margin, 1088–1089,
1094–1096, 1119, 1122
Contribution margin ratio, 1089,
1130
Control listing, 320
Controllable fixed costs, 1124
Controller, 33
Controlling account, 225
Coors Company (Adolph), 392
Convertible bonds payable, 762–
764
Copyrights, 478
Corporations:
characteristics of, 26, 650–651
closely held, 669
defined, 26, 650
formation of, 652–654
publicly owned, 6
stockholders' liability for debts
of, 26, 241, 650
stockholders' equity in balance
sheet, 27, 656, 672,
Cost accounting:
chapter coverage of, 1020–1050
defined, 34, 988
Cost accounting systems:
flow of costs in, 1026–1027,
1031
job-order, 1022–1030
objectives of, 1021–1022
process cost, 1022, 1030–1042
Cost behavior, 1080, 1082–1086
Cost centers, 1115–1116
Cost drivers, 997–999, 1078
Cost of finished goods manufactured, 992–993, 1000
Cost of goods sold:
cost flow assumptions, 408–415
defined, 223
estimating techniques, 424–426
in an income statement, 224
in a periodic inventory system,
233–234
in a perpetual inventory system, 230
Cost principle, 16–17, 229, 406,
456–458, 606–607
Cost variances, 1168–1177
Cost-effective information, 171, 274
Cost-volume-profit (CVP) analysis:
assumptions underlying, 1096
basic formula, 1085
chapter coverage of, 1077–1096
graph, 1087
sales volume and target income, 1089–1092
summary of formulas, 1096
CPA (*see* Certified Public Accountant)
Credit balance, 60–61
Credit card sales, 368–369

Credit losses, 358–366
Credit risk, 374–375
Credit terms, 247–248, 251
Creditors:
as users of financial statements, 27–28
defined, 27
interest in solvency, 27–28,
316–319, 939–944
Current assets, 236–241
Current liabilities:
accounts payable, 513–514
accrued expenses, 517–520
current portion of long-term
debt, 517, 521–524
defined, 236–241
notes payable (*see* Notes payable)
payroll tax liabilities, 520, 533–
541
unearned revenue, 521
Current ratio, 238–240, 513, 943–
944
Cycle time, 1049

Data base systems, 77–78, 279–282
Debit balance, 60
Debit and credit entries, 59–61
equality of, 61
rules of, 61, 111
Debit and credit memoranda, 291
Debt ratio, 525–526, 757–758, 940
Deferred income taxes, 754–755,
852–855
Default (of a note receivable), 372
Defects-per-million, 1050
Deferred charges, 478
Deficit, 656
Deming, W. Edwards, 1050
Depletion, 479–480
Depreciation:
accumulated (*see* Accumulated
depreciation)
causes of, 461
as a cost allocation process,
459–461
defined, 119–120, 459–460
for fractional periods, 467, 470
for income tax purposes, 469–
470, 480–485
management's responsibility for
estimates, 467–469
methods of:
Modified Accelerated Cost
Recovery System
(MACRS), 480–485
straight-line, 462–463
units-of-output, 463–464
declining-balance, 464–465
sum-of-the-years'-digits,
465–466
selecting a method, 467
Differential analysis (*see* Incremental analysis)
Digital Equipment Corporation, 396
Direct costing (*see* Variable costing)
Direct costs, 996